Farnsworth on Contracts

Third Edition

by E. Allan Farnsworth

Farnsworth on Contracts, Third Edition, is the cornerstone of every commercial law attorney's library. Praised for its usefulness in litigation, arbitration, and practice, it has been cited by courts at every level. Considered the greatest authority of his time on contract law, Professor Farnsworth, Reporter for the Restatement (Second) of Contracts, draws on all statutory and judicial sources for the underlying law as he advises you on the drafting of specific clause language.

Highlights of the 2017-3 Cumulative Supplement

Among the highlights of the 2017-3 Cumulative Supplement are:

- In *Taylor v. University of the Cumberlands*, the court held that the agreement was not an invalid as based on past consideration despite language in agreement that the parties "agree that the compensation and benefits contained in this agreement is/are for the past decades of duties and/or work performed." See §2.7.
- In *Vitacost.com, Inc. v. McCants*, the court held that the purchaser was not on notice that the sale was subject to an arbitration agreement because, among other reasons, the check out page linked to "'terms and conditions,' not 'terms and conditions of *sale*.'" See §3.7.
- The Third Circuit applied "browsewrap" principles to agreements for sale of telephone services to inmates, where the transaction could be completed by telephone but the agreement was available only online. *See James v. Global Tellink Corp.*, §3.7.

Wolters Kluwer

- The Second Circuit found no contractual offer in a grocery chain's advertisements that it would make charitable donations for every code (up to a maximum amount) entered on its website. *See McCabe v. ConAgra Foods*, §3.10.
- A party asserting that "brain fog" rendered him incompetent to execute a real estate contract had submitted sufficient evidence to survive summary judgment. *See Gray v. Jung*, §4.6.
- Discussion of *Great Lakes Insurance SE v. Queen*, in which the district court judge appeared suspicious of the insurance company's claim that a misrepresentation was material but was bound by Georgia law "that summary judgment may be granted on the materiality issue based on the uncontroverted affidavit of an insurance company's representative." See §4.12.
- In *Schnuck Markets, Inc. v. First Data Merchant Services Corp.*, the Eighth Circuit narrowly construed a Master Services Agreement's limitation of liability provision in the context of a data breach and imposition of fines by MasterCard and Visa against the bank and data processor responsible for facilitating a grocery chain's credit card transactions. See §4.28a.
- The federal Consumer Review Fairness Act became effective in March, prohibiting form contracts that restrict consumer from criticizing the product in reviews or that transfer intellectual property in reviews to the company. See §5.5.
- A contract interpretation case that hinged on the Oxford comma became a social media hit. *See O'Connor v. Oakhurst Dairy*, §7.8.
- The court in *Under Armour, Inc. v. Ziger/Snead* discussed the role of ambiguity in contracts, and held that "losses incurred" in a prevailing party fee-shifting provision in the contract was broad enough to include diverted employee time. See §7.8.
- In *Janati v. University of Nevada Las Vegas School of Dental Medicine*, the court discussed doctrines that have

developed for evaluating alleged breaches of procedures required by student manuals, questioning whether such doctrines are "really 'contractual' in nature." See §7.10.

- In *Wilson v. New York State Thruway Authority*, the court held that the Authority was not required to pay retirees' health insurance premiums under the contract, declining to look to extrinsic evidence—the past practice of paying those premiums for more than four decades. See §7.13.
- The Seventh Circuit declined to accept a would-be class plaintiff's characterization of claims as simple contract claims, holding that they were in fact securities law claims that cannot be litigated as a class under a federal statute. *See Holtz v. JPMorgan Chase Bank*, §7.17b.
- The Second Circuit noted a circuit split but held to its rule that an arbitration clause is unenforceable if the parties envisioned a specific arbiter that is no longer available. *See Moss v. First Premier Bank*, §9.7.

As part of the 2017-3 Cumulative Supplement, the tables and the index have been completely updated to make all of the news readily accessible.

7/17

For questions concerning this shipment, billing, or other customer service matters, call our Customer Service department at 1-800-234-1660.

For toll-free ordering, please call 1-800-638-8437.

FARNSWORTH ON CONTRACTS

VOLUMES I-III

2017-3 Cumulative Supplement

E. ALLAN FARNSWORTH
Late Alfred McCormack Professor of Law
Columbia University
Reporter, Restatement (Second) of Contracts

This supplement supersedes all previous supplements.

Wolters Kluwer

Published by Wolters Kluwer in New York.

Wolters Kluwer Legal & Regulatory U.S. serves customers worldwide with CCH, Aspen Publishers and Kluwer Law International products.

Printed in the United States of America
Library of Congress Catalog Card No. 90-60589
ISBN 978-1-4548-8460-6

1 2 3 4 5 6 7 8 9 0

SUSTAINABLE FORESTRY INITIATIVE Certified Sourcing
www.sfiprogram.org
SFI-00756

About Wolters Kluwer Legal & Regulatory U.S.

Wolters Kluwer Legal & Regulatory U.S. delivers expert content and solutions in the areas of law, corporate compliance, health compliance, reimbursement, and legal education. Its practical solutions help customers successfully navigate the demands of a changing environment to drive their daily activities, enhance decision quality and inspire confident outcomes.

Serving customers worldwide, its legal and regulatory portfolio includes products under the Aspen Publishers, CCH Incorporated, Kluwer Law International, ftwilliam.com and MediRegs names. They are regarded as exceptional and trusted resources for general legal and practice-specific knowledge, compliance and risk management, dynamic workflow solutions, and expert commentary.

WOLTERS KLUWER SUPPLEMENT NOTICE

This product is updated on a periodic basis with supplements and/or new editions to reflect important changes in the subject matter.

If you would like information about enrolling this product in the update service, or wish to receive updates billed separately with a 30-day examination review, please contact our Customer Service Department at 1-800-234-1660 or email us at: *customer.service@wolterskluwer.com*. You can also contact us at:

Wolters Kluwer
Distribution Center
7201 McKinney Circle
Frederick, MD 21704

Important Contact Information

- To order any title, go to *www.wklawbusiness.com* or call 1-800-638-8437.
- To reinstate your manual update service, call 1-800-638-8437.
- To contact Customer Service, e-mail *customer.service@wolterskluwer.com*, call 1-800-234-1660, fax 1-800-901-9075, or mail correspondence to: Order Department — Wolters Kluwer, PO Box 990, Frederick, MD 21705.
- To review your account history or pay an invoice online, visit *www.WKLawBusiness.com/payinvoices.*

Wolters Kluwer

SUMMARY OF CONTENTS

VOLUME I

PART I
INTRODUCTION

PART II
ENFORCEABILITY OF PROMISES

VOLUME II

PART III
SCOPE AND EFFECT OF PROMISES

VOLUME III

PART IV
RIGHTS OF THIRD PARTIES

PART V
ENFORCEMENT OF PROMISES

VOLUME I

PART I

INTRODUCTION

CHAPTER 1

CONTRACTS AND CONTRACT LAW IN GENERAL

§1.1 THE MEANING OF *CONTRACT*

§1.1 n.1 p.4 Add the following at the end: This last points toward an occasional attempt to enforce promises made by electoral candidates during campaigns, as witness the "Contract with America" in the 1994 congressional elections. Attempts to enforce these "contracts" almost invariably come to naught. *See* Wrona & Cissna, Switching Sides: Is Party Affiliation a Tie That Binds?, 28 Ariz. St. L.J. 735 (1996); Note, Read My Lips: Examining the Legal Implications of Knowingly False Campaign Promises, 90 Mich. L. Rev. 428 (1991). *See infra* §3.7. There is, however, a remarkable doctrine called "contract with the voters" stemming from the Contracts Clause of the Texas Constitution. This requires that funds from a voter-approved tax be used for the approved purpose and that lands purchased for that project be dedicated to that purpose. *See* Gallagher Headquarters Ranch Dev. v. City of San Antonio, 269 S.W.3d 628 (Tex. Civ. App. 2008) (recognizing doctrine but finding it susceptible to abrogation by state statutes), *review granted and judgment vacated pursuant to settlement agreement*, No. 08-0773 (Tex. Jun. 18, 2010). Social contract theorists should take note.

§1.2 THE ROLE OF EXCHANGE

§1.2 n.3 p.7 Add the following at the end: Korn & Decktor Korn, Where People Don't Promise, 93 Ethics 445 (1983) (study of Tonga).

§1.2 p.8 In the first full paragraph, add a note to the end of the second to last sentence: . . . efficient use of economic resources.[7a]

[7a] In 2016, two professors were awarded the Nobel Prize in Economic Sciences for their work on "analysis of optimal contractual arrangements." Binyamin Appelbaum, "Oliver Hart and Bengt Holmstrom Win Nobel in Economics for Work on Contracts," N.Y. Times, Oct. 10, 2016.

§1.4 THE ENFORCEMENT OF PROMISES IN ROMAN LAW

§1.4 n.1 p.11 Add the following at the end: R. Zimmermann, The Law of Obligations (1990).

The enforcement of bilateral promises was not, however, new to Roman law. *See* R. VerSteeg, Early Mesopotamian Law 172-81 (2000) (Laws of Hammurabi and of Lipit-Ishtar recognized bailments, warranties); R. VerSteeg, Law in Ancient Egypt 192-201 (2002) (19th and 20th Dynasties had contracts of bailment, purely executory contracts for the sale of goods).

§1.4 p.12 In the third full paragraph, add the following at the end of the last sentence: . . . sale, hire, partnership, and mandate.[2a]

[2a] The sales contract, *emptio venditio*, had its roots in the *stipulatio*, as did the other consensual contracts. F. de Zulueta, The Roman Law of Sale 1-6 (1945).

§1.4 n.3 p.13 Add the following to the list after **"See also":** L. Friedman, Contract Law in America (1965); D. Ibbetson, A Historical Introduction to the Law of Obligations (1999).

§1.5 THE ENFORCEMENT OF PROMISES IN EARLY ENGLISH LAW

§1.5 n.1 p.13 ***Add the following at the end:*** ; Note, Supply versus Demand for Efficient Legal Rules: Evidence from Early English "Contract" Law and the Rise of Assumpsit, 73 U. Pitt. L. Rev. 161 (2011).

§1.5 p.14 ***In the final paragraph, after the second sentence, add the following:*** . . . made by merchants.[3a]

[3a] *But see* Kadens, The Myth of the Customary Law Merchant, 90 Tex. L. Rev. 1153 (2012).

§1.6 THE DEVELOPMENT OF A GENERAL BASIS FOR ENFORCING PROMISES

§1.6 p.22 ***Add the following at the end of the carryover sentence at the top of the page:*** . . . exchanges of promises.[11a]

[11a] Assumpsit continues to make appearances in the courts, notwithstanding the existence of the cause of action for breach of contract. *See, e.g.*, Hall v. Laroya, 238 P.3d 714 (Haw. App. 2010) (for the purposes of a fee-shifting statute, a suit to collect attorney's fees is "in the nature of assumpsit"). Day v. Heller, 653 N.W.2d 475 (Neb. 2002) (action in assumpsit for misrepresentation of paternity); Coleman v. Duane Morris, LLP, 58 A.3d 833 (Pa. Super. 2012) (legal malpractice claim brought as "action in assumpsit"). Assumpsit appears most often as the source of the modern doctrine of money had and received, which, if anything, is restitutionary rather than contractual. *See, e.g.*, Avidor v. Sutter's Place, Inc., 151 Cal. Rptr. 3d 804 (Ct. App. 2013) (tracing cause of action for money had and received to "an alleged duty to make restitution under an assumpsit theory"); Town of Stratford v. Castater, 46 A.3d 945 (Conn. App. 2012) (discussing at length the roots of money had and received in the action of *indebitatus assumpsit*); Citibank (S.D.) v. Graham, 726 S.E.2d 617 (Ga. App. 2012) ("the right to sue for a refund arose at common law under the theory of *indebitatus assumpsit* for money had and received"); H.E.B., L.L.C. v. Ardinger, 369 S.W.3d 496 (Tex. Civ. App. 2012) (courts use "money had and received" interchangeably with other terms, such as assumpsit).

§1.7 CONTRACT INTO THE TWENTY-FIRST CENTURY

***§1.7 n.1 p.23 Add the following after* "See" *and before* "VerSteeg":** Graveson, The Movement from Status to Contract, 4 Modern L. Rev. 261 (1941);

§1.7 n.13 p.24 Add the following at the end of the second sentence: ; Preston & McCann, Llewellyn Slept Here: A Short History of Sticky Contracts and Feudalism, 91 Or. L. Rev. 129 (2012).

§1.7 n.14 p.25 Add the following at the end: The worldwide wave of privatization over the last decade or two has produced its own Thurn und Taxis families, predictably enough to the student of history.

§1.7 n.19 p.26 Add the following at the end: Another area where contract and tort exist in uneasy companionship is promissory fraud. *See* I. Ayres & G. Klass, Insincere Promises (2005); Bridgeman & Sandrik, Bullshit Promises, 76 Tenn. L. Rev. 379 (2009).

§1.7 n.26 p.28 Add the following after the second sentence: On the impact of Coase's work, *see* Symposium, Markets, Firms, & Property Rights: A Celebration of the Research of Ronald Coase, 54 J.L. & Econ. S1-S401 (2011).

§1.7 p.29 Add in place of the second, third, and fourth sentences on the page: One should note, though, that the American Law Institute has underway projects that will likely provide special rules for parts of contract law. The Restatement (Third) of Consumer Contracting, just underway, the Restatement (Third) of Employment Law, now within sight of completion, and the Principles of the Law of Software Contracts, now complete, deal with areas of contract law that have shown significant non-uniformity. The Restatement (Third) of Restitution and Unjust Enrichment, recently approved by ALI, also addresses a number of contract rules.

§1.7 p.29 In the final paragraph, add four lines from the bottom: For *most* substitute *forty-seven.*

§1.7 n.38 p.29 Add the following at the end: Since then, in 2005, UNCITRAL promulgated a Convention on the Use of Electronic Communications in International Commerce. It has been signed by 18 nations and ratified by 2. The National Conference of Commissioners on Uniform State Laws has completed a project on the implementation of the Convention in the United States, however, and it is anticipated that the Convention will be ratified by Congress in the not too distant future. The Convention is almost entirely consistent with UETA.

§1.7 n.40 p.30 Add the following at the end: These provisions, like much else in Amended Article 2, have drawn criticism. *See* Braucher, Under the Surrounding Circumstances: Amended Article 2's Redundant (or Worse) Electronic Commerce Provisions, 68 Ohio St. L.J. 115 (2007).

§1.8 TREATISES, RESTATEMENTS, AND SCHOLARSHIP

§1.8 n.5 p.32 Add the following at the end: ; Wells, Langdell and the Invention of Legal Doctrine, 58 Buff. L. Rev. 551 (2010).

§1.8 n.13 p.34 Add the following to the list in the third sentence: Adams, Blaming the Mirror: The Restatements and the Common Law, 40 Ind. L. Rev. 205 (2007); Adams, The Folly of Uniformity? Lessons from the Restatement Movement, 33 Hofstra L. Rev. 423 (2004).

§1.8 n.13 p.34 Add the following to the list in the final sentence: Hull, Restatement and Reform: A New Perspective on the Origins of the American Law Institute, *in* The American Law Institute Seventy-fifth Anniversary 49 (1998).

More generally on private attempts to unify state law, *see* Snyder, Molecular Federalism and the Structures of Private Lawmaking, 14 Ind. J. Global Legal Stud. 419 (2007).

§1.8 n.14 p.34 Replace the fourth sentence with the following: As of March 1, 2004, the last time the figures were published, the contracts Restatements had been cited 28,739 times out of a total for all Restatements of 161,486, according to the American Law Institute's 2004 Annual Reports.

§1.8 n.14 p.34 Add the following at the end: There are no plans to begin a Restatement (Third) of Contracts to accompany the many Restatement Thirds already completed or now in progress. Traynor, The First Restatements and the Vision of the American Law Institute, Then and Now, 32 S. Ill. L.J. 145, 148 (2007). As mentioned earlier, though, the ALI is in the middle of preparing a series of Restatements or Principles that deal with most areas in contract law that have proved controversial. When these projects are complete, it will be an interesting challenge to figure out what types of contracts are still dealt with only by the Restatement Second.

§1.8 n.16 p.35 Replace the citations to **Calamari & Perillo**, **Murray**, **Atiyah**, **Furmston**, **Treitel**, *and* **Chitty** *with the following:* J. Perillo, Calamari & Perillo on Contracts (6th ed. 2009); J. Murray, Murray on Contracts (5th ed. 2011); S. Smith, Atiyah's Introduction to the Law of Contract (6th ed. 2006); M. Furmston, Cheshire, Fifoot & Furmston's Law of Contract (16th ed. 2012); G. Treitel, The Law of Contract (11th ed. 2003); Chitty on Contracts (H. Beale gen. ed. 30th ed. 2011).

§1.8 n.16 p.35 Add the following to the list in the first sentence: M. Chen-Wishart, Contract Law (2010).

§1.8 n.19 p.35 Add the following to the list after **"See generally":** P. Alces, A Theory of Contract Law: Empirical Insights and Moral Philosophy (2011); F. Buckley, Just Exchange (2005); D. Kimel, From Promise to Contract (2003); S. Smith, Contract Theory (2004); S. Waddams, Principle and Policy in Contract Law: Competing or Complementary Concepts? (2011).

§1.8 n.19 p.35 Add the following at the end: For an interesting defense of theoretical heterodoxy, *see* Trakman, Pluralism in Contract Law, 58 Buff. L. Rev. 1031 (2010).

§1.8 n.20 p.36 Add the following at the end of the first sentence: , though Fuller, Consideration and Form, 41 Colum. L. Rev. 799 (1941) is not too far behind.

§1.8 n.21 p.36 Add the following at the end: Those in search of a balanced statement of the history of contract or a sound set of predictions on contract's future might profitably look elsewhere.

§1.8 n.24 p.37 Add the following to the list after **"See also":** Dobbins, The Hidden Costs of Contracting: Barriers to Justice in the Law of Contracts, 7 J. L. Soc'y 116 (2005); Florestal, Is a Burrito a Sandwich? Exploring Race, Class, and Culture in Contracts, 14 Mich. J. Race & L. 1 (2008); Gordon, Unfreezing Legal Reality: Critical Approaches to Law, 15 Fla. St. U.L. Rev. 195 (1987); Hart, Contract Formation and the Entrenchment of Power, 41 Loy. U. Chi. L.J. 175 (2009).

§1.8 n.24 p.37 Add the following at the end: ; Post, Contract and Dispossession, 1 Col. J. Race & L. 418 (2012).

§1.8 n.25 p.37 Add the following to the list after **"See also":** Feminist Perspectives on Contract Law (L. Mulcahy & S. Wheeler eds. 2005); Ertman, Legal Tenderness: Feminist Perspectives on Contract Law, 18 Yale J.L. & Feminism 545 (2006); Post, Outsider Jurisprudence and the "Unthinkable" Tale: Spousal Abuse and the Doctrine of Duress, 26 U. Haw. L. Rev. 469 (2004); Quinn, Feminist Legal Realism, 35 Harv. J.L. & Gender 1 (2012); Rounds, The Common Law Is Not Just About Contracts: How Legal Education Has Been Short-Changing Feminism, 43 U. Rich. L. Rev. 1185 (2009).

§1.8 n.26 p.37 Add the following to the list after **"See generally":** L. Kalman, Legal Realism at Yale, 1927-60 (1986); B. Leiter, Naturalizing Jurisprudence (2007); J. Schlegel, American Legal Realism & Empirical Social Science (1995); Gordon, Professors and Policymakers: Yale Law School Faculty in the New Deal and After, in History of the Yale Law School 75 (A. Kronman ed. 2004); Engle, The Fake Revolution: Understanding Legal Realism, 47 Washburn L.J. 653 (2008); Leiter, In Praise of Realism (And against "Nonsense" Jurisprudence), 100 Geo. L.J. 865

(2012); Tamanaha, Understanding Legal Realism, 87 Tex. L. Rev. 731 (2009); Ursin, The Missing Normative Dimension in Brian Leiter's "Reconstructed" Legal Realism, 49 San Diego L. Rev. 1 (2012).

§1.8 n.26 p.37 Add the following at the end: For two contrasting assessments of the post-Realist enterprise, *see* Kronman, Jurisprudential Responses to Legal Realism, 73 Cornell L. Rev. 335 (1988); Miles & Sunstein, The New Legal Realism, 75 U. Chi. L. Rev. 831 (2008).

***§1.8 n.27 p.37 Add the following to the list after* "See":** R. Kreitner, Calculating Promises (2007).

§1.8 n.27 p.37 Add the following to the end: ; Note, Supply versus Demand for Efficient Legal Rules: Evidence from Early English "Contract" Law and the Rise of Assumpsit, 73 U. Pitt. L. Rev. 161 (2011).

***§1.8 n.28 p.37 In the second sentence, add the following to the list after* "see":** Revisiting the Contracts Scholarship of Stewart Macaulay (J. Braucher, J. Kidwell, & W. Whitford eds., 2013);

***§1.8 n.28 p.37 In the third sentence, add the following to the list after* "see":** Geis, Automating Contract Law, 83 N.Y.U. L. Rev. 450 (2008); Smith & King, Contracts as Organizations, 51 Ariz. L. Rev. 1 (2009).

***§1.8 p.37 Add the following to the third sentence in the first paragraph after* "sociology":** or psychology[28a]

[28a] *See, e.g.*, Bar-Gill, The Law, Economics and Psychology of Subprime Mortgage Contracts, 94 Cornell L. Rev. 1073 (2009); Bar-Gill, The Behavioral Economics of Consumer Contracts, 92 Minn. L. Rev. 749 (2008); Becher & Unger-Aviram, The Law of Standard Form Contracts: Misguided Intuitions and Suggestions for Reconstruction, 8 DePaul Bus. & Com. L.J. 199 (2010); Benoliel, The Behavioral Law and Economics of Franchise Tying Contracts, 41 Rutgers L.J. 527 (2010); Eisenberg, The Limits of Cognition and the Limits of Contract, 47 Stan. L. Rev. 211 (1995); Garvin, Adequate Assurance of Performance: Of Risk, Duress, and Cognition, 69 U. Colo. L. Rev. 71 (1998); Garvin, Disproportionality and the Law of Consequential Damages: Default Theory and Cognitive Reality, 59 Ohio St. L.J.

339 (1998); Garvin, Small Business and the False Dichotomies of Contract Law, 40 Wake Forest L. Rev. 295 (2005); Hollander-Blumoff, Social Psychology, Information Processing, and Plea Bargaining, 91 Marq. L. Rev. 163 (2007); Korobkin, Bounded Rationality, Standard Form Contracts, and Unconscionability, 70 U. Chi. L. Rev. 1203 (2003); Wilkinson-Ryan, Do Liquidated Damages Encourage Breach? A Psychological Experiment, 108 Mich. L. Rev. 633 (2010). *But see* Wright & Ginsburg, Behavioral Law and Economics: Its Origins, Fatal Flaws, and Implications for Liberty, 106 Nw. U. L. Rev. 1033 (2012).

***§1.8 n.29 p.37 Add the following to the list after* "See also":** Bagchi, Distributive Injustice and Private Law, 60 Hastings L.J. 105 (2008); Bridgeman, Why Contracts Scholars Should Read Legal Philosophy: Positivism, Formalism, and the Specification of Rules in Contract Law, 29 Cardozo L. Rev. 1443 (2008); Bridgeman, Reconciling Strict Liability with Corrective Justice in Contract Law, 75 Fordham L. Rev. 3013 (2007); Klass, Three Pictures of Contract: Duty, Power, and Compound Rule, 83 NYU L. Rev. 1726 (2008); Kordana & Tabachnick, Rawls and Contract Law, 73 Geo. Wash. L. Rev. 598 (2005); Oman, Consent to Retaliation: A Civil Recourse Theory of Contractual Liability, 96 Iowa L. Rev. 529 (2011); Shiffrin, Must I Mean What You Think I *Should* Have Said?, 98 Va. L. Rev. 159 (2012).

***§1.8 n.29 p.37 In the third sentence, add the following to the list after* "see":** Kraus, The Correspondence of Contract and Promise, 109 Colum. L. Rev. 1603 (2009); Pratt, Contract: Not Promise, 35 Fla. St. U.L. Rev. 801 (2008); Shiffrin, The Divergence of Contract and Promise, 120 Harv. L. Rev. 709 (2007).

§1.8 n.29 p.37 Add the following before the last sentence: On the effect Fried's work has had on contract theory (and an overview of contract theory generally), *see* Symposium, Contract as Promise at 30: The Future of Contract Theory, 45 Suffolk U.L. Rev. 601-978 (2012).

***§1.8 n.31 p.38 Add the following to the list after* "See also":** V. Goldberg, Framing Contract Law (2006); M. Kovac, Comparative Contract Law and Economics (2011).

§1.8 n.31 p.38 Add the following at the end: For an attempt to reconcile economic and deontological approaches to contract, *see* Zamir & Richman, Law, Morality, and Economics: Integrating Moral Constraints with Economic Analysis of Law, 96 Cal. L. Rev. 323 (2008). *See also* Oman, Markets as a Moral Foundation for Contract Law, 98 Iowa L. Rev. 183 (2012); Shavell, Is Breach of Contract Immoral?, 56 Emory L.J. 439 (2006).

§1.8a UNIDROIT PRINCIPLES OF INTERNATIONAL COMMERCIAL CONTRACTS

§1.8a n.1 p.38 Add the following to the list after **"See generally"**: Zimmermann, The Present State of European Private Law, 57 Am. J. Comp. L. 479 (2009); Zimmermann, The UNIDROIT Principles of International Commercial Contracts 2004 in Comparative Perspective, 21 Tul. Eur. & Civ. L.F. 1 (2006).

§1.8a p.39 Add the following at the end of the third sentence of the first full paragraph: . . . well received by arbitrators.[2a]

[2a] A recent review of cases on the UNILEX database shows hundreds of arbitral decisions that invoke the UNIDROIT Principles. They are seldom cited to by American courts, and then normally only in passing. *See, e.g.*, Chien v. Commw. Biotechnologies, 484 B.R. 659, (E.D. Va. 2012) (UNIDROIT Principles relied upon by plaintiff; court finds them unilluminating; collecting cases); Kyle Winnick, International Commercial Arbitration, Anticipatory Repudiation, and the Le Mercatoria, 15 Cardozo J. Conflict Resol. 847, 862 (2014) (collecting cases and concluding "Whether or not the CISG and/or UNIDROIT Principles are an articulation of the lex mercatoria and, thus, represent an 'international consensus,' is a question that myriad tribunals have answered in the affirmative.").

§1.8a n.4 p.39 Add the following at the end: See generally Reich, A European Contract Law: Ghost or Host for Integration?, 24 Wis. Int'l L.J. 425 (2006).

§1.8a n.8 p.40 Add the following at the end: See generally Bonell, Policing the International Commercial Contract Against Unfairness under the UNIDROIT Principles, 3 Tul. J. Int'l & Comp. L. 73 (1995).

§1.8a n.10 p.40 Add the following at the end: *See generally* Steven D. Walt, The Modest Role of Good Faith in Uniform Sales Law, 33 B.U. Int'l L.J. 37, 69 (2015) (criticizing the provision as "boilerplate" and ill-defined, and arguing that "Because UNCITRAL and UNIDROIT conventions must be interpreted autonomously, a good faith standard cannot be supplied by domestic legal terms and concepts. Nor does the good faith directive in the UNCITRAL and UNIDROIT conventions provide a principle of good faith by which contracting parties' performances can be measured.").

§1.9 UNIFORM COMMERCIAL CODE

***§1.9 n.1 p.42 In the last sentence of the first paragraph, add the following to the list after* "see":** B. Leiter, Naturalizing Jurisprudence (2007); Nyquist, Llewellyn's Code as a Reflection of Legal Consciousness, 40 New Eng. L. Rev. 419 (2006).

***§1.9 n.1 p.42 In the last sentence of the first paragraph, add the following to the list after the citation to* "Gedid, U.C.C. Methodology":** Grisé et al., Rudolf von Jhering's Influence on Karl Llewellyn, 48 Tulsa L. Rev. 93 (2012);

***§1.9 n.1 p.42 In the third paragraph, add the following to the list after* "See also":** Ribstein & Kobayashi, An Economic Analysis of Uniform State Laws, 25 J. Legal Stud. 131 (1996); Snyder, Clouds of Mystery: Dispelling the Realist Rhetoric of the Uniform Commercial Code, 68 Ohio St. L.J. 11 (2007).

***§1.9 p.43 In the first full paragraph, add the following to the second sentence after* "a few provisions of":** Article 3 on accord and satisfaction by check and

§1.9 p.43 In the second full paragraph, add the following at the end of the second sentence: . . . the Code's sponsors in 2001.[4a]

[4a] Article 1 has since been enacted in 43 states, with three more considering it in the 2013 legislative session.

§1.9 n.11 p.44 Add the following at the end: ; Symposium, Amended Article Two: Reversing the Curse?, 52 S. Tex. L. Rev. 471-614 (2011).

§1.9 p.45 Add the following at the end of the carryover sentence: . . . to neuter the gender.[13a]

[13a] Amended Article 2 has been enacted in no states. Indeed, it was introduced as a bill in very few, and in those met with much opposition. Accordingly, the National Conference of Commissioners on Uniform State Laws, with the agreement of the American Law Institute, has removed Amended Article 2 from its list of legislative priorities. Moreover, the amendments are no longer part of the official text of the Code. For a perhaps overoptimistic discussion of Amended Article 2's prospects and significance, *see* Symposium, Amended Article Two: Reversing the Curse?, 52 S. Tex. L. Rev. 471-614 (2011).

***§1.9 n.17 p.45 Add the following to the list after* "Accord":** Specialty Beverages, L.L.C. v. Pabst Brewing Co., 537 F.3d 1165 (10th Cir. 2008) ("In the UCC context, decisions from other jurisdictions are particularly persuasive due to the uniform nature of the UCC"); Purina Mills, L.L.C. v. Less, 295 F. Supp. 2d 1017 (N.D. Iowa 2003) (decisions from other jurisdictions are "instructive" and "authoritative"). Fariba v. Dealer Servs. Corp., 100 Cal. Rptr. 3d 219 (Ct. App. 2009) ("Case law from other jurisdictions applying California's Commercial Code, the Uniform Commercial Code, or the uniform code of other states, are considered good authority in litigation arising under the California act.");

§1.9 n.17 p.45 Add the following at the end: *Cf.* Arthur Glick Truck Sales v. Stuphen E. Corp., ___ F. Supp. 2d ___, 2012 WL 6592343 (S.D.N.Y. Dec. 18, 2012) (using decisions from other jurisdictions to help make an "*Erie* guess" on how New York's courts would read the UCC).

***§1.9 n.19 p.46 Add the following to the list after* "See":** First State Bank v. Clark, 635 N.W.2d 29 (Iowa 2001) (consulting history of UCC 9-306).

§1.9 n.19 p.46 Add the following to the end of the first sentence: ; HSBC Bank USA v. Thompson, 2010 WL 3451130 (Ohio App. Sept. 3, 2010) (consulting drafts of Article 3, as cited to by other court).

§1.9 n.23 p.47 Add the following to the list after **"Accord":** Jones v. Wells Fargo Bank, 666 F.3d 955 (5th Cir. 2012) (commentary "is an authoritative interpretation of the Code"); McCarthy v. BMW Bank of N. Am., 509 F.3d 528 (D.C. Cir. 2007) (comments "persuasive"); Strojny v. PermaDri, Inc., 78 UCC Rep. Serv. 2d 690 (D. Haw. Sept. 30, 2012) (comments "highly persuasive"); Intelogic Trace Texcom Grp. v. Merchs. Nat'l Bank, 626 N.E.2d 839 (Ind. App. 1993) (fn. 7: official comments "persuasive in interpreting the language of the Code"); Fisher Sand & Gravel Co. v. Neal A. Sweebe, Inc., 810 N.W.2d 277 (Mich. App. 2011) ("Although the official comments to the UCC do not have the force of law, they are useful aids to the interpretation and construction of the UCC."); Volvo Pers. Fin. v. Wells Fargo Bank, 163 P.3d 723 (Utah App. 2007) (comments "persuasive, but not controlling").

§1.9 n.24 p.47 Add the following to the list after the citation to **American Natl. Bank v. Tina Marie Homes:** American Ins. Co. v. Ohio Dep't of Admin. Servs., 778 N.E.2d 1135 (Ohio Ct. Cl. 2002) (comments "have not been enacted into law," so "the court may not refer to the comments under circumstances where the legislative intent is clear from the plain language of the statute");

§1.9a SCOPE OF CODE PROVISIONS

§1.9a n.1 p.48 Add the following at the end of the first sentence: ; Melson v. Traxler, 356 S.W.3d 264 (Mo. App. 2011) (using Code definitions in real property dispute; "While these definitions are found in Missouri's adaptation of the Uniform Commercial Code . . . , they are equally applicable to contracts that do not fall under the UCC.").

§1.9a n.2 p.48 Replace the citation to **Mieske v. Bartell Drug Co. with the following:** 593 P.2d 1308 (Wash. 1979).

§1.9a n.2 p.48 Add the following at the end: ; Estate of Kriefall v. Sizzler USA Franchise, 816 N.W.2d 853 (Wis. 2012) (Article 2 applies to restaurant franchisor's arrangements for its franchisees to buy meat).

§1.9a n.3 p.48 Add the following to the first sentence after "distinguished in": BMC Indus. v. Barth Indus., 160 F.3d 1322 (11th Cir. 1998) (contract to design and manufacture machinery within Article 2; contract allocated most of price to goods, and machinery was complete when it left the seller's plant) and in

§1.9a n.3 p.48 Add the following at the end: This opens the question whether a transaction is a sale. UCC 2-106 ("the passing of title from the seller to the buyer for a price"); UCC 2-304 (defining price). *See* Sec. Nat'l Bank v. Abbott Labs., 76 U.C.C. Rep. Serv. 2d 796 (N.D. Iowa 2012) (sale encompasses hospital getting samples of formula from manufacturer to be put into gift bags for new mothers); Pennsy Supply v. Am. Ash Recycling Corp., 895 A.2d 595 (Pa. Super. 2006) ("sale" encompasses exchange of goods for relieving seller of disposal costs). *Cf.* Cosy Goose Hellas v. Cosy Goose USA, Ltd., 581 F. Supp. 2d 606 (S.D.N.Y. 2008) (shoe importer not "buyer" for the purpose of creating the implied warranty of merchantability, UCC 2-314). Along similar lines, several provisions of the Code, including UCC 2-107 on goods to be severed from realty, refer specifically to a "contract for the sale of goods." *See* Epstein v. Coastal Timber Co., 711 S.E.2d 912 (S.C. 2011) (UCC 2-107 does not convert standing timber to goods in the absence of a contract for sale; a mortgage of property including standing timber thus need not satisfy Article Nine requirements for perfecting an interest in personal property).

§1.9a n.6 p.49 Add the following after the second sentence: *Foster* and *Hirschfeld* were in turn followed in TK Power, Inc. v. Textron, Inc., 433 F. Supp. 2d 1058 (N.D. Cal. 2006) (test for whether different bodies of law should be applied to different causes of action: "1. Whether the non-goods aspect of the

transaction is clearly distinct and easily separable from the goods aspect"; "2. Whether the alleged performance or non-performance pertains solely to the non-goods aspect of the transaction"; "3. Whether it makes sense to apply the UCC to the non-goods aspect of the transaction and whether applying non-UCC law accords with the parties' intent.").

§1.9a n.7 p.49 Insert the following in place of the citations to **Baker** *and* **Data Processing Servs.:** Insul-Mark Midwest, Inc. v. Modern Materials, Inc., 612 N.E.2d 550 (Ind. 1993) (adopting predominant thrust test because it "preserves parties' expectations regarding their agreement" and rejecting bifurcation because it "could lead to difficulties when the substantive issue at trial . . . is related to the enforceability of the agreement."), followed in Lamell Lumber Corp. v. Newstress Int'l, 938 A.2d 1215 (Vt. 2007);

§1.9a n.7 p.49 Add the following to the last sentence, before the citation to **Field:** C9 Ventures v. SVC-West, 136 Cal. Rptr. 3d 550 (Ct. App. 2012) (lease of helium-filled tanks predominantly a lease transaction, not a sales transaction, and thus was not governed by Article 2);

§1.9a n.8 p.50 In the first paragraph, add the following at the end of the third sentence: , distinguished in Bluefield Gas Co. v. Abbs Valley Pipeline, 76 U.C.C. Rep. Serv. 2d 540 (S.D.W. Va. 2012) (*Elkins Manor* decision "is limited solely to the application of the UCC to construction contracts"; court applies *Bonebrake* test to contract for sale of gas that included the building of a pipeline).

§1.9a n.8 p.50 Add the following at the end of the first paragraph: The ALI's recent project on software contracts adopts the predominant purpose test to determine what law governs mixed transactions in goods and embedded software. Principles of the Law of Software Contracts §1.07(a) & cmt. b (2010).

§1.9a n.8 p.50 In the second paragraph, add the following to the list after the citation to **"Coakley":** , followed in Trevillyan v. APX Alarm Sec. Sys., 2011 WL 11611 (D.S.C. Jan. 3, 2011) (contract

for alarm system not within Article 2; fees paid were for alarm services, not alarm equipment); C9 Ventures v. SVC-West, 136 Cal. Rptr. 3d 550 (Ct. App. 2012) (indemnification clause in invoice referred specifically to "the items rented," which points toward the application of UCC Article 2A rather than Article 2);

§1.9a n.8 p.50 ***In the second paragraph, add the following to the list after the second* "See":** Mecanique v. Durr Envt'l, 304 F. Supp. 2d 971 (S.D. Ohio 2004) (question is ordinarily one of fact for jury and burden of proof is on party who asserts that UCC governs).

§1.9a n.9 p.50 ***Add the following after the citation to* ITT:** , followed in Olé Mexican Foods v. Hanson Staple Co., 676 S.E.2d 169 (Ga. 2009) ("the parties' aim to settle [whether the goods were merchantable and fit for a particular purpose] creates strong doubt that the primary purpose of their agreement was a sale of goods subject to application of the same implied warranties of Article 2"); Golden v. Den-Mat Corp., 276 P.3d 773 (Kan. App. 2012) (applies predominant purpose test to contract between patient and dentist for whitening teeth; held that application of veneers was the predominant purpose of the transaction, so Article 2 applied); Aliki Foods v. Otter Valley Foods, 726 F. Supp. 2d 159 (D. Conn. 2010) ("If the 'dominant purpose' of the contract as a whole was for the sale of goods, then the entire agreement is governed by Article 2.");

§1.9a n.9 p.50 ***Delete the citation to* Brandt; *add the following after the citation to* Akrosil:** , followed in Double AA Builders v. Grand State Constr., 114 P.3d 835 (Ariz. App. 2005) ("Determining the predominant purpose of the contemplated contract is often a question of fact."); Lohman v. Wagner, 862 A.2d 1042 (Md. App. 2004) (applying Article 2 to agreement because "services were all incidental . . . and did not constitute the main thrust or predominant purpose of the agreement").

§1.9a n.10 p.51 ***Add the following to the list in the first sentence:*** Paramount Contracting Co. v. DPS Indus., 709 S.E.2d 288 (Ga. App. 2011) (contract to sell and haul dirt; worthwhile analysis of how the parties characterized the contract before litigation).

§1.9a n.10 p.51 Add the following after the citation to **"City of Lennox":** , followed in Blesi-Evans Co. v. W. Mech. Serv., 72 U.C.C. Rep. Serv. 2d 115 (D.S.D. 2010) (boilers)

§1.9a n.10 p.51 Add the following after the first paragraph: A similar rule applies when the choice is between Article 2 and federal maritime law. In a mixed transaction, maritime jurisdiction applies to the whole action only if "the contract is primarily maritime and the non-maritime elements of the contract are incidental to that primary purpose." In contrast. courts are willing to apply the gravamen test "if a contract's maritime obligations are separable from its non-maritime aspects and can be tried separately without prejudice to the other." Alphamate Commodity GmbH v. CHS Europe SA, 627 F.3d 183 (5th Cir. 2010).

§1.9a n.11 p.51 Add the following to the list in the first sentence: Crider, Inc. v. Keystone Foods, 75 U.C.C. Rep. Serv. 2d 856 (S.D. Ga. 2011) (contract for one chicken processor to process chickens for another not governed by Article 2; the overall purpose of the transaction was to cook chicken, not to sell it, and the contract refers to the agreement as for "supply, custom processing and contract packing," not for buying or selling); Bamcor LLC v. Jupiter Aluminum Corp., 767 F. Supp. 2d 959 (N.D. Ind. 2011) (contract to rebuild industrial equipment not within Article Two; the main tasks listed in the contract were services, and "the parts Bamcor had to purchase to complete these tasks were incidental to rebuilding the equipment"); Franklin Publ'ns v. Gen'l Nutrition Corp., 63 U.C.C. Rep. Serv. 2d 662 (S.D. Ohio 2007) (contract to publish and distribute magazines predominantly for the publisher's skill, judgment, and expertise, not for the physical magazines themselves, so contract not governed by Article 2); AES Puerto Rico, L.P. v. Alstom Power, Inc., 429 F. Supp. 2d 713 (D. Del. 2006) (contract to "furnish and construct two boilers and pollution control equipment" not within Article Two because it was not "primarily for the sale of goods"); Wall Street Network v. N.Y. Times Co., 80 Cal. Rptr. 3d 6 (Ct. App. 2008) (agreement to solicit newspaper subscriptions through Internet advertising not within Article Two; majority approach, with many illustrative cases); Brandt v. Boston Scientific Corp., 792 N.E.2d 296 (Ill. 2003) (following majority of jurisdictions that "hold that a

hospital's provision of a defective medical device is primarily a transaction for services"), erroneously followed in *In re* Yasmin & Yaz (Drospirenone) Mktg., Sales Practices & Prod. Liab. Litig., 692 F. Supp. 2d 1012 (S.D. Ill. 2010) (sale of prescription medication by pharmacy predominantly a services transaction, notwithstanding the substantially ministerial role played by the pharmacist), *aff'd on other grounds sub nom.* Walton v. Bayer Corp., 643 F.3d 994 (7th Cir. 2011); U.S. Neurosurgical v. St. Luke's Cancer Inst., 328 S.W.3d 234 (Mo. App. 2010) (supply of surgical equipment to hospital a lease, not a service transaction; were it otherwise, "it is likely that USN's compensation would have been based on the services rendered" rather than as a percentage of the take); Lamell Lumber Corp. v. Newstress Int'l, 938 A.2d 1215 (Vt. 2007) (contract for kiln: "the purchase and sale of the component materials . . . were incidental to the overall objective of designing, engineering, and erecting the kiln," so not within Article 2), followed in Openaire, Inc. v. L.K. Rossi Corp., 940 A.2d 724 (Vt. 2007) (contract to build swimming pool enclosure; "the contract included much more than simply the production of a specially manufactured good and the attachment of that good to the premises").

§1.9a n.11 p.51 Add the following after the citation to **"Kirkpatrick":** , followed in Janke v. Brooks, 77 U.C.C. Rep. Serv. 2d 352 (D. Colo. 2012) (Article 2 did not apply to contract to restore a classic auto; though the cost of the parts was a bit more than half of the cost, the "overarching purpose [was] to craft a wholly remodeled car")

§1.9a n.12 p.52 Add the following after the citation to **J.O. Hooker & Sons:** , followed by Peavey Elec. Corp. v. Baan U.S.A., 10 So. 3d 945 (Miss. App. 2009) (dispute as to the quality of services supplied with software governed by common law under the gravamen test).

§1.9a n.14 p.53 Add the following to the list: Leno v. K & L Homes, 803 N.W.2d 543 (N.D. 2011) (sale of home affixed to real property not within Article 2, even though the house may contain some goods); Jannusch v. Naffziger, 883 N.E.2d 711 (Ill. App. 2008) (sale of concession business: applies predominant purpose

test, and "significant tangible assets were involved in this case"); MBH, Inc. v. John Otte Oil & Propane, 727 N.W.2d 238 (Neb. App. 2007) (Article Two inapplicable when the majority of the purchase price is for non-goods and when "the heart of the contract is the goodwill and the real estate").

§1.9a n.15 p.53 Add the following to the list: Specialty Beverages, L.L.C. v. Pabst Brewing Co., 537 F.3d 1165 (10th Cir. 2008) (following majority; collecting cases), followed in Precision Fitness Equip. v. Nautilus, Inc., 73 U.C.C. Rep. Serv. 2d 699 (D. Colo. 2011) ("if the primary purpose of the Agreement at issue here was not the sale of Nautilus's goods, the Court is at a loss to determine what it might have been") but distinguished in Eureka Water Co. v. Nestle Waters N. Am., 690 F.3d 1139 (10th Cir. 2012) (supply of goods "only an incidental, and perhaps nonexistent . . . component of the contractual relationship"); Medline Indus. v. Ram Medical, 892 F. Supp. 2d 957 (N.D. Ill. 2012) (predominant purpose of distributorship contract "plainly relates to the sale of goods," so Article Two applies); Executone of Columbus v. Inter-Tel, Inc., 665 F. Supp. 2d 899 (S.D. Ohio 2009) (following majority); AutoChlor Sys. v. JohnsonDiversey, 328 F. Supp. 2d 980 (D. Minn. 2004) (following majority); East Hill Marine, Inc. v. Rinker Boat Co., 229 S.W.3d 813 (Tex. Civ. App. 2007) (following majority; collecting cases).

***§1.9a n.15 p.53 Add the following after the citation to* Watkins:** , distinguished in MidAmerican Distrib. v. Clarification Tech., 807 F. Supp. 2d 646 (E.D. Ky. 2011) (distributorship not within Article 2; unlike normal distributorships, here the seller contracts with the customer and then instructs the manufacturer to produce the product contracted for), *aff'd*, 485 Fed. Appx. 779 (6th Cir. 2012)

§1.9a n.16 p.54 Add the following to the list: Duncan Servs. v. ExxonMobil Oil Corp., 722 F. Supp. 2d 640 (D. Md. 2010) (somewhat questionably holding that Article Two applies to dispute regarding the assignability of franchise agreements); Wolverine World Wide v. Wolverine Canada, 653 F. Supp. 2d 747 (W.D. Mich. 2009) ("distributorship agreements lacking quantity terms do not constitute a contract for the sale of goods"); Carcorp, Inc. v. Chesrown Oldsmobile-GMC Truck, Inc., 823 N.E.2d 34 (Ohio App. 2004) (applying common law to sale of distributorship because "the substantial majority of items . . . are of an intangible and immovable character").

§1.9a n.16 p.54 ***Add the following at the end:*** *Cf.* Prima Int'l Trading v. Wyant, 68 U.C.C. Rep. Serv. 2d 279 (E.D. Ky. 2009) (equipment broker not liable for breach of express warranty because he did not own the equipment and thus was not a seller).

§1.9a n.17 p.54 ***Add the following after the first sentence:*** As to the inclusion of "specially manufactured goods," *see* Propulsion Techs. v. Attwood Corp., 369 F.3d 896 (5th Cir. 2004) (transaction is one in goods even if "production of goods is labor-intensive and the cost of goods is relatively inexpensive").

§1.9a n.17 p.54 ***Add the following after the second sentence:*** *Cf.* Singletary v. P & A Invs., 712 S.E.2d 681 (N.C. App. 2011) (mobile home a good unless so firmly rooted that it cannot be removed without material harm to the realty).

§1.9a n.18 p.54 ***Add the following to the beginning of the first sentence, replacing the word "See":*** *See* MWI Veterinary Supply Co. v. Wotton, ___ F. Supp. 2d ___, 2012 WL 4061222 (D. Idaho Sept. 14, 2012) (sale of firm's assets primarily sale of patent rights, which are intangibles not subject to Article Two); Lansing Trade Grp. v. OceanConnect, LLC, 77 U.C.C. Rep. Serv. 2d 966 (D. Kan. 2012) (renewable fuel identification numbers are "intangible rights . . . more properly categorized as choses (or things) in action"). *But*

§1.9a n.19 p.54 ***Correct the citation to* Keck *to read as follows:*** 830 So. 2d 1

§1.9a n.19 p.54 ***Add the following to the list in the final sentence:*** Hodges v. John F. Jenkins Contracting, 252 S.W.3d 152 (Ark. App. 2007) (distinguishing contract to sell unsevered dirt, which would be within Article 2, with contract to sever the dirt, which was not).

§1.9a n.20 p.54 Add the following at the end of the third sentence: , regrettably reaffirmed in Lezell v. Forde, 891 N.Y.S.2d 606 (Sup. Ct. Kings Cnty. 2009) (shares in a cooperative apartment governed by Article Two). It is difficult to see why this type of transaction should be governed by Article Two, when other methods of transferring interests in real property quite plainly are not.

***§1.9a n.22 p.55 Delete the citation to* Encogen Four Partners.**

***§1.9a n.22 p.55 Add the following to the list after* "Cf.":** Exelon Corp. v. Dep't of Revenue, 917 N.E.2d 899 (Ill. 2009) (for the purposes of personal property taxation, electricity is tangible personal property).

§1.9a n.22 p.55 Add the following before the second-to-last sentence: *Cf. In re* Pilgrim's Pride Corp., 397 B.R. 828 (Bankr. N.D. Tex. 2009) (electricity is not a good, but gas and water are), disagreed with in GFI Wis. v. Reedsburg Utility Comm'n, 440 B.R. 791 (W.D. Wis. 2010) (electricity is a good, because it moves, it occupies space, it can be handled, it can be stored, and it is not merely a medium of delivering something else; "For the purpose of determining administrative priority under the Bankruptcy Code, the meaning of 'good' should not depend on quantum physics . . .").

***§1.9a n.22 p.55 Add the following to the list after* "See generally":** Stuart, Electricity and UCC Article 2: A Regulatory and Contractual Pyramid of Mismatched Liabilities, 40 UCC L.J. 217 (2007).

§1.9a n.23 p.55 Add the following to the list in the second sentence: Dealer Mgmt. Sys. v. Design Auto. Grp., 822 N.E.2d 556 (Ill. App. 2005) ("courts have generally recognized that computer software qualifies as a 'good' for purposes of the UCC"), followed in Bruel & Kjaer v. Village of Bensenville, 969 N.E.2d 445 (Ill. App. 2012) (contract to supply radar systems was for provision of goods, even though it entailed providing some original software).

§1.9a n.23 p.55 ***Add the following after the second sentence:*** *Cf.* Dechert LLP v. Com., 998 A.2d 575 (Pa. 2010) (mass-market software considered personal property for the purposes of sales tax).

§1.9a n.23 p.55 ***Add the following at the end of the fifth sentence:*** ; Princeton Healthcare Sys. v. Netsmart N.Y., 29 A.3d 361 (N.J. Super. App. Div. 2011) (distinguishing between mass-market software and custom-made software for the purpose of determining the scope of the New Jersey Consumer Fraud Act).

§1.9a n.23 p.55 ***Add the following at the end:*** A recently completed ALI project on software contracting distinguishes among embedded software, software that accompanies goods, and free-standing software. The first is governed by goods law if the goods aspect predominates; the second's software component, but not its goods component, would be within the scope of the project; and the last would be within the scope of the project. Principles of the Law of Software Contracts §§1.06-1.08 (2010).

§1.9a n.24 p.56 ***Correct the cross-reference as follows:*** note 3 to §1.9 *supra*.

§1.9a n.32 p.57 ***Add the following after the first sentence:*** For criticism of UCC 2-725, *see* Garvin, Uncertainty and Error in the Law of Sales: The Article Two Statute of Limitations, 83 B.U. L. Rev. 345 (2003).

§1.9a n.33 p.57 ***Add the following to the beginning of the first sentence:*** B & B Hardware v. Fastenal Co., 688 F.3d 917 (8th Cir. 2012) (contract to supply fasteners was for sale, not brokerage; "the agreement repeatedly refers to Fastenal's duty to 'purchase' goods from B & B and 'resell' them to third party customers");

§1.9b UNITED NATIONS CONVENTION ON CONTRACTS FOR THE INTERNATIONAL SALE OF GOODS

§1.9b n.6 p.60 ***Replace the text of the footnote with the following:*** The Vienna sales convention has now been adopted by more than 75 countries, including Argentina, Australia, Austria, Brazil, Canada, Chile, China, Colombia, the Czech Republic, Denmark, Ecuador, Egypt, Finland, France, Germany, Greece, Honduras, Hungary, Iraq, Israel, Italy, Japan, Mexico, the Netherlands, New Zealand, Norway, Poland, Romania, Russia, Singapore, South Korea, Spain, Sweden, Switzerland, Turkey, Ukraine, the United States, Uruguay, and Zambia. It has not yet been adopted by India or the United Kingdom.

§1.9b n.7 p.60 Replace the citation to Schlechtriem with the following: Commentary on the UN Convention on the International Sale of Goods (CISG) (P. Schlechtriem & I. Schwenzer eds., 2d English ed. 2005).

§1.9b n.7 p.60 Add the following to the list in the second sentence: Schwenzer & Hachem, The CISG — Successes and Pitfalls, 57 Am. J. Comp. L. 457 (2009).

§1.9b n.7 p.60 Add the following at the end: For assessments of how the United States has dealt with CISG, *see* Reimann, The CISG in the United States: Why It Has Been Neglected and Why Europeans Should Care, 71 Rabels Zeitschrift für Ausländisches und Internationales Privatrecht 115 (2007); Note, The Development of a Federal CISG Common Law in U.S. Courts: Patterns of Interpretation and Citation, 61 U. Miami L. Rev. 509 (2007); Survey, Global Sales Law: An Analysis of Recent CISG Precedents in U.S. Courts, 2004-2012, 67 Bus. Law. 1351 (2012). For a somewhat jaundiced view of the enterprise, *see* Cuniberti, Is the CISG Benefiting Anybody?, 39 Vand. J. Transnat'l L. 1511 (2006). For a look at its fit with the UNIDROIT Principles, *see* Bonell, The CISG, European Contract Law and the Development of a World Contract Law, 56 Am. J. Comp. L. 1 (2008). *Cf.* Hondius, CISG and a European Civil Code: Some Reflexions, 71 Rabels Zeitschrift für Ausländisches und Internationales Privatrecht 99 (2007). On the borderline between CISG and domestic law, *see* Lookofsky, Not Running Wild With the CISG, 29 J.L. & Com. 141 (2011).

§1.9b n.8 p.61 Add the following at the end: *See* Prime Start Ltd. v. Maher Forest Prods. Ltd., 442 F. Supp. 2d 1113 (W.D.

Wash. 2006) ("Because not all parties are from countries that signed the CISG, the CISG cannot apply to this dispute").

§1.9b n.9 p.61 Add the following at the end of the first sentence: , distinguished in Caterpillar, Inc. v. Usinor Industeel, 393 F. Supp. 2d 659 (N.D. Ill. 2005) (CISG does not preempt state law for suit between buyer's subsidiary and seller, because by its terms CISG applies only to contracts between buyer and seller).

§1.9b n.9 p.61 Add the following at the end: *Accord:* Forestal Guarani, S.A. v. Daros Int'l, 67 U.C.C. Rep. Serv. 2d 18 (D.N.J. 2008); Geneva Pharm. Tech. Corp. v. Barr Labs., 201 F. Supp. 2d 236 (S.D.N.Y. 2002), *aff'd in part and rev'd in part on other grounds*, 386 F.3d 485 (2d Cir. 2004); Mitchell Aircraft Spares v. Eur. Aircraft Serv. AB, 23 F. Supp. 2d 915 (N.D. Ill. 1998). CISG, like Article 2, does not occupy the field of sales law, so some questions in CISG cases will be governed by the sales law or the general contract law of the relevant jurisdiction. *See* CISG 4 (CISG does not apply to "the validity of the contract or of any of its provisions or of any usage" or "the effect which the contract may have on the property in the goods sold"). *See also* U.S. Nonwovens Corp. v. Nuspark Eng'g, Inc., 4 N.Y.S.3d 868 (2015) ("The CISG is a self-executing treaty that preempts contrary provisions of Article 2 of the UCC and other state contract law to the extent that those causes of action fall within the scope of the CISG. Outside the scope of the CISG, otherwise applicable state law governs the dispute") (citing U.S. Const., Art. VI; Medellin v. Texas, 552 U.S. 491, 504-05, 128 S. Ct. 1346, 170 L. Ed. 2d 190 (2008), American Mint LLC v. GOSoftware, Inc., No. 1:05-cv-650, 2005 U.S. Dist. LEXIS 45003, 2005 WL 2021248, at *2-3 (M.D. Pa. Aug. 16, 2005) (noting that if the CISG applies to the contract at issue, it will preempt domestic sale laws that otherwise would govern the contract), and Caterpillar Inc. v. Usinor Industeel, 393 F.Supp.2d 659, 676 (N.D. Ill. 2005)).

§1.9b n.10 p.61 Add the following at the beginning: *See* CISG Advisory Council, Opinion No. 4: Contracts for the Sale of Goods to be Manufactured or Produced and Mixed Contracts (Article 3 CISG), 17 Pace Int'l L. Rev. 79 (2005).

§1.9b n.10 p.61 ***Add the following at the end:*** The issue seems not to have arisen in U.S. courts. *See* S.r.l. Orintix v. NV Fabelta Ninove, No. 1998/AR/2613 (App. Ct. Nov. 24, 2004) (Belg.) (available at http://cisgw3.law.pace.edu/cases/041124b1.html) (looks to relative value of goods and services to determine whether whole contract falls under CISG). A related problem arises when one looks at non-privity actions. If the contract between seller and buyer is subject to domestic law, but the contract between buyer and sub-buyer is subject to CISG, what body of law governs a direct action by the sub-buyer against the seller? *See* Carette, Direct Contractual Claim of the Sub-Buyer and International Sale of Goods: Applicable Law and Applicability of the CISG, 16 Eur. Rev. Private L. 583 (2008).

§1.9b p.62 ***Add the following to the end of the first full sentence of the carryover paragraph:*** . . . injury (CISG 5).[12a]

[12a] Nor has CISG been held to include distributorship or franchise agreements, in contrast to most of the decisions under Article 2. *See* Gruppo Essenziero Italiano v. Aromi D'Italia, 2011 WL 3207555 (D. Md. July 27, 2011); Multi-Juice, S.A. v. Snapple Beverage Corp., 2006 WL 1519981 (S.D.N.Y. June 1, 2006); Amco Ukrserv. v. Am. Meter Co., 312 F. Supp. 2d 681 (E.D. Pa. 2004);Viva Vino Import Corp. v. Farnese Vini S.r.l., 2000 WL 1224903 (E.D. Pa. Aug. 29, 2000) (CLOUT No. 420).

§1.9b p.63 ***Add the following at the end of the carryover sentence from p.62:*** . . . a New York court.[13]

[13] *See* BP Oil Int'l v. Empresa Estatal Petroleos de Ecuador, 332 F.3d 333 (5th Cir. 2003) (contract states that law of Ecuador applies; "Given that the CISG *is* Ecuadorian law, a choice of law provision designating Ecuadorian law merely confirms that the treaty governs the transaction."); Microgem Corp. v. Homecast Co., 2012 WL 1608709 (S.D.N.Y. Apr. 27, 2012) ("Stating only that a contract will be governed by a particular jurisdiction's laws is generally insufficient to opt out of the CISG when the CISG has been incorporated into that jurisdiction's laws."); Easom Automation Sys. v. Thyssenkrupp Fabco, 64 U.C.C. Rep. Serv. 2d 106 (E.D. Mich. 2007) (parties specified "laws of Canada"; CISG applies, "as the Convention is the law of Canada"); Travelers Prop. Cas. Co. v. Saint-Gobain Technical Fabrics Can. Ltd., 474 F. Supp. 2d 1075 (D. Minn. 2007) ("shall be governed by the laws of the State of Minnesota" failed to exclude CISG; "absent an express statement that the CISG does not apply, merely referring to a particular state's law does not opt out of the CISG"); American Mint LLC v. GOSoftware, Inc., 2006 WL 42090 (M.D. Pa. Jan. 6, 2006); Valero Mktg. & Supply Co. v. Greeni

Oy, 373 F. Supp. 2d 475 (D.N.J. 2005), *rev'd on other grounds*, 242 Fed. Appx. 840 (3d Cir. 2007)); *cf.* Asante, *supra* note 9 (choice of laws of British Columbia insufficient to displace CISG). *See generally* Johnson, Understanding Exclusion of the CISG: A New Paradigm of Determining Party Intent, 59 Buff. L. Rev. 213 (2011).

The symmetric case — opting out of domestic law and into CISG — seems not to have been litigated in the United States. There the main issue would be whether CISG was an appropriate body of law for a contract not otherwise subject to it. If the parties to a contract can choose as their governing law the contract rules of an arbitral body or of a trade association, it would seem logical that they could choose any other body of law instead, whatever the source might be — CISG, the Restatement Second, the UNIDROIT Principles, the *lex talionis*, the customary law of the Lower Snodsbury piepowder court in 1432. It is possible to fall into a body of law by a sort of estoppel; if the parties to a contract litigate as though one source of law governs their relations, there comes a point at which it becomes too late for one of them to have a juridical epiphany and invoke the one true law. *See* Ho Myung Moolsan Co. v. Manitou Mineral Water, 73 U.C.C. Rep. Serv. 2d 313 (S.D.N.Y. 2010) (parties litigated as though New York's domestic law governed their action all the way to a pretrial order, so neither could suddenly insist on litigating under CISG).

§1.10 ADAPTABILITY OF CONTRACT LAW

***§1.10 n.2 p.64 Add the following to the list after* "See also":** Smith v. Anderson, 632 F.3d 277 (6th Cir. 2011) (applying parol evidence rule to plea agreement); United States v. Gibson, 530 F.3d 606 (7th Cir. 2008) (contract to commit murder); Parrish v. Brownlee, 335 F. Supp. 2d 661 (E.D.N.C. 2004) (ROTC enlistment); Kashmiri v. Regents of Univ. of Cal., 67 Cal. Rptr. 3d 635 (Ct. App. 2007) (implied, though unenforceable, contract created by university catalogue and website); T.F. v. B.L., 813 N.E.2d 1244 (Mass. 2004) (implied agreement by domestic partner to act as parent in exchange for mother's conceiving and bearing child); Reid v. McLeary, 706 N.Y.S.2d 179 (App. Div. 2000) (contract to get married); Gallagher Headquarters Ranch Dev. v. City of San Antonio, 269 S.W.3d 628 (Tex. Civ. App. 2008) ("contract with the voters" limiting local government uses of voted taxes and resulting purchases), *review granted and judgment vacated pursuant to settlement agreement*, No. 08-0773 (Tex. Jun. 18, 2010); Jud. Inquiry & Rev. Comm'n v. Elliott, 630 S.E.2d 485

(Va. 2006) (supervision agreement between judge and Judicial Inquiry & Review Commission).

***§1.10 n.2 p.64 Add the following to the list after* "But cf.":** Tran v. State Sys. of Higher Educ., 986 A.2d 179 (Pa. Commw. 2009) (student handbook for state university not a contract; "[r]ather, the Handbook set forth the administrative procedures and remedies available").

***§1.10 n.2 p.64 In the final sentence, add the following to the list after* "see":** Bibas, Regulating the Plea-Bargaining Market: From Caveat Emptor to Consumer Protection, 99 Cal. L. Rev. 1117 (2011); Cicchini, Broken Government Promises: A Contract-Based Approach to Enforcing Plea Bargains, 38 N.M. L. Rev. 159 (2008).

§1.10 n.2 p.64 Add the following at the end: *Cf.* Puckett v. United States, 129 S. Ct. 1423 (2009) (Scalia, J.) ("Although the analogy may not hold in all respects, plea bargains are essentially contracts."); United States v. Heatley, 39 F. Supp. 2d 287 (S.D.N.Y. 1998) (Sotomayor, J.) ("a defendant's rights are grounded in more than contract, and thus contract principles, while useful, do not completely define the obligations of the parties"); People v. Alfaro, 896 N.E.2d 1077 (Ill. App. 2008) ("Plea agreements are governed to some extent by principles of contract law, keeping in mind that the 'contract' right is constitutionally based and reflects concerns that are fundamentally different from and wider than those of commercial contract law.").

***§1.10 n.11 p.66 Add the following to the last sentence after* "See":** Note, eBay Sellers and Article 2: Selling a Broader Merchant Concept, 56 Case W. Res. L. Rev. 1199 (2006).

§1.10 n.11 p.66 Add the following at the end: As to the desirability of a contract law for firms, *see* Schwartz & Scott, Contract Theory and the Limits of Contract Law, 113 Yale L.J. 541 (2003). As to the desirability of a contract law for small firms, see Garvin, Small Business and the False Dichotomies of Contract Law, 40 Wake Forest L. Rev. 295 (2005).

§1.10 n.12 p.66 Add the following to the list after the first **"Accord":** *In re* Montagne, 431 B.R. 94 (Bankr. D. Vt. 2010) (a couple, as dairy farmers, were merchants with respect to the purchase of goods in connection with the operation of their dairy farm);

§1.10 n.12 p.66 Add the following to the list after the citation to **Currituck Grain:** Brooks Cotton Co. v. Williams, 381 S.W.3d 414 (Tenn. Civ. App. 2012) (farmer may be merchant if the farmer has sufficient expertise in the sale of crops, not just the growing of crops);

§1.10 n.12 p.66 Add the following to the list after the second **"Accord":** R.F. Cunningham & Co. v. Driscoll, 790 N.Y.S.2d 368 (City Ct. 2005) (farmer "is experienced in the selling of his grain products and therefore has the necessary knowledge and skill" to be a merchant).

§1.10 n.14 p.67 Add the following to the list after **"But cf.":** Mfrs. & Traders Trust Co. v. Malick, 857 N.Y.S.2d 350 (App. Div. 2008) (silent partner in auto dealership who routinely used dealer plates not a merchant for the purposes of her purchase of a personal vehicle).

§1.10 n.26 p.69 Add the following to the list after **"Accord":** Gallagher v. S. Source Packaging, 564 F. Supp. 2d 503 (E.D.N.C. 2008) (using UCC 2-210 to help resolve whether anti-assignment clause should be enforced); Estate of Polushkin *ex rel.* Polushkin v. Maw, 170 P.3d 162 (Alaska 2007) (applying UCC 2-208 by analogy to settlement agreement for oil spill damages); Murray, Under the Spreading Analogy of Article 2 of the Uniform Commercial Code, 39 Fordham L. Rev. 447 (1971).

§1.10 n.26 p.69 Add the following to the third sentence after the citation to **Whitney Bros.:** Belmont Ptnrs. v. China YiBai United Guar. Int'l Holding, 73 U.C.C. Rep. Serv. 2d 753 (W.D. Va. 2011) (applying Article 2 damage rules to sale of securities);

***§1.10 n.26 p.69 Add the following to the third sentence after the citation to* J.L. Teel Co.:** Melson v. Traxler, 356 S.W.3d 264 (Mo. App. 2011) (using Code definitions in real property dispute; "While these definitions are found in Missouri's adaptation of the Uniform Commercial Code . . . , they are equally applicable to contracts that do not fall under the UCC.");

PART II

ENFORCEABILITY OF PROMISES

CHAPTER 2

CONSIDERATION AND OTHER GROUNDS FOR RECOVERY

§2.2 THE BARGAIN TEST OF CONSIDERATION

§2.2 n.1 p.77 ***Add the following after the first sentence:*** *Accord:* Margeson v. Artis, 776 N.W.2d 652 (Iowa 2009) ("it has been an essential part of the development of our contract law . . . that contract law exists to enforce mutual bargains, not gratuitous promises") (citing to treatise) (noting as well that "the enforceability of some promises has proven malleable as courts and scholars have rethought the theoretical underpinnings of the element of consideration") (citing to treatise).

§2.2 n.2 p.78 ***Add the following to the list after "See also":*** Cohen, The Basis of Contract, 46 Harv. L. Rev. 553, 575-78 (1932).

§2.2 n.4 p.78 ***Add the following to the list after "See generally":*** Pretorius, The Basis of Contractual Liability in American Law, 37 Comp. & Int'l L.J. of S. Afr. 226 (2004).

§2.2 n.6 p.78 ***Add the following at the end:*** The promisee must establish the existence of consideration or a substitute as part of its case-in-chief, as is true of any other element of its cause of action. In some jurisdictions, this proof is eased by the

presumption that written contracts are supported by consideration. *See* Frequent Flyer Depot v. Am. Airlines, 281 S.W.3d 215 (Tex. Civ. App. 2009).

§2.2 n.9 p.79 Add the following at the end: For an example, *see* Laredo Coca-Cola Bottling Co. v. Combs, 317 S.W.3d 735 (Tex. Civ. App. 2010) (court found no benefit or detriment where agreement required that customer purchase minimum quantity of syrup, carbon dioxide, and cups from bottler, because price unchanged and bottler applied alternative remedy if minimum not met). The court's benefit-detriment analysis is a little strained, to be sure. But this is an easy bargain case, because minimum purchase agreements are routinely the subject of bargain and because alternative performances can provide consideration if the alternatives would each provide consideration. *See infra* §2.15.

***§2.2 n.11 p.79 Add the following to the list after* "See":** Teeven, The Advent of Recovery on Merchant Transactions in the Absence of a Bargain, 39 Am. Bus. L.J. 289 (2002).

§2.3 WHAT CAN CONSTITUTE CONSIDERATION

§2.3 n.1 p.80 Add the following after the first sentence: Ind. Dep't of State Revenue v. Belterra Resort Ind., 935 N.E.2d 174 (Ind. 2010) (although no consideration given for conveyance of riverboat, consideration present because the transactions associated with its conveyance "were so interdependent that it is unreasonable to conclude that any of the transactions would have been undertaken except with a view to completing the whole series of transactions"), *aff'd on rehearing*, 942 N.E.2d 796 (Ind. 2011).

§2.3 n.2 p.80 Add the following to the first sentence: Thiesing v. Dentsply Int'l, 748 F. Supp. 2d 932 (E.D. Wis. 2010) (Minnesota law: "a promise is not rendered unenforceable by the fact that part of the consideration for it is invalid"; cites to Restatement Second §80(2)); Gen. Elec. Capital Corp. v. Transp. Logistics Corp., 893 A.2d 467 (Conn. App. 2006) (mix of past and future consideration sufficient to enforce guaranty).

*§2.3 n.4 p.80 **Add the following to the list after*** **"Accord"*:*** *In re* Marriage of Tabassum & Younis, 881 N.E.2d 396 (Ill. App. 2007) (refraining from filing divorce petition consideration for post-marital agreement); Midwest Land Inv. Co. v. Veach, 135 P.3d 1263 (Kan. App. 2006) (giving up right to bid on property consideration); Pulley v. Short, 261 S.W.3d 701 (Mo. App. 2008) ("The mutual waiver of rights to the other spouse's assets is sufficient consideration to support an antenuptial agreement.").

*§2.3 n.6 p.80 **Add the following to the first sentence:*** A promise is sufficient even if the promisor silently intended to fulfill the promise only under certain conditions. Trans-Western Petroleum, Inc. v. United States Gypsum Co., 830 F.3d 1171, 2016 U.S. App. LEXIS 13561 (10th Cir. 2016) ("Consideration does not require an actual payment, only a promise to pay." Claim that one party "intended to obtain a legal opinion about the status of the Trans-Western lease before he paid . . . does not change the draft's validity or obviate Trans-Western's promise to pay.").

*§2.3 n.6 p.80 **Add the following at the end:*** For an unusual application, *see* United States v. Gibson, 530 F.3d 606 (7th Cir. 2008) (promise to commit murder; for purposes of federal' murder-for-hire statute, 18 U.S.C. §1958(a), consideration requires "that the murder must have been solicited in exchange for something of pecuniary value," here a promised share of profits from drug proceeds).

*§2.3 n.8 p.81 **In the first paragraph, add the following to the list in the first sentence:*** Thompson v. Allstate Ins. Co., 673 S.E.2d 227 (Ga. 2009) (insured's release of her own claims could serve as consideration for insurer's payment to husband of the liability limits for his bodily injury claim); Wyatt v. Pezzin, 589 S.E.2d 250 (Ga. App. 2003) (purchase of property from owner's son consideration for option contract covering owner's adjoining property); Meincke v. Nw. Bank & Trust Co., 756 N.W.2d 223 (Iowa 2008) (bank making additional loans to business owned by daughter and nephew consideration for mother's/aunt's entering into a subordination agreement).

***§2.3 n.8 p.81 In the first paragraph, add the following to the list after* "See also":** Sterling Sav. Bank v. JHM Props., 717 F. Supp. 2d 1142 (D. Or. 2010) ("Sterling's agreement as the lender to extend future credits and loans to JHM, the debtor, requires no further consideration for the [guaranty] to be effective.").

§2.3 n.8 p.81 In the second paragraph, add the following to the list in the third sentence: United States v. Morrison, 28 So. 3d 94 (Fla. App. 2009) (consideration found where bank agreed to a mortgage with a married couple; wife bound, even though she neither received nor used any of the loan proceeds).

§2.4 EXAMPLE OF CONSIDERATION

§2.4 n.9 p.84 Add the following to the list in the third sentence: Swimelar v. Baker (*In re* Baker), 604 F.3d 727 (2d Cir. 2010) (citing to *Hamer* in support of its holding that settlement of a wrongful death claim provides consideration for an annuity contract).

§2.4 n.9 p.84 Add the following at the end: *Cf.* Price v. Taylor, 575 F. Supp. 2d 845 (N.D. Ohio 2008) ("Valid consideration requires that the parties bargain for performances or return promises. . . . Valid consideration may consist of either a benefit to the promisor or a detriment to the promisee."); Steiner v. Thexton, 226 P.3d 359 (Cal. 2010) ("It is not enough . . . to confer a benefit or suffer prejudice for there to be consideration. . . . the second requirement is that the benefit or prejudice must actually be bargained for as the exchange for the promise."); Davis v. Paepke, 3 So. 3d 131 (Miss. App. 2009) (invoking both bargained-for exchange and benefit-detriment approaches, but ultimately applying benefit-detriment); McLellan v. Charly, 758 N.W.2d 94 (Wis. App. 2008) ("Consideration may be either a benefit to the promisor or a detriment to the promisee. . . . In either case, the benefit or the detriment must be bargained for."). The courts that require both benefit or detriment and bargain over-egg the pudding. There are agreements that satisfy only one of these two tests, a good many of which are routinely enforced — including by courts in the jurisdictions above.

§2.4 n.10 p.85 Add the following to the list in the second sentence: Barfield v. Commerce Bank, 484 F.3d 1276 (10th Cir. 2007) (consideration in exchange of small bills for large; "Consideration does not need to have a quantifiable financial value"); Pennsy Supply v. Am. Ash Recycling Corp., 895 A.2d 595 (Pa. Super. 2006) (consideration in promise to supply unwanted ash free of charge in order to avoid paying disposal costs).

§2.4 n.10 p.85 Add the following to the list after **"But cf.":** Smith v. Wachovia Bank, 33 So. 3d 1191 (Ala. 2009) (wife's exercise of power of attorney not consideration for the granting of the power of attorney).

§2.4 n.11 p.85 Add the following to the list after **"See generally":** Gamage & Kedem, Commodification and Contract Formation: Placing the Consideration Doctrine on Stronger Foundations, 73 U. Chi. L. Rev. 1299 (2006).

§2.5 EXCHANGE LACKING: GRATUITOUS PROMISES

§2.5 n.2 p.86 Add the following after the first sentence: *See also* Estate of Tahilan v. Friendly Care Home Health Servs., 731 F. Supp. 2d 1000 (D. Haw. 2010) (promise to forgive loan upon death is a gift *causa mortis* rather than a contract).

§2.5 n.6 p.87 Add the following to the list after **"See also":** Prentice, "Law &" Gratuitous Promises, 2007 U. Ill. L. Rev. 881; Wessman, Recent Defenses of Consideration: Commodification and Collaboration, 41 Ind. L. Rev. 9 (2008).

§2.5 n.7 p.87 Replace the cross-reference in the last sentence with the following: §2.18a *infra*.

§2.7 PAST CONSIDERATION

§2.7 n.1 p.90 Add the following after the second sentence: But see Taylor v. Univ. of the Cumberlands, 2017 U.S. Dist. LEXIS 17005 (E.D. Ky. Feb. 7, 2017) (language in agreement that the employer "agree[s] that the compensation and benefits contained in this agreement is/are for the past decades of duties and/or work performed" did not render the agreement invalid as based on past consideration where the agreement contained other promises (such as to work for the employer until he decided to retire), and moreover, the language and past actions of unusually successful fundraising for the employer also suggests indebtedness, which would be valid consideration and subject to the business judgment rule).

§2.7 n.1 p.90 Add the following to the list after the third sentence: Take It Away v. Home Depot, 374 Fed. Appx. 47 (1st Cir. 2010) (Souter, J., sitting by designation) (no consideration for confidentiality agreement when secret disclosed before agreement entered into); Blackmon v. Iverson, 324 F. Supp. 2d 602 (E.D. Pa. 2003) (past acts of friendship and disclosure of marketing idea not consideration for basketball star's promise of royalties); Bratton v. Bratton, 136 S.W.3d 595 (Tenn. 2004) (wife's promise to forgo career as dentist was not consideration for postnuptial agreement because she had already reached this decision at time of marriage), followed in Barton v. Sclafani Invs., 320 S.W.3d 453 (Tex. Civ. App. 2010) (work performed before sale of real estate not consideration for agreement to pay commission in sales document, because there was no agreement before the work was done that the broker would receive a commission); Simmons v. Simmons, 249 S.W.3d 843 (Ark. App. 2007) ("an existing marriage is past consideration and will not support a postnuptial agreement"); Jackson v. Luellen Farms, 877 N.E.2d 848 (Ind. App. 2007) (surety unsupported by consideration of promise to pay past debt of another).

Heather Mills, the ex-wife of Sir Paul McCartney, allegedly told her publicist that she could not afford to pay her full usual fee, so would pay a smaller amount and would "take care of you when I get the big money." Parapluie v. Mills, 555 Fed. Appx. 679,

682, 2014 U.S. App. LEXIS 2808 (9th Cir. 2014). The Ninth Circuit held that there was insufficient evidence that the statements about being unable to pay more were false when she uttered them, at 681 ("Mills's $30,000 charity bid on a cruise in March 2007 might create a genuine issue of triable fact, except that Mills's credit card payment for the cruise was declined"), and further held that the promise was "too vague to support a concrete promise to pay," at 682.

§2.8 MORAL OBLIGATION

§2.8 n.1 p.92 Add the following to the third sentence: Konica Minolta Bus. Solutions v. Allied Office Prods., 724 F. Supp. 2d 861 (S.D. Ohio 2010) ("a note given as security for an antecedent debt is sufficient consideration to establish a valid obligation under a promissory note") (internal quotation marks omitted); Branch Banking & Trust Co. v. Morrison, 661 S.E.2d 784 (N.C. App. 2008) (grant of credit consideration for both the debtor's obligation to pay back the debt and the guarantor's obligation to pay on a defaulted obligation; irrelevant that credit provided before guaranty executed, as long as part of the same transaction); Jackson v. Luellen Farms, 877 N.E.2d 848 (Ind. App. 2007) (earlier consideration effective if "(1) The guaranty was executed pursuant to an understanding had before and was an inducement to the execution of the principal contract; or (2) The guaranty was delivered before any obligation or liability was incurred under the principal contract; or (3) The guaranty was made pursuant to a contract provision; or (4) The principal contract does not become operative until the execution of a guaranty; or (5) The guaranty expressly refers to a previous agreement between the principal debtor and creditor which is executory in its character and embraces prospective dealings between the parties.").

§2.8 n.17 p.95 Add the following at the end: See Dess Props. v. Sheridan Truck & Heavy Equip., 185 P.3d 1113 (Or. App. 2008) (following Restatement Second; defining void contracts as "agreements actually entered into that are unenforceable by reason of their failure to comply with some other legal requirement").

§2.8 n.24 p.97 Add the following at the end: For a more theological vantage, see Pryor, Consideration in the Common Law of Contracts: A Biblical-Theological Critique, 18 Regent U.L. Rev. 1 (2005-2006).

§2.8 n.29 p.98 Add the following to the list after* "See generally"*: Teeven, Moral Obligation Promise for Harm Caused, 39 Gonzaga L. Rev. 349 (2003/04).

§2.8 n.30 p.99 Add the following to the end of the first sentence: ; *see* United Res. Recovery Corp. v. Ramko Venture Mgmt., 584 F. Supp. 2d 645 (S.D.N.Y. 2008) (requirements of §5-1105 not met when consideration recited is vague and meaningless); Braka v. Travel Assistance Int'l, 807 N.Y.S.2d 372 (App. Div. 2006) (applying §5-1105 to written promise to repay costs of air evacuation).

§2.8 n.36 p.100 Add the following as a second paragraph: In Baxter v. Wing, 2016 Ark. App. 589 (2016), the decedent left a will providing for equal distribution of his estate among four stepchildren, but additionally purchased a life insurance policy that named only one of them as the sole beneficiary. He reportedly had asked that beneficiary to share it with the other stepchildren, but only after he had taken out the policy and there was no evidence that he secured a promise from her to follow his wishes. The Arkansas Court of Appeals held that "his instructions do not constitute an oral contract," and noted that "even if Susannah had a moral obligation to do what her stepfather asked of her, she did not have a legal obligation to do so under the facts of this case."

§2.9 UNSOLICITED ACTION

§2.9 n.2 p.101 Add the following to the list after* "Accord"*: Blackmon v. Iverson, 324 F. Supp. 2d 613 (E.D. Pa. 2003) ("no allegation that the move was required in exchange for any promise by the defendant to pay," so no consideration); Weed v. Weed, 968 A.2d 310 (Vt. 2008) (caretaking by son and daughter-in-law not consideration for transfer of real property; "There is no indication in the record that either party regarded the caretaking as consideration, or that [the mother] transferred the Enosburg land to [the son and daughter-in-law] in exchange for their caretaking."), distinguished by Ferrisburgh Realty Invs. v. Schumacher, 992 A.2d 1042 (Vt. 2010) (promise to execute prior financing agreement consideration where prior agreement oral and thus unenforceable unless reduced to writing).

§2.9 n.6 p.103 Add the following at the end: On the problems arising from continued at-will employment as consideration, see §2.10a *infra*.

***§2.9 n.7 p.104 Add the following to the list after* "See":** Carey v. FedEx Ground Package Sys., 321 F. Supp. 2d 902 (S.D. Ohio 2004) (as in Williston's example of the tramp, plaintiff "established the existence merely of a conditional gratuitous promise"); Carlisle v. T & R Excavating, Inc., 704 N.E.2d 39 (Ohio App. 1997) (giving Williston's example; "a condition for a promise. . . . does not induce the promise, is not bargained for, and is not reasonably understood as consideration").

***§2.9 n.7 p.104 Add the following to the list after* "But see":** Dorman v. Publix-Saenger-Sparks Theatres, Inc., 184 So. 886 (Fla. 1938) (distinguishing Williston's tramp hypothetical; registration and presence at theatre were consideration for lottery prize).

§2.9 n.8 p.105 Add the following at the end: This issue arises when open-source software is transferred. By itself, the transfer would seem purely donative. If, however, the transferor requires that the transferee do "more than is necessary to transfer a gift," such as provide source code, agree to maintenance services, or distribute derivative software on the same terms as the original software, then the transfer is supported by consideration. *See* Principles of Software Contracts §1.06 cmt. d & rptrs. Notes cmt. d (2010). *See also* Jacobsen v. Katzer, 535 F.3d 1373 (Fed. Cir. 2008) ("The lack of money changing hands in open source licensing should not be presumed to mean that there is no economic consideration, however. There are substantial benefits, including economic benefits, to the creation and distribution of copyrighted works under public licenses that range far beyond traditional license royalties. For example, program creators may generate market share for their programs by providing certain components free of charge. Similarly, a programmer or company may increase its national or international reputation by incubating open source projects. Improvement to a product can come rapidly and free of charge from an expert not even known to the copyright holder. . . . The choice to exact consideration in the form of compliance with the open source requirements of disclosure and explanation of changes, rather than as a dollar-denominated fee, is entitled to no less legal recognition.").

§2.9 n.9 p.105 ***Add the following at the end:*** On its history, *see* Casto & Ricks, "Dear Sister Antillico . . .": The Story of *Kirksey v. Kirksey*, 94 Geo. L.J. 321 (2006).

§2.9 n.11 p.105 ***Add the following after the fourth sentence:*** *But cf.* Estate of Shapiro v. United States, 634 F.3d 1055 (9th Cir. 2011) ("homemaking services can be adequate consideration for a property-sharing agreement between cohabitants"); Estate of Fallon v. Fallon, 30 So. 3d 1281 (Miss. App. 2010) ("It cannot reasonably be argued that love and affection cannot serve as sufficient consideration to support a conveyance by deed."); Williams v. Ormsby, 944 N.E.2d 699 (Ohio App. 2010), *appeal allowed*, 941 N.E.2d 803 (Ohio 2011) ("moving into a home with another and resuming a relationship can constitute consideration sufficient to support a contract"). The holding in *Estate of Fallon* is, perhaps fortunately, dictum; the court held that a writing that recites consideration is presumed to have it, and the party challenging consideration failed to produce contrary evidence. The quote from *Williams v. Ormsby* is, alas, holding, not dictum. But the Ohio Supreme Court has sensibly granted review of this decision, which casts considerable doubt upon its survival.

§2.9 n.11 p.105 ***Add the following at the end:*** *See generally* Keren, Considering Affective Consideration, 40 Golden Gate U.L. Rev. 165 (2010).

§2.9 n.13 p.106 ***Add the following at the start:*** *Cf.* Samra v. Shaheen Bus. & Inv. Grp., 355 F. Supp. 2d 483 (D.D.C. 2005) (intent of promisor to make gratuitous promise irrelevant, if promisor required or accepted consideration in exchange for it).

§2.9 p.106 In the first paragraph, add the following at the end of the second sentence: . . . assumes that it was part of a bargain.[13a]

[13a] The reverse is also true. *See* Barnes v. Michalski, 925 N.E.2d 323 (Ill. App. 2010) ("The law presumes a gift if someone transfers property to his or her spouse or family member . . . but not if someone transfers property to a friend. . . . If someone writes a friend a check, the law presumes the check is not a gift but the payment of an antecedent debt.").

§2.10 ACTION NOT TAKEN IN RESPONSE

§2.10 n.1 p.107 Add the following to the list after* "See also"*: Young v. Allstate Ins. Co., 198 P.3d 666 (Haw. 2008) (insured agreed not to seek counsel and insurer pledged to handle insured's claim fairly, but insurer's promise was not conditioned upon the insured's pledge).

§2.10 n.4 p.108 Add the following after the reference to* Schlesinger *in the second paragraph: *See also* Lerner, Promises of Rewards in a Comparative Perspective, 10 Ann. Surv. Int'l Comp. L. 53 (2004).

§2.10 n.6 p.109 Add the following after the first sentence: *Accord:* Vanegas v. Am. Energy Servs., 302 S.W.3d 299 (Tex. 2009) ("[A]ny promise to pay sale or merger proceeds became an enforceable unilateral contract when the employees performed.").

§2.10 n.10 p.109 In the first paragraph, add the following to the list after* "Accord"*: Cobaugh v. Klick-Lewis, Inc., 561 A.2d 1248 (Pa. Super. 1989) (finding consideration where golfer knew of offer to award car "to anyone who made a hole-in-one at the ninth hole" before hitting hole-in-one).

§2.10 n.10 p.109 In the third paragraph, add the following to the list after* "Accord"*: Aon Risk Servs. v. Meadors, 267 S.W.3d 603 (Ark. App. 2007) (employee who began brokering a deal before learning of an offered bonus accepted the offer by completing the deal).

§2.10a EMPLOYER HANDBOOKS

§2.10a n.1 p.110 Add the following after the second sentence: The current draft of the Restatement (Third) of Employment Law adopts at-will employment as the default rule. Restatement (Third) of Employment Law §2.01 (T.D. No. 2, Apr. 3, 2009).

§2.10a n.3 p.111 In the first paragraph, add the following to the list after **"see"*:*** Peters v. Gilead Scis., 533 F.3d 594 (7th Cir. 2008) (Indiana law: although not clear whether employment handbook's provisions "may be enforceable as a contract under Indiana law[,] at the least, they are promises giving rise to recovery under promissory estoppel.").

§2.10a n.3 p.111 Add the following to the list after **"Contra"*:*** DeFranco v. Storage Tech. Corp., 622 F.3d 1296 (10th Cir. 2010) (Colorado law: claim that promissory estoppel supports permanent employment available only if special consideration or an express stipulation as to the length of employment; court does not discuss the incongruity of requiring special consideration when promissory estoppel is largely a substitute for consideration); Balmer v. Elan Corp., 599 S.E.2d 158 (Ga. 2004) (no promissory estoppel "where the promise relied upon was for employment for an indefinite period"); Ross v. May Co., 880 N.E.2d 210 (Ill. App. 2007) (no expectation of reasonable reliance on manager's promises of discharge only for cause "where disclaimers in every handbook plaintiff received since 1990 contained an explicit disclaimer informing employees that the only person who could alter their at-will employment status was the senior vice president of human resources").

§2.10a n.3 p.111 Add the following at the end: The Restatement (Third) of Employment Law provides that promissory estoppel is a means for altering the at-will employment relation. Restatement (Third) of Employment Law §2.02(b) (T.D. No. 2, Apr. 3, 2009).

§2.10a n.4 p.112 Add the following after the first sentence: *Accord:* Parrish v. Valero Retail Holdings, 727 F. Supp. 2d 1266 (D.N.M. 2010) ("The bargained-for exchange is the offer of employment in exchange for signing an agreement to participate in the [arbitration] plan.").

§2.10a n.4 p.112 Add the following at the end: It follows that the employer may not unilaterally modify the terms of a contract thus created without providing consideration. Ross v. May Co., *supra* note 3 (continued employment insufficient to support modification of handbook; consequence would have been to change discharge only for cause to at-will employment).

§2.10a n.7 p.112 Add the following to the list in the first sentence: DeFranco v. Storage Tech. Corp., 622 F.3d 1296 (10th Cir. 2010) (Colorado law: forgoing the opportunity to look for other jobs not special consideration); Turner v. Newsom, 3 So. 3d 913 (Ala. Civ. App. 2008) (accepting promotion not relinquishment sufficient to constitute independent consideration).

§2.10a n.15 p.115 Add the following to the list in the first sentence: Guz v. Bechtel Nat'l, 8 P.3d 1089 (Cal. 2000) ("employee's mere passage of time in the employer's service . . . cannot atone for an implied-in-fact contract that the employee is no longer at will"), distinguished by McCollum v. xCare.net, 212 F. Supp. 2d 1142 (N.D. Cal. 2002) (invoking *Guz* dictum that "the covenant [of good faith and fair dealing] might be violated if termination of an at-will employee was a mere pretext to cheat the worker out of another contract benefit to which the employee was clearly entitled"); Morrow v. Hallmark Cards, 273 S.W.3d 15 (Mo. App. 2008) ("[I]n these cases, the courts generally, we submit, fail to see that at-will employment does not provide legal consideration . . . a term or condition of employment ends when the employment ends."), in turn followed in Frye v. Speedway Chevrolet Cadillac, 321 S.W.3d 429 (Mo. App. 2010) ("the mere continuation of at-will employment provided no consideration for [the employees'] waiver of the right to access to the courts").

§2.10a n.16 p.115 Add the following to the list: Kauffman v. Int'l Bhd. of Teamsters, 950 A.2d 44 (D.C. 2008) ("neither party to at-will employment is bound to continue performance, and thus courts properly view future performance by each as valid consideration for the change in terms"), followed in Baldonado v. Wynn Las Vegas, LLC, 194 P.3d 96 (Nev. 2008) ("the employee's continued employment constitutes sufficient consideration for the modification"); Melena v. Anheuser-Busch, Inc., 847 N.E.2d 99 (Ill. 2006) ("continued employment is sufficient consideration for the enforcement of employment agreements"); Brown v. Louisville Jefferson County Redev. Auth., 310 S.W.3d 221 (Ky. App. 2010) (no additional reciprocal consideration needed for promise of continued employment; continued work sufficient); LeMaitre v. Mass. Turnpike Auth., 876 N.E.2d 888 (Mass. App. 2007) (following *Pine River*), *vacated and remanded on other grounds*, 897 N.E.2d 1218 (Mass. 2008), distinguished by Day v. Staples, Inc., 555 F.3d 42 (1st Cir. 2009) (did not follow *LeMaitre* because the handbook at issue expressly stated that it was "not a contract of employment"); Vanegas v. Am. Energy Servs., 302 S.W.3d 299 (Tex. 2009) ("[A]ny promise to pay sale or merger proceeds became an enforceable unilateral contract when the employees performed.").

§2.10a n.16 p.115 Add the following after the citation to **Duldulao***:* distinguished by Ross v. May Co., *supra* note 3 (no consideration for continued employment when employee could be discharged only for cause) and by Stoll v. United Way, 883 N.E.2d 575 (Ill. App. 2008) (memorandum of understanding between employer and union created no enforceable rights for employee).

§2.10a n.16 p.115 Add the following at the end: Indeed, one study found that 38 states recognize some form of implied contract claim based on employer representations. Walsh & Schwarz, State Common Law Wrongful Discharge Doctrines: Update, Refinement, and Rationales, 33 Am. Bus. L.J. 645 (1996).

Consistent with the requirements of mutual assent, though, the employee needs some opportunity to consider whether to remain employed before continued employment will amount to acceptance. *See* Kauffman v. Int'l Bhd. of Teamsters, *supra*. As a corollary to this, modifications to the employment relation are prospective only. *See* Gebhardt v. Time Warner Entertainment-Advance/Newhouse, 726 N.Y.S.2d 534 (App. Div. 2001) ("Although plaintiff was an at-will employee, defendant nevertheless was entitled to change the terms of the employment agreement only prospectively, subject to plaintiff's right to leave the employment if the new terms were unacceptable.").

§2.10a n.20 p.116 Add the following at the end: The *Toussaint* rationale has been linked to the importance of preserving relational contracts. Bird, Employment as a Relational Contract, 8 U. Pa. J. Lab. & Emp. L. 149 (2005).

§2.10a n.24 p.117 Add the following after the citation to **Rowe***:* Mannix v. County of Monroe, 348 F.3d 526 (6th Cir. 2003) (an expressly at-will employment relation may not "be turned into a just-cause relationship by no more than a legitimate expectation on the part of the employee," citing *Toussaint* to that effect), distinguished by Horton v. 48th Dist. Ct., 446 F. Supp. 2d 756 (E.D. Mich. 2006) (handbook, unlike that in *Mannix*, inexplicit in its attempt to reserve the right to terminate employment at will, and thus may have created a legitimate expectation of discharge only for just cause).

§2.10a n.24 p.117 Add the following to the list after **"See"***:* Slawson, Unilateral Contracts of Employment: Does Contract Law Conflict With Public Policy, 10 Tex. Wesleyan L. Rev. 9 (2003).

§2.10a n.24 p.117 Add the following before the last sentence: That it is possible to make a traditional unilateral employment contract in Michigan, *see* Sniecinski v. Blue Cross & Blue Shield, 666 N.W.2d 186 fn. 9 (Mich. 2003) ("generally employment contracts are unilateral").

§2.10a n.25 p.118 Add the following at the end: The Restatement (Third) of Employment Law follows *Toussaint* as well. Restatement (Third) of Employment Law §2.04 & rptr. cmt. b (T.D. No. 2, Apr. 3, 2009).

§2.10a n.26 p.118 Add the following to the list after **"Accord"***:* Caley v. Gulfstream Aerospace Corp., 428 F.3d 1359 (11th Cir. 2005) (Georgia law; consideration where employer "can modify the [arbitration agreement] only upon notice and is bound by the [arbitration agreement] in effect at the time it receives a claim"), declined to follow in Morrow v. Hallmark Cards, 273 S.W.3d 15 (Mo. App. 2008) (arbitration clause unenforceable when employer could modify it retroactively and without notice), in turn followed in Frye v. Speedway Chevrolet Cadillac, 321 S.W.3d 429 (Mo. App. 2010) (clause might be

acceptable if prospective and effective only upon advance notice, but here the clause "***does not*** require Speedway to provide its employees any ***advance*** notice of an amendment" and thus is illusory) (emphasis in original) and declined to follow in Soto v. State Indus. Prods., 642 F.3d 67 (1st Cir. 2011) (continued employment after agreement to arbitrate "sufficient consideration to render the agreement enforceable"); Douglass v. Pflueger Hawaii, 135 P.3d 129 (Haw. 2006) (clause in arbitration agreement allowing the employer to modify it without notice "renders the purported arbitration agreement illusory"), distinguished by Vickery v. Hastert, 201 P.3d 628 (Haw. 2009) (*Douglass* distinguishable because it "concerned arbitration agreements that were not part of a larger contract, whereas the arbitration provision in this case was part of the Agreement"); Sisneros v. Citadel Broad. Co., 142 P.3d 34 (N.M. App. 2006) ("Citadel gives up its right to change or terminate its agreement to arbitrate disputes upon accrual of an employee's claim. This constitutes consideration . . ."); *In re* Halliburton Co., 80 S.W.3d 566 (Tex. 2002) (arbitration agreement enforceable because of required ten-day notice to amend and the inapplicability of changes to disputes of which Halliburton had notice at the time of amendment), distinguished by Morrison v. Amway Corp., 517 F.3d 248 (5th Cir. 2008) (arbitration clause unenforceable where no limits on Amway's ability to amend, in particular "no *Halliburton* type savings clauses which preclude application of such amendments to disputes which arose (or of which Amway had notice) before the amendment"), by *In re* Datamark, Inc., 296 S.W.3d 614 (Tex. Civ. App. 2009) (arbitration clause unenforceable where employer can modify it at any time without notice, as long as modification in a signed writing), and by *In re* Bunzi USA, 155 S.W.3d 202 (Tex. Civ. App. 2004) (unlike the agreement in *Halliburton*, this agreement did not specify that "employment is contingent upon the Agreement, nor does it provide that employment constitutes acceptance of the Agreement."), but followed in *In re* Polymerica, LLC, 296 S.W.3d 74 (Tex. 2009) (enforcing arbitration clause where may be changed, but only upon giving notice to employees and only prospectively).

§2.10a n.26 p.118 Add the following at the end: The most recent draft of the new Restatement on employment law adopts this approach. Restatement (Third) of Employment Law §2.05(a) (T.D. No. 2, Apr. 3, 2009).

Modification of employee manuals became especially important after Supreme Court cases upholding mandatory arbitration agreements against claims of unconscionablility or the vindication of rights doctrine, see §4.28 note 52 *infra*, as employers sought to create or modify a delegation clause for current employees. *See, e.g.*, Davis v. Nordstrom, Inc., 755 F.3d 1089, 1094 (9th Cir. 2014) (holding that arbitration agreement met "minimal requirements under California law for providing employees with reasonable notice of a change to its employee handbook by sending a letter to Davis and other employees informing them of the modification, and not seeking to enforce the arbitration provision during the 30 day notice period"), citing, Schachter v. Citigroup, Inc., 218 P.3d 262 (Cal. 2009) (continuing employment after notice constitutes acceptance of new terms).

§2.10a n.27 p.119 Add the following to the list: DeArmond v. Halliburton Energy Servs., 81 P.3d 573 (N.M. App. 2003) (distinguishing decisions holding employees bound when they continued to work after receiving arbitration agreements on ground that they acknowledged looking at what they received).

§2.10a n.27 p.119 Add the following as a second paragraph: When the New York University School of Medicine began requiting medical faculty to generate external funding sufficient to cover 60% of the portion of their salary allocated to research or face salary cuts, some faculty brought suit alleging this was inconsistent with the concept of tenure and in violation of the Faculty Handbook. Their suit was initially dismissed by the lower court, which relied on New York precedent that "Routinely issued employee manuals, handbooks and policy statements should not lightly be converted into binding employment agreements . . . upon the mere allegation of reliance on a particular provision." Matter of Monaco v. New York Univ. & N.Y. Univ. Sch. of Med., 18 N.Y.S.3d 580 (N.Y. Sup. Ct. 2015), quoting Lobosco v. NY Tel. Co./NYNEX, 96 N.Y.2d 312, 317 (N.Y. 2001). Moreover, the faculty relied upon the definition of tenure as guaranteeing "freedom of research and economic security," although there was no provision specifically addressing diminutions in salary. But the

Appellate Division reversed, holding that "[f]or the purpose of surviving respondents' cross motion to dismiss, petitioners . . . have sufficiently alleged that the policies contained in respondent's Faculty Handbook, which 'form part of the essential employment understandings between a member of the Faculty and the University,' have the force of contract. Further, for the purposes of surviving respondents' cross motion to dismiss, petitioners have sufficiently alleged that they had a mutual understanding with respondent that tenured faculty members' salaries may not be involuntarily reduced," (citing *see* O'Neill v New York Univ., 97 A.D.3d 199, 208-10, 944 N.Y.S.2d 503 [1st Dep't 2012]).

§2.10a n.28 p.119 Add the following after the citation to **Asmus***:* , distinguished in McCaskey v. Cal. State Auto Ass'n, 118 Cal. Rptr. 3d 34 (Ct. App. 2010) (no power to terminate unilaterally right to reduced sales quotas at different levels of seniority; promise was for definite period, and proposed termination was before benefit had taken effect).

§2.10a n.29 p.120 Add the following to the list after **"But cf."***:* Quiles v. Financial Exchange Co., 879 A.2d 281 (Pa. Super. 2005) ("without receipt or delivery of the Handbook which was the only document containing the relevant arbitration provisions, Quiles was unable to knowingly and voluntarily waive all other means of dispute resolution"), distinguished by Lynn v. Gen. Elec. Co., 407 F. Supp. 2d 1257 (D. Kan. 2006) (employee had adequate notice of the arbitration agreement where included in separation agreement and available on employer's website).

§2.10b EMPLOYEE COVENANTS

§2.10b n.1 p.121 Add the following to the list after **"See generally"***:* Lord, The At-Will Relationship in the 21st Century: A Consideration of Consideration, 58 Baylor L. Rev. 707 (2006); Note, Where Have You Gone, Law and Economics Judges? Economic Analysis Advice to Courts Considering the Enforceability

of Covenants Not to Compete Signed After At-Will Employment Has Commenced, 66 Ohio St. L.J. 1105 (2005).

§2.10b n.2 p.121 Add the following at the end: Labriola v. Pollard Grp., Inc., 100 P.3d 791 (Wash. 2004) ("consideration exists if the Employee enters into a noncompete agreement when he or she is first hired."). For an interesting variation, *see* Trilogy Software, Inc. v. Callidus Software, Inc., 143 S.W.3d 452 (Tex. Civ. App. 2004) (no consideration for nondisclosure agreement executed at time of hiring, even though there would have been immediately upon starting work).

§2.10b n.3 p.121 Add the following to the list in the first sentence: Mayer Hoffman McCann, P.C. v. Barton, 614 F.3d 893 (8th Cir. 2010) (stock buy-back agreement consideration for noncompete covenant); Access Organics v. Hernandez, 175 P.3d 899 (Mont. 2008) ("The non-compete agreement is simply a condition of employment which the employee takes into account when accepting or rejecting the employment offer."); Wright v. Sports Supply Grp., 137 S.W.3d. 289 (Tex. Civ. App. 2004) (in return employer undertook "to provide confidential information and training and . . . did so").

§2.10b n.3 p.121 Add the following to the list after **"But cf.":** Glisson v. Global Sec. Servs., 653 S.E.2d 85 (Ga. App. 2007) (continued employment not consideration for covenant not to compete because employer already obliged to employ the worker; "a promise to perform a preexisting contractual obligation does not constitute consideration for a new agreement").

§2.10b n.3 p.121 Add the following at the end: As with other promises, the courts do not look to the adequacy of the consideration, but rather only that it was new, separate, and bargained-for. *See* Hejl v. Hood, Hargett & Assocs., 674 S.E.2d 425 (N.C. App. 2009) (upholding three-year non-compete agreement procured for consideration of $500).

Massachusetts has an interesting variation on this theme. Whenever there is a material change in the job such that the employer and employee have entered into a new employment relation, the old covenant is considered abandoned and rescinded and the employer must secure a new restrictive covenant. F.A. Bartlett Tree Expert Co. v. Barrington, 233 N.E.2d 756 (Mass. 1968) (salesman to district sales manager; employer proffered new contract, which employee did not sign), followed in AFC Cable Sys. v. Clisham, 62 F. Supp. 2d 167 (D. Mass. 1999) (sales consultant to sales manager; changes in remuneration, sales area, and responsibilities; employer proffered new agreement, which employee did not sign) and distinguished by Astro-Med, Inc. v. Nihon Kohden Am., 591 F.3d 1 (1st Cir. 2009) ("job change from product specialist to district sales manager does not reflect a mutual abandonment and rescission of the non-competition provision," given absence of intent to revoke or supersede the prior relation and failure to proffer new agreement); Scafuri v. Lumenis, Ltd., 831 N.E.2d 959 (Mass. App. 2005) (CEO to COO; employer refused to sign changed agreement proffered by employee).

§2.10b n.5 p.122 Add the following to the list after **"But cf.":** Ikon Office Solutions v. Am. Office Prods., 178 F. Supp. 2d 1154 (D. Or. 2001) (seventeen days was too long since no published Oregon case has enforced a covenant "signed more than three days after the employee commenced work or was promoted"), *aff'd*, 61 Fed. Appx. 378 (9th Cir. 2003).

§2.10b n.5 p.122 Add the following at the end: These timing issues also arise in determining the exact time of promotion; if the promotion precedes the covenant, then, as with these other cases, the promotion could not provide consideration for the covenant. *See* Softchoice, Inc. v. Schmidt, 763 N.W.2d 660 (Minn. App. 2009) (promotion effective, not "when an employee is informally told that he has been selected for promotion," but "when the terms of the promotion have been defined and the promotion has been formally offered and accepted in writing.").

§2.10b n.6 p.122 Add the following at the end: *But see* Thiesing v. Dentsply Int'l, 748 F. Supp. 2d 932 (E.D. Wis. 2010) (Minnesota law: "had he not signed the Employment Agreement, Thiesing would have lost his job, which . . . indicates that the agreement was not bargained for"). This flagrantly misreads Minnesota law. Continued employment, with no more, does not yield

consideration, true. But when coupled with a threat of discharge, continued employment clearly is consideration. Nor is the court correct to state that because the threat of discharge was made *en masse*, that it was not bargained for. There was no negotiation, but bargained-for exchange does not require actual negotiation, nor has it ever. Perhaps it is just as well that this is a diversity decision from an out-of-state court and hence of no precedential value. (And ultimately the court concludes that the covenant is enforceable, so justice was done between the parties.).

§2.10b n.7 p.122 Add the following to the list in the first sentence: Piano v. Premier Distrib. Co., 107 P.3d 11 (N.M. App. 2004) (arbitration agreement signed after employment began was illusory if no additional consideration); Franco v. Liposcience, Inc., 676 S.E.2d 500 (N.C. App.) ("additional agreements must be supported by consideration," and "mere continued employment by the employee is insufficient"; anti-retaliation letter secured by father in exchange for father's agreement not to sue employer for his own discharge also not consideration, even though forbearance from suit is consideration in the context of debtor-creditor contracts; "Though in general, employment contracts are guided by the general principles of contract, we decline to extend the principles from the debtor cases . . . to defeat the application of the at-will doctrine here."), *aff'd per curiam*, 686 S.E.2d 152 (N.C. 2009), distinguished in Elliott v. Enka-Candler Fire & Rescue Dep't, ___ S.E. 2d ___, 2011 WL 2732244 (N.C. App. July 5, 2011) (additional consideration required, but present here where employee gave up right to leave at any time in exchange for employment for a term); Labriola v. Pollard Grp., Inc., *supra* note 2, (no consideration where employee "received no additional benefits" for signing the noncompete agreement).

§2.10b n.7 p.122 Replace the citation to* Poole *in the first sentence with the following: Poole v. Incentives Unlimited, 548 S.E.2d 207 (S.C. 2001) ("when a covenant is entered into after the inception of employment, separate consideration, in addition to continued at-will employment, is necessary for the covenant to be enforceable").

§2.10b n.7 p.122 Add the following after the citation to **Gibson***:* , followed in Morrow v. Hallmark Cards, 273 S.W.3d 15 (Mo. App. 2008) (non-mutual arbitration clause unenforceable where sole basis for consideration the continued offer of employment; distinguishing arbitration from covenants not to compete because the latter "are more about equity than about contracts" and have as consideration the employee's continued access to protected assets and relationships).

§2.10b n.8 p.123 In the first sentence, delete the citation to **Canter** *and add the following to the list:* Lake Land Emp't Grp. v. Columber, 804 N.E.2d 27 (Ohio 2004) ("subsequent employment alone [is] sufficient consideration to support a covenant not to compete"), followed in Summits 7, Inc. v. Kelly, 886 A.2d 365 (Vt. 2005) ("[C]ontinued employment alone is sufficient consideration to support a covenant not to compete entered into during an at-will employment relationship.") and extended in Whisman v. Ford Motor Co., 157 Fed. Appx. 792 (6th Cir. 2005) (applying *Lake Land* reasoning to changes in overtime and annual incentive policies).

§2.10b n.8 p.123 Add the following to the list in the first sentence: Lucht's Concrete Pumping v. Horner, 255 P.3d 1058 (Colo. 2011) ("an employer's forbearance of the right to terminate an existing at-will employee constitutes adequate consideration to support a noncompetition agreement"); Access Organics v. Hernandez, *supra* note 3 (where noncompete signed four months after employment began, the initial offer was past consideration; "Non-compete agreements entered into by existing employees may be supported by independent consideration."); Alex Sheshunoff Mgmt. Serv. v. Johnson, 209 S.W.3d 644 (Tex. 2006) (requiring that employer's consideration "give rise to the employer's interest in restraining the employee from competing"; promise to disclose confidential information and provide specialized training adequate to support nondisclosure covenant), followed in Mann Frankfort Stein & Lipp Advisors v. Fielding, 289 S.W.3d 844 (Tex. 2009) (client purchase clause "was designed to hinder Fielding's ability to use the confidential information to compete against Mann Frankfort" and so was ancillary to or part of the otherwise enforceable agreement), interpreted by

Valley Diagnostic Clinic, P.A. v. Dougherty, 287 S.W.3d 151 (Tex. Civ. App. 2009) (*Sheshunoff* held that "[a] compensation provision made only in exchange for a non-compete promise is precisely the sort of restraint of trade that Texas law prohibits" and that non-compete agreements must be ancillary to an already enforceable agreement) and in Vanegas v. Am. Energy Servs., 302 S.W.3d 299 (Tex. 2009) (offer to enter into unilateral contract may give rise to enforceable obligation if supported by consideration at time of enforcement, even if in at-will employment context; promise by corporation to provide bonuses to workers who remained with corporation until sold thus enforceable, even though unsupported by consideration when made), itself followed in Mendez v. New Bell Gen. Servs., 727 F. Supp. 2d 585 (W.D. Tex. 2010) (upholding arbitration clause added to contract by employer; even though illusory when made, promise ultimately supported by provision of benefits to worker), and distinguished by Powerhouse Prods. v. Scott, 260 S.W.3d 693 (Tex. Civ. App. 2008) (offer of work in position already long-held did not constitute new consideration for a non-compete agreement and thus did not satisfy *Sheshunoff*'s test).

§2.10b n.8 p.123 Add the following after the citation to* Curtis 1000*: , followed in Bires v. WalTom, LLC, 662 F. Supp. 2d 1019 (N.D. Ill. 2009) (less than one year employment after restrictive covenant insufficient consideration).

§2.10b n.8 p.123 Add the following at the end: Some states have made a showing of additional consideration a statutory requirement for a noncompete agreement to be enforced after employment has started. *See* Nike, Inc. v. McCarthy, 379 F.3d 576 (9th Cir. 2004) (construing Oregon statute requiring "subsequent bona fide advancement"). In contrast, the current Restatement project allows continued employment alone to serve as consideration for a noncompete agreement. Restatement (Third) of Employment Law §6.05 (P.D. No. 2, May 17, 2004).

§2.11 PEPPERCORNS AND PRETENSE OF BARGAIN

***§2.11 n.2 p.124 In the second paragraph, add the following to the list after* "See":** Brown & Brown, Inc. v. Mudron, 887 N.E.2d 437 (Ill. App. 2008) ("even a peppercorn of consideration is sufficient to support a finding of adequate consideration"); Currid v. Meeting House Rest., Inc., 869 A.2d 516 (Pa. Super. 2005) (finding lack of "a peppercorn").

§2.11 n.2 p.124 In the second paragraph, add the following at the end: *See generally* Comment, 97 Nw. U. L. Rev. 1809 (2003).

§2.11 n.3 p.125 Add the following to the list at the end: Quilling v. Trade Ptnrs., 572 F.3d 293 (6th Cir. 2009) ("valuable consideration"); Wallace v. Frontier Bank, N.A., 903 So. 2d 792 (Ala. 2004) ("adequate consideration"); Harley v. Indian Spring Land Co., 3 A.3d 992 (Conn. App. 2010) ("adequate consideration"); Glisson v. Global Sec. Sys., 653 S.E.2d 85 (Ga. App. 2007) ("valuable consideration" and "sufficient consideration"); Justad v. Ward, 211 P.3d 118 (Idaho 2009) ("sufficient consideration"); Melena v. Anheuser-Busch, 847 N.E.2d 99 (Ill. 2006) ("sufficient consideration"); Bank of N.Y. v. Nally, 820 N.E.2d 644 (Ind. 2005) ("valuable consideration"); Cannon v. Cannon, 865 A.2d 563 (Md. 2005) ("sufficient consideration" and "valuable consideration"); Weaver v. Harpster, 975 A.2d 555 (Pa. 2009) ("adequate consideration"); Hall v. Prosero, Inc., 774 S.E.2d 216 (Ga. App. 2015) (finding purchase of stock for $1.25 per share to constitute "full consideration" because, at time of purchase, the stock held at least nominal market value of $0.01 per share).

***§2.11 n.4 p.125 Add the following to the list after* "see":** Sirius LC v. Erickson, 244 P.3d 224 (Idaho 2010) (" 'this Court will not inquire into the adequacy of consideration as bargained for by parties to an agreement' so long as some consideration is provided") (quoting from Boise Tower Assocs. v. Hogland, 215 P.3d 494 (Idaho 2009); McLellan v. Charly, 758 N.W.2d 94 (Wis. App. 2008) ("courts are not concerned with the adequacy of consideration")).

§2.11 n.4 p.125 Add the following at the end: Factors outside contract law may, however, oblige a court to look at the adequacy of consideration, not merely its presence. *See* Turken v. Gordon, 224 P.3d 158 (Ariz. 2010) ("courts do not ordinarily examine the proportionality of consideration between parties contracting at arm's length, leaving such issues to the market place. . . . In contrast, our Gift Clause [of Arizona constitution] quite appropriately focuses on adequacy of consideration because paying far too much for something effectively creates a subsidy from the public to the seller."). And at times courts will frame substantive unconscionability in terms of inadequate consideration. *See* Potts v. Potts, 303 S.W.3d 177 (Mo. App. 2010) (" 'An ante-nuptial agreement requires more consideration than that necessary for a simple contract, in that the consideration moving to the spouse or prospective spouse surrendering marital rights must be fair and equitable in the particular circumstances.' ") (quoting from *In re* Marriage of Thomas, 199 S.W.3d 847, 852 (Mo. App. 2006)). For the sake of conceptual tidiness, if nothing else, it might be better not to use the language of consideration here. The real point is substantive fairness, and that is policed elsewhere.

§2.11 n.5 p.125 Add the following at the end: See generally Eisenberg, Probability and Chance in Contract Law, 45 UCLA L. Rev. 1005 (1998).

§2.11 n.9 p.127 Add the following to the list after **"Cf."***:* Kells v. Missouri Mountain Props., 247 S.W.3d 79 (Mo. App. 2008) ($500 for rights to $76,025 "adequate consideration": "Even a small consideration is sufficient to support a contract.").

§2.11 n.9 p.127 Add the following to the list after **"But cf."***:* Take It Away v. Home Depot, 374 Fed. Appx. 47 (1st Cir. 2010) (Souter, J., sitting by designation) (disclosed business plan lacked "anything of value not readily imaginable that might be protected" by confidentiality agreement and thus did not provide consideration).

§2.11 n.12 p.128 Add the following after the second sentence: Accord: Weed v. Weed, 968 A.2d 310 (Vt. 2008) (promise to pay $10 in exchange for 103.4 acres of land was "a pretense"),

distinguished in Ferrisburgh Realty Investors v. Schumacher, 992 A.2d 1042 (Vt. 2010) (exchange of actual financing for supplemental covenants supported by consideration, even though earlier oral promise to finance; prior promise unenforceable until note executed).

§2.12 SETTLEMENT OF INVALID CLAIMS AS CONSIDERATION

§2.12 n.2 p.129 Add the following at the end: Some courts have apparently put up procedural hurdles to the enforcement of settlement agreements, though in practice the courts generally disregard them. *See* Muilenberg, Inc. v. Cherokee Rose Design & Build, 250 S.W.3d 848 (Mo. App. 2008) (requiring that existence of settlement agreement be proved "by clear, convincing and satisfactory evidence" but then giving effect to somewhat dubious agreement).

§2.12 n.7 p.130 Add the following to the list after "Accord": Dobson v. Portrait Homes, 117 P.3d 1200 (Wyo. 2005) (claim "must involve doubt or uncertainty" and be the subject of "a good-faith dispute").

§2.12 n.10 p.131 Add the following at the end: *Cf.* O'Connell-Starkey v. Starkey, 944 A.2d 897 (Vt. 2007) (upholding provisions of divorce decree that granted child support even though DNA tests showed that the ex-husband was not the father of the child; collecting cases) (3-2). Those suspecting fraud on Ms. Boehm's part may take comfort in the possibility that fraud would preclude paternity by estoppel. Glover v. Severino, 946 A.2d 710 (Pa. Super. 2008), analyzed in R.W.E. v. A.B.K., 961 A.2d 161 (Pa. Super. 2008).

§2.12 n.11 p.131 Add the following at the end: *But cf.* Neuhoff v. Marvin Lumber & Cedar Co., 370 F.3d 197 (1st Cir. 2004) (though claim "need only be 'well founded and made in good faith and not frivolous, vexatious or unlawful,' " mere forbearance to sue on claim without any promise to forbear is not sufficient).

§2.12 n.12 p.131 Add the following to the list after **"Accord"***:* Kalis v. Colgate-Palmotive Co., 787 N.E.2d 182 (Ill. App. 2003) ("A promise to forego pursuit of a legal claim will be determined to be adequate consideration to support formation of a contract even if the claim is invalid, provided that it is asserted in good faith.").

§2.13 ILLUSORY PROMISES AS CONSIDERATION

§2.13 n.1 p.133 Add the following in front of the citation to **Graphic Arts Finishers***:* Thiesing v. Dentsply Int'l, 748 F. Supp. 2d 932 (E.D. Wis. 2010) (Minnesota law: promise to make employee's salary whole after departure consideration for non-compete agreement, though promise to make additional payments entirely at the employer's discretion not consideration because illusory).

§2.13 n.1 p.133 Add the following before the final sentence: In addition, apparently illusory language will not render the contract unenforceable for lack of consideration if the party in fact has provided something of value. In Stokes v. DISH Network, LLC, 838 F.3d 948, 951 (8th Cir. 2016), subscribers of satellite television sued when the provider ceased to carry Fox stations or provide compensation, and argued that the contract was illusory when the provider relied upon a provision that "WE RESERVE THE RIGHT TO CHANGE PRICES, PACKAGES, AND PROGRAMMING AT ANY TIME, INCLUDING WITHOUT LIMITATION, DURING ANY TERM AGREEMENT PERIOD TO WHICH YOU HAVE AGREED." Although the subscribers were successful at the trial court level, the appellate court made short work of this claim, calling it a "classic red herring" and explaining:

> the district court concluded that, if the Subscription Agreements provided "that DISH cannot be held liable for any interruption or

> delay of any or all programs for any period of time . . . such an interpretation would of course render the contract illusory." We disagree. An illusory contract is unenforceable from its inception. Here, the Subscription Agreement between Stokes and DISH had been in effect for years when the Turner and FOX News service interruptions occurred. Both parties had provided substantial performance of their respective contractual promises, and DISH continued to provide many uninterrupted channels to its subscribers. Under Colorado law, a contract is not illusory for lack of consideration where a party with seemingly unlimited discretion in performing has at least partially performed and thereby "incurred a sufficient detriment to provide consideration."

Id. at 952 (quoting United Press Int'l, Inc. v. Sentinel Publ'g Co., 166 Colo. 47, 441 P.2d 316, 318-19 (1968)). The court also considered and rejected an argument that compensation was required under the implied covenant of the duty of good faith and fair dealing, as discussed in §7.17b, *infra*.

§2.13 n.1 p.133 Add the following to the list after* "Cf."*: *In re* 24R, Inc., 324 S.W.3d 564 (Tex. 2010) (stand-alone arbitration agreement enforceable because both parties bound to arbitrate and agreement did not give employer any right to change it unilaterally).

§2.13 n.4 p.134 Add the following after the citation to* Dumais*: Walker v. Ryan's Family Steak Houses, Inc., 400 F.3d 370 (6th Cir. 2005) (applying *Floss* to attempted correction of arbitration agreement, again finding an illusory promise).

§2.13 n.4 p.134 Add the following to the cases following* Floss*: Cheek v. United Healthcare, 835 A.2d 656 (Md. 2003) (provision giving employer power to change or revoke its arbitration policy in its "sole and absolute discretion" made its " 'promise' to arbitrate . . . entirely illusory"), distinguished in Holloman v. Circuit City Stores, 894 A.2d 547 (Md. 2006) (where employer "is bound to the terms of the arbitration agreement for 364 days, must provide thirty-days notice prior to any modification and may only alter the agreement on a single day out of the year," the restrictions "create a binding obligation on Circuit City's part to submit to arbitration"), which was followed in turn by Harby v. Wachovia

Bank, 915 A.2d 462 (Md. App. 2007) (deposit agreement allowing bank to change with notice of at least 30 days not illusory).

§2.13 n.4 p.134 Add the following to the list after **"Accord"***:* Zamora v. Swift Transp. Corp., 547 F. Supp. 2d 699 (W.D. Tex. 2008) ("If a party possesses the right to modify or terminate an arbitration agreement without notice, its promise is illusory, and the agreement is unenforceable."), *aff'd per curiam* 319 Fed. Appx. 333 (5th Cir. 2009); Davis v. Gen. Foods Corp., 21 F. Supp. 445 (S.D.N.Y. 1937) (where manufacturer promised to examine idea for food product, with any use or compensation "resting solely in our discretion," use created "no legal obligation whatever"); Office Pavillion S. Fla. v. ASAL Prods., 849 So. 2d 367 (Fla. App. 2003) (where seller agreed to sell buyer "any chairs it choose to order" at price in price list and buyer may have agreed, "its acceptance involved no promised performance"); Douglass v. Pfleuger Haw., 135 P.3d 129 (Haw. 2006) (where employee handbook allowed employer to change it "at any time and without notice," arbitration clause therein was illusory); Frye v. Speedway Chevrolet Cadillac, 321 S.W.3d 429 (Mo. App. 2010) (no consideration for promise to take part in dispute resolution program because "the Program ***does not*** require Speedway to provide its employees any ***advance*** notice of an amendment") (emphasis in original).

§2.13 n.4 p.134 Add the following after the citation to ***Blair:*** and in Iberia Credit Bureau v. Cingular Wireless, 379 F.3d 159 (5th Cir. 2004) (where cable provider was "required to give the customer notice of the proposed change" of terms this was not a situation in which company "has not really bound itself at all").

§2.13 n.4 p.134 Add the following to the list after **"But cf."***:* *In re* Polymerica, LLC, 296 S.W.3d 74 (Tex. 2009) (dispute resolution provision not illusory because it "requires notice to employees and applies prospectively only").

§2.13 n.6 p.135 Add the following to the list after **"Accord"***:* Princeton Homes v. Virone, 612 F.3d 1324 (11th Cir. 2010) (promise to complete construction within two years illusory because it was conditioned upon the builder obtaining a building

permit on some undetermined date; query whether an implied reasonable efforts/reasonable time requirement might have given this promise substance).

§2.13 n.7 p.135 Add the following to the list after **"Accord"***:* Armstrong Paint & Varnish Works v. Cont'l Can Co., 133 N.E. 711 (Ill. 1921) ("While consideration is essential to the validity of a contract, mutuality of obligation is not.").

§2.13 n.7 p.135 Add the following at the end: For a curious and atavistic adherence to mutuality, *see* Tyson Foods v. Archer, 147 S.W.3d 681 (Ark. 2004) (requiring "mutual obligations" as an essential element of contract), followed in Hot Spring Cnty. Med. Ctr. v. Ark. Radiology Affiliates, 288 S.W.3d 676 (Ark. App. 2008) ("[M]utuality of obligation means that an obligation must rest on each party to do or permit to be done something in consideration of the act or promise to be bound; thus, neither party is bound unless both are bound," but court goes on to define mutuality in terms of illusory promises: "A contract, therefore, that leaves it entirely optional with one of the parties as to whether or not he will perform his promise would not be binding on the other.").

§2.13 n.8 p.136 Add the following after the second sentence: See also Ziotas v. Reardon Law Firm, 959 A.2d 1013 (Conn. App. 2008) (promise of a bonus of unstated amount not illusory; "[t]hat promise was supported by consideration in the form of the plaintiff's acceptance of a lower salary" and the history of increasing bonuses made the lack of a specified amount "not too indefinite to be enforceable"), *aff'd in part, rev'd in part on other grounds*, 997 A.2d 453 (Conn. 2010).

§2.13 n.9 p.136 Add the following to the list after **"Accord"***:* Furrer v. Southwest Ore. Cmty. Coll., 103 P.3d 118 (Or. App. 2004) (promise of early retirement subject to discretion of board not illusory "because defendant was obligated to exercise its discretion . . . in good faith").

§2.13 n.10 p.137 In the first paragraph, add the following to the list after **"Cf."***:* Saddleridge Estates v. Ruiz, 323 S.W.3d 427 (Mo. App. 2010) (contract with realtor provided for exclusive listing

rights; "[t]hat same language implies [the realtor's] obligation to market the property, sell it, and give the proceeds to the [owners]").

§2.13 n.10 p.137 Add the following after the third sentence: *But cf.* Moran v. Erk, 901 N.E.2d 187 (N.Y. 2008) (real estate contract subject to attorney approval; no duty of good faith and fair dealing applied to attorney, who "may timely disapprove the contract for any reason or for no reason," but the contract nevertheless exists).

§2.13 n.11 p.137 Add the following to the list after "see": Bird, An Employment Contract "Instinct with an Obligation": Good Faith Costs and Contexts, 28 Pace L. Rev. 409 (2008).

§2.13 n.11 p.137 Add the following at the end: For a provocative tracing of the history of this case, see V. Goldberg, Framing Contract Law ch. 2 (2006). More generally, *see* Symposium, The Enduring Legacy of *Wood v. Lucy, Lady Duff-Gordon*, 28 Pace L. Rev. 161 (2008).

§2.13 n.12 p.137 Add the following after the second sentence in the second paragraph: *Cf.* Hinc v. Lime-O-Sol Co., 382 F.3d 716 (7th Cir. 2004) (Indiana law; where contract states that it is a "best efforts agreement" to market Lime-O-Sol "in a manner that seems appropriate," the reference to best efforts makes the promise not illusory).

§2.13 n.12 p.137 Add the following at the end: On the consequences of implying a best efforts clause in order to make an otherwise illusory promise enforceable, see Goldberg, Desperately Seeking Consideration: The Unfortunate Impact of U.C.C. Section 2-306 on Contract Interpretation, 68 Ohio St. L.J. 103 (2007).

§2.13 n.16 p.138 Add the following to the list after "Accord": Mendez v. New Bell Gen. Servs., 727 F. Supp. 2d 585 (W.D. Tex. 2010) (arbitration clause in employment contract illusory when made because of no limits on employer's termination rights, including no notice, but unilateral contract made when employer provided benefits and employee accepted them);

Steiner v. Thexton, 226 P.3d 359 (Cal. 2010) (option rendered irrevocable when optionee began performance under agreement benefitting both itself and optionor, notwithstanding its right not to continue with the transaction); Flagship Resort Dev. Corp. v. Interval Int'l, 28 So. 3d 915 (Fla. App. 2010) (where developer and time-share exchange company had done business for over 15 years, "even if the [contract] lacked mutuality at its formation, the [contract] has been performed by both sides. . . . any purported lack of mutuality . . . has been cured by the parties' subsequent performance according to the terms of the agreement"); Guest v. Allstate Ins. Co., 205 P.3d 844 (N.M. App. 2009) (performance may substitute for consideration, but the "actions must have been something for which [the promisee] bargained"), *rev'd on other grounds*, 244 P.3d 342 (N.M. 2010); Pozament Corp. v. AES Westover, LLC, 812 N.Y.S.2d 154 (App. Div. 2006) (agreement giving right to acquire fly ash without a minimum quantity not illusory; "plaintiff's partial performance by removal of fly ash . . . before it was stopped by defendant, supplied the necessary consideration"); Frequent Flyer Depot v. Am. Airlines, 281 S.W.3d 215 (Tex. Civ. App. 2009) ("[E]ven if an illusory promise renders a contract unilateral, consideration can still be established by part performance by the promisee.").

§2.13 n.18 p.139 Add the following at the end: *Cf.* Devine v. Notter, 753 N.W.2d 557 (Wis. App. 2008) (attorney approval option does not render promise illusory, because one alternative — going ahead as is — is consideration, and "[e]ven assuming that consulting with an attorney is not a sufficient detriment to serve as consideration, the five-day limit here serves to eliminate this alternative very quickly, so that the party is left with the remaining option: performance of the deal as written."); Restatement Second §77 (alternative promises not consideration unless . . . "(b) one of the alternative performances would have been consideration and there is or appears to the parties to be a substantial possibility that before the promisor exercises his choice events may eliminate the alternative which would not have been consideration") (relied upon in *Devine*, *supra*).

§2.13 n.19 p.139 Add the following to the end: *See also* Marshall Durbin Food Corp. v. Baker, 909 So. 2d 1267 (Miss. App.

2005) (promise to at-will employee that would get extended compensation if certain triggering events occurred; promise illusory when made, but created a unilateral contract which could be accepted by performance); Metro. Ventures, LLC v. GEA Assocs., 717 N.W.2d 58 (Wis. 2006) (sale-purchase agreement for partnership not illusory, despite financing clause that gave one party "sole discretion to approve the financing" and "exclusive authority to waive the contingency," where "the subsequent actions of *both* parties rendered the financing clause definite") (emphasis in original).

§2.14 TERMINATION CLAUSES

§2.14 n.2 p.140 Add the following to the list after **"Accord"***:* Succession of Rhodes, 918 So. 2d 626 (La. App. 2005) (agreement between decedent and companion providing for a cash payment on death, but terminable at will by either party, was unenforceable as illusory; "a condition that depends solely on the whim of both parties makes the obligation null"); Thompson v. Bar-S Foods Co., 174 P.3d 567 (Okla. 2007) ("the reservation of a unilateral right to cancel the entire agreement is so broad that it negates the existence of consideration; the promise is essentially empty or illusory"); Frequent Flyer Depot v. Am. Airlines, 281 S.W.3d 215 (Tex. Civ. App. 2009) ("A promise is illusory when it fails to bind the promisor who retains the option of discontinuing performance without notice.").

§2.14 n.3 p.140 Add the following to the list after **"See"***:* Outback/Empire I v. Kamitis, Inc., 825 N.Y.S.2d 747 (App. Div. 2006) (contract not illusory where lessee had to give written notice of termination within specific time frame); *In re* Odyssey Healthcare, 310 S.W.3d 419 (Tex. 2010) (arbitration clause terminable only upon 14 days' notice, and effective only prospectively; "[B]ecause of these limitations on Odyssey's right to amend or terminate the agreement, the arbitration agreement did not contain an illusory promise by Odyssey.").

§2.14 n.4 p.141 Add the following after the first sentence: *Accord:* Thrifty Payless, Inc. v. Mariners Mile Gateway, 111 Cal. Rptr. 3d 173 (Ct. App. 2010) (contract containing mutual termination rights upon the giving of written notice if the lease term had not started by a particular date not illusory, even without resort to the duty of good faith and fair dealing; "a contract with a mutual termination provision is not illusory when conditioned on notice").

§2.14 n.5 p.141 Add the following to the list after **"Accord"*:*** Askinuk Corp. v. Lower Yukon Sch. Dist., 214 P.3d 259 (Alaska 2009) (lease of real property for one dollar a year, subject to renegotiation, the lease rate to remain at one dollar a year until a new rate is determined; "Because the covenant of good faith and fair dealing is implied in all contracts in Alaska, this provision is not illusory. The covenant prevents each party from doing anything that would injure the right of the other to receive the benefits of the agreement. Askinuk can therefore rely on the school district's express promise to renegotiate the rate and its implied promise to renegotiate in good faith."); Questar Builders v. CB Flooring, 978 A.2d 651 (Md. 2009) ("termination for convenience rights . . . may be enforceable, subject to the implied limitation that they be exercised in good faith and in accordance with fair dealing").

§2.14 n.6 p.141 Add the following at the end: , somewhat unconvincingly distinguished in Flood v. ClearOne Commc'ns, 634 F. Supp. 2d 1257 (D. Utah 2009) (provision in *Resource Management* "amenable to an objective standard," whereas provision in *Flood* — whether ClearOne's board decided in good faith that expenses incurred in the defense of a former officer were reasonable, that ClearOne could make payment, and that ClearOne's resources should not be directed elsewhere — is not). The issue is not whether the board of directors could in good faith decide that the corporation's monies could be better spent on something other than paying criminal defense lawyers to represent a corporate officer. The issue is whether, having made a promise to indemnify, the board could in good faith retract it. The resulting focus should thus be on a change in position. This is capable of objective determination, in the same manner as force majeure clauses or material adverse change clauses.

§2.15 REQUIREMENTS AND OUTPUT CONTRACTS

§2.15 n.1 p.143 In the first paragraph, add the following at the start: *See* Mid-S. Packers v. Shoney's, 761 F.2d 1117 (5th Cir. 1985) ("an essential element of a requirements contract is the promise of the buyer to purchase exclusively from the seller either the buyer's entire requirements or up to a specified amount"). *Accord:* Brooklyn Bagel Boys v. Earthgrains Refrig. Dough Prods., 212 F.3d 373 (7th Cir. 2000); Rosenthal v. Nat'l Produce Co., 573 A.2d 365 (D.C. 1990); Kirkwood-Easton Tire Co. v. St. Louis County, 568 S.W.2d 267 (Mo. 1978).

***§2.15 n.1 p.143 In the first paragraph, add the following to the list after* "Accord":** G.B. "Boots" Smith Corp. v. Cobb, 860 So. 2d 774 (Miss. 2003) ("no reason to include the wording 'all fill dirt for project' unless [road builder] intended to buy all the fill dirt needed for the project from these particular sellers"), *opinion after remand* 911 So. 2d 421 (Miss. 2005).

***§2.15 n.1 p.143 In the second paragraph, add the following to the list after* "See":** City of Louisville v. Rockwell Mfg. Co., 482 F.2d 159 (6th Cir. 1973); PMC Corp. v. Houston Wire & Cable Co., 797 A.2d 125 (N.H. 2002).

***§2.15 n.1 p.143 In the second paragraph, add the following after the citation to* Bruckel:** discussed in Comment, 39 Tulsa L. Rev. 711 (2004); *see also* Blair, "You Don't Have to be Ludwig Wittgenstein": How Llewellyn's Concept of Agreement Should Change the Law of Open-Quantity Contracts, 37 Seton Hall L. Rev. 67 (2006).

§2.15 n.4 p.144 Add the following at the end: *Cf.* Laredo Coca-Cola Bottling Co. v. Combs, 317 S.W.3d 735 (Tex. Civ. App. 2010) (no consideration for agreement to provide soda fountain equipment, even though customer had to use supplier's products in connection with equipment and had to purchase a minimum quantity of those products). The court reasoned that the first requirement was not consideration because the customer did not have to use any of the supplier's products, and could sell anyone else's products if it chose. As for the minimum, it concluded that this did not provide consideration, because if the customer did not buy the minimum amount the supplier in practice did not bill it for the shortage, but rather either charged rent or repossessed the equipment. Both points seem questionable. The court's conclusion is questionable. Had the supplier required payment of a rental fee, consideration would have been beyond doubt. Instead, it sought profits from the sale of its products for use in the machine. Had there been no minimum purchase requirement, consideration might have been in doubt. But there was. And the practice of either repossessing or charging rental hardly disqualifies the minimum clause as consideration. There was no argument that the supplier had waived its right to insist upon payment.

§2.15 n.12 p.147 Add the following to the list after **"Accord"***:* Vulcan Materials Co. v. Atofina Chems., 355 F. Supp. 2d 1214 (D. Kan. 2005) ("the 'unreasonably disproportionate' language of 2-306(1) restricts the ability of the buyer to increase purchases, not to decrease them: the buyer can decrease its purchases, subject to the limitation not of reasonableness, but of good faith").

§2.15 n.12 p.147 Add the following at the end: A twist on the conventional output or requirements contract comes when the two coincide — that is, when the parties make an output contract subject to the buyer's requirements. *See* Griffith v. Clear Lakes Trout Co., 200 P.3d 1162 (Idaho 2009) (Clear Lakes agreed to sell the Griffiths enough small trout to enable them to grow up to two million pounds of market-size trout per year, and Clear Lake agreed to repurchase the trout once they reached market size). Then it is possible to have both a stated estimate and a stated maximum, with only the latter subject to a requirement of good faith.

§2.15 n.13 p.147 Add the following after the first sentence: *Accord:* Structural Polymer Grp. v. Zoltek Corp., 543 F.3d 987 (8th Cir. 2008) (the implied duty of good faith and fair dealing "is enough to avoid finding a contract null and void due to an illusory promise"; consequently, "[a]n assertion of bad faith . . . is an argument that SP *breached* the agreement, not that the agreement lacked mutuality or consideration in the first place.") (quoting from Magruder Quarry & Co. v. Briscoe, 83 S.W.3d 647 (Mo. App. 2002)) (emphasis in original).

§2.15a DRAFTING CONDITIONS TO ACCELERATE NEGOTIATIONS

§2.15a n.9 p.149 Add the following at the end: For a more complete discussion of conditions of satisfaction, see §8.4 *infra*.

§2.15a n.13 p.150 Add the following at the end of the second paragraph: For an alternative reading of *Mattei* and satisfaction clauses generally, *see* V. Goldberg, Framing Contract Law ch. 4 (2006).

§2.15a n.19 p.152 Add the following to the list after **"But cf.":** Moran v. Erk, 901 N.E.2d 187 (N.Y. 2008) (real estate contract subject to attorney approval; no duty of good faith and fair dealing applied to attorney, who "may timely disapprove the contract for any reason or for no reason," but the contract nevertheless exists).

§2.15a n.20 p.152 Add the following at the end: *Cf.* Devine v. Notter, 753 N.W.2d 557 (Wis. App. 2008) (clause permitting cancellation within five days of accepting offer if attorney disapproved; held enforceable because (1) one of the alternatives, going ahead with the deal, is consideration, and the other possibility would likely be eliminated in short order, invoking Restatement Second §77; and (2) the obligations to consult with an attorney and provide notice within five days "though not onerous, are enough to save the deal from being illusory.").

§2.16 FORM: THE SEAL

§2.16 n.3 p.154 ***Add the following to the end:*** Jewish law of the Talmudic and post-Talmudic eras similarly used form to make promises enforceable without consideration. The institution of the *kinyan* — the passing of an object, commonly a handkerchief, from the buyer to the seller, or the donee to the donor, followed by its return — has this effect, and indeed is the only way to make a bilateral executory promise enforceable. *See* 2 I. Herzog, The Main Institutions of Jewish Law 33-42, 110-111 (2d ed. 1967); 6 E. Quint, A Restatement of Rabbinic Civil Law 127-135 (1995).

§2.16 p.154 In the first full paragraph, add the following at the end of the fourth sentence: . . . sealed by the promisor.[4a]

[4a] Merely attaching a seal to an amendment does not retroactively make the contract sealed. Perkins v. M & M Office Holdings, 695 S.E.2d 82 (Ga. App. 2010) ("If the parties desired to alter the status of their Agreement in that manner, they could have expressly incorporated the prior Agreement by reference and stated their intention to place it under seal along with the amendments.").

§2.16 n.5 p.154 ***Add the following after the first sentence:*** *See also* Burton v. Williams, 689 S.E.2d 174 (N.C. App. 2010) ("[A]n instrument under seal 'imports consideration' to support that instrument, or, stated differently, the presence of a seal raises a presumption that the instrument is supported by consideration") (quoting from Justus v. Deutsch, 303 S.E.2d 571 (N.C. App. 1983)); Mitchell Bank v. Schanke, 676 N.W.2d 849 (Wis. 2004) (where contract was executed, seal was conclusive evidence of consideration, though seal is only presumptive evidence in case of executory contract). This may not merely shift the burden of proof. *See* Loman-Garrett Supply Co. v. Dudney, 289 S.E.2d 600 (N.C. App. 1982) (this presumption "must be rebutted by clear and convincing evidence").

§2.16 p.155 Add the following footnote to the end of the third sentence: . . . to serve as a seal.[9a]

[9a] *See* Whittington v. Dragon Grp., 991 A.2d 1 (Del. 2009) ("in the case of an individual . . . the presence of the word 'seal' next to an individual's signature is all that is necessary to create a sealed instrument"); Collins v. Tracy Grill & Bar Corp., 19 A.2d 617 (Pa. Super. 1941) ("Any kind of a flourish or mark will be sufficient if it be intended for a seal."). *Cf. In re* Polkowski, 303 B.R. 585 (Bankr. M.D. Pa. 2003) (presence of a seal, word, scrawl, or other sign essential, regardless of the intent of the parties); McCalla v. Stuckey, 504 S.E.2d 269 (Ga. App. 1998) (party bound by extended statute of limitations for sealed instruments only if its signature bore a seal; fact that others on the same document did irrelevant).

§2.16 n.10 p.155 Add the following at the end: This continues to be a point for litigation. *See, e.g.*, Whittington v. Dragon Grp., 991 A.2d 1 (Del. 2009) (if word "seal" present next to an individual's signature, unnecessary to state in the body of the obligation that it was intended to be a sealed document); Dist. of Col. Water & Sewer Auth. v. Delon Hampton & Assocs., 851 A.2d 410 (D.C. 2004) (longer statute of limitations for sealed instruments inappropriate; even though the word seal appears on the signature page, there was no actual seal, and the word did not appear next to the signatures, so there is no evidence that the parties intended the document to be under seal); Carolina Marine Handling v. Lasch, 609 S.E.2d 548 (S.C. App. 2005) (longer statute of limitations for sealed instruments inappropriate; recitation of setting hands and seals too "generic" to satisfy requirement of intent).

§2.17 RECITALS

§2.17 n.6 p.157 Add the following to the end: The reverse is true as well; a recital that a transfer of ownership is without consideration does not preclude a jury from finding the contrary. *See* Ind. Dep't of State Revenue v. Belterra Resort Ind., 935 N.E.2d 174 (Ind. 2010) (such a declaration "is not dispositive"), *aff'd on reh'g*, 942 N.E.2d 796 (Ind. 2011).

***§2.17 n.8 p.158 Add the following to the list after* "But see":** Network Prot. Sciences v. Fortinet, Inc., 2013 U.S. Dist. LEXIS 118105 at *21-22 (N.D. Cal. Aug. 20, 2013) (applying

Texas law, "the assignment agreement itself acknowledges the receipt of good and valuable consideration, stating that MHP assigns the patents to NPS '[f]or good and valuable consideration, the receipt of which is hereby acknowledged' (Neukom Decl. Exh. 13 at 1). This recital is conclusive. Even if no actual consideration were paid, moreover, NPS's agreement to be bound by the choice-of-law provision would be deemed adequate consideration."; Smith v. Mountjoy, 694 S.E.2d 598 (Va. 2010) (court gives weight to caption "deed of gift" when determining whether transaction contract or gift, though noting that the caption is "not controlling").

§2.17 n.8 p.158 Add the following after the citation to **Daniel***:* , followed in Estate of Fallon v. Fallon, 30 So. 3d 1281 (Miss. App. 2010) (because administrator of estate presented no evidence that a deed lacked consideration, the recital contained in the deed goes unrebutted and establishes consideration).

§2.17 n.8 p.158 Add the following after the citation to **Lemaire***:* , followed in Blockbuster, Inc. v. C-Span Entm't, 276 S.W.3d 482 (Tex. Civ. App. 2008) ("A written contract reciting a consideration is deemed to import one.").

§2.17 n.8 p.158 Add the following after the fourth sentence: *Cf. In re* Rudell Estate, 780 N.W.2d 884 (Mich. App. 2009) ("a deed's recital of consideration is only prima facie evidence 'of the slightest kind.' ") (quoting from Mowrey v. Mowrey, 9 Mich. 39, 41 (1860)).

§2.17 n.11 p.159 Add the following at the end: Even that may not always be necessary, though it would be desirable. In some jurisdictions, the simple fact of making a written contract is enough to shift the burden of proof as to consideration. *See* Margeson v. Artis, 776 N.W.2d 652 (Iowa 2009) ("[W]e presume a written and signed agreement is supported by consideration."); Blockbuster, Inc. v. C-Span Entm't, *supra* note 8 ("[T]he existence of a written contract presumes consideration for its execution.").

§2.18 REFORM OF THE BASES FOR ENFORCEMENT

§2.18 n.4 p.160 Add the following after the third sentence: The Uniform Law Commissioners withdrew the Written Obligations Act as obsolete in July of 2009. Minutes of Exec. Comm., July 13, 2009 at 6 (available at http://www.uniformlaws.org/Shared/Docs/Executive/ExecMin071309.pdf).

§2.18 n.4 p.160 Add the following after the sixth sentence: See also Kia v. Imaging Sciences Int'l, 735 F. Supp. 2d 256 (E.D. Pa. 2010) (statement that "This Agreement shall be binding upon me, my heirs, executors, assigns and administrators and is for the benefit of the Company and its successors and assigns" sufficient to express intent to be bound for the purposes of the Written Obligations Act).

§2.18a GIFTS, GIFT PROMISES, AND PATERNALISM

§2.18a n.4 p.162 Add the following at the end: On the other hand, another medieval legal system, Talmudic and rabbinic law, did allow gratuitous promises to be enforced if they were accompanied by the form of a *kinyan*. *See* §2.16 note 3.

§2.18a n.18 p.165 Add the following at the end: The Uniform Law Commissioners withdrew the Written Obligations Act as obsolete in July of 2009. Minutes of Exec. Comm., July 13, 2009 at 6 (available at http://www.nccusl.org/Update/Docs/Executive/ExecMin071309.pdf).

§2.18a n.19 p.166 Add the following at the end: More generally on civil law approaches to the enforceability of promises, *see* Farnsworth, Comparative Contract Law, in Oxford Handbook of Comparative Law 899, 907-15 (M. Reimann & R. Zimmermann eds. 2007); Philippe, French and American Approaches to Contract Formation and Enforceability: A Comparative Perspective, 12 Tul. J. Comp. & Int'l L. 357 (2005).

§2.18a n.21 p.167 Add the following at the end: We need not go far afield to see revocation for ingratitude at work. Louisiana, like the other civilian jurisdictions above, generally makes inter vivos donations irrevocable. But by statute, "[r]evocation on account of ingratitude may take place only in the following cases: (1) If the donee has attempted to take the life of the donor; or (2) If he has been guilty towards him of cruel treatment, crimes, or grievous injuries." La. Civ. Code art. 1557. The bases for revocation mentioned above are generally found in Louisiana law as well. *See* Salassi v. Salassi, 13 So. 3d 670 (La. App. 2009) (allegations that the donee had threatened that his pregnant wife would be thrown out of house along with two-year-old child and given no means of support unless she signed a declaration of gift; qualified as cruel treatment and grievous injury); Bello v. Bello, 3 So. 3d 559 (La. App. 2009) (donor able to argue ingratitude for matrimonial transfer of interest in real property, where couple had since divorced); Sanders v. Sanders, 768 So. 2d 739 (La. App. 2000) (donee denied that donor was his father and told others that he wished his father and mother would die; held to be cruel treatment and grievous injury and hence ingratitude); Whitman v. Whitman, 730 So. 2d 1048 (La. App. 1999) (donee's adultery was cruel treatment and grievous injury to donor). *Cf.* Manichia v. Mahoney, 45 So. 3d 618 (La. App. 2010) (divestiture of entire estate not a basis for revoking a gift unless the donor was unable to sustain himself when the promise was made, so evidence of a current inability to pay obligations irrelevant).

§2.19 RELIANCE AS A GROUND FOR RECOVERY: PROMISSORY ESTOPPEL

§2.19 n.2 p.168 Add the following at the end of the first sentence: , followed in LeMaitre v. Mass. Turnpike Auth., 897 N.E.2d 1218 (Mass. 2008).

§2.19 n.4 p.168 Add the following at the end: On the growth of assumpsit generally, *see* Ames, The History of Assumpsit, 2 Harv. L. Rev. 1 (1888). *Cf.* Barnes v. Yahoo!, Inc., 570 F.3d 1096

(9th Cir. 2009) (noting common origin of contract and promissory estoppel in assumpsit).

§2.19 n.15 p.170 Add the following to the list after* "See"*: Bridgeman, *Allegheny College* Revisited: Cardozo, Consideration, and Formalism in Contract, 39 U.C. Davis L. Rev. 150 (2005).

§2.19 n.20 p.171 Add the following to the list after* "See also"*: Grover v. Wadsworth, 205 P.3d 1196 (Idaho 2009) (in the absence of a promise, promissory estoppel does not apply; however, where the plaintiffs relied to their disadvantage on the defendant's statements about the amounts owing on a note, the defendant was (equitably) estopped from claiming that the plaintiffs owed him more than the amount originally stated); Ford Motor Credit Co. v. Ryan, 939 N.E.2d 891 (Ohio App. 2010) ("equitable estoppel arises from a misrepresentation of fact, while promissory estoppel arises from a promise . . . Moreover, equitable estoppel is a defense to a legal or equitable claim, while promissory estoppel is a cause of action."); Youngblood v. Auto-Owners Ins. Co., 158 P.3d 1088 (Utah 2007) (extended and helpful analysis of differences between promissory estoppel and equitable estoppel).

§2.19 n.20 p.171 Add the following at the end: The historical relation of equitable estoppel and promissory estoppel has caused some jurisdictions to apply the clear and convincing proof standard of equitable estoppel in promissory estoppel actions. *See* Lord v. Souder, 748 A.2d 393 (Del. 1999); W.R. Grace & Co. v. Geodata Servs., 547 So. 2d 919 (Fla. 1989); Blackburn v. Habitat Dev. Co., 57 S.W.3d 378 (Mo. App. 2001); Dailey v. Craigmyle & Son Farms, 894 N.E.2d 1301 (Ohio App. 2008). *Cf.* K.C. Props. of N.W. Ark. v. Lowell Inv. Partners, 280 S.W.3d 1 (Ark. 2008) (a party relying on promissory estoppel "must prove it strictly, there must be certainty to every intent, the facts constituting it must not be taken by argument or inference, and nothing can be supplied by intendment").This ought not be encouraged; promissory estoppel is normally treated as an alternative to conventional contract, so the standard of proof should be the same.

§2.19 n.21 p.171 Add the following to the list after **"Accord"***:* Kim v. Dean, 135 P.3d 978 (Wash. App. 2006).

§2.19 n.21 p.171 Add the following at the end: *Cf.* Vila v. Inter-Am. Inv. Corp., 570 F.3d 274 (D.C. Cir. 2009) (showing parallels between promissory estoppel and unjust enrichment; "unjust enrichment — like promissory estoppel — is not a contract remedy"); Double AA Builders v. Grand State Constr., 114 P.3d 835 (Ariz. App. 2005) ("Promissory estoppel provides an equitable remedy and is not a theory of contract liability," so statute providing for attorneys' fees for breaches of express or implied contracts does not apply); Medistar Corp. v. Schmidt, 267 S.W.3d 150 (Tex. Civ. App. 2008) (Statute of Frauds defense unavailable in an action invoking promissory estoppel as the basis for affirmative relief).

§2.19 n.23 p.172 Add the following to the list after **"See"***:* Ngugi, Promissory Estoppel: The Life History of an Ideal Legal Transplant, 41 U. Rich. L. Rev. 425 (2007); Teeven, A History of Promissory Estoppel: Growth in the Face of Doctrinal Resistance, 72 Tenn. L. Rev. 1111 (2005); Teeven, Origins of Promissory Estoppel: Justifiable Reliance and Commercial Uncertainty Before Williston's Restatement, 34 U. Memphis L. Rev. 499 (2004).

§2.19 n.24 p.172 In the first paragraph, add the following to the list after **"See generally"***:* Chung, Promissory Estoppel and the Protection of Interpersonal Trust, 56 Clev. St. L. Rev. 37 (2008); Jimenez, The Many Faces of Promissory Estoppel: An Empirical Analysis Under the Restatement (Second) of Contracts, 57 UCLA L. Rev. 669 (2010); Powers, Promissory Estoppel and Wagging the Dog, 59 Ark. L. Rev. 841 (2007); Pretorius, The Basis of Contractual Liability in American Law, 37 Comp. & Int'l L.J. of S. Afr. 226 (2004); Wilkinson-Ryan & Hoffman, Breach Is For Suckers, 63 Vand. L. Rev. 1003 (2010).

§2.19 n.25 p.173 In the first paragraph, add the following after the citation to **Virginia School of the Arts***:* , reaffirmed in Mongold v. Woods, 677 S.E.2d 288 (Va. 2009) ("promissory estoppel is not a cognizable cause of action in Virginia").

***§2.19 n.25 p.173 In the first paragraph, insert the following after the sentence beginning* "But see":** Other jurisdictions have allowed a cause of action resting on promissory estoppel, but have sought to limit its incursion. *See* Suddith v. Univ. of So. Miss., 977 So. 2d 1158 (Miss. App. 2007) (promissory estoppel " 'may arise . . . if a refusal to enforce [the promise] would be virtually to sanction the perpetuation of fraud or would result in other injustice' ") (quoting from C.E. Frazier Constr. Co. v. Campbell Roofing & Metal Works, 373 So. 2d 1036 (Miss. 1979)); Clevenger v. Oliver Ins. Agency, 237 S.W.3d 588 (Mo. 2007) ("in Missouri, promissory estoppel is not a favorite of the law"); AHA Sales v. Creative Bath Prods., 867 N.Y.S.2d 169 (App. Div. 2008) (promissory estoppel limited to cases in which the promisee suffered an unconscionable injury); Barnes & Robinson Co. v. Onesource Facility Servs., 195 S.W.3d 637 (Tenn. App. 2006) ("Tennessee does not liberally apply the doctrine of promissory estoppel. To the contrary, it limits application of the doctrine to exceptional cases."), followed in Chavez v. Broadway Elec. Serv. Corp., 245 S.W.3d 398 (Tenn. App. 2007) ("its application is limited to exceptional cases where the circumstances border on actual fraud").

***§2.19 n.25 p.173 In the second paragraph, add the following to the list after* "See":** Boon Rawd Trading Int'l Co. v. Paleewong Trading Co., 688 F. Supp. 2d 940 (N.D. Cal. 2010) (because defendant alleged in its answer that the promises in question were bargained for, those promises amounted to consideration and thus exclude a claim in promissory estoppel); Skallerup v. City of Hot Springs, 309 S.W.3d 196 (Ark. 2009) ("Promissory estoppel applies when the elements of a contract cannot be shown."); LoPresti v. Rutland Reg'l Health Servs., 865 A.2d 1102 (Vt. 2004) (following "the well-established rule that promissory estoppel will not apply when the relationship of the parties is governed by a contract"). *Cf.* Local 107 Office & Prof'l Employees Int'l Union v. Offshore Logistics, 380 F.3d 832 (5th Cir. 2004) (dictum: where union had right to sue under Railway Labor Act, "promissory estoppel need not be invoked").

§2.19 n.25 p.173 In the second paragraph, add the following at the end: For a flagrant misapplication of this principle, *see* Bybee Farms v. Snake River Sugar Co., 563 F. Supp. 2d 1184 (E.D. Wash.

2008) (reliance on promise constitutes bargained-for forbearance, which means there is a contract and thus no promissory estoppel claim — but the promise was unauthorized, so actually there is no promise after all and thus there would be no promissory estoppel). The court seems to ignore the fact that if there is no promise, then there is no contract. In any event, as one judge has pointed out, regrettably in dissent, the Restatement Second itself contains illustrations that involve promises made in connection with a written contract. Restatement Second §90 ills. 2 & 5; Coral Reef Drive Land Dev. v. Duke Realty L.P., 45 So. 3d 897 (Fla. App. 2010) (Cope, J., dissenting). *Cf.* ConAgra Trade Grp. v. Fuel Exploration, 636 F. Supp. 2d 1166 (D. Colo. 2009) ("a promissory estoppel theory . . . does not apply when the terms of a written contract contravene the alleged oral promise."). It is not entirely clear whether this is meant to make the point above, or that there is in essence a statute of frauds for promissory estoppel, or that the parol evidence rule applies with special force to oral promises invoked in promissory estoppel cases.

Possibly, there is some general confusion at work. *See id.* ("Fuel Ex misconstrues the theory of promissory estoppel. As the cited cases make clear, promissory estoppel is an affirmative claim for relief ple[]d in the absence of a written agreement; it is not a defense to enforcement of a contract."). Other courts are clearer that the issue is one of parol evidence and integration — namely, that it is inherently unreasonable to rely upon oral representations when there exists a fully integrated writing covering the same subject. This is especially so when the oral representations partly preceded the drafting of the integrated agreement. *See* Executone of Columbus v. Inter-Tel, Inc., 665 F. Supp. 2d 899 (S.D. Ohio 2009); White Constr. Co. v. Martin Marietta Materials, 633 F. Supp. 2d 1302 (M.D. Fla. 2009). This result is not inevitable, because the oral representations might have been omitted through a scrivener's error, through fraud in the inducement, or because they amounted to a collateral agreement. But it seems natural that contracting parties, especially sophisticated ones, should disdain reliance upon oral promises when they have executed a fully integrated writing covering the same subject. See *infra* §7.3 at notes 46-47 (parol evidence rule and promissory estoppel). *See generally* Epstein, Arbuckle, & Flanagan, Contract Law's Two "P.E.'s": Promissory Estoppel and the Parol Evidence Rule, 62 Baylor L. Rev. 397 (2010); Metzger, The Parol Evidence Rule: Promissory Estoppel's Next Conquest?, 36 Vand. L. Rev. 1383 (1983).

In any case, it is difficult to understand why breach of contract and promissory estoppel must be mutually exclusive at the pleading stage. Pleading in the alternative is hardly a novelty. True, if promissory estoppel is a substitute for consideration, then it has no role when the plaintiff has proved consideration. If promissory estoppel is considered a cause of action of its own, then awarding damages for it and for breach of contract would be double-dipping. But those points are germane only after the facts have been found, not until. *See* Shahata v. W Steak Waikiki, 721 F. Supp. 2d 968 (D. Haw. 2010) (where there are genuine issues of material fact surrounding the existence of a contract, inappropriate to dismiss promissory estoppel claim); House of Flavors v. TFG-Mich., 674 F. Supp. 2d 306 (D. Me. 2009) (promissory estoppel does not apply when there is an enforceable contract, but if the contract is voidable then promissory estoppel may be relevant upon avoidance).

§2.19 n.26 p.174 Add the following at the end: For a venturesome proposal to extend promissory estoppel's reach, *see* Hartzog, Promises and Privacy: Promissory Estoppel and Confidential Disclosure in Online Communities, 82 Temple L. Rev. 891 (2009).

§2.19 n.27 p.174 Add the following at the end: *Accord:* Fiebelkorn v. IKON Office Solutions, 668 F. Supp. 2d 1178 (D. Minn. 2009). *But see* Marquardt v. Perry, 200 P.3d 1126 (Colo. App. 2008) ("Whether a plaintiff has justifiably relied on a defendant's promise is an issue of law for the trial court.").

§2.19 n.29 p.174 Add the following at the end as a new paragraph: Conditional promises have been the subject of some contention. Restatement Second §91 allows them to be enforced in the same manner as other promises, but performance is due only upon the occurrence of the condition. This has generally, though not uniformly, been accepted. *See* Advanced Marine Tech. v. Burnham Sec., 16 F. Supp. 2d 375 (S.D.N.Y. 1998); Garcia v. World Sav., FSB, 107 Cal. Rptr. 3d 683 (Ct. App. 2010); Nelson

v. Elway, 908 P.2d 102 (Colo. 1995); Kemira, Inc. v. Williams Investigative & Sec. Servs., 450 S.E.2d 427. *But see* Gore v. Flagstar Bank, 711 N.W.2d 330 (Mich. 2006) (Taylor, C.J., concurring) ("plaintiff cannot construct a detrimental reliance or estoppel theory on a conditional promise, especially when the condition did not take place") (quoting Bivans Corp. v. Cmty. Nat'l Bank, 166 N.W.2d 270 (Mich. App. 1968)).

***§2.19 n.30 p.175 Add the following to the list after* "Accord":** Garwood Packaging v. Allen & Co., 378 F.3d 698 (7th Cir. 2004) (Posner, J.) ("while the promise relied upon to trigger an estoppel must be definite in the sense of being clearly a promise and not just a statement of intentions . . . its terms need not be as clear as a contractual promise would have to be in order to be enforceable").

***§2.19 n.30 p.175 Add the following after the citation to* Whorley v. First Westside Bank:** and Blinn v. Beatrice Cmty. Hosp., 708 N.W.2d 235 (Neb. 2006)

***§2.19 n.31 p.175 In the first paragraph, add the following to the list after* "Accord":** Norton v. McOsker, 407 F.3d 501 (1st Cir. 2005) (in palimony case, a promise to "take care of" the paramour was insufficiently "clear and unambiguous"); Garwood Packaging v. Allen & Co., *supra* note 30 (Posner, J.) ("the vaguer the alleged promise the less likely it is to be held a promise"); Cosgrove v. Bartolotta, 150 F.3d 729 (7th Cir. 1998) (if a promise "is vague and hedged about with conditions. . . . [the promisee] cannot plead promissory estoppel"); Nelson v. Long Lines Ltd., 335 F. Supp. 2d 944 (N.D. Iowa 2004) ("clear and definite," which has as its focus " 'a clear understanding by the promisor that the promisee was seeking an assurance upon which he could rely and without which he would not act.' ") (quoting from Nat'l Bank of Waterloo v. Moeller, 434 N.W.2d 887, 889 (Iowa 1989)); ATS v. State Dep't of Fish & Game, 172 P.3d 764 (Alaska 2007) (requiring that the promise be "definitive," "very clear," and "must use precise language," and must also "manifest an unequivocal intent to be bound") (following Simpson v. Murkowski, 129 P.3d 435 (Alaska 2006)); Univ. Hotel Dev. v. Dusterhoft Oil, 715 N.W.2d 153 (N.D. 2006) ("definite, clear, and unambiguous terms");

Chavez v. Broadway Elec. Serv. Corp., *supra* note 25 (statements to prospective employees about robust state of job market "too ambiguous, vague, and nonspecific to support Plaintiffs' claims for damages").

***§2.19 n.31 p.175 In the second paragraph, add the following to the list after the first* "See":** Barnes v. Yahoo!, Inc., *supra* note 4 ("ordinary contract principles usually apply," including that the promises giving rise to promissory estoppel be as clear as those giving rise to a contract supported by consideration); Armstrong v. Rohm & Haas Co., 349 F. Supp. 2d 71 (D. Mass. 2004) (for the purpose of vagueness, "an action based on reliance is equivalent to a contract action"); Garcia v. World Sav., FSB, 107 Cal. Rptr. 3d 683 (Ct. App. 2010) (applying general contract test for indefiniteness to promissory estoppel claim); Jackson v. Ford, 555 S.E.2d 143 (Ga. App. 2001) (promise too vague to support breach of contract action also too vague to support promissory estoppel action), followed in Ga. Invs. Int'l v. Branch Banking & Trust Co., 700 S.E.2d 662 (Ga. App. 2010) (alleged promise of loan vague and indefinite because of missing interest rate).

§2.19 n.31 p.175 In the second paragraph, add the following after the citation to* Nappi*: , followed in Harvey v. Dow, 962 A.2d 322 (Me. 2008) (implied promise sufficient; here, derived from the "acquiescence, support, and encouragement of [Harvey's] construction of a house on the property").

§2.19 n.31 p.175 In the third paragraph, add the following at the end: *But cf.* Donna Ind. Sch. Dist. v. Gracia, 286 S.W.3d 392 (Tex. Civ. App. 2008) (sovereign immunity bars promissory estoppel actions, save in "exceptional cases where the circumstances clearly demand its application," primarily zoning and permitting cases "where sovereign immunity was not a central issue").

§2.19 n.32 p.176 Add the following at the end: Similarly, a statement of fact with no future implications does not amount to a promise. *See* Pappas v. Ippolito, 895 N.E.2d 610 (Ohio App. 2008) (allegedly misleading rent rolls insufficient; "Because appellants' claim is not based upon an enforceable promise, but rather upon a misrepresentation of an existing or past fact, it fails to satisfy the first element of promissory estoppel"). *Cf.* MMK Grp. v. SheShells Co., 591 F. Supp. 2d 944 (N.D. Ohio 2008) (where promise contingent on uncertain events, the claimant "cannot establish the presence of a clear and unambiguous promise").

§2.19 n.33 p.176 Add the following to the list after* "Accord"*: City of Clinton v. Pilgrim's Pride Corp., 632 F.3d 148 (5th Cir. 2010) (Arkansas law: business's promise that it "will not go off and leave you holding the bag" and that it would "have a long-term commitment to the City of Clinton" so "vague and attenuated" that they "cannot be considered to be promises that the defendant would reasonably expect to induce action").

§2.19 n.33 p.176 Add the following after the second sentence: *Cf.* Chism v. Curtner, 619 F.3d 979 (8th Cir. 2010) (Arkansas law: city cannot be estopped by the unauthorized actions of its officers, so it would not reasonably expect reliance on those acts, nor would it be reasonable to rely upon them), *abrogated on other grounds*, Torgerson v. City of Rochester, 643 F.3d 1031 (8th Cir. 2011). On the intersection between governmental liability and contract principles more generally, see §5.1 *infra*.

§2.19 n.33 p.176 Add the following as a new paragraph at the end: It is growing relatively common for promisors to insert anti-reliance clauses in their agreements, such as "This is provided for informational purposes and no reliance should be placed thereon" (taken from a bid letter). So far these have been quite effective in stopping plaintiffs at the second element of promissory estoppel, or sometimes the third when framed as reasonable reliance. *See* Fletcher-Harlee Corp. v. Pote Concrete Contractors, 482 F.3d 247 (3d Cir. 2007) (industry practice "cannot justify relying on a submission that specifically directs the recipient not to rely on it"); Barnes & Robinson Co. v. Onesource Facility Servs., *supra* note 25 (no reliance reasonable when letter of intent stated that "the parties shall have no liability in the event the transaction was not completed for any reason whatsoever"); Finch v. Farmers Co-Op. Oil Co., 109 P.3d 537 (Wyo. 2005) (disclaimers of continued employment in handbook "prevented Mr. Finch from establishing that he reasonably relied on Mr. Nelson's statement").

§2.19 n.34 p.177 Add the following to the list after "See": Binkley v. Entergy Operations, 602 F.3d 928 (8th Cir. 2010) (Arkansas law; plaintiff has the "burden of showing that he suffered a detriment"; no harm in inability to appeal discharge where final decision made by person who fired him).

§2.19 n.34 p.177 Add the following at the end: It may, however, be too early to write off reliance; whether it is the key to promissory estoppel, it very much remains an element. *See* Nationwide Mut. Ins. Co. v. Regency Furniture, 963 A.2d 253 (Md. App. 2009) (where insured responded to insurer's statement exactly as it would had the insurer not made the statement, there is "no evidence whatsoever that Regency changed its position in reliance on Nationwide's statement" and thus no basis for estoppel, whether equitable or promissory).

§2.19 n.36 p.177 Add the following to the list after "Accord": Hartford Fire Ins. Co. v. City of Mont Belvieu, 611 F.3d 289 (5th Cir. 2010) (city's reliance on implied promise by surety not to assert statute of limitations unreasonable; city "is a legally sophisticated party and, as a municipality, knowledgeable in Texas's law of public project bonds"); Gilmour v. Am. Nat'l Red Cross, 385 F.3d 1318 (11th Cir. 2004) (where employment manual provided for additional insurance coverage at the discretion of employer's national headquarters, reliance by worker on supervisor's assurances "unreasonable as a matter of law"); Local 107 Office & Prof'l Employees Int'l Union v. Offshore Logistics, 380 F.3d 832 (5th Cir. 2004) (federal common law) (where union relied upon assurances of pay increases in electing not to sue, but did not first get a letter of agreement, it did not establish "why its reliance was reasonable"); Barnes & Robinson Co. v. Onesource Facility Servs., 195 S.W.3d 637 (Tenn. App. 2006) ("the plaintiff must show not only that a promise was made, but also that the plaintiff *reasonably relied* on the promise to his detriment"); Hess v. Johnston, 163 P.3d 747 (Utah App. 2007) (fiancé did not act "with prudence and in reasonable reliance" upon promise to marry by paying for trips, giving money to son, and having a vasectomy;

"the engagement period is, in essence, a test period, mak[ing] reliance on the promise of marriage inherently problematic").

§2.19 n.36 p.177 Add the following at the end: For an interesting analysis of the relation of reasonable reliance and promissory intent, *see* Garwood Packaging v. Allen & Co., *supra* note 30 (Posner, J.) ("the essence of the doctrine of promissory estoppel is not that the plaintiff have reasonably relied on the defendant's promise, but that he have reasonably relied on its *being* a promise in the sense of a legal commitment, and not a mere prediction or aspiration or bit of puffery").

§2.19 n.38 p.178 Add the following after the first sentence: *Accord:* Sandel v. ATP Oil & Gas Corp., 243 S.W.3d 749 (Tex. Civ. App. 2007) (continuing to work after receiving letter promising stock options not detrimental reliance; "[f]ailure to seek another job is insufficient because Sandel must show that but for the letter, he would have stopped working for ATP").

§2.19 n.40 p.180 Add the following to the list after **"Accord"***:* Knauf Realty v. Prudential Real Estate Affiliates, 486 F. Supp. 2d 855 (W.D. Wis. 2007) (same).

§2.19 n.41 p.180 Add the following after the first sentence: *Accord:* Local 107 Office & Prof'l Employees Int'l Union v. Offshore Logistics, *supra* note 36 (federal common law) (no injustice in failing to enforce promised pay increases when union could have asserted its rights to sue under the Railway Labor Act); Hinkel v. Sataria Distrib. & Packaging, 920 N.E.2d 766 (Ind. App. 2010) (promise of a year's salary and insurance coverage if employment terminated voluntarily; "Hinkel was provided with a period of employment at Sataria [four months], a substantial salary, and six weeks of severance. Hinkel has not shown an injury so independent and severe that injustice could only be avoided by enforcement of [the defendant's] alleged promise."); Peluso v. Kistner, 970 A.2d 530 (Pa. Commw. Ct. 2009) (dictum: "there is 'no injustice in being deprived of a gratuitous benefit.' ") (quoting from Stelmack v. Glen Alden Coal Co., 14 A.2d 127 (Pa. 1940)).

§2.19 n.41 p.180 Add the following to the list in the last sentence: Norton v. Hoyt, 278 F. Supp. 2d 214 (D.R.I. 2003) ("public policy would frown on enforcing" promise to divorce wife and marry and support another woman even if other requirements for promissory estoppel were met).

§2.19 n.41 p.180 Add the following at the end: For the potential relevance of equitable concepts, *see* Garcia v. World Sav., FSB, 107 Cal. Rptr. 3d 683 (Ct. App. 2010) (considering the application of unclean hands doctrine, but concluding that it wasn't relevant given the facts). For a peculiar application of this element, see Clevenger v. Oliver Ins. Agency, *supra* note 25 (where insurance agent misrepresented contents of policy, no action in promissory estoppel; there was an adequate remedy at law, a negligence suit, so injustice would not be avoided through the use of the equitable remedy of promissory estoppel).

§2.19 n.42 p.180 In the first paragraph, add the following to the list after* "Accord"*: Newton Tractor Sales v. Kubota Tractor Corp., 906 N.E.2d 520 (Ill. 2009) ("courts may appropriately limit relief to only those damages suffered as a result of justifiably relying on the other party's promise").

§2.19 n.42 p.180 Add the following at the end of the first paragraph: Professor Hillman has surveyed promissory estoppel cases and found a roughly even split between expectation and reliance damages, with the balance shifting somewhat for different causes of action. *See* Hillman, *supra* note 24. *See also* Jackson v. Morse, 871 A.2d 47 (N.H. 2005) (collecting cases). *But see* Jimenez, The Many Faces of Promissory Estoppel: An Empirical Analysis Under the Restatement (Second) of Contracts, 57 UCLA L. Rev. 669 (2010) (more recent empirical study, showing expectation more common than reliance).

§2.19 n.43 p.181 Add the following to the list after the first* "Accord"*: Toscano v. Greene Music, 21 Cal. Rptr. 3d 732 (Ct. App. 2004) (allowing reliance damages, including lost wages from the old job, where employee resigned on the basis of a promised job that was then withdrawn).

§2.19 n.43 p.181 In the second paragraph, add the following to the list after* "See generally"*: Comment, Using Promissory Estoppel to Preserve Traditional Contract Principles and Protect Employee Rights, 2005 Mich. St. L. Rev. 1235.

§2.19 p.182 Add the following to the text after the second full sentence: Indeed, it would follow as well that equitable remedies would be available in promissory estoppel actions whenever they would in actions over contracts formed with consideration.[45a]

[45a] *See* Jackson v. Morse, *supra* note 42 ("in some instances, the appropriate remedy may be specific performance"); Skebba v. Kasch, 724 N.W.2d 408 (Wis. App. 2006) ("a court, in fashioning a remedy, can consider any equitable *or* legal remedy which will 'prevent injustice.' ") (emphasis in original).

§2.19 n.47 p.182 Add the following after the second sentence: *Cf.* Curtis Lumber Co. v. La. Pac. Corp., 618 F.3d 762 (8th Cir. 2010) (Arkansas law: relief under promissory estoppel not limited to restitution by promisor to promisee, but includes reliance costs incurred by third parties).

§2.19 n.48 p.182 Add the following to the end: On the presumption that the expectation measure should be applied, see Jackson v. Morse, *supra* note 42.

§2.19 n.51 p.183 Add the following after the first sentence: *Accord:* Jackson v. Morse, *supra* note 42 ("damages in the case of an indefinite or unclear promise 'will be limited to expenses incurred in reasonable reliance on the vague promise' ") (quoting Garwood Packaging v. Allen & Co., *supra* note 30); Clifford R. Gray, Inc. v. LeChase Constr. Servs., 857 N.Y.S.2d 347 (App. Div. 2008) ("Plaintiff is not asking Supreme Court to enforce a contract that would otherwise be enforceable but for lack of consideration . . . but to provide a remedy where the underlying agreement fails for indefiniteness. . . . The doctrine is not being used defensively in support of contract rights, but, instead, to create a new right in the interests of justice with relief designed to achieve equity . . . Under these circumstances, plaintiff is not entitled to the benefit of the bargain because there was no bargain.") (citations and internal quotation marks omitted).

§2.19 n.56 p.184 ***Add the following at the end:*** Another possibility is also tort-like: in promissory estoppel cases the promisee is partly at fault for not securing a properly binding contract, so justice is served by restoring the promisee to its pre-promise condition but no more. *See* Bechtel Corp. v. CITGO Prods. Pipeline Co., 271 S.W.3d 898 (Tex. Civ. App. 2008).

§2.20 NATURE AND ROLE OF RESTITUTION

§2.20 n.3a p.185 ***Add the following new note after the second sentence in the second paragraph:*** [3a] *See* Restatement (Third) of Restitution & Unjust Enrichment §6 cmt. a (identifying "[m]istaken payment of money not due" as "one of the core cases of restitution."); *In re* APA Assessment Fee Litig., 766 F.3d 39 (D.C. Cir. 2014) (holding allegations of misleading dues statement sufficient to state claim for unjust enrichment).

§2.20 n.4 p.186 ***Add the following after the second sentence:*** *See* Town of New Hartford v. Conn. Resources Recovery Auth., 970 A.2d 592 (Conn. 2009) ("an implied in law contract is another name for a claim for unjust enrichment").

§2.20 n.5 p.186 ***Add the following to the list after "See":*** River Park Hosp. v. BlueCross BlueShield of Tenn., 173 S.W.3d 43 (Tenn. App. 2002) (finding implied-in-law contract where hospital was obliged to take emergency patients under federal law and insurer was obliged to pay for emergency care under its contract with the state; "while neither of these parties may have wanted to deal with the other, both were left with no choice").

§2.20 n.6 p.186 ***Add the following to the list after "Accord":*** Lindquist Ford v. Middleton Motors, 557 F.3d 469 (7th Cir. 2009) ("[Q]uantum meruit and unjust enrichment are quasi-contract actions (obligations imposed by law in the absence

of a contract). . . . The Wisconsin Supreme Court distinguishes quantum meruit/contracts implied by law from unjust enrichment, where there is no implied contract at all . . . In contrast to quantum meruit, an implied-in-fact contract is governed by general contract principles."); Confold Pac. v. Polaris Enters., 433 F.3d 952 (7th Cir. 2006) (Posner, J.) (seeking to disentangle this "bewildering array of terms"); Mid-Hudson Catskill Rural Migrant Ministry v. Fine Host Corp., 418 F.3d 168 (2d Cir. 2005) (Sotomayor, J.) ("Applying New York law, we may analyze quantum meruit and unjust enrichment together as a single quasi contract claim."); Boon Rawd Trading Int'l Co. v. Paleewong Trading Co., 688 F. Supp. 2d 940 (N.D. Cal. 2010) ("unjust enrichment . . . is synonymous with restitution. . . . As such, a claim for unjust enrichment is properly pled as a claim for a contract implied-in-law.") (internal quotation omitted); Ellipso, Inc. v. Mann, 460 F. Supp. 2d 99 (D.D.C. 2006) ("action in *quantum meruit* is an action on a contract implied in fact," while "[a]n unjust enrichment action . . . involves a quasi-contract, a contract implied in law"); Gray v. Tri-Way Constr. Servs., 210 P.3d 63 (Idaho 2009) ("quantum meruit is a remedy for an implied-in-fact contract . . ." and "[u]njust enrichment, or restitution, is the measure of recovery under a contract implied in law"); Hayes Mechanical v. First Indus., L.P., 812 N.E.2d 419 (Ill. App. 2004) ("In a *quantum meruit* action, the measure of recovery is the reasonable value of work and material provided, whereas in an unjust enrichment action, the inquiry focuses on the benefit received and retained as a result of the improvement provided by the contractor"); Johnson v. Larson, 779 N.W.2d 412 (S.D. 2010) ("Quantum meruit implies a contract where none exists and awards restitution for the value of the services provided under that implied contract. . . . Further, damages may be awarded even if the plaintiff's services conferred no benefit. Unjust enrichment, on the other hand, allowed an award of restitution for the value of the benefit unjustly received, rather than the value of the service provided. The defendant must be unjustly *enriched.* However, the reasonable cost of the services provided can be evidence of the value of the benefit conferred.") (citations omitted); R.M. Dudley Const. Co. v. Dawson, 258 S.W.3d 694 (Tex. Civ. App. 2008) ("Quantum meruit is an equitable theory of recovery intended to prevent unjust enrichment when there is an implied agreement to pay for goods or services provided" while "Unjust enrichment, itself, is not an independent cause of action" but instead is the result of a failure to make restitution of benefits received under circumstances "that give rise to an implied or quasi-contractual obligation to repay"); Young v. Young, 191 P.3d 1258 (Wash. 2008) ("Unjust enrichment is the method of recovery for the value of the benefit retained absent any contractual relationship because notions of fairness and justice require it. . . . In such situations a quasi contract is said to exist between the parties. . . . 'Quantum meruit,' on the other hand, is the method of recovering the reasonable value of services provided under a contract implied in fact.").

§2.20 n.6 p.186 Add the following at the end: The legal or equitable basis for these causes of action has more than merely academic import. *See* Cummings v. Bean, 853 A.2d 221 (Me. 2004) ("Unlike the theory of unjust enrichment, which is firmly rooted in equity, quantum meruit is 'an issue triable of right by a jury' and is, therefore, an action sounding in law, not equity."); Pepi Corp. v. Galliford, 254 S.W.3d 457 (Tex. Civ. App. 2007) (different statutes of limitations apply to actions for quantum meruit and for unjust enrichment). *Cf.* Shum v. Intel Corp., 630 F. Supp. 2d 1063 (N.D. Cal. 2009) ("unjust enrichment is an equitable claim," but because there exists "a factual question common to both unjust enrichment and breach of contract, the unjust enrichment claim was properly tried to the jury.").

The new Restatement attacks vigorously the law-equity dichotomy commonly applied to restitution, stating that "[l]iabilities and remedies within the law of restitution and unjust enrichment may have originated in law, in equity, or in a combination of the two." Restatement Third of Restitution & Unjust Enrichment §4(1) (2011). Going further, the comment states that "[t]he most widespread error is the assertion that a claim in restitution or unjust enrichment is by its nature equitable rather than legal. From this false premise a court may conclude, depending on the problem at hand, (i) that there is no right to jury trial of a particular issue; (ii) that the remedy in question is available where it might otherwise not be, because the relevant statute authorizes 'equitable relief'; or (iii) that the claim in question may be dismissed because the plaintiff has an adequate remedy at law. The first two conclusions may be justifiable for other reasons, but courts frequently reach them by mischaracterizing the law of restitution and unjust enrichment. . . . The third conclusion is simply wrong." *Id.* at cmt. *c*.

§2.20 n.8 p.187 Insert the following in place of the second sentence: The American Law Institute has approved the new Restatement (Third) of Restitution and Unjust Enrichment, and its final text has just been published. On the new Restatement, *see* Kovacic-Fleischer, Quantum Meruit and the Restatement (Third) of Restitution and Unjust Enrichment, 27 Rev. Litig. 127 (2007); Rendleman, Restating Restitution: The Restatement Process and Its Critics, 65 Wash. & Lee L. Rev. 933 (2008).

§2.20 n.8 p.187 Add the following to the list after "See": T. Baloch, Unjust Enrichment and Contract (2009); P. Birks, Unjust Enrichment (2d ed. 2005); A. Burrows, The Law of Restitution (2011); H. Dagan, The Law and Ethics of Restitution (2004). Both Birks and Dagan are discussed in Gergen, A Thoroughly Modern Theory of Restitution, 84 Tex. L. Rev. 173 (2005).

§2.20 n.8 p.187 Add the following to the last sentence: Roundtable, 65 Wash. & Lee L. Rev. 889 (2008).

§2.20 n.21 p.188 Add the following at the start: Thus it is not enough that the claimant's loss was the product of injustice; the other party's gains must themselves have come about through circumstances that make their retention unjust. *See* Casstevens v. Smith, 269 S.W.3d 222 (Tex. Civ. App. 2008) (defrauded homeowner has no restitution action against buyer at proper foreclosure sale; action is against the people whose fraud caused the foreclosure). Similarly, in many states restitution requires a direct economic transaction between the parties. *In re* Whirlpool Corp. Front-Loading Washer Prods. Liability Litig., 684 F. Supp. 2d 942 (N.D. Ohio 2009) (no restitution claim where plaintiffs bought washing machines from retailers, who in turn bought them from the defendant/manufacturer; although there are indirect benefits, the parties engaged in no economic transactions). *Cf.* Sheet Metal Workers Local 441 Health & Welfare Plan v. GlaxoSmithKline, PLC, 737 F. Supp. 2d 380 (E.D. Pa. 2010) (surveying law in many states). On the other hand, the party against which restitution is sought need not have behaved wrongfully. The injustice central to unjust enrichment is not injustice wrought by the defendant's bad acts; it is the general injustice of the situation. *In re* Whirlpool Corp. Front-Loading Washer Prods. Liability Litig., 684 F. Supp. 2d 942, at 959 ("[T]he plaintiff must plead merely that it would be inequitable for the defendant to retain the benefit or that retention of the benefit without payment therefor would be unjust.") (internal quotes omitted).

§2.20 n.22 p.188 Add the following at the end: These grounds do not include the more general defenses to restitution, such as unclean hands, passing on, change of position, laches, and the like. *See generally* Restatement Third of Restitution & Unjust Enrichment §§62-70 (2011). *Cf.* Phillips v. Brink's Co., 632 F. Supp. 2d 563 (W.D. Va. 2009) (no restitution for overpaid disability benefits because beneficiary "rationally planned his life based on the amount stated in his benefit letter . . . and as a result he changed his position," and plan took almost seven years to discover overpayments).

§2.20 n.23 p.188 Add the following at the end: *See also* Royal Inv. Grp. v. Wang, 961 A.2d 665 (Md. App. 2008) (contractor demolished old house and built new one, even though it had breached its contract to buy the property and the owner had repeatedly objected to the construction; "[A]lthough Royal may have conferred a benefit on Mr. Wang, it was conferred against Mr. Wang's wishes and express directions. . . . Accordingly, even though Mr. Wang may be enriched by improvements made to the Property, there was no **UNJUST** enrichment in this case.") (emphasis in original).

§2.20 n.27 p.190 Add the following at the end: *See also* Restatement (Third) of Restitution and Unjust Enrichment §20 (2011) (ratifying *Cotnam* and similar cases).

§2.20 n.28 p.190 Add the following at the end: This approach is largely ratified in the new Restatement of Restitution, which "presum[es] that rescue by a nonprofessional is a gratuitous act." Restatement (Third) of Restitution and Unjust Enrichment §20 cmt. b (2011). As the comment states, "[t]he imposition of restitutionary liability in such circumstances . . . transforms an act of self-sacrifice into a contentious exchange of values." *Id.*

§2.20 n.29 p.190 Add the following to the list after **"Accord"***:* Estate of Goth v. Tremble, 873 N.Y.S.2d 364 (App. Div. 2009) ("defendant's candid admissions that he voluntarily provided services to decedent out of friendship without expectation of any compensation would defeat the claim that plaintiff possesses property rightfully belonging to defendant"); Chambers v. Hunt Petroleum Corp., 320 S.W.3d 578 (Tex. Civ. App. 2010) (lessees unable to recover maintenance costs from lessor; lessor stated that "they told him that he was being so nice that they would clean up the brush," so lessor treated the work as gratuitous); Hess v. Johnston, 163 P.3d 747 (Utah App. 2007) (no unjust enrichment for gifts given a fiancée before she broke off the engagement; the donor intended nothing "other than an unconditional gift").

§2.20 n.31 p.191 Add the following at the end: Both the holding in *Webb* and the law of marine salvage are approved of by the draft Restatement. Restatement (Third) of Restitution and Unjust Enrichment §§20 ill. 7 *(Webb)* & 21 cmt. e (2011).

§2.20 n.33 p.191 Add the following to the list after **"Accord"***:* Kia v. Imaging Sciences Int'l, 735 F. Supp. 2d 256 (E.D. Pa. 2010) (no recovery in restitution where contract exists; even if jury ultimately rejects existence of contract, no recovery, because "in the absence of this contract, Kia could have no expectation that he would be provided any of the proceeds from the sale of ISI"); *In re* New Motor Vehicles Can. Export Antitrust Litig., 350 F. Supp. 2d 160 (D. Me. 2004) ("unjust enrichment ordinarily does not furnish a basis for liability where parties voluntarily have negotiated, entered into and fully performed their bargain"); David M. Somers & Assocs. v. Busch, 927 A.2d 832 (Conn. 2007) ("A party may not recover the reasonable value of services rendered, pursuant to the doctrine of *quantum meruit*, when the actions for which it seeks relief were governed by an express contract."); Town of New Ross v. Ferretti, 815 N.E.2d 162 (Ind. App. 2004) ("where the rights of parties are controlled by an

express contract, recovery cannot be based upon a theory implied in law").

§2.20 n.33 p.191 Add the following to the list after "Cf.": Town of New Hartford v. Conn. Res. Recovery Auth., 970 A.2d 592 (Conn. 2009) (" 'when an express contract does not fully address a subject, a court of equity may impose a remedy to further the ends of justice' ") (quoting from Klein v. Arkoma Prod. Co., 73 F.3d 779 (8th Cir. 1996)); Morris Pumps v. Centerline Piping, 729 N.W.2d 898 (Mich. App. 2006) (suppliers to insolvent subcontractor sued general contractor: while there is no action in *quantum meruit* if there is an express contract between the same parties on the same subject matter, there are no such limits if the defendant was not a party to that contract); Ron Medlin Constr. v. Harris, 681 S.E.2d 807 (N.C. App. 2009) ("[T]he focus, in the *quantum meruit* context, is on whether there is an express contract *on the subject matter at issue* and not on whether there was a contract between the parties.") (emphasis in original), *aff'd*, 704 S.E.2d 486 (N.C. 2010); Mongold v. Woods, 677 S.E.2d 288 (Va. 2009) (rule barring quantum meruit claims applies only when there is an express contract "covering the services for which quantum meruit recovery is claimed"; because additional work not dealt with under original contract, quantum meruit action available for it).

§2.20 n.33 p.191 Add the following after the third sentence: This point is nicely made in Johnson v. Larson, 779 N.W.2d 412 (S.D. 2010). There Johnson arranged that Larson would remove rock from his land in exchange for the value of the rock, with a later agreement that Larson could store the rock on Johnson's land in exchange for installing drain tile. Some time later, Penny asked whether he could have the rock; believing that Larson had abandoned the rock, Johnson said yes, and Penny removed the rock gratis. Naturally, Larson then showed up, demanding the rock. Left rockless, he sued Johnson and Penny. The court held that Larson had no cause of action in unjust enrichment against Johnson; "there was no room for a court to imply a promise by Larson to pay Johnson, as the parties expressly fixed their rights and obligations: Johnson's remedy lay in a claim for breach of contract." 779 N.W.2d at 416. In contrast, the court held that there was no contract between Larson and Penny, so an unjust enrichment action was available — indeed, "[t]he transfer between Johnson and Penny is the very type of event contemplated by the doctrine of unjust enrichment." 779 N.W.2d at 417.

§2.20 n.33 p.191 Add the following to the list after **"But cf.":** Exxon Corp. v. Central Gulf Lines, 500 U.S. 603 (1991) (maritime jurisdiction: unjust enrichment claim may proceed when based on a maritime contract); Boon Rawd Trading Int'l Co. v. Paleewong Trading Co., 688 F. Supp. 2d 940 (N.D. Cal. 2010) (" 'Restitution may be awarded in lieu of breach of contract damages when the parties had an express contract, but it was procured by fraud or is unenforceable or ineffective for some reason.' ") (quoting McBride v. Boughton, 20 Cal. Rptr. 3d 115 (Ct. App. 2004)); MMK Grp. v. SheShells Co., 591 F. Supp. 2d 944 (N.D. Ohio 2008) (unjust enrichment "may also be maintained despite the existence of an express contract where there is evidence of fraud, bad faith, or illegality").

§2.20 n.33 p.191 Add the following at the end: It is important to bear in mind that merely alleging the existence of a contract does not foreclose pleading restitution in the alternative. Ultimately, of course, these counts may prove inconsistent, but until the facts are established or conceded there is no need to choose. *See In re* Checking Account Overdraft Litig., 694 F. Supp. 2d 1302 (S.D. Fla. 2010) ("[W]hile the law does not permit a party to simultaneously prevail on an unjust enrichment theory and a contractual theory, it does not require the dismissal (at the motion to dismiss stage) of an unjust enrichment claim merely because an express contract exists that arguably governs the conduct complained of."); Hickman v. Wells Fargo Bank, 683 F. Supp. 2d 779 (N.D. Ill. 2010) ("While a party may plead a claim for unjust enrichment in the alternative where the existence of a valid contract is questioned, if there is no dispute over the existence of a contract, a claim for unjust enrichment necessarily fails."; here, defendant concedes existence of valid, enforceable contract, so the claim for unjust enrichment must be dismissed). Nor is the mere presence of a contract enough. If the contract proves invalid or unenforceable, then its existence will not foreclose a claim

sounding in restitution. *But see* Arena Res. v. OBO, Inc., 238 P.3d 357 (N.M. App. 2010) (claimant had itself breached the contract with the other party, but was held unable to recover in restitution because the contract covered the same subject matter).

The draft Restatement of Restitution recognizes this line of cases, while doubting its antecedents. Restatement (Third) of Restitution and Unjust Enrichment, ch. 4, topic 2, rptr's note to intro. note (2011). More trenchantly, the Restatement states elsewhere: "[t]he most widespread error is the assertion that a claim in restitution or unjust enrichment is by its nature equitable rather than legal. From this false premise a court may conclude . . .(iii) that the claim in question may be dismissed because the plaintiff has an adequate remedy at law. . . . The third conclusion is simply wrong." Restatement Third of Restitution & Unjust Enrichment §4 cmt. c (2011).

§2.20 p.192 Add the following to the end of the carryover sentence: . . . rendered under the contract.[33a]

[33a] *See* Total Recycling Servs. v. Conn. Oil Recycling Servs., 970 A.2d 807 (Conn. App. 2009) (Peters, J.) (quoting from treatise) (no inconsistency between finding that plaintiff substantially performed its contract with the defendant and finding that plaintiff was entitled to recover in unjust enrichment).

§2.20 n.35 p.193 Add the following at the end: As to restitution as a remedy when a contract is unenforceable, see §6.11 *infra.*

§2.20 n.35 p.193 Add the following after the citation to* DCB Construction*: followed in Hayes Mech. v. First Indus., L.P., 812 N.E.2d 419 (Ill. App. 2004) (contractor that performed work on building at request of tenant could not recover from owner where there was "no indication that the landlord enticed the contractor to complete the renovation work requested by the tenant").

§2.20 n.36 p.193 Add the following to the list after the first* "Cf."*: Jewett v. Boihem, 23 So. 3d 658 (Ala. 2009) (seller of interest in company liable in restitution to buyer even though buyer's payments were made to the company, rather than to the seller; the money "was paid to the company *at the instance of*

Jewett. To the extent that the *company* is in Jewett's hands, the *money* is in his hands," and seller was the "sole owner and manager of the company"); Town of New Hartford v. Conn. Resources Recovery Auth., *supra* note 4 (" 'when an express contract does not fully address a subject, a court of equity may impose a remedy to further the ends of justice' ") (quoting from Klein v. Arkoma Prod. Co., 73 F.3d 779 (8th Cir. 1996)); Wagner & Brown, Ltd. v. Sheppard, 282 S.W.3d 419 (Tex. 2008) (co-tenant permitted to recover share of drilling costs from former co-tenant when incurred during term of co-tenant's lease).

§2.20 n.36 p.193 Add the following after the citation to* Green Quarries*: , distinguished away *sub silentio* in Unerstall Founds. v. Corley, 328 S.W.3d 305 (Mo. App. 2010) (permitting suit by unpaid subcontractor against owner, but only where "the owner failed to pay not only the subcontractor but also the general contractor for the work performed by the subcontractor," lest the owner have to pay twice for the same work).

§2.20 n.36 p.193 Add the following at the end: The *common fund doctrine* falls generally under this heading. Under this doctrine, where an attorney has successfully asserted the rights of one beneficiary and recovered funds, the attorney's fee may be recovered pro rata from other beneficiaries who had taken no part in paying the attorney up to the value of their shares in the common fund, provided the attorney's efforts increased the value of the beneficiary's claim to the common fund more than the prorated amount of the attorney's fee. Restatement (Third) of Restitution & Unjust Enrichment §29 (2011). *See* Stevens v. Country Mut. Ins. Co., 903 N.E.2d 733 (Ill. App. 2008) (common fund doctrine applies against injured party's insurer where injured party's lawyer secured settlement from tortfeasor's insurer). An example is a class action suit where there is no statutory fee-shifting provision; very likely most of the class members have not engaged class counsel, but class counsel is entitled to a reasonable fee paid pro rata by all class members. *See* Victor v. Argent Classic Convertible Arbitrage Fund, 623 F.3d 82 (2d Cir. 2010) ("[T]he common fund doctrine permits attorneys whose work created a common fund for the benefit of a group of plaintiffs to receive reasonable attorneys' fees from the fund. . . . Class action lawsuits are the prototypical example of instances where the common fund doctrine can apply."). *Cf.* 21st Century Ins. Co. v. Super. Ct., 213 P.3d 972 (Cal. 2009) (in suit against tortfeasor, insurer must pay pro rata share of policyholder's attorney fees; effectively, "the insurer pays all the attorney fees attributable to recovering the . . . expenses for which it seeks reimbursement, while the insured — like any other litigant — pays fees incurred in pursuing recovery for additional damages (such as for pain and suffering).").

If the third party expressly agrees to pay, then the problem would be one of past consideration, not restitution. Nevertheless, courts do allow enforcement of those promises notwithstanding the presence of only past consideration. Generally they do so, however, on basically restitutionary grounds. *See* Edson v. Poppe, 124 N.W. 441 (S.D. 1910) (owner agreed to pay well-driller hired by former tenant; held that the promise "is supported by a sufficient consideration if the services were beneficial, and were not intended to be gratuitous."). On the use of past consideration in similar cases, see §2.8 *supra*.

Though contract and unjust enrichment may be close relations, they are not twins, much less alter egos. Pleading one thus should not ordinarily mean that one has pleaded the other. But one does sometimes find easygoing courts to the contrary, notwithstanding their different elements and approaches to damages. *See* Hernandez v. Lopez, 103 Cal. Rptr. 3d 376 (Ct. App. 2009) ("The Hernandezes' detailed cause of action for breach of contract fully raised all the facts and circumstances in which equity could contemplate a quasi-contractual remedy to prevent Lopez and his wife from being unjustly enriched at the expense of the Hernandezes."). *Cf.* Lauriedale Assocs. v. Wilson, 9 Cal. Rptr. 2d 774 (Ct. App. 1992) ("The phrase 'Unjust Enrichment' does not describe a theory of recovery, but an effect: the result of a failure to make restitution under circumstances where it is equitable to do so.").

§2.20 n.38 p.195 Add the following at the end: The Colorado Supreme Court recently set forth a new test in this setting, holding that "when close family members or confidants act with a mutual purpose, unjust enrichment occurs when one party benefits from an action that is a significant deviation from that mutual purpose." Lewis v. Lewis, 189 P.3d 1134 (Colo. 2008). This stems from the confidential nature of the relationship, which requires something less than the degree of malfeasance ordinarily required to make enrichment unjust.

§2.20 n.42 p.196 Add the following to the list after **"Accord":** Hansen Bancorp v. United States, 367 F.3d 1297 (Fed. Cir. 2004) (quoting Restatement Second §371 and holding that exchange of stock in healthy thrift institution for stock in new thrift institution " 'advanced' the government's 'interests' " by enabling it to "avoid the high cost of bailing out another insolvent thrift").

§2.20 n.43 p.196 Add the following to the list after **"Accord":** Miller v. Horn, 254 S.W.3d 920 (Mo. App. 2008) (where construction for which $193,665 had already been paid resulted in a partially completed building, and the building and land sold for $100,000, the contractor failed to show any benefit from unpaid-for work); Ludyjan v. Cont. Cas. Co., 747 N.W.2d 745 (Wis. App. 2008) (buildings constructed by tenants on land with the understanding that they would be removed when the tenants vacated, where the tenants vacated, left the buildings behind, and sought restitution; no recovery because landlord not at fault, "so it was proper to value the buildings according to their 'use value' to [the defendant]: nothing.").

§2.20 n.43 p.196 Add the following to the list after **"But cf.":** Dellagrotta v. Dellagrotta, 873 A.2d 101 (R.I. 2005) ("Plaintiffs realized the difference between the fair market value of the house in its unimproved state and with the improvements," which was the appropriate measure for restitution).

§2.20 n.43 p.196 Add the following at the end: Cf. Young v. Young, *supra* note 6 (when using the cost of improvements method, "the award may not be reduced by the claimant's actual cost absent fault by the claimant or inconsequential relationship to the benefit conferred to the defendant.").

Complicating the choice between methods of measurement is how courts tease apart the various causes of action falling generally under restitution. For example, some courts distinguish *quantum meruit*, for which the measure is the value of services provided, from unjust enrichment, for which the measure is the value of the benefit unjustly received. Sullivan v. Leor Energy, 600 F.3d 542 (5th Cir. 2010); Johnson v. Larson, *supra* note 6.

§2.20 n.46 p.197 Add the following after the first sentence: For an interesting application to contingent fee contracts, *see* Liss v. Studeny, 879 N.E.2d 676 (Mass. 2008) (where lawyer sought restitution for work done on contingent case, but contingency never occurred, no recovery in *quantum meruit*).

§2.20 p.198 Add the following footnote: . . . business or profession.[47]

[47] Estate of Mueller v. Karns, 873 N.E.2d 652 (Ind. App. 2007) (basing conservator's fee on amounts charged for similar projects and offer by conservatorship for his services); Mongold v. Woods, *supra* note 36 (hourly rate allowed for quantum meruit claim was the same as that already contracted for by the parties for similar but distinct work).

CHAPTER 3

THE BARGAINING PROCESS: OFFER AND ACCEPTANCE

§3.3 OFFER AND ACCEPTANCE

§3.3 n.1 p.203 Add the following after the first sentence: On computer-to-computer contracting, *see generally* J. Winn & B. Wright, Law of Electronic Commerce ch. 5 (4th ed. 2001); Chopra & White, Artificial Agents and the Contracting Problem: A Solution Via an Agency Analysis, 2009 J. L. Tech. & Pol'y 363.

§3.3 n.2 p.203 Add the following to the list after **"See generally"***:* Ben-Shahar, Contracts without Consent: Exploring a New Basis for Contractual Liability, 152 U. Penn. L. Rev. 1829 (2004); Eisenberg, The Revocation of Offers, 2004 Wis. L. Rev. 271.

§3.3 n.2 p.203 Add the following to the list in the fifth sentence: Philippe, French and American Approaches to Contract Formation and Enforceability: A Comparative Perspective, 12 Tul. J. Comp. & Int'l L. 357 (2005).

§3.3 n.3 p.204 Add the following to the end of the fifth sentence: and in R.I. Council 94, AFSCME, AFL-CIO v. State, 714 A.2d 584 (R.I. 1998) (agreement between two state agencies not a violation of collective bargaining agreement, because both agencies are part of a single entity and thus cannot make their agreements into enforceable contracts).

§3.4 BILATERAL AND UNILATERAL CONTRACTS

§3.4 n.4 p.206 Add the following to the list after "See"*:* Conference Am. v. Conexant Sys., 508 F. Supp. 2d 1005 (M.D. Ala. 2007); Mitri v. Arnel Mgmt. Co., 69 Cal. Rptr. 3d 223 (Ct. App. 2007); Scoular Co. v. Denney, 151 P.3d 615 (Colo. App. 2006); Auto Glass Exp. v. Hanover Ins. Co., 975 A.2d 1266 (Conn. 2009); Newton Tractor Sales v. Kubota Tractor Corp., 906 N.E.2d 520 (Ill. 2009); *In re* Certified Question (Bankey v. Storer Broad. Co.), 443 N.W.2d 112 (Mich. 1989) ("definitions of unilateral and bilateral contracts were not included in the Second Restatement of Contracts . . . Nevertheless, . . . unilateral contract theory has not only persisted, its use by appellate courts has increased . . ."); Weinstein v. KLT Telecom, 225 S.W.3d 413 (Mo. 2007); Vanegas v. Am. Energy Servs., 302 S.W.3d 299 (Tex. 2009); Duncan v. Alaska USA Fed. Credit Union, 199 P.3d 991 (Wash. App. 2008) ("Notwithstanding [the Restatement Second], we recognize that Washington cases in this area of employment law still use these distinctions to characterize the nature of the employment relationship.").

§3.4 n.4 p.206 Add the following at the end: For a particularly lively account of the pointlessness of the distinction, *see* Epstein & Liebesman, Bearded Ladies Walking on the Brooklyn Bridge, 59 Ark. L. Rev. 267 (2006). The status of unilateral contracts is still emphasized in some tax cases, however. *See* Giant Eagle, Inc. v. Comm'r of Internal Revenue, 822 F.3d 666 (3d Cir. 2016) (under accrual accounting method and the "all events" test, taxpayer could claim expenses based on gas rewards program earned by shopping at affiliated grocery story; grocery customers were "a party to a unilateral contract with Giant Eagle. Liability therefore attached upon her performance, *i.e.*, at checkout.").

§3.5 ANOTHER VIEW OF THE AGREEMENT PROCESS

§3.5 n.1 p.207 Add the following to the list after "See": Guidry v. Charter Comm'ns, 269 S.W.3d 520 (Mo. App. 2008) ("A

contractual relationship may arise without the formalities of offer and acceptance.").

§3.5 n.2 p.207 Add the following at the beginning: See Gregory v. Dillard's, Inc., 565 F.3d 464 (8th Cir. 2009) (Murphy, J., dissenting) ("The steps toward contract formation will vary with context. The purchase of a standardized commercial product — a can of soda or a packet of chewing gum — from a low service convenience store requires virtually no interaction between customer and clerk aside from the tender of payment. Mere seconds may elapse between the formation of a customer's intent to purchase and the final exchange of cash for goods. . . . On the other hand, a consumer's purchase of expensive durable goods — a new washer and dryer or a new car — often involves significant customer education, inspection of wares, comparison of prices and features, negotiation of financing agreements, and extended assistance by informed sales agents. In such circumstances the process of contract formation may be quite lengthy, and the customer's specific intentions may wax and wane throughout.").

§3.6 SUBJECTIVE AND OBJECTIVE THEORIES

§3.6 n.2 p.209 Add the following to the list after **"See also"***:* Navair, Inc. v. IFR Americas, 519 F.3d 1131 (10th Cir. 2008) ("IFR makes the far-too-common error of construing too literally the phrase 'the meeting of the minds.' Contracts are not formed by comparing mental states; they are formed by what the parties *communicate*." (emphasis in original)); Hildenbrand v. Capital RV Ctr., 794 N.W.2d 733 (N.D. 2011) (" 'The invocation of the shorthand expression 'meeting of the minds' is more misleading than helpful in deciding contract cases. . . . It is the words of the contract and the manifestations of assent which govern, not the secret intentions of the parties . . . ' ") (quoting from Delzer v. United Bank, 527 N.W.2d 650, 655 n.3 (N.D. 1995)).

§3.6 n.2 p.209 Add the following at the end: But see Sprout v. Bd. of Educ. of County of Harrison, 599 S.E.2d 764 (W. Va. 2004) (apparently using subjective intent as element of contract formation).

§3.6 n.4 p.209 Add the following to the list after **"See generally"***:* Barnes, The Objective Theory of Contracts, 76 U. Cin. L. Rev. 1119 (2008); Pretorius, The Basis of Contractual Liability in American Law, 37 Comp. & Int'l L.J. of S. Afr. 226 (2004).

§3.6 n.4 p.209 Add the following to the end: For a particularly vigorous defense of subjective intent as both normatively and descriptively superior to objective intent, *see* Solan, Contract as Agreement, 83 Notre Dame L. Rev. 353 (2007). *See also* Whittier, The Restatement of Contracts and Mutual Assent, 17 Cal. L. Rev. 441 (1929). Other legal systems, in particular the French, are predominantly subjective, though one may ask whether this matters in most cases. *See* Barnes, The French Subjective Theory of Contract: Separating Rhetoric from Reality, 83 Tul. L. Rev. 359 (2008); Valcke, Convergence *and* Divergence of the English, French, and German Conceptions of Contract, 16 Eur. Rev. Private L. 29 (2008). *See generally* Beever, Agreements, Mistakes, and Contract Formation, 20 King's L.J. 21 (2009) (contrasting civil law and common law approaches; finds neither either pure or adequately descriptive).

§3.6 n.6 p.210 Add the following at the end of the second sentence: and in Newkirk v. Village of Steger, 536 F.3d 771 (7th Cir. 2008) (one must "look first to the written records, not to mental processes," ignoring "hidden doubts or questions").

§3.6 n.6 p.210 Add the following to the list after **"Accord"***:* Loppert v. WindsorTech, Inc., 865 A.2d 1282 (Del. Ch. 2004) ("the parties' overt manifestation of assent — not subjective intent — controls the result"); Hanson v. Maxfield, 23 So. 3d 736 (Fla. App. 2009) (" 'The making of a contract depends not on the agreement of two minds in one intention, but on the agreement of two sets of external signs — not on the parties having meant the same thing but on their having said the same thing.' ") (quoting from Blackhawk Heating & Plumbing Co. v. Data Lease Fin. Corp., 302 So. 2d 404 (Fla. 1974), itself quoting from Gendzier v. Bielecki, 97 So. 2d 604 (Fla. 1957), itself quoting from Holmes, The Path of the Law, 10 Harv. L. Rev. 457 (1897)); Amann v. Frederick, 257 N.W.2d 436 (N.D. 1977) ("Assent, in the

sense of the law, is a matter of overt acts, not of inward unanimity in motives, design, or the interpretation of words.").

§3.6 n.6 p.210 ***Add the following at the end:*** Who this reasonable person is has occasioned a measure of debate. For one thoughtful approach, *see* Pagnani-Braga-Kimmel Urologic Assoc. v. Chappell, 968 A.2d 1242 (N.J. Super. L. Div. 2009) ("When looking for mutual assent, a court will take these outward manifestations and ask 'what meaning the words should have conveyed to a *reasonable person* cognizant of the relationship between the parties and all of the antecedent and surrounding facts and circumstances.' ") (quoting from Esslinger's Inc. v. Alachnowicz, 172 A.2d 433 (N.J. Super. App. Div. 1961)), followed in *In re* Nickels Midway Pier, 348 Fed. Appx. 781 (3d Cir. 2009). Such a definition does edge toward subjectivism, though, insofar as it is highly contextualized. For a less sober approach, *see* A. P. Herbert, *Fardell v. Potts,* in Uncommon Law 1 (1935) ("All solid virtues are his, save only that peculiar quality by which the affection of other men is won. . . . He is one who invariably looks where he leaps . . . who in the way of business looks only for that narrow margin of profit which twelve men such as himself would reckon to be 'fair,' and contemplates his fellow-merchants, their agents, and their goods, with that degree of suspicion and distrust which the law deems admirable . . . Devoid, in short, of any human weakness, with not one single saving vice, *sans* prejudice, procrastination, ill-nature, avarice, and absence of mind, as careful for his own safety as he is for that of others, this excellent but odious character stands like a monument in our Courts of Justice, vainly appealing to his fellow-citizens to order their lives after his own example.").

§3.6 n.10 p.210 ***Add the following at the end of the first sentence:*** Colton v. Colton, 244 P.3d 1121 (Alaska 2010) (defendant's "unexpressed intentions and mental reservations do not override his objective and unequivocal manifestations of assent to the terms of the agreement"); Zimmerman v. McColley, 826 N.E.2d 71 (Ind. App. 2005) ("Hall manifested a willingness to settle the claim for a lump sum of $115,000 at the moment she asked Chamberlain whether the McColleys would accept that amount; whether or not Hall actually intended to do so is

immaterial."); Dobson v. Portrait Homes, 117 P.3d 1200 (Wyo. 2005) ("a contract can be formed where one party lacks subjective intent, but nevertheless proceeds as if there were a contract").

§3.6 n.12 p.211 Add the following at the end: See also Stewart v. Cendant Mobility Servs. Corp., 837 A.2d 736 (Conn. 2003) ("promise must reflect a present intent to commit as distinguished from a mere statement to contract in the future"); Universal Health Servs. v. Renaissance Women's Grp., 121 S.W.3d 742 (Tex. 2003) ("language that the project 'will be composed of a women's hospital . . . and medical offices and clinic' is only a general description of the project, not an obligation on either party"); Bubble Pony, Inc. v. Facepunch Studios Ltd., 2015 U.S. Dist. LEXIS 163718 (D. Minn. Dec. 7, 2015) (parties had a contract governing some work, but never formed a contract with regard to the work in dispute because, as to the latter, the defendant "used vague and indefinite terms such as 'eventually' and 'something like 60%.' . . . At most, the emails reflect an intention to explore such an agreement at a later time. Because the parties never reached such an agreement, there is no contract covering Glynn's work on RUST and his contract claim fails as a matter of law."). *Cf.* Garwood Packaging v. Allen & Co., 378 F.3d 698 (7th Cir. 2004) (Posner, J.: "what is a reasonable, and indeed actual, understanding will often depend on the knowledge that the promisee brings to the table").

§3.6 n.13 p.211 Add the following to the list after **"Accord":** Bayview Hunters Point Cmty. Advocates v. Metro. Transp. Comm'n, 366 F.3d 692 (9th Cir. 2004) (agreement "to establish a ridership 'target' is simply not the same as promising to attain that target").

§3.6 n.15 p.212 Add the following to the list after **"Accord":** Lovely v. Percy, 826 N.E.2d 909 (Ohio App. 2005) (allegations that plastic surgeon promised patient that her breasts would be particular size stated cause of action).

§3.6 n.16 p.212 Add the following to the list after **"See":** Price Bros. Co. v. Philadelphia Gear Corp., 649 F.2d 416 (6th Cir. 1981) (to determine whether a statement is a warranty or merely

puffing, "the court should consider the reasonableness of the buyer in believing the seller").

§3.6 n.16 p.212 ***Add the following at the end:*** *See generally* Hoffman, The Best Puffery Article Ever, 91 Iowa L. Rev. 1395 (2006).

§3.7 INTENTION TO BE BOUND OR NOT

§3.7 n.1 p.213 ***Add the following at the end:*** An important application of this principle arises with the various forms of on-line contracting. As one court recently summarized:

> There are two primary means of forming contracts on the internet: (1) "clickwrap" agreements, "in which website users typically click an 'I agree' box after being presented with a list of terms and conditions of use," and (2) "browsewrap" agreements, in which "the terms and conditions of use for a website or other downloadable product are posted on the website typically as a hyperlink at the bottom of the screen."

Nicosa v. Amazon.com, 84 F. Supp. 3d 142 (E.D.N.Y. 2015) (quoting Hines v. Overstock.com, Inc., 668 F. Supp. 2d 362, 366 (E.D.N.Y. 2009)). Another court reduced this to a chart:

	"Clickwrap" agreements	**"Browsewrap" agreements**
Notice provided by offeror — how terms are presented to the user	On the same webpage/user is forced to scroll through	Hyperlink; user not required to open or review
Manifestation of assent by offeree	Click on "I agree" box/expressly manifest assent	Silence/use of website or service

In re Facebook Biometric Information Litig., 185 F. Supp. 3d 1155, 2016 U.S. Dist. LEXIS 60046, at *22 (N.D. Cal. 2016). "Although there is no per se rule of validity or invalidity on either end, [the 9th] Circuit has recognized that the closer digital agreements are to the clickwrap end of the spectrum, the more often they have been upheld as valid and enforceable." *Id.*

In general, the courts have had no difficulty enforcing promises made through clickwrap agreements. *See* Bassett v. Electronic Arts, 93 F. Supp. 3d 95, 104 (E.D.N.Y. 2015) ("Plaintiff manifested assent to the agreement to arbitrate when he clicked 'I Accept' during both the registration process and when later confronted with updated Terms of Service"); Starke v. Gilt Grp., Inc., 2014 U.S. Dist. LEXIS 58006 (S.D.N.Y. Apr. 24, 2014) ("Regardless of whether he actually read the contract's terms, Starke was directed exactly where to click in order to review those terms, and his decision to click the 'Shop Now' button represents his assent to them."). The Fourth Circuit has even held that copyright can be assigned with a click. Metro. Reg'l Info. Sys., Inc. v. Am. Home Realty Network, Inc., 722 F.3d 591, 602 (4th Cir. 2013) (clicking yes on a Terms of Use notice prior to uploading a photograph "effect[s] a valid transfer of copyright interests under Section 204 of the Copyright Act."). In a 2015 case, the Second Circuit likened e-mails containing links to terms and conditions to promotional materials noting that terms and conditions were available elsewhere or upon request. Starkey v. G Adventures, Inc., 796 F.3d 193 (2d Cir. 2015) (following Effron v. Sun Line Cruises, Inc., 67 F.3d 7, 8-9 (2d Cir. 1995) and holding that "G Adventures' emails thus sufficiently directed Starkey's attention to the Booking Terms and Conditions by means of a hyperlink and language advising Starkey to click on the hyperlink. This method serves the same function as the method of cross-referencing language in a printed copy promotional brochure and sufficed to direct Starkey's attention to the Booking Terms and Conditions. Both methods may be used to reasonably communicate a forum selection clause.").

Nevertheless, click agreements are only valid if the user is on notice that she is agreeing to a contract. The Seventh Circuit, in setting aside an arbitration agreement with TransUnion, explained:

> Translated to the Internet, we might ask whether the web pages presented to the consumer adequately communicate all the terms and conditions of the agreement, and whether the circumstances support the assumption that the purchaser receives reasonable notice of those terms. This is a fact-intensive inquiry: we cannot presume that a person who clicks on a box that appears on

> a computer screen has notice of all contents not only of that page but of other content that requires further action (scrolling, following a link, etc.) Indeed, a person using the Internet may not realize that she is agreeing to a contract at all, whereas a reasonable person signing a physical contract will rarely be unaware of that fact. We need, therefore, to look more closely at both the law and the facts to see if a reasonable person . . . would have realized that he was assenting to [a contract].

Sgouros v. TransUnion Corp., 817 F.3d 1029, 1034-35 (7th Cir. 2016). In that case, the consumer was purchasing his credit score and the click box was adjacent to bold text stating that the user was authorizing the use of personal information to obtain a credit report; the arbitration agreement was contained deep within an agreement that appeared in a scroll box that showed only three lines at a time. The Seventh Circuit characterized this as misleading and found that "TransUnion undid whatever notice it might have been furnishing in its bold text block by explicitly stating that a click on the button constituted assent for TransUnion to obtain access to the purchaser's personal information. That text distracted the purchaser from the Service Agreement by informing him that clicking served a particular purpose unrelated to the Agreement."

Browsewrap agreements present even more complexities than clickwrap contracts. To hazard a generalization, the browsewrap cases usually turn on whether "the website user . . . had actual or constructive knowledge of the site's terms and conditions, and have manifested assent to them." Cvent, Inc. v. Eventbrite, Inc., 739 F. Supp. 2d 927, 937 (E.D. Va. 2010). Constructive knowledge may prove especially important in routine cases. If, for example, the pertinent text is available only through a hyperlink, but the buyer must click on a button in order to assent to the hyperlinked term, that text is likely to become part of the contract. Even though the buyer may not have read the text, it has had constructive notice of its terms, just as a buyer of a ticket has constructive knowledge of the terms, not only on the front, but also on the back. *See* Fteja v. Facebook, Inc., 841 F. Supp. 2d 829 (S.D.N.Y. 2012). However, the terms must be sufficiently brought to the party's attention, and will not be enforced if "buried or 'submerged' in multiple layers of web-pages." Jerez v. JD Closeouts.com, Inc., 36 Misc. 3d 161; 943 N.Y.S.2d 392 (Nassau

Dist. Ct. 2012); *accord*: Lee v. Intellius, 737 F.3d 1254, 1259 (9th Cir. 2013) (design of agreement buttons and location of terms and conditions appeared "designed to deceive"); Hines v. Overstock .com, 668 F. Supp. 2d 362 (E.D.N.Y. 2009) (terms and conditions not part of browsewrap agreement "the website did not prompt [the plaintiff] to review the Terms and Conditions and because the link to the Terms and Conditions was not prominently displayed so as to provide reasonable notice of the Terms and Conditions"); Unif. Computer Info. Transactions Act §§111-112 (requiring that the terms be "available in a manner that ought to call [them] to the attention of a reasonable person" or that the website "disclose the availability of the standard terms in a prominent place" and "does not take affirmative acts to prevent printing or storage of the standard terms"), *aff'd per curiam*, 380 Fed. Appx. 22 (2d Cir. 2010); Nguyen v. Barnes & Noble Inc., 763 F.3d 1171, 1178-79 (9th Cir. 2014) ("where a website makes its terms of use available via a conspicuous hyperlink on every page of the website but otherwise provides no notice to users nor prompts them to take any affirmative action to demonstrate assent, even close proximity of the hyperlink to relevant buttons users must click on — without more — is insufficient to give rise to constructive notice"); Long v. Provide Commerce, Inc, 245 Cal. App. 4th 855 (2016) (browsewrap agreement unenforceable where court found that it was "difficult it is to find the Terms of Use hyperlinks in the checkout flow *even when one is looking for them*") (emphasis in original); Vitacost .com, Inc. v. McCants, 210 So. 3d 761, 763 (Fla. Ct. App. 2017) (terms and conditions, including arbitration agreement, not enforceable where the link was at the bottom of most pages and even on the check out page was situated to the side and "labeled 'terms and conditions,' not 'terms and conditions of *sale*.' " The enforceability of browsewrap agreements, particularly where they require arbitration, has gained both scholarly and popular attention in recent years. *See* Jeremy B. Merrill, *Online, It's Easy To Lose Your Right to Sue*, N.Y. Times Oct. 23, 2014, quoting Nancy S. Kim, Wrap Contracts: Foundations and Ramifications (Oxford Univ. Press 2013).

Of course, many websites do not clearly fall into either category of clickwrap or browsewrap, and the court must examine the specific design to determine whether the customer was on notice. Cf. Nicosia v. Amazon.com, 84 F. Supp. 3d 142 (E.D.N.Y.

2015) (characterizing Amazon's 2012 Conditions of Use agreement as "a hybrid between a clickwrap and a browsewrap agreement" and finding its arbitration clause enforceable based on inquiry notice to plaintiff), *aff'd in part and rev'd in part*, 834 F.3d 220, 2016 U.S. App. LEXIS 15656 (2d Cir. 2016) ("In a seeming effort to streamline customer purchases, Amazon chose not to employ a clickwrap mechanism" and the webpage design was such that "that reasonable minds could disagree on the reasonableness of notice," so the issue was not suitable to summary disposition); Savetsky v. Pre-Paid Legal Servs., Inc., 2015 U.S. Dist. LEXIS 17591 (N.D. Cal. Feb. 12, 2015) (noting that the website design "do[es] not fit neatly into any of these categories" and holding that the arbitration clause was not enforceable, where the agreement was not visible unless the user "clicked through two optional links and read to page seven," and the first such link was labeled "more plan details" and appeared after a list of other plan features such that "a reasonable person could easily conclude that 'More Plan Details' are simply an even fuller list of features LegalShield offers to its members, not the member contract or additional terms and conditions.").

In re Facebook Biometric Information Litig., 185 F. Supp. 3d 1155, 2016 U.S. Dist. LEXIS 60046 (N.D. Cal. 2016), involved two plaintiffs that had affirmatively checked an "I agree" box and another, Licata, who had registered at a time when there was no separate box but only "a single 'Sign Up' click to activate an account and accept the terms of service," *Id.* at *25. The judge there commented that "this Court were deciding those questions on a clean slate, it might find that users in Licata's situation did not form a contract with Facebook. But our [Ninth] Circuit has indicated a tolerance for the single-click 'Sign Up' and assent practice. . . . What appears to save the approach is that a user like Licata had to take some action — a click of a dual-purpose box — from which assent might be inferred. A contract was not foisted upon him simply by passively viewing a website." The court further found that the combination of direct emails and the "jewel notification" within Facebook was valid to alter the terms to their current form.

It is also worth noting that the standard for contract formation, even if the terms are deemed too hidden to be enforceable, is different from a *mens rea* of false advertising and similar laws. In

Handy v. LogMeIn, Inc., 2015 U.S. Dist. LEXIS 97021 (E.D. Cal. July 24, 2015), the plaintiff asserted that he would not have purchased software if he had known that a related, free product could be discontinued in the future, and that the "Terms and Conditions of Use," with a statement that the company could "modify or discontinue" the product was too inconspicuous and behind too many "clicks" to be enforceable. The court concluded that the plaintiff's arguments concerning enforceability of browsewrap terms "misses the point," because the issue is not whether the contract is enforceable, but whether the defendant had an affirmative duty to direct the plaintiff to available information related to a different product.

In a putative class action case in 2015, a district court found that a "sign-in wrap agreement" to arbitrate disputes was not consented to by consumers who were not adequately informed of the agreement based on the design of that website. Berkson v. Gogo, LLC, 97 F. Supp. 3d 359 (E.D.N.Y. 2015). The court collected cases and articulated a set of general principles:

> Lower courts upholding sign-in-wrap arrangements . . . have done so under three circumstances. They emphasized notice and an effective opportunity to access terms and conditions.
>
> First, where the hyperlinked "terms and conditions" is next to the only button that will allow the user to continue use of the website. See, e.g., Crawford v. Beachbody, LLC, No. 14-CV-1583, 2014 U.S. Dist. LEXIS 156658, 2014 WL 6606563, at *3 (S.D. Cal. Nov. 5, 2014) (forum selection clause binding where consumer clicked on button marked "Place Order" and above button was statement informing user that by clicking the button user was subject to the website's "terms and conditions," which were available in the same screen via hyperlink); Starke v. Gilt Group, Inc., No. 13-CV-5497, 2014 U.S. Dist. LEXIS 58006, 2014 WL 1652225, at *2-3 (S.D.N.Y. Apr. 24, 2014) (arbitration clause in "terms of use" binding where consumer clicked "Shop Now" button next to statement that informed user that "the consumer will become a Gilt member and agrees to be bound by the 'Terms of Membership,' " which were available next to the button as a hyperlink); Swift v. Zynga Game Network, Inc., 805 F. Supp. 2d 904, 908, 912 (N.D. Cal. 2011) (arbitration clause enforceable where user clicked on button marked "accept," below which was statement in small grey font indicating that clicking on the button meant accepting the hyperlinked "terms of service").

Second, where the user "signed up" to the website with a clickwrap agreement and was presented with hyperlinks to the "terms of use" on subsequent visits. See, e.g., Nicosia v. Amazon.com, Inc., No. 14-CV-4513, 84 F. Supp. 3d 142, 2015 WL 500180, at *7 (E.D.N.Y. Feb. 4, 2015) (arbitration clause enforceable where user clicked box acknowledging terms at initial signup to website and was presented with hyperlink at top of webpage to "terms of use" multiple times after completing purchases), appeal filed, No. 15-CV-0423 (2d Cir. Feb. 13, 2015); Zaltz v. JDATE, 952 F. Supp. 2d 439, 454 (E.D.N.Y. 2013) (forum selection clause binding where user had to assent to clickwrap agreement and clicked button marked "accept," next to which was hyperlink to "terms of use," to sign up to website and to renew her membership).

Third, where notice of the hyperlinked "terms and conditions" is present on multiple successive webpages of the site. See, e.g., Major v. McCallister, 302 S.W.3d 227, 230-31 (Mo. Ct. App. S. Dist. 2009) (forum selection clause enforceable where hyperlink to "terms and conditions" was presented on multiple successive webpages and the final step in the website's signup process was to click a button next to which was the phrase: "By submitting you agree to the Terms of Use").

At 400-01.

In 2012, the Tenth Circuit considered a variation on this common practice: the technician installing TV/Voice service provides a "welcome kit" with terms and conditions, then asks the customer if she accepts, and that acceptance is indicated on the *technician's* laptop. The court found this general practice to constitute acceptance, and it found that the single declaration that a customer never agreed to the terms to be inadequate. Hancock v. AT&T, 701 F.3d 1248, 1253 (10th Cir. 2012). For further discussion, see *infra* §4.26.

In a case involving factually unique circumstances — sale of telephone services to inmates — the Third Circuit applied browsewrap principles to sales completed in what it characterized as "an unusual hybrid of technology — offering services via one medium (an interactive telephone voice-response system) and purporting to bind users of those services to terms that are accessible only through a different medium (the internet)." James v. Global Tellink Corp., 2017 U.S. App. LEXIS 5448 (3d Cir. Mar. 29, 2017). When signing up by telephone, customers would hear an audio notice to "[p]lease note that your account, and any transactions you complete . . . are governed by the terms of use and the privacy statement posted at www.offenderconnect.com." However, the Circuit noted that "[t]hey neither received GTL's terms of use, nor were they informed that merely using GTL's telephone service would constitute assent to those terms. Under these circumstances, Appellees did not assent to the terms of use or the arbitration provision contained therein." *Id.* at *11.

A clickwrap agreement may be tied with or independent of the purchase of a separate, physical item, as was the case with home DNA testing kits. Tompkins v. 23andMe, 2014 U.S. Dist. LEXIS 88068 (N.D. Cal. June 25, 2014). Customers first purchased a kit online, to be shipped to them. The court found that this transaction did not bind the purchaser to arbitrate disputes, because the agreement would have been visible only had the purchaser "scroll[ed] through a significant amount of information to view the TOS hyperlink at the bottom of the homepage." The district court found that the agreement therefore "would have been ineffective to bind website visitors or customers who only purchased a DNA kit without creating an account or registering a kit." However, purchasers also had to create an account and send the kit back to the company in order to receive results from the home test. At the point of registration, the customer had to click on an "I ACCEPT THE TERMS OF SERVICE" button, with a prominent link to the TOS. The district court found that this constituted acceptance. It also considered and rejected claims of lack of consideration at the registration stage and inadequacy of notice, and distinguished this situate from a shrinkwrap agreement. *Id.* at *20-32. The court went on to find that the arbitration agreement was procedurally unconscionable because "[b]y the time those customers create accounts and register their DNA kits — when 23andMe first requires them to acknowledge the arbitration provision — they have already paid 23andMe, and the cancellation period may have long expired." *Id.* at *54-55. Moreover, the arbitration agreement is "at the very end of the TOS as a subparagraph to the final section titled 'Miscellaneous' " and, furthermore, incorporates by reference the American Arbitration Association rules, which the customer would then have to research in order to fully understand the scope of the agreement. This finding of procedural unconscionablility, however, was without effect in this case because California law provides that arbitration agreements are enforceable unless the court finds both procedural and substantive unconscionablility; the court found that this agreement was not substantively unconscionable. *Id.* at *66-67.

§3.7 n.2 p.213 Add the following at the beginning: Jordan Panel Sys. Corp. v. Turner Constr. Co., 841 N.Y.S.2d 561 (App. Div. 2007) ("if Jordan knew or had reason to know that Turner did not intend to be bound by the conduct the complaint alleges to have constituted Turner's manifestation of assent, there was no manifestation of mutual assent and, therefore, no contract") (citing treatise).

Block v. eBay, Inc., 747 F.3d 1135 (9th Cir. 2014) involved an allegation that the "automatic bidding system," under which the software places new bids in increments up to a set amount, violated the terms of a contract that specified that it was "not involved in the actual transaction" and the "no agency" provision. The Ninth Circuit held that these provisions were "general descriptions" of eBay's services and did not constitute an "enforceable promise."

§3.7 n.3 p.213 Add the following to the list after "Accord": Fletcher-Harlee Corp. v. Pote Concrete Contractors, 421 F. Supp. 2d 831 (D.N.J. 2006) (clause in a bid stating that the bidder "will not be responsible or liable in any manner pending execution of a written agreement" means that it "did not manifest an intention to be bound to the amount in the bid"), *aff'd*, 482 F.3d 247 (3d Cir. 2007) ("because the submission expressly disclaimed Pote's intention to be bound, it could not be an offer"); Medistar Corp. v. Schmidt, 267 S.W.3d 150 (Tex. Civ. App. 2008) (proposal letter stated that it was "preliminary" and "for discussion only"; held not to be a contract as a matter of law).

§3.7 n.19 p.218 In the second paragraph, add the following to the list in the first sentence: Tom-Lin Enters. v. Sunoco, 349 F.3d 277 (6th Cir. 2003) (where there was no evidence of industry pricing standards and gasoline distributor's pricing practices did not differ from that of a competitor, there was no material factual dispute as to whether distributor's pricing practices were commercially unreasonable).

§3.8 INTENTION NOT TO BE BOUND UNTIL LATER WRITING

§3.8 n.1 p.220 ***Add the following to the list after "see":*** Sullivan v. William A. Randolph, Inc., 504 F.3d 665 (7th Cir. 2007) (Posner, J.) ("If you behave in a way that you would not have done had you not thought you were bound on a contract — such as by making the payments called for by it — the fact that you omitted to sign it will not allow you to deny that you are bound."); Toledano v. O'Connor, 501 F. Supp. 2d 127 (D.D.C. 2007) ("defendants' subjective motives for not signing the contract are irrelevant to the question whether the lack of a signature precluded the formation of a contract, and there simply is no general requirement under California law that all parties must sign an agreement before a contract is formed"); BDO Seidman, LLP v. Bee, 970 So. 2d 869 (Fla. App. 2007) ("a contract may be binding on a party even without that party's signature where assent may be shown by the acts or performance of the party"); Moorman v. Blackstock, Inc., 661 S.E.2d 404 (Va. 2008) ("[W]here parties intend to culminate their agreement with a signed contract, there is a strong presumption that no contract exists until a contract is formally signed and in writing.").

§3.8 n.2 p.221 ***Add the following at the end:*** *Accord:* Gray v. Tri-Way Constr. Servs., 210 P.3d 63 (Idaho 2009) ("If the parties view the written draft as merely a record, then the oral agreement is valid. However, if the parties view the written draft a consummation of the negotiation, then the oral agreement is not valid.").

§3.8 n.3 p.221 ***Add the following after the first sentence:*** As one court put it, "It is necessary that agreement shall have been expressed on all essential terms, such that the final document is understood to be a mere memorial of the agreement already reached and may not contain a material term that is not already agreed upon . . . Thus, we consider the parties' 'intent to be bound' as a question separate from but related to the definiteness of terms." Block v. Magura, 949 N.E.2d 1261, 1266 (Ind. App. 2001).

§3.8 n.4 p.221 In the first paragraph, add the following to the list after* "See also"*: Shoels v. Klebold, 375 F.3d 1054 (10th Cir. 2004) ("though letter clearly contemplates working out a more detailed agreement, nowhere does it state that the existence of a binding contract is conditioned on successfully completing that process").

§3.8 n.4 p.221 In the first paragraph, add the following at the end: *Cf.* Gray v. Tri-Way Constr. Servs., *supra* note 2 (" 'The burden of proof is on the party asserting that the contract was binding before the written draft was signed.' ") (quoting from Intermountain Forest Mgmt. v. La. Pac. Corp., 31 P.3d 921 (Idaho 2001)).

§3.8 n.4 p.221 In the second paragraph, add the following to the list after* "See"*: PFT Roberson, Inc. v. Volvo Trucks N. Am., 420 F.3d 728 (7th Cir. 2005) (parties may "reach[] agreement in stages without taking the risk that courts will enforce a partial bargain that one side or the other would have rejected as incomplete").

§3.8 n.5 p.222 Add the following after the citation to* Doll*: , followed in White Constr. Co. v. Martin Marietta Materials, 633 F. Supp. 2d 1302 (M.D. Fla. 2009) ("Unless the Parties intended to be bound by the [letter of intent], they did not enter into a contract . . . regardless of the level of detail set forth in the [letter of intent]; no such intent to be bound here, where the document states that 'This letter is not intended to create nor should it be construed as creating any legal obligation . . .' ").

§3.8 n.5 p.222 Add the following to the list after* "Cf."*: Dennis v. Kaskel, 950 N.E.2d 68 (Mass. App. 2011) (memorandum not final where it states that the parties intend to "enter into a legally binding agreement" within three weeks and, if they did not, that one party would have the option either to extend the time to do so or demand immediate repayment of money he had advanced).

§3.8 n.5 p.222 Add the following at the end: Statutes or judicial decisions may also limit the ability of a contracting party — primarily, but not exclusively, a governmental entity — to be bound before the execution of a formal agreement.

See Ry-Tan Constr. v. Wash. Elem. Sch. Dist., 111 P.3d 1019 (Ariz. 2005) (common law rule that "a public agency that accepts a bid on a public contract is not bound until a formal contract exists").

***§3.8 n.6 p.222 In the first paragraph, add the following to the list after* "Accord":** Rivera v. Alaimo, 863 N.Y.S.2d 452 (App. Div. 2008) (payments and other material terms of a lease and contract to sell fixtures "were dependent upon the preparation and execution of a 'final lease agreement' "; the result "was a mere agreement to agree, which is unenforceable"); Jordan Panel Sys. Corp. v. Turner Constr. Co., 841 N.Y.S.2d 561 (App. Div. 2007) ("the inception paragraph plainly stated that Turner would be contractually bound only by its own signature on a written agreement; absent that, Turner would not be bound") (citing treatise).

§3.8 n.6 p.222 In the first paragraph, add the following at the end: *Cf.* Vacold LLC v. Cerami, 545 F.3d 114 (2d Cir. 2008) (finding document showed intent to be bound; "[T]he early drafts expressly and conspicuously stated that they were not intended to be binding, but this language is absent from the April 9 agreement.").

***§3.8 n.6 p.222 In the second paragraph, add the following to the list after* "Cf.":** Turner Broad. Sys. v. McDavid, 693 S.E.2d 873 (Ga. App. 2010) (letter of intent stated expressly that neither party would be bound until definitive agreements executed; after letter of intent expired, though, parties were free to make oral contracts, especially in light of the lack of a survival provision in the letter of intent); Union Sav. Bank v. White Family Cos., 916 N.E.2d 816 (Ohio App. 2009) (use of the word "tentative" in a writing created an ambiguity as to the degree of finality of that writing).

§3.8 n.6 p.222 In the second paragraph, replace the citation to Treitel with the following: G. Treitel, The Law of Contract 53 (11th ed. 2003).

§3.8 n.7 p.223 Add the following to the list: First Nat'l Mtg. Co. v. Fed. Realty Inv. Trust, 631 F.3d 1058 (9th Cir. 2011) (agreement enforceable even though it contemplated a final writing; the agreement stated that its terms "are hereby accepted by the parties subject only to approval of the terms and conditions of a formal agreement," and the successive drafts of the document were in turn called a "Counter Proposal," a "Revised Proposal," and a "Final Proposal").

***§3.8 n.9 p.223 Add the following to the list after* "Accord":** Cochran v. Norkunas, 919 A.2d 700 (Md. 2007) ("letter of intent" for sale of real property saying that the seller will receive a standard form contract within 48 hours, "[t]he contract will contain a financing requirement" and the buyers "will delete the standard home inspection contingency" is non-binding).

§3.8 n.9 p.223 Add the following at the end: *Cf.* APS Capital Corp. v. Mesa Air Grp., 580 F.3d 265 (5th Cir. 2009) (Texas law "does not require non-binding language as a per-se rule or even as a general principle. Rather, the thrust is that in the absence of such language a party may hazard being bound."), distinguished in Bissada v. Ark. Children's Hosp., 639 F.3d 825 (8th Cir. 2011) (statement in e-mail from lawyer for plaintiff to lawyer for defendant stating that the plaintiff "will agree" to a settlement is an offer, not merely an invitation to offer). *See generally* Ben-Shahar, Pre-Closing Liability, 77 U. Chi. L. Rev. 977 (2010) (extended analysis of *Empro v. Ball-Co*).

***§3.8 n.10 p.224 Add the following to the list after* "Accord":** Vacold LLC v. Cerami, *supra* note 6 (use of phrase "letter agreement" suggests finality; in addition, "all five previous drafts were styled a 'summary of discussions' or the like"); Block v. Magura, 949 N.E.2d 1261 (Ind. App. 2011) (letter of intent stated that it was to "confirm" the terms of an agreement and used the terms "offer made" and "accepted" to describe the consequences of the parties' signatures; showed an intent to be bound); Basis Tech. Corp. v. Amazon.com, 878 N.E.2d 952 (Mass. App. 2008) (where e-mail states that it "confirms the essential business terms of the settlement" and that the parties "agree that they promptly will take all reasonable steps to memorialize" those terms, the agreement was enforceable without a final writing), followed in Targus Grp. Int'l v. Sherman, 922 N.E.2d 841 (Mass. App. 2010) (agreement in principle enforceable where it states that it is complete "as to form and content" and where it frequently uses the term "agree" in the present tense).

***§3.8 n.12 p.224 Add the following to the list after* "See also":** PFT Roberson, Inc. v. Volvo Trucks N. Am., Inc., 420 F.3d 728 (7th Cir. 2005) (lack of agreement on clauses that ultimately required lengthy negotiation and documentation makes earlier e-mail "principally . . . a discussion tool listing the subjects that the parties agree must be agreed on in the future"), followed in Citadel Grp. v. Wash. Reg'l Med. Ctr., 784 F. Supp. 2d 949 (N.D. Ill. 2011) (continued negotiation after "Authorization to Proceed" and vague statements within the authorization provide evidence that this was "a starting point rather than an ending point for lease negotiations"); Diesel Power Equip. v. ADDCO, 377 F.3d 853 (8th Cir. 2004) (lack of agreement on "vital term" of payment schedule shows lack of intent to be bound, as does subsequent negotiation over material terms); Gardner v. Marcum, 665 S.E.2d 336 (Ga. App. 2008) (failure to agree on whether advanced funds were a loan or an equity interest means "there was no assent by the parties to the essential terms of the contract, but only an unenforceable agreement to agree").

But see Beverly v. Abbott Labs., 817 F.3d 328 (7th Cir. 2016) (signed, handwritten document prepared at end of mediation session provided "my client will communicate to its internal business client the fact that Abbott/AbbVie has offered $200,000 + Abbott/AbbVie pays cost of mediation to resolve this matter and that Martina Beverly has demanded $210,000 + Abbott/AbbVie pays cost of mediation to resolve this matter. Both parties committ [sic] that their offer and demand will remain open until Tuesday, July 22, 2014, 3:00 PM central." Abbott then accepted the offer and the court found this to be an enforceable agreement. The plaintiff had argued that it was unenforceable because it lacked certain material terms, most notably any waiver-and-release language. The court disagreed: "Though perhaps inartful, this phrase ["to resolve this matter"] adequately conveys Beverly's offer to abandon her claims against Abbott; the use of formal terms such as 'waiver,' 'release,' and 'covenant not to sue' was unnecessary. . . ." *Id.* at 335.

§3.8 n.12 p.224 Add the following after the citation to* Plumbing Shop*: followed in Keystone Land & Dev. Co. v. Xerox Corp., 353 F.3d 1070 (9th Cir. 2003) (if "parties intended their legal obligations to be deferred until the execution of the formal writing, the preliminary writings and negotiations cannot constitute a contract").

§3.8 n.13 p.224 Add the following to the first sentence: Strauss v. Newmarket Global Consulting Grp., 5 A.3d 1027 (D.C. 2010) ("a written contract can memorialize an oral agreement if the document is understood as a 'mere memorial' of the oral agreement . . . but no oral contract exists if the document is to contain any material term that the parties did not previously agree upon"); Lambert v. Fleet Nat'l Bank, 865 N.E.2d 1091 (Mass. 2007) (discussion in which plaintiff said that he "would expect some cooperation from [the bank]" and "was expecting a new first mortgage" too indefinite: "not only does the extreme vagueness of the purported 'agreement' make its enforcement impossible, . . . it indicates that there was no intent to be bound, and thus no agreement, in the first place.").

§3.8 n.13 p.224 Add the following at the end: Because the degree of completeness is relevant to these issues of intent, a court should first determine what the terms of the agreement are and only then determine whether and to what extent the parties intended to be bound to those terms. *See* Roberts v. City of St. Louis, 254 S.W.3d 280 (Mo. App. 2008).

§3.8 n.14 p.225 Add the following to the list after* "Accord"*: Janky v. Batistatos, 559 F. Supp. 2d 923 (N.D. Ind. 2008) (term "mutual global release" "does not come close to adequately describing how the parties intended to complete the complicated task of terminating at least four separate lawsuits, each in various stages of litigation and jurisdictions. . . . Add to this the past history of bitter acrimony between the parties and sanctionable attorney conduct, and I must conclude that the email lacked the definiteness required to address the parties' obvious concerns over continued legal battles").

§3.8 n.15 p.225 Add the following to the list after **"Accord"***:* APS Capital Corp. v. Mesa Air Grp., *supra* note 9 ("The language of a contract must be read in the light cast by industry practice in which it arises . . . [A]greement as to central, carefully negotiated terms in a time-sensitive context need not lead to a contract, when complex, high-value assets such as trade claims are at issue . . . "); Fairbrook Leasing v. Mesaba Aviation, 295 F. Supp. 2d 1063 (D. Minn. 2003) (though "presence of open terms . . . suggests the parties do not intend to be bound," the "suggestion can be overcome when the open terms are insignificant to the parties"), *aff'd*, 519 F.3d 421 (8th Cir. 2008); Leeds v. First Allied Conn. Corp., 521 A.2d 1095 (Del. Ch. 1986) ("while it is certainly possible to make a binding contract to sell a $3.5 million business . . . on a single page, it would be extraordinary to do so"); Conwell v. Gray Loon Outdoor Mktg. Grp., 906 N.E.2d 805 (Ind. 2009) ("All that is required to render a contract enforceable is reasonable certainty in the terms and conditions of the promises made . . . ; absolute certainty in all terms is not required. Only essential terms need be included to render a contract enforceable. . . . A court will not find that a contract is so uncertain as to preclude specific enforcement where a reasonable and logical interpretation will render the contract valid.").

§3.8 n.15 p.225 Add the following after the citation to **Miller***:* and in Learning Annex Holdings v. Whitney Educ. Grp., 765 F. Supp. 2d 403 (S.D.N.Y. 2011) (applying four-part test; no Type I agreement because the document stated that "this Memorandum is not a binding legal obligation").

§3.8 n.15 p.225 Add the following at the end: *Cf.* CoMentis, Inc. v. Purdue Research Found., 765 F. Supp. 2d 1092 (N.D. Ind. 2011) (it is "certainly plausible that the non-material issues that the parties left for another day were procedural — merely dotting i's and crossing t's. Why else would the parties give themselves just three weeks to 'execute' the final agreement, despite negotiating the terms of the license agreement for over six months?").

§3.8 n.17 p.225 Add the following to the list after **"Accord"***:* Vacold LLC v. Cerami, *supra* note 6 ("nothing in the record reveals that the parties left anything for further negotiation"; though terms remained open, these were "standard"

and filling them in was merely "formalizing contract documentation").

§3.8 n.19 p.226 Add the following to the list after **"Accord"***:* Steven R. Perles, P.C. v. Kagy, 473 F.3d 1244 (D.C. Cir. 2007) ("It strains credulity to suggest that Perles and Kagy, both of whom are attorneys, intended a single, undocumented telephone conversation to give rise to a mutually binding agreement giving a junior attorney the potential right to millions of dollars in compensation for her work."); Spencer Trask Software & Info. Servs. LLC v. RPost Int'l Ltd., 383 F. Supp. 2d 428 (S.D.N.Y. 2003) ("complex, multi-stage package deal" for venture capital financing not the type of contract that would be made orally); Strauss v. Newmarket Global Consulting Grp., 5 A.3d 1027 (D.C. 2010) ("the lack of a written agreement raises serious questions as to why experienced businessmen engaged in a complex business transaction did not clarify in writing exactly what the subject matter, scope, duration, and terms of the agreement were"); Lambert v. First Nat'l Bank, *supra* note 13 ("it is inconceivable that such a major modification to a large commercial loan would be made informally and in general terms rather than in a finely detailed written agreement").

§3.8 n.20 p.226 Add the following to the list after **"But cf."***:* Forte Sports v. Toy Airplane Gliders of Am., 371 F. Supp. 2d 648 (E.D. Pa. 2004) ("while a signed settlement agreement is certainly customary when resolving legal disputes, the failure to execute such a document here does not negate the existence of a legally binding settlement"); Willey v. Willey, 912 A.2d 441 (Vt. 2006) (declining to adopt per se rule that settlement agreements be unenforceable without a writing).

§3.8 n.21 p.227 Add the following after the first sentence: Accord: Gray v. Tri-Way Constr. Servs., *supra* note 2.

§3.8 n.22 p.227 Add the following after the citation to **R.G. Group***:* , followed in McElroy v. Germark Alloy Ref'g Corp., 592 F. Supp. 2d 508 (S.D.N.Y. 2008) (no binding obligation where part performance equally consistent with duties under contract and duties as employee, many terms were yet to be settled, and

the agreement was for transferring an interest in a multi-million dollar venture).

§3.8 n.22 p.227 Add the following to the list after **"see"***:* Brown v. Cara, 420 F.3d 148 (2d Cir. 2005); Ciaramella v. Reader's Digest Ass'n, 131 F.3d 320 (2d Cir. 1997) (oral settlement agreements); Cont'l Labs. v. Scott Paper Co., 759 F. Supp. 538 (S.D. Iowa 1990), *aff'd mem.*, 938 F.2d 184 (8th Cir. 1991).

§3.8 n.23 p.227 Add the following to the list after **"Accord"***:* Brown v. Cara, *supra* note 22 ("while [the intentions of the parties are] frequently a source of persistent disputes of fact, '[w]here a question of intention is determinable by written agreements, the question is one of law, appropriately decided on a motion for summary judgment.' ") (quoting Arcadian Phosphates, Inc. v. Arcadian Corp., 884 F.2d 69 (2d Cir. 1989)); Gray v. Tri-Way Constr. Servs., *supra* note 2 ("mutual assent is a question of fact"); Willey v. Willey, *supra* note 20 ("Whether husband and wife will be bound by their oral settlement agreement depends on their intent at the time of the oral settlement, which is a question of fact."); Highland Capital Mgmt., LP v. Bank of Am., 698 F.3d 202 (5th Cir. 2012) (oral agreement followed by e-mail stating agreement was "subject to appropriate consents and documentation" did not establish, at least at summary judgment stage, intent not to be bound until later writing; use of standard terms and reference to industry custom and practice left the language ambiguous); Douglas v. University of Pittsburgh, 2016 U.S. Dist. LEXIS 147584 (W.D. Pa. Oct. 24, 2016) (jury question whether oral agreement had sufficient terms to create a two-year employment contract where employee began performance but was later presented with a written contract with additional terms, which he refused to sign; "[f]urther . . . there is a genuine factual dispute as to whether Plaintiff was fulfilling his obligations under an oral agreement or acquiescing to the alleged modified terms that were later proposed in writing, such that the entry of summary judgment is precluded").

§3.8 n.30 p.228 Add the following to the end: AGA Shareholders, LLC v. CSK Auto, Inc., 467 F. Supp. 2d 834 (N.D. Ill. 2006) (where the parties "routinely acted in accordance with the [contract] and considered the [contract] to be the baseline for their relationship," the contract was held enforceable notwithstanding a clause requiring that both parties execute the contract and the failure of one to do so); U.S. Fid. & Guar. Co. v. Delmar Dev. Partners, LLC, 788 N.Y.S.2d 252 (App. Div. 2005) (after execution of preliminary letter of agreement, "the parties acted as if their disputes had been resolved, supporting plaintiff's position that the terms of the letter were intended to be binding" notwithstanding the letter's statement that it was subject to a binding written document).

§3.8 n.31 p.229 Add the following to the list after "Accord": Steven R. Perles, P.C. v. Kagy, *supra* note 19 (repeated attempts to get defendant to "work out" compensation after the oral agreement "suggests that no final agreement had been reached"); Aveta Inc. v. Bengoa, 986 A.2d 1166 (Del. Ch. 2009) (agreement held not binding in part because "[t]he parties did not treat it as a binding agreement or amendment" and "[n]egotiations over a potential settlement continued for months after" its execution); Dennis v. Kaskel, 950 N.E.2d 68 (Mass. App. 2011) (memorandum on terms of investment in franchise operation not final when one party afterward proposed a very different and complex investment structure and the parties negotiated for two years further, suggesting that the party seeking enforcement "himself viewed the memorandum as simply the first step in negotiations ultimately designed to yield a completed product").

§3.8 n.36 p.230 Add the following to the list after "Accord": Int'l Casings Grp. v. Premium Std. Farms, 358 F. Supp. 2d 863 (W.D. Mo. 2005) ("merely because parties intend a written memorialization of the agreed upon terms does not demonstrate that they intend the writing to be a condition precedent to the formation of a contract"); Loppert v. WindsorTech, Inc., 865 A.2d 1282 (Del. Ch. 2004) ("the fact that the parties . . . manifest an intention to prepare and adopt a written memorial will not prevent contract formation if the evidence reveals manifestations of assent that are in themselves sufficient to conclude a contract").

§3.8a PRELIMINARY AGREEMENTS

§3.8a n.2 p.231 ***Replace the citation to Fontaine & De Ly with the following:*** M. Fontaine & F. De Ly, Drafting International Contracts: An Analysis of Contract Clauses (2006).

§3.8a n.2 p.231 ***Add the following to the list after* "See generally"*:*** R. Feldman & R. Nimmer, Drafting Effective Contracts §1.05 (2d ed. 1999); Torsello, Preliminary Agreements and CISG Contracts, in Drafting Contracts Under the CISG 191 (H. Flechtner et al. eds. 2008).

§3.8a n.4 p.231 ***Add the following at the beginning:*** *See, e.g.*, Block v. Magura, 949 N.E.2d 1261 (Ind. App. 2011) ("it is the substance of an agreement that controls whether it is enforceable, not the title of a document as a letter of intent or something else").

§3.8a n.6 p.231 ***Replace the current text with the following:*** For a tripartite division of these way-stations, *see* Keystone Land & Dev. Co. v. Xerox Corp., 94 P.3d 945 (Wash. 2004) (distinguishing among agreement to agree, agreements with open terms, and contracts to negotiate). *See also* IDT Corp. v. Tyco Grp., 863 N.Y.S.2d 30 (App. Div. 2008), *aff'd*, 918 N.E.2d 913 (N.Y. 2009) (describing "contingent Type I agreement," in which the agreement is incomplete and requires the parties to negotiate in good faith, but also provides a set of standard terms that will fill in any remaining gaps if either party insists they do so).

§3.8a n.7 p.232 ***Add the following at the end:*** For representative decisions following this categorization, *see* Fairbrook Leasing v. Mesaba Aviation, 519 F.3d 421 (8th Cir. 2008); Burbach Broad. Co. v. Elkins Radio Corp., 278 F.3d 401 (4th Cir. 2002); Trianco, LLC v. IBM Corp., 583 F. Supp. 2d 649 (E.D. Pa. 2008), *aff'd*, 347 Fed. Appx. 808 (3d Cir. 2009); Learning Annex Holdings v. Whitney Educ. Grp., 765 F. Supp. 2d 403 (S.D.N.Y. 2011); Fickes v. Sun Expert, 762 F. Supp. 998 (D. Mass. 1991); Stouffer Hotel Co. v. Teachers Ins. & Annuity Assn., 737 F. Supp. 1553 (M.D. Fla. 1990); Ziegler Furniture & Funeral Home, Inc. v. Cicmanec, 709 N.W.2d 350 (S.D. 2006) (quoting this treatise). *But see* IDT Corp.

v. Tyco Grp., 918 N.E.2d 913 (N.Y. 2009) ("While we do not disagree with the reasoning in federal cases, we do not find the rigid classifications into 'Types' useful.").

§3.8b A PRELIMINARY AGREEMENT SAMPLER

§3.8b n.3 p.236 Add the following at the end: *See also* Garnot v. LaDue, 845 N.Y.S.2d 555 (App. Div. 2007) (purchase offer agreement enforceable because "it contains all essential terms of a complete agreement, notwithstanding the parties' intention to later sign a more detailed contract").

§3.8b n.5 p.237 Add the following at the end: *Cf.* Diesel Power Equip. v. ADDCO, 377 F.3d 853 (8th Cir. 2004) (potential buyer "could have easily protected itself by including a good-faith or similar provision in the Letter of Intent that would have precluded ADDCO from entertaining other offers until the continuing negotiations between them broke down").

§3.8b p.237 Add a new footnote 5a on line 22: . . . the letter is binding or nonbinding.[5a]

[5a] *See* John Wood Grp. v. ICO, 26 S.W.3d 12 (Tex. Civ. App. 2000) (quoting this section of this treatise).

***§3.8b n.7 p.238 Add the following to the list after* "Cf.":** W. Beach Marina v. Erdeljac, 94 S.W.3d 248 (Tex. Civ. App. 2002) ("Appropriate documentation to be entered into recognizing the validity and scope of [the] easement" . . . "does not conclusively establish that the parties had no intent to be immediately bound").

***§3.8b n.9 p.239 Add the following to the list after* "But cf.":** 50 Pine Co. v. CapitalSource Fin. LLC (*In re* 50 Pine Co.), 317 B.R. 276 (Bankr. S.D.N.Y. 2004) (term sheet stating that it was "for discussion purposes only" and was "not a commitment to extend credit in any form" did not obligate the lender to move forward in good faith).

§3.8c DRAFTING AGREEMENTS WITH OPEN TERMS

§3.8c n.3 p.243 ***Add the following at the end:*** R. Lake & U. Dretta, Letters of Intent and Other Precontractual Documents: Comparative Analysis and Forms (2d ed. 1994).

§3.8c n.15 p.247 ***Add the following at the end:*** and in COC Servs. v. CompUSA, Inc., 150 S.W.3d 654 (Tex. Civ. App. 2004).

§3.8c n.16 p.247 ***Add the following at the end:*** *See also* Network Enters., Inc. v. APBA Offshore Prods., Inc., 427 F. Supp. 2d 463 (S.D.N.Y. 2006) (giving effect to contractual clause requiring "a written instrument duly executed by all parties"), *aff'd*, 264 Fed. Appx. 36 (2d Cir. 2008) (per curiam). For a particularly vehement denial of binding effect, *see* White Constr. Co. v. Martin Marietta Materials, 633 F. Supp. 2d 1302 (M.D. Fla. 2009) (on the first page, with emphasis as indicated: "This non-binding letter describes the basic terms of the proposed transaction, along with various examinations of [the seller] that must be concluded to the satisfaction of [the buyer] prior to the execution of a legally binding agreement. ***THIS LETTER EXPRESSES THE INTENT OF THE PARTIES FOR DISCUSSION PURPOSES ONLY FOR USE IN DRAFTING A DEFINITIVE CONTRACT. THIS LETTER IS NOT INTENDED TO CREATE NOR SHOULD IT BE CONSTRUED AS CREATING ANY LEGAL OBLIGATION TO CONCLUDE THIS TRANSACTION UNDER THE TERMS OUTLINED HEREIN OR ON ANY OTHER TERMS OR CONDITIONS NOR IS IT INTENDED TO CREATE ANY OTHER OBLIGATIONS EXCEPT FOR THOSE SET FORTH IN PARAGRAPHS E AND F.***"). It should be noted, however, that even the clearest statement that a letter of intent is not binding may be circumvented by subsequent assurances that there would be a contract. *See* 1861 Grp. v. Wild Oats Mkts., 728 F. Supp. 2d 1052 (E.D. Mo. 2010) (assurances may supersede the disclaimer language in a non-binding letter of intent, but may not themselves create promises to negotiate).

§3.8c p.247 ***In the first full paragraph, add the following at the end of the first sentence:*** . . . controlling as to intent.[17a]

[17a] *See, e.g.*, PFT Roberson, Inc. v. Volvo Trucks N. Am., 420 F.3d 728 (7th Cir. 2005) ("Illinois is averse to enforcing tentative agreements that are expressly contingent on the signing of formal or final documents.").

§3.8c n.19 p.247 Add the following at the end: Dalton v. Robert Jahn Corp., 146 P.3d 399 (Or. App. 2006) ("That those additional documents needed to be finalized was not a bar to the existence of a binding contract but, rather, a term of the contract in the sense that the parties had agreed to create the documents").

§3.8c n.22 p.248 Add the following after the first sentence: *Cf.* CoMentis, Inc. v. Purdue Research Found., 765 F. Supp. 2d 1092 (N.D. Ind. 2011) ("The distinction is admittedly a bit slippery.").

§3.8c n.24 p.248 Add the following after the first sentence: More generally, *see* Block v. Magura, 949 N.E.2d 1261 (Ind. App. 2011) (holding incomplete agreement enforceable: "to the extent more terms were not included in the Letter of Intent, they were either irrelevant to the sale of Block's partnership or, even if customary or desirable, inessential to the performance of the agreement").

§3.10 WHAT IS AN OFFER

***§3.10 n.4 p.251 Add the following to the list after* "See also":** Kashmiri v. Regents of Univ. of Cal., 67 Cal. Rptr. 3d 635 (Ct. App. 2007) (specific fee information in university catalogues yielded implied-in-fact contract when students entered into contract by accepting offer of admission); Stepp v. Freeman, 694 N.E.2d 510 (Ohio App. 1997) (where workplace group collectively purchased lottery tickets, circumstances made it "inferable that a contract existed as a matter of tacit understanding"), distinguished by Dickerson v. Deno, 770 So. 2d 63 (Ala. 2000) (unlike *Stepp*, the parties here held individually owned tickets even though they were purchased at the same time).

§3.10 n.4 p.251 Add the following at the end: *Cf.* Boudreaux v. Van Kerkhove, 993 So. 2d 725 (La. App. 2008) ("Whereas the consent of the parties is established through offer and acceptance, such a process is not a ritual that should be regarded as indispensable for the formation of a valid contract.").

***§3.10 n.5 p.252 Add the following to the list after* "Accord":** Warner Bros. Int'l Television Distrib. v. Golden Channels & Co., 522 F.3d 1060 (9th Cir. 2008) ("Mutual assent is essential to an implied contract, the distinction from an express contract being merely that the promise is implied by conduct rather than expressed in words."); Al's Serv. Ctr. v. BP Prods. N. Am., 599 F.3d 720 (7th Cir. 2010) (an implied-in-fact contract "is treated just like an express contract"; citing to treatise); Confold Pac. v. Polaris Enters., 433 F.3d 952 (7th Cir. 2006) (Posner, J.) ("a 'contract implied in fact' is thus a species of express contract").

***§3.10 n.5 p.252 In the second paragraph, add the following to the list after* "See":** Guidry v. Charter Comm'ns, 269 S.W.3d 520 (Mo. App. 2008) (where the parties continue to behave as they did before their contract terminated, they may continue to have a contractual obligation; what the terms of that obligation are, however, depends on other indicia of mutual assent).

§3.10 n.5 p.252 In the second paragraph, add the following at the end: For an interesting variation, *see* Ramsey v. Allstate Ins. Co., 416 Fed. Appx. 516 (6th Cir. 2011) (after death of insured, son and heir continued making payments for property insurance on insured's home, insurer accepted those payments, insurer issued renewed insurance policies, and insurer took possession of house after casualty; held that this created a genuine issue of material fact on the question of implied-in-fact contract, notwithstanding the expiration of the insured's contract).

***§3.10 n.6 p.252 Add the following to the list after* Barker:** *Accord:* McQuiston v. K-Mart Corp., 796 F.2d 1346 (11th Cir. 1986) ("placing goods on a shelf in a self-service store for customer inspection and selection constitutes an offer to sell such goods at the stated price, and the customer's act of taking physical possession of the goods with intent to pay for them constitutes a reasonable mode of acceptance"; no acceptance here because customer lacked the intent to purchase at the time the goods were removed from the shelf); Fender v. Colonial Stores, 225 S.E.2d 691 (Ga. App. 1976) ("the retailer's act of placing [the goods] on the shelf with the price stamped upon them manifested an intent to offer them for sale" and "the plaintiff's act of taking physical possession of the goods with the intent to purchase them manifested an intent to accept the offer and a promise to take them to the check-out counter and to there pay for them").

§3.10 n.6 p.252 Add the following at the end: *Cf.* Del Real v. N.E. Ill. Reg'l Commuter R.R. Corp., 934 N.E.2d 574 (Ill. App. 2010) (no contract for carriage when prospective passenger purchased ticket and presented herself at the platform with the intent to board the train; no offer until the passenger presented herself at the proper place with the intent to be transported, and no acceptance until the carrier takes the passenger on board for transportation).

***§3.10 n.10 p.253 Add the following to the list after* "Accord":** Roznowski v. Bozyk, 251 N.W.2d 606 (Mich. App. 1977) (factors to consider when determining whether presumption of gratuity rebutted include "the type of services rendered, duration of services, closeness of relation of the parties, and the expressed expectations of the parties").

***§3.10 n.12 p.254 Add the following to the list after* "Accord":** Lambert v. Don M. Barron Contractor, 974 So. 2d 198 (La. App. 2008) (where parties were friends and advice had been given freely before the alleged contract, the finder of fact must overcome "the competing implications of a benefit extended by one to a friend for a gratuitous reason without obtaining any advantage in return").

***§3.10 n.20 p.256 Add the following to the list after* "Cf.":** Lowery v. Cnty. of Riley, 738 F. Supp. 2d 1159 (D. Kan. 2010) ("there are no magic words that must be uttered in order to constitute either an offer or an acceptance sufficient to create a binding contract").

§3.10 n.21 p.256 Add the following to the list in the second sentence: Ace Am. Ins. Co. v. Wendt, LLP, 724 F. Supp. 2d 899 (N.D. Ill. 2010) (price quotation with sufficient detail may be offer; "[m]oreover, the fact that defendant prominently identified a specific means of acceptance (in bold, capitalized text in the first line of the proposal) suggests that it indeed intended to create a legally operative offer").

§3.10 n.22 p.257 Add the following at the end of the first sentence: Restatement Second §26 cmt. c ("In determining whether an offer is made[,] relevant factors include . . . the completeness of the terms of the suggested bargain.").

§3.10 n.22 p.257 Add the following to the list after **"See"***:* J.D. Fields & Co. v. U.S. Steel Int'l, 426 Fed. Appx. 271 (5th Cir. 2011) ("a price quote, if detailed enough, can constitute an offer capable of acceptance").

§3.10 n.22 p.257 Add the following after the citation to **Heartland Express***:* , followed in Hinshaw v. Ligon Indus., 551 F. Supp. 2d 798 (N.D. Iowa 2008) (letter from employee proposing resignation an offer, even though it stated that the employee "would be more than willing to sign" a non-compete agreement and a confidentiality agreement "under the proper terms"; the employee had not been subject to these before, and the employer stated that it was not interested in them, so the terms were not essential and the letter's failure to state the terms of those agreements did not make it fatally indefinite).

§3.10 n.24 p.258 In the first paragraph, add the following to the list after **"Accord"***:* Kraft Foods N. Am. v. Banner Eng'g & Sales, 446 F. Supp. 2d 551 (E.D. Va. 2006) (price quotation stating that all orders are subject to seller's acceptance is not an offer; "If Banner's quotation were an offer, which empowered Kraft to form a contract through acceptance, then Kraft's purchase order would not be subject to Banner's acceptance at its home office. Rather, a contract would already have been formed."); Leavell v. Dep't of Nat. Res., 923 N.E.2d 829 (Ill. App. 2010) (request that plaintiff's attorney prepare settlement documents for defendant's review

not an offer, but rather an invitation to offer, because the defendant reserved a right of review); Rios v. State, 974 A.2d 366 (Md. App. 2009) (plea agreement, where defense attorney made a proposal subject to his client's approval; "An 'offer' that requires a third party's approval before it becomes effective is no offer at all.").

§3.10 n.24 p.258 In the first paragraph, add the following to the list after "**Cf.**"*:* Volker Court v. Santa Fe Apartments, 130 S.W.3d 607 (Mo. App. 2004) (no offer where prospective vendor said "I want to have a signed, secure contract to stick under [my brother's] nose").

§3.10 n.24 p.258 Add the following as a third paragraph: The precise language of the reservation can be the key. In a case that received much public attention, Prof. Steven Salaita signed an offer letter for a tenured faculty position with the University of Illinois, resigned his former job, and began moving, with the University paying most of his moving expenses. Salaita v. Kennedy, 118 F. Supp. 3d 1068 (N.D. Ill. 2015). He then issued a series of tweets on his personal Twitter account that were critical of Israel and garnered national media coverage. The University's Board then voted to deny Prof. Salaita's appointment. Prof. Salaita brought suit and, as relevant here, the issue arose as to whether a contract was formed. The offer letter stated "I am pleased to offer you a faculty position." It then recited essential terms, and closed with the sentence, "[t]his recommendation for appointment is subject to approval by the Board of Trustees of the University of Illinois." In denying a motion to dismiss, the district court held that the University's performance on the contract may have been subject to approval by the Board, but the offer itself was not conditional and therefore a contract was formed, with obligations of good faith and fair dealing. The court distinguished cases where the communication specified that "the offer" was conditional. *Id.* at 1077-78, citing Lutz v. Purdue Univ., 133 F. Supp. 2d 1101, 1109 (N.D. Ind. 2001) (granting summary judgment in favor of Purdue when a professor's contract stated that he was "not officially employed until a completed and signed contract has been approved by the President of Purdue University"); Allen v. Cedar Real Estate Grp., LLP, 236 F.3d 374, 381 (7th Cir. 2001) (finding

that the contract drafter's "choice of the word 'offer' is telling" when he drafted a provision that said "this offer is subject to" a certain condition). Rather, the court in *Salaita* concluded that "at the very least, there is a reasonable argument that the condition went to performance and not formation, which precludes dismissal." *Id.* at 1079. Two months after this ruling, the parties reportedly settled the case for $875,000. *See* Jodi S. Cohen, University of Illinois OKs $875,000 Settlement to End Steven Salaita Dispute, Chicago Tribune (Nov. 12, 2015); Center for Constitutional Rights, Press Release, Settlement Reached in Case of Professor Fired for "Uncivil" Tweets (Nov. 12, 2015).

§3.10 n.30 p.260 Add the following to the list after **"Accord"***:* La Bo J P'ship v. La. Lottery Corp., 6 So. 3d 191 (La. App. 2009) (advertisement for lottery which didn't state that grand prizes were payable over 20 years).

§3.10 n.31 p.261 Add the following at the end: The same principle applies to promotions that involve charitable contributions up to a specified maximum. McCabe v. ConAgra Foods, Inc., 2017 U.S. App. LEXIS 3755 (2d Cir. Mar. 2, 2017) (no contractual offer where grocery chain advertised it would donate to an anti-poverty nonprofit for every code entered on its website, up to an annual maximum, because "[a]n individual entering a code would have no knowledge whether the maximum donation had been reached" and thus had "no power of acceptance.") For a general critique of the reluctance to find that advertisements are offers, *see* Feinman & Brill, Is an Advertisement an Offer? Why it is, and Why it Matters, 58 Hastings L.J. 61 (2006).

§3.10 n.32 p.261 Add the following at the end: See also H. Beale et al., Cases, Materials & Text on Contract Law 185-87 (2002) (comparative treatment of Dutch, English, French, and German law).

§3.10 n.34 p.262 Add the following at the end: Hyperbolic statements to the public are not offers when circumstances would not objectively indicate that the person intends to enter a contract. In Kolodziej v. Mason, 774 F.3d 736 (11th Cir. 2014), the Eleventh Circuit considered a claim by a law student who heard a

televised interview with a man who had been convicted of murder despite appearing on surveillance tapes away from the scene of the crime a short time later and attempted to take him up on what he asserted was a unilateral offer. Mason asserted that the prosecution's theory was invalid because it would be impossible to make the trip in the required timeframe, and the stated, "I challenge anybody to show me — I'll pay them a million dollars if they can do it." *Id.* at 739. The Eleventh Circuit held that this does not suggest intent to offer to enter into a contract, and commented that "we find it neither prudent nor permissible to impose contractual liability for offhand remarks or grandstanding." *Id.* at 746.

§3.10 n.35 p.262 In the second paragraph, add the following after the second sentence: *Accord:* Young v. Hefton, 173 P.3d 671 (Kan. App. 2007) (UCC 2-328 "is instructive although not technically applicable to auction sales of real estate") (collecting cases).

§3.10 n.36 p.263 Add the following at the end: There is a third type of auction, one not discussed in UCC 2-328 — a *conditional* auction, in which "the seller reserves the right to accept or reject bids *after* the close of bidding." *Young, supra* note 35 (emphasis in original).

§3.10 n.37 p.263 Add the following to the list after **"Accord":** Lal v. Ameriquest Mortg. Co., 858 A.2d 119 (Pa. Super. 2004) ("once the hammer falls and bidding is closed, the winning bidder has entered into a binding contract and may no longer retract his or her bid").

§3.11 WHO CAN ACCEPT AN OFFER

§3.11 n.2 p.264 Add the following at the end: In one unusual case, a legal recruitment firm sent a résumé of an attorney to a partner in a law firm's New York office, accompanied by a term sheet with the fee for successful placement. The firm had no practice in that field at the New York office, and the partner ignored the e-mail. Shortly after, a partner in the firm's Washington office received the same résumé from another recruitment firm, interviewed the candidate, and offered employment. The candidate accepted and began work in the New York office. The original recruitment firm sought damages for breach of an implied-in-fact contract. It lost. The court observed that "[a]s it is undisputed both that the New York partner did not know that the candidate was being interviewed by the Washington office, and that the Washington office did not know prior to interviewing the candidate that his résumé had been sent to the New York partner, the required assent necessary to establish an implied contract cannot be inferred." Sivin-Tobin Assocs. v. Akin Gump Strauss Hauer & Feld LLP, 892 N.Y.S.2d 71, 73 (App. Div. 2009). The result is at least intuitively reasonable. *Quaere* whether the result would be the same had the partners been in the same office, or if there had been only two partners.

§3.11 n.5 p.265 Add the following at the end: An allied problem arises when an agent purports to contract on behalf of a nonexistent principal. Is there no contract, or is the agent personally bound? From the vantage of offer and acceptance, the most obvious answer is that it depends on the objective intent of the parties. *See generally* Macgregor, Acting on Behalf of a Non-Existent Principal, 14 Edinburgh L. Rev. 92 (2010). It may be, however, that the aggrieved seller would have recourse against the buyer for misrepresentation, whether fraudulent or negligent.

§3.12 OFFER MAY INVITE ACCEPTANCE BY A PROMISE OR BY PERFORMANCE

§3.12 n.5 p.267 Change the cross-reference in the second sentence to: §3.14a *infra*.

§3.12 n.6 p.267 Add the following at the end: As to rewards, *see* Lerner, Promises of Rewards in a Comparative Perspective, 10 Ann. Surv. Int'l & Comp. L. 53 (2004).

§3.12 p.268 Add a new footnote 9a on line 25: . . . the goods are nonconforming.[9a]

[9a] *See* Dubrofsky v. Messer, 31 U.C.C. Rep. Serv. 907 (Mass. App. 1981) ("the plaintiff's subsequent shipment of conforming and non-conforming goods constituted an acceptance of the defendant's offer").

§3.13 WHAT IS AN ACCEPTANCE

§3.13 n.3 p.269 Add the following after But cf.: Augstein v. Leslie, 2012 U.S. Dist. LEXIS 149517 (S.D.N.Y. Oct. 17, 2012) (promise by hip hop artist via YouTube to pay $1 million for return of his laptop is enforceable as an offer that was accepted by performance; promisor was precluded from claiming the laptop lacked essential data because he returned the hard drive to the manufacturer and caused it to be erased, despite being on notice that it would be relevant to future litigation).

§3.13 n.8 p.270 Add the following at the end: *See* Int'l Bus. Mach. Corp. v. Johnson, 629 F. Supp. 2d 321 (S.D.N.Y.) (following Restatement Second §19(2); where employee repeatedly signed non-compete agreement on employer's line, the signatures created ambiguity, which employer in fact interpreted as lack of assent), *aff'd per curiam* 355 Fed. Appx. 454 (2d Cir. 2009). But *cf.* Martin v. Comcast, 146 P.3d 380 (Or. App. 2006) (no modification by continued receipt of services where notice sent in a "bill stuffer," and "a subscriber could easily have continued using Comcast's service without ever being aware of the arbitration clause;" hence, "inaction did not signify acceptance.").

§3.13 p.270 In the second full paragraph, add the following to the second sentence: . . . a nod of the head,[9a]

[9a] Lowery v. County of Riley, 738 F. Supp. 2d 1159 (D. Kan. 2010) ("objective manifestation of assent need not be expressed in words"; nod of assent sufficient to manifest offeror's assent to settlement offer proposed by third party).

§3.13 n.10 p.270 In the first paragraph, add the following to the list after "Accord": Porter v. Gen'l Boiler Casing Co., 396 A.2d 1090 (Md. 1979) (acceptance can be "by acts as well as words;

no formal acceptance is required"); Haufler v. Zotos, 845 N.E.2d 322 (Mass. 2006) ("written contract, signed by only one party, may be binding and enforceable even without the other party's signature if the other party manifests acceptance"); Horton v. DaimlerChrysler Fin. Servs. Ams., 262 S.W.3d 1 (Tex. Civ. App. 2008) (tendering first payment due under offer of settlement constitutes acceptance of settlement agreement, even though second payment not timely).

§3.13 n.10 p.270 Add the following after the citation to* American Bronze*: , distinguished in E.C. Styberg Eng'g Co. v. Eaton Corp., 492 F.3d 912 (7th Cir. 2007) (no contract formed by two orders, one of them cancelled, where the parties neither had "repeated and ongoing conduct manifesting an agreement" nor "an established course of dealing to which they adhered").

§3.13 n.10 p.270 Add the following at the end of the first paragraph: For an example of mixed promise and performance, *see* DeClaire v. G & B McIntosh Family Ltd. P'ship, 260 S.W.3d 34 (Tex. Civ. App. 2008) (note called for signatures from both lender and borrower; only borrower signed, but "[b]y taking possession of the Note, acting on it, and not objecting to any part of it, McIntosh accepted its terms on behalf of the Partnership.").

§3.13 n.10 p.270 Add the following at the end of the third paragraph: , in Byrd v. Simmons, 5 So. 3d 384 (Miss. 2009) (arbitration agreement and admission agreement separate, and nursing home did not sign the former), and in Masteller v.Champion Home Bldrs., 723 N.W.2d 561 (S.D. 2006) (homeowners never expressly agreed to later-arriving warranty, and did not accept the benefits of that warranty).

§3.13 n.12 p.272 Add the following at the end: *See* Empire Mach. Co. v. Litton Bus. Tel. Sys., 566 P.2d 1044 (Ariz. App. 1977) ("this section was an attempt to simplify the common law rule that an acceptance of a contract could only be made in the manner and medium of the offer").

§3.13 n.13 p.272 Add the following at the end: *Cf.* Hanson v. Maxfield, 23 So. 3d 736 (Fla. App. 2009) (offer stating requirements for insurance policy provided as part of settlement accepted by promise, even though accompanying insurance policy allegedly did not conform with the terms of the offer).

§3.13 n.15 p.272 Add the following at the end: A corollary is that one party's understandings or impressions will not suffice to make a contract; being sure that the other side would accept does not substitute for acceptance, however justifiable the belief. *See* Dynegy Mktg. & Trade v. Multiut Corp., 648 F.3d 506 (7th Cir. 2011) ("Unilateral 'understandings' are not enough to give rise to an enforceable oral contract . . .").

§3.13 n.21 p.275 Add the following to the list after **"Accord"**: Janky v. Batistatos, 559 F. Supp. 2d 923 (N.D. Ind. 2008) (purported acceptance of settlement agreement adds global release term prefaced by "Although not explicitly mentioned in your proposal"; "even though the Defendants wrote 'accept' in the December 2 email, the inclusion of additional terms from the initial offer turns the email into a counter-offer").

§3.13 n.25 p.275 Add the following at the beginning: All Am. Roofing v. Zurich Am. Ins. Co., 934 N.E.2d 679 (Ill. App. 2010) ("where the parties make a writing and its execution conditions precedent to its completion, there is no contract until this occurs"; although documents did not state expressly that both parties had to sign before the agreement was binding, both parties behaved as though that was the case).

§3.13 n.28 p.276 Add the following to the list after **"Accord"**: Carroll v. Fremont Inv. & Loan, 636 F. Supp. 2d 41 (D.D.C. 2009) (plaintiffs' signatures on first page of four-page contract do not manifest intent to be bound where they "signed only at the bottom of the first page despite the fact that the contract had initial or signature lines on each of the four pages" and "they struck through paragraph three of the contract").

§3.13 n.29 p.277 Add the following to the list after **"Accord"***:* Restatement Second §60; Suss Pontiac-GMC v. Boddicker, 208 P.3d 269 (Colo. App. 2008) (although option contract calls for notice of exercise by certified mail, return receipt requested, notice by first-class mail acceptable; "an alternative delivery method is sufficient if it serves the same function as the method specified," at least where "the parties did not attach special significance to the method of delivery") (collecting cases).

§3.13 p.277 In the first full paragraph, add the following at the end of the second sentence: . . . with those requirements.[30a]

[30a] An interesting example of this uncommon argument arose in Auto Glass Express v. Hanover Ins. Co., 975 A.2d 1266 (Conn. 2009). There an insurer periodically sent pricing letters to auto glass repair companies, giving its pricing schedule and stating that "[b]ills that are accurate and not more than this pricing structure will be paid promptly as submitted." The companies submitted claims to the insurer for more than the pricing structure. The insurer reimbursed the glass companies for the amount in the pricing structure. When the glass companies sued for breach of contract, the insurer argued that by performing the glass repairs the glass companies had accepted the terms of the pricing letters. The supreme court held that the letters contained offers, not of prompt payment at the given rate, but of prompt payment at the given rate of invoices not exceeding that given rate. Consequently, the glass companies did not accept the offer by sending invoices for higher amounts, and they were thus free to assert their own breach of contract actions.

§3.14 PROMISE INFERRED FROM SILENCE OR EXERCISE OF DOMINION

§3.14 n.3 p.278 Add the following at the end: A common example of an implied-in-fact contract occurs when parties continue to perform after a contract has expired. *See* Luden's v. Local Union No. 6, 28 F.3d 347 (3d Cir. 1994) ("when a contract lapses but the parties to the contract continue to act as if they are performing under a contract, the material terms of the prior contract will survive" absent a contrary indication). Some courts, especially in collective bargaining disputes, are reluctant to draw

even this inference. *See* Williamsbridge Manor Nursing Home v. Local 144 Div. of 1199, Nat'l Health & Human Servs. Employees Union, AFL-CIO, 107 F. Supp. 2d 222 (S.D.N.Y. 2000) (rejecting proposition that optional terms, such as arbitration agreements, survive the expiration of the underlying contract); Teamsters Local Union No. 122 v. August A. Busch & Co., 932 F. Supp. 374 (D. Mass. 1996) (rejecting *Luden's* because "postexpiration conduct may reflect nothing more than compliance with the unilateral change doctrine" rather than a desire to carry the contract terms forward).

§3.14 n.4 p.278 In the first paragraph, add the following at the end: The Code's approach to acceptance is identical. U.C.C. 2-606(1)(c); *see* Hines v. Mercedes-Benz USA, 358 F. Supp. 2d 1222 (N.D. Ga. 2005) (buyer who revoked acceptance of defective automobile re-accepted it by continuing to drive it, despite having another vehicle).

§3.14 n.4 p.278 In the second paragraph, add the following at the end: Grosso v. Miramax Film Corp., 400 F.3d 658 (9th Cir. 2005) (cause of action for implied-in-fact contract for conveying idea for screenplay where "the plaintiff prepared the work, disclosed the work to the offeree for sale, and did so under circumstances from which it could be concluded that the offeree voluntarily accepted the disclosure knowing the conditions on which it was tendered and the reasonable value of the work").

§3.14 n.10 p.280 Add the following to the list after "See also": J. Sheldon & C. Carter, Unfair & Deceptive Acts & Practices §5.8.4 (6th ed. 2004) (discussing FTC and state UDAP provisions); UMG Recordings v. Augusto, 558 F. Supp. 2d 1055 (C.D. Cal. 2008) (promotional compact discs are gifts under federal law, so the recipient's sale of them was protected under the first sale doctrine of copyright law).

§3.14 n.11 p.280 Add the following to the list after "Accord": Memberworks v. Yance, 899 So. 2d 940 (Ala. 2004) (re-enrollment in discount club sufficient to show assent to arbitration clause, even though clause provided after oral contract made); Nationwide Mut. Fire Ins. Co. v. Royall, 588 F. Supp. 2d

1306 (M.D. Fla. 2008) (insurer's recovery of costs and fees incurred while defending suit on behalf of insured; "In the limited circumstances in which acquiescence may constitute acceptance, the law appears to require, at a minimum, that there at least be some reasonable time for the offeree to reject the offer before acquiescence will be deemed an acceptance.") (relying upon Restatement Second §69). *But see* Chase Bank USA v. Leggio, 999 So. 2d 155 (La. App. 2008) (where credit card issuer could not prove that cardholder had received notice of an arbitration clause, the cardholder's continued use of the card did not constitute an acceptance of the arbitration clause); Martin v. Comcast, 146 P.3d 380 (Or. App. 2006) (continued receipt of services not assent to modification of arbitration agreement, where notice was obscure and therefore there was "no objectively manifested meeting of the minds").

A contract modification may be accepted by conduct ratifying the new agreement. In *NECA-IBEW Rockford Local Union 364 Health & Welfare Fund v. A&A Drug Co.*, 736 F.3d 1054 (7th Cir. 2013), a local union negotiated and executed an agreement with Sav-Rx to provide prescription drug benefits to its members. Thereafter, the IBEW national union negotiated an agreement with Sav-Rx in which all its locals were invited to join, that would provide better pricing and services, but contained an arbitration clause. The local's Board of Trustees never voted to join the national agreement, but for eight years the local accepted services from Sav-Rx under the terms of that national agreement. When a dispute arose, Sav-Rx sought to enforce the arbitration clause, while the local asserted that it never agreed to arbitration. Both the District Court and the Seventh Circuit held that because the local "knew it was accepting benefits under the National Agreement, the Fund therefore ratified that agreement" and was bound by the arbitration clause. *Id.* at 1056. Although the local's Board of Trustees was the only body with authority to enter into a contract on behalf of this Fund, and no other party had implied or apparent authority, nevertheless "[a] principal like the Fund can ratify a contract when the principal enjoys the benefits of the contract and does not repudiate it." *Id.* at 1059.

§3.14 n.12 p.280 Add the following after the first sentence: *Accord:* Roger's Backhoe Serv. v. Nichols, 681 N.W.2d 647 (Iowa

2004) (though property owner told excavator that extra work should not be done, "he was bound to call off the digging" done in his presence and with his knowledge "if he did not intend to pay for it").

§3.14 n.12 p.280 Add the following to the list after **"But cf.":** Estate of Mueller v. Karns, 873 N.E.2d 652 (Ind. App. 2007) (where consultant had performed in full when it sent a letter requesting payment, no opportunity to reject and silence not acceptance).

§3.14 p.280 Correct the second marginal header to read: Rules severely tested

§3.14 n.14 p.281 Add the following at the end of the paragraph: In an interesting case, the Ninth Circuit held that no contract had been formed where the purchaser of a vehicle that came with a free trial for Sirius Satellite Radio continued to use the service after receiving a contract in the mail providing "that failure to cancel the subscription within three business days of activation legally binds the customer to the agreement." Knutson v. Sirius XM Radio Inc., 771 F.3d 559, 562 (9th Cir. 2014). Sirius attempted to analogize the case to shrinkwrap agreements, under which the license or contract terms are not known until after the purchase of software or other product, or other instances in which use has been approved by the courts as constituting assent to be bound by the terms. The Circuit found all such cases distinguishable because here, the plaintiff "purchased his vehicle from Toyota, he did not receive any documents from Sirius XM, and he did not know that he was entering into a contractual relationship with Sirius XM by using the service. Instead, he believed that Sirius XM's trial subscription was a complimentary service 'provided for marketing purposes.'" *Id.* at 566. Thus, he had no reason to treat the letter in the mail a month later as anything to which he had to respond or even open and read. Because there was no mutual assent, the arbitration agreement was unenforceable and the plaintiff could go forward with his Telephone Consumer Protection Act for unsolicited phone calls from Sirius.

§3.14 n.16 p.281 ***Add the following at the beginning:*** In an interesting illustration, a lawyer rented space from a co-owner of a building. The second co-owner, seeing the lawyer present, demanded that the lawyer agree to pay him rent or vacate the building. The lawyer remained in the offices and continued paying rent to the first co-owner. The second co-owner sued to evict the lawyer on the basis of the lawyer's assent to his proposed agreement. The court held that the lawyer's "remaining in his office on the premises was not an action indicative of acceptance under the circumstances. He was already there pursuant to his agreement with [the first co-owner]. Therefore, [the second co-owner] could not assume that [the lawyer's] refusing to vacate indicated acceptance of his offer." Bruscato v. Oswalt, 975 So. 2d 120 (La. App. 2008).

§3.14 n.16 p.281 ***Add the following to the list after "Cf.":*** Kauffman v. Int'l Bhd. of Teamsters, 950 A.2d 44 (D.C. 2008) (change in housing allowance for at-will employee enforceable where employee continued working for three years; continued employment amounts to assent, at least after "a brief period of time . . . while considering whether to accept the change or leave the employment").

§3.14 n.17 p.281 ***Add the following at the end of the first paragraph:*** The Restatement Second approach was rejected in Manigault v. Macy's E., 318 Fed. Appx. 6 (2d Cir. 2009) (per curiam) (even though the employee didn't intend to be bound, "Manigault continued to work after receiving notice of the SIS program. Manigault therefore agreed to arbitration by continuing with her employment.").

§3.14 n.23 p.283 ***In the second paragraph, add the following at the end of the first sentence:*** and followed in Bell, Inc. v. IFS Indus., 742 F. Supp. 2d 1049 (D.S.D. 2010) (use of forum-selection clause in order confirmations for eight years sufficient to bind buyer "at least tacitly . . . through its course of dealing").

§3.14a EMPLOYEE RIGHTS AND EMPLOYER HANDBOOKS

§3.14a n.2 p.284 Add the following at the end of the first paragraph: This also operates to restrict the rights or benefits due an employee. *See* Conner v. Celanese, Inc., 428 F. Supp. 2d 628 (S.D. Tex. 2006) (posting of lowered pay rate for at-will employees; "When the employer notifies the employee of the change in terms, the employee must either accept the new terms or quit.").

***§3.14a n.5 p.286 In the first paragraph, add the following to the list after* "see":** Kern v. Palmer Coll. of Chiropractic, 757 N.W.2d 651 (Iowa 2008) (following *Toussaint* approach, so that finder of fact is to apply the stated definition of good cause; rejecting "the narrower role of the judicial fact-finder prevailing in the jurisdictions that review the reasonableness of an employer's termination decision").

***§3.14a n.6 p.286 In the first paragraph, add the following after the citation to* Shebar:** , followed in Lapidoth v. Telcordia Techs., 22 A.3d 11 (N.J. Super. App. Div. 2011) (letters authorizing maternity leave with a guarantee of reinstatement sufficient to create genuine issue on terms of employment, especially where defendant had given plaintiff nine earlier maternity leaves and reinstated her after each);

§3.14a n.7 p.287 In the first paragraph, add the following to the list in the first sentence: DeFranco v. Storage Tech. Corp., 622 F.3d 1296 (10th Cir. 2010) (promise of permanent employment is merely employment for an indefinite term, and thus terminable at will by either party, unless there is special consideration for the promise of permanent employment); Ledgerwood v. Nat'l Amusements, 625 F. Supp. 2d 466 (E.D. Mich. 2007) (statements that "we'll always have a job for you," "come in, do your job, keep doing a good job . . . and the promotions will come and we'll always take care of you," "managers were exempt from layoffs because of the theater closings," and that worker was a "lifer" insufficient to "reasonably instill a legitimate expectation of just cause employment because there is no evidence the alleged promises were made to anyone other than him").

§3.14a n.8 p.289 Add the following to the list in the first sentence: Cundiff v. Dollar Loan Ctr., 726 F. Supp. 2d 1232 (D. Nev. 2010) (schedule of salary for the next 15 years does not make the employment contract for a term of fifteen years, where language referred to salary after the 15-year period).

§3.14a n.8 p.289 Add the following to the list after **"Contra"*:*** Mathis v. Brown & Brown of S.C., 698 S.E.2d 773 (S.C. 2010) (reference to salary for first and second years sufficient to support finding that contract was for a term of at least two years).

§3.14a n.9 p.289 Add the following at the end of the first paragraph: The current draft of the new Restatement of Employment Law adopts this position, though recognizing that it has not been popular. Restatement (Third) of Employment Law §2.03(a)(2) & cmt. h (T.D. No. 2, Apr. 3, 2009).

§3.14a n.11 p.290 In the first paragraph, add the following to the list in the second sentence: McNamara v. Yellow Transp., 570 F.3d 950 (8th Cir. 2009) (South Dakota law; "continued employment after an employer imposes a term or condition upon employment demonstrates the acceptance and consideration necessary to form an enforceable contract"); Seawright v. Am. Gen'l Fin. Servs., 507 F.3d 967 (6th Cir. 2007) (where handbook stated that continued employment constituted acceptance of the arbitration agreement, "Seawright expressed a valid assent when she continued to work"); Kunzie v. Jack-in-the-Box, Inc., 330 S.W.3d 476 (Mo. App. 2010) (continued work insufficient to establish the employee's assent to changed terms; the employee's failure to sign the proposed agreement could have been a rejection and counter-offer, which the employer would have accepted by continuing to employ the worker).

§3.14a n.11 p.290 In the first paragraph, add the following after the citation to **Feges*:*** , in turn followed in Alexandria Housing & Redev. Auth. v. Rost, 756 N.W.2d 896 (Minn. App. 2008) (handbook stated that "[a]n employee who gives unsatisfactory service or who is guilty of substantial violation of regulations shall be subject to dismissal without notice" insufficiently definite, because "unsatisfactory," "substantial," and "regulations" are vague and undefined).

§3.14a n.11 p.290 In the first paragraph, add the following at the end: *See also* Brown v. St. Paul Travelers Cos., 559 F. Supp. 2d 288 (W.D.N.Y. 2008) (arbitration policy sought to be enforced by employer; "while there is no signed acknowledgment of plaintiff's receipt of the handbook, the arbitration policy is a written policy, plaintiff was advised that compliance with the arbitration policy was a condition of continued employment, she was advised that it was her responsibility to 'read and understand' all of the company policies including the arbitration policy, and she continued her employment with defendant."), *aff'd*, 331 Fed. Appx. 68 (2d Cir. 2009).

§3.14a n.12 p.291 Add the following to the list in the first sentence: Lawson v. N.Y. Billiards Corp., 331 F. Supp. 2d 121 (E.D.N.Y. 2004) (no evidence that the plaintiff relied on the manual's termination clause to his detriment, and continued employment not "sufficient to create a binding obligation").

§3.14a n.14 p.292 Add the following after the first sentence: If limited distribution is troublesome, not distributing at all to the employee is more so. Quiles v. Fin. Exch. Co., 879 A.2d 281 (Pa. Super. 2005) ("Without being given information explaining the company's policy to exclusively arbitrate any workplace disputes, Quiles could not accept the terms of the agreement to arbitrate"), followed in Kirleis v. Dickie, McCamey & Chilcote, P.C., 560 F.3d 156 (3d Cir. 2009) (shareholder in law firm not bound by arbitration clause in bylaws when had never received a copy of the bylaws; as a result, she could not have agreed explicitly to the arbitration clause, as required under Pennsylvania arbitration law). *Cf.* Thompson v. Bar-S Foods Co., 174 P.3d 567 (Okla. 2007) (no valid arbitration agreement where arbitration clause in a document not distributed to worker).

§3.14a n.15 p.292 Add the following after the citation to* Gilbert*: and in Lapidoth v. Telcordia Techs., 22 A.3d 11 (N.J. Super. App. Div. 2011) (giving effect to the reasonable expectations of an employee, not of the particular employee in question);

§3.14a n.17 p.293 Add the following to the list after **"Contra"***:* Dahlberg v. Lutheran Soc. Servs., 625 N.W.2d 241 (N.D. 2001) (whether handbook modified at-will relation ("a question of law")).

§3.14a n.19 p.294 In the first paragraph, add the following to the list in the first sentence: Dodge v. CDW-Gov't, Inc., 415 Fed. Appx. 485 (4th Cir. 2011) (giving effect to disclaimers in handbook stating that its "contents . . . are presented as a matter of information only and do not create a contract" and that "[n]one of the . . . benefits described in this or any other handbook are intended to . . . confer any rights or privileges."); Alexandria Housing & Redevelopment Auth. v. Rost, *supra* note 11 (handbook stated that the employer "shall consider all employees to be employed at will. There shall be no employment contracts with any employee" "clearly expresses [the employer's] intent to retain at-will employment relationships with its employees" and "will prevent the formation of a contractual right to continued employment"), followed in Coursolle v. EMC Ins. Grp., 794 N.W.2d 652 (Minn. App. 2011) (handbook contained section called "Employee Handbook Disclaimer," which stated that "[t]his handbook is a guide for your general background and knowledge only. It does not constitute a contract." and that "this handbook is not intended to become expressly or implicitly a part of any agreement or contract of employment. The statements contained in this handbook do not limit the right of either the company or the employee to terminate employment at any time with or without cause."); Baldonado v. Wynn Las Vegas, 194 P.3d 96 (Nev. 2008) ("employee handbook expressly stated that 'any' policies were subject to unilateral modification").

§3.14a n.19 p.294 In the first paragraph, add the following after the citation to **Orr***:* , followed in Hayes v. Trustees of Ind. Univ., 902 N.E.2d 303 (Ind. App. 2009) (giving effect to disclaimer language: "[t]he language used in this manual should not be construed as creating a contract of employment," and "[a]t any time," the University "reserves the right to modify, to change, to suspend, or to cancel all or any part of the policies, procedures, and programs contained in this manual.").

§3.14a n.19 p.294 In the first paragraph, add the following after the citation to* Federal Express*: followed in *In re* 24R, Inc., 324 S.W.3d 564 (Tex. 2010) (giving effect to disclaimer in employee manual stating that "[t]he policies and procedures in this manual are not intended to be contractual commitments by The Boot Jack"; as a result, employee manual's unlimited right for employer to amend arbitration clause did not render an arbitration clause contained in a separate document illusory), extended precariously in Sun Fab Contracting v. Lujan, 361 S.W.3d 147 (Tex. Civ. App. 2011) (giving effect to similar disclaimer in employee manual; as a result, validating arbitration clause found in agreement contained within handbook, but not listed in the table of contents and not referring to handbook).

§3.14a n.19 p.294 In the first paragraph, add the following after the citation to* Johnson*: distinguished in Cabaness v. Thomas, 232 P.3d 486 (Utah 2010) (disclaimer in employee manual covered only some aspects of employment, leading to the inference that the employer intended to make a contract with its employees as to all other aspects.

§3.14a n.19 p.294 In the second paragraph, add the following after the citation to* Loghry*: followed in Finch v. Farmers Co-Op. Oil Co., 109 P.3d 537 (Wyo. 2005) ("the existence of these disclaimers prevented Mr. Finch from establishing that he reasonably relied").

§3.14a n.19 p.294 Add the following after the first paragraph: The current draft of the new Restatement of Employment Law gives weight to disclaimers, though pointing out that a disclaimer "should be viewed . . . in the context of the entire statement, other employer policies, and the employer's course of conduct." Restatement (Third) of Employment Law §2.04 & cmt. c (T.D. No. 2, Apr. 3, 2009).

§3.14a n.20 p.295 In the first paragraph, add the following to the list after* "See"*: Lapidoth v. Telcordia Techs., 22 A.3d 11 (N.J. Super. App. Div. 2011) (disclaimer in handbook does not preclude company from creating other than at-will employment through letters to employee containing company policy).

§3.14a n.20 p.295 Add the following after the citation to **Conner***:* *on remand*, 611 S.E.2d 905 (S.C. 2005).

§3.14a n.21 p.296 Add the following after the first sentence: Accord: Navlet v. Port of Seattle, 194 P.3d 221 (Wash. 2008) (reserved right to terminate retirement benefit plan ineffective to deprive eligible retirees of benefits; "An employer cannot expect to accept the benefit of continued service from its employees while reserving the right not to compensate those employees once it has received the full benefit of their service.").

§3.15 NOTICE OF ACCEPTANCE

§3.15 n.1 p.298 Add the following at the end: See Oliva v. Amtech Reliable Elevator Co., 851 N.E.2d 256 (Ill. App. 2006) (in the absence of an express notice requirement for the renewal of a lease, "[t]he holding over by the tenant operates as sufficient notice to the landlord that the tenant has elected to exercise its option").

§3.15 n.5 p.300 Add the following to the list after **"Accord"***:* Baraliu v. Vinya Capital, 765 F. Supp. 2d 289 (S.D.N.Y. 2011) (failure to communicate acceptance to offeror is "more than a mere formality" and is "fatal to [the plaintiff's] claim"); Cochran v. Norkunas, 919 A.2d 700 (Md. 2007) ("Signing the contract in private without transmitting the documents or otherwise communicating acceptance to the Buyers or their agent does not create an enforceable agreement").

§3.15 n.11 p.301 Add the following at the beginning: See Oliva v. Amtech Reliable Elevator Co., *supra* note 1 ("by accepting the increased rental [required under the option], [landlords] waived any notice to which they might have been entitled").

§3.16 WAYS OF TERMINATION

§3.16 n.1 p.303 ***Add the following after the first sentence:*** For an example, see Family Video Movie Club v. Home Folks, 827 N.E.2d 582 (Ind. App. 2005) ("the destruction by fire of the structure subject to Home Folks' leasehold terminated Home Folks' time to accept Family Video's offer").

§3.17 REVOCATION OF THE OFFER

§3.17 p.303 ***Add a new footnote 2a on line 11:*** . . . revocable as to any part not accepted.[2a]

[2a] *Cf.* Barnett Millworks v. Guthrie, 974 So. 2d 952 (Ala. 2007) (continuing guaranty agreement amounts to "an offer to guarantee payment for future specified acts . . . and this offer is not accepted until such extensions of credit are made. . . . [so] this Court has recognized a guarantor's right to unilaterally revoke an agreement to guarantee the payment of another regarding future acts.").

§3.17 n.4 p.304 ***Add the following at the end:*** *Accord:* Cent. Puget Sound Reg'l Transit Auth. v. Eastey, 144 P.3d 322 (Wash. App. 2006).

§3.18 OFFEROR'S DEATH OR INCAPACITY

§3.18 n.2 p.308 ***Add the following at the end:*** *See generally* Ricks, The Death of Offers, 79 Ind. L.J. 667 (2004).

§3.18 n.5 p.308 ***Add the following to the list after* "But cf.":** Dep't of Revenue v. Estate of Shea, 885 N.E.2d 866 (Mass. App. 2008) (offer of settlement made by husband and wife survived husband's death; the wife's joint liability was unaffected by her husband's death, and in any case the offer contained a waiver of the statute of limitations and thus was more like a completed contract).

§3.19 LAPSE OF THE OFFER

§3.19 n.5 p.310 Add the following at the end: *Cf.* Taylor v. Carbajal, 304 S.W.3d 585 (Tex. Civ. App. 2010) (when option contract fails to state a time for performance, the courts will imply a reasonable time; although ordinarily time is of the essence for option contracts, that is not necessarily true, particularly where, as here, the option was part of a bilateral contract, and where a provision creating a time for the exercise of the option was left blank).

§3.19 n.6 p.310 Add the following to the list after* "See"*: Sherrod *ex rel.* Cantone v. Kidd, 155 P.3d 976 (Wash. App. 2007) (time for accepting settlement offer lapsed when arbitrator rendered judgment; issue of fact).

§3.19 n.16 p.312 Add the following after the citation to* Hapka*: followed in Perry v. Ronan, 234 P.3d 617 (Ariz. App. 2010) (expressly adopting Restatement Second §49; acceptance possible after deadline has passed if: "(1) there is a delay in the delivery of the offer due to the fault of the offeror or the means of transmission adopted by the offeror; (2) the offeree neither knows nor has reason to know of the delay; and (3) the offeree accepts within *the same period of time* that would have been permissible if there was no delay") (emphasis in original).

§3.19 n.17 p.313 Add the following to the list after* "Accord"*: Reny v. Sneed, 647 S.E.2d 379 (Ga. App. 2007) ("[a]n acceptance of an offer after the time limited is binding on the offeror if he assents to the acceptance after it is made") (quoting W.B. Leedy & Co. v. Shirley, 104 S.E.2d 580 (Ga. App. 1958)); Starlite Ltd. P'ship v. Landry's Rest., 780 N.W.2d 396 (Minn. App. 2010) ("an offeror cannot waive a term of an offer and create a valid agreement because there was no longer an offer that the offeree could accept"); Restatement Second §70 & cmt. b.

§3.20 REJECTION BY THE OFFEREE

§3.20 n.4 p.314 Add the following at the end: *See generally* Ayres, Never Say No: The Law, Economics, and Psychology of Counteroffers, 25 Ohio St. J. on Disp. Resol. 603 (2010).

§3.20 n.6 p.314 Add the following at the end: *Cf.* People v. Henderson, 809 N.E.2d 1224 (Ill. 2004) (accused's "counteroffer operated as a rejection of the State's offer" of plea agreement).

§3.20 n.7 p.315 Add the following after the first sentence: *Accord:* Rios v. State, 974 A.2d 366 (Md. App. 2009) (offer of plea agreement; defense lawyer's response "Would you consider allowing a nolo plea to reckless?" "was a mere inquiry regarding the possibility of different plea agreement terms, not a counteroffer"; quoting from Restatement Second §39).

§3.21 BATTLE OF THE FORMS

§3.21 n.2 p.315 Add the following to the list after "Accord": Bedford Care Ctr.-Monroe Hall v. Lewis, 923 So. 2d 998 (Miss. 2006) (conservator's refusal to sign arbitration clause in admission agreement, followed by nursing home's admission of the conservatee, operated as an acceptance of the conservator's terms).

§3.21 n.2 p.315 Add the following to the list after "But cf.": Amedisys, Inc. v. Kingwood Home Healthcare, LLC, 437 S.W.3d 507, 57 Tex. Sup. Ct. J. 547 (Tex. May 9, 2014) (defendant offered to settle claims "asserted or which could have been asserted" but the plaintiff's acceptance referenced only the claims "asserted"; "under the summary judgment record in this case, the variation in language . . . is not material and did not convert [plaintiff's] acceptance into a counteroffer.").

§3.21 n.6 p.317 Add the following to the list after "Accord": Grant v. Lyons, 17 So. 3d 708 (Fla. App. 2009) (insurer's acceptance of insured's offer to settle may add a requirement that the insured sign the usual settlement documents; if, however, "the release contains objectionable, not 'usual' terms, no acceptance of the offer occurs").

§3.21 n.11 p.319 In the second paragraph, add the following to the list after **"See"***:* Eiselen & Bergenthal, The Battle of Forms: A Comparative Analysis, 39 Comp. & Int'l L.J. S. Afr. 214 (2006); Stemp, A Comparative Analysis of the "Battle of the Forms," 15 Transnat'l & Contemp. Probs. 243 (2005); Stephens, Escape from the Battle of the Forms: Keep it Simple, Stupid, 11 Lewis & Clark L. Rev. 233 (2007).

§3.21 n.13 p.320 In the second paragraph, add the following to the end: Judge Easterbrook's statement has been much criticized by commentators. *See* Hillman, Rolling Contracts, 71 Fordham L. Rev. 743 (2002) ("Easterbrook was plainly wrong about §2-207's applicability"); Murray, Contract Theories and the Rise of Neoformalism, 71 Fordham L. Rev. 869 (2002) ("the superficial notion that UCC §2-207 applies only where there are two conflicting forms"); White, Default Rules in Sales and the Myth of Contracting Out, 47 Loyola L. Rev. 53 (2002) ("When Judge Easterbrook in ProCD states that §2-207 does not apply to transactions that involve only one document, he is wrong"). Judge Easterbrook seems unrepentant, continuing to assert this even in cases governed by UCC Article 2A — which does not have a battle of the forms provision. IFC Credit Corp. v. United Bus. & Indus. Credit Union, 512 F.3d 989 (7th Cir. 2008) ("there was only one form . . . so §2-207 need not be consulted" in case of personal property leasing).

§3.21 n.14 p.321 In the first paragraph, change the citation to **White & Summers** *to the following:* J. White & R. Summers, 1 Uniform Commercial Code §1-3, at 60-61 (5th ed. 2006).

§3.21 n.14 p.321 In the first paragraph, add the following to the list after **"See also"***:* Flender Corp. v. Tippins Int'l, 830 A.2d 1279 (Pa. Super. 2003) (joining "majority of courts" that have adopted " 'knockout' rule").

§3.21 n.15 p.321 Add the following to the list after **"Accord"*:*** Gage Prods. Co. v. Henkel Corp., 393 F.3d 629 (6th Cir. 2004) (the seller's shipments "were based on such fundamentally different [price] terms than those proposed in the purchase orders, [thus] arguably manifesting the parties' intent not to be bound"); Parker Drilling Co. v. Romfor Supply Co., 316 S.W.3d 68 (Tex. Civ. App. 2010) (purported acceptance changed number of items to be purchased, total price, price for main items, and identity of ultimate purchaser; "[b]y changing the material terms of the offer, [the seller's] e-mail constitutes a rejection of [the buyer's] offer and a counteroffer").

§3.21 n.18 p.323 Add the following at the end of the first sentence: . . . despite clear statements to the contrary in the comments to both sections. UCC-O 2-201 cmt. 3; UCC-O 2-207 cmt. 6.

§3.21 n.19 p.323 Add the following at the end: *See generally* Marks, The Limits of Limiting Liability in the Battle of the Forms: U.C.C. Section 2-207 and the "Material Alteration" Inquiry, 33 Pepp. L. Rev. 501 (2006).

§3.21 n.20 p.324 In the first paragraph, add the following to the list in the second sentence: ICC Chem. Corp. v. Vitol, Inc., 425 Fed. Appx. 57 (2d Cir. 2011) (" '[S]urprise includes both the subjective element of what a party knew and the objective element of what a party should have known. To carry the burden of showing surprise, a party must establish that, under the circumstances, it cannot be presumed that a reasonable merchant would have consented to the original term' ") (quoting from Coosemans Specialties v. Gargiulo, 485 F.3d 701, 708 (2d Cir. 2007)).

§3.21 n.20 p.324 In the first paragraph, add the following after the citation to **Waukesha Foundry*:*** and in Paul Gottlieb & Co. v. Alps S. Corp., 985 So. 2d 1 (Fla. App. 2007) (agreeing with Judge Posner in *Union Carbide* that the basic test is whether agreement to the additional term cannot be presumed).

§3.21 n.20 p.324 In the first paragraph, add the following at the end: *Cf.* Marvin Lumber & Cedar Co. v. PPG Indus., 401 F.3d 901 (8th Cir. 2005) (discussing argument that hardship is not a criterion).

***§3.21 n.21 p.324 Add the following to the list after* "Accord":** Marvin Lumber & Cedar Co. v. PPG Indus., *supra* note 20, (clause limiting damages for breach to purchase price); Trans-Tec Asia v. M/V Harmony Container, 435 F. Supp. 2d 1015 (C.D. Cal. 2005) (choice-of-law clause).

***§3.21 n.22 p.324 In the first paragraph, add the following to the list after* "Accord":** Paul Gottlieb & Co. v. Alps S. Corp., *supra* note 20 (provision excluding consequential damages).

***§3.21 n.22 p.324 In the second paragraph, add the following to the list after* "See":** Paul Gottlieb & Co. v. Alps S. Corp., *supra* note 20 ("a party seeking the exclusion of a contractual term or provision . . . as constituting a material alteration, has the burden of proof").

***§3.21 n.23 p.325 Add the following to the list after* "Accord":** Trans-Tec Asia v. M/V Harmony Container, *supra* note 21 (choice-of-law clause); Oakley Fertilizer v. Cont'l Ins. Co., 276 S.W.3d 342 (Mo. App. 2009) (risk of loss).

§3.21 n.25 p.326 In the first paragraph, add the following after the citation to* Standard Bent Glass*: and in ICC Chem. Corp. v. Vitol, Inc., 425 Fed. Appx. 57 (2d Cir. 2011) (requiring case-by-case analysis of arbitration clauses; no surprise here where evidence was that some traders in the pertinent field arbitrate and others do not).

***§3.21 n.25 p.326 Add the following to the list in the second paragraph after* "Accord":** Colo.-Ark.-Tex. Distrib. v. Am. Eagle Prods., 525 F. Supp. 2d 428 (S.D.N.Y. 2007) (whether arbitration clause is a material alteration must be determined case-by-case; here, buyer familiar with language and arbitration common in industry, so not a material alteration).

§3.21 n.25 p.326 Add the following at the end: Current case law in this area may be shifting. Recently the American Arbitration Association and the National Arbitration Forum announced their departure from some or all of the consumer arbitration arena. The American Arbitration Association, citing concerns about due process, has stopped taking consumer debt collection arbitration cases until it can determine "that adequate and broadly acceptable due process protocols are in place." Am. Arbitration Ass'n, AAA Announces Moratorium on Consumer Debt Collection Arbitration Cases, July 27, 2009, http://www.adr.org/sp.asp?id=36432. The National Arbitration Forum agreed to cease administering consumer arbitration disputes as part of a consent decree entered into with the Attorney General of Minnesota, resolving an action alleging that the NAF "hid from the public its extensive ties to the collection industry." Office of Minn. Att'y Gen'l, National Arbitration Forum Barred from Credit Card and Consumer Arbitrations under Agreement with Attorney General Swenson (July 20, 2009), http://www.ag.state.mn.us/Consumer/PressRelease/090720NationalArbitrationAgremnt.asp. *See also* Nat'l Arbitration Forum, National Arbitration Forum to Cease Administering All Consumer Arbitrations in Response to Mounting Legal and Legislative Challenges (July 19, 2009), http://www.adrforum.com/newsroom.aspx?itemID=1528. Other arbitral bodies have changed their rules in ways that call into question the parties' initial consent to arbitration. For example, the American Health Lawyers Association Alternative Dispute Resolution Service now will administer a claim only if the parties agreed to arbitration after the injury has occurred. Bedford Health Props. v. Estate of Davis, 50 So. 3d 362 (Miss. App. 2010). These departures and their causes give ammunition to those seeking to have arbitration clauses deemed material alterations for the purposes of UCC 2-207(2)(b). They may also require the redrafting of much boilerplate; given the importance of the AAA and NAF, it is not unlikely that one or the other is named in a stock arbitration clause, and the AHLA body is mentioned in a good many pre-dispute arbitration clauses. The typical clause does not provide for a backup arbitrator. Doing so might be prudent under the circumstances. Alternatively, an agreement might provide a mechanism by which the parties could choose an arbitrator should the original choice be unavailable. If the parties do not do so, the result depends on the jurisdiction. In some, the court has the statutory authority under state law to select an arbitrator. *See* BallenIsles Country Club v. Dexter Realty, 24 So. 3d 649 (Fla. App. 2009) (applying Fla. Stat. §682.04 to permit choosing replacement arbitrator). In others, there is no such state statutory authority, which generally means that the arbitration clause fails as hopelessly indefinite (at least, given the leading approach to reading the pertinent clause of the Federal Arbitration Act). *See* Jones v. GGNSC Pierre LLC, 684 F. Supp. 2d 1161 (D.S.D. 2010) (§5 of Federal Arbitration Act does not permit court to appoint new arbitrator where the original forum was "an integral part of the arbitration clause," though itself finding the clause not integral; collecting authorities); Carr v. Gateway, Inc., 918 N.E.2d 598 (Ill. App. 2009) (clause integral, so arbitration clause unenforceable); Stewart v. GGNSC-Canonsburg, 9 A3d 215 (Pa. Super. 2010) (same), followed in Rivera v. Am. Gen'l Fin. Servs., 259 P.3d 803 (N.M. 2011) (same), both in turn followed in Geneva-Roth Capital v. Edwards, 956 N.E.2d 1195 (Ind. App. 2011) (same); Grant v. Magnolia Manor-Greenwood, 678 S.E.2d 435 (S.C. 2009) (same). *Cf.* Bedford Health Props. v. Estate of Davis, 50 So. 3d 362 (Miss. App. 2010) (pre-dispute consent to AHLA arbitration vitiated when AHLA changed its rules to permit arbitration only after post-dispute consent, so no arbitration provided for). *But cf.* Estate of Perez v. Life Care Ctrs., 23 So. 3d 741 (Fla. App. 2009) (choice of arbitrator not integral, so court may appoint replacement); Wright v. GGNSC Holdings, 808 N.W.2d 114 (S.D. 2011) (same); *In re* Brock Specialty Servs., 286 S.W.3d 649 (Tex. Civ. App. 2009) (same). Relatedly, the Dodd-Frank Wall Street Reform and Consumer Protection Act of 2010 prohibits mandatory arbitration of whistleblower claims. 7 U.S.C.S. §26(n)(2). However, arbitration agreements need not explicitly carve out whistleblower claims to be otherwise enforceable. Santoro v. Accenture, 748 F.3d 217, 222 (4th Cir. 2014) ("an agreement to arbitrate whistleblower claims is not 'valid or enforceable.' This language represents a clear Congressional command that Dodd-Frank whistleblower claims are not subject to predispute arbitration. It does not follow, however, that Dodd-Frank likewise prohibits the arbitration of non-whistleblower claims simply because an arbitration agreement does not carve-out Dodd-Frank whistleblower claims. Instead, we think the language, context, and enactment of the statute lead to the opposite conclusion.").

§3.21 n.28 p.327 In the first paragraph, add the following to the list after **"See"***:* Scientific Components Corp. v. ISIS Surface Mounting, 539 F. Supp. 2d 653 (E.D.N.Y. 2008) (acceptance stating in capital letters that "acceptance of your company's order is expressly made conditional on your company's assent to the terms and conditions on the face and reverse side of this acknowledgment; these terms and conditions are also contained on the reverse side of Mini-Circuits' invoice" was sufficient to come within the "my way or the highway" exception in subsection (1)).

§3.21 n.28 p.327 In the first paragraph, add the following to the list after **"But cf."***:* Manitowoc Marine Grp. v. Ameron Int'l Corp., 424 F. Supp. 2d 1119 (E.D. Wis. 2006) (offeree's use of "subject to its terms and conditions" insufficient to avoid contract formation, but "Any conduct by Buyer which recognizes the existence of a contract . . . shall constitute acceptance by Buyer of all of the following terms and conditions. Acceptance is limited to acceptance of the express terms contained on the face and back hereof" does limit acceptance to the seller's terms); Polytop Corp. v. Chipsco, Inc., 826 A.2d 945 (R.I. 2003) (not sufficient to say "additional or different terms proposed by seller are rejected unless expressly assented to").

§3.21 n.28 p.327 In the first paragraph, complete the citation to **Idaho Power** *as follows:* 596 F.2d 924 (9th Cir. 1979).

§3.21 n.28 p.327 In the first paragraph, add the following to the list after **"But cf."***:* Stemcor USA v. Trident Steel Corp., 471 F. Supp. 2d 362 (S.D.N.Y. 2006) ("This contract reflects in its entirety all details as agreed between the parties thereto" not an unambiguous assertion that the acceptance was expressly made conditional on assent).

§3.21 n.28 p.327 In the third paragraph, add the following after the citation to **Uniroyal***:* , followed in Belden Inc. v. Am. Elec. Components, 885 N.E.2d 751 (Ind. App. 2008) (where acceptance is "expressly made conditional upon Buyer's assent solely to the terms of such acknowledgment," performance by parties creates contract under §2-207(3)).

§3.21 n.31 p.329 In the first paragraph, add the following to the list after* "Accord"*: Glasstech, Inc. v. Chicago Blower Corp., 675 F. Supp. 2d 752 (N.D. Ohio 2009) (in spite of a "my way or the highway" clause in the offer and in the purported acceptance, the parties formed a contract; variant warranty provisions in the offer and the acceptance were knocked out).

§3.21 n.31 p.329 In the first paragraph, add the following after the citation to* Coastal & Native Plant Specialties*: , followed in Belden Inc. v. Am. Elec. Components, *supra* note 28 ("we rely solely on Section 2-207(3) to determine what terms are included in the contract").

§3.21 n.31 p.329 Add the following as a new paragraph: Whether a contract is formed by conduct may bc asked only after one has determined that no contract was made by the exchange of writings. Section 2-207(3) thus is irrelevant if a contract has been formed through writings, a point that is at times missed by litigants and law students. *See* Oakley Fertilizer v. Cont'l Ins. Co., *supra* note 23 ("In this case, however, Section 2-207(3) is inapplicable because . . . Seller's sales contract and Buyer's purchase agreement established a valid written contract under Section 2-207(1).").

§3.21 n.32 p.329 Add the following after the citation to* Diamond Fruit Growers*: , followed in Tacoma Fixture Co. v. Rudd Co., 174 P.3d 721 (Wash. App. 2008) (where contract made by shipping goods in response to order, terms in invoices that followed not part of contract under 2-207(3)); Scientific Components Corp. v. ISIS Surface Mounting, *supra* note 28 (course of dealing in which parties performed despite the "my way or the highway" clause in the acceptance and in which the offeror and offeree negotiated over open orders amounts to an acceptance under UCC-O 2-207(3)).

§3.21 p.332 Add the following footnote at the end of the second paragraph: . . . a completely recast UCC-R 2-207.[40a]

[40a] *See generally* Thatcher, The Long Awaited Official Overhaul of U.C.C. Section 2-207: An Essay on the Limits of Improvement, 51 S. Dak. L. Rev. 296 (2006).

§3.21 n.43 p.333 Add the following at the end: The new Principles of the Law of Software Contracts adopts the formulation of UCC-R 2-207 on how to determine what the terms of the contract are. Principles of the Law of Software Contracts §2.01(b) & cmt. d (2010).

§3.21a WINNING THE BATTLE OF THE FORMS

§3.21a n.4 p.334 Add the following at the end: This approach will not, however, work in jurisdictions employing the knock-out rule. In those, a contract would be formed by the exchange of documents, and additional terms would not get in because of UCC 2-207(2)(a), but different terms would merely yield knock-out and the default terms. In practice, however, even knock-out jurisdictions seem to ignore the knock-out rule when UCC 2-207(2)(a) applies, thus permitting the offeror to insist upon its own terms.

§3.21a n.5 p.334 Add the following at the end: This result is hard to square with the statute. If a "my way or the highway" clause appears in the offer, and if it prevents a contract from being formed by anything other than meek acceptance of the offeror's terms, then why is UCC 2-207(2)(a) in the statute at all? If the offeree accepts, then we do not refer to §2-207(2) at all. If the offeree sends a variant acceptance, then a contract would be formed, if at all, by conduct, which means we would go to §2-207(3) to find the terms. In neither case would 2-207(2)(a) have any effect. For that section to have a function, it must be possible to form a contract by responding to an offer containing a "my way or the highway" clause with a variant acceptance.

§3.22 CONTRACTS BY CORRESPONDENCE

§3.22 n.1 p.337 In the first paragraph, add the following at the end: For a helpful discussion of how one proves dispatch in the context of a mass mailing, *see* Olson v. The Bon, 183 P.3d 359 (Wash. App. 2008).

§3.22 n.1 p.337 In the second paragraph, add the following at the end: For a comparative analysis, *see* Yamaguchi, The Problem of Delay in the Contract Formation Process: A Comparative Study of Contract Law, 37 Cornell Int'l. L.J. 357 (2004).

§3.22 n.5 p.338 Add the following after the first sentence: *Accord:* U.S. Life Ins. Co. v. Wilson, 18 A.3d 110 (Md. App. 2011) (acceptance through dispatch occurred when bank sent check upon instruction of offeree, not when offeree instructed bank to send the check; until the bank sent the check, the offeree "had set in motion the means to accept the offer . . .but still had the power to reverse course").

***§3.22 n.5 p.338 Add the following to the list after* "See also":** Duron v. Albertson's LLC, 560 F.3d 288 (5th Cir. 2009) (proof of dispatch may be circumstantial, "including customary mailing practices used in the sender's business"); Envtl. Equip. & Serv. Co. v. Wachovia Bank, 741 F. Supp. 2d 705 (E.D. Pa. 2010) (insufficient detail in supporting affidavit to invoke presumption; thorough analysis of necessary degree of proof); Hartford Underwriters Ins. Co. v. Reed, 57 So. 3d 742 (Ala. 2010) (detailed testimony about standard business practice constituted "clear and convincing evidence" that cancellation notice was properly sent, and thus that the sender would gain a presumption that the notice was received); *In re* Rural Route Neighbors, 960 A.2d 856 (Pa. Cmmw. 2008) ("Evidence concerning the customary procedures for mailing of letters is generally accepted as sufficient to establish that a letter was mailed.").

§3.22 n.6 p.338 Add the following at the end: , followed in U.S. Life Ins. Co. v. Wilson, 18 A.3d 110 (Md. App. 2011) (quoting with approval from comment a).

§3.22 n.12 p.340 Add the following to the list after **"See"**: Raymond, Manner, Method, Receipt or Dispatch: The Use of Electronic Media is Nothing New to the Law, 52 Loy. L. Rev. 1 (2006); Watnick, The Electronic Formation of Contracts and the Common Law "Mailbox Rule," 56 Baylor L. Rev. 175 (2004).

§3.22 n.15 p.340 ***In the first paragraph, add the following to the end:*** CISG and the UNIDROIT Principles differ from this. They make acceptance effective upon receipt, with a modest allowance made when the dispatch was timely but the transmission delayed. CISG 18(2), 21(2); UNIDROIT Principles 2.6(2), 2.9(2). Once the acceptance has been sent, though, the offer becomes irrevocable. CISG 16(1); UNIDROIT Principles 2.4(1).

§3.22 n.26 p.343 ***Add the following after the first sentence:*** *Accord:* Tippett v. Daly, 964 A.2d 606 (D.C. 2009) (adopting approach of Restatement Second §63(b), described as the majority rule); Meadows v. Midland Super Block Join Venture, 255 S.W.3d 739 (Tex. Civ. App. 2008) (mailbox rule does not apply where option calls for actual delivery).

§3.22 n.26 p.343 ***Add the following at the end:*** *Cf.* Scoville v. Shop-Rite Supermarkets, 863 A.2d 211 (Conn. App. 2004) ("parties to an option contract may make an agreement that does not require actual notice for effective acceptance"), declined to extend by Camphor Technologies v. Biofer, S.P.A., 916 A.2d 142 (Conn. Super. 2007) (not permitting parties to modify "service of process, or any other court action" by contract).

Quaere whether the rule might differ if the owner were unavailable during much of the option period or otherwise frustrated its exercise. *See* Tippett v. Daly, *supra* (raising question and citing to authority that suggests reversion to the usual mailbox rule).

§3.22 n.27 p.343 ***In the second paragraph, add the following to the list in the second sentence:*** Cortez v. Cortez, 203 P.3d 857 (N.M. 2009) (depositing a check in the mail constitutes payment, where "the contract was silent with regard to mailing, and the parties had no established pattern of mailing").

§3.23 *OPTIONS, OPTION CONTRACTS,* AND *FIRM OFFERS*

§3.23 n.1 p.344 Replace the citation to **Bristol** *with the following:* Bristol, Cardiff, & Swansea Aërated Bread Co. v. Maggs, 44 Ch. Div. 616 (1890).

§3.23 n.4 p.344 Add the following to the list after **"See"***:* U.S. Gen'l v. Jenson, 128 P.3d 56 (Utah App. 2005) (where real estate contract allowed buyers "to change their minds about purchasing the property and walk away," the contract "was not a bilateral contract, but an option contract"). *See generally* Katz, The Option Element in Contracting, 90 Va. L. Rev. 2187 (2004) (economic analysis of options).

§3.23 n.8 p.345 Add the following to the list after **"But see"***:* McLamb v. T.P. Inc., 619 S.E.2d 577 (N.C. App. 2005) ($500 refundable deposits not consideration for option; "consideration which may be withdrawn on a whim is illusory consideration which is insufficient to support a contract").

§3.23 n.9 p.346 Add the following to the list after **"Accord"***:* Gulf Coast Realty Co. v. Prof'l Real Estate Partners, 926 So. 2d 992 (Ala. 2005) (enforcing option contained in a lease); Restatement Second §80(1).

§3.23 n.11 p.346 Add the following to the list after **"Accord"***:* Steiner v. Thexton, 226 P.3d 359 (Cal. 2010) (option to sell real property enforceable after optionee undertook to have parcel split, an action benefitting the optioner).

§3.23 n.15 p.347 Add the following at the end: Where a contract merges an option with a lease, though, failure of consideration for the lease means failure of consideration for the option. *See* Estate of Ryan v. Shuman, 655 S.E.2d 644 (Ga. App. 2007) (not citing to *Smith v. Wheeler, supra*).

§3.23 n.17 p.347 Add the following at the end: See Knott v. Racicot, 812 N.E.2d 1207 (Mass. 2004) (abrogation of common law rule that consideration was not required for option contracts

under seal did not retroactively invalidate right of first refusal under seal where Restatement Second §87(1) was complied with.); 1464-Eight, Ltd. v. Joppich, 154 S.W.3d 101 (Tex. 2004) (abandoning consideration requirement and adopting Restatement Second §87(1)). Interestingly, a concurrence in *1464-Eight* suggests that it would be preferable to abandon even the form of consideration–a position reminiscent of Lord Mansfield's attempt to do away with the consideration requirement in commercial contracting. *1464-Eight, supra* (Jefferson, C.J., concurring). In any case, it is important that the purported consideration really be consideration if the offer is to become irrevocable. *See* Sandel v. ATP Oil & Gas Corp., 243 S.W.3d 749 (Tex. Civ. App. 2007) (neither past service nor work that was not bargained for constitute purported consideration for the purposes of Restatement Second §87(1)(a)). And it is fair to say that the Restatement Second approach is far from universally accepted; for example, it remains the majority view that the consideration for an option contract must be separate from that for the underlying purchase. *See* McLellan v. Charly, 758 N.W.2d 94 (Wis. App. 2008) (collecting cases).

§3.23 n.22 p.348 In the first paragraph, add the following after the first sentence: *Accord:* Cornish Coll. of the Arts v. 1000 Va. Ltd. P'ship, 242 P.3d 1 (Wash. App. 2010) (permitting both specific performance and damages for consequential loss, provided the latter are merely complements of the former).

§3.23 n.24 p.349 In the first paragraph, add the following to the list in the second sentence: Luccia v. Ross, 274 S.W.3d 140 (Tex. Civ. App. 2008) (failed attempt to exercise option does not cause option to expire, absent language to the contrary).

§3.23a OPTIONS AND *RIGHTS OF FIRST REFUSAL*

***§3.23a n.1 p.350 Add the following to the list after* "See":**
Faucette v. Chantos, 322 S.W.3d 901 (Tex. Civ. App. 2010) (provision in option that buyers must "purchase" the shares "only in a lump sum" did not mean that tender of payment was a

requirement for exercising the option; rather, the option was accepted by notice and the resulting bilateral contract was the source of the payment requirement) (strong dissent on interpreting the option).

§3.23a n.2 p.350 Add the following at the end: Some modest exceptions may, however, be allowed the holder of the option. *See* Elderkin v. Carroll, 941 A.2d 1127 (Md. 2008) (non-matching terms in attempted exercise of option will not prevent its effect if (a) the owner waives exact matching, (b) the difference is in the proper names of the parties, or (c) the difference is merely an inquiry, request, or suggestion that clearly is not a condition of acceptance). *Accord:* S.E. Cinema Entm't v. P.B. Realty, 585 F. Supp. 2d 754 (D.S.C. 2008) (request for leeway in closing date "does not mean that [the option holder] . . . varied the terms of acceptance . . . Nowhere in that [request] did SE Cinema suggest that it would not be exercising its option if PB Realty did not agree to give it 'leeway' on a closing date"). *Cf.* Besteman v. Pitcock, 272 S.W.3d 777 (Tex. Civ. App. 2008) ("Except in rare cases of equity, acceptance of an option must be unqualified, unambiguous, and strictly in accordance with the terms of the agreement."; 49-day delay in giving notice not excused by any resulting unconscionable hardship). *Accord:* Langer v. Bartholomay, 745 N.W.2d 649 (N.D. 2008).

At times the courts have strained to make an apparently variant exercise effective. In one recent case, the option provided that the holders of the option would have the right to buy the remaining shares in a closely held firm, "but only in a lump sum wherein Buyers purchase all remaining shares." The term "Buyers" was defined. The alleged acceptance called for the named buyers plus the company itself to make the purchase. This certainly looks like an attempt at a variant exercise. The appellate court did not see it that way, though, reasoning that "[t]he arrangement to equalize the share ownership and to have the company itself buy the remaining shares merely goes to the manner in which the other shareholders would accomplish the agreed-upon purpose of buying out [optionor's] ownership interest." Faucette v. Chantos, 322 S.W.3d 901, 909 (Tex. Civ. App. 2010). To reach this result required that the court employ a particularly vigorous sort of purposive interpretation. Given the usual rules of strictness in the interpretation of options, this approach seems at least incongruous. Nor is it at all clear that the court properly determined the purpose of the option. As the dissent observes, another very plausible reading is that the optionor wanted these particular buyers, not the company, to put up the needed funds.

§3.23a p.350 In the first paragraph, add the following to the end of the third sentence: . . . and the duty of good faith.[3a]

[3a] *See* Brunswick Hills Racquet Club v. Route 18 Shopping Ctr. Assocs., 864 A.2d 387 (N.J. 2005) (landlord breached duty of good faith and fair dealing with respect to tenant's option though "a series of evasions and delays, that lulled plaintiff into believing it had exercised the lease option properly").

§3.23a n.6 p.350 In the first paragraph, add the following at the end: *Cf.* Langer v. Bartholomay, *supra* note 2 ("Time is generally of the essence in exercising an option . . .").

§3.23a n.9 p.351 Add the following to the list in the first sentence: Creque v. Texaco Antilles Ltd., 409 F.3d 150 (3d Cir. 2005) ("Where . . . a corporation conveys property from one of its wholly-owned subsidiaries to another in good faith for a legitimate business purpose, there has been no bona fide third party offer sufficient to trigger a right of first refusal on the property."); Webster v. Ocean Reef Cmty. Ass'n, 994 So. 2d 367 (Fla. App. 2008) (right of first refusal not triggered by gifts; "[w]ere we to construe 'sale' or 'purchase' to include [the donative] transfer, the Association would have a right of first refusal to acquire the residence for nothing, nada, zero."); Rucker Props. v. Friday, 204 P.3d 671 (Kan. App. 2009) ("a transfer among co-owners without payment doesn't trigger a right of first refusal when the owner must have a 'desire to sell the property' to trigger it") (collecting cases).

§3.23a n.9 p.351 In the first paragraph, add the following to the list after "See generally": Naudé, Which Transactions Trigger a Right of First Refusal or Preferential Right to Contract?, 123 S. African L.J. 461 (2006).

§3.23a n.10 p.351 In the first paragraph, add the following at the end of the first paragraph: *Cf.* Schroeder v. Duenke, 265 S.W.3d 843 (Mo. App. 2008) ("a transfer of property by gift from one family member to another does not trigger a right of first refusal"; a transfer for purported consideration may or may not be a bona fide offer, depending on whether "the price was set with at least some reference to its fair market value").

§3.23a n.10 p.351 In the first paragraph, add the following to the list in the first sentence: Uno Rests. v. Boston Kenmore Realty, 805 N.E.2d 957 (Mass. 2004) ("requirement that triggering offers be bona fide serves to disable property owners from extinguishing a right of first refusal by simply relaying vague offers" and "offer is bona fide if it was made 'honestly and with serious intent' ").

§3.23a n.10 p.352 In the first paragraph, add the following after the citation to* West Texas Transmission*: , followed in Bischoff v. Bletz, 998 A.2d 705 (Vt. 2010) (where right of first refusal required the holder to buy "on the same terms and conditions as the original bona fide offer," it was not sufficient merely to tender the same price), and distinguished in St. George's Dragons v. Newport Real Est. Grp., 971 A.2d 1087 (N.J. Super. App. Div. 2009) (rightholder need only match the third party's offering price, not the net that would be received by the owner).

§3.23a n.12 p.352 In the second paragraph, add the following to the list after* "see"*: Bayer v. Showmotion, Inc., 973 A.2d 1229 (Conn. 2009) ("The fact that the parties [after the exercise of the right of first refusal] were unable to agree on the nonessential terms of the purchase and sale agreement has no bearing on the existence of a binding contract between them."); Wilson v. Wilson, 53 So. 3d 865 (Miss. App. 2011) (holder of first refusal's persistent refusal to meet the offered purchase price and instead secure a much lower price do not necessarily amount to counteroffers, but they do yield a failure to exercise the holder's rights).

§3.23a n.12 p.352 In the second paragraph, add the following to the list after* "But cf."*: 7-Eleven, Inc. v. Stin, L.L.C., 961 So. 2d 977 (Fla. App. 2007) (where holder of right of first refusal timely notified the owner of its intent to exercise its right, holder could submit variant contract without losing its right; "it would have been unreasonable to require 7-Eleven to have only one opportunity to proffer a formal contract because the [other] offer contemplated a different use and some conditions were irrelevant if 7-Eleven purchased"); IH Riverdale v. McChesney Capital Partners, 633 S.E.2d 382 (Ga. App. 2006) ("If the offers were in fact different, whether the difference in terms is material is determinative.").

§3.23a n.12 p.352 Add the following at the end: The duty of good faith and fair dealing, present generally in contracts, may be implicated if the holder acts badly. *See* LDC-728 Milwaukee v. Raettig, 727 N.W.2d 82 (Wis. App. 2006) (tenant breached duty of good faith when he exercised his right of first refusal when he had "no reasonable chance of . . . actually completing that transaction and . . . knew, or should have known, that this was so").

§3.23a n.13 p.353 In the second sentence, add the following to the list after* "see"*: Van Dam v. Spickler, 968 A.2d 1040 (Me. 2009) (buyer of property subject to right of first refusal is "subject to the possibility of a decree of specific performance," if the buyer purchases with knowledge of the right and fails to inquire whether the right holder wishes to exercise that right).

§3.23a n.13 p.353 In the third sentence, add the following to the list after* "see"*: Kaiser v. Bowlen, 200 P.3d 1098 (Colo. App. 2008) (right of first refusal triggered by sale of stock is not triggered by sale of stock in the parent company, provided the parent company does not exist in order to avoid the right of first refusal) (collecting cases); Pecora v. Berlin, 62 So. 3d 28 (Fla. App. 2011) (right of first refusal does not apply to court-supervised sale procured by a court-appointed receiver pursuant to a statutory dissolution).

§3.23a n.15 p.353 Add the following to the list in the first sentence: Kaiser v. Bowlen, *supra* note 13 ("Colorado, like a majority of states, construes a [right of first refusal] clause strictly.").

§3.23a n.15 p.353 Add the following after the first sentence: Also a matter of interpretation is whether the owner, after the holder exercises its right of first refusal, may then go back to the original offeror, elicit a higher offer, and come back to the holder demanding that higher amount. Mamo v. Skvirsky, 960 A.2d 595 (D.C. 2008).

§3.23a n.15 p.353 Replace the citation to **Fontaine & De Ly** *with the following:* M. Fontaine & F. De Ly, Drafting International Contracts: An Analysis of Contract Clauses ch.10 (2006).

§3.23a n.15 p.353 Add the following to the list after **"See"**: Torsello, Preliminary Agreements and CISG Contracts, in Drafting Contracts Under the CISG 191 (H. Flechtner et al. eds. 2008).

§3.23a n.17 p.354 Add the following at the end: But see Advanced Recycling Sys. v. S.E. Props. Ltd. P'ship, 787 N.W.2d 778 (S.D. 2010) (states that majority rule is that "[i]f the owner has not manifested an intention to sell the leased premises apart from the whole, the right of first refusal dies not ripen into an enforceable option contract to purchase the lease premises"; collects cases, follows the majority). *Cf.* Navasota Resources, L.P. v. First Source Tex., 249 S.W.3d 526 (Tex. Civ. App. 2008) (collecting cases that show substantial split; sides with those holding that the right of first refusal is invoked by a package transaction). Consistent with the cases above, however, the holder of this right of first refusal "cannot be compelled to purchase assets beyond those included within the scope of the agreement subject to the preferential right in order to exercise that right." *Id.* If the other assets are closely related, though, "whether the holder of a preferential right must purchase the additional assets turns on whether the condition that requires the purchase of additional assets is commercially reasonable, imposed in good faith, and not specifically designed to defeat the preferential right." FWT, Inc. v. Haskin Wallace Mason Prop. Mgmt., 301 S.W.3d 787, 801-02 (Tex. Civ. App. 2009). Along similar lines, there remains some question how the presence of a right of first refusal affects the ability of the owner to sell parts of the larger parcel. Certainly the owner may not circumvent the right of first refusal by selling off the subject

property piecemeal—i.e., by asserting that the right of first refusal applies only to the property as a whole. *See* Whiteface Resort Holdings v. McCutchen, 860 N.Y.S.2d 308 (App. Div. 2008). But it is less clear whether the owner may sell a portion of the property subject to the right of first refusal, or whether the holder of the right may prevent the sale of less than the whole property. *See* Hicks v. Castille, 313 S.W.3d 874 (Tex. Civ. App. 2010) (right of first refusal for whole property does not preclude selling a part of the property, as long as the seller gives the right-holder proper notice of the proposed sale and thus the opportunity to exercise the right of first refusal). The prudent drafter will answer this question one way or the other in the document creating the right.

§3.23a n.18 p.354 Add the following after the first sentence: *See In re* Smith Trust, 745 N.W.2d 754 (Mich. 2008) (once bona fide offer received and notice given, "the option in the lease agreement became operative. As a result, the [owner] did not have the right to revoke her offer to sell the property to [the option holders] until after the option period expired . . ."). *Cf.* Glick v. Chocorua Forestlands Ltd. P'ship, 949 A.2d 693 (N.H. 2008) (whether the option survives the withdrawal of the third-party offer depends on the precise language of the right of first refusal).

§3.23a n.20 p.354 Correct the citation to* Comeaux *to read as follows: 93 S.W.3d 215.

§3.23a n.20 p.354 Add the following at the end: The grantor must, of course, act in good faith when giving the holder notice of its right. Dyrdal v. Golden Nuggets, 689 N.W.2d 779 (Minn. 2004) ("the lessor need provide only reasonable notice of the essential terms of an offer of sale to trigger the lessee's obligation to timely respond"; while this may require inquiry on the lessee's part, "such an inquiry must be done within a reasonable time and . . . both the lessee, in making inquiry, and the lessor, in responding to the inquiry, must act timely, reasonably and in good faith").

§3.23a n.21 p.355 Add the following to the list after **"But cf."***:* Bauermeister v. Waste Mgmt. Co., 783 N.W.2d 594 (Neb. 2010) (rule against perpetuities does not apply to contractual option to repurchase property).

§3.23a n.21 p.355 Add the following at the end: *Cf.* Unif. Rule against Perpetuities Act §4(1) (1990) ("Section 1 (statutory rule against perpetuities) does not apply to: (1) a nonvested property interest or a power of appointment arising out of a nondonative transfer . . .") (adopted in 31 states).

§3.23a n.23 p.355 Add the following to the list: IH Riverdale v. McChesney Capital Partners, *supra* note 12 (where right of first refusal states no time for its exercise, "a reasonable time for performance will be implied").

§3.23a n.23 p.355 Add the following at the end: *Cf.* Van Dam v. Spickler, *supra* note 13 (indefinite right of first refusal against purchaser who was not a bona fide purchaser limited by laches, where right holder waited five years before seeking to exercise the right, during which purchaser had paid taxes and property had significantly increased in value).

§3.24 RELIANCE ON OFFER THAT INVITES PERFORMANCE

§3.24 n.7 p.357 Add the following after the first sentence: *See* Cascade Auto Glass v. Progressive Cas. Ins. Co., 145 P.3d 1253 (Wash. App. 2006) (insurer's pricing policy toward windshield company treated as a standing offer modifiable at will; "Cascade created binding unilateral contracts each time it repaired or replaced auto glass for Progressive's insureds after receiving Progressive's new offer.").

§3.24 n.11 p.358 Add the following to the list after **"Accord"***:* Ford v. Am. Express Fin. Advisors, 98 P.3d 15 (Utah 2004) (benefits contributions for financial planners).

§3.24 n.14 p.359 Add the following at the beginning: Devlin v. Empire Blue Cross & Blue Shield, 274 F.3d 76 (2d Cir. 2001) (retirement plan; when workers began working to attain necessary years for pension, and where the employer had not reserved the right to revoke the offer, it lost the right on the start of performance), distinguished by Robinson v. Sheet Metal Workers' Nat'l Pension Fund, 441 F. Supp. 2d 405 (D. Conn. 2006) (a provision allowing the employer to "amend or terminate benefits at any time" put workers on notice that their benefits were subject to modification), *aff'd*, 515 F.3d 93 (2d Cir. 2008). Revocation notwithstanding reliance may also further a social policy, such as the Uniform Arbitration Act's strong preference for written arbitration agreements. *See* Heider v. Knautz, 919 N.E.2d 1058 (Ill. App. 2009) ("an oral agreement to submit a dispute to arbitration is revocable by either party at any time prior to the entry of an award").

§3.25 RELIANCE ON OFFER THAT INVITES A PROMISE

§3.25 n.5 p.364 Add the following after the first sentence: *Cf.* Complete Gen. Constr. Co. v. Kard Welding, 911 N.E.2d 959 (Ohio App. 2009) ("A general contractor's mere use of a subcontractor's quote in formulating a bid for a general contract does not constitute acceptance of the subcontractor's offer.").

§3.25 n.7 p.365 Add the following at the end: Electro-Lab v. Sharp Constr. Co., 593 S.E.2d 170 (S.C. App. 2004) ("general contractor's mere use of a subcontractor's bid . . . does not constitute acceptance").

***§3.25 n.10 p.365 Add the following to the list after* "Accord":** Double AA Bldrs. v. Grand State Constr., 114 P.3d 835 (Ariz. App. 2005) (following *Drennan*).

§3.25 n.10 p.365 Add the following after the citation to* Wargo Builders*: , followed in Complete Gen. Constr. Co. v. Kard Welding, *supra* note 5 (subcontractor's attempted bid revocation half an hour before the general contractor's sealed bid was due was ineffective; the subcontractor was obligated to keep its original quote open for acceptance for a reasonable time after the general contractor was notified of its award).

§3.25 n.11 p.366 Add the following to the list after **"Accord"***:* *Drennan, supra* note 7 ("a general contractor is not free to delay acceptance after he has been awarded the general contract in the hope of getting a better price. Nor can he reopen bargaining with the subcontractor and at the same time claim a continuing right to accept the original offer"); Complete Gen. Constr. Co. v. Kard Welding, *supra* note 5 (general contractor "continued to negotiate bids submitted by other structural contractors in the hope that those subcontractors would reduce their bids," and this bid-shopping "renders it unfair to hold the subcontractor to its bid.").

§3.25 n.12 p.366 Add the following at the start: *See* Fletcher-Harlee Corp. v. Pote Concrete Contractors, 482 F.3d 247 (3d Cir. 2007) (where bid stated that it was for informational purposes only and should not be relied upon, reliance was unreasonable and promissory estoppel unavailable).

§3.25 n.17 p.367 Add the following at the end of the first paragraph: *Accord:* Double AA Bldrs. v. Grand State Constr., *supra* note 10 (applying §90(1) to *Drennan*-like facts).

§3.26 PRECONTRACTUAL LIABILITY

§3.26 n.1 p.369 Add the following to the list after **"See"***:* McClain v. Octagon Plaza, 71 Cal. Rptr. 3d 885 (Ct. App. 2008) ("the implied covenant is a supplement to an existing contract, and thus it does not require parties to negotiate in good faith prior to any agreement"); Barnes & Robinson Co. v. OneSource Facility Servs., 195 S.W.3d 637 (Tenn. App. 2006) ("Tennessee courts . . . have not recognized a duty to negotiate in good faith absent an express contractual agreement to do so.").

§3.26 n.7 p.370 Add the following at the beginning: Keystone Land & Dev. Co. v. Xerox Corp., 94 P.3d 945 (Wash. 2004) (rejecting argument that negotiations might have advanced to point where there was "duty to go forward" and declining to impose such a duty "in the absence of an enforceable contract" to negotiate).

§3.26 n.16 p.371 Add the following to the list after* "Accord"*: Miami-Dade County Sch. Bd. v. J. Ruiz Sch. Bus Serv., 874 So. 2d 59 (Fla. App. 2004); Ritchie Paving v. City of Deerfield, 67 P.3d 843 (Kan. 2003); Paul Sardella Constr. Co. v. Braintree Hous. Auth., 329 N.E.2d 762 (Mass. App. 1975); Mech. Contractors Ass'n v. Univ. of Cincinnati, 788 N.E.2d 670 (Ohio App. 2003).

§3.26 n.19 p.372 Add the following to the list after* "Accord"*: Planning & Design Solutions v. City of Santa Fe, 885 P.2d 628 (N.M. 1994) (city's acts . . . "introducing a locality requirement after the bids were opened, awarding the contract to the fourth-ranked bidder, and rejecting the proposals after making a contract award . . . were arbitrary and capricious").

§3.26 n.20 p.372 Add the following to the list after* "See also"*: Kostritsky, Uncertainty, Reliance, Preliminary Negotiations and the Holdup Problem, 61 SMU L. Rev. 1377 (2008); Schwartz & Scott, Precontractual Liability and Preliminary Agreements, 120 Harv. L. Rev. 661 (2007).

§3.26 n.29 p.376 Add the following to the list after* "But cf."*: Copeland v. Baskin-Robbins USA, 117 Cal. Rptr. 2d 875 (Ct. App. 2002) (unjust enrichment unsuitable "where . . . the subject matter of the contract is not an idea nor does the potential seller typically confer a precontractual service on the potential buyer").

§3.26 n.39 p.380 Add the following at the end: discussed in Duhl, *Red Owl's* Legacy, 87 Marq. L. Rev. 297 (2003), Scott, *Hoffman v. Red Owl Stores* and the Myth of Precontractual Reliance, 68 Ohio St. L.J. 71 (2007), Whitford & Macaulay, *Hoffman v. Red Owl Stores:* The Rest of the Story, 61 Hastings L.J. 801 (2010), and, in a rejoinder to Whitford and Macaulay, Scott, *Hoffman v.*

Red Owl Stores and the Limits of the Legal Method, 61 Hastings L.J. 859 (2010). For an interesting economic analysis of *Red Owl, see* Grosskopf & Medina, Regulating Contract Formation: Precontractual Reliance, Sunk Costs, and Market Structure, 39 Conn. L. Rev. 1977 (2007).

§3.26 n.40 p.380 In the first paragraph, add the following to the list after **"Accord"***:* 1861 Grp. v. Wild Oats Mkts., 728 F. Supp. 2d 1052 (E.D. Mo. 2010) (reliance on promises that the defendant would enter into a lease agreement was unreasonable as a matter of law; the plaintiff was a sophisticated landlord and thus knew the importance of having an enforceable lease agreement in hand before relocating other tenants, making its reliance on mere promises unreasonable).

§3.26 n.40 p.380 In the first paragraph, add the following at the end: But see Thompson v. Floyd, 713 S.E.2d 883 (Ga. App. 2011) (promissory estoppel potentially applies when employee left earlier job because of a promised fee on the completion of the new employer's sale to another firm, despite a possible lack of definiteness in the employment agreement).

§3.26 n.41 p.381 Add the following at the end: But cf. Birt v. Wells Fargo Home Mortg., 75 P.3d 640 (Wyo. 2003) (statements "preparatory to the signing of long-term financing agreements do not constitute a clear and definite promise where the terms of the proposed agreement are not to be finally determined until a formal closing").

§3.26b AGREEMENTS TO NEGOTIATE

§3.26b n.2 p.391 Add the following to the list after **"See generally"***:* Sanders, Looking for Faith in All the Wrong Places: Rethinking Agreements to Negotiate in Good Faith, 7 U.C. Davis Bus. L.J. 199 (2006); Note, Integrating Preliminary Agreements into the Interference Torts, 110 Colum. L. Rev. 1253 (2010).

§3.26b n.4 p.392 In the third paragraph, add the following at the end: *Accord:* IDT Corp. v. Tyco Grp., 918 N.E.2d 913 (N.Y. 2009) (giving effect to agreement to negotiate in good faith, but determining that the negotiations in fact were in good faith even though no final agreement resulted).

§3.26b n.7 p.394 Add the following to the list in the first sentence: Bacou Dalloz USA v. Cont'l Polymers, 344 F.3d 22 (1st Cir. 2003) (error to rule "that all agreements to agree are unenforceable in Rhode Island").

§3.26b n.7 p.394 Add the following after the citation to* A/S Apothekernes*: distinguished in Jenkins v. County of Schuylkill, 658 A.2d 380 (Pa. Super. 1995) (clearly "not a detailed letter of intent").

§3.26b n.7 p.394 Add the following to the list in the first sentence: Keystone Land & Dev. Co. v. Xerox Corp., 94 P.3d 945 (Wash. 2004).

§3.26b n.8 p.394 Add the following to the second paragraph after* "to negotiate in"*: Network Enters. v. APBA Offshore Prods., 427 F. Supp. 2d 463 (S.D.N.Y. 2006), *aff'd*, 264 Fed. Appx. 36 (2d Cir. 2008) and

§3.26b n.9 p.394 In the first paragraph, add the following to the list in the first sentence: Warner Bros. Int'l Television Distrib. v. Golden Channels & Co., 522 F.3d 1060 (9th Cir. 2008) (statement in contract that parties agreed to discuss security as part of contract extension read to make agreement on security an implied condition of performance).

§3.26b p.396 Add the following after the fourth sentence of the first full paragraph: . . . the agreement to negotiate.[12a]

[12a] *See* Logan v. D.W. Sivers Co., 169 P.3d 1255 (Or. 2007) ("plaintiff may be able to charge defendant with any expenses that she incurred (and wasted) in attempting to negotiate a final agreement . . . But, because defendant never agreed . . . even to negotiate in good faith . . . plaintiff

cannot, under this contract, charge defendant with losses that flowed from her inability to finally purchase it.").

§3.26b n.19 p.397 ***Add the following to the list in the first sentence:*** Network Enters. v. APBA Offshore Prods., *supra* note 8 (appropriate measure of damages for purchaser of network time's failure to negotiate in good faith is the exhibition fee multiplied by the number of episodes that the parties "would have . . . agreed upon" if the defendant had negotiated in good faith).

§3.26c MEANING OF *FAIR DEALING*

§3.26c n.47 p.409 ***Add the following at the end:*** followed in Supervalu Inc. v. Associated Grocers, 428 F. Supp. 2d 985 (D. Minn. 2006) (no duty to disclose competing negotiations).

§3.26c n.54 p.411 ***Add the following at the end:*** Nor does it follow that there is a duty to negotiate in good faith. *See* Logan v. D.W. Sivers Co., 169 P.3d 1255 (Or. 2007) ("Defendant's obligation not to solicit or sell to others for 60 days did *not* include any promise to negotiate in good faith — or at all — during that 60-day period") (emphasis in original).

§3.26c n.62 p.413 ***Add the following at the end:*** One should be careful not to assume that any attempt to renegotiate terms agreed upon is in bad faith. It may be that to reach an agreement on an open term, it is necessary for one party to adjust an agreed-upon term — for example, a seller might lower the price if it gets more flexibility on shipping dates. It is hard to see why this sort of give-and-take would be perfectly acceptable before terms are agreed upon and forbidden after.

§3.27 DEFINITENESS IN GENERAL

§3.27 n.1 p.417 ***Add the following at the end:*** *See generally* Geis, An Embedded Options Theory of Indefinite Contracts, 90

Minn. L. Rev. 1665 (2006); Scott, A Theory of Self-Enforcing Indefinite Agreements, 103 Colum. L. Rev. 1641 (2003).

§3.27 n.5 p.418 Add the following to the list after **"Accord"***:* Coe v. Chesapeake Energy Corp., 695 F.3d 311, 322 (5th Cir. 2012) (natural gas lease agreement not indefinite despite lack of final lease schedule, agreement on revenue interest, or miscellaneous final agreement terms); Dye v. Mech. Enters., 708 S.E.2d 24 (Ga. App. 2011) (where the parties agreed that an employee would be paid a commission and that they had agreed on how that commission would be calculated, "[t]he fact that the evidence concerning the method they agreed upon is conflicting did not render the agreement unenforceable, but instead required that this issue be submitted to a jury for resolution"); Smith v. Smith, 597 S.E.2d 250 (Va. 2004) (quoting *Heyman Cohen*).

§3.27 n.6 p.418 Add the following to the list after **"See"***:* Behrens v. S.P. Constr. Co., 904 A.2d 676 (N.H. 2006) (no contract where parties failed to reach agreement on financing term in sale of real estate).

§3.27 p.419 In the second full paragraph, add the following at the end of the first sentence: . . . all of the problems that may arise.[12a]

[12a] As Judge Posner colorfully put it, "The fact that a contract is incomplete, presents interpretive questions, bristles with unresolved contingencies, and in short has as many holes as a Swiss cheese does not make it unenforceable for indefiniteness. Otherwise there would be few enforceable contracts. Complete contingent contracts are impossible. The future, over which contractual performance evolves, is too uncertain." Haslund v. Simon Prop. Grp., 378 F.3d 653 (7th Cir. 2004). *Accord:* Fransmart, LLC v. Freshii Dev., 768 F. Supp. 2d 851 (E.D. Va. 2011) ("It is well-settled that courts will enforce exclusive dealings contracts with broad performance obligations. . . . With these contracts, it is often impractical to reduce performance obligations to well-defined terms because the parties do not foresee all of the possible contingencies that might arise during the course of contract performance.") (citations omitted).

§3.27 n.14 p.420 Add the following to the beginning of the note: Boardwalk at Daytona Dev., LLC v. Paspalakis, 2016 Fla. App. LEXIS 17366, 41 Fla. L. Weekly 2605 (Fla. Dist. Ct. App. Nov. 18,

2016) (where settlement agreement's terms could have described any of three distinct plots of land, with lot sizes ranging from 7,682 to 17,350 square feet, "neither the amended agreement alone nor the amended agreement as supplemented by the trial evidence established a meeting of the minds on what real estate was being bought and sold. Thus, the trial court erred in granting specific performance.")

§3.27 n.14 p.420 Add the following as a new paragraph at the end: One New York Civil Court judge described what he characterized as "a very unfortunate trend" in certain businesses inducing a customer to apply for credit for a item, but without specifying terms — then informing the customer that her credit was approved and the items is being delivered, and asserting that all sales are final should the customer attempt to reject the terms later. As the judge describes the typical case, "[t]he financing company pays the store and, when inevitably the poor quality, shoddily constructed furniture, appliances, or whatnot, begin to break, the buyer calls the store — unhelpful since they were already paid — and the financing company which argues that it is merely a lender and has no obligations as to the merchandise." Capitol Discount Corp. v. Rivera, 38 Misc. 3d 1226(A) (N.Y. Civ. Ct. 2013). In this case, the terms of the agreement were left blank at the time of the application. As a result, the court found, "there was no offer to sell the furniture or at a minimum no price was given, she did not accept an offer to sell the furniture, she did not assent to the terms of the contract, and she did not intend to be bound. It is undisputed that she received consideration — the furniture. Nonetheless, no contract was formed in the absence of most of the elements for forming a contract. By accepting the furniture, Defendant still did not enter into a contract to pay. Material terms, most notably the price, were still not agreed upon and, when she learned what they were thereafter, Defendant called the store and expressed her unwillingness to enter into the agreement." The court went on to find that the contract would be unconscionable if one were deemed to have existed.

§3.28 EXAMPLES OF INDEFINITENESS

§3.28 n.1 p.420 Add the following to the list after **"Accord"***:* Gutkowski v. Steinbrenner, 680 F. Supp. 2d 602 (S.D.N.Y. 2010) (agreement that employee would be "fairly compensated for his idea and efforts" insufficiently definite, absent proof of a "fixed and invariable" usage of trade on the meaning of fair compensation); Armstrong v. Rohm & Haas Co., 349 F. Supp. 2d 71 (D. Mass. 2004) (agreement to provide "all the work they could handle" "too imprecise to be enforceable"); Knowles v. Wright, 288 S.W.3d 136 (Tex. Civ. App. 2009) (partnership agreement in which one partner would receive 50% of the shares in exchange for "conceiving this idea . . . and in exchange for my further consulting work at a reduced rate of payment" too indefinite "as to what exactly [the plaintiff] was obligated to do and what specific services he was required to provide"; proof of what typical worker would do unhelpful in absence of proof that parties made that the standard), distinguished in Hoffman v. L & M. Arts, 774 F. Supp. 2d 826 (N.D. Tex. 2011) (finding sufficiently definite a promise to keep all aspects of a transaction confidential indefinitely); Chavez v. McNeely, 287 S.W.3d 840 (Tex. Civ. App. 2009) (divorce decree providing that wife "will provide as much toward the care and providing for the needs of [quadriplegic husband] as possible, limited only by her personal financial condition" contains three indefinite terms, with no way to determine their meaning, and thus the clause is unenforceable); Prince, Yeates & Geldzahler v. Young, 94 P.3d 179 (Utah 2004) (agreement to allocate legal fee in a "fair and equitable" manner "too indefinite to create an express contract").

§3.28 n.1 p.420 Add the following after the citation to **Academy Chicago Publishers***:* followed in Bus. Sys. Eng'g v. Int'l Bus. Mach. Corp., 547 F.3d 882 (7th Cir. 2008) (description of work to be performed as "services," "software," "provid[ing] development resources" too indefinite; the documents "do not state, with any reasonable specificity, what services, software, and 'development resources' Business Systems was to provide. Beyond that, there is no mention of when and where Business Systems was to provide those services, software, and 'development resources'; what set of criteria was to be used to establish that Business

Systems satisfactorily provided them; and when and how the parties were to handle payment. . . . Without the provision of such terms, we lack the ability to enforce any agreement between the parties, since we would not be able to determine what each party had agreed to do."); Assoc. Benefit Servs. v. Caremark Rx, 493 F.3d 841 (7th Cir. 2007) (agreement with "no statement whatsoever of the consideration ABS will provide for the receipt of commissions" is "insufficiently definite"), but

§3.28 n.1 p.420 Add the following after the citation to* Dawson*: and in Jannusch v. Naffziger, 883 N.E.2d 711 (Ill. App. 2008) (sale of business: where price and items to be transferred were settled, "[n]o essential terms remained to be agreed upon," even though among the open terms were "allocating a price for good will, a covenant not to compete, allocating a price for the equipment, how to release liens, what would happen if there was no loan approval, and other issues").

§3.28 n.1 p.420 In the first paragraph, add the following at the end: Implied-in-fact contracts are subject to the same problems with indefinite terms. *See* Baer v. Chase, 392 F.3d 609 (3d Cir. 2004) (agreement giving "true value" of services unenforceable as vague and indefinite).

§3.28 n.5 p.421 Add the following to the end: For useful overviews of methods to cure indefiniteness, *see* APS Capital Corp., v. Mesa Air Grp., 580 F.3d 265, 271-73 (5th Cir. 2009); Dalton v. Robert Jahn Corp., 146 P.3d 399, 411 (Or. App. 2006).

§3.28 p.421 In the second paragraph, line nine, replace the reference to The Supreme Court of California with: The California Court of Appeals

§3.28 n.6 p.421 Add the following to the list after* "See also"*: Korff v. Corbett, 794 N.Y.S.2d 374 (App. Div. 2005) (letter containing basic terms about consideration and timing sufficient; terms that remain "ambiguous, indefinite or uncertain" may be determined by extrinsic or parol evidence).

§3.28 n.6 p.421 Add the following at the end: Incorporation by reference normally poses no difficulties, as long as the drafter is unambiguous about what is incorporated. *See, e.g.* Naturipe Foods, LLC v. Siegel Egg Co., Inc., 2016 Mich. App. LEXIS 1653 (Sept. 8, 2016) (contract provision providing that sale was "subject to Seller's Terms and Conditions" was enforceable even though buyer was never provided with a copy of those terms and conditions. "[I]t was defendant's duty to obtain an explanation of the contract term. Defendant's apparent failure to do so constitutes negligence and estops it from asserting that the Terms and Conditions do not apply on the grounds of ignorance."). *But see* Gilbert St. Devs. v. La Quinta Homes, 94 Cal. Rptr. 3d 918 (Ct. App. 2009) (rejecting provision that applies the American Arbitration Association rules "existing at the date" of filing, at least for the purposes of determining jurisdiction; "[W]hat is being incorporated must *actually exist at the time of the incorporation*, so the parties can know exactly what they are incorporating."; "Incorporating the *possibility* of a *future* rule by reference simply doesn't even meet the basic requirements for a valid incorporation by reference under simply state contract law."), followed in Taubman Cherry Creek Shopping Ctr. v. Neiman-Marcus Corp., 251 P.3d 1091 (Colo. App. 2010) ("[W]e are aware of no precedent holding that parties can clearly know of and assent to contract terms that do not yet exist when, as here, the term is in abrogation of statutorily expressed public policy, the parties do not expressly agree to be bound by future amendments, neither party has any control over subsequent amendments, and there is no ascertainable standard for the promulgation of amendments or new rules.").

§3.28 n.7 p.422 Add the following at the end: distinguished in Lexington Heights Dev. v. Crandlemire, 92 P.3d 526 (Idaho 2004) (issue in *Thorn Springs Ranch* was whether "parties had reached an oral agreement for the transfer," not whether the statute of frauds had been satisfied).

§3.28 n.8 p.422 Add the following to the list after **"Accord":** T.G. Slater & Son, Inc. v. Donald P. & Patricia A. Brennan LLC, 385 F.3d 836 (4th Cir. 2004) (contract providing for "a customary real estate commission" enforceable if custom or trade usage proved and if promisor knew or should have known

of the custom); Askinuk Corp. v. Lower Yukon Sch. Dist., 214 P.3d 259 (Alaska 2009) (agreement that parties would renegotiate price in ten years, the old price continuing until they reached agreement, was not illusory because the parties were obliged to negotiate in good faith); Honeywell Int'l v. Air Prods. & Chems., 872 A.2d 944 (Del. 2005) (New York law: "[A] contract may be valid and enforceable even if some of its terms are left to future negotiation . . . The terms of the Agreement and the parties' course of performance also provide a reasonably certain basis for the Court to craft a remedy."); Reebaa Constr. v. Chong, 657 S.E.2d 826 (Ga. 2008) (Sears, C.J., concurring) (construction contract with many upgrades requested by owner, but no firm price actually set; "although the price of the work beyond that envisioned in the parties' original contract was initially indefinite, once that work was completed pursuant to the parties' general agreement, the price of the work became definite and the modification of the initial contract enforceable"); Sony Ericsson Mobile Commc'ns USA v. Agere Sys., 672 S.E.2d 763 (N.C. App. 2009) (absent terms in master agreement do not make it indefinite, where the terms appropriate for a master agreement are present); Helpin v. Trustees of Univ. of Pa., 969 A.2d 601 (Pa. Super. 2009) (although the original offer of employment had many open or undefined terms, "the parties reduced their agreement to a course of conduct based on a comprehensive understanding of the [offer]," after performing under the terms of the offer for 13 years), *aff'd*, 10 A.3d 267 (Pa. 2010); Consignment Sales v. Tucker Oil Co., 705 S.E.2d 73 (S.C. App. 2010) (although sale of supply contracts did not specify how net profits were to be calculated, the buyer "calculated net profit and paid [the seller] for eighteen months without objection," so price term sufficiently certain); Metro. Ventures v. GEA Assocs., 717 N.W.2d 58 (Wis. 2006) (even if agreement so indefinite that interpretation is uncertain, "the parties' subsequent conduct and practical interpretation can cure this defect"; course of performance here provided missing financing terms for business purchase agreement).

§3.28 n.11 p.423 Add the following at the end: If, however, the promisor reserves unlimited rights to alter an agreement, rights not expressly subject to reasonableness, language or a duty of good faith, then the agreement will likely be found fatally indefinite (just as it would be found illusory for the purposes of consideration). *See* OfficeMax, Inc. v. Sousa, 773 F. Supp. 2d 190 (D. Me. 2011).

***§3.28 n.11 p.423 Add the following to the list after* "Accord":** Fransmart, LLC v. Freshii Dev., 768 F. Supp. 2d 851 (E.D. Va. 2011) (lack of specificity in franchise agreement not fatal, because the agreement "provides alternate mechanisms for [the franchisor] to monitor and control [the franchisee's] performance," such as a duty of reasonable efforts on the part of the franchisee, the right of the franchisor to approve any proposed franchisees, and a minimum number of franchises to be procured every year); 8621 Ltd. P'ship v. LDG, Inc., 900 A.2d 259 (Md. App. 2006) (clause requiring an access route if it "can reasonably be provided" enforceable in light of case law and duty of good faith).

§3.28 n.13 p.423 Add the following at the end: There is some question how to determine whether a price set under UCC 2-305 is reasonable. In particular, it has been argued that the price must pass both objective and subjective tests, the latter particularly important when the price has allegedly been set for bad motives. *See* Marcoux v. Shell Oil Prods. Co., 524 F.3d 33 (1st Cir. 2008), *aff'd in part, rev'd in part and remanded on other grounds sub nom.* Mac's Shell Serv. v. Shell Oil Prods., 130 S. Ct. 1251 (2010). Most courts and commentators agree that reasonableness is subject only to an objective test, the better to promote certainty. This is consistent with UCC 2-305 cmt. 3, which states that "in the normal case a 'posted price' or a future seller's or buyer's 'given price,' 'price in effect,' 'market price,' or the like satisfies the good faith requirement." *See* Casserlie v. Shell Oil Co., 902 N.E.2d 1 (Ohio 2009) (the subjective test "would eviscerate the safe harbor [in comment 3] in any action in which the plaintiff alleges circumstantial evidence of an improper motive.").

***§3.28 n.14 p.424 Add the following to the list after* "Accord":** Haslund v. Simon Prop. Grp., 378 F.3d 653 (7th Cir. 2004) (term providing for grant of equity omitted whether stock would be voting or non-voting and whether there would be restrictions on vesting; "Important details, to be sure; but their absence did not necessarily make the contract indefinite. A court might be able to fill them in without shouldering an inordinate burden of inquiry or creating an inordinate risk of error. . . . Evidence of trade usage is admissible to supply the answers to such questions."); Dalton v. Robert Jahn Corp., *supra* note 5 (agreement to use "fair market value discounted for applicable discounts for minority interests, lack of marketability, and any other discount available" sufficiently definite, particularly because "[t]he parties in this case agreed to hire jointly selected appraisers").

§3.28 n.15 p.424 Add the following to the list after **"But cf.":** Connor v. Harless, 626 S.E.2d 755 (N.C. App. 2006) (purchase option for "fair market value . . . based on at least two appraisals" indefinite, as "there were no additional provisions stating how to proceed if the appraisals produced vastly different values"); Playoff Corp. v. Blackwell, 300 S.W.3d 451 (Tex. Civ. App. 2009) ("fair market value" of privately held business insufficiently definite; "even [the plaintiff] contemplated that fair market value of the entities would be determined by a specific formula yet to be determined by additional negotiation and agreement between the parties," and the parties never agreed upon a definition), declined to follow in Abatement Inc. v. Williams, 324 S.W.3d 858 (Tex. Civ. App. 2010) (method of calculating profit not necessary for agreement to be enforceable; "there is no evidence that the particular method of calculating profits was important to the parties at the time of the agreement").

§3.28 n.16 p.424 Add the following at the beginning: Conwell v. Gray Loon Outdoor Mktg. Grp., 906 N.E.2d 805 (Ind. 2009) (contract to modify website had no price, but where the buyer accepted the invoice price the contract was ultimately definite enough); Inimitable Grp., L.P. v. Westwood Grp. Dev. II, Ltd., 264 S.W.3d 892 (Tex. Civ. App. 2008) (contract for interior finish-out of building lacked a definite price, but "when the parties have done everything else necessary to make a binding agreement for services, their failure to specify a price does not leave the contract so incomplete that it cannot be enforced").

***§3.28 n.17 p.424 Add the following to the list after* "See also":** A.T.N. v. McAirlaid's Vliestoffe GmbH & Co., 557 F.3d 483 (7th Cir. 2009) (exclusivity clause of indefinite duration is terminable at will); Patel v. Liebermensch, 197 P.3d 177 (Cal. 2008) (escrow period not an essential term of a contract for sale; "a reasonable time for payment may be implied in a contract for the sale of real property"); Inimitable Grp., L.P. v. Westwood Grp. Dev. II, Ltd., *supra* note 16 ("If no time for performance is stated in the contract, the law may imply a reasonable one if the contract is sufficiently definite for a court to be able to fix the time when it can be enforced."; here, parties "intended for the interior finish-out to be completed within a reasonable time after construction of, and closing on, the exterior part of the building, so as to provide [the buyer] with the maximum savings of time and money").

***§3.28 n.18 p.425 Add the following to the list after* "See":** Navair, Inc. v. IFR Ams., 519 F.3d 1131 (10th Cir. 2008) (end date for distribution agreement absent, but contract not fatally indefinite, because the contract would therefore continue for a reasonable time; quoting from treatise); Dambrowski v. Champion Int'l Corp., 76 P.3d 1080 (Mont. 2003) (reasonableness "hinges upon the underlying circumstances," and 45 days was reasonable time for performance of settlement agreement). Herder Hallmark Consultants v. Regnier Consulting Grp., 685 N.W.2d 564 (Wis. App. 2004) (reasonable compensation for transfer of assets of actuarial business).

§3.28 n.22 p.425 Add the following to the list in the first sentence: Arbitron, Inc. v. Tralyn Broad., 400 F.3d 130 (2d Cir. 2005) (Calabresi, J.) (agreement for listener demographic data: unclear whether UCC 2-305 applies, but term allowing promisor to fix price enforceable if price consistent with duties of good faith or fair dealing in any case), *on remand* 526 F. Supp. 2d 441 (S.D.N.Y. 2007) (invalidating agreement allowing supplier of data to set price requires showing that there is a bad motive, discriminatory pricing, or pricing unfair or unreasonable when compared with that charged others similarly situated), *aff'd*, 328 Fed. Appx. 755 (2d Cir. 2009) (per curiam).

§3.28 n.43 p.429 Add the following to the list: EastBanc, Inc. v. Georgetown Park Assocs. II, L.P., 940 A.2d 996 (D.C. 2008) (joint venture to purchase and redevelop a shopping mall; "This was an emerging situation and details would be worked out if East Banc acquired the Mall. The specifics of any future joint venture were not central to the agreement to cooperate in acquiring the property.").

§3.28 n.46 p.430 Add the following to the list after **"See"***:* King v. Stanley, 197 P.2d 321 (Cal. 1948) (proposed real estate purchase agreement may be supplemented with "[t]he usual and reasonable conditions of such a contract" if the essential features can otherwise be determined), disapproved of in part by Patel v. Liebermensch, 197 P.3d 177 (Cal. 2008) (not agreeing that manner of payment is a material term and cannot be supplied with reference to custom). Even where the terms of the agreement provide for considerable unilateral changes, the courts look to standard real estate practice in determining whether the changes are enforceable. In Goldberg v. 401 N. Wabash Venture LLC, 2013 U.S. Dist. LEXIS 76367 (N.D. Ill. May 31, 2013), *aff'd*, 755 F.3d 456 (7th Cir. June 10, 2014), the contract for purchase of condominium units provided the builder with "sole and absolute discretion, to modify the Condominium Documents." After the purchaser provided $516,457 in earnest money, the builder modified the documents to remove "the ballrooms, meeting rooms, and function rooms from the Common Elements." The purchaser then sued, alleging breach of the implied covenant of good faith and fair dealing. The district court, and later, Judge Posner in the Seventh Circuit, relied upon the sophistication of the purchaser and the determination that the modifications were "not outside the bounds of the customs and practices within the hotel condominium industry."

§3.28 n.46 p.430 Add the following at the end: On the degree of completeness normally required, see Quenneville v. Buttolph, 833 A.2d 1263 (Vt. 2003) (oral agreement was enforceable where it contained "property to be sold, total price, amount financed and terms of financing, including the interest rate, amount of balloon note, assumption of farm debt, and amount of cash payment, and the closing date").

§3.28 n.47 p.430 ***Add the following at the end:*** *Accord:* Bus. Specialists v. Land & Sea Petroleum, 25 So. 3d 693 (Fla. App. 2010) (financing term essential to agreement for the sale of land, so its absence rendered the agreement unenforceable); Zukerman v. Montgomery, 945 N.E.2d 813 (Ind. App. 2011) (real property transaction fatally indefinite when identified property was owned by a range of individuals and businesses, but agreement did not state whether the sellers "signed the Settlement Agreement in their individual capacities or on behalf of the various businesses in which they may have had some interest" and where it was unclear to what extent each of the parties had the authority to act on behalf of those businesses).

§3.28 n.48 p.430 ***Add the following to the list after* "But cf.":** Garnot v. LaDue, 845 N.Y.S.2d 555 (App. Div. 2007) (specific performance available where parties had signed a purchase offer agreement with "all essential terms of a complete agreement").

§3.28 n.50 p.431 ***Add the following to the list after* "See also":** Tractebel Energy Mktg. v. AEP Power Mktg., 487 F.3d 89 (2d Cir. 2007) (for long-term power marketing agreement: "Where, as here, the parties have agreed on all material terms of the contract and clearly manifested their intent to be bound by these terms, but have left the practical implementation of certain terms to be resolved in good faith negotiations at a future date, the contract will be enforced."); Dalton v. Robert Jahn Corp., *supra* note 5 (identification of property on which timber would be cut not material in the context of a global settlement; "Terms that are material to one kind of contract are not necessarily material to another kind of contract.").

§3.29 INDEFINITENESS IN AGREEMENTS WITH OPEN TERMS

§3.29 n.2 p.432 ***In the second paragraph, add the following at the end:*** *See generally* Ben-Shahar, "Agreeing to Disagree": Filling Gaps in Deliberately Incomplete Contracts, 2004 Wis. L. Rev. 389.

***§3.29 n.5 p.432 Add the following to the list after* "Cf.":** GRB Farm v. Christman Ranch, 108 P.3d 507 (Mont. 2005) (lease provided for renewal "upon such terms and conditions as Lessor and Lessee shall agree to"; court held this an "agreement to agree," with the parties merely "to contemplate negotiating," and thus was unenforceable).

***§3.29 n.7 p.433 Add the following to the list after* "Accord":** Hughes v. Misar, 76 P.3d 111 (Or. App. 2003) (a court may use "courageous common sense" to imply fair and reasonable terms if necessary to give effect to the intent of the parties).

Indian Harbor Ins. Co. v. F&M Equip. Ltd., 804 F.3d 310 (3d Cir. 2015), involved an insurance policy with a ten-year period of coverage and a renewal option, specifying reasons the policy could be canceled or not renewed and promising that the company "shall not cancel nor non-renew this Policy except for the reasons stated above." At the expiration of the ten-year coverage period, the insurance company sent "its version of a renewal offer," at 312, which was a one-year term and omitted coverage for the one site that had a prior claim. The insured rejected that offer and attempted to renew its policy, sending a check for the amount of the premium under the first policy, which the insurance company rejected and instead brought suit seeking a declaratory judgment. The Third Circuit held that the insurance company breached the renewal clause of the insurance agreement. "On the question of what constitutes a renewal, it is clear under our precedent that a renewal need not be identical to the original. But to hold that it can be any modification at all would not give effect to the parties' intentions," at 315. The court held that "a reasonable change in price should not alone render a new contract a nonrenewal," but the change in coverage period, coverage amount, and properties covered are not "recognizable extensions of the initial Policy." Failure to "offer a contract that is either the same or nearly the same," at 316, constituted a breach of the promise to offer a renewal. However, this breach did not mean that the insured could simply send a check for the old premium amount to effect a renewal. Rather, the insurance company "must offer a contract that can be considered a renewal, and then the parties can negotiate the details." The insurance company's final objection, that renewal on the same terms would include another promise to renew and lock the company into an obligation to "recursively renew the contract in perpetuity" received little sympathy from the court: "To the extent Indian Harbor argues that a contract it drafted was not careful enough, we are unmoved." But the court left the possibility of changing this clause in future contracts; whether such a renewal offer would meet the "nearly the same" standard was "a question for another day."

§3.30 MITIGATING DOCTRINES

§3.30 n.1 p.436 Add the following after the first sentence: *Cf.* Fedynich v. Massood, 342 S.W.3d 887 (Mo. App. 2011) (recognizing severability, but not applying it because the party seeking to invoke it had not pleaded, even in the alternative, that the contract was enforceable only in part).

Oryann, Ltd. v. SL & MB, LLC, 2015 Ohio 5461 (Ohio Ct. App. 2015), involved sale of a horse farm, including real estate and business assets. The contract provided that the assets to be transferred were listed in Exhibit A, but that exhibit was left blank. When a dispute arose between the parties, the trial court "found there was no meeting of the minds with respect to the asset purchase agreement and that it was illusory because it failed to identify with sufficient clarity the assets to which it applied." The Ohio Court of Appeals reversed, holding "that both contracts were part of the same transaction and that the parties intended to be bound by both." The Court of Appeals looked to cross-references in both contracts and criticized the trial court's reasoning as one that would render parts of the agreement meaningless, holding that the asset purchase agreement was enforceable.

§3.30 n.3 p.436 Add the following to the list in the first sentence: Wenning v. Calhoun, 827 N.E.2d 627 (Ind. App. 2005) (contract to sell land fatally indefinite because it lacked a description of the property to be sold, but restitution available): Northeast Fence & Iron Works v. Murphy Quigley Co., 933 A.2d 664 (Pa. Super. 2007) (allowing unjust enrichment claim when no contract because no agreed-upon price).

§3.30 n.3 p.436 Add the following at the end: *But see* City of Clinton v. Pilgrim's Pride Corp., 632 F.3d 148 (5th Cir. 2010) (no restitution to city for construction of expanded water system on basis of vague and ambiguous promises to keep factory open; vagueness of promises prevents any enrichment from becoming unjust).

§3.30 n.4 p.437 Add the following at the end: *Cf.* Wenning v. Calhoun, *supra* note 3 (to effect restitution, owner of land must return to buyer/occupant any payments made, but buyer/tenant must pay to owner "the reasonable value of her occupation of the land until now"; analogizing to sale of goods) (citing this treatise).

§3.30 n.7 p.437 Add the following to the end: *Cf.* Thompson v. Floyd, 713 S.E.2d 883 (Ga. App. 2011) (applying promissory estoppel as means of making an otherwise indefinite promise enforceable); Clifford R. Gray, Inc. v. LeChase Constr. Servs., LLC, 819 N.Y.S.2d 182 (App. Div. 2006) (promise to award a subcontract too indefinite to enforce as a contract, but potentially allows a promissory estoppel claim).

CHAPTER 4

POLICING THE AGREEMENT

§4.1 THREE PERSPECTIVES

§4.1 n.5 p.441 Add the following after the citation to **Bethlehem Steel***:* The history of *Bethlehem Steel* is nicely laid out in Parrillo, "The Government at the Mercy of Its Contractors": How the New Deal Lawyers Reshaped the Common Law to Challenge the Defense Industry in World War II, 57 Hastings L.J. 93 (2005).

§4.2 INCAPACITY IN GENERAL

§4.2 n.2 p.443 Add the following to the list after **"See generally"***:* Speth, The Married Women's Property Acts, 1839-1865: Reform, Reaction, or Revolution?, in 2 Women and the Law: The Social Historical Perspective 69 (D. Kelly Weisberg ed. 1982); Benson, *Fisher v. Allen*: The Southern Origins of the Married Women's Property Acts, 6 J. S. Legal Hist. 97 (1998); Chused, Married Women's Property Law: 1800-1850, 71 Geo. L.J. 1359 (1983).

§4.2 p.443 In the first full paragraph, add the following at the end of the final sentence: . . . mixed blessing at best.[4]

[4] As Arthur Leff put it, "the typical has a tendency to become stereotypical, with what may be unpleasant results even for the beneficiaries of the

judicial benevolence." Leff, Unconscionability and the Code — The Emperor's New Clause, 115 U. Pa. L. Rev. 485, 556 (1967).

§4.3 THE TEST OF IMMATURITY

§4.3 n.1 p.443 In the first paragraph, add the following to the list at the end: *But see* Gomes v. Hameed, 184 P.3d 479 (Okla. 2008) (majority is "calculated from the first minute of the day on which a person is born to the same minute of the corresponding day"). The Restatement (Second) favors the former view. Restatement Second §14.

§4.3 n.1 p.443 Add the following to the list after* "See generally"*: Cunningham, A Question of Capacity: Towards a Comprehensive and Consistent Vision of Children and Their Statute under Law, 10 U.C. Davis J. Juv. L. & Pol'y 275 (2006); Daniel, Virtually Mature: Examining the Policy of Minors' Incapacity to Contract Through the Cyberscope, 43 Gonz. L. Rev. 239 (2007-2008); Note, The Infancy Defense in the Modern Contract Age: A Useful Vestige, 34 Seattle U.L. Rev. 613 (2011).

§4.3 n.3 p.444 Add the following after the fourth sentence: *See also* S.B. v. Saint James Sch., 959 So. 2d 72 (Ala. 2006) (person reaches majority at age 19 or upon marriage). *But see* Bramley's Water Conditioning v. Hagen, 501 N.E.2d 38 (Ohio App. 1985) ("A married sixteen-year-old is no more mature and no less imprudent than an unmarried one.").

§4.3 n.5 p.444 Add the following at the end: The same beneficent impulse actuates modern courts. *See* Berg v. Traylor, 56 Cal. Rptr. 3d 140 (Ct. App. 2007) ("The law shields minors from their lack of judgment and experience"); Michaelis v. Schori, 24 Cal. Rptr. 2d 380 (Ct. App. 1993) ("It is the policy of the law to protect a minor against himself and his indiscretions and immaturity as well as against the machinations of other people and to discourage adults from contracting with an infant."); Iverson v. Scholl

Inc., 483 N.E.2d 893 (Ill. App. 1985) ("The public policy of Illinois is to protect minors and their property from the consequences of dealing with others."); Douglass v. Pflueger Hawaii, 135 P.3d 129 (Haw. 2006) ("law should protect children from the detrimental consequences of their youthful and improvident acts"); Dodson v. Shrader, 824 S.W.3d 545 (Tenn. 1992) ("[T]he underlying purpose of the infancy doctrine . . . is to protect minors from their lack of judgment and from squandering their wealth through improvident contracts with crafty adults who would take advantage of them in the marketplace."); Statler v. Dodson, 466 S.E.2d 497 (W. Va. 1995) ("the policy of the law [is] to protect infants against their own mistakes or improvidence, and from designs of others, and to discourage adults from contracting with an infant").

§4.3 n.6 p.444 Add the following to the list at the end: Berg v. Traylor, *supra* note 5.

§4.3 n.7 p.444 Add the following at the end: *Accord:* Sheller v. Frank's Nursery & Crafts, 957 F. Supp. 150 (N.D. Ill. 1997) ("[I]f the Court were to allow the minor Plaintiffs to disaffirm the contract [of employment] . . . Plaintiffs would be retaining the advantage of the contract — employment, which entitled them to bring this suit — while repudiating that very same contract. The Court cannot permit such a result. . . ."); Scott Eden Mgmt. v. Kavovit, 563 N.Y.S.2d 1001 (Sup. Ct. 1990) ("If the infant may rescind the contract with the manager immediately after a lucrative performance contract is signed, yet still retain the benefits of the performance contract, no reputable manager will expend any efforts on behalf of an infant."). On this particular point, see note 11 *infra*.

§4.3 n.11 p.445 In the first paragraph, add the following at the end: *Cf.* Deville v. Fed. Sav. Bank of Evangeline Parish, 635 So. 2d 195 (La. 1994) (dictum: "Contracts with minors are relatively null and may be rescinded at the minor's request, unless the purpose of the contract was to provide the minor with necessities for support or education, or was for a purpose related to his business.").

§4.4 EFFECTS OF MINORITY

§4.4 n.2 p.446 Add the following at the end: This opinion has been overturned by statute as to exculpation agreements signed by parents. Colo. Rev. Stat. §13-22-107.

§4.4 n.5 p.447 Add the following at the end: *Accord:* Grange Mut. Cas. Co. v. Kay, 589 S.E.2d 711 (Ga. App. 2004) (insurance company cannot assert infancy in attempt to avoid enforcement of a settlement agreement). *Cf.* Shumate v. Twin Tier Hospitality, 655 F. Supp. 2d 521 (M.D. Pa. 2009) ("The appointment of an agent by a minor is not void, but merely voidable.").

§4.4 n.8 p.447 Add the following after the first sentence: *Accord:* Iverson v. Scholl Inc., 483 N.E.2d 893 (Ill. App. 1985) ("the filing of suit is sufficient evidence of plaintiff's desire to disaffirm any purported discharge given by her under the cajoling influence of her father"); G.E.B. v. S.R.W., 661 N.E.2d 646 (Mass. 1996) ("the child has unequivocally disaffirmed her mother's purported release in the settlement agreement by instigating the instant suit").

§4.4 n.9 p.447 Add the following at the end: *Accord:* Sarmiento v. Grange Mut. Cas. Co., 835 N.E.2d 692 (Ohio 2005) (minor beneficiary cannot seek benefits of insurance policy while avoiding its period of limitations). *But see* J.T. *ex rel.* Thode v. Monster Mountain, 754 F. Supp. 2d 1323 (N.D. Ala. 2010) (infant entitled to avoid release signed by representative of parents before motocross riding); Franco v. Neglia, 776 N.Y.S.2d 690 (App. Div. 2004) (infant entitled to disaffirm release signed before starting kick-boxing class). In an interesting decision, one court held that the system of child labor laws of the state provided all the protection of the common law of infancy, so a minor would not have the right to disaffirm the arbitration clause in his employment contract as part of an employment discrimination action. Douglass v. Pflueger Hawaii, 135 P.3d 129 (Haw. 2006).

Arbitration agreements entered into by a minor and later disaffirmed raise interesting issues, given the Federal Arbitration Act and concern that employers may be reluctant to hire minors if they cannot be held to arbitration agreements. In Lopez v. Kmart

Corp, 2015 U.S. Dist. LEXIS 58328 at *19, 24 Wage & Hour Cas. 2d (BNA) 1610 (N.D. Cal. May 4, 2015), the court distinguished California law from other states that had considered the question. Because California provides minors with the right of disaffirmance by statute, Cal. Family Code §6710, that court declined to consider equitable principles, and instead recognized the plaintiff's right to disaffirm, and ruled that he did so by filing suit one month after turning 18. The court distinguished Douglass v. Pflueger Haw., Inc., 110 Haw. 520, 135 P.3d 129, 145 (2006), and Sheller v. Frank's Nursery & Crafts, Inc., 957 F. Supp. 150, 154 (N.D. Ill. 1997), characterizing those decisions as relying upon common law "infancy doctrine," which allowed those courts to consider equitable principles where statutory rights prohibited California courts from doing so.

§4.4 n.12 p.448 Add the following at the end: Suing on a contract may thus ratify it, just as suing to avoid the contract disaffirms it. *See* Sheller v. Frank's Nursery & Crafts, 957 F. Supp. 150 (N. D. Ill. 1997) (Title VII suit on employment contract); Value Auto Credit v. Talley, 727 So. 2d 61 (Ala. 1999) (minor sues for breach of contract and thus cannot avoid a related arbitration agreement); Foss v. Circuit City Stores, 477 F. Supp. 2d 230 (D. Me. 2007) (filing of a lawsuit on statutory grounds not an affirmance, though suing on the contract would have been).

§4.4 n.13 p.448 Add the following after the third sentence: *But cf.* Foss v. Circuit City Stores, *supra* note 12 (punching and turning in time card not ratification).

§4.4 n.16 p.449 Add the following at the end: *Accord: In re* Estate of Duran, 66 P.3d 326 (N.M. 2003) (no need to disaffirm if no benefit to infant; "[a]fter all, there would be no reason to repudiate a contract when the party would be in the same position, whether the contract remains in force or not"). In contrast, *see* Muller v. CES Credit Union, 832 N.E.2d 80 (Ohio App. 2005) (disaffirmance of liability as cosignor of loan not permitted when 14 had passed from cosignor's eighteenth birthday to the time of attempted disaffirmance). Some states have, however, made contracts with minors automatically effective upon attaining majority unless they are promptly disaffirmed, with no reference at all to reliance. Kan. Stat. Ann. §38-102; *see also* State v. Bishop, 240 P.3d 614 (Kan. App. 2010) (applying statute to give effect to diversion agreement for purpose of sentencing).

§4.5 RESTITUTION ON MINOR'S AVOIDANCE

§4.5 n.2 p.450 Add the following after the first sentence: *Accord:* State v. Bishop, 240 P.3d 614 (Kan. App. 2010) (to disaffirm, minor must "restore[] to the other party all benefits received by the minor under the contract that remain in the minor's possession at any time after attaining majority"); Gillis v. Whitley's Auto Sales, 319 S.E.2d 661 (N.C. App. 1984) (infant need return only whatever part of the consideration remains under his control); Halbman v. Lemke, 298 N.W.2d 562 (Wis. 1980) ("The minor will not be required to give up what he does not have."); Swalberg v. Hannegan, 883 P.2d 931 (Utah App. 1994) (infant not liable for any "waste of property received under a contract").

§4.5 n.2 p.450 Add the following at the end: *Accord:* Mullen v. Tucker, 510 N.E.2d 771 (Ind. Ct. App. 1987).

§4.5 n.4 p.451 In the citation to Valencia, change the following: Ariz. to Ariz. App.

§4.5 n.4 p.451 Add the following to the list after **"Accord"*:*** Dodson v. Schrader, 824 S.W.2d 545 (Tenn. 1992) (holding infants accountable for full restitution would "encourage honesty and integrity" and "lead them to a good and useful business future"; a contrary policy would "only lead to the corruption of principles and encourage young people in habits of trickery and dishonesty"). On the latter, see note 21 *infra.*

§4.5 n.5 p.451 Add the following at the end: For another justification, *see* Yale Diagnostic Radiology v. Estate of Fountain, 838 A.2d 179 (Conn. 2004) ("most apt theory is that of an implied in law contract" arising from "equitable considerations, including the law's disfavor of unjust enrichment"). *Accord: In re* Estate of Reed, 201 P.3d 1264 (Colo. App. 2008) (restitution permitted

" 'not on the ground of any liability to pay on the part of the child, but upon equitable principles' ") (quoting from Perkins v. Westcoat, 33 P. 139, 140 (Colo. App. 1893)).

§4.5 n.6 p.451 ***Add the following at the end:*** Haw. Rev. Stat. §577A-4 (medical care).

§4.5 n.7 p.451 ***Add the following at the end:*** *Cf.* Young v. Weaver, 883 So. 2d 234 (Ala. Civ. App. 2003) ("whether the subject of the contract is generally considered a necessity" is a question of law; if it is, "whether the subject of the contract is, in fact, a necessity to that minor" is a question of fact).

§4.5 n.9 p.452 ***Add the following after the citation to*** **Webster Street Partnership***:* followed in Young v. Weaver, *supra* note 7 (where parents willing and able to furnish housing, a rented apartment was not a necessity).

§4.5 n.11 p.452 ***Add the following to the list after*** **"Accord"***:* *In re* Estate of Reed, *supra* note 5 (psychological care for minor suffering from post-traumatic stress disorder; "provider is entitled to recover only the fair and reasonable value of the services provided, which may or may not be the same as the amount of the provider's bill"); MN Medinvest Co. v. Estate of Nichols, 908 So. 2d 1178 (Fla. App. 2005) (care in nursing home for severely injured infant).

§4.5 n.11 p.452 ***Add the following at the end:*** *But cf.* Berg v. Traylor, 56 Cal. Rptr. 3d 140 (Ct. App. 2007) (personal management services for child actor not a necessity).

Whether attorneys are necessaries has occasioned some debate. Certainly, there is much respectable authority to the effect that legal assistance can qualify as needed to protect the infant's rights. Often, this is accompanied by requirements that the fees be reasonable and the services reasonably necessary. *See* Goldberg v. Super. Ct., 28 Cal. Rptr. 2d 613 (Ct. App. 1994) (requiring judicial review); Statler v. Dodson, 466 S.E.2d 496 (W. Va. 1995). If the legal work can safely await majority, though, it is not a necessary. Zelnick v. Adams, 561 S.E.2d 711 (Va. 2002). And some courts unaccountably do not consider their fellow attorneys necessary, to the point of nullifying any settlements or dismissals they may obtain when purportedly hired by minors. Miller v. Miller, 677 A.2d 64 (Me. 1996).

Health care may yield fewer objections than legal services, but nevertheless has brought on some. Whether and to what extent parents may be held liable is actively disputed. *See In re* Estate of Reed, *supra* note 5 ("parents were responsible in the first instance," but "if a parent cannot or will not pay for a child's 'necessaries' — including necessary medical care — the provider of the necessaries may look to the child"); Primax Recoveries v. Atherton, 851 N.E.2d 639 (Ill. App. 2006) (parents solely liable on implied contract theory); Johns Hopkins Hosp. v. Pepper, 697 A.2d 1358 (Md. 1997) (parents liable unless "absent from the minor child's life" and "contribute nothing"). The area has thus yielded legislation to remove the disability of minority from at least some health care contracts. For representative decisions construing these statutes, *see* Michaelis v. Schori, 24 Cal. Rptr. 2d 380 (Ct. App. 1993); Sharon v. City of Newton, 796 N.E.2d 738 (Mass. 2002). When infants are liable for health care costs, they generally may recover them in tort despite the normal vesting of that right in their parents. Schmidt v. Prince George's Hosp., 784 A.2d 1112 (Md. 2001).

§4.5 n.14 p.453 Add the following at the end: In some jurisdictions, a minor may disaffirm a contract for the purchase of an automobile but must compensate the seller for any depreciation or damage. Bobby Floars Toyota v. Smith, 269 S.E.2d 320 (N.C. App. 1980).

§4.5 n.17 p.453 Add the following as a new paragraph at the end: If the goods or services supplied under the contract have been held to be necessaries, the infant may be held to other terms of the contract. MN Medinvest Co. v. Estate of Nichols, *supra* note 11 (infant bound by arbitration clause). One may ask whether this is entirely consistent with the idea that the minor is obligated in restitution, not in contract.

§4.5 n.20 p.454 Add the following at the end: *But see* Webster St. P'ship v. Sheridan, *supra* n.7 ("Because the parties then stand as if no contract had ever existed, the infant can recover payments made to the adult, and the adult is entitled to the return of whatever was received by the infant."; true even if the child can return nothing).

§4.5 n.21 p.454 Add the following to the list in the final sentence: Foss v. Circuit City Stores, 477 F. Supp. 2d 230 (D. Me. 2007) (minor's misrepresentation of age irrelevant; "This immature and false representation is exactly why the law acts to protect the infant.").

§4.6 THE TEST OF MENTAL INCOMPETENCY

§4.6 n.1 p.456 Add the following to the list after **"See generally"***:* Blumenthal, The Default Legal Person, 54 UCLA L. Rev. 1135, 1219-44 (2007).

§4.6 n.3 p.457 Add the following to the list after **"See"***:* Proctor v. Classic Automotive, 20 So. 3d 1281 (Ala. Civ. App. 2009) (person suffering from depression, manic depression, and bipolar disorder not necessarily incapable of entering into a contract, and was held to do so where she knew what type of contract she had signed); *In re* Mildred M.J., 844 N.Y.S.2d 539 (App. Div. 2007) ("there is no presumption that a person suffering from dementia is wholly incompetent"); Gaddy v. Douglass, 597 S.E.2d 12 (S.C. App. 2004) ("we in no way suggest that all people suffering some degree of dementia . . . invariably lack contractual capacity").

§4.6 n.4 p.457 Add the following to the list after **"Accord"***:* Wilcox Mfg. Grp. v. Mktg. Servs. of Ind., 832 N.E.2d 559 (Ind. App. 2005) ("able to understand in a reasonable manner the nature and effect of his act" or "have had no reasonable understanding of the contract's terms due to his instability"); Nelson v. Holland, 776 N.W.2d 446 (Minn. App. 2009) ("A person is mentally competent to enter into a contract if the contracting party can understand the nature and effect of the party's actions when executing the contract."); Jennings v. Reed, 885 A.2d 482 (N.J. Super. App. Div. 2005) ("unable to comprehend the nature

and extent of his acts"); Bailey v. Bailey, 677 S.E.2d 56 (Va. App. 2009) ("While a contracting party must 'understand the nature and consequences' of entering into the agreement, the 'law does not require that one have the ability to make a reasoned judgment' concerning it.") (quoting from Drewry v. Drewry, 383 S.E.2d 12, 17-18 (Va. App. 1989)).

§4.6 n.4 p.457 Add the following to the list after* "see"*: Maimonides School v. Coles, 881 N.E.2d 778 (Mass. App. 2008) (standard for contractual capacity "more demanding" than that for testamentary capacity).

§4.6 n.4 p.457 Add the following to the list after* "But see"*: Nichols v. Estate of Tyler, 910 N.E.2d 221 (Ind. App. 2009) ("Evaluating mental capacity to contract for the sale of real property is closely akin to evaluating the mental capacity necessary to make a will.").

§4.6 n.5 p.457 Add the following to the list in the first sentence: Barbee v. Johnson, 665 S.E.2d 92 (N.C. App. 2008).

§4.6 n.9 p.458 Add the following after the citation to* McGovern*: and in *In re* Marriage of Davis, 89 P.3d 1206 (Or. App. 2004) (rejecting "affective test" of §15 because "cognitive test is the test that Oregon courts appear to follow").

§4.6 n.9 p.458 Add the following after the second sentence: *Cf.* Skannal v. Bamburg, 33 So. 3d 227 (La. App. 2010) (one "who was deprived of reason at the time of contracting, may obtain rescission of an onerous contract upon the ground of incapacity only upon showing that the other party knew or should have known that person's incapacity").

§4.6 n.15 p.460 Add the following to the list after* "see"*: Skannal v. Bamburg, 33 So. 3d 227 (La. App. 2010) ("The presumption is that all persons have capacity to contract; lack of capacity must be shown by clear and convincing evidence."); Sears v. First Pioneer Farm Credit, 850 N.Y.S.2d 219 (App. Div. 2007) ("the burden of proving incompetence rests with the party asserting incapacity"), quoting Matter of Obermeier, 540 N.Y.S.2d 613

(App. Div. 1989); Bailey v. Bailey, *supra* note 4 ("The law presumes competency and places the burden on the challenging party to demonstrate incompetency by clear and convincing evidence."). In denying summary judgment, the court in Gray v. Jung, 54 Misc. 3d 1207(A) (N.Y. Sup. Ct. 2017) characterized proof as "a difficult task" but held it was sufficient at the summary judgment stage that the party had submitted an affidavit from a board certified attending physician that "sets forth details about Koock Jung's condition, including that his diagnosis included, 'Borreliosis Complex with neuroborreliosis' and further that 'he is especially impacted with regards to short-term memory, concentration, and overall mentation ("brain fog"); he also reported auditory hallucinations' " and opining "to a reasonable degree of medical certainty, that [Koock] Jung's condition was severe enough to preclude him from fully understanding or entering into a contract for the sale of his home."

§4.6 n.16 p.460 Add the following at the end: Alternatively, some states provide that an adjudication of incapacity makes all subsequent attempts to contract void, but that a certificate from a treating physician that the person has regained the ability to reason creates a presumption of capacity even absent a further judicial proceeding. Idaho Code §32-108; *see also* Rogers v. Household Life Ins. Co., 250 P.3d 786 (Idaho 2011) (construing statute).

§4.7 EFFECTS OF MENTAL INCOMPETENCY

§4.7 n.3 p.461 Add the following after the first sentence: *Accord:* Delsas *ex rel.* Delsas v. Centex Home Equity Co., 186 P.3d 141 (Colo. App. 2008) (stating majority (voidable) and minority (void) rules, though noting that fraud in the factum yields a void contract). See *infra* §4.10 (types of fraud).

§4.7 n.4 p.461 Add the following after the first sentence: *Accord:* Rogers v. Household Life Ins. Co., 250 P.3d 786 (Idaho 2011) (applying Idaho Code §32-108; contracts made before a judicial finding of incapacity are voidable, but contracts made after are void).

§4.7 n.6 p.462 Add the following to the list after **"Accord"***:* Delsas *ex rel.* Delsas v. Centex Home Equity Co., *supra* note 3 (next friend); Nelson v. Holland, 776 N.W.2d 446 (Minn. App. 2009) (personal representative); Weaver v. St. Joseph of the Pines, 652 S.E.2d 701 (N.C. App. 2007) (heirs).

§4.7 n.7 p.462 Add the following after the first sentence: Accord: Wilcox Mfg. Grp. v. Mktg. Servs. of Ind., 832 N.E.2d 559 (Ind. App. 2005) (payments on loan agreements for a year and a half after regaining lucidity constitute ratification); Weaver v. St. Joseph of the Pines, *supra* note 6 (payments to nursing home by heirs was "undisputed evidence of ratification").

§4.10 THE ELEMENTS OF MISREPRESENTATION

§4.10 n.1 p.468 Add the following to the list after **"see"***:* McCaddin v. S.E. Marine, 567 F. Supp. 2d 373 (E.D.N.Y. 2008) (same; quoting from treatise).

§4.10 n.2 p.468 Add the following to the list after **"Accord"***:* McCaddin v. S.E. Marine, *supra* note 1 (quoting Restatement Second §163 ill. 2: "This is an example of fraud in the execution which would result in a void contract"); Village Northridge Homeowners Ass'n v. State Farm Fire & Cas. Co., 237 P.3d 598 (Cal. 2010) ("If the fraud goes to the execution or inception of the contract, so that the promisors do not know what they are signing, the contract lacks mutual assent and is void."); Lewis v. Mathes, 829 N.E.2d 318 (Ohio App. 2005) ("A release obtained by fraud in factum is void ab initio," while "[w]hen a release is obtained through fraud in the inducement, it is merely voidable.").

§4.10 n.3 p.468 Add the following at the end: The new Restatement (Third) of Restitution and Unjust Enrichment usefully abandons contract language here and instead refers to

rescinding a *transfer*. Restatement (Third) of Restitution and Unjust Enrichment §13(1) & cmt. a (T.D. No. 1, Apr. 6, 2001) ("Where contract is concerned with the effectiveness of the agreement, the focus of restitution is on the effectiveness of any resulting transfer.").

§4.10 n.5 p.469 Add the following at the beginning: Delsas *ex rel.* Delsas v. Centex Home Equity Co., 186 P.3d 141 (Colo. App. 2008) ("A void deed is a nullity, invalid ab initio, or from the beginning, for any purpose. It does not, and cannot, convey title, even if recorded. . . . In contrast, a voidable deed conveys property and creates legal title unless, and until, it is set aside by the court."). *See* Restatement (Third) of Restitution and Unjust Enrichment §13 cmt. d (T.D. No. 1, Apr. 6, 2001) ("As between transferor and transferee, the distinction between void and voidable transfers is rarely of any consequence.").

§4.10 n.5 p.469 Add the following at the end of the first paragraph: In addition, the recipient of a misrepresentation ordinarily may choose between suing on the contract or off, the latter requiring rescission and restitution. When the misrepresentation amounts to fraud in the factum, however, there is no contract in the first place, and so logically there is no requirement of rescission. Village Northridge Homeowners Ass'n v. State Farm Fire & Cas. Co., 237 P.3d 598 (Cal. 2010). This does not, however, mean that the promisor may entirely avoid restitution. As the Restatement (Third) of Restitution and Unjust Enrichment points out, the issue is whether a transfer should be undone, not whether a contract should be undone. Consequently, even though there is no contract to rescind, there is a transfer to rescind, and this rescission results in restitution. Restatement (Third) of Restitution and Unjust Enrichment §13 cmt. a (T.D. No. 1, Apr. 6, 2001) ("the essence of the relief sought is simply the reversal of a transfer induced by misrepresentation").

§4.10 n.5 p.469 Add the following at the end of the second paragraph: , followed in Hotels Nev. v. L.A. Pac. Ctr., 50 Cal. Rptr. 3d 700 (Ct. App. 2006) ("If the entire contract is void at its inception because of fraud, then the parties have not agreed to anything, including the arbitration of any controversy.") and in

Duffens v. Valenti, 74 Cal. Rptr. 3d 311 (Ct. App. 2008) ("an arbitration clause will not be enforced if it is found within an agreement that may properly be judicially determined to be void for fraud in the execution or fraud in the inception, such that there was never any existing agreement in the first place, and this determination includes any arbitration clause within the basic agreement; fraud in the execution voids the entire agreement"). *Accord:* Boyd v. Allied Home Mtg. Capital Corp., 523 F. Supp. 2d 650 (N.D. Ohio 2007) ("there cannot be fraud in the factum where the complaining party had an opportunity to read the document"); BankCherokee v. Insignia Dev., 779 N.W.2d 896 (Minn. App. 2010) ("[O]ne party's misrepresentation as to the nature of a proposed contract does not amount to fraud in the execution if the other party had a reasonable opportunity to acquaint himself with the contract and failed to do so."). *See also* Restatement Second §163 cmt. b (same). On the so-called duty to read and its limits, see §4.26 at notes 8-22 *infra.*

§4.10 n.6 p.469 Add the following at the end of the first sentence: Dartmouth Mot. Sales v. Wilcox, 517 A.2d 804 (N.H. 1986) (buyer misrepresented himself as auto dealer; under UCC §2-403(1), nevertheless took voidable title).

§4.10 n.7 p.469 Add the following to the list after "Accord": Sisneros v. Citadel Broad. Co., 142 P.3d 34 (N.M. App. 2006).

§4.11 ASSERTION NOT IN ACCORD WITH FACTS

§4.11 n.1 p.470 Add the following at the end: By using the passive voice, much of what follows avoids discussing whose misrepresentation to whom gives rise to this defense. In particular, what about misrepresentations made through third parties? Obviously, agents may make misrepresentations that bind their principals. But if the third party is not culpable, but rather is a mere conduit? The tort approach may be useful. There "a plaintiff can rely upon the third-party communication of a defendant's fraudulent misrepresentation if the plaintiff shows that the defendant intended the plaintiff to learn of and rely on it in the transaction or type of transaction involved, or had a particular reason to believe that the plaintiff would do so." Knights of Columbus Council 3152 v. KFS BD, Inc., 791 N.W.2d 317, 327 (Neb. 2010).

§4.11 n.4 p.471 Add the following to the list after **"Accord"***:* Sisneros v. Citadel Broad. Co., 142 P.3d 34 (N.M. App. 2006) (quoting this treatise).

§4.11 n.8 p.471 Replace the text of the footnote with the following: For example, some courts have held that drawing a check amounts to a representation that there are sufficient funds in the account on which it is drawn. *Compare* Amoco Pipeline Co. v. Admiral Crude Oil Corp., 490 F.2d 114 (10th Cir. 1974) (misrepresentation); Klockner v. Keser, 488 P.2d 1135 (Colo. App. 1971) (same), *and* Liles Bros. & Son v. Wright, 638 S.W.2d 383 (Tenn. 1982) (same) *with* Williams v. United States, 458 U.S. 279 (1982) (no misrepresentation), Val-Land Farms v. Third Nat'l Bank, 937 F.2d 1110 (6th Cir. 1991) (same), *and* Dixie Bonded Whse. & Grain Co. v. Allstate Fin. Corp., 755 F. Supp. 1543 (M.D. Ga.), *aff'd sub nom.* Graniteville Co. v. Bleckley Lumber Co., 944 F.2d 819 (11th Cir. 1991) (same). *Cf. In re* Creative Bldgs., 498 F.2d 1 (7th Cir. 1974) (question of fact, depending largely on reliance). In contrast, the act of ordering goods on credit has been held not to be a misrepresentation of one's ability to pay, at least barring fraudulent intent or fraudulent concealment of insolvency. Rochford v. N.Y. Fruit Auction Corp., 116 F.2d 584 (2d Cir. 1940) (Clark, J.) ("[M]erely continuing business in the not unnatural hope 'that better times would come — that tomorrow should be as this day and much more abundant,' is not enough.") (quoting from Nichols v. Pinner, 18 N.Y. 295 (1858)).

§4.11 n.10 p.471 Add the following to the list after **"Accord"***:* Bradley v. Kryvicky, 574 F. Supp. 2d 210 (D. Me. 2008) (tort: statement that leaky windows were being remedied inadequate when windows had caused problems since construction and repairs were unlikely to fix leaking; "one who voluntarily elects to make a partial disclosure is deemed to have assumed a duty to tell the whole truth"); Knights of Columbus Council 3152 v. KFS BD, Inc., 791 N.W.2d 317 (Neb. 2010) (tort: "When a party

makes a partial or fragmentary statement that is materially misleading because of the party's failure to state additional or qualifying facts, the statement is fraudulent.").

§4.11 n.11 p.472 Add the following at the end: *Cf.* Simone v. Homecheck Real Estate Servs., 840 N.Y.S.2d 398 (App. Div. 2007) (for sale of real property, only active concealment such that "the seller thwarted the buyer's efforts to fulfill the buyer's responsibilities fixed by the doctrine of caveat emptor" can impose tort liability for nondisclosure), followed in Daly v. Kochanowicz, 884 N.Y.S.2d 144 (App. Div. 2009) ("The plaintiff is under the mistaken impression that the sellers and their real estate brokers . . . had an affirmative duty to disclose the water intrusion history of the subject property."; citing *Simone* to the effect that active concealment required, potentially including false representations in mandatory disclosure statements).

§4.11 n.12 p.472 Add the following at the end: *Cf.* Knights of Columbus Council 3152 v. KFS BD, Inc., 791 N.W.2d 317 (Neb. 2010) (tort: "We note that an overlap exists between fraudulent concealment claims and misrepresentation claims based on half-truths or ambiguities. That is, if a defendant's partial or ambiguous representation is materially misleading, then the defendant has a duty to disclose known facts that are necessary to prevent the representation from being misleading.").

§4.11 n.15 p.473 Add the following at the end: *See generally* Kaye, Disclosure, Information, the Law of Contracts, and the Mistaken Use of Laidlaw v. Organ, 79 Miss. L.J. 577 (2010).

§4.11 n.15 p.473 In the first paragraph, add the following to the list after* "See generally"*: R. Cooter & T. Ulen, Law & Economics 280-286 (4th ed. 2004); Borden, Mistake and Disclosure in a Model of Two-Sided Informational Inputs, 73 Mo. L. Rev. 667 (2008); Charnock, The Linguistics of Misrepresentation: Intentions and Truth Values, 23 Int'l J. for Semiotics L. 427 (2010); Craswell, Taking Information Seriously: Misrepresentation and Nondisclosure in Contract Law and Elsewhere, 92 Va. L. Rev. 565 (2006); Eisenberg, Disclosure in Contract Law, 91 Calif. L. Rev. 1645 (2003); Grosskopf & Medina, A Revised Economic Theory of Disclosure Duties and Break-Up Fees in Contract Law, 13 Stan. J.L. Bus. & Fin. 148 (2007); Harrison, Rethinking Mistake and Nondisclosure in Contract Law, 17 Geo. Mason L. Rev. 335 (2010); Johnson, An Economic Analysis of the Duty to Disclose Information: Lessons Learned from the Caveat Emptor Doctrine, 45 San Diego L. Rev. 79 (2008); Krawiec & Zeiler, Common-Law Disclosure Duties and the Sin of Omission: Testing the Meta-Theories, 91 Va. L. Rev. 1795 (2005); Oberman, Sex, Lies, and The Duty to Disclose, 47 Ariz. L. Rev. 871 (2005).

§4.11 p.474 In the carryover paragraph, add the following at the end of the first full sentence: . . . the fact does not exist.[17a]

[17a] Restatement Second §161. *See* Cannon Techs. v. Sensus Metering Sys., 734 F. Supp. 2d 753 (D. Minn. 2010) (tort: following Restatement exceptions).

§4.11 n.18 p.474 Add the following to the list after "Accord": Calemine v. Samuelson, 89 Cal. Rptr. 3d 495 (Ct. App. 2009) ("where the seller knows of facts materially affecting the value or desirability of the property . . . and also knows that such facts are not known to, or within the reach of the diligent attention and observation of the buyer, the seller is under a duty to disclose them to the buyer"); Nichols v. Minnick, 885 N.E.2d 1 (Ind. 2008) ("A real estate broker representing a seller has the duty to [disclose] to the seller . . . adverse material facts or risks actually known by the [broker] concerning the real estate transaction.").

§4.11 n.18 p.474 Add the following at the end: Duties to disclose may arise from statute. *See* Throckmartin v. Century 21 Top Realty, 226 P.3d 793 (Wyo. 2010) (real estate broker has statutory duty to disclose all material adverse facts).

§4.11 n.19 p.474 In the first paragraph, add the following to the list after "Accord": Glover v. Severino, 946 A.2d 710 (Pa. Super. 2008) (duty of mother to disclose possibility of alternative paternity to alleged father; failure to do so precludes application of paternity by estoppel).

§4.11 n.19 p.474 Add the following at the end of the first paragraph: *But see* Mallen v. Mallen, 622 S.E.2d 812 (Ga. 2005) (no confidential relationship between people who have agreed to marry) (4-3). On nondisclosure and the enforceability of premarital agreements, see §5.4 *infra.*

§4.11 n.19 p.474 In the second paragraph, add the following after the third sentence: As to marine insurance, *see* Certain Underwriters at Lloyds v. Inlet Fisheries Inc, 518 F.3d 645 (9th Cir. 2008) (doctrine of *uberrimae fidei* — "a duty of utmost good faith" — requires that " 'the party procuring insurance, is not, at the time, in possession of any fact material to the risk, which he does not disclose' ") (quoting from McLanahan v. Universal Ins. Co., 26 U.S. 170 (1828) (Story, J.)).

§4.11 n.19 p.474 In the second paragraph, add the following to the list after "But cf.": Brass Metal Prods. v. E-J Enters., 984 A.2d 361 (Md. App. 2009) ("[A] confidential relationship may exist in a business relationship. Certain factors above and beyond a typical business relationship must exist, however."; here, no independent relationship, no special confidences, and no common business objectives, for " '[t]he fact that one businessman trusts another and relied on another to perform a contract does not give rise to a confidential relationship, because something apart from the transaction between the parties is required.' ") (quoting from Williams v. Dresser Indus., 120 F.3d 1163 (11th Cir. 1997)); Am. Bank Ctr. v. Wiest, 793 N.W.2d 172 (N.D. 2010) (bank ordinarily not a fiduciary of its customers, but special circumstances may exist which yield trust and confidence; here, loan officer helped make fraudulent transaction, the upshot of which was improving the financial position of another bank customer at the defrauded customer's expense).

§4.11 n.23 p.476 Add the following to the list after "Accord": Mid-Am. Real Estate Co. v. Iowa Realty Co., 385 F. Supp. 2d 828 (S.D. Iowa 2005) (failure to disclose imminent news story based on interview when executing settlement that included confidentiality clause not going to a basic assumption of the contract, and not known to correct a mistake of that sort); Yazd v.

Woodside Homes Corp., 143 P.3d 283 (Utah 2006) (tort: builder-contractor failed to disclose information about soil conditions).

§4.11 n.23 p.476 Add the following after the second sentence: For a variation on this theme, *see* Precision Enters. v. Duffack Enters., 710 N.W.2d 348 (Neb. App. 2006) (duty to disclose "facts basic to the transaction when [party] knows another party is about to enter into the transaction under a mistake as to those facts and that the other party would reasonably expect a disclosure of those facts because of the relationship between the parties, the customs of the trade, or other objective circumstances"). There is some reason to lessen the consequences of nondisclosure when litigation is underway; disclosing information may discourage settlement, and in any event discovery may make that information available and thus would mitigate the effects of nondisclosure. *See* Hardin v. KCS Int'l, 682 S.E.2d 726 (N.C. App. 2009) ("One of the reasons that a party may choose to settle before discovery has been completed is to avoid the opposing party's learning of information that might adversely affect settlement negotiations. The opposing party assumes the risk that he or she does not know all of the facts favorable to his or her position when choosing to enter into a settlement prior to discovery.").

§4.11 n.23 p.476 Add the following at the end of the first paragraph: For an interesting case at the borderline of misrepresentation and nondisclosure — and with a questionable result — *see* Poe v. Summers, 11 So. 3d 129 (Miss. App. 2009) (seller of land mistakenly thought that person who bought property was daughter of intended buyer, but in fact was daughter of seller's psychiatrist, and introduced her as intended buyer's daughter within her earshot; held that the actual buyer "had no underlying fiduciary duty to the appellants to speak" and that she "did not participate in suppressing her identity to deceive the appellants," so no duty to disclose identity; 5-3 with strong dissent). If a buyer's failure to disclose that she is the agent of another can be grounds for rescission, *a fortiori* a buyer's failure to disclose that she is not even the person she is thought to be is as well.

§4.11 n.26 p.476 Add the following at the end of the first paragraph: *But cf.* Qualls v. Rumsfeld, 412 F. Supp. 2d 40 (D.D.C. 2006) (Army recruiter failed to disclose stop-loss policy to re-enlistee; stop-loss's uses are "rare occurrences" and the enlistee was a veteran, so non-disclosure not tantamount to misrepresentation).

§4.11 n.26 p.476 In the second paragraph, add the following to the list after **"Accord"***:* White v. Bowman, 304 S.W.3d 141 (Mo. App. 2009) (tort: "a duty to disclose arises only if the material fact is not discoverable through the exercise of ordinary diligence," so no duty with respect to mold visible at time of final inspection of house).

§4.11 n.26 p.476 In the second paragraph, add the following after the third sentence: *Cf.* Los Angeles Unified Sch. Dist. v. Great Am. Ins. Co., 234 P.3d 490 (Cal. 2010) (recognizing liability when public entity fails to disclose pertinent information to a prospective bidder, but noting limitation that the public entity does not "have any duty to disclose information that is reasonably available or that the contractor knew or had a realistic opportunity to discover").

§4.12 FRAUDULENT OR MATERIAL

§4.12 n.1 p.479 Add the following after the first sentence: *See, e.g.*, Yazd v. Woodside Homes Corp., 143 P.3d 283 (Utah 2006) (cause of action for fraudulent concealment requires proof "(1) that the nondisclosed information is material, (2) that the nondisclosed information is known to the party failing to disclose, and (3) that there is a legal duty to communicate.").

§4.12 n.2 p.479 Add the following to the list after **"Accord"***:* *In re* Estate of McKenney, 953 A.2d 336 (D.C. 2008) (quoting from treatise).

§4.12 n.2 p.479 Add the following at the end: *But cf.* Eigen v. Textron Lycoming Reciprocating Engine Div., 874 A.2d 1179 (Pa.

Super. 2005) (elements of fraud in the inducement include both that it be "material to the transaction at hand" and "made falsely, with knowledge of its falsity or recklessness as to whether it was false").

§4.12 n.5 p.479 Add the following after the first sentence: *See* Restatement Second §162(1)(b).

§4.12 n.7 p.480 Add the following to the list after **"Accord"*:*** Knights of Columbus Council 3152 v. KFS BD, Inc., 791 N.W.2d 317 (Neb. 2010) (tort: "a plaintiff can rely upon the third-party communication of a defendant's fraudulent misrepresentation if the plaintiff shows that the defendant intended the plaintiff to learn of and rely on it in the transaction or type of transaction involved, or had a particular reason to believe that the plaintiff would do so.").

§4.12 n.9 p.480 Add the following to the list after **"Accord"*:*** *In re* Estate of McKenney, *supra* note 2 (quoting from treatise); Fogel v. Enter. Leasing Co., 817 N.E.2d 1135 (Ill. App. 2004) (material "if the party seeking rescission would have acted differently had it been aware of the misrepresentation"); Eigen v. Textron Lycoming Reciprocating Engine Div., *supra* note 2 ("A misrepresentation is material if the party would not have entered into the agreement but for the misrepresentation."); Yazd v. Woodside Homes Corp., *supra* note 1 (tort: material if "important," and importance "can be gauged by the degree to which the information could be expected to influence the judgment of a person buying property or assenting to a particular purchase price").

§4.12 n.9 p.480 Add the following after the third sentence: For another approach, *see* Venture Props. v. Parker, 195 P.3d 470 (Or. App. 2008) (adapting factors from Restatement Second §241). Factors used to determine the materiality of breach do not fit well with formation, because issues about curing or compensating for harm would not arise at the time the contract is being made. Hence the *Venture Properties* decision, in which the court reaches a sound conclusion by ignoring two of the five factors and reading another very freely. The court's focus on whether the injured party would be deprived of the benefit it reasonably expected and whether the behavior was consistent with standards of good faith and fair dealing is appropriate, but these reduce to whether the offeree would, if it knew the facts, go forward; surely it would not if it knew that it would not get its anticipated benefit or be dealt with in good faith.

§4.12 n.9 p.480 Add the following at the end: Materiality is generally a question of fact. Calemine v. Samuelson, 89 Cal. Rptr. 3d 495 (Ct. App. 2009). However, at summary judgment, the party challenging materiality must offer evidence to rebut claims of materiality. In Great Lakes Ins., SE v. Queen, 2017 U.S. Dist. LEXIS 8491 (M.D. Ga. Jan. 23, 2017), a homeowner checked "no" on a questionnaire for insurance coverage that asked if the property to be insured was on more than five acres, although the address of the property was over eight acres, apparently because he intended to insure only one of the tracts. When the insurance company disclaimed the policy, he argued that it was not a misrepresentation and in any event was not material, since the damage occurred on the smaller tract. The judge appeared sympathetic, opining that the insurance official's "affidavit is not particularly persuasive as to why the additional three acres would have made much difference from an underwriting increased risk perspective. Great Lakes knew it was insuring the building that contained the contents that were damaged. That building, along with Queen's house, sat on less than five acres. Had Queen produced an affidavit from a qualified person that contradicted the Brennan affidavit, it is likely that a genuine dispute would have been created and summary judgment avoided." *Id.* at *11. However, in the absence of such evidence, the district court was bound by state law, and "Georgia courts generally find that summary judgment may be granted on the materiality issue based on the uncontroverted affidavit of an insurance company's representative establishing that the policy would not have been written as issued had the insurance company known of the misrepresentation." *Id.* at *11-*12, citing T.J. Blake Trucking, Inc. v. Alea London, Ltd., 284 Ga. App. 384, 643 S.E.2d 762, 762-63 (Ga. Ct. App. 2007) (finding, based on an uncontroverted affidavit, that the insurer would not have issued the truck insurance policy as written had the insured disclosed that one of her dump truck drivers had a number of driving violations, including a suspended license and several reckless driving charges); Graphic Arts Mut. Ins. Co. v. Pritchett, 220 Ga. App. 430, 469 S.E.2d 199, 202 (Ga. Ct. App. 1995) (approving summary judgment in favor of insurer where insurer presented uncontroverted evidence that under its underwriting guidelines, the insurer would not have issued a policy to an applicant who failed to disclose that two other insurers had canceled the applicant's policies); Davis v. John Hancock Mut. Life Ins. Co., 202 Ga. App. 3, 413 S.E.2d 224, 226 (Ga. Ct. App. 1991) (affirming summary judgment where the insurer presented uncontroverted evidence that it would not have issued the insured's life insurance policy had she disclosed that she suffered from incurable leukemia).

§4.13 RELIANCE

§4.13 n.1 p.482 ***Add the following at the end:*** It is not necessary that the relied-upon statement come directly from the offeree. As one court put it, "a plaintiff can rely upon the third-party communication of a defendant's fraudulent misrepresentation if the plaintiff shows that the defendant intended the plaintiff to learn of and rely on it in the transaction or type of transaction involved, or had a particular reason to believe that the plaintiff would do so." Knights of Columbus Council 3152 v. KFS BD, Inc., 791 N.W.2d 317, 327 (Neb. 2010) (tort).

§4.13 n.4 p.482 ***Add the following at the end:*** Undertaking independent investigation has even been held *by itself* to undercut reliance, because the decision to investigate further means that one is not content with reliance on the promisor's statements. Pleasant v. Bradford, 260 S.W.3d 546 (Tex. Civ. App. 2008) (discussing this doctrine, but ultimately not applying it because the buyer did not seek out additional information about the square footage of a house, but rather received it in the course of other, unrelated investigation). This approach suggests a Manichaean view of reliance, which fits neither with cognitive psychology nor with sound business practice. One may seek confirmation of one's

decision by looking for consistent information and dismissing that which is inconsistent. One may also rely mainly on one source, even though other sources support the same conclusion. Neither undercuts the merits of a reliance claim.

§4.13 n.5 p.483 Add the following after the citation to **Jefferson Assocs.***:* followed in Bynum v. Prudential Servs., 129 S.W.3d 781 (Tex. Civ. App. 2004) (declining to set aside "as is" clause on grounds that "terms were inconspicuous boiler-plate provisions that were agreed to by unsophisticated purchasers").

§4.13 n.5 p.483 Add the following after the citation to **Pairett***:* and in Cherry v. McCall, 138 S.W.3d 35 (Tex. Civ. App. 2004) (there was "no evidence to support the . . . argument that the "as is" provision was not freely negotiated").

§4.13 n.5 p.483 Add the following to the list after **"Accord"***:* Kopley Grp. V. v. Sheridan Edgewater Props., 876 N.E.2d 218 (Ill. App. 2007) (tort: "as is" clause in contract to purchase property, together with "ample opportunity to discover whether the building was in good condition," prevents buyer from proving reasonable reliance).

§4.13 n.6 p.483 Add the following to the list after **"Accord"***:* Napcor Corp. v. JP Morgan Chase Bank, 938 N.E.2d 1181 (Ill. App. 2010) (tort: "as is" clause in contract to purchase property "did not preclude plaintiff from claiming that it relied on the alleged misrepresentations," even though the buyer was sophisticated; refers to approach as the majority view, and observes that "a purchaser of real property is entitled to rely on the truthfulness and accuracy of the statements contained in a disclosure report").

§4.13 n.7 p.483 Add the following after the citation to **Danann Realty***:* , distinguished in DNJ Logistic Grp. v. DHL Express (USA), 727 F. Supp. 2d 160 (E.D.N.Y. 2010) ("Although the contract states that it is 'not to be considered a guarantee of shipment volumes,' . . . it does not explicitly state that DNJ disclaims reliance on any previous representations made to it about anticipated volumes."; as a result, the contract might supplement, not

supplant, the earlier representations, which would leave unaffected whether reliance on those representations was justifiable).

§4.13 n.7 p.483 Add the following to the list after **"Accord"***:* Abry Partners V., L.P. v. F & W Acquisition, LLC, 891 A.2d 1032 (Del. Ch. 2006) (following *Danann*).

§4.13 n.7 p.483 Add the following after the citation to **Rissman***:* , distinguished by Westerfield v. Quizno's Franchise Co., 2008 WL 2512467 (E.D. Wis. Apr. 16, 2008) (*Rissman* and similar cases giving effect to anti-reliance clauses do not require *per se* denial of claimed reasonable reliance).

§4.13 n.7 p.483 Add the following to the list after **"See"***:* Blankenship v. USA Truck, 601 F.3d 852 (8th Cir. 2010) (a no-reliance clause "is not an absolute bar to Blankenship's fraud claim," though noting that his "acquiescence to the no-reliance clause . . . betrays a lack of justifiable reliance on his part"); Extra Equipamentos e Exportação Ltda. v. Case Corp., 541 F.3d 719 (7th Cir. 2008) (Posner, J.: "In the trade, no-reliance clauses are called 'big boy' clauses (as in 'we're big boys and can look after ourselves'). But if someone who is *not* a big boy — indeed is not even represented by counsel — signs a big-boy clause, there can be a problem . . ."); CERAbio LLC v. Wright Med. Tech., 410 F.3d 981 (7th Cir. 2005) (construing Delaware law and finding anti-reliance clauses in stock purchase contracts made between sophisticated parties *per se* valid); Forest Oil Corp. v. McAllen, 268 S.W.3d 51 (Tex. 2008) (enforcing an anti-reliance clause where: "(1) the terms of the contract were negotiated, rather than boilerplate, and during negotiations the parties specifically discussed the issue which has become the topic of the subsequent dispute; (2) the complaining party was represented by counsel; (3) the parties dealt with each other in an arm's-length transaction; (4) the parties were knowledgeable in business matters; and (5) the release language was clear."), followed in Worldwide Asset Purchasing v. Rent-A-Center E., 290 S.W.3d 554 (Tex. Civ. App. 2009) (enforcing anti-reliance clause under these factors with a clause that was "a clear and unequivocal expression of the parties' intent to disclaim reliance"; pertinent clause read "[Worldwide Asset] has relied solely on its own investigation and it has not relied

upon any oral or written information promised by [Rent-A-Center] and acknowledges that no employee of [Rent-A-Center] has been authorized to make, and that [Worldwide Asset] has not relied upon, any written statements other than those specifically contained in this Agreement.") and distinguished in Duke Energy Int'l v. Napoli, 748 F. Supp. 2d 656 (S.D. Tex. 2010) (contractual "as-is" and merger clauses ineffective to waive fraudulent inducement claim; the provisions were "not as all encompassing as" those in *Forest Oil*, and the contract was not negotiated at arm's length).

§4.13 n.7 p.483 Add the following after the fourth sentence: For particularly worthwhile analyses of the competing interests involved, *see* Extra Equipamentos e Exportação Ltda. v. Case Corp., *supra* (Posner, J.); Abry Partners V, L.P. v. F & W Acquisition LLC, *supra* (Strine, V.C.).

§4.13 n.7 p.483 Add the following to the list after* "See generally"*: Blair, A Matter of Trust: Should No-Reliance Clauses Bar Claims for Fraudulent Inducement of Contract?, 92 Marq. L. Rev. 423 (2009).

§4.13 n.7 p.483 In the second paragraph, add the following after the first sentence: For illustrations, *see* Petrakopoulou v. DHR Int'l, 590 F. Supp. 2d 1013 (N.D. Ill. 2008) (tort: "integration clauses do not preclude claims for fraudulent inducement"); Airborne Health v. Squid Soap, 984 A.2d 126 (Del. Ch. 2009) (referring to a merger clause: "This is a standard integration clause, albeit a wordy one. Nothing in this provision resembles anti-reliance language. It defines the parties' agreement. It does not disclaim reliance."). *But cf.* Mitec Partners v. U.S. Bank Nat'l Ass'n, 605 F.3d 617 (8th Cir. 2010) ("In general . . . 'contractual disclaimers are ineffective to bar a plaintiff from asserting a claim for fraudulent inducement.' But the case before us is different. The alleged fraudulent misrepresentation was made in a document that was itself subject to a subsequent, integrated contract that contained multiple, unambiguous disclaimers") (quoting from N.W. Bank & Trust Co. v. First Ill. Nat'l Bank, 354 F.3d 721, 726 (8th Cir. 2003)); Rose v. ADT Security Servs., 989 So. 2d 1244 (Fla. App. 2008) (the plaintiffs "cannot claim that they justifiably relied upon oral representations when the terms of the subsequent written agreement expressly and conspicuously contradict the oral statements"); Pollman v. Swan, 699 S.E.2d 582 (Ga. App. 2010) (merger clause bars evidence of misrepresentations outside contract, but does not bar evidence of fraudulent concealment), *cert. granted,* No. S10G1989 (Ga. Apr. 18, 2011); Masingill v. EMC Corp., 870 N.E.2d 81 (Mass. 2007) ("It is unreasonable as a matter of law to rely upon prior oral representations that are (as a matter of fact) specifically contradicted by the terms of a written contract.").

§4.13 n.8 p.484 ***Add the following to the list after* "Accord"*:*** I-var v. Elk River Partners, 705 F. Supp. 2d 1220 (D. Colo. 2010) (although claims for misrepresentation may be waived by contract, "a standard integration clause or generic 'non-reliance' provision is not enough; the disclaimer must be 'couched in clear and specific language' to be effective") (quoting from Keller v. A.O. Smith Harvestor Prods., 819 P.2d 69, 74 (Colo. 1991)); Nahigian v. Juno Loudoun, LLC, 684 F. Supp. 2d 731 (E.D. Va. 2010) ("[I]f an individual is duped into entering an agreement that same agreement cannot take away the individual's right to sue for fraud."); Scantek Medical v. Sabella, 583 F. Supp. 2d 477 (S.D.N.Y. 2008) (tort: where anti-reliance clause " 'is an omnibus statement,' as opposed to a specific disclaimer," was drafted entirely by the debtor's lawyers, and were not negotiated, and where the creditor concealed information in order to induce the debtor's asset, information solely within the creditor's knowledge, it would be inappropriate to dismiss a claim for misrepresentation); Farnham v. Electrolux Home Care Prods., Ltd., 527 F. Supp. 2d 584 (W.D. Tex. 2007) ("Whether a disclaimer of reliance is binding depends on the language of the release and the circumstances surrounding its formation."; finding release ineffective because there was insufficient evidence of an express bargain to disclaim reliance, particularly because of the lack of knowledge and sophistication of one party and the lack of arm's-length dealing); McClain v. Octagon Plaza, 71 Cal. Rptr. 3d 885 (Ct. App. 2008) (anti-reliance clause "does not insulate Octagon from liability for fraud or prevent McClain from demonstrating justifiable reliance"); Hinesley v. Oakshade Town Ctr., 37 Cal. Rptr. 3d 364 (Ct. App. 2005) (specific anti-reliance clause "certainly a factor to

consider in determining whether Hinesley justifiably relied"); Osterhaus v. Toth, 187 P.3d 126 (Kan. App. 2008) ("Releasing the seller from any liability just because the buyer signed the buyer's acknowledgement and agreement is too simplistic. The district court must consider the disclosure statement, whether there was an inspection, and all the facts surrounding the sale before concluding there was a waiver of the seller's untruths."; here not enforceable because the "seller [was] untruthful about material facts in its disclosure statement, the material fact is not discoverable in a reasonable inspection, and the seller [did] not correct the untruth before selling").

***§4.13 n.8 p.484 Add the following to the list after* "Cf.":** Sacred Heart Health Sys. v. Humana Military Healthcare Servs., 601 F.3d 1159 (11th Cir. 2010) (reviewing treatment of anti-waiver clauses in multiple states for purposes of class action certification; notes variations); MBIA Ins. Corp. v. Royal Indem. Co., 426 F.3d 204 (3d Cir. 2005) (Alito, J.) (predicting that Delaware would enforce anti-disclaimer clauses "clearly inconsistent with reasonable reliance on extracontractual representations"), distinguished by Shelby Elec. Co. v. Forbes, 205 S.W.3d 448 (Tenn. App. 2005) (declining to enforce a general waiver clause against a fraud claim, where the fraud was not specifically waived); Slack v. James, 614 S.E.2d 636 (S.C. 2005) ("A general non-reliance clause . . . does not prevent one from proceeding on tort theories of negligent misrepresentation and fraud," but suggesting that a non-reliance clause with "the required specificity" would).

§4.13 n.15 p.486 Add the following at the end: This issue arose with interesting facts in Koehlinger v. State Lottery Comm'n, 933 N.E.2d 534 (Ind. App. 2010). The state lottery erred greatly in listing the unclaimed prizes for a scratch-off game, leading those who viewed the website to think that the aggregate return to player was quite high. Disappointed ticket purchasers sued as a class to rescind their contracts. In holding that the rescission count could go forward, the court stated that it was necessary for the plaintiffs to show detrimental reliance. The court went on:

> Proof that one purchased a Cash Blast ticket in reliance on the misinformation is not sufficient, standing alone, to show prejudice.

> After all, if the player simply diverted money to Cash Blast away from a game of chance with a lower [return to player] than Cash Blast, he was actually better off, although perhaps not as well-off as he thought he was. On the other hand, a class member who can establish that he bought Cash Blast tickets in reliance on the misinformation using money that would not otherwise have been spent has shown prejudice. Additionally, a class member who can prove that he diverted funds to Cash Blast that would have otherwise been spent on a game of chance with a higher [return to player] has shown prejudice.

933 N.E.2d at 540 n.5. This illustrates the potential difficulty in establishing detrimental reliance where the misrepresentation occurs in a world of uncertainty. The court's analysis seems quite sound. One might ask, though, about a buyer who otherwise would have spent the money on something other than a lottery ticket but worth even less than the chance purchased — say, a bad dinner or a ticket to a rotten movie. Looked at abstractly, buying the lottery ticket could be said to have increased the buyer's net wealth. But one must give some weight to the preferences of the buyer, even if ultimately they were disappointed.

§4.14 RELIANCE MUST BE JUSTIFIED

§4.14 n.1 p.486 ***Add the following after the sixth sentence:*** "Justified" is not a synonym of reasonable, at least for tortious misrepresentation. Spreitzer v. Hawkeye State Bank, 779 N.W.2d 726 (Iowa 2009) ("While the terms 'justifiable' and 'reasonable' are often used interchangeably in addressing the element of reliance, they can describe different approaches. We simply clarify that the justified standard followed in Iowa means the reliance does not necessarily need to conform to the standard of a reasonably prudent person, but depends on the qualities and characteristics of the particular plaintiff and the specific surrounding circumstances."). *See* Field v. Mans, 516 U.S. 59 (1995) (surveying state law as of 1978; thirty-six jurisdictions used justifiable reliance, five required reasonable reliance, and five required reliance in fact).

§4.14 n.2 p.487 In the first paragraph, add the following to the list after* "See"*: Am. Gen. Life Ins. v. Goldstein, 741 F. Supp. 2d 604 (D. Del. 2010) ("Plaintiff cannot claim to have relied upon the misrepresentation of Goldstein's income when plaintiff obtained the true amount from another source before the Policy issued. . . . Once plaintiff knew Goldstein's true income, the misrepresentation could no longer induce plaintiff into issuing the Policy."); Addison v. Carballosa, 48 So. 3d 951 (Fla. App. 2010) ("Justifiable reliance, however, does not permit the recipient of a fraudulent misrepresentation to blindly rely on it."); Baxter v. Fairfield Fin. Servs., 704 S.E.2d 423 (Ga. App. 2010) (reliance on other party's statement about the appraised value of property not justifiable, given lack of due diligence; "Blind reliance precludes a fraud claim as a matter of law."); Sunset Beach Dev. v. AMEC, Inc., 675 S.E.2d 46 (N.C. App. 2009) (tort: no reasonable reliance when sophisticated developers entering into purchase of property including wetlands knew "that the Master Wetlands Map [from the Army Corps of Engineers] was dated more than two years prior to the date it was delivered, and that the map was signed by an individual who no longer worked for the Corps" and failed to inspect the land themselves).

§4.14 n.2 p.487 Add the following at the end: Whether reliance is justifiable depends on a good many factors. One list devised initially for securities fraud but then imported for common-law fraud is: " '(1) the sophistication and expertise of the plaintiff in financial . . . matters; (2) the existence of long-standing business or personal relationships; (3) access to the relevant information; (4) the existence of a fiduciary relationship; (5) concealment of the fraud; (6) the opportunity to detect the fraud; (7) whether the plaintiff initiated the . . . transaction or sought to expedite the transaction; and (8) the generality or specificity of the misrepresentations.' " Spreitzer v. Hawkeye State Bank, 775 N.W.2d 573, 585 (Iowa 2009) (quoting from Davidson v. Wilson, 973 F.2d 1391, 1400 (8th Cir. 1992)).

§4.14 p.487 Add the following after the first full sentence: . . . could not be expected to be taken seriously.[2a]

[2a] Rodi v. S. New Eng. Sch. of Law, 532 F.3d 11 (1st Cir. 2008) (unreasonable for a student to rely on a dean's statement that the school "had remedied accreditation problems significant enough to derail its application in just four weeks" and that the school would be accredited before the student was graduated; catalog disclaimed statements about accreditation, accreditation was in the hands of a third party, and the dean "had been exposed as a flawed prognosticator"); *In re* Estate of McKenney, 953 A.2d 336 (D.C. 2008) ("It may be unreasonable to rely on a misrepresentation when the statement is preposterous and obviously false . . ."). *Rodi* also supports the unremarkable proposition that law school deans are not to be trusted.

§4.14 n.3 p.487 Add the following after the second sentence: *Cf.* Kinsey v. Cendant Corp., 588 F. Supp. 2d 516 (S.D.N.Y. 2008) (tort: "the sophistication of a party is relevant to the reasonableness of his asserted reliance on a defendant's representations"); Hoyt Props. v. Prod. Res. Grp., 716 N.W.2d 366 (Minn. App. 2006) ("an experienced businessperson is entitled to rely on statements by an opposing party to a transaction, unless his or her experience makes the truth or falsity of the representation apparent").

§4.14 n.3 p.487 Add the following to the list after **"But cf."*:*** Metavante Corp. v. Emigrant Sav. Bank, 619 F.3d 748 (7th Cir. 2010) (reliance on oral representations not reasonable where the sophisticated parties had negotiated extensively over the issues in question, and these had been dealt with in the subsequent writing); Mitec Partners v. U.S. Bank Nat'l Ass'n, 605 F.3d 617 (8th Cir. 2010) (tort: reliance upon bank's misstatement of loan priority unjustified; borrower was represented by counsel, was a sophisticated entity, and had access to the pertinent information, so its "failure to conduct basis due diligence . . . was akin to blindly relying on U.S. Bank's alleged misrepresentation"); Pollman v. Swan, 699 S.E.2d 582 (Ga. App. 2010) (tort: buyer's reliance on misrepresentations of builder and broker unjustified where the buyer's inspector warned them of potential problems and recommended further investigation), *cert. granted*, No. S10G1989 (Ga. Apr. 18, 2011); Harshman II Dev. Co. v. Meijer Stores Ltd. P'ship, 938 N.E.2d 53 (Ohio App. 2010) (tort: where buyer of commercial real estate knew that the land had several wet areas and "had an unimpeded opportunity to inspect the property prior to its purchase," it could not reasonably rely upon the seller's assertion that the property had no wetlands issues); Precision Enters. v. Duffack Enters., 710 N.W.2d 348 (Neb. App. 2006) (auto dealership "had a duty of reasonable prudence," and an experienced dealer "would not be reasonable in relying on a buyer's representation that a trade-in vehicle had not sustained prior injury when such vehicle is covered in mud and the hood is out of alignment"); Rapid Demolition Co. v. State, 864 N.Y.S.2d 503 (App. Div. 2008) (claimant alleged that it incurred added costs on a contract to demolish a bridge because the concrete deck was thicker than indicated in the plans; because the claimant did not inspect the deck, and "even a visual inspection of the concrete overlay would have revealed its true thickness," no recovery).

§4.14 n.4 p.487 Add the following at the end: *Accord:* Sisneros v. Citadel Broad. Co., 142 P.3d 34 (N.M. App. 2006) (quoting Restatement Second approvingly).

§4.14 n.5 p.488 Add the following after the citation to* Spiess*: , followed in Northstar Indus. v. Merrill Lynch & Co., 558 F. Supp. 2d 944 (D. Minn. 2008) ("the listener is under no obligation to conduct an investigation so long as it is not known by the listener that a representation is false and it is not obviously false"), *rev'd on other grounds*, 576 F.3d 827 (8th Cir. 2009).

§4.14 n.5 p.488 Add the following to the list after* "Accord"*: Hammes v. JCLB Props., 764 N.W.2d 552 (Iowa App. 2008) (for purchase of home, "to rule plaintiffs did not justifiably rely on a disclosure statement that is legally required for the protection of purchasers defies logic"); Phelps-Dickson Builders v. Amerimann Partners, 617 S.E.2d 664 (N.C. App. 2005) (builder relied on statement by developer about number of homes sold, demand, and capacity of current builders potentially justifiable: "[t]he law does not require a prudent man to deal with everyone as a rascal") (quoting Johnson v. Owens, 140 S.E.2d 311 (N.C. 1965)); Bowman v. Presley, 212 P.3d 1210 (Okla. 2009) ("The very fact of the material representation is itself enough to justify a buyer's reasonable reliance upon its accuracy").

§4.14 n.5 p.488 Add the following at the end: *But see* Meyer v. Waite, 606 S.E.2d 16 (Ga. App. 2004) (failure to disclose faults in stucco, and indeed concealment by patching and painting, excused where buyers had expressly retained the right to void the sales agreement upon an unfavorable stucco inspection and then chose not to have that inspection); Dickerson v. Strand, 904 N.E.2d 711 (Ind. App. 2009) (where the buyers "had a reasonable opportunity to inspect the house . . . the fact that [they] did not actually inspect the house is irrelevant; . . . it is the opportunity to inspect that matters"). It should be added that the court in *Dickerson* commented about its precedential authority that "we had to dust it off" and stated that "We encourage our supreme court to reevaluate the social value of a rule allowing a seller of property to lie with impunity as long as the prospective buyer had a reasonable opportunity to inspect the property." *But see* Vanderwier v. Baker, 937 N.E.2d 396 (Ind. App. 2010) (rejecting *Dickerson* because Indiana statute requiring disclosure by seller abrogated common law).

The New York Court of Appeals recently issued an important decision in support of this principle. In DDJ Mgmt. v. Rhone Grp., 931 N.E.2d 87 (N.Y. 2010), the court was faced with a borrower that had falsified its financial statements to its lenders in order to avoid default. The borrower had warranted that its statements were accurate, but a careful analysis of them would have shown worrisome discrepancies. The lenders did not make any further investigation of the statements. In a subsequent fraud action, the borrower asserted as a defense that the lenders could not have relied reasonably on its statements, given their facial implausibility and the lenders' failure to investigate further. The court of appeals rejected this argument. It observed that the rule requiring the exercise of ordinary intelligence as a prerequisite to a fraud action "serves to rid the courts of cases in which the claim of reliance is likely to be hypocritical." Additionally, "the rule rejects the claims of plaintiffs who have been so lax in protecting themselves that they cannot fairly ask for the law's protection. . . . Where, however, a plaintiff has taken reasonable steps to protect itself against deception, it should not be denied recovery merely because hindsight suggests that it might have been possible to detect the fraud when it occurred. In particular, where a plaintiff has gone to the trouble to insist upon a written representation that certain facts are true, it will often be justified in accepting that representation rather than making its own inquiry."

Although "there were hints from which plaintiffs might have been put on their guard . . . plaintiffs made a significant effort to protect themselves against the possibility of false financial statements . . ." Consequently, the court could not find as a matter of law that the plaintiffs were unjustified in relying upon the borrower's assertions.

This principle is tested in the realm of settlement agreements when the underlying dispute involves claims of fraud and dishonesty. Can the releasing party then seek rescission on the grounds that the released party made misrepresentations in the course of settlement negotiations? Some courts find it "unreasonable to rely on the representations of the allegedly dishonest party," thus making any reliance unjustifiable. Metrocall of Del. v. Cont'l Cellular Corp., 437 S.E.2d 195 (Va. 1993). *See* Indus. Comm'l Elec. v. McLees, 101 P.3d 593 (Alaska 2004) (Bryner, J., dissenting) (collecting cases). Other courts, in contrast, prefer not to decide this as a matter of law, on the grounds that the degree of fraud in the underlying dispute is less likely to be relevant to justified reliance than is "the course of dealings between the parties before and after the dispute." Indus. Comm'l Elec., *supra*.

§4.14 n.7 p.488 Add the following to the end of the first sentence: ; Crandall v. Grbic, 138 P.3d 365 (Kan. App. 2006) (home buyer whose father attended home inspection and whose home inspection mentioned the potential for roof problems could not justifiably rely on fraudulent concealment of results of other inspection).

§4.14 n.9 p.488 Add the following to the list after "Accord": Addison v. Carballosa, 48 So. 3d 951 (Fla. App. 2010) (failure to read not excused; "Because the changes to the document were obvious, with the exercise of ordinary diligence, any misrepresentation as to its content was easily discoverable."); Oelze v. Score Sports Venture, 927 N.E.2d 137 (Ill. App. 2010) (disclaimer in tennis club membership agreement: "Had plaintiff read the agreement, she would have seen the release . . . Her failure to read the release should not be held against defendant."); Ballard v. Commercial Bank of DeKalb, 991 So. 2d 1201 (Miss. 2008) (where seller had an opportunity to read the deed before signing and was competent to make financial decisions, he is "responsible for reading the instruments that he clearly signed"); Sorenson v. Bridge Capital Corp., 861 N.Y.S.2d 280 (App. Div. 2008) ("Plaintiff's negligent failure to read the agreements prevents him from establishing justifiable reliance").

§4.14 n.9 p.488 ***Add the following after the citation to* Smith*:*** , followed in Arko v. Cirou, 700 S.E.2d 604 (Ga. App. 2010) (rejecting argument that failure to read excused because did not have reading glasses when the pertinent documents were signed).

§4.14 n.9 p.488 ***Add the following after the second sentence:*** *Cf.* All Am. Roofing v. Zurich Am. Co., 934 N.E.2d 679 (Ill. App. 2010) ("[A] contracting party is not obligated to advise the other party of the contents of the agreement they are signing.").

§4.14 n.9 p.488 ***Add the following to the list in the third sentence:*** Massey Auto. v. Norris, 895 So. 2d 215 (Ala. 2004) (temporary inability to read communicated to seller).

§4.14 n.9 p.488 ***Add the following after the third sentence:*** Greater forgiveness may be appropriate when the failure to read is the consequence of both fraud in the factum and the recipient's inability to read. Bassett v. Jasper Banking Co., 629 S.E.2d 434 (Ga. App. 2006) ("Where, however, one who can not read is induced to sign an instrument by the misrepresentations of the other party as to its character and contents, he is not bound thereby.") (quoting Pirkle v. Gurr, 128 S.E.2d 490 (Ga. 1962)).

§4.14 n.10 p.489 ***Add the following to the list after* "Accord"*:*** Arko v. Cirou, 700 S.E.2d 604 (Ga. App. 2010) (presence of confidential relationship could excuse failure to read because of reliance upon the representations of the other party, but mere friendship insufficient to constitute a confidential relationship); Sisneros v. Citadel Broad. Co., *supra* note 4 ("a contract may be voidable even when a party fails to use care in reading the writing"); Restatement Second §172 (ignorance of facts "does not make his reliance unjustified unless it amounts to a failure to act in good faith and in accordance with reasonable standards of fair dealing").

§4.14 n.10 p.489 In the second paragraph, add the following to the list: Martinez v. Freedom Mtg. Team, 527 F. Supp. 2d 827 (N.D. Ill. 2007) ("contracting parties generally have a duty to become aware of the contents of their contracts, but one party may justifiably rely on the representations of another when (as here) the parties lack equal knowledge or further inquiry into the contract terms has been blocked . . . Here Martinez justifiably relied on Funes' representation because the document was provided to him only in a language foreign to him: English.").

§4.14 n.13 p.490 Add the following to the list after **"Accord"*:*** Sindecuse v. Katsaros, 541 F.3d 801 (8th Cir. 2008) ("a statement about the future actions of third parties is really a prediction rather than a promise"; statement that there would be a market for stock held inadequate for misrepresentation claim); NPS, LLC v. Ambac Assur. Corp., 706 F. Supp. 2d 162 (D. Mass. 2010) ("[A]ll commercial puffing and sales talk is, to some extent, intended to induce reliance. It is meant to entice potential customers to buy or potential shareholders to invest. The puffing crosses the line into misrepresentation when it is 'an *integral* part of a representation of *material fact.*' ") (quoting from Bergeron v. Ridgewood Sec. Corp., 610 F. Supp. 2d 113 (D. Mass. 2009)) (emphasis in original).

§4.14 n.13 p.490 Add the following at the end: *See generally* Hoffman, The Best Puffery Article Ever, 91 Iowa L. Rev. 1395 (2006).

§4.14 n.14 p.490 Add the following after the first sentence: *Accord:* Trans-Spec Truck Serv. v. Caterpillar Inc., 524 F.3d 315 (1st Cir. 2008) (statement that seller "bragg[ed] that engine up like there was no tomorrow" "recounts classic seller's talk, which is not actionable as a misrepresentation"); Gentry v. Harborage Cottages-Stuart, 602 F. Supp. 2d 1239 (S.D. Fla. 2009) (antifraud provisions of land sales disclosures statute: statements that condominiums "(1) are a luxury development; (2) are extraordinary; (3) blend tropical charm with contemporary elegance; (4) combine materials and finishes of exceptional quality with timeless craftsmanship; (5) provide spacious patios from which to enjoy glorious sunrises over the water; and (6) that Altman Development Corporation consistently delivers products and services of the highest caliber to clients and residents, fall squarely within the scope of opinions, exaggerations and general characterizations that constitute puffery"); Hanson-Suminski v. Rohrman Midwest Motors, 898 N.E.2d 194 (Ill. App. 2008) (" 'Puffery' denotes the exaggerations reasonably to be expected of a seller as to the degree of quality of his or her product, the truth or falsity of which cannot be precisely determined."; statement that the car has had neither accidents nor repairs not mere puffery).

§4.14 n.16 p.491 Add the following at the end: *Cf.* Ragsdale v. Kennedy, 209 S.E.2d 494 (N.C. 1974) (question for jury whether statements by corporate president with special knowledge of facts, including business's loss of money, to the effect that the corporation was a "gold mine" and a "going concern" were opinion or material fact).

§4.14 n.20 p.492 Add the following after the citation to* Scott*: and in Gordon, Unfreezing Legal Reality: Critical Approaches to Law, 15 Fla. St. U.L. Rev. 195 (1987).

§4.14 p.492 Add the following at the end of the third sentence of the first full paragraph: . . . incompatible with that opinion.[22a]

[22a] Hoyt Props. v. Prod. Res. Grp., *supra* note 3 ("Although abstract statements of law or pure legal opinions are not actionable, statements of law that imply knowledge of facts are actionable.").

§4.14 n.23 p.492 Add the following to the list after* "Accord"*: Richardson v. Weatherford, 997 So. 2d 1254 (Fla. App. 2009) (tort: no duty on debtor's lawyer to disclose to creditor, after the parties agreed to add loan extension fees in place of foreclosure, "that the transactions 'might' be usurious").

§4.14 n.29 p.494 Add the following after the second sentence: *See* Zoltek Corp. v. Structural Polymer Grp., 592 F.3d 893 (8th Cir. 2010) (tort: unreasonable to rely on buyer's stated intentions to purchase when "the parties were both sophisticated entities," their contract "required individual orders be in writing," putting the oral orders in question perhaps within UCC §2-201, and "the representations at issue were made in the midst of contentious litigation between the parties," particularly when the estimates in question were made "to bolster a future lost profits claim").

§4.14 n.31 p.494 Add the following to the list after **"Accord"***:* Strange v. Davis, 44 So. 3d 1109 (Ala. Civ. App. 2010) (promise to prepare writing amounts to promissory fraud where promisor had no intention at the time of the promise to have the agreement reduced to writing, thus making it easier to argue that the parties had reached a contrary agreement); Lumpkin v. Deventer N. Am., 672 S.E.2d 405 (Ga. App. 2008) (tort: though a promise normally does not amount to actionable fraud, it may if "made without a present intent to perform," which normally is proved inferentially; here, builder's promise to repair home amounted to fraud when evidence that builder told subcontractor not to fix problems, but to make only cosmetic repairs); Sabo v. Delman, 143 N.E.2d 906 (N.Y. 1957) ("if a promise was made with a preconceived and undisclosed intention of not performing it, it constitutes a misrepresentation of a 'material existing fact' "), explained in Int'l Cabletel v. Le Groupe Videotron Ltee, 978 F. Supp. 483 (S.D.N.Y. 1997) (Sotomayor, J.); Traders Bank v. Dils, 704 S.E.2d 691 (W. Va. 2010) (ordinarily "fraud cannot be predicated on a promise not performed," but there is an exception "where the device used to accomplish the fraud is the promise itself," in particular one which at the time of promising the promisor had no intention of performing).

§4.14 n.31 p.494 Add the following to the list after **"See generally"***:* I. Ayres & G. Klass, Insincere Promises (2005).

§4.14 n.31 p.494 Add the following after the first paragraph: Rarely is proof of promissory fraud direct. There is, however, an innate difficulty with much circumstantial evidence. One method of indirect proof of fraudulent intent is to see whether the subsequent actions of the promisor are consistent with the intent to perform the promise. But it is entirely possible that later, inconsistent acts merely reflect an honest change of

mind, so that the original statement of intent was entirely accurate. Because this type of evidence can support opposite hypotheses, much ultimately will depend upon the nature and quantity of the later evidence. It is fair to say that the more remote the evidence from the promise, the less likely it will be found satisfactory proof of promissory fraud. *See* Erickson v. Erickson, 782 N.W.2d 346 (N.D. 2010) (rejecting 2007 evidence of 1998 intent; constructive fraud "cannot be a basis to rescind a contract formed with free and effective consent because a contracting party changes his or her mind after entering the contract").

§4.15 EFFECTS OF MISREPRESENTATION

§4.15 n.1 p.495 Add the following at the end: Insurance contracts take a somewhat different tack. There it may be true that the contract is void, not voidable, "because of a variety of behaviors by an insured, when the materiality of a misrepresentation strikes at the core of the agreement to insure"; not in the case quoted from, though, where a father did not list his minor daughter as part of his household when applying for auto insurance. Rutgers Cas. Ins. Co. v. LaCroix, 946 A.2d 1027 (N.J. 2008).

§4.15 p.496 Add the following to the end of the carryover sentence: . . . avoidance (or "rescission") of the contract.[1a]

[1a] Restatement Second §380; Eigen v. Textron Lycoming Reciprocating Engine Div., 874 A.2d 1179 (Pa. Super. 2005) (affirmance of a contract does not bar the right to recover; it bars only rescission). Rescission's grounding in equity may affect whether it is available. Unclean hands in particular may preclude rescission, leaving only an action for damages. Isaacs v. Bishop, 249 S.W.3d 100 (Tex. Civ. App. 2008) (plaintiff held partly responsible for the fraud perpetrated on him, so no rescission). *Accord:* Am. Bank Ctr. v. Wiest, 793 N.W.2d 172 (N.D. 2010) ("Rescission of a contract is not a matter of absolute right, but instead is committed to the district court's sound discretion."; considered unclean hands argument, but concluded that the promisor was highly culpable and allowed rescission).

§4.15 n.2 p.496 Add the following after the second sentence: *Accord:* Turner v. Wakefield, 481 So. 2d 846 (Miss. 1985) (those who receive the benefit of performance may not then sue for deceit; "otherwise one might, with knowledge of fraud, speculate upon the advantages or disadvantages of an agreement, receive its benefits, and thereafter repudiate all its obligations"); Shaw v. Raymond, 196 S.W.3d 655 (Mo. App. 2006) (unavailability of rescission after full performance "well established") (quoting Roberts v. Anderson, 254 S.W. 723 (Mo. App. 1923)).

§4.15 n.3 p.496 Add the following at the end: *See generally* Garvin, Credit, Information, & Trust in the Law of Sales: The Credit Seller's Right of Reclamation, 44 UCLA L. Rev. 247 (1996).

§4.15 n.4 p.496 Add the following as a new paragraph at the end: Just as the victim of misrepresentation loses the right to rescind the contract if it ratifies it, so too does it lose the right to bring an action for breach of contract if it prevails on its request for rescission; if the contract has been rescinded, there is nothing left to enforce. Awada v. Shuffle Master, 173 P.3d 707 (Nev. 2007) ("When the district court rescinded the agreement, it eliminated the basis for Awada's claims for breach of contract").

§4.15 n.5 p.497 Add the following to the list after "Accord": Leisure Resort Tech. v. Trading Cove Assocs., 889 A.2d 785 (Conn. 2006) ("plaintiff's disavowal of its right of rescission and its remedy of restitution have foreclosed as a proper measure of damages the current value of the beneficial interest received by the defendants"); Megel v. Donaldson, 654 S.E.2d 656 (Ga. App. 2007) (suit for damages in tort means that plaintiff affirmed the contract and may not seek rescission); Harkins v. Channell, 618 S.E.2d 129 (Ga. App. 2005) (suit for reformation means that plaintiff affirmed the contract and may not seek rescission); Allianz Ins. Co. v. Guidant Corp., 884 N.E.2d 405 (Ind. App. 2008) ("When a party elects to affirm a contract induced by fraudulent misrepresentations, the party may only seek tort damages.").

§4.15 n.5 p.497 Add the following at the end: Similarly, a party to a settlement agreement who sues in fraud affirms the agreement and can recover damages only for the "fair compromise value of the claim at the time of the settlement"; to allow the full amount of potential damages would effectively grant both the rescission remedy and the fraud remedy. Exotics Haw.-Kona v. E.I. du Pont de Nemours & Co., 172 P.3d 1021 (Haw. 2007).

§4.15 n.6 p.497 Add the following after the fifth sentence: *Accord*: Shaw v. Raymond, *supra* note 2 ("Because . . . rescission was not an available remedy . . . Raymond did not in fact have two remedies from which to elect, and thus, the doctrine of election of remedies does not operate to bar Raymond from seeking damages").

§4.15 n.8 p.498 Add the following to the list after* "Accord"*: Colburn Family Found. v. Chabad's Children of Chernobyl, 739 F. Supp. 2d 614 (S.D.N.Y. 2010) (even if settlement agreement procured through misrepresentation, "the Chabad defendants complied with the terms of the Agreement for nearly two and [one-] half years, thereby ratifying the contract"); Honeycutt v. Honeycutt, 701 S.E.2d 689 (N.C. App. 2010) (no avoidance where spouse accepted benefits of separation agreement for over a year after she retained counsel and sued for its rescission).

§4.15 n.8 p.498 Add the following after the citation to* Restatement Second*: , followed in Newcastle Homes v. Thye, 241 P.3d 988 (Kan. 2010) (developer lost ability to avoid a rescission agreement with a buyer because very shortly after the time of contracting, the developer should have discovered the alleged fraud and damages it invoked in its attempt to avoid the agreement, but did not act for over a year).

§4.15 n.9 p.498 Add the following after the first sentence: Brown v. City of S. Burlington, 393 F.3d 337 (2d Cir. 2004) ("Avoiding a contract of release on the grounds of fraudulent misrepresentation, then, requires not only manifestation of an intent to avoid the release within a reasonable time after the discovery of the fraud but also return of any consideration received by the releaser within a reasonable time.").

§4.15 n.14 p.499 Add the following to the list after **"Cf."***:* Isaacs v. Bishop, *supra* note 1a ("An inability to return the parties to their former position should be considered in determining whether rescission would be equitable.").

§4.15 n.15 p.499 Add the following to the list after **"Accord"***:* Lumsden v. Lawing, 451 S.E.2d 659 (N.C. App. 1995) (allowing rescission without disgorgement under "extraordinary circumstances"; real property that was the subject of the action had been foreclosed upon and sold to a third party).

§4.15 n.19 p.500 Add the following to the list after **"Accord"***:* Honeycutt v. Honeycutt, 701 S.E.2d 689 (N.C. App. 2010) (insufficient to state that one is prepared to disgorge benefits received under the contract).

§4.15 n.19 p.500 Add the following at the end: If the recipient refuses to rescind the contract, restitution is therefore unavailable, and the recipient must seek benefit-of-the-bargain damages in tort or contract. Leisure Resort Tech. v. Trading Cove Assocs., *supra* note 5 (plaintiff unable to prove benefit-of-the-bargain damages).

§4.15 n.20 p.500 Add the following at the end: The equitable grant of reasonable time has been rendered statutory in some jurisdictions. Cal. Civ. Code §1693 ("A party who has received benefits by reason of a contract that is subject to rescission and who in an action or proceeding seeks relief based upon rescission shall not be denied relief because of a delay in restoring or in tendering restoration of such benefits before judgment unless such delay has been substantially prejudicial to the other party; but the court may make a tender of restoration a condition of its judgment."); *see also* Village Northridge Homeowners Ass'n v. State Farm Fire & Cas. Co., 237 P.3d 598 (Cal. 2010) (tracing history of this exception and this statute).

§4.16 THE ELEMENTS OF DURESS

§4.16 n.1 p.501 Add the following to the list after* "See generally"*: Giesel, A Realistic Proposal for the Contract Duress Doctrine, 107 W. Va. L. Rev. 443 (2005); Hill, A Utilitarian Theory of Duress, 84 Iowa L. Rev. 275 (1999); Shavell, Contractual Holdup and Legal Intervention, 36 J. Legal Stud. 325 (2007).

§4.16 n.1 p.501 Add the following at the end: For a comparative analysis of duress and undue influence, *see* Philippe, French and American Approaches to Contract Formation and Enforceability: A Comparative Perspective, 12 Tul. J. Comp. & Int'l L. 357 (2005).

§4.16 p.502 Add the following at the end of the second sentence of the second full paragraph: . . . inflict some loss or harm on another.[3a]

[3a] Thus pressure from one's own attorney cannot be duress, whatever else it may be. Bistany v. PNC Bank, 585 F. Supp. 2d 179 (D. Mass. 2008) (threat to withdraw unless the client agreed to a settlement).

§4.16 n.8 p.503 Add the following to the list after* "Accord"*: ConAgra Trade Grp. v. Fuel Exploration, 636 F. Supp. 2d 1166 (D. Colo. 2009) ("[T]he terms of the [contracts] are not shocking or surprising enough to indicate that ConAgra's threats actually subjugated Fuel Ex's free will in signing those contracts.").

§4.17 THE IMPROPRIETY OF THE THREAT

§4.17 n.3 p.504 Add the following after the first sentence: *Accord:* Bailey v. Estate of Kemp, 955 So. 2d 777 (Miss. 2007) (dominant party must have "threatened to do something which [it] had no legal right to do"); Madey v. Carman, 858 N.Y.S.2d 784 (App. Div. 2008) ("There is no actionable duress, however, where, as here, the alleged menace was to exercise a legal right."); Cummings Inc. v. Dorgan, 320 S.W.3d 316 (Tenn. App. 2009) ("the assertion of a legal right . . . would not constitute duress").

An interesting variation on this principle is Olmsted v. Saint Paul Pub. Sch., 830 F.3d 824, 2016 U.S. App. LEXIS 13868, 41 I.E.R. Cas. (BNA) 899 (8th Cir. 2016), which rejected a teacher's claim that the threat to report his misconduct to state authorities unless he resigned was an unlawful threat because the schools had no discretion to decline to report misconduct of the nature it was alleging, under Minn. Stat. §122.A.20. The court credited the district's evidence that "it did not make a report every time a teacher was suspended." *Id.* at *9. Applying state law, the Eighth Circuit held that "[u]nder Minnesota law, it is 'undisputed that duress is coercion by means of physical force or unlawful threats which destroys the victim's free will and compels him to comply with some demand of the party exerting the coercion.'" *Id.* at *7, citing Wise v. Midtown Motors, 231 Minn. 46, 42 N.W.2d 404, 407 (1950). Moreover, any possible threat "was cured" because he "had full knowledge of all the facts, advice from an attorney, and ample time for reflection." *Id.* at *10.

§4.17 n.4 p.504 Add the following to the list after* "But see"*: Wright Therapy Equip. v. Blue Cross & Blue Shield of Ala., 991 So. 2d 701 (Ala. 2008) (exercising one's contractual right to withhold remittances in order to recover allegedly overbilled amounts is not duress; quaere whether that would be true were the contractual right exercised in bad faith).

§4.17 n.7 p.505 Add the following at the end: The threat need not come from the party against whom the defense is asserted, "so long as the duress is causally tied to the defendant." Curtis Lumber Co. v. La. Pac. Corp., 618 F.3d 762 (8th Cir. 2010). *But see* Kalyanaram v. Burck, 225 S.W.3d 291 (Tex. Civ. App. 2006) (no duress after party forwarded information to prosecutor, as threat then arose from non-party). The Restatement Second recognizes third-party duress, with the important exception that the defense is not available if "the other party to the transaction in good faith and without reason to know of the duress either gives value or relies materially on the transaction." Restatement Second §175(2) & cmt. e. *See* Chan v. Lund, 116 Cal. Rptr. 3d 122 (Ct. App. 2010) (following Restatement; counsel's threat to withdraw on the eve of trial not duress where the attorney was not a party to the resulting settlement agreement, "the defendants were not responsible for any alleged acts of economic duress and were not aware of [the] allegation . . . until after the contract was entered into").

§4.17 n.12 p.506 ***Add the following at the end:*** *Accord:* Cont'l Cas. Co. v. Huizar, 740 S.W.2d 429 (Tex. 1987) ("[a] threat to institute a civil suit or even the actual institution of suit does not, as a matter of law, constitute duress").

§4.17 n.13 p.506 ***Add the following at the end:*** *Cf.* Medical Recovery Servs. v. Carnes, 230 P.3d 760 (Idaho App. 2010) ("the threat of civil proceedings does not constitute duress if made in good faith and without other oppressive circumstances").

§4.17 n.16 p.507 ***Add the following at the end:*** On the background of *Austin Instruments*, see Miller, Revisiting *Austin v. Loral*: A Study in Economic Duress, Contract Modification and Framing, 2 Hastings Bus. L.J. 357 (2006).

§4.17 n.17 p.507 ***Add the following to the list after* "But cf.":** ConAgra Trade Grp. v. Fuel Exploration, 636 F. Supp. 2d 1166 (D. Colo. 2009) ("Fuel Ex cannot show that ConAgra's threats to withhold future business were improper or unreasonably coercive.").

§4.17 n.17 p.507 ***Add the following at the end:*** It is important, however, to remember that other doctrines may impose limits on the scope of duress. Consider, for example, the late-arriving non-compete agreement. Most often, these are offered to at-will employees, and very often, the consideration is their continued employment. Duress? Certainly not if the jurisdiction does not recognize the duty of good faith and fair dealing as part of at-will employment contracts. See *infra* §7.17a. Even if the jurisdiction does recognize this implied duty, it seems unlikely that conditioning further employment upon assent to a non-compete agreement would amount to duress. Purely as a matter of description, these non-compete covenants seem ingrained in modern employment practice. Once one accepts the freedom-of-contract premise of at-will employment doctrine, it follows that ordinary threats to discharge would not amount to duress, implicit as they

are in the basic employment relation. *See* Cummings Inc. v. Dorgan, 320 S.W.3d 316 (Tenn. App. 2009) (threat to discharge not duress when used to revise commission agreement). This may not, however, be true when the employer enters into the employment relationship with the intent to spring a non-compete agreement on the employee shortly after employment begins. The employee's case would be still stronger if taking the job entailed considerable costs expended in reliance on the employment, or concomitant threats to impair one's prospects for future employment, or other instances of opportunistic behavior on the part of the employer. The increasing use of non-compete agreements in low-wage jobs has received some attention in recent years, and could lead to legislative responses. *See e.g,.* Mobility and Opportunity for Vulnerable Employees Act, S. 1504 (114th Cong.) (would prohibit covenants not to compete for employees whose base salary is below $15/hour, adjusted for inflation, or the applicable minimum wage, if higher); Lydia DePillis, "Can the Senate Stop Low-Wage Employers from Tying up Workers with Non-Competes?," *Washington Post*, June 2, 2015.

§4.17 n.18 p.507 Add the following at the end: *See* Bank of Am. v. 108 N. State Retail, 928 N.E.2d 42 (Ill. App. 2010) ("the term 'wrongful' is not limited to acts that are criminal, tortious, or in violation of a contractual duty. They must extend to acts that are wrongful in a moral sense as well.").

§4.17 n.21 p.508 Add the following after the citation to* Vail/ Arrowhead*: , followed in ConAgra Trade Grp. v. Fuel Exploration, *supra* note 17 ("courts may look to the nature of the bargain that the parties strike").

§4.17 n.23 p.508 Add the following to the list after* "See"*: ConAgra Trade Grp. v. Fuel Exploration, *supra* note 17 (no duress where buyer could not show that seller was the only vendor available and, in fact, that other vendors would have been available in a month and that buyer took over a month to consider whether to agree to seller's terms); Hall v. Martin Eng'g Co., 597 F. Supp. 2d 651 (S.D.W. Va. 2009) ("Because the Halls were responsible in large part for their own monetary troubles, Martin cannot be held liable for economic duress."); Int'l Paper Co. v.

Whilden, 469 So. 2d 560 (Ala. 1985) ("The entering into a contract with reluctance or even dissatisfaction with its terms because of economic necessity does not, of itself, constitute economic duress invalidating the contract."); Swindle v. Harvey, 23 So. 3d 562 (Miss. App. 2009) ("any duress the Harveys were under resulted from the changes required by [non-parties], not the Bank's actions").

§4.17 n.23 p.508 Add the following at the end: *Cf.* Schoeps v. Museum of Modern Art, 594 F. Supp. 2d 461 (S.D.N.Y. 2009) (applying German duress law, which requires threat or a combination of distinct disadvantage and lopsided terms; triable issue where Jewish plaintiff in Germany transferred ownership of paintings in 1935 "only because of threats and economic pressures by the Nazi government").

§4.17 n.26 p.509 Add the following at the end: *But cf.* Colello v. Colello, 780 N.Y.S.2d 450 (App. Div. 2004) (fiancé's threat to cancel wedding if fiancée refused to sign prenuptial agreement was not duress).

***§4.17 n.27 p.509 Add the following to the list after* "Accord":** ConAgra Trade Grp. v. Fuel Exploration, *supra* note 17 ("[A] financial bind created by a party's own doing will not support a finding of duress.").

§4.17 n.28 p.510 Add the following at the end: *But cf.* Edwards v. Kia Motors of Am., 486 F.3d 1229 (11th Cir. 2007) (no duress when, after its failure to make payments due and to award promised franchise, franchisor did not approve sale of franchise but instead submitted release to franchisee).

***§4.17 n.29 p.510 Add the following to the list after* "Accord":** Traystman, Coric & Keramidas v. Daigle, 855 A.2d 996 (Conn. App. 2004) (lawyer threatened to withdraw after the first day of trial unless client signed promissory note for fee); Comcast of Ore. v. City of Eugene, 155 P.3d 99 (Or. App. 2007) (city's threat to terminate cable franchise unless franchisee paid invalid permit fees); Holler v. Holler, 612 S.E.2d 469 (S.C. App. 2005) (fiancé would not marry pregnant fiancée unless she signed a pre-nuptial agreement, knowing that she would be deported unless she married, where she did not understand the agreement and lacked money for an attorney or translator), distinguished by Biliouris v. Biliouris, 852 N.E.2d 687 (Mass. App. 2006) (upholding pre-nuptial agreement entered into by pregnant fiancée where other coercive circumstances not present).

§4.18 THE GRAVITY OF THE THREAT

§4.18 n.2 p.510 Add the following at the end: For an early critique of this approach, *see* Union Pac. R. Co. v. Pub. Serv. Comm'n, 248 U.S. 67, 70 (1918) (Holmes, J.) ("It always is for the interest of a party under duress to choose the lesser of two evils. But the fact that a choice was made according to interest does not exclude duress. It is the characteristic of duress properly so called.").

§4.18 n.3 p.511 Add the following after the first sentence: *Accord:* ConAgra Trade Grp. v. Fuel Exploration, 636 F. Supp. 2d 1166 (D. Colo. 2009) (same); Dobson v. Portrait Homes, 117 P.3d 1200 (Wyo. 2005) (same).

§4.18 n.3 p.511 Add the following at the end: *Cf.* Cabot Corp. v. AVX Corp., 863 N.E.2d 503 (Mass. 2007) (using both "free will" and "no reasonable alternative" tests); Gainey v. Gainey, 675 S.E.2d 792 (S.C. App. 2009) (same). That the question is one of law, *see* Anselmo v. Mfrs. Life Ins. Co., 771 F.2d 417 (8th Cir. 1985) (whether "facts are sufficient to constitute duress is a matter of law for the court," while whether the facts exist is a matter of fact). *But see* Gainey v. Gainey, *supra* ("[w]hether duress exists in a particular case is a question of fact"). *See generally* Bar-Gill & Ben-Shahar, The Law of Duress and the Economics of Credible Threats, 33 J. Legal Stud. 391 (2004).

§4.18 n.4 p.511 Add the following to the list after "See": Hampton Island v. HAOP, LLC, 702 S.E.2d 770 (Ga. App. 2010) (threatened civil suit not duress; recipient "made an informed decision on advice of counsel to settle . . . rather than defend against those claims in court and seek the alternative remedy of attorney fees to the extent that those claims were deemed frivolous").

§4.18 n.5 p.511 ***Add the following at the end:*** An analogous situation arises when a taxpayer pays a tax and then challenges its legitimacy. If it seeks to recover its payments, ordinarily it will not succeed under the *voluntary payments* doctrine. See *infra* §§4.23 & 9.4. An exception to that doctrine is, however, duress. Of particular importance is whether the taxpayer had a reasonable alternative to paying the tax — for example, doing business in a tax-free venue. *See* Raintree Homes v. Village of Long Grove, 906 N.E.2d 751 (Ill. App. 2009) (impact fees paid by developer as a prerequisite to issuing building permits; developer did a significant part of its business in the village and without the permits would have gone out of business).

§4.18 n.9 p.512 ***Add the following after the first sentence:*** *Accord:* ConAgra Trade Grp. v. Fuel Exploration, *supra* note 3 (other crude oil vendors available).

§4.18 n.10 p.512 ***Add the following to the list after "Accord":*** Osborne v. Howard Univ. Physicians, 904 A.2d 335 (D.C. 2006) (no duress where plaintiff failed to proffer "evidence of particularized economic harm that would result from choosing termination (and litigation) over signing the [settlement] contract").

§4.18 n.11 p.512 ***Add the following to the list after "Accord":*** Curtis Lumber Co. v. La. Pac. Corp., 618 F.3d 762 (8th Cir. 2010) (refusal to pay rebates to the customers of the recipient of threats; although the recipient had the option not to make good on the rebates, its options, "in reality, would not have afforded relief," because the result would have been "severe repercussions in its overall revenue"); *In re* RLS Legal Solutions, 156 S.W.3d 160 (Tex. Civ. App. 2005) (law firm withheld paycheck to employee until she signed a non-compete agreement with an arbitration clause; employee was the household's sole provider and could not pay her bills otherwise).

§4.18 n.11 p.512 Add the following at the end: *But cf.* Edwards v. Kia Motors of Am., 486 F.3d 1229 (11th Cir. 2007) (no duress where franchisor withheld payment before presenting unfavorable contractual terms); Cabot Corp. v. AVX Corp., *supra* note 3 (no duress where customer could have secured injunction against supplier rather than succumb to threats to withhold goods); Bank of Am. v. 108 N. State Retail, 928 N.E.2d 42 (Ill. App. 2010) (no duress when bank refused to continue lending after default without countervailing modifications to the loan agreement; mere "financial pressure" insufficient); Dobson v. Portrait Homes, *supra* note 3 (refusal to pay $3,645.18 when total price $380,000 means "that risk imbalance does not exist").

§4.18 n.12 p.513 Add the following at the end: *But see* Oxxford Clothes XX v. Expeditors Int'l of Wash., 127 F.3d 574 (7th Cir. 1997) (Posner, J.) (no duress even where goods withheld wrongfully and injunction denied; no attempt to seek appellate review, and in any event the duress defense does not protect against judicial error: "The hallmark of duress or extortion is that the victim has no feasible legal remedy."), analyzed in Baird, The Young Astronomers, 74 U. Chi. L. Rev. 1641 (2007).

§4.18 n.13 p.513 Add the following to the list after **"Accord"***:* Cabot Corp. v. AVX Corp., *supra* note 3 (where disputants "are sophisticated and substantial commercial parties" "represented by highly competent counsel," "we will strictly construe the requirements of economic duress against the party asserting it"); ChampionsWorld LLC v. U.S. Soccer Fed'n, 726 F. Supp. 2d 961 (N.D. Ill. 2010) (no duress where parties negotiated over terms for three years; "ChampionsWorld was in a position from the beginning to reject USSF's terms and do business elsewhere."); Hampton Island v. HAOP, LLC, 702 S.E.2d 770 (Ga. App. 2010) (duress defense unavailable where recipient of threat "was a sophisticated businessman who consulted with legal counsel before executing the Agreement"); Holler v. Holler, 612 S.E.2d 469 (S.C. App. 2005) (pre-nuptial agreement procured by duress even though made available three months before the wedding where fiancée unable to translate into her native language, pregnant, under threat of deportation unless married, and completely dependent on fiancé for support), distinguished by

Mallen v. Mallen, 622 S.E.2d 812 (Ga. 2005) (pregnant fiancée's pre-nuptial agreement not procured by duress; fiancée negotiated for changes, and "had already demonstrated her willingness to terminate the pregnancy").

§4.18 n.15 p.514 Add the following to the list after **"But cf."***:* Feuer v. Darkanot, 829 N.Y.S.2d 164 (App. Div. 2007) (duress in court's threat to hold party in contempt if he did not agree on the record to settlement agreed to off the record).

§4.19 EFFECTS OF DURESS

§4.19 n.4 p.515 Add the following to the list after **"Accord"***:* Cabot Corp. v. AVX Corp., 863 N.E.2d 503 (Mass. 2007) (ratification where delay of 18 months before asserting duress).

§4.20 UNDUE INFLUENCE

§4.20 n.1 p.516 Add the following to the list after **"See generally"***:* Bell, Abuse of a Relationship: Undue Influence in English Law and French Law, 15 Eur. Rev. Private L. 555 (2007).

§4.20 n.3 p.516 Add the following after the first sentence: For example, a party subject to undue influence while making an agreement may ratify that agreement once the undue influence is lifted. *See* Gengaro v. City of New Haven, 984 A.2d 1133 (Conn. App. 2009) ("because the plaintiff had seven days to rescind . . . after the signing of the agreement, took actions to confirm that he would receive the benefits of the agreement, accepted and enjoyed the benefits of the agreement and did not bring an action claiming that the agreement was void until at least ten months after it was signed, he effectively ratified the agreement").

§4.20 n.3 p.516 Add the following as a separate paragraph at the end: Though undue influence may give rise to a claim in restitution, it does not give rise to a claim at law. Lavoie v. N.E. Knitting, 918 A.2d 225 (R.I. 2007); Restatement Second ch. 7, topic 2, intro. note at 474 ("the victim of duress or undue influence is usually limited to avoidance and does not have an affirmative action for damages"). In addition, where a modification of an otherwise unexceptionable contract was procured through undue influence, the modification, not the unmodified contract, becomes voidable. *Ex parte* Estelle, 982 So. 2d 1086 (Ala. 2007) ("[A] change in beneficiary resulting from undue influence is void; thus, the original policy would remain in effect, and the original beneficiary's interest would vest upon the policyholder's death.").

§4.20 p.517 Add the following after the first sentence: . . . such a relationship existed.[4a]

[4a] *Ex parte* Estelle, *supra* note 3 ("[A]n insurance policy that has been changed as a result of undue influence is void for the same reason that an insurance policy that has been changed while the policyholder was mentally incompetent is void: the act of changing the beneficiary was not meaningfully the act of the policyholder."); Hooten v. Jensen, 227 S.W.3d 431 (Ark. App. 2006) ("The questions of undue influence and mental capacity are so closely interwoven that they can be considered together."); Nichols v. Estate of Tyler, 910 N.E.2d 221 (Ind. App. 2009) ("Complete unsoundness of mind is not necessary to support a finding of undue influence; rather, weakness of mind when combined with other factors is sufficient."); Landers v. Sgouros, 224 S.W.3d 651 (Mo. App. 2007) ("mental capacity and undue influence are intertwined").

§4.20 n.5 p.517 Add the following at the end: *See also* Estate of Parfitt v. Parfitt, 672 S.E.2d 827 (Va. 2009) (by statute, an agency relationship creates a fiduciary duty and thus may support shifting the burden of proof); Endicott v. Saul, 176 P.3d 560 (Wash. App. 2008) ("A confidential relationship exists when one person has gained the confidence of the other and purports to act or advise with the other's interest in mind."; power of attorney coupled with false or misleading counsel described as in the best interest of the vulnerable adult); Comeau v. Nash, 233 P.3d 572 (Wyo. 2010) (former grandson-in-law part of confidential relationship because of long-term friendship, and where promisor in declining health and lived with the former grandson-in-law).

§4.20 n.6 p.517 Add the following to the list: Nelson v. Holland, 776 N.W.2d 446 (Minn. App. 2009) (presence of confidential relationship only a factor in determining whether conduct resulted from undue influence); *In re* Mildred M.J., 844 N.Y.S.2d 539 (App. Div. 2007) (family relationship "does not, per se, create a presumption of undue influence").

§4.20 n.7 p.517 In the second paragraph, add the following to the list after **"see"***:* Trent v. Nat'l City Bank, 918 N.E.2d 646 (Ind. App. 2009) (bank not a dominant party "simply because it provided services to her as a financial institution as to her other investments or because it administered [a trust] to which she was a beneficiary").

§4.20 n.10 p.518 Add the following after the second sentence: *Cf.* Miller v. Dunn, 184 S.W.3d 122 (Mo. App. 2006) ("To establish undue influence, it is not necessary to establish the existence of a confidential relationship between the donor and the donee.").

§4.20 n.12 p.518 Add the following to the list after **"Accord"***:* Nichols v. Estate of Tyler, *supra* note 4a ("When transactions occur between a dominant and a subordinate party which benefit the dominant party, 'the law imposes a presumption that the transaction was the result of undue influence exerted by the dominant party, constructively fraudulent, and, thus void.' ") (quoting from Hamilton v. Hamilton, 858 N.E.2d 1032 (Ind. App. 2006)); Basham v. Duffer, 238 S.W.3d 304 (Tenn. App. 2007) (defendant "exercised his status as [decedent's] power of attorney, placing the burden on him to prove by clear and convincing evidence that any of the transactions were fair"); Endicott v. Saul, *supra* note 5 ("Because the trial court correctly concluded that [the defendants] had a confidential relationship with [the plaintiff], as a matter of law they have the burden to prove a gift was not a result of undue influence.").

§4.20 n.12 p.518 In the first paragraph, add the following to the list after **"Cf."***:* Friendly Ice Cream Corp. v. Beckner, 597 S.E.2d 34 (Va. 2004) (burden "shifts when weakness of mind *and* grossly inadequate consideration or suspicious circumstances are shown *or* when a confidential relationship is established").

§4.20 n.12 p.518 In the fifth sentence of the first paragraph, add the following to the list after "**see**"*:* Nichols v. Estate of Tyler, *supra* note 4a ("To rebut the presumption of undue influence, a dominant party has to demonstrate by clear and unequivocal proof that the transaction in question was made at arm's length and is therefore valid.").

§4.20 n.12 p.518 Add the following after the fifth sentence of the first paragraph: Indiana's common-law burden shifting has in part been abrogated by a statute that eliminates the burden shift for attorneys-in-fact who do not exercise their powers of attorney. Ind. Code §30-5-9-2(b); *see In re* Estate of Compton, 919 N.E.2d 1181 (Ind. App. 2010) (construing statute).

§4.20 n.12 p.518 In the second paragraph, add the following to the list after "**See**"*:* Comeau v. Nash, 233 P.3d 572 (Wyo. 2010) (party seeking to invalidate transfer must prove undue influence by a preponderance of the evidence). *Cf.* Krueger v. Ary, 205 P.3d 1150 (Colo. 2009) (thorough analysis: rebuttable presumption shifts only the burden of going forward; the burden of proof remains on the party asserting the defense, with the result that the initial burden-shifting is a question of law, not a question of fact).

§4.20 n.13 p.519 Add the following to the list after "**see**"*:* Bailey v. Turnbow, 639 S.E.2d 291 (Va. 2007) ("[W]here great weakness of mind concurs with gross inadequacy of consideration, or circumstances of suspicion, the transaction will be presumed to have been brought about by undue influence."); Endicott v. Saul, *supra* note 5 ("Even though no directly false statements are made, if there appears to be a studied effort to produce a false impression upon the mind of the party from whom land is being purchased, this, together with inadequacy of price, will be sufficient to authorize relief.") (quoting from Downing v. State, 115 P.2d 972 (Wash. 1941)).

§4.20 n.14 p.519 Add the following after the first sentence: See Kelly v. Provident Life & Accident Ins. Co., 734 F. Supp. 2d 1085 (S.D. Cal. 2010) (following *Odorizzi;* also noting that these factors are not exhaustive, and finding a triable issue when the source of unjust enrichment was bad-faith denial of coverage, instigating a

law-enforcement investigation, and suing to recover benefits paid, all while aware that the plaintiff was mentally ill). *Cf.* Nelson v. Holland, 776 N.W.2d 446 (Minn. App. 2009) ("Whether conduct resulted from undue influence involves the weighing of factors, including whether the third-party influencer had the opportunity to exercise influence; whether the third-party influence actively participated in the transaction; whether the transferor and third-party influencer had a confidential relationship; and whether there was an unreasonable or unusual disposition of property."). For another list, perhaps more applicable to wills than contracts, *see* Barbee v. Johnson, 665 S.E.2d 92, 99 (N.C. App. 2008) ("'1. Old age and physical and mental weakness of the person executing the instrument. 2. That the person signing the paper is in the home of the beneficiary and subject to his constant association and supervision. 3. That others have little or no opportunity to see him. 4. That the instrument is different and revokes a prior instrument. 5. That it is made in favor of one with whom there are no ties of blood. 6. That it disinherits the natural objects of his bounty. 7. That the beneficiary has procured its execution.' ") (quoting from Hardee v. Hardee, 309 S.E.2d 243 (N.C. 1983)).

§4.21 MODIFICATION AND THE PRE-EXISTING DUTY RULE

§4.21 n.2 p.521 Add the following at the end: Because the legal duty rule applies only to modifications of existing contracts, one way to avoid its strictures is to show that the purported modification is actually just part of the original contract and thus that the original consideration does double duty. Of course, this is difficult to apply to secondary agreements remote in time from the original agreement. *See* Hall v. Perry, 211 P.3d 489 (Wyo. 2009) (treating release of liability as "an addendum to the original contract" to outfit the plaintiff for a mule deer hunt, so it "did not require additional consideration").

§4.21 n.4 p.522 Add the following after the citation to **Threedy**: amplified in Threedy, Labor Disputes in Contract Law: The Past and Present of *Alaska Packers' Ass'n v. Domenico*, 10 Tex. Wesleyan L. Rev. 65 (2003).

§4.21 n.4 p.522 Add the following to the list after **"Accord"**: Schneir v. State, 43 So. 3d 135 (Fla. App. 2010) (revised plea agreement unenforceable where defendant's promise to testify truthfully at a trial was present in the prior contract as well); Stefano Arts v. Sui, 690 S.E.2d 197 (Ga. App. 2010) (promise to cooperate in the performance of existing contract unsupported by consideration); Emigrant Mktg. Co. v. Chicago Fin. Servs., 898 N.E.2d 1069 (Ill. App. 2007) (New York law: where independent contractor hired at will, consideration for modification of contract in favor of employer is "the continued relationship between the parties"); Hinkel v. Sataria Distrib. & Packaging, 920 N.E.2d 766 (Ind. App. 2010) (severance package promised after execution of employment contract; continued work under original contract not consideration because the worker "had assumed those duties and employment obligations as consideration for the original agreement").

§4.21 n.4 p.522 Add the following at the end: The legal duty rule may also render attempts to change an employee's status unenforceable. Mathis v. Brown & Brown of S.C., 698 S.E.2d 773 (S.C. 2010) (employee originally under term contract, but later agreement provided for at-will employment; held that "[a]ny subsequent agreement must be supported by consideration and [the employer] has shown no separate consideration to support the Employment Agreement," so the later agreement was unenforceable and the employee remained on a term contract). For more on modification in the context of employment, see §2.10b *supra*.

§4.21 n.5 p.522 Add the following at the end: The preexisting duty rule for the sale of goods was, however, eliminated by the enactment of Article Two of the UCC. UCC §2-209(1); see §4.22 *infra*.

§4.21 n.7 p.523 Add the following to the list after **"Accord"***:* Brodeur v. Claremont Sch. Dist., 626 F. Supp. 2d 195 (D.N.H. 2009) (student handbook for public high school not a contract supported by consideration; "Given the compulsory nature of [the student's] attendance . . . [her] attendance, or continued attendance, at [the school] could not have furnished the consideration necessary to make the handbook a contract"); Hooks v. State, 668 So. 2d 718 (Ga. 2008) (sentencing agreement illusory where the criminal "received only that to which he was already entitled as a matter of law" — here, a promise to seek sentences that turned out to be "the most severe punishment possible"); Jankowski v. Monclova-Maumee-Toledo Joint Econ. Dev. Zone Bd. of Dirs., 924 N.E.2d 932 (Ohio App. 2010) ("Because the contract between the township and the JEDZ is premised on the consideration of the township performing services that it is already legally obligated to provide, the contract fails for want of consideration.").

§4.21 n.8 p.523 Add the following to the list after **"Cf."***:* *In re* Marriage of Dargan, 13 Cal. Rptr. 3d 522 (Ct. App. 2004) (where husband's "sole consideration . . . was his promise to refrain from using illegal drugs, a crime," it was not consideration for post-marital agreement).

§4.21 n.12 p.524 Add the following after the first sentence: See Cent. Ceilings v. Nat'l Amusements, 873 N.E.2d 754 (Mass. App. 2007) ("Central's bargained-for promise to perform rather than repudiate any contractual obligation to Old Colony was sufficient consideration to support National's agreement to pay for Central's work.").

§4.21 n.15 p.525 Add the following to the list in the second paragraph: Harley v. Indian Spring Land Co., 3 A.3d 992 (Conn. App. 2010) (extension of deadlines in land sales contract supported by consideration, because seller was able to retain the deposit for that extended period); Harris v. A.G. Edwards & Sons, 273 S.W.3d 540 (Mo. App. 2008) (arbitration agreement added ability for arbitrators to choose venue and consent to jurisdiction for enforcing judgment; "The consideration here may be slight, but it is still present.").

§4.21 n.15 p.525 Add the following at the end of the second paragraph: For a bizarrely narrow reading of this exception, *see* Coral Reef Drive Land Dev. v. Duke Realty Ltd. P'ship, 45 So. 3d 897 (Fla. App. 2010) (developer's agreement not to refinance or sell property subject to an option held by the mortgagee in exchange for a promise to exercise the option not supported by consideration, because "there is no evidence whatsoever that Coral Reef ever attempted to refinance or sell the property, much less that it could have done so"). As the dissent properly points out, forbearance qualifies as consideration, and whether the developer had immediate prospects to refinance or sell the land is immaterial: it had the legal right to do so, it gave that right up, and that right is something that might plausibly have been sought by the mortgagee/option-holder in exchange for its own promise.

§4.22 REFORM OF THE RULE

§4.22 n.3 p.528 In the fourth paragraph, add the following to the list after **"See generally"***:* Note, Terms Subject to Change: Assent and Unconscionability in Contracts that Contemplate Amendment, 31 Cardozo L. Rev. 545 (2009).

§4.22 n.4 p.529 Add the following after the citation to **Quigley***:* and followed in Margeson v. Artis, 776 N.W.2d 652 (Iowa 2009) (proposed modification of financing terms in contract to sell business not supported by consideration where only the buyer's performance was modified; discussing Restatement Second §89 but not addressing whether it might be used in this case); Zhang v. Dist. Ct., 103 P.3d 20 (Nev. 2004) (finding no consideration merely in rescission followed by a simultaneous new agreement).

§4.22 n.4 p.529 Add the following to the list after **"Accord"***:* United States v. Novosel, 481 F.3d 1288 (10th Cir. 2007) (referring to §89 as "[a] well-established exception to the preexisting duty rule"); Guesthouse Int'l v. Shoney's N. Am. Corp., 330 S.W.3d 166 (Tenn. Ct. App. 2010) (applying Restatement Second §89; giving effect to modification of hotel license

agreement in order to allow non-franchisor restaurants when chain had closed more than half of franchise restaurants).

§4.22 n.6 p.529 Add the following to the list in the first sentence: Mont. Code Ann. §28-1-1403.

§4.22 n.6 p.529 Add the following after the first sentence: *See* Adell Broad. Corp. v. Apex Media Sales, 708 N.W.2d 778 (Mich. App. 2005) (construing Mich. Comp. Laws §566.1); Mungas v. Great Falls Clinic, 221 P.3d 1230 (Mont. 2009) (construing Mont. Code Ann. §28-1-1403).

§4.22 n.9 p.530 Add the following at the end of the fourth paragraph: *Cf.* State Street Bank & Trust Co. v. Inversiones Errazuriz Limitada, 246 F. Supp. 2d 231 (S.D.N.Y. 2002) ("Nor does the covenant apply to settlement negotiations, extensions, or modifications of the existing contract."); Copeland v. Baskin Robbins U.S.A., 117 Cal. Rptr. 2d 875 (Ct. App. 2002) ("When two parties under no compulsion to do so engage in negotiations to form or modify a contract, neither party has any obligation to continue negotiating or to negotiate in good faith.").

§4.22 n.18 p.532 Add the following at the end of the first paragraph: One recent decision has affirmed the availability of damages for a failure to negotiate modifications in good faith. Rand-Whitney Containerboard Ltd. P'ship v. Town of Montville, 289 F. Supp. 2d 62 (D. Conn. 2003). *Cf.* Morton v. Allstate Ins. Co., 58 F. Supp. 2d 325 (D. Vt. 1999) ("If a modification of [the contract] is fraudulently obtained, the aggrieved party may have a claim for breach of the covenant [of good faith and fair dealing], as well as a fraud claim.").

§4.22 n.19 p.533 Add the following at the beginning of the note: *Cf.* Copeland v. Baskin Robbins U.S.A., *supra* note 9 ("The appropriate remedy for a breach of a contract to negotiate is not damages for the injured party's lost expectations under the prospective contract but damages caused by the injured party's reliance on the agreement to negotiate.").

§4.23 CLAIMS SETTLEMENTS

§4.23 n.1 p.533 ***Insert second paragraph:*** The venue provision in a settlement agreement has been found to constitute a waiver of sovereign immunity, permitting a federal court to exercise supplemental jurisdiction to enforce the agreement. Pettigrew v. Oklahoma, 722 F.3d 1209 (W.D. Okla. 2013).

§4.23 n.3 p.534 ***In the first paragraph, add the following after the first sentence:*** *Accord:* Petty v. Citibank (S.D.) N.A., 218 S.W.3d 242 (Tex. Civ. App. 2007) (partial payment of liquidated credit card debt by customer not consideration for an accord and satisfaction).

§4.23 n.3 p.534 ***Add the following at the end of the first paragraph:*** *See generally* O'Sullivan, In Defence of *Foakes v. Beer*, 55 Cambridge L.J. 219 (1996).

§4.23 n.5 p.534 ***Add the following at the end:*** though detriment may arise from the lessee's reliance on a lower rent charge, and thus improved cash flow for other activities. *But cf.* Barinaga v. JP Morgan Chase & Co., 749 F. Supp. 2d 1164 (D. Or. 2010) ("Barinaga's payment of amounts already due under the Loan is not sufficient consideration to support the enforcement of the alleged oral agreement to permanently modify the terms of the Loan."); Dennis v. First Nat'l Bank, 668 S.E.2d 479 (Ga. App. 2008) (suit for fraud: "The alleged oral promise of First National to release appellants' debt in return for less than the amount owed on the renewed note was without consideration, and, therefore, was unenforceable. As such, appellants could not reasonably rely upon that promise, and summary judgment thus was appropriate on appellants' fraud claim."). *See generally* Pearce, *Foakes v. Beer* and Promissory Estoppel: A Step Too Far, 19 King's L.J. 630 (2008). Another approach is to divide the contract into fully performed parts and executory parts, only the latter of which could be rendered unenforceable by the legal duty rule. Double H Housing Corp. v. David, 947 A.2d 38 (D.C. 2008) (treating each lowered payment under a periodic tenancy in a month-to-month lease as an accord and satisfaction).

§4.23 n.7 p.535 Add the following at the end: For an example of a plain, not to say rigid application of the rule of *Foakes v. Beer, see* Lamb v. Fulton-DeKalb Hosp. Auth., 677 S.E.2d 328 (Ga. App. 2009) (agreement to settle disputed hospital bill for less than the amount concededly due unsupported by consideration and thus unenforceable).

§4.23 n.13 p.536 Add the following to the list after "Accord": Petty v. Citibank (S.D.) N.A., *supra* note 3 ("no evidence or allegation that the amount of the debt . . . was unliquidated or subject to a bona fide dispute").

§4.23 n.16 p.537 In the first paragraph, add the following to the list after "Accord": Hoerstman Gen. Contracting v. Hahn, 711 N.W.2d 340 (Mich. 2006) ("Defendants' concession of part of the debt has no effect on the question whether the claim was liquidated.").

§4.23 n.16 p.537 In the second paragraph, add the following to the list in the second sentence: Matlack Coal & Iron Corp. v. N.Y. Quebrancho Extract Co., 30 F.2d 275 (2d Cir. 1929) (L. Hand, J.) ("when there are two claims arising upon separate promises, though in the same contract, payment of the amount concededly due upon one will not be a good consideration for the release of damages upon breach of the other"); Brucato v. Ezenia! Inc., 351 F. Supp. 2d 464 (E.D. Va. 2004) ("where . . . a debtor offers payment for one or more undisputed claims such payment does not operate to discharge by accord and satisfaction other explicitly disputed claims arising out of separate and distinct transactions") Restatement Second §74 cmt. c.

§4.23 n.16 p.537 Add the following at the end: There is a curious counterpart to accord and satisfaction when the payment is made, not in a conscious attempt to resolve a dispute, but in response to knowledge of the material facts or ignorance of the law. Under the *voluntary payment doctrine*, payments of such claims "are deemed voluntary and cannot be recovered . . ." absent fraud, duress, or compulsion. Ga. Code Ann. §13-1-13; *see also* Miga v. Jensen, 299 S.W.3d 98 (Tex. 2009) (doctrine exists to prevent recipient from thinking the matter closed and then have the other party seek return of the payment). *See generally* §9.4 *infra*. The doctrine has its limits, most notably for the payment of judgments during the pendency of appeal and when payment is made because of a mistake of fact. Miga v. Jensen, *supra*; *see also* Restatement (Third) of Restitution and Unjust Enrichment §18 cmt. c (T.D. No. 1, 2001). Its basic contradiction of the principles of unjust enrichment has narrowed its scope in practice. *See* Ellison v. Southstar Energy Servs., 691 S.E.2d 203 (Ga. 2010) (payments made to gas company not subject to voluntary payments doctrine because of statutory private right of action). Nevertheless, the doctrine persists, and may still entrap the incautious party too accustomed to the norms of accord and satisfaction. *Cf.* S. Mut. Church Ins. Co. v. ARS Mech., 703 S.E.2d 363 (Ga. App. 2010) (insurer acquires no right of subrogation merely because it pays its insured, if it was not legally obliged to do so).

§4.23a SETTLEMENT BY CHECK

§4.23a n.3 p.538 Add the following after the first sentence: *Accord:* Mossing v. Demlow Prods., 782 N.W.2d 780 (Mich. App. 2010) (letter from claimant's attorney stated that "The memo on the check also indicated that it was a final payment. As you know, the issue of future payment is in dispute in this matter and therefore, the check is being cashed with the understanding that it is not, in fact, a final payment . . ."; accord and satisfaction effective). The claimant's strategy in *Mossing* is precisely what UCC §3-311 was designed to prevent, which makes the claimant's letter more than a little ill-advised.

***§4.23a n.4 p.538 Add the following to the list after* "But cf.":** Springwell Corp. v. Falcon Drilling Co., 16 F. Supp. 2d 300 (S.D.N.Y. 1998) (Sotomayor, J.; "The mere crossing out of the words 'annual retainer' and insertion of the words 'Falcon-Def Fin costs-DLJ' on the return invoice falls far short of the type of 'unequivocal expression' required to establish an accord and satisfaction."); Double H Housing Corp. v. David, 947 A.2d 38 (D.C. 2008) (besides notation on check, "other manners of conveying the debtor's intent in tendering the check may be a sufficient basis for application of the doctrine," so long as "the debtor 'must intend the amount paid as a liquidation of [the creditor's] claim, and the [creditor] in accepting it must understand that it is so intended.' ") (quoting Andrews v. Haller, 32 App. D.C. 398 (D.C. Cir. 1909)); United Am. Ins. Co. v. Merrill, 978 So. 2d 613 (Miss. 2007) (disputed insurance claim: "Neither the letter from United, nor the refund check, establish that the check was in satisfaction of the claim," so the insured "neither believed nor understood that cashing the check would serve as release or waiver of her claim" and thus cashing it was not an accord and satisfaction).

§4.23a n.6 p.539 Add the following to the list after **"But see"***:* Auto Glass Exp. v. Hanover Ins. Co., 912 A.2d 513 (Conn. App. 2006) (explanation of benefits form accompanying checks stated "FAIR AND REASONABLE PAYMENT" and "REASONABLE & CUSTOMARY ADJ."; failed "to state that the payment is full and final").

§4.23a n.8 p.540 Add the following after the citation to **Webb***:* *Ex parte* Meztista, 845 So. 2d 795 (Ala. 2001) ("parties are sophisticated business people, who were aware of their rights and of the nature of their dispute").

§4.23a n.8 p.540 Add the following at the end: For an interesting treatment of good faith in a transaction between an unsophisticated customer and a bank, see both the majority and dissenting opinions in Johnston v. First Union Nat'l Bank, 624 S.E.2d 10 (Va. 2006).

§4.23a n.9 p.540 Add the following after citation to **Jones***:* distinguished by Auto Glass Exp. v. Hanover Ins. Co., *supra* note 6 (good faith when "in *every* case the payment was less than the amount the plaintiffs had submitted").

§4.23a n.12 p.540 Add the following at the end: See IFC Cred. Corp. v. Bulk Petrol. Corp., 403 F.3d 869 (7th Cir. 2005) (though check sent to one other than designated agent, "notice was given to the correct party within a reasonable time before collection of the instrument," so accord and satisfaction valid).

§4.23a n.13 p.541 Add the following to the list in the first sentence: IFC Cred. Corp. v. Bulk Petrol. Corp., *supra* note 12 ("retention of a tender conspicuously identified as an accord and satisfaction effectively dooms a claimant's case"); MKL Pre-Press Elecs./MKL Computer Media Supplies v. La Crosse Litho Supply, 840 N.E.2d 687 (Ill. App. 2005) ("the act of knowingly accepting and depositing a check upon which conditional language has been added indicates the existence of an accord and satisfaction").

§4.23a n.13 p.541 Add the following at the end of the first paragraph: In Ass'n Res. v. Wall, 2 A.3d 873 (Conn. 2010), the court essentially ignored the teaching of *County Fire Door Corp.* regarding the acts effective to accept a tendered payment. There an employee and an employer disputed the size of a bonus due the employee. The employer offered to pay part of the sum to resolve the dispute and keep open the possibility of continued employment; otherwise, the employer would pay the full bonus requested and not renew the employee's contract. The employee accepted the smaller payment, but stated that he "in no way agreed to that being the full satisfaction of his claim," and took the payment because he needed cash. The court inexplicably bought this argument and held that there was no satisfaction. This completely misses the point of accord and satisfaction. Who cares whether the employee made mental reservations when he cashed the check? Nor is his need for money germane to accord and satisfaction; insofar as it provides a defense, that would fall under duress, at least if the employee's need arose from the bad-faith behavior of the employer. It is hard to explain the court's ruling as a principled statement of law. Certainly the court did not state that it was overruling *County Fire Door*, which it did not even seek to distinguish. One may hope that this decision will be treated as the *lusus naturae* it assuredly is.

§4.23a n.14 p.541 Add the following to the list after "See": Am. Nat'l Prop. & Cas. Co. v. Nersesian, 689 N.W.2d 922 (Wis. App. 2004) (no acceptance where the claimants chose not to return the required release and within a month notified the debtor that they "were putting the settlement 'on hold' ").

§4.23a n.16 p.541 Add the following to the list in the first sentence: Alpine Haven Prop. Owners Ass'n v. Deptula, 830 A.2d 78 (Vt. 2003) (homeowner who had litigated claim several times and lost "no longer was raising a 'bona fide dispute' ").

§4.23a n.16 p.541 Add the following at the end: For an unusual illustration of this issue, *see* Milton M. Cooke Co. v. 1st Bank & Trust, 290 S.W.3d 297 (Tex. Civ. App. 2009) (debtor sought to offset amount paid by bank on forged checks against its debts by sending checks in full satisfaction of those debts that set off the amount lost via forgery; held that UCC §3-311(c) did not apply because it may be invoked only in favor of "a person against whom a claim is asserted," and no claim had been asserted against the debtor, which was current on its debts). This decision also uses UCC §1-302 to allow the parties to contract around UCC §3-311, in this case by designating a particular office as the recipient for all disputed payments.

One instance where the parties need not have a bona fide dispute comes with partial payment in lieu of filing bankruptcy, provided the threat of filing bankruptcy is not manufactured for the purpose of accomplishing an accord and satisfaction. This falls within the catch-all exception of comment 4. Citibank (S.D.) v. Perz, 947 N.E.2d 191 (Ohio App. 2010) ("The right of an insolvent debtor to file bankruptcy and seek a discharge of the debt is a thing of significant value, and its relinquishment is more than what the debtor was already bound to do."; thorough discussion of exception).

§4.23a n.18 p.542 Add the following to the list in the first sentence: Hoerstman Gen. Contracting v. Hahn, 711 N.W.2d 340 (Mich. 2006) (crossing out language on check on attorney's advice ineffective; §3-311 "contains no exception for a mistaken understanding of the law"); Case Funding Network v. Anglo-Dutch Petroleum Int'l, 264 S.W.3d 38 (Tex. Civ. App. 2007) ("With all rights reserved against all Parties and under protest," when inscribed on check, ineffective to prevent accord and satisfaction).

§4.24 DISCHARGE SUPPORTED BY CONSIDERATION

§4.24 n.3 p.544 Add the following to the list after **"See also"***:* Margeson v. Artis, 776 N.W.2d 652 (Iowa 2009) (dictum: "When a rescission is followed by a subsequent contract, the consideration for the two contracts can be identical."); Haskell v. Versyss Liquidating Trust, 815 N.E.2d 225 (Mass. App. 2004) (quoting this section of the treatise).

§4.24 n.4 p.544 Add the following to the list after **"See"***:* Power-Tek Solutions Servs. v. Techlink, Inc., 403 F.3d 353 (6th Cir. 2005) (following §280); K & K Recycling v. Alaska Gold Co., 80 P.3d 702 (Alaska 2003) (following §280).

§4.24 n.4 p.544 Add the following to the list after **"But see"***:* Langhoff Props. v. BP Prods. N. Am., 519 F.3d 256 (5th Cir. 2008) (Louisiana law: "novation is the extinguishment of an existing obligation by the substitution of a new one" (quoting La. Civ. Code art. 1879)); Fanucchi & Limi Farms v. United Agri Prods., 414 F.3d 1075 (9th Cir. 2005) (novation includes "the substitution of a new debtor or new creditor" or "the substitution of a new obligation between the same parties"); Cincinnati Ins. Co. v. Leighton, 403 F.3d 879 (7th Cir. 2005) ("A novation is the substitution of a new obligation for an existing one, which is thereby extinguished."); Lumsden v. Williams, 704 S.E.2d 458 (Ga. App. 2010) ("an amendment does not automatically result in a novation of a prior contract"); Wells REIT II — 80 Park Plaza v. Dir., Div. of Taxation, 999 A.2d 489 (N.J. Super. App. Div. 2010) ("a novation substitutes a new contract and extinguishes the old one"); Med. Staffing Network v. Ridgway, 670 S.E.2d 321 (N.C. App. 2009) (among the methods of discharge is "a novation, which is the substitution of a new contract"); Weaver v. Am. Power Conversion Corp., 863 A.2d 193 (R.I. 2004) (novation, substituted contract, and accord and satisfaction "essentially intertwined," so court will "overlook[] fine common law distinctions"); *In re* Bath Junkie Franchise, 246 S.W.3d 356 (Tex. Civ. App. 2008) ("Novation occurs if a contract evidences an intention to relinquish and extinguish pre-existing claims and rights of action; in lieu of the old obligation, a party accepts the promise of

performance of the new obligation instead of the performance itself."). *Cf.* Lauderdale v. Eugene Water & Elec. Bd., 177 P.3d 13 (Or. App. 2008) ("An accord and satisfaction is a type of executed, substituted contract which extinguishes a previous obligation."). This inchoate use of very distinct terms may thus lead to considerable confusion. Rather than rely upon one of these terms to convey meaning, the prudent drafter would instead make clear the actions and consequences; once those are in place, the label is of modest import.

§4.24 n.5 p.545 Add the following at the end: *Cf.* Utica Mut. Ins. Co. v. Vigo Coal Co., 393 F.3d 707 (7th Cir. 2004) ("proof of a novation must be 'clear and definite' or 'clear and satisfactory' or words to that effect"). *But cf.* Fitness Experience v. TFC Fitness Equip., 355 F. Supp. 2d 877 (N.D. Ohio 2004) (novation not implied from continued employment after corporate succession and assignment of employment contract); *In re* Bath Junkie Franchise, *supra* note 4 ("It must clearly appear that the parties intended a novation; novation is never presumed."). Whether an agreement is a modification, a substituted agreement, or a novation depends principally on the intent of the parties, so the issue is one of fact for the jury. Wells REIT II — 80 Park Plaza v. Dir., Div. of Taxation, 999 A.2d 489 (N.J. Super. App. Div. 2010).

§4.24 n.9 p.546 Add the following after the fourth sentence: The promise or performance must qualify as consideration for the accord to have effect. Barinaga v. JP Morgan Chase & Co., 749 F. Supp. 2d 1164 (D. Or. 2010) (agreement merely to pay a portion of an acknowledged debt not consideration for an accord); Barnett v. Quinn, 979 So. 2d 816 (Ala. App. 2007) (no accord where alleged consideration consists entirely of performing actions already required by contract); Shore v. Peterson, 204 P.3d 1114 (Idaho 2009) (no requirement of a bona fide dispute, as is necessary for accord and satisfaction by check, as long as there is consideration). *Cf.* Riley v. Pierson, 13 A.3d 732 (Conn. Super. 2009) ("If the defendants were acting in good faith when making their demand, then the plaintiff received consideration for his payment"), *aff'd*, 12 A.3d 581 (Conn. App. 2011) ("we adopt [the trial court's] decision as a statement of the facts and the applicable law on these issues"); Lumsden v. Williams, 704 S.E.2d 458

(Ga. App. 2010) ("An accord and satisfaction also requires that parties have a bona fide dispute prior to the tender of any amount less than that due under their contract."). Perhaps obviously, an accord and satisfaction requires that the debtor have conveyed to the creditor that the payment tendered is in full satisfaction of a particular debt; simply making the payment is inadequate, whatever the debtor's subjective intent might have been. *In re* Marriage of Thompson, 48 Cal. Rptr. 2d 721 (Ct. App. 1996); Coburn v. Auto-Owners Ins. Co., 938 N.E.2d 400 (Ohio App. 2010) (genuine issue of material fact where insurer presented checks to injured party before the injured party had made a claim against the insurer).

§4.24 n.10 p.547 Add the following after the first sentence: *Accord:* Am. Seating Co. v. Kawahara Design, 575 F. Supp. 2d 822 (W.D. Mich. 2008) (following Restatement Second 281(2), so that if the obligor breaches the accord, the obligee may choose to enforce either the accord or the original obligation; if the former, however, the obligee "must refund any consideration that it has received from the other party").

§4.24 n.12 p.547 Add the following to the list in the first sentence: Fanucchi & Limi Farms v. United Agri Prods., *supra* note 4 (to tell whether an agreement is a substituted agreement, "California courts seek to determine the parties' intent," starting with "the substance of the change or changes between the old and new agreements" and looking as well to "the conduct of the parties"). Other questions arise where the agreements contain conflicting provisions as to arbitrability of claims. *Compare* Dasher v. RBC Bank, 745 F.3d 1111 (11th Cir. 2014) (no Federal Arbitration Act presumption of arbitrability where dispute is over whether an arbitration agreement has been superseded by subsequent agreement) with Terminix Int'l Co. v. Palmer Ranch Ltd. P'ship, 432 F.3d 1327, 1332 (11th Cir. 2005) and U.S. Nutraceuticals LLC v. Cyanotech Corp., 769 F.3d 1308 (11th Cir. 2014) (although subsequent contract contained clear carve-out from arbitration for type of dispute at issue, whether earlier contract should govern this dispute is question for the arbitrator); *see also* Sharpe v. AmeriPlan Corp., 769 F.3d 909 (5th Cir. 2014) (holding that, for three of the four plaintiffs, the earlier agreement, requiring mediation then litigation rather than arbitration, was not effectively superseded because provisions for amendments to the original agreements were not followed).

§4.24 n.12 p.547 Add the following at the end of the first sentence: *See* Weaver, *supra* note 4; Ford v. Am. Express Fin. Advisors, 98 P.3d 15 (Utah 2004). *Cf.* Baylor Health Care Sys. v. Employers Reins. Corp., 492 F.3d 318 (5th Cir. 2007) (Texas law; "to confect an accord and satisfaction, parties must agree to a discharge of existing obligations in terms that are 'plain, definite, certain, clear, full, explicit, not susceptible of any other interpretation, and accompanied by acts and declarations that [the parties are] sure to understand.' ") (quoting Christian v. Univ. Fed. Sav. Ass'n, 792 S.W.2d 533, 534 (Tex. Civ. App. 1990)).

§4.24 n.13 p.548 Add the following to the list after* "See also"*: Rosen v. Ascentry Techs., 177 P.3d 765 (Wash. App. 2008) ("To overcome the presumption that a settlement agreement is an executory accord [rather than a substituted contract], the parties' intent to do so must be clear.").

§4.24 p.548 Add the following at the end of the third sentence of the second paragraph: . . . relation of debtor and creditor.[13a]

[13a] Ryan Graphics v. Bailin, 833 N.Y.S.2d 448 (App. Div. 2007) (account stated "cannot be used to create liability where none otherwise exists").

§4.24 n.14 p.549 Add the following at the end: *Accord:* Richburg v. Palisades Collection, 247 F.R.D. 457 (E.D. Pa. 2008) ("This final tally, once assented to, becomes the 'account stated,' and any further cause of action is based on this 'account stated' rather than on any of the underlying transactions.").

§4.24 n.15 p.549 Add the following at the end: *Accord:* Assoc'd Petroleum Prods. v. N.W. Cascade, 203 P.3d 1077 (Wash. App. 2009) (following Restatement Second). As with other promises, the standard contract defenses apply to accounts stated. Restatement Second §282 cmt. c; Assoc'd Petroleum Prods. v. N.W. Cascade, *supra* (unilateral mistake and fraudulent concealment).

§4.24 n.17 p.549 Add the following to the list after **"See also"***:* Brad Foot Gear Works v. Delta Brands, 332 F. Supp. 2d 1123 (N.D. Ill. 2004) (letter from buyer's director of business operations that acknowledged the amount of liability was an account stated).

§4.24 n.18 p.549 Add the following to the list after **"Accord"***:* Delta Consulting Grp. v. R. Randle Constr., 554 F.3d 1133 (7th Cir. 2009) (Illinois law; paid invoices and acknowledged the amount owed, with objections only after more than a year, so invoices became account stated); EMI Music Mktg. v. Avatar Records, 317 F. Supp. 2d 412 (S.D.N.Y. 2004) (failure to object to account statements over three-year span, coupled with repeated acknowledgments of the amounts owed, bound the debtor); Credit One v. Head, 977 A.2d 767 (Conn. App. 2009) (retention of statements for up to six years was for an unreasonable time, "which, in an action that was based on account stated, is prima facie evidence of the correctness of the account"); Mintz & Gold v. Hart, 852 N.Y.S.2d 248 (App. Div. 2008) (where defendant "had not only received and retained, without objection, invoices for legal services . . . but also made partial payments on the invoices" account stated is suitable cause of action); Paul, Weiss, Rifkind, Wharton & Garrison v. Koons, 780 N.Y.S.2d 710 (Sup. Ct. 2004) (where "[d]efendant never objected to the bills, acknowledged in writing that they were fair and reasonable, and explicitly promised to pay them," and did pay them in part, account stated doctrine prevails over claim that fees charged were unethically high).

§4.24 n.18 p.549 Add the following to the list after **"But cf."***:* Whitaker v. J R Produce Corp. (*In re* Gulf N. Transp.), 340 B.R. 111 (Bankr. M.D. Fla. 2006) ("A party's failure to object, standing alone, is not always proof of liability on the part of the defendant."); Eagle Maint. Servs. v. D.C. Contract Appeals Bd., 893 A.2d 569 (D.C. 2006) (no assent to correctness of balance, because party sought additional costs; consequently, account stated inapplicable); M & A Constr. Corp. v. McTague, 800 N.Y.S.2d 235 (App. Div. 2005) ("Where either no account has been presented or there is any dispute regarding the correctness of the account, the cause of action fails."); Morrison Cohen Singer

& Weinstein v. Brophy, 798 N.Y.S.2d 379 (App. Div. 2005) (where law firm sent invoices "years after services were rendered" in "clear violation of the billing procedure described in the retainer agreement," and could not even establish that the invoices were properly addressed and mailed, "defendant's claimed silence cannot be interpreted as an unequivocal assent to the balance stated").

§4.24 n.21 p.550 Add the following to the list after* "See also"*: Bischoff v. Cook, 185 P.3d 902 (Haw. App. 2008) (extensive discussion of history and nature of rescission); Zuba v. Pawtucket Credit Union, 941 A.2d 167 (R.I. 2008) (adopting definition; quotes treatise).

§4.24 n.22 p.550 Add the following to the list after* "Accord"*: O'Brien & Gere Technical Servs. v. Fru-Con/Fluor Daniel Joint Venture, 380 F.3d 447 (8th Cir. 2004) (abandonment inferred from the parties' inability to keep up with their construction schedule, agree on the scope of the work to be performed, or agree on the pricing for change work); Coburn v. Auto-Owners Ins. Co., 938 N.E.2d 400 (Ohio App. 2010) (insurer's offer of additional payments for settled insurance claim potentially abandonment of existing release); Zuba v. Pawtucket Credit Union, *supra* note 21 (execution of deed in lieu of foreclosure effectively yielded a rescission); Eldridge v. Farnsworth, 166 P.3d 639 (Utah App. 2007) (parties failed to perform obligations under real estate purchase contract, including no tender of funds or seller disclosures and a cancelled closing with no objections).

§4.24 n.24 p.551 Add the following at the end: To play one last variation on this theme, the parties may execute a *conditional release*, under which mutual releases take place "only upon the satisfaction of certain obligations"; should those obligations not be satisfied, the parties would be free to sue on the old agreement. *In re* Bath Junkie Franchise, *supra* note 4.

§4.25 DISCHARGE UNSUPPORTED BY CONSIDERATION

§4.25 n.13 p.554 Add the following at the end: *Cf.* Ohio Rev. Code §1303.44 ("no consideration is necessary for an instrument or obligation thereon given in payment of or as security for an antecedent obligation of any kind"); Konica Minolta Bus. Solutions v. Allied Office Prods., 724 F. Supp. 2d 861 (S.D. Ohio 2010) (applying statute, so that pre-existing debt was consideration for later promissory note).

§4.26 STANDARDIZED AGREEMENTS

§4.26 n.2 p.557 Add the following after the first sentence: For a selection of recent scholarship, *see* Symposium, "Boilerplate": Foundations of Market Contracts Symposium, 104 Mich. L. Rev. 821 (2006). *See generally* Becher & Unger-Aviram, The Law of Standard Form Contracts: Misguided Intuitions and Suggestions for Reconstruction, 8 DePaul Bus. & Com. L.J. 199 (2010).

§4.26 n.3 p.557 Add the following at the end: *See also* Carbajal v. H & R Block Tax Servs., 372 F.3d 903 (7th Cir. 2004) (Easterbrook, J.; "Forms reduce transactions costs and benefit consumers because, in competition, reductions in the cost of doing business show up as lower prices . . ."), followed in Taylor Bldg. Corp. of Am. v. Benfield, 884 N.E.2d 12 (Ohio 2008). *See generally* Fairfield, The Cost of Consent: Optimal Standardization in the Law of Contract, 58 Emory L.J. 1401 (2009).

§4.26 p.558 Add the following at the end of the carryover sentence: . . . a form slanted in its favor.[3a]

[3a] *But see* Marotta-Wurgler, Competition and the Quality of Standard Form Contract: The Case of Software License Agreements, 5 J. Empirical Legal Stud. 447 (2008) (negative relation between difficulty of access by buyers and tilting of terms toward sellers).

§4.26 n.7 p.558 ***Add the following at the end:*** *See generally* Barnes, Rediscovering Subjectivity in Contracts: Adhesion and Unconscionability, 66 La. L. Rev. 123 (2005); Eigen, The Devil is in the Details: The Interrelationship Among Citizenship, Rule of Law and Form-Adhesive Contracts, 41 Conn. L. Rev. 381 (2008); Patterson, Standardization of Standard-Form Contracts: Competition and Contract Implications, 52 Wm. & Mary L. Rev. 327 (2010); Smith, Reforming the Law of Adhesion Contracts: A Judicial Response to the Subprime Mortgage Crisis, 14 Lewis & Clark L. Rev. 1035 (2010); Note, Disciplining Standard Form Contract Terms Through Online Information Flows: An Empirical Study, 85 N.Y.U.L. Rev. 1618 (2010).

§4.26 n.8 p.559 ***Add the following to the list after "Accord":*** W.K. v. Farrell, 853 N.E.2d 728 (Ohio App. 2006) ("If a person can read and is not prevented from reading what he signs, then he alone is responsible for his omission to read what he signs."); Vera v. North Star Dodge Sales, 989 S.W.2d 13 (Tex. Civ. App. 1998) ("[a]bsent proof of mental incapacity, a person who signs a contract is presumed to have read and understood the contract, unless he was prevented from doing so by trick or artifice"), followed in *In re* Big 8 Food Stores, 166 S.W.3d 869 (Tex. Civ. App. 2005) but distinguished by Prevot v. Phillips Petroleum Co., 133 F. Supp. 2d 937 (S.D. Tex. 2001) ("the Texas Supreme Court would hold that while illiteracy of the person making a contract does not by itself make the contract unconscionable, when . . . there is also a language barrier and the person was pressured into signing the agreement quickly, the Court would be well within its discretion to find the contract to be procedurally unconscionable. Moreover, this is not a case where a party seeking to avoid arbitration simply claims not to have read the contract, though having had the opportunity and ability to do so."); Polzin v. Appleway Equip. Leasing, 191 P.3d 476 (Mont. 2008) ("Failure to read and understand a clear and unambiguous agreement, absent mistake, is not a defense to its enforcement."); Herron v. Century BMW, 693 S.E.2d 394 (S.C. 2010) (plaintiffs may not "invalidate the enforceability of the arbitration agreement by claiming they did not read it"), *vacated and remanded on other grounds*, 131 S. Ct. 2872 (2011); Molina v. Scandinavian Designs, Inc., 2014 U.S. Dist. LEXIS 55863, 22 Wage & Hour Cas. 2d

(BNA) 979 (N.D. Cal. Apr. 21, 2014) ("even if Molina could read very little English, Molina's signature on the Arbitration Agreement manifests his assent to its terms, binding him to the contract.").

§4.26 n.8 p.559 Add the following to the list after **"But cf."***:* Hennig v. Ahearn, 601 N.W.2d 14 (Wis. App. 1999) (whether employer "had a duty to point out his last-minute alteration" of executive compensation agreement by insertion of nine words "in the middle of a paragraph-long, multi-part definition" was jury question).

§4.26 n.9 p.559 Add the following to the list after **"Accord"***:* Hartland Computer Leasing Corp. v. The Ins. Man, 770 S.W.2d 525 (Mo. App. 1989) (standard form contracts are "natural concomitant of our mass production — mass consumer society" and "rule automatically invalidating adhesion contracts would be completely unworkable"), followed in Greenpoint Credit, L.L.C. v. Reynolds, 151 S.W.3d 868 (Mo. Ct. App. 2004) (enforcing arbitration clause in form contract as being within the reasonable expectations of the contracting parties); Hinkal v. Pardoe, 133 A.3d 738 (Pa. Super. 2016) (rejecting claim that waiver of liability was ineffective because "the waiver language appeared on the back of the agreement, she never read or was told to read the back of the agreement, and the clause was not 'brought home' to her in a way that could suggest she was aware of the clause and its contents" because "failure to read her agreement does not render it either invalid or unenforceable," and moreover, the agreement "included an unambiguous directive not to sign before reading both sides, a clear pronouncement that the terms on both sides of the form are part of the agreement, and a straightforward statement that the agreement constitutes the entire agreement between the parties.").

§4.26 n.10 p.559 Add the following to the list after **"Accord"***:* Morales v. Sun Constructors, 541 F.3d 218 (3d Cir. 2008) ("In the absence of fraud, the fact that an offeree cannot read, write, speak, or understand the English language is immaterial to whether an English-language agreement the offeree executes is enforceable."); Wash. Mut. Fin. Grp. v. Bailey, 364 F.3d

260 (5th Cir. 2004) ("an individual's inability to understand a contract because of his or her illiteracy is not a sufficient basis for concluding that a contract is unenforceable"), followed in Am. Gen. Fin. Servs. v. Griffin, 327 F. Supp. 2d 678 (N.D. Miss. 2004) (blindness) and Bolden v. Ky. Fin. Co., 316 F. Supp. 2d 406 (S.D. Miss. 2004) (lack of sophistication).

§4.26 p.560 Add the following at the end of the carryover sentence: . . . they have developed several techniques.[10a]

[10a] This list is hardly exhaustive; indeed, courts have used virtually every tool they can adapt to the purpose in order to invalidate or limit noxious standard forms. One common technique is waiver; a party that proceeds too far in litigation may be deemed to have waived its right to demand arbitration. Abramson v. Wildman, 964 A.2d 703 (Md. App. 2009) (among the relevant factors are whether an answer directed to the merits is filed, participation in extensive discovery (particularly using discovery tools unavailable in arbitration), the filing of suit, and the simple passage of time). Another is lack of authority, common, for example, in nursing home cases. *See* Barker v. Evangelical Lutheran Good Samaritan Soc'y, 720 F. Supp. 2d 1263 (D.N.M. 2010) (daughter lacked authority to bind father to arbitration agreement; father was third-party beneficiary of admission agreement, but not of arbitration agreement); Miss. Care Ctr. v. Hinyub, 975 So. 2d 211 (Miss. 2008) (daughter lacked power of attorney needed to bind her father when she signed admissions documents containing arbitration provisions), followed in Lujan v. Life Care Ctrs., 222 P.3d 970 (Colo. App. 2009) ("'medical treatment' in the context of a health care proxy is to be narrowly construed and does not include the authority to sign an arbitration agreement on behalf of an incapacitated patient") and in Monticello Cmty. Care Ctr. v. Estate of Martin *ex rel.* Peyton, 17 So. 3d 172 (Miss. App. 2009) (arbitration agreement followed admission agreement and thus outside third-party beneficiary relation), but distinguished in Forest Hill Nursing Ctr. v. McFarlan, 995 So. 2d 775 (Miss. App. 2008) (although no power of attorney, resident bound by arbitration agreement as third-party beneficiary, where arbitration clause integral to care agreement). Still another is lack of consideration, where the agreement is illusory because one party can alter it at will. *See* Morrow v. Hallmark Cards, 273 S.W.3d 15 (Mo. App. 2008) (Hallmark "may at its sole discretion modify or discontinue the [arbitration agreement] at any time"; in addition, continuing employment is not consideration because at-will employment is not a legally enforceable contract), rejected by Soto v. State Indus. Prods., 642 F.3d 67 (1st Cir. 2011) (rejecting argument that continued employment is not consideration for an arbitration agreement). *See also* the concurrence of Ahuja, J., in *Morrow*, which develops nicely the illusory aspect of this agreement. *But cf.* Rivera v. Am.

Gen. Fin. Servs., 242 P.3d 351 (N.M. App. 2010) (even though arbitration provision asymmetrical, each party did give up a partial right to litigate and so there was consideration), *rev'd on other grounds*, ___ P.3d ___, 2011 WL 3687624 (N.M. July 27, 2011); Hayes v. Oakridge Home, 908 N.E.2d 408 (Ohio 2009) (no lack of consideration where both parties gave up their rights to trial).

***§4.26 n.11 p.560 Add the following to the list after* "Cf.":** Woolums v. Nat'l RV, 530 F. Supp. 2d 691 (M.D. Pa. 2008) ("Adhesion contracts are not per se invalid, but courts strictly construe them against the drafting party, who holds a position of superior bargaining power and can dictate the agreement's terms."); Person v. Google, Inc., 456 F. Supp. 2d 488 (S.D.N.Y. 2006) ("Such contracts [of adhesion] require a more 'refined' scrutiny for fairness."); Huverserian v. Catalina Scuba Luv, 110 Cal. Rptr. 3d 112 (Ct. App. 2010) (broad disclaimer of liability held inapplicable because caption did not encompass the type of injury incurred); Ravetto v. Triton Thalassic Techs., 941 A.2d 309 (Conn. 2008) (finding that employee need not return advance, reasoning in part "that, because the employer generally enjoys superior bargaining power in the employment relationship, it is incumbent upon the employer to make any obligation for reimbursement explicit in the employment agreement"); Zahn v. Kroger Co. of Mich., 764 N.W.2d 207 (Mich. 2009) (interpreting indemnification clause routinely, but noting that it does so in part because "[t]hese are business entities with equal bargaining power").

§4.26 n.11 p.560 Add the following after the second sentence: *But cf.* Brockmann v. Brockmann, 938 N.E.2d 831 (Ind. App. 2010) ("Generally, when construing arbitration agreements, doubts are resolved in favor of arbitration . . . However, parties are only bound to arbitrate those issues that by clear language they have agreed to arbitrate, and arbitration agreements will not be extended by construction or implication to cover any other matters.").

The Third Circuit determined that a dispute between an insurer and a health service provider fell outside the arbitration agreement because the alleged misconduct would have given rise to a cause of action even if there were no agreement between the parties. In Cardionet, Inc. v. Cigna Health Corp., 751 F.3d 165,

169 (3d Cir. 2014), the insurer for several years had covered outpatient cardiac telemetry services ("OCT," which allows for monitoring of cardiac arrhythmias outside the hospital), but then announced in a Physician Update that it would no long do so "because it is considered [experimental, investigational, and unproven]." By its terms, the agreement required arbitration of disputes "regarding the performance or interpretation of the Agreement." *Id.* at 173. The court rejected the insurer's argument that the claims "unavoidably implicate Cigna's contractual obligation to treat as 'Covered Services' any services that participants are entitled to receive under their benefits plans." *Id.* at 175. Rather, the court held that "the adjudication of CIGNA's direct claims depends on whether the Physician Update — a document completely distinct from the Agreement — is deceptive and misleading, and whether any deceptions therein caused a cognizable injury to the Providers. The resolution of these claims does not require construction of, or even reference to, any provision in the Agreement." *Id.* The court noted that such claims may fall within the scope of arbitration agreements, but found that the language of this particular agreement was distinguishable from cases that had required arbitration of Lanham Act, tort, and trade disparagement. *Id.* at 176. In addition to these direct claims, the provider also brought a derivative claim on behalf of insured. The court concluded that those claims, too, fall outside the scope of the agreement, since the dispute was to whether the plan is obligation to pay for OCT services is governed by ERISA, not the Agreement. *Id.* at 177. Going further, the court express policy concerns with requiring a provider to arbitrate derivative claims: "[w]ere we to prevent providers that have promised to arbitrate their own claims against an insurer from bringing patients' claims in court, these providers would be less likely to accept patients' claims in exchange for services. This, in turn, would make it more difficult for patients to receive necessary services where their insurers have denied coverage." *Id.* at 178.

Arnold v. Burger King, 2015-Ohio-4485 (Ohio Ct. App. 2015) involved a mandatory arbitration agreement as a condition of employment that submitted to arbitration "any and all disputes, claims or controversies for monetary or equitable relief arising out of or relating to [Arnold's] employment" as well as "claims or controversies relating to events *outside the scope of your employment*," at ¶4 (alterations in original). The employee then brought suit, alleging she was raped by her supervisor in the Burger King bathroom during working hours, and the defendant moved to compel arbitration. The Ohio Court of Appeals noted that "[w]hile there are a number of cases on the enforceability of arbitration agreements and clauses, particularly in the consumer and employment realm, there are distinctly fewer on claims involving coworker criminal violence such as sexual assault." At ¶36. After considering a number of cases, citing Smith v. Captain D's, LLC, 963 So. 2d 1116 (Miss. 2007) (holding arbitration provision unconscionable where claim related to rape that was related to, but outside the scope of, employment), Jones v. Halliburton, 583 F.3d 228 (5th Cir. 2009) (holding that employee did not agree to arbitrate claims related to gang rape by coworkers), and Doe v. Princess Cruise Lines, Ltd., 657 F.3d 1204 (11th Cir. 2011) (holding that broadly drafted arbitration clause did not reach claims for sexual assault by coworkers because "the claims were not an immediately, foreseeable result of the employment and thus, were not within the scope of the clause"), the Ohio court held that the overarching issue was whether it was "reasonably foreseeable that the arbitration contract encompassed the conduct in question," at ¶45. The court held that it was not. The claims "exist independent of the employment relationship," at ¶65, and "ongoing verbal and physical contact culminating in sexual assault as well as retaliation, harassment, or other detrimental acts against Arnold based on the unlawful conduct is not a foreseeable result of the employment," at ¶67. The court went on to find the clause procedurally unconscionable because of the disparity in bargaining power combined with a Policy Notice it found to be misleading and inconsistent with the arbitration agreement, at ¶¶80-82, and substantively unconscionable because the agreement incorporated by reference a website that contained "a true labyrinth of information with links to rules, forms, ethics, discovery protocols, etc. There is nothing to direct an arguably unsophisticated individual through the maze of information in order to ascertain which of the multiple documents apply to pursuing arbitration," at ¶¶92-95.

§4.26 n.11 p.560 Add the following after the third sentence: For an unequivocal and rather oblivious rejection, *see* Rory v. Cont'l

Ins. Co., 703 N.W.2d 23 (Mich. 2005) ("it is of no legal relevance that a contract is or is not described as 'adhesive' ").

§4.26 n.15 p.561 Add the following after the second sentence: *Cf.* Jazz Photo Corp. v. Int'l Trade Comm'n. 264 F.3d 1094 (Fed. Cir. 2001) (notations that camera available only for single use contained in a list of warnings "instructions and warnings of risk, not mutual promises or a condition placed on the sale," and thus was "not in the form of a contractual agreement by the purchaser to limit reuse of the camera."), distinguished in Static Control Components v. Lexmark Int'l, 487 F. Supp. 2d 830 (E.D. Ky. 2007) (language on outside of package "clearly set form contractual terms. . . . This is exactly the sort of adhesion licensing agreement that has been held to be valid."), *motion to reconsider granted on other grounds*, 615 F. Supp. 2d 575 (E.D. Ky. 2009); RealPage, Inc. v. EPS, Inc., 560 F. Supp. 2d 539 (E.D. Tex. 2007) (terms of license agreement enforceable even though end user did not have to scroll through them in order to download the program); Metters v. Ralphs Grocery Co., 74 Cal. Rptr. 3d 210 (Ct. App. 2008) (arbitration agreement "was not contained in an employment contract, where it might have been expected, but in a form on which Metters was directed to submit his grievance. The context of this form did not alert him he was agreeing to anything, let alone arbitration.").

§4.26 n.17 p.562 Add the following at the end: *Cf.* Kortum-Managhan v. Herbergers NBGL, 204 P.3d 693 (Mont. 2009) ("making a change in a credit agreement by way of a 'bill stuffer' does not provide sufficient notice to the consumer on which acceptance of the unilateral change to a contract can be expressly or implicitly found"; moreover, "attempting to change the terms of a contract through the use of a 'bill stuffer' is 'sneaky and unfair' ").

***§4.26 n.19 p.562 Add the following to the list after* "Accord":** Thompson v. Toll Dublin, 81 Cal. Rptr. 3d 736 (Ct. App. 2008) (procedural unconscionability where "the arbitration provisions, on their face, applied to a limited category of actions — Title 7 claims — and were included in approximately 800 pages of documents . . . which together comprised the purchase agreement"); Palm Beach Mot. Cars v. Jeffries, 885 So. 2d 990 (Fla. App. 2004) (arbitration clause unenforceable because of "the organization of the contract provisions; the exceptionally small size of the type of the provision alerting the customer to the terms on the back of the agreement; the lack of initials on the back page of the agreement; and the customary practice of the employees in *not* calling attention to the provisions on the back of the form"), distinguished in Murphy v. Courtesy Ford, 944 So. 2d 1131 (Fla. App. 2006) ("[T]he agreement was not procedurally unconscionable because the agreement appeared in the same type-face as did the rest of the provisions of the purchase contract, the contract was signed by Murphy, and there was no evidence indicating that Courtesy Ford actively discouraged or prevented Murphy from knowing and understanding the disputed contract terms . . ."); D.R. Horton, Inc. v. Green, 96 P.3d 1159 (Nev. 2004) (arbitration clause unenforceable when placed on back page in fine print and when "nothing ever drew attention" to it), distinguished by Lawrence v. Household Bank (SB), N.A., 397 F. Supp. 2d 1332 (M.D. Ala. 2005) ("In contrast to the *Horton* agreement, the word 'ARBITRATION' is written in bold, capital letters").

***§4.26 n.19 p.562 Add the following to the list after* "But cf.":** Tortoriello v. Gerald Nissan, 882 N.E.2d 157 (Ill. App. 2008) (adhesion contracts presented in fine print and difficult-to-understand language "are not *per se* unconscionable from a procedural standpoint. Some added coercion or overreaching is necessary.") Forest Hill Nursing Ctr. v. McFarlan, 995 So. 2d 775 (Miss. App. 2008) (although arbitration clause found on page five of an eight-page document, the section heading was in bold type, it was the only section that had to be initialed, the language was not complex and legalistic, and a preceding paragraph "written in bold-faced letters draws attention to the fact that the parties are giving up their constitutional right to have a claim decided before a judge and jury"; not procedurally unconscionable).

***§4.26 n.20 p.563 Add the following to the list after* "Accord":** Baker v. Osborne Dev. Corp., 71 Cal. Rptr. 3d 854 (Ct. App. 2008) (arbitration clause for contract to build home contained only in application to obtain warranty was unenforceable; reference not "clear and unequivocal" and was not "called to the attention of the other party," and owner was not provided with it before the close of escrow); Chestnut Hills Condo. Assn. v. Pasquinelli, Inc., 822 N.E.2d 12 (Ill. App. 2004) (limited warranty in separate document not part of purchase agreement when agreement did not expressly incorporate it, but rather "refer[red] only to the *existence* of the Limited Warranty"), followed in Clarendon Am. Ins. Co. v. 69 W. Washington Mgmt. LLC, 870 N.E.2d 978 (Ill. App. 2007) ("[T]he two agreements were not entered into by the same parties nor were they executed in the course of the same transaction."); Byrd v. Simmons, 5 So. 3d 384 (Miss. 2009) (nursing home admissions agreement and arbitration agreement separate, and assent to arbitration not required as prerequisite for admission).

***§4.26 n.20 p.563 Add the following to the list after* "But cf.":** Herron v. Century BMW, 693 S.E.2d 394 (S.C. 2010) (arbitration agreement enforced; in a separate document included in a packet of documents to sign, labeled plainly as an arbitration agreement, and placing key provisions in capital letters just above the signature line), *vacated and remanded*, 131 S. Ct. 2872 (2011).

§4.26 n.21 p.564 Add the following after the second sentence: In contrast, an arbitration clause contained in the only underlined paragraph in the whole agreement and placed directly above the petitioners' signatures was deemed part of the contract and not procedurally unconscionable. Walther v. Sovereign Bank, 872 A.2d 735 (Md. 2005).

§4.26 n.23 p.564 In the first paragraph, add the following after the second sentence: *See* Westfield Ins. Co. v. Birkey's Farm Store, 924 N.E.2d 1231 (Ill. App. 2010) ("The question before the court is not whether the disclaimer at issue could have been made more conspicuous but, rather, whether the disclaimer at issue was presented in a manner reasonably sufficient to draw attention to it.").

§4.26 n.23 p.564 In the first paragraph, add the following after the third sentence: *See* LDT Keller Farms v. Brigitte Holmes Livestock Co., 722 F. Supp. 2d 1015 (N.D. Ind. 2010) (disclaimer not conspicuous when "at the bottom of the page, in type much smaller than the rest of the contract," and "the text was not presented in bold font or in contrasting color"); Tague v. Autobahn Motors, 914 N.E.2d 710 (Ill. App. 2009) (disclaimer conspicuous where lower right-hand corner of contract contains paragraph entitled "Disclaimer of Warranties" in bold capital letters, the following text is underlined, and the paragraph appears immediately above the signature line).

***§4.26 n.23 p.564 In the second paragraph, add the following to the list after* "See":** Tague v. Autobahn Motors, 914 N.E.2d 710 (Ill. App. 2009) ("question of law, which we review *de novo*").

§4.26 n.23 p.564 Add the following to the list in the second sentence of the third paragraph: Tortoriello v. Gerald Nissan, *supra* note 19 ("even an arbitration clause hidden in a maze of fine print . . . may be considered part of the bargain if it was brought to the consumer's attention . . .").

§4.26 n.23 p.564 Add the following new paragraph at the end: Waiver of constitutional or statutory rights are often subject to a further requirement that the waiver be conspicuous, clear, and unambiguous. For example, in 2014, the New Jersey Supreme Court considered an arbitration clause that clearly required all disputes to go to binding arbitration but did not explicitly provide that such a clause effected a waiver of the right to sue, and it found that the clause was therefore not enforceable under New Jersey Law. Atalese v. U.S. Legal Servs. Grp., L.P., 219 N.J. 430, 99 A.3d 306 (2014). The New Jersey Supreme Court "ha[s] repeatedly stated that '[t]he point is to assure that the parties know that in electing arbitration as the exclusive remedy, they are waiving their time-honored right to sue.' " Garfinkel v. Morristown Obstetrics & Gynecology Assocs., 168 N.J. 124, 132, 773 A.2d 665 (2001) (quoting Marchak v. Claridge Commons, Inc., 134 N.J. 275, 282, 633 A.2d 531 (1993); Hirsch v. Amper Fin. Servs., LLC, 215 N.J. 174, 187, 71 A.3d 849 (2013)).

See also the discussion of insistence on informed consent in §4.29a *infra*.

***§4.26 n.25 p.565 Add the following to the list after* "See":** DJ Coleman, Inc. v. Nufarm Americas., 693 F. Supp. 2d 1055 (D.N.D.

2010) (statement on label that seller "warrants that this product . . . is reasonably fit for the purposes stated on the Directions for Use" inconsistent with statement in those directions that "NUFARM MAKES NO WARRANTIES OF MERCHANTABILITY OR OF FITNESS FOR A PARTICULAR PURPOSE, NOR ANY OTHER EXPRESS OR IMPLIED WARRANTIES WITH RESPECT TO THE SELECTION, PURCHASE OR USE OF THIS PRODUCT," so the language of the express warranty prevails).

§4.26 n.26 p.566 Add the following at the end: U.C.C. §2-316(3)(a) provides another means of excluding or limiting implied warranties — the use of language "which in common understanding calls the buyer's attention to the exclusion of warranties and makes plain that there is no implied warranty." This subsection has no requirement of conspicuous disclaimer, but the courts have generally read one into the statute. *See* Fairchild Indus. v. Maritime Air Serv., 333 A.2d 313 (Md. 1975); Lumber Mut. Ins. Co. v. Clarklift of Detroit, 569 N.W.2d 681 (Mich. App. 1997); Gindy Mfg. Corp. v. Cardinale Trucking Corp., 268 A.2d 345 (N.J. Super. 1970), *overturned in part on other grounds*, Ramirez v. Autosport, Inc., 440 A. 2d 1345 (N.J. 1982); Patton v. McHone, 822 S.W.2d 608 (Tenn. App. 1991). *But see* Smith v. Sharpensteen, 521 P.2d 394 (Okla. 1974) (no requirement that a disclaimer under UCC §2-316(3)(a) be conspicuous).

§4.26 n.28 p.566 Add the following at the end: *See generally* J. Sheldon & C. Carter, Unfair & Deceptive Acts & Practices §5.2.2 (5th ed. 2001) (collecting statutes).

The ALI's Principles of the Law of Software Contracts deals with this for standard-form transfers of generally available software. For these, the standard terms are enforceable if reasonably comprehensible. Principles of the Law of Software Contracts §2.02(d) (2010).

§4.26 n.29 p.566 Add the following at the end: The laws of many EU states contain similar provisions. *See, e.g.*, AGBG §3 (Germany).

§4.26 n.30 p.566 Add the following after the sentence beginning **"Cf."***:* Indeed, some courts go further and refuse to enforce contracts of adhesion "against the weaker party if it is . . . not within their reasonable expectations." Zigrang v. U.S. Bancorp Piper Jaffray, 123 P.3d 237 (Mont. 2005); *see also* Woodruff v. Bretz, Inc., 218 P.3d 486 (Mont. 2009) (same). *Accord:* Bruni v. Didion, 73 Cal. Rptr. 3d 395 (Ct. App. 2008) (applying reasonable expectations test to hold arbitration provisions in adhesive contract unenforceable); Dairy Farm Leasing Co. v. Hartley, 395 A.2d 1135 (Me. 1978) ("where a standard-form, printed contract is submitted to the other on a 'take it or leave it' basis, upon equitable principles the provisions of the contract are generally construed to meet the reasonable expectations of the party in the inferior bargaining position, because the parties are in vastly unequal bargaining positions"); Swain v. Auto Servs., 128 S.W.3d 103 (Mo. App. 2003) (contracts of adhesion "are not inherently sinister and automatically unenforceable"; rather, "[o]nly those provisions that fail to comport with [the individual's] reasonable expectations and are unexpected and unconscionably unfair are unenforceable"), distinguished in Grossman v. Thoroughbred Ford, 297 S.W.3d 918 (Mo. App. 2009) (where terms not shown to be non-negotiable and other auto dealers were available, the contract's arbitration provision was not a contract of adhesion); Obstetrics & Gynecologists v. Pepper, 693 P.2d 1259 (Nev. 1985) ("An adhesion contract need not be unenforceable if it falls within the reasonable expectations of the weaker or 'adhering' party and is not unduly oppressive."). *But cf.* Dugan v. R.J. Corman R.R. Co., 344 F.3d 662 (7th Cir. 2003) (Posner, J.: while "boilerplate will sometimes be irrelevant to the document in which it has been unthinkingly inserted," there is "no 'mere boilerplate' defense to a suit for breach of contract").

Tennessee has taken a more refined position. There "the party who signs a printed form furnished by the other party will be bound by the provisions in the form over which the parties actually bargained and such other provisions that are not unreasonable in view of the circumstances surrounding the transaction." Parton v. Mark Pirtle Oldsmobile-Cadillac-Isuzu, *supra* note 21, at 637-38. These circumstances include the size and location of the provisions, how understandable they are, how long they are, how accurately the reader is alerted to their existence, how sophisticated the reader is, whether the reader had the opportunity to review the document before assenting, how substantively fair the provision is, and whether the reader should reasonably have expected the provision. Tennessee has thus taken up Llewellyn's critique of assent to standardized forms. K. Llewellyn, The Common Law Tradition, *infra* note 40. For a careful exposition of this approach, *see* Lloyd, The "Circle of Assent" Doctrine: An Important Innovation in Contract Law, 7 Transactions: Tenn. J. Bus. L. 237 (2006). *See also* Note, The Circle of Assent: How "Agreement" Can Save Mandatory Arbitration in Long-Term Care Contracts, 62 Vand. L. Rev. 1017 (2009).

§4.26 n.30 p.566 Add the following to the list in the last sentence: Barnes, Toward a Fairer Model of Consumer Assent to Standard Form Contracts: In Defense of Restatement Subsection 211(3), 82 Wash. L. Rev. 227 (2007).

§4.26 n.32 p.567 Add the following to the end: *But see* Memberworks v. Yance, 899 So. 2d 940 (Ala. 2004) (arbitration clause in package enforceable when goods ordered via telephone and arbitration clause was not mentioned during the conversation; "Yance maintained his relationship with Memberworks by continuing to pay his annual membership fee" and thus "manifested his assent to abide by the terms of the arbitration agreement").

§4.26 n.35 p.568 Add the following after the citation to **ProCD*:*** which was distinguished in Motise v. Am. Online, 346 F. Supp. 2d 563 (S.D.N.Y. 2004) (*ProCD* relevant only where the purchaser had the option to read the terms before use; where no such opportunity, the putative licensee not bound unless notice provided by other means); Wachter Mgmt. Co. v. Dexter & Chaney, Inc., 144 P.3d 747 (Kan. 2006) (buyer in *ProCD* did not negotiate with seller before purchase, so contract would be formed later); Rico v. Cappaert Mfd. Housing, 903 So. 2d 1284 (La. App. 205) (warranty not binding where no accept-or-return policy); and DeFontes v. Dell, Inc., 984 A.2d 1061 (R.I. 2009) (adopting *ProCD* ("It is simply unreasonable to expect a seller to apprise a consumer of every term and condition at the moment he or she makes a purchase. A modern consumer neither expects nor desires to wade through such minutia, particularly when making a purchase over the phone, when full disclosure of the terms would border on the sadistic") but also holding that the seller did not adequately apprise the buyer of her right to reject the proffered terms by returning the goods, so the buyer was not bound by the late-arriving terms and conditions), and followed in Spivey v. Adaptive Mktg., 660 F. Supp. 2d 940 (S.D. Ill. 2009) (purchaser of membership in buying service agreed to terms sent after oral conversation by receiving them in the mail and not rejecting them in the 30 days given), *aff'd on other grounds*, 622 F.3d 816 (7th Cir. 2010) (O'Connor, J., sitting by designation).

§4.26 n.35 p.568 Add the following at the end of the list after "Accord": rejected by Wachter Mgmt. Co. v. Dexter & Chaney, Inc., *supra*, ("we disagree with the *Mortenson* court's analysis of when the contract was formed," instead choosing "traditional contract principles"); Static Control Components v. Lexmark Int'l, *supra* note 15 (following *ProCD* where terms of agreement printed on box and provide for return if undesirable); Schultz v. AT & T Wireless Servs., 376 F. Supp. 2d 685 (N.D.W. Va. 2005) ("agrees with the *Zeidenberg* and *Hill* analyses"); i.Lan Sys. v. NetScout Serv. Level Corp., 183 F. Supp. 2d 328 (D. Mass. 2002) (applying *ProCD* in context of clickwrap); Bess v. DirecTV, Inc., 885 N.E.2d 488 (Ill. App. 2008) ("Although Bess did not receive the Customer Agreement at the time she ordered the service, she was not bound by its terms until after she had read the Customer Agreement and continued to receive the service."); Stenzel v. Dell, Inc., 870 A.2d 133 (Me. 2005) ("by accepting delivery of the computers, and then failing to exercise their right to return the computers as provided by the agreement, [the plaintiffs] expressly manifested their assent to be bound").

§4.26 n.35 p.568 Add the following to the list after "Contra": followed in Lively v. Ijam, Inc., 114 P.3d 487 (Okla. Civ. App. 2005) (under UCC §2-207, terms on invoice are merely proposals for addition and thus "only became a part of the contract if the buyer expressly agreed to the terms"), but distinguished in Davidson & Assocs. v. Internet Gateway, 334 F. Supp. 2d 1164 (E.D. Mo. 2004) (not applicable where plaintiffs had actual notice of existence of terms on box for software and where had actual notice of terms before software installed).

§4.26 n.35 p.568 In the second paragraph, add the following to the list after* "See generally"*: Friedman, Text and Circumstance: Warranty Disclaimers in a World of Rolling Contracts, 46 Ariz. L. Rev. 677 (2004); Friedman, Improving the Rolling Contract, 56 Am. U.L. Rev. 1 (2006); Lawrence, Rolling Contracts Rolling Over Contract Law, 41 San Diego L. Rev. 1099 (2004); White, Autistic Contracts, 45 Wayne L. Rev. 1693 (2000).

§4.26 n.35 p.568 In the second paragraph, add the following at the end: For a Canadian perspective, *see* Lawson & de Lima, "Browse-Wrap" Contracts and Unfair Terms: What the Supreme Court Missed in *Dell Computer Corporation v. Union des consommateurs et Dumoulin*, 37 Rev. Gen. de Droit 445 (2007).

§4.26 n.36 p.569 Add the following at the end: The ALI Principles of the Law of Software Contracts takes a different approach. Rather than focusing on the time of contract formation, they provide simply that "[a] transferee adopts a standard form as a contract when a reasonable transferor would believe the transferee intends to be bound by the form." §2.02(b) (2010). The Principles then provide a safe harbor if the standard form is reasonably accessible before the transfer began, the transferee has reasonable notice of the form before payment or completion, the transferee has signified its agreement at the close of the transaction or does not return the unopened software within a reasonable time, and the standard form can be stored and reproduced. *Id.* at §2.02(c). This seeks to overcome barriers to information while providing certainty for transferors. The safe harbor is not exclusive, though the Reporters' statement that "failure to comply does not absolutely bar a transferor from otherwise proving transferee assent" suggests that they hold a parsimonious view of the exceptions. *Id.* at §2.02 cmt. c.

§4.26 n.37 p.569 Add the following to the end of the first sentence: *Accord:* CoStar Realty Info. v. Field, 737 F. Supp. 2d 496 (D. Md. 2010) (enforcing internet terms of use contracts "when a website provider requires its users to affirmatively click an 'Agree' button before entering the website"); RealPage, Inc. v. EPS, Inc., *supra* note 15 (clickwrap license agreements enforceable even though it was not necessary for end user to scroll through the agreements before downloading); Siebert v. Amateur Athletic Union, 422 F. Supp. 2d 1033 (D. Minn. 2006) (following *Hill* in enforcing a clickwrap clause; "the 'click' represents assent to the contract"); i.Lan Sys. v. NetScout Serv. Level Corp., *supra* note 35 ("If *ProCD* was correct to enforce a shrinkwrap license agreement, where any assent is implicit, then it must also be correct to enforce a clickwrap license agreement, where the assent is explicit.").

§4.26 n.37 p.569 Add the following at the end: *See generally* Principles of the Law of Software Contracts §2.02 Reporters' notes to cmt. b (2010) (collecting shrinkwrap cases and stating that "[c]ourts generally enforce clickwrap terms and similar processes on the theory that a transferee's clicking on an 'I agree' icon forms a contract"); Nancy S. Kim, *Wrap Contracts: Foundations and Ramifications* (surveying history of shrinkwrap, clickwrap, and browsewrap agreements and proposing doctrinal solutions such as the duty to draft reasonably, specific assent, and a reconceptualization of unconscionability). A 2012 study by researchers at Carnegie Mellon found that "reading all of the privacy policies an average Internet user encounters in a year would take 76 work days." Keith Wagstaff, "You'd Need 76 Work Days to Reach All Your Privacy Policies Each Year," *Time*, Mar. 6, 2012.

§4.26 n.38 p.569 Add the following after the citation to* Register.com*: , *aff'd*, 356 F.3d 393 (2d Cir. 2004), followed in Major v. McCallister, 302 S.W.3d 227 (Mo. App. 2009) (browsewrap enforceable where site gave notice of license terms right next to the button to be clicked, with a link to those terms visible on the same page without scrolling and similar links present on every other page; terms were thus not "so inconspicuous that a reasonably prudent internet user could not know or learn of their existence, or assent to them without a 'click' "), both distinguished in Hoffman v. Supplements Togo Mgmt., 18 A.3d 210 (N.J. Super App. Div. 2011) (browsewrap not enforceable where visible only if buyer scrolled down to a submerged portion of the webpage containing the disclaimer; the clause "was unreasonably masked from the view of the prospective purchasers because of its circuitous mode of presentation"). The opinion of the Second Circuit draws a useful distinction between the first contact and subsequent contacts. A late-arriving term might well not bind its recipient where that recipient had no reason to understand that it would be bound. After repeated exposure, though, it was "well aware" of the term, so its "choice was either to accept the offer of contract, taking the information subject to the terms of the offer, or, if the terms were not acceptable, to decline to take the benefits." *Cf.* Cvent, Inc. v. Eventbrite, Inc., 739 F. Supp. 2d 927 (E.D. Va. 2010) ("Most courts which have considered the issue . . . have held that in order to state a plausible claim for relief based upon a browsewrap agreement, the website user must have had actual or constructive knowledge of the site's terms and conditions, and have manifested assent to them."). Somewhat in contrast is Guadagno v. E*Trade Bank, 592 F. Supp. 2d 1263 (C.D. Cal. 2008), in which the court held, applying Virginia law, that an clickwrap agreement sufficiently presented an arbitration clause when the agreement itself was available via a link on the page for assent, with a note to the effect that the agreement contained "important information about your account(s)," and the agreement itself called attention to the arbitration clause at the top of the document and again at the clause itself. The court asserted that "[a] reasonably prudent offeree would have noticed the link and reviewed the terms before clicking on the acknowledgement icon." This is empirically false, unless only a small minority of offerees is prudent.

Much seems to hinge upon whether the court, in assessing the design of the page and links, believes that the page was "designed to deceive," in the words of the Ninth Circuit in a case that involved both an arbitration agreement and an agreement to enroll in the services of another company. Lee v. Intellius, 737 F.3d 1254, 1259 (9th Cir. 2013). There, the plaintiff provided the credit card number for a one-time purchase of a background report from Intelius from a website clearly branded as that company. A year later, he discovered monthly credit card charges from a different company. The website was designed so that, after a series of clicks, the user was presented with a prominent "YES And show my report," or a less apparent "no, show my report"; the "YES" button included purchase of a subscription service from Adaptive Marketing. *Id.* at 1257. The Ninth Circuit was "skeptical that Lee 'objectively manifested assent' to the contract," *id.* at 1259, but ultimately relied upon the fact that the party was not clearly identified:

> When Lee entered his e-mail address and clicked on the large orange "YES" button, he had completed his purchase of the background check from Intelius but had not yet received a copy of his promised report. He did not re-enter his credit card number on the new webpage. The language on the "YES" button told him that the effect of clicking on that button would allow him to see the report he had already purchased. The critical text on the new webpage was written in small, light-colored print. We are skeptical that, under such circumstances, Lee objectively manifested assent to a contract. Nevertheless, because of the lack of clarity in Washington law surrounding whether and under what circumstances a click may constitute an objective manifestation of assent, we do not rest our conclusion that Lee did not enter into a contract on the ground that he did not manifest assent. We rest our conclusion on another ground. Washington law requires that the "essential elements" of the contract be set forth in writing. An essential element is identification of the parties to the contract.

Id. at 1260. These "data-pass" mechanisms, providing billing information to a third party, were made unlawful by the 2010 Restore Online Shoppers' Confidence Act, 15 U.S.C. §8402(b). The opinion has ongoing significance, therefore, with regard to its "skepticism" of whether a click under these circumstances manifests intent to be bound, as well as its determination that the arbitration agreement was not agreed to because that clause was several "clicks" away and apparently related to the subscription service rather than to the intended purpose. *Lee*, 737 F.3d at 1261-62.

It would in any case seem more prudent to place the assent icon below a list of terms, as in A.V. v. iParadigms, 544 F. Supp. 2d 473 (E.D. Va. 2008), *aff'd in part, rev'd in part on other grounds* 562 F.3d 630 (4th Cir. 2009). Alternatively, the offeror could require that the offeree scroll through the terms in order to reach the icon for assent, or place the terms on the assent screen in a scroll-through box and require clicking on a special icon showing assent to those terms before going ahead with the contract. These likely would have the effect of increasing the percentage of offerees actually reading, deliberating over, and consciously assenting to the click-through terms all the way from infinitesimal to minuscule. At least they would lower the costs of securing the information as far as practicable, leaving the decision whether to trust or verify in the hands of the offeree.

***§4.26 n.38 p.569 Add the following to the list after* "See":** Mann & Siebeneicher, Just One Click: The Reality of Internet Retail Contracting, 108 Colum. L. Rev. 984 (2008).

§4.26 n.38 p.569 Add the following at the end: *See generally* Principles of the Law of Software Contracting §2.02 Reporters' Notes to cmt. b (2010) (browsewrap is "more problematic" than clickwrap "because it does not require transferees to see the terms before 'agreeing' to them," but at least some courts will enforce it "when the transferee should have knowledge of the standard form from previous visits to a site or based on reasonable notice"). In that vein, the Uniform Computer Information Transactions Act (UCITA) permits a breach of contract claim if a person has both an opportunity to review the terms and engages in statements or conduct that either show or lead another to infer assent. Under UCITA, this opportunity to review exists only when the term is displayed in a manner that would call it to the attention of a reasonable person, or if the website prominently states that the terms are available and does not prevent the viewer from storing or printing those terms. UCITA §§112 & 211; *see also* Cvent, Inc. v. Eventbrite, Inc., 739 F. Supp. 2d 927 (E.D. Va. 2010) (applying UCITA; pleadings insufficient to state a plausible claim for relief).

§4.26 n.40 p.570 Add the following at the end: For more recent explorations of assent in standardized contracting, see Alces, Guerilla Terms, 56 Emory L.J. 1511 (2007); Wedemaier, Disputing Boilerplate, 82 Temple L. Rev. 1 (2009). For a critique of Llewellyn, see Rakoff, Contracts of Adhesion: An Essay in Reconstruction, 96 Harv. L. Rev. 1174 (1983).

§4.27 PRECURSORS OF UNCONSCIONABILITY

§4.27 n.1 p.572 Add the following at the end of the first paragraph: Certain types of bargains, most notably in the family setting, do receive more searching substantive scrutiny. *See* Potts v. Potts, 303 S.W.3d 177 (Mo. App. 2010) (" 'An ante-nuptial agreement requires more consideration than that necessary for a simple contract, in that the consideration moving to the spouse or prospective spouse surrendering marital rights must be fair and equitable in the particular circumstances.' ") (quoting from *In re* Marriage of Thomas, 199 S.W.3d 847, 852 (Mo. App. 2006)); Santini v. Robinson, 891 N.Y.S.2d 100 (App. Div. 2009) (property settlement as part of separation agreement is to "be closely scrutinized" to ensure that it was "arrived at fairly and equitably" and to avoid enforcing terms that are "manifestly unjust") (internal quotations omitted). See *infra* §4.28 on price unconscionability.

§4.27 n.4 p.573 Add the following to the list after **"Accord"***:* Kenda Corp. v. Pot O' Gold Money Leagues, 329 F.3d 216 (1st Cir. 2003) (non-compete agreement, the only consideration for which were business plans that were "no more than a series of mispresentations").

§4.27 n.7 p.574 Add the following at the end: Accord: Soc'y of Lloyd's v. Reinhart, 402 F.3d 982 (10th Cir. 2005); U.S. Welding v. Battelle Energy Alliance, 728 F. Supp. 2d 1110 (D. Idaho 2010); Morris v. Castle Rock Entm't, 246 F. Supp. 2d 290 (S.D.N.Y. 2003); Norwest Fin. Miss. v. McDonald, 905 So. 2d 1187 (Miss. 2005); Swain v. Auto Servs., 128 S.W.3d 103 (Mo. App. 2003); Taylor v. Butler, 142 S.W.3d 277 (Tenn. 2004). *But see* Cordova v. World Fin. Corp., 208 P.3d 901 (N.M. 2009) ("The repetition of this unhelpful terminology from a bygone age only serves to confuse the unconscionability issues without serving any constructive purpose. We specifically disapprove of its use as a controlling standard of unconscionability analysis . . .").

§4.27 p.574 In paragraph three and in the margin, replace **Wooliums** *with:* Woollums

§4.27 n.10 p.575 Add the following after the first sentence: (There is some difference of opinion about the defendant's name. The Official Reporter spells it *Woollums,* while the West Reporter spells it *Wollums*. *Compare* 93 Ky. 582 *with* 20 S.W. 781. The world awaits resolution of this mystery.)

§4.27 n.10 p.575 Add the following to the list after **"Accord"***:* Pleasant Hollow Homeowners Ass'n v. Webster, 285 S.W.3d 421 (Mo. App. 2009) (sheriff's sale of home grossed $10 where market price was between $110,000 and $160,000; set aside sale because the consideration was "grossly inadequate" and amounted to constructive fraud); Swayne v. Beebles Invests., 891 N.E.2d 1216 (Ohio App. 2008) (contract unenforceable where client of mortgage brokers "was unfamiliar with financial matters, as she was a recent widow whose husband had managed the couple's finances").

§4.27 p.575 In line fifteen, replace **Wooliums** *with:* Woollums

§4.27 n.15 p.577 Add the following to the list after **"See"***:* Brown v. Wells Fargo Bank, 85 Cal. Rptr. 3d 817 (Ct. App. 2008) (fiduciary relationship between customers and bank, where bank officer knew that client "had limited vision and that his declining health rendered him 'a little slow,' " worked biweekly at the customers' home office, managed their financial paperwork, introduced the customers to an estate attorney and an accountant, gave the customers investment advice, and repeatedly urged the customers to give their brokerage account to a broker working for the bank); Perry v. Estate of Carpenter, 918 N.E.2d 1156 (Ill. App. 2009) (attorney's proposed sale of estate property held unenforceable; "the probate court historically has been the repository of equitable powers" and "where the contract price is grossly inadequate, slight circumstances indicating fraud or unfairness in the transaction may well suffice as a ground to set aside the sale"); *In re* Rudder, 217 P.3d 183 (Or. App. 2009) ("the relationship between the parties to a premarital agreement is fiduciary in character if entered into in contemplation of marriage").

§4.27 n.15 p.577 Add the following after the third sentence: Cf. McMullen v. Kutz, 985 A.2d 769 (Pa. 2009) (fee-shifting clause in contract: "courts may consider reasonableness when making a counsel fee award, regardless of the precise verbiage of the document authorizing such award" because "the potential for abuse is too high"; collecting cases).

§4.28 UNCONSCIONABILITY

§4.28 n.5 p.578 In the first paragraph, add the following to the list after* "See generally"*: Friedman, Giving Unconscionability More Muscle: Attorney's Fees as a Remedy for Contractual Overreaching, 44 Ga. L. Rev. 317 (2010); Schmitz, Embracing Unconscionability's Safety Net Function, 58 Ala. L. Rev. 73 (2006).

§4.28 n.5 p.578 In the first paragraph, add the following to the list after* "See also"*: Gilo & Porat, Viewing Unconscionability through a Market Lens, 52 Wm. & Mary L. Rev. 133 (2010); Marrow, Squeezing Subjectivity from the Doctrine of Unconscionability, 53 Clev. St. L. Rev. 187 (2005-2006); Saprai, Against Equality of Exchange, 21 King's L.J. 71 (2010).

§4.28 n.5 p.578 In the second paragraph, add the following to the list: Barnes, Consumer Assent to Standard Form Contracts and the Voting Analogy, 112 W. Va. L. Rev. 839 (2010); Korobkin, Bounded Rationality, Standard Form Contracts, and Unconscionability, 70 U. Chi. L. Rev. 1203 (2003).

§4.28 n.9 p.579 Add the following to the list after* "See"*: Unif. Computer Info. Transactions Act §111; Unif. Consumer Leases Act §110.

§4.28 n.9 p.579 In the first sentence, make the following correction: For Uniform Consumer Credit Code read Model Consumer Credit Code.

§4.28 n.9 p.579 In the final sentence, make the following correction: For note 52 read note 63.

§4.28 n.10 p.579 Add the following after the citation to* Cheshire Mortgage Co.*: , followed in New England Retail Properties v. Maturo, 925 A.2d 1151 (Conn. 2007)

§4.28 n.10 p.579 Add the following to the list after* "See also"*: *In re* Poly-Am., 262 S.W.3d 337 (Tex. 2008) ("Whether a contract is contrary to public policy or unconscionable at the time it is formed is a question of law."); Scott v. Cingular Wireless, 161

P.3d 1000 (Wash. 2007) ("We review trial court decisions on motions to compel arbitration de novo.").

§4.28 n.14 p.580 Add the following after the third sentence: *Accord: In re* Poly-Am., *supra* note 10 ("The burden of proving . . . fraud, unconscionability or voidness under public policy — falls on the party opposing the contract.").

§4.28 n.15 p.581 Add the following at the end: A court should look at the contract as a whole when determining whether any particular provision is procedurally or substantively sound. *See* Tortoriello v. Gerald Nissan, 882 N.E.2d 157 (Ill. App. 2008).

§4.28 n.16 p.581 Add the following after the first sentence: *Accord:* Davis v. LaFontaine Motors, 719 N.W.2d 890 (Mich. App. 2006) (where failure of a remedy came after the contract was made, but the remedy had been sufficient, no unconscionability); Vintage Health Res. v. Guiangan, 309 S.W.3d 448 (Tenn. App. 2009) (common law: "Whether a contract is unconscionable is determined based on the circumstances as they existed at the time the parties executed the contract.").

§4.28 n.16 p.581 Add the following after the citation to **Industralease*:*** rejected in Dallas Aerospace v. CIS Air Corp., 352 F.3d 775 (2d Cir. 2003) (citing this treatise and stating that treatises "dutifully cite *Industrialease* as the lone exception").

§4.28 n.16 p.581 Add the following at the end: Contingent fee agreements may similarly be unconscionable either as of when they are entered into or when they ripen. *See* Lawrence v. Miller, 901 N.E.2d 1268 (N.Y. 2008) (contingent fee agreement may be rendered unconscionable and unenforceable "where the amount of the fee, combined with the large percentage of the recovery it represents, seems disproportionate to the value of the services rendered"). Premarital agreements and contingent fee agreement have in common a history of close judicial scrutiny on their substantive and procedural fairness, so there is at least consistency in the dual methods of invalidation.

§4.28 n.17 p.581 Add the following at the end: The Principles of European Contract Law divides this defense differently. Article 4:109 allows a party to avoid a contract if: (a) it had a relationship of trust with the other party, was in economic distress, or was improvident, ignorant, inexperienced, or lacking in bargaining skill; and (b) the other party should have known of this and took advantage of the situation in a grossly unfair manner or took an excessive benefit. This sweeps in part of the law of undue influence as well as much of unconscionability, though it omits a good deal of the procedural aspect. That is found in Article 4:110 on unfair terms in standardized contracts, which encompasses the EU Directive on Unfair Terms in Consumer Contracts and extends it to all other contracts.

§4.28 n.20 p.582 Replace **Wooliums** *with:* Woollums.

§4.28 n.22 p.582 Add the following at the end: See generally Korobkin, A "Traditional" and "Behavioral" Law-and-Economics Analysis of *Williams v. Walker-Thomas Furniture Company*, 26 U. Haw. L. Rev. 441 (2004).

§4.28 n.23 p.582 Add the following at the end of the first sentence: , followed in Taylor Bldg. Corp. of Am. v. Benfield, 884 N.E.2d 12 (Ohio 2008) and in Vintage Health Res. v. Guiangan, 309 S.W.3d 448 (Tenn. App. 2009).

§4.28 n.23 p.582 Add the following at the end: Cf. Wisconsin Auto Title Loans v. Jones, 714 N.W.2d 155 (Wis. 2006) (setting forth nine factors for determining procedural unconscionability; citing to treatise) (Abrahamson, C.J.).

§4.28 n.24 p.583 Add the following to the list after **"See"**: D.R. Horton, Inc. v. Green, 96 P.3d 1159 (Nev. 2004); Tillman v. Comm'l Credit Loans, 655 S.E.2d 362 (N.C. 2008); Adler v. Fred Lind Manor, 103 P.3d 773 (Wash. 2004).

§4.28 n.25 p.583 Add the following after the second sentence: Gatton v. T-Mobile USA, 61 Cal. Rptr. 3d 344 (Ct. App. 2007) ("Whether the challenged provision is within a contract of

adhesion pertains to the oppression aspect of procedural unconscionability.").

§4.28 n.25 p.583 Add the following to the list after **"See"***:* Ostroff v. Alterra Healthcare Corp., 433 F. Supp. 2d 538 (E.D. Pa. 2006) (where nursing home presented daughter of potential resident with 31-page agreement the day of admission, did not allow her to consult an attorney, and told her that unless she signed the agreement that day, her mother would not be admitted, contract was procedurally unconscionable); M & T Mtg. Corp. v. Miller, 323 F. Supp. 2d 405 (E.D.N.Y. 2004) (procedural unconscionability encompasses "high pressure commercial tactics" and "deceptive practices and language in the contract"); Discover Bank v. Superior Ct., 113 P.3d 1100 (Cal. 2005) ("when a consumer is given an amendment to its cardholder agreement in the form of a 'bill stuffer' that he would be deemed to accept if he did not close his account, an element of procedural unconscionability is present"), distinguished by *In re* Yahoo! Litigation, 251 F.R.D. 459 (C.D. Cal. 2008) (*Discover*'s holding does not apply to disputes involving large sums of money); Mattingly v. Palmer Ridge Homes, 238 P.3d 505 (Was. App. 2010) (limitation of liability in home warranty procedurally unconscionable when not made available to the buyers until after they entered into the contract; "documents incorporated by reference usually must be reasonably available, at the least, so that the essentials of a contract can be discerned by the singer"); Coady v. Cross County Bank, 729 N.W.2d 732 (Wis. App. 2007) (failure to provide credit card agreements until cards arrived, rather than when plaintiffs signed up, "weigh[s] in favor of procedural unconscionability").

§4.28 n.25 p.583 Add the following at the end: Cf. Kortum-Managhan v. Herbergers NBGL, 204 P.3d 693 (Mont. 2009) ("making a change in a credit agreement by way of a 'bill stuffer' does not provide sufficient notice to the consumer on which acceptance of the unilateral change to a contract can be expressly or implicitly found"; moreover, "attempting to change the terms of a contract through the use of a 'bill stuffer' is 'sneaky and unfair' ").

§4.28 n.26 p.583 Add the following to the list after **"Accord"***:* Skirchak v. Dynamics Research Corp., 508 F.3d 49 (1st Cir. 2007) (finding waiver of class rights procedurally unconscionable where contained in an e-mail sent to employees the Tuesday before Thanksgiving which "did not state it represented a modification to their employment contract at all"); Geoffroy v. Wash. Mut. Bank, 484 F. Supp. 2d 1115 (S.D. Cal. 2007) (arbitration clause in checking account contract unconscionable when contained on signature card, traditionally "used simply for the purpose of maintaining a specimen of an account-holder's signature," put in fine print (where depositors demonstrated difficulty in reading larger print), not called attention to by the bank, and ambiguously phrased); Gonski v. Second Judicial Dist. Ct., 245 P.3d 1164 (Nev. 2010) (arbitration clauses substantively unconscionable even though initialed, when they are "not particularly called out on the pages" and nowhere "drew [the buyer's] attention to the importance of what those pages contained," and when the provisions were included in a large number of documents given the buyers to review within a brief time frame); Thibodeau v. Comcast Corp., 912 A.2d 874 (Pa. Super. 2006) (change in broadband contract unconscionable where the old and new agreements "were virtually identical in terms of style, font size, type and layout," save that, "buried on page 8 of the 10-page document was a new and substantially different arbitration clause").

§4.28 n.26 p.583 Add the following after the second ***sentence:*** *But cf.* Fallo v. High-Tech Inst., 559 F.3d 874 (8th Cir. 2009) (although arbitration provision on the back of the contract, the contract "consisted of a single sheet of paper printed on both sides that set out basic terms" and thus was not procedurally unconscionable); Novak v. Overture Servs., 309 F. Supp. 2d 446 (E.D.N.Y. 2004) (though window on computer screen allowed viewing of only ten lines at a time, no unconscionability where forum selection clause appeared "more than three hundred lines into the document").

§4.28 n.27 p.583 Add the following after the citation to **Weaver***:* *Accord:* Swayne v. Beebles Invs., 891 N.E.2d 1216 (Ohio App. 2008) (plaintiff "was unfamiliar with financial matters, as

she was a recent widow whose husband had managed the couple's finances"); Coady v. Cross County Bank, *supra* note 25 (resting procedural unconscionability holding in part on fact that not all the plaintiffs had finished high school, and that none of them "have any particular business acumen or experience").

***§4.28 n.27 p.583 In the first paragraph, add the following to the list after* "But cf.":** Miller v. Cotter, 863 N.E.2d 537 (Mass. 2007) (plaintiff, a regional claims manager for an insurance company, was "an intelligent and educated man whose professional experience gave him sophistication in dealing with contracts," and so should have been aware of the nature of the documents he signed); Hayes v. Oakridge Home, 908 N.E.2d 408 (Ohio 2009) (plaintiff's "age, in and of itself, is not a sufficient basis for finding the agreement procedurally unconscionable").

§4.28 n.27 p.583 In the first paragraph, add the following at the end: *See generally* Barnes, Rediscovering Subjectivity in Contracts: Adhesion and Unconscionability, 66 La. L. Rev. 123 (2005).

§4.28 n.27 p.583 In the second paragraph, add the following at the end: *Accord:* Martinez v. Freedom Mtg. Team, 527 F. Supp. 2d 827 (N.D. Ill. 2007) ("'Disclosing' the true terms of a document written in a foreign language is tantamount to no disclosure at all. . . . Martinez reasonably believed that he had been informed of the meaning of what he was signing, but unfortunately for him his interpreter [an employee of the defendant] spoke with forked tongue in providing the English-to-Spanish translation."); Hialeah Auto. v. Basulto, 22 So. 3d 586 (Fla. App. 2009) (although it is generally true that a party to a contract is bound by it even if he or she does not read it, "in this case the dealer's personnel undertook to explain the contracts to the [non-English-speaking] buyers in Spanish. Having done so, they were obliged to do so accurately."). *Cf.* Advanta Bus. Servs. Corp. v. Colon, 782 N.Y.S.2d 502 (Sup. Ct. App. Term 2004) (question of fact whether defendant, not a native speaker of English, was the subject of unconscionable behavior; English proficiency relevant to that determination).

***§4.28 n.28 p.584 In the second paragraph, add the following to the list after* "See generally":** Barnhizer, Inequality of Bargaining Power, 76 U. Colo. L. Rev. 140 (2005); Kim, Bargaining Power and Background Law, 12 Vand. J. Ent. & Tech. L. 93 (2009).

***§4.28 n.28 p.584 Add the following to the list after* "Accord":** Vasquez-Lopez v. Beneficial Or., 152 P.3d 940 (Or. App. 2007) (unequal bargaining power combined with affirmative concealment of arbitration terms made those terms procedurally unconscionable); Vintage Health Res. v. Guiangan, 309 S.W.3d 448 (Tenn. App. 2009) (unequal bargaining power insufficient to establish unconscionability, but it is a factor; disparity in size similarly "is not enough in and of itself to find that the parties had substantially unequal bargaining power," as true here, where employee was in high-demand occupation); Wisconsin Auto Title Loans v. Jones, *supra* note 23 (indigent borrower in a weak bargaining position as against subprime lender).

***§4.28 n.29 p.584 Add the following to the list after* "Accord":** Creighton Univ. v. Gen. Elec. Co., 636 F. Supp. 2d 940 (D. Neb. 2009) (finding no procedural unconscionability where university "sought proposals from other vendors" and where the contract recites that "the terms and conditions of this Agreement have been the subject of active and complete negotiations"); Westerfield v. Quizno's Franchise Co., 527 F. Supp. 2d 840 (E.D. Wis. 2007) (not unconscionable where "[t]he very facts alleged in the complaint belie the suggestion that [the plaintiffs] are unsophisticated or vulnerable individuals of whom advantage is easily taken"), *vacated on other grounds*, 2008 WL 2512467 (E.D. Wis. Apr. 16, 2008).

§4.28 n.30 p.584 Add the following after the second sentence: *Cf.* Taylor Bldg. Corp. of Am. v. Benfield, *supra* note 23 ("inequality of bargaining power alone is insufficient to invalidate an otherwise enforceable arbitration contract").

***§4.28 n.31 p.585 Add the following after the citation to* Armendariz:** , followed in Gonski v. Second Judicial Dist. Ct., 245 P.3d 1164 (Nev. 2010) ("a strong showing of procedural unconscionability mean[s] that less substantive unconscionability

[is] required . . . The reverse is true also: the stronger the showing of substantive unconscionability, the less necessary is a strong showing of procedural unconscionability.").

§4.28 n.31 p.585 Add the following to the list after **"Accord"***:* Tillman v. Comm'l Credit Loans, *supra* note 24 ("while the presence of both procedural and substantive problems is necessary for an ultimate finding of unconscionability, such a finding may be appropriate when a contract presents pronounced substantive unfairness and a minimal degree of procedural unfairness, or vice versa"); Wisconsin Auto Title Loans v. Jones, *supra* note 23 ("a sufficient quantum of both procedural and substantive unconscionability" required) (citing to treatise).

§4.28 n.32 p.585 In the first paragraph, add the following after the second sentence: *Cf.* Awuah v. Coverall N. Am., 554 F.3d 7 (1st Cir. 2009) (unconscionability "essentially a fairness issue") (citing to treatise).

§4.28 n.32 p.585 In the second paragraph, add the following at the end: *See* Marrow, Crafting a Remedy for the Naughtiness of Procedural Unconscionability, 34 Cumb. L. Rev. 1 (2003).

§4.28 n.33 p.586 Add the following to the list after **"Accord"***:* Awuah v. Coverall N. Am., *supra* note 32 ("the fact that an agreement is a contract of adhesion . . . does not alone make the document invalid") (citing to treatise); Hollins v. Debt Relief of Am., 479 F. Supp. 2d 1099 (D. Neb. 2007) ("adhesion contracts are not automatically unconscionable or void"); Ostroff v. Alterra Healthcare Corp., *supra* note 25 ("Procedural unconscionability is generally found where the agreement is a contract of adhesion" . . . but "[a] contract of adhesion is not necessarily unenforceable"); Tortoriello v. Gerald Nissan, *supra* note 15 ("[C]ontracts of adhesion, . . . are not *per se* unconscionable from a procedural standpoint. Some added coercion or overreaching is necessary."); Walther v. Sovereign Bank, 872 A.2d 735 (Md. 2005) ("A contract of adhesion is not automatically deemed *per se* unconscionable."); Taylor Bldg. Corp. of Am. v. Benfield, *supra* note 23 ("simply showing that a contract is preprinted and that the arbitration clause is a required term, without more, fails to

demonstrate the unconscionability of the arbitration clause"); *In re* AdvancePCS Health, 172 S.W.3d 603 (Tex. 2005) ("Adhesion contracts are not automatically unconscionable") followed in *In re* U.S. Home Corp., 236 S.W.3d 761 (Tex. 2007); Adler v. Fred Lind Manor, *supra* note 24 ("the fact that an agreement is an adhesion contract does not necessarily render it procedurally unconscionable"); Wisconsin Auto Title Loans v. Jones, *supra* note 23 ("Standardized form contracts are suspect . . . Ordinarily, however, adhesion contracts are valid.") (citing to treatise).

§4.28 n.33 p.586 Add the following after the second sentence: *Cf.* Muhammad v. Cnty. Bank of Rehoboth Beach, 912 A.2d 88 (N.J. 2006) ("A sharpened inquiry concerning unconscionability is necessary when a contract of adhesion is involved."); Strand v. U.S. Nat'l Bank Nat'l Ass'n ND, 693 N.W.2d 918 (N.D. 2005) ("a consumer transaction which is essentially a contract of adhesion will be examined by the courts with special scrutiny"), followed in Quality Bank v. Cavett, 788 N.W.2d 629 (N.D. 2010) ("Courts presume adhesion contracts are procedurally unconscionable."); Simpson v. MSA of Myrtle Beach, 644 S.E.2d 663 (S.C. 2007) (consumer contract with auto dealer adhesive; though "not per se unconscionable," they are looked at "with 'considerable skepticism' ") (quoting Eagle v. Fred Martin Motor Co., 809 N.E.2d 1161 (Ohio App. 2004)).

§4.28 n.33 p.586 Add the following at the end: California has gone to the extreme of suggesting that all adhesion contracts are procedurally unconscionable, leaving only substantive unconscionability to be determined. Gentry v. Superior Ct., 165 P.3d 556 (Cal. 2007) ("Ordinary contracts of adhesion . . . contain a degree of procedural unconscionability even without any notable surprises"); Little v. Auto Stiegler, Inc., 63 P.3d 979 (Cal. 2003) ("The procedural element of an unconscionable contract generally takes the form of a contract of adhesion"), followed in Murphy v. Check 'N Go, 67 Cal. Rptr. 3d 120 (Ct. App. 2007) ("the agreement was a contract of adhesion, and thus procedurally unconscionable"). *Accord* Nagrampa v. MailCoups, Inc., 469 F.3d 1257 (9th Cir. 2006) ("When the weaker party is presented the clause and told to 'take it or leave it' without the opportunity for meaningful negotiation, oppression, and therefore procedural unconscionability,

are present."); Bragg v. Linden Research, 487 F. Supp. 2d 593 (E.D. Pa. 2007) ("A contract or clause is procedurally unconscionable if it is a contract of adhesion."); Gatton v. T-Mobile USA, *supra* note 25 ("the procedural element [is] satisfied where the agreement containing the challenged provision was a contract of adhesion"); Martinez v. Master Prot. Corp., 12 Cal. Rptr. 3d 663 (Ct. App. 2004) ("An arbitration agreement that is an essential part of a 'take it or leave it' employment condition, without more, is procedurally unconscionable."). *But see* Arguelles-Romero v. Superior Ct., 109 Cal. Rptr. 3d 289 (Ct. App. 2010) (distinguishing between *Discover Bank* and *Gentry*; the latter is not primarily an unconscionability case, but instead deals with the enforceability of class action waivers as potential violations of statutory rights); Roman v. Super. Ct., 92 Cal. Rptr. 3d 153 (Ct. App. 2009) ("The adhesive nature of the contract will not always make it procedurally unconscionable. When bargaining power is not grossly unequal and reasonable alternatives exist, oppression typically inherent in adhesion contracts is minimal."); Morris v. Redwood Empire Bancorp, 27 Cal. Rptr. 3d 797 (Ct. App. 2005) ("courts often reflexively conclude the finding of an adhesion contract alone satisfies the procedural prong . . . Consequently, other procedural issues, including surprise, often are ignored . . . Undue reliance on any one procedural factor to the exclusion of others may produce analytical myopia and obscure the larger unconscionability picture."); Crippen v. Cent. Valley RV Outlet, 22 Cal. Rptr. 3d 189 (Ct. App. 2004) ("there is no general rule that a form contract used by a party for many transactions is procedurally unconscionable").

See generally Warkentine, Beyond Unconscionability: The Case for Using "Knowing Assent" as the Basis for Analyzing Unbargained-For Terms in Standard Form Contracts, 31 Seattle U. L. Rev. 469 (2008).

§4.28 n.35 p.587 In the first paragraph, add the following at the end of the second sentence: , in Davis v. O'Melveny & Myers, 485 F.3d 1066 (9th Cir. 2007) ("the availability of other employment" cannot "defeat a claim of procedural unconscionability when an employee is faced with a 'take it or leave it' condition of employment"), in Nagrampa v. MailCoups, Inc., *supra* note 33 (plaintiff "a first-time franchise owner" with "no specialized education or training in the field") and in Gatton v. T-Mobile USA, *supra* note 25 ("there are provisions so unfair or contrary to public policy that the law will not allow them to be imposed in a contract of adhesion, even if theoretically the consumer had an opportunity to discover and use an alternate provider"), rejected in Shroyer v. New Cingular Wireless Servs., 498 F.3d 976 (9th Cir. 2007) ("we have consistently followed the courts that reject the notion that the existence of 'marketplace alternatives' bars a finding of procedural unconscionability"), and followed in Morris v. Redwood Empire Bancorp, *supra* note 33 (merchant's contract with credit card companies: plaintiff "failed to allege he could not have obtained credit card services from another source on different terms" and "was under no . . . compulsion ['not to seek out alternative sources'] in attempting to start his business").

***§4.28 n.35 p.587 In the first paragraph, add the following to the list after* "Accord":** Cooper v. MRM Inv. Co., 367 F.3d 493 (6th Cir. 2004) (to find employment contract adhesive "there must be evidence that [employee] would be unable to find suitable employment if she refused to sign"); Lovey v. Regence Blueshield of Idaho, 72 P.3d 877 (Idaho 2003) (no showing that insured "was prevented by market factors, timing, or other pressure from being able to contract with another [health insurer] on more favorable terms or to refrain from contracting at all"); Freedman v. Comcast Corp., 988 A.2d 68 (Md. App. 2010) (not a contract of adhesion because of a "clear and conspicuous (and convenient) opt-out provision, so that the term was not offered on a 'take-it-or-leave-it' basis with respect to the entire agreement," so that "appellee's customers could reject the Arbitration Provision with *no effect* on the rest of the agreement") (emphasis in original); Hayes v. Oakridge Home, *supra* note 27 (where patient did not show lack of nursing home alternatives and where "the agreement clearly delineated in several places that it was voluntary and not a condition of her admission," no procedural unconscionability); W.K. v. Farrell, 853 N.E.2d 728 (Ohio App. 2006) ("When a candidate for employment is free to look elsewhere for employment and is not otherwise forced to consent to the arbitration agreement, the agreement to arbitrate is not unconscionable."); Livingston v. Metro. Pediatrics, 227 P.3d 796 (Or. App. 2010) (no procedural unconscionability when prospective employee, "who is highly educated, had an opportunity to review the employment agreement for two weeks, and he signed and returned it without making any changes").

§4.28 n.35 p.587 In the first paragraph, add the following at the end: *But cf.* Taylor Bldg. Corp. v. Benfield, 860 N.E.2d 1058 (Ohio App. 2006) (presence of alternative sources of supply "weighs against procedural unconscionability," but is only one factor), *aff'd in part, rev'd in part on other grounds*, 884 N.E.2d 12 (Ohio 2008); Coady v. Cross County Bank, *supra* note 25 (presence of other options "far from a dispositive factor" and plaintiffs "are not necessarily required to demonstrate to a factual certainty that they could not have obtained the desired product or service elsewhere under more favorable terms").

§4.28 n.35 p.587 In the second paragraph, add the following to the list in the first sentence: Lloyd v. Sugarloaf Mountain Corp., 833 A.2d.1 (Me. 2003) (mountain bike race entitled "Widowmaker Challenge").

***§4.28 n.35 p.587 In the second paragraph, add the following after the citation to* Collins:** followed in Hurst v. Enterprise Title Agency, 809 N.E.2d 689 (Ohio App. 2004) (escrow agreement).

***§4.28 n.36 p.588 Add the following to the list after* "Accord":** Strand v. U.S. Nat'l Bank Nat'l Ass'n ND, *supra* note 33 ("a party alleging unconscionability must demonstrate some quantum of both procedural and substantive unconscionability").

***§4.28 n.36 p.588 Add the following after the citation to* Resource Mgt. Co.:** , followed in Ryan v. Dan's Food Stores, 972 P.2d 395 (Utah 1998) ("substantive unconscionability alone may support a finding of unconscionability"), in Burton Lumber & Hardware Co. v. Graham, 186 P.3d 1012 (Utah App. 2008); and in Owner-Operator Indep. Drivers Ass'n v. C.R. England, Inc., 325 F. Supp. 2d 1252 (D. Utah 2004).

***§4.28 n.36 p.588 Add the following to the list after* "But cf.":** Batory v. Sears, Roebuck & Co., 456 F. Supp. 2d 1137 (D. Ariz. 2006) ("substantive unconscionability alone is sufficient to render a contract unconscionable"); Vicksburg Partners v. Stephens, *supra* note 33 (holding limitations on remedies clauses unenforceable despite the absence of procedural unconscionability; court decided "whether [the clauses] are substantively unconscionable and therefore unenforceable," though also using adhesive nature of contract as "mak[ing] a facially oppressive term presumptively invalid"), *rev'd on other grounds sub nom.* Covenant Health & Rehab. of Picayune v. Estate of Moulds, 14 So. 3d 695 (Miss. 2009); *In re* Poly-Am., *supra* note 10 ("in general, a contract will be found unconscionable if it is grossly one-sided"); Potts v. Potts, 303 S.W.3d 177 (Mo. App. 2010) ("even without any specific procedural unconscionability, a court can refuse to enforce a highly unconscionable (that is, *substantively* unconscionable) provision."; ante-nuptial agreement held both substantively and procedurally unconscionable) (emphasis in original); Adler v. Fred Lind Manor, *supra* note 24 ("substantive unconscionability alone can support a finding of unconscionability"), followed in Scott v. Cingular Wireless, *supra* note 10 ("Because we find the class action waiver substantively unconscionable, we find it unnecessary to address plaintiffs' claims of procedural unconscionability.").

§4.28 n.37 p.588 Add the following after the citation to* Gillman*: recognized as New York law in Hottle v. BDO Seidman, 846 A.2d 862 (Conn. 2004) (arbitration clause not "so unreasonable as to render it unenforceable solely on the ground of substantive unconscionability" under the exception).

§4.28 n.38 p.588 Add the following to the list after* "See"*: Kinkel v. Cingular Wireless, 857 N.E.2d 250 (Ill. 2006) ("[T]he doctrine of unconscionability should be at least as protective of individual consumers who enter into contract with commercial entities as it is of one business that enters into a contract with another business."); Knudsen v. Lax, 842 N.Y.S.2d 341 (Co. Ct. 2007) (abandonment clause in lease unconscionable when invoked after tenant and children left building because registered sex offender had moved next door); Wisconsin Auto Title Loans v. Jones, *supra* note 23 ("Substantive unconscionability has usually been successfully raised against commercial interests dealing with consumers, especially poor and disadvantaged consumers.") (citing to treatise).

§4.28 n.38 p.588 Add the following at the end: This may in part be caused by legislative action that calls into question certain types of contractual behavior. *See In re* Poly-Am., *supra* note 10 (finding liability limitation in employment contract unconscionable and void as against public policy because it contravened the purposes of the Texas Workers' Compensation Act).

§4.28 n.39 p.588 Add the following to the list after **"Accord"***:* Spectrum Networks v. Plus Realty, 878 N.E.2d 1122 (Ohio C.P. 2007) (realtor avoiding consulting agreement with telecommunications firm).

§4.28 n.39 p.588 Add the following to the list after **"See generally"***:* Garvin, Small Business and the False Dichotomies of Contract Law, 40 Wake Forest L. Rev. 295 (2005).

§4.28 n.40 p.589 Add the following to the list after **"See"***:* Nagrampa v. MailCoups, Inc., *supra* note 33 (arbitration clause unconscionable; "franchise agreements have some characteristics of contracts of adhesion because of the 'vastly superior bargaining strength' of the franchisor"); Indep. Ass'n of Mailbox Ctr. Owners v. Superior Ct., 34 Cal. Rptr. 3d 659 (Ct. App. 2005) (provision banning group arbitration not enforceable).

§4.28 n.41 p.589 Add the following to the list after **"Accord"***:* Indep. Ass'n of Mailbox Ctr. Owners v. Superior Ct., *supra* note 40 ("franchise agreements, in some cases, have the same qualities of adhesion contracts as do certain consumer contracts . . . . These franchise agreements also resemble employment agreements to the extent that the franchisees' livelihoods are involved").

§4.28 n.41 p.589 In the second paragraph, add the following to the list after **Carter***:* Arnott v. Am. Oil Co., 609 F.2d 873 (8th Cir. 1979) ("franchisor and franchisee of a service station operation are involved in a fiduciary franchise relationship"), limited by Bain v. Champlin Petroleum Co., 692 F.2d 43 (8th Cir. 1982) ("*Arnott* does not stand for the proposition that the grant of a franchise of itself in all instances imposes on the franchisor all the

duties and responsibilities which traditionally pertain to a true fiduciary").

§4.28 n.41 p.589 ***In the second paragraph, add the following after the second sentence:*** *Cf.* Larese v. Creamland Dairies, 767 F.2d 716 (10th Cir. 1985) ("the franchisor-franchisee relationship is one which requires the parties to deal with one another in good faith and in a commercially reasonable manner").

§4.28 n.43 p.590 ***Add the following to the list after "Accord":*** U.S. Welding v. Battelle Energy Alliance, 728 F. Supp. 2d 1110 (D. Idaho 2010) (rejecting unconscionability argument because the plaintiff "is a sophisticated corporate entity, complete with in-house counsel, and obtained this procurement contract after voluntarily submitting a bid . . . Moreover, [the plaintiff] subsequently extended the duration of the contract performance period on several occasions. This is not a situation in which a powerless consumer is forced into a contract in order to obtain a necessary benefit."); BDO Seidman v. Bee, 970 So. 2d 869 (Fla. App. 2007) (partner in accounting firm bound by arbitration clause requiring that panel consist entirely of firm's partners); Miller v. Cotter, *supra* note 27 (plaintiff, a regional claims manager for an insurance company, was "an intelligent and educated man whose professional experience gave him sophistication in dealing with contracts," and so should have been aware of the nature of the documents he signed).

§4.28 n.46 p.591 ***Add the following at the end of the second sentence:*** , itself followed in Gibson v. Nye Frontier Ford, 203 P.3d 1091 (Alaska 2009) (identical $50,000 threshold; "the cases in which arbitration will be sought by an employer against an employee are so much less frequent than cases in which the employee is pursuing a claim that this possibility does not serve to refute Gibson's charge of one-sidedness"), and in Gentry v. Superior Ct., *supra* note 33 (citing liberally to *Armendariz*); Geoffroy v. Wash. Mut. Bank, *supra* note 26 (arbitration clause in checking account contract unconscionable when bank had right to offset or exercise a security interest without going to arbitration, but all of depositor's claims would go to arbitration); Bragg v. Linden Research, *supra* note 33 (where the terms of service "provide [the

drafter] with a variety of one-sided remedies to resolve disputes, while forcing its customers to arbitrate any dispute" and where the drafter had a unilateral right to modify the agreement at any time, the terms were substantively unconscionable) and in Zuver v. Airtouch Commc'ns, 103 P.3d 753 (Wash. 2004) (provision barring employee, but not employer, from recovering exemplary or punitive damages "so one-sided and harsh" as to be substantively unconscionable); but distinguished in Irwin v. UBS Painewebber, 324 F. Supp. 2d 1103 (C.D. Cal. 2004) (arbitration clause enforceable except for imposition of fees; though a contract of adhesion, it did not lack mutuality and it provided for full discovery) and vigorously rejected in Oblix, Inc. v. Winiecki, 374 F.3d 488 (7th Cir. 2004) (Easterbrook, J.) ("It is in the end irrelevant whether the Supreme Court of California wants to treat arbitration less favorably than other promises in form contracts; no state can apply to arbitration (when governed by the Federal Arbitration Act) any novel rule. Under normal rules of contract, the promises Winiecki made in order to be hired and paid are enforceable. Thus she must arbitrate."). *See also* Merkin v. Vonage Am., Inc., 2014 U.S. Dist. LEXIS 14055 (C.D. Cal. Feb. 3, 2014) (arbitration agreement was procedurally unconscionable because it was contract of adhesion and unilaterally modified 36 times, and was substantively unconscionable because it lacked mutuality in that collection, intellectual property, and unauthorized use disputes could be litigated in court); Nishimura v. Gentry Homes, Ltd., 338 P.3d 524 (Haw. 2014) (holding arbitration agreement unenforceable because "the arbitrator-selection provision at issue in this appeal was fundamentally unfair, because it gave the defendant's agent 'sole discretion' to select an arbitration service") (following McMullen v. Meijer, Inc., 355 F.3d 485 (6th Cir. 2004)).

§4.28 n.46 p.591 Add the following at the end of the first paragraph: *See generally* Estlund, Between Rights and Contracts: Arbitration Agreements and Non-Compete Covenants as a Hybrid Form of Employment Law, 155 U. Pa. L. Rev. 379 (2006).

§4.28 n.47 p.592 Add the following to the list after "Accord": Harper v. Ultimo, 7 Cal. Rptr. 3d 418 (Ct. App. 2003) (Better Business Bureau arbitration rules not attached to homeowners' property repair contract were unconscionable), explained in Lucas v. Gund, Inc., 450 F. Supp. 2d 1125 (C.D. Cal. 2006) ("[T]he problem [in *Harper*] wasn't just that the rules were not attached, but that it was done to hide the fact that the weaker party was giving up significant rights"); Arnold v. Burger King, 2015-Ohio-4485 (arbitration clause procedurally and substantively unconscionable, and rape by coworker fell outside scope of agreement; discussed *supra* note 11).

§4.28 n.47 p.592 Add the following to the list after* "See generally"*: Bruhl, The Unconscionability Game: Strategic Judging and the Evolution of Federal Arbitration Law, 83 N.Y.U.L. Rev. 1420 (2008); Gavin, Unconscionability Found: A Look at Pre-Dispute Mandatory Arbitration Agreements 10 Years After *Doctor's Associates, Inc. v. Casarotto*, 54 Clev. St. L. Rev. 249 (2006); Marrow, Determining if Mandatory Arbitration is "Fair": Asymmetrically Held Information and the Role of Mandatory Arbitration in Modulating Uninsurable Contract Risks, 54 N.Y.L.S. L. Rev. 187 (2009-2010); Miller, Contracting Out of Process, Contracting Out of Corporate Accountability: An Argument Against Enforcement of Pre-Dispute Limits on Process, 75 Tenn. L. Rev. 365 (2008). The rise of arbitration agreements is also gaining considerable public attention and criticism. See Jessica Silver-Greenberg and Robert Gebeloff, "Arbitration Everywhere, Stacking the Deck of Justice," New York Times (Oct. 31, 2015), Silver-Greenberg and Gebeloff, "In Arbitration, a 'Privatization of the Justice System,'" New York Times (Nov. 1, 2015).

§4.28 n.47 p.592 Add the following at the end: Franchisees successfully challenged an arbitration clause as illusory in Druco Rest. Inc. v. Steak N Shake Enters., Inc., 765 F.3d 776, 779 (7th Cir. 2014). The original agreement did not require arbitration but provided that the franchisor "reserve[d] the right to institute at any time a system of nonbinding arbitration or mediation." *Id.* at 779. When a group of franchisees initiated a lawsuit, the franchisor then modified the agreement to require arbitration. The Seventh Circuit found "that the arbitration clauses are illusory and unenforceable under Indiana law." *Id.* at 784.

The Supreme Court of Louisiana refused to enforce an arbitration clause in a contract between a trampoline park and a patron, finding that the formatting of the form contract made it adhesionary and unenforceable. Duhon v. ActiveLaf, LLC, 2016-0818 (La. Oct. 19, 2016). The court found:

> looking at the Agreement as a whole, the arbitration language appears to be the only specific provision not relegated to a separate paragraph or set apart in some explicit way. Here, the two-sentence provision mandating arbitration is camouflaged within the confines of an eleven sentence paragraph, nine of which do not discuss arbitration. The effect of the placement of the arbitration language is to cloak it within a blanket of boilerplate language regarding rules and risks of participating in the Sky Zone activities. Thus, . . . we find Mr. Duhon did not truly consent to the arbitration provision

Id. at 10. The court further found that only the customer, and not the company, were bound to submit claims to arbitration, and held that this "lack of mutuality in the arbitration clause fortifies our finding that it is adhesionary." *Id.*

A threshold issue has divided the courts: whether the Federal Arbitration Act (FAA) preempts state law on unconscionability. The Supreme Court has held that "generally applicable contract defenses, such as fraud, duress, or unconscionability, may be applied to invalidate arbitration agreements without contravening [FAA §2]." Doctor's Assocs. v. Casarotto, 517 U.S. 681 (1996). In parsing general applicability, the Court also has stated that "[a] state-law principle that takes its meaning precisely from the fact that a contract to arbitrate is at issue does not comport with this requirement of [FAA] §2" and that a court may not "rely on the uniqueness of an agreement to arbitrate as a basis for a state-law holding that enforcement would be unconscionable." Perry v. Thomas, 482 U.S. 483 (1987). Lower courts have divided when applying these principles to unconscionability claims, with some concluding that applicable state law applies neutrally across contracts and other concluding that across-the-board holdings that types of arbitration clauses are unconscionable fall afoul of the FAA. *Compare* Lowden v. T-Mobile USA, 512 F.3d 1213 (9th Cir. 2008) (state law not preempted), Kinkel v. Cingular Wireless, *supra* note 38 (same), Discover Bank v. Superior Ct., *supra* note 25 (same) and Wisconsin Auto Title Loans v. Jones, *supra* note 23 (same) *with* Gay v. Credit *Inform*, 511 F.3d 369 (3d Cir. 2007) (state law preempted) and Schultz v. AT & T Wireless Servs., 376 F. Supp. 2d 685 (N.D.W. Va. 2005) (same). THI of New Mexico v. Patton, 741

F.3d 1162 (10th Cir. 2014) considered a doctrine from the New Mexico Court of Appeals that held all one-sided arbitration agreements to be unconscionable. The district court held the agreement unenforceable on the basis of that state law doctrine, finding this outcome consistent with the American Arbitration Act provision that arbitration agreements can be held unenforceable on generally applicable state law grounds that apply to any contract. 851 F. Supp. 2d 1281 (D.N.M. 2011). The Tenth Circuit reversed, finding that the state common law was necessarily premised on an assumption that arbitration is inferior to litigation, which the AAA was designed to overcome. "[J]ust as the FAA preempts a state statute that is predicated on the view that arbitration is an inferior means of vindicating rights, it also preempts state common law — including the law regarding unconscionability — that bars an arbitration agreement because of the same view." 741 F.3d at 1167.

The courts holding that there is no preemption are in the majority, and in any case generally have the better of the argument. A court could apply its universal unconscionability provisions and find that all arbitration agreements of a certain type — for example, agreements barring class actions — were unconscionable, just as it could find all contracts to commit murder to be void as against public policy without making individualized determinations.

To some degree the Supreme Court resolved this in Buckeye Check Cashing v. Cardegna, 546 U.S. 440 (2006). There it distinguished between challenges to the validity of an arbitration clause and challenges to the validity of the contract as a whole. The former may be resolved in court; the latter must go to the arbitrator. This does not address whether a state's courts could hold a particular type of arbitration clause universally unconscionable, but it does make clear who may make what determination. *Cf.* Townsend v. Quadrant Corp., 224 P.3d 818 (Wash. App. 2009) (arbitration clause not procedurally unconscionable; parties challenging the clause alleged facts relating to the agreement as a whole, not the arbitration clause in particular, which was held insufficient to establish procedural unconscionability), *review granted*, 238 P.3d 1252 (Wash. 2010).

The holding in *Buckeye Check Cashing* was narrowed materially in Rent-A-Center W. v. Jackson, 130 S. Ct. 2772 (2010). The

Court continued the *Buckeye* distinction between the validity of the arbitration clause and the validity of the agreement as a whole, but focused more tightly on the arbitration clause. It held that courts may determine the validity, not of the arbitration agreement as a whole, but only of the "delegation provision — the provision that gave the arbitrator exclusive authority to resolve any dispute relating to the enforceability of this Agreement." *Id.* at 2779 (internal quotations and ellipses omitted). The balance of the arbitration agreement is, like the substantive parts of the contract, within the arbitrator's exclusive scope to adjudicate, including questions of validity. It is safe to say that fewer disputes will be heard by the courts, which will increase the risk that the law as applied by arbitrators and the law as applied by courts will diverge; after all, arbitral decisions are seldom published and need not in any case be supported by detailed legal analysis, unless the pertinent arbitral rules require that. Perhaps more important, it is difficult to tell which challenges may still be heard in courts and which not. The Court acknowledged that many of the challenges Jackson raised — for example, to fee-splitting and discovery limitations provisions — would be more difficult to establish if directed toward only the delegation provision, i.e., the specific agreement to arbitrate. *Id.* at 2780. Fee-splitting is on its face one sort of dispute that will seldom be heard by courts, because the fees involved with the delegation provision itself will be fairly modest compared to those for the arbitration as a whole. But it is far too early to give up on judicial challenges to arbitration clauses. One issue unaddressed by the Court is to what extent an attack on the delegation provision permits a look at what the consequences of delegation would be. To take an extreme case, a delegation provision stating that the plaintiff would have to post a $10 million bond as a condition of arbitration would presumably be open to judicial attack, even after *Rent-A-Center.* Beyond these threshold issues rest some pertaining to the arbitration itself. Put otherwise, can a delegation provision be unconscionable because the underlying arbitration would itself be unconscionable? To answer this question requires at least a sidelong glance at the substance of the arbitration clause — not, perhaps, the clause-by-clause attack that is so common now, but an attack on the proceeding as a whole. One would anticipate fewer successes when one has to kill the whole provision rather than lop off unwelcome bits, to be sure. But sufficiently noxious arbitration agreements should still be subject to judicial challenge by this means.

§4.28 n.48 p.592 Add the following after the citation to **Ting***:* , followed in Nagrampa v. MailCoups, Inc., *supra* note 33 (arbitration clause in franchise contract unconscionable where it is "far more likely" that the franchisee would raise issues subject to arbitration than would the franchisor, and the franchisor would have access to court to obtain any provisional remedy); Baker v. Osborne Dev. Corp., 71 Cal. Rptr. 3d 854 (Ct. App. 2008) (arbitration clause in home sales contract unenforceable when the seller "would have no conceivable reason to institute legal proceedings" but "virtually every claim the homeowners might raise against . . . [those] in any way involved in the construction of plaintiffs' homes would be subject to arbitration") Morrow v. Hallmark Cards, 273 S.W.3d 15 (Mo. App. 2008) (only employment-related claims against the company subject to arbitration; "[t]his does not necessarily mean that there could be no enforceable contract to arbitrate claims," for there could be an enforceable underlying contract, or a special reason for a one-sided contract, or specific consideration for the imbalance. "However, the lack of mutual promises to submit claims must be considered in determining whether there is an enforceable agreement, particularly if it is adhesive in nature."); and in Wisconsin Auto Title Loans v. Jones, *supra* note 23 ("The doctrine of substantive unconscionability limits the extent to which a stronger party to a contract may impose arbitration on the weaker party without accepting the arbitration forum for itself.").

§4.28 n.48 p.592 Add the following to the list after the citation to **The Money Place v. Barnes***:* , Tyson Foods v. Archer, 147 S.W.3d 681 (Ark. 2004) (arbitration clause permitting only one party to litigate lacked mutuality and hence unenforceable), and Asbury Auto. Used Car Ctr. v. Brosh, 220 S.W.3d 637 (Ark. 2005) ("Mutuality within the arbitration agreement itself is required.").

§4.28 n.48 p.592 Add the following to the list after **"Accord"***:* Abramson v. Juniper Networks, 9 Cal. Rptr. 3d 422 (Ct. App. 2004) (mutuality is "key factor" and if "only the weaker

party's claims are subject to arbitration, and there is no reasonable justification for that lack of symmetry, the agreement lacks the requisite degree of mutuality"); Covenant Health Rehab. of Picayune v. Brown, 949 So. 2d 732 (Miss. 2007) (clause in nursing home contract that required alternative dispute resolution except for issues of payment or refund "was one-sided, oppressive, and unconscionable"), *overruled on other grounds*, Covenant Health Rehab. of Picayune v. Estate of Moulds, *supra* note 36; Rivera v. Am. Gen. Fin. Servs., ___ P.3d ___, 2011 WL 3687624 (N.M. July 27, 2011) (lending agreement required arbitration except for foreclosure or repossession actions; "American General's ability under the arbitration clause to seek judicial redress of its likeliest claims while forcing Rivera to arbitrate any claim she may have is unreasonably one-sided."); Tillman v. Comm'l Credit Loans, *supra* note 24 (where the exceptions to an arbitration clause "appear to be designed for more for the benefit of defendants than for plaintiffs," "[t]he one-sidedness of the clause therefore contributes to our overall conclusion that it is unconscionable"); Taylor v. Butler, 142 S.W.3d 277 (Tenn. 2004) (finding arbitration clause "oppressive" where it obliged the buyer to arbitrate while preserving the seller's right to litigate "for practically all claims that it could have"); Owner-Operator Indep. Drivers Ass'n v. C.R. England, Inc., *supra* note 36 (where drafter may "act unfettered by any requirement to arbitrate" but the agreements "purport to bind the drivers to submit any and all claims to an expensive arbitration proceeding in a distant and inconvenient forum," the clause is substantively unconscionable).

§4.28 n.48 p.592 Add the following after the second sentence: *Cf.* Motsinger v. Lithia Rose-FT, 156 P.3d 156 (Or. App. 2007) (mutuality not relevant to the enforceability of arbitration clauses; rather, "we must determine on a case-by-case basis whether, given the unequal bargaining power, the effect of the arbitration clause makes the parties' respective obligations so unbalanced as to be unconscionable"; fact of one-sided arbitration by itself not sufficient to yield an unconscionable effect).

§4.28 n.49 p.592 Add the following after the citation to **Green Tree Fin. Corp.***:* , followed in State *ex rel.* Vincent v. Schneider, 194 S.W.3d 853 (Mo. 2006).

***§4.28 n.49 p.592 Add the following to the list after* "Accord":** Caley v. Gulfstream Aerospace Corp., 428 F.3d 1359 (11th Cir. 2005) (no unconscionability where "both parties are required to arbitrate covered claims, and neither is required to arbitrate non-covered claims"); Iberia Credit Bureau v. Cingular Wireless, 379 F.3d 159 (5th Cir. 2004) (clause permitting cable provider to change terms of agreement upon notice to customer did not make arbitration clause unconscionable); Tortoriello v. Gerald Nissan, *supra* note 15 (mutuality of obligation relevant only to the extent of finding consideration; here, "the promise to arbitrate is part of a clause within a larger contract. . . . As plaintiff has never questioned that [this contract] is supported by consideration, the arbitration clause does not suffer for lack of mutuality of obligation."). *Cf.* Salley v. Option One Mortg. Corp., 925 A.2d 115 (Pa. 2007) (subprime loan contract allowing lender to litigate foreclosure, but providing only arbitration for borrower's claims, "does not, in and of itself, render the arbitration agreement substantively unconscionable").

§4.28 n.49 p.592 Add the following after the citation to* Conseco*: , followed in Walther v. Sovereign Bank, *supra* note 33 ("Mutuality . . . does not require an exactly even exchange of identical rights and obligations").

§4.28 n.49 p.592 Add the following at the end: As a rationale, some courts have held that there is no problem with mutuality when "the underlying contract . . . is supported by adequate consideration." Stenzel v. Dell, Inc., 870 A.2d 133, 144 (Me. 2005). *Accord:* Oblix, Inc. v. Winiecki, *supra* note 46 (Easterbrook, J.) ("Winiecki does not deny that the arbitration clause is supported by consideration — her salary. Oblix paid her to do a number of things; one of the things it paid her to do was agree to non-judicial dispute resolution. It is hard to see how the arbitration clause is any more suspect, or any less enforceable, than the others — or, for that matter, than her salary."); Harris v. Green Tree Fin. Corp., 183 F.3d 173 (3d Cir. 1999) ("As long as the requirement of consideration is met, mutuality of obligation is present"); Price v. Taylor, 575 F. Supp. 2d 845 (N.D. Ohio 2008) (excluding claims from arbitration clause which the plaintiff would be more likely to bring "is not a question of mutuality, but of adequacy of consideration"); State *ex rel.* Vincent v. Schneider, *supra*; DEX Media v. Nat'l Mgmt. Servs., 150 P.3d 1093 (Or. App. 2007) ("not every contractual obligation need be mutual as long as each party has provided some consideration for the contract"); *In re* FirstMerit Bank, 52 S.W.3d 749 (Tex. 2001). ("[A]n arbitration clause does not require mutuality of obligation, so long as the underlying contract is supported by adequate consideration."). *Cf.* Zuver v. Airtouch Comm'ns, 103 P.3d 753 (Wash. 2004) (*First Merit* holding is the majority approach). This seems consistent with the frequent hostility of modern contract law toward mutuality of obligation. Restatement Second §79; see §3.2 *supra*. As long as the contract as a whole is supported by consideration, it should not matter for the purposes of consideration whether one party or the other has greater rights in a particular area of the contract. *But see* Motsinger v. Lithia Rose-FT, *supra* note 48 ("[I]t is possible for a contractual term to be supported by adequate consideration and yet be so unreasonable as to be unconscionable in the context of a contract of adhesion.").

§4.28 n.50 p.592 Add the following after the citation to* Circuit City Stores*: , rejected by Gentry v. Superior Ct., *supra* note 33 (despite opt-out right to arbitration clause in employment contract, agreement "was, at the very least, not entirely free from procedural unconscionability").

§4.28 n.50 p.592 Add the following to the list after* "Cf."*: Wash. Mut. Fin. Grp. v. Bailey, 364 F.3d 260 (5th Cir. 2004) (rejecting contention that arbitration agreement was unconscionable because lender did not inform borrowers that they were signing arbitration agreement after they had informed lender of their inability to read); Marcus & Millichap Real Estate Inv. Servs. of Seattle, Inc. v. Yates, Wood & MacDonald, Inc., 192 Wn. App. 465 (Wash. App. 2016) ("voluntary membership in a professional organization gives rise to a corresponding obligation to comply with that organization's bylaws. Where those bylaws contain an agreement to arbitrate, this principle applies with equal force. Under such circumstances, a binding agreement to arbitrate is adequately evidenced by proof of membership in the organization; a signed agreement is not required."); Salameno v. GoGo LLC, 2016 U.S. Dist. LEXIS 88166 (E.D.N.Y. July 7, 2016) (in dispute involving quality of in-flight Internet service, court enforced arbitration agreement because "[i]n order to purchase Gogo's product, plaintiffs were presented with a webpage that required them to click a button near the statement 'By clicking this button, you agree to Gogo's privacy & cookie policy and terms of use.' The 'terms of use' were hyperlinked so that plaintiffs could review the terms before making their purchase. This constituted a clickwrap agreement. Then, each time plaintiffs signed-in to use Gogo's product, they were again presented with a webpage that contained the terms of use hyperlink. This constituted a sign-in-wrap agreement. Additionally, upon purchase, plaintiffs were sent a confirmation e-mail that also contained a hyperlink to Gogo's terms of use. Similar combinations of clickwrap and sign-in-wrap agreements are enforceable.") (citation omitted).

§4.28 n.50 p.592 Add the following to the list after **"But cf.":** Douglas v. U.S. Dist. Ct., 495 F.3d 1062 (9th Cir. 2007) (long-distance telephone company could not change terms of agreement without providing "proper notice of the changes" proposed; posting on the company's website insufficient); Fitz v. NCR Corp. 13 Cal. Rptr. 3d 88 (Ct. App. 2004) (employee "could either quit her job of 14 years or agree to the terms by merely remaining employed . . . for one month"); Sgouros v. TransUnion Corp., 817 F.3d 1029 (7th Cir. 2016) (*see also* §3.7 *supra*) (where consumer purchased credit score online, there was no agreement to arbitrate where arbitration clause appeared online deep within a scroll box and, moreover, "TransUnion undid whatever notice it might have been furnishing in its bold text block by explicitly stating that a click on the button constituted assent for TransUnion to obtain access to the purchaser's personal information. That text distracted the purchaser from the Service Agreement by informing him that clicking served a particular purpose unrelated to the Agreement.").

§4.28 n.50 p.592 Add the following to the end: There have been some efforts to limit mandatory arbitration of employment disputes by federal law. In 2014, President Obama issued the Fair Pay and Safe Workplaces Executive Order, requiring that companies with contracts worth over $1 million facing employee

disputes arising under the Civil Rights Act or alleging sexual assault or harassment may send those disputes to arbitration only "with the voluntary consent of employees or independent contractors after such disputes arise." Section 6(a). Exec. Order No. 13,673, 79 Fed. Reg. 45,309, 45,314 (July 23, 2014). Similar legislative efforts received some support but appear to have stalled. *See, e.g.*, Arbitration Fairness Act, S. 878, 113th Cong. (2013).

Related to consent, a minor's right to disaffirm a contract raises interesting issues for arbitration clauses. *See supra* §4.4 note 9; *compare* Douglass v. Pflueger Haw., Inc., 110 Haw. 520, 135 P.3d 129, 145 (2006) (17-year-old employee competent to consent to arbitration agreement; "by relaxing the requirements for sixteen- and seventeen-year-olds to obtain employment, the legislature clearly viewed minors in this particular age group — being only one to two years from adulthood — as capable and competent to contract for gainful employment and, therefore, should be bound by the terms of such contracts"), *and* Sheller *ex rel.* Sheller v. Frank's Nursery & Crafts, Inc., 957 F. Supp. 150, 154 (N.D. Ill. 1997) (arbitration agreement enforceable because "[p]ermitting the minor Plaintiffs to void their contract would be inconsistent with the public policy reasons underlying the infancy law doctrine."), *with* Lopez v. Kmart Corp., 2015 U.S. Dist. LEXIS 58328, 24 Wage & Hour Cas. 2d (BNA) 1610 (N.D. Cal. May 4, 2015) (statutory right to disaffirm is absolute; minor disaffirmed arbitration agreement by filing suit one month after turning 18).

§4.28 n.51 p.593 Add the following after the citation to* Mendez*: , followed in Walters v. A.A.A. Waterproofing, 211 P.3d 454 (Wash. App. 2009) (particularized proof of income and expenses such that the plaintiff "plausibly declares that [he and his family] have nothing left from their paychecks after paying [their] expenses"; "This information establishes a prima facie case that the costs of arbitration are prohibitive," and the employer did not come forward with facts to rebut the plaintiff's case).

§4.28 n.51 p.593 Add the following to the list after* "Accord"*: Clark v. Renaissance West, LLC, 307 P.3d 77, 81 (Ariz. Ct. App. 2013) (skilled nursing facility could not enforce arbitration clause against plaintiff, where "it would cost Plaintiff approximately $22,800 in arbitrator's fees to arbitrate the case" and there was no provision for waiver or reduction of fees); State *ex rel.* Vincent v. Schneider, *supra* note 49 ("It is unconscionable to have a provision in an arbitration clause that puts all fees for arbitration on the consumer . . . particularly . . . when the cost-shifting terms could work to grant one party immunity from legitimate claims"); Covenant Health Rehab. of Picayune v. Brown, *supra* note 48 (finding unconscionable a clause requiring that nursing-home resident pay all enforcement costs if the resident challenges the process or an award under it); Tillman v. Comm'l Credit Loans, *supra* note 24 (where "[p]laintiffs simply do not have the resources to risk facing" arbitral fees, which helps "create[] a barrier to pursuing arbitration that is substantially greater than that present in the context of litigation"); Gonski v. Second Judicial Dist. Ct., 245 P.3d 1164 (Nev. 2010) (unconscionable to require that party initiating arbitration pay the necessary fees, especially because "the plan administrator is to determine the arbitration organization"); Delta Funding Corp. v. Harris, 912 A.2d 104 (N.J. 2006) (provision requiring each party to bear its own costs and fees and potentially the costs of the winner unconscionable as "deterrent to the vindication of [the plaintiff's] statutory rights" and contrary to "the statutory remedy of attorney's fees and costs"); McNulty v. H & R Block, 843 A.2d 1267 (Pa. Super. 2004) (clause requiring consumer to pay $50 fee to arbitrate claim that would not exceed $37 was unconscionable); McKee v. AT&T Corp., 191 P.3d 845 (Wash. 2008) (where merchant gives itself the right to collect attorney fees against the consumer, but the consumer is barred from collecting attorney fees unless "expressly authorized by statute," the provision "contravenes the policy of this state" by making fee recovery non-reciprocal and thus is substantively unconscionable).

§4.28 n.51 p.593 Add the following to the list after "Cf.": Awuah v. Coverall N. Am., *supra* note 32 (the concern is "whether the arbitration regime here is structured so as to *prevent* a litigant from having access to the arbitrator to resolve claims. . . . The standard for such a showing of illusoriness would also be high — all formal dispute resolution involves costs and inconvenience."; remanding for further fact-finding on whether the arbitration clause is illusory); Nagrampa v. MailCoups, Inc., *supra* note 33 (clause requiring arbitration in Boston unconscionable where franchisee in California and franchisor in Massachusetts); Bragg v. Linden Research, *supra* note 33 (clause requiring arbitration in San Francisco unconscionable where customers are located all over the country and the average transaction involves a modest amount); Hollins v. Debt Relief of Am., *supra* note 33 (clause requiring arbitration in Texas for Nebraska resident unconscionable; it "is arguably a calculated decision by the defendant to insulate itself from its malfeasance"); Owner-Operator Indep. Drivers Ass'n v. C.R. England, Inc., *supra* note 36 (where fees "effectively deter use of [] arbitration" and the arbitration must take place in Salt Lake City, "a distant and inconvenient forum," arbitration clause substantively unconscionable); Wisconsin Auto Title Loans v. Jones, *supra* note 23 (fee-splitting provision unconscionable in subprime lending contract; "the borrowers are, in all likelihood, strapped for cash").

§4.28 n.51 p.593 Add the following to the list after **"But cf.":** Green Tree Fin. Corp.-Ala. v. Randolph, 531 U.S. 79 (2000) (federal causes of action under FAA: "arbitration agreement's silence on [arbitration costs] . . . is plainly insufficient to render it unenforceable"; mere risk that a plaintiff will be foreclosed from having her case heard is too speculative to justify invalidating arbitration clause), followed in Taylor Bldg. Corp. of Am. v. Benfield, *supra* note 23 (state causes of action: "an arbitration clause will not be held unenforceable based on unsupported allegations of prohibitive costs"); Motsinger v. Lithia Rose-FT, *supra* note 48 ("We will not invalidate the arbitration clause simply because of the possibility that plaintiff, if she were to lose, would bear some undetermined costs of arbitration."), itself followed in Livingston v. Metro. Pediatrics, 227 P.3d 796 (Or. App. 2010) ("[I]n the absence of evidence that the fee-shifting provision, in fact, results in the arbitration forum not providing a reasonable alternative forum for this plaintiff, we conclude that the fee-shifting provision is not substantively unconscionable") and distinguished in Parada v. Super. Ct., 98 Cal. Rptr. 3d 743 (Ct. App. 2009) (proof that cost of three-arbitrator panel unnecessary and prohibitive), itself distinguished in Monex Deposit Co. v. Gilliam, 671 F. Supp. 2d 1137 (C.D. Cal. 2009) (same provision, but with only one arbitrator; held not procedurally unconscionable for reasons of cost); Gibson, *supra* note 46 (generally applicable

bar on waiver of substantive rights under state Wage and Hour Act covers attempt to split costs of arbitration) and in Walters, *supra* (fee-shifting provision "is an enormous deterrent to an employee contemplating a suit to vindicate the right to overtime pay"; "where the governing statutes provide that only a prevailing employee will be entitled to recover fees and costs, a reciprocal attorney fees provision is unconscionable"); Vasquez-Lopez v. Beneficial Or., *supra* note 28 (where arbitration agreement does allocate costs, using the plaintiff's estimate of costs sufficient); Nagrampa v. MailCoups, Inc., *supra* note 33 (fee-splitting clause not substantively unconscionable per se); Faber v. Menard, 367 F.3d 1048 (8th Cir. 2004) (party seeking to avoid arbitration "bears burden of showing that arbitrators' fees will be cost-prohibitive" by "specific evidence" and "more than just a hypothetical inability to pay"); Bess v. DirecTV, Inc., 885 N.E.2d 488 (Ill. App. 2008) ("An arbitration provision is not rendered inherently unconscionable because some of the arbitration costs will be imposed on the customer."); Stenzel v. Dell, Inc., *supra* note 49 (fee-shifting provision in arbitral rules prevents cost from supporting unconscionability claim); Feeney v. Dell, Inc., 908 N.E.2d 753 (Mass. 2009) ("We decline to enforce a prohibition on class actions in a consumer contract where to do so would in effect sanction a waiver of the right to proceed in a class action under [the Massachusetts UDAP statute]"; to do so "creates the potential for countless customers to be without an effective method to vindicate their statutory rights, a result clearly at odds with our public policy"); *In re* Poly-Am., *supra* note 10 (requires "*some evidence* that a complaining party will likely incur arbitration costs in such an amount as to deter enforcement of statutory rights in the arbitral forum" (emphasis in original)); Torres v. Simpatico, Inc., 781 F.3d 963, 969 (8th Cir. 2015) (franchisees failed to provide sufficient evidence that arbitration costs would be prohibitively expensive; parties challenging the agreement "bear the burden of showing that individual arbitration would be prohibitively expensive, and that it is likely, as opposed to merely speculative, that the prohibitive costs will actually be incurred").

§4.28 n.52 p.593 Add at beginning of note: In 2011, the U.S. Supreme Court held that arbitration agreements that prohibited class actions were not unconscionable, and that the Federal

Arbitration Act, 9 U.S.C §2, preempts any state law doctrine to the contrary. AT&T Mobility LLC v. Concepcion, 131 S. Ct. 1740, 179 L. Ed. 2d 742, 2011 U.S. LEXIS 3367 (2011). Some courts continued to strike down class action waivers, not on unconscionability grounds but under the vindication of rights doctrine, which held that a party could avoid arbitration if it could show that arbitration would not be an effective means of vindicating statutory rights. But, in 2013, the U.S. Supreme Court held that the Federal Arbitration Act does not permit a court to refuse to enforce a class action waiver provision in an arbitration agreement under that doctrine, either. Am. Express Co. v. Italian Colors Rest., 133 S. Ct. 2304, 186 L. Ed. 2d 417, 2013 U.S. LEXIS 4700 (2013). *See also* Johnmohammadi v. Bloomingdale's, Inc., 755 F.3d 1072 (9th Cir. 2014) (class action waiver was not unenforceable as contrary to employee rights under Norris-LaGuardia Act or National Labor Relations Act to engage in "concerted activities"). These two holdings are contrary to a considerable weight of holdings and rationale in earlier state and lower federal court rulings, which are discussed further below.

AT&T Mobility was a preemption case. Under California law, contracts of adhesion that contained class action waivers were unconscionable. The Supreme Court held that, where this doctrine prevented arbitration on the terms specified in an agreement, it frustrated the purposes of the FAA and was thus preempted by the federal law. The majority opinion reasoned that "[a]lthough §2's saving clause preserves generally applicable contract defenses, it does not suggest an intent to preserve state-law rules that stand as an obstacle to the accomplishment of the FAA's objectives. *Cf.* Geier v. Am. Honda Motor Co., 529 U.S. 861, 872, 120 S. Ct. 1913, 146 L. Ed. 2d 914. The FAA's overarching purpose is to ensure the enforcement of arbitration agreements according to their terms so as to facilitate informal, streamlined proceedings." *AT&T Mobility LLC*, 131 S. Ct. at 1743.

Technically, this holding on preemption grounds did not resolve whether federal common law such as the effective vindication of rights doctrine could invalidate class action waivers in arbitration agreements, although in his majority opinion in *American Express*, Justice Scalia wrote, "[t]ruth to tell, our decision in *AT&T Mobility* all but resolves this case." *American Express Co.*, 133 S. Ct. at 2312. When the Court considered that specific issue just two years later, it reasoned that the vindication of rights doctrine is inapplicable to waivers of class action. Addressing the reasoning from other courts that the practicalities of individual cases and low damages in many instances meant that class action was the only viable means of resolving certain types of alleged violations of rights, the Court held that "the fact that it is not worth the expense involved in proving a statutory remedy does not constitute the elimination of the right to pursue that remedy. The class-action waiver merely limits arbitration to the two contracting parties." *Id.* at 2311 (citation omitted).

These recent Supreme Court cases rejected the reasoning in a great number of cases to have considered the issue of class action waivers. Most recently, however, a new rationale for invalidating class action waivers (in arbitration agreements and elsewhere) is gaining traction, at least in the context of an employment contract. In August 2016, in Morris v. Ernst & Young, LLP, 834 F.3d 975, 2016 U.S. App. LEXIS 15638, 167 Lab. Cas. (CCH) P10,936, 26 Wage & Hour Cas. 2d (BNA) 1460 (9th Cir. 2016), the Ninth Circuit held that a class action waiver in an employment contract was unenforceable because it conflicted with employee rights under the National Labor Relations Act to engage in "concerted action." The court was careful to explain that the Federal Arbitration Act was inapplicable because "the arbitration requirement is not the problem. The same provision in a contract that required court adjudication as the exclusive remedy would equally violate the NLRA. The NLRA obstacle is a ban on initiating, in any forum, concerted legal claims — not a ban on arbitration." *Id.* at *16. The case is discussed further at §5.5 n.6, *infra*.

DirecTV, Inc. v. Imburgia, 136 S. Ct. 463 (2015) involved a clause that specified that all aspects the arbitration agreement would be unenforceable "[i]f . . . the law of your state would find this agreement to dispense with class arbitration procedures unenforceable." The California courts interpreted this clause to mean "the law of your state without considering the preemptive effect, if any of the [Federal Arbitration Act]." The Supreme Court reversed, holding that "framing the question in such terms" suggests a different treatment of arbitration clauses, not placing them, as the FAA requires, "on equal footing with all other contracts," Buckeye Check Cashing, Inc. v. Cardegna, 546 U.S. 440, 443, 126 S. Ct. 1204, 163 L. Ed. 2d 1038 (2006). Ultimately, the

Court concluded "that California courts would not interpret contracts other than arbitration contracts the same way," *DirecTV*, 136 S. Ct. at 373, and instead the contract clause was to be read as "the valid law of your state," as modified by Supreme Court decisions on FAA preemption.

In Holick v. Cellular Sales of New York LLC, 802 F.3d 391 (2d Cir. 2015), two named class representatives signed an employment contract that included an agreement to arbitrate "[a]ll claims, disputes, or controversies arising out of, or in relation to this document or Employee's employment with [Defendant]." They then sued, alleging that their "independent contractor" status prior to this employment agreement was in violation of the Fair Labor Standards Act (FLSA) because they were statutory employees. The defendant moved to compel arbitration, and the plaintiffs asserted that the employment contract did not cover the period before the defendant acknowledged them as employees. The Second Circuit reiterated that it "has held that broad arbitration provisions that contain no express temporal limitation can apply to claims that arose prior to the execution of the arbitration agreement." At 397. However, it looked to indicators of the parties' intent at the time of signing the contract that contained the arbitration agreement. Prior to signing that agreement, the parties executed an independent contractor agreement and behaved differently. Accordingly, "[i]t would be inconsistent with the parties' conduct to construe the Compensation Agreement, which referenced 'employment,' to apply to a period when the parties themselves did not contemplate such a relationship." At 398. The court recognized that the allegations in the complaint are that plaintiffs were employees at the time the dispute arose and called defendant's argument to compel arbitration on that basis "superficially appealing," but held that whether a party is an employee for FLSA purposes is a different question from a determination of the parties' intent. "After Defendants-Appellants affirmatively stated that Pratt and Burrell were not employees for over a year, it rings hollow for them to now argue that the parties intended the word 'employment' in the Compensation Agreements to apply retroactively as to this dispute."

In May 2016, the Consumer Financial Protection Board (CFPB) proposed regulations that would prohibit providers of consumer financial products and services from using a pre-dispute arbitration agreement to block consumer class actions in court and would require providers to insert language into their arbitration agreements reflecting this limitation. (Bureau of Consumer Fin. Prot., *Proposed Rule with Request for Public Comment*, CFPB-2016-0020, RIN 3170-AA51 (2016), available at http://files.consumerfinance.gov/f/documents/CFPB_Arbitration_Agreements_Notice_of_Proposed_Rulemaking.pdf.) This followed a CFPB study, released in 2015. (Bureau of Consumer Fin. Prot., *Arbitration Study: Report to Congress, Pursuant to Dodd-Frank Wall Street Reform and Consumer Protection Act §1028(a)* (2015), available at http://files.consumerfinance.gov/f/201503_cfpb_arbitration-study-report-to-congress-2015.pdf.) The rules proposed in 2016 are "based on the Bureau's preliminary findings — which are consistent with the Study — that pre-dispute arbitration agreements are being widely used to prevent consumers from seeking relief from legal violations on a class basis, and that consumers rarely file individual lawsuits or arbitration cases to obtain such relief." (Bureau of Consumer Fin. Prot., *Proposed Rule with Request for Public Comment*, CFPB-2016-0020, RIN 3170-AA51 (2016) at 3, available at http://files.consumerfinance.gov/f/documents/CFPB_Arbitration_Agreements_Notice_of_Proposed_Rulemaking.pdf.) Its press release called the arbitration waivers a "contract gotcha" under which "companies can sidestep the legal system, avoid accountability, and continue to pursue profitable practices that may violate the law and harm countless consumers" (Bureau of Consumer Fin. Prot., Press Release, "CFPB Proposes Prohibiting Mandatory Arbitration Clauses that Deny Groups of Consumers their Day in Court," May 5, 2016, available at http://www.consumerfinance.gov/about-us/newsroom/consumer-financial-protection-bureau-proposes-prohibiting-mandatory-arbitration-clauses-deny-groups-consumers-their-day-court/) and it quickly received considerable support from advocacy groups and academics. (Jean Sternlight of the University of Nevada at Las Vegas organized signatures for a letter from law professors in support of the regulations, available at https://bsl.app.box.com/v/CFPBletter.) The proposed rules would create a new 12 C.F.R. part 1040. 81 Fed. Reg. 32830 (May 24, 2016).

After the November 2016 Presidential election, there was rampant speculation as to whether the CFPB will finalize regulations before Donald Trump takes office. *See e.g.*, Jessica Karmasek, "Attorney: 'Very Likely' CFPB Will Finalize Proposed Arbitration Rules before Obama's Departure," Legal News Line, Dec. 29, 2016; Andrew Ackerman, "Financial Regulators Scramble to Complete Postcrisis Rules: Republicans urge policy makers not to rush new regulations before President-elect Trump takes office," Wall Street Journal, Nov. 21, 2016. In the end, the CFPB did not publish final rules before January 20, 2017. The speculation then moved to Congress, where 23 members sent a letter to Trump, "caution[ing] . . . against entering into a protracted — and likely unsuccessful — legal battle to oust [CFPB] Director Richard Cordray . . . before his term expires in July 2018," in part because "the CFPB is well on its way to completing rulemakings to . . . rein in forced arbitration clauses that deny consumers their day in court." Letter from Maxine Waters et al. to Donald Trump, Jan. 9, 2017, available on https://www.cfpbmonitor.com/wp-content/uploads/sites/5/2017/01/cmw_cfpb_letter_-_01.09.2017.pdf. Of course, CFPB still must contend with the prospect of the Republican Congress reversing any final rule. See Gregory Roberts, "CFPB's Assault on Arbitration Stuck Between Rock, Hard Place," Bloomberg Law, Mar. 7, 2017, https://www.bna.com/cfpbs-assault-arbitration-n57982084833/.

§4.28 n.52 p.593 Add the following at the end of the paragraph: *Accord: In re* Am. Express Merchs. Litig., 634 F.3d 187 (2d Cir. 2011) (antitrust: class action waiver unconscionable, based on expert affidavit about massive cost and extreme statutory limits on expert reimbursement; enforcing it would "effectively depriv[e] plaintiffs of the statutory protections of the antitrust laws") Skirchak v. Dynamics Research Corp., 508 F.3d 49 (1st Cir. 2007) (FLSA case; class waiver unconscionable because "[t]he timing, the language, and the format of the presentation of the [waiver] obscured, whether intentionally or not, the waiver of class rights."); Dale v. Comcast Corp., 498 F.3d 1216 (11th Cir. 2007) (class action waiver, and thus whole arbitration clause, unconscionable because otherwise the cable subscribers "would effectively be precluded from suing" for a violation of the Cable Act, for "[t]he cost of vindicating an individual subscriber's claim, when compared to his or her potential recovery, is too great"); Kristian v. Comcast Corp., 446 F.3d 25 (1st Cir. 2006) (class action waiver unconscionable because "[p]laintiffs [would] be unable to vindicate their statutory rights . . . because of the 'enforcement gap' created by the de facto liability shield"); Leonard v. Terminix Int'l Co., 854 So. 2d 529 (Ala. 2002) (pesticide company's arbitration clause was unconscionable because it foreclosed consumers from "practical redress through a class action" and restricted them to "disproportionately expensive individual arbitration"), followed in Kinkel v. Cingular Wireless, *supra* note 38 (class action waiver coupled with lack of mutuality and high liquidated damages clause unconscionable; "[t]hese provisions operate together to create a situation where the cost of vindicating the claim is so high that the plaintiff's only reasonable, cost-effective means of obtaining a complete remedy is as either the representative or a member of a class.") and in Whitney v. Alltel Commc'ns, 173 S.W.3d 300 (Mo. App. 2005) (upholding a class action waiver "would unfairly allow companies like Alltel to insulate themselves from the consumer protection laws of this State"), but distinguished in Gipson v. Cross Country Bank, 294 F. Supp. 2d 1251 (M.D. Ala. 2003) (credit card holder "may not have to pay any money out of her own pocket to initiate" arbitration, "need not worry about having her damages reduced by . . . costs or attorneys fees," and is not barred from "substantive remedies"); S.D.S. Autos v. Chrzanowski, 976 So. 2d 600 (Fla. App. 2007) (even though UDAP statute provides for attorney's fees, they are evaluated in light of the actual damages; consequently, barring class actions will chill the private enforcement scheme and is unconscionable); Muhammad v. Cnty. Bank of Rehoboth Beach, *supra* note 33 (class action waiver unconscionable; " 'rational' consumers may decline to pursue individual consumer-fraud suits because it may not be worth the time spent prosecuting the suit," and the waivers "can functionally exculpate wrongful conduct by reducing the possibility of attracting competent counsel"); Fiser v. Dell Computer Corp., 188 P.3d 1215 (N.M. 2008) (class waiver unconscionable; "[E]nforcing the class action ban would be tantamount to allowing Defendant to unilaterally exempt itself from New Mexico consumer protection laws."); Tillman v. Comm'l Credit Loans, *supra* note 24 (bar of class actions and joinder of claims "contributes to the financial inaccessibility of the arbitral forum" and "to the one-sidedness of the clause because the right to join claims and pursue class actions would benefit only borrowers"); Vasquez-Lopez v. Beneficial Or., *supra* note 28 ("the class action ban is unilateral in effect and, more significantly, it gives defendant a virtual license to commit, with impunity, millions of dollars' worth of small-scale fraud"); Thibodeau v. Comcast Corp., *supra* note 26 ("It is clearly contrary to public policy to immunize large corporations from liability by allowing them to preclude all class action litigation or [] arbitration."); Scott v. Cingular Wireless, *supra* note 10 (where "claims as small as those in this case are impracticable to pursue on an individual basis," a class action ban "functions to exculpate the drafter from liability," making the ban substantively unconscionable as "denying any meaningful remedy"), followed in McKee v. AT&T Corp., *supra* note 51 ("the individual claims here are extremely small, under $2 per month" so "[w]ithout access to class-wide relief, competent counsel would not be available to redress many meritorious claims; moreover, the agreement here is even less favorable than that in *Scott*, because *Scott* provided for fee-shifting for a prevailing plaintiff and the agreement here barred the arbitrator from awarding them unless statutorily required to do so") and in Lowden v. T-Mobile USA, *supra* note 47; Coady v. Cross County Bank, *supra* note 25 ("a waiver of class-wide relief is a significant factor . . . in invalidating an arbitration provision as unconscionable" . . . "particularly . . . when the damages involved are comparatively small for each individual consumer").

Cf. Gentry v. Superior Ct., *supra* note 33 (class action waiver void as against public policy if it would "disadvantage employees in vindicating their rights" under California's overtime statute); Klussman v. Cross Country Bank, 36 Cal. Rptr. 3d 728 (Ct. App. 2005) (for choice of law purposes, California's rejection of class action waivers is "a fundamental public policy interest" outweighing interest in uniform regulation of banks), followed in Hoffman v. Citibank (S.D.), 546 F.3d 1078 (9th Cir. 2008) (enforcing class arbitration waiver under South Dakota law "would be contrary to a fundamental public policy of California"); Brady v. Williams Capital Grp., 928 N.E.2d 383 (N.Y. 2010) (whether class arbitration waiver procedurally unconscionable as too costly depends, inter alia, on "(1) whether the litigant can pay the arbitration fees and costs; (2) what is the expected cost differential between arbitration and litigation in court; and (3) whether the cost differential is so substantial as to deter the bringing of claims in the arbitral forum"); Bilbrey v. Cingular Wireless, 164 P.3d 131 (Okla. 2007) (it is "unconscionable to apply a class action waiver to the lawsuit currently being prosecuted").

The Supreme Court has also held that the default provision in arbitration agreements — at least, arbitration agreement between sophisticated parties — is not to allow class-wide arbitration. Stolt-Nielsen S.A. v. AnimalFeeds Int'l Corp. 130 S. Ct. 1758 (2010). Because arbitration is a creature of contract, the Court held, if an agreement is silent about class-wide arbitration then only individual arbitration may result, barring some agreement to the contrary. If this approach extends outside the purely commercial realm, it will become very hard for consumers to pursue class arbitrations; the merchant, who almost invariably drafts the agreement, will simply remain silent about the availability of a class action. The Court's ruling was, however, over a dispute between merchants, and the Court did mention this dual merchant status in the course of justifying its result.

That agreement to permit class actions, however, need not be explicit; it need only be found by the arbitrator to be the intent of the parties in drafting the contract. Just a few years after *Stolt-Nielsen*, the Court let stand an arbitrator's decision that the agreement did permit class actions, despite the fact that the terms of the agreement appeared to be silent on that issue. Oxford Health Plans LLC v. Sutter, 133 S. Ct. 2064 (2013). There, the arbitrator relied on a broad requirement to arbitrate to conclude that the "intent of the clause" was "to vest in the arbitration process everything that is prohibited from the court process." *Id.* at 2067. Since court actions could include class actions, the parties, the arbitrator reasoned, must have intended to send class actions to arbitration. The majority held that this meant the arbitrator was determining the intent of the parties and meaning of the agreement, which are powers reserved to the arbitrator that a court (even the Supreme Court) may not set aside, even if unreasonable. Justice Kagan, in her majority opinion, explained the distinction:

> In *Stolt-Nielsen*, the arbitrators did not construe the parties' contract, and did not identify any agreement authorizing class proceedings. So in setting aside the arbitrators' decision, we found not

> that they had misinterpreted the contract, but that they had abandoned their interpretive role. Here, the arbitrator did construe the contract (focusing, per usual, on its language), and did find an agreement to permit class arbitration. So to overturn his decision, we would have to rely on a finding that he misapprehended the parties' intent. But §10(a)(4) bars that course: It permits courts to vacate an arbitral decision only when the arbitrator strayed from his delegated task of interpreting a contract, not when he performed that task poorly. *Stolt-Nielsen* and this case thus fall on opposite sides of the line that §10(a)(4) draws to delimit judicial review of arbitral decisions.

Id. at 2070.

However, whether courts or the arbitrator should decide whether the agreement permits classwide arbitration is still, at least arguably, unresolved. Courts should decide "gateway" matters of arbitrability, while the arbiter should decide "subsidiary" questions. The Supreme Court plurality treated class arbitrability as a subsidiary question in *Green Tree Fin. Corp. v. Bazzle*, 539 U.S. 444, 452 (2003), but the question was characterized as "fundamental" in Stolt-Nielsen S.A. v. Animalfeeds Int'l Corp., 559 U.S. 662, 681-82 (2009); and in 2013, the Court acknowledged explicitly that it "has not yet decided whether the availability of class arbitration is a question of arbitrability." Oxford Health Plans LLC v. Sutter, 133 S. Ct. 2064, 2068 n.2 (2013). However, the Sixth Circuit reasoned that "recently the Court has given every indication, short of an outright holding, that classwide arbitrability is a gateway question rather than a subsidiary one." Reed Elsevier, Inc. v. Crockett, 734 F.3d 594, 598 (6th Cir. 2013). Reviewing the relevant criteria, the Circuit concluded that "whether an arbitration agreement permits classwide arbitration is a gateway matter, which is reserved 'for judicial determination unless the parties clearly and unmistakably provide otherwise.' " *Id.* at 599 (quoting Howsam v. Dean Witter Reynolds, Inc., 537 U.S. 79, 83 (2002)). The Third Circuit noted in 2014 that the Sixth was the only other circuit to address this question directly, and "join[ed] the Sixth Circuit Court of Appeals in holding that the availability of class arbitration is a 'question of arbitrability' " to be decided by the court rather than the arbitrator. Opalinski v. Robert Half Int'l, Inc., 761 F.3d 326, 335 (3d Cir. 2014). It reasoned that "we read the Supreme Court as characterizing the permissibility of classwide arbitration not solely as a question of procedure or contract interpretation but as a substantive gateway dispute qualitatively separate from deciding an individual quarrel. Traditional individual arbitration and class arbitration are so distinct that a choice between the two goes, we believe, to the very type of controversy to be resolved," *id.* at 334.

The gateway question of arbitrability also arises outside the class action context, of course. Some courts have held that the courts need not send an issue to arbitration if the claim that the dispute is covered by the arbitration provision is not plausible or is "wholly groundless." *See* Agere Sys., Inc. v. Samsung Elecs. Co., 560 F.3d 337 (5th Cir. 2009); Qualcomm Inc. v. Nokia Corp., 466 F.3d 1366, 1371 (Fed. Cir. 2006). In Douglas v. Regions Bank, 757 F.3d 460 (5th Cir. 2014), the Fifth Circuit declined to send a dispute to arbitration where the delegation provision was in a contract for checking account which she closed years before the current dispute, involving embezzlement of settlement funds from a car accident. The court rejected the notion that "no matter how untenable the argument that there is some connection between the dispute and the agreement, an arbitrator must decide first," holding instead that no delegation clause had been agreed to because the party "meant only to bind herself to arbitrate gateway questions of arbitrability if the argument that the dispute falls within the scope of the agreement is not wholly groundless," *id.* at 464. The dissenting judge was sympathetic, but found that Supreme Court precedent does not allow the Circuit to adopt such a rule; "when the parties clearly and unmistakably agree to arbitrate arbitrability, questions regarding the scope of the parties' agreement to arbitrate must be addressed in the first instance by the arbitrator, not a court," *id.* at 467 (Dennis, C.J., dissenting). *Cf.* Al Rushaid v. Nat'l Oilwell Varco, Inc., 757 F.3d 416 (5th Cir. 2014) (reference to another document in price quotation was sufficient to incorporate arbitration delegation provision; co-defendant's pursuit of discovery did not waive moving defendant's right to invoke arbitration).

§4.28 n.52 p.593 Add the following after the citation to **AutoNation USA Corp.***:* , followed in Stenzel v. Dell, Inc., *supra* note 49 ("an arbitration provision that precludes the use of class actions is not necessarily substantively unconscionable").

§4.28 n.52 p.593 In the first paragraph, add the following to the list after **"But cf."***:* Pleasants v. Am. Express Co., 541 F.3d 853 (8th Cir. 2008) (class action waiver not unconscionable where statute provides for attorney's fees, costs, statutory damages, and actual damages); Caley v. Gulfstream Aerospace Corp., *supra* note 49 (preclusion of class actions consistent with goals of "simplicity, informality, and expedition"), distinguished in Dale v. Comcast Corp., *supra* (in *Caley*, plaintiffs had available fee-shifting statutes, unlike in *Dale*); Schultz v. AT & T Wireless Servs., *supra* note 47 (where plaintiff alleged injury sufficient to surmount diversity threshold, "the plaintiff can effectively and cost-efficiently vindicate his rights through arbitration"), greatly extended in Strawn v. AT & T Mobility, 593 F. Supp. 2d 894 (S.D.W. Va. 2009) (individual claims of roughly $5,000 "a significant amount of damages" so that class action waivers would not prevent pursuing individual claims); Freedman v. Comcast Corp., 988 A.2d 68 (Md. App. 2010) (class action waiver enforceable; ipse dixit); Delta Funding Corp. v. Harris, *supra* note 51 (preclusion not unconscionable where plaintiff seeks over $100,000; this is "adequate incentive to bring her claim as an individual action," and the pertinent statutes "provide for attorney's fees and costs to prevailing plaintiffs"); Strand v. U.S. Nat'l Bank Nat'l Ass'n ND, *supra* note 33 (plaintiff failed to prove that no attorney would take individual cases, arbitration would be in plaintiff's home jurisdiction, fees and costs would be advanced by the defendant, and the plaintiff could recover his fees if successful, so plaintiff failed to establish substantive unconscionability). One might ask whether, as in *Strawn*, a claim for $5,000 would make individual arbitration cost-effective.

§4.28 n.52 p.593 Add the following at the end of the first paragraph: *Ting*, *Szetela*, and related cases were largely superseded by Discover Bank v. Superior Ct., *supra* note 25, and by Gentry v. Superior Ct., *supra* note 33. *Discover Bank* held that class action waivers were unconscionable "when the waiver is found in

a consumer contract of adhesion in a setting in which disputes between the contracting parties predictably involve small amounts of damages, and when it is alleged that the party with the superior bargaining power has carried out a scheme to deliberately cheat large numbers of consumers out of individually small sums of money." *Discover Bank* has been followed, and perhaps extended, in Shroyer v. New Cingular Wireless Servs., *supra* note 35 (class arbitration waiver in cellular telephone service contract unconscionable); Oestreicher v. Alienware Corp., 502 F. Supp. 2d 1061 (N.D. Cal. 2007) (class action against computer manufacturer for breach of warranty, unfair trade practices, and untrue advertising; bar held unconscionable), *aff'd,* 322 Fed. Appx. 489 (9th Cir. 2009) (per curiam); Cohen v. DirecTV, Inc., 48 Cal. Rptr. 3d 813 (Ct. App. 2006) (class action against satellite broadcasting company for inadequate signal quality, invoking state unfair practices law); Murphy v. Check 'N Go, *supra* note 33 (class action against employer for violation of state labor laws); and Indep. Ass'n of Mailbox Ctr. Owners v. Superior Ct., *supra* note 40 (class action against franchisor challenging conversion of stores to new format). *But see* Omstead v. Dell, Inc., 533 F. Supp. 2d 1012 (N.D. Cal.. 2008) ($4,000 large enough to warrant enforcing class action waiver for sale of high-end electronics), *rev'd on other grounds*, 594 F.3d 1081 (9th Cir. 2010).

A clearer extension was found in *Gentry*, which ratified the earlier decisions in the context of a claim for overtime pay to which the workers were entitled under statute. The arbitration clause would have required individual arbitration and limited the recovery of both direct and punitive damages permitted by the statute. The court found this clause potentially void on public policy grounds. More important for present purposes, the court found that the presence of an opt-out provision did not prevent the adhesion contract from being "at the very least, not entirely free from procedural unconscionability." And although the employer contained a plain and accurate description of the arbitration clause, which contained the reminder that an employee "may consult with an attorney," the description was one-sided and "touted the virtues of arbitration," which made it "likely that Circuit City employees felt at least some pressure not to opt out of the arbitration agreement." The court was careful to reaffirm its holding in *Discover Bank* that some class action waivers might well prove enforceable, but its decision here suggests the number will be very modest. *Cf.* Arguelles-Romero v. Super. Ct., 109 Cal. Rptr. 3d 289 (Ct. App. 2010) ("While *Discover Bank* and *Gentry* were applications of the same general principle, it is also apparent that they involved different legal theories. *Discover Bank* is based on unconscionability, which is a legal determination subject to de novo review, while *Gentry* is based on whether a class arbitration (or action) is a significantly more effective practical means of vindicating unwaivable statutory rights, which is a discretionary determination subject to abuse of discretion review.").

But this line of doctrine was rendered largely moot by the Supreme Court's recent decision in *AT&T Mobility v. Concepcion*, 131 S. Ct. 1740 (2011). The question there was whether California's unconscionability doctrine improperly singled out bans on class-wide arbitration, which would be improper under *Prima Paint* and its successors. Certainly, the court below was clear on this issue, though it was dealt with somewhat cursorily. Laster v. AT & T Mobility, 584 F.3d 849 (9th Cir. 2009). Judge Easterbrook's attack on California's jurisprudence in this area may have encouraged the Court to grant review. Oblix, Inc. v. Winiecki, 374 F.3d 488 (7th Cir. 2004). *Pace* Judge Easterbrook, however, the California Supreme Court had never set forth an absolute ban on class-action waivers; indeed, it has been careful to state otherwise. If one traces the history of these class-action waiver decisions, it becomes apparent that the California courts arrived at their current law by applying pre-existing principles of unconscionability law, principles it applies in all other cases as well. There is a profound logical error at work here in confusing cause with effect. Those challenging the current law on class-action waivers conclude from the fairly consistent striking of these clauses that the courts must have singled them out. But it is facially just as likely that the courts have applied neutral principles to consistently extreme facts. Just because the courts consistently find that shooting someone constitutes battery does not mean that they harbor a unique bias against guns. Nor is it clear why a doctrine barring the enforcement of class-action waivers in both litigation and arbitration unfairly penalizes arbitration. Nor, for that matter, was it obvious why the Court would reach out to decide a matter of California's domestic law in the aftermath of *Erie*.

But it did. In what has already become a notorious decision, the Court held that the FAA preempts California's unconscionability doctrine concerning class arbitration waivers in consumer contracts, thus abrogating *Discover Bank*. This may puzzle anyone who takes seriously the Court's repeated assertion that "courts must place arbitration agreements on an equal footing with other contracts." AT&T Mobility v. Concepcion, 131 S. Ct. 1740, 1745 (2011). The Court solved this puzzle by creating a new standard for FAA preemption: whether the law in question "interferes with fundamental attributes of arbitration," in particular the "overarching purpose" of "facilitat[ing] streamlined proceedings." AT&T Mobility v. Concepcion, 131 S. Ct. 1740, 1748 (2011). Class arbitration serves as such an "obstacle" because it impinges on the main advantages of arbitration, such as informality, speed, and low cost, and imposes risks upon defendants that they would not likely choose without the substantive review afforded in judicial proceedings. *Discover Bank* is thus preempted by the FAA because it stands in the way of individual arbitration.

There are many odd things about this decision. For example, the Court reaches its conclusions about the relative merits of individual arbitration and class arbitration with very little empirical basis, as phrases like "we find it unlikely" or "we find it hard to believe" suggest. We also see a strange lack of faith in arbitration by a court apparently devoted to its use. The Court bases its statement that "class arbitration greatly increases risks to defendants" on the observations that "[t]he absence of multilayered review makes it more likely that errors will go uncorrected," which matters much more in class arbitrations than in individual arbitrations. AT&T Mobility v. Concepcion, 131 S. Ct. 1740, 1752 (2011). So much, it would seem, for the outcome-neutrality of arbitration so often invoked by the Court. And, as the dissent points out, the Court uses the wrong comparison for assessing the effects of class arbitrations upon the efficiency of arbitration. Instead of comparing individual arbitration with class arbitration, the dissent observes that the Court should have compared class arbitration with litigation. In the words of the dissent, "if incentives are at issue, the *relevant* comparison is not 'arbitration with arbitration' but a comparison between class arbitration and judicial class actions. After all, in respect to the relevant set of contracts, the *Discover Bank* rule similarly and equally sets aside clauses that forbid class procedures — whether arbitration procedures or ordinary judicial procedures are at issue." AT&T Mobility v. Concepcion, 131 S. Ct. 1740, 1759 (2011) (Breyer, J., dissenting).

More important for us is what this means for the enforceability of anti-class-arbitration clauses or other provisions that at some level burden arbitration. One problem is the slippery nature of the new analysis. Presumably, a state law or policy that turns arbitration into something other than arbitration is preempted. But what is this Platonic ideal of arbitration to which all versions are compared? And, even more to the point, how far away can arbitration get from this ideal before it is no longer real arbitration? Another problem arises from the procedural posture of this case. *Concepcion* came through the federal courts. Justice Thomas has from time to time stated that he does not think the FAA applies in state court. So if a similar decision came from the California Supreme Court, would it be upheld, with Justice Thomas's hands-off approach effectively providing the fifth vote? For that matter, Justice Thomas's concurrence rested on his view that the FAA allows states to regulate defects in the making of an agreement, not in its enforceability. AT&T Mobility v. Concepcion, 131 S. Ct. 1740, 1753 (2011) (Thomas, J., concurring). There is some reason to question his apparent assumption that unconscionability goes to enforcement rather than formation. But, as Justice Thomas also observed, this reading "has not been fully developed by any party . . . and could benefit from briefing and argument in an appropriate case." AT&T Mobility v. Concepcion, 131 S. Ct. 1740, 1754 (2011) (Thomas, J., concurring). So if the Court grants certiorari in an appropriate case, we may well see a different approach take root.

A very big question is what remains of the law of unconscionability when applied to arbitration clauses. Under state arbitration law, probably quite a lot — but that will likely matter less and less as contract drafters work through the consequences of *Concepcion*. Under the FAA, however, a good deal of current caselaw is suspect. For example, consider the line of cases holding discovery limitations unconscionable. As the Court stated in *Concepcion*, among the charms of bilateral arbitration is lessened discovery. Presumably, then, a rule that invalidates discovery limits would unduly burden arbitration and as a result be preempted by the FAA. (At some point, though, questions of due process might enter the equation.)

Still another question is the remaining pertinence of class action waivers in other aspects of analysis. Suppose a court undertakes a standard unconscionability analysis, one that looks closely at the specific contract and contracting process rather than more generally at a type of contract or clause. In such an analysis, could the presence of a class arbitration/class action waiver still play a part? Some of the Court's rhetoric suggests not. But its actual holding does not match its rhetoric. The Court objected to *Discover Bank*'s general rule against class arbitration waivers. It did not object to employing unconscionability analysis to arbitration agreements, but rather to its blanket application to class-arbitration waivers. That door remains open, at least by a crack and at least for the moment.

And we should consider the current state of affairs for consumer grievances. In some industries, such as cell phones and credit cards, class arbitration waivers are universal. In others, however, such as auto sales and home construction, they are patchy, and they are nonexistent or all but for real estate brokerage agreements. Drahozal & Zyontz, An Empirical Study of AAA Consumer Arbitrations, 25 Ohio St. J. on Disp. Resol. 843 (2010). These percentages may change in the wake of *Concepcion*, but for now, anyway, class arbitration remains an option in some parts of the consumer world. Additionally, we must not underestimate the role of non-legal sanctions, most notably reputation. For every consumer who is denied what she was promised, how many get it in the first place — and how many get it, not initially, but after complaining? This is not to say that class arbitration is unimportant. As its advocates properly point out, its threat may well keep firms from engaging in small-scale chiseling, especially of a sort that is difficult to find or prove and modest in size for the individual consumer. And many, perhaps most consumers are not able to pursue claims with the tenacity and expertise of, say, law professors — in particular, the poor and poorly educated, who need protection the most. But *Concepcion* is not likely to result in a world of *caveat emptor*.

Still, *Concepcion* does make a difference, and a big one. In the short run, it seems likely that courts will tend to apply it mechanically to validate class arbitration waivers, or rather to hold that they are not unconscionable. Possibly this will change if venturesome courts test *Concepcion*'s outer bounds. But as the courts commonly observe, it would be the height of folly for an individual to seek piddling damages, whatever the forum. If class-arbitration and class-action waivers are broadly validated, then the combination of *Stolt-Nielsen, Rent-A-Center*, and *Concepcion* will almost entirely eliminate the ability to pursue small claims in adversary proceedings, at least for those who are neither vindictive nor lunatic.

Going further, the Ninth Circuit held that the reasoning of *Concepcion* ends the so-called *Broughton-Cruz* rule, a California Supreme Court doctrine (developed in *Broughton v. Cigna Healthplans of California*, 21 Cal. 4th 1066, 90 Cal. Rptr. 2d 334, 988 P.2d 67 (Cal. 1999) and *Cruz v. PacifiCare Health Sys., Inc.*, 30 Cal. 4th 303, 133 Cal. Rptr. 2d 58, 66 P.3d 1157, 1164-65 (Cal. 2003)) that that had exempted claims for "public injunctive relief" from the reach of mandatory arbitration agreements. Ferguson v. Corinthian Colleges, Inc., 733 F.3d 928 (9th Cir. 2013). There, the plaintiffs sought injunctive relief under California's unfair competition law, false advertising law, and Consumer Legal Remedies Act, but the Circuit held that "the FAA preempts" state precedents that it would be unconscionable to enforce arbitration agreements where the plaintiffs seek injunctive relief under such consumer protection laws. *Id.* at 934-37.

The same Ninth Circuit panel, however, found an arbitration agreement in an employment contract unconscionable under the circumstances of *Chavarria v. Ralphs Grocery Co.*, 733 F.3d 916 (9th Cir. 2013). The Circuit emphasized the reasoning of recent Supreme Court cases that unconscionability cannot invalidate an arbitration agreement if what makes the agreement unconscionable is something that only or disproportionately applies to arbitration agreements, but if "[n]o single rule of unconscionability uniquely applicable to arbitration is at issue in this case [, the court] must therefore apply California's general principle of contract unconscionability." *Id.* at 921-22. The Circuit was particularly concerned with the fact that the employee signed a contract of adhesion containing the arbitration provision but did not receive the details of the agreement, including method of selecting and arbitrator and costs, until some weeks later. It found the agreement both procedurally and substantively unconscionable. *Id.* at 922-26.

The careful drafter for a seller or supplier of services might therefore want to reconsider class arbitration waivers, if hitherto they were omitted because of their futility. More generally, the Court's apparent friendliness toward largely unregulated arbitration may embolden drafters in industries where arbitration has real potential, if undertaken with discovery limits and similar cost-saving constraints. The continuing existence of unconscionability, even though circumscribed, may, however, put some limits on drafting, lest an arbitration clause be stricken as a whole.

See generally Clancy & Stein, An Uninvited Guest: Class Arbitration and the Federal Arbitration Act's Legislative History, 63 Bus. Law. 55 (2007); Gilles, Opting Out of Liability: The Forthcoming, Near-Total Demise of the Modern Class Action, 104 Mich. L. Rev. 373 (2005); Sternlight & Jensen, Using Arbitration to Eliminate Consumer Class Actions: Efficient Business Practice or Unconscionable Abuse?, 67 Law & Contemp. Probs. 75 (2004); Note, Buyer Beware: Why the Class Arbitration Waiver Clause Presents a Gloomy Future for Consumers, 58 Duke L.J. 103 (2008); Note, Come One, Come All: The New and Developing World of Nonsignatory Arbitration and Class Arbitration, 62 U. Miami L. Rev. 95 (2007); Note, Beyond Unconscionability: Class Action Waivers and Mandatory Arbitration Agreements, 59 Vand. L. Rev. 1735 (2006).

For other bases for holding an arbitration clause substantively unconscionable, see Davis v. O'Melveny & Myers, *supra* note 35 (abridgement of statute of limitations for employment-related statutory claims substantively unconscionable, particularly because it would "bar a 'continuing violations' theory"; confidentiality provision unconscionable because it "would handicap if not stifle an employee's ability to investigate and engage in discovery" and "prevent others from building cases"); Walker v. Ryan's Family Steak Houses, 400 F.3d 370 (6th Cir. 2005) (severe restrictions on discovery); Bragg v. Linden Resources, *supra* note 33 (confidentiality provision unconscionable because the company "places itself in a far superior legal posture by ensuring that none of its potential opponents have access to precedent while, at the same time, the company accumulates a wealth of knowledge"); Ostroff v. Alterra Healthcare Corp., *supra* note 25 (allowing plaintiff to depose only the defendant's experts substantively unconscionable, because the "[p]laintiff's limited information will put her at a distinct disadvantage in arbitration"); Ontiveros v. DHL Express (USA), 79 Cal. Rptr. 3d 471 (Ct. App. 2008) (giving arbitrator exclusive authority to resolve enforceability issues "is unconscionable and, therefore, unenforceable"; in addition, where there were severe limits on discovery, "the permitted amount of discovery is so low while the burden for showing a need for more discovery is so high that plaintiff's ability to prove her claims would be unlawfully thwarted by the discovery provision in the agreement."). State *ex rel.* Vincent v. Schneider, *supra* note 49 (clause in home purchase contract giving president of local home builder association sole discretion to pick arbitrator "requires that an individual in a position of bias be the sole selector of an arbitrator, who must be unbiased"); Covenant Health Rehab. of Picayune v. Brown, *supra* note 48 (abridgement of statute of limitations, waiver of punitive damages, and limit on liability all unconscionable); Estate of Ruszala v. Brookdale Living Communities, 1 A.3d 806 (N.J. Super. App. Div. 2010) (bar on deposing fact witnesses as part of arbitration unconscionable but severable); Simpson v. MSA of Myrtle Beach, *supra* note 33 (bar on award of punitive or exemplary damages, including damages under unfair trade practices statutes, unconscionable; barring statutory damages "violates statutory law" and "runs contrary to the underlying statutes' very purposes of punishing acts that adversely affect the public interest"); *In re* Poly-Am., *supra* note 10 ("if the discovery limitations the arbitration agreement imposes operate to prevent effective presentation of [the plaintiff's] claim they would be unenforceable," but leaves that determination to the arbitrator as discovery proceeds) (quaere whether a draconian limit on discovery might invalidate the whole arbitration clause, a matter within the competence of the court).

The Supreme Court is not the only entity busily upending arbitration law and practice. Two of the leading arbitration organizations, the American Arbitration Association and the National Arbitration Forum, have announced that they are immediately leaving much or all of the consumer arbitration business — all in the case of the National Arbitration Forum, consumer debt collection cases for the American Arbitration Association. The American Arbitration Association did so because of concerns about due process issues, while the National Arbitration Forum did so as part of a consent decree entered into with the Attorney

General of Minnesota, who had alleged in a lawsuit that the National Arbitration Forum "hid from the public its extensive ties to the collection industry." Office of the Attorney General, National Arbitration Forum Barred from Credit Card and Consumer Arbitrations under Agreement with Attorney General Swanson (July 20, 2009), http://www.ag.state.mn.us/Consumer/PressRelease/090720NationalArbitrationAgremnt.asp; *see also* National Arbitration Forum, National Arbitration Forum to Cease Administering All Consumer Arbitrations in Response to Mounting Legal and Legislative Challenges (July 19, 2009) http://www.adrforum.com/newsroom.aspx?itemID=1528; American Arbitration Association, AAA Announces Moratorium on Consumer Debt Arbitration Cases (July 27, 2009) http://www.adr.org/sp.asp?id=36432.

This will have a significant effect on contracts that specified one or the other as the arbitrator. For a recent example, *see* Rivera v. Am. Gen. Fin. Servs., ___ P.3d ___, 2011 WL 3687624 (N.M. July 27, 2011) (contract provided for NAF arbitration; as a matter of contract interpretation, held that choice of NAF was integral to the arbitration agreement, so a court may not appoint a replacement and the arbitration provision fails). See §7.16 *infra*. It also gives ammunition to those who consider arbitration clauses material alterations of offers for the purposes of the "battle of the forms." See §3.21 *supra*. For our purposes, it strengthens the hands of those who would attack arbitration clauses root and branch. If the leading not-for-profit arbitration organization has due process concerns about a significant part of its arbitral work and the leading for-profit arbitration firm has quit the whole field under pressure from Congress and the courts, it becomes much easier to argue that a particular arbitration provision is unconscionable. It remains to be seen whether other arbitration organizations will follow suit; if so, this whole area may fall into desuetude for lack of arbitrators. It also is possible that Congress will pass one or more of the bills pending that would radically curtail mandatory arbitration, though the politics of arbitration reform changed greatly in the last election. The recent financial reform legislation has this effect. See §3.21 *supra*. Outside the judicial realm, those attacking arbitration clauses are at present in the ascendant. Within the courts, however . . .

*§4.28 n.52 p.593 **In the second paragraph, complete the citation to*** **Bazzle** ***as follows:*** Green Tree Fin. Corp. v. Bazzle, 539 U.S. 444 (2003).

*§4.28 n.52 p.593 **Replace the citation to*** **Pedcor** ***with the following:*** Pedcor Mgt. Co. Welfare Benefit Plan v. Nations Personnel of Tex., 343 F.3d 355 (5th Cir. 2003) (arbitration agreement "as in *Green Tree* does not clearly forbid class action").

*§4.28 n.52 p.593 **In the second paragraph, add the following at the end:*** *Bazzle* contains an important exception, permitting a court to decide "whether the parties have a valid arbitration agreement at all." 539 U.S. at 452. If the clause is sufficiently clear, then there is no issue of contract interpretation that *Bazzle* would otherwise give to the arbitrator; in that case, the court may pass on its validity. *See* Muhammad v. Cnty. Bank of Rehoboth Beach, *supra* note 33; Simpson v. MSA of Myrtle Beach, *supra* note 33.

*§4.28 n.53 p.593 **In the first paragraph, add the following to the list after*** **"Cf.":** Bhim v. Rent-A-Center, 655 F. Supp. 2d 1307 (S.D. Fla. 2009) (although employer and employee had a disparity in bargaining power, and employer required all of its employees to sign arbitration agreements, employee failed to show "that she lacked employment alternatives" and the agreement was not procedurally deficient otherwise, so the arbitration agreement was enforceable); Brown v. Wells Fargo Bank, 85 Cal. Rptr. 3d 817 (Ct. App. 2008) (limitations on appeals and on discovery not unconscionable, as they favor "expeditious, binding and final resolutions of disputes" and in any event apply to all non-personal-injury arbitrations); Freedman v. Comcast Corp., 988 A.2d 68 (Md. App. 2010) (limits on discovery in consumer telecommunications contract not unconscionable; reference to arbitral rules does not itself mean too limited a scope of discovery, and limited discovery is not inherently unconscionable); Covenant Health Rehab. v. Brown, *supra* note 48; Quigley v. KPMG Peat Marwick, 749 A.2d 405 (N.J. Super. App. Div. 2000) (courts "have consistently determined that the economic coercion of obtaining or keeping a job, without more, is insufficient to overcome an agreement to arbitrate statutory claims"); Horrocks v. Keepers, Inc., 2016 Conn.

Super. LEXIS 14, 25 Wage & Hour Cas. 2d (BNA) 1897 (Jan. 4, 2016) ("plaintiffs argue that the arbitration agreement is procedurally unconscionable because the defendants presented an adhesion contract that they knew was a misrepresentation of employment law, violating their duty of good faith and fair dealing as an employer. . . . The plaintiffs also provide no specific evidence that the defendants knowingly presented the plaintiffs with a contract containing an illegal purpose. Even if proffering this contract with a known illegal purpose makes the arbitration agreement procedurally unconscionable, the court is not aware of any Connecticut precedent that would allow the court to void a contract based solely on procedural unconscionablility").

Nevertheless, each aspect of the arbitration agreement must be considered. For example, in 2013, the Ninth Circuit held that an agreement to submit disputes to "binding, non-appealable arbitration" did not deprive the court of jurisdiction because "non-appealable" is ambiguous and, if read broadly, would run contrary to the statutory appealability of arbitration awards under §10 of the Federal Arbitration Act. *In re* Wal-Mart Wage & Hour Emp't Practices Litig., 737 F.3d 1262, 1266-68 (9th Cir 2013).

§4.28 n.54 p.594 Add the following to the end: Because contracts infected with unconscionability are voidable, but not void, it should be possible to ratify them. This would not be done easily, given the shady or oppressive acts that gave rise to the unconscionability defense. Still, under the right circumstances a party to a contract may be in a sufficiently strong bargaining position and have a sufficient command of the facts to be able to ratify an otherwise unenforceable contract. For an application of this in the special setting of attorney-client relations, *see* King v. Fox, 851 N.E.2d 1184 (N.Y. 2006) ("Where a fully informed client with equal bargaining power knowingly and voluntarily affirms an existing fee arrangement that might otherwise be considered voidable as unconscionable, ratification can occur so long as the client has both a full understanding of the facts that made the agreement voidable and knowledge of his or her rights as a client.").

§4.28 n.55 p.594 Add the following after the citation to* Little*: , followed in Gibson, *supra* note 46 (rejecting employee's anti-severability argument; this was "the first case decided by this court involving an attempt to force an unconscionable arbitration remedy on an employee," and "[w]e have no reason to think that . . . employers will ignore the precedent"; "[i]f in future cases similar unconscionable clauses are sought to be enforced despite our ruling in this case, severance might not be appropriate").

§4.28 n.55 p.594 Add the following to the list after **"Accord":** Roman v. Super. Ct., 92 Cal. Rptr. 3d 153 (Ct. App. 2009) (severing cost-shifting provision from balance of arbitration clause); Kristian v. Comcast Corp., *supra* note 52 (severing class arbitration waiver from balance of arbitration clause); Irwin v. UBS Painewebber, *supra* note 46 (finding fee provision of arbitration clause unenforceable but severable from the balance of the clause, which was not "tainted with illegality"); Kinkel v. Cingular Wireless, *supra* note 38 ("the existence of a severability clause and the strong public policy in favor of enforcing arbitration clauses weigh in favor of enforcing the arbitration clause without the offending class action waiver"), followed in Tortoriello v. Gerald Nissan, *supra* note 15 (disclaimer of punitive damages unconscionable; if stricken, "the intent of the arbitration clause remains essentially fulfilled," and there is also a severability clause) and in Keefe v. Allied Home Mktg. Corp., 912 N.E.2d 310 (Ill. App. 2009) (enforcing arbitration clause after severing prohibition on class actions); Muhammad v. Cnty. Bank of Rehoboth Beach, *supra* note 33 (severing class action waiver from rest of arbitration clause), followed in Estate of Ruszala v. Brookdale Living Communities, 1 A.3d 806 (N.J. Super. App. Div. 2010) (severing bar on deposing fact witnesses, cap on compensatory damages, and bar on punitive damages, but otherwise enforcing arbitration clause); Walters, *supra* note 51 (severing venue and fee-shifting provisions from rest of arbitration clause; "[w]hat remains is simply the basic agreement to arbitrate").

§4.28 n.55 p.594 Add the following to the end of the first paragraph: Interestingly, in many of these cases the defendant, invariably the drafter, seeks to avoid arbitration if the class waiver fails, while the plaintiff wants to arbitrate and thus merely sever the class waiver. *See* Oestreicher v. Alienware Corp., *supra* note 52; Scott v. Cingular Wireless, *supra* note 10. Presumably arbitration loses its charms for a defendant when the arbitrator can give class-wide

relief, even though the cost savings and efficiency of arbitration would remain. *See generally* Eisenberg, Miller & Sherwin, Arbitration's Summer Soldiers: An Empirical Study of Arbitration Clauses in Consumer and Nonconsumer Contracts, 41 U. Mich J. L. Reform 871 (2008) (large businesses favor arbitration in their dealings with consumers but not with one another), critiqued in Kim & Lin, Arbitration's Summer Soldiers Marching into Fall: Another Look at Eisenberg, Miller, and Sherwin's Empirical Study of Arbitration Clauses in Consumer and Nonconsumer Contracts, 34 Vt. L. Rev. 597 (2010). On the consequences of severability on the inclination of contracting parties to use dubiously proper terms, *see* Sullivan, The Puzzling Persistence of Unenforceable Contract Terms, 70 Ohio St. L.J. 1127 (2009).

§4.28 n.55 p.594 In the second paragraph, complete the citation to* Anders *as follows: Anders v. Hometown Mtg. Servs., 346 F.3d 1024 (11th Cir. 2003).

§4.28 n.55 p.594 In the second paragraph, add the following to the end: *Cf. In re* Poly-Am., *supra* note 10 ("An illegal or unconscionable provision of a contract may generally be severed so long as it does not constitute the essential purpose of the agreement. . . . [T]he intent of the parties, as expressed by the severability clause, is that unconscionable provisions be excised where possible.").

§4.28 n.56 p.595 Add the following to the second sentence: , in Thompson v. Toll Dublin, 81 Cal. Rptr. 3d 736 (Ct. App. 2008) (where scope and mutuality aspects are unconscionable, "[i]n light of the pervasiveness of the unconscionable provisions related to arbitration and the fact that the purported scope of the arbitration provisions exceeded the plaintiffs' reasonable expectations, there are no isolated provisions that can be severed and the arbitration provisions as a whole are unenforceable against plaintiffs"); Ontiveros v. DHL Express (USA), *supra* note 52 (provisions for arbitrator determinations of enforceability, partial payment of costs by plaintiff, and severe limits on discovery support the conclusion that the agreement as a whole is "permeated with unconscionability and will not be enforced"); Davis v. O'Melveny &

Myers, *supra* note 35 (four unconscionable provisions in arbitration clause "cannot be stricken or excised without gutting the agreement," and "a court cannot rewrite the arbitration agreement for the parties," so the whole agreement was held unconscionable), Nagrampa v. MailCoups, Inc., *supra* note 33 (lack of mutuality of remedy and oppressive forum selection clause render the arbitration clause "so permeated by substantive unconscionability that it cannot be cured by severance"), Murphy v. Check 'N Go, *supra* note 33 (invalidating clause because the provisions for arbitral determination of unconscionability and class action waiver were unconscionable)

§4.28 n.56 p.595 Add the following to the list after "Accord": Dale v. Comcast Corp., *supra* note 52 (concluding without discussion that "[b]ecause the class action waiver cannot be severed from the Agreement, the entire arbitration provision is rendered unenforceable."); Covenant Health & Rehab. of Picayune v. Estate of Moulds, *supra* note 36 (invalidating entire contract where arbitration clause itself unconscionable and additionally contains terms outside of arbitration that are unconscionable); Vasquez-Lopez v. Beneficial Or., *supra* note 28 (where severing unconscionable terms meant that "the trial court would have had to rewrite the contract," not an abuse of discretion for court to hold entire clause unenforceable); Simpson v. MSA of Myrtle Beach, *supra* note 33 (in spite of severability clause, entire arbitration clause held unenforceable; courts do not "rewrite contracts for parties," and this clause was so "grossly unconscionable" that public policy would best be served by its complete unenforceability).

§4.28 n.56 p.595 Add the following at the end: At times arbitration clauses will contain anti-severability provisions, which generally are enforceable. *See* Shroyer v. New Cingular Wireless Servs., *supra* note 35 (enforcing nonseverability clause); Hollins v. Debt Relief of Am., *supra* note 33 ("the court has no choice but to strike the arbitration provision in its entirety" in light of its partial unconscionability).

§4.28 n.58 p.595 Add the following after the first sentence: *Accord:* Carey v. Lincoln Loan Co., 125 P.3d 814 (Or.

App. 2005) (court remedied unconscionability of prepayment term in lending agreement by limiting it to circumstances in which "the provision will fail to achieve its essential purpose if it is not enforced and that, even then, that its enforcement will not deprive plaintiffs of . . . their ability to sell the house and receive all or the major portion of its increased value"), *aff'd*, 157 P.3d 775 (Or. 2007).

***§4.28 n.59 p.595 Add the following to the list after* "Accord":** Poff v. Brown, 288 S.W.3d 620 (Ark. 2008) (unconscionability is an affirmative defense, so "the failure to plead the affirmative defense may be determinative of the issue"); Arthur v. Microsoft Corp., 676 N.W.2d 29 (Neb. 2004) (UCC §2-302 "was not intended to create a cause of action and cannot be used as a basis for damages"); Carey v. Lincoln Loan Co., *supra* note 58 ("unconscionability is not a basis for a separate claim for relief"); Nygaard v. Sioux Valley Hosps., 731 N.W.2d 184 (S.D. 2007) (plaintiffs "have no right to recover damages simply because they *entered into* an unconscionable contract" (emphasis in original)).

§4.28 n.62 p.596 In the first paragraph, add the following to the list in the third sentence: Swayne v. Beebles Invs., *supra* note 27 (interest rate on mortgage 41.657%, with 31% of proceeds used for closing costs and fees, some of them unlawful; "these numbers, on their face, are one-sided in favor of Beebles").

§4.28 n.62 p.596 In the second paragraph, add the following to the start: The UNIDROIT Principles provide for avoidance in the face of gross disparity, a concept familiar in civilian jurisdictions as *laesio enormis*. UNIDROIT Principles art. 3.10; *see* C. civ. art. 1674 (French statement of *laesio enormis*). Our only civilian jurisdiction has the principle of lesion beyond moiety, under which a buyer who purchased of an immovable for less than half the fair market price may either return the immovable to the seller or keep the immovable and pay the difference between fair market value and the price paid. La. Civ. Code arts. 2589-2591; Joiner v. Abercrombie, 968 So. 2d 1184 (La. App. 2007) (applying principle).

Nor is price unconscionability at all a new phenomenon. Roman law, though generally unreceptive to arguments that a price was unfair, did at times recognize what we would now call price unconscionability. C. 4, 44, 2. *See generally* R. Zimmermann, The Law of Obligations 259-270 (1990). The doctrine took strongest hold in religious law. Medieval legal theorists, most notably Aquinas, advanced notions of the *pretium justum*, or just price. *See* J. Gordley, *supra*, at 65-67; Johnson, Just Price, Aquinas, and the Labor Theory of Value, in The Medieval Tradition of Natural Law 75 (1987). Talmudic law also imposed strict limits on price, which could not vary by more than one-sixth from the correct price. Bava Metzia 50b; Shulchan Aruch 227:2 et seq. *See generally* Lifshitz, Oppressive-Exploitative Contracts: A Jewish Law Perspective, 23 J.L. & Relig. 425 (2007-2008).

***§4.28 n.65 p.597 Add the following to the list after* "See":** Stoll v. Chong Lor Xiong, 241 P.3d 301 (Okla. Civ. App. 2010) (clause in farm purchase agreement providing that seller retains right to chicken litter for 30 years, which was projected to generate roughly double the sales price bargained for; court found this clause unconscionable and refused to enforce it without otherwise invalidating the contract).

***§4.28 n.66 p.597 In the second paragraph, add the following to the list after* "See":** Pleasant Hollow Homeowners Ass'n v. Webster, 285 S.W.3d 421 (Mo. App. 2009) (sheriff's sale of home grossed $10 where market price was between $110,000 and $160,000; set aside sale because the consideration was "grossly inadequate" and amounted to constructive fraud).

§4.28 n.67 p.598 Add as a second paragraph: A variation on price unconscionability is excessive returns on an investment; although "typically the subject of usury challenges, the unconscionability doctrine may also apply." Ow v. Oropeza, 2016 Bankr. LEXIS 2857 (N.D. Cal. Aug. 5, 2016). A man who "was homeless, distraught over the pending trustee's sale, and desperate to save his childhood home" agreed to transfer a significant interest in the home in exchange for payments to keep current on the mortgage, which under the circumstances meant that "in exchange for $38,960.50, [the offeror] expected a return of $105,000 in a matter of months." *Id.* at *12. The court held that "[t]hese facts demonstrate significant substantive unconscionability, with enough procedural unconscionability to render the [agreements] unenforceable." *Id.* at *14.

§4.28a LIMITATION OF REMEDIES

§4.28a n.1 p.599 Add the following after the citation to* Valhal Corp.*: ; and Fort Knox Self Storage v. W. Techs., 142 P.3d 1 (N.M. App. 2006) (distinguishing between exculpatory or indemnity clauses and limitations on liability; while the former are disfavored, the latter can be "a reasonable allocation of risk").

§4.28a n.1 p.599 Add the following to the list after* "See"*: Trans-Spec Truck Serv. v. Caterpillar Inc., 524 F.3d 315 (1st Cir. 2008) ("both Caterpillar and Trans-Spec are sophisticated commercial parties who negotiated the contract . . . at arm's length"; giving effect to limitation of liability for negligence); 1800 Ocotillo v. WLB Grp., 196 P.3d 222 (Ariz. 2008) ("We also decline to hold that liability-limitation clauses are generally unenforceable as contrary to a judicially identified public policy. Such clauses may desirably allow the parties to allocate as between themselves the risks of damages in excess of the agreed-upon cap, which could preserve incentives for one party to take due care while assigning the risk of greater damages to another party that might be better able to mitigate or insure against them."); Rhino Fund v. Hutchins, 229 P.3d 1186 (Colo. App. 2008) ("As a general rule, courts will uphold an exculpatory provision in a contract between two established and sophisticated business entities that have negotiated their agreement at arm's length."); Evans v. Lima Lima Flight Team, 869 N.E.2d 195 (Ill. App. 2007) ("Although exculpatory agreements are not favored and are strictly construed against the party they benefit . . . parties may allocate the risk of negligence as they see fit, and exculpatory agreements do not violate public policy as a matter of law.").

§4.28a n.1 p.599 Add the following after the first sentence: *Cf.* Schenkel & Shultz, Inc. v. Hermon F. Fox & Assocs., 658 S.E.2d 918 (N.C. 2008) (distinguishing between "exculpatory provisions, whereby a party seeks to protect itself from liability arising from its *own* negligence . . . that this Court has strictly construed" and "a standard contract of indemnity," which " 'will be construed to cover all losses, damages, and liabilities which reasonable appear to have been within the contemplation of the parties' ") (quoting Dixie Container Corp. v. Dale, 160 S.E.2d 708 (N.C. 1968)); Zuver v. Airtouch Commc'ns, 103 P.3d 753 (Wash. 2004) (employment contract: clause barring employee, but not employer, from recovering exemplary or punitive damages invalidated as unconscionable), distinguished by Torgerson v. One Lincoln Tower, 210 P.3d 318 (Wash. 2009) ("Buyers cannot compare the remedies limitation in their purchase and sale agreements, negotiated with their expertise as agents, with the clauses at issue in *Zuver*, . . . which were deemed to effectively foreclose legal action for one side."). *But see* Uncle Joe's v. L.M. Berry & Co., 156 P.3d 1113 (Alaska 2007) ("the law disfavors — and sometimes positively forbids — contractual exculpatory clauses"); Queen Villas Homeowners Ass'n v. TCB Prop. Mgmt., 56 Cal. Rptr. 3d 528 (Ct. App. 2007) ("Where a two-party contract purportedly releases one side from liability to the other . . . courts must look for clear, unambiguous and explicit language not to hold the released party liable."); Murphy v. YMCA of Lake Wales, 974 So. 2d 565 (Fla. App. 2008) ("Exculpatory clauses are disfavored and will be strictly construed against the party claiming to be relieved of liability."); Laeroc Waikiki Parkside v. K.S.K. (Oahu) Ltd. P'ship, 166 P.3d 961 (Haw. 2007) (exculpatory clauses "are generally valid," but "are strictly construed against the promisee" and "will be held void if the agreement is (1) violative of a statute; (2) contrary to a substantial public interest, or (3) gained through inequality of bargaining power"); Zerjal v. Daech & Bauer Constr., 939 N.E.2d 1067 (Ill. App. 2010) ("While generally disfavored under Illinois law . . . exculpatory clauses are enforceable unless (1) enforcement would be against a settled public policy of the state and (2) something in the social relationship of the parties militates against enforcement."); United Servs. Auto. Ass'n v. ADT Sec. Servs., 241 S.W.3d 335 (Ky. App. 2006) ("Contracts exempting from liability for negligence are not favored and are strictly construed against the parties relying upon them."); Yang v. Voyagaire Houseboats, 701 N.W.2d 783 (Minn. 2005) ("Exculpatory clauses are 'not favored,' and they are 'strictly construed against the benefited party.' "); Pitts v. Watkins, 905 So. 2d 553 (Miss. 2005) (limitations on liability "are given strict scrutiny"); Caballero v. Stafford, 202 S.W.3d 683 (Mo. App. 2006) (" 'Although exculpatory clauses in contracts releasing an individual from his or her own future negligence are disfavored, they are not prohibited as against public policy.' " . . . "Exculpatory clauses are strictly construed against the party seeking their enforcement."); Rainbow Country Rentals & Retail v. Ameritech Publ'g, 706 N.W.2d 95 (Wis. 2005) ("Wisconsin case law does not favor exculpatory agreements"); Espinoza v. Arkansas Valley Adventures, LLC, 809 F.3d 1150 (10th Cir. 2016) (under Colorado law, "while businesses providing, say, water, electricity, or sanitary services usually may not shield themselves from claims of negligence, recreational service providers often can. . . . This relatively permissive public policy toward recreational releases may not be unique to Colorado common law but it does seem to be one of its distinguishing features").

In Severn Peanut Co., Inc. v. Industrial Fumigant Co., 807 F.3d 88 (4th Cir. 2015), the Fourth Circuit considered a contract's exclusion of consequential damages where the fumigant company allegedly misapplied the pesticide, resulting in fire that burned down a structure. Severn Peanut alleged that the fumigation company "dumped approximately 49,000 tablets of Fumitoxin into Severn's peanut dome through a single access hatch," causing them to pile up, despite required product labeling instructing not to allow piling and a contractual obligation to fumigate "in a manner consistent with instructions . . . and precautions." The contract also provided that the fumigator was not "assuming any risk of incidental or consequential damages" to Severn's "property, product, equipment, downtime, or loss of business." The Fourth Circuit gave effect to this clause, observing that "[e]nforcement of contractual liability limitations and damages exclusions is one aspect of this freedom of contract." The court observed that "both parties are experienced businesses" and disagreed with Severn's arguments that the limitation should be unenforceable as unconscionable or against public policy: "We are not presently considering the plight of a vulnerable member of the public adrift among the variegated hazards of a complex commercial world. Instead, we are considering a rather typical agreement among two commercial entities, and we may hold them to the contract's terms." Severn also sued for negligence, but applying state law, the Circuit concluded that "North Carolina's economic loss principles prevent Severn from transforming its breach of contract claim into tort."

In Schnuck Mkts., Inc. v. First Data Merch. Servs. Corp., 852 F.3d 732 (8th Cir. 2017), the Eighth Circuit narrowly construed a Master Services Agreement's limitation of liability provision in the context of a data breach and imposition of fines by MasterCard and Visa against the bank and data processor responsible for facilitating a grocery chain's credit card transactions. Credit card companies have the contractual right to impose fines and assess costs associated with reimbursing cardholders and monitoring or canceling at-risk cards. After a cyber-attack against the market compromised cardholder data, the credit card companies assessed fees against the authorizing bank, which in turn began withholding funds from the market. The market then sued, relying on a contract provision limiting its liability to $500,000, with exceptions for "third party fees" and "fees, fines or penalties" imposed by the credit card associations. The Eighth Circuit looked to other provisions to construe these exceptions narrowly. "Third party fees," the court reasoned, includes only payment for services, not reimbursement for losses. Similarly, the exclusion of "fines or penalties" was inapplicable because "[t]he assessments for issuer losses are more accurately defined as 'compensation or reparation for an injury' and not as 'a sum imposed as punishment.' " The Circuit also rejected the argument that such a narrow reading of the limitation of liability would result in "the commercially unreasonable result of requiring Defendants to act as Schnucks's insurer." It reasoned that "the underlying business arrangement, which represents Defendants' choice to vouch for Schnucks's compliance with data-security standards, is not rendered commercially unreasonable merely because the limitation on Schnucks's liability is broader than Defendants now wish it to be."

§4.28a n.2 p.599 In the second paragraph, add the following to the list in the first sentence: Doty Commc'ns v. L.M. Berry & Co., 417 F. Supp. 2d 1355 (N.D. Ga. 2006) ("Limitations of liability clauses . . . are enforceable under Georgia law unless the defendants' conduct gives rise to a tort claim for gross negligence or wanton or willful conduct.")

§4.28a n.2 p.599 In the third paragraph, add the following after the citation to* Discount Fabric*: , distinguished in Rainbow Country Rentals & Retail v. Ameritech Publ'g, *supra* note 1 (clause enforceable because directory publisher no longer had a monopoly and because the clause was a stipulated damages clause rather than exculpatory clause)

§4.28a n.3 p.600 Add the following to the list in the second sentence: United Servs. Auto. Ass'n v. ADT Sec. Servs., *supra* note 1 (upholding clause: "there is a broad public policy of freedom of contract in Kentucky and permitting alarm companies to limit their liability does not leave consumers unprotected"); Synnex Corp. v. ADT Sec. Servs., 928 A.2d 37 (N.J. Super. App. Div. 2007) ("Other jurisdictions also generally uphold the validity of exculpatory clauses in alarm company contracts.").

§4.28a n.3 p.600 Add the following at the end: *Cf.* Adler v. Columbia Sav. & Loan Ass'n, 811 N.Y.S.2d 737 (App. Div. 2006) ("[p]ublic policy considerations protect alarm companies for injuries to non-contracting plaintiffs"). *But see* U.S. Fire Ins. Co. v. Sonitrol Mgmt. Corp., 192 P.3d 543 (Colo. App. 2008) (limitation of damages clause properly protects alarm company against its own negligence, but not against willful and wanton conduct).

§4.28a n.4 p.600 Add the following to the list in the third sentence: Law Co. v. Mohawk Constr. & Supply Co., 523 F. Supp. 2d 1276 (D. Kan. 2007) ("even if exculpatory to one party, such 'contracts freely arrived at and fairly made are favorites of the law' ") (quoting from Kansas City Structural Steel Co. v. L.G. Barcus & Sons, Inc., 535 P.2d 419 (Kan. 1975)), *rev'd on other grounds*, 2009 WL 2488140 (10th Cir. Aug. 17, 2009).

§4.28a n.4 p.600 Add the following after the citation to* William Elec.*: followed in J.A. Jones Constr. Co., v. Lehrer McGovern Bovis, 89 P.3d 1009 (Nev. 2004) (describing exceptions of fraud, misrepresentation, concealment or other bad faith, delays amounting to abandonment, and delays caused by active interference as giving rise to "violation of the duty of good faith and fair dealing" as "logical extension of existing law" and as "adopted by a majority of jurisdictions," but rejecting the failure to contemplate exception).

§4.28a n.4 p.600 Add the following after the citation to **Evergreen Pipeline Constr. Co.***:* , in Comm'l Elec. Contractors v. Pavarini Constr. Co., 856 N.Y.S.2d 46 (App. Div. 2008) (*Corinno* exceptions (bad faith or willful, malicious, or grossly negligent conduct; lack of contemplation; intentional abandonment; fundamental breach) do not apply; "inept administration or poor planning" insufficient), and in Blue Water Envt'l v. Inc. Village of Bayville, 843 N.Y.S.2d 681 (App. Div. 2007) ("no claim for delay" provision not contrary to public policy, and in any event bars only claims for delays which are reasonably foreseeable, arise from the contractor's work during performance, or otherwise are mentioned in the contract).

§4.28a n.4 p.600 Add the following to the list following **"But cf."***:* Tricon Kent Co. v. LaFarge N. Am., 186 P.3d 155 (Colo. App. 2008) (" 'no-damages-for-delay' clauses are valid and enforceable in Colorado, but they are to be strictly construed against the owner or contractor"); James Corp. v. N. Allegheny Sch. Dist., 938 A.2d 474 (Pa. Commw. Ct. 2007) (no-damages-for-delay clauses "[o]rdinarily . . . enforceable," but not "where (1) there is an affirmative or positive interference by the owner with the contractor's work, or (2) there is a failure on the part of the owner to act upon some essential ma[tt]er necessary to the prosecution of the work").

§4.28a n.4 p.600 Add the following at the end: There have been legislative responses to the general validation of no-damages-for-delay clauses. *See* Wash. Rev. Code §4.24.360 ("Any clause in a construction contract . . . which purports to waive, release, or extinguish the rights of a contractor, subcontractor, or supplier to damages or an equitable adjustment arising out of unreasonable delay in performance which delay is caused by the acts or omissions of the contractee or persons acting for the contractee is against public policy and is void and unconscionable.").

This deference to limitation of liability clauses appears in other parts of the construction process as well. *See* Jordan v. Diamond Equip. & Supply Co., 207 S.W.3d 525 (Ark. 2005) (upholding strictly construed exculpatory clause in lease contract for heavy landscaping equipment); Zerjal v. Daech & Bauer Constr., 939 N.E.2d 1067 (Ill. App. 2010) (liquidated damages clause in home inspection contract upheld; although the clause was in a form contract, "the plaintiffs were under no economic or other compulsion to sign the inspection contract"). *Cf.* Fort Knox Self Storage v. W. Techs., *supra* note 1 (survey of subsurface conditions; "there is a significant difference between contracts that insulate a party from any and all liability and those that simply limit liability," with the latter "enforceable as long as they are 'reasonable and not so drastic as to remove the incentive to perform with due care.' ") (quoting from Valhal Corp. v. Sullivan Assocs., *supra* note 1). *But cf.* Gonski v. Second Judicial Dist. Ct., 245 P.3d 1164 (Nev. 2010) (limitation of remedies unconscionable where the provisions "impliedly waive . . . statutory rights" afforded owners in construction defect disputes).

§4.28a n.5 p.601 Add the following to the list in the first sentence: Canal Elec. Co. v. Westinghouse Elec. Co., 973 F.2d 988 (1st Cir. 1992) (Breyer, J.) ("the liability limitation clause simply reflects a decision by highly sophisticated business entities about how to allocate certain risks"); Dry Dock v. Godfrey Conveyor Co., 717 F. Supp. 2d 825 (W.D. Wis. 2010) ("there is little need for the court to protect the interests of savvy commercial parties in dealings with each other"); Zaremba v. Marvin Lumber & Cedar Co., 458 F. Supp. 2d 545 (N.D. Ohio 2006) (" 'where there is no great disparity of bargaining power between the parties, a contractual provision which excludes liability for consequential damages and limits the buyer's remedy to repair or replacement of the defective product is not unconscionable' ") (quoting Chemtrol Adhesives v. Am. Mfrs. Mut. Ins. Co., 537 N.E.2d 624 (Ohio 1989)); Star-Shadow Prods. v. Super 8 Sync Sound Sys., 730 A.2d 1081 (R.I. 1999) (defective film supplied to motion picture producer; "plaintiffs received what they bargained for, and the risk of equipment failure properly lay on them, not defendant").

§4.28a n.7 p.602 Add the following to the list after **"Contra"***:* DJ Coleman, Inc. v. Nufarm Ams., 693 F. Supp. 2d 1055 (D.N.D. 2010) (pesticide; consequential damages disclaimer unconscionable where disclaimer part of contract of adhesion between parties with "a substantial inequality in bargaining power," even though the farmer had long used the pesticide, and where limiting the remedy to replacement or refund would cause the loss of a whole year's crop); Nomo Agroindus. v. Enza Zade N. Am., 492 F. Supp. 2d 1175 (D. Ariz. 2007) (seed tomatoes; remedy failed of its essential purpose because "[a] farmer's lost growing season and the accompanying loss of expected profits due to defective seeds clearly is not compensated by simply replacing or refunding the price of the defective seeds").

§4.28a n.8 p.603 Add the following after the first sentence: Accord: Bernath v. Potato Servs. of Mich., 300 F. Supp. 2d 175 (D. Me. 2004) (shipment of incorrect seed potatoes not a "novel circumstance[] not contemplated by the parties"); Proto Const. & Dev. Corp. v. Superior Precast, 52 U.C.C. Rep. Serv. 2d 921 (E.D.N.Y. 2002) ("Given that both parties were aware that there was a substantial risk of delay when they entered into the contract, and that the parties, both of whom are sophisticated companies, allocated the risk of that delay to the plaintiff, plaintiff is not deprived of the substantial value of the bargain by enforcing the Limitation of Liability clause."); Computerized Radiological Servs. v. Syntex Corp., 595 F. Supp. 1495 (S.D.N.Y. 1984) ("A limited remedy fails of its essential purpose when the circumstances existing at the time of the agreement have changed"), *aff'd in part, rev'd in part on other grounds*, 786 F.2d 72 (2d Cir. 1986).

§4.28a n.9 p.603 Replace the citation to **White & Summers** *with the following:* 1 J. White & R. Summers, Uniform Commercial Code §12.10, at 832 (5th ed. 2006).

§4.28a n.9 p.603 In the first paragraph, add the following to the list after **"See"***:* Dynamic Recycling Servs. v. Shred Pax Corp., 569 N.E.2d 570, 577 (Ill. App. 1991); Goddard v. Gen. Motors Corp., 396 N.E.2d 761 (Ohio 1979).

§4.28a n.10 p.603 Add the following at the end: *Wilson Trading* has been much assailed by courts and commentators. *See* G. Travalio et al., Nordstrom on Sales §4.08[E][1], at 495-96 (2d ed. 2000) ("there is no basis in the Code for the categorical exemption of cases involving latent defects . . . In fact, consequential damages are generally excluded by sellers to avoid liability in precisely those circumstances."); J. White & R. Summers, *supra* note 9, §12-10 at 834 ("In *Wilson Trading*, the exclusive remedy might have been unreasonable, but it did not fail of its essential purpose."); Arkwright-Boston Mut. Mfrs. Ins. Co. v. Westinghouse Elec. Corp., 844 F.2d 1174 (5th Cir. 1988) ("In twenty intervening years no other court has followed this decision and commentators have roundly criticized it.").

§4.28a n.11 p.603 Add the following after the citation to **Boston Helicopter Charter***:* , followed in Baptists Mem'l Hosp. v. Argo Constr. Corp., 308 S.W.3d 337 (Tenn. App. 2009) ("the fact that the alleged defect . . . was latent does not cause the contractually limited remedy to fail of its essential purpose").

§4.28a n.12 p.604 Add the following at the end: All this applies only if the clause in question is clearly exclusive. If it is not, then the courts will read it to be cumulative, not exclusive, and will allow the buyer its full remedies under Article Two. *See* Advanced Bodycare Solutions v. Thione Int'l, 615 F.3d 1352 (11th Cir. 2010) ("The statutory language and comment show a strong reluctance to construe a contractual remedy as exclusive."; clause providing for termination, renegotiation, or removal of exclusivity as sole remedies for breach of installment contract; because the clause "does not clearly express that the listed remedies are the exclusive remedies available to Thione, regardless of what the parties' intentions may have been, the Agreement did not effectively limit Thione's remedies"); Creative Extruded Prods. V. Amity Mold Co., 902 N.E.2d 531 (Ohio App. 2008) (provision that "[c]redit in full will be rendered on all defective moldings" does not mean that credit is the only available remedy).

§4.28a n.13 p.604 Add the following at the end: In contrast, a limitation on liability clause that provides for repair, replacement, or refund is almost invariably upheld. *See* Figgie Int'l v. Destileria

Serrales, 190 F.3d 252 (4th Cir. 1999); Dow Corning Corp. v. Capitol Aviation, 411 F.2d 622 (7th Cir. 1969); White v. Microsoft Corp., 454 F. Supp. 2d 1118 (S.D. Ala. 2006); Taylor Inv. Corp. v. Weil, 169 F. Supp. 2d 1046 (D. Minn. 2001); *In re* Access Cardiosystems, 361 B.R. 626 (Bankr. D. Mass. 2007); Arcata Graphics Co. v. Heidelberg Harris, Inc., 874 S.W.2d 15 (Tenn. App. 1993). Clauses providing for refund ordinarily fail only where the seller has either refused to provide a refund or has provided it only after hugely extended delays. *See* Webco Indus. V. Thermatool Corp., 278 F.3d 1120 (10th Cir. 2002); Ragen Corp. v. Kearney & Trecker Corp., 912 F.2d 619 (3d Cir. 1990); Marr Enters. V. Lewis Refrigeration Co., 556 F.2d 951 (9th Cir. 1977).

§4.28a n.14 p.605 In the first paragraph, add the following at the end: At the risk of stating the obvious, UCC §2-719 applies to contract damages. If, therefore, a limitation of liability fails of its essential purpose "the effect of this failure would be to revive other *contractual* remedies. . . . Such a revival would have no effect on the exclusion of *tort* liability by means of a negligence disclaimer." Trans-Spec Truck Serv. V. Caterpillar Inc., *supra* note 1.

***§4.28a n.14 p.605 In the second paragraph, add the following to the list after* "See generally":** Williams, Getting What You Bargained For: How Courts Might Provide a Coherent Basis for Damages that Arise When Remedies Fail of Their Essential Purpose, 5 Va. L. & Bus. Rev. 131 (2010); Wladis et al., Sales, 55 Bus. Law. 1951, 1966-68 (2000).

***§4.28a n.15 p.606 Add the following to the list after* "Accord":** Razor v. Hyundai Motor Am., 854 N.E.2d 607 (Ill. 2006) (following *Chatlos*).

***§4.28a n.16 p.606 Add the following to the list after* "Accord":** AES Tech. Sys. v. Coherent Radiation, 583 F.2d 933 (7th Cir. 1978) ("courts must peer into the particular factual circumstances of each case to determine if indeed the contract met its purpose").

§4.28a n.16 p.606 Add the following at the end: The best efforts of this treatise and some others notwithstanding, most jurisdictions that have addressed this issue, and a large majority of those that have done so in the last two decades, have chosen the independent approach exemplified by *Chatlos* rather than either the dependent or case-by-case approaches. The most thorough recent review of the literature is in *Razor, supra* note 15. This author is unrepentant in his preference for the case-by-case approach, which avoids the Procrustean assumptions either of independence or of dependence. But he realizes that he is dog-paddling against a rather powerful current.

§4.28a n.18 p.607 Add the following to the end of the first paragraph: It should be remembered that UCC §2-316(2) provides only one means of disclaiming implied warranties — the "safe harbor" approach containing language certain to work. Under section 2-316(3)(a), other language may suffice as well, if that language "in common understanding calls the buyer's attention to the exclusion of warranties and makes plain that there is no implied warranty." *See* Star-Shadow Prods. V. Super 8 Sync Sound Sys., *supra* note 5 ("Section [2-316] does not mandate that a limitation of liability clause expressly mention the implied warranty of merchantability in order to effectively waive this implied warranty.").

§4.28a n.18 p.607 Add the following after the citation to **Tolmie Farms** *in the second paragraph:* , followed in R.O.W. Window Co. v. Allmetal, Inc., 856 N.E.2d 55 (Ill. App. 2006) (even though disclaimer sent with goods, still part of contract because "there was a course of dealing that took place over several years").

§4.28a n.18 p.607 Add the following to the list in the second paragraph after **"See"***:* Desouza v. Lauderdale, 928 So. 2d 1035 (Ala. 2005) (applying UCC §2-316(2) by analogy); Kirkman v. Parex, Inc., 632 S.E.2d 854 (S.C. 2006) ("disclaimer can be permitted only if strict conditions are met": the disclaimer " 'must be (1) conspicuous, (2) known to the buyer, and (3) specifically bargained for,' and [t]his standard is to be applied strictly and will be met only in rare circumstances") (quoting Burbo v. Harley C. Douglass, Inc., 106 P.3d 258 (Wash. App. 2005), itself followed in

Mattingly v. Palmer Ridge Homes, 238 P.3d 505 (Wash. App. 2010)); Heath v. Palmer, 915 A.2d 1290 (Vt. 2006) (disclaimers of the implied warranties of habitability and good workmanship must be "conspicuous," "clear and unambiguous").

§4.28a n.18 p.607 Add the following at the end of the third paragraph: Some states have dealt with this by statute, typically by requiring disclosure of the presence or absence of warranties. *See* Conn. Gen. Stat. §47-118(d); Haw. Rev. Stat. §514A-61.

§4.28a n.20 p.608 Add the following at the end: As with current Article 2, it also is possible to disclaim the implied warranties without using the safe harbor language, following the same test as current law except that in consumer contracts the disclaimers must, if in a record, be conspicuous.

§4.28a n.24 p.608 Add the following after the first paragraph: This line of cases rests on three points. First, in the comments to UCC §2-302 many of the cases cited to deal with disclaimers. Second, 2-302 states expressly that it applies to "any clause" of a contract. Third, comment 1 to §2-302 refers both to oppression and unfair surprise. A term may be oppressive even if the buyer is unsurprised — if, for example, it is in a contract of adhesion and it is substantively unfair. This debate may, however, prove unimportant in most cases. If a term complies with §2-316(2) or (3), it is unlikely to be held procedurally unconscionable, save by those courts attaching very high weight to the degree of adhesion of a contract.

***§4.28a n.24 p.608 Add the following to the list in the second paragraph following* "See generally":** G. Travalio et al., Nordstrom on Sales §4.07[C][4] (2d ed. 2000); Wright, Your Mileage May Vary: A General Theory of Legal Disclaimers, 7 Pierce L. Rev. 85 (2008).

§4.29 CONSUMER LEGISLATION

§4.29 n.2 p.609 Add the following at the end of the first paragraph: Even less successful so far has been the Uniform Consumer Lease Act, proposed by the Uniform Law Commissioners in 2001; at this writing it has but one adoption.

§4.29 n.2 p.609 In the second paragraph, add the following at the end of the third sentence: and in UCC 2A-103(1)(e) (*consumer lease* is lease made to a lessee "who takes under the lease primarily for a personal, family, or household purpose").

§4.29 n.4 p.610 Add the following in place of the text after the first sentence: European law has undergone great change in the last decade as a result of EC Directive 93/13/EEC on Unfair Terms in Consumer Contracts. Most of the implementing legislation in the member states has contained lists of proscribed terms, lists of presumptively invalid terms, or both. *See generally* Comm'n. of the European Communities, Report from the Commission on the Implementation of Council Directive 93/13/EEC of 5 April 1993 on Unfair Terms in Consumer Contracts (2000); Nebbia, Reforming the UK Law on Unfair Terms: The Draft Unfair Contract Terms Bill, 23 J. Contract L. 228 (2007); Whittaker, The Language or Languages of Consumer Contracts, 8 Camb. Y.B. Eur. Legal Studies 229 (2005-2006).

§4.29 n.14 p.611 Add the following to the list after **"See"***:* Willis, Against Financial-Literacy Education, 94 Iowa L. Rev. 197 (2008).

§4.29 n.14 p.611 Add the following to the end: Butler & Johnston, Reforming State Consumer Protection Liability: An Economic Approach, 2010 Colum. Bus. L. Rev. 1; Hillman, Online Consumer Standard Form Contracting Practices: A Survey and Discussion of Legal Implications, in Consumer Protection in the Age of the "Information Economy" 283 (J. Winn ed. 2006); Garvin, Small Business and the False Dichotomies of Contract Law, 40 Wake Forest L. Rev. 295 (2005); Gillette, Rolling Contracts as an Agency Problem, 2004 Wis. L. Rev. 679; Hadfield et al., Information-Based Principles for Rethinking Consumer

Protection Policy, 21 J. Consumer Poly. 131 (1998); Hillman & Rachlinski, Standard-Form Contracting in the Electronic Age, 77 N.Y.U. L. Rev. 429 (2002); Silber, Observing Reasonable Consumers: Cognitive Psychology, Consumer Behavior and Consumer Law, 2 Loy. Consumer L. Rep. 69 (1990).

§4.29 n.17 p.612 Add the following at the end: For a good comprehensive treatment of Magnuson-Moss and related statutes, see C. Carter & J. Sheldon, Consumer Warranty Law (2006).

§4.29a DRAFTING DISCLAIMERS AND OTHER LIMITATIONS OF LIABILITY

§4.29a n.2 p.614 Replace the citation to **Fontaine & De Ly** *with the following:* M. Fontaine & F. De Ly, Drafting International Contracts: An Analysis of Contract Clauses ch. 7 (2006).

§4.29a n.2 p.614 In the final sentence, Add the following to the list after **"See"***:* R. Feldman & R. Nimmer, Drafting Effective Contracts §5.05 (2d ed. 1999); J. Klotz, International Sales Agreements: An Annotated Drafting and Negotiating Guide ch. 13 (Int'l ed. 1998); Lookofsky, Tooling Up for Warranties with the CISG Case Digest, in Drafting Contracts Under the CISG 343 (H. Flechtner et al. eds. 2008); Warranties & Disclaimers (M. Kurer et al. eds. 2002).

§4.29a n.4 p.614 Add the following to the list after **"See"***:* Kunz, The Ethics of Invalid and "Iffy" Contract Clauses, 40 Loy. L.A. L. Rev. 487 (2006); Schmitz, Ethical Considerations in Drafting and Enforcing Consumer Arbitration Clauses, 49 S. Tex. L. Rev. 841 (2008); Sullivan, The Puzzling Persistence of Unenforceable Contract Terms, 70 Ohio St. L.J. 1127 (2009).

§4.29a n.7 p.615 Add the following at the end: See Morningstar v. Hallett, 858 A.2d 125 (Pa. Super. 2004) ("as is" disclaimer "insufficient to disclaim the express warranty that the horse was 11 years old"). For a common-law application, *see* Jewelers Mut. Ins. Co. v. Firstar Bank, 820 N.E.2d 411 (Ill. 2004) (rental of safety

deposit box: exculpatory clause invalidated in light of promise to exercise ordinary care to prevent unauthorized people from opening the box). Note, however, that UCC §2-316(1) is subject to the parol evidence rule; it is thus possible for a seller to make an oral express warranty and effectively disclaim it in a later integrated writing. *See* St. Croix Printing Equip. v. Rockwell Int'l Corp., 428 N.W.2d 877 (Minn. App. 1988); Rawson v. Conover, 20 P.3d 876 (Utah 2001). Moreover, to make a remedy exclusive one must clearly say so; simply laying out a remedy without more makes the remedy cumulative. *See* Creative Extruded Prods. v. Amity Mold Co., 902 N.E.2d 531 (Ohio App. 2008) (provision that "[c]redit in full will be rendered on all defective moldings" does not mean that credit is the only available remedy).

§4.29a n.11 p.615 Add the following at the beginning: *See* Nester Comm'l Roofing v. Am. Builders & Contractors Supply Co., 250 Fed. Appx. 852 (10th Cir. 2007) (disclaimer on buckets of roofing material conspicuous even though in smaller type than surrounding text; it was in a separate paragraph and in capital letters).

§4.29a n.11 p.615 Add the following to the list after **"See"**: Nomo Agroindus. v. Enza Zade N. Am., 492 F. Supp. 2d 1175 (D. Ariz. 2007) (disclaimer of implied warranties in seed invoice ineffective where found on back, where only warning on front is a statement in "micro print that is tiny compared with the rest of the information on the invoice" that the buyer agrees to the disclaimers on the back).

§4.29a n.13 p.616 Add the following to the list after **"But cf."**: Pidcock v. Ewing, 371 F. Supp. 2d 870 (E.D. Mich. 2005) (warranty disclaimer on back of sales agreement effective where in capital letters and contrasting type, and where front stated in capital letters and contrasting type that warranties and exclusions were on the reverse); Parsley v. Monaco Coach Corp., 327 F. Supp. 2d 797 (W.D. Mich. 2004) (warranty disclaimer on back of purchase agreement effective where there were many references to exclusions on the front in capital letters, bold print, and contrasting color); Perry v. Gulf Stream Coach, 814 N.E.2d 634 (Ind. App. 2004) (warranty disclaimer on back of sales agreement effective

where in capital letters and underlined, and where front of agreement alerted purchases to read the reverse side).

§4.29a n.15 p.616 Add the following at the end: For an illustration under the common law, *see* Atkins v. Swimwest Family Fitness Ctr., 691 N.W.2d 334 (Wis. 2005) (invalidating disclaimer where part of registration form and with no separate signature; "the waiver in this case could have been a separate document, providing . . . more adequate notice," and "a separate signature line could have been provided, but was not"), distinguished by Rainbow Country Rentals & Retail v. Ameritech Pub., 706 N.W.2d 95 (Wis. 2005) (notice of indemnity provision adequate where "[d]irectly above the signature line was a warning that terms and conditions, including the separately numbered indemnity provision, were on the back of the form").

§4.29a n.16 p.616 Add the following to the list in the first sentence: Wilson v. Royal Motor Sales, 812 N.E.2d 133 (Ind. App. 2004) (warranty disclaimer on back conspicuous where in bold and capital letters, and front refers to material on back).

§4.29a n.21 p.618 Add the following to the list: Thompson v. Hi Tech Motor Sports, 945 A.2d 368 (Vt. 2008) ("Although [an express mention of negligence] is not essential, in its absence there must be words that convey a similar intent"; failure to refer to release for negligence, but rather to dangers inherent in activity, makes disclaimer ineffective against negligence claim), distinguished by Provoncha v. Vt. Motocross Ass'n, 974 A.2d 1261 (Vt. 2009) (exculpatory clause encompassing injury "in anyway arising . . . from any cause what so ever . . . sufficiently clear as to operate as a release"); Ketler v. PFPA, LLC, 132 A.3d 746 (Del. 2016) (gym membership agreement that gym "will not be liable for any injury, including, without limitation, personal, bodily, or mental injury . . . resulting from the negligence of Planet Fitness or anyone on Planet Fitness' behalf whether related to exercise or not" effective release of negligence claim and enforceable as not against public policy).

§4.29a n.22 p.618 Add the following after the citation to **Green Intl.:** followed in turn in Storage & Processors v. Reyes, 134 S.W.3d 190 (Tex. 2004) (applying doctrine to "agreement which does anything less than totally exculpate a party . . . would radically expand the doctrine," but "unique status" justifies its application to employer's nonsubscriber workers' compensation benefits plan).

§4.29a n.22 p.618 Add the following to the list in the first sentence: Starr v. Dow Agroscis., 339 F. Supp. 2d 1097 (D. Or. 2004) (disclaimer of "consequential, special, or indirect damages" insufficiently specific to disclaim damages for negligence, where negligence never mentioned and consequences never explained); Applbaum v. Golden Acres Farm & Ranch, 333 F. Supp. 2d 31 (N.D.N.Y. 2004) (agreement to hold defendant "harmless from every and all claim which may arise from injury" insufficient to show the necessary "clear and unequivocal intent of the parties to absolve the defendant from injury"); Cohen v. Five Brooks Stable, 72 Cal. Rptr. 3d 471 (Ct. App. 2008) (waiver of negligence must be "clear, unambiguous, and explicit"); Murphy v. YMCA of Lake Wales, 974 So. 2d 565 (Fla. App. 2008) (invalidating attempted disclaimer that did mention negligence where same clause promised that would take "every reasonable precaution"); Yang v. Voyagaire Houseboats, 701 N.W.2d 783 (Minn. 2005) ("[a]n exculpatory clause is unenforceable if it is ambiguous in scope"); Markel Am. Ins. Co. v. Dagmar's Marina, 161 P.3d 1029 (Wash. App. 2007); (clause must "clearly and unequivocally exculpate" party from its own negligence; clause said only that defendant "shall not be liable or responsible in any manner for [the vessel's] safekeeping"); Walters v. YMCA, 96 A.3d 323, 328 (N.J. Super. Ct. App. Div. 2014) (general "hold harmless" exculpatory clause unenforceable as against public policy; "Given the expansive scope of the exculpatory clause here, we hold that if applied literally, it would eviscerate the common law duty of care owed by defendant to its invitees, regardless the nature of the business activity involved. Such a prospect would be inimical to the public interest because it would transfer the redress of civil wrongs from the responsible tortfeasor to either the innocent injured party or to society at large, in the form of taxpayer-supported institutions.").

§4.29a n.23 p.619 Add the following at the end: *Cf.* Courbat v. Dahana Ranch, 141 P.3d 427 (Haw. 2006) (upholding broad disclaimer of liability for ordinary negligence, but invalidating it for gross negligence). As to federal maritime law, *see* Hopkins v. The Boat Club, 866 So. 2d 108 (Fla. App. 2004) (state laws requiring specific reference conflict with federal courts, which "have consistently refused to hold that words such as 'negligence' . . . are indispensable").

§4.29a n.25 p.620 Add the following at the end: When "Superstorm Sandy" struck the New York City area in October 2012, some artwork was damaged in the Christie's Fine Art Storage Services facility in the Red Hook area of Brooklyn, prompting a legal test to its subrogation and disclaimer of liability clauses with those who had stored their artwork there. Christie's offered the option to buy insurance from them or, the option plaintiffs selected, sign a loss/damage waiver, obtain adequate insurance, and waive any rights of subrogation. XL Specialty Insurance Co. v. Christie's Fine Art Storage Services, Inc., 137 A.D.3d 563, 564 (N.Y. App. 2016). When Christie's was sued by the insurance company as subrogee for the party that lost artwork during the storm, it moved to dismiss the claim on the basis of the waiver. The Appellate Division held that the waiver of liability and waiver of subrogation was unenforceable under UCC Article 7. UCC §7-204(a) provides that a "warehouse is liable for damages for loss of or injury to the goods caused by its failure to exercise care with regard to the goods that a reasonably careful person would exercise under similar circumstances" and §7-202(c) states that any limitation of liability may not "impair [that] duty of care." The court followed Kimberly-Clark Corp. v. Lake Erie Warehouse, Div. of Lake Erie Rolling Mill, 49 A.D.2d 492 (1975), *appeal dismissed* 39 N.Y.2d 888 (1976), which considered a less explicit subrogation waiver but held that "the implied waiver of subrogation in that case was nothing more than another attempt by defendant to exempt itself from all liability, which 'would defeat the statute and must be held void.' "

§4.29a n.27 p.620 Add the following at the end: *Cf. In re* Enron Corp., 367 B.R. 384 (Bankr. S.D.N.Y. 2007) (giving effect to clause that "[u]nder no circumstances shall any warranty or

remedy contained in this Agreement be deemed to have failed of its essential purpose so long as [Marathon] has the right to provide [Enron Wind] with a refund"; issue open whether by delay Marathon lost that right).

§4.29a n.29 p.621 ***In the first paragraph, add the following to the list in the first sentence:*** In Biotronik A.G. v. Conor Medsystems Ireland, Ltd., 22 N.Y.3d 799 (N.Y. 2014), the New York Court of Appeals held that lost profits could be recovered as general damages under the circumstances of the arrangement between the parties in that case. The parties' agreement provided that there would be no liability for "indirect, special, consequential, incidental, or punitive damage." *Id.* at 803 However, the court noted that this "was not a simple resale contract," *id.*; rather, "[t]The agreement reflects defendant's anticipation and dependence on the resale, and, as such, the agreement reflects an arrangement significantly different from a situation where the buyer's resale to a third party is independent of the underlying agreement," *id.* at 810. Thus, "[t]he contract clearly contemplated that plaintiff would resell defendant's stents. That was the very essence of the contract. Any lost profits resulting from a breach would be the 'natural and probable consequence' of that breach." *Id.* at 808. *Accord:* Penncro Assocs. v. Sprint Spectrum, 499 F.3d 1151 (10th Cir. 2007) ("Lost profits, under appropriate circumstances, can be recoverable as a component of either (or both) direct and consequential damages."); Creighton Univ. v. Gen. Elec. Co., 636 F. Supp. 2d 940 (D. Neb. 2009) (uncollected claims resulting from an inadequate health care technology system consequential damages, not direct).

§4.29a n.29 p.621 ***Add the following to the list in the second paragraph:*** Lamell Lumber Corp. v. Newstress Int'l, 938 A.2d 1215 (Vt. 2007) (repair-or-replace limited remedy "by its terms deals exclusively with the remedies available for 'defective materials' and thus does not limit remedies for improper design").

§4.29a n.30 p.622 ***Add the following at the end:*** *See also* the discussion of severability as a means of saving partly unconscionable contracts in §4.28 *supra.* For representative severability

clauses, *see* Tortoriello v. Gerald Nissan, 882 N.E.2d 157 (Ill. App. 2008); *In re* Poly-Am., 262 S.W.3d 337 (Tex. 2008).

§4.29a p.622 Add the following at the end of the second full sentence of the carryover paragraph: . . . recitals can sometimes be helpful.[32]

[32] *See* Creighton Univ. v. Gen. Elec. Co., 636 F. Supp. 2d 940 (D. Neb. 2009) (finding no procedural unconscionability where university "sought proposals from other vendors" and where the contract recites that "the terms and conditions of this Agreement have been the subject of active and complete negotiations").

VOLUME II

CHAPTER 5

UNENFORCEABILITY ON GROUNDS OF PUBLIC POLICY

§5.1 PUBLIC POLICY AS A GROUND FOR UNENFORCEABILITY

§5.1 n.1 p.2 Add the following at the end: *Cf.* Sanchez v. Cnty. of San Bernardino, 98 Cal. Rptr. 3d 96 (Ct. App. 2009) (confidentiality provision of severance agreement with government; where "broad, general public policy in favor of open government . . . must be balanced against the broad, general public policy in favor of privacy" the court lacks the firm guidance needed to find that a contract violates public policy).

§5.1 n.2 p.2 Add the following at the end: For examples in residential lease agreements, *see* Furth-Matzkin, Meirav, On the Surprising Use of Unenforceable Contract Terms: Evidence from the Residential Rental Market (May 22, 2016), Harvard John M. Olin Center for Law, Economics, and Business, Discussion Paper No. 61, 2015, available at SSRN: http://ssrn.com/abstract=2782987 ("the study analyzes a sample of 70 leases in terms of Massachusetts Landlord and Tenant Law. The paper's findings reveal that landlords frequently use legally dubious — as well as clearly invalid — provisions in their contracts.").

Although arbitration is a creature of contract, whether arbitral awards are unenforceable as contrary to public policy is beyond the scope of this treatise. Certainly the public policy exception exists under federal and state arbitration law, though the Court has warned that the exception "is limited to situations where the contract as interpreted would violate 'some explicit public policy' that is 'well defined and dominant, and is to be ascertained "by reference to the laws and legal precedents and not from general considerations of supposed public interests." ' " United Paperworkers v. Misco, Inc., 484 U.S. 29, 43 (1987); *see also* Eastern Associated Coal Corp. v. United Mine Workers, 531 U.S. 57 (2000); W.R. Grace & Co. v. Int'l Nat'l Union of United Rubber Workers, 461 U.S. 757 (1983). For a thoughtful explication of this body of law, *see* State v. Henderson, 762 N.W.2d 1 (Neb. 2009) (declining to enforce arbitral award of reinstatement to state trooper who had been terminated for membership in group affiliated with Ku Klux Klan; 3-2). *See also* Kitsap Cnty. Deputy Sheriff's Guild v. Kitsap Cnty., 219 P.3d 675 (Wash. 2009) (enforcing arbitral award reinstating deputy sheriff who had been found to be untruthful and insubordinate, in the absence of "an explicit, well defined, and dominant public policy" to the contrary; strong dissent by J.M. Johnson, J.), cited to approvingly in Alaska v. Pub. Safety Employees Ass'n, 257 P.3d 151 (Alaska 2011) (enforcing arbitral award of reinstatement of state trooper after instance of dishonesty during training program); Cedar Fair, L.P. v. Falfas, 140 Ohio St. 3d 447, 19 N.E.3d 893 (OH 2014) (reversing arbitral award of reinstatement because, under Ohio law, reinstatement "is not an available remedy for breach of an employment contract unless it is explicitly provided for in the contract or by an applicable statute and . . . the arbitration panel in this case exceeded its authority by holding otherwise"). The First Circuit has held that the contractual right to require arbitration can be waived by conduct, such as pursuing litigation until it appears that the party may lose in court. Joca-Roca Real Estate, LLC v. Brennan, 772 F.3d 945 (1st Cir. 2014) ("we do not condone the use of an arbitration clause as a parachute when judicial winds blow unfavorably.").

***§5.1 n.3 p.2 Add the following to the list after* "See":** Katun Corp. v. Clarke, 484 F.3d 972 (8th Cir. 2007) (distinguishing contract to indemnify against past criminal acts from contract to indemnify against future criminal acts; "a party may not insure itself against penalties for conduct not yet committed, since legal sanctions are an important means by which society discourages future misconduct"); Carter v. Cohen, 116 Cal. Rptr. 3d 303 (Ct. App. 2010) ("'Knowing that they will receive no help from the courts and must trust completely to each other's good faith, the parties are less likely to enter an illegal arrangement in the first place.'") (quoting from Lewis & Queen v. N.M. Ball Sons, 308 P.2d 713 (Cal. 1957)); J & K Plumbing & Heating Co. v. William H. Lane, Inc., 786 N.Y.S.2d 253 (App. Div. 2004) ("pay-when-paid" clause in subcontractor's agreement with general contractor, purporting to transfer risk of owner's default from general contractor to subcontractor, void as against public policy).

§5.1 n.3 p.2 Add the following at the end: One setting that raises this somewhat obliquely is estoppel against the government. Here, the behavior of the party seeking enforcement is not unsavory or blameworthy; rather, the problem lies with the prospect of governmental actors exceeding their statutory or constitutional powers. The courts have thus not only refused to find estoppel, but also have refused to grant recovery in quantum meruit to the supplier. As one court put it, "deference to legislative policy should trump individual acts or statements of a government official that may be contrary to such policy. Otherwise, protections afforded the public interest are thwarted." Sullivan v. Chief Justice for Admin. & Mgmt., 858 N.E.2d 699 (Mass. 2006). *Accord:* Lumbermens Mut. Cas. Co. v. United States, 654 F.3d 1305 (Fed. Cir. 2011) (federal government's waiver of sovereign immunity under the Tucker Act does not extend to implied-in-law contracts or actions in quantum meruit); Chism v. Curtner, 619 F.3d 979 (8th Cir. 2010) (no equitable estoppel against city; mayor's promise of employment contract not authorized, nor did the mayor have authority to bind the city thus), *abrogated on other grounds*, Torgerson v. City of Rochester, 643 F.3d 1031 (8th Cir. 2011); Int'l Salt Co. v. City of Boston, 590 F. 3d 1 (1st Cir. 2009) (denying recovery in equitable estoppel or quantum meruit: "a party seeking to enter into a municipal contract has the responsibility of knowing the limitations on a municipality's contracting power, and such party cannot recover on a contract that does not comply"; as for estoppel, "Unfortunately for International Salt, it experienced an inherent risk of doing business with the City, and the fact that the City benefited from International Salt's acquiescence is now of no consequence."); P & D Consultants v. City of Carlsbad, 119 Cal. Rptr. 3d 253 (Ct. App. 2010) (where contract contained no-oral-modifications clause, contractor could not recover for oral change orders, whether under breach of contract, breach of implied contract, or quantum meruit; "the party contracting with a public agency is charged with the knowledge of public contracting law," and implied-in-law contracts or quantum meruit are unavailable because these "are based on quantum meruit or restitution considerations which are outweighed by the need to protect and limit a public entity's contractual obligations") (nested quotation marks omitted), followed in G. Voskanian Constr. v. Alhambra Unified Sch. Dist., 139 Cal. Rptr. 3d 286 (Ct. App. 2012) ("the instant contractual requirement that change orders be in writing could not be waived or orally modified") Biello v. Town of Watertown, 953 A.2d 656 (Conn. App. 2008) (refusal to pay promised salary; "implied contract claims in the public sector would invite endless litigation on the basis of misinformation by employees, thereby drawing down the public fisc," so "courts have consistently refused to give effect to government-fostered expectations that, had they arisen in the private sector, might well have formed the basis for a contract or an estoppel") (quoting Fennell v. City of Hartford, 681 A.2d 934 (Conn. 1996)), followed in Ferrucci v. Town of Middlebury, 25 A.3d 728 (Conn. App. 2011) (rejecting promissory estoppel claim; "Because the law charges the plaintiff with notice that neither [of the officials] had the authority to modify the terms of the plan, any reliance on [an official's letter] cannot be deemed reasonable."); Village of Angel Fire v. Bd. of Cnty. Comm'rs, 242 P.3d 371 (N.M. App. 2010) (sovereign immunity encompasses actions in quantum meruit); Md. Transp. Auth. Police Lodge #34 v. Md. Transp. Auth., 5 A.3d 1174 (Md. App. 2010) (no estoppel, whether equitable or promissory, against the state, barring "an extraordinary case presenting particularly compelling equitable grounds"; but "we are unaware of any Maryland case so holding"), *rev'd on other grounds*, 21 A.3d 1098 (Md. 2011); JFK Holding Co. v. City of New York, 891 N.Y.S.2d 32 (App. Div. 2009) (dismissing claim for breach of oral contract to assume obligations under lease; "estoppel does not generally lie against municipalities"); Transp. Servs. of N.C. v. Wake Cnty. Bd. of Ed., 680 S.E.2d 223 (N.C. App. 2009) (no estoppel against government to enforce contract made ultra vires); Union Stock Yards Co. v. City of Hillsboro, 947 N.E.2d 183 (Ohio App. 2010) (promise cannot rely reasonably upon promise made ultra vires; "Persons seeking to enter into a contractual relationship with a governmental entity are on constructive notice of the statutory limitations on the power of the entity's agent to contract. . . . Protection of the public's resources in this context sometimes comes with a cost to misinformed parties."); Bowen v. Pub. Employees Ret. Bd., 206 P.3d 232 (Or. App. 2009) ("As a matter of law, a party's reliance on a state agency's false representation is not reasonable if the state actor had no authority to make it."). *Cf.* Wayne Moving & Storage of N.J. v. Sch. Dist. of Philadelphia, 625 F.3d 148 (3d Cir. 2010) (estoppel against government permissible only if actions rise to the level of a "fundamental injustice," where estoppel invoked to avoid proscriptions on contracting behavior); City of Bridgeport v. C.R. Klewin N.E., 971 A.2d 864 (Conn. Super. 2007) (permitting conventional defenses of laches and ratification where city seeking disgorgement of profits under illegal contract, where illegality unknown to contractor); Poteau Valley Improvement Auth. v. Okla. Pub. Employees Ret. Sys., 233 P.3d 423 (Okla. Civ. App. 2010) (permitting estoppel against government, but only if it would advance a "stronger, more compelling public policy or interest," an obstacle the court calls "formidable").

§5.1 n.4 p.3 Add the following to the list after **"Accord"***:* Morris-Griffin Corp. v. C & L Serv. Corp., 731 F. Supp. 2d 488 (E.D. Va. 2010) ("'If a party has been engaged in an illegal business and been cheated, equity will not help him.' . . . Under the circumstances, the Court must invoke the unclean hands doctrine not for [the defendant's] sake, but for its own.") (quoting from Wheeler v. Sage, 68 U.S. 518, 529 (1863)).

§5.1 n.5 p.3 Add the following to the list after **"Accord"***:* Sabia v. Mattituck Inlet Marina & Shipyard, 805 N.Y.S.2d 346 (App. Div. 2005) (purchase agreement stated false seller to evade sales tax, but buyer now asserts breach of warranty claims against the true seller; "Since no right of action can arise from an illegal contract, plaintiffs are barred, as a matter of law, from suing on the alleged agreement").

§5.1 n.9 p.4 In the first paragraph, add the following at the end: *Cf.* Packard v. OCA, Inc., 624 F.3d 726 (5th Cir. 2010) ("Texas law distinguishes between a party who must rely on an illegal contract to establish his right to recover and a party that merely needs to refer to an illegal contract to explain the transaction, allowing the latter to recover."). Courts continue to refer to contracts void as against public policy, though generally when they do so they then find ways to categorize some contracts violating public policy as merely voidable. *See* Ockey v. Lehmer, 189 P.3d 51 (Utah 2008) ("Contracts that offend an individual . . . are voidable. Only contracts that offend public policy or harm the public are void ab initio."; court then narrows class of void contracts to those that harm the general public, rather than individuals, and that without doubt offend public policy). Still, the void versus voidable distinction retains a good deal of force. *See In re* Estate of Molino, 81 Cal. Rptr. 3d 512 (Ct. App. 2008) (contract with heir hunter containing "an element of legal representation" void as against public policy; consequently, the contract cannot be ratified; PHL Variable Ins. Co. v. Price Dawe 2006 Ins. Trust, 28 A.3d 1059 (Del. 2011)) ("if a life insurance policy lacks an insurable interest at inception, it is void *ab initio* because it violates Delaware's clear public policy against wagering"; consequently, none of the terms of the policy came into effect, including its incontestability clause, with the result that the insurer could challenge the enforceability of the policy after the incontestability period); State v. Steele, 236 P.3d 161 (Utah App. 2010) (following *Ockey*, *supra*, but finding void as against public policy a hunting license procured by misrepresenting residency).

§5.1 n.9 p.4 In the second paragraph, add the following at the end: *Cf.* N.J. Dental Ass'n v. Metro. Life Ins. Co., 36 A.3d 1066 (N.J. Super. App. Div. 2012) (dental association could bring declaratory judgment action seeking to invalidate clauses in its members' contracts involved with creating an unwanted insurance program; "One questioning the legality of a contract provision may obtain a judicial determination of the issue and injunctive relief. Such an action is not one to enforce the law, it is one to determine whether courts will enforce the contract.").

§5.1 n.9 p.4 ***In the third paragraph, add the following after the citation to* NCH Corp.*:*** , followed in AMX Int'l v. Battelle Energy Alliance, 744 F. Supp. 2d 1087 (D. Idaho 2010) ("Because an unreasonable covenant not to compete violates public policy, it follows that an unreasonable noncompete agreement is void ab initio." Thus, the defendant "may assert the unenforceability of

the underlying noncompete agreements as a complete defense to AMX's tortious interference action *if* the noncompete provisions are found unreasonable and violative of public policy").

§5.1 n.10 p.4 Add the following to the list: 12 Havemeyer Place Co. v. Gordon, 820 A.2d 299 (Conn. App. 2003) ("agreements contrary to public policy, that is those that negate laws enacted for the common good, are illegal and therefore unenforceable"); Bank of the W. v. Kline, 782 N.W.2d 453 (Iowa 2010) (contracts "arose out of an illegal act and enforcement would be contrary to public policy").

§5.1 p.4 In the first full paragraph, add the following at the end of the third sentence: . . . or even usually so.[10a]

[10a] For example, "operating a nightclub or bar is not illegal in itself, [but] operation of a nightclub or bar at this particular premises is illegal regardless of who operates it"; as a result, a contract leasing this property for use only as a nightclub or bar is unenforceable. Merry Homes v. Chi Hung Luu, 312 S.W.3d 938, 948 (Tex. Civ. App. 2010).

As states have begun to legalize the growth, possession, and distribution of marijuana, courts have sometimes had to grapple with whether contracts regarding such activities are unenforceable as against public policy as reflected in federal statutes (if not current federal enforcement practice). Green Earth Wellness Ctr., LLC v. Atain Specialty Ins. Co., 163 F. Supp. 3d 821, 2016 U.S. Dist. LEXIS 19768 (D. Colo. 2016) involved an insurance claim by a marijuana distributor, which suffered damage from smoke and ash from a nearby wildfire. After parsing the contract to determine whether plants were covered "stock" within the meaning of the agreement, the court turned to the insurance company's "indirect invitation to declare the Policy void on public policy grounds." The court noted 21 U.S.C. §841(a)(1) and (b)(1)(D), but said that "the nominal federal prohibition against possession of marijuana conceals a far more nuanced (and perhaps even erratic) expression of federal Policy." *Id.* at *28. In response to the company's request that the court rule on "[w]hether, in light of [federal and state law], it is legal for Atain to pay for damage to marijuana plants and products, and if so, whether the Court can order Atain to pay for these damages," the court crafted a very precise line: "Any judgment issued by this Court will be recompense to Green Earth based on Atain's failure to honor its contractual promises, not an instruction to Atain to 'pay for damages to marijuana plants and products.' " *Id.* at *34. Ultimately, it held that the parties knew what they were doing when they specifically contracted for coverage for a marijuana business and the court would not invalidate that contract on the basis of the inconsistent federal approach to state-licensed marijuana businesses. It distinguished Tracy v. USAA Cas. Ins. Co., 2012 U.S. Dist.

LEXIS 35913, 2012 WL 928186 (D. Haw. Mar. 16, 2012), which had granted summary judgment to the insurer because enforcement of the contract "would be contrary to federal law and public Policy," citing the "several additional years evidencing a continued erosion of any clear and consistent federal public policy in this area," *id.* at *36.

§5.1 n.13 p.5 Add the following to the list after "Accord": Isles Wellness v. Progressive N. Ins. Co., 725 N.W.2d 90 (Minn. 2006) (violation of corporate practice of medicine doctrine did not make contract with insurer avoidable; "categorically voiding the contracts would not serve the public policy reasons underlying the corporate practice of medicine doctrine."), followed in Cal. Physicians' Serv. v. Aoki Diabetes Res. Inst., 78 Cal. Rptr. 3d 646 (Ct. App. 2008) ("The ban on the corporate practice of medicine is meant to protect patients, not health care service plans . . . . Blue Shield would be unjustly enriched if it were allowed to retain the benefit of services bestowed on its subscribers without compensating ADRI."), in turn followed in Wald v. Truspeed Motorcars, 108 Cal. Rptr. 3d 542 (Ct. App. 2010) (dispute between salesperson and dealership about unpaid commission: "Nothing in this salesperson-dealer dispute implicates the real reason for the dealer licensing statutes . . . which is to protect *the public* from unscrupulous dealers. . . . It would upend that statutory goal to allow a dealer to use the licensing statute to get away with not paying for services actually rendered.").

§5.1 n.13 p.5 Add the following at the end: For a particularly striking instance of this balancing, see Tenet v. Doe, 544 U.S. 1 (2005), in which the Court held unenforceable an agreement between the CIA and foreign agents on the grounds of state security.

§5.1 n.14 p.5 Add the following at the end: *Cf.* Rodgers v. Rodgers, 988 So. 2d 1041 (Ala. Civ. App. 2007) (construing statute that renders voidable any conveyance of realty for which a material part of the consideration is agreeing to support the grantor during life, save against good faith purchasers for value; intended "to cure the twin evils of injustice and fraud when the elderly and infirm are lured into executing conveyances upon promises of lifetime support").

§5.1 n.18 p.6 ***Add the following at the end:*** For an application of those principles outside the realm of legislation, see Isles Wellness v. Progressive N. Ins. Co., *supra* note 13 (refusing to render insurance contract avoidable by the insurer because of the corporate practice of medicine by the provider; "[w]e will not void a contract unless it is established that the corporation's actions show a knowing and intentional failure to abide by state and local law," and here the promise sought legal advice before entering into the contracts).

§5.1 n.23 p.7 ***Add the following to the list after "See":*** Baugh v. Novak, 340 S.W.3d 372 (Tenn. 2011) ("We must, if possible, interpret contracts in a way that upholds their validity."); Ross v. Union Carbide Corp., 296 S.W.3d 206 (Tex. Civ. App. 2009) ("When two constructions of a contract are possible, we must apply the one that does not result in a violation of law. . . . We therefore conclude that the parties intended the release to be as broad and comprehensive as the law allows, but not more so.").

§5.1 n.29 p.8 ***Add the following to the list after "Accord":*** Yoo v. Jho, 55 Cal. Rptr. 3d 243 (Ct. App. 2007) ("In order to prevent the judicial system from lending its assistance to a party who sought to obtain the benefit of an illegal bargain . . . the trial court should have raised the issue of illegality on its own motion in order to dispose of the matter."); Baugh v. Novak, 340 S.W.3d 372 (Tenn. 2011) ("whether a contract is contrary to public policy is an issue that trial and appellate courts may raise sua sponte. . . . However, it would have been better practice for the court to give the parties an opportunity to address this issue before the filing of the opinion.").

§5.2 SOME JUDICIALLY DEVELOPED POLICIES

§5.2 n.4 p.9 ***In the first paragraph, add the following to the list after "Accord":*** Neve v. Davis, 775 N.W.2d 80 (S.D. 2009) ("if *any part of the consideration* for a note is for the repayment of money lost in gambling, the entire note is absolutely void") (emphasis in original).

§5.2 n.6 p.10 Add the following to the list after **"See"***:* McDonald's Corp. v. Rappaport, 532 F. Supp. 2d 264 (D. Mass. 2008) ("any ambiguity in a restrictive covenant must be resolved in favor of the freedom of land from servitude, meaning the less restricted use"); Shaffer v. Bellows, 260 P.3d 1064 (Alaska 2011) (perpetual right of first refusal giving holder right to purchase at fixed price plus inflation may be held unenforceable on remand; the largely fixed price means that owners of the property "will have an incentive not to sell it so long as it has a value greater than the bargain price [the holder of the option] would be able to pay — even if another potential buyer would be willing to pay far more and put the island to far more beneficial use"); Smurfit-Stone Container Enters. v. Zion Jacksonville Ltd. P'ship, 52 So. 3d 55 (Fla. App. 2010) (right of first refusal not unreasonable restraint on alienability; although right was unlimited, it did not unduly restrict marketability — indeed, "this type of provision creates a constant prospective purchaser for land, a condition most sellers do not have the good fortune to enjoy").

§5.2 n.6 p.10 Add the following after the first sentence: Cf. Malad, Inc. v. Miller, 199 P.3d 623 (Ariz. App. 2008) (applying rule against perpetuities to commercial real estate sales agreement); Hensley-O'Neal v. Metro. Nat'l Bank, 297 S.W.3d 610 (Mo. App. 2009) (applying rule against perpetuities to contract giving a prospective purchaser a preemptive right to purchase property in foreclosure).

§5.2 n.7 p.10 Add the following after the first sentence: But see Fitzpatrick v. Kenneth J. Allen & Assocs., 913 N.E.2d 255 (Ind. App. 2009) (fee-splitting agreement enforceable where the additional attorney "performed the work required of him under the parties' contract"; permitted by professional responsibility rules under these circumstances). *Cf.* Davis v. Scott, 320 S.W.3d 87 (Ky. 2010) (settlement agreement included assignment of malpractice claim; the assignment was impermissible, but the agreement as a whole was nevertheless enforceable, so the remedy was to dismiss the enforcement action without prejudice in order to allow the real party in interest to refile); Trust for Certificate Holders of Merrill Lynch Mtg. Invs. v. Love Funding Corp., 918 N.E.2d 889 (N.Y. 2009) (champerty prohibition "does not apply when the

purpose of an assignment is the collection of a legitimate claim"; focus is on "the difference between one who acquires a right in order to make money from litigating it and one who acquires a right in order to enforce it"), followed in SB Schwartz & Co. v. Levine, 918 N.Y.S.2d 171 (App. Div. 2011) ("Willingness to resort to litigation, however, will not render a transaction champertous if the primary purpose of the transaction is to enforce a legitimate claim, or if the party obtaining the claim or debt does so as part of a larger transaction and the intent to commence litigation is incidental to that larger transaction"; transfer of claim as part of corporate dissolution not champertous) Odell v. Legal Bucks, 665 S.E.2d 767 (N.C. App. 2008) (assignment of proceeds of personal injury action not champertous; "an outsider's involvement in a lawsuit does not constitute champerty or maintenance merely because the outsider provides financial assistance to the litigant and shares in the recovery" unless the lender "attempted to control the resolution of her claim for the purpose of stirring up strife and continuing litigation"). *But cf.* W. Broad Chiropractic v. American Family Ins., 912 N.E.2d 1093 (Ohio 2009) (barring the assignment of proceeds of tort claims; such an assignment gives the claim to one who "expects full payment and lacks interest in negotiating the amount of the debt," "opens the door for other creditors to seek debt protection through [such] assignments," and, thanks to the possibility of priority battles among assignees of the same claim, would put the insurer "into a credit situation that is completely unrelated to the underlying accident, [so that] the unrelated third party becomes a de facto collection agent that must prioritize and pay debts to avoid personal liability"); A. Unruh Chiropractic Clinic v. De Smet Ins. Co., 782 N.W.2d 367 (S.D. 2010) (assignment of proceeds of personal injury claim prohibited; like assignment of the claims themselves, assignments discourage settlement, promote maintenance, and create the possibility of priority battles among assignees).

§5.2 n.7 p.10 Add the following to the list after **"See generally"***:* Radin, Maintenance by Champerty, 24 Cal. L. Rev. 48 (1936).

§5.2 n.8 p.10 In the first paragraph, add the following after the second sentence: *Cf.* Unami v. Roshan, 659 S.E.2d 724 (Ga. App. 2008) (agreement not to disclose settlement void as against public policy when a duty to disclose to financial backer already existed).

§5.2 n.9 p.11 Add the following at the end of the first paragraph: For a fascinating exploration of political influence and contract law during the rise of classical contract theory, see Teachout, The Unenforceable Corrupt Contract: Corruption and Nineteenth-Century Contract Law, 35 N.Y.U. Rev. L. & Soc. Change 681 (2011).

§5.2 n.10 p.12 In the third paragraph, add the following at the end: *Cf.* Perricone v. Perricone, 972 A.2d 666 (Conn. 2009) (upholding confidentiality agreement in marital settlement against First Amendment challenge on grounds of prior restraint).

§5.2 n.13 p.13 Add the following after the first sentence: *Accord:* Morris-Griffin Corp. v. C & L Serv. Corp., 731 F. Supp. 2d 488 (E.D. Va. 2010) (contract with government based upon misrepresentation of small business status; "To be sure, not every contract that is procured by fraud is *per se* illegal. But in the present case, the parties' fraudulent conduct relates directly to their noncompliance with applicable federal regulations."); Sabia v. Mattituck Inlet Marina & Shipyard, 805 N.Y.S.2d 346 (App. Div. 2005) (purchase agreement that listed false seller in order to evade paying sales tax was unenforceable).

§5.2 n.16 p.13 Add the following after the first sentence: *Accord:* Buenz v. Frontline Transp. Co., 882 N.E.2d 525 (Ill. 2008) (contract for indemnification against one's own negligence enforceable if not contrary to statute and provides "clearly and explicitly" for indemnification); George L. Brown Ins. Agency v. Star Ins. Co., 237 P.3d 92 (Nev. 2010) (adopting majority rule that "an express or explicit reference to the indemnitee's own negligence is required to indemnify an indemnitee for his or her own negligence"; general reference in indemnification clause to "any and all damages" insufficiently specific).

§5.2 n.16 p.13 Add the following to the list after **"Cf."***:* Katun Corp. v. Clarke, 484 F.3d 972 (8th Cir. 2007) (contract to indemnify for past wrongful acts; "Because the indemnification provision at issue in this case did not create the kind of negative incentives normally associated with attempts to insure against penal sanctions and because a contract should not be voided absent an unmistakable violation of public policy, we cannot conclude that the claim for indemnification was an illegal demand or patently in violation of public policy."), followed in Brown v. Gallagher, 902 N.E.2d 1037 (Ohio App. 2008) (permitting enforcement of contract indemnifying a party for consequences of past criminal acts; not a contract which "indemnifies appellant for prospective acts or in any way encourages future illegal behavior"); Fairfield Ins., Co. v. Stephens Martin Paving, 246 S.W.3d 653 (Tex. 2008) (reviewing caselaw; most states find punitive damages insurance not void against public policy; Texas goes with majority in generally allowing this insurance, providing that the underlying public policy does not provide otherwise, as it would if the insurance was intended to protect against misfeasance or nonfeasance by senior corporate officers).

§5.2 n.17 p.13 Add the following to the list after **"Accord"***:* U.S. Fire Ins. Co. v. Sonitrol Mgmt. Corp., 192 P.3d 543 (Colo. App. 2008) ("Exculpatory clauses insulating a party from its own negligence, though disfavored, are permitted in Colorado if one party is not at a significant disadvantage in bargaining. . . . However, an exculpatory clause is against public policy if it enforces a release from willful and wanton misconduct."; applies both to exculpatory clauses and to limitations of liability), distinguished in Perrine v. E.I. du Pont de Nemours & Co., 694 S.E.2d 815 (W. Va. 2010) (public policy issues germane only to pre-injury releases, not to post-injury releases) Farina v. Mt. Bachelor, 66 F.3d 233 (9th Cir. 1995) (under Oregon law, attempt to exculpate skiing facility "from liability for more than ordinary negligence, including gross negligence and wanton or willful misconduct" rendered entire release clause invalid), disapproved in Harmon v. Mt. Hood Meadows, 932 P.2d 92 (Or. App. 1997) ("Ninth Circuit cited no authority substantiating its 'overbreadth/anti-severability' analysis"); City of Santa Barbara v. Super. Ct., 161 P.3d 1095 (Cal. 2007) (invalidating exculpatory

clause including gross negligence: "public policy generally precludes enforcement of an agreement that would remove an obligation to adhere to even a *minimal* standard of care") (emphasis in original); Hymel v. Eagle, Inc., 7 So. 3d 1249 (La. App. 2009) ("it is against public policy to permit a party to obtain a license for the commission of future bad acts"); Finch v. Southside Lincoln-Mercury, 685 N.W.2d 154 (Wis. App. 2004) (clause in dealership facility lease that exculpated lessor invalid as to claim for tortious interference with contract, as an otherwise valid exculpatory clause "cannot operate to relieve a party from the consequences of intentional or reckless conduct").

§5.2 n.17 p.13 Add the following at the end: Not all provisions that allocate risk are similarly suspect. *See* Great Am. Ins. Co. v. SimplexGrinnell LP, 874 N.Y.S.2d 465 (App. Div. 2009) (waiver of subrogation clause in sprinkler service agreement not unconscionable; "'[a] distinction must be drawn between contractual provisions which seek to exempt a party from liability . . . and contractual provisions . . . which in effect simply require one of the parties to the contract to provide insurance for all of the parties'") (quoting from Board of Educ. v. Valden Assocs., 389 N.E.2d 798 (N.Y. 1979)).

***§5.2 n.18 p.14 Add the following to the list after* "Cf.":** Sylva Shops Ltd. P'ship v. Hibbard, 623 S.E.2d 785 (N.C. App. 2006) (upholding clause relieving landlord of need to mitigate damages: "If a party may . . . contract to insulate itself from liability for a failure to exercise due care, we can perceive no basis for precluding a party from contracting to relieve itself from a duty of due care to minimize its damages.").

§5.2 n.18 p.14 Add the following after the fourth sentence: For example, *see* Ariz. Rev. Stat. §32-1159 (declaring indemnity agreements in construction or architectural settings against the public policy of the state). Indemnity agreements are more suspect than limitations of liability. "Because an indemnity provision eliminates all liability for damages, it also eliminates much of the incentive to exercise due care. . . . Although it is possible that a limitation of liability provision could cap the potential recovery at a dollar amount so low as to effectively eliminate the incentive to take precautions, that is not the case here." 1800 Ocotillo v. WLB Grp., 196 P.3d 222 (Ariz. 2008). On this last point, *see* Speedway SuperAmerica v. Erwin, 250 S.W.3d 339 (Ky. App. 2008) ("[W]here a party uses an indemnification provision to defend against its own negligence, any distinction between a pre-injury release and an indemnification provision can become, as it has in this case, analytically negligible.").

§5.2 n.19 p.14 Add the following at the end: *Accord:* Brown v. Soh, 909 A.2d 43 (Conn. 2006) (invalidating exculpatory agreements in the employment context; "[i]f employers were permitted to obtain broad waivers of their liability, an important incentive to manage risk would be removed."), distinguished by Merrick v. Cumin, 919 A.2d 495 (Conn. App. 2007) (holding that there was no "Connecticut public policy prohibiting equally sophisticated business partners from signing a settlement agreement providing for the waiver of future claims regarding breach of fiduciary duty") and by Bowman v. Sunoco, Inc., 986 A.2d 883 (Pa. Super. 2009) (permitting release by employee of claims against customers of security company when workplace injury covered by workers' compensation; third-party releases "do not impede the ultimate goal of the [Workers' Compensation Act] — to enable an employee hurt at work to receive from his or her employer compensation benefits for all work-related injuries suffered"), *appeal granted*, 17 A.3d 920 (Pa. 2011). *Cf.* Speedway SuperAmerica v. Erwin, *supra* note 18 (invalidating exculpatory agreement for independent contractor, who had only an eighth-grade education; "[t]he predominant fact of *this* case is the disparity in bargaining power existing between these two parties").

§5.2 n.20 p.15 Add the following to the list after "see": Wartsila NSD N. Am. v. Hill Int'l, 530 F.3d 269 (3d Cir. 2008) (Maryland law: courts would not conclude "that construction consulting has the same broad public impact as other business that have been found essential to the public good, such as innkeepers, public utilities, common carriers, or schools"); Johanns v. Minn. Mobile Storage, 720 N.W.2d 5 (Minn. App. 2006) (self-storage facility neither a public nor an essential service; the facility operator was not required to accept these patrons, and "self-storage facilities are widely available . . . Assuming the damage limitation was unacceptable to respondents, they could have selected a different facility.").

§5.2 n.20 p.15 Add the following at the end: For a successful attempt, see Yang v. Voyagaire Houseboats, 701 N.W.2d 783 (Minn. 2005) (renter of houseboats is "an innkeeper providing a public service," making its broad exculpatory clause unenforceable), distinguished in Myers v. Lutsen Mountain Corp., 587 F.3d 891 (8th Cir. 2009) (skiing is purely recreational, not a public service, so release signed by skier does not violate public policy).

§5.2 n.21 p.15 Add the following to the list after **"Accord"***:* Jesse v. Lindsley, 233 P.3d 1 (Idaho 2008) (public policy "for landlords to provide safe habitation for their tenants" means that exculpatory clause covering all injuries or accidents incurred by the tenant is overbroad and unenforceable).

§5.2 n.21 p.15 Add the following to the list after **"Cf."***:* Marcinczyk v. State of N.J. Police Training Comm'n, 5 A.3d 785 (N.J. 2010) (refusing to enforce limitation of liability provision in contract between police trainee and police academy because "it contravenes our public policy as expressed in the Tort Claims Act, which occupies the field of public entity liability"); Lucier v. Williams, 841 A.2d 907 (N.J. Super. 2004) (refusing to enforce limitation of liability provision in home inspection contract).

§5.2 p.16 Add the following at the end of the first full sentence: . . . payment of "additional reasonable fees."[21a]

[21a] On contracts of adhesion, see §4.26 *supra*. Courts show some disagreement in defining just what adhesion means. Generally the term refers to the ability to bargain over specific terms. Occasionally, however, a court defines it as not merely that one has no ability to negotiate the terms of a contract, but that one is "under compulsion" to sign because the contract "relate[s] to essential services." Chepkevich v. Hidden Valley Resort, 2 A.3d 1174 (Pa. 2010) (but cf. the dissent by Saylor, J., which argues for the traditional definition).

§5.2 n.22 p.16 Add the following to the list after* "Accord"*: Jones v. Dressel, 623 P.2d 370 (Colo. 1981) (following *Tunkl*, though concluding that exculpatory clause in contract to skydive valid because of a lack of a duty to the public).

§5.2 n.22 p.16 Add the following after the citation to* Olson*: qualified in Russell v. Bray, 116 S.W.3d 1 (Tenn. App. 2003) (application of *Olson* criteria "should be limited to situations involving a contract with a professional person, rather than a tradesman") and in turn followed in Carey v. Merritt, 148 S.W.3d 912 (Tenn. App. 2004) (housing inspector a professional) and in Henderson v. Quest Expeditions, 174 S.W.3d 730 (Tenn. App. 2005) (whitewater rafting business "is not a 'professional' trade, which affects the public interest").

§5.2 n.22 p.16 Add the following after the citation to* Wagenblast*: , followed in Hanks v. Grace, 273 P.3d 1029 (Wash. App. 2012) (invalidating release of claims against realtor put into rescission agreement).

§5.2 n.23 p.16 Add the following after the citation to* Wolf*: , followed in Hanks v. Powder Ridge Rest. Corp., 885 A.2d 734 (Conn. 2005) ("[O]ur analysis is guided, but not limited, by the *Tunkl* factors, and is informed by any other factors that may be relevant given the factual circumstances of the case and current societal expectations.").

§5.2 n.24 p.16 In the first sentence of the second paragraph, add the following to the list after* "see"*: Gentry v. Super. Ct., 165 P.3d 556 (Cal. 2007) (statutory right to receive overtime pay is unwaivable because the right is "mandated by statute and is based on an important public policy"; class arbitration waiver in this case yields a de facto waiver), *overturned on other grounds by* AT&T Mobility v. Concepcion, 131 S. Ct. 1740 (2011) Brown v. Soh, *supra* note 19 (clause exculpating employer infirm: "workplace safety and compensation for workplace injuries are areas subject to public regulation . . . and the law expressly provides that [employers] cannot contract away their statutory obligations."); Carey, *supra* note 22 (statutory regulation of inspections for new buildings makes inspections of old buildings a field "suitable for public regulation").

§5.2 n.24 p.16 In the first paragraph, add the following to the list after **"But see"***:* Zerjal v. Daech & Bauer Constr., 939 N.E.2d 1067 (Ill. App. 2010) ("It takes more than the legislature's regulation of an industry, however, for a public policy interest to be found."; declining to invalidate clause exculpating home inspector, where legislation addressed the licensing and regulation of home inspectors but not their liability), rejected by Finch v. Inspectech, LLC, 727 S.E.2d 823 (W. Va. 2012) (following majority approach and invalidating exculpatory clause in home inspection service contract; collecting cases).

§5.2 n.25 p.17 Add the following to the list after **"Accord"***:* McGrath v. SNH Dev., 969 A.2d 392 (N.H. 2009) (snowboarding); Stelluti v. Casapenn Enters., 1 A.3d 678 (N.J. 2010) (health club; "By its nature, exercising entails vigorous physical exertion. Injuries from exercise are common. . . . [I]t is not unreasonable to encourage patrons of a fitness center to take proper steps to prepare . . . before engaging in a foreign activity for the first time."); Chepkevich v. Hidden Valley Resort, 2 A.3d 1174 (Pa. 2010) (skiing); Pearce v. Utah Athletic Fed'n, 179 P.3d 760 (Utah 2008) (bobsledding).

§5.2 n.25 p.17 Add the following to the list after **"But see"***:* City of Santa Barbara v. Super. Ct., *supra* note 17 (recreational camp for developmentally disabled children: invalidating exculpatory clause encompassing gross negligence); Tayar v. Camelback Ski Corp., 957 A.2d 281 (Pa. Super. 2008) (snowtubing; invalidating release against employee for reckless acts and against employer for acts of employee), *appeal granted*, 8 A.3d 299 (Pa. 2010).

§5.2 n.25 p.17 Add the following after the citation to **Berlangieri***:* and in Hanks v. Powder Ridge Rest. Corp., *supra* note 23 (snowtubing accident caused by improper course design; invalidating waiver of negligence to the extent harm could be avoided by the exercise of reasonable care by the owner, in part because "this court has previously recognized the public policy interest of promoting vigorous participation in such activities," and because the owner did not inform potential patrons in advance of the liability limitations, "the plaintiff . . . was faced

with the dilemma of either signing the defendants' proffered waiver of prospective liability or forgoing completely the opportunity to snowtube"; 4-3 court with strong dissent).

§5.2 n.25 p.17 Add the following after the citation to **Behr***:* and in Thompson v. Hi Tech Motor Sports, 945 A.2d 368 (Vt. 2008) (test-driving dealership's motorcycle; unlike *Dalury*, here "public policy concerning motorcycle safety places the burden of safe driving on the operator of the motorcycle"), in turn followed by Provoncha v. Vt. Motocross Ass'n, 974 A.2d 1261 (Vt. 2009) (enforcing an exculpatory agreement for a car racing club, as it "is neither of great importance to the public nor open to the public at large" and thus does not implicate public policy).

§5.2 n.25 p.17 Add the following to the last sentence of the first paragraph: Woodman v. Kera, LLC, 760 N.W.2d 641 (Mich. App. 2008) (opinion of Talbot, J.; "preinjury waivers effectuated by parents on behalf of their minor children are not presumptively enforceable"), *aff'd*, 785 N.W.2d 1 (Mich. 2010) (five separate opinions; majority (see opinions of Young, J., and Hathaway, J.) appear to retain the traditional rule against enforcing pre-injury releases executed by parents o behalf of children); Hojnowski v. Vans Skate Park, 901 A.2d 381 (N.J. 2006) (invalidating parents' waiver of negligence by commercial entity; holding "in agreement . . . with the overwhelming majority of jurisdictions"), followed in J.T. v. Monster Mountain, LLC, 754 F. Supp. 2d 1323 (M.D. Ala. 2010) (pre-injury release signed by coach on the authority of the parent and on behalf of the minor does not bind minor in personal injury action against motocross park operator), Kirton v. Fields, 997 So. 2d 349 (Fla. 2008) (pre-injury release executed by parent on behalf of child unenforceable in tort action arising from commercial activity), and Rosen v. BJ's Wholesale Club, 51 A.3d 100 (Md. App. 2012) (approach in *Hojnowski* followed as to commercial enterprises by virtually all states, though some disagreement whether it applies to claims against governmental entities or non-profit organizations). Gomes v. Hameed, 184 P.3d 479 (Okla. 2008) ("an agreement not to sue which is negotiated on behalf of a minor or incapacitated person must be approved by the court to be enforceable").

§5.2 n.26 p.18 Add the following at the end: This issue is dealt with to some degree in UCC 2-719(3). Consequential damages, which include physical harm arising from a breach of contract, "may be limited or excluded unless the limitation is unconscionable." For sales of consumer goods, limitations on personal injury damages are prima facie unconscionable, but that is not true for commercial losses.

§5.2 n.28 p.18 Add the following after the second sentence: *Cf.* Abry Partners V. v. F & W Acquisition, 891 A.2d 1032 (Del. Ch. 2006) (Strine, V.C.) (anti-reliance clause enforced as to representations made outside the contract, but unenforceable on public policy grounds as to fraudulent misrepresentations made within the contract), adopted in RAA Mgmt. v. Savage Sports Holdings, 45 A.3d 107 (Del. 2012) (anti reliance clause effective against claims of misrepresentations made during negotiations for deal that was never consummated); Rose v. ADT Sec. Servs., 989 So. 2d 1244 (Fla. App. 2008) (giving effect to anti-reliance clause, which effectively eliminated justifiable reliance).

§5.2 n.28 p.18 Add the following at the end: As to the effects of anti-reliance clauses on misrepresentation claims, see §4.13 *supra*. *See generally* Blair, A Matter of Trust: Should No-Reliance Clauses Bar Claims for Fraudulent Inducement of Contract?, 92 Marq. L. Rev. 423 (2009).

Courts have also prevented parties from effectively delegating important statutory responsibilities by contract. In Chicago Hous. Auth. v. DeStefano & Partners, Ltd., 45 N.E.3d 767 (Ill. App. Ct. 2015) (*appeal denied*, 50 N.E.3d 1138 (Ill. 2016)), the Chicago Housing Authority (CHA) hired DeStefano to provide professional architectural and engineering services for seven multifamily residential buildings owned and operated by CHA. The contract required DeStefano to "certify that all work . . . conforms to . . . all applicable Federal, State and local building codes, as amended, including, but not limited to, the Uniform Federal Accessibility Standards, the American with Disabilities Act of 1990 [(ADA) [and] Section 504 of the Rehabilitation Act of 1973." When Housing and Urban Development (HUD) advised CHA that the work was not in compliance with accessibility laws, "CHA hired a new architecture firm to perform the work necessary to comply with its obligations under the voluntary compliance agreement. According to CHA, it incurred over $4.3 million to bring the seven buildings into compliance with the federal accessibility standards." *Id.* at 770. CHA then sued DeStefano for these costs, alleging breach of contract. The Chicago circuit court and appellate court disallowed those claims, reasoning that CHA had a non-delegable obligation under federal law and "any attempt to seek indemnity for lack of compliance with Section 504 and the ADA would frustrate Congress' purpose in enacting the statutes." *Id.* at 776. Likewise, some common law duties are also non-delegable in contract. Floyd v. City of Sanibel, 2017 U.S. Dist. LEXIS 2667 (M.D. Fla. Jan. 9, 2017) (city could be sued by tenant despite its contract with a private company to act as landlord because, under Florida law, "the City, as the Unit owner, cannot delegate its duty to provide a reasonably safe premises").

The appellate court recognized a "distinction between a state-law claim seeking indemnification or contribution related to . . . violations and a state-law contract claim arising from a breach of a duty imposed by the particular terms of the contract." *Id.* at 774. However, CHA did not act until HUD stepped in, which appeared to be the court's central concern:

> If not for HUD's compliance review, CHA would not have been issued a preliminary noncompliance letter and would not have negotiated a voluntary compliance agreement with HUD. In turn, CHA would not have incurred the costs associated with reworking the subject premises to bring them into compliance with the federal accessibility standards. Overall, no matter the label of CHA's cause of action, the breach of contract claim was a *de facto* indemnity claim and, therefore, was preempted.

Id. at 775. "CHA's failure to appropriately supervise the construction of the subject premises was not conduct Section 504 and the ADA were intended to protect." *Id.* at 776.

§5.2 n.31 p.19 Add the following to the end: *Cf.* Mr. Sign Sign Studios v. Miguel, 877 So. 2d 47 (Fla. App. 2004) (option to purchase property included within a lease enforceable, as "it was not for an unlimited duration and was not an unreasonable restraint on alienation"); RTS Landfill v. Appalachian Waste Sys., 598 S.E.2d 798 (Ga. App. 2004) (preemptive right of first refusal at price lower than that offered by third party unenforceable, taking into consideration "its duration, price, and the purpose for which it was imposed"). There is a somewhat perverse line of cases apparently denying any role for reasonableness in assessing whether a contract violates public policy. *See* DeFrain v. State Farm Mut. Auto Ins. Co., 817 N.W.2d 504 (Mich. 2012) ("That a contract provision fails to comport with the personal predilections of the majority of the deciding tribunal about what is reasonable or fair does not make the provision violative of law or public policy. Judicial notions of reasonableness are not clearly rooted in the law and are therefore not a valid basis for refusing to enforce an unambiguous contract provision."). One can hardly cavil at a rejection of unmoored judicial musings on what feels reasonable. But the law is shot through with tests of reasonableness, and whether a provision is reasonable is often a judicial task. Rejecting reasonableness tests as part of a public policy determination therefore seems unnecessarily rigid. Declaring this a boost to freedom of contract similarly seems peculiar, unless one's conception of contract has not advanced much beyond Christopher Columbus Langdell.

§5.3 THE POLICY AGAINST RESTRAINT OF TRADE

§5.3 p.19 Add the following new note in the second sentence: . . . and agreements fixing prices[1a]

[1a] A recent case casts doubt on at least some uses of so-called "most favored nation" clauses, which had long been thought safe. These clauses (taking their name from international trade agreements; also known as "price parity agreements") require the seller to offer the buyer the lowest price it offers to any competitor. Apple required MFN clauses in its contracts with publishers in order to ensure that prices for e-books available through its online outlet would be no more expensive than e-books at other online retailers. In 2013, a U.S. District Court in New York found that "the MFN protected Apple from retail price competition as it punished a Publisher if it failed to impose agency terms on other e-tailers." United States v. Apple Inc., 952 F. Supp. 2d 638, 2013 U.S. Dist. LEXIS 96424, at *63 (S.D.N.Y. July 10, 2013). The court was explicit that MFN agreements were not found to be unlawful in themselves; "[w]hat was wrongful was the use of those components to facilitate a conspiracy with the Publisher

Defendants." *Id.* at *184. The AAG who oversees the Antitrust Division later told the *Wall Street Journal* that "[w]hile most favored-nation clauses can be competitively benign, when they are used as a tool to engage in anticompetitive conduct that harms consumers, the Antitrust Division will take enforcement action." "Apple Ruling Heaps Doubt on 'MFN' Clauses," *Wall Street Journal* July 14, 2013 (quoting Assistant Attorney General Bill Baer).

In 2015, the U.S. Supreme Court declined to revisit the rule that a contract cannot provide for royalty payments after the expiration of the patent. Kimble v. Marvel Entm't, LLC, 135 S. Ct. 2401 (2015). The rule announced in Brulotte v. Thys Co., 379 U.S. 29, 85 S. Ct. 176, 13 L. Ed. 2d 99 (1964) was grounded upon a view that a patent holder should not be able to leverage its monopoly power to extend the benefits of the monopoly after the statutory expiration of patent rights. Unaware of this case, Marvel settled a lawsuit with the holder of a patent on a toy that shoots "webs" from the wrist, setting "no end date for royalties, apparently contemplating that they would continue for as long as kids want to imitate Spider-Man (by doing whatever a spider can)." At 2406. Marvel later discovered the Brulotte rule, and sought declaratory judgment that the company could cease payments at the end of the patent term. The Court accepted certiorari on "the sole question presented [of] whether we should overrule Brulotte." The Court acknowledged that the rule "prevents some parties from entering into deals they desire," at 2408, but ultimately held that principles of *stare decisis* require adherence to that restriction.

§5.3 p.20 Add the following to the end of third sentence in first full paragraph: . . . including general economic conditions.[3a]

[3a] Some jurisdictions have avoided this imprecision by barring noncompetition agreements entirely, save for a few closely defined exceptions. Cal. Bus. & Prof. Code §§16600-16602.5; Edwards v. Arthur Andersen LLP, 189 P.3d 285 (Cal. 2008) ("California . . . rejected the common law 'rule of reasonableness'; covenants not to compete are void, subject to several exceptions").

§5.3 n.6 p.21 Add the following at the end: *See also* Restatement (Third) of Employment Law §8.07 cmt. *e* (T.D. No. 4, Apr. 11, 2011) ("An employer may have many economic reasons to attempt to restrict what its employees can do after termination of their employment. Some of these reasons, however, will not support an otherwise reasonable restrictive covenant because they are not sufficiently weighty to justify the social and individual costs inherent in restrictions on competition. For example, an interest in recouping investments in the training of employees may justify repayment obligations but would not justify a restriction on competition.").

§5.3 n.7 p.21 Add the following after the citation to **Crystal City***:* followed in H & M Commercial Driver Leasing v. Fox Valley Containers, 805 N.E.2d 1177 (Ill. 2004) (rejecting *Heyde*) and in turn distinguished by VL Systems v. Unisen, Inc., 61 Cal. Rptr. 3d 818 (Ct. App. 2007) (because the no-hire clause in *H&M* "was expressly limited to employees that the plaintiff had provided to the defendant," it was "less broad and impacted a substantially smaller number of employees").

§5.3 n.14 p.22 Add the following at the end of the first paragraph: Accord: Dicen v. New Sesco, Inc., 839 N.E.2d 684 (Ind. 2005) (covenants not to compete arising from sales of businesses "stand in better stead" than do ordinary covenants). Even California, normally resolute against noncompetition agreements, permits them as part of the sale or dissolution of corporations, partnerships, and limited liability corporations. Cal. Bus. & Prof. Code §§16601-16602.5.

§5.3 n.18 p.24 Add the following to the list after **"See generally"***:* Estlund, Between Rights and Contract: Arbitration Agreements and Non-Compete Agreements as a Hybrid Form of Employment Law, 155 U. Pa. L. Rev. 379 (2006); Stone, Knowledge at Work: Disputes Over the Ownership of Human Capital in the Changing Workplace, 34 Conn. L. Rev. 721 (2002).

§5.3 n.18 p.24 Add as a new paragraphs: Restrictive covenants that condition employment on an agreement not to compete with the business after the end of the employment relationship are viewed quite differently depending upon the specific circumstances and the jurisdiction. A 2014 New York Appellate Division case considering such a clause and a choice of law provision brings the differences into stark relief. In addition to finding a broad non-solicitation covenant unenforceable under New York law, the court acknowledged that Florida law would enforce it but found that the choice-of-law provision was "unenforceable because it is 'truly obnoxious' to New York public policy." Brown & Brown, Inc. v. Johnson, 115 A.D.3d 162, 980 N.Y.S.2d 631 (N.Y. App. Div. 2014).

In 2015, Hawaii became particularly concerned with the effects of non-competition and non-solicitation agreements in the technology sector, and amended its antitrust law to provide that "it shall be prohibited to include a noncompete clause or a nonsolicit clause in any employment contract relating to an employee of a technology business. The clause shall be void and of no force and effect." Haw. Rev. Stat. §480-4(d).

The increasing use of non-compete agreements in low-wage jobs has received some attention in recent years, and could lead to legislative responses. *See e.g.*, Mobility and Opportunity for Vulnerable Employees Act, S. 1504 (114th Cong.) (would prohibit covenants not to compete for employees whose base salary is below $15/hour, adjusted for inflation, or the applicable minimum wage, if higher); Lydia DePillis, "Can the Senate Stop Low-Wage Employers from Tying up Workers with Non-Competes?," *Washington Post*, June 2, 2015.

§5.3 n.19 p.24 In the second paragraph, add the following at the end: On the other hand, that information has value to an employer does not perforce make it protectable. Nor does experience acquired through employment constitute protectable information, leaving aside specific knowledge of trade secrets or the like. *See* Bendinger v. Marshalltown Trowel Co., 994 S.W.2d 468 (Ark. 1999). For an attempt to delimit the scope of this protectable interest, *see* Restatement (Third) of Employment Law §8.02 (T.D. No. 4, Apr. 11, 2011) (defining "confidential information").

§5.3 n.20 p.25 Add the following after the first sentence: *Accord:* Mayer Hoffman McCann, P.C. v. Barton, 614 F.3d 893 (8th Cir. 2010) (Missouri law: upholding agreement not to contract former clients for two years); RLM Commc'ns Inc. v. Tuschen, 831 F.3d 190 (4th Cir. 2016) (agreement to "not directly or indirectly participate in a business that is similar to a business now or later operated by Employer in the same geographical area" found by the court to be "largely unmoored from RLM's legitimate business interests" and so overly broad as to be unenforceable); Grillea v. United Natural Foods, Inc., 2016 U.S. Dist. LEXIS 118322 (E.D.N.Y. Aug. 31, 2016) (one year non-compete agreement was reasonable because plaintiff was a highly placed employee with "specialized knowledge of defendant's internal structure and business, marketing and pricing strategies"). Customer lists or databases may not be protectable, though, if they were easily compiled, readily ascertainable, insufficiently guarded, or marginally valuable. *See* Restatement (Third) of Employment Law §8.02 cmt. *f* (T.D. No. 4, Apr. 11, 2011).

§5.3 n.22 p.25 In the first paragraph, add the following to the list after **"Accord"***:* Dominic Wenzell, D.M.D. P.C. v. Ingrim, 228 P.3d 103 (Alaska 2010) (a high "level of scrutiny is not applied to covenants ancillary to the sale of a business because the contracting parties are more likely to be of equal bargaining power"); Edwards v. Arthur Andersen LLP, *supra* note 3a (excepting sales of corporations and partnership dissolutions from California's general ban on restrictive covenants); H & G Ortho v. Neodontics Int'l, 823 N.E.2d 718 (Ind. App. 2005) ("non-competition agreements ancillary to the sale of a business are not as 'ill-favored at law' as employee covenants") (quoting Kladis v. Nick's Patio, 735 N.E.2d 1216 (Ind. App. 2000)); Missett v. Hub Int'l Pa., 6 A.3d 530 (Pa. Super. 2010) ("Post-employment restrictive covenants . . . are subject to a more stringent test of reasonableness than covenants ancillary to the sale of a business. . . . This heightened scrutiny stems from a historical reluctance on the part of our courts to enforce any contracts in restraint of trade, particularly where they restrain an individual from earning a living at his trade.").

§5.3 n.22 p.25 In the first paragraph, add the following after the third sentence: The borderline cases — for example, the sale of a business that functionally is a post-employment restraint, as in a professional practice — can yield interesting results. *See* Sheehan & Sheehan v. Nelson Malley & Co., 117 P.3d 219 (Nev. 2005) (sale of accounting practice; court strictly construes the language and applies *contra proferentem* in holding the covenant unenforceable).

§5.3 n.22 p.25 In the first paragraph, delete the citation to **Habif** *and add the following to the list after* **"Cf."***:* OnBrand Media v. Codex Consulting, 687 S.E.2d 168 (Ga. App. 2009) (three levels of scrutiny for non-compete agreements: (1) covenants ancillary to the sale of a business "are viewed with the least degree of scrutiny"; (2) covenants ancillary to professional partnerships are subject to a "middle level of scrutiny"; and (3) covenants ancillary to an employment contract "receive close scrutiny to ensure that

they are strictly limited in duration, territory, and prohibited activities"; applying intermediate level of scrutiny to agreements ancillary to a proposed joint venture).

§5.3 n.22 p.25 In the third paragraph, delete the citation to **Maw** *and add the following to the list after* **"But cf.":** Maw v. Advanced Clinical Communications, 846 A.2d 604 (N.J. 2004) (where there was "no violation of a clear mandate of public policy," if employee "could not negotiate terms that were to her liking, she was free to dispute the reasonableness of those terms if and when her employer attempted to enforce the agreement").

§5.3 n.23 p.26 Add the following after the citation to **Justin Belt:** followed in Cranston Print Works v. Pothier, 848 A.2d 213 (R.I. 2004) (covenant was ancillary to "otherwise valid contract" where it was "subordinate to a settlement agreement and to a mutual release resolving contested litigation" between former employer and employee).

§5.3 n.23 p.26 Add the following to the list after **"See also":** Mayer Hoffman McCann, P.C. v. Barton, 614 F.3d 893 (8th Cir. 2010) ("a stockholder's agreement between a professional corporation and a shareholder falls within the class of contracts wherein restrictive covenants are appropriate").

§5.3 n.26 p.26 Add the following to the list after **"Accord":** Boulanger v. Dunkin' Donuts, 815 N.E.2d 572 (Mass. 2004) ("franchise agreement was akin to the sale of a business"; legitimate business interest where franchisee received "confidential information such as financial data and profitability of particular stores, new product development, and marketing and promotion strategies").

§5.3 n.26 p.26 Add the following to the list after **"Cf.":** Atlanta Bread Co. v. Lupton-Smith, 679 S.E.2d 722 (Ga. 2009) ("[T]here is no distinction to be made as to the level of scrutiny applied to a noncompetition clause in a franchise or distributorship agreement based on its status as being active during the term of the agreement, and this Court declines to adopt a lesser standard of scrutiny.").

§5.3 n.28 p.27 ***Add the following at the beginning:*** *See* Thiesing v. Dentsply Int'l, 748 F. Supp. 2d 932 (E.D. Wis. 2010) (continued employment after agreeing to covenant not consideration, but promise to make up any loss in pay due to covenant was consideration).

§5.3 n.28 p.27 ***Add the following at the end:*** *See* Restatement (Third) of Employment Law §8.06 cmt. *e* (T.D. No. 4, Apr. 11, 2011).

§5.3 n.29 p.27 ***Add the following after the citation to* Guy Carpenter & Co.*:*** and limited in Alex Sheshunoff Mgmt. Servs. v. Johnson, 209 S.W.3d 644 (Tex. 2006) (abrogating *Light*'s holding that unilateral contracts must be enforceable at the time of formation, instead holding that the ancillary agreement is enforceable if performance eventually supplies consideration), in Mann Frankfort Stein & Lipp Advisors v. Fielding, 289 S.W.3d 844 (Tex. 2009) (where "the nature of the employment for which the employee is hired will reasonably require the employer to provide confidential information to the employee . . . then the employer impliedly promises to provide confidential information"), and in Marsh USA v. Cook, 354 S.W.3d 764 (Tex. 2011) (defining "ancillary" as "reasonably related to an interest worthy of protection," rather than giving rise to the employer's interest).

§5.3 n.31 p.29 ***Add the following at the end:*** *See generally* Restatement (Third) of Employment Law §8.07(b)(iii) & cmt. *c* (T.D. No. 4, Apr. 11, 2011).

§5.3 n.32 p.29 ***In the first paragraph, add the following to the list after* "Accord"*:*** Ecology Servs. v. Clym Envt'l Servs., 952 A.2d 999 (Md. App. 2008) ("covenants not to compete are not justified if the harm caused by service to another consists merely in the fact that the former employee becomes a more efficient competitor just as the former employer did through having a competent and efficient employee . . . In contrast, covenants not to compete are justified if a part of the compensated services of the former employee consisted in the creation of the good will of customers and clients . . ."); Columbus Med. Servs. v. Thomas, 308 S.W.3d 368 (Tenn. App. 2009) (staffing agency has legitimate business

interest in preventing "opportunistic disintermediation," that is, cutting out the staffing agency as the middleman between employer and employee; collecting cases).

§5.3 n.32 p.29 In the second paragraph, add the following after the fourth sentence: This "legitimate business interest" test recently, came under fire from within the Illinois courts. *See* Sunbelt Rentals v. Ehlers, 915 N.E.2d 862 (Ill. App. 2009) ("courts at any level, when presented with the issue of whether a restrictive covenant should be enforced, should evaluate only the time-and-territory restrictions contained therein"). The Illinois Supreme Court has put an end to the back-and-forth squabbling of the lower courts by resoundingly affirming the "legitimate business interest" test. Reliable Fire Equip. Co. v. Arredondo, 965 N.E.2d 393 (Ill. 2011) ("this court . . . has repeatedly recognized the three-dimensional rule of reason, specifically including the element of the legitimate business interest of the promisee"). The legitimate business interest test may remain vital in New York. See Kelly v. Evolution Mkts., 626 F. Supp. 2d 364 (S.D.N.Y. 2009) (determining as a threshold matter that the employer had a legitimate business interest in enforcing its restrictive covenants before reaching whether those covenants were reasonable). Florida has made the test statutory. Fla. Stat. Ann. §542.335(1)(b); *see also* GPS Indus. v. Lewis, 691 F. Supp. 2d 1327 (M.D. Fla. 2010) (applying statute).

§5.3 n.33 p.30 Add the following at the end: *See generally* Restatement (Third) of Employment Law §8.06 (T.D. No. 4, Apr. 11, 2011).

§5.3 n.34 p.30 In the first paragraph, add the following at the end: *Cf.* Fine v. Commc'n Trends, 699 S.E.2d 623 (Ga. App. 2010) (covenant barring former employee from soliciting business similar to that of employer, and not even to "contact, call upon, communicate with or attempt to communicate with any such person or entity"; clause would in effect bar employee from even accepting unsolicited business and thus is unenforceable).

§5.3 n.36 p.30 Add the following at the end: *Accord:* Sharvelle v. Magnante, 836 N.E.2d 432 (Ind. App. 2005) (employee's promise not to provide "health care of every nature and kind" overbroad where practice had been limited to ophthalmology); Scanline Med. v. Brooks, 259 P.3d 911 (Okla. Civ. App. 2011) (salesperson's promise not to sell any medical devices competing with the employer's products unenforceable as overbroad; not limited to particular type of medical device or to established customers of employer).

§5.3 n.37 p.30 Add the following after the first sentence: Accord: Atlanta Bread Co. v. Lupton-Smith, *supra* note 26 (clause prohibiting franchisee from taking any part in similar businesses during the life of the franchise agreement overbroad because it lacked any territorial restriction); Cent. Ind. Podiatry v. Krueger, 882 N.E.2d 723 (Ind. 2008) (clause prohibiting podiatrist from working anywhere the employer had maintained an office was overbroad; "noncompetition agreements justified by the employer's development of patient relationships must be limited to the area in which the physician has had patient contact"); Hejl v. Hood, Hargett & Assocs., 674 S.E.2d 425 (N.C. App. 2009) (nonsolicitation agreement geographically overbroad because it "encompasses two states regardless of whether Plaintiff had any personal knowledge of Defendant's customers in those areas").

§5.3 n.38 p.30 Add the following to the list after **"Accord"***:* Friemuth v. Fiskars Brands, 681 F. Supp. 2d 985 (W.D. Wis. 2010) ("the lack of any time limitation renders a restrictive covenant unreasonable per se"); Applied Materials v. Advanced Micro-Fabrication Equip. (Shanghai) Co., 630 F. Supp. 2d 1084 (N.D. Cal. 2009) (invalidating clause requiring employee to assign rights to any inventions created for one year after employment, even if developed entirely after employment; "Since the Court finds that the Assignment Clause touches post-employment inventions, regardless of when they were conceived or whether they were based on Applied's confidential information, the Clause necessarily operates as a restriction on employee mobility."). *But see* Brainware, Inc. v. Mahan, 808 F. Supp. 2d 820 (E.D. Va. 2011) (rejecting per se invalidity of indefinite nondisclosure provisions; this one is enforceable because it "is narrowly limited to actual confidential information").

§5.3 n.41 p.31 Add the following to the list after **"See"**: Coleman v. Retina Consultants, 687 S.E.2d 457 (Ga. 2009) (question of law subject to de novo review).

§5.3 n.44 p.32 Add the following after the third sentence: Cf. Missett v. Hub Int'l Pa., 6 A.3d 530 (Pa. Super. 2010) ("the circumstances of termination are but one of many factors").

§5.3 n.44 p.32 Add the following at the end: The draft Restatement takes the manner of the employee's departure into account in determining whether a covenant is enforceable by disallowing enforcement where "(a) the employer discharges the employee on a basis that makes enforcement of the covenant inequitable; (b) the employer acted in bad faith in requiring or invoking the covenant; [or] (c) the employer materially breached the underlying employment agreement." Restatement (Third) of Employment Law §8.06 & cmts. f & g (T.D. No. 4, Apr. 11, 2011) (see also the Reporters' Notes for exhaustive discussions of the leading case authority).

§5.3 n.45 p.32 ***In the first paragraph, add the following to the second sentence:*** and in Law Offices of Ronald J. Palagi v. Howard, 747 N.W.2d 1 (Neb. 2008) ("While the restrictive language in paragraph 12 of the Attorney's Agreement [requiring that all fees from clients of former employer be paid to former employer] does not directly restrict a departing lawyer from practicing in competition with the firm, it provides a strong financial disincentive for that lawyer to perform services for a former client, and accordingly, it restricts the client's right to retain the lawyer.").

§5.3 n.45 p.32 Add the following after the citation to **Pettingell:** , in turn distinguished in Pierce v. Morrison Mahoney LLP, 897 N.E.2d 562 (Mass. 2008) (unlike in *Pettingell*, where the unenforceable partnership agreement distinguished between partners who left to compete and those who did not, the amended agreement made no such distinction; accordingly, a partner "who voluntarily withdraws and competes . . . may accept the representation of any client without triggering a financial forfeiture").

§5.3 n.45 p.32 In the first paragraph, add the following before the next-to-last sentence: For this argument in another setting, *see* Garfinkel v. Mager, 57 So. 3d 221 (Fla. App. 2010) (giving effect to settlement agreement in which lawyer promised not to represent clients with respect to suing the former employer; parties stated specifically that "every effort was made to limit the restrictions . . . to those that are reasonable and necessary to protect the legitimate business interests of [the employer]" and no restrictions otherwise placed on lawyer's ability to represent clients of employer).

§5.3 n.46 p.33 Add the following to the end of the second sentence: and in Mohanty v. St. John Heart Clinic, *supra* note 32 (upholding covenants barring cardiologists from "the practice of medicine" within a two or five-mile radius for three and five years; "[r]estrictive covenants protect the business interests of established physicians and, in this way, encourage them to take on younger, inexperienced doctors. . . . It is possible that patients would be more adversely affected if we were to ban reasonable restrictive covenants in physician employment contracts."), followed in Cent. Ind. Podiatry v. Krueger, 882 N.E.2d 723 (Ind. 2008) (in light of the "substantial majority" of jurisdictions adhering to this approach, "[a]ny decision to ban physician noncompetition agreements altogether should be left to the legislature").

§5.3 n.46 p.33 In the second paragraph, add the following to the list in the second sentence: Mercho-Roushdi-Shoemaker-Dilley Thoraco-Vascular Corp. v. Blatchford, 900 N.E.2d 786 (Ind. App. 2009) (public interest against enforcement of non-compete agreement where there were no or few suitable alternatives in the pertinent area, and indeed where some patients would die without the care provided by these physicians); Murfreesboro Med. Clinic v. Udom, 166 S.W.3d 674 (Tenn. 2005) (relying on AMA opinion discouraging covenants not to compete; invalidating essentially all physician noncompetition agreements) (decision countermanded by legislature two years later), followed in Columbus Med. Servs. v. Thomas, 308 S.W.3d 368 (Tenn. App. 2009) (substantial public interest in retaining therapists working with disabled people, given the "very serious" effect of losing continuity of care to these "vulnerable" and "fragile" patients).

§5.3a DRAFTING RESTRICTIVE COVENANTS

§5.3a n.1 p.34 Add the following to the list after the first **"See"**: Bishara, Fifty Ways to Leave Your Employer: Relative Enforcement of Covenants Not to Compete, Trends, and Implications for Employee Mobility Policy, 13 U. Pa. J. Bus. L. 751 (2011); McDonald, Noncompete Contracts: Understanding the Cost of Unpredictability, 10 Tex. Wesleyan L. Rev. 137 (2003).

§5.3a n.1 p.34 Add the following after the second sentence: For a thorough review of the pertinent caselaw, *see* B. Malsberger, Covenants Not to Compete: A State-by-State Survey (7th ed. 3 vol. 2010).

§5.3a n.1 p.34 Replace the citation to **Fontaine & De Ly** *with the following:* M. Fontaine & F. De Ly, Drafting International Contracts: An Analysis of Contract Clauses chs. 5, 13 (2006).

§5.3a n.3 p.35 Add the following at the end: *See also* Restatement (Third) of Employment Law §8.06 & cmt. *e* (T.D. No. 4, Apr. 11, 2011) (consideration not required).

§5.3a p.35 Add the following at the end of the sixth sentence of the carryover paragraph: . . . again with an appropriate recital.[4a]

[4a] Marsh USA v. Cook, 354 S.W.3d 764 (Tex. 2011) ("Consideration for a noncompete that is reasonably related to an interest worthy of protection . . . satisfies the statutory nexus."; protecting goodwill is such an interest).

§5.3a n.8 p.36 Add the following at the end: For characterization in the middle, *see* OnBrand Media v. Codex Consulting, 687 S.E.2d 168 (Ga. App. 2009) (ordinarily using intermediate level of scrutiny for professional partnership agreements, but here applying it to nondisclosure agreements ancillary to a planned joint venture).

§5.3a n.14 p.37 Add the following at the end of the second paragraph: *But see* Allen, Gibbs & Houlik, L.C. v. Ristow, 94 P.3d 724 (Kan. App. 2004) (administrator of employee benefit plans

did not receive training "out of the ordinary or unique" that would warrant enforcing a covenant not to compete). On the range of interests legitimate enough to warrant protection, *see* Restatement (Third) of Employment Law §8.07 cmt. *e* (T.D. No. 4, Apr. 11, 2011) ("An employer may have many economic reasons to attempt to restrict what its employees can do after termination of their employment. Some of these reasons, however, will not support an otherwise reasonable restrictive covenant because they are not sufficiently weighty to justify the social and individual costs inherent in restrictions on competition. For example, an interest in recouping investments in the training of employees may justify repayment obligations but would not justify a restriction on competition."). More specifically on the types of information falling in or out of this category, *see also* Restatement (Third) of Employment Law §8.02 (T.D. No. 4, Apr. 11, 2011).

§5.3a n.15 p.38 Add the following to the list in the first sentence: Softchoice Corp. v. MacKenzie, 636 F. Supp. 2d 927 (D. Neb. 2009) ("A list of the customers that a large reseller of computer software would target in a town the size of Omaha could essentially be put together from the phone book.").

§5.3a n.15 p.38 Add the following at the end of the first paragraph: *See generally* Restatement (Third) of Employment Law §8.02(b)(i-ii) & cmt. *f* (T.D. No. 4, Apr. 11, 2011) (information not confidential if it is "(i) generally known to the public or in the employer's industry; [or] (ii) readily obtainable by others through proper means").

§5.3a n.17 p.38 Add the following at the end: The draft Restatement similarly abandons the "common calling" approach; the relevant question is whether the employer has a protectable right in the information, not on who possesses the information. To that end, the Restatement excludes from the definition of "confidential information" information "acquired by employees in increasing their general experience, knowledge, and skills during the ordinary course of their employment." Restatement (Third) of Employment Law §8.02(b)(iii) (T.D. No. 4, Apr. 11, 2011). What job the employee held is not, of course, irrelevant. For example, the scope of a duty of loyalty depends greatly on the extent of one's managerial status. Restatement (Third) of Employment Law §§8.01 & cmt. *a*, 8.04(c) (T.D. No. 4, Apr. 11, 2011).

***§5.3a n.19 p.39 Add the following to the list after* "But cf.":** Edwards v. Arthur Andersen LLP, 189 P.3d 285 (Cal. 2008) (suggesting that there is no trade secret exception to California's broad prohibition of non-competition agreements, but not reaching the issue), interpreted in Dowell v. Biosense Webster, Inc., 102 Cal. Rptr. 3d 1 (Ct. App. 2009) ("we doubt the continued viability of the common law trade secret exception to covenants not to compete") and in Retirement Grp. v. Galante, 98 Cal. Rptr. 3d 585 (Ct. App. 2009) (California's statute "bars a court from specifically enforcing (by way of injunctive relief) a *contractual* clause" but still permits courts to enjoin tortuous conduct).

***§5.3a n.20 p.39 Add the following to the list after* "Accord":** Pathfinder Commc'ns Corp. v. Macy, 795 N.E.2d 1103 (Ind. App. 2003) (radio station had "legitimate protectible interest in . . . its former on-air personality").

§5.3a n.21 p.39 Add the following at the end of the first paragraph: *But see* GPS Indus. v. Lewis, 691 F. Supp. 2d 1327 (M.D. Fla. 2010) ("The mere identity of clients or pricing terms related to GPSI's projects may not be sufficient to justify a restrictive covenant. . . . This is especially true where, as here, GPSI has not shown its customer and pricing lists or business plans derive economic value from not being readily ascertained by others who can obtain economic value from their disclosure or use or that they are the subject of reasonable efforts to maintain their security."). *See generally* Restatement (Third) of Employment Law §8.02 cmt. *f* (T.D. No. 4, Apr. 11, 2011) (distinguishing between customer information developed in the course of customer relationships (rarely protected) and information consciously developed (potentially protected)).

***§5.3a n.22 p.40 Add the following to the list after* "See":** Mayer Hoffman McCann, P.C. v. Barton, 614 F.3d 893 (8th Cir. 2010) (giving effect to two-year ban on departing accountants contacting former clients; the accountants "had substantial contact with, and influence over, their clients"); Hejl v. Hood, Hargett & Assocs., 674 S.E.2d 425 (N.C. App. 2009) (covenant barring insurance account executive from offering insurance to "any person, firm or entity to whom [Defendant] has sold any product or service, or quoted any product or service" overbroad because it "includes any person, firm, or entity to whom Defendant had merely quoted a product or service"; "Defendant's attempt to prevent Plaintiff from obtaining clients where Defendant had failed to do so, is an impermissible restraint on Plaintiff.").

***§5.3a n.24 p.40 In the first paragraph, add the following to the list after* "see":** GPS Indus. v. Lewis, 691 F. Supp. 2d 1327 (M.D. Fla. 2010) ("The mere identity of clients or pricing terms related to GPSI's projects may not be sufficient to justify a restrictive covenant. . . . This is especially true where, as here, GPSI has not shown its customer and pricing lists or business plans derive economic value from not being readily ascertained by others who can obtain economic value from their disclosure or use or that they are the subject of reasonable efforts to maintain their security.").

***§5.3a n.24 p.40 In the first paragraph, add the following to the list after* "Cf.":** Natural Organics v. Kirkendall, 860 N.Y.S.2d 142 (App. Div. 2008) ("'an employee's recollection of information pertaining to specific needs and business habits of particular customers is not confidential'") (quoting from Walter Karl, Inc. v. Wood, 528 N.Y.S.2d 94 (App. Div. 1988)).

§5.3a n.24 p.40 In the second paragraph, add the following at the end: *But see* GPS Indus. v. Lewis, 691 F. Supp. 2d 1327 (M.D. Fla. 2010) (no protectable interest where information in question had been obtained by new employer independently and before the formation of the former employer).

§5.3a p.41 In the first full paragraph, add the following in the second sentence: . . . than in the case of a restraint ancillary to a sale of a business,[27a]

[27a] *See generally* Restatement (Third) of Employment Law §8.07 cmt. *d* (T.D. No. 4, Apr. 11, 2011) (the basic enforceability test applies to sales of

businesses, but "the tailoring can have a more generous fit because the policy concerns counseling narrow tailoring are less compelling").

§5.3a n.28 p.41 Add the following to the list in the first sentence: Cambridge Eng'g, Inc. v. Mercury Partners 90 Bi, 879 N.E.2d 512 (Ill. App. 2007) (provision barring "any activity for or on behalf of Employer's competitors" encompasses work "in an entirely non-competitive capacity" and thus displays "blatant overbreadth"); Sharvelle v. Magnante, 836 N.E.2d 432 (Ind. App. 2005) (promise not to solicit "former, current or future" patients or employees overbroad; blue-penciled to remove "former" and "future").

§5.3a n.28 p.41 Add the following to the list after **"But see"**: Star Direct v. Dal Pra, 767 N.W.2d 898 (Wis. 2009) (upholding non-compete covenant barring post-termination solicitation of current or recent past customers, even if employee had not dealt with them at all; the employee's "special knowledge of customer needs, pricing, and profit margins means that there was real danger in him seeking Star Direct's current and past customers. . . . Even if Dal Pra was not the recent servicer of a customer, he would still have some relationship with that customer, important knowledge about that customer, or maybe most significantly, special knowledge about Star Direct's business and methods"). *See* Burke v. Cumulus Media, Inc., 2016 U.S. Dist. LEXIS 91880 (E.D. Mich. July 15, 2016) (interpreting agreement prohibiting former radio show host from "appearing, performing, or allowing Employee's voice or picture to be heard, broadcast, used, or transmitted live or by recording in or on any radio station located within the Restricted Area" to not reach an Internet version of the show, after emphasizing that although non-compete agreements "are expressly authorized by statute, they are disfavored in Michigan as restraints on commerce.").

§5.3a n.31 p.42 Add the following to the list in the first sentence: H & R Block Tax Servs. v. Kutzman, 681 F. Supp. 2d 1248 (D. Mont. 2010) (franchisee barred from competing for one year within a 45-mile radius of her franchise; held reasonable because she may still serve any such clients at a distance, and barring her competition would allow franchisor to "retain its

goodwill and sell the franchises without competition from the [franchisee]"); Boulanger v. Dunkin' Donuts, 815 N.E.2d 572 (Mass. 2004) (two-year ban on operating doughnut shop within five miles of any of franchisor's stores held reasonable; "what the covenant not to compete was protecting was the defendant's franchise system").

§5.3a n.31 p.42 Add the following to the list after **"See"***:* Mayer Hoffman McCann, P.C. v. Barton, 614 F.3d 893 (8th Cir. 2010) (upholding ban on client contact with no geographic limits, because "a customer restriction may substitute for an explicit geographical restriction"; "it only prohibits appellants from soliciting MHM clients — not from performing services for MHM's clients whom the appellants did not solicit. Furthermore . . . the appellants would still be free to provide accounting services to all non-MHM clients anywhere."); Kelly v. Evolution Mkts., 626 F. Supp. 2d 364 (S.D.N.Y. 2009) (upholding nationwide ban on soliciting former clients; the former employer's business is conducted largely by telephone and by travel to conferences and networking events, so "any geographic limitation on the covenant's scope would obviate its usefulness").

§5.3a n.31 p.42 Add the following at the end: Recitals that a geographic restriction is fair and reasonable, and why, may make the non-compete agreement more palatable to the court. *See* Singas Famous Pizza Brands v. N.Y. Advertising, 468 Fed. Appx. 43 (2d Cir. 2012) (pointing to similar recitals as evidence that the non-compete clause was enforceable).

§5.3a n.32 p.43 Add the following after the citation to **American Software USA***:* and reaffirmed in Palmer & Cay v. Lockton Cos., 629 S.E.2d 800 (Ga. 2006) (upholding geographically unlimited non-solicitation agreement when limited temporally to two years after termination and substantively to customers served by the employees during their terms of employment).

§5.3a n.32 p.43 Add the following to the list in the first sentence: GPS Indus. v. Lewis, 691 F. Supp. 2d 1327 (M.D. Fla. 2010) (global non-compete agreement "patently unreasonable" even if former employer operates worldwide; suggests that clause might be enforceable if limited to those areas where the plaintiff

had actual operations); Cambridge Eng'g v. Mercury Partners 90 Bi, *supra* note 28 (territorial scope overbroad where it included areas in which the employer had never done business); Payroll Advance v. Yates, 270 S.W.3d 428 (Mo. App. 2008) (covenant not to compete that prohibits competition in any business within a 50-mile radius overbroad because (a) the geographic limit includes branch offices, so that "[r]espondent would be greatly limited in the geographic area she could work," and (b) competition is not defined, which makes the covenant overly broad as to scope); Hejl v. Hood, Hargett & Assocs., *supra* note 22 (invalidating non-compete agreement for insurance account executive that "encompasses two states regardless of whether Plaintiff had any personal knowledge of Defendant's customers in those areas").

§5.3a n.34 p.44 Add the following to the list in the first sentence: Friemuth v. Fiskars Brands, 681 F. Supp. 2d 985 (W.D. Wis. 2010) ("the lack of any time limitation renders a restrictive covenant unreasonable per se"), followed in Metso Minerals Indus. v. FLSmidth-Excel LLC, 733 F. Supp. 2d 980 (E.D. Wis. 2010) (absence of temporal limitations on non-disclosure covenant renders it unenforceable).

§5.3a n.35 p.44 In the first paragraph, add the following to the list after* "See"*: H & R Block E. Enters. v. Swenson, 745 N.W.2d 421 (Wis. App. 2007) (provision extending two-year noncompete agreement "by any period(s) of violation" unenforceable as overly uncertain and unpredictable and thus renders the two-year period itself unreasonable).

§5.3a n.36 p.44 Add the following at the end: *See* Restatement (Third) of Employment Law §8.06 cmt. *c* (T.D. No. 4, Apr. 11, 2011) ("The provision of compensation to the former employee during the term of the restrictive covenant (sometimes called 'garden leave') may be a factor in favor of finding it reasonable.").

§5.3a n.37 p.45 In the first paragraph, add the following to the list after* "Accord"*: *In re* Citigroup, Inc., 535 F.3d 45 (1st Cir. 2008) (upholding employment contract calling for the forfeiture of unvested stock if employee left company voluntarily; not a covenant against competition, because the "forfeiture provision becomes operative when one voluntarily leaves the company, regardless of any future employment decision he makes. In other words, the forfeiture occurs whether the participant chooses to work for a competitor or not."), followed in Weems v. Citigroup, Inc., 961 A.2d 349 (Conn. 2008).

***§5.3a n.37 p.45 In the first paragraph, add the following to the list after* "Cf.":** Drennen v. ExxonMobil Corp., 367 S.W.3d 288 (Tex. Civ. App. 2012) (New York law upholds "employee's choice" provision, but Texas law invalidates them).

§5.3a n.37 p.45 Add the following after the citation to* Eastern Carolina*: *aff'd mem.*, 572 S.E.2d 780 (N.C. 2002).

§5.3a n.37 p.45 Add the following at the end of the second paragraph: and elaborated on by Morris v. Schroder Capital Mgmt., 859 N.E.2d 503 (N.Y. 2006) (federal constructive discharge law applies to "employee choice" doctrine; if employee's work environment is made "so intolerable that it compels him to leave, that choice is essentially taken away from the employee," so the employer may not invoke the doctrine to enforce the clause and deny the benefit).

§5.3a n.37 p.45 Add the following to the list after* "Accord"*: Deming v. Nationwide Mut. Ins. Co., 905 A.2d 623 (Conn. 2006) (forfeiture of deferred compensation upon competition "does not differ meaningfully from a covenant not to compete"; "subjecting the employee to an economic loss undoubtedly is designed to deter competition.").

§5.3a n.38 p.46 Add the following to the list in the first sentence: Mayer Hoffman McCann, P.C. v. Barton, 614 F.3d 893 (8th Cir. 2010) (upholding ban on client contact with no geographic limits, because "a customer restriction may substitute for an explicit geographical restriction"); Wood v. Accordia of W. Va., 618 S.E.2d 415 (W. Va. 2005) ("non-piracy provisions, which ordinarily do not include territorial limits, are less restrictive on the employee and the economic forces of the marketplace [than are covenants not to compete]").

§5.3a n.38 p.46 Add the following after the first sentence: But *see* Freiburger v. J-U-B Eng'rs, 111 P.3d 100 (Idaho 2005) (rejecting the distinction between anti-piracy clauses and covenants not to compete, instead asking for either "whether or not the clause is no more restrictive than necessary to protect the employer's legitimate business interests").

§5.3a n.38 p.46 Add the following at the end: Even California, notoriously reluctant to uphold restraints on competition, permits non-solicitation agreements directed toward the customers and employees of a sold business. That far, and no further; a non-solicitation agreement directed toward the customers and employees of the buyer, not merely the sold business, is unenforceable. *See* Strategix, Ltd. v. Infocrossing W., 48 Cal. Rptr. 3d 614 (Ct. App. 2006).

§5.3a n.39 p.47 Add the following to the list in the first sentence: Softchoice Corp. v. MacKenzie, *supra* note 15 (non-compete agreement unenforceable for overbreadth; "[t]he agreement covers Softchoice's and its predecessor's present and potential customers and is not limited only to the customers that were contacted by [the employee]").

§5.3a n.40 p.47 In the second paragraph, add the following at the end: *Accord:* Applied Materials v. Advanced Micro-Fabrication Equip. (Shanghai) Co., 630 F. Supp. 2d 1084 (N.D. Cal. 2009) (invalidating clause requiring employee to assign rights to any inventions created for one year after employment, even if developed entirely after employment; "Since the Court finds that the Assignment Clause touches post-employment inventions, regardless of when they were conceived or whether they were based on Applied's confidential information, the Clause necessarily operates as a restriction on employee mobility."). *But cf.* Milliken & Co. v. Morin, 731 S.E.2d 288 (S.C. 2012) (upholding assignment clause that excluded from its scope "inventions for which no equipment, supplies, facility, or proprietary information of Milliken were used; that were developed entirely on an employee's own time; that did not relate directly to the current or anticipated business of Milliken; or that were not the result of any work performed for Milliken"; employee entitled to any invention not

based on his work for employer, and "[a]n employer therefore has a legitimate interest in protecting inventions that are the fruits of its employee's efforts while working for the company"); Preston v. Marathon Oil Co., 277 P.3d 81 (Wyo. 2012) (finding enforceable a clause assigning all intellectual property rights in inventions to employer, including a presumption that inventions conceived within one year after the end of employment would be presumed to have been conceived during employment; transfers of intellectual property not as fundamental as restrictive covenants). In the picturesque words of one court, "A naked assignment or agreement to assign, in gross, a man's future labors as an author or inventor, — in other words, a mortgage on a man's brain, to bind all its future products, — does not address itself favorably to our consideration." Aspinwall Mfg. v. Gill, 32 F. 697, 700 (C.C.D.N.J. 1887) (Bradley, J.). *See generally* Restatement (Third) of Employment Law §§8.09-8.11 (T.D. No. 4, Apr. 11, 2011) (employee's rights to inventions created during and after employment).

In re Facebook Biometric Information Litig., 185 F. Supp. 3d 1155, 2016 U.S. Dist. LEXIS 60046, at *19 (N.D. Cal. 2016), involved a choice of law provision that "[t]he laws of the State of California will govern this Statement, as well as any claim that might arise between you and us, without regard to conflict of law provisions." The plaintiffs had brought suit under the Illinois Biometric Information Privacy Act, 740 Ill. Comp. Stat. 14/1 *et seq.* and the parties agreed to transfer the case to California. The court found that the parties had entered into a valid contract with a choice of law agreement, *see* §3.7, but held that it would not be enforced. The court applied California law regarding enforceability of choice of law provisions. *Id.* at *28-29 (quoting Atl. Marine Const. Co. v. U.S. Dist. Court for W. Dist. of Texas, 134 S. Ct. 568, 582, 187 L. Ed. 2d 487 (2013)) ("federal court sitting in diversity ordinarily must follow the choice-of-law rules of the State in which it sits."). Although Facebook met the initial factors (the clause was broad enough to encompass this dispute; Facebook had considerable contacts with California), the fact that the Illinois Biometric Information Privacy Act was a "fundamental policy" and it had "materially greater interest . . . in determination of the issue" was determinative. *Id.* at *31-32 (following Washington Mutual Bank, FA v. Superior Court, 24 Cal. 4th 906, 103 Cal. Rptr. 2d 320, 15 P.3d 1071 (2001) and Restatement (Second) of Conflict of Laws

§187). The court held that "if California law is applied, the Illinois policy of protecting its citizens' privacy interests in their biometric data, especially in the context of dealing with 'major national corporations' like Facebook, would be written out of existence. That is the essence of a choice-of-law conflict." *Id.* at *34.

§5.3a n.44 p.49 Add the following after the citation to* Kolani*: , followed in Applied Materials v. Advanced Micro-Fabrication Equip. (Shanghai) Co., *supra* note 40 ("The Court is not permitted to apply any narrowing construction to limit the application of the Assignment Clause. . . .").

§5.3a n.44 p.49 Add the following to the list after* "But see"*: Sharvelle v. Magnante, 836 N.E.2d 432 (Ind. App. 2005) (noting, but giving no effect to, severability clause).

§5.3a n.48 p.50 Add the following to the list in the first sentence: Mayer Hoffman McCann, P.C. v. Barton, 614 F.3d 893 (8th Cir. 2010) (upholding liquidated damages, in part because lost fees from former clients difficult to measure precisely).

§5.3a n.48 p.50 Add the following to the list in the second sentence: Technical Aid Corp. v. Allen, 591 A.2d 262 (N.H. 1991) (damages may not be difficult to estimate if loss "relates to a specific client" since "injured party may point to the history of revenues").

§5.3a n.48 p.50 Add the following after the third sentence: Failing to include a liquidated damages clause has its own perils; damages for breach of a non-compete agreement are often difficult to prove, so the breached-against party may recover nothing. Blase Indus. Corp. v. Anorad Corp., 442 F.3d 235 (5th Cir. 2006) (defense verdict; because employee was at-will, "it is impossible to determine [damages] with the amount of certainty required").

§5.4 THE POLICY AGAINST IMPAIRMENT OF FAMILY RELATIONS

§5.4 n.3 p.52 Add the following at the end: However, a Georgia appellate court held in 2013 that a promise to marry is enforceable as a contract and a sufficiently deceptive promise to marry can be grounds for recovery in fraud. Kelley v. Cooper, 751 S.E.2d 889 (Ga. App. 2013). Although Georgia law prohibits enforcement of contracts relating to meretricious relationships such as unmarried cohabitation, a promise to marry represents the end of such a relationship and therefore is enforceable. *Id.* at 892 ("the fact that the parties were living together both before and after the marriage proposal is only collateral to the promise to marry"). Moreover, evidence that the defendant never intended to marry the woman, but only to induce her to remain in the relationship, supports recovery in fraud. *Id.* at 892-93.

§5.4 n.4 p.52 ***In the first paragraph, add the following to the list after* "See also"*:*** *In re* Marriage of Best, 901 N.E.2d 967 (Ill. App. 2009).

§5.4 n.4 p.52 ***In the third paragraph, add the following to the list after* "See"*:*** *In re* Marriage of Rife, 878 N.E.2d 775 (Ill. App. 2007) (invalidating clause in marital settlement agreement that ended wife's right to receive funds from IRA if she petitioned court for change in support or visitation; "because its intent and natural effect are to deter petitioner from seeking modifications to the child-related provisions of the judgment, it is tantamount to an agreement not to modify child custody, child support, or visitation"), followed in *In re Joshua S.*, 973 N.E.2d 1046 (Ill. App. 2012) (invalidating clause in plea bargain in child abandonment prosecution in which state agreed not to use existing evidence to terminate parental rights; state's public policy is that the courts and prosecutors "have the duty to act in the best interest of the minor and for the minor's own protection"); Court v. Kiesman, 850 A.2d 330 (Me. 2004) ("Allowing parents to circumvent the modification process by entering into contracts that are only facially separate from the issue of child support frustrates the ability to enforce child support orders."); Laffin v. Laffin, 760 N.W.2d 738 (Mich. App. 2008) (reciprocal alimony provision "would

deprive the parties' children of the child support they are entitled to by law, and, therefore, the reciprocal alimony provision is void as against public policy, because parties cannot bargain away their children's right to support.").

§5.4 n.4 p.52 ***In the third paragraph, add the following to the list after*** **"Cf.":** *In re* Marriage of Best, 901 N.E.2d 967 (Ill. App. 2009) (clause in pre-nuptial agreement banning fee-shifting "is not enforceable as to child-related issues, because it violates public policy by discouraging both parents from pursuing litigation in their child's best interests").

§5.4 n.5 p.53 ***In the first paragraph, add the following after the fourth sentence:*** *Cf.* J.F. v. D.B., 879 N.E.2d 740 (Ohio 2007) (Ohio has no public policy concerning gestational surrogacy, so gestational surrogacy contracts do not violate public policy, even when one of the provisions requires the surrogate not to assert parental rights); Ferguson v. McKiernan, 940 A.2d 1236 (Pa. 2007) (agreement between mother and sperm donor that donor would not seek visitation and mother would not seek child support enforceable; facts resemble anonymous sperm donation far more closely than traditional parenthood, and no legislative mandate regarding this "constantly evolving science of reproductive technology"); *In re* Paternity of F.T.R, 2013 WI 66, ¶ 28 (2013) (in general paternity agreements are "a valid, enforceable contract unless enforcement is contrary to the best interests of the child.").

§5.4 n.5 p.53 ***In the second paragraph, add the following to the list after*** **"See":** *In re* Marriage of Witten, 672 N.W.2d 768 (Iowa 2003) ("no transfer, release, disposition, or use of the embryos can occur without the signed authorization of both donors"); Roman v. Roman, 193 S.W.3d 40 (Tex. Civ. App. 2006) ("allowing the parties voluntarily to decide the disposition of frozen embryos in advance of cryopreservation, subject to mutual change of mind, jointly expressed, best serves the existing public policy of this State and the interests of the parties").

§5.4 n.5 p.53 ***In the second paragraph, add the following after the first sentence:*** *See generally* Matsumura, Binding Future Selves, 75 La. L. Rev. 71 (2014) (collecting cases and arguing that judicial

reluctance to enforce some intimate agreements, such as surrogacy and disposition of frozen embryos, is premised upon an unsound "different selves rationale" that privileges the party's intent at the time of dispute rather than at the time of contract formation); Collett, Whose Life is it Anyway?: Texas Public Policy and Contracts to Kill Embryonic Children, 50 S. Tex. L. Rev. 371 (2009).

***§5.4 n.5 p.53 In the third paragraph, add the following to the list after* "See generally":** Yehezkel Margalit, In Defense of Surrogacy Agreements: A Modern Contract Law Perspective, 20 Wm. & Mary J. Women & L. 1 (2013).

§5.4 n.8 p.54 Add the following to the list in the second sentence: Ureneck v. Cui, 798 N.E.2d 305 (Mass. App. 2003) ("agreement falls squarely within the categorical prohibition against marriage brokerage contracts").

§5.4 n.16 p. 56 Add the following at the end: *Cf.* UPMAA §6 (these agreements are enforceable without consideration); Restatement (Third) of Property §9.4 (same).

§5.4 n.17 p.56 Add the following after the second sentence: Along these lines, spouses may enter into enforceable contracts regarding student support, though these contracts may have to await divorce for enforcement. Ashby v. Ashby, 227 P.3d 246 (Utah 2010).

§5.4 n.18 p.56 Add the following at the end: *But see* Potts v. Potts, 303 S.W.3d 177 (Mo. App. 2010) (invalidating antenuptial contract because of one-sided property division; "The agreement . . . allowed Raymond to generate a large estate of non-marital property while limiting the distribution to Susan (upon dissolution) exclusively to a formula to be in lieu of maintenance, even after a twenty year marriage in which Susan had devoted her efforts to raising the children and running the household and thereby supporting Raymond's business."); *In re* Marriage of Bernard, 204 P.3d 907 (Wash. 2009) (invalidating property division as substantively unfair where it "overall made provisions for [wife] disproportionate to the means of [husband],

and limited [wife's] ability to accumulate her separate property while precluding her common law or statutory claims on [husband's] property").

§5.4 n.19 p.56 Add the following at the end: *Cf.* Diosdado v. Diosdado, 118 Cal. Rptr. 2d 494 (Ct. App. 2002) (provision imposing damages for infidelity unenforceable). This is not necessarily true for more procedural matters. Decisions to arbitrate, for example, or decisions to waive fault rules, may well be enforceable. *See* Massar v. Massar, 652 A.2d 219 (N.J. Super. App. Div. 1995) (enforcing agreement not to use fault grounds for divorce); Eason v. Eason, 682 S.E.2d 804 (S.C. 2009) (enforcing agreement to waive adultery as defense to alimony claim). On arbitration, see §5.4a *infra*.

§5.4 n.21 p.57 Add the following to the list after "Accord": Barber v. Barber, 38 So. 3d 1046 (La. App. 2010) (voiding premarital agreement that waived alimony rights in the event of separation, but upholding the provisions of that agreement waiving the right to alimony after divorce).

§5.4 n.22 p.57 Add the following after the second sentence: *Cf.* Hoyt v. Hoyt, 372 S.W.2d 300 (Tenn. 1963) (because "marriage settlement . . . in contemplation of divorce is not against public policy" reconciliation agreement in similar circumstances was not). *But cf.* Bratton v. Bratton, 136 S.W.3d 595 (Tenn. 2004) (adopting "proposition that marital partners may validly contract to divide property or set support in the event of a divorce by post nuptial agreement, even without it being incident to a contemplated separation or divorce"), followed in Ansin v. Craven-Ansin, 929 N.E.2d 955 (Mass. 2010) ("Marital contracts are not the product of classic arm's-length bargaining, but that does not make them necessarily coercive."), in turn followed in Bedrick v. Bedrick, 17 A.3d 17 (Conn. 2011) ("Postnuptial agreements are consistent with public policy; they realistically acknowledge the high incidence of divorce and its effect upon our population.").

§5.4 n.23 p.57 Add the following to the list after "Accord": Crews v. Crews, 989 A.2d 1060 (Conn. 2010) (prenuptial agreements generally enforceable, but that depends on "whether the circumstances at the time of dissolution were so 'beyond the contemplation' of the parties at the time the antenuptial agreement was signed that enforcement of the agreement would work an injustice"; this test "is analogous to determining whether enforcement of an agreement would be unconscionable") (quoting from McHugh v. McHugh, 436 A.2d 8 (Conn. 1980)); Lane v. Lane, 202 S.W.3d 577 (Ky. 2006) ("[A]nte-nuptial agreements are not per se invalid as against public policy. However, courts retain the right to analyze such agreements for unconscionability . . ."); Mamot v. Mamot, 813 N.W.2d 440 (Neb. 2012) (assent to prenuptial agreement not voluntary where agreement was first presented one week before the wedding, agreement did not contain disclosure of assets, fiancé threatened to cancel wedding if not signed, parties had great disparity in assets, and there was no real opportunity given to consult with independent counsel); *In re* Marriage of Bernard, 204 P.3d 90 (Wash. 2009) (agreement unenforceable when significantly revised version presented three days before wedding); Cioffi-Petrakis v. Petrakis, 103 A.D.3d 766, 960 N.Y.S.2d 152 (N.Y. App. Div. 2013) (upholding trial court decision to set aside prenuptial agreement on grounds of fraudulent inducement, and noting general principle in New York that "while 'there is a heavy presumption that a deliberately prepared and executed written instrument manifests the true intention of the parties' (Brassey v Brassey, 154 A.D.2d 293, 295, 546 N.Y.S.2d 370), an agreement between spouses or prospective spouses may be invalidated if the party challenging the agreement demonstrates that it was the product of fraud, duress, or other inequitable conduct (see Christian v Christian, 42 N.Y.2d 63, 73, 365 N.E.2d 849, 396 N.Y.S.2d 817; Petracca v Petracca, 101 A.D.3d 695, 956 N.Y.S.2d 77; Weinstein v Weinstein, 36 A.D.3d 797, 798, 830 N.Y.S.2d 179; Lombardi v. Lombardi, 235 A.D.2d 400, 652 N.Y.S.2d 549).").

§5.4 n.23 p.57 Add the following after the citation to **Scherer***:* , somewhat oddly applied in Mallen v. Mallen, 622 S.E.2d 812 (Ga. 2005) (no confidential relationship between parties to prenuptial agreement; wife's failure "to verify representations regarding the meaning and content of the agreement" prevents her from invalidating pre-nuptial agreement, even in the face of nondisclosure of husband's income), in turn criticized

in Younger, Lovers' Contracts in the Courts: Forsaking Even Minimum Decencies, 13 Wm. & Mary J. Women & L. 349 (2007), limited by Blige v. Blige, 656 S.E.2d 822 (Ga. 2008) (no duty of inquiry for pre-nuptial agreements), and explained in Lawrence v. Lawrence, 687 S.E.2d 421 (Ga. 2009) (in *Mallen*, lack of formal disclosure untroubling because parties had cohabited for four years, information disclosed showed husband to be wealthy, and wife knew husband to have large income; in *Blige*, inadequate disclosure where couple did not cohabit and husband concealed wealth by modest standard of living; here, no formal disclosure required because husband gave wife expensive gifts, told her about his real estate dealings, including the amounts borrowed, and told her which businesses he owned).

§5.4 n.23 p.57 ***In the second paragraph, add the following to the list after*** **"See generally"*:*** Note, Reviewing Premarital Agreements to Protect the State's Interest in Marriage, 91 Va. L. Rev. 535 (2005).

§5.4 n.23 p.57 ***Add the following at the end:*** For comparative perspectives, *see* Marital Agreements and Private Autonomy in Comparative Perspective (J. Scheppe ed., 2012).

§5.4 n.24 p.58 ***Add the following to the list after*** **"Accord"*:*** Oldani v. Oldani, 34 A.3d 407 (Conn. App. 2011) ("the law places no duty or burden on either party to inquire as to the requisite disclosure of the other party, only a duty on each to inform"); Ansin v. Craven-Ansin, 929 N.E.2d 955 (Mass. 2010) ("Before a marital agreement is sanctioned by a court, careful scrutiny by the judge should determine at a minimum whether (1) each party has had an opportunity to obtain separate legal counsel of each party's own choosing; (2) there was fraud or coercion in obtaining the agreement; (3) all assets were fully disclosed by both parties before the agreement was executed; (4) each spouse knowingly and explicitly agreed in writing to waive the right to a judicial equitable division of assets and all marital rights in the event of a divorce; and (5) the terms of the agreement are fair and equitable at the time of execution and at the time of divorce."); *In re* Marriage of Bernard, *supra* note 18 (two-prong test; first prong requires "substantive fairness," while second prong, applicable

only if the agreement is not substantively fair, requires that the agreement be procedurally fair, including an inquiry "whether the spouses made a full disclosure of the amount, character, and value of the property involved").

§5.4 n.25 p.58 Add the following at the end: *Cf.* Binek v. Binek, 673 N.W.2d 594 (N.D. 2004) (following other jurisdictions in which "full disclosure clause has been held to create a rebuttable presumption of full disclosure"); Sims v. Sims, 685 S.E.2d 869 (Va. App. 2009) (same). Georgia's courts, though not requiring a formal pre-execution disclosure, nevertheless encourage it as a way to ensure that the necessary information has been disclosed. Lawrence v. Lawrence, *supra* note 23 ("attaching to the antenuptial agreement financial statements showing both parties' assets, liabilities, and income, while not necessary, 'is the most effective method of satisfying the statutory [disclosure] obligation in most circumstances' ") (quoting from Blige v. Blige, *supra* note 23 (in turn quoting from Friezo v. Friezo, 914 A.2d 533, 550 (Conn. 2007))).

§5.4 n.26 p.58 Add the following to the list after "Accord": Bedrick v. Bedrick, 17 A.3d 17 (Conn. 2011) (reviewing marital agreement for enforceability, in part by asking whether injustice would result from enforcement because of significant changes in circumstances after the agreement was signed); Ansin v. Craven-Ansin, 929 N.E.2d 955 (Mass. 2010) ("Where one spouse challenges the enforceability of the agreement, the spouse seeking to enforce the agreement shall bear the burden of satisfying" the criteria listed *supra* note 24, including whether "the terms of the agreement are fair and equitable at the time of execution and at the time of divorce") (citing to ALI Principles of Family Dissolution §7.04(2) (2002)).

§5.4 n.26 p.58 Add the following after the citation to Gentry: , followed in Lane v. Lane, *supra* note 23 ("a trial court may modify or invalidate all or part of an ante-nuptial agreement where enforcement is unconscionable in its application").

§5.4 n.26 p.58 Add the following to the list in the last sentence: *In re* Marriage of Bernard, *supra* note 18 (same).

§5.4 n.26 p.58 Add the following at the end: *But see* Baker v. Baker, 622 So. 2d 541 (Fla. App. 1993) (enforcing antenuptial agreement which waived alimony and left the wife a pauper; although the substance of the agreement was unfair, there was no procedural unconscionability), followed in McNamara v. McNamara, 40 So. 3d 78 (Fla. App. 2010) (Florida law provides that "[a]n inadequate provision for the impecunious spouse . . . raises a presumption of concealment or that the challenging spouse lacked knowledge of the proponent's finances at the time the agreement was made," but that presumption was rebutted here despite detailed disclosure only the night before the wedding; wife had a "general and approximate knowledge of the proponent's property," was herself a consultant specializing in the review of defense contracts, and had entered into a similar prenuptial agreement with her former spouse; furthermore, the wedding had no guests and thus could have been postponed easily). *Cf.* Potts v. Potts, 303 S.W.3d 177 (Mo. App. 2010) (applying substantive and procedural unconscionability analysis to premarital agreement).

§5.4 n.27 p.58 Add the following after the second sentence: *See also In re* Marriage of Balcof, 47 Cal. Rptr. 3d 183 (Ct. App. 2006) (marital agreement unenforceable because of undue influence); Bakos v. Bakos, 950 So. 2d 1257 (Fla. App. 2007) (same). It follows that a relationship of trust and confidence exists during a marriage; hence the usual strict scrutiny of postnuptial agreements. *See* Ansin v. Craven-Ansin, 929 N.E.2d 955 (Mass. 2010) (in contrast to the confidential relationship that exists between those engaged to be married, "[t]he obligation is greater with respect to marital agreements because each spouse owes a duty of absolute fidelity to the other"); *In re* Estate of Smid, 756 N.W.2d 1 (S.D. 2008) ("postnuptial agreements are subjected to close scrutiny because of the confidential relationship between husband and wife").

§5.4 n.28 p.59 Add the following after the citation to **Simeone***:* followed in Crews v. Crews, 989 A.2d 1060 (Conn. 2010) ("general contract principles apply to antenuptial

agreements," though these agreements are also subject to added scrutiny to ensure their basic justice).

§5.4 n.28 p.59 Add the following after the citation to* Yannalfo*: distinguished in *In re* Estate of Hollett, 834 A.2d 348 (N.H. 2003) (where there was neither "sufficient time" nor "reasonable opportunity" to make use of advice of recent law school graduate, wife's signature did not, given complexity of finances and agreement and disparity of bargaining power, meet "heightened standard applied to prenuptial agreements").

§5.4 n.30 p.59 Add the following at the end of the first paragraph: In July of 2012, the Uniform Law Commissioners approved the Uniform Premarital and Marital Agreements Act (UPMAA), which is meant to replace the Uniform Premarital Agreement Act of 1983 and extend its coverage to marital agreements. The UPMAA permits the parties to premarital or marital agreements to affirm, modify, or waive their rights to support and to many other rights arising from marital status, mainly rights to property and responsibility for liabilities (in either case also when arising from separation, marital dissolution, or death). UPMAA §2(2), (4), & (5). Such an agreement must be in a record signed by both parties. UPMAA §6. As with the original act, the agreement may not be enforced if consent to it was involuntary or if the agreement, or part of it, was unconscionable — either at the time of contracting or after, if material changes in the circumstances of one of the parties would make enforcement of the term yield substantial hardship. UPMAA §9(a) & (c). The disclosure requirements under UPMAA are more stringent than those under UPMA, particularly regarding the associated rights to counsel. There is, however, safe harbor language that should allow careful drafters to avoid most problems with procedural unconscionability. UPMAA §9(f).

§5.4 n.30 p.59 In the third paragraph, add the following to the list after* "see"*: Younger, Lovers' Contracts in the Courts: Forsaking the Minimal Decencies, 13 Wm. & Mary J. Women & L. 349 (2007).

§5.4 n.32 p.60 In the first paragraph, add the following after the first sentence: Wright v. Wright, 761 N.W.2d 443 (Mich. App. 2008) (postnuptial contract granting virtually all marital property to husband in the event of a divorce void as against public policy; "a couple that is maintaining a marital relationship may not enter into an enforceable contract that anticipates and encourages a future separation or divorce," with those agreements receiving "much stricter legal scrutiny than postnuptial, postseparation agreements that essentially settled property issues arising in ongoing or imminent divorce litigation"); Sims v. Sims, *supra* note 25 (invalidating property settlement in which wife "waived spousal support and relinquished to [husband] almost 100% of the marital estate — including the marital residence, all retirement benefits and deferred compensation"; the agreement "literally left her penniless with no practical means for supporting herself," and indeed "wife had in fact already become a public charge, receiving food stamps"; this last implicates the state's interest in ensuring that a spouse not become a public charge).

§5.4 n.32 p.60 Add the following at the end: *See generally* Atwood, Marital Contracts and the Meaning of Marriage, 54 Ariz. L. Rev. 1 (2012); Williams, Postnuptial Agreements, 2007 Wis. L. Rev. 827.

§5.4 n.33 p.61 Add the following at the end: Some courts have held that antenuptial agreements, which allow for a significant property settlement or significant alimony even after a short-lived marriage, may be unenforceable as promoting divorce, regardless of which party seeks the divorce. Gross v. Gross, 464 N.E.2d 500 (Ohio 1984), explained in Gartrell v. Gartrell, 908 N.E.2d 1019 (Ohio App. 2009) ("the validity of the agreement does not depend upon which party benefits under the terms of the agreement, or upon which party abandons the marriage or disregards the marriage vows"). It is difficult to see why an agreement providing for a significant property transfer should be unenforceable by the recipient if the *other* party seeks dissolution of the marriage; if anything, a clause of this sort would tend to dissuade that party from ending the marriage, given the financial consequences of doing so. Courts have thus far stated no policy against holding together troubled marriages, which would seem to be the consequence of the decisions in *Gross* and *Gartrell*. On the other hand, agreements simply barring divorce, particularly if only one party is prohibited from doing so, are also unenforceable, given that it is "socially and morally undesirable to compel parties to a dead marriage to retain an illusory and deceptive status." P.B. v. L.B., 855 N.Y.S.2d 836 (Sup. 2008) (invalidating portion of separation agreement barring husband from seeking divorce without wife's written consent for five years, with no reciprocal provision). The line may perhaps be drawn between ailing marriages and fundamentally dead ones, with a sort of juridical triage providing life support to the former and interring the latter.

§5.4 n.35 p.62 Add the following as a new paragraph: Underscoring the extent to which attitudes have changed, in 2013 the New York Appellate Court reinstated a claim of breach of an oral cohabitation agreement between two women who had been in a committed same-sex relationship for nearly 18 years. Dee v. Rakower, 112 A.D.3d 204; 976 N.Y.S.2d 470 (N.Y. App. 2013). Their relationship predated New York recognition of same-sex marriages, but the plaintiff alleged that the two had an oral "oral 'joint venture/partnership' agreement whereby she would share in assets, including the defendant's retirement contributions and earnings, in exchange for leaving her full-time job to care for the parties' children." *Id.* at 206. In reversing dismissal, the Appellate Division held that "[t]here is no reason, on this record, at this early stage of the litigation to conclude, as the Supreme Court did, that the oral agreement between the parties cannot serve as the basis for a breach of contract cause of action." *Id.* at 211.

§5.4 n.37 p.63 Add the following after the first sentence: *Accord:* Norton v. Hoyt, 278 F. Supp. 2d 214 (D.R.I. 2003) (Rhode Island "has not recognized palimony").

§5.4 n.39 p.63 In the second paragraph, add the following after the second sentence: *But cf.* Chiba v. Greenwald, 67 Cal. Rptr. 3d 86 (Ct. App. 2007) (palimony agreement itself enforceable, but was combined with unlicensed work as agent; court declined to sever and found the entire agreement unenforceable).

§5.4 n.40 p.63 Add the following after the citation to **Doe***:* *Contra:* T.F. v. B.L., 813 N.E.2d 1244 (Mass. 2004) (implied contract between mother and her former domestic partner that the partner would take responsibilities of parent in exchange for the mother's conceiving and bearing child held unenforceable).

§5.4a DRAFTING INTIMATE AGREEMENTS

§5.4a n.1 p.65 Substitute the following for the first sentence: Lindey and Parley on Separation Agreements and Antenuptial Contracts (2d ed. A. Lindey & L. Parley eds. 2 vols. 1999); L. Ravdin, Premarital Agreements: Drafting and Negotiation (2011); S. Schlissel, E. Karabatos & R. Poepplein, Separation Agreements and Marital Contracts (2d ed. 2 vols. 1997); G. Skoloff, R. Singer & R. Brown, Drafting Prenuptial Agreements (1994); Turner & Morgan, Attacking and Defending Marital Agreements (2d ed. 2012).

§5.4a n.2 p.65 Add the following at the end: *Cf.* UPMAA §3(d) (Act does not affect waivers of property rights if the recipient of the right is either "a bona fide purchaser for value or a donee that establishes good faith reliance.").

§5.4a n.3 p.66 Add the following at the end: The same is true under the Uniform Premarital and Marital Agreements Act. More precisely, if the requirements of the Act are satisfied, the duty of support may be modified if other state law would otherwise allow this, except to the extent that the modification would cause a party to the agreement to be eligible for public assistance. UPMAA §§5 & 9(b) & (c).

§5.4a p.66 Add the following after the third sentence in the carryover paragraph: . . . failure to make full disclosure is imprudent.[3a]

[3a] To that end, it is prudent to attach to the antenuptial agreement a full listing of assets, liabilities, and income in order to avoid an attack on the grounds of nondisclosure. *See* Lawrence v. Lawrence, 687 S.E.2d 421 (Ga. 2009) ("attaching to the antenuptial agreement financial statements showing both parties' assets, liabilities, and income, while not necessary, 'is the most

effective method of satisfying the statutory [disclosure] obligation in most circumstances' ") (quoting from Blige v. Blige, *supra* note 23 (in turn quoting from Friezo v. Friezo, 914 A.2d 533, 550 (Conn. 2007))). It may also be prudent to avoid incentives to divorce, such as by granting one spouse a large increase in wealth over the premarital assets upon divorce, even if that spouse is the moving party. *See* Stern v. Stern, 243 A.2d 319 (Pa. 1968) (postnuptial agreement; husband would make payments to wife and give her a share in the proceeds of the marital home upon divorce, even if she was the movant). In principle, a clause granting such an increase to the non-movant should be unexceptionable, but at least in some jurisdictions it may not be. In those, some sort of link between the length of marriage and the amount granted may be in order, somewhat in the manner of avoiding liquidated damages clauses that are invariant to the gravity of the breach. *See* Gartrell v. Gartrell, 908 N.E.2d 1019 (Ohio App. 2009) ("the validity of the agreement does not depend upon which party benefits under the terms of the agreement, or upon which party abandons the marriage or disregards the marriage vows"). And if a jurisdiction enacts the new Uniform Act, the agreement will be unenforceable if, before signing the agreement, "the party did not receive a reasonably accurate description and estimate of value of the property, liabilities, and income of the other party." UPMAA §9(a)(4)(A).

§5.4a n.4 p.66 Add the following after the first sentence: *Cf.* Ware v. Ware, 687 S.E.2d 382 (W. Va. 2009) ("one attorney may not represent, nor purport to counsel, both parties to a prenuptial agreement"; as a consequence of the husband's attorney representing to the wife that he represented both her interest and his, the wife "was divested of her opportunity to consult with independent counsel" and so the resulting agreement was unenforceable). The UPMAA provides that the agreement will be unenforceable if the party seeking avoidance "did not have access to independent legal representation," which entails having sufficient time to decide whether to hire a lawyer, to do so, and to secure and consider the resulting advice. UPMAA §9(a)(2) & (f).

§5.4a n.13 p.68 Add the following after the second sentence: The Restatement (Second) position was adopted in the Uniform Act. UPMAA §4.

§5.4a n.13 p.68 Add the following after the third sentence: *See also* Gamache v. Smurro, 904 A.2d 91 (Vt. 2006) (applying California law to agreement signed in California); Bradley v. Bradley, 164 P.3d 567 (Wyo. 2007) (choice of law provision selecting Minnesota law enforced, causing an amendment to the agreement to become unenforceable because it did not comply with Minnesota law on modification).

§5.4a n.14 p.68 ***Add the following at the end:*** For limits on the right of review, *see* Burke v. Burke, 662 S.E.2d 622 (Va. App. 2008) (property settlement agreement's term banning appellate review not against public policy; "A no-appeal clause . . . forces the parties to realize that the litigation must end and that the ruling of the trial court is final. Given the contentious nature of some of these cases, such provisions protect both parties by resolving the dispute more quickly and minimizing costs.").

§5.5 JUDICIAL DERIVATION OF POLICIES FROM LEGISLATION

§5.5 n.6 p.69 ***In the second paragraph, add the following to the list after "see":*** King v. Riedl, 58 So. 3d 190 (Ala. Civ. App. 2010) (statute requires that contractors be licensed, and that residential home builders may not bring suit under any contracts entered into when they were unlicensed); Parente v. Pirozzoli, 866 A.2d 629 (Conn. App. 2005) (statute explicitly prohibited transfer of liquor license to convicted felon); Master Tech Satellite v. Mastec N. Am., 49 So. 3d 789 (Fla. App. 2010) (statute requires that electrical contractors be licensed, and that the contracts of unlicensed contractors "shall be unenforceable in law or equity by the unlicensed contractor"); Bank of the W. v. Kline, 782 N.W.2d 453 (Iowa 2010) (permitting guarantors to assert violations of the Equal Credit Opportunity Act as affirmative defense); Timber Ridge, Inc. v. Hunt Country Asphalt & Paving, 671 S.E.2d 789 (W. Va. 2008) (statutes barring unlicensed appraisers and unlicensed realtors from suing to collect fees).

Legislation can also alter the normal rules for offer and acceptance. For example, in 2015 PayPal announced that it was altering the terms of its User Agreement, in accordance with contractual provisions for alteration and amendment, to provide, "You consent to receive autodialed or prerecorded calls and text messages from PayPal." The Federal Communications Commission sent a letter, cautioning that the amendments "raise serious concerns for the Enforcement Bureau," and noting that regulations implementing the Telephone Consumer Protection Act (TCPA, or more commonly, the Do-Not-Call Act) requires, among other things, that consent to receive automated calls be in writing, bear the signature of the person who will receive the calls, and not be a condition of purchasing any goods or services. FCC, letter to Louise Pentland, General Counsel, PayPal, Inc., June 11, 2015, available on http://transition.fcc.gov/Daily_Releases/Daily_Business/2015/db0611/DOC-333875A1.pdf. A few months later, the FCC issued a formal Citation and Order to Lyft (a "ride sharing" company) relating to the "terms of service" users must agree to upon signing up with Lyft, which included a statement of consent to automated and prerecorded messages. *In re* Lyft, Inc., DA 15-997 (Sept. 11, 2015). The FCC found "that Lyft (1) unlawfully conditioned consumers' ability to use Lyft's services on their agreement to receive marketing text messages, and (2) illegally circumvented the FCC's disclosure requirements for prior express written consent."

So-called gag clauses, aimed primarily at negative online reviews, also have been rendered unenforceable in consumer contracts by recent legislation. The federal Consumer Review Fairness Act became effective in 2017, prohibiting form contracts that restrict consumer from criticizing the product in reviews or that transfer intellectual property in reviews to the company. Consumer Review Fairness Act of 2016, Pub. L. No. 114-258, 130 Stat. 1355 (2017), to be codified at 15 U.S.C. §45b. Such clauses were already illegal in California under a 2014 law. Cal Civ Code §1670.8 (Prohibition against provision waiving consumer's right to make statement regarding seller or lessor, or concerning goods or services, in specified consumer contract). The specific federal legislation also follows a 2015 Federal Trade Commission action against a company that had sought to enforce the non-disparagement clause in its contract with consumers, asserting attempts to enforce that contractual provision "constitute unfair acts or practices in violation of Section 5 of the FTC Act, 15 U.S.C. §45(a) and (n)." Complaint at ¶66, Federal Trade Comm'n v. Roca Labs., Inc, 15-CV-2231 (M.D. Fla. Sept. 24, 2015). The FTC claimed that the marketer of weight-loss products not only "made baseless claims" about the effectiveness of the products but also "threatened to enforce 'gag clause' provisions against consumers to stop them from posting negative reviews and testimonials online." FTC, Press Release, "FTC Sues Marketers Who Used 'Gag Clauses,' Monetary Threats, and Lawsuits to Stop Negative Consumer Reviews for Unproven Weight-Loss Products," Sept. 28, 2015. The "terms and conditions," contained in package inserts and online, included a broad non-disparagement clause, that "regardless of your personal experience with RL, you will **not** disparage RL and/or any of its employees, products or services. This means that you will not speak, publish, cause to be published, print, review, blog, or otherwise write negatively about RL, or its products or employees in any way. This encompasses all forms of media, including and especially the internet." Compl. at ¶ 46. The court issued a stipulated temporary restraining order that, among other things, prohibited the company from "[p]urporting to bind, including through any notice, warning, threat to enforce or attempt to enforce, any purchaser of a Covered Product — regardless of when purchased — to any contractual provision that purports to prohibit purchasers from speaking or publishing truthful or non-defamatory negative comments or reviews about Defendants, their products, or their employees." Stipulated Temporary Restraining Order with Other Equitable Relief and Order to Show Cause Why a Preliminary Injunction Should Not Issue, at 4, Federal Trade Comm'n v. Roca Labs, Inc, 15-CV-2231 (M.D. Fla. Sept. 29, 2015). A month later, the court issued a preliminary injunction that included the same prohibition and required disclosure of all its lawsuits "and a statement of whether Roca Labs. asserts the authority and right to continue to pursue such litigation consistent with . . . this Order." Preliminary Injunction and Order for Other Equitable Relief, at 12, Federal Trade Comm'n v. Roca Labs., Inc, 15-CV-2231 (M.D. Fla. Oct. 29, 2015).

In 2016, the Ninth Circuit held that a class action waiver in an employment contract was unenforceable because it conflicted with employee rights under the National Labor Relations Act to engage in "concerted action." Morris v. Ernst & Young, LLP, 834 F.3d 975, 2016 U.S. App. LEXIS 15638, 167 Lab. Cas. (CCH) P10,936, 26 Wage & Hour Cas. 2d (BNA) 1460 (9th Cir. 2016). The court held that the NLRA "Section 7's 'mutual aid or protection clause' includes the substantive right to collectively 'seek to improve working conditions through resort to administrative and judicial forums.' " *Id.* at *14, quoting Eastex, Inc. v. NLRB, 437 U.S. 556, 566 (1978). In the employment contracts before it, "[t]he 'separate proceedings' clause prevents concerted activity by employees in arbitration proceedings, and the requirement that employees only use arbitration prevents the initiation of concerted legal action anywhere else. The result: interference with a protected §7 right in violation of §8. Thus, the 'separate proceedings' terms in the Ernst & Young contracts cannot be enforced." *Id.* at *15. Although these clauses were part of an arbitration agreement, the Ninth Circuit noted that "the arbitration requirement is not the problem. The same provision in a contract that required court adjudication as the exclusive remedy would equally violate the NLRA. The NLRA obstacle is a ban on initiating, in any forum, concerted legal claims — not a ban on arbitration." *Id.* at *16.

§5.5 n.9 p.70 Add the following to the list after "Accord": Chubb Lloyds Ins. Co. v. Andrew's Restoration, 323 S.W.3d 564 (Tex. Civ. App. 2010) (requirement that home improvement contractors provide warning to potential clients; the statute "does not provide that omission of the required warning makes a contract invalid or void," and "[g]iven the numerous remedies available . . . we conclude that the statutory consequence of noncompliance is 'apparently ample' to insure observance," so violation of the statute does not render the contract unenforceable) (quoting from New Boston Gen. Hosp. v. Tex. Workforce Comm'n, 47 S.W.3d 34, 40 (Tex. Civ. App. 2001)), *aff'd in part, rev'd in part on other grounds sub nom.* Cruz v. Andrew's Restoration, 364 S.W.3d 817 (Tex. 2012).

In recent years, there have been some news accounts of businesses attempting to prohibit negative online reviews as a term of their contract or online agreement, *see, e.g.*, Kate Cox, "Lawmakers Propose Bill to Prevent Businesses from Suing You for Complaining About Them," Consumerist, May 18, 2015. In apparent response, California enacted legislation, effective January 2015, that prohibits a contract from containing "a provision waiving the consumer's right to make any statement regarding the seller or lessor or its employees or agents, or concerning the goods or services." Cal. Civil Code §1670.8. The law makes such clauses "unlawful" and provides for fines and actions by the attorney general, but does not specify that such provisions are unenforceable, but instead states only that the statute "does not affect any other relief or remedy provided by law." Similar legislation was introduced in Congress in May 2015. Securing Participation, Engagement, and Knowledge Freedom by Reducing Egregious Efforts Act of 2015 or the SPEAK FREE Act of 2015, H.R. 2304, 114th Congress (2015).

§5.5 n.10 p.70 Add the following to the list in the first sentence: Cal. Physicians' Serv. v. Aoki Diabetes Res. Inst., 78 Cal. Rptr. 3d 646 (Ct. App. 2008) (ban on corporate practice of medicine does not allow insurer to avoid paying provider; "a contract for the provision of medical services by licensed professionals is plainly not malum in se"), followed in Wald v. Truspeed Motorcars, 108 Cal. Rptr. 3d 542 (Ct. App. 2010) (ban on auto sales by unlicensed salespersons does not allow auto dealer to avoid paying salesperson; "Nothing in *Wald* being able to receive compensation for his efforts is 'malum in se.' ") (emphasis in original); Simaee v. Levi, 802 N.Y.S.2d 493 (App. Div. 2005) ("the violation of a statute that is merely malum prohibitum will not necessarily render a contract illegal and unenforceable"); Unger v. Leviton, 787 N.Y.S.2d 625 (Super. Ct. Nassau Cnty. 2004) (rule of unenforceability "may not apply where the illegality in question is not *malum in se*, but is merely *malum prohibitum*").

§5.5 n.12 p.71 Add the following after the citation to* Continental Basketball Ass'n*: and in Imperial Ins. Restoration & Remodeling v. Costello, 965 N.E.2d 723 (Ind. App. 2012) (failure of home improvement contractor to supply to owner all information required by statute did not warrant invalidating the contract; the contractor supplied the requested services, the owner signed a certificate of satisfaction, and the owner's insurer had paid the owner for the contractor's services).

§5.5 n.12 p.71 Add the following at the end: *Cf.* R.A.C. v. Bd. of Ed. of City of N.Y., 799 N.Y.S.2d 559 (App. Div. 2005) (statute forbidding former public servants from appearing before their old agencies for one year after employment; although statute *malum prohibitum*, still bars recovery; strong public policy against fraud and immoral conduct, and evidence that former employee had unclean hands). For a similar list, *see* Frishman v. Maginn, 912 N.E.2d 468 (Mass. App. 2009) ("'the nature of the subject matter of the contract; what was the extent of the illegal behavior; was that behavior a material or only an incidental part of the performance of the contract . . . ; what was the strength of the public policy underlying the prohibition; how far would effectuation of the policy be defeated by denial of an added sanction; how serious or deserved would be the forfeiture suffered by the plaintiff, how gross or undeserved the defendant's windfall.'") (quoting from Town Planning & Engr. Assocs. v. Amesbury Specialty Co., 342 N.E.2d 706 (Mass. 1976)); Baugh v. Novak, 340 S.W.3d 372 (Tenn. 2011) ("'the objects and reach of the statute, its subject-matter, the mischiefs aimed to be corrected, the class of persons sought to be controlled, and whether the legislative intention will be subserved by holding the policy contract valid or invalid'") (quoting from Biggs v. Reliance Life Ins. Co., 195 S.W. 174 (Tenn. 1917)). *See also* Restatement Second §178 (another, similar list), followed in Alaska v. Pub. Safety Employees Ass'n, 257 P.3d 151 (Alaska 2011) and K. Miller Constr. Co. v. McGinnis, 938 N.E.2d 471 (Ill. 2010).

§5.5 n.13 p.71 Add the following after the first sentence: *Cf.* K. Miller Constr. Co. v. McGinnis, 938 N.E.2d 471 (Ill. 2010) (normally "an amendatory change in the language of a statute creates a presumption that it was intended to change the law as it previously existed," but legislative history may show otherwise; here, that history states that the amendment "is a clarification of the prior statute and must be accepted as a legislative declaration of the meaning of the original Act.").

§5.5 n.13 p.71 Add the following at the end: For an extreme insistence upon legislative history, *see* Penunuri v. Sundance Partners, 257 P.3d 1049 (Utah App. 2011) (construing statute on liability for risks of equine activities; in absence of legislative history, declines to "pluck a principle of public policy from the text of a statute"; distinguishes contrary interpretation of almost identical statute on skiing injuries on the grounds that the skiing statute "includes a declaration of public policy" which became "the centerpiece" of the state supreme court's review) (quoting from Rothstein v. Snowbird Corp., 175 P.3d 560 (Utah 2007) (reading skiing statute as intended to allow ski area operators to purchase liability insurance at reasonable rates; accordingly, resorts could not use pre-injury releases to pare back or even eliminate the cause for that insurance)), *cert. granted*, No. 20110565 (Utah Oct. 20, 2011).

§5.5 n.14 p.71 Add the following to the list after **"Accord"***:* Fleissner v. Fitzgerald, 937 N.E.2d 1152 (Ill. App. 2010) (statute requiring that home improvement contracts over a certain size be in writing; "we cannot say that the oral contract in this case violated the public policy behind the Act, as we do not have a consumer who was deceived by a 'fly by night' contractor. Rather, the case involves an honest contractor seeking payment for performed services, which the consumer contends were devalued by alleged damage incurred during the work."); Simaee v. Levi, 802 N.Y.S.2d 493 (App. Div. 2005) (statute requiring that sales of substantial interests in hospitals be approved by a regulator did not warrant holding such a contract unenforceable; "the statute does not expressly provide that its violation will deprive parties to a contract of their right to sue for enforcement, and regulatory sanctions are in place in the event that a violation occurs").

§5.5 n.17 p.72 Add the following after the citation to **Pearsall***:* *Cf.* Unger v. Leviton, *supra* note 10 (where partner asserted illegal filling out of HUD form as defense to suit by other partner for share of resale profit, "the relief from this contractual burden would reflect a legal climate in which crime does, in fact, pay"). *But see* Neve v. Davis, 775 N.W.2d 80 (S.D. 2009) (pursuant to statute, refusing to enforce promissory note for loan used in modest part to pay a gambling debt).

Although it arises in an unusual factual context, the California Appellate Court's handling of a challenge to "tiered" rates for water usage is instructive. California was facing severe water supply challenges in 2015 when the court decided Capistrano Taxpayers Assn., Inc. v. City of San Juan Capistrano, 235 Cal. App. 4th 1493 (2015), in which water customers challenged a tiered system under which high-volume users paid more per cubic-foot of water used, relying on a state constitutional provision (adopted by voter initiative, "Proposition 218") that requires service fees to be proportional to use. The court recognized the difficulties in supplying adequate water to Southern California, *id.* at 1496-97, but held that the water district had not demonstrated that its pricing system was consistent with the state constitution, which "requires public water agencies to calculate the actual costs of providing water at various levels of usage," *id.* at 1497. However, it essentially invited the water districts to redesign a tiered system that would accomplish the same disparate pricing for high-volume users if they could demonstrate that they were in fact "passing on the true, marginal cost of water to those consumers whose extra use of water forces water agencies to incur higher costs to supply that extra water," *id.* at 1516.

§5.5 n.20 p.73 Add the following after the first sentence: *Accord:* Coma Corp. v. Kans. Dep't of Labor, 154 P.3d 1080 (Kan. 2007) (undocumented worker's employment contract fully enforceable via the state's pay act; collecting cases); Jara v. Strong Steel Door, 871 N.Y.S.2d 363 (App. Div. 2009) ("neither the contract at issue nor the work . . . performed was illegal").

Cuellar-Aguilar v. Deggeller Attractions, Inc., 812 F.3d 614 (8th Cir. 2015) involved workers who were lawfully employed in the United States under the H2-B visa program. Because H2-B regulations, unlike those applicable to the H2-A program, did not provide for a contractual relationship with the employer, the district court had concluded that, under federal law, there was no contract and dismissed their breach of contract claim that alleged failure to pay the minimum wage. The Eighth Circuit reversed, holding that existence of a contract is a question of state law and need not be found in federal regulations (even if other aspects of the transaction are governed by federal law). *Id.* at 618.

***§5.5 n.20 p.73 Add the following to the list after* "See":** Carter v. Cohen, 116 Cal. Rptr. 3d 303 (Ct. App. 2010) ("a plaintiff's awareness that he or she may be participating in improper conduct does not bar relief under a statute if raising such a barrier would defeat the aim of the statute"); Maudlin v. Pac. Decision Sci. Corp., 40 Cal. Rptr. 3d 724 (Ct. App. 2006) (allowing employer not to pay agreed-upon deferred compensation because the original agreement was structured to avoid taxes would yield "staggering" unjust enrichment, given that the employee's conduct "involved little, if any, moral turpitude" and the employer "was clearly guilty of the greater moral fault").

§5.5 n.20 p.73 Add the following after the second sentence: *Cf.* Packard v. OCA, Inc., 624 F.3d 726 (5th Cir. 2010) ("The focus of the public policy exception to the rule general[ly] prohibiting recovery by parties to illegal contracts is properly on the *public's* interest, not the parties'.") (emphasis in original).

§5.5 n.20 p.73 Add the following at the end: *But cf.* R.A.C. v. Bd. of Educ. of City of N.Y., 799 N.Y.S.2d 559 (App. Div. 2005) (refusal to enforce contract between former public employee and contractor, where former employee unlawfully steered business to contractor; "although barring the [former employee] from recovering under the subject contract may result in a windfall to [the contractor], precluding such recovery is consistent with the public policy sought to be served by imposing post-employment restrictions . . .").

§5.5 n.22 p.74 Add the following after the citation to* Cohen*: , followed in Perricone v. Perricone, 972 A.2d 666 (Conn. 2009) (upholding confidentiality agreement as part of marital settlement against First Amendment challenge; "we conclude that a party's contractual waiver of the first amendment's prohibition on prior restraints on speech constitutionally may be enforced by the court even if the contract is not narrowly tailored to advance a compelling state interest").

§5.5 n.23 p.74 Add the following at the end: *Accord:* Frishman v. Maginn, *supra* note 12 (contract for the sale of unregistered securities violated Regulation D, 17 C.F.R. §§230.501-230.506, issued pursuant to the Securities Act of 1933, because not all investors were accredited; contract unenforceable as to all investors).

§5.5 n.24 p.74 Add the following to the list after* "Accord"*: Hickey v. Scott, 738 F. Supp. 2d 55 (D.D.C. 2010) (waiver of malpractice claim unenforceable as violation of Rule of Professional Conduct 1.8(g)(1)); McIntosh v. Mills, 17 Cal. Rptr. 3d 66 (Ct. App. 2004) (lawyer's fee-sharing agreement with non-lawyer violated Rules of Professional Conduct and thus was unenforceable on public policy grounds); Morrison v. West, 30 So. 3d 561 (Fla. App. 2010) (lawyer's contingent fee agreement unenforceable when not admitted in Florida and not associated with Florida lawyer, because of both the Rules of Professional Conduct and Florida statutory law); Law Offices of Ronald J. Palagi v. Howard, 747 N.W.2d 1 (Neb. 2008) (requirement that departing lawyer forfeit all fees earned from former clients violated Code of Professional Responsibility and Rules of Professional Conduct and thus was unenforceable); Cardillo v. Bloomfield 206 Corp., 988 A.2d 136 (N.J. Super. App. Div. 2010) (agreement in which attorney agreed not to represent any clients against litigants in the future violated Rules of Professional Conduct and thus was unenforceable on public policy grounds); LoPresti v. Rutland Regional Health Servs., 865 A.2d 1102 (Vt. 2004) (allegations that medical group violated AMA Principles of Medical Ethics stated a claim for wrongful discharge in violation of public policy); Rich v. Simoni, 2014 U.S. Dist. LEXIS 257 (N.D. W.Va. Apr. 10, 2015) (rule of professional ethics prohibiting fee sharing with non-lawyer is a statement of public policy with the force of law equal to that given to statutes), 2014 U.S. Dist. LEXIS 138352, at *45 (N.D. W.Va. Apr. 10, 2015) ("Since any claim to compensation by Simoni is based on a fee-splitting agreement, if the agreement was void ab initio because it violated West Virginia public policy, Simoni could not reasonably have relied on Rich's promise, and therefore could not have any reasonable expectation of receiving compensation, whether under a theory of unjust enrichment, quantum meruit, or breach of implied contract."), 772 S.E.2d 327 (W. Va. 2015) (professional conduct rule that "proscribes the sharing of fees between lawyers or law firms and non-lawyers, is an explicit judicial declaration of West Virginia public policy with the force and effect of law. Accordingly, a fee-sharing agreement between a lawyer or a law firm and a non-lawyer that violates the provisions of Rule 5.4 of the West Virginia Rules of Professional Conduct is void as against public policy and wholly unenforceable.").

§5.5 n.24 p.74 ***Add the following after the second sentence of the first paragraph:*** *But see* Mohanty v. St. John Heart Clinic, 866 N.E.2d 85 (Ill. 2006) (opinion of the AMA Council on Ethical and

Judicial Affairs "while informative, is not the equivalent of an Illinois statute or rule of professional conduct and, for that reason, does not provide a clear expression of the public policy of this state.").

***§5.5 n.26 p.75 Add the following to the list after* "Accord":** Cabot Oil & Gas Corp. v. Huffman, 705 S.E.2d 806 (W. Va. 2010) ("Typically, the law that is in effect at the time a contract is executed is the law that thereafter applies to and governs the parties' agreement."; change in law barring permits for oil and gas rights did not apply to land already conveyed by state under deed reserving oil and gas rights).

§5.5 n.26 p.75 Add the following new paragraph after the first paragraph: In a curious decision arising from odd facts, one court held that a contract rendered illegal by subsequent referenda remained unenforceable even after the referenda were held unconstitutional, as the short-lived referenda invalidated the contracts, and the contracts could not then be resuscitated even after the death of the referenda. White v. J.M. Brown Amusement Co., 601 S.E.2d 342 (S.C. 2004). For unconstitutional acts to have this effect is surprising, at least in the absence of reliance upon the transitory illegality by the other contracting party.

§5.5 n.30 p.76 Add the following at the end: Contracts with the federal government are subject to the *unmistakability doctrine* and the *sovereign acts doctrine.* Under the former, the government has a defense against contract claims "where existing terms of a contract to which the United States is a party conflict with subsequently enacted federal legislation." NRDC v. Kempthorne, 621 F. Supp. 2d 954, 984 (E.D. Cal. 2009). In other words, federal contracts prevail over the decisions of later Congresses "only if those contracts contain an unmistakable promise." Kimberly Assoc. v. United States, 261 F.3d 864, 869 (9th Cir. 2001). The doctrine does not apply when the government acts as a private party, or where the legislation is directed toward particular contract rights. United States v. Winstar Corp., 518 U.S. 839 (1996) (private party). The complementary sovereign acts doctrine "provides that government as contractor cannot be held liable for the acts of government as regulator." Far W. Fed. Bank v. Office of Thrift Supervision, 119 F.3d 1358 (9th Cir. 1997).

§5.6 APPLICATION TO COMMERCIAL BRIBERY, UNLICENSED CLAIMANTS, AND IMPROPER USE

§5.6 n.6 p.77 Add the following to the list after **"Accord"***:* S.E.L. Maduro (Fla.) v. M/V Santa Lucia, 116 F.R.D. 289 (D. Mass. 1987) (kickback by stevedoring company to agent for shipper; on attempt by stevedoring company to secure payment, "it is beyond doubt that commercial bribery clearly contravenes a strong public policy and that the Court, in the due administration of justice, cannot enforce a contract that is obtained by that means").

§5.6 n.14 p.79 In the first paragraph, add the following to the list after **"Accord"***:* Tradewinds Envtl. Restoration v. St. Tammany Park, LLC, 578 F.3d 255 (5th Cir. 2009) (unlicensed mold remediation contractor unable to recover for work performed, as the licensing statutes "were enacted to protect an interest vital to the public order") McIntosh v. Mills, 17 Cal. Rptr. 3d 66 (Ct. App. 2004) (the public policy against "the unwholesome spectre of attorneys soliciting professional liaisons with laypersons" strong enough to warrant finding fee-splitting agreement illegal); Wachovia Bank v. Coffey, 698 S.E.2d 244 (S.C. App. 2010) (lender unable to enforce mortgage because its preparation of legal documents in connection with the loan was unauthorized practice of law), extended in Matrix Fin. Servs. v. Frazer, 714 S.E.2d 532 (S.C. 2011) (equitable subordination unavailable to lender because its preparation of legal documents in connection with the loan was unauthorized practice of law).

§5.6 n.14 p.79 Add the following after the citation to **Solomon***:* , distinguished by D'Angelo Dev. & Constr. Co. v. Cordovano, 897 A.2d 81 (Conn. 2006) (unlike *Solomon*, the cumulative penalties applying to unlicensed contractors "are adequate to deter noncompliance with the act's provisions").

§5.6 n.19 p.82 In the first paragraph, add the following to the list after **"Accord"***:* D'Angelo Dev. & Constr. Co. v. Cordovano, *supra* note 14 (contractor unaware of licensing requirements and, on learning of them, sought certificate immediately and did not begin work until the certificate was received; "the purpose of the contract was not to violate the law but to effectuate an otherwise legal transaction"); Lutz Homes v. Weston, 19 So. 3d 60 (Miss. 2009) ("Once a license has been obtained, the disqualification is removed and an action may be brought to enforce a residential building or sales contract, regardless of whether the contract was made before or after the license was acquired."); Ron Medlin Constr. v. Harris, 704 S.E.2d 486 (N.C. 2010) (unlicensed contractor a general partner of business which held license, but signed contract as an individual rather than on behalf of the business; "a contract for the construction of a home or building executed by a partner in a licensed partnership . . . is the contract of the partnership unless the remaining partners can show that the partner was not authorized to act on behalf of the partnership," so the partnership did have a contract with the owner and could not recover in quantum meruit).

§5.6 n.19 p.82 Add the following after the citation to **DeReggi Constr. Co.***:* , followed in Baltimore St. Bldrs. v. Stewart, 975 A.2d 271 (Md. App. 2009) ("substantial compliance with the licensing statute entitles a contractor to enforce a home improvement contract"; no recovery here because contractor never secured license).

§5.6 n.19 p.82 In the first paragraph, add the following to the list after **"But see"***:* Milloy v. Woods, 23 So. 3d 48 (Ala. Civ. App. 2009) (home builder completed project in 2002 but was not issued a license until 2005; because the builder was unlicensed "when he contracted to perform work on Milloy's house . . . [the builder] was statutorily barred from maintaining a breach-of-contract action against Milloy"); ParkWest Homes v. Barnson, 238 P.3d 203 (Idaho 2010) ("Although work done by ParkWest while unregistered was illegal, work done after it registered was certainly legal. . . . Thus, ParkWest is entitled to a lien for work or labor it provided and materials it supplied during the time that it was duly registered.").

§5.6 n.20 p.82 Add the following to the list after **"Accord"***:* D'Angelo Dev. & Constr. Co. v. Cordovano, *supra* note 14 (where statute regulating home improvement contractors provided for invalidation but statute regulating home construction silent, this "suggests that the legislature did not intend for non-compliant new home construction contracts to be deemed invalid or unenforceable"); Timber Ridge, Inc. v. Hunt Country Asphalt & Paving, 671 S.E.2d 789 (W. Va. 2008) (where real estate appraisers and real estate brokers are statutorily barred from seeking compensation if unlicensed, implying a similar bar for unlicensed home contractors "would clearly exceed our mandate as a judicial body").

Legislative responses to the "sharing economy" may spark public attention to these doctrines. For example, in May 2015 the City of Santa Monica, California, passed an ordinance to define any short-term (under 30 days) use of a home for compensation without the owner's presence as a "vacation rental" and prohibited, while short-term use of the home with the owners in residence was permissible "home sharing" only if homeowner obtained a license and paid a transient occupancy tax. Santa Monica Muni. Code §§6.20.010-6.20.100. It provides for fines, imprisonment, and reimbursement for investigative costs (which are planned to include surveying the streets to find homes that match images of AirBnB listings, NPR, "Santa Monica Cracks Down On Airbnb, Bans 'Vacation Rentals' Under a Month," May 13, 1015), and remittance of "all illegally obtained rental revenue to the City," Santa Monica Muni. Code §6.20.100, but does not explicitly provide that the contracts are unenforceable. Taking a somewhat different approach, in April 2016, the Los Angeles City Council proposed an ordinance that would permit "home sharing" rentals if the host registered with the city, obtained a license, operated according to various restrictions, and revealed all platforms being used. Hosting platforms also would have to register with the city and cooperate in identifying any listings that did not comply with the ordinance. Los Angeles City Council, Draft Ord. No. CPC-2016-12435-CA (Apr. 15, 2016), available at http://planning.lacity.org/ordinances/docs/HomeSharing/STROrdinancePublicDraft.pdf; *see also* Emily Alpert Reyes, L.A. Plan Would Demand Airbnb Hand Over Information So City Can Track Down Illegal Rentals, Los Angeles Times, Apr. 15, 2016; Dakota Smith, From

Immigration to Short-Term Housing to Street Vendors, L.A. City Hall Faces a Heavy Agenda, Los Angeles Times, Jan. 2, 2017 (at some point in 2017, the LA "City Council is expected to finally pass a law to regulate short-term housing rentals"). *See also* Liam Dillon, California Lawmakers Can't Figure Out What To Do With Airbnb. Here's Why, Los Angeles Times, May 7, 2017.

§5.6 n.21 p.83 Add the following to the list after **"Accord"***:* Carter v. Cohen, 116 Cal. Rptr. 3d 303 (Ct. App. 2010) (tenant allowed to recover excess rent payments even though property rented lacked certificate of occupancy: "Courts have . . . permitted parties to obtain benefits under a law enacted for their protection, despite their participation in transactions that contravened the law."); Medina v. Safe-Guard Prods., 78 Cal. Rptr. 3d 672 (Ct. App. 2008) ("holding an insurance contract *void* because the insurer was not licensed is about the worst possible remedy for the illegality of the insurer's unlicensed status"; therefore, "[i]n the case of a contract issued by an unlicensed insurer, where the *only* taint of illegality is the unlicensed status of the insurer itself, and the Legislature has already provided a scheme of penalties against that insurer, the contract is readily severable as to any claims that the innocent consumer might present"); Dist. Bd. of Trustees v. Morgan, 890 So. 2d 1155 (Fla. App. 2004) (association of architects lacked required certificate of authorization, but architects themselves had licenses; knowing about the lack of certification, employer fired architects after most of the work had been performed and asserted public policy defense; allowing enforcement of contract by architects, because "there was no risk that professional architectural services would be foisted on the public, in general, and on the [employer], in particular, by unlicensed persons").

§5.6 n.22 p.83 Add the following to the list after **"Cf."***:* White v. Cridlebaugh, 100 Cal. Rptr. 3d 434 (Ct. App. 2009) (not only can an owner seek the disgorgement of any amounts paid to an unlicensed contractor, but the unlicensed contractor cannot reduce the recovery authorized by asserting claims of offset, indemnity, or contribution arising out of the unlicensed work), extended in Alatriste v. Cesar's Exterior Designs, 108 Cal. Rptr. 3d 277 (Ct. App. 2010) (California statute bars recovery by

unlicensed contractor even if the owner knew at the time of contracting or performance that the contractor was unlicensed).

§5.6 n.22 p.83 Add the following to the list after **"But see":** Van Zanen v. Qwest Wireless, 522 F.3d 1127 (10th Cir. 2008) (insurance supplied by unlicensed entity, and client seeks restitution; "it is *granting* restitution to the Van Zanens that would effect an injustice . . . Indeed, if the unlicensed party has performed but has not been paid, that party may have a claim in restitution for the benefit conferred."); Restatement (Third) of Restitution and Unjust Enrichment §32 & cmts. e & f (2011).

§5.6 n.22 p.83 Add the following at the end: But unjust enrichment goes only so far. One who pays for unlicensed services may not be able to recover those fees in a subsequent legal action against a third party whose conduct created the need for the services unlawfully rendered, whether directly or via restitution. Webb *ex rel.* Webb v. Clark Cnty. Sch. Dist., 218 P.3d 1239 (Nev. 2009) (unlicensed psychologist treated student injured by teacher; fees unrecoverable in suit against school district). Presumably the injured student may bring an action sounding either in contract or in unjust enrichment against the unlicensed provider, though whether that right is hollow is another question.

§5.6 n.27 p.84 Add the following after the citation to **Carroll:** , explored in Spanbauer, Selling Sex: Analyzing the Improper Use Defense to Contract Enforcement through the Lens of Carroll v. Beardon, 59 Clev. St. L. Rev. 693 (2011).

§5.6 n.27 p.84 Add the following after the citation to **Potomac Leasing:** , followed by De Lage Landen Fin. Servs. v. Cricket's Termite Control, 942 So. 2d 1001 (Fla. App. 2006) (contract for sale of automatic dialing equipment enforceable, even though the equipment was put to an unlawful use; the equipment had some lawful uses and the equipment was not used in "flagrant violation of the fundamental rights of man and society").

§5.6 n.27 p.84 Add the following at the end: *But cf.* Zenon v. R.E. Yeagher Mgmt. Corp., 748 A.2d 900 (Conn. App. 2000) (as part of attempt to evade liquor licensing laws, true owner arranged

for false owner to make application, and true owner executed a note to the false owner; when false owner sought to collect on the note, owner was denied recovery, because "[t]he execution of this note was integral to the implementation of the unlawful operation of the facility" and "the liquor licensing requirements are for the protection of the public and common good").

§5.7 MITIGATION IN GENERAL

§5.7 n.2 p.86 Add the following at the end: Cf. Baugh v. Novak, 340 S.W.3d 372 (Tenn. 2011) ("Tennessee courts should be particularly hesitant to decline to enforce an otherwise valid contract when the party seeking to avoid its contractual obligations has already received the benefit of the other party's performance."; purchaser of stock cannot be allowed to benefit from a declaration that an indemnification agreement it made was unenforceable, when the purchaser had already received his share of the profits and the business had closed with no assets).

§5.7 n.3 p.86 Add the following to the list after **"But cf.":** Baugh v. Novak, 340 S.W.3d 372 (Tenn. 2011) (parties made contract to avoid stock transfer restraints contained in earlier agreement with different party).

§5.7 n.3 p.86 Substitute the following for the parenthetical following the citation to **Korea Life Ins.**: ("evidence shows that *both* parties intended to engage in a transaction in violation of Korean law and structured transaction to escape eyes of regulators").

§5.8 DIVISIBILITY

§5.8 n.2 p.87 Add the following at the end: See Trilegiant v. Orbitz, LLC, 993 N.Y.S.2d 462 (N.Y. Sup. Ct. 2014) (data-pass agreement, under which customer credit card information was conveyed to business partner, was made illegal by Restore Online Shopper Confidence Act three years after Orbitz canceled the

agreement, but Orbitz was required to continue making termination payments under the Master Services Agreement (MSA); "if these sophisticated parties to the original MSA wanted Orbitz's promise to pay each quarterly termination payment to be contingent on Trilegiant's continued use of DataPass and subsequent forfeiture of revenues, they could have so stipulated in the MSA (see NYSCEF Doc. No. 89 at p 6, Entered 10/7/2013). This Court finds that Orbitz's promise to pay all quarterly termination payments is supported by the same bargained-for consideration given by Trilegiant in exchange for Orbitz's various promises in the MSA as a whole.").

***§5.8 n.4 p.87 In the first paragraph, add the following to the list after* "Accord":** Venturi & Co. v. Pac. Malibu Dev. Corp., 92 Cal. Rptr. 3d 123 (Ct. App. 2009) (unlicensed real estate broker performed both brokerage services and non-brokerage services, such as helping develop a marketing strategy and give financial advice; remanding for trial court to determine which services required no license and thus would be compensable); Junho Hyon v. Selten, 60 Cal. Rptr. 3d 896 (Ct. App. 2007) (where single fee provided for all activities, including for unlawful attorney referrals, "[b]y statute, the contract is therefore void in its entirety").

§5.8 n.4 p.87 Add the following to the end of the second paragraph: *Accord*: Booker v. Robert Half Int'l, 413 F.3d 77 (D.C. Cir. 2005) (Roberts, J.) (presence of severability clause supports enforcement of arbitration clause less an illegal ban on punitive damages); ManorCare Health Servs. v. Stiehl, 22 So. 3d 96 (Fla. App. 2009) (enforcing arbitration provision in nursing home agreement because remedial limitations potentially severable by arbitrator); *In re* Poly-Am., 262 S.W.3d 337 (Tex. 2008) ("An illegal or unconscionable provision of a contract may generally be severed so long as it does not constitute the essential purpose of the agreement. . . . The relevant inquiry is whether or not parties would have entered into the agreement absent the unenforceable provisions. . . . the intent of the parties, as expressed by the severability clause, is that unconscionable provisions be excised where possible"; provisions barring punitive damages or reinstatement excised and rest of arbitration clause enforced). For an unusual application, *see In re* Wolf and Taylor, 197 P.3d 585 (Or. App. 2008) (dissolution of domestic partnership, where dissolution agreement provided for dog visitation rights, and one party sought to rescind based on the illegality of the dog visitation provision; "[W]hether an agreement regarding visitation of a dog is illegal certainly is an interesting question," but one unnecessary to reach, because a severability clause would at most require that the offending provision be severed and the rest of the agreement enforced). More broadly, courts dealing with contracts here as elsewhere seek to give effect to the intent of the parties. A severability clause obviously is an important indicator of intent, but its absence is not necessarily fatal. *See* Mousa v. Saba, 218 P.3d 1038 (Ariz. App. 2009) ("A contract may be severed, however, only if its terms clearly show the parties intended it to be severable."; unlicensed broker unable to establish any specific amount he was promised for his non-brokerage services). And, like other contractual rights, severability can be waived by the parties to the agreement. Thus, for example, the parties to a contract with a generally enforceable arbitration clause that included an unenforceable class action waiver and a severability clause were free not to sever the infirm waiver from the rest of the arbitration clause, with the result that the whole arbitration clause was rendered unenforceable. Herron v. Century BMW, 693 S.E. 394 (S.C. 2010).

§5.8 n.5 p.88 Add the following after the first sentence: *Accord:* Orthodontic Ctrs. of Ill. v. Michaels, 403 F. Supp. 2d 690 (N.D. Ill. 2005) (although business management agreement between orthodontist and corporation unenforceable because it violated laws against the corporate practice of dentistry, promissory notes for advances from the corporation to the orthodontist so that the orthodontist could open her practice enforceable "so long as [the corporation] 'can establish [its] claim without requiring the aid or proof of the illegal contract' ") (quoting from Cent. Repub. Trust Co. v. Evans, 37 N.E.2d 745, 751 (Ill. 1941)); MKB Mgmt. v. Melikian, 108 Cal. Rptr. 3d 899 (Ct. App. 2010) (unlicensed real estate broker allowed to recover for services for which broker's license not needed, but not otherwise).

§5.8 n.6 p.88 Add the following at the end of the second sentence: and in Huskinson & Brown v. Wolf, 84 P.3d 379 (Cal. 2004) (attorney's fees: "Where services are rendered under a contractual compensation arrangement that is unenforceable as against public policy, but the subject services are not otherwise prohibited, quantum meruit may be allowed."), in turn followed in Fair v. Bakhtiari, 125 Cal. Rptr. 3d 765 (Ct. App. 2011) ("Attorneys who violate a rule of professional conduct *may* recover in quantum meruit where they do not act in violation of an express statutory prohibition when providing legal services and where the subject services are not otherwise prohibited."; no recovery where attorney entered into business transactions adverse to his clients without first obtaining consent, thus breaching an absolute prohibition of this type of relationship every time he performed legal services).

§5.8 n.6 p.88 Add the following to the list after* "Cf."*: Santoro v. Accenture, 748 F.3d 217, 222 (4th Cir. 2014) ("[despite legislative prohibition of mandatory arbitration of whistleblower claims, i]t does not follow, however, that Dodd-Frank likewise prohibits the arbitration of non-whistleblower claims simply because an arbitration agreement does not carve-out Dodd-Frank whistleblower claims. Instead, we think the language, context, and enactment of the statute lead to the opposite conclusion.").

§5.8 n.8 p.88 Add the following at the end: *Cf.* Illinois v. Schlabach, 965 N.E.2d 585 (Ill. App. 2012) (plea bargain, in which the agreement as to one charge was unenforceable; the whole plea agreement was rendered voidable, because the plea bargain implicitly linked the proposed sentence on one charge to the proposed sentence on the other).

§5.8 n.11 p.89 Add the following to the list after* "Accord"*: *In re* OCA, Inc. (Woehrle v. Orthalliance New Image), 552 F.3d 413 (5th Cir. 2008) (business service agreements with orthodontists under which corporation "conducted the financial and marketing activity of the practices, . . . maintained the facilities, equipment, and support personnel required to operate the practices . . . stipulated how much each Orthodontist was required to work, and greatly restricted their ability to perform services outside" violated laws banning the corporate practice of dentistry; illegal provisions were essential parts of the contract and thus could not be severed); MKB Mgmt. v. Melikian, 108 Cal. Rptr. 3d 899 (Ct. App. 2010) (for purposes of motion to dismiss, "we cannot conclude, based on the complaint alone, that the property management agreement had a single, unlawful object or that the violation of the real estate licensing statutes so permeated the entire agreement as to render the entire agreement void"); Duffens v. Valenti, 74 Cal. Rptr. 3d 311 (Ct. App. 2008) (dating services contracts lacking mandatory disclosures and containing contrary language about refunds of deposits; arbitration clause not severable because "[t]he defects in these agreements are central to the policy of the statutes"); Chiba v. Greenwald, 67 Cal. Rptr. 3d 86 (Ct. App. 2007) (cohabitation agreement contained agreement to serve as agent; agent was unlicensed, and court found the agency and the cohabitation sufficiently entwined that the agreement as a whole was enforceable); Ga. Props. v. Dalsimer, 835 N.Y.S.2d 41 (App. Div. 2007) (portion of agreement that waived provisions of rent control law not severable from the rest; "[w]here the main objective of an agreement is illegal, courts will not sever and enforce incidental legal clauses"); Star Direct v. Dal Pra, 767 N.W.2d 898 (Wis. 2009) ("In the context of multiple non-compete provisions in a contract, indivisibility will usually be seen by an intertwining, or inextricable link, between the various provisions via a textual reference such that one provision cannot be read or interpreted without reference to the other."), followed in Frank D. Gillitzer Elec. Co. v. Andersen, 780 N.W.2d 542 (Wis. App. 2010) (concededly reasonable training reimbursement provision divisible from concededly unreasonable non-compete provision; these provisions "can be independently read and understood" and "do not share identical factual triggers").

§5.8 n.11 p.89 Add the following at the end: *Cf.* Barber v. Barber, 38 So. 3d 1046 (La. App. 2010) (illegality of part of a contract does not render the whole unenforceable unless it can be presumed that the contract would not have been made without the unenforceable part).

§5.8 n.14 p.90 Add the following after the first sentence: *Accord:* Prusky v. Reliastar Life Ins. Co., 445 F.3d 695 (3d Cir. 2006) (insurance policy enforceable even after insurer barred illegal late trading; "the primary purpose of the contract or an essential part of the agreed exchange [was] not affected by disregarding the illegal provision").

§5.8 n.15 p.90 In the first paragraph, add the following to the list after **"Accord"***:* Ross v. Union Carbide Corp., 296 S.W.3d 206 (Tex. Civ. App. 2009) ("an invalid release and assignment of workers' compensation claims can be severed from the remainder without doing violence to the parties' agreement," where "there is no evidence that the parties would have declined to execute a Release that did not dispose of claims for statutory workers' compensation benefits").

§5.8 n.19 p.91 Add the following to the list in the first sentence: *In re* Martin, 596 F. Supp. 2d 142 (D. Mass. 2009) (deleting "any" and "including but not limited to" list from exculpatory clause and enforcing the balance).

§5.8 n.20 p.91 Add the following to the list after **"Accord"***:* Dicen v. New Sesco, Inc., 839 N.E.2d 684 (Ind. 2005) (striking entire employment covenant because geographic limitation "unreasonably broad"; "[w]e decline to utilize a blue pencil to strike the geographical limitation, because the result would be no geographical limitation at all"); Eastern Bus. Forms v. Kistler, 189 S.E.2d 22 (S.C. 1972) (provision of 100-mile radius "furnishes no basis for dividing this territory"), applied in Rockford Mfg. v. Bennet, 296 F. Supp. 2d 681 (D.S.C. 2003) ("First . . . the contract must be severable. Second, the severability must be apparent from the contract itself — in language and subject matter"; holding that a list of companies is severable, while a 100-mile radius emphatically is not).

§5.8 n.20 p.91 Add the following to the list after **"Cf."***:* Sharvelle v. Magnante, 836 N.E.2d 432 (Ind. App. 2005) (wielding blue pencil to strike words in overbroad non-solicitation clause, but not using it to rewrite scope of non-competition clause).

§5.8 n.20 p.91 Add the following at the end: The consequence may thus be that the employer ends up with less

protection than it would have had if it had drafted more conservatively. *Cf.* Cent. Ind. Podiatry v. Krueger, 882 N.E.2d 723 (Ind. 2008) (bluepenciling geographic scope written in terms of counties; consequence is to exclude some close-by areas where the county as a whole extends too far).

***§5.8 n.21 p.92 In the first paragraph, add the following to the list after* "Accord":** Freiburger v. J-U-B Eng'rs, 111 P.3d 100 (Idaho 2005) (whole clause unenforceable where "it would be necessary not only to strike some of the words . . . but in addition, to add clauses . . . This is far more than a 'blue pencil' approach to an unreasonable word or two . . ."); Class Action Claim Servs. v. Clark, 892 So. 2d 595 (La. App. 2004) ("when a non-compete clause is overbroad in its geographical boundaries, the Court should delete the overbroad portions and enforce the remainder of the geographic restriction"); Cobb v. Caye Publ'g Grp., 322 S.W.3d 780 (Tex. Civ. App. 2010) ("If the trial court in a suit to enforce a covenant not to compete determines that the limitations as to time, geographic area, or scope of activity in the covenant are unreasonable, the court shall reform the covenant to the extent necessary to cause the limitations to be reasonable and to impose a restraint that is not greater than necessary to protect the goodwill or other business interest of the promisee and enforce the covenant as reformed."; limiting geographic scope to area in which employee actually worked and not area in which employer had targeted for expansion).

***§5.8 n.21 p.92 In the first paragraph, add the following after the citation to* Bess:** , more or less followed in Thiesing v. Dentsply Int'l, 748 F. Supp. 2d 932 (E.D. Wis. 2010) (Minnesota law: cites to *Bess* in dictum supporting the court's ability to revise obnoxious clauses, not just blue-pencil them, but then employs traditional blue-penciling).

***§5.8 n.21 p.92 In the first paragraph, add the following after the citation to* Fullerton Lumber Co.:** abrogated by Wis. Stat. §103.465 ("Any covenant . . . imposing an unreasonable restraint is illegal, void and unenforceable even as to any part of the covenant that would be a reasonable restraint."), in turn applied in Star Direct v. Dal Pra, *supra* note 11 ("This statute was passed in 1957 in response to our decision[] in *Fullerton Lumber Co. . . .*").

§5.8 n.21 p.92 ***In the second paragraph, add the following to the list in the second sentence:*** Keener v. Convergys Corp., 342 F.3d 1264 (11th Cir. 2003) (Georgia "applies strict scrutiny to restrictive covenants in employment contracts").

§5.8 p.93 ***In the first full paragraph, add the following to the end of the first sentence:*** . . . and then uphold them.[22a]

[22a] *See* Cambridge Eng'g v. Mercury Ptnrs. 90 BI, 879 N.E.2d 512 (Ill. App. 2007) ("Such reformation, if permitted by courts, would give employers an incentive to draft restrictive covenants as broadly as possible, since the courts would automatically amend and enforce them to the extent that they were reasonable in the particular circumstances of each case. This could have a severe chilling effect on employee post-termination activities; an employee unschooled in the law cannot be expected to know to what extent such a covenant is enforceable, particularly since courts apply a multifactor reasonableness standard rather than a bright-line rule.").

§5.8 n.23 p.93 ***Add the following to the list after "Accord":*** Broadley v. Mashpee Neck Marina, 471 F.3d 272 (1st Cir. 2006) (citing to treatise; declining to narrow overbroad exculpatory clause because of "the extreme overbreadth of the clause and the plainness of its illegality, the boilerplate character of the contract and lack of specific negotiation, the absence of an explicit reference to negligence which would provide better warning, and the attorney's fees clause"); Applied Materials v. Advanced Micro-Fabrication Equip. (Shanghai) Co., 630 F. Supp. 2d 1084 (N.D. Cal. 2009) ("The Court is not permitted to apply any narrowing construction to limit the application of the Assignment Clause"); Cambridge Eng'g v. Mercury Partners 90 BI, *supra* note 22a ("when deciding whether modification is appropriate, the fairness of the restraints contained in the contract is a key consideration"); Payroll Advance v. Yates, 270 S.W.3d 428 (Mo. App. 2008) ("We are not convinced . . . that a trial court is compelled to take action to modify an agreement it finds broader than necessary. The issuance and terms of an injunction rest largely in the sound discretion of the trial court . . ."); Poynter Invs. v. Century Bldrs. of Piedmont, 694 S.E.2d 15 (S.C. 2010)

("the restrictions in a non-compete clause cannot be rewritten by a court or limited by the parties' agreement, but must stand or fall on their own terms").

§5.8 n.23 p.93 Add the following at the end: *Cf.* Atlanta Bread Co. Int'l v. Lupton-Smith, 679 S.E.2d 722 (Ga. 2009) ("Since in-term restraints contained in franchise agreements are subject to strict scrutiny, they cannot be blue-penciled if found to be unreasonable as to time, territory or scope."); H & R Block E. Enters. v. Swenson, 745 N.W.2d 421 (Wis. App. 2007) (where time periods in noncompetition and nonsolicitation clauses are unreasonable, "each clause is void and unenforceable even if each is otherwise reasonable"). For a scholarly defense of this technique, *see* Ben-Shahar, Fixing Unfair Contracts, 63 Stan. L. Rev. 869 (2011). *See generally* Restatement (Third) of Employment Law §8.08 (T.D. No. 4, Apr. 11, 2011) (allowing judicial modification of otherwise unenforceable restrictive covenants, subject to the duty of good faith; lack of good faith may be shown by "its gross overbreadth alone, or by overbreadth coupled with other evidence that the employer sought to do more than protect its legitimate interests").

§5.9 RESTITUTION

§5.9 n.1 p.94 Add the following to the list after **"Accord"***:* Morrison v. West, 30 So. 3d 561 (Fla. App. 2010) (no recovery in quantum meruit for work done under contingent fee agreement by lawyer unlicensed in Florida; noting that quantum meruit might be available to Florida lawyer working under unenforceable contingent fee agreement, because the representation is not itself unlawful); Local 798 Realty Corp. v. 152 W. Condo., 866 N.Y.S.2d 51 (App. Div. 2008) (no recovery in restitution for work done as part of scheme to defraud; "plaintiff never sought, or agreed to accept, the work that defendants were performing on the property, and the services were rendered strictly to benefit defendants").

§5.9 n.1 p.94 Add the following after the third sentence: *Cf.* Cohen v. Brown, 93 Cal. Rptr. 3d 24 (Ct. App. 2009) (permitting *quantum meruit* recovery under unlawful fee-splitting arrangement by attorney who had done work); Strong v. Beydoun, 83 Cal. Rptr. 3d 632 (Ct. App. 2008) (attorney engaged through unlawful fee-splitting arrangement may not recover in quantum meruit from client; recourse is against the attorney with whom she made the arrangement).

§5.9 n.2 p.95 Add the following to the list after "Accord": King v. Riedl, 58 So. 3d 190 (Ala. Civ. App. 2010) (statute requiring that building contractors be licensed, and that residential home builders may not bring suit under any contracts entered into when they were unlicensed, also disallows actions based on non-contractual theories); Castillo v. Barrera, 53 Cal. Rptr. 3d 494 (Ct. App. 2007) (unlicensed boxing manager: "The Boxing Act is a regulatory statute, and recovery on a quantum meruit theory in the absence of compliance with the act would be inconsistent with its regulatory purpose."); TTSI Irrevocable Trust v. ReliaStar Life Ins. Co., 60 So. 3d 1148 (Fla. App. 2011) (owner of policy lacked insurable interest, and sought restitution of premiums paid; "[A]s a general rule, contracts that are void as contrary to public policy will not be enforced by the courts and the parties will be left as the court found them. . . . We see no reason to depart from the general rule where, as in the instant case, the party seeking to enforce the contract is the only party who engaged in deceptive and misleading conduct at the time the contract was entered into.").

§5.9 n.3 p.95 Add the following at the end: *Accord:* Van Zanen v. Qwest Wireless, 522 F.3d 1127 (10th Cir. 2008) (denying restitution of payments made to unlicensed insurance agent when clients received the agreed-upon insurance; this denial serves the rationales "(1) that recognizing a claim for unjust enrichment would provide a remedy not intended by the licensing statute; (2) that restitution would itself be inequitable by affording a windfall to the plaintiff; (3) that a plaintiff has adequate remedies at law if performance by the unlicensed person is substandard; and (4) that a party who has rendered performance under a contract is not unjustly enriched because it has not retained a benefit without paying for it") (citations omitted); Fausnight v. Perkins, 994 So. 2d 912 (Ala. 2008) (no restitution for clients of unlicensed home builder; statute already provides for penalties, so "the legal maxim *expressio unius est exclusio alterius* applies"; in addition, "we do not believe that creating an inequitable situation where one does not already exist is a proper use of the courts") (quoting from Schank v. Schuchman, 106 N.E. 127 (N.Y. 1914) (Cardozo, J.: "The law may at times refuse to aid a wrongdoer in getting that which good conscience permits him to receive; it will not for that reason aid another in taking away from him that which good conscience entitles him to retain.")). *See generally* Restatement (Third) of Restitution and Unjust Enrichment §32(2) & cmt. *f* (2011) ("There is no unjust enrichment if the claimant receives the counter performance specified by the parties' unenforceable agreement.").

§5.9 n.5 p.95 Add the following to the list after* Edwards*: Wald v. Truspeed Motorcars, 108 Cal. Rptr. 3d 542 (Ct. App. 2010) (allowing recovery in restitution against dealer for unlicensed salesperson's commissions; the licensing statute is to protect members of the public, not employers, and the employer in any case bears the greater moral fault, because "[i]t knew of the licensing statutes, it seeks to enjoy a tangible windfall based on Wald's work and deny him all recompense for it"); Barry v. Pac. W. Constr., 103 P.3d 440 (Idaho 2004) (allowing recovery in restitution for unlicensed contractor, as to do otherwise "is a harsh result, particularly where the public entity has not sought any remedy for the breach of the public policy" and where the general contractor had already been compensated for the work done by the unlicensed subcontractor), distinguished in Farrell v. Whiteman, 200 P.3d 1153 (Idaho 2009) (architect unlicensed in Idaho but licensed elsewhere allowed to recover in unjust enrichment for work done for client; "it would be contrary to the public interest to allow a developer to avoid any payment for architectural services when the work performed was not sub-standard, the building was actually constructed, and several units were sold"); Fleissner v. Fitzgerald, 937 N.E.2d 1152 (Ill. App. 2010) (owner invoked statute requiring that home improvement contracts of a certain size be in writing; restitution available because "[t]o hold otherwise would allow a consumer to renege on an otherwise valid oral contract after work is performed and enjoy the benefits of his improved property at the expense of the contractor.").

§5.9 n.5 p.95 Add the following after the first sentence: Cf. Town of Gilbert Prosecutor's Office v. Downie, 189 P.3d 393 (Ariz. 2008) (restitution in criminal proceeding against unlicensed contractor; rejecting a rule of total disgorgement by the contractor, instead holding that "determining a victim's 'loss' requires consideration of any benefits conferred on the victim").

§5.9 n.6 p.95 Add the following after the first sentence: Accord: Carlton at the Lake, Inc. v. Barber, 928 N.E.2d 1266 (Ill. App. 2010) (Nursing Home Care Act's requirement of signature of patient or guardian on contract to provide services would not bar a claim in quantum meruit; "only an issue of *execution* caused the contract to be unenforceable," and allowing the home to recover in quantum meruit "will not defeat the purposes of the act"); Shafer Elec. & Constr. v. Mantia, 96 A.3d 989, 996 (Pa. 2014) (where home improvement contract failed to provide toll-free consumer protection hotline number, specify start date, or comply with other technical requirements of the Home Improvement Consumer Protection Act, contractor could bring claim in quantum meruit; "[i]t is well-settled at common law, however, that a party shall not be barred from bringing an action based in *quantum meruit* when one sounding in breach of express contract is not available."). How this applies to the attorney-client relation has yielded a large and not always coherent body of authority. In general, a fairly technical problem with the attorney-client relation may bar a breach of contract action by the attorney against the former client, but generally allows recovery in restitution — if without good cause, perhaps under any prior contingent fee agreement as well. Hoover Slovacek LLP v. Walton, 206 S.W.3d 557 (Tex. 2006). Sufficient infirmities in performance may, however, result in no recovery under any theory for the breaching lawyer. Restatement (Third) of Restitution and Unjust Enrichment §32 cmt. *e*. If the problem arises in a contract between successive attorneys, the outgoing attorney still has only a right in restitution. However, the attorney may elect either a standard restitutionary recovery or a reasonable contingent fee, determined either at the time of substitution or the end of the case. Nabi v.

Sells, 892 N.Y.S.2d 41 (App. Div. 2009). *But cf.* Eichholz Law Firm v. Tate Law Grp., 714 S.E.2d 413 (Ga. App. 2011) (discharged attorney and replacement attorney entered into fee-splitting agreement based on contingent fee arrangement; the contract is unenforceable, but the discharged law firm "may seek to recover in quantum meruit for services it provided to the Tate firm pursuant to their joint venture"). And substantial infirmities in a contract for legal representation may bar any recovery, including recovery in restitution. *See* Restatement (Third) of Restitution and Unjust Enrichment §32 ill. 7.

§5.9 n.12 p.97 Add the following to the list after "Accord": Medina v. Safe-Guard Prods., 78 Cal. Rptr. 3d 672 (Ct. App. 2008) ("obviously an innocent consumer who buys an insurance contract from an unlicensed insurance company is far 'less morally blameworthy' than the company that does not disclose its unlicensed status prior to contracting").

§5.9 n.16 p.97 Add the following to the list after "Accord": Gamboa v. Alvarado, 941 N.E.2d 1012 (Ill. App. 2011) (fraudulent agreement to procure legal immigration documents by bribing officials to expedite the paperwork; the plaintiffs here were not *in pari delicto* with the defendants, because they "spoke little English, did not know defendants were lying/unable to deliver on their promises and would not necessarily know the agreement was illegal or that . . . they had recourse under" a part of the consumer protection statute directed specifically at fraudulent immigration services; furthermore, that statute "was clearly passed for the protection of persons such as plaintiffs and would be best served if plaintiffs are allowed to proceed with their claims" under restitution, inter alia).

§5.9 n.20 p.98 Add the following at the end: The *locus poenitentiae* is perhaps more familiar from criminal law, as the time during which a conspirator may withdraw from a conspiracy and thus secure an affirmative defense if charged with any substantive crimes later carried out by her former conspirators. The basic rule here is much like that in contract, suitably tweaked to allow for context. "What is required is an 'affirmative act bringing home the fact of his withdrawal to his confederates,' made in time for his companions to effectively abandon the conspiracy and in a way which would be sufficient to inform a reasonable man of the withdrawal." 2 W. LaFave, Substantive Criminal Law §12.4(b) (2011) (quoting from Loser v. Super. Ct., 177 P.2d 320 (Cal. App. 1947)). *Cf.* Model Penal Code §5.03(7)(c) (withdrawal occurs "only if and when he advises those with whom he conspired of his abandonment or he informs the law enforcement authorities of the existence of the conspiracy and of his participation therein").

CHAPTER 6

THE REQUIREMENT OF A WRITING: THE STATUTE OF FRAUDS

§6.1 HISTORY AND FUNCTIONS OF THE STATUTE

§6.1 n.3 p.102 Add the following after the third sentence: *Cf.* Lindsay v. McEnearney Assocs., 531 S.E.2d 573 (Va. 2000) ("The purposes of [the Statute of Frauds] are to provide reliable evidence of the existence and terms of certain types of contracts and to reduce the likelihood that contracts within the scope of this statute can be created or altered by acts of perjury or fraud.").

§6.1 n.5 p.103 Add the following at the end: , discussed in Beaver v. Brumlow, 231 P.3d 628 (N.M. App. 2010).

§6.1 n.9 p.104 Add the following after the first sentence: *See* Chateau des Charmes Wines Ltd. v. Sabaté USA, 328 F.3d 528 (9th Cir. 2003) ("Within such a framework, the oral agreements between Sabaté USA and Chateau des Charmes as to the kind of cork, the quantity, and the price were sufficient to create complete and binding contracts. . . . In this respect, the regime of the C.I.S.G. differs from that of the Uniform Commercial Code, which would require a contract for the sale of corks for the value involved here to be evidenced by a writing. *See* U.C.C. §2-201.").

§6.1 n.9 p.104 Add the following at the end: *See* Forestal Guarani, S.A. v. Daros Int'l, 613 F.3d 395 (3d Cir. 2010) (contract between U.S. firm and Argentinian firm; because Argentina made an Art. 96 reservation, the forum state's court must use its own choice-of-law rules to determine which forum's law applies, and then apply the law of the forum designated by that analysis).

§6.1 p.105 Add the following footnote at the end of the second sentence of the first complete paragraph: . . . perform this function to some degree.[13a]

[13a] It is, however, important not to take this evidentiary purpose too far. "Although the Statute of Frauds was designed to serve an evidentiary purpose, it is not a rule of evidence. In cases of loss or destruction, the contents of a memorandum may be shown by an unsigned copy or by oral evidence." Restatement Second §137 cmt. *a.* See *infra* §6.7 n.58.

§6.1 n.14 p.105 Add the following after the second sentence: *Accord:* Waddle v. Elrod, 367 S.W.3d 217 (Tenn. 2012) (a purpose of the land contract statute of frauds "is to protect property owners against 'hasty or inconsiderate agreements concerning a valuable species of property' and 'misunderstandings as to the nature and extent of such agreements' ") (quoting from Brandel v. Moore Mtg. & Inv. Co., 774 S.W.2d 600, 604 (Tenn. App. 1989)).

§6.1 n.15 p.105 Add the following at the end: *See* N. Coast Cookies v. Sweet Temptations, 476 N.E.2d 388 (Ohio App. 1984) ("This statute serves to ensure that transactions involving a transfer of realty interests are commemorated with sufficient solemnity. A signed writing provides greater assurance that the parties and the public can reliably know when such a transaction occurs. It supports the public policy favoring clarity in determining real estate interests and discourages indefinite or fraudulent claims about such interests.").

§6.1 n.16 p.105 Add the following at the end: *Accord:* Ohanian v. Avis Rent A Car Sys., 779 F.2d 101 (2d Cir. 1985) ("Whatever may be the fact with regard to the history of the statute, and whatever may have been the difficulties arising from proof that all sides agree brought about the enactment of the statute of frauds over 300 years ago, it is an anachronism today. The reasons that prompted its passage no longer exist. And, far from serving as a barrier to fraud-in the case of a genuinely aggrieved plaintiff barred from enforcing an oral contract-the statute may actually shield fraud.").

§6.1 n.19 p.106 Add the following to the list after **"See also"***:* Burns v. McCormick, 135 N.E. 273 (N.Y. 1922) (Cardozo, J.) ("The peril of perjury and error is latent in the spoken promise.").

§6.1 n.19 p.106 Add the following to the list after the third sentence: For a plainer statement of this idea, *see* Kluver v. PPL Mont., 293 P.3d 817 (Mont. 2012) ("[T]he purpose of the statute of frauds is to prevent fraud.").

§6.1 n.20 p.106 Add the following at the end of the first paragraph: On Lord Kenyon's willingness to let morality dictate the law and his mistrust of markets, *see* Hay, Lloyd Kenyon, in Oxford Dictionary of National Biography (online ed. 2009; accessed Jan. 20, 2013) ("Concern for moral principle appeared to govern Kenyon's decisions at least as much as concern for the letter of law."; refers to "Kenyon's hostility to market reasoning"); on Lord Kenyon's general abilities, *see* 4 J. Campbell, Lives of the Chief Justices 48 (1881) ("[H]e had not acquired enough general knowledge to make him ashamed or sensible of his ignorance, and without the slightest misgiving he blurted out observations which exposed him to ridicule.").

§6.1 n.20 p.106 Add the following at the end of the second paragraph: As one treatise-writer dryly put it, the Statute of Frauds "has been most productive of litigation." E. Harriman, Elements of the Law of Contracts 193 (1896).

§6.1 n.21 p.106 In the second sentence, replace the citation to **Bernstein** *with the following:* Braunstein, Remedy, Reason, and the Statute of Frauds: A Critical Economic Analysis, 1989 Utah L. Rev. 383.

§6.1 n.22 p.107 Add the following after the second sentence: *See generally* Classic Cheesecake Co. v. JPMorgan Chase Bank, 546 F.3d 839 (7th Cir. 2008) (Posner, J.: "the statute of frauds has long been controversial"; citing to treatise).

§6.2 SCOPE OF THE STATUTE

§6.2 n.1 p.108 Add the following at the end: *Accord:* MP Innovations v. Atl. Horizon Int'l, 899 N.Y.S.2d 213 (App. Div. 2010) (the statute of frauds, "by its own terms, applies to implied as well as express contracts"). At the risk of stating the obvious, the Statute of Frauds is relevant only if there is a contract of some sort. Hanson v. Legasus of N.C., 695 S.E.2d 499 (N.C. App. 2010) ("An agreement is a pre-requisite to a contract and thus also a pre-requisite to a contract which is compliance with the Statute of Frauds."). As a corollary, whether there is a contract is not the same question as whether a contract is enforceable. If it were, then there would be no statute of frauds. *But see* Thomas J. Sibley, P.C. v. Brentwood Inv. Dev. Co., 356 S.W.3d 659 (Tex. Civ. App. 2011) (unsigned writing not a bar to forming a contract where the parties performed according to its terms; because the fact that the writing was unsigned did not prevent a contract from being formed, it also would not prevent that contract from being enforced; court seems blithely unaware of its horrible non sequitur).

§6.2 n.2 p.108 Add the following to the end: The original Statute of Frauds placed the limit at £10, an amount equal to roughly $2,000 today.

§6.2 n.3 p.108 Add the following to the end of the second sentence: , taking into account the probable inflation between the time of the amendment and the time of any subsequent amendment.

§6.2 n.10 p.109 Add the following to the list in the first sentence: Tex. Occ. Code Ann. §1101.806(c).

§6.2 n.10 p.109 Add the following to the list in the second sentence: Duncan v. F-Star Mgmt., 281 S.W.3d 474 (Tex. Civ. App. 2008) (insufficiently detailed description of real property to satisfy the statute, and part performance exception not satisfied because alleged performance not unequivocally referable to the contract).

§6.2 n.14 p.110 Add the following after the citation to the* Ohio Revised Code*: *See also* Brocail v. Detroit Tigers, 268 S.W.3d 90 (Tex. Civ. App. 2008) (Michigan statute requires that promises of cures relating to medical care or treatment be in writing, apart from actions in negligence). (So much for *Hawkins v. McGee*!).

§6.2 n.14 p.110 Add the following to the list in the final sentence: Green v. Midland Mtg. Co., 342 S.W.3d 686 (Tex. Civ. App. 2011) ("Under Tex. R. Civ. P. 11, no agreement between the attorneys or parties to a suit is enforceable unless it is in writing, signed, and filed with the papers as part of the record, or unless it is made in open court and entered of record."); Affordable Erecting v. Neosho Trompler, 715 N.W.2d 620 (Wis. 2006) (under Wis. Stat. §807.05, settlement agreements must be in a signed writing or recorded in the minutes of the court).

§6.2 n.14 p.110 Add the following at the end: An increasingly important writing requirement applies to promises relating to commercial lending, enacted in response to a wave of lender liability litigation. Cal. Civ. Code §1624(a)(7); Fla. Stat. Ann. §687.0304; Ind. Code §26-2-9-4; Ky. Rev. Stat. §371.010; La. Rev. Stat. §1122; Minn. Stat. §513.33, subd. 2; Mo. Stat. Ann. §432.047; Neb. Rev. State. §§45-1,112 & 1,113; Ohio Rev. Code §1335.02. For representative decisions construing these, see Fortress Sys. v. Bank of the W. 559 F.3d 848 (8th Cir. 2009) (Nebraska law); Thomas & Wong Gen. Contr. v. Lake Bank, 553 F.3d 650 (8th Cir. 2009) (Minnesota law); Metro Bldg. Materials v. Republic Nat'l Bank, 919 So. 2d 595 (Fla. App. 2006); Sees v. Bank One, 839 N.E.2d 154 (Ind. 2005); Farmers Bank & Trust Co. v. Willmott Hardwoods, 171 S.W.3d 4 (Ky. 2005); Bailey v. Hawthorn Bank, 382 S.W.3d 84 (Mo. App. 2012). These statutes are at times considerably more stringent than the general Statute of Frauds. For example, some require that the writing actually be received from the party to be charged, and some expressly eliminate the usual exceptions to the statute. *See, e.g.*, S.C. Code Ann. §37-10-107 (both). Some also extend well outside enforcement of the lending agreement. Colorado's statute, for example, requires a sufficient writing for any action or claim *relating to* a credit agreement above $25,000. Colo. Rev. Stat. §38-10-124(2). For an illustration of its scope, *see* Dalton v. Countrywide Home Loans, 828 F. Supp. 2d 1242 (D. Colo. 2011) (lending statute of frauds bars claims for fraudulent misrepresentation, promissory estoppel, unjust enrichment, breach of fiduciary duty, breach of the implied covenant of good faith and fair dealing, and outrageous conduct insofar as they are based on the lender's alleged oral representations).

Furthermore, not all writing requirements are statutory. For example, in Georgia "at-will employees cannot enforce oral promises." Goddard v. City of Albany, 684 S.E.2d 635, 640 (Ga. 2009).

§6.2 n.15 p.110 Add the following to the list in the first sentence: Unif. Arbitration Act §6(a); Conn. Rev. Stat. §52-408; 710 Ill. Comp. Stat. §5/1.

***§6.2 n.21 p.111 Add the following to the list after* "Accord":** ; Automated Cutting Technologies v. BJS N. Am. E, Inc., 78 U.C.C. Rep. Serv. 2d 93 (E.D. Ky. 2012) (same).

§6.2 n.24 p.112 Add the following after the first sentence: *Accord:* Battalino v. Van Patten, 917 A.2d 595 (Conn. App. 2007) ("The rent specified in a written lease may be reduced by oral agreement, at least between the original lessor and lessee, without violating the statute of frauds. . . . The agreement may be proved by the lessee's offer and the lessor's acceptance without protest of the reduced payment."); Apple's Mobile Catering v. O'Dell, 233 P.3d 142 (Idaho 2010) (oral agreement to modify sale of goods contract within UCC 2-201(1) enforceable where original contract was in writing and contract as modified was fully performed). *Contra:* Plasma Centers of Am. v. Talecris Plasma Res., 731 S.E.2d 837 (N.C. App. 2012) (the rule allowing a party to avoid enforcement if there is no written memorandum "also applies to the modification of contracts that must be in writing");

Linton v. E.C. Cates Agency, 113 P.3d 26 (Wyo. 2005) ("if the original agreement was required to comply with the statute of frauds, any material modification of that agreement must also conform to the statute of frauds").

***§6.2 n.26 p.112 In the first paragraph, add the following to the list after* "Contra":** Upperline Equip. Co. v. J & M, Inc., 724 F. Supp. 2d 883 (E.D. Tenn. 2009) (applying UCC 2-209(3) to oral modification of date deposit was due); Woodland Harvesting v. Ga. Pac. Corp., 693 F. Supp. 2d 732 (E.D. Mich. 2010) ("all contracts and contract modifications must be signed and in writing if the contract is subject [to] the statute of frauds").

***§6.2 n.26 p.112 In the second paragraph, add the following to the list after* "See":** McCann v. U.S. Bank, 873 F. Supp. 2d 823 (E.D. Mich. 2012) (applying Michigan statute barring the oral modification of lending agreements); Labrant v. Mortgage Elec. Registration Sys., 870 F. Supp. 2d 671 (D. Minn. 2012) (lender statute of frauds applies to loan modifications); Kelmor, LLC v. Ala. Dynamics, 20 So. 3d 783 (Ala. 2009) (contract for sale of land: oral modification of closing date was a substantive change, particularly because the writing stated that time was of the essence, so it would have had to meet the requirements of the statute of frauds); Best v. Edwards, 176 P.3d 695 (Ariz. App. 2008) ("[A]n amendment to a real estate option purchase agreement that modifies a material term, such as the option's expiration date, must comply with the statute of frauds."); Secrest v. Sec. Nat'l Mtg. Loan Trust, 84 Cal. Rptr. 3d 275 (Ct. App. 2008) (agreement to forbear from exercising foreclosure right is a modification of a contract within the statute of frauds and thus is itself within the statute of frauds), followed in Clark v. Countrywide Home Loans, 732 F. Supp. 2d 1038 (E.D. Cal. 2010) (oral modification of loan agreement barred by Statute of Frauds); Plasma Centers of Am. v. Talecris Plasma Res., 731 S.E.2d 837 (N.C. App. 2012) (writing requirement "also applies to the modification of contracts that must be in writing"); Am. Garment Props. v. CB Richard Ellis-El Paso, 155 S.W.3d 431 (Tex. Civ. App. 2004) (real estate brokerage contract; oral modification to lower commission "materially [a]ffects the obligations of the underlying agreement" and thus is unenforceable absent a writing); Iota, LLC v. Davco

Mgmt. Co., 284 P.3d 681 (Utah App. 2012) ("'[W]hen a contract is required to be in writing, the same requirement applies with equal force to any alteration or modification thereof.'") (quoting from Fisher v. Fisher, 907 P.2d 1172, 1176 (Utah App. 1995)).

***§6.2 n.28 p.113 In the first paragraph, add the following to the list after* "Accord":** Dolansky v. Frisillo, 939 N.Y.S.2d 210 (App. Div. 2012) ("a parol discharge of a contract for the sale of land is valid"; even though written contract contains no-oral-modifications clause, "the word 'changed' does not include cancellation or termination," so an oral termination is barred neither by the statute of frauds nor by the NOM clause);

§6.2 n.28 p.113 Add the following at the end of the first paragraph: *Dolansky* raises an important point for drafting. Parties to a contract may put in place their own statute of frauds by requiring that modifications to the contract must be in writing in order to be enforceable. If they do so, however, they should be careful about the scope of the no-oral-modifications clause — in particular, about whether the clause encompasses only modifications, or also cancellation or termination.

§6.3 CONTRACTS TO ANSWER FOR THE DUTY OF ANOTHER

***§6.3 n.1 p.114 In the fourth paragraph, add the following to the list after* "See":** P. Alces, The Law of Suretyship and Guaranty (2d ed. 2003).

§6.3 n.2 p.114 Add the following after the first sentence: *Accord:* Hartford Fire Ins. Co. v. C. Springs 300, Ltd., 287 S.W.3d 771 (Tex. Civ. App. 2009) (quoting from Restatement; in addition, "A contract to enter a contract covered by the statute of frauds must also meet the statute of frauds.").

§6.3 n.9 p.116 Add the following at the end: *But see* E. Harriman, Elements of the Law of Contract 195 (1896) (defending majority approach; "The better rule, however, is that such contracts are not within the statute, because [B].'s promise is really a promise to [C]. to pay any claim that [X] may have against [C].; so that the promise is to the debtor, [C]., and not to the creditor, [X]. It is in reality not the contingent liability of [A] to [C]. but the liability of [C]. to [X] for which [B]. agrees to be answerable to [C].").

§6.3 p.118 Add the following to the end of the carryover sentence at the top of the page: . . . loan is to be repaid.[11a]

[11a] Consequently, older cases invoking the so-called "preexisting debt rule" as a limit on the application of the statute of frauds are unsound. Rosewood Care Ctr. v. Caterpillar, Inc., 877 N.E.2d 1091 (Ill. 2007) ("there is no preexisting debt rule").

§6.3 n.15 p.119 In the second sentence, add the following to the list after "Accord": *In re* Stout, 474 B.R. 803 (Bankr. S.D. Tex. 2012) (agreement between president of company and lender not within statute, where president made clear that he wanted to borrow individually, that he would pay back the money, that the money should be wired to his personal bank account, and that he had spent some of the money on personal items; even though president apparently signed in his official capacity, the debtor "orally assumed primary liability for the loan, not a guaranty liability"); Abadie v. Bacino, 91 So. 3d 1220 (La. App. 2012) (parents' promise to pay client's legal fees in child custody dispute was original between parents and attorney, not a guarantee of a contract between attorney and client);

§6.3 n.15 p.119 Add the following at the end: *Cf.* Concordia Gen. Contracting v. Peltz, 782 N.Y.S.2d 848 (App. Div. 2004) (subcontractor's promise to perform its work despite general contractor's default provided consideration for the owner's oral promise to pay, and the parties intended that the owner should be a principal debtor; consequently, the oral contract fell outside the suretyship statute of frauds).

§6.3 n.38 p.124 In the first paragraph, add the following to the list after "See": ; Cruz v. Andrews Restoration, 364 S.W.3d 817 (Tex. 2012) ("[T]he question is not who was the primary *beneficiary*, but whether [the promisor's] primary *purpose* in promising to pay was to benefit itself.") (emphasis in original).

§6.3 n.38 p.124 In the second paragraph, add the following after the citation to* Heese Produce Co.*: , reaffirmed by Garnett v. Genetic Improvement Servs. (*In re* Estate of Dueck), 736 N.W.2d 720 (Neb. 2007) (quoting parenthetical passage with approval).

§6.3 n.38 p.124 In the second paragraph, add the following to the list after* "But see"*: Shelton v. Kennedy Funding, 622 F.3d 943 (8th Cir. 2010) ("The surety prong of the Arkansas Statute of Frauds only applies when the would-be surety does not receive new consideration for his promise.").

§6.3 n.39 p.125 Add the following after the citation to* Burlington Indus.*: , distinguished in Terrell v. Kaplan, 613 S.E.2d 526 (N.C. App. 2005) (guarantor was president of original debtor; modification of note stated that she had agreed to become a guarantor of the note, and that the modification was made in consideration of her promise; and guarantor was primary beneficiary of estate of co-owner of original debtor). For one version of the test, *see* Cruz v. Andrews Restoration, 364 S.W.3d 817 (Tex. 2012) ("The main purpose doctrine requires that: (1) the promisor intended to create primary responsibility in itself to pay the debt; (2) there was consideration for the promise; and (3) the consideration given for the promise was primarily for the promisor's own use and benefit — that is, the benefit it received was the promisor's main purpose for making the promise.")

§6.3 n.40 p.125 Add the following to the list after* "Accord"*: America's Floor Source v. Joshua Homes, 946 N.E.2d 799 (Ohio App. 2010) (leading object exception applies where guarantor of corporation's debt was the sole shareholder of the corporation; "[the guarantor's] promise to personally pay a portion of his company's debt was clearly in his own best interest, since he wanted [the creditor] to continue providing [the company] with labor and materials, from which [the guarantor] and his company were deriving revenue"), cited to but otherwise ignored in Lind Stoneworks v. Top Surface, 954 N.E.2d 1256 (Ohio App. 2011) (promise by owner of company that he would "take care of" company's debt was within statute of frauds; "[n]o evidence was offered at trial to the effect that [the owner]'s agreement to guarantee [his company]'s debt would have subserved some pecuniary or business purpose of [the owner]'s own or would have benefited him individually");

§6.3 n.41 p.125 Add the following after the citation to **Haas Drilling Co.:** , followed in Cruz v. Andrews Restoration, 364 S.W.3d 817 (Tex. 2012) (main purpose of insurer's agreement to pay repair bills incurred by its insured was for the insurer "to buy time to decide how to proceed with the claim").

§6.3 n.45 p.126 In the first paragraph, add the following to the list in the second sentence: Christian v. Smith, 759 N.W.2d 447 (Neb. 2008) (where surety's interest was "the ownership of the cattle and the potential profits from the sale of the cattle" and the ostensible obligee got only a commission on sale, the leading object exception applied and the oral contract was outside the statute of frauds).

§6.4 CONTRACTS NOT TO BE PERFORMED WITHIN A YEAR

§6.4 n.1 p.129 In the second paragraph, add the following at the end: , followed in McElroy v. Gemark Alloy Ref. Corp., 592 F. Supp. 2d 508 (S.D.N.Y. 2008) (joint venture subject to statute of frauds). *Accord:* Olson v. Halvorsen, 986 A.2d 1150 (Del. 2009) ("Because we can construe the statute of frauds and the LLC Act together and the General Assembly did not clearly intend the LLC Act to render the statute of frauds inapplicable, there is no implied repeal of the statute of frauds."); Olympic Holding Co. v. Ace Ltd., 909 N.E.2d 93 (Ohio 2009) ("a joint-venture agreement that does not comply with the statute of frauds is unenforceable").

§6.4 n.3 p.130 Add the following to the list after* "Accord"*: ; Holloway v. Dekkers, 380 S.W.3d 315 (Tex. Civ. App. 2012) (one-year employment contract was within statute where employee was to begin on August 5 and the contract was made on July 23)

§6.4 n.8 p.131 Add the following to the first sentence, after **"puzzlement among commentators"***:* ; it "no longer seems to serve any purpose very well, and today its only remaining effect is arbitrarily to forestall the adjudication of possibly meritorious claims. For this reason, the courts have for many years looked on the provision with disfavor, and have sought constructions that limited its application"

§6.4 n.8 p.131 Add the following to the list after **"Accord"***:* Leon v. Kelly, 618 F. Supp. 2d 1334 (D.N.M. 2008) ("a contract is incapable of being performed within one year only if it is genuinely impossible that it be performed within one year"; quotes from treatise); Prof'l Bull Riders v. Autozone, Inc., 113 P.3d 757 (Colo. 2005) ("we have long construed the one-year provision narrowly"; citing to treatise).

§6.4 n.8 p.131 Add the following to the end: *But see* LaRue v. Kalex Constr. & Dev., 97 So. 3d 251 (Fla. App. 2012) (the statute of frauds "should be strictly construed").

§6.4 n.9 p.132 Add the following to the list after **"Accord"***:* Loan Modification Grp. v. Reed, 694 F.3d 145 (1st Cir. 2012) (loan modification partnership not of fixed duration and thus not within statute of frauds; although the parties contemplated that the partnership would last for four years, "it could be fully performed within one year and need not last the entire four-year duration"); McElroy v. Gemark Alloy Ref. Corp., *supra* note 1 (joint venture contract not within statute of frauds, because it provided for ending the venture upon reaching a certain level of profitability, which could be reached within one year); Barnes v. Michalski, 925 N.E.2d 323 (Ill. App. 2010) (loan contract not within one-year provision where it was "theoretically possible for [the borrower] to perform the alleged contract within a year," even though loan was for more than half the borrower's annual income); Coady v. Wellfleet Marine Corp., 816 N.E.2d 124 (Mass. App. 2004) (indefinite contract to lease boat slip not within one-year provision; "because the contract here was indefinite, it could

have been performed within one year"); Moses v. Savedoff, 947 N.Y.S.2d 419 (App. Div. 2012) ("The statute of frauds is inapplicable to an agreement to create a joint venture or partnership because an oral agreement for an indefinite period creates a partnership or joint venture at will."); Abatement Inc. v. Williams, 324 S.W.3d 858 (Tex. Civ. App. 2010) (contract with indefinite term of employment not within one-year provision, despite the expectations of the employee; "hopes and expectations are not enough to show performance within a year is impossible"), followed in Kalmus v. Oliver, 390 S.W.3d 586 (Tex. Civ. App. 2012) ("expectation" that performance would take two years insufficient to bring contract within statute of frauds); Browning v. Poirier, 165 So. 3d 663 (Fla. 2015) (oral agreement to purchase and share proceeds of any winning lottery tickets could have been performed within one year and was not within statute of frauds).

§6.4 n.9 p.132 Add the following at the end: *But see* S. Cherry St., LLC v. Hennessee Grp. LLC, 573 F.3d 98 (2d Cir. 2009) (where "the possibility existed that the agreement would not be performed within one year, the duration of the defendant's right and obligation was thus unlimited," so the contract fell within the statute of frauds).

§6.4 n.10 p.132 Add the following after the citation to* C.R. Klewin, Inc.*: , followed in Johnson v. Walden Univ., 839 F. Supp. 2d 518 (D. Conn. 2011) (graduate of doctoral program in psychology alleged that his advisor promised him that he would be able to practice psychology if he earned the degree, which the program in fact did not do; contract not within the statute of frauds, even though completing his coursework and dissertation could not imaginably be completed within one year, because "the implied contract alleged by the plaintiff did not say in express terms that performance would have a specific duration beyond one year")

§6.4 n.10 p.132 In the first paragraph, add the following to the list after* "Accord"*: Warner v. Tex. & Pac. Ry. Co., 164 U.S. 418 (1896) ("The question is not what [the] probable, or expected, or actual performance of the contract was, but whether the contract, according to the reasonable interpretation of its terms, required that it should not be performed within the year."), followed in Morgenweck v. Vision Capital Advisors, 410 Fed. Appx. 400 (2d Cir. 2011) (contract to distribute annual profits by its terms cannot be performed within one year); Lester v. TMG, Inc., 896 F. Supp. 2d 482 (E.D. Va. Sept. 13, 2012) ("at-will employment contracts are not within the Statute of Frauds"); Rudinsky v. Harris, 290 P.3d 1218 (Ariz. App. 2012) (the one-year provision does not apply to oral contracts "when there is a possibility of performance within one year"); Prof'l Bull Riders v. Autozone, Inc., *supra* note 8 (statute covers "only those agreement that exclude, by their very terms, the possibility of performance within one year"); Mackay v. Four Rivers Packing Co., 179 P.3d 1064 (Idaho 2008) (contract to work until retirement not within one-year provision, because "Mackay could have retired within one year under the terms of the alleged contract"); Tobin v. Ruman, 819 N.E.2d 78 (Ind. App. 2004) (at-will employment contract not within statute; "only if it is impossible for an oral contract to be completed within one year does it fall within the Statute of Frauds"); Gelman v. Buehler, 936 N.Y.S.2d 154 (App. Div. 2012) (even though anticipated duration of contract was four to seven years, "it cannot be said that there was absolutely no possibility that performance could not be completed within one year," so the agreement was not within the statute of frauds), *rev'd on other grounds*, 20 N.Y.3d 534, 986 N.E.2d 914 (App. Div. 2013); Cathy Daniels, Ltd. v. Weingast, 936 N.Y.S.2d 44 (App. Div. 2012) (indemnification contract not within statute, even though its actual performance was more than a year after the agreement was made; "the question is not what the actual performance of the contract was, but whether the contract required that it should not be performed within a year"); Birdwell v. Psimer, 151 S.W.3d 916 (Tenn. App. 2004) (loan with five-year payment schedule not within statute; "no proof that the parties agreed that this loan would absolutely not be repaid within one year").

§6.4 n.10 p.132 In the second paragraph, add the following to the list after* "Contra"*: Nasso v. Bio Reference Labs., 892 F. Supp. 2d 439 (E.D.N.Y. 2012) (contract to pay commissions on earnings from accounts procured by plaintiff; the contract had no ending point, so it "is exactly the type of service contract of indefinite and unlimited duration to which the New York courts have held that the Statute of Frauds applies."); Tydir v. Williams, 89 So. 3d 1129 (Fla. App. 2012) (issue is whether it is clear from the object of the contract and the circumstances surrounding its formation "that the agreement between the parties at issue was intended to extend longer than one year"; whether the agreement could be performed within a year is not important); Harriman v. United Dominion Indus., 693 N.W.2d 44 (S.D. 2005) (contract for employment until retirement within one-year provision, for "the contract was intended to be more than one year in duration").

§6.4 n.10 p.132 Add the following at the end: For an ironic application of this rule, *see* Bithoney v. Fulton-DeKalb Hosp. Auth., 721 S.E.2d 577 (Ga. App. 2011) (oral contract with indefinite term within statute of frauds because its termination clause provided for severance payments spread over 15 months).

§6.4 n.11 p.133 Add the following to the list after **"Accord"*:*** Sheehy v. Clifford Chance Rogers & Wells, 822 N.E.2d 763 (N.Y. 2004) (oral agreement to make supplemental retirement payments starting in the fifth year after retirement within Statute of Frauds, as the performance "could not possibly have been completed within one year of the agreement"); Knudson v. Kyllo, 819 N.W.2d 511 (N.D. 2012) (unsigned partnership dissolution agreement provided for allocating the partnership's leased farmland for "each year" after its effective date; held that this agreement could not be performed within one year); Monasco v. Gilmer Boating & Fishing Club, 339 S.W.3d 828 (Tex. Civ. App. 2011) ("The statute of frauds does not apply if performance could conceivably be completed within one year of the agreement's making.").

§6.4 n.13 p.133 Add the following after the first sentence: *Accord:* Prof'l Bull Riders v. Autozone, Inc., *supra* note 8 ("a promise of two or more performances, in the alternative, does not fall within the one-year provision if any one of the alternatives could be fully performed within one year," so option to sponsor events for either one or two years not within statute) (citing to treatise).

§6.4 n.13 p.133 Add the following to the list after **"But cf.":** Sawyer v. Mills, 295 S.W.3d 79 (Ky. 2009) (agreement to make payments monthly for ten years within statute of frauds; "The appropriate inquiry thus is whether . . . the parties contemplated that the contract at issue would be performed within a year, and if, by its terms, it could be. It is irrelevant whether performance would be possible under different terms. A contrary rule — that if it is possible to perform a contract within a year even though such completion is not contemplated by the parties — would eviscerate the Statute of Frauds' requirement that agreements not to be performed within one year be in writing.").

§6.4 n.13 p.133 Add the following to the list after the citation to **"Learning Works":** , followed in Kohanowski v. Burkhardt, 821 N.W.2d 740 (N.D. 2012) (contract to pay money in 36 installments within one-year provision of statute of frauds, in part because it had no express prepayment term)

§6.4 n.15 p.134 Add the following after the citation to **Freedman:** , followed in Gelman v. Buehler, 936 N.Y.S.2d 154 (App. Div. 2012) (venture capital partnership agreement not within statute of frauds; "although the estimated time to achieve a liquidity event was to be four to seven years, it cannot be said that there was absolutely no possibility that performance could not be completed within one year"), *rev'd on other grounds*, 20 N.Y.3d 534, 986 N.E.2d 914 (2013).

§6.4 n.15 p.134 Add the following to the list after **"Accord":** Acoustic Innovations v. Schafer, 976 So. 2d 1139 (Fla. App. 2008) ("[The defendant] could have transferred the shares to [the plaintiff] immediately after forming the oral agreement, had [the plaintiff] requested that he do so. The fact that [the plaintiff] waited until a year had passed to request the shares is of no import."); Mackay v. Four Rivers Packing Co., 179 P.3d 1064 (Idaho 2008) (oral contract of employment "until retirement" not within statute of frauds, "[s]ince Mackay could have retired within one year under the terms of the alleged contract").

§6.4 n.17 p.134 Add the following at the end: *But cf.* Northrup v. Brigham, 826 N.E.2d 239 (Mass. App. 2005) (contract to make will falls within statute of frauds).

***§6.4 n.18 p.135 Add the following to the list after* "Accord":** Laudano v. 214 S. St. Corp., 608 F. Supp. 2d 185 (D. Mass. 2009) ("lifetime employment contracts are an exception to the statute of frauds").

***§6.4 n.22 p.136 Add the following to the list after* "Cf.":** Johnson v. Diamond Shine, Inc., 890 F. Supp. 2d 763 (W.D. Ky. 2012) (oral contract to pay a percentage of gross sales for life not within one-year provision; collecting cases);

§6.4 n.27 p.137 Add the following at the end: *See generally* O'Gorman, The Statute of Frauds and Oral Promises of Job Security: The Tenuous Distinction Between Performance and Excusable Nonperformance, 40 Seton Hall L. Rev. 1023 (2010).

***§6.4 n.28 p.137 Add the following to the list after* "Accord":** Sullivan v. Leor Energy, 600 F.3d 542 (5th Cir. 2010) (Texas law; contract of employment for two and one-half years within the statute of frauds notwithstanding a clause permitting termination upon 30 days' written notice); Tobin v. Ruman, 819 N.E.2d 78 (Ind. App. 2004) (at-will employment contract not within one-year provision, as the employee "could have tendered his resignation or been fired at any time").

***§6.4 n.30 p.138 In the first paragraph, add the following after the citation to* Ohanian:** , followed in Pearce v. Manhattan Ensemble Theater, 528 F. Supp. 2d 175 (S.D.N.Y. 2007) (contract to star in play not within the statute even though it contemplated performance over more than one year; contract also provided for 15 weeks' salary even if the show closed, so it may be "that the parties contemplated termination . . . even before the fifteen-week mark . . . [which] would remove the agreement from the ambit of the Statute of Frauds.").

***§6.4 n.30 p.138 In the first paragraph, add the following after the citation to* Cron:** , followed in Ryan v. Kellogg Ptnrs. Inst'l Servs., 968 N.E.2d 947 (N.Y. 2012) (agreement to extend time for payment of bonus beyond one year not within statute; bonus had vested within one year, employer was entitled to discharge employee within one year, and in any event was for the benefit of the party asserting the statute) but distinguished in Velez v. Sanchez, 693 F.3d 308 (2d Cir. 2012) (agreement to pay for college tuition in exchange for labor within statute of frauds, because the amount to be paid was not fixed within one year).

§6.4 n.30 p.138 In the first paragraph, add the following at the end: The tangles of this case law have ensnared some courts and lawyers. For example, in Robins v. Zwirner, 713 F. Supp. 2d 367 (S.D.N.Y. 2010), a confidentiality agreement between two people was of "unlimited duration." The court held that this agreement was within the Statute of Frauds because the agreement could be terminated within one year only if the party maintaining the confidence breached. But if the agreement was in fact personal, then the obligation of confidentiality would presumably die with the promisor (though it is possible to imagine a contract that would place obligations on the promisor's estate, for example). The court might have reached the same result by relying upon the lifetime provision of the New York Statute of Frauds, discussed at note 25 *supra*. That statute includes any contract the performance of which cannot be completed "before the end of a lifetime," which should include any contracts of unlimited duration.

§6.4 n.30 p.138 In the second paragraph, add the following at the end of the third sentence: , followed in Bennett v. Atomic Prods. Corp., 903 N.Y.S.2d 154 (App. Div. 2010) (agreement to develop and market medical equipment not within statute of frauds, because the defendant had the right to terminate it at will by ceasing its sale of the products; distinguishing *Shirley Polykoff Advertising* because there the agreements required annual payments).

§6.4 n.30 p.138 In the second paragraph, add the following after the third sentence: *Accord:* Gersten-Hillman Agency v. Heyman, 892 N.Y.S.2d 209 (App. Div. 2009) (oral promise to pay renewal commissions after the termination of an at-will employee relation within statute of frauds); distinguished away by *Bennett, supra*, because in *Gersten-Hillman* the duration of performance was determined by the customer, who was not a party to the contract at issue.

§6.4 n.30 p.138 In the second paragraph, add the following at the end of the last sentence: , followed in Rudinsky v. Harris, 290 P.3d 1218 (Ariz. App. 2012) (continuing promise to pay commission on any sales ever made to the customers brought in by the broker; arrangement is indefinite and contemplates performance over extended period, and contract contains no termination clause; collects cases and notes split among courts)

§6.4 n.32 p.139 Add the following at the end: *But cf.* Sullivan v. Leor Energy, 600 F.3d 542 (5th Cir. 2010) (Texas law; notes Restatement approach, but concludes that Texas has nevertheless shown itself "'definitely committed'" to termination clause as irrelevant to scope of one-year provision) (quoting from Gilliam v. Kouchoucos, 340 S.W.2d 27, 29 (Tex. 1960)).

§6.4 n.33 p.139 Add the following to the list after "Accord": Dalkilic v. Titan Corp., 516 F. Supp. 2d 1177 (S.D. Cal. 2007) (oral contract for employment for a minimum of five years not within one-year provision of statute of frauds; contract could have been terminated within one year, even though the contract had no early termination option);

§6.4 n.33 p.139 Add the following at the end: The holding in *Dalkilic* seems overbroad, though its facts and thus its scope are unclear. If, as it would seem, the court found the possibility of termination within one year enough even with no termination clause, then all employment contracts are outside the statute of frauds — that is, all employment contracts that do not forbid termination in the first year, even for cause, a qualification that will exclude few, if any, contracts. Indeed, the same reasoning would go to a contract governed by the common law that is materially breached, or one under Article Two that falls afoul of the perfect tender rule. Those hostile to the one-year provision of the statute of frauds, a very large and respectable group, may applaud the result. But it is hard to imagine that any legislature that has ever enacted this statute of frauds provision meant anything like this reading.

§6.5 CONTRACTS FOR THE SALE OF AN INTEREST IN LAND

§6.5 n.2 p.140 Add the following to the list after **"See also"***:* 200 N. Gilmor, LLC v. Capital One, 863 F. Supp. 2d 480 (D. Md. 2012) ("The statute of frauds was intended to avoid claims to land based on allegations of parol transactions, with the incidental uncertainties and weakening of record titles . . ."); N. Coast Cookies v. Sweet Temptations, 476 N.E.2d 388 (Ohio App. 1984) ("This statute serves to ensure that transactions involving a transfer of realty interests are commemorated with sufficient solemnity. A signed writing provides greater assurance that the parties and the public can reliably know when such a transaction occurs. It supports the public policy favoring clarity in determining real estate interests and discourages indefinite or fraudulent claims about such interests.").

§6.5 n.7 p.141 Add the following at the beginning: See, e.g., Waddle v. Elrod, 367 S.W.3d 217 (Tenn. 2012) ("sale" includes any alienation of real property, including donations of realty).

§6.5 n.7 p.141 Add the following at the end: Nor is an agreement to discharge a contract for the sale of land. Dolansky v. Frisillo, 939 N.Y.S.2d 210 (App. Div. 2012).

§6.5 n.8 p.141 Add the following to the list after **"Accord"***:* Owens v. M.E. Schepp Ltd. P'ship, 182 P.3d 664 (Ariz. 2008) ("an oral partition agreement among tenants in common is 'for the sale of real property' and thus within the scope of [the statute of frauds]"); Quimby v. Myers, 895 A.2d 128 (Vt. 2005) ("a writing is required to transfer real property, already owned by one partner, to another partner or to the partnership") (collecting cases). *See also* Restatement Second §128(2).

§6.5 n.8 p.141 Add the following at the end: Contra: Meyer v. Christie, 634 F.3d 1152 (10th Cir. 2011) (Kansas law: noting existence of *Filippi*, but concluding that, "Although the statute of frauds would apply to a land purchase agreement as between the seller and the purchaser of the property, it does not [a]ffect the

relationship between the parties to the joint venture agreement or their obligations under that agreement.").

§6.5 n.9 p.142 Add the following after the first sentence: *Accord:* Plumitallo v. Hudson Atl. Land Co., 903 N.Y.S.2d 127 (App. Div. 2010) (statute of frauds does not apply to "oral joint venture agreements to deal in real property. . . . The plaintiff is not seeking to acquire an interest in real property, but rather, is asserting an alleged interest in joint venture assets"); Sewing v. Bowman, 371 S.W.3d 321 (Tex. Civ. App. 2012) ("Merely because a partnership agreement contemplates transactions in real estate does not transform the partnership itself into a transaction for the sale of real estate, bringing it under the statute of frauds.").

***§6.5 n.9 p.142 Add the following to the list after* "See":** Lairsen v. Figuerado, 466 Fed. Appx. 480 (6th Cir. 2012) (shares in limited liability company which owned a marina were personal property, not real property);

***§6.5 n.10 p.142 In the first paragraph, add the following to the list after* "Accord":** Ardmore, Inc. v. Rex Grp., Inc., 377 S.W.3d 45 (Tex. Civ. App. 2012) (statute of frauds applies to purchase option in sublease). Pardee v. Jolly, 182 P.3d 967 (Wash. 2008) ("An option to purchase real estate is subject to the statute of frauds."); Tangipahoa Dev. Co. v. Bedico Junction, LLC, 5 So. 3d 238 (La. App. 2008) (agreement extending option period was within statute).

***§6.5 n.11 p.142 Add the following to the list after* "Cf.":** Davis v. Sperry, 288 P.3d 26 (Utah App. 2012) (correcting scrivener's error in option agreement not barred by statute of frauds; testimony went to intent of parties on writing, not to terms of side agreement that would itself require a writing);

§6.5 n.12 p.142 Add the following after the first sentence: *Accord:* DeFriece v. McCorquodale, 998 So. 2d 465 (Ala. 2008) (oral promises made by mother to distribute potential inheritance of real property among children upon her death within the real property statute of frauds); Cragle v. Gray, 206 P.3d 446 (Alaska 2009) ("oral succession contracts that are not reduced to writing are unenforceable"); Ogden v. Griffith, 236 P.3d 1249 (Idaho 2010) (settlement agreement requiring the creation of a deed of trust within the real property statute of frauds).

§6.5 n.12 p.142 Add the following to the list after* "Cf."*: Johnson v. DeKalb Cnty., 726 S.E.2d 102 (Ga. App. 2012) (settlement agreement requiring transfer of land not within the land contract statute of frauds); Grisham v. Grisham, 289 P.3d 230 (Nev. 2012) (stipulated agreement in court not within statute of frauds; "The formality, publicity, and solemnity of an open court proceeding . . . protects parties against hasty and improvident settlement agreements by impressing upon them the seriousness and finality of the decision to settle.") (internal quotation marks omitted).

§6.5 n.12 p.142 Add the following at the end: *But cf.* Waddle v. Elrod, 367 S.W.3d 217 (Tenn. 2012) (settlement agreement requiring the transfer of land is within the land contract statute of frauds)

§6.5 n.15 p.143 Add the following to the list after* "Accord"*: Ogden v. Griffith, 236 P.3d 1249 (Idaho 2010) (settlement agreement requiring the creation of a deed of trust within the real property statute of frauds).

§6.5 n.18 p.143 Add the following at the end: *But cf.* Grant v. Donelson, 79 So. 3d 569 (Miss. App. 2012) (agreement that buyer would have title placed in lender's name in exchange for loan was not within the statute of frauds).

§6.5 n.20 p.144 Add the following to the list in the fifth sentence: ; Dolansky v. Frisillo, 939 N.Y.S.2d 210 (App. Div. 2012) ("a parol discharge of a contract for the sale of land is valid"; even though written contract contains no-oral-modifications clause, "the word 'changed' does not include cancellation or termination," so an oral termination is barred neither by the statute of frauds nor by the NOM clause)

§6.5 n.24 p.144 Add the following to the list after **"Accord"***:* Machado v. Ryan, 280 P.3d 715 (Idaho 2012) (same); Allen v. Allen, 280 S.W.3d 366 (Tex. Civ. App. 2008) (same).

§6.5 n.26 p.144 Add the following at the end: Accord: B & C Investors v. Vojak, 79 So. 3d 42 (Fla. App. 2011) (claims for breach of fiduciary duty and legal malpractice arising from an oral contract to convey real property are not within the land contract provision of the statute of frauds; "they are separate claims which stand on their own based on Vojak's failure to act in BCI's best interests"); Am. Pension Servs. v. Cornerstone Home Bldrs., 213 P.3d 1038 (Idaho 2009) (loan to builder: oral agreement that builder would pay lender $750 per lot sold not within statute; "[a]lthough the parties' agreement contemplated that Cornerstone would enter into agreements with third parties for the sale of real property, as between the parties to this contract, the contract merely defined the terms of loan repayment"); Mangum v. Turner, 255 S.W.3d 223 (Tex. Civ. App. 2008) (oral settlement agreement of dispute over the transfer of deeds not within the real property statute of frauds where the terms involved only the payment of money, as "a real estate transaction is merely incidentally involved.").

§6.5 n.28 p.145 Add the following after the first sentence: Accord: Snyder v. HSBC Bank, 873 F. Supp. 2d 1139 (D. Ariz. 2012) ("A loan modification agreement and deed of trust agreement must be in writing and signed by the party to be charged to be enforceable."); *In re* Whatever, LLC, 478 B.R. 700 (Bankr. W.D. Pa. 2012) ("an interest in land includes mortgages"); Greenstein v. Wells Fargo Bank, N.A., 2017 U.S. Dist. LEXIS 46498 (D. Nev. Mar. 29, 2017) ("Nevada's statute of frauds requires that any agreement related to an interest in land — such as a loan modification — be in writing . . . .") (citing Sarro v. Nev. State Bank, 2016 U.S. Dist. LEXIS 162988 (D. Nev. Nov. 23, 2016) and Hampton v. Countrywide Home Loans, Inc., 2011 U.S. Dist. LEXIS 53715 (D. Nev. May 11, 2011)).

§6.5 n.28 p.145 Add the following to the list in the third sentence: Granadino v. Wells Fargo Bank, N.A., 236 Cal. App. 4th 411 (2015) ("the alleged promise that no foreclosure sale was

scheduled is unenforceable absent a signed writing"); Clark v. Countrywide Home Loans, 732 F. Supp. 2d 1038 (E.D. Cal. 2010) ("Absent a written agreement to modify the loan, any claim based upon an oral contract to modify the loan is barred by the statute of frauds."); Strausser v. Pramco, III, 944 A.2d 761 (Pa. Super. 2008) ("An agreement to forbear from foreclosure, between mortgagor and mortgagee, has been held to represent an interest in land such that the agreement is subject to the Statute of Frauds . . .").

§6.5 n.29 p.145 ***In the second paragraph, add the following to the list in the second sentence:*** Shelton v. Kennedy Funding, 622 F.3d 943 (8th Cir. 2010) ("an oral or unsigned agreement to satisfy a mortgage does not fall within the Arkansas Statute of Frauds" because "it neither creates nor conveys an interest in land").

§6.5 n.30 p.145 ***Add the following at the end:*** *Cf. In re* Whatever, LLC, 478 B.R. 700 (Bankr. W.D. Pa. 2012) (settlement agreement for satisfaction of borrower's obligations under mortgage loan by paying reduced payoff amount was subject to the land contract statute of frauds); Berdick v. Costilla, 97 So. 3d 316 (Fla. App. 2012) (assignment or sublease with a term of more than one year falls within the statute of frauds for real property).

§6.5 n.31 p.146 ***Add the following at the end:*** *See also* Samarasinghe v. C.I.R., T.C. Memo 2012-23, 2012 WL 162716 (T.C. 2012) (construing New Jersey statute providing that lease with term exceeding three years must be in writing and signed by both landlord and tenant). Note that *both* parties must sign, not merely the party against whom performance is sought.

§6.6 CONTRACTS FOR THE SALE OF GOODS

§6.6 n.14 p.148 ***In the second paragraph, add the following after the second sentence:*** One can reconcile these cases by distinguishing between rights of first refusal, which do not fall within Article Two, and option contracts, which do. *See* Johnny Ray Sports v. Wachovia Bank, 982 So. 2d 1067 (Ala. 2007). *But see* Robins v.

Zwirner, 713 F. Supp. 2d 367 (S.D.N.Y. 2010) ("Rights of first refusal and agreements to agree on the sale of a good are both governed by the U.C.C. . . . ").

§6.6 n.19 p.150 Add the following at the end: It should be noted that UCC 2A-201 does contain a Statute of Frauds governing leases of personal property. It requires a writing unless "the total payments to be made under the lease contract . . . are less than $1,000." UCC 2A-201(1)(a).

§6.6 n.21 p.150 Add the following at the end: For a curious non-Code application, see Carcorp, Inc. v. Chesrown Oldsmobile-GMC Truck, 823 N.E.2d 34 (Ohio App. 2004) (where Statute of Frauds governs transactions of over $5,000, "the statute merely limits potential enforceability to $5,000, if its writing requirement is not satisfied").

§6.7 NATURE AND CONTENTS OF WRITING REQUIRED

§6.7 p.152 Add the following at the end of the first paragraph: . . . commonly called a "memorandum."[2a]

[2a] A memorandum is not the same as a contract. The purpose of a memorandum is to show that there is a contract; although of course this will be done if the memorandum contains the entire contract, a memorandum need not have been intended to serve as a contract, and may even be a repudiation of the contract, as discussed later in this section. *See* Hern Family Ltd. P'ship v. Compass Bank, 863 F. Supp. 2d 613 (S.D. Tex. 2012) ("The Statute of Frauds does not require, however, that the contract be in writing; rather, 'the written agreement merely furnishes written evidence of a contract and its essential terms.' ") (quoting from Maginn v. Norwest Mtg., 919 S.W.2d 164 (Tex. Civ. App. 1996)).

§6.7 n.3 p.153 Add the following to the list after ***"Accord":*** Preston Exploration Co. v. GSF, L.L.C., 669 F.3d 518 (5th Cir. 2012) (reading three purchase and sale agreements together, including the exhibits they refer to).

§6.7 n.3 p.153 Add the following after the second sentence: In the words of one treatise-writer, the writings must be "connected, consistent and complete." E. Harriman, Elements of the Law of Contracts 207 (1896).

§6.7 n.3 p.153 Add the following at the end: There is some disagreement whether determining the sufficiency of a writing is a matter of law, of fact, or both, though most jurisdictions treat it as a question of law. *Compare* Public Health Equip. & Supply Co. v. Clarke Mosquito Control Prods., 410 Fed. Appx. 738 (5th Cir. 2010) (Texas law; law), Sterling v. Taylor, 152 P.3d 420 (Cal. 2007) (same), Brown Dev. Corp. v. Hemond, 956 A.2d 104 (Me. 2008) (same), and Blair v. Brownson, 197 S.W.3d 681 (Tenn. 2006) (same) *with* McInnis v. Lind, 108 P.3d 578 (Or. App. 2005) (mixed). *But see* Public Health Equip. & Supply Co. v. Clarke Mosquito Control Prods., *supra* (whether a writing falls within an exception to the statute of frauds is usually a question of fact); Kalmus v. Oliver, 390 S.W.3d 586 (Tex. Civ. App. 2012) ("The question of whether an agreement falls within the statute of frauds is one of law. . . . But determining whether an exception to the statute of frauds applies is generally a question of fact.").

§6.7 n.4 p.153 Add the following at the end: For an observation that misses this point entirely, *see* May Trucking Co. v. N.W. Volvo Trucks, 241 P.3d 729 (Or. App. 2010) ("It is difficult to understand how emails to which plaintiff was not even a party satisfy the requirement of a signed writing evidencing an intention to be bound to an agreement *with plaintiff.*"). *Pace* the court, it is very easy to imagine that an e-mail signed by the party against whom enforcement is sought might satisfy the statute of frauds. If the memorandum is sufficiently detailed, is signed by the party against whom enforcement is sought, and makes clear that the party considers itself bound to an agreement, it does not matter whether the memorandum is sent to the other party, sent to a third party, or not sent at all.

§6.7 n.5 p.153 Add the following to the list after "Accord": Uhar & Co. v. Jacob, 710 F. Supp. 2d 45 (D.D.C. 2010) (written lease agreement satisfies statute for agreement between owner and broker to procure tenants).

§6.7 n.7 p.153 Add the following to the end: , followed in Gillis v. Wells Fargo Bank, 875 F. Supp. 2d 728 (E.D. Mich. 2012) (lender statute of frauds; collecting cases); Int'l Casings Grp. v. Premium Std. Farms, 358 F. Supp. 2d 863 (W.D. Mo. 2005) (collecting cases); Gleneagle Civic Ass'n v. Hardin, 205 P.3d 462 (Colo. App. 2008), followed in PayoutOne v. Coral Mtg. Bankers, 602 F. Supp. 2d 1219 (D. Colo. 2009).

This result is required under UETA §7 ("A contract shall not be denied legal effect or enforceability solely because an electronic record was used in its formation."). *See* Gillis v. Wells Fargo Bank, 875 F. Supp. 2d 728 (E.D. Mich. 2012); Crestwood Shops v. Hilkene, 197 S.W.3d 641 (Mo. App. 2006); Kluver v. PPL Mont., 293 P.3d 817 (Mont. 2012). The parties to a transaction may agree, however, that e-mails will not constitute writings for the purposes of the statute of frauds. *See* Dhillon v. Zions First Nat'l Bank, 462 Fed. Appx. 880 (11th Cir. 2012) (e-mails insufficient where parties signed a negotiation agreement stating that "(1) 'email messages originating from either party or their respective agents during the negotiation process shall be considered verbal in nature and shall not be binding on either party,' (2) any 'verbal offer, acceptance or agreement . . . is not a binding agreement until both Parties execute a written contract,' and (3) a contract must be signed by both parties to be valid").

This principle was extended to text messages in a case in the Massachusetts Land Court. St. John's Holdings, LLC v. Two Elecs., LLC, 2016 Mass. LCR LEXIS 49 (Mass. Land Ct. Apr. 14, 2016) (finding "that the February 3rd text message is a writing and that, read in the context of exchanges between the parties, it contains sufficient terms to state a binding contract"), *dismissed on other grounds*, 24 LCR 654 (2016) (the issue of "actual or apparent authority to bind Two Electronics was not decided in the [earlier decision,]" but evidence at trial showed he did not have the requisite authority).

§6.7 n.11 p.154 Add the following to the list after **"But cf.":** Sawyer v. Mills, 295 S.W.3d 79 (Ky. 2009) (checks contain no references to terms of contract).

§6.7 n.16 p.154 Add the following after the second sentence: *Cf.* Vittiglio v. Vittiglio, 824 N.W.2d 591(Mich. App. 2012) (tape recording of settlement reached in mediation sufficient because of statute providing that settlements are binding if acknowledged on a recording, thus satisfying the statute of frauds' requirement that an estate in land may be conveyed either in a sufficient writing or by operation of law).

§6.7 n.17 p.155 Add the following to the list after "Accord": Sawyer v. Mills, *supra* note 11 (no electronic signature on tape made surreptitiously).

§6.7 n.17 p.155 Add the following at the end: *Sawyer* is problematic in its choice of law. The transaction in question occurred after the effective date of Kentucky's enactment of UETA, which would govern this transaction. Ky. Rev. Stat. §369.104. For this transaction, however, E-SIGN and UETA provide the same result; the tape recording lacks an electronic signature, and the parties to the transaction did not consent to have their transactions occur through electronic means.

§6.7 n.20 p.155 Add the following to the list: Royal Inv. Grp. v. Wang, 961 A.2d 665 (Md. App. 2008) ("[T]he Statute of Frauds is not a bar to enforcing an oral contract when there is a subsequent writing confirming the agreement, even if the writing is signed after a breach of the agreement.") (quoting treatise); Gen. Metal Fabricating Corp. v. Stergiou, ___ S.W.3d ___, 2013 WL 561466 (Tex. Civ. App. Feb. 14, 2013) ("The description of the land may be obtained from documents that are prepared in the course of the transaction, even if those documents are prepared after the parties' contract for sale.").

§6.7 n.21 p.155 Add the following to the list after "Accord": McInnis v. Lind, *supra* note 3 (a letter offering a compromise satisfies the statute because it "indicates defendant's willingness to enter into an agreement on certain terms and thereby provides some evidence that the parties in fact did enter into such an agreement").

§6.7 n.21 p.155 Add the following after the citation to **Farrow***:* , disagreed with by Cent. Ill. Light Co. v Consolidation Coal Co., 349 F.3d 488 (7th Cir. 2003) (disagreeing with "suggestion in *Farrow* . . . that a written offer can be the confirmation that satisfies the statute of frauds even when the acceptance is oral").

§6.7 n.21 p.155 Add the following as a new paragraph at the end: An interesting variation on this theme comes when the writings that the plaintiff would offer to satisfy the statute of frauds are privileged and inadmissible. In Fesmire v. Digh, 683 S.E.2d 803 (S.C. App. 2009), the plaintiff sought to satisfy the writing requirement for a land contract with letters written between the attorneys to the parties in the course of settlement negotiations. The appellate court ruled that these letters could not be used to satisfy the writing requirement, taking into account (a) the importance and delicacy of the settlement process and (b) that the statements in those letters were assumptions for the purpose of negotiating a settlement.

§6.7 n.22 p.156 Add the following to the list after **"Accord"***:* White Constr. Co. v. Martin Marietta Materials, 633 F. Supp. 2d 1302 (M.D. Fla. 2009) (letter of intent that was executed well before the alleged oral contract and expired before those promises were made not sufficient to satisfy the statute of frauds; "the LOI and the alleged oral contract are two separate and independent events").

§6.7 n.26 p.157 Add the following to the list after **"Accord"***:* Jones v. Baran Co., 660 S.E.2d 420 (Ga. App. 2008) (answer and deposition of defendant); Glacial Plains Co-Op. v. Lindgren, 759 N.W.2d 661 (Minn. App. 2009) (sale of goods; admission in deposition and summary judgment papers); Performance Mach. Co. v. Yellowstone Mountain Club, 169 P.3d 394 (Mont. 2007) (UCC 2A statute of frauds: admission in an answer and in a deposition).

§6.7 n.27 p.158 Add the following at the end of the first paragraph: For a helpful discussion of what constitutes a judicial admission, albeit in a different context, *see* Zapp v. CSX Transp., 300 S.W.3d 219 (Ky. App. 2009) ("A judicial admission is a formal

statement concerning a disputed fact, made by a party during a judicial proceeding, that is adverse to that party, and that is deliberate, clear, and uncontradicted."). *See also* Transcontinental Realty Invs. v. John T. Lupton Trust, 286 S.W.3d 635 (Tex. Civ. App. 2009) (a judicial admission must be "(1) a statement made during the course of a judicial proceeding; (2) that is contrary to an essential fact or defense asserted by the person making the admission; (3) that is deliberate, clear, and unequivocal; (4) that, if given conclusive effect, would be consistent with public policy; and (5) that is not destructive of the opposing party's theory of recovery").

§6.7 n.28 p.158 Add the following to the end: ; James L. Gang & Assocs. v. Abbott Labs., 198 S.W.3d 434 (Tex. Civ. App. 2006) ("To constitute an admission of a party, the statement must be made by a party's agent concerning a matter within the scope of his employment and made *during* the existence of the employment relationship.") (emphasis in original). *Quaere* whether an agent fired because she would admit to a contract should still be deemed an agent

§6.7 n.29 p.158 Add the following to the list after **"Accord"*:*** Jones v. Baran Co., *supra* note 26 ("[W]here the Dealer admitted that a contract existed for the sale of a specific quantity of goods . . . but on different terms and conditions than those alleged by [the buyer], the oral agreement between [the buyer] and the Dealer was enforceable . . .").

§6.7 n.30 p.158 Add the following to the list after **"Accord"*:*** Peterson v. Shore, 197 P.3d 789 (Idaho App. 2008) (no admission when "the agreement alleged in [the plaintiff's] pleadings did not contain the same material terms as the agreement admitted to by [the defendant] in his deposition"); Packgen v. BP Exploration & Prod., Inc., 957 F. Supp. 2d 58, 93 (D. Me. 2013), *aff'd*, 754 F.3d 61 (1st Cir. 2014) (e-mail complaining that "I do not understand why we keep placing orders with suppliers like this" did not admit to any specific agreement; failure to cite specific portions of the record in denying opposing party's statement of facts did not, in light of consistent record of denials supported by declarations, constitute admission).

§6.7 n.32 p.159 Add the following to the list after "Accord": Gibson v. Arnold, 288 F.3d 1242 (10th Cir. 2002) (collecting cases; "virtually every court that has addressed the issue during the last twenty-five years has held that judicial admissions are an exception to the statute of frauds"); Concordia Gen. Contracting v. Peltz, 782 N.Y.S.2d 848 (App. Div. 2004) (judicial admission exception applied to suretyship statute of frauds).

§6.7 n.32 p.159 Add the following after the fifth sentence: For a vigorous extension of this exception, *see* Powell v. City of Newton, 703 S.E.2d 723 (N.C. 2010) (applying exception to unsworn settlement agreement made in open court; "Holding parties to their in-court statements made on the record reinforces the solemnity of the courtroom and the reliability of the proceedings therein."). *Accord:* Pietrobon v. Libarle, 40 Cal. Rptr. 3d 718 (Ct. App. 2006) (assent to settlement agreement in open court sufficient, at least when the agreement is placed on the record).

§6.7 n.32 p.159 Add the following before the last sentence: This exception was turned on its head in Bithoney v. Fulton-DeKalb Hosp. Auth., 721 S.E.2d 577 (Ga. App. 2011) (promisee admitted in deposition that the termination clause of his oral employment contract provided for severance payments over 15 months; even though contract itself was indefinite and therefore not otherwise within statute of frauds, the termination provision was enough to pull the contract within the statute).

§6.7 n.33 p.159 Add the following to the list after "Accord": ; Kluver v. PPL Mont., 293 P.3d 817 (Mont. 2012) (uncontroverted evidence that defendant had admitted the existence of a contract; "it would be a fraud on the defendant to allow plaintiffs to admit to the contract, and then allow them to avoid its obligations by asserting the statute of frauds") (quoting from Hayes v. Hartelius, 697 P.2d 1349, 1353 (Mont. 1985)).

§6.7 n.35 p.160 Add the following as a third paragraph to the end: In Walker v. Carter, 210 F. Supp. 3d 487, 2016 U.S. Dist. LEXIS 131557, at *24-25; Copy. L. Rep. (CCH) P30,993 (S.D.N.Y. 2016), the district court noted that "[w]hen faced with this situation — where the Statute of Frauds is alleged to be satisfied by a missing writing — New York's courts have not been entirely consistent" and provided a survey of different approaches to missing contracts by various appellate divisions in New York:

> For instance, the Third Department has adopted a bright-line rule, holding that "[e]xcept where the party invoking the protection of the Statute of Frauds admits the unproduced agreement was indeed entered into, the Statute of Frauds shelters certain transactions from the uncertainty of witness memory and the danger of fraud by immunizing them from parol evidence." Matter of Talco Contractors Inc. v. New York State Tax Commission, 140 A.D.2d 834, 528 N.Y.S.2d 219, 220 (3d Dept. 1988). The Fourth Department, too, has constrained the types of evidence that may be used to prove the existence of a missing writing. It held that "a party may elicit parol evidence to prove the existence and terms of a written agreement, thereby satisfying the requirements of the Statute of Frauds, when the failure to produce the original is adequately explained." Nicosia v. Muller, 229 A.D.2d 964, 645 N.Y.S.2d 385, 386 (4th Dept. 1996). That "parol evidence may consist of the admission of an adversary," as in the Third Department, "or the testimony of others who have first-hand knowledge of the existence of the writing and its terms." *Id.* (internal citations omitted).
>
> The First and Second Departments have adopted looser rules. The Second Department held that "[t]he loss or destruction of a written instrument does not deprive it of effect under the Statute of Frauds. Therefore, even if no signed copy of the lease can be found, the appellants could still prove its existence by extrinsic evidence." Lynch v. Savarese, 217 A.D.2d 648, 629 N.Y.S.2d 804 (2d Dept. 1995) (internal citations omitted). Similarly, the First Department has held that claims based on lost writings are "not barred by the Statute of Frauds, since the plaintiff is entitled to the opportunity to prove, if she can, the existence and the contents of the lost writing by parol and circumstantial evidence" Love v. Spector, 215 A.D.2d 733, 733, 627 N.Y.S.2d 87, 88 (1st Dept. 1995) (citations and internal quotation marks omitted).

Walker involved a plaintiff who claimed rights related to the creation of the logo for Carter's (aka Jay-Z's) Roc-A-Fella Records. He claimed he was to receive payments over ten years, and that there was a contract but that he lost the only copy. The court held that "even by the more permissive standards used by the First and Second Departments, Plaintiff does not present evidence of the existence of the writing sufficient to create a triable issue of material fact. Defendants do not admit to the existence of the writing. And the testimony presented by Plaintiff of the alleged writing is alternately contradictory, self-serving, and not based on first-hand knowledge." *Id.* at *28.

§6.7 n.37 p.161 In the second paragraph, add the following to the list after **"see"**: CQ, Inc. v. TXU Mining Co., 565 F.3d 268 (5th Cir. 2009) (writing stated that "[t]he intent was to 'eventually' form an agreement 'if the Alliance [was] determined to be a "go project" ' "; "This type of contingent language does not satisfy the statute of frauds because it is not confirmatory of a contract already in existence."); SS-II, LLC v. Bridge St. Assocs., 977 A.2d 189 (Conn. 2009) ("A mere statement that the parties will mutually determine the future purchase price does not mean that the parties will, in fact, agree."); William J. Jenack Estate Appraisers & Auctioneers v. Rabizadeh, 952 N.Y.S.2d 197 (App. Div. 2012) (memorandum of sale inadequate because it had only the consignor's identification number, not the consignee's).

§6.7 n.38 p.161 Add the following to the list after **"But cf."**: Yellow Book Sales & Dist. Co. v. Valle, 35 A.3d 1082 (Conn. App. 2012) (writing insufficient when ambiguous whether president of obligor signed in his corporate capacity or in his individual capacity as guarantor), *cert. granted in part*, 41 A.3d 661 (Conn. 2012); Greene v. McLeod, 942 A.2d 1254 (N.H. 2008) (blank warranty deeds signed by seller insufficient; "[t]hey did not indicate the purchase price, the identities of both parties to the transaction or describe the real estate in question.").

§6.7 n.39 p.161 Add the following at the end: *Cf.* Tampa Inv. Grp. v. Branch Banking & Trust Co., 723 S.E.2d 674 (Ga. 2012) (guaranties sufficient because they identified the notes to which they applied by category and timing, even though they did not identify the individual notes), *on remand sub nom*. Legacy Communities Grp. v. Branch Banking & Trust Co., 729 S.E.2d 612 (Ga. App. 2012) (guaranties here insufficient against a guarantor not specifically named in the documents and not necessarily included without the use of parol evidence); Hartford Fire Ins. Co. v. C. Springs 300, Ltd., 287 S.W.3d 771 (Tex. Civ. App. 2009) ("a

memorandum of a guaranty or suretyship must contain (1) the parties involved, (2) a manifestation of intent to guarantee the obligation, and (3) a description of the obligation being guaranteed").

§6.7 n.40 p.162 Add the following to the list after **"Accord"***:* Price v. Willbanks, 374 S.W.3d 28 (Ark. App. 2009) ("if a writing furnishes a means by which the realty can be identified, it need not describe the property with the particularity required for deed. . . . Further, although extrinsic evidence may not be used to add or change a deficient description, it may be used to decipher or make intelligible the terms of the contract so long as the writing itself provides the key to the description."); Sterling v. Taylor, *supra* note 3 ("while the properties were identified in the memorandum only by street address, neither party displayed any confusion over their actual location . . . [and] extrinsic evidence may be consulted to locate property described in imprecise terms"); Park Regency Partners v. Gruber, 608 S.E.2d 667 (Ga. App. 2004) (for sale of parking units in condominium, set of plans identifying units by number sufficient; "while a perfect description is not required, the contract must furnish the key to identifying the land intended to be conveyed"); Machado v. Ryan, 280 P.3d 715 (Idaho 2012) ("language in a deed providing that the conveyance is 'subject to' easements of record does not in itself reserve an easement"); Del Pozo v. Impressive Homes, 945 N.Y.S.2d 368 (App. Div. 2012) ("the description of real property in a contract of sale 'need not be as detailed and exact as the description in a deed' . . . Where the property is described with such definiteness and exactness as will permit it to be identified with reasonable certainty, 'parol evidence would then be admissible to enable the court to identify precisely the property to which the contract relates' ") (quoting from Elias v. Serota, 480 N.Y.S.2d 344 (App. Div. 1984) and Boyajian v. Casey, 383 N.Y.S.2d 714 (App. Div. 1976), respectively); Zuk v. Zuk, 55 A.3d 102 (Pa. Super. 2012) (signed writing stating that the agreement was to sell 30 acres from an 84 and one-eighth acre parcel sufficient, even though the writing did not specify which 30 acres were to be sold; parol evidence available to establish boundaries); Gen. Metal Fabricating Corp. v. Stergiou, ___ S.W.3d ___, 2013 WL 561466 (Tex. Civ. App. Feb. 14, 2013) (references to "White Buildings" and

"Blue Building" in promise to make a security agreement sufficient; "the various deeds of trust and the security agreements circulated as drafts between the parties contain sufficient legal descriptions of those properties");

§6.7 n.40 p.162 Add the following at the end: *Cf.* Callies v. O'Neal, 216 P.3d 130 (Idaho 2009) (real estate brokerage contract statute of frauds: "a legally enforceable property description . . . need not be as specific as a property description contained in a real estate sale agreement." Rather, "[s]o long as the description 'enable[s] the broker to locate the property, show it, and point out its boundaries to the prospective purchaser,' it meets the requirements of the statute.") (quoting from Central Idaho Agency v. Turner, 442 P.2d 442 (Idaho 1968)). *Cf.* Ardmore, Inc. v. Rex Grp., Inc., 377 S.W.3d 45 (Tex. Civ. App. 2012) ("While we apply a strict application of the statute of frauds, we allow for a liberal construction of the words describing the land.").

The party asserting the defense may not withhold necessary information and then argue that the proffered documents are insufficient because they lack the withheld information. *See* Thornhill, Inc. v. NVR, Inc., 422 F. Supp. 2d 646 (N.D. W. Va. 2006) (applying "prevention doctrine"). It is not entirely clear whence this principle arose; possibly from the same place as the prevention doctrine in the law of conditions. See *infra* §8.15.

§6.7 n.41 p.162 Add the following to the list after "Accord": Preston Exploration Co. v. GSF, L.L.C., 669 F.3d 518 (5th Cir. 2012) (description insufficient to the extent that the documents do not contain recording information sufficient to identify the properties in question); McClung v. Atlanta Real Estate Acquisitions, 639 S.E.2d 331 (Ga. App. 2006) (reference to acreage insufficient where part of a larger parcel), followed in O'Dell v. Pine Ridge Invs., 667 S.E.2d 912 (Ga. App. 2008) (description of land as "187.5 acres in Land Lot 170" inadequate, containing "neither a legal description of the subject property, nor any language that would allow the introduction of extrinsic evidence to supply such a description") and in Salim v. Solaiman, 691 S.E.2d 389 (Ga. App. 2010) (address inadequate without extrinsic evidence connecting the address to a particular tract, providing "the same degree of certainty as that required in a deed conveying realty") (internal quotation omitted); Greene v. McLeod, *supra* note 38 (blank warranty deed insufficiently detailed; although parol may be used to clarify vague terms, it may not be used where "the only writings fail to contain *any* of the essential terms of the real estate contract") (emphasis in original); Fears v. Tex. Bank, 247 S.W.3d 729 (Tex. Civ. App. 2008) ("20 acres off of the West end" of a 100-acre tract insufficient, "standing alone, to determine where, or at what angle, or series of angles, the property was divided from the main part"), followed in May v. Buck, 375 S.W.3d 568 (Tex. Civ. App. 2012) (description inadequate because "[t]he terms of the letter agreement give rise to several possible configurations of tracts that may be said to be 'identified' by the letter agreement, existing writings referenced therein, or both"); 303, LLC v. Born, 823 N.W.2d 269 (Wis. App. 2012) ("remaining acreage" fatally indefinite in right of first refusal; not clear whether this means all the remaining acreage or some of the remaining acreage, and if the latter what part of the remaining acreage would be subject to that right; "A clear distinction must be drawn between the proper admission of extrinsic evidence for the purpose of applying the description to identified property versus the improper supplying of a description or adding to a description that on its face is insufficient.").

§6.7 n.41 p.162 Add the following to the list after **"See"***:* TR-One, Inc. v. Lazz Dev. Co., 945 N.Y.S.2d 416 (App. Div. 2012) (statement that "[t]he exact size and location of the parcel subject to this option is located primarily in the Village of Pawling and is to be defined and determined by a Survey to be obtained by Optionee at its expense and which description will be agreed upon by the parties and then added as an exhibit to the contract of sale" insufficient "to identify the subject property with the degree of certainty necessary to satisfy the statute of frauds");

§6.7 n.43 p.163 Add the following after the second sentence: Cf. MacThompson Realty v. City of Nashua, 993 A.2d 773 (N.H. 2010) (price is essential term, but "a contract which sets a price by a future appraisal is sufficiently definite to satisfy the statute of frauds"); Ardmore, Inc. v. Rex Grp., Inc., 377 S.W.3d 45 (Tex. Civ. App. 2012) ("The purpose of a description in a written

conveyance is not to identify the land, but to afford a means of identification.").

§6.7 n.44 p.163 In the second paragraph, add the following to the list after **"See also"**: Shellabarger v. Shellabarger, 317 S.W.3d 77 (Mo. App. 2010) (date for performance of option to purchase real estate not essential, when context made clear that the exact timing was not critical, and in any case, "if no time is agreed upon, the law will imply a reasonable time"; quoting from and relying upon Restatement Second §131 illus. 15).

§6.7 n.45 p.164 Add the following to the list after **"See"**: Sterling v. Taylor, *supra* note 3 ("if a memorandum includes the essential terms of the parties' agreement, but the meaning of those terms is unclear, the memorandum is sufficient under the statute of frauds if extrinsic evidence clarifies the terms with reasonable certainty"); Botkin v. Sec. State Bank, 130 P.3d 92 (Kan. 2006) ("only reasonable certainty of the terms is required and . . . extrinsic evidence is admissible merely to help clarify the essential, albeit ambiguous, terms"); Bailey v. Hawthorn Bank, 382 S.W.3d 84 (Mo. App. 2012) (written credit agreement's lack of an interest rate does not make the writing insufficient; interest rate not essential in credit statute of frauds, and in any case the interest rate "fluctuates day to day so it would not be unreasonable to set a specific percentage at a later date").

§6.7 n.45 p.164 Add the following after the third sentence: *Cf.* Westlake Petrochems. v. United Polychem, 688 F.3d 232 (5th Cir. 2012) (payment and credit terms not essential; "the industry norm is to negotiate payment and credit terms *after* formation of the contract") (emphasis in original).

§6.7 n.47 p.164 Add the following to the list after **"Accord"**: First Nat'l Mtg. Co. v. Fed. Realty Inv. Trust, 631 F.3d 1058 (9th Cir. 2011) (California law: absence of express lease term not fatal if the term could be implied from the writing, if necessary with the help of extrinsic evidence); Omar v. Rozen, 867 N.Y.S.2d 458 (App. Div. 2008) (writing sufficient where "identifies the parties, describes the subject property, and provides a reasonably certain method of determining a purchase price and the

terms of financing"; "While some terms, such as the closing date, the quality of title to be conveyed, and the risk of loss between contract and closing, are not included within the agreement, the law will serve to fill in those missing provisions."), followed in Triple A Supplies v. WPA Acquisition Corp., 944 N.Y.S.2d 757 (App. Div. 2012) (although writing for contract conveying real property did not set forth the quality of title to be conveyed, default rules would fill that gap).

§6.7 n.48 p.164 Add the following at the end: The memorandum must state, not only that consideration was given, but also that it was given in exchange for the return promise or performance. This can be a problem when the memorandum was one of a collection of writings. *See* Southland Bank v. A & A Drywall Supply Co., 21 So. 3d 1196 (Ala. 2008) (requirement not met when writing that expressed consideration did not state that the consideration was paid for the loan commitment at issue, where payment was made to a third party and there was no evidence that the third party's actions were required by the lender).

§6.7 n.52 p.166 Add the following at the end: Lohman v. Wagner, 862 A.2d 1042 (Md. App. 2004) (agreement unenforceable in absence of quantity term; rejecting argument that UCC 2-201 does not require quantity term, but merely limits enforcement to the extent of any quantity term).

§6.7 n.54 p.166 Add the following to the list after "Accord": MEMC Elec. Materials v. BP Solar Int'l, 9 A.3d 508 (Md. App. 2010) (quantity sufficiently defined when contract states a specific minimum quantity with a right of first refusal of output).

§6.7 n.58 p.167 Add the following after the first sentence: Monetti, S.P.A. v. Anchor Hocking Co., 931 F.2d 1178 (7th Cir. 1991) ("end of the statute of frauds thus is substantive (albeit the means is procedural)").

§6.7 n.58 p.167 Add the following after the second sentence: Monetti, S.P.A. v. Anchor Hocking Co., *supra* ("use of oral evidence to get round the requirement of a writing would be bootstrapping"); Bazak Int'l Corp. v. Mast Indus., 535 N.E.2d 633 (N.Y. 1989) (use of parol evidence would "undermine the very reason for a Statute of Frauds in the first instance").

§6.7 n.58 p.167 Add the following at the end: *Accord:* Sterling v. Taylor, *supra* note 3 (where "the extrinsic evidence . . . is at odds with the writing . . . the evidence is insufficient to show with reasonable certainty that the parties understood and agreed to the price alleged by the plaintiffs. . . . The price terms stated in the memorandum, considered together with the extrinsic evidence of the contemplated price, leave a degree of doubt that the statute of frauds does not tolerate.").

§6.7 p.168 In the first paragraph, add the following to the last sentence: . . . precluding reformation of that term.[59]

[59] As the UCC makes clear in the comment. *See* UCC 2-201 cmt. 1 ("such material terms as are stated need not be precisely stated").

§6.8 REQUIREMENT OF SIGNATURE

§6.8 n.1 p.168 Add the following at the end as new paragraphs: For an example of a court that confused contract formation with the sufficiency of a writing, *see* Thomas J. Sibley, P.C. v. Brentwood Inv. Dev. Co., 356 S.W.3d 659 (Tex. Civ. App. 2011). There, a law firm failed to pay rent on its leased offices. The landlord sued for breach of contract. Among the law firm's defenses were (1) that there was no contract because there was no signed writing and (2) that even if there were such a contract, it would be unenforceable under the statute of frauds. The court properly disposed of the first argument by finding a contract by conduct; the law firm occupied the space and paid some of the rent, and the landlord maintained the building as required by the lease. The court dealt with the statute of frauds question by stating that "[a]s we have concluded that the omission of the lessor's signature was not fatal to the lease's enforceability, Sibley, P.C.'s statute of frauds argument is without merit." 356 S.W.3d at 664. The court's reasoning rested on a non sequitur. Whether there was a contract and whether the contract was enforceable are two very different inquiries. If the statute of frauds is satisfied whenever the parties to a contract act as though they have one, even if the writings proffered do not themselves satisfy the statute of frauds, then the signature requirement — and much else in the statute of frauds — is effectively gone for all contracts not purely executory. More to the point, statute of frauds analysis requires first that there be a contract. The parties' performance was relevant to this issue, given the lack of a signature as an expression of assent. But once there is an actual contract, then the question is whether the contract satisfies the formal requirements of the statute.

It is possible that the parties' performance could have brought the contract under the part-performance exception to the land contract statute of frauds, or perhaps under a more general reliance-based exception. But that wasn't the holding, and the opinion does not mention that the argument was made. It is mildly ironic that a law firm that did not keep its promise was held to that promise in spite of its perfectly correct technical defense, perhaps because the firm itself didn't make the argument convincingly. Irony aside, though, the opinion rather badly misstates the law here, effectively eviscerating the signature requirement of the statute of frauds. It is fortunate that this part of the court's opinion was not assigned a headnote and key number, making it more likely that it will leave the law largely undisturbed.

§6.8 n.6 p.169 Add the following to the list after* "See"*: Gen. Trading Int'l v. Wal-Mart Stores, 320 F.3d 831 (8th Cir. 2003) (signed e-mail could satisfy statute); Roger Edwards, LLC v. Fiddes & Son, Ltd., 245 F. Supp. 2d 251 (D. Me. 2003); Cent. Ill. Light Co. v. Consolidation Coal Co., 235 F. Supp. 2d 916 (C.D. Ill. 2002), *aff'd*, 349 F.3d 488 (7th Cir. 2003); Green v. Midland Mtg. Co., 342 S.W.3d 686 (Tex. Civ. App. 2011).

§6.8 n.6 p.169 Add the following at the end: The signature requirement, like other aspects of electronic communication, has been affected greatly by the enactment of UETA and E-Sign. *See* UETA 7(c) & (d) (legal requirements of writings or signatures satisfied by electronic records or signatures); E-Sign 101(a) (same). *See* SN4, LLC v. Anchor Bank, fsb, 848 N.W.2d 559, 567 (Minn. Ct. App. 2014) ("while contracting parties may agree to negotiate and form a contract by electronic means, doing so does not mean that they have also agreed to electronically subscribe to whatever agreement may result from their electronic negotiations"). For other applications of UETA, *see In re* Marriage of Weiss, 239 P.3d 123 (Mont. 2010) (giving effect to electronic transfer of funds, notwithstanding a writing requirement in a premarital agreement, because of UETA 7); Int'l Casings Grp. v. Premium Std. Farms, 358 F. Supp. 2d 863 (W.D. Mo. 2005) (UETA makes electronic signatures effective to satisfy UCC 2-201, provided that the signators "had the present intention to authenticate the document"). The parties may, of course, make clear their intention *not* to authenticate the document, whether in the document itself or in a master agreement or other contract governing negotiation. *See* Dhillon v. Zions First Nat'l Bank, 462 Fed. Appx. 880 (11th Cir. 2012) (e-mails insufficient where parties signed a negotiation agreement stating that "(1) 'email messages originating from either party or their respective agents during the negotiation process shall be considered verbal in nature and shall not be binding on either party,' (2) any 'verbal offer, acceptance or agreement . . . is not a binding agreement until both Parties execute a written contract,' and (3) a contract must be signed by both parties to be valid"); SN4, LLC v. Anchor Bank, fsb, 848 N.W.2d 559, 562 (Minn. Ct. App. 2014) ("no reasonable fact-finder could determine that [e-mail block] electronic signatures are logically associated with the [email attachment]," given that the e-mail body stated that the attachment "needs to be signed").

For perhaps an overenthusiastic application, *see* Powell v. City of Newton, 684 S.E.2d 55 (N.C. App. 2009) (signature requirement satisfied under UETA by plaintiff's counsel's signatures on e-mails concerning the transaction, even though those e-mails never acknowledged the existence of a contract; strong dissent). *Cf.* Buckles Mgmt. v. InvestorDigs, LLC, 728 F. Supp. 2d 1145 (D. Colo. 2010) (e-mail of settlement terms satisfies writing requirement, but not signed within the meaning of the Statute of Frauds when electronic signature was from employee without authority to bind principal); Young v. Rose, 286 P.3d 518 (Ariz. App. 2012) (whether "thank you e-mail qualifies as an electronic signature necessarily entails review of matters outside the pleadings" and therefore cannot be resolved by a motion to dismiss). It is important to note that UETA does not provide the rules of contract formation, but rather addresses only how any writing requirements might be satisfied by electronic communications. *See* Alliance Laundry Sys. v. Thyssenkrupp Materials, 570 F. Supp. 2d 1061 (E.D. Wis. 2008). For international commercial contracts, the United Nations recently adopted the Convention on the Use of Electronic Communications in International Contracts. It has not taken effect yet, but the United States is looking closely at possible ratification, and the Uniform Law Commissioners have completed work on the implementing legislation. For a highly skeptical view of the virtues of the Convention, *see* Mik, "Updating" the Electronic Transactions Act? — Australia's Accession to the UN Convention on the Use of Electronic Communications in International Contracts 2005, 26 J. Contract L. 184 (2010).

§6.8 n.8 p.169 Add the following after the citation to **Parma Tile***:* distinguished in Rosenfeld v. Zerneck, 776 N.Y.S.2d 458 (Sup. Ct. 2004) ("in contradistinction to the fax imprint in *Parma*, we have the defendant's typewritten name upon an e-mail which the defendant acknowledges that he sent"), in turn declined to follow by Vista Developers Corp. v. VFP Realty, 847 N.Y.S.2d 416 (Sup. Ct. 2007) (New York Statute of Frauds provision permitting use of electronic signatures does not apply to contracts concerning real property), which itself was rejected in Naldi v. Grunberg, 908 N.Y.S.2d 639 (App. Div. 2010) (even before E-SIGN and UETA, New York Statute of Frauds for real property transactions permitted the use of electronic signatures), followed in Newmark & Co. Real Estate v. 2615 E. 17th St. Realty, 914 N.Y.S.2d 162 (App. Div. 2011) ("An e-mail sent by a party, under which the sending party's name is typed, can constitute a writing for purposes of the statute of frauds"), in turn followed in Hakim v. Hakim, 953 N.Y.S.2d 1 (App. Div. 2012) (e-mails that were authenticated by in-house counsel "constitute the requisite 'writing signed by the party to be charged' ").

§6.8 n.17 p.170 Add the following to the end: The Massachusetts Land Court held that typing a first name at the end of a text message can constitute a signature under some circumstances. St. John's Holdings, LLC v. Two Elecs., LLC, 2016 Mass. LCR LEXIS 49 (Mass. Land Ct. Apr. 14, 2016) ("Typing their

names at the end of certain messages containing material terms, but declining to do so for more informal discussions, is indicative that the parties chose to be bound by those signed communications. In the context of these exchanges between the parties, the court infers that the text message sent by Barry was intended to be authenticated by his deliberate choice to type his name at the conclusion of his text message."), *dismissed on other grounds*, 24 LCR 654 (2016) (the issue of "actual or apparent authority to bind Two Electronics was not decided in the [earlier decision,]" but evidence at trial showed he did not have the requisite authority).

***§6.8 n.19 p.171 In the first paragraph, add the following to the list after* "See":** Grabill Cabinet Co. v. Sullivan, 919 N.E.2d 1162 (Ind. App. 2010) (creditor need not sign guaranty, as only the guarantor was to be charged).

§6.8 n.21 p.172 Add the following at the end: *Cf.* Helmus v. Chase Home Fin., 890 F. Supp. 2d 806, 2012 WL 3704977 (W.D. Mich. 2012) (requirement that writing be signed by an "authorized representative" not met with cover letter signed "CHASE HOME FINANCE LLC," so contract not enforceable).

***§6.8 n.22 p.172 Add the following to the list after* "But cf.":** Kluver v. PPL Mont., 293 P.3d 817 (Mont. 2012) (exception where execution by the agent is in the presence of the principal);

§6.8 n.24 p.172 Add the following after the first sentence: For an extension of this principle, *see* Westlake Petrochem. v. United Polychem., 688 F.3d 232 (5th Cir. 2012) (broker acting on behalf of both buyer and seller sent them written confirmations of an unwritten contract; these confirmations satisfy the statute of frauds, even though neither party to the contract actually signed them).

§6.8 n.26 p.173 Add the following at the end: Contemporaneous records may stand on a special footing; if they collectively contain the necessary terms, the writings may not need any relation apart from execution as part of the same transaction.

Dabbs v. Key Equip. Fin., 694 S.E.2d 161 (Ga. App. 2010) (ten-day interval between execution of lease and guaranty sufficiently contemporaneous, but they do not clearly relate to the same transaction; parol inadmissible for that purpose), distinguished with considerable strain in LaFarge Bldg. Materials v. Pratt, 706 S.E.2d 131 (Ga. App. 2011) (application and guaranty not construed together, even though part of the same two-page document; guaranty did not incorporate the terms of the application expressly, its scope is not identical to that in the application, and the application is not signed and does not reflect "that the parties formed a binding contract regarding the extension of credit") and followed in Patterson v. Bennett St. Properties, 726 S.E.2d 147 (Ga. App. 2012) (assignment, lease amendment, and guaranty read together, with parol admissible, because all were signed and each made reference to the others).

§6.8 n.28 p.173 Add the following to the list after **"Accord"***:* Coe v. Chesapeake Exploration, 695 F.3d 311 (5th Cir. 2012) (signed conveyance of oil and gas leases described only as "certain oil and gas leases" sufficient; signed writing contained "a sufficient nucleus of description" to permit the use of parol in the form of a map designated as Exhibit A to the conveyance and attached to it);

§6.8 n.31 p.174 Add the following at the end: *But see* William J. Jenack Estate Appraisers & Auctioneers v. Rabizadeh, 952 N.Y.S.2d 197 (App. Div. 2012) (applying *Crabtree* to statute of frauds for goods sold at public auction, N.Y. Gen. Oblig. L. §5-701(a)(6)).

§6.8 n.32 p.175 Add the following to the list after **"Accord"***:* Trustmark Ins. Co. v. Gen. & Cologne Life Re of Am., 424 F.3d 542 (7th Cir. 2005) ("the multiple documents . . . fall short, for they neither state essential terms, refer expressly to each other, nor connect in such a way as to reflect relation to a particular contract"); McInnis v. Lind, 108 P.3d 578 (Or. App. 2005) ("One document need not expressly incorporate the other by reference if the connection between them is unmistakable," a connection that can be established by testimony).

***§6.8 n.33 p.175 Add the following to the list after* "Accord":** Dabbs v. Key Equip. Fin., 694 S.E.2d 161 (Ga. App. 2010) ("where the statute of frauds is applicable, a party may not rely on parol evidence to establish that the documents were executed in the course of the same transaction"); Wells Fargo Bank v. Tippecanoe Assocs., 923 N.E.2d 423 (Ind. App. 2010) (when one document signed and another not signed, linking them occurs only when the signed document "clearly and definitely refers to the unsigned [document]"; if not, "we would have to resort to parol evidence, which is not permitted when engaging in this type of analysis"); Home Realty Lynnwood v. Walsh, 189 P.3d 253 (Wash. App. 2008) (though multiple writings may collectively satisfy the statute of frauds, this is subject to "the rule that bars reliance on parol evidence to satisfy the statute of frauds").

***§6.8 n.40 p.177 Add the following to the list after* "Cf.":** Delta Star, Inc. v. Michael's Carpet World, 666 S.E.2d 331 (Va. 2008) (proposals insufficient because "by definition . . . a proposal is an offer presented for acceptance or rejection. In submitting its proposals, Michael's sought to form a contract, rather than to confirm a contract.").

***§6.8 n.43 p.178 Add the following to the list after* "Accord":** Tubelite Co. v. Original Sign Studio, 891 N.E.2d 820 (Ohio App. 2008) ("Although the failure to object to a confirmatory writing eliminates a statute of frauds defense, it does not establish the existence of a contract. A party who sends a confirmatory writing still bears the burden of persuading the trier of fact that the receiving party actually agreed to the oral contract memorialized in the confirmatory writing.").

§6.8a USE OF CONFIRMATION TO SATISFY UCC 2-201

§6.8a n.6 p.179 Add the following before the first sentence: As, for instance, in Apex LLC v. Sharing World, Inc., 142 Cal. Rptr. 3d 210 (Ct. App. 2012) (giving effect to documents entitled "Sales Contract — Flat").

§6.8a n.7 p.179 Add the following to the list after* "But see"*: Delta Star, Inc. v. Michael's Carpet World, 666 S.E.2d 331 (Va. 2008) (invoice sufficient for goods listed, but not for balance of alleged contract).

§6.8a n.8 p.179 Add the following after the first sentence: Electronic communications can satisfy UCC 2-201(2). *See* Alliance Laundry Sys. v. Thyssenkrupp Materials, 570 F. Supp. 2d 1061 (E.D. Wis. 2008) (e-mails satisfy 2-201 "if the jury finds that the e-mails formed a contract").

§6.8a n.10 p.180 Add the following at the end: More generally, whether this exception applies is a question of fact; as a result, it is not futile for a plaintiff to amend its complaint to counter the assertion of this defense, because doing so would render the issue unfit for resolution with a motion to dismiss. Public Health Equip. & Supply Co. v. Clarke Mosquito Control Prods., 410 Fed. Appx. 738 (5th Cir. 2010) (Texas law).

§6.9 SATISFACTION BY PART PERFORMANCE

§6.9 p.180 In the first paragraph, add the following at the end of the fourth sentence: . . . reliable evidence of an agreement.[2a]

[2a] Losh Family, LLC v. Kertsman, 228 P.3d 793 (Wash. App. 2010) ("Three factors are typically considered in determining whether there is sufficient evidence of part performance: (1) delivery and assumption of actual and exclusive possession; (2) payment or tender of consideration; and (3) the making of permanent, substantial, and valuable improvements, referable to the contract. . . . These three factors serve an evidentiary function allowing the court to be certain the contract existed and [of] its terms.").

§6.9 n.3 p.180 In the first paragraph, add the following at the end: *Cf.* Kiernan v. Creech, 268 P.3d 312 (Alaska 2012) ("The part performance doctrine is a particular application of promissory estoppel in the context of land transfer contracts that do not comply with the statute of frauds."). *See also* Ficke v. Wolken, 291 Neb. 482, 868 N.W.2d 305 (2015) ("[t]he part performance exception entails an onerous burden of proof — a plaintiff must prove not only that the alleged performance is referable to the oral contract, but also that the performance 'cannot be accounted for on any other reasonable hypothesis' " and moreover, "the alleged acts of performance must speak for themselves" and not rely solely on testimony of the party claiming the act was intended as part performance) (quoting Crnkovich v. Crnkovich, 144 Neb. 904, 907, 15 N.W.2d 66, 68 (1944) and citing Owens v. M.E. Schepp Ltd. P'ship, 218 Ariz. 222, 182 P.3d 664 (2008) and Glazer v. Dress Barn, Inc., 274 Conn. 33, 873 A.2d 929 (2005)).

§6.9 n.8 p.182 Add the following after the second sentence: *Cf.* Upperline Equip. Co. v. J & M, Inc., 724 F. Supp. 2d 883 (E.D. Tenn. 2009) (where only performance completed was the inspection of the goods, the part performance exception was not satisfied).

§6.9 n.13 p.183 Add the following at the beginning: *See* Dallas Aerospace v. CIS Air Corp., 352 F.3d 775 (2d Cir. 2003) (statute not satisfied where acceptance of payment "was entirely consistent with . . . pre-existing rights and duties under the unmodified agreement").

§6.9 n.14 p.183 In the first paragraph, add the following to the list after "See": Hern Family Ltd. P'ship v. Compass Bank, 863 F. Supp. 2d 613 (S.D. Tex. 2012) (partial performance " 'must be such as could have been done with no other design than to fulfill the particular agreement sought to be enforced' "; paying off existing debt in reliance on oral promise to lend not sufficient, because paying off debt is itself a routine activity) (quoting from Bank of Texas v. Gaubert, 286 S.W.3d 546, 554 (Tex. Civ. App. 2009) (in turn quoting from Exxon Corp. v. Breezevale Ltd., 82 S.W.3d 429, 439-40 (Tex. Civ. App. 2002))); Hemispherx Biopharma v. Mid-S. Capital, 690 F.3d 1216 (11th Cir. 2012) ("The act performed must be consistent with the existence of a contract, inconsistent with the lack of a contract, and essential to the contract, such that it resulted in both a loss or injury to the party seeking to enforce the unsigned contract and a benefit to the other party."; quaere whether this goes more to restitution than contract); SS-II, LLC v. Bridge St. Assocs., 977 A.2d 189 (Conn. 2009) (no role for part performance exception where underlying agreement left price to be determined).

§6.9 n.14 p.183 In the first paragraph, add the following after the citation to* Nashan*: followed in Beaver v. Brumlow, 231 P.3d 628 (N.M. App. 2010) (rejecting "the suggestion that the 'unequivocally referable' concept means that outside of the contract, there can be no other plausible explanation for the part performance"; instead, reading *Nashan* to hold that "the performance must lead an outsider to 'naturally and reasonably' conclude that the contract alleged actually exists"); Kazlauskas v. Emmert, 275 P.3d 171 (Or. App. 2012) (managing properties not unequivocally referable to contract for sale, because buyer/manager was paid for those services; living on property similarly not referable, because buyer had lived there before alleged agreement; but remodeling house was unequivocally referable and thus was sufficient evidence of part performance). *But cf.* Long v. City of Glendale, 93 P.3d 519 (Ariz. App. 2004) (not requiring that performance by vendor be "unequivocally referable" to the contract where the vendor completed his performance by transferring the land).

§6.9 n.14 p.183 Add the following at the end of the second paragraph: For an instance where a typographical error may have caused the ambiguity that ultimately prevented the use of this exception, *see* Bauchman-Kingston P'ship v. Haroldsen, 233 P.3d 18 (Idaho 2008) (contract stated that "purchase price shall be based on appraisal [sic] acceptable to both seller and buyer"; error yielded ambiguity on whether the contract called for the appraisal or the appraiser to be acceptable, so unclear whether condition met; with no price established, "any attempted performance . . . was not full performance").

§6.9 n.16 p.184 Add the following to the end: For an undue narrowing of the part performance exception, see Sullivan v. Porter, 861 A.2d 625 (Me. 2004) (requiring that "the other party made misrepresentations that induced that partial performance").

§6.9 n.17 p.184 In the first paragraph, add the following to the list after **"Accord"***:* White Constr. Co. v. Martin Marietta Materials, 633 F. Supp. 2d 1302 (M.D. Fla. 2009) ("'the doctrine of part performance does not apply to actions for the recovery of damages for alleged breach of an oral contract within the operation of the statute of frauds'") (quoting from LynkUs Comm'ns v. WebMD Corp., 965 So. 2d 1161 (Fla. App. 2007)); Snyder v. HSBC Bank, 873 F. Supp. 2d 1139 (D. Ariz. 2012) (part performance exception "is an equitable one which is only available to a party seeking equitable relief"); Sparks Assocs. v. N. Hills Holding Co. II, 941 N.Y.S.2d 695 (App. Div. 2012) ("Part performance by the party seeking to enforce the contract may be sufficient in some circumstances to overcome the statute of frauds, but only in an action for specific performance.").

§6.9 n.17 p.184 Substitute the following in the second line of the second paragraph for the citation to **Wolfe** *in the first paragraph:* Glazer v. Dress Barn, 873 A.2d 929 (Conn. 2005) ("this distinction is no longer warranted with the merger of actions in law and equity").

§6.9 n.17 p.184 In the first paragraph, add the following after the citation to **Phillips***:* , followed in Trustmark Ins. Co. v. Gen. & Cologne Life Re of Am., 424 F.3d 542 (7th Cir. 2005) ("in order for the plaintiff to invoke the doctrine of partial performance, it must first establish entitlement to equitable relief. And to be entitled to equitable relief, Trustmark must show that it has no adequate remedy at law.").

§6.9 n.18 p.184 Add the following to the end of the first sentence: *Accord:* Long v. City of Glendale, *supra* note 14 (seller avoids statute of frauds defense by full performance). This may, however, be an inadvertent extension of the full-performance exception for the one-year statute to the land contract realm.

§6.9 n.19 p.184 Add the following to the list after **"Accord"***:* Winecellar Farm, Inc. v. Hibbard, 27 A.3d 777 (N.H. 2011) (whether part performance withdraws an oral contract for the sale of land from the statute of frauds depends in part on whether restitution would be adequate; if it is, "this weighs against

allowing the contract to be specifically enforced because, in that circumstance, the award of a monetary recovery provides adequate relief"); Strausser v. Pramco, III, 944 A.2d 761 (Pa. Super. 2008) (monthly payments insufficient to qualify as part performance, because the performance is compensable in damages).

§6.9 n.19 p.184 Add the following to the list after **"Cf."***:* Crossroads Church v. County of Dakota, 800 N.W.2d 608 (Minn. 2011) (partial payment may, coupled with the taking of possession, constitute part performance; payment did not occur when check paid to escrow agent, but rather at time of closing).

§6.9 n.20 p.185 Add the following at the end: For a thoughtful analysis using the traditional indicia of reliance, *see* Losh Family, LLC v. Kertsman, 228 P.3d 793 (Wash. App. 2010) ("Three factors are typically considered in determining whether there is sufficient evidence of part performance: (1) delivery and assumption of actual and exclusive possession; (2) payment or tender of consideration; and (3) the making of permanent, substantial, and valuable improvements, referable to the contract. . . . The making of substantial and valuable improvements is the strongest factor . . . , while payment alone is the weakest."). *Accord:* Zuk v. Zuk, 55 A.3d 102 (Pa. Super. 2012) (reciting test of "possession, payment and improvement"). *Cf.* Wilberg v. Hyatt, 285 P.3d 1249 (Utah App. 2012) ("the requirements of the part performance doctrine are malleable in that strong proof of one requirement may somewhat diminish the strength of the showing needed for another requirement"); Iota, LLC v. Davco Mgmt. Co., 284 P.3d 681 (Utah App. 2012) ("The requirements of [the reliance] prong are most stringent where the existence of the oral contract is uncertain, that is, where neither independent acts nor an admission of the contract affirmatively demonstrate that an oral contract existed.").

§6.9 n.21 p.185 Add the following to the list after **"Accord"***:* Bradley v. Bauldree, 101 So. 3d 221 (Ala. Civ. App. 2012) (partial performance exception applies where buyer tendered a down payment and took possession); Harvey v. Dow, 962 A.2d 322 (Me. 2008) ("It is beyond question that construction of a $200,000 immobile house constitutes an irretrievable change

in position; therefore the statute of frauds is not a bar to enforcement . . ."); Hurtubise v. McPherson, 951 N.E.2d 994 (Mass. App. 2011) (following Restatement Second §129; estoppel appropriate when buyer "occupied a parcel of [seller's] land and undertook the expense of construction . . . [The seller] watched [the buyer's] reliance unfold through seven to eight weeks of construction and $39,690 of expenditures."); Brice v. Hrdlicka, 206 P.3d 265 (Or. App. 2009) (contract to convey half-interest in property which was, to be reconveyed later, sufficiently performed when the plaintiff executed the deed conveying the half-interest), distinguished in part and followed in part in Kazlauskas v. Emmert, 275 P.3d 171 (Or. App. 2012) (managing properties and living on one property not unequivocally referable to the asserted contracts to convey an interest in real property; breached-against party was paid separately for managing properties, and was already living in that house when the agreement were made-however, remodeling the house was entirely after the agreement and was unequivocally referable to it).

§6.9 n.21 p.185 Add the following to the list after* "But cf."*: Crossroads Church v. County of Dakota, 800 N.W.2d 608 (Minn. 2011) ("The mere act of taking possession of land . . . is insufficient to avoid application of the statute of frauds.").

§6.9 n.22 p.186 Add the following to the list after* "See"*: Rentz v. Grant, 934 So. 2d 368 (Ala. 2006) (tenant "has not demonstrated that her possession of the house relates exclusively to an agreement to purchase the house and not to her agreement to lease the house; thus, [she] cannot rely on her possession as lessee to save her oral agreement to purchase the house from the operation of the Statute of Frauds"); Owens v. M.E. Schepp Ltd. P'ship, 182 P.3d 664 (Ariz. 2008) (payment to landscaping contractor and withdrawal of objection to tree removal not unequivocally referable to a contract for sale; either is consistent with continued co-tenancy); 151 Mulberry St. Corp. v. Italian American Museum, 957 N.Y.S 2d 698 (App. Div. 2013) (oral option for purchase of realty by tenant in oral agreement; although the putative buyer had made improvements to the property, that wasn't unequivocally referable to the contract, because it was also consistent with a lease contract).

§6.9 n.22 p.186 Add the following after the second sentence: *Cf.* Kiernan v. Creech, 268 P.3d 312 (Alaska 2012) ("It is true that we generally require exclusive and notorious possession. But we are persuaded by the opinions of courts from other jurisdictions that have waived these requirements when faced with oral contracts providing that the parties were to share the property. Those courts hold that, in such cases, the party asserting part performance must have possessed the property to the full extent of the alleged oral contract.").

***§6.9 n.23 p.186 Add the following to the list after* "Accord":** Greene v. McLeod, 942 A.2d 1254 (N.H. 2008) ("the payment of the purchase price, in conjunction with the payment of over thirty years of taxes, is sufficient for part performance"; no possibility of restitution from decedent).

***§6.9 n.24 p.186 In the first paragraph, add the following to the list after* "See":** *In re* Estate of Thompson, 752 N.W.2d 624 (N.D. 2008) (part performance for land contracts requires clear and convincing evidence).

***§6.9 n.25 p.187 Add the following to the list after* "Accord":** ; Harding Co. v. Sendero Resources, 365 S.W.3d 732 (Tex. Civ. App. 2012) ("When a party accepts assignments of mineral leases, the statute of frauds cannot be raised as a defense to payment.").

§6.9 n.25 p.187 Add the following at the end: *Cf.* Ala v. Chesser, 5 So. 3d 715 (Fla. App. 2009) ("the statute of frauds does not defeat recovery where the party seeking redress proves full performance on his part of an oral agreement for the conveyance of land," including an action in restitution).

***§6.9 n.26 p.187 In the first paragraph, add the following to the list after* "Accord":** LaRue v. Kalex Constr. & Dev., 97 So. 3d 251 (Fla. App. 2012) ("Full performance of an oral agreement . . . may remove the agreement from the statute of frauds if the agreement is capable of being performed within a year and was, in fact, performed within one year.");

§6.9 n.26 p.187 Add the following as a new paragraph after the second paragraph: As with part performance of land contracts, even full performance by one party must be unequivocally referable to the contract. Holloway v. Dekkers, 380 S.W.3d 315 (Tex. Civ. App. 2012) (employee who worked as promised under the oral contract did not perform in a manner unequivocally referable to the contract; he was paid a salary, so the work he did could easily be explained as nothing more than working for money, rather than as performance of a broader employment agreement not in a writing that satisfies the statute of frauds).

§6.9 n.26 p.187 In the third paragraph, add the following to the list after* "See"*: Fresh Capital Fin. Servs. v. Bridgeport Capital Servs., 891 So. 2d 1142 (Fla. App. 2005) (commission agreement for client referrals; "referral of each client . . . amounted to a separate contract which [the plaintiff] fully performed at the time of the referral"), declined to extend by Metro Bldg. Materials Corp. v. Republic Nat'l Bank, 919 So. 2d 595 (Fla. App. 2006) ("We cannot accept the proposition that submitting a completed application for credit constitutes full performance on the borrower's side so as to take the transaction out of the statute of frauds.").

§6.9 n.27 p.188 Add the following to the list after* "Accord"*: Arnold & Associates v. Misys Healthcare Sys., 275 F. Supp. 2d 1013 (D. Ariz. 2003) ("part performance is inapplicable because Plaintiff does not seek equitable remedies"); Robinson v. BDO Seidman, LLP, 854 N.E.2d 767 (Ill. App. 2006) (unless otherwise impracticable to return the parties to the status quo or compensate the promisee for his service, statute of frauds applies; "plaintiff was compensated for his partial performance and therefore the statute of frauds remains in effect"); Coca-Cola Co. v. Babyback's Int'l, 841 N.E.2d 557 (Ind. 2006) (allowing a part performance exception to the one-year provision "would invite persons to concoct and seek enforcement of fictitious contracts on grounds that the existence of an agreement would provide the only explanation for such persons' conduct," and "the nature of evidentiary facts potentially asserted to show part performance of an agreement not performable within one year would be vague, subjective, imprecise, and susceptible to fraudulent application").

§6.9 n.27 p.188 Add the following to the list after **"Contra"***:* Sullivan v. Leor Energy, 600 F.3d 542 (5th Cir. 2010) (Texas law; part-performance exception available, but not applicable here because the proffered performance was explicable by the written part of the contract, and thus was not unequivocally referable to the oral part, and also because denial of performance would not have yielded a virtual fraud); CQ, Inc. v. TXU Mining Co., 565 F.3d 268 (5th Cir. 2009) ("a court may enforce an oral contract that has been partially performed if enforcement is necessary to prevent a virtual fraud"; not present here, because the performance in question was consistent with purely preparatory work done in advance of a possible contract, as well as with the contract itself); Nelson v. Elway, 908 P.2d 102 (Colo. 1995) (applying part performance doctrine to contracts within the one-year provision if the part performance is "(1) substantial; and (2) required by, and fairly referable to no other theory besides that allegedly contained within the oral agreement"); Biko v. Siemens Corp., 246 S.W.3d 148 (Tex. Civ. App. 2007) (routine labor not unequivocally referable to a special bonus plan, where workers were paid regular wages and bonuses).

§6.9 n.27 p.188 Add the following to the list after **"See"***:* Glazer v. Dress Barn, *supra* note 17 ("we never have intended that the doctrine of equitable estoppel and the doctrine of part performance operate as independent exceptions to the statute of frauds. . . . Rather, part performance is an essential element of the estoppel exception").

§6.9 n.33 p.189 Add the following at the beginning: United Resource Recovery Corp. v. Ramko Venture Mgmt., 584 F. Supp. 2d 645 (S.D.N.Y. 2008) (part performance not an exception to brokerage statute of frauds); Johnson v. McPhee, 210 P.3d 563 (Idaho App. 2009) ("we doubt that a common law doctrine exempting partially performed contracts from a statute of frauds may be applied to alter the operation of a comprehensive statutory regulatory scheme").

§6.10 EFFECTS IN GENERAL

§6.10 n.2 p.190 Add the following to the list in the first sentence: Ala. Code §8-9-2 ("void").

§6.10 n.3 p.190 Add the following after the first sentence: The statute of frauds thus creates no duties, but merely provides a defense when their breach is asserted. Consequently, attempts to create a cause of action for violating the statute of frauds are invariably fruitless. *See* Hawa Constr. v. Pollock, 674 F. Supp. 2d 256 (D.D.C. 2009) (specialized statute of frauds for home improvements; "a statute of frauds . . . is not normally a source for affirmative relief").

§6.10 n.4 p.190 In the first paragraph, add the following at the beginning: Heritage Bldg. Prop. v. Prime Income Asset Mgmt., 43 So. 3d 1138 (Miss. App. 2009) ("[T]he statute of frauds does not make a contract void or prevent the contract from being formed. Rather, the statute only allows the defense to its enforcement[,] which defense is personal to the defendant.").

§6.10 n.9 p.191 Add the following to the list at the beginning: Waddle v. Elrod, 367 S.W.3d 217 (Tenn. 2012) ("parol agreements within the Statute of Frauds are not void ab initio, and enforcement of such agreements may be barred only if a party pleads the Statute of Frauds");

§6.10 n.19 p.193 In the third paragraph, add the following to the list after* "Accord"*: Marvin Inc. v. Albstein, 386 F. Supp. 2d 247 (S.D.N.Y. 2005) (following *DF Activities*); Owens v. M.E. Schepp Ltd. P'ship, 182 P.3d 664 (Ariz. 2008) (following *DF Activities*).

§6.10 n.19 p.193 Add the following at the end: Still, there is something to be said as well for permitting one round of discovery; it may be that deposing agents of the defendant will yield the requisite admission, or that documents found in discovery will collectively satisfy the statute. In addition, the affiant is probably not a lawyer, and thus may not be competent to say whether the facts of which he is aware amount to a contract. A sworn affidavit, after all, reflects only the knowledge and authority of its author, who may not have a monopoly on either. *See* Dennco, Inc. v. MacNeill Eng'g Co., 2005 WL 3578132 (D.N.H. Dec. 29, 2005) (allowing depositions of most important agents of defendant "[i]n order to balance the protection afforded to MacNeill by the statute of frauds against Dennco's need for a reasonable opportunity to show whether the admission exception of §2-201(3)(b) might apply"); Gooch v. Farmers Mktg. Ass'n, 519 So. 2d 1214 (Miss. 1988) (reversible error to grant summary judgment when statute of frauds pleaded because the non-moving party "might have been able to obtain an admission by [the other party] or one of its agents that a contract for sale was made . . . In this regard, it is conceivable that [the non-moving party] could obtain testimony relating to the parties' course of dealing, if any, or the usage of trade observed in the filing of such [agreements].") The *Gooch* court may, however, have swung too far in the other direction. The effect of *Gooch* is to eliminate summary judgment in cases involving oral contracts, or indeed any ruling on a statute of frauds defense until after the parties have introduced their evidence.

Possibly we need a standard here rather than a rule. If the plaintiff has no factual basis whatever to think it can obtain an admission from the defendant, then summary judgment seems appropriate. If the plaintiff has attempted in vain to gain a factual basis for its optimistic belief that an admission is just around the corner, then there seems little reason to proceed. If there is some factual basis, however, it may be that further discovery is in order. If the factual basis is substantial but not conclusive, then the plaintiff should have the right at trial to wrest the admission from the obdurate defendant. Trial courts should be able to sort these cases appropriately. *See generally* Herbert, Procedure and Promise: Rethinking the Admissions Exception to the Statute of Frauds under U.C.C. Article 2, 2A, and 8, 45 Okla. L. Rev. 203 (1992).

§6.10 n.22 p.194 Add the following to the list after "Accord": Nasso v. Bio Reference Labs., 892 F. Supp. 2d 439 (E.D.N.Y. 2012) ("Fraud by a party to a contract may permit a plaintiff to avoid the application of the Statute of Frauds. . . . [but] the defendant's failure to keep its promises is insufficient to constitute fraud under the exception to the Statute of Frauds doctrine."); Crowley v. Adams & Edens, P.A., 731 F. Supp. 2d 628

(S.D. Miss. 2010) ("an action for misrepresentation may be maintained, even when the promise itself is unenforceable by the statute of frauds"; described as majority rule); Sovereign Bank v. Licata, 977 A.2d 228 (Conn. App. 2009) ("A negligent misrepresentation does not seek to *enforce* the underlying contract; rather, it seeks damages for reliance on misrepresentations that may have been made in relation to that contract."); Holloway v. Holloway, 726 S.E.2d 198 (N.C. App. 2012) (statute of frauds bars only enforcement of the contract; it does not bar other claims, including a claim for restitution); Lam v. Phuong Nguyen, 335 S.W.3d 786 (Tex. Civ. App. 2011) ("the Statute of Frauds does not bar a claim for fraud or negligent misrepresentation to the extent a party seeks to recover reliance or out-of-pocket damages because such damages are not part of the benefit of the alleged bargain between the parties"); Transcontinental Realty Invs. v. John T. Lupton Trust, 286 S.W.3d 635 (Tex. Civ. App. 2009) ("[A] claim of negligent misrepresentation may not be used to circumvent the statute of frauds . . . The statute of frauds does not bar the recovery of out-of-pocket damages for fraud, however.").

§6.10 n.22 p.194 Add the following to the list after* "Contra"*: Brochu v. Santis, 939 A.2d 449 (R.I. 2008) ("mere allegations of fraud, without accompanying evidence, are insufficient to remove an oral contract from" the statute of frauds).

§6.10 n.24 p.195 In the first paragraph, add the following to the list after* "Accord"*: Palmer v. Bahm, 128 P.3d 1031 (Mont. 2006) ("a stranger to a contract lacks standing to enforce compliance with the statute of frauds") (collecting cases); Comet Energy Servs. v. Powder River Oil & Gas Ventures, 239 P.3d 382 (Wyo. 2010) (purpose of the statute of frauds is to give a party "the right to assert the statute as a defense to his or her own liability," so "[a] third party should not be able to assert the invalidity of such transaction . . .") followed in Cash v. Granite Springs Retreat Ass'n, 248 P.3d 614 (Wyo. 2011) ("While generally privies to a contracting party may assert the statute of frauds defense, that is not the case after the contract has been fully performed by the contracting parties."); Restatement Second §144.

***§6.10 n.25 p.196 In the first paragraph, add the following to the list after* "But see":** Preston Exploration Co. v. GSF, L.L.C., 669 F.3d 518 (5th Cir. 2012) ("To the extent that certain leases are listed on Exhibit A of the [purchase and sale agreements] but contain no corresponding recording information on the Assignment Exhibit A that is part of Exhibit C, enforcement is limited to those leases identified by recording information.");

§6.11 RESTITUTION

§6.11 n.1 p.197 In the first paragraph, add the following to the list in the first sentence: ; Smestad v. Harris, 820 N.W.2d 363 (N.D. 2012) (oral contract to repay loans)

***§6.11 n.5 p.198 Add the following to the list after* "Accord":** B & B Wrecker Serv. v. City of Citronelle, 90 So. 3d 743 (Ala. Civ. App. 2011) (special statute of frauds applying to contracts entered into by municipalities; though oral contract between city and towing company falls within the statute, the statute of frauds does not bar an action in quasi-contract or constructive contract by the towing company for the reasonable value of its services); Holloway v. Holloway, 726 S.E.2d 198 (N.C. App. 2012) (oral agreement to sell property and pay mortgage and taxes on new property within the statute, but here the plaintiff sought only return of the money used to pay mortgage, so motion to dismiss denied).

§6.11 n.5 p.198 Add the following at the end: Indeed, the presence of a right in restitution has served as an obstacle to asserting the reliance exception to the Statute of Frauds, because injustice can be avoided via restitution. *See* Yoost v. Zalcberg, 925 N.E.2d 763 (Ind. App. 2010). *Cf.* Brace v. Comfort, 2 So. 3d 1007 (Fla. App. 2008) ("a statute of frauds defense is inapplicable to such equitable claims as unjust enrichment, restitution, and imposition of a constructive trust"). On the reliance exception, see *infra* §6.12.

§6.11 n.12 p.200 In the first paragraph, add the following to the list after **"Accord"***:* Home Realty Lynnwood v. Walsh, 189 P.3d 253 (Wash. App. 2008) (even if land sale contract unenforceable because of statute of frauds, seller may retain earnest money if the buyer defaulted and the seller "remained ready, willing, and able to perform").

§6.11 n.20 p.202 Add the following to the list after **"Accord"***:* Brochu v. Santis, 939 A.2d 449 (R.I. 2008) ("an oral agreement precludes recovery of a commission 'irrespective of whether the action is based on the contract, on quantum meruit for services rendered, or on a theory of estoppel' ") (quoting Zexter v. Cerrone, 265 A.2d 328, 328-29 (R.I. 1970)).

§6.11 n.20 p.202 Add the following at the end: See Snyder v. Bronfman, 921 N.E.2d 567 (N.Y. 2009) (applying this statute to claim for reasonable compensation for services; statute refers specifically "to a contract implied in fact or in law"); MP Innovations v. Atl. Horizon Int'l, 899 N.Y.S.2d 213 (App. Div. 2010) (same). The courts often impose lesser writing requirements upon restitutionary claims — for example, by requiring only that the signed writing "evidence that fact of plaintiff's employment to render the alleged services." Morris Cohon & Co. v. Russell, *supra* note 4, followed in Springwell Corp. v. Falcon Drilling Co., 16 F. Supp. 2d 300 (S.D.N.Y. 1998) (Sotomayor, J.; "courts have been particularly willing to entertain quantum meruit claims where despite its other shortcomings or ambiguities, a defendant's writing expressly acknowledges that the plaintiff performed requested services").

§6.12 RELIANCE

§6.12 n.1 p.202 Replace the citation to **Bernstein** *with the following:* Braunstein, Remedy, Reason, and the Statute of Frauds: A Critical Economic Analysis, 1989 Utah L. Rev. 383.

§6.12 n.3 p.203 Add the following at the end: Accord: Thompson v. First Am. Nat'l Bank, 19 So. 3d 784 (Miss. App. 2009) ("the

statute of frauds, having been enacted for the purpose of preventing fraud, shall not be the instrument of shielding, protecting, or aiding the party who relies upon it in the perpetration of a fraud or in the consummation of a fraudulent scheme") (internal quotations omitted), followed in Crowley v. Adams & Edens, P.A., 731 F. Supp. 2d 628 (S.D. Miss. 2010) (statute of frauds does not bar claims for estoppel).

§6.12 n.4 p.203 Add the following at the end: For an instance of the convergence of these doctrines, aided by judicial recognition of the availability of remedies in both law and equity, see Glazer v. Dress Barn, 873 A.2d 929 (Conn. 2005) ("we never have intended that the doctrine of equitable estoppel and the doctrine of part performance operate as independent exceptions to the statute of frauds. . . . Rather, part performance is an essential element of the estoppel exception"). For a valiant attempt to distinguish among these exceptions, *see* Kolkman v. Roth, 656 N.W.2d 148 (Iowa 2003).

§6.12 n.5 p.203 Add the following to the list after **"Accord"***:* Ogden v. Griffith, 236 P.3d 1249 (Idaho 2010) (equitable estoppel applies where party sent attorneys to negotiate settlement agreement and those attorneys agreed on the general terms).

§6.12 n.5 p.203 Add the following to the list after **"But cf.":** *after the citation to* **Seymour***:* , overturned on other grounds by Sterling v. Taylor, 152 P.3d 420 (Cal. 2007).

§6.12 n.5 p.203 Add the following to the list after **"But cf.":** *after the citation to* **"Southmark Corp."***:* Helmus v. Chase Home Fin., 890 F. Supp. 2d 806 (W.D. Mich. 2012) (credit statute of frauds: no equitable estoppel because agreement states that it would not become effective until signed by both parties and lender supplied signed copy to borrower, so that it would have been unreasonable for the borrowers to move forward on purchasing property even though they had not received a signed copy of the agreement to lend);

§6.12 n.6 p.204 Add the following at the end: *Contra:* Crowley v. Adams & Edens, P.A., 731 F. Supp. 2d 628 (S.D. Miss. 2010) ("while the putative oral agreement may not be enforceable under the statute of frauds, it may be enforceable under a theory of promissory estoppel, which will support a claim for damages"). Some courts in contrast have lessened the traditional requirements for equitable estoppel. *See* Allen v. Allen, 280 S.W.3d 366 (Tex. Civ. App. 2008) (no requirement of misrepresentation); Affordable Erecting v. Neosho Trompler, 715 N.W.2d 620 (Wis. 2006) (same). Others have dispensed with that requirement in certain contexts. *See* Powell v. City of Newton, 684 S.E.2d 55 (N.C. App. 2009) (invoking doctrine of "judicial estoppel" to prevent use of Statute of Frauds defense against settlement agreement assented to in court).

§6.12 n.8 p.205 In the first paragraph, add the following to the list after the citation to* Chambers*: , followed in Control Solutions v. Oshkosh Corp., 78 U.C.C. Rep. Serv. 2d 239 (N.D. Ill. 2012) (manufacture of prototypes not sufficient, especially because parties continued to negotiate over the design even after the prototypes were made) and in Automated Cutting Technologies v. BJS N. Am. E, Inc., 78 U.C.C. Rep. Serv. 2d 93 (E.D. Ky. 2012) (purchasing equipment not a substantial beginning; in addition, "completing 30% of an expressly stipulated initial quantity [cannot] qualify as substantially beginning manufacture of goods in putative years 2-5 of a contract.").

§6.12 n.8 p.205 In the first paragraph, add the following to the list after the citation to* Webcor*: , followed in Woodland Harvesting v. Ga. Pac. Corp., 693 F. Supp. 2d 732 (E.D. Mich. 2010) ("the purchase of specialized sorting equipment and investment in inventory cannot convert otherwise ordinary pine wood chips into specially manufactured goods") and distinguished in RIJ Pharm. Corp. v. Ivax Pharm., 322 F. Supp. 2d 406 (S.D.N.Y. 2004) (silk-screened bottles for pharmaceuticals an "essential part of the agreement," as they were contracted for specifically and their manufacture was responsible for much of the structure of the agreement); Packgen v. BP Exploration & Prod., Inc., 957 F. Supp. 2d 58 (D. Me. 2013), *aff'd*, 754 F.3d 61, 68 (1st Cir. 2014) (oil containment boom was not specially manufactured good because manufacturer sold the boom on the open market for $2/sq. ft. after failure of talks to sell to BP for $21.75/sq. ft. in immediate aftermath of Deepwater Horizon accident; "It is the nature of the goods themselves that matters, not the circumstances under which Packgen tried to do business with BP.")

§6.12 n.8 p.205 ***In the first paragraph, add the following to the list after* "But Cf.":** Company Image Knitware v. Mothers Work, 909 A.2d 324 (Pa. Super. 2006) (knockoff goods contracted for by knockoff goods specialty shop within exception; though by definition knockoff goods resemble goods for which there is a market, they also are not suitable for sale in that market by those vendors, and the market for these knockoff goods was limited to this particular buyer);

§6.12 n.8 p.205 ***Add the following to the end of the first paragraph:*** For an extremely narrow reading of this exception, *see* Epprecht v. IBM Corp., 36 U.C.C. Rep. Serv. 391 (E.D. Pa. 1983) (manufacture of 7,000 specially manufactured machine parts not a substantial beginning of a contract for 50,000 parts; "Under [that] reasoning, production of seven thousand specially made parts would allow proof of an oral contract for ten thousand parts or fifty thousand parts or one million parts.").

§6.12 n.12 p.207 ***Add the following at the end:*** *Accord:* Yoost v. Zalcberg, 925 N.E.2d 763 (Ind. App. 2010) (injustice avoidable other than by enforcement of oral promise; forgoing claims arising from oral contract "does nothing to prevent Yoost from receiving the reasonable value of his services based on his remaining claim for quantum meruit").

§6.12 n.16 p.208 ***In the second paragraph, add the following to the list after* "See generally":** Epstein, Starbird, & Vincent, Reliance on Oral Promises: Statute of Frauds and "Promissory Estoppel," 42 Tex. Tech. L. Rev. 913 (2010).

§6.12 n.18 p.209 ***Add the following to the list after the citation to* C.G. Campbell & Son:** , approved in Farmers Bank & Trust Co. v. Willmott Hardwoods, 171 S.W.3d 4 (Ky. 2005).

§6.12 n.19 p.209 Replace the citation to UCC-R 20201(1) with the following: UCC-R 2-201(1).

§6.12 n.20 p.209 In the first paragraph, add the following after the citation to **Valdez Fisheries Dev. Ass'n***:* itself distinguished in Kiernan v. Creech, 268 P.3d 312 (Alaska 2012) (promissory estoppel germane when oral contract lacked material ambiguous terms).

§6.12 n.20 p.209 In the second paragraph, add the following to the list after **"with"***:* State v. Hinojos, 713 S.E.2d 351 (S.C. App. 2011) (applying estoppel to bar Statute of Frauds defense to action on bail bond).

§6.12 n.20 p.209 In the second paragraph, add the following to the list after **"See"***:* Brochu v. Santis, 939 A.2d 449 (R.I. 2008) (promissory estoppel applied to brokerage agreements "would, in the absence of fraud, defeat the very purpose for which [the brokerage exception] was enacted") (quoting Heyman v. Adeack Realty, 228 A.2d 578, 580 (R.I. 1967)).

§6.12 n.20 p.209 In the second paragraph, add the following after the citation to **Everett***:* , followed in Hoover v. Moran, 662 S.E.2d 711 (W. Va. 2008) (applying to UCC §8-319 (now repealed)).

§6.12 n.20 p.209 In the third paragraph, add the following to the list in the first sentence: Kiernan v. Creech, 268 P.3d 312 (Alaska 2012) ("we thus join the many jurisdictions that recognize some form of promissory estoppel as an exception to the statute of frauds in land transactions; collecting cases").

§6.12 n.20 p.209 In the third paragraph, add the following after the citation to **Brown***:* , followed in Coca-Cola Co. v. Babyback's Int'l, 841 N.E.2d 557 (Ind. 2006), in turn followed in Hrezo v. City of Lawrenceburg, 934 N.E.2d 1221 (Ind. App. 2010) (damages limited to the reliance interest, and in any event this exception requires that the reliance injury be independent from the benefit of the bargain, and be so large as to amount to an unjust and unconscionable injury) and in Yoost v. Zalcberg, 925 N.E.2d

763 (Ind. App. 2010) (not satisfied where reliance was continued work at a very low wage in reliance on a promise to release a mortgage; the plaintiff "continued to perform the same duties that he had always performed . . . and was paid essentially the same amount he had always been paid, albeit a low amount, for merely continuing his employment"; quaere whether this result would have come about had the plaintiff threatened to quit without the promise of other compensation).

***§6.12 n.20 p.209 In the third paragraph, add the following to the list after* "But cf.":** Bradley v. Sanchez, 943 So. 2d 218 (Fla. App. 2006) ("the statute of frauds prohibits the oral modification of a contract for the sale of land under the doctrine of promissory estoppel"); E. Tangipahoa Dev. Co. v. Bedico Junction, LLC, 5 So. 3d 238 (La. App. 2008) (reliance on an oral promise almost always unreasonable, because the law requires that they be in writing — especially, as here, where the party seeking to avoid the statute was a sophisticated businessman and an attorney).

§6.12 n.20 p.209 In the third paragraph, add the following at the end: Special statutes of frauds may also be subject to the reliance exception. *See* Affordable Erecting v. Neosho Trompler, *supra* note 2 (statute of frauds for settlement agreements subject to estoppel exception); Bank of Tex. v. Gaubert, 286 S.W.3d 546 (Tex. Civ. App. 2009) (applying reliance exception to statute of frauds for loan agreements). *But see* Farmers Bank & Trust Co. v. Willmott Hardwoods, *supra* note 18 (refusing to find an equitable estoppel exception to a lending statute of frauds); Fortress Sys. v. Bank of the W., 559 F.3d 848 (8th Cir. 2009) (Nebraska law; same); Labrant v. Mortgage Elec. Registration Sys., 870 F. Supp. 2d 671 (D. Minn. 2012) (Minnesota law; same). And some special statutes of frauds expressly eliminate that exception. *See, e.g.*, S.C. Code Ann. §37-10-107(2)(b).

§6.12 n.20 p.209 Add the following after the third paragraph: For a wholesale and antediluvian rejection of the promissory estoppel exception, *see* Olympic Holding Co. v. Ace Ltd., 909 N.E.2d 93 (Ohio 2009). This is very much a minority position; as the dissent in *Olympic Holding Co.* points out, "an overwhelming majority of jurisdictions recognize that promissory estoppel may bar a party from asserting a defense under the statute of frauds in certain circumstances." *Olympic Holding Co., supra* (O'Donnell, J., dissenting) (collecting cases; 26 jurisdictions recognize a reliance exception, while only eight do not). *See also* McCann v. U.S. Bank, 873 F. Supp. 2d 823 (E.D. Mich. 2012) (promissory estoppel does not apply to a statute of frauds case involving the sale of real property).

§6.12 n.22 p.210 Add the following to the list after "Accord": Transcontinental Realty Invs. v. John T. Lupton Trust, 286 S.W.3d 635 (Tex. Civ. App. 2009) ("'Since the promisee in such cases is partially responsible for his failure to bind the promisor to a legally sufficient contract, it is reasonable to conclude that all that is required to achieve justice is to put the promisee in the position he would have been in had he not acted in reliance upon the promise.'"; plaintiff sought only expectation damages, so its estoppel counter-defense was ineffectual).

§6.12 n.22 p.210 Add the following at the end: *Cf.* State v. Hinojos, 713 S.E.2d 351 (S.C. App. 2011) (estopping bail bondsmen from denying liability on the bond, in essence estreating their portion of the bond).

§6.12 n.23 p.211 Add the following to the list after "See": Darby Trading v. Shell Int'l Trading & Shipping Co., 568 F. Supp. 2d 329 (S.D.N.Y. 2008) (New York requires showing of "unconscionable injury" to invoke promissory estoppel exception; "the demonstration of . . . typical expectation damages, without more, does not demonstrate an unconscionable injury"); Secrest v. Sec. Nat'l Mtg. Loan Trust, 84 Cal. Rptr. 3d 275 (Ct. App. 2008) ("[T]he party seeking to enforce the contract must have changed position in reliance on the oral contract to such an extent that application of the statute of frauds would result in an unjust or unconscionable loss, amounting in effect to a fraud."); Robinson v. BDO Seidman, LLP, 854 N.E.2d 767 (Ill. App. 2006) (promissory estoppel bars application of the statute of frauds only where "the performing party would otherwise be without remedy and the other party would be unjustly enriched"); Coca-Cola Co. v. Babyback's Int'l, *supra* note 20 (requiring that "the reliance injury must be not only (1) independent from the benefit of the bargain and resulting incidental expenses and inconvenience, but also (2) so substantial as to constitute an unjust and unconscionable injury"), followed in Classic Cheesecake Co. v. JPMorgan Chase Bank, 546 F.3d 839 (7th Cir. 2008) (Posner, J.: Indiana rule really not rooted in moral judgments, but rather "is to require a party that wants to get around the statute of frauds to prove an *enhanced* promissory estoppel, and the enhancement consists of proving a kind or amount of reliance unlikely to have been incurred had the plaintiff not had a good-faith belief that he had been promised consideration").

§6.12 n.23 p.211 Add the following after the citation to* Philo Smith & Co.*: followed in Robins v. Zwirner, 713 F. Supp. 2d 367 (S.D.N.Y. 2010) (promissory estoppel exception applies only if the plaintiff "suffer[s] a greater injury than one that is both predictable and, to a certain degree, the consequence[] of the Plaintiff's own choices").

§6.12 n.23 p.211 Add the following to the list after* "see"*: City of Orlando v. W. Orange Country Club, 9 So. 3d 1268 (Fla. App. 2009) ("the law is well-settled that '[t]he doctrine of promissory estoppel cannot be used to circumvent the statute of frauds' ") (quoting from Harris v. School Bd. of Duval Cnty., 921 So. 2d 725 (Fla. App. 2006)); May Trucking Co. v. N.W. Volvo Trucks, 241 P.3d 729 (Or. App. 2010) ("a party asserting estoppel to avoid the statute of frauds must show that the party asserting the statute of frauds made a misrepresentation beyond the contractual promise itself and gained an advantage from the misrepresentation and detrimental reliance").

§6.12 n.23 p.211 Add the following at the end: *Cf.* Sawyer v. Mills, 295 S.W.3d 79 (Ky. 2009) (declining to decide whether promissory estoppel exception exists).

§6.12 n.27 p.212 Add the following to the list after* "Accord"*: Olympic Holding Co. v. Ace Ltd., *supra* note 20 ("promissory estoppel is an adequate remedy for a fraudulent oral promise or breach of an oral promise, absent a signed agreement"); Medistar Corp. v. Schmidt, 267 S.W.3d 150 (Tex. Civ. App. 2008) ("The statute of frauds . . . is not a defense to an action for affirmative relief under the doctrine of promissory estoppel."); Barrie-Chivian v. Lepler, 87 Mass. App. Ct. 83, 34 N.E.3d 769 (2015) ("doctrinal developments reflected in more recent cases make clear that the Statute of Frauds does not bar recovery on a promissory estoppel theory").

§6.12 n.27 p.212 Add the following after the citation to* Architectural Metal Sys.*: , followed in Trustmark Ins. Co. v. Gen. & Cologne Life Re of Am., 424 F.3d 542 (7th Cir. 2005) (quoting language in parenthetical).

§6.12 n.29 p.212 In the second paragraph, add the following at the end: *See* Richmond v. EBI, Inc., 53 So. 3d 859 (Miss. App. 2011) ("Although modification of an agreement that falls under the statute of frauds must be in writing, a waiver is not required to be in writing.").

§6.12 n.31 p.213 Add the following to the list after* "Accord"*: Valley Bank of Commerce v. Hilburn, 105 P.3d 294 (N.M. App. 2004) (following Restatement Second §150; paying off note a material change in position on bank's promise to return a guaranty).

PART III

SCOPE AND EFFECT OF PROMISES

CHAPTER

7

THE LAW OF THE CONTRACT: INTERPRETATION AND OMITTED CASES

§7.1 SIGNIFICANCE OF THE LAW OF THE CONTRACT

§7.1 n.2 p.218 ***Add the following at the end:*** Also, note that while courts will interpret contracts by references to statues and common law, and are subject to review by higher courts, an increasing number of contracts require that disputes instead be settled by arbitration, and courts generally are powerless to review the substance of an arbitrator's decision. Even where questions of law are central to interpretation of the contract, an arbitrator's decision cannot be overturned if it was even arguably interpreting the contract. For example, in *BNSF Ry. Co. v. Alstom Transp., Inc.*, 777 F.3d 785 (5th Cir. 2015), the Fifth Circuit reversed a district court decision that had set aside an arbitration panel's decision that found a breach of the contract, which had imposed a good faith and fair dealing obligation (erroneously under applicable state law, in the court's view) upon a contract that allowed for termination of the agreement "without cause." The arbitration panel said it was interpreting the contract terms, albeit by reference to Illinois common law, and accordingly was "arguably interpreting" the contract and thus its decision could not be reversed by the courts. The circuit explained that the fact that "we

might interpret the Agreement differently than the Panel is entirely beside the point because it is not our interpretation that the parties bargained for." *Id.* at 789.

§7.1 n.3 p.219 Add the following at the end: In Andermann v. Sprint Spectrum, LP, 785 F.3d 1157 (7th Cir. 2015) (Posner, J.), the issue was whether the arbitration agreement in a cellular telephone services contract could be enforced when suit was filed over actions that occurred after the contract was terminated. The plaintiffs signed a contract with U.S. Cellular, which assigned the contract to Sprint, which then canceled the contract because the plaintiffs' phone was not compatible with its network. The plaintiffs filed suit alleging that later sales calls from Sprint violated the Telephone Consumer Protection Act, and Sprint moved to compel arbitration. The district court held that the agreement to arbitrate did not apply to this dispute because the calls occurred after the contract was terminated, so the dispute over the legality of those calls did not arise from the contract, but Judge Posner reversed. "It was to prevent the loss of all these customers because of the incompatibility that Sprint had told them in the calls that it could offer them a substitute service. The calls gave rise to the dispute; and so the Andermanns were required to arbitrate the dispute."

***§7.1 n.4 p.219 Add the following to the list after* "See":** C. Fox, Working with Contracts (2002); L. Kaplow & S. Shavell, Contracting (2004); T. Stark, Drafting Contracts (2007).

§7.2 THE RATIONALE OF THE PAROL EVIDENCE RULE

***§7.2 n.1 p.220 In the second paragraph, add the following to the list after* "See generally":** Mitchell, Contract Interpretation: Pragmatism, Principle and the Plain Meaning Rule, 26 J. Contract L. 134 (2010); E. Posner, The Parol Evidence Rule, the Plain Meaning Rule, and the Principles of Contractual Interpretation, 146 U. Pa. L. Rev. 533 (1998).

§7.2 n.4 p.221 Add the following to the list after **"Accord"***:* Kenney v. Vansittert, 277 S.W.3d 713 (Mo. App. 2008) ("The parol evidence rule . . . exists to preserve the sanctity of written contracts.").

§7.2 n.5 p.221 Add the following at the end: Furthermore, CISG has no parol evidence rule. CISG art. 8(3) ("In determining the intent of a party or the understanding a reasonable person would have had, due consideration is to be given to all relevant circumstances of the case including the negotiations, any practices which the parties have established between themselves, usages and any subsequent conduct of the parties."). *See also* Principles of Eur. Contract L. art. 5:102 ("In interpreting the contract, regard shall be had, in particular, to: (a) the circumstances in which it was concluded, including the preliminary negotiations . . ."); UNIDROIT Principles of Int'l Comm'l Contracts art. 4.3 (in giving effect to the intent of the parties, "regard shall be had to all the circumstances, including (a) preliminary negotiations between the parties . . ."). Merger clauses are treated variously. Some jurisdictions ignore them entirely. Others give them effect, but only if individually negotiated for. Still others take them into account, but do not give them conclusive weight. Principles of Eur. Contract L. art. 2:105 & notes. The sentence in the text to the effect that "[t]he parol evidence rule is universally recognized" should be taken to refer only to the United States and other common-law nations — and, as the preceding paragraph notes, the parol evidence rule has not escaped attack even within the sheltering arms of the common law.

§7.2 n.8 p.222 Change the title of **First State Bank in Durant** *to:* First Nat'l Bank in Durant.

§7.2 n.8 p.222 Add the following at the end: *Accord:* Kenney v. Vansittert, 277 S.W.3d 713 (Mo. App. 2008) ("The parol evidence rule is a substantive rule of contract law . . ."); Conway v. 287 Corp. Ctr. Assocs., 901 A.2d 341 (N.J. 2006) ("the parol evidence rule is a rule of substantive law, not a rule of evidence"); Baroid Equip. v. Odeco Drilling, 184 S.W.3d 1 (Tex. Civ. App. 2005) ("The parol evidence rule is not a mere rule of evidence, but a rule of substantive contract law.").

§7.2 n.10 p.222 Add the following after the first sentence: For an interesting exploration of the history of this case, see Keren, Textual Harassment: A New Historicist Reappraisal of the Parol Evidence Rule with Gender in Mind, 13 Am. U. J. Gender Soc. Pol'y & L. 251 (2005).

§7.2 n.13 p.223 Add the following to the list after "Contra": Prattville Mem. Chapel v. Parker, 10 So. 3d 546 (Ala. 2008) ("'where evidence violative of the parol evidence rule is admitted without objection, it may be considered and allowed such force and effect as its weight entitles it in construing the agreement of the parties'").

§7.2 n.17 p.225 Add the following at the beginning: Extra Equipamentos e Exportação Ltda. v. Case Corp., 541 F.3d 719 (7th Cir. 2008) (Posner, J.: "Drafters of contracts worry lest in the event of a dispute one of the parties ask the court to depart from the terms of the written contract on the ground that it is not the parties' entire agreement — there are additional terms to which they had agreed during the negotiations leading up to the making of the contract. If such a claim enabled the party making it to obtain a jury trial on the meaning of the contract, the contractual process would be riven by uncertainty."; quoting from treatise).

§7.3 THE APPLICATION OF THE PAROL EVIDENCE RULE

§7.3 n.3 p.226 Add the following at the beginning: Bank of America v. C.D. Smith Motor Co., 106 S.W.3d 425 (Ark. 2003) ("merger clause did not preclude course of dealing evidence" where it "did not contradict the terms of the parties' agreement").

§7.3 n.3 p.226 Substitute the following for the second sentence: The inclusion of course of performance seems unnecessary because course of performance is subsequent to the agreement.

§7.3 n.9 p.227 In the first paragraph, add the following after the first sentence: *But cf.* Kenney v. Vansittert, 277 S.W.3d 713 (Mo. App. 2008) (because writing unsigned, "there is no objective indication of mutual assent within [its] four corners" and so "[w]e cannot conclude solely from the document that [it] is the final and complete expression of the parties' agreement," so parol is admissible).

***§7.3 n.13 p.227 Add the following to the list after* "Accord":** Utica Mut. Ins. Co. v. Vigo Coal Co., 393 F.3d 707 (7th Cir. 2004) (in the absence of a merger clause, "a party can ask the judge to look at extrinsic evidence, though initially just for the limited purpose of deciding whether the contract really is integrated").

§7.3 n.22 p.230 Add the following at the end of the first sentence: , followed in Morgan Bldgs. & Spas v. Humane Soc'y of S.E. Tex., 249 S.W.3d 480 (Tex. Civ. App. 2008) ("In determining whether an agreement is integrated, the parol evidence rule does not bar the consideration of any evidence.").

***§7.3 n.24 p.230 Add the following after the citation to* J & B:** followed in Davis v. G.N. Mortg. Corp., 396 F.3d 869 (7th Cir. 2005) (barring supplemental parol if the writing is complete on its face).

***§7.3 n.24 p.230 Add the following to the list after* "Accord":** Kenney v. Vansittert, 277 S.W.3d 713 (Mo. App. 2008) ("In Missouri, to determine if a writing is integrated, we look to the face of the document itself — without looking to the surrounding facts and circumstances.").

***§7.3 n.27 p.231 Add the following to the list after* "Accord":** Hinkel v. Sataria Distrib. & Packaging, 920 N.E.2d 766 (Ind. App. 2010) ("The preliminary question of integration, either complete or partial, requires the court to hear all relevant evidence, parol or written."; follows Restatement Second); S.D. Deacon Corp. v. Gaston Bros. Excavating, 206 P.3d 689 (Wash. App. 2009) ("A court may consider evidence of negotiations and circumstances surrounding the formation of the contract, and if the agreement is not completely integrated, additional terms may be proved to the extent they are consistent with the written terms.").

§7.3 n.27 p.231 Delete the citation to **Cobb State Bank.**

§7.3 n.27 p.231 Add the following at the end: The Wisconsin Supreme Court recently brought confusion to what had been a clear body of parol evidence doctrine. Until recently, Wisconsin was unambiguously in the Restatement Second camp. *See* Dairyland Equip. Leasing v. Bohen (*In re* Spring Valley Meats), 288 N.W.2d 852 (Wis. 1980) ("'Parol evidence is always admissible with respect to the issue of integration.'") (quoting from FDIC v. First Mortg. Invs., 250 N.W.2d 362 (Wis. 1977)). Indeed, the opinion that did the damage quotes the sentence above with approval. Town Bank v. City Real Estate Dev., 793 N.W.2d 476, 485 (Wis. 2010). But then the *Town Bank* court blithely stated that evidence relating to integration "is not 'parol evidence' at all." To support this astonishing statement, the court observed that "we are merely invoking an already recognized and well-defined rule of contract law: when a contract is ambiguous, a court may consider extrinsic evidence to resolve the parties' intent." Well, yes, but that conflates the parol evidence rule with the rules on parol evidence and interpretation. Whether an agreement is ambiguous depends critically on its precise terms, which are determined only after application of the parol evidence rule. Making clear that this comment was not merely a *lapsus calami*, the court inverted the all-but-universal law in this area when it stated that "[i]f and once it is determined that the parties intended the contract to be integrated, only then does the parol evidence rule go into effect."

Pretty bad? Just wait. The next paragraph begins with the statement that "when the contract contains an unambiguous merger or integration clause, the court is barred from considering evidence of any prior or contemporaneous understandings or agreements between the parties, even as to the issue of integration" because "if the contract is unambiguous, the court's attempt to determine the parties' intent ends with the language of the contract, without resort to extrinsic evidence." Let us leave aside the narrow approach espoused by the court to determine ambiguity — a common one, but not therefore unimpeachable.

See *infra* §7.12. Does the court mean that it uses the Restatement Second approach, thus admitting parol to determine the degree of integration — except when the contract contains an unambiguous merger clause, which absolutely excludes parol, and whose ambiguity is determined without recourse to extrinsic evidence? That isn't how it began its discussion. Or has it overturned a long string of cases *sub silentio*, putting Wisconsin on the Williston side of the parol evidence debate? Or has it redefined the parol evidence rule to leave the earlier authority intact, while at the same time depriving it of most of its effect? Surely Wisconsin lawyers and contract drafters would like to know which — but they can't look to *Town Bank* for assistance. As the dissent properly observes, "the majority's inconsistency is demonstrated not only from paragraph to paragraph, but also the inconsistency exists within the very same paragraph." Town Bank v. City Real Estate Dev., 793 N.W.2d 476, 493 (Wis. 2010) (Bradley, J., dissenting). Had the court not confused the parol evidence rule with the use of parol in contract interpretation, it might well have avoided this mess. But it did, and so we can but await a later attempt to clarify what had been clear.

§7.3 n.32 p.232 Add the following to the list after **"Accord"***:* Alliance Laundry Sys. v. Thyssenkrupp Materials, 570 F. Supp. 2d 1061 (E.D. Wis. 2008) ("Although the parties' e-mails may constitute a final expression of their agreement with respect to the items to be purchased and the price, nothing in the e-mails indicates that the parties intended them to constitute a complete and exclusive statement of the agreement's terms.").

§7.3 n.32 p.232 Add the following at the end of the first paragraph: *Cf.* Withers v. City of Lake St. Louis, 318 S.W.3d 256 (Mo. App. 2010) ("When a written contract omits an essential term to the agreement, it is considered incomplete . . ."; agreement by which city annexed land was missing an exhibit containing the development plans, which were at issue).

§7.3 n.32 p.232 In the second paragraph, add the following to the list after **"see"***:* Digitech Computer v. Trans-Care, 583 F. Supp. 2d 984 (S.D. Ind. 2008) (part of "ample evidence that the parties did not intend a complete integration" was that "[t]here was no integration clause"); America's Floor Source v. Joshua

Homes, 946 N.E.2d 799 (Ohio App. 2010) (document only partial integration because, among other things, it "lacks the usual contract language that expressly states that the agreement is the complete contract"); City of Grantsville v. Redev. Agency, 233 P.3d 461 (Utah 2010) ("[I]n the absence of an integration clause, when a party to a contract insists that the contract is not integrated, a court must determine as a question of fact whether the writing constituted a final and complete expression of their bargain.") (internal quotes omitted).

§7.3 n.32 p.232 In the second paragraph, add the following to the list after **"But see"***:* Massey v. Town of Branford, 985 A.2d 335 (Conn. App. 2009) ("The plaintiffs have cited no authority, and we know of none, that holds that the absence of a merger clause is evidence that a contract is incomplete or ambiguous.") (Peters, J.); Sees v. Bank One, 839 N.E.2d 154 (Ind. 2005) (Boehm, J., concurring and dissenting) ("[T]he absence of an integration clause is not conclusive as to whether parties intend a writing to be completely integrated."; cites to Restatement Second §209 cmt. *b*).

§7.3 n.32 p.232 In the second paragraph, add the following after the citation to **Jake C. Byers, Inc.***:* , followed in Richards v. JTL Grp., 212 P.3d 264 (Mont. 2009) (absence of merger clause "is not necessarily fatal to JTL's argument that the Sale Agreement was final and complete").

§7.3 n.35 p.233 Add the following to the end: *See also* Davis v. G.N. Mortg. Corp., 396 F.3d 869 (7th Cir. 2005) (finding fully integrated loan agreement in combination of 24 documents executed at loan closing). *But see* Digitech Computer v. Trans-Care, 583 F. Supp. 2d 984 (S.D. Ind. 2008) ("the reference to writings outside of the [integrated document] . . . is substantial evidence that Digitech did not intend a complete integration"); Scovill Fasteners v. N. Metals, 692 S.E.2d 840 (Ga. App. 2010) (finding only partial integration where the purportedly final writing "anticipated that necessary terms such as material specifications, quantities, pricing information, and delivery dates would be supplied as part of the bidding and ordering process").

§7.3 n.36 p.233 In the first paragraph, add the following to the list after **"Accord"***:* Howard v. Perry, 106 P.3d 465 (Idaho 2005) ("the merger clause is not merely a factor to consider in deciding whether the agreement is integrated; it proves the agreement is integrated"); Phelps-Dickson Builders v. Amerimann Partners, 617 S.E.2d 664 (N.C. App. 2005) ("the merger clause bars the parol evidence"); Davis v. KB Home, 713 S.E.2d 799 (S.C. App. 2011) (facially unambiguous merger clause conclusive as to integration); City of Grantsville v. Redev. Agency, 233 P.3d 461 (Utah 2010) ("When a contract includes an integration clause, the contract is presumed to contain the whole agreement and parties may not rely on extrinsic evidence in attempting to prove that the contract is not integrated."); Town Bank v. City Real Estate Dev., 793 N.W.2d 476 (Wis. 2010) ("when the contract contains an unambiguous merger or integration clause, the court is barred from considering evidence of any prior or contemporaneous understandings or agreements between the parties, even as to the issue of integration").

§7.3 n.36 p.233 Add the following at the end of the first paragraph: For an unusual application of this principle, *see* Smith v. Anderson, 632 F.3d 277 (6th Cir. 2011), raising it in the context of a petition for a writ of habeas corpus. The petitioner and the state entered into a plea agreement which was memorialized, complete with integration clause, and stated on the record in open court. The written agreement did not include a promise made by the prosecutor not to send letters of recommendation to the parole board. A subsequent prosecutor broke that promise. Though the court found the petitioner's arguments appealing and the prosecutor's behavior appalling, it nevertheless affirmed the exclusion of evidence of the terms of the prior agreement, given the presence of a "fully integrated, written plea agreement which did not discuss the promise at issue" and the failure of the parties to respond when asked by the court whether there were any additional terms.

§7.3 n.36 p.233 Add the following at the end of the second paragraph: On the comparatively restrictive approaches used in other common-law jurisdictions, *see* Bayley, Prior Negotiations and Subsequent Conduct in Contract Interpretation: Principles and Practical Concerns, 28 J. Contract L. 179 (2012).

§7.3 n.37 p.234 In the second paragraph, add the following after the citation to **Tallmadge***:* followed in Alstom Power v. Balcke-Durr, 849 A.2d 804 (Conn. 2004) (language of merger clause between two corporations was "conclusive evidence of the parties' intent to create a fully integrated agreement").

§7.3 n.37 p.234 Add the following to the list after **"Accord"***:* Jenkins v. Eckerd Corp., 913 So. 2d 43 (Fla. App. 2005) ("Although the existence of a merger clause does not *per se* establish that the integration of the agreement is total . . . a merger clause is a highly persuasive statement that the parties intended the agreement to be totally integrated . . ."); Green v. Vanguard Med. Assocs., 944 N.E.2d 184 (Mass. App. 2011) ("even apparently straightforward contractual language asserting integration will not always compel a conclusion that a writing reflects a complete and integrated agreement"); Behrens v. S.P. Constr. Co., 904 A.2d 676 (N.H. 2006) ("Though not dispositive, an integration clause is evidence that parties intended a writing to be a total integration."); Bellman v. Am. Int'l Grp., 865 N.E.2d 853 (Ohio 2007) ("Whether a contract is integrated . . . is not dependent upon the existence of an integration clause to that effect, and '[t]he presence of an integration clause makes the final written agreement no more integrated than does the act of embodying the complete terms into the writing.' "); Traders Bank v. Dils, 704 S.E. 2d 691 (W. Va. 2010) ("we do not find the integration clause that is purportedly contained in the promissory note to exclude the possibility of a fraudulent inducement claim"; argument that no sophisticated business person would enter into a big contract without reducing all the terms to writing "is certainly one that Traders Bank may use to try to convince a jury") (footnotes omitted); S.D. Deacon Corp. v. Gaston Bros. Excavating, 206 P.3d 689 (Wash. App. 2009) ("While boilerplate integration clauses can provide strong evidence of integration, they are not operative if they are premised on incorrect statements of fact.").

§7.3 n.38 p.235 Add the following at the end: Evan v. Poe & Assocs., 873 N.E.2d 92 (Ind. App. 2007) (the parol evidence rule "does not apply to a controversy between a third party and one of the parties to the instrument"; nevertheless, "when a [contract] is unambiguous we need not look at any other evidence to

determine the parties' intent.") (quoting from Cooper v. Cooper, 730 N.E.2d 212 (Ind. App. 2000)), followed in Bowman v. Int'l Bus. Mach. Corp., 853 F. Supp. 2d 766 (S.D. Ind. 2012) (third parties expressly and unambiguously excluded in contract, so parol evidence regarding the intent of the parties inadmissible).

§7.3 n.39 p.236 Add the following at the end: *Cf.* ERI Consulting Eng'rs v. Swinnea, 318 S.W.3d 867 (Tex. 2010) (permitting evidence of collateral agreement that was the consideration for the principal agreement).

§7.3 n.40 p.236 Add the following to the list after* "See also"*: Baroid Equip. v. Odeco Drilling, 184 S.W.3d 1 (Tex. Civ. App. 2005) (requiring that the agreement not be inconsistent with the integrated contract "and (a) is made for separate consideration, or (b) is such an agreement as might naturally be made as a separate agreement by parties situated as were the parties to the written contract"), followed in DeClaire v. G & B McIntosh Family Ltd. P'ship, 260 S.W.3d 34 (Tex. Civ. App. 2008) (oral contract unenforceable because its contents largely overlapped those of the writing, but with one different term).

§7.3 n.40 p.236 Add the following after the second sentence: For somewhat different formulations, see Ala. Elec. Co-op. v. Bailey's Constr. Co., 950 So. 2d 280 (Ala. 2006) (asking whether "the alleged collateral oral agreement was one the parties would naturally have included in the written agreement") (quoting from treatise); Hinkel v. Sataria Distrib. & Packaging, 920 N.E.2d 766 (Ind. App. 2010) (the court "'must compare . . . the alleged oral and written agreements and must determine whether the parties, situated as were the ones to the contract, would naturally and normally include the one in the other if it were made'") (quoting Steinke v. Sungard Fin. Sys., 121 F.3d 763 (1st Cir. 1997)).

§7.3 n.45 p.237 Add the following at the end: *Accord:* Suburban Leisure Ctr. v. AMF Bowling Prods., 468 F.3d 523 (8th Cir. 2006) (later e-commerce agreement on marketing, though containing a merger clause, "does not address" the subject of the prior oral agreement to franchise and therefore the latter is not merged into it).

§7.3 n.46 p.237 In the first paragraph, add the following to the list after **"Contra"***:* All-Tech Telecom v. Amway Corp., 174 F.3d 862 (7th Cir. 1999) (Posner, J.); "When there is an express contract governing the relationship out of which the promise emerged, and no issue of consideration, there is no gap in the remedial system for promissory estoppel to fill. To allow it to be invoked becomes in those circumstances gratuitous duplication or, worse, circumvention of carefully designed principles of contract law."); Kia v. Imaging Sciences Int'l, 735 F. Supp. 2d 256 (E.D. Pa. 2010) ("Although Kia formulates [his] claim as one for 'promissory estoppel,' it is actually an improper attempt to vary the terms of an integrated, written agreement based on alleged oral statements ma[d]e prior to his signing it."); Davis v. Siemens Med. Solutions USA, 399 F. Supp. 2d 785 (W.D. Ky. 2005) ("To allow oral promises otherwise inadmissible under the parol evidence rule to form the basis of a promissory estoppel claim would eviscerate the rule and disregard at least 140 years of jurisprudence."), *aff'd*, 278 Fed. Appx. 378 (6th Cir. 2008).

§7.3 n.46 p. 237 In the second paragraph, add the following to the list after **"See generally"***:* Epstein, Arbuckle, & Flanagan, Contract Law's Two "P.E.'s": Promissory Estoppel and the Parol Evidence Rule, 62 Baylor L. Rev. 397 (2010).

§7.3 n.48 p.238 Add the following to the list after **"Accord"***:* Digitech Computer v. Trans-Care, 583 F. Supp. 2d 984 (S.D. Ind. 2008) ("whether or not the parties intended a complete integration is a question of law for the court"); Harbor Village Home Ctr. v. Thomas, 882 So. 2d 811 (Ala. 2003) ("whether a contract is integrated is ordinarily a question of law for the court"); Green v. Vanguard Med. Assocs., 944 N.E.2d 184 (Mass. App. 2011) ("Whether an agreement is integrated 'is an issue of fact for the decision of the trial judge' ") (quoting from Wang Labs. v. Docktor Pet Ctrs., 422 N.E.2d 805 (Mass. App. 1981)); Tangren Family Trust v. Tangren, 182 P.3d 326 (Utah 2008) ("Whether a contract is integrated is a question of fact" to be resolved by the trial judge).

§7.3 n.48 p.238 ***In the second paragraph, add the following to the list after* "see":** Baroid Equip. v. Odeco Drilling, 184 S.W.3d 1 (Tex. Civ. App. 2005) ("As a question of law, the standard of review is de novo.").

§7.3 n.55 p.239 ***Add the following at the end:*** It is important to remember that the use of parol for interpretation, associated with the plain meaning rule and the like, is conceptually distinct from the parol evidence rule. The parol evidence rule determines whether parol can add a term to a contract. Contract interpretation takes the language of the contract as given and tries to assign it a meaning. Courts and commentators do much mischief when they blur these concepts. For a recent opinion drawing the distinction neatly, see Burlison v. United States, 533 F.3d 419 (6th Cir. 2008) (quoting from Corbin, The Parol Evidence Rule, 53 Yale L.J. 603, 622 (1944): "Even if a written document has been assented to as the complete and accurate integration of the terms of a contract, it must still be interpreted and all those factors that are of assistance in this process may be proved by oral testimony."). For a recent opinion mixing these separate concepts together, with predictably dire results, *see* Town Bank v. City Real Estate Dev., 793 N.W.2d 476, 485 (Wis. 2010), discussed at §7.3 n.27 *supra*. *See generally* Kniffin, Conflating and Confusing Contract Interpretation and the Parol Evidence Rule: Is the Emperor Wearing Someone Else's Clothes?, 62 Rutgers L. Rev. 75 (2009).

§7.3 n.56 p.239 ***In the second paragraph, add the following to the list in the second sentence:*** Thompson v. Allstate Ins. Co., 673 S.E.2d 227 (Ga. 2009) ("[T]he parol evidence rule is applicable only to the parties to a release or other contract and to their privies, so that parol evidence is admissible in favor of or against a stranger to the release."); Bank One Nat'l Ass'n v. Surber, 899 N.E.2d 693 (Ind. App. 2009) (parol evidence rule does not apply to "a controversy between a third party . . . and a party to the settlement agreement"); Podraza v. New Century Physicians, 789 N.W.2d 260 (Neb. 2010) ("the parol evidence rule cannot be invoked by a stranger to the agreement to prevent a party to the writing from adducing extraneous evidence as to its terms, even if that evidence varies or contradicts the written agreement," though noting that this exception does not apply to intended beneficiaries of the

contract); Baroid Equip. v. Odeco Drilling, 184 S.W.3d 1 (Tex. Civ. App. 2005) ("The general rule is that, before one contract is merged into another, the last contract *must be between the same parties* as the first . . . However, in some instances, the third party has been so involved with the creation of the written contract, or is claiming rights under the contract such that he is bound to abide by its terms, i.e., he is no longer a stranger to the contract.") (emphasis in original), distinguished by Crockett & Myers, Ltd. v. Napier, Fitzgerald, & Kirby, LLP, 440 F. Supp. 2d 1184 (D. Nev. 2006) (parol evidence rule applies where oral fee-splitting agreement between two law firms and later written retainer agreement between those parties and client; in contrast, *Baroid* dealt with an agreement involving a complete non-party).

§7.3 n.56 p.239 In the second paragraph, add the following at the end: Corbin thought this limitation unsound. Corbin, The Parol Evidence Rule, 53 Yale L.J. 603, 661-62 (1944) ("If two parties have by a complete written integration discharged and nullified antecedent negotiations between them, they are so discharged and nullified without regard to the identity of the person who may be asserting or denying the fact.").

§7.4 EVIDENCE TO SHOW NO VALID WRITTEN AGREEMENT

***§7.4 n.2 p.240 Add the following to the list after* "Cf.":** Alliance Laundry Sys. v. Thyssenkrupp Materials, 570 F. Supp. 2d 1061 (E.D. Wis. 2008) ("nothing in the e-mails indicates that the parties intended them to constitute a complete and exclusive statement of the agreement's terms," so parol admissible to determine whether the parties formed a contract and what the terms might be); CFC Inv. v. McLean, 900 N.E.2d 716 (Ill. App. 2008) (where writings did not show an intent to make them the final writing, parol evidence admissible to determine whether and to what extent the writings were final; quoting treatise); Wiencek & Assocs. Architects & Planners, PC v. Community Homes Hous., Inc., 2016 Md. App. LEXIS 1441 (Md. Ct. Spec. App. July 12, 2016) ("The justification asserted by Wiencek for refusing to consider parol evidence to determine whether a contract exists is misplaced because it suggests that we must enforce the merger clause of the contract in order to determine whether the contract in which the merger clause is found is valid. Accordingly, we reject the contention that a merger clause precludes a party from presenting parol evidence to determine whether a document constitutes an integration").

§7.4 n.7 p.242 Add the following to the list after **"Accord"***:* Brown Dev. Corp. v. Hemond, 956 A.2d 104 (Me. 2008) (agreement that contract to convey real property was to become effective only when the buyer purchased a neighboring lot; quotes from Restatement Second §217); Union Sav. Bank v. White Family Cos., 916 N.E.2d 816 (Ohio App. 2009) (parol evidence rule does not apply when determining whether the parties intended to make a contract).

§7.4 n.8 p.242 ***Add the following after the first sentence:*** *Accord:* Beatley v. Knisley, 917 N.E.2d 280 (Ohio App. 2009) ("Courts admit extrinsic evidence of a condition precedent because satisfaction of such a condition must occur before a contract comes into existence.").

§7.4 n.9 p.242 ***Add the following at the end:*** *Accord:* Apex LLC v. Sharing World, 206 Cal. App. 4th 999, 142 Cal. Rptr. 3d 210 (Ct. App. 2012) (barring proffered evidence of condition that buyers would not have to take delivery unless its customers issued a letter of credit; "The asserted condition here was at most a condition to [buyer's] obligation to accept delivery. . . . The condition did not affect contract validity or formation inasmuch as the sales contracts imposed upon [seller] the obligation to tender the cottonseed to [buyer] before the condition was satisfied.").

§7.4 n.13 p.243 Add the following to the list after **"Accord"***:* Sunset Pointe at Silver Lakes Assocs. v. Vargas, 881 So. 2d 12 (Fla. App. 2004) (oral representations that loan would be approved without requirement of sale of existing home "directly contradicted the financing contingency provision in the written agreement and were accordingly not admissible"); Brown Dev. Corp. v. Hemond, 956 A.2d 104 (Me. 2008) ("Consideration of oral conditions is not barred by the parol evidence rule unless they

'in a real sense contradict' or are 'repugnant to the conditions or terms' of the written contract"); Beatley v. Knisley, 917 N.E.2d 280 (Ohio App. 2009) ("a party may not introduce extrinsic evidence of an oral condition precedent when the written contract addresses the subject matter of the condition precedent and the contractual terms are inconsistent with the condition precedent"); Tangren Family Trust v. Tangren, 182 P.3d 326 (Utah 2008) (oral promise of condition precedent inadmissible in light of integration clause; "To argue that the Lease is not the complete agreement of the parties is to argue in direct contradiction to the clear integration clause").

***§7.4 n.16 p.244 Add the following to the list after* "Accord":** Diamond v. Scudder, 845 N.Y.S.2d 452 (App. Div. 2007) (recital that "the purchasers had given the sum of $4,600 to the seller and the seller had received that sum from the purchaser").

§7.4 n.18 p.245 Add the following after the first sentence: *Accord:* Voracek v. Crown Castle USA, 907 A.2d 1105 (Pa. Super. 2006) ("extrinsic evidence is admissible for the purpose of showing that by reason of mistake, fraud or accident, the written instrument does not express the actual intention of the parties").

***§7.4 n.19 p.245 Add the following to the list after* "Accord":** Radman v. Flanders Corp., 172 P.3d 668 (Utah App. 2007) (allowing proof of precontractual statements to establish breach of warranty that there had been no material misstatements of fact or omissions of material fact).

***§7.4 n.20 p.245 In the first paragraph, add the following to the list after* "Accord":** Extra Equipamentos e Exportação Ltda. v. Case Corp., 541 F.3d 719 (7th Cir. 2008) (Posner, J.: tort action for fraudulent misrepresentation against distributor; citing to treatise); 3Com Corp. v. Capital 4, Inc., 626 F. Supp. 2d 428 (S.D.N.Y. 2009) (tort action for fraudulent inducement); C & Vantage Leasing v. Wolfe, 795 N.W.2d 65 (Iowa 2011) (tort action for fraudulent misrepresentation and defense of fraudulent inducement); Phelps-Dickson Builders v. Amerimann Partners, 617 S.E.2d 664 (N.C. App. 2005) (tort action for fraudulent misrepresentation against builder and realtor); Slack v. James, 614 S.E.2d 636 (S.C. 2005) (tort action against vendor of house).

§7.4 n.20 p.245 In the first paragraph, add the following to the list after **"But see"***:* Gulf Liquids New River Project v. Gulsby Eng'g, 356 S.W.3d 54 (Tex. Civ. App. 2011) ("the merger clause expressly covers [pre-contractual statements of fact and promises] and prohibits evidence of additional pre-contract terms from serving as the basis for a fraudulent inducement claim").

§7.4 n.20 p.245 In the second paragraph, add the following at the end of the second sentence: and reaffirmed and restated by Toy v. Metro. Life Ins. Co., 928 A.2d 186 (Pa. 2007) (*Bardwell's* holding was "to deny the fraud exception to a party who only alleges that he was induced by fraud into entering into an agreement, but to allow it to a party who also alleges that a misrepresentation was fraudulently omitted from the parties' written contract." Put otherwise, "[W]hile the fraud exception to the parol evidence rule potentially applies in two scenarios — fraud in the inducement, where a party alleges that he was induced into entering the agreement through the other's fraud, and fraud in the execution, where a party alleges that he was mistaken as to the terms and the actual contents of the agreement he executed due to the other's fraud — the Court has determined that in Pennsylvania, only fraud in the execution . . . is excepted from the parol evidence rule's operation."). *Id.* at 206.

§7.4 n.20 p.245 In the second paragraph, add the following at the end: For a plaintive response to these cases, see Cabot Oil & Gas Corp. v. Jordan, 698 F. Supp. 2d 474 (M.D. Pa. 2010) (noting that "whether claims of fraudulent inducement based on misrepresentations not related to subjects specifically addressed in the written contract are barred by the parol evidence rule" remains unresolved in Pennsylvania; court therefore declines jurisdiction over declaratory judgment action).

§7.4 n.23 p.246 Add the following to the list after **"Accord"***:* Weatherly v. Weatherly, 665 S.E.2d 922 (Ga. App. 2008) ("'[p]arol evidence shall be admissible to show that a writing either was originally void or subsequently became so'";

applied to allow evidence that party did not sign instrument with knowledge of its effect) (quoting Ga. Code Ann. §24-6-8).

§7.4 n.23 p.246 Add the following after the citation to **Galmish***:* and in turn followed in Takis, L.L.C. v. C.D. Morelock Props., 905 N.E.2d 204 (Ohio App. 2008) ("Parties may not prove fraud by claiming the inducement to enter into an agreement was a promise that was within the scope of the integrated agreement but ultimately was not included in it.").

§7.4 n.24 p.246 Add the following after the first sentence: *Accord:* Richards v. JTL Grp., 212 P.3d 264 (Mont. 2009) ("the fraud exception 'only applies when the alleged fraud does not relate directly to the subject of the contract.' "); Slack v. James, 614 S.E.2d 636 (S.C. 2005) ("breach of contract claims based on pre-contract statements or representations are precluded by the parol evidence rule").

§7.4 n.24 p.246 Add the following at the end of the second sentence: and followed in Glazer v. Lehman Bros., Inc., 394 F.3d 444 (6th Cir. 2005) (promise that arbitration provisions would not be enforced was "directly contradictory to the terms of the signed written agreements" and thus was inadmissible parol evidence) and Micrel, Inc. v. TRW, Inc., 486 F.3d 866 (6th Cir. 2007) (parol evidence rule does not bar proof of promissory fraud unless the promise . . . contradicts an integrated written agreement).

§7.4 n.24 p.246 Add the following at the end: *Pendergrass* has been the subject of substantial criticism and often grudging and narrow application, and has now been rejected by the California Supreme Court. Riverisland Cold Storage Inc. v. Fresno-Madera Prod. Credit Ass'n, 55 Cal. 4th 1169, 1172; 291 P.3d 316, 317 (2013) ("The *Pendergrass* limitation finds no support in the language of the statute codifying the parol evidence rule and the exception for evidence of fraud. It is difficult to apply. It conflicts with the doctrine of the Restatements, most treatises, and the majority of our sister-state jurisdictions. Furthermore, while intended to prevent fraud, the rule established in *Pendergrass* may actually provide a shield for fraudulent conduct. Finally, *Pendergrass* departed from established California law at the time it

was decided, and neither acknowledged nor justified the abrogation. We now conclude that *Pendergrass* was ill considered, and should be overruled.") (affirming judgment and modifying lower court opinion, 119 Cal. Rptr. 3d 380 (Ct. App. 2011)), that *Pendergrass* applies only to promissory fraud, and not "where the party seeking admission of the parol evidence has alleged that the other party misinterpreted the content of the written contract and thereby induced execution of the contract"; collecting cases. *See also* Continental Airlines v. McDonnell Douglas Corp., 264 Cal. Rptr. 779 (Ct. App. 1989) (presenting attacks on *Pendergrass*, but then stating that "while the *Pendergrass* rule may be subject to criticism, and even questioned, it is still the law and we are bound by it").

§7.4 n.25 p.246 Add the following after the citation to* Sound Techniques*: distinguished in Shawmut-Canton LLC v. Great Spring Waters of Am., 816 N.E.2d 545 (Mass. App. 2004) (*Sound Techniques* rationale does not apply to cases of fraudulent inducement, so merger clause ineffective "even where the parties are sophisticated and their bargaining powers are equal").

§7.4 n.25 p.246 Delete the citation to* Greenfield *and add the following at the end: *Cf.* Greenfield v. Heckenbach, 797 A.2d 63 (Md. App. 2002) (though where avoidance is sought parol evidence rule may bar evidence of unintentional representation, "mere presence of a general integration clause" does not bar tort claim for negligent misrepresentation), applied in Carroll Co. v. Sherwin-Williams Co., 848 F. Supp. 2d 557 (D. Md. 2012) (general anti-reliance clause "operates like a general merger clause, in that it indicates, without specifically disclaiming representations as to a particular subject matter, that the parties, in making the agreement, will not rely on anything outside of the four corners of the agreement" and so does not pretermit a claim for fraudulent or negligent misrepresentation).

§7.4 n.26 p.247 Add the following to the list after* "Accord"*: Extra Equipamentos e Exportação Ltda. v. Case Corp., 541 F.3d 719 (7th Cir. 2008) (Posner, J.: "most courts . . . hold that neither the [parol evidence] rule nor the [merger] clause prevents a disappointed party to the contract from basing a tort suit on proof that in the course of the negotiations the other party made fraudulent representations"; citing to treatise); W.W. Vincent & Co. v. First Colony Life Ins. Co., 814 N.E.2d 960 (Ill. App. 2004) ("the parol evidence rule, as a doctrine of contract law, has no application to cases sounding in tort"; integration clause thus does not bar fraud action); Tru-Cal, Inc. v. Conrad Kacsik Instrument Sys., 905 N.E.2d 40 (Ind. App. 2009) ("a party can overcome the effect of an integration clause and bring a fraud in the inducement claim to rescind the contract"), applied in Michiana Dairy Processors v. All Star Beverage, 744 F. Supp. 2d 790 (N.D. Ind. 2010) ("[A] claim of fraudulent inducement may be barred by a contract's integration clause if based on oral misrepresentations made prior to the execution of the contract. . . . A party may overcome the effect of such an integration clause if the party can show that it had a right to rely on the alleged misrepresentations and did in fact rely on them in executing the integration clause.").

§7.4 n.26 p.247 Add the following to the list after **"But cf."**: Giacomantonio v. Romagnoli, 701 S.E.2d 510 (Ga. App. 2010) (when allegedly defrauded party affirms a contract containing a merger clause, it is estopped from asserting that it relied upon the other party's misrepresentations; bars all tort claims based on those misrepresentations, including breach of fiduciary duty); Springs Window Fashions Div. v. Blind Maker, 184 S.W.3d 840 (Tex. Civ. App. 2006) ("merger clauses could . . . operate to negate the reliance element even of fraudulent-inducement claims arising from the same contract containing the merger clause").

§7.4 n.26 p.247 Add the following after the citation to **One-O-One Enters.**: (R.B. Ginsburg, J.), followed in Cent. Truck Ctr. v. Cent. GMC, 4 A.3d 515 (Md. App. 2010) (lengthy and detailed contract for sale of business that "no doubt [was] the product of considerable negotiation and bargaining by sophisticated businesspeople represented by experienced advisors" contained integration clause; as a result, "reliance on extra-contractual documents was unreasonable," vitiating claim of fraud in the inducement).

§7.5 REFORMATION AND THE PAROL EVIDENCE RULE

§7.5 n.1 p.248 ***Add the following at the end:*** *See generally* Ohlendorf, Textualism and the Problem of Scrivener's Error, 64 Me. L. Rev. 119 (2011).

§7.5 n.2 p.248 ***Add the following at the end:*** Wells Fargo Bank Minn. v. Mowery, 931 N.E.2d 1121 (Ohio App. 2010) (assignee of mortgagee lacked privity and could not seek reformation of the deed conveying the property to the mortgagee; attempt to get an order in equity transferring the land to the intended owner a vain attempt to "circumvent longstanding rules of equity").

§7.5 n.3 p.248 ***Add the following at the end of the first paragraph:*** This idea was nicely stated in Urick v. Burge, 86 N.W.2d 543, 548-49 (Mich. 1957) (Smith, J., concurring):

> A strictly formal system of law knows no contrast between the will and the utterance, and no possibility of a contradiction between the two. This is thoroughly the conception of the Germanic law. The utterance is the law's embodiment. No more, and yet no less, than what is uttered can bind or loose. Hence the minute precision with which obligations of debt were written out. * * * Hence the legal proverbs, 'one man one word,' 'the word stands,' 'words make the bargain,' and the like. A necessary result is that mistake in contractual relations receives but scanty considerations. * * * All that a man does is judged alone by its external manifestations and its objective effect, not by his inward motive. The law concedes nothing either to good or to bad faith, as long as it is concerned with the legal consequences of conduct.
>
> We do not dispute the seductive simplicities of this doctrine. At one stroke we remove from the law all the vexing and confounding questions about what goes on in the mind of man. Who cares? There stands the scroll.
>
> But it has never been doubted, from the very beginnings of what we know as equity, that the chancellor does indeed concern himself with the intent of people. Specifically, as to the situation confronting us, that he will amend an instrument to represent the actual agreement of the parties, regardless of the content of the parchment.

To state what may be obvious, "in order to reform a written agreement to correct a mutual mistake, some form of an agreement in writing must have existed." Garnett v. Genetic Improvement Servs. (*In re* Estate of Dueck), 736 N.W.2d 720 (Neb. 2007) (declining to reform document to add signature of decedent).

§7.5 n.3 p.248 In the second paragraph, add the following to the list in the second sentence: *In re* Estate of Munawar, 981 A.2d 584 (D.C. 2009) (deed failed to provide for joint tenancy with right of survivorship).

§7.5 n.5 p.248 Add the following at the end: Nat'l Austl. Bank v. United States, 452 F.3d 1321 (Fed. Cir. 2006) (requiring that "the mistake [have] had a material effect on the bargain" to grant reformation).

§7.5 n.9 p.249 Add the following at the end: *Accord:* KT Holdings USA v. Akerman, Senterfitt & Eidson, 34 So. 3d 61 (Fla. App. 2010) (sale of corporate assets mistakenly included corporate jet not part of transaction).

§7.5 n.10 p.249 Add the following to the list after* "Accord"*: Young v. Verizon's Bell Atl. Cash Balance Plan, 615 F.3d 808 (7th Cir. 2010) (federal common law: pension plan repeated an element in a formula for determining the balance); Drake v. Hance, 673 S.E.2d 411 (N.C. App. 2009) (property description included property not to be sold); Katsam Holdings v. 419 W. 55th St. Corp., 870 N.Y.S.2d 324 (App. Div. 2009) (lease prepared using residential form rather than commercial form); Local Mktg. Corp. v. Prudential Ins. Co., 824 N.E.2d 122 (Ohio App. 2004) (lease agreement stated that net rentable area was approximately 5,845 square feet, rather than the actual 5,393); Sikora v. VanderPloeg, 212 S.W.3d 277 (Tenn. App. 2006) (duration of warranty of amount of business receipts listed as six months instead of seven); James Clark, Inc. v. Vitro Am., 269 S.W.3d 681 (Tex. Civ. App. 2008) (personal guaranty listed creditor both in line for creditor and in line for debtor).

§7.5 n.10 p.249 Add the following at the end: A rather appalling illustration came in 1986, when in the course of restructuring a loan to U.S. Lines the first mortgage, held by Prudential, for $92,885,000 was carelessly rendered as $92,885, with no one involved catching the error (repeated on almost one hundred documents) until the documents had been executed. After U.S. Lines went bankrupt, other creditors and the bankruptcy trustee wanted to enforce the mortgage as written. To resolve the trustee's claim, Prudential paid $11,400,000 of the $65,400,000 raised from the sale of the encumbered ships. GE Credit, the holder of the second mortgage, made a similar demand, but Prudential here resisted and the matter was litigated — one hopes to no one's surprise, in favor of the holder of the first mortgage. Prudential Ins. Co. of Am. v. S.S. Am. Lancer, 686 F. Supp. 469 (S.D.N.Y. 1988), *aff'd*, 870 F.2d 867 (2d Cir. 1989). According to one estimate, the cost to the first mortgagor of settlements, legal fees, and retaining the ships — the collateral — which otherwise it would have liquidated, was some $31,000,000. Margolick, At the Bar: How Three Missing Zeros Brought Red Faces and Cost Millions of Dollars, N.Y. Times, Oct. 4, 1991, at B16.

§7.5 n.11 p.250 ***Add the following at the start of the first sentence:*** Hearn v. Hearn, 936 A.2d 400 (Md. App. 2007) ("[I]t is within the power of a court of equity to revise a consent order to make it conform with the actual mutual intent of the parties.")

§7.5 n.13 p.250 ***Add the following at the beginning:*** Apple Tree Ridge Neighborhood Ass'n v. Grandfather Mountain Heights Prop. Owners Corp., 697 S.E.2d 468 (N.C. App. 2010) (rejects reformation of settlement agreement where relocated right-of-way required in it was impracticable; "we refuse to permit a trial court to use reformation to essentially create a new agreement between the parties and impose upon [one of them] a liability which she had not assumed, or an obligation which she had not undertaken").

§7.5 n.14 p.250 ***Add the following at the end:*** On the other hand, at times courts have declined to use reformation to add language to a contract, instead treating the issue much in the manner of a court supplying omitted terms or interpreting existing ones. *See* Rogal v. UTA Peters Randall, 971 A.2d 796 (Conn. App. 2009) (court supplies missing prohibitory language in non-solicitation agreement; "[W]e do not believe that the contract at hand needed to be reformed for the court to be empowered to

supply an obvious missing term consistent with the clear intent expressed in the balance of the contract language.").

§7.5 n.17 p.251 Add the following at the beginning: Restatement Second §166 & cmt. *a*. *See*

***§7.5 n.17 p.251 Add the following to the list after* "Accord":** Protective Life Ins. Co. v. Hansen, 632 F.3d 388 (7th Cir. 2011) ("Reformation is an equitable remedy that is available only when a document fails to fully or accurately reflect the contracting parties' actual agreement either because the contracting parties made a mutual mistake or because one party made a mistake while the other party committed a fraud."; not available for double reformation, on theory that if original error had not occurred, a subsequent transfer would have taken place); NOLM v. County of Clark, 100 P.3d 658 (Nev. 2004) (reformation allowed "where one party makes a unilateral mistake and the other party knew about it but failed to bring it to the mistaken party's attention," thus allowing reformation of conveyance from 0.92 acre to 0.49 acre).

§7.5 n.20 p.252 Add the following at the beginning of the first paragraph: Restatement Second §161. *See*

§7.5 n.20 p.252 Add the following at the end of the first paragraph: On the other hand, consistent with the ordinary law of non-disclosure, it has been held that a duty to disclose arises only in the course of a fiduciary or confidential relationship. *See* Travelers Indem. Co. v. CDL Hotels USA, 322 F. Supp. 2d 482 (S.D.N.Y. 2004) (Mukasey, J.) (no reformation where party against which reformation was sought dealt at arm's length with party seeking reformation, and there was no information as to which the party seeking reformation was ignorant, the other party was knowledgeable, and the other party knew of the ignorance of the party seeking reformation). This applies New York's *special funds* doctrine, which "recognizes that, sometimes, even commercial transactions may be 'inherently unfair' when they are conducted with a sufficient imbalance of relevant information." Newbro v. Freed, 409 F. Supp. 2d 386, 401 (S.D.N.Y. 2006).

§7.5 n.22 p.253 Add the following to the end: Accord: Poly Trucking v. Concentra Health Servs., 93 P.3d 561 (Colo. App. 2004) ("where a party's unilateral mistake is the result not of fraud, but of its own failure to use due diligence in reading the contract before signing it, that party will be held to the terms of the contract"), distinguished by Level 3 Comm'ns v. Liebert Corp., 535 F.3d 1146 (10th Cir. 2008) (allowing fraudulent concealment claim where, unlike *Poly Trucking*, the "defendant triggered the duty to disclose by making an ambiguous statement capable of misleading"); Oelze v. Score Sports Venture, 927 N.E.2d 137 (Ill. App. 2010) (even if employee had misled plaintiff as to whether an agreement was only about her financial obligation, "plaintiff had a duty to read the agreement before she signed it. She did not read it. She was not prevented from reading it. It was her own decision not to read it. . . . Her failure to read the release should not be held against defendant."); Westgate at Williamsburg Condo. Ass'n v. Philip Richardson Co., 621 S.E.2d 114 (Va. 2005) ("The error in this case was not that of the scrivener's transcription of the real estate description, but in the review processes of the parties."), analyzed in and followed by Tiger Fibers v. Aspen Specialty Ins. Co., 594 F. Supp. 2d 630 (E.D. Va. 2009).

§7.5 n.23 p.253 Add the following to the list after **"Accord"***:* Traders Bank v. Dils, 704 S.E.2d 691 (W. Va. 2010) (parol evidence rule did not bar fraud claim based on misrepresentation of contemporaneous intent to perform).

§7.5 n.24 p.253 Add the following to the list after **"Accord"***: In re* Estate of Munawar, 981 A.2d 584 (D.C. 2009) ("'[T]he fact that the person seeking reformation did not read the document to ascertain the error, or that the person had constructive notice of the defect, does not deny that person the right to reformation. . . . [I]f the rule were to the contrary, it is difficult to imagine any case where the remedy would ever be available.'") (quoting from 14 Powell on Real Property §81A.07[3][e]).

§7.5 n.25 p.253 Add the following to the list after **"See"***:* Howmedica Osteonics Corp. v. Wright Med. Tech., 540 F.3d 1337 (Fed. Cir. 2008) (New Jersey law; reformation available to a

mistaken party "unless that party's 'fault amounts to a failure to act in good faith and in accordance with reasonable standards of fair dealing' ") (quoting from Restatement Second §157 & cmt. *a*); Goodall v. Whispering Woods Ctr., 990 So. 2d 695 (Fla. App. 2008) ("it is a plaintiff's *gross* negligence that will prevent him from obtaining reformation from a court of equity") (emphasis in original); Sikora v. VanderPloeg, 212 S.W.3d 277 (Tenn. App. 2006) ("reformation is denied only in 'extreme cases' where a party's fault 'amounts to a failure to act in good faith and in accordance with reasonable standards of fair dealing' "; mere "inattention" insufficient, short of "gross negligence") (quoting from Restatement Second §157 & cmt. *a*)

***§7.5 n.28 p.254 Add the following to the list after* "Accord":** Long v. City of Glendale, 93 P.3d 519 (Ariz. App. 2004) ("the parol evidence rule does not apply to reformation claims"); Goodall v. Whispering Woods Ctr., 990 So. 2d 695 (Fla. App. 2008) (the doctrine of merger in deed "is inapplicable in an action seeking the equitable remedy of reformation").

§7.5 n.28 p.254 Add the following after the second sentence: *Contra:* Tiger Fibers v. Aspen Specialty Ins. Co., 594 F. Supp. 2d 630 (E.D. Va. 2009) ("whether there is a scrivener's error must be decided based on the [contract] itself and not any parol evidence"). Virginia distinguishes between scrivener's errors and mistake. The former requires that the error be contradicted by all other documents and be proved without parol evidence. The latter requires proof by clear and convincing evidence, but may be proved with the aid of parol. The basis for the distinction is not entirely clear, but seems to turn on the difference between proof of faulty expression and proof of mistaken belief.

§7.5 n.36 p.256 Add the following at the beginning: Protective Life Ins. Co. v. Hansen, 632 F.3d 388 (7th Cir. 2011) (equities do not favor reformation when girlfriend of embezzling employee sought to be made beneficiary of key man insurance policy after employee's suicide; employee's attempt to transfer ownership of the policy was "an effort to swindle even more" from the employer, the girlfriend seeks a "windfall" from the key man policy even as creditors of the employer remain unpaid, and neither the girlfriend nor the employee had ever paid any premium on the policy).

§7.5 n.36 p.256 Add the following after the second sentence: Similarly, reformation is barred to those with unclean hands. Hardy v. Hardy, 910 N.E.2d 851 (Ind. App. 2009).

§7.5 n.38 p.257 Add the following to the list after **"Accord"***:* Howmedica Osteonics Corp. v. Wright Med. Tech., 540 F.3d 1337 (Fed. Cir. 2008) ("clear and convincing evidence"); Nat'l Austl. Bank v. United States, 452 F.3d 1321 (Fed. Cir. 2006) ("the elements of a claim for reformation must be proved by clear and convincing evidence"); *In re* Estate of Munawar, 981 A.2d 584 (D.C. 2009) ("[A]lthough the trial court's factual determinations were generally not without basis in the record, the trial court erred as a matter of law in holding that those findings amounted to clear and convincing evidence that the deed did not express the parties' mutual agreement."); Nissan Autos. of Marlborough v. Glick, 816 N.E.2d 161 (Mass. App. 2004) ("a party seeking recovery for a unilateral mistake must present full, clear, and decisive proof that a mistake occurred"); Barclay Arms, Inc. v. Barclay Arms Assoc., 540 N.E.2d 707 (N.Y. 1989) ("right to reformation must be demonstrated by clear, positive and convincing evidence").

§7.5 n.38 p.257 Add the following after the second sentence: Cf. Young v. Verizon's Bell Atl. Cash Balance Plan, 615 F.3d 808 (7th Cir. 2010) (federal common law for ERISA: equitable reformation requires clear and convincing evidence — evidence "that is 'clear, precise, convincing and of the most satisfactory character that a mistake has occurred and that the mistake does not reflect the intent of the parties.' ") (quoting from Int'l Union of Electronic, Elec. Salaried, Mach. & Furniture Workers v. Murata Erie N. Am., 980 F.2d 889 (3d Cir. 1992)).

§7.6 ORAL MODIFICATIONS AND NO-ORAL-MODIFICATION CLAUSES

§7.6 n.1 p.257 Add the following at the end of the first paragraph: *See generally* Crespi, Clarifying the Boundary Between the Parol Evidence Rule and the Rules Governing Subsequent Oral Modifications, 34 Ohio N. Univ. L. Rev. 71 (2008).

§7.6 n.5 p.258 Substitute the following for the citation to* Fontaine & De Ly*: M. Fontaine & F. De Ly, Drafting International Contracts: An Analysis of Contract Clauses ch.3 (2006).

§7.6 n.7 p.258 Add the following to the list after* "Accord"*: DeFranco v. Storage Tech. Corp., 622 F.3d 1296 (10th Cir. 2010) (Colorado law: in face of written employment agreement containing a no-oral-modifications clause, "a subsequent oral agreement could still modify the at-will employment provision of that agreement"); *Ex parte* Coleman, 861 So. 2d 1080 (Ala. 2003) (proof of oral modification serves "as proof as a waiver of the requirement for a writing"); Coral Reef Drive Land Dev. v. Duke Ltd. Realty Ltd. P'ship, 45 So. 3d 897 (Fla. App. 2010) ("oral modifications are permitted despite [no-oral-modifications clauses] when one party provides additional consideration for the modification accepted by the other party"; expressing hope that "[o]ur Supreme Court or legislature may someday recede from this outdated common law concept"); Husky Rose, Inc. v. Allstate Ins. Co., 19 So. 3d 1085 (Fla. App. 2009) (written agreements with no-oral-modifications clauses may be modified orally, among other circumstances, "(1) where it would be a fraud on one party to refuse to perform the oral modification, or (2) where subsequent conduct of the parties indicates the acceptance of the oral modification"); Seneca Waste Solutions v. Sheaffer Mfg. Co., 791 N.W.2d 407 (Iowa 2010) ("Although the written contract states that any modifications must be in writing, a written contract may be modified by a subsequent oral contract having the essential elements of a binding contract."); Fleming v. JE Merit Constructors, 985 So. 2d 141 (La. App. 2008) ("[W]ritten contracts may be modified by oral contracts or by the conduct of the parties, even when the written contract contains the provision that it must be modified in writing."); KC Excavating &

Grading v. Crane Constr. Co., 141 S.W.3d 401 (Mo. App. 2004) ("parties can waive a change order requirement by orally agreeing to the work").

§7.6 n.7 p.258 Add the following after the citation to **Cambridgeport Sav. Bank***:* , amplified in Wells Fargo Bus. Credit v. Environamics Corp., 934 N.E.2d 283 (Mass. App. 2010) ("[I]n order to support the existence of an oral modification, the parol evidence must be sufficiently weighted and of competent probity to present a material issue for trial; that is, the parol evidence must be of sufficient strength to present an ambiguity between the actual conduct of the parties and the contract.").

§7.6 n.7 p.258 Add the following at the end: *See generally* Davis, The Demand for Immutable Contracts: Another Look at the Law and Economics of Contract Modifications, 81 N.Y.U. L. Rev. 487 (2006); Schmitz, Should Contractual Clauses that Forbid Renegotiation Always be Enforced?, 21 J.L. Econ. & Org. 315 (2005).

§7.6 n.8 p.259 Add the following at the end of the last sentence: , quoted from and followed in Hovnanian Land Inv. Grp. v. Annapolis Towne Centre, 25 A.3d 967 (Md. 2011) ("[T]he freedom to contract is not limited to the contract as written. Instead, the freedom to contract includes the freedom to alter that contract.").

§7.6 n.10 p.260 Add the following to the list after **"Accord"***:* Prof'l Ins. Corp. v. Cahill, 90 So. 2d 916 (Fla. 1956) ("[a] written contract . . . may be altered or modified by an oral agreement if the letter has been accepted and acted upon by the parties in such manner as would work a fraud on either party to refuse to enforce it . . . even though there was in the written contract a provision prohibiting its alteration except in writing"), followed in J. Lynn Constr. v. Fairways at Boca Golf & Tennis Condo. Ass'n, 962 So. 2d 928 (Fla. App. 2007) and WSOS-FM v. Hadden, 951 So. 2d 61 (Fla. App. 2007); Wells Fargo Bus. Credit v. Environamics Corp., 934 N.E.2d 283 (Mass. App. 2010) ("[I]n order to support the existence of an oral modification, the parol evidence must be sufficiently weighted and of competent probity to present

a material issue for trial; that is, the parol evidence must be of sufficient strength to present an ambiguity between the actual conduct of the parties and the contract."); Smith-Hunter Constr. Co. v. Hopson, 616 S.E.2d 419 (S.C. 2005) (where "Homeowners had authorized the work done pursuant to those invoices, knew the work was being done, and accepted the benefits of the work," the "Homeowners had waived" the requirement that modifications be in a signed writing).

§7.6 n.10 p.260 Add the following at the end: Waiver may not be so readily available to those contracting with the government, particularly when the government official purportedly authorizing the change order without requiring that it be written lacks the power to do so. *See* G. Voskanian Constr. v. Alhambra Unified Sch. Dist., 139 Cal. Rptr. 3d 286 (Ct. App. 2012) (oral modification ineffective, even as a waiver, when the official granting the modification did so outside his statutory authority).

§7.6 n.11 p.260 Add the following at the end: *Cf.* Supermarket Merch. & Supply v. Marschuetz, 196 S.W.3d 581 (Mo. App. 2006) (unilateral modifications of employment agreement unenforceable where agreement had no-oral-modifications clause and the employee never signed a writing, even though the employee continued to work after those modifications had been proposed).

§7.6 n.12 p.260 Add the following after the first sentence: The court of appeals has made clear that this statute essentially overturns *Beatty, supra* note 8. Israel v. Chabra, 906 N.E.2d 374 (N.Y. 2009).

***§7.6 n.12 p.260 Add the following to the list after* "But cf.":** Baraliu v. Vinya Capital, 765 F. Supp. 2d 289 (S.D.N.Y. 2011) ("The party seeking to avoid the effect of this provision . . . can only do so by showing either partial performance or equitable estoppel.").

§7.6 n.12 p.260 Add the following to the last sentence: , followed in Penava Mech. Corp. v. Afgo Mech. Servs., 896 N.Y.S.2d 349 (App. Div. 2010) (no-oral-modifications clause ineffective because the owner "waived such right by directing [contractor] to perform overtime work and not to bother with the [written modifications]"), and in Israel v. Chabra, *id.* ("[S]ection 15-301(1) does not compel the enforcement of a 'no oral modification' clause at the expense of other aspects of the parties' agreement.").

***§7.6 n.13 p.261 Add the following to the list after* "But cf.":** Martinsville Nylon Emps. Council Corp. v. NLRB, 969 F.2d 1263 (D.C. Cir. 1992) (choosing UCC 2-209 over the common law as the source for the federal common law of collective bargaining agreements; "The drawback of the common law rule is that it denies to all contracting parties, no matter how sophisticated, the ability to decide from themselves whether to restrict the manner in which their agreement may be modified. The UCC rule, on the other hand, enables those parties who mutually value certainty in their relations to have it"), rejected in Mechanical Contractors Ass'n v. Greater Bay Area Ass'n, 78 Cal. Rptr. 2d 225 (Ct. App. 1998) (need for flexibility in collective bargaining agreements makes adoption of the UCC rule undesirable); Krispy Kreme Doughnut Corp. v. Satellite Donuts, 725 F. Supp. 2d 389 (S.D.N.Y. 2010) (applying UCC 2-209(2) to franchise agreement).

§7.6 n.13 p.261 Add the following after the citation to Snyder article: commented on in Brinkley, The Regulation of Contractual Change: A Guide to No Oral Modification Clauses for North Carolina Lawyers, 81 N.C. L. Rev. 2239 (2003).

§7.6 n.17 p.262 Add the following at the end: *See generally* Valspar Refinish v. Gaylord's, Inc., 764 N.W.2d 359 (Minn. 2009) (collecting cases on waiver and UCC §2-209).

***§7.6 n.18 p.262 In the first paragraph, add the following to the list after* "See also":** Thermal Design v. M & M Bldrs., 698 S.E.2d 516 (N.C. App. 2010) (under UCC 2-209, "a party asserting waiver must demonstrate, in addition to a promise made by the waiving party, either: (1) additional consideration; (2) material change in position by the promisee based on the alleged oral contract; or (3) [for the purposes of 2-209(3)] conduct on the part of the party offering the statute of frauds as a defense sufficient to show that an oral agreement was reached").

§7.6 n.18 p.262 Add the following at the end of the first paragraph: *Wisconsin Knife* has proved a controversial decision, with many other cases following Judge Easterbrook's dissent. *See* BMC Indus. v. Barth Indus., 160 F.3d 1322 (11th Cir. 1998) (finding reliance unnecessary and expressly rejecting the majority opinion in *Wisconsin Knife*: "While subsection (4) states that an attempted modification that fails may still constitute a waiver, subsection (5) provides that the waiver may be retracted *unless* the non-waiving party relies on the waiver. Consequently, the statute recognizes that waivers may exist in the absence of detrimental reliance — these are the retractable waivers referred to in subsection (5). Only this interpretation renders meaning to subsection (5), because reading subsection (4) to require detrimental reliance for all waivers means that waivers would *never* be retractable.").

§7.6a DRAFTING MERGER AND NO-ORAL-MODIFICATION CLAUSES

§7.6a n.2 p.263 Add the following after the first sentence: *Accord:* Madey v. Duke Univ., 336 F. Supp. 2d 583 (M.D.N.C. 2004) (passage in letter from prospective employer stating that the employee's "agreement will complete the acceptance of [the employer's] offer of a position as Professor of Physics" not a merger clause; it "merely indicates that signing the letter is the last formal step necessary for Dr. Madey to join Duke as a Professor of Physics").

§7.6a n.5 p.264 Add the following at the end: Atlantic Pier Assocs. v. Boardakan Rest. Partners, 647 F. Supp. 2d 474 (E.D. Pa. 2009) ("Where prior fraudulent representations are alleged, the parol evidence rule bars such representations where the written agreement: (1) contains terms which directly deal with the subject matter of the alleged oral representation; and (2) represents the entire contract between the parties, particularly where the written agreement also contains an integration clause. . . . To satisfy the 'same subject matter' requirement, the written contract need not directly contradict the prior representation, but rather need only 'relate to subjects that were specifically addressed in the written contract.' ") (quoting from HCB Contractors v. Liberty Place Hotel Assocs., 652 A.2d 1278, 1279 (Pa. 1995)).

§7.6a n.8 p.264 Add the following at the beginning: *See* 3Com Corp. v. Capital 4, Inc., 626 F. Supp. 2d 428 (S.D.N.Y. 2009) ("New York law does not permit the mere inclusion of merger language in a contract to provide an automatic, categorical defense against any claim of fraud."). *See also* the discussion of no-reliance clauses and merger clauses in §4.13 *supra*.

§7.6a p.266 Add the following at the end of the first sentence of the first full paragraph: . . . both parties or their agents."[14a]

[14a] *See* Krispy Kreme Doughnut Corp. v. Satellite Donuts, 725 F. Supp. 2d 389 (S.D.N.Y. 2010) (giving effect to clause stating that "[e]xcept as otherwise expressly provided herein, there are no other oral or written agreement, understandings, representations, or statements relating to the subject matter of this Agreement. . . . This Agreement shall not be modified except by written agreement signed by both parties.") (citing to treatise); BDI Laguna Holdings v. Marsh, 689 S.E.2d 39 (Ga. App. 2009) (giving effect to clause stating that "This Agreement contains the entire agreement of the parties with respect to the subject matter hereof, and supersedes all prior agreements and understandings, oral or written, between the parties hereto with respect to the subject matter hereof. This Agreement may be amended, changed, modified, extended or rescinded only by a writing signed by the party against whom any such amendment, change, modification, extension or rescission is sought.").

§7.6a n.16 p.266 In the first paragraph, add the following to the list in the first sentence: C. Brown Trucking Co. v. Henderson, 700 S.E.2d 882 (Ga. App. 2010) ("[A] modification of the agreement is not equivalent to a rescission or cancellation of the agreement. And if the parties had desired to require that the rental agreement could only be rescinded in writing, they could have done so.")

§7.6a n.16 p.266 In the second paragraph, add the following to the list in the last sentence: Supermarket Merch. & Supply v. Marschuetz, 196 S.W.3d 581 (Mo. App. 2006) (giving effect to clause providing that "no modification shall be binding upon the Employee or Supermarket Merchandising unless made in writing and signed by the Employee and an authorized officer of Supermarket Merchandising.").

§7.6a n.17 p.266 Add the following at the beginning: For an example of an omnibus no-oral-modification and anti-waiver clause, *see* Wireless Properties v. CC Fin., 10 A.3d 613 (Del. 2010) ("'neither [the contract] nor any portion or provisions hereof may be changed, modified, amended, waived, supplemented, discharged, cancelled, or terminated orally or by any course of dealing, or in any manner other than by an agreement in writing, signed by the party to be charged'"). The clause might prudently have mentioned a course of performance as well as a course of dealing; indeed, a course of performance is more likely to give rise to a claim of waiver than is a course of dealing.

§7.6a n.18 p.266 Add the following to the list in the first sentence: Awards.com v. Kinko's, 834 N.Y.S.2d 147 (App. Div. 2007) (an "unambiguous non-waiver clause" is "uniformly enforced").

§7.6a n.18 p.266 Add the following to the list after **"But cf.":** Hovnanian Land Inv. Grp. v. Annapolis Towne Centre, 25 A.3d 967 (Md. 2011) ("[O]ur caselaw shows a persistent unwillingness to give dispositive and preclusive effect to contractual limitations on future changes to that contract. This approach applies to the entire catalogue of possible alterations in contractual rights and obligations, whether it is mutual modification, novation, waiver of remedies, or, as here, a waiver of condition precedent."), followed in 42 E. v. D.R. Horton, Inc., 722 S.E.2d 1 (N.C. App. 2012) (non-waiver clause does not preclude finding that a party to the contract waived a "time is of the essence" clause).

§7.7 THE PROCESS OF INTERPRETATION

§7.7 n.1 p.267 Add the following to the list after **"See generally":** S. Burton, Elements of Contract Interpretation (2009); K. Greenawalt, Legal Interpretation (2010); G. McMeel, The Construction of Contracts (2011); A. Scalia & B. Garner, Reading Law: The Interpretation of Legal Texts (2012), bludgeoned by Posner, The Spirit Killeth, But the Letter Giveth Life, The New Republic, Sept. 13, 2012, at 18 (starting an avalanche of

essays and blog postings pro and contra); Katz, The Economics of Form and Substance in Contract Interpretation, 104 Colum. L. Rev. 496 (2004); Posner, The Law and Economics of Contract Interpretation, 83 Tex. L. Rev. 1581 (2005).

§7.7 n.3 p.267 ***Add the following at the end:*** For a linguistic analysis of the harms wrought by ambiguity and vagueness, whether common or separate, *see* Solan, Pernicious Ambiguity in Contracts and Statutes, 79 Chi.-Kent L. Rev. 859 (2004).

§7.7 n.5 p.267 ***Add the following at the end:*** Carter, Commercial Construction and Contract Doctrine, 25 J. Contract L. 83 (2009).

§7.7 p.269 ***In the first full paragraph, line eight, make the following substitution:*** For *parol evidence* read *plain meaning*.

§7.8 VAGUENESS AND AMBIGUITY

§7.8 n.3 p.270 ***Add the following after the first sentence:***

Accord: Cashin v. Cashin, 681 N.W.2d 255 (Wis. App. 2004) ("ambiguity is defined as language that is subject to two or more reasonable interpretations, either on its face or as applied to the extrinsic facts to which it refers"); North River Mews Assocs. LLC v. Alcoa Corp., 2016 U.S. Dist. LEXIS 65918 (D.N.J. May 19, 2016) (agreement that "Buyer expressly releases Seller and agrees to waive all rights that it may have to seek contribution from Seller" was ambiguous because "Moving Defendants argue that 'contribution' should not be given its technical meaning as a term of art, but rather its common meaning. The technical meaning would not release the claims here; the common meaning would. This is a textbook example of contractual ambiguity. In such circumstances, the Court will construe the contract in the light most favorable to the non-moving party.").

Horizon Pools & Landscapes, Inc. v. Sucarichi, 2016 Tex. App. LEXIS 13024 (Dec. 8, 2016), involved a form contract for constructing a pool and spa that included blanks after "lights(s)" [sic], "Pool Light," and another "lights" in the spa section of the form. The salesperson filled in "(2) L.E.D." on the first line, something illegible next to "Pool Light," and "100 watt" in the section relating to spa lights. The parties disputed whether the agreement was to install two total lights or two LED pool lights and a third light in the spa. The Texas Court of Appeals explained that "a court generally must decide whether a contract is ambiguous by determining the parties' intent as expressed within the four corners of the agreement. Mere lack of clarity or poor draftsmanship does not make a contract ambiguous, unless its provisions are susceptible to more than one reasonable interpretation." *Id.* at *7, citing Guggenheim Corporate Funding, LLC v. Valerus Compression Serv., 465 S.W.3d 673, 681 (Tex. App. 2015). The court held that the contract was ambiguous and the lower court properly relied upon extrinsic evidence to determine the parties' intent. The contact's "terms do not explicitly state the total number of lights in a combined structure. In addition, the two sections pertaining to the pool confuse the matter by providing two separate blanks relating to lighting: 'Lights(s)' and 'Pool Light.' The handwritten notation accompanying the latter of these is illegible, which ultimately renders it impossible to say what the contract specifies with respect to lighting." *Id.* at *10, citing Guzman v. Acuna, 653 S.W.2d 315, 319 (Tex. App. 1983) (holding that illegibility of essential handwritten terms in form contract made it uncertain and ambiguous).

***§7.8 n.6 p.270 Add to the list after* "See":** Miller v. Miller, 1 So. 3d 815 (La. App. 2009) (joint custody agreement provided that father "begin setting funds aside" for college).

§7.8 n.6 p.270 Add the following at the end: A professor at a state university who was terminated under the "civility" clause in his employment contract lost his challenge when the Eighth Circuit determined the obligation to discharge his "duties civilly, constructively and in an informed manner" was not unconstitutionally vague. Keating v. Univ. of South Dakota, 569 Fed. Appx. 469 (8th Cir. 2014).

***§7.8 n.11 p.271 Add the following to the list after* "See also":** Superior Ice Rink v. Nescon Contracting Corp., 861 N.Y.S.2d 362 (App. Div. 2008) (if policy mandates coverage if required by "written contract, agreement or permit," would an oral agreement suffice?).

§7.8 n.14 p.271 ***Add the following at the end:*** A contract interpretation case that hinged on the Oxford comma became a social media hit in 2017. The First Circuit considered a statutory exclusion from overtime regulations for employees engaged in "[t]he canning, processing, preserving, freezing, drying, marketing, storing, packing for shipment or distribution of [specified goods." Me. Rev. Stat. Ann. tit. 26 §664(3)(F). When a diary company denied overtime to drivers, asserting that they were involved in "distribution," the drivers responded that they were not involved in "packing for . . . distribution." The First Circuit held that "if that exemption used a serial comma to mark off the last of the activities that it lists, then the exemption would clearly encompass an activity that the drivers perform," but in the absence of the Oxford comma, the clause was ambiguous and so the rule of construction under Maine law that ambiguous wage and hour laws should be construed to favor the employee controlled. O'Connor v. Oakhurst Dairy, 851 F.3d 69 (1st Cir. 2017).

§7.8 p.272 ***In the first paragraph, add the following at the end of the first sentence:*** . . . inclusive disjunctive (P *or else* Q, *or else both*).[16a]

[16a] Southtrust Bank v. Copeland One, 886 So. 2d 38 (Ala. 2003) (viewing the use of "or" in "shall have the exclusive right during the term of this lease . . . to operate an ATM or any other type of banking facility" at a particular location as ambiguous, given the possible exclusive and inclusive senses of "or").

§7.8 n.17 p.272 ***Add the following to the list after "see":*** Sanders v. Molla, 985 A.2d 439 (D.C. 2009) (finding "and" ambiguous in the phrase "[l]andlord and tenant shall have the option to renew this lease," because the "and" can be read as either conjunctive or disjunctive; cites to hornbook).

§7.8 n.19 p.272 ***Add the following at the end:*** Ionata v. Allstate Ins. Co., 2016 U.S. Dist. LEXIS 116776 (E.D. Pa. Aug. 30, 2016) involved an insurance policy covering a "dwelling," defined as "where you reside." The insured had moved out, but disputed

whether it remained one of her "residences." More importantly, the court determined that other clauses in the policy seemed to envision the insured not residing at the property, at least not on a permanent basis. "Here, where the Policy does not attempt to define what it means to 'reside' at the Property, and the definition that Allstate advances in support of its Motion cannot be reconciled with the explicit permission the Policy confers to leave it vacant or rent it to third parties, I cannot hold as a matter of law that the language is unambiguous." *Accord:* Burns v. Smith, 303 S.W.3d 505 (Mo. 2010) ("If a contract promises something at one point and takes it away at another, there is an ambiguity.").

§7.8 n.21 p.272 Add the following after the second sentence: *See also* McKeever v. Rushing, 41 So. 3d 920 (Fla. App. 2010) (body of agreement contains general release but title is "Property Damage Release": does the release cover personal injury claims?); Soncoast Cmty. Church v. Travis Boating Ctr., 981 So. 2d 654 (Fla. App. 2008) (In release, "defendants" used broadly (Travis Boating included) and narrowly ("the DEFENDANTS have filed Third-Party Complaints against Travis Boating . . ."; Travis Boating excluded); is Travis Boating covered by the release?); Watkins v. Schexnider, 31 So. 3d 609 (La. App. 2010) (home purchase agreement states that it is for the sale of the house, but elsewhere refers to the address at which the house is located and to the need to insure the property; is the agreement for the sale of the house alone, or is it for the house and land?).

§7.8 n.22 p.273 Add the following to the list after* "See"*: Cachil Dehe Band of Wintun Indians v. California, 618 F.3d 1066 (9th Cir. 2010) (court finds proffered interpretation of both parties unreasonable; devises own interpretation of "opaquely drafted and convoluted formula").

In Under Armour, Inc. v. Ziger/Snead, LLP, 2017 Md. App. LEXIS 418 (Md. Ct. Spec. App. Apr. 27, 2017), the contract included what the parties ultimately agreed was to be construed as a prevailing party expense-shifting clause, under which Ziger was entitled to "attorneys' fees, costs, expenses, and losses incurred" related to enforcement of the contract. Ziger claimed losses in the form of diverted employee time. Under Armour claimed the terms losses was "not sufficiently specific to support a contractual undertaking to pay Ziger for garden variety litigation tasks." In holding the contract does require payment of such losses, the court took the occasion to discuss the role of ambiguity in contracts:

> Like "expenses" and unlike attorneys' fees and costs, the word "losses" is a general term that legitimately can cover a variety of things. To appellant, that is its weakness, but, assessing its purpose in an objective manner, that is its value — to avoid the need for the contract to specify each and every conceivable kind of "loss" not covered by the other terms that may result from a default by appellant. Adoption of appellant's view would achieve precisely what should be avoided. The word "losses" is no less definite or specific with respect to the provable diversion of employee time than it is to any other kind of harm not covered by "expenses" that may accrue from a breach of the contract.

§7.8 n.26 p.274 Add the following at the end: *Cf.* Choi & Triantis, Strategic Vagueness in Contract Design: The Case of Corporate Acquisitions, 119 Yale L.J. 848 (2010). On national differences in drafting techniques, *see* Hill & King, How Do German Contracts Do As Much with Fewer Words?, 79 Chi.-Kent L. Rev. 889 (2004).

§7.9 THE CHOICE OF MEANING

§7.9 n.7 p.276 Add the following to the list after "see": Whiting v. AARP, 637 F.3d 355 (D.C. Cir. 2011) (rejecting suggestion that "the court should take into account the probable educational attainment and sophistication of the target audience" of a mass solicitation by an insurer; rather, proffered interpretations "must be consistent with the meaning which common speech imports") (internal quotations omitted); Micro Focus (U.S.) v. Bell Canada, 686 F. Supp. 2d 564 (D. Md. 2010) (contract clauses "are construed in an ordinary and popular sense by reasonable persons and full effect is given to the intention of the parties"); Chance v. McCann, 966 A.2d 29 (N.J. Super. App. Div.

2009) (parol evidence inadmissible to show that when parties wrote $630,000, they actually meant $160,000).

§7.9 n.7 p.276 Add the following at the end of the first paragraph: *Cf.* Prentis Family Found. v. Karmanos Cancer Inst., 698 N.W.2d 900 (Mich. App. 2005) ("courts are not permitted to discern the parties' reasonable expectations and rewrite contracts accordingly"; clause stating that "in further recognition and appreciation" for creating a fund, a center would be named after the foundation's founders held not to be supported by consideration, even though "plaintiff may have expected that the naming provision was bargained consideration").

§7.9 n.12 p.278 Add the following to the end of the first paragraph: Walker v. Trailer Transit, Inc., 824 F.3d 688 (7th Cir. 2016) involved a dispute over the meaning of "reimburse." Drivers contracted for 71% of gross revenue, "less any insurance related surcharge and all items intended to reimburse [Trailer Transit] for special services," but alleged that the company was making a profit on its "special services." *Id.* at 689. The Seventh Circuit rejected the drivers' interpretation, explaining that "reimburse" in the sense of recovering actual costs is a common meaning but "is not the *only* possible meaning of 'reimburse.' The word also is used to mean 'compensate' or 'pay.' If the contract had said 'reimburse *the expense of* special services,' that would limit the word's meaning to recovery of actual costs. But those italicized words aren't in the contract." The court explained why this interpretation was reasonable and noted that the result might have been different if there were an allegation that the company was trying to "take opportunistic advantage" by, for example, transferring revenue to "special services" from "the portion of the bill subject to their 71% share," but there was no such allegation. It also noted that the representative plaintiff worked with the defendant for seven years and only brought suit two years after ending that relationship; "[t]he judiciary does not rewrite contracts after the fact to favor one side." *Id.* at 690.

§7.9 n.12 p.278 Add the following at the end: *Contra:* Farmers Auto Ins. Ass'n v. Wroblewski, 887 N.E.2d 916 (Ill. App. 2008) (court applies plain meaning of release, despite affidavits from the attorneys who drafted it that they intended a different meaning by the language they chose; "[W]here we have found that the contractual terms in the . . . release are unambiguous, we are constrained to the language contained in that release itself and cannot consider the parol evidence advanced by [one party].") This shows an excessive attachment to objective interpretation, the court here applying it even when it is a palpably inferior means to discern the intent of the parties at the time of contracting.

§7.9 n.17 p.280 Add the following to the list after "Accord": Bull Motor Co. v. Murphy, 270 S.W.3d 350 (Ark. App. 2007) (applying Restatement Second §201(2); auto dealer had reason to know both general definition of "new vehicle" and that in the Motor Vehicle Code, but buyer had reason to know only the general definition, so buyer's meaning prevails); United Rentals v. RAM Holdings, 937 A.2d 810 (Del. Ch. 2007) (Strine, V.C.) (applying Restatement Second §201(2); in merger agreement, where "the extrinsic evidence presented at trial does not lead to an obvious, reasonable interpretation," but only one party had reason to know the meaning attached by the other, the meaning of the other applies); Chisos, Inc. v. JKM Energy, 258 P.3d 1107 (N.M. App. 2011) (applying Restatement Second §201(2); conveyance interpreted in favor of buyer where seller should have known the meaning attached by buyer, but buyer had no reason to know meaning attached by seller).

§7.9 n.17 p.280 In the second paragraph, add the following at the end: *See generally* Cohen, The Fault That Lies Within Our Contract Law, 107 Mich. L. Rev. 1445 (2009); Eisenberg, The Role of Fault in Contract Law: Unconscionability, Unexpected Circumstances, Interpretation, Mistake, and Nonperformance, 107 Mich. L. Rev. 1413 (2009).

§7.9 p.280 Add the following to the fifth sentence: . . . a more attenuated kind of fault.[18a]

[18a] United Rentals v. RAM Holdings, *supra* note 17 (the party that knew or should have known about the conflicting interpretations "had an affirmative duty to clarify its position in the face of an ambiguous contract with glaringly conflicting provisions").

§7.9 n.19 p.281 In the first paragraph, add the following after the second sentence: Not all courts consider this approach objective. *See* United Rentals v. RAM Holdings, 937 A.2d 810 (Del. Ch. 2007) ("where an examination of the extrinsic evidence does not lead to an obvious, objectively reasonable solution . . . the Court considers the evidence of what one party *subjectively* 'believed the obligation to be, coupled with evidence that the other party knew or should have known of such belief.' ") (quoting U.S. West v. Time Warner, 1996 WL 307445, at *11 (Del. Ch. June 6, 1996)). The evidence of this will doubtless be objective, lest it be dismissed as self-serving, but the objective evidence will be of a subjective belief.

§7.9 n.22 p.282 In the third paragraph, add the following to the list after "Accord": Duck Dog, L.C. v. Brownstar Props., 990 So. 2d 525 (Fla. App. 2008) (definition of "certified" as qualifying a special assessment disputed between the parties, and no guidance present in the contract, so no contract formed: "Without a meeting of the minds on this clearly essential term of the sales contract, the trial court erred in finding that there was an enforceable contract . . .").

§7.9 n.27 p.284 In the second paragraph, add the following to the end of the final sentence: and in Miller v. Miller, 1 So. 3d 815 (La. App. 2009) ("Since [plaintiff] is demanding performance of this obligation, she bears the burden of proving its existence."; lack of evidence leads to invalidation of vague term). *Accord:* Shay v. Creative Poolscapes & Gardens, 25 So. 3d 155 (La. App. 2009) (where neither party met the burden of showing that its terms prevailed, neither party prevails on its claim).

§7.10 FUNDAMENTAL PRINCIPLES OF INTERPRETATION

§7.10 n.1 p.286 Add the following to the list after "Accord": Zahn v. Kroger Co., 764 N.W.2d 207 (Mich. 2009) (indemnity agreements).

§7.10 n.1 p.286 Add the following new paragraph at the end: In the student-university context, the courts have adopted a flexible approach in evaluating breach of contract claims premised on violations of student handbooks. In Janati v. Univ. of Nev. Las Vegas Sch. of Dental Med., 2017 U.S. Dist. LEXIS 46497 (D. Nev. Mar. 29, 2017) the district court applied Nevada law, which required that departures from procedures in student manuals must be "arbitrary, capricious, or in bad faith," Lucey v. State ex rel. Bd. of Regents of the Nev. Sys. of Higher Educ., 2009 U.S. Dist. LEXIS 30132 (D. Nev. Apr. 8, 2009), in order to constitute a breach of contract, and provided a helpful overview of the approach to student-university breach of contract disputes in general:

> It is questionable whether the *Lucey* test is really "contractual" in nature because it does not require reference to any contract or agreement. However, many cases have recognized the need for flexibility when analyzing the contractual relationship between the student and university, and that "hornbook rules cannot be applied mechanically" in such situations. *See, e.g.,* Amaya v. Brater, 981 N.E.2d 1235, 1240 (Ind. Ct. App. 2013) (citation omitted). "Courts have applied contract law flexibly to actions involving academic and disciplinary decisions by educational institutions because of the lack of a satisfactory standard of care by which to evaluate these decisions." Kashmiri v. Regents of Univ. of Calif., 156 Cal. App. 4th 809, 826, 67 Cal. Rptr. 3d 635 (Cal. Ct. App. 2007) (*cited with approval by* Robinson v. Nev. Sys. of Higher Educ., No. 3:15-cv-00169-MMD-VPC, 2015 U.S. Dist. LEXIS 167567 (D. Nev. Dec. 15, 2015)). The *Amaya* court reconciled the standards by laying out the broad or crucial procedural protections listed in the university's policy and evaluating whether the university "substantially followed" them. 981 N.E.2d at 1241 ("Literal adherence by a university to its internal rules will not be required when the dismissal of a student rests upon expert judgments as to academic or professional standards and such judgments are fairly and nonarbitrarily arrived at.") (citation omitted).

Janati, 2017 U.S. Dist. LEXIS 46497, at *14. *Accord:* Walker v. Presidents & Fellows of Harvard Coll., 840 F.3d 57 (1st Cir. 2016) (in Massachusetts, "the standard of reasonable expectation applies" in disputes between students and private colleges regarding contracts such as student conduct handbooks; "[u]nder this reasonable expectation standard, courts ask, in interpreting the contractual terms, 'what meaning the party making the manifestation, the university, should reasonably expect the other party[, the student,] to give it.' " (quoting Schaer v. Brandeis Univ., 432 Mass. 474, 735 N.E.2d 373, 378 (2000)).

***§7.10 n.4 p.286 Add the following to the list after* "Accord":** Fishman v. LaSalle Nat'l Bank, 247 F.3d 300 (1st Cir. 2001) ("Common sense is as much a part of contract interpretation as is the dictionary or the arsenal of canons."); Sembler Family P'ship v. Brinker Fla., 660 F. Supp. 2d 1307 (M.D. Fla. 2009) (rejecting as "absurd" interpretation of notice provision that would not only set an ending date for the notice period but also a starting date only five days before).

§7.10 n.5 p.287 Add the following at the end: *Accord:* State *ex rel.* Petro v. R.J. Reynolds Tobacco Co., 820 N.E.2d 910 (Ohio 2004) (interpreting contract in terms of "common usage").

§7.10 n.6 p.287 Add the following at the end: *Accord:* Klein v. Chevron U.S.A., 137 Cal. Rptr. 3d 293 (Ct. App. 2012) (using state weight and measurement laws to provide definition of "gallon"); Bonvillain Builders v. Gentile, 29 So. 3d 625 (La. App. 2009) ("laws that exist at the time of execution of a contract form a part of that contract and are incorporated in it"). Though perhaps it should go without saying, the interests of planning and certainty require that a contract "be construed as of the date on which it was made." Bowdoin Square v. Winn-Dixie Montgomery, 873 So. 2d 1091, 1101 (Ala. 2003). *Accord:* Behrens v. S.P. Constr. Co., 904 A.2d 676 (N.H. 2006) (interpretation requires "considering the circumstances and the context in which the agreement was negotiated"); Mullinnix LLC v. HKB Royalty Trust, 126 P.3d 909 (Wyo. 2006) ("we look to the meaning of terms at the time of execution").

Moreover, parties may not escape the legal significance of what is being contracted for by labeling the arrangement something else, as is particularly relevant in the employment context. Regarding employee or independent contractor status, *see* Alexander v. FedEx Ground Package Sys., Inc., 765 F.3d 981 (9th Cir. 2014) (operating agreement between FedEx and a class of delivery drivers characterized them as independent contractors, but Ninth Circuit found that the material terms of their contractual relationship and control rendered them employees as a matter of state law); O'Connor v. Uber Tech., Inc., 82 F. Supp. 3d 1133 (N.D. Cal. 2015) ("contracts explicitly provide that the relationship between the transportation providers and Uber/Raiser 'is solely that of independent contracting parties,' " but the court held that drivers are "presumptive employees" and "whether an individual should ultimately be classified as an employee or an independent contractor under California law presents a mixed question of law and fact" that could not be resolved at summary judgment). Regarding joint employer status when contracting with a staffing agency, *see* Browning-Ferris Indus. of Cal., Inc., 362 NLRB 186 (2015) (although BFI's contract with a staffing agency provided that the staffing agency was "the sole employer of the personnel it supplies" and responsible for matters such as selecting and hiring, the Board applied a restated standard that "two or more statutory employers are joint employers of the same statutory employees if they 'share or codetermine those matters governing the essential terms and conditions of employment' " to find that BFI was a joint employer) (citing NLRB v. Browning-Ferris Indus. of Pennsylvania, Inc., 691 F.2d 1117 (3d Cir. 1982)).

§7.10 n.7 p.287 Add the following after the first sentence: *See also* Confold P. v. Polaris Indus., 433 F.3d 952 (7th Cir. 2006) (Posner, J.) (where agreement copied from other contract, the scope of that contract informed the reading of the disputed contract).

§7.10 n.8 p.287 Add the following to the list in the second sentence: Employers Reinsurance Corp. v. Am. S.W. Ins. Managers, 261 S.W.3d 432 (Tex. Civ. App. 2008) ("courts construe contracts from a utilitarian standpoint, bearing in mind the particular business activity sought to be served").

§7.10 n.11 p.287 Add the following to the list after **"See":** Hess v. Kanoski & Assocs., 668 F.3d 446 (7th Cir. 2012) ("Under Illinois law, undefined terms are generally given their plain, ordinary, and popular meanings as found in dictionary definitions. Resort to dictionary definitions often, however, does not settle the question; that is the case here.") (citations and internal quotes omitted).

§7.10 n.11 p.287 Add the following to the list after **"See also"***:* Fleet Nat'l Bank v. H & D Entm't, 96 F.3d 532 (1st Cir. 1996) ("In short, words matter; but the words are to be read as elements in a practical working document and not as a crossword puzzle.").

§7.10 n.12 p.288 Add the following to the list after **"Accord"***:* Bukuras v. Mueller Grp., 592 F.3d 255 (1st Cir. 2010) (rejecting dictionary definition of "bonus" in favor of contextual definition; "the scope of a party's obligations cannot 'be delineated by isolating words and interpreting them as though they stood alone.' ") (quoting from Starr v. Fordham, 648 N.E.2d 1261 (Mass. 1995), in turn quoting from Comm'r of Corps. & Taxation v. Chilton Club, 61 N.E.2d 335 (Mass. 1945)).

In *Hess v. Kanoski Bresney*, 784 F.3d 1154 (7th Cir. 2015), the Seventh Circuit considered a terminated attorney's employment contract that provided that he was entitled to a tiered bonus structure of 15 percent over fees "generated" over base salary and 25 percent of fees "received" over $750,000. The firm argued that the attorney was entitled to nothing from a case that he had worked on extensively but settled after he was terminated, because fees were not generated until they were received. The Seventh Circuit acknowledged that " 'generate' has a common-usage definition that is different from the term 'received,' " *id.* at 1159, citing *Webster's Third New International Dictionary*, but nevertheless held that, in the context of an attorney employment contract, it was not practical to attempt to determine when fees were generated other than treating them as generated when received. Because of the great complexity that would follow from the attorney's interpretation, the court held that the simpler understanding was more "plausible."

Capital City Cmty. Urban Dev. v. Columbus City, 2015 Ohio Misc. LEXIS 15172 (Sept. 17, 2015) involved a historic theater and an agreement to "provide Saturday movies for children once the theater is operational, and for as long as feasible. The cost is to be $ 1.00 or less for a double feature." When operation and ownership changed hands, subject to this original agreement, a protracted disagreement regarding the meaning of "as long as feasible" ensued. The court held that it "must allot the phrase "for as long as feasible" some meaning that gives the phrase vitality," observed that the defendant is "a business and must take into consideration the economic vitality of its programs in order to remain open and beneficial to the public," and accordingly adopted the defendant's proposed, dictionary-based definition of " 'reasonable assurance of success' and 'capable of being done' with economic viability being a key feature of feasibility."

§7.10 n.14 p.288 Add the following after the second sentence: *But see* Chance v. McCann, 966 A.2d 29 (N.J. Super. App. Div. 2009) (parol evidence inadmissible to show that when parties wrote $630,000, they actually meant $160,000).

§7.10 n.15 p.288 Add the following to the list in the second sentence: Ocean Petroleum Co. v. Yanek, 5 A.3d 683 (Md. 2010) ("Because the relevant provisions of the lease agreement contemplate a transaction between a landlord and a tenant rather than an ordinary property owner and potential buyer, [the option provisions] indicate that the parties contemplated a transaction in which the property is sold free of the tenant's encumbrance thereon."); Kirby Lake Dev. v. Clear Lake City Water Auth., 320 S.W.3d 829 (Tex. 2010) ("[W]e must evaluate the overall agreement to determine what purposes the parties had in mind at the time they signed the Agreements."); Cavan v. Maron, 2016 U.S. Dist. LEXIS 112299 (D. Ariz. Aug. 22, 2016) ("The Court, drawing on its judicial experience and common sense . . . concludes that the plaintiff has plausibly pleaded that the parties intended that the rare watch that the plaintiff purchased, which was valued at more than $2,000,000, would have all of its original parts absent a disclosure to the contrary.") (citing Ashcroft v. Iqbal, 556 U.S. 662, 679, 129 S. Ct. 1937, 173 L. Ed. 2d 868 (2009)).

§7.10 n.15 p.288 Add the following at the end: For an extreme statement of purposive interpretation, *see* Krajacich v. Great Falls Clinic, 276 P.3d 922 (Mont. 2012) ("[C]ontract terms that are inconsistent with the general nature of the contract or the primary intention of the parties are to be rejected."). In a particularly interesting fact pattern, a physician leased office space, with a right to cancel the lease "for cause other than Undertenant's relocation of her medical practice within the New York City Metropolitan area." Because of her terminal illness, she joined a medical group in Manhattan that would allow her to maintain health insurance. The landlord sued for breach, invoking the exception to the termination clause; the physician defended by pointing to the purpose behind that clause. The appellate court found the clause ambiguous because "the extent to which the cancellation right turns on the consequences of rather than the reasons for a decision to cancel" and thus remanded for trial. Adams v. Lewin, 899 N.Y.S.2d 215 (App. Div. 2010).

§7.10 n.16 p.289 Add the following at the end: quoted approvingly in Estate of Polushkin v. Maw, 170 P.3d 162 (Alaska 2007).

***§7.10 n.20 p.289 In the second paragraph, add the following to the list after* "Accord":** Whetstone Candy Co. v. Kraft Foods, 351 F.3d 1067 (11th Cir. 2003) ("'whereas' clauses are not binding when the contract is otherwise unambiguous"); Hagene v. Derek Polling Constr., 902 N.E.2d 1269 (Ill. App. 2009) ("The contract recitals create a context through which the operational portion of the contract can be better understood, because they indicate the relevant circumstances to its execution."); Clarkson & Co. v. Cont'l Res., 806 N.W.2d 615 (S.D. 2011) (interpreting agreement in light of statement in prefatory section).

§7.10 n.20 p.289 In the second paragraph, add the following after the citation to* Abraham Zion Corp.*: , followed and extended by Devan Motors v. Infiniti Div. of Nissan N. Am., 579 F. Supp. 2d 294 (D. Conn. 2008) ("The description of a contract's purposes is analogous to a 'whereas' clause.").

§7.10 p.290 Add the following to the sixth sentence: Most judges would probably agree with Hand.[22a]

[22a] For a rare illustration, see Chance v. McCann, 966 A.2d 29 (N.J. Super. App. Div. 2009) (written contract stated price for building as $630,000, but one party sought to prove that they actually meant that the price should be $160,000; court declines to admit parol because the parol would contradict a term of the writing).

§7.10a DRAFTING RECITALS

§7.10a n.2 p.291 Add the following after the second sentence: For a careful analysis of how recitals and promises interrelate, *see In re* Universal Serv. Fund Tel. Billing Practice Litig., 619 F.3d 1188 (10th Cir. 2010).

§7.10a n.4 p.291 Add the following at the end: *Accord:* Clarkson & Co. v. Cont'l Res., 806 N.W.2d 615 (S.D. 2011) (interpreting agreement in light of statement in prefatory section).

§7.11 RULES IN AID OF INTERPRETATION

***§7.11 n.1 p.292 Add the following to the list after* "See":** Nat'l Tax Inst. v. Topnotch at Stowe Resort & Spa, 388 F.3d 15 (1st Cir. 2004) ("agreements, especially commercial arrangements, are designed to make sense"), followed in Utica Mut. Ins. Co. v. Vigo Coal Co., 393 F.3d 707 (7th Cir. 2004) ("good sense, or such synonyms as commercial reasonableness, provides sound guidance for interpreting ambiguous contracts"); Ramlall v. MobilePro Corp., 30 A.3d 1003 (Md. App. 2011) ("A contract should not be construed to produce a result that is absurd, commercially unreasonable[,] or contrary to the reasonable expectations of the parties."); Girgenti v. Girgenti, 917 N.Y.S.2d 258 (App. Div. 2011) (contracts should be interpreted to give "a practical and reasonable interpretation to the language employed"); Clarkson & Co. v. Cont'l Res., 806 N.W.2d 615 (S.D. 2011) (rejecting interpretation as illogical that would freeze payments for road use for 25 years).

***§7.11 n.2 p.293 Add the following to the list after* "Accord":** Fix v. Quantum Indus. Partners, 374 F.3d 549 (7th Cir. 2004) (noting "strong presumption against reading into contracts provisions that easily could have been included but were not"); Rowe v. Great Atlantic & Pacific Tea Co., 385 N.E.2d 566 (N.Y. 1978) (though lessee "might have agreed to include a provision limiting its right to assign the lease had [lessor] insisted on such a clause, we may safely assume that [lessor] would have had to pay a price for that concession" and "courts should be extremely reluctant to interpret an agreement as impliedly stating something which the parties have neglected to specifically include").

§7.11 n.5 p.293 Add the following at the end: *See generally* Hoffheimer, Conflicting Rules of Interpretation and Construction in Multi-Jurisdictional Disputes, 63 Rutgers L. Rev. 599 (2011).

***§7.11 n.7 p.294 In the first paragraph, add the following to the list after* "Accord":** Dover Village Ass'n v. Jennison, 119 Cal. Rptr. 3d 175 (Ct. App. 2010) (condominium covenants provide that patio and garage are exclusive use common areas, so that definition will be interpreted not to include sewer lines); Azat v. Farruggio, 875 A.2d 778 (Md. App. 2005) ("silence creates ambiguity when it involves a matter naturally within the scope of the contract"); Bentley Funding Grp. v. SK & R Grp., 609 S.E.2d 49 (Va. 2005) (because defined term "Property" did not include escrows, it will not be read to include them).

§7.11 n.7 p.294 In the first paragraph, add the following after the second sentence: *Cf.* Clarkson & Co. v. Cont'l Res., 806 N.W.2d 615 (S.D. 2011) (because contract uses the phrase "owned and/or leased," use elsewhere of the term "owned" excludes leases; "[I]f the parties intended to include leased land for the payment at issue, they would have used the term 'leased' as they did in other parts of the contract.").

***§7.11 n.8 p.294 Add the following to the list after* "Accord":** Maxim Techs. v. City of Dubuque, 690 N.W.2d 896 (Iowa 2005) (indemnification clause must "be read in context" of terms referring to environmental liability "and limited to environmental-type claims"); Jensen v. Bd. Of Regents of the Univ. of Neb., 684 N.W.2d 537 (Neb. 2004) (term "any other source whatsoever" "is modified by the specific words and terms surrounding it," and thus is restricted to insurance recovery); Team Mktg. USA Corp. v. Power Pact, 839 N.Y.S.2d 242 (App. Div. 2007) ("When the event that prevents performance is not enumerated, but the clause contains an expansive catch-all phrase in addition to specific events, 'the precept of *ejusdem generis* as a construction guide is appropriate' "; therefore, force majeure clause listing, inter alia, war, Acts of God, riots and restraints of public authority held not to cover one party's decision to change a marketing schedule); Hilco Elec. Coop. v. Midlouthian Butane Gas Co., 111 S.W.3d 75 (Tex. 2003) ("phrase 'any lawful purpose' . . . is limited to purposes similar in kind or class to the twenty-one identified categories"); Café Rio v. Larkin-Gifford-Overton, LLC, 207 P.3d 1235 (Utah 2009) ("the general term 'obstruction' . . . should be construed according to the specific enumerations of 'fence, wall, [and] barricade' " that precede it).

***§7.11 n.8 p.294 Add the following to the list after* "But cf.":** Nova Cas. Co. v. Waserstein, 424 F. Supp. 2d 1325 (S.D. Fla. 2006) ("[A] court is not permitted to use the rule of *ejusdem generis* to discern the plain language of a contract. It may only use the rule to construe the contract *after* it determines that the plain language of the contract is ambiguous.") (emphasis in original); Clinical Research Inst. v. Kemper Ins. Cos., 84 P.3d 147 (Or. App. 2004) ("Depending on how the common characteristics of a group are defined, the rule can lead to different results."); Hirschhorn v. Auto-Owners Ins. Co., 809 N.W.2d 529 (Wis. 2012) ("waste" within a pollution exclusion clause unambiguously includes bat guano; *ejusdem generis* does not apply because "we will not apply rules of construction to rewrite the plain terms of the policy's definition of 'pollutants' ").

***§7.11 n.9 p.295 In the first paragraph, add the following to the list after* "Accord":** Penncro Assocs. v. Sprint Spectrum, 499 F.3d 1151 (10th Cir. 2007) (general term "consequential damages" to be read in terms of "lost profits, lost revenues and lost business opportunities," thus not including lost profits that are not consequential damages); Chunn v. Whisenant, 877 So. 2d 595 (Ala. 2003) (general term "inventory" to be read in terms of "goodwill, office supplies, inventory, and attachments," and thus not to include interests in real estate); Com. ex rel. Fisher v. Philip Morris, Inc., 4 A.3d 749 (Pa. Commw. 2010) (in consent decree barring the use of certain cartoons in cigarette advertising, "unnatural or extrahuman abilities" to be read in light of examples, such as "imperviousness to pain or injury"; "Photographs of a radio with a propeller floating in the sky or speakers perched on stems growing out of the ground are a far cry from the unnatural or superhuman 'powers' of those listed."); Mylan Labs. v. Am. Motorists Ins. Co., 700 S.E.2d 518 (W. Va. 2010) (insurance coverage against "discrimination" did not encompass antitrust price discrimination; the context for the term is a list of "offenses against the liberty, emotional well-being, reputation, or peaceful possession of property of the plaintiff as opposed to economic injury").

In Atlantic Cas. Ins. Co. v. Gustafson, 2016 Mich. App. LEXIS 1092 (May 26, 2016) a property owner contracted with a company for landscaping and drainage work and was injured by flying debris. The insurance company denied coverage because the policy excluded injury to contractors, which were defined to "include but is not limited to any independent contractor or subcontractor of any insured, any general contractor, any developer, *any property owner*, any independent contractor or subcontractor of any general contractor, any independent contractor or subcontractor of any general developer, any independent contractor or subcontractor of any property owner and any and all persons providing services or materials of any kind for these persons or entities mentioned herein." The court first noted that the exclusion of "any property owner" could be understood as "encompassing virtually the entire world (except perhaps for a newborn baby) [which would render] the policy illusory." It then applied the principle of *noscitur a sociis* and found that the exclusion should extend only to "the contractor, any subcontractors, or any vendors supplying materials or services, or who otherwise are involved from a commercial standpoint."

§7.11 n.12 p.295 Add the following to the list after "Accord": Jaffe v. Jaffe, 17 So. 3d 1251 (Fla. App. 2009) (in marital settlement agreement, reading duration of term requiring payment of education-related expenses is consistent with the term providing for tuition; to do otherwise "contravenes a unified interpretation of the entire agreement and circumvents its stated meaning and purpose").

In Gorog v. Best Buy Co., 760 F.3d 787 (8th Cir. 2014), the former CEO of Napster was terminated without cause and the company was then sold to Best Buy. His contract provided for a Performance Award at a Target Date based on performance criteria. One provision of the contract provided that if he were terminated without cause before the Target Date, he would be paid an Award pro-rated to his period of employment, but another provided that he would be entitled to 100% of the Award if the company were sold prior to the Target Date. After the sale, former CEO Gorog sued, relying solely on the later clause and without pleading achievement of performance criteria that would entitle him to an award under the former clause. The Eighth Circuit held that "[t]he forfeiture and acceleration provisions are mutually exclusive and thus Gorog is not entitled to a performance award" under the sale clause. The court reasoned that Gorog's reading would lead to clearly unintended results in certain circumstances, such as if he were terminated for cause prior to a sale, but by instead "interpreting the forfeiture and acceleration provisions as mutually exclusive, sections 2.4(a) through 2.4(d) are harmonized and will be applied without causing absurd results," *Id.* at 794.

§7.11 n.13 p.296 In the first paragraph, add the following to the list after* "Accord"*: Equity Lifestyle Props. v. Fla. Mowing & Landscape Serv., 556 F.3d 1232 (11th Cir. 2009) ("We must read the contract to give meaning to each and every word it contains, and we avoid treating a word as redundant or mere surplusage if any meaning, reasonable and consistent with other parts, can be given to it.") (internal quotation omitted); Baldwin Piano v. Deutsche Wurlitzer GmbH, 392 F.3d 881 (7th Cir. 2004) ("interpreting contracts so that major clauses fall out usually is not a sensible way to understand the parties' transaction"); United Rentals v. RAM Holdings, 937 A.2d 810 (Del. Ch. 2007) (Strine, V.C.) (invoking "the canon of construction that requires harmonization of seemingly conflicting contract provisions").

§7.11 n.13 p.296 Add the following after the citation to* Iowa Fuel & Minerals*: , followed in Seneca Waste Solutions v. Sheaffer Mfg. Co., 791 N.W.2d 407 (Iowa 2010) (rejecting proffered interpretation that would render one provision superfluous).

§7.11 n.13 p.296 Add the following at the end of the first paragraph: *But cf.* Krajacich v. Great Falls Clinic, 276 P.3d 922 (Mont. 2012) ("[C]ontract terms that are inconsistent with the general nature of the contract or the primary intention of the parties are to be rejected.").

§7.11 n.13 p.296 In the second paragraph, add the following at the end: *Accord:* BP Prods. N. Am. v. Stanley, 669 F.3d 184 (4th Cir. 2012) (Virginia law: "[W]hen two constructions may be given a contract, one of which would render it valid and the other of which would destroy it, the former construction will be given it, if [it is] reasonable.") (internal quotations omitted).

§7.11 n.16 p.297 Add the following to the list after* "Accord"*: Northrop Grumman Info. Tech. v. United States, 535 F.3d 1339 (Fed. Cir. 2008) (government contract; "[T]he language used in a contract to incorporate extrinsic material by reference must explicitly, or at least precisely, identify the written material being incorporated and must clearly communicate that the purpose of the reference is to incorporate the referenced material into the contract (rather than merely to acknowledge that the referenced material is relevant to the contract, e.g., a background law or negotiating history.")); Allstate Life Ins. Co. v. BFA L.P., 948 A.2d 318 (Conn. 2008) ("When parties execute a contract that clearly refers to another document, there is an intent to make the terms and conditions of the other document a part of their agreement, so long as both parties are aware of the terms and conditions of that other document."); C.L.D.F. Inc. v. Aramore LLC, 659 S.E.2d 695 (Ga. App. 2008) ("As a matter of contract law, we must consider the Lease and the Guaranty together, as contemporaneous writings, in an effort to derive their intended meaning."); Whitemaine v. Aniskovich, 183 P.3d 137 (Nev. 2008) ("[T]wo instruments are presumed to be a single contract if (1) they are contemporaneously executed, (2) they concern the same subject matter, and (3) one of the instruments refers to the other."; particularly thorough analysis); Dietrich v. Chem. Bank, 454 N.Y.S.2d 490 (Sup. 1981), *aff'd*, 459 N.Y.S.2d 1016 (App. Div. 1983) ("A contract can be comprised of separate writings or documents if the writings make it clear that they are to be read in conjunction with other writings to determine the intent of the parties."); *In re* Lisa Laser USA, 310 S.W.3d 880 (Tex. 2010) ("Because neither document could be considered 'this Agreement' by itself, the common sense approach is to read the two documents as multiple documents describing a sing[le] transaction . . .").

§7.11 n.16 p.297 Add the following to the list after **"But cf.":** Peterson v. Residential Alternatives, 932 N.E.2d 1 (Ill. App. 2010) ("Parties may not incorporate another agreement into a contract without an express 'reference' demonstrating an intent to incorporate another agreement into the contract."; nursing home care agreement and arbitration agreement contained no internal links and so were unrelated, meaning that the latter lacked consideration and was unenforceable); Hoover v. Holbert, 51 So. 3d 251 (Miss. App. 2011) (promissory note separate from contemporaneous asset purchase agreement; note made no reference to agreement, and stated that it "represents a complete contract and does not require any further documentation for payment due"); Ledaura, LLC v. Gould, 237 P.3d 914 (Wash. App. 2010) (although lease and option contain cross-references, they are independent agreements because "the parties supported each agreement with an independent source and amount of consideration" and the agreements "contained contradictory assignment clauses," so in the absence of express language demonstrating their interdependence, the contracts are considered separate).

§7.11 n.16 p.297 Add the following at the end: By definition, incorporation by reference requires that the thing to be incorporated exist at the time of the incorporation. If not, then the result is not incorporation but delegation and very likely a fatally indefinite agreement. As one court observed, this is not even buying a pig in a poke; then "there was at least *some thing* in the bag that the parties could look at. Here, by contrast, the bag was empty at the time of the transaction and *might* or might *not* be later filled with a pig. Or a cat or rat or, for that matter, nothing." Gilbert St. Developers v. La Quinta Homes, 94 Cal. Rptr. 3d 918, 925 (Ct. App. 2009).

There are no "magic words" needed in one document to incorporate part or all of another document. But a prudent drafter would heed the advice of the Federal Circuit on how to avoid litigating this issue, which one may do "by simply adopting widely-used and judicially-approved language of incorporation, such as 'is hereby incorporated by reference' or 'is hereby incorporated as though fully set forth herein,' and by including specific and sufficient information identifying a particular document, such as the title, date, parties to, and section headings of any document to be incorporated." *Northrop Grumman, supra*, at 1346.

§7.11 p.297 Add the following after the carryover sentence: Also according to the Eighth Circuit, however, "when courts construe a sequence of written agreements, a subsequent contract that applies more specifically to the . . . work in question is controlling."[16a]

[16a] Thornton Drilling Co. v. Nat'l Union Fire Ins. Co., 537 F.3d 943, 947 (8th Cir. 2008).

***§7.11 n.20 p.299 In the second paragraph, add the following to the list after* "see":** Viera v. Life Ins. Co. of N. Am., 642 F.3d 407 (3d Cir. 2011) ("[T]he last-antecedent rule is not an absolute and can assuredly be overcome by other indicia of meaning. . . . Where the meaning of the contract language is clear, the last-antecedent rule should not be used to create ambiguity.") (internal quotations omitted); Nat'l Tax Inst. v. Topnotch at Stowe Resort & Spa, 388 F.3d 15 (1st Cir. 2004) (last antecedent rule "formally applies, but it is not conclusive; and anyway the opaque sentence in question — inserted seemingly at random between unrelated provisions — was not drafted with any noticeable precision"); Am. Music Co. v. Higbee, 103 P.3d 518 (Mont. 2004) (applying "basic grammatical construction rule that, absent a contrary intention, qualifying words and phrases should be applied only to the words or phrases immediately preceding"); Whitebox Convertible Arbitrage Partners v. Fairfax Fin. Holdings, 900 N.Y.S.2d 56 (App. Div. 2010) (finding ambiguity because of unclear placement of qualifying phrase); Wohl v. Swinney, 888 N.E.2d 1062 (Ohio 2008) ("the rule applies only when no contrary intention otherwise appears").

***§7.11 n.23 p.300 Add the following to the list after* "Accord":** Sutter Ins. Co. v. Applied Sys., 393 F.3d 722 (7th Cir. 2004) ("commercial reasonableness is a useful guide to the interpretation of an ambiguous contract"); Baldwin Piano v. Deutsche Wurlitzer GmbH, 392 F.3d 881 (7th Cir. 2004) ("when there is a choice among plausible interpretations, it is best to choose a reading that makes commercial sense, rather than a reading that makes the deal one-sided"); 7-Eleven, Inc. v. Stin, LLC, 961 So. 2d 977 (Fla. App. 2007) ("Contracts should receive a construction that is reasonable, practical, sensible, and just."); ERC 16W Ltd. P'ship v. Xanadu Mezz Holdings, 943 N.Y.S.2d 493 (App. Div. 2012) ("[A] construction of a contract that would give one party an unfair and unreasonable advantage over the other, or that would place one party at the mercy of the other, should, if at all possible, be avoided."); Employers Reinsurance Corp. v. Am. S.W. Ins. Managers, 261 S.W.3d 432 (Tex. Civ. App. 2008) (courts "will avoid when possible and proper a construction which is unreasonable, inequitable, and oppressive").

§7.11 n.26 p.300 In the first paragraph, add the following to the list after* "Accord"*: Tri-State Fin. v. First Dakota Nat'l Bank, 538 F.3d 920 (8th Cir. 2008) (South Dakota law: "ambiguities are to be construed against the drafter"); Southtrust Bank v. Copeland One, 886 So. 2d 38 (Ala. 2003) ("any ambiguity in a contract must be construed against the drafter"); RAM Mut. Ins. Co. v. Rohde, 820 N.W.2d 1 (Minn. 2012) ("when language is ambiguous, it should be construed against the drafter"); Austin v. Carpenter, 3 So. 3d 147 (Miss. App. 2009) (construing condition precedent against drafter, which results in the failure of the condition and the unenforceability of the contract); City of Bismarck v. Mariner Constr., 714 N.W.2d 484 (N.D. 2006) ("If a contract is uncertain, the language of the contract should be interpreted most strongly against the party who caused the uncertainty to exist").

§7.11 n.26 p.300 In the second paragraph, add the following after the first sentence: *Cf.* City of Bismarck v. Mariner Constr., *supra* ("for contracts between a public entity and a private party, it is presumed that all uncertainty was caused by the private party").

§7.11 n.26 p.300 In the second paragraph, add the following after the second sentence: *Accord:* States Roofing Corp. v. Winter, 587 F.3d 1364 (Fed. Cir. 2009) ("A 'patent ambiguity' is one that is 'obvious, gross, glaring, so that plaintiff contractor had a duty to inquire about it at the start.' ") (quoting from H & M Moving v. United States, 499 F.2d 660 (Ct. Cl. 1974)), followed in Armour of

Am. v. United States 96 Fed. Cl. 726, 2011 WL 86475 (2011) (if ambiguity were patent, then it "should have been raised by plaintiff and clarified . . . prior to signing the contract" so that its "failure to inquire and clarify what it perceived was an apparent discrepancy . . . precludes its argument").

§7.11 n.26 p.300 ***Add the following at the end:*** This canon has special force when the contract in question is between an attorney and a client. As the Restatement (Third) of the Law Governing Lawyers puts it, "A tribunal should construe a contract between client and lawyer as a reasonable person in the circumstances of the client would have construed it." Restatement (Third) of the Law Governing Lawyers §18(2). Lawyers normally draft their own fee contracts, they are in better positions to find and correct errors, and they should let clients know about the obligations and risks created by representation — hence this maxim. Restatement (Third) of the Law Governing Lawyers at §18 cmt. *h*. *See also* Weiner v. Burr, Pease & Kurtz, P.C., 221 P.3d 1 (Alaska 2009) (applying Restatement).

§7.11 n.28 p.302 ***In the first paragraph, add the following after the first sentence:*** *See generally* Horton, Flipping the Script: *Contra Proferentem* and Standard Form Contracts, 80 U. Colo. L. Rev. 431 (2009).

§7.11 n.28 p.302 ***In the first paragraph, add the following to the list in the third sentence:*** Royal Maccabees Life Ins. Co. v. James, 146 S.W.3d 340 (Tex. Civ. App. 2004) (in the face of "more than one reasonable interpretation, we will find the contract is ambiguous and adopt the interpretation that most favors coverage for the insured"); N. Sec. Ins. Co. v. Doherty, 987 A.2d 253 (Vt. 2009) ("Because the policy language is ambiguous, we construe it in favor of providing coverage . . .").

§7.11 n.29 p.302 ***Add the following to the list after "Accord":*** Barrett v. McDonald Invs., 870 A.2d 146 (Me. 2005) ("where an individual with little leverage is entering into an agreement with a larger entity that offers its services on a 'take it or leave it' basis, we conclude that the balance tips in favor of applying the equitable rule favoring the construction of the

contract against the drafter" versus the presumption in favor of arbitration).

***§7.11 n.30 p.303 Add the following to the list after* "Accord":** Royal Ins. Co. of Am. v. Orient Overseas Container Line, 525 F.3d 409 (6th Cir. 2008) ("Even when this and other circuits have not termed bills of lading contracts of adhesion, federal appellate courts have nonetheless resolved ambiguities in admiralty contracts against the drafters of these contracts."); City of Hope Nat'l Med. Ctr. v. Genentech, Inc., 181 P.3d 142 (Cal. 2008) (rejecting argument that *contra proferentem* applies only to adhesion contracts; rather, it is "a general rule of contract interpretation").

***§7.11 n.30 p.303 Add the following to the list after* "But cf.":** Rexam Beverage Can Co. v. Bolger, 620 F.3d 718 (7th Cir. 2010) (rejecting argument that lease should be construed against the "sophisticated businessman" who drafted the lease, noting that "Rexam is not unsophisticated, nor was its predecessor in interest that signed the lease"); Alberto-Culver Co. v. Aon Corp., 812 N.E.2d 369 (Ill. App. 2004) (where the insured "is a sophisticated corporate entity familiar with aviation insurance . . . application of the *contra [proferentem]* rule here is inappropriate"); Zahn v. Kroger Co., 764 N.W.2d 207 (Mich. 2009) (construing indemnification clause: "We cannot assume that the parties in this case, given their equal bargaining power, agreed to a clause that has no meaning or that we should ignore it because the language was part of a form contract."); Westfield Family Physicians v. HealthNow N.Y., 873 N.Y.S.2d 793 (App. Div. 2009) (*contra proferentem* "is not applicable where, as here, the party seeking to apply it participated in negotiating the terms of the document").

***§7.11 n.32 p.304 Add the following to the list after* "Accord":** Viera v. Life Ins. Co. of N. Am., 642 F.3d 407 (3d Cir. 2011) ("[W]e must construe ambiguous policy provisions against the drafter of the contract once a determination of ambiguity has been made . . ."); Mary J. Baker Revocable Trust v. Cenex Harvest States Coops., 164 P.3d 851 (Mont. 2007) ("the general maxim that a court should construe contract language against the party that drafted it presupposes that the language is reasonably susceptible to more than one construction").

***§7.11 n.33 p.304 Add the following to the list after* "Accord":** Swift & Co. v. Elias Farms, 539 F.3d 849 (8th Cir. 2008) (*contra proferentem* "applies only as a last resort, after all other evidence fails to demonstrate the intent of the parties"; citing to treatise); Nat'l Tax Inst. v. Topnotch at Stowe Resort & Spa, 388 F.3d 15 (1st Cir. 2004) (*contra proferentem* "has little to do with actual intentions and should only be used, as a last resort, if other aids to construction leave the case in equipoise"), followed by McAdams v. Mass. Mut. Life Ins. Co., 391 F.3d 287 (1st Cir. 2004) ("there is no need to turn to a last resort canon"); United States v. Ins. Co. of N. Am., 131 F.3d 1037 (D.C. Cir. 1997) (rule "is traditionally used only in cases of doubt where other factors are not decisive"); Petrucelli v. Palmer, 596 F. Supp. 2d 347 (D. Conn. 2009) ("the doctrine of *contra proferentem* works as a tiebreaker in close cases"); Alberto-Culver Co. v. Aon Corp., 812 N.E.2d 369 (Ill. App. 2004) (rule is to be used "only as a last resort, when other techniques of interpretation and construction have not resolved . . . which of two or more possible reasonable meanings the court should choose"); Fire Ins. Exchange v. Oltmanns, 285 P.3d 802 (Utah App. 2012) ("the last resort in contract interpretation is to construe the provision *against* the drafter") (emphasis in original).

§7.11 n.34 p.304 Add the following at the start: Restatement Second §207. *Accord:* Time Warner Entmt. Co. v. Everest Midwest Licensee, 381 F.3d 1039 (10th Cir. 2004) ("this license agreement affects the public interest and should therefore be liberally construed, where appropriate, to favor the public").

However, in 2015, the Supreme Court rebuked the Sixth Circuit for "placing a thumb on the scale in favor of vested retiree benefits in all collective-bargaining agreements." M&G Polymers v. Tackett, 135 S. Ct. 926, 935, 90 L. Ed. 2d 809, 818 (2015). The contract in that case provided certain retired employees and their dependents with lifetime health insurance contributions, but another provision limited contributions to "the duration of the agreement." The Sixth Circuit found that the health care benefits were vested rights, relying on the context of labor negotiations and observing that the provision would otherwise be illusory. The Supreme Court held that the circuit relied on previous circuit cases (Yard-Man and its progeny, International Union, United Auto, Aerospace, & Agricultural Implement Workers of Am. v. Yard-Man, Inc., 716 F. 2d 1476 (6th Cir. 1983)) that are "inconsistent with ordinary principles of contract law" and reversed and remanded with instructions to "apply ordinary principles of contract law" without those public policy considerations.

§7.11 n.36 p.305 ***In the first paragraph, add the following to the list after*** **"Accord"*:*** Wilson v. Travelers Ins. Co., 605 P.2d 1327 (Okla. 1980) ("Insurance contracts are contracts of adhesion, and where the contract is susceptible of two constructions, the construction most favorable to the insured must be adopted."); Fire Ins. Exch. v. Oltmanns, 285 P.3d 802 (Utah App. 2012) ("As a practical matter . . . there is a different protocol in the case of insurance and surety contracts, where it is seen as appropriate to jump immediately to what is usually viewed as the 'last resort,' 'tie-breaker' rule of interpretation, namely construction against the drafter. . . . This is due to the probable dearth of relevant extrinsic evidence in these contracts" thanks to their almost always adhesive nature); Co-op. Fire Ins. Ass'n v. White Caps, 694 A.2d 34 (Vt. 1997) ("we routinely construe insurance policies in favor of the insured, and in accord with the reasonable expectations of the purchaser").

§7.11 n.36 p.305 ***In the first paragraph, add the following to the list after*** **"Contra"*:*** Wilkie v. Auto-Owners Ins. Co., 664 N.W.2d 776 (Mich. 2003) ("rule of reasonable expectations has no application in Michigan").

§7.11 n.36 p.305 ***In the first paragraph, add the following at the end:*** *See* Nat'l Mut. Ins. Co. v. McMahon & Sons, 356 S.E.2d 488 (W. Va. 1987) ("doctrine of reasonable expectations is limited to those instances . . . in which the policy language is ambiguous").

§7.12 EVIDENCE OF PRIOR NEGOTIATIONS

§7.12 n.4 p.306 Add the following to the list after **"See also":** Listokin, Bayesian Contractual Interpretation, 39 J. Legal Stud. 375 (2010); Note, The Use of Parol Evidence in Interpretation of Plea Agreements, 110 Colum. L. Rev. 840 (2010).

§7.12 n.11 p.308 Add the following to the list after **"See":** 3-D & Co. v. Tew's Excavating, 258 P.3d 819 (Alaska 2011) ("Courts may always examine extrinsic evidence in determining what a contract means."); Estate of Polushkin v. Maw, 170 P.3d 162 (Alaska 2007) ("It is not necessary to find that an agreement is ambiguous before looking to extrinsic evidence as an aid in determining what it means.").

§7.12 n.11 p.308 Add the following at the end: New Jersey has similarly followed Corbin and done away with the plain meaning rule. Conway v. 287 Corp. Ctr. Assocs., 901 A.2d 341, 347 (N.J. 2006) ("Extrinsic evidence may be used to discover the true meaning of contractual terms. It is only after the meaning of the contract is discerned that the parol evidence rule comes into play to prohibit the introduction of extrinsic evidence to vary the terms of the contract."), following Atl. N. Airlines v. Schwimmer, 96 A.2d 652 (N.J. 1953) ("Evidence of the circumstances is always admissible in aid of the interpretation of an integrated agreement. This is so even when the contract on its face is free from ambiguity. . . . The admission of evidence of extrinsic facts is not for the purpose of changing the writing, but to secure light by which to measure its actual significance.").

§7.12 n.12 p.308 Add the following to the list after **"Accord":** LPP Mtg. v. Sugarman, 565 F.3d 28 (1st Cir. 2009) ("The thin end of the wedge was the view, now quite common, that extrinsic evidence can be offered to show that seemingly plain language, in the circumstances, conceals an ambiguity. From there, it is not a long leap to a 'peek' at extrinsic evidence even where it does not focus directly on ambiguity."; cites to treatise).

§7.12 p.309 Add the following at the end of the first sentence: . . . there is a two stage process.[12a]

[12a] Mississippi has a three-stage process. Between the first and second stages below it uses the canons of construction to try to dispel ambiguity. Only if those prove unavailing will the court examine the parol. Dalton v. Cellular S., 20 So. 3d 1227 (Miss. 2009). This may raise the canons above their station. As noted earlier, the canons normally are used as a last resort, not as something in the middle. *See supra* §7.11. In practice, however, judges searching for plain meaning will at least unconsciously employ many of the conventions of language.

***§7.12 n.13 p.309 Add the following to the list after* "Accord":** Am. Fed'n of Gov't Employees v. FLRA, 470 F.3d 375 (Fed. Cir. 2006) ("Resort to parol evidence may only be had where the language of an agreement is ambiguous on its face."); Peach State Roofing v. 2224 S. Trail Corp., 3 So. 3d 442 (Fla. App. 2009) ("Without a finding of ambiguity, the trial court erred in holding that the contract included an implied term based on custom and practice.").

§7.12 n.13 p.309 Add the following after the citation to* Air Safety*: , explained in River's Edge Homeowners' Ass'n v. City of Naperville, 819 N.E.2d 806 (Ill. App. 2004) (*Air Safety* rejected provisional admission only for contracts containing a merger clause, but prior Illinois Supreme Court precedent adopted four corners rule generally) and limited in Bright Horizons Children's Ctrs. v. Riverway Midwest II, 931 N.E.2d 780 (Ill. App. 2010) (allowing provisional admission to determine whether contract ambiguous), and given full effect in Thompson v. Gordon, 948 N.E.2d 39 (Ill. 2011) ("If the contract language is ambiguous, a court can consider extrinsic evidence to determine the parties' intent.").

§7.12 n.14 p.310 Add the following to the list after* "See also"*: States Roofing Corp. v. Winter, 587 F.3d 1364 (Fed. Cir. 2009) ("A 'patent ambiguity' is one that is 'obvious, gross, glaring, so that plaintiff contractor had a duty to inquire about it at the start.' ") (quoting from H & M Moving v. United States, 499 F.2d 660 (Ct. Cl. 1974)); Jenkins v. Eckerd Corp., 913 So. 2d 43 (Fla. App. 2005) ("A latent ambiguity arises when a contract on its face appears clear and unambiguous, but fails to specify the rights or duties of the parties in certain situations."); Swanson v. BECO Constr. Co., 175 P.3d 748 (Idaho 2007) ("To determine whether a contract is patently ambiguous, a court looks at the face of the document and gives the words or phrases used their established definitions in common use or settled legal meanings."); City of Grosse Pointe Park v. Mich. Mun. Liability & Prop. Pool, 702 N.W.2d 106 (Mich. 2005) (opinion of Cavanagh, J.) ("resort to extrinsic evidence is unnecessary to detect a patent ambiguity"); Withers v. City of Lake St. Louis, 318 S.W.3d 256 (Mo. App. 2010) ("Latent ambiguities which are not apparent on the face of the contract must be developed by extrinsic evidence to demonstrate the real intent of the parties.").

***§7.12 n.16 p.310 Add the following to the list after* "Accord":** McAdams v. Mass. Mut. Life Ins. Co., 391 F.3d 287 (1st Cir. 2004) ("contextual evidence is not the kind of evidence that is intended to be barred by the parol evidence if no ambiguity is found; rather, context should be used as a tool to find unambiguous meaning in the first instance"); Bank of N.Y. Trust v. Franklin Advisers, 674 F. Supp. 2d 458 (S.D.N.Y. 2009) (ambiguity exists "where a contract 'suggest[s] more than one meaning when viewed objectively by a reasonably intelligent person who has examined the context of the entire integrated agreement and who is cognizant of the customs, practices, usages and terminology as generally understood in the particular trade or business.' ") (quoting from British Int'l Ins. Co. v. Seguros La Republica, S.A., 342 F.3d 78, 82 (2d Cir. 2003)); Ocean Petroleum Co. v. Yanek, 5 A.3d 683 (Md. 2010) (disputed language "must be considered within the context of the lease agreement and the circumstances under which it was executed"); Mary J. Baker Revocable Trust v. Cenex Harvest States Coops., 164 P.3d 851 (Mont. 2007) ("for the purpose of aiding the court in determining, as a preliminary matter, whether the instrument contains an ambiguity, objective evidence of 'the circumstances under which [the instrument] was made, including the situation of the subject of the instrument and of the parties to it,' may be shown and considered.") (quoting from Mont. Code §1-4-102) (citing to treatise); Behrens v. S.P. Constr. Co., 904 A.2d 676 (N.H. 2006) ("we give the language used by the parties its reasonable meaning, considering the circumstances and context in which the agreement was negotiated"); Mullinnix LLC v. HKB Royalty Trust, 126 P.3d 909 (Wyo. 2006) ("By allowing evidence of the circumstances surrounding execution . . . courts are more apt to arrive at the parties' true intent at the time of the execution") (citing to treatise).

§7.12 n.16 p.310 Add the following after the second sentence: *Cf.* Ultra Resources v. Hartman, 226 P.3d 889 (Wyo. 2010) (emphasizing "the importance of interpreting contracts at the time and place of execution").

§7.12 n.16 p.310 Add the following at the end: The Michigan Supreme Court has divided evenly on an unusual restrictive rule: the standard of proof of latent ambiguity. *Compare* City of Grosse Pointe Park v. Mich. Mun. Liability & Prop. Pool, 702 N.W.2d 106 (Mich. 2005) (opinion of Cavanagh, J.) (rejecting clear and convincing standard), *with id.* (opinion of Young, J.) (proposing clear and convincing standard). It is hard to justify heightened proof of ambiguity except by a rather touching belief in the abilities and resources of contract drafters.

§7.12 n.17 p.311 Add the following at the end of the second sentence: and followed in Wright v. Dave Johnson Ins., 275 P.3d 339 (Wash. App. 2012).

§7.12 n.17 p.311 Add the following to the list after "Accord": Fleet Bus. Credit v. Enterasys Networks, 816 N.E.2d 619 (Ill. App. 2004) ("a contract does not exist in a vacuum; its terms must be understood in light of the commercial context within which it was drawn").

§7.12 n.18 p.312 In the first paragraph, add the following to the list after "See": Chance v. McCann, 966 A.2d 29 (N.J. Super. App. Div. 2009) (parol evidence inadmissible to show that when parties wrote $630,000, they actually meant $160,000).

§7.12 n.18 p.312 Add the following at the end of the first paragraph: *But see* Penncro Assocs. v. Sprint Spectrum, 499 F.3d 1151 (10th Cir. 2007) ("[P]arties to a contract are free to define their terms in any manner they wish. . . . But, while the parties may depart from the meanings associated with ordinary English and existing law, courts will recognize and give effect to such private definitions only where the parties' intention to deviate from common usage is manifest.").

§7.12 n.20 p.312 In the first paragraph, add the following at the end of the first sentence: , but reaffirmed in S. Road Assocs. v. IBM, 826 N.E.2d 806 (N.Y. 2005) ("extrinsic evidence may not be considered unless the document itself is ambiguous").

***§7.12 n.20 p.312 In the first paragraph, add the following to the list after* "Accord":** HOP Energy v. Local 553 Pension Fund, 678 F.3d 158 (2d Cir. 2012) (New York law: "Extrinsic evidence cannot be used to vary the terms of a facially unambiguous contract. . . . With unambiguous contracts, a party's subjective intent and understanding of the terms is irrelevant."); Artuso v. Vertex Pharms., 637 F.3d 1 (1st Cir. 2011) (Massachusetts law; "Only in the event of linguistic uncertainty may a court refer to antecedent negotiations as a method of clarifying the meaning of contractual terms.").

§7.12 n.20 p.312 Add the following at the end of the first paragraph: Somewhat curiously, the Federal Circuit has stated that, "[a]lthough extrinsic evidence may not be used to interpret an unambiguous contract provision, we have looked to it to confirm that the parties intended for the term to have its plain and ordinary meaning." Evidently, then, whether language is ambiguous must initially be determined using a restrictive approach, with possible confirmation in the manner of the more liberal approach coming later. That the court will use evidence to decide on ambiguity late but not early seems both less certain than the restrictive approach and less accurate than the liberal approach. TEG-Paradigm Envtl. v. United States, 465 F.3d 1329, 1338 (Fed. Cir. 2006). *Cf.* Flores v. Earnshaw, 209 P.3d 428 (Utah App. 2009) (extrinsic evidence admissible to determine validity of facial ambiguity, but the initial finding of facial ambiguity must be made without that evidence), rightly contradicted by Watkins v. Henry Day Ford, 239 P.3d 526 (Utah App. 2010) (court determines whether contract is ambiguous by looking "to the evidence presented regarding the facts known to the parties and the circumstances present at the time the parties were contracting"), *cert. granted*, 247 P.3d 774 (Utah 2011); Town Bank v. City Real Estate Dev., 793 N.W.2d 476 (Wis. 2010) ("if the contract is unambiguous, the court's attempt to determine the parties' intent ends with the language of the contract, without resort to extrinsic evidence"; unclear whether the initial finding of ambiguity may derive from extrinsic evidence).

§7.12 n.22 p.313 Add the following to the list after **"See"***:* Confold P. v. Polaris Indus., 433 F.3d 952 (7th Cir. 2006) (Posner, J.) (a plain meaning rule, by "minimizing both contractual transaction costs and uncertainty increases the value of contracts as means of conducting business").

§7.12 n.22 p.313 In the second paragraph, add the following after the first sentence: The relative merits of purposive and formal interpretation have of late occasioned much scholarly debate. *See* Schwartz & Scott, Contract Theory and the Limits of Contract Law, 113 Yale L.J. 541 (2003) (stating generally formal approach); Bayern, Rational Ignorance, Rational Closed-Mindedness, and Modern Economic Formalism in Contract Law, 97 Cal. L. Rev. 943 (2009) (attacking Schwartz & Scott approach); Kostritsky, Plain Meaning vs. Broad Interpretation: How the Risk of Opportunism Defeats a Unitary Default Rule for Interpretation, 96 Ky. L.J. 43 (2007) (same); Schwartz & Scott, Contract Interpretation Redux, 119 Yale L.J. 926 (2010) (rebutting attackers). *See generally* Kostritsky, Interpretive Risk and Contract Interpretation: A Suggested Approach for Maximizing Value, 2 Elon L. Rev. 109 (2011).

§7.12 n.24 p.314 Add the following after the first sentence: Cf. Nat'l Tax Inst. v. Topnotch at Stowe Resort & Spa, 388 F.3d 15 (1st Cir. 2004) (the restrictive approach "should be taken with a grain of salt, partly because extrinsic evidence may in fact reveal an ambiguity not otherwise patent . . . but also because language may point only slightly in one direction and extrinsic evidence strongly in another").

§7.12 n.25 p.314 Add the following to the list after **"Accord"***:* E. Ridge v. Larimer & Weld Irrigation Co., 109 P.3d 969 (Colo. 2005) ("extrinsic evidence may be conditionally admitted to determine whether the contract is ambiguous"); Pillsbury Co. v. Wells Dairy, 752 N.W.2d 430 (Iowa 2008) (follows Restatement Second); Richards v. JTL Grp., 212 P.3d 264 (Mont. 2009) ("the circumstances under which an instrument was made may be considered to aid the court in determining, as a preliminary matter, whether the instrument 'contains an ambiguity' "); Conway v. 287 Corp. Ctr. Assocs., 901 A.2d 341 (N.J. 2006) ("We consider all of the relevant evidence that will assist in determining the intent and meaning of the contract."); Mark V, Inc. v. Mellekas, 845 P.2d 1232 (N.M. 1993) ("[E]ven if the language of the contract appears to be clear and unambiguous, 'a court may hear evidence of the circumstances surrounding the making of the contract and of any relevant usage of trade, course of dealing, and course of performance,' in order to decide whether the meaning of a term or expression contained in the agreement is actually unclear.") (quoting C.R. Anthony Co. v. Loretto Mall Partners, 817 P.2d 238 (N.M. 1991)); Batzer Constr. v. Boyer, 129 P.3d 773 (Or. App. 2006) ("[T]o determine whether a contractual provision is ambiguous, the trial court can properly consider the text of the provision in the context of the agreement as a whole and in light of the circumstances underlying the formation of the contract."); Berthel Land & Livestock v. Rockies Exp. Pipeline, 275 P.3d 423 (Wyo. 2012) ("[E]ven when a contract's language is unambiguous, this Court may consider the facts and circumstances surrounding the making of the contract to determine the parties' intent and the plain meaning of the terms used."; course of negotiation used to help determine intent of the parties); Berg v. Hudesman, 801 P.2d 222 (Wash. 1990) (adopting Restatement Second approach; "We now hold that extrinsic evidence is admissible as to the entire circumstances under which the contract was made, as an aid in ascertaining the parties' intent."), followed in Spectrum Glass Co. v. Pub. Utility Dist. No. 1, 119 P.3d 854 (Wash. App. 2005) ("The court may consider (1) the subject matter and objective of the contract, (2) the circumstances surrounding the making of the contract, (3) the subsequent conduct of the parties to the contract, (4) the reasonableness of the parties' respective interpretations, (5) statements made by the parties in preliminary

negotiations, (6) usages of trade, and (7) the course of dealing between the parties"), in turn followed in Wash. State Republican Party v. Wash. State Grange, 676 F.3d 784 (9th Cir. 2012) (using e-mail sent during settlement negotiations to determine whether the ultimate settlement preserved a right to reimbursement for attorneys' fees and costs), but limited somewhat in Hearst Comm'ns v. Seattle Times, 115 P.3d 262 (Wash. 2005) ("when interpreting contracts, the subjective intent of the parties is generally irrelevant if the intent can be determined from the actual words used"; evidence as to the parties' stated intent was thus irrelevant, "[b]ecause extrinsic evidence may be used only to determine the meaning of specific words in the agreement") and in Brogan & Anensen LLC v. Lamphiear, 202 P.3d 960 (Wash. 2009) ("[A] party may offer extrinsic evidence in a contract dispute to help the fact[-]finder interpret a contract term and determine the contracting parties' intent regardless of whether the contracts terms are ambiguous. . . . Extrinsic evidence is not admissible, however, to show intention independent of the contract.").

§7.12 n.25 p.314 Add the following at the end: At least one court, however, has interpreted the language to justify allowing everything *but* evidence of negotiations, which it characterizes as "subjective" and therefore unusable. Mary J. Baker Revoc. Trust v. Cenex Harvest States Coops., 164 P.3d 851 (Mont. 2007) (quoting Restatement Second §212 cmt. *b* at length and approvingly, but then rejecting evidence of promises made by one party during negotiations as "subjective evidence of ambiguity").

§7.12 n.26 p.315 Add the following at the end: On the importance of distinguishing between the parol evidence rule, which does potentially permit actual changes in the language of the contract, and contract interpretation, which does not, see generally Kniffin, Conflating and Confusing Contract Interpretation and the Parol Evidence Rule: Is the Emperor Wearing Someone Else's Clothes?, 62 Rutgers L. Rev. 75 (2009).

§7.12 n.28 p.316 Add the following at the end: Not all California courts seem at ease with this expansive view of extrinsic evidence. *See* Klein v. Chevron U.S.A., 137 Cal. Rptr. 3d 293

(Ct. App. 2012) ("When the contract is clear and explicit, the parties' intent is determined solely by reference to the language of the agreement.").

§7.12 n.36 p.318 Add the following at the end: *Pacific Gas & Electric* also faces attack from within. The California Supreme Court recently reaffirmed it, but two concurring justices applauded *Trident* and stated that "it may be time for a fuller reconsideration of the meaning and scope of *Pacific Gas*." Dore v. Arnold Worldwide, 139 P.3d 56, 63 (Cal. 2006) (Baxter, J., & Corrigan, J. concurring).

§7.12 n.37 p.318 Add the following at the end: *Accord:* Cachil Dehe Band of Wintun Indians v. California, 618 F.3d 1066 (9th Cir. 2010) (applying "reasonably susceptible" test and concluding that the contract term was not thus susceptible and so not permitting the admission of parol evidence). At least some California courts have interpreted *Pacific Gas & Electric* similarly. Abers v. Rounsavell, 116 Cal. Rptr. 3d 860 (Ct. App. 2010) ("Ambiguities arise when contractual language reasonably may be susceptible to more than one interpretation based upon the offered evidence regarding the material facts. Under these circumstances, trial judges, acting as a gatekeeper, may take a 'preliminary look' at proffered extrinsic evidence to determine ambiguity . . . ") (citations omitted).

§7.12a DETERMINING WHETHER LANGUAGE IS AMBIGUOUS

§7.12a n.7 p.320 Add the following to the list in the first sentence: Swanson v. BECO Constr. Co., 175 P.3d 748 (Idaho 2007) ("For a contract term to be ambiguous, there must be at least two different reasonable interpretations of the term . . ."); City of Bismarck v. Mariner Constr., 714 N.W.2d 484 (N.D. 2006) ("An ambiguity exists when rational arguments can be made in support of contrary provisions as to the meaning of the language in question.").

§7.12a n.7 p.320 Add the following at the end of the first paragraph: Even under a liberal approach to interpretation, the contents of the writing itself are paramount. Pillsbury Co. v. Wells Dairy, 752 N.W.2d 430 (Iowa 2008) ("[A]lthough we allow extrinsic evidence to aid in the process of interpretation, the words of the agreement are still the most important evidence of the [parties'] intentions at the time they entered into the contract.").

§7.12a n.8 p.320 Add the following to the list in the first sentence: Richards v. JTL Grp., 212 P.3d 264 (Mont. 2009) ("Mere disagreement as to the interpretation of a written instrument does not automatically create an ambiguity."), following Mary J. Baker Revoc. Trust v. Cenex Harvest States Coops., 164 P.3d 851 (Mont. 2007) ("an ambiguity exists only if the language is susceptible to at least two reasonable but conflicting meanings") (citing to treatise).

§7.12a n.9 p.320 Add the following to the list: McHugh v. DLT Solutions, 618 F.3d 1375 (Fed. Cir. 2010) ("replace"); Mountainview Landowners Coop. Ass'n v. Cool, 86 P.3d 484 (Idaho 2004) (quoting Webster's definition of "swimming"); Estate of Moor *ex rel.* Moor v. State, 46 So. 3d 849 (Miss. App. 2010) ("construct"); State *ex rel.* Petro v. R.J. Reynolds Tobacco Co., 820 N.E.2d 910 (Ohio 2004) (adopting definition of "merchandise" drawn from "a battle of dictionaries, statutes, and case law"). In Gilman v. Marsh & McLennan Co., Inc., 826 F.3d 69 (2d Cir. 2016), the Second Circuit looked to statutory definitions of "cause" as one indicator that the employees' dismissal for failure to cooperate in an internal investigation was "for cause" within the meaning of agreements that controlled whether or not they were entitled to stock and other benefits upon termination of employment.

§7.12a n.15 p.322 Add the following at the end of the first sentence: W.W. Vincent & Co. v. First Colony Life Ins. Co., 814 N.E.2d 960 (Ill. App. 2004) ("a court will not consider parol evidence of prior negotiations to create an 'extrinsic ambiguity' where the parties to a contract have included an integration clause").

§7.13 EVIDENCE OF COURSE OF DEALING, USAGE, AND COURSE OF PERFORMANCE

§7.13 n.1 p.322 In the first paragraph, add the following after the third sentence: *See* Treibacher Industrie, A.G. v. Allegheny Techs., 464 F.3d 1235 (11th Cir. 2006) (CISG: "the parties' usage of a term in their course of dealings controls that term's meaning in the face of a conflicting customary usage of the term").

§7.13 n.1 p.322 In the second paragraph, add the following to the list after* "See generally"*: Gillette, The Perils of Article 2: Strategies of Interpretation, 6 Va. J. 38 (2003); Graffi, Remarks on Trade Usages and Business Practices in International Sales Law, 29 J.L. & Com. 273 (2011).

§7.13 n.4 p.323 In the first paragraph, add the following to the list after* "See"*: L.F. Brands Mktg. v. Dillard's, Inc., 314 S.W.3d 736 (Ark. App. 2009) (using course of performance and course of dealing to determine gross profit margin for dickered contract containing merger clause; "there is no requirement that the writing be declared ambiguous before evidence of the parties' course of dealing and course of performance is admissible").

§7.13 n.4 p.323 Add the following after the citation to* Altronics*: , PCS Nitrogen Fertilizer v. Christy Refractories, 225 F.3d 974 (8th Cir. 2000) ("Moreover, the fact that Christy repeatedly sent its customer acknowledgment form to PCS does not establish a course of dealing; the multiple forms merely demonstrated Christy's desire to include the arbitration clause as a term of the contract."), and Belden Inc. v. Am. Elec. Components, 885 N.E.2d 751 (Ind. App. 2008) ("the repeated exchange of forms does not in and of itself establish a course of dealing between the parties that incorporates the terms of those forms into the parties' contract");

§7.13 p.324 Add the following at the end of the first full sentence: . . . mere interpretation of those terms.[4a]

[4a] But, as with all contracts, a course of dealing gives way to a contrary express term. UCC 1-303(e)(1); Chicago United Indus. v. City of Chicago,

685 F. Supp. 2d 791 (N.D. Ill. 2010) ("[A] course of dealing may not be used to contradict the express terms of a written contract."; course of dealing granting contract extensions inadmissible in the face of express terms giving discretion in whether to grant them).

§7.13 n.5 p.324 Add the following to the list after **"Accord"***:* Browning-Ferris Indus. v. Casella Waste Mgmt., 945 N.E.2d 964 (Mass. App. 2011) (using course of dealing over four years to lend meaning to ambiguous waste disposal agreement; "'There is no surer way to find out what parties meant, than to see what they have done.'") (quoting from Brooklyn life Ins. Co. v. Dutcher, 95 U.S. 269, 273 (1877)).

§7.13 n.5 p.324 Add the following at the end: Cf. One Beacon Ins. Co. v. Crowley Marine Servs., 648 F.3d 258 (5th Cir. 2011) (federal maritime law: "[T]erms and conditions contained in subsequently-issued purchase orders may supplement an oral agreement if there is evidence of a prior course of dealing between the parties from which a court may infer that the parties were aware of and consented to those additional contractual terms."); Monzingo v. Alaska Air Grp., 112 P.3d 655 (Alaska 2005) (course of dealing "provide[s] an additional indication of [Monzingo's] reasonable expectations at the time of drafting"). *But see* Wilson v. New York State Thruway Auth., 54 Misc. 3d 1212(A), 2016 N.Y. slip op. 51857(U) (N.Y. Sup. Ct. 2016) (Authority had paid 100% of retiree health insurance premiums from 1973 until 2015, pursuant to contract that required "retirement benefits"; nevertheless, in the absence of express language regarding insurance premiums and cost sharing, language was not ambiguous so court would not look to extrinsic evidence of past practice, and case by retirees was dismissed as a matter of law).

§7.13 n.8 p.325 Add the following to the list after the fifth sentence: Employment Television Enters. v. Barocas, 100 P.3d 37 (Colo. App. 2004) ("even if a term is not facially ambiguous, evidence of industry standards may be used to demonstrate the parties' intent," thus allowing evidence of meaning of "program" in television industry) (citing to treatise); Law Debenture Trust Co. v. Maverick Tube Corp., 595 F.3d 458 (2d Cir. 2010) (Kearse, J.) ("An ambiguity exists where the terms of the contract 'could

suggest more than one meaning when viewed objectively by a reasonably intelligent person who has examined the context of the entire integrated agreement and who is cognizant of the customs, practices, usages and terminology as generally understood in the particular trade or business.' ") (quoting from Int'l Multifoods Corp. v. Commercial Union Ins. Co., 309 F.3d 76 (2d Cir. 2002), applied in FCCD Ltd. v. State Street Bank & Trust Co., 2011 WL 519228 (S.D.N.Y. Feb. 15, 2011) (admitting expert testimony to explain meaning of change of control provision in commercial real estate agreement); Sun Am. Bank v. Fairfield Fin. Servs., 690 F. Supp. 2d 1342 (M.D. Ga. 2010) (usage of trade may be used to determine whether a writing is ambiguous, even under a plain-meaning approach); Mullinnix LLC v. HKB Royalty Trust, 126 P.3d 909 (Wyo. 2006) (courts "allow[] the use of . . . custom and usage at the time of execution of the contract, in order to arrive at the plain meaning of the agreement, with the goal of more closely effectuating the parties' true intent").

***§7.13 n.8 p.325 Add the following to the list after* "Contra":** Swanson v. BECO Constr. Co., 175 P.3d 748 (Idaho 2007) ("Usage of trade cannot supplant the express terms of a contract."); Polyfusion Elecs. v. Airsep Corp., 816 N.Y.S.2d 783 (App. Div. 2006) ("defendant was not entitled to rely upon that extrinsic evidence of industry custom and practice to alter the terms of the otherwise unambiguous agreement").

§7.13 n.8 p.325 Add the following after the next-to-last sentence: For an unusual intermediate approach, see TEG-Paradigm Envtl. v. United States, 465 F.3d 1329 (Fed. Cir. 2006) (evidence of trade practice may be used to interpret otherwise unambiguous language, but only where the language was "reasonably susceptible of differing interpretations at the time of contracting") (quoting from Metric Constructors v. NASA, 169 F.3d 747, 752 (Fed. Cir. 1999)).

§7.13 n.13 p.327 Add the following at the end: More recently, Professor Lisa Bernstein has found that some trade associations reject the use of trade usage and the like when settling disputes among their members, instead relying upon rather formal interpretative techniques. Bernstein, *supra* note 1. This may reflect the relative ability of different types of contracting parties to draft complete contracts, as has recently been suggested, rather than as a wholesale adoption of formal contracting methods. Badawi, Interpretive Preferences and the Limits of the New Formalism, 6 Berkeley Bus. L.J. 1 (2009).

§7.13 n.16 p.328 In the second paragraph, add the following after the second sentence: *But cf.* Law Debenture Trust Co. v. Maverick Tube Corp., 595 F.3d 458 (2d Cir. 2010) ("'A custom, in order to become a part of a contract, must be so far established and so far known to the parties, that it must be supposed that their contract was made in reference to it. For this purpose the custom must be established, and not casual, uniform and not varying, general and not personal, and known to the parties.'") (quoting from Belasco Theatre Corp. v. Jelin Prods., 59 N.Y.S.2d 42 (App. Div. 1945)); SR Int'l Bus. Ins. Co. v. World Trade Ctr. Props., 467 F.3d 107 (2d Cir. 2006) ("Under New York law, evidence of custom and usage must establish that . . . the term in question has a fixed and invariable usage . . .").

***§7.13 n.17 p.328 Add the following to the list after* "See":** SR Int'l Bus. Ins. Co. v. World Trade Ctr. Props., 467 F.3d 107 (2d Cir. 2006) (requiring proof "that the party sought to be bound was aware of the custom, or that the custom's existence was so notorious that it should have been aware of it") (internal quotations omitted); Akassy v. William Penn Apts. Ltd. P'ship, 891 A.2d 291 (D.C. 2006) ("a party to an agreement is bound by usages of the terms which he or she had reason to know"; tenant had reason to know that rent control laws permitted periodic rent increases).

***§7.13 n.21 p.329 Add the following to the list after* "Accord":** Bank of N.Y. Trust v. Franklin Advisers, 674 F. Supp. 2d 458 (S.D.N.Y. 2009) ("'The [parties'] interpretation of the contract in practice, prior to litigation, is compelling evidence of the parties' intent.'") (quoting from Ocean Transp. Line v. Am. Philippine Fiber Indus., 743 F.2d 85, 91 (2d Cir. 1984)); Novelis Corp. v. Anheuser-Busch, Inc., 559 F. Supp. 2d 877 (N.D. Ohio 2008) ("the parties themselves know best what they have meant by their words or agreement and their action under that agreement is the best indication of what that meaning was"; failure to object to disclosures of information is course of performance defining scope of confidentiality agreement) (quoting from UCC §2-208 cmt. 1); Auto-Chlor Sys. v. JohnsonDiversey, 328 F. Supp. 2d 980 (D. Minn. 2004) ("the course of actual performance by the parties is considered the best indication of what they intended the writing to mean") (quoting from UCC 2-202 cmt. 2).

§7.13 n.22 p.330 In the first paragraph, add the following after the third sentence: *See generally* Graves, Course of Performance as Evidence of Intent or Waiver . . . , 52 Drake L. Rev. 235 (2004).

§7.13 n.26 p.331 Add the following to the list after* "Accord"*: LPP Mtg. v. Sugarman, 565 F.3d 28 (1st Cir. 2009) ("Course of conduct testimony, for obvious reasons, troubles courts less than other testimony, and is widely considered."; citing to treatise); City of Hope Nat'l Med. Ctr. v. Genentech, Inc., 181 P.3d 142 (Cal. 2008) ("A party's conduct occurring between execution of the contract and a dispute about the meaning of the contract's terms may reveal what the parties understood and intended those terms to mean.").

§7.13 n.26 p.331 Add the following at the end: A course of performance may be proved only through evidence of the parties' behavior between the time of contracting and the time a dispute arose. This is implicit in the Code's definition of course of performance, which requires that "the other party, with knowledge of the nature of performance and opportunity for objection to it, accepts the performance or acquiesces in it without objection." UCC §1-303(a)(2); City of Hope Nat'l Med. Ctr. v. Genentech, Inc., 181 P.3d 142 (Cal. 2008); Employers Reinsurance Co. v. Superior Court, 74 Cal. Rptr. 3d 733 (Ct. App. 2008) (course of performance antedates a dispute).

§7.13 n.28 p.331 Add the following after the first sentence: *See* Dallas Aerospace v. CIS Air Corp., 352 F.3d 775 (2d Cir. 2003) ("a single act of accepting payment is not a course of performance"); Estate of Polushkin v. Maw, 170 P.3d 162 (Alaska 2007) ("Course of performance evidence to be relevant requires repeated occasions.").

§7.13 n.28 p.331 Add the following to the list after the first **"See"***:* Meiners v. University of Kansas, 359 F.3d 1222 (10th Cir. 2004) (communications between parties showed mutual understanding).

§7.13 n.30 p.332 Add the following after the third sentence: See generally Bayley, Prior Negotiations and Subsequent Conduct in Contract Interpretation: Principles and Practical Concerns, 28 J. Contract L. 179 (2012).

§7.13 n.30 p.332 Add the following at the end: For a rare U.S. application, see 10 Perry St. v. Unionville Water Co., 987 A.2d 1009 (Conn. 2010) (rejecting evidence of course of performance in favor of the language of the lease; "'In determining the meaning and effect of the controverted language in the lease, the inquiry must focus on the intention expressed in the lease and not on what intention existed in the minds of the parties.'") (quoting from Tinaco Plaza v. Freebob's, Inc., 814 A.2d 403 (Conn. App. 2003)).

§7.13 n.32 p.333 In the second paragraph, add the following to the list after **"see"***:* Monzingo v. Alaska Air Grp., 112 P.3d 655 (Alaska 2005) (course of dealing prevails over industry practice).

§7.13 n.36 p.334 In the first paragraph, add the following to the list after **"Accord"***:* Chicago United Indus. v. City of Chicago, 685 F. Supp. 2d 791 (N.D. Ill. 2010) ("a course of dealing may not be used to contradict the express terms of a written contract"; course of dealing of automatic contract extensions inadmissible where express agreement gives discretion whether to extend).

§7.14 QUESTION OF LAW OR FACT

§7.14 n.1 p.337 Add the following to the end: For a sobering study of psychological bias in this area, see Solan, Rosenblatt, & Osherson, False Consensus Bias in Contract Interpretation, 108 Colum. L. Rev. 1268 (2008).

***§7.14 n.5 p.338 Add the following to the list after* "Accord":** Whitney Holding Corp. v. Terry, 270 P.3d 662 (Wyo. 2012) (whether a contract is ambiguous is a matter of law; "We determine whether a written contract term is ambiguous by independently reviewing the disputed term in light of the actual language of the contract.") (internal quotations omitted).

***§7.14 n.7 p.338 Add the following to the list after* "Accord":** 10 Perry St. v. Unionville Water Co., 987 A.2d 1009 (Conn. 2010) ("'Ordinarily the parties' intent is a question of fact. . . . Where a party's intent is expressed clearly and unambiguously in writing, however, the determination of what the parties intended . . . is a question of law.'") (quoting from Auto Glass Express v. Hanover Ins. Co., 975 A.2d 1266 (Conn. 2009)).

§7.14 n.7 p.338 Add the following after the second sentence: *Cf.* Confold P. v. Polaris Indus., 433 F.3d 952 (7th Cir. 2006) (Posner, J.) ("if there is tension between [extrinsic] evidence and the words of the contract, or if for any other reason the meaning of the contract remains uncertain even after the extrinsic evidence is presented, there must be a trial to determine the contract's meaning").

§7.14 n.9 p.339 Correct the citation to* Dillon *to read as follows: 819 A.2d 703.

***§7.14 n.9 p.339 Add the following to the list after* "Accord":** First Nat'l Mortg. Co. v. Fed. Realty Inv. Trust, 631 F.3d 1058 (9th Cir. 2011) (California law; "'Where the interpretation of contractual language turns on a question of the credibility of *conflicting* extrinsic evidence, interpretation of the language is not solely a judicial function.'") (quoting from Morey v. Vannucci, 75 Cal. Rptr. 2d 573 (Ct. App. 1998)). McAdams v. Mass. Mut. Life Ins. Co., 391 F.3d 287 (1st Cir. 2004) ("Ordinarily, contracts are construed by a court as a matter of law unless there are material disputes as to extrinsic facts bearing on the correct interpretation."); City of Hope Nat'l Med. Ctr. v. Genentech, Inc., 181 P.3d 142 (Cal. 2008) ("Interpretation of a written instrument becomes solely a judicial function only when it is based on the words of the instrument alone, when there is no conflict in the extrinsic evidence, or when a determination was made based on incompetent evidence."), followed in Cachil Dehe Band of Wintun Indians v. California, 618 F.3d 1066 (9th Cir. 2010) ("[W]hen there is a material conflict in extrinsic evidence supporting competing interpretations of ambiguous contract language the court may not use the evidence to interpret the contract as a matter of law, but must instead render the evidence to the factfinder for evaluation of its credibility.").

§7.14 n.11 p.339 Add the following to the list after "Accord": Cherne Contracting Corp. v. Marathon Petroleum Co., 578 F.3d 735 (8th Cir. 2009) (Minnesota law: "[A] court is to determine whether a written contract is ambiguous, and if it is unambiguous, the court is to construe the contract as a matter of law. . . . If reference to disputed extrinsic facts is required to resolve an ambiguity in a contract, a jury is to determine the relevant facts."), followed in Rios v. Jennie-O Turkey Store, 793 N.W.2d 309 (Minn. App. 2011) (granting summary judgment where plaintiffs failed to bring forth extrinsic facts supporting their interpretation of the ambiguous language); City of Bismarck v. Mariner Constr., 714 N.W.2d 484 (N.D. 2006) ("the court . . . initially determine[s] if the contract is ambiguous, which is a question of law. . . . if the contract is unambiguous, the court interprets the meaning of the contract as a matter of law . . . If a contract is ambiguous, the trier of fact may consider extrinsic evidence about the parties' intent to determine the meaning of the contract."); Glenn v. Reese, 225 P.3d 185 (Utah 2009) ("Because the plain language of the contract allows no other reasonable interpretation, we hold that the [contract] is unambiguous and can be interpreted as a matter of law.").

§7.14 n.13 p.340 Add the following after the first sentence: *Accord:* 10 Perry St. v. Unionville Water Co., 987 A.2d 1009 (Conn. 2010) ("'the trial court's interpretation of a contract, being a determination of the parties' intent, is a question of fact that is subject to reversal on appeal only if it is clearly erroneous'") (quoting from Poole v. City of Waterbury, 831 A.2d 211 (Conn. 2003)).

§7.14 n.13 p.340 Add the following to the list after **"Contra"***:* Suburban Leisure Ctr. v. AMF Bowling Prods., 468 F.3d 523 (8th Cir. 2006) ("We review *de novo* the district court's denial of a motion to compel arbitration based on contract interpretation."); N. Sec. Ins. Co. v. Doherty, 987 A.2d 253 (Vt. 2009) ("The interpretation of an insurance policy, like other contracts, is a question of law over which our review is nondeferential and plenary.").

§7.14 n.14 p.341 In the second paragraph, add the following to the list after* "Accord"*: Batzer Constr. v. Boyer, 129 P.3d 773 (Or. App. 2006) ("[W]here the court must determine whether a contractual term is ambiguous, and the parties have presented evidence of the circumstances underlying the formation of the contract, the court must first find the historical facts before resolving the legal question whether the term is ambiguous. . . . [W]e review the court's explicit and implicit findings of fact for any evidence in the record to support them, and the legal consequences of those facts for legal error.").

§7.14 n.15 p.341 Add the following to the list after **"Accord"***:* Behrens v. S.P. Constr. Co., 904 A.2d 676 (N.H. 2006) ("we review a trial court's interpretation of a contract *de novo*. . . . Where, however, . . . the fact finder has properly looked to extrinsic evidence to determine the intent of the parties, our standard of review is more deferential."); Wright v. Dave Johnson Ins., 275 P.3d 339 (Wash. App. 2012) ("When interpretation depends on factual determinations . . . we review the fact finder's determinations of such matters for substantial evidence. . . . Otherwise contract interpretation is a question of law, which we review de novo.").

§7.14 n.15 p.341 Add the following after the citation to **Parsons***:* , followed in Abers v. Rounsavell, 116 Cal. Rptr. 3d 860 (Ct. App. 2010) ("While we defer to a trial court's resolution of factual disputes, including factually disputed extrinsic evidence, we independently determine whether the contract is reasonably susceptible to different meanings.").

§7.15 REASONS FOR OMISSION

§7.15 n.11 p.344 Add the following at the end: Sometimes the omissions are more direct. *See* Bickham v, Standley, 917 N.E.2d 330 (Ohio App. 2009) (meaning of blanks in financing contingency clause section of form contract; interpreted as met if buyer secured any type of financing).

§7.15 n.12 p.344 Add the following at the end: *See also* Haslund v. Simon Prop. Grp., 378 F.3d 653 (7th Cir. 2004) (Posner, J.) ("The fact that a contract is incomplete, presents interpretive questions, bristles with unresolved contingencies, and in short has as many holes as a Swiss cheese does not make it unenforceable for indefiniteness. Otherwise there would be few enforceable contracts. Complete contingent contracts are impossible. The future, over which contractual performance evolves, is too uncertain. . . . If contracting parties had to provide for every contingency that might arise, contract negotiations would be interminable. Contracts can be shorter and simpler and cheaper when courts stand ready to fill gaps and resolve ambiguities in the minority of contracts that get drawn into litigation.").

***§7.15 n.14 p.345 Add the following to the list after* "See":** Welles v. Turner Entm't Co., 503 F.3d 728 (9th Cir. 2007) (whether assignment of television and film rights to *Citizen Kane* included home video; contract held ambiguous, with court choosing neutrality on whether older technologies encompass future ones).

§7.15 n.14 p.345 Add the following at the end: *Boosey & Hawkes* was itself followed in Intersport, Inc. v. NCAA, 885 N.E.2d 532 (Ill. App. 2008) (dispute whether trademark license applies to video-enabled wireless communication devices, even though the technology for those devices did not exist at the time of contracting).

§7.16 THE PROCESS BY WHICH A COURT SUPPLIES A TERM

§7.16 n.2 p.346 Add the following after the citation to **Mohawk Maintenance***:* , followed in Bessemer Trust Co. v. Branin, 949 N.E.2d 462 (N.Y. 2011) (unanimously reaffirming *Mohawk Maintenance*).

§7.16 n.6 p.348 Add the following to the list after **"Accord"***:* Downtown Barre Dev. v. C & S Whsl. Grocers, 857 A.2d 263 (Vt. 2004) ("[W]e may not insert terms into an agreement by implication unless the implication arises from the language employed or is indispensable to effectuate the intention of the parties.").

§7.16 n.6 p.348 Add the following at the end: The identity of the parties may also affect a court's willingness to imply terms. In particular, courts are reluctant to use implication freely in contracts with governments acting in their governmental capacities. *See* H.D. Goodall Hosp. v. Dep't of Health & Human Servs., 951 A.2d 828 (Me. 2008) ("Were this a contract between private parties, we might be able to infer an intent to be bound to pay by a reasonable time. . . . We do not infer such an intent where the party to be bound is the State discharging its governmental duties."). This may share a cause with the similar reluctance to apply estoppel — namely, a concern about binding a government to a contractual term that has not been assented to by the pertinent body. The worry should be less here than in estoppel, though, because here the implication is to fill in the blanks of an otherwise authorized agreement, rather than to create an agreement that had not otherwise been authorized.

§7.16 n.8 p.348 Add the following after the first sentence: Accord: Reiss v. Fin. Performance Corp., 764 N.E.2d 958 (N.Y. 2001) (court may not "imply term where the circumstances surrounding the formation of the contract indicate that the parties, when the contract was made, must have foreseen the contingency at issue and the agreement can be enforced according to its terms"), followed in Pentech Pharm. v. Par Pharm., 597 F. Supp. 2d 758 (N.D. Ill. 2009) (declining to interpolate limits on division of settlement proceeds).

In *Zelnick v. Morristown-Beard School*, 2015 N.J. Super. LEXIS 222 (Dec. 22, 2015), the plaintiffs asked the court to find an implied agreement to provide a "safe learning environment" in a contract between parents and a private school, which the school allegedly breached when it allowed a teacher to have a sexual relationship with their underage daughter. The court rejected this claim, finding "no legal authority that creates such an implied term as a matter of law" and holding that, in any event, the damages sought were not related to what would have been contemplated by the parties if there were a breach of such a term. *Id.* at *10. The court observed that "[g]enerally, failure to abide by a contractual term does not create liability in tort." *Id.* at *8. (The plaintiffs also pursued tort claims, but they lacked standing and those counts, too, were dismissed because the daughter had since reached the age of majority and did not support the lawsuit.)

§7.16 n.10 p.349 Add the following after the second sentence: *See* Pac. Gas & Elec. Co. v. United States, 536 F.3d 1282 (Fed. Cir. 2008) (adopting Restatement Second §204 and its terminology).

§7.16 n.15 p.350 Add the following to the list after "Accord": Vita v. Berman, Devalerio & Pease, LLP, 967 N.E.2d 1142 (Mass. App. 2012) (using course of performance under client referral agreement to supply missing referral fee; "'[I]n an ordinary contract, where matters are left open, the court may imply terms either that are reasonable or that may be gathered from the subsequent course of performance.'") (quoting from Lawrence v. City of Cambridge, 664 N.E.2d 1 (Mass. 1996)).

§7.16 n.17 p.350 Add the following to the list after "See": Duncan v. TheraTx, 775 A.2d 1019 (Del. 2001) ("default damages rules . . . should generally reflect the contract term that most parties would have bargained for"); Browning-Ferris Indus. v. Casella Waste Mgmt., 945 N.E.2d 964 (Mass. App. 2011) (inserting curative term to deal with parties' omission: "The equitable insertion here treats the parties even-handedly and serves the professed business objectives of both."); Giessow Rests. v. Richmond Rests., 232 S.W.3d 576 (Mo. App. 2007) ("[W]hen parties reduce their agreements to writing we presume that the instrument contains the entire contract, and we will not imply additional provisions unless necessary to effectuate the parties' clear intentions. . . . It is not enough to conclude that an implied covenant is necessary to make the agreement fair or that without it, an agreement is unwise or will operate unjustly.").

§7.16 n.17 p.350 Add the following at the end: On the different ways to determine what terms should be implied, see Davis v. Devon Energy Corp., 218 P.3d 75 (N.M. 2009) ("In implying a covenant, courts may either be effectuating the parties' intentions by interpreting the written terms of an agreement and analyzing the parties' conduct, or they may be stating that a duty imposed by law creates an obligation on one or more of the parties to the agreement."); *see also In re* Target Corp. Customer Data Security Breach Litig., 2014 U.S. Dist. LEXIS 175768, at *52-55 (D. Minn. Dec. 18, 2014) (dismissing claims under trade practice laws and for unjust enrichment, but allowing claim for breach of implied contract to go forward; whether there was an implied contract — "in which Plaintiffs agreed to use their credit or debit cards to purchase goods at Target and Target agreed to safeguard Plaintiffs' personal and financial information" — is a question of fact for trial) (settlement approved, 2015 U.S. Dist. LEXIS 34554 (D. Minn. Mar. 19, 2015)).

§7.16 n.21 p.351 Add the following to the list after "See": Bank of N.Y. v. Janowick, 470 F.3d 264 (6th Cir. 2006) (using "community standards of fairness" to determine what term is reasonable under the circumstances); Disotell v. Stiltner, 100 P.3d 890 (Alaska 2004) ("[W]here there is in fact no agreement, the court should supply a term which comports with community standards of fairness and policy rather than analyze a hypothetical model of the bargaining process.") (quoting from Restatement Second §204 cmt. *d*); Browning-Ferris Indus. v. Casella Waste Mgmt., 945 N.E.2d 964 (Mass. App. 2011) (inserting curative term to deal with parties' omission: "The equitable insertion here treats the parties even-handedly and serves the professed business objectives of both.") (also referring to Restatement Second §204 cmt. d). *Cf.* Solomon v. U.S. Healthcare Sys., 797 A.2d 346 (Pa. Super. 2002) ("A court may imply a missing term in a . . . contract only when it is necessary to prevent injustice and it is *abundantly clear* that the parties intended to be bound by such term.") (emphasis in original).

§7.17 EXAMPLES OF TERMS SUPPLIED BY COURTS

§7.17 n.2 p.355 Add the following at the end: *Cf.* N. Ins. Co. v. Point Judith Marina, 579 F.3d 61 (1st Cir. 2009) (supplying implied warranty of workmanlike performance, which is "inherent in federal maritime law"); Lofts at Fillmore Condo. Ass'n v. Reliance Commercial Constr., 190 P.3d 733 (Ariz. 2008) (implied warranties of workmanship and habitability for non-privity purchasers); Speight v. Walters Dev. Co., 744 N.W.2d 108 (Iowa 2008) (implied warranty of workmanlike construction); Scott v. Garfield, 912 N.E.2d 1000 (Mass. 2009) (implied warranty of habitability for visitors); Davencourt at Pilgrims Landing Homeowners Ass'n v. Davencourt at Pilgrims Landing, 221 P.3d 234 (Utah 2009) (implied warranty of habitability; collects cases); Carlile v. Harbour Homes, 194 P.3d 280 (Wash. App. 2008) (implied warranty of habitability).

§7.17 n.3 p.355 In the first paragraph, add the following to the list after **"Contra"***:* Thompson v. Miles, 741 F. Supp. 2d 296 (D. Me. 2010) (Maine law recognizes the duty of good faith and fair dealing only in contracts involving insurance or within the scope of the UCC); WFND, LLC v. Fargo Marc, LLC, 730 N.W.2d 841 (N.D. 2007) ("In North Dakota the doctrine of an implied covenant of good faith and fair dealing has only been applied to insurance contracts.") (quoting Dalan v. Paracelsus Healthcare Corp., 640 N.W.2d 726 (N.D. 2002)).

§7.17 n.3 p.355 In the first paragraph, add the following after the fifth sentence: For two somewhat unusual applications, see Cole v. State, 922 A.2d 354 (Del. 2005) ("a covenant of good faith and fair dealing applies to plea bargains as well as to any agreement between a criminal defendant and the State") (collecting cases), and City of St. Joseph v. Lake Contrary Sewer Dist., 251 S.W.3d 362 (Mo. App. 2008) (city's passage of ordinance

burdening other members of a sewer system at minimal benefit to itself was a breach of the covenant of good faith and fair dealing). For recognition that this duty takes different forms under different circumstances, see Centronics Corp. v. Genicom Corp., 562 A.2d 187 (N.H. 1989) (there is "not merely one rule of implied good faith in New Hampshire's law of contract, but a series of doctrines, each of them speaking in terms of an obligation of good faith but serving markedly different functions.") (Souter, J.), followed in Livingston v. 18 Mile Point Drive, 972 A.2d 1001 (N.H. 2009) ("The various implied good-faith obligations fall into three general categories: (1) contract formation; (2) termination of at-will employment agreements; and (3) limitation of discretion in contractual performance.").

§7.17 n.3 p.355 In the third paragraph, add the following to the list after* "See generally"*: Munukka, Harmonisation of Contract Law: In Search of a Solution to the Good Faith Problem, in 48 Scandinavian Studies in Law 229 (Peter Wahlgren ed. 2005); Hofmann, Interpretation Rules and Good Faith as Obstacles to the UK's Ratification of the CISG and to the Harmonization of Contract Law in Europe, 22 Pace Int'l L. Rev. 145 (2010); Hunter, Good Faith and the Construction of Terms in Commercial Contracts: The American Perspective, 25 J. Contract L. 39 (2009); Imwinkelried, The Implied Obligation of Good Faith in Contract Law: Is It Time to Write Its Obituary?, 42 Tex. Tech L. Rev. 1 (2009); Loewenstein, The Diverging Meaning of Good Faith, 34 Del. J. Corp. L. 433 (2009); Pargendler, Modes of Gap Filling: Good Faith and Fiduciary Duties Reconsidered, 82 Tul. L. Rev. 1316 (2008); Russi, Can Good Faith Performance Be Unfair? An Economic Framework for Understanding the Problem, 29 Whittier L. Rev. 565 (2008).

§7.17 n.4 p.356 Add the following after the third sentence: *See* Brunswick Hills Racquet Club v. Rte. 18 Shopping Ctr. Assocs., 864 A.2d 387 (N.J. 2005) (following Restatement Second §205; "Every party to a contract . . . is bound by a duty of good faith and fair dealing in both the performance and enforcement of the contract.").

§7.17 n.6 p.356 ***Add the following at the end:*** This approach to good faith even appears in fields related to, but distinct from, contracts. *See* Goldman v. Capital City Mortg. Corp. (*In re* Nieves), 648 F.3d 232 (4th Cir. 2011) (using objective good faith standard in determining whether the bankruptcy trustee may avoid transfers under Bankruptcy Code §550(b)(1); discusses UCC standard approvingly and at length).

The U.S. Supreme Court held that common law claims for breach of the implied covenant of good faith and fair dealing are preempted by the Airline Deregulation Act "if it seeks to enlarge the contractual obligations that the parties voluntarily adopt." Northwest, Inc. v. Ginsberg, 134 S. Ct. 1422, 1426 (2014). In this case, Northwest Airlines had revoked Ginsberg's membership in the frequent flyer rewards program, citing "abuse" of the program based on Ginsberg apparent success with frequent complaints (contacting the office 24 times) generating "1,925.00 in travel credit vouchers, 78,500 WorldPerks bonus miles, a voucher extension for your son, and $491.00 in cash reimbursements." at 1427. Ginsberg's suit alleged the cancelation on the basis of the "abuse" clause "contravened his reasonable expectations with respect to the manner in which Northwest would exercise its discretion." *Id.* First, the Court broadly held that "the [Airline Deregulation Act's] phrase 'other provision having the force and effect of law' includes common-law claims," at 1430, and that the frequent flyer program falls within the Act's coverage of "rates," at 1431. Striking somewhat of a middle ground between the parties positions (that the covenant is either never or always preempted), the Court held that "[a] State's implied covenant rules will escape pre-emption only if the law of the relevant State permits an airline to contract around those rules in its frequent flyer program agreement, and if an airline's agreement is governed by the law of such a State, the airline can specify that the agreement does not incorporate the covenant." at 1433. The Court further noted that Ginsberg could have pursued a breach-of-contract claim on the theory that the contract did not give Northwest unfettered discretion to determine when membership could be terminated for "abuse," but he chose to pursue an appeal only as to the implied covenant claim. *Id.*

In a remarkable factual context, the Court of Claims held that the Drug Enforcement Administration (DEA) breached its duty of good faith and fair dealing in an implied-in-fact contract with an informant, identified as "the Princess," when it failed to protect her from being kidnapped and held captive for three months. SGS-92-X003 v. United States, 118 Fed. Cl. 492 (2014). The court had previously determined that the "DEA sent the Princess on a mission to Colombia without following its own procedures," 85 Fed. Cl. 678 (2009), and found that later-produced documents "echo the conclusion that DEA owed a duty to protect informants" generally and, moreover, "demonstrate that DEA willingly assumed and regularly acknowledged its duty to protect the Princess," 118 Fed. Cl. at 518. In finding liability under these circumstances, the court surveyed recent cases and distinguished cases that rested liability on violation of regulations, finding liability here because the conduct undermined the parties' bargain and established expectations. 118 Fed Cl. at 522-24 (citing Agredano v. United States, 595 F.3d 1278, 1280 (Fed. Cir. 2010), *rev'g* 82 Fed. Cl. 416 (2008), Precision Pine & Timber, Inc. v. United States, 596 F.3d 817 (Fed. Cir. 2010), and Metcalf Constr. Co. v. United States, 742 F.3d 984, 990-94 (Fed. Cir. 2014)). The court went on to award expectancy damages sufficient to cover the costs of a course of treatment for the plaintiff's medical conditions resulting from the kidnapping and captivity, extending to multiple sclerosis. See §12.8, *infra*.

However, "Texas law does not impose a generalized contractual duty of good faith and fair dealing and, in fact, rejects it in almost all circumstances." Hux v. Southern Methodist Univ., 819 F.3d 776, 781 (5th Cir. 2016), citing English v. Fischer, 660 S.W.2d 521, 522 (Tex. 1983). Only in "an extremely narrow class of cases," notably involving insured-insurer relationships, have Texas courts held that a "special relationship may give rise to a tort duty of good faith and fair dealing." *Id.*, citing Arnold v. Nat'l Cnty. Mut. Fire Ins. Co., 725 S.W.2d 165, 167 (Tex. 1987). In 2016, the Fifth Circuit considered and rejected a claim by a student that his multiple meetings with administrators and University Chaplains in which his mental health was discussed gave rise to such a special relationship, finding that "claims demonstrate at most the sort of unilateral, purely subjective sense of trust that Texas courts have determined is insufficient to convert an ordinary arm's-length relationship into a special or confidential relationship." *Id.*. The Fifth Circuit held that "given the Texas courts' decades-long refusal to extend the special-relationship doctrine beyond the insurance context, we are confident that the Texas Supreme Court would hold that there is no duty of good faith and fair dealing in the student-university relationship." *Id.* at 783.

§7.17 n.11 p.357 Add the following to the list after "Accord": C & E Servs. v. Ashland Inc., 601 F. Supp. 2d 262 (D.D.C. 2009) ("The breach of the duty of good faith and fair dealing must necessarily arise out of the performance or enforcement of the contract, not out of the contract negotiations."); Travelers Indem. Co. v. CDL Hotels USA, 322 F. Supp. 2d 482 (S.D.N.Y. 2004) (Mukasey, J.) ("[T]here can be no breach of the duty of good faith and fair dealing where there is no 'valid and binding contract from which such a duty would arise.' ") (quoting from Am.-Eur. Art Assocs. v. Trend Galleries, 641 N.Y.S.2d 835, 836 (App. Div. 1996)); McClain v. Octagon Plaza, 71 Cal. Rptr. 3d 885 (Ct. App. 2008) ("the implied covenant is a supplement to an existing contract, and thus it does not require parties to negotiate in good faith prior to any agreement"), followed in Newsom v. Countrywide Home Loans, 714 F. Supp. 2d 1000 (N.D. Cal. 2010) (no cause of action for breach of the duty of good faith and fair dealing results from the withholding of required disclosures before the execution of a trust deed); J & M Lumber & Constr. Co. v. Smyjunas, 20 A.3d 947 (N.H. 2011) (declining invitation to extend implied duty of good faith and fair dealing outside of contract to cover business dealings generally; plaintiff "does not contend that this claim is recognized in any other jurisdiction . . .").

§7.17 n.11 p.357 Add the following at the end of the first paragraph: For a comparative perspective, *see* Botchway & Choong, Not Ready for Change? The English Courts and Pre-Contractual Negotiations, 45 Int'l Law. 625 (2011). On precontractual liability more generally, see §3.26 *supra*.

§7.17 n.13 p.358 Add the following to the list after "Accord": McAdams v. Mass. Mut. Life Ins. Co., 391 F.3d 287 (1st Cir. 2004) ("The purpose of the covenant is not to add terms to a contract; indeed, it may not do so."); Ziegler v. Findlay Indus., 464 F. Supp. 2d 733 (N.D. Ohio 2006) (Ohio law; "While breach of a duty of good faith and fair dealing is not an independent claim, it can be raised as part of a breach of contract action."); Casey v. Semco Energy, 92 P.3d 379 (Alaska 2004) (because "covenant of good faith and fair dealing 'will not create a duty where one does not exist,' " employer did not breach covenant by not including former employees in early retirement plan where their inclusion was conditional on finding by employer's counsel); UNO Restaurants v. Boston Kenmore Realty Corp., 805 N.E.2d 957 (Mass. 2004) ("[t]he covenant may not . . . be invoked to create rights and duties not otherwise provided for in the existing contractual relationship, as the purpose of the covenant is to guarantee that the parties remain faithful to the intended and agreed expectations of the parties in their performance."), followed by Eigerman v. Putnam Invs., 877 N.E.2d 1258 (Mass. 2007) ("the implied covenant of good faith and fair dealing cannot create rights and duties that are not already present in the contractual relationship"); Cavendish Farms v. Mathiason Farms, 792 N.W.2d 500 (N.D. 2010) (although there is no independent claim for breach of the duty of good faith and fair dealing, good faith is relevant when determining whether a party has exercised its discretion reasonably).

§7.17 n.13 p.358 Add the following after the second sentence: *Cf.* Harris v. Provident Life & Accident Ins. Co., 310 F.3d 73 (2d Cir. 2002) ("New York law . . . does not recognize a separate cause of action for breach of the implied covenant of good faith and fair dealing when a breach of contract claim, based on the same facts, is also pled."), followed in Travelers Indem. Co. v. CDL Hotels USA, 322 F. Supp. 2d 482 (S.D.N.Y. 2004) (no cause of action for breach of implied covenant when breach of contract action for failure to secure approval for insurance policy revisions was "based on precisely the same allegations"). There is some doubt whether this accurately captures New York law. *See, e.g.*, Forman v. Guardian Life Ins. Co., 908 N.Y.S.2d 27 (App. Div. 2010) (allowing cause of action for breach of the duty of good faith and fair dealing where insurer was alleged to have "frustrated the basic purpose of the parties' contracts" by sending the plaintiff claims to investigate on a contingent fee contract even though it had contracted with some of those claimants not to pursue claim audits against them).

§7.17 p.358 Add the following to the end of the last sentence: . . . have felt so constrained.[14a]

[14a] *See, e.g.*, Forman v. Guardian Life Ins. Co., 908 N.Y.S.2d 27 (App. Div. 2010); Excel Constr. v. HKM Eng'g, 228 P.3d 40 (Wyo. 2010) (discussing "a suit based on the implied covenant").

§7.17 n.15 p.359 Add the following at the end: Insurance contracts yield a special case; there the duty of good faith creates obligations on the part of the insurer to bargain and settle in good faith with the insured. Christiansen v. Farmers Ins. Exch., 116 P.3d 259 (Utah 2005) (declining to "condition discovery in litigation of a bad faith claim on violation of the express terms of the contract," because "the refusal to bargain or settle, standing alone, may, under appropriate circumstances, be sufficient to prove a breach") (quoting from Beck v. Farmers Ins. Exch., 701 P.2d 798, 801 (Utah 1985)).

***§7.17 n.16 p.359 In the first paragraph, add the following to the list after* "Accord":** Bohne v. Computer Assocs. Int'l, 514 F.3d 141 (1st Cir. 2008) ("The doctrine of good faith and fair dealing 'concerns the manner in which existing contractual duties are performed', not the lawfulness of the agreement itself.") (quoting from Eigerman v. Putnam Invs., 877 N.E.2d 1258 (Mass. 2007)); Limbert v. Miss. Univ. for Women Alumnae Ass'n, 998 So. 2d 993 (Miss. 2008) ("a party has not breached the implied covenant of good faith and fair dealing when the party took only those actions which were duly authorized by the contract"); Paxi, LLC v. Shiseido Ams. Corp., 636 F. Supp. 2d 275 (S.D.N.Y. 2009) ("[T]he obligation of good faith and fair dealing does not negate an expressly bargained-for clause that allows a party to exercise its discretion, unless that clause imposes a limit on the discretion to be exercised or explicitly states that the duty of good faith and fair dealing applies."); Shoney's LLC v. MAC E., LLC, 27 So. 3d 1216 (Ala. 2009) (a contract granting a party sole discretion as to the exercise of a right "is not mitigated by an implied covenant of good faith and fair dealing in contracts because an unqualified reservation of a right in the sole discretion of one of the parties to a contract expresses the intent of the parties to be subject to terms that are inconsistent with any such implied covenant"); Nemec v.

Shrader, 991 A.2d 1120 (Del. 2010) ("The implied covenant [of good faith and fair dealing] only applies to developments that could not be anticipated, not developments that the parties simply failed to consider — particularly where the contract authorizes the Company to act exactly as it did here."); WFND, LLC. v. Fargo Marc, LLC, *supra* note 3 ("the implied covenant of good faith and fair dealing . . . does not operate to alter the material terms of a contract"); Nygaard v. Sioux Valley Hosps. & Health Sys., 731 N.W.2d 184 (S.D. 2007) ("The covenant of good faith does not create an amorphous companion contract with latent provisions to stand at odds with or in modification of the express language of the parties' agreement.") (quoting from Farm Credit Servs. of Am. v. Dougan, 704 N.W.2d 24, 28 (S.D. 2005)).

***§7.17 n.16 p.359 In the first paragraph, add the following to the list after* "But cf.":** Fleming v. Civil Serv. Comm'n, 792 N.W.2d 871 (Neb. 2011) ("[T]he scope of protection offered by the [covenant of good faith and fair dealing] is curtailed by the purposes and express terms of the contract. In other words, the nature and extent of the covenant's protections are measured by the justifiable expectations of the parties.") (citation omitted).

§7.17 n.17 p.360 Add the following at the end: *Accord:* Estate of Draper v. Bank of Am., 205 P.3d 698 (Kan. 2009) (agreement by couple that wife would leave three-quarters of her probate estate to his sons by a previous marriage, but wife put almost all funds into an irrevocable trust for the benefit of charities; court imposed constructive trust creating a life estate for the widow, even though not a term of the contract, because "[g]ifts cannot be made . . . if the main purpose is defeating the agreement and preventing it from operating for the benefit of those designated"). *Cf.* Metavante Corp. v. Emigrant Sav. Bank, 619 F.3d 748 (7th Cir. 2010) (Wisconsin law: "It is, of course, possible to breach the implied duty of good faith even while fulfilling all of the terms of the written contract.")

§7.17 p.361 Add the following at the end of the second full sentence: . . . according to the nature of the agreement.[22a]

[22a] Justice Souter has suggested that there is "not merely one rule of implied good faith in New Hampshire's law of contract, but a series of

doctrines, each of them speaking in terms of an obligation of good faith but serving markedly different functions." Centronics Corp. v. Genicom Corp., 562 A.2d 187 (N.H. 1989).

§7.17 n.23 p.361 Add the following to the end of the first paragraph: *See also* Brunswick Hills Racquet Club v. Rte. 18 Shopping Ctr. Assocs., 864 A.2d 387 (N.J. 2005) (where plaintiff mistakenly thought payment to renew option due at time of closing, rather than at earlier deadline, for 19 months after the plaintiff gave notice of renewal "defendant, through its agents, engaged in a pattern of evasion, sidestepping every request by plaintiff to discuss the option and ignoring plaintiff's repeated verbal and written entreaties to move forward," so that the defendant "acted in total disregard of the harm caused to plaintiff, unjustly enriching itself with a windfall increase in rent at plaintiff's expense."). But merely obnoxious or repellent behavior, however commercially unreasonable, does not amount to lack of good faith or fair dealing without a clear link to a term of the contract. Ament v. One Las Olas, Ltd., 898 So. 2d 147 (Fla. App. 2005) (seller of condominium unit sought to terminate sales agreement because the buyer's conduct was "grossly abusive, profane, and obnoxious" and "by any reasonable measure, beyond insufferable"; but "[n]either a claim nor a defense may be based only upon rudeness," and the seller did not establish that "the purchaser's objectionable conduct related to the performance of an express term of the purchase agreement.").

§7.17 n.27 p.362 Add the following at the end: *Accord:* Hometown Folks v. S & B Wilson, Inc., 643 F.3d 520 (6th Cir. 2011) ("Passive non-cooperation, as well as active non-cooperation, may constitute breach of the duty of good faith and fair dealing."); Tractebel Energy Mktg. v. AEP Power Mktg., 487 F.3d 89 (2d Cir. 2007) (quoting this section of the treatise); Waste Connections v. Ritchie Corp., 228 P.3d 429 (Kan. App. 2010) ("Parties shall not intentionally and purposely do anything which will have the effect of destroying or injuring the right of the other party to receive the fruits of the contract."); Ferrara v. Walters, 919 So. 2d 876 (Miss. 2005) ("The covenant imposes a duty not to prevent or hinder the other party's performance, but may also impose a duty 'to take some affirmative steps to cooperate in achieving those goals.' ") (quoting from Cenac v. Murry, 609 So. 2d 1257, 1272 (Miss. 1992));

City of Gillette v. Hladky Constr., 196 P.3d 184 (Wyo. 2008) ("A breach of the implied covenant occurs when a party interferes or fails to cooperate in the other party's performance.").

§7.17 n.28 p.362 Add the following at the end: *Accord:* Clancy v. King, 954 A.2d 1092 (Md. 2008) (author Tom Clancy could not withdraw his name from a venture with his ex-wife in order to make it less profitable; "One certainly breaches the promise of good faith owed in contract . . . by working actively to decrease directly the profits of the business venture.").

§7.17 n.29 p.362 Add the following to the list after **"Accord"*:*** Hometown Folks v. S & B Wilson, Inc., 643 F.3d 520 (6th Cir. 2011) (Tennessee law: "Parties have a duty of good faith and fair dealing not only in executing the transaction ultimately contemplated by the contract, but also in fulfilling the preconditions and contingencies set forth in the contract."; accordingly, seller's delays in providing needed financial documents and allowing access to the properties for sale constituted breach of the covenant); Anchorage Chrysler Ctr. v. DaimlerChrysler Motors Corp., 221 P.3d 977 (Alaska 2009) (auto manufacturer breached the covenant through its fraudulent misrepresentations to dealer in the course of negotiation that it would not grant a rival franchise; objective standard of fairness met "because no reasonable person would regard [the manufacturer's] willful misrepresentation as fair," and subjective standard was met "because [the dealer] believed that it was contracting for peace in the form of assurances that [the manufacturer] would not open new dealerships . . ."); Brehm v. 21st Century Ins. Co., 83 Cal. Rptr. 3d 410 (Ct. App. 2008) (insurer's refusal to attempt settlement before demanding arbitration; "[B]y making lack of agreement as to the value of the claim an express precondition to demanding arbitration, the policy itself contemplates the parties will first make an affirmative effort to resolve their dispute, in effect creating a contractual duty to discuss the claim to which the implied covenant of good faith and fair dealing properly attaches."); Ferrara v. Walters, 919 So. 2d 876 (Miss. 2005) (when the sellers of land learned that the warranty deed had title defects, the duty of good faith meant "they were duty bound to take affirmative steps to cure the defect in an effort to allow both parties to receive their bargain under the contract"); Century Partners v. Lesser Goldsmith Enters., 958 A.2d 627 (Vt. 2008) (landlord's refusal to sign certificate of occupancy, which created a continuing violation of city ordinances, and refusal to meet in order to discuss alterations were breaches of the covenant of good faith and fair dealing; "tenant was entitled to landlord's good-faith cooperation").

§7.17 n.29 p.362 Add the following after the third sentence: *Contra:* Elderkin v. Carroll, 941 A.2d 1127 (Md. 2008) (exercise of option to purchase real property, where option holder made repeated errors in its failed attempts; "[T]he good faith requirement does not impose upon the seller an additional duty to make the sale easier for the buyer, but rather that a seller cannot act in a manner that improperly attempts to defeat the exercise of the purchaser's contract rights.").

§7.17 n.31 p.363 Add the following to the list after* "Accord"*: Handle Constr. Co. v. Norcon, Inc., 264 P.3d 367 (Alaska 2011) (following *Spearin* by recognizing an implied warranty of adequate design specifications).

§7.17 n.31 p.363 Add the following to the list after* "But cf."*: Dugan & Meyers Constr. Co. v. Ohio Dep't of Admin. Servs., 864 N.E.2d 68 (Ohio 2007) (*Spearin* does not apply to delay occasioned by plan changes, nor does it invalidate an express contractual provision allocating risk).

§7.17 n.32 p.364 Add the following after the citation to* Dalton*: , followed in Fishoff v. Coty Inc., 634 F.3d 647 (2d Cir. 2011) (*post hoc* devaluation of former employee's stock options violated duty of good faith and fair dealing) and in Lonner v. Simon Prop. Grp., 866 N.Y.S.2d 239 (App. Div. 2008) (class action against gift card provider that charged dormancy fees; allegations that "the terms of the fee disclosure are not clear and conspicuous, but rather, unclear and hidden, [are] sufficient to maintain a claim based upon a breach of the implied covenant of good faith and fair dealing"; in addition, "[e]ven were the defendant entitled to charge dormancy fees, it is still precluded under the implied covenant of good faith and fair dealing from setting such fees at grossly excessive amounts."). This reads the covenant of good faith and fair dealing too broadly; that covenant applies to contract performance and enforcement, not to the means by which obnoxious terms became part of the contract. *See, e.g.*, Renovator's Supply v. Sovereign Bank, 892 N.E.2d 777 (Mass. App. 2008) (the implied duty of good faith and fair dealing "governs the performance of contracts but not their formation"). Unconscionability or misrepresentation would seem better bases for questioning whether a contract was formed. *Dalton* was distinguished away by the court of appeals in Moran v. Erk, 901 N.E.2d 187 (N.Y. 2008). There a contract for the sale of real property provided that it was contingent upon approval by attorneys for the seller and buyer. The buyers instructed their attorney to disapprove the contract. The sellers argued that those instructions constituted a breach of the duty of good faith and fair dealing as laid out in *Dalton*. The court of appeals thought otherwise. The sellers were not deprived of the fruits of their contract by the attorney's failure to approve it; rather, "any 'fruits' of the contract were *contingent* on attorney approval, as any reasonable person in the [sellers'] position should have understood." And a requirement of good faith in the exercise of an attorney approval clause in a contract for the sale of real estate would make refusals into disputed questions of fact, requiring that an attorney testify as to the communications she had with her client. *Moran* is of interest because of its subject and jurisdiction, naturally, but it is also of interest because it shows that courts are willing to give effect to unbridled grants of discretion without the limits imposed by the duty of good faith.

***§7.17 n.32 p.364 Add the following to the list after* "But cf.":** Allworth v. Howard Univ., 890 A.2d 194 (D.C. 2006) (promotion and tenure dispute; "to create triable issues of fact on her claim of bad faith or unfair dealing, Dr. Allworth had to present evidence not simply of negligence or lack of diligence by the university, but of arbitrary and capricious action on its part").

§7.17 n.33 p.364 Add the following at the end of the first sentence: , followed in Brunswick Hills Racquet Club v. Rte. 18 Shopping Ctr. Assocs., 864 A.2d 387 (N.J. 2005) (failure to respond to plaintiff's requests for 19 months until time for renewal of lease had passed "was a demonstrable course of conduct, a series of evasions and delays, that lulled plaintiff into believing it had exercised the lease option properly. Defendant acted in total disregard of the harm caused to plaintiff, unjustly enriching itself with a windfall increase in rent at plaintiff's expense."), and in Knudsen v. Lax, 842 N.Y.S.2d 341 (Jefferson Co. Ct. 2007) (landlord behaved opportunistically by refusing to permit an early termination of a family's apartment lease because a Level 3 sex offender had moved into the next apartment). *See also* Livingston v. 18 Mile Point Drive, 972 A.2d 1001 (N.H. 2009) (exercise of option required notice by certified mail, but plaintiff gave premature oral notice and continued corresponding on the uncorrected assumption that the option had been exercised; taking advantage of this amounted to "evasion of the spirit of the bargain and failure to cooperate in the other [party's] performance" and thus breached the covenant of good faith and fair dealing); Salas v. Mountain States Mut. Cas. Co., 202 P.3d 801 (N.M. 2009) (insurer knew insured's status, her personal injury action, her need to secure insurer's consent before settlement in order to preserve her benefits, and her likely ignorance of this requirement; "Defendant's silence in the face of Plaintiff's apparent ignorance was inequitable, unfair, and inconsistent with the covenant of good faith and fair dealing.").

§7.17 n.33 p.364 Add the following at the end: *See generally* Rakoff, Good Faith in Contract Performance: *Market Street Associates Ltd. Partnership v. Frey*, 120 Harv. L. Rev. 1187 (2007).

§7.17 n.34 p.365 Add the following to the list after "Accord": Auto-Chlor Sys. v. JohnsonDiversey, 328 F. Supp. 2d 980 (D. Minn. 2004) (applying UCC 2-305; referring approvingly to *Allapattah Servs.*).

§7.17 n.34 p.365 Add the following after the citation to HRN: , *rev'd*, 144 S.W.3d 429 (Tex. 2004) (reversing appellate court and rejecting *Mathis*, instead looking only to objective evidence of price discrimination; "Premising a breach of contract claim solely on assumed subjective motives injects uncertainty into the law of contracts and undermines one of the UCC's primary goals — to promote certainty and predictability in commercial transactions."), followed in Exxon Mobil Corp. v. Gill, 299

S.W.3d 124 (Tex. 2009) (claim that supplier recouped promised rebates by raising prices; because prices charged were the posted market prices, they were in objective good faith and thus not contrary to UCC §2-305);

***§7.17 n.34 p.365 Add the following to the list after* "But cf.":** Tom-Lin Enters. v. Sunoco, 349 F.3d 277 (6th Cir. 2003) (rejecting *Mathis* under Ohio law, which requires a showing "that the price was not fixed in a commercially reasonable manner" and also "that the pricing was commercially unjustifiable"; subjective element irrelevant, and objective element satisfied if supplier did not use discriminatory pricing); Flagler Auto. v. Exxon Mobil Corp., 582 F. Supp. 2d 367 (E.D.N.Y. 2008) (distinguishing *Allapattah* on the facts; even if UCC 2-305 requires only a subjective showing, the plaintiffs did not provide the requisite facts; takes no position on the role of objectivity; collecting cases).

§7.17 n.35 p.365 Add the following at the end: followed in Wilson v. Amerada Hess Corp., 773 A.2d 1121 (N.J. 2001) (party with discretion in setting price breaches duty of good faith and fair dealing if it "exercises its discretionary authority arbitrarily, unreasonably, or capriciously, with the objective of preventing the other party from receiving its reasonably expected fruits under the contract"). *See* Locke v. Warner Bros., Inc., 66 Cal. Rptr. 2d 921 (Ct. App. 1997) ("[W]here a contract confers on one party a discretionary power affecting the rights of the other, a duty is imposed to exercise that discretion in good faith and in accordance with fair dealing."), followed in Peak-Las Positas Partners v. Bollag, 90 Cal. Rptr. 3d 775 (Ct. App. 2009) (term providing for escrow extensions upon mutual consent, "which mutual consent shall not be unreasonably withheld or delayed"; "Bollag was bound by an implied covenant of good faith and fair dealing not to do anything that would destroy or injure PLP's rights under the purchase agreement."); Littlejohn v. Parrish, 839 N.E.2d 49 (Ohio App. 2005) (term giving holder of mortgage the right to approve prepayment subject to the implied covenant of good faith and fair dealing, which "requires not only honesty but also reasonableness in the enforcement of the contract"); Cavendish Farms v. Mathiason Farms, 792 N.W.2d 500 (N.D. 2010) (contractual right to reject potatoes "'at any time' accorded significant discretion to [the buyer] in determining when it would formally reject the [sellers'] potatoes and allow them to be sold to other buyers. The [UCC] mandated that it exercise that discretion in good faith and in a commercially reasonable manner"; accordingly, withholding notice of rejection for five months even though buyer knew the delay would harm the sellers was breach of duty of good faith and thus a breach of the underlying contract term); Eggett v. Wasatch Energy Corp., 94 P.3d 193 (Utah 2004) ("the more leeway a party has under the terms of the contract, the more contracting parties may invoke the protection of the covenant of good faith and fair dealing in the exercise of that discretion").

§7.17 n.36 p.365 Add the following after the first sentence: *Accord:* McAdams v. Mass. Mut. Life Ins. Co., 391 F.3d 287 (1st Cir. 2004) ("lack of good faith can be inferred from 'unreasonable[ness] under all the circumstances") (quoting from Nile v. Nile, 734 N.E.2d 1153 (Mass. 2000)).

§7.17 n.37 p.365 Add the following after the first sentence: *But cf.* Abels v. JPMorgan Chase Bank, 678 F. Supp. 2d 1273 (S.D. Fla. 2009) (bank used its discretion to buy insurance where borrower's lapsed to buy exorbitantly priced insurance from an affiliate); Wolf v. Walt Disney Pictures & Television, 76 Cal. Rptr. 3d 585 (Ct. App. 2008) ("if the express purpose of the contract is to grant unfettered discretion, and the contract is otherwise supported by adequate consideration, then the conduct is, by definition, within the reasonable expectation of the parties and can never violate an implied covenant of good faith and fair dealing," so studio's decision to enter into promotional agreements for which it received no monetary consideration did not violate the implied covenant contained within its licensing agreement with the licensor), distinguished in Best Buy Stores v. Manteca Lifestyle Ctr., 859 F. Supp. 2d 1138 (E.D. Cal. 2012) (contract gave developer discretion when to build the various parts of a shopping center, but not "as to *whether* to construct the shopping center," so the developer's decision not to build some sections was subject to the implied duty of good faith).

§7.17 p.366 Add the following at the end of the carryover sentence: . . . as to which the buyer has some discretion.[37a]

[37a] A single contract may be both an output contract and a requirements contract. For example, in Griffith v. Clear Lakes Trout Co., 200 P.3d 1162 (Idaho 2009), a hatchery entered into a contract with a trout grower under which the hatchery agreed to sell the grower enough small trout to enable the grower to grow up to two million pounds of trout per year, which the growers agreed to sell back to the hatchery once they reached marketable size. The court held that this was a hybrid output/requirements contract because "the quantity of fish under the agreement was not only subject to the [grower's] good-faith output of market-size trout, up to the stated maximum of two million pounds, but was also subject to [the hatchery's] good-faith requirements for trout in its resale market."

§7.17 n.38 p.366 In the first paragraph, add the following after the first sentence: *See* Structural Polymer Grp. v. Zoltek Corp., 543 F.3d 987 (8th Cir. 2008) ("The Supply Agreement bound SP to order product from Zoltek in good faith, and if SP failed to purchase anything from Zoltek during the term of the agreement, then the contract allowed Zoltek to allege that SP acted in bad faith by failing to make purchases.").

§7.17 n.38 p.366 In the first paragraph, add the following at the end: The party alleging bad faith carries the burden of proof. Chicago United Indus. v. City of Chicago, 685 F. Supp. 2d 791 (N.D. Ill. 2010) (seller failed to meet burden; although it proved that the buyer had reduced its requirements, "the reduction itself is not evidence of bad faith").

§7.17 n.38 p.366 Add the following at the end: ____ The duty of good faith applies as well to a buyer's decision to purchase goods outside the requirements contract. *See* Structural Polymer Grp. v. Zoltek Corp., *id.* (buyer may have breached requirements contract when it "contracts to purchase its requirements for a product from a particular seller, but then — without a 'good faith' basis to do so — purchases an interchangeable product from a third party instead").

§7.17 n.41 p.367 Add the following at the start of the footnote: Reyelt v. Danzell, 533 F.3d 28 (1st Cir. 2008) (implying best efforts clause where purchaser had agreed to seek a zoning variance) (quoting from treatise).

§7.17 n.41 p.367 Add the following to the list after **"Accord"**: Samica Enters. v. Mail Boxes Etc. USA, 637 F. Supp. 2d 712 (C.D. Cal. 2008) (adopting approach from treatise and Farnsworth, On Trying to Keep One's Promises: The Duty of Best Efforts in Contract Law, 46 U. Pitt. L. Rev. 1 (1984): "Courts [and Plaintiffs] sometimes confuse the standard of best efforts with that of good faith. . . . Good faith is a standard that has honesty and fairness at its core and that is imposed on every party to a contract. Best efforts is a standard that has diligence as its essence and is imposed only on those contracting parties that have undertaken such performance. The two standards are distinct and that of best efforts is the more exacting.").

§7.17 n.42 p.368 Add the following at the end of the first paragraph: , followed in Mark Techs. Corp. v. Utah Res. Int'l, 147 P.3d 509 (Utah App. 2006) ("an express best efforts clause imposes obligations that are different than those implied under the covenant of good faith and fair dealing").

§7.17 n.45 p.369 Add the following at the end: Cf. Third Story Music v. Waits, 48 Cal. Rptr. 2d 747 (Ct. App. 1995) (best efforts term implied in exclusive contract to make, sell, and distribute recordings).

§7.17 n.48 p.369 Add the following at the end: Cf. Concorde Res. Corp. v. Kepco Energy, 254 P.3d 734 (Okla. Civ. App. 2011) (oil and gas leases contain an implied covenant to market the product); Occidental Permian Ltd. v. Helen Jones dn., 333 S.W.3d 392 (Tex. Civ. App. 2011) (same).

§7.17 n.54 p.371 Add the following to the list after **"Accord"**: Jaffe v. Jaffe, 17 So. 3d 1251 (Fla. App. 2009) (marital settlement agreement provided no termination date for paying son's education-related expenses, but cut off regular expenses at particular ages; held that would imply ending date of end of education),

§7.17 n.54 p.371 Add the following at the end: But cf. Bell v. Leven, 90 P.3d 1286 (Nev. 2004) (though "courts should avoid construing contracts to impose a perpetual obligation, when the

language of a contract clearly provides that a contract is to have a perpetual duration, the courts must enforce the contract according to its terms"), followed in S. Wine & Spirits v. Mountain Valley Spring Co., 646 F.3d 526 (8th Cir. 2011) (Nevada law: although indefinite durations are favored over perpetual durations, a contract providing for termination only by mutual consent or default is perpetual).

§7.17 n.55 p.371 Add the following to the list in the final sentence after* "see"*: Mid-W. Energy Consultants v. Covenant Home, 815 N.E.2d 911 (Ill. App. 2004) ("A contract of indefinite duration such as the one here is not deemed perpetual and, thus, is terminable at will."); Cascade Auto Glass v. Progressive Cas. Ins. Co., 145 P.3d 1253 (Wash. App. 2006) (pricing agreement between insurer and auto repairer; "When a contract for a continuing performance fails to specify the intended duration, we construe it to be terminable-at-will by either party after a reasonable notice.").

§7.17 n.55 p.371 Add the following after the citation to* Trient Partners I*: , in turn followed in Jespersen v. Minn. Mining & Mfg. Co., 700 N.E.2d 1014 (Ill. 1998) ("Advances in technology, changes in consumer taste and competition mean that once-profitable businesses perish regularly. Today's fashion will tomorrow or the next day inevitably fall the way of the buggy whip, the eight-track tape and the leisure suit. Men and women of commerce know this intuitively and achieve the flexibility needed to respond to market demands by entering into agreements terminable at-will."), in its turn followed in A.T.N., Inc. v. McAirlaid's Vliesstoffe GmbH, 557 F.3d 483 (7th Cir. 2009) ("a contract permitting one party to terminate based on a material breach by the other party is deemed terminable at will") and distinguished in Dermesropian v. Dental Experts, 718 F. Supp. 2d 143 (D. Mass. 2010) (Illinois law: contract not perpetual, even if indefinitely renewable, "because the Contract explicitly provides for termination upon the occurrence of specific, objective events").

§7.17 n.56 p.372 Add the following to the list after* "Accord"*: Unterberger v. Red Bull N. Am., 75 Cal. Rptr. 3d 368 (Ct. App. 2008) ("where there was no agreement that distributing arrangements would last for a fixed term of years, such contracts 'were of indefinite duration, making them terminable at will . . .' ") (quoting from Varni Bros. Corp. v. Wine World, 41 Cal. Rptr. 2d 740 (Ct. App. 1995)).

§7.17 n.57 p.372 Add the following to the list after **"But cf."**: Fitzpatrick v. Teleflex, Inc., 763 F. Supp. 2d 224 (D. Me. 2011) (no fiduciary duty owed distributor by manufacturer).

§7.17 n.58 p.373 Add the following to the list after **"Accord"**: City of E. Chicago v. E. Chicago 2nd Century, 878 N.E.2d 358 (Ind. App. 2007) ("A contract that provides for continuing performance and has no ending date, or that provides it will last indefinitely, is terminable at will by either party." But the contract contained a provision terminating the agreement upon revocation of a license, which "might amount to an 'implied durational term' that would prevent the agreement from being terminable at will"), *aff'd in part, rev'd in part on other grounds*, 908 N.E.2d 611 (Ind. 2009).

§7.17 n.58 p.373 Add the following at the end: Courts have been willing to extend equitable concepts to the franchise relation, at least to the extent consistent with any pertinent statutory scheme. Maintainco, Inc. v. Mitsubishi Caterpillar Forklift Am., 975 A.2d 510 (N.J. Super. App. Div. 2009) (recognizing constructive termination of franchisee).

§7.17 n.60 p.373 Add the following to the list after **"Accord"**: Navair, Inc. v. IFR Americas, 519 F.3d 1131 (10th Cir. 2008) (termination of distributorship; absence of agreed-upon end date "means that Navair would be protected only for a reasonable time"); Boland, Inc. v. Rolf C. Hagen (USA) Corp., 685 F. Supp. 2d 1094 (E.D. Cal. 2010) (distributorship contract "could only be terminated after a reasonable time and with reasonable notice" if the distributor had incurred significant expenses in connection with the contract).

§7.17 n.60 p.373 In the second paragraph, add the following after the citation to **Cherick**: distinguished in Boyle v. Douglas Dynamics, 99 Fed. Appx. 243 (1st Cir. 2004) ("*Cherick* does not

hold that a manufacturer must provide notice to its current distributors before appointing a new distributor.").

§7.17 n.62 p.375 Replace the citation to **Fontaine & De Ly** *with the following:* M. Fontaine & F. De Ly, Drafting International Contracts: An Analysis of Contract Clauses ch.12 (2006).

§7.17 n.63 p.375 Add the following after the citation to **Teitelbaum***:* followed in RGJ Assocs. v. Stainsafe, Inc., 300 F. Supp. 2d 250 (D. Mass. 2004) ("amount of damages following the termination date is limited to the time period of what constitutes reasonable notice").

§7.17 n.66 p.377 Add the following at the end of the first paragraph: See also Giusti v. Sterling Wentworth Corp., 201 P.3d 966 (Utah 2009) ("[W]e presume that employment contracts are at-will. When an employer intends to alter the at-will arrangement and guarantee employment for a specified period, we require the employer to make that promise clear and definite . . ."). Promises other than duration will, however, be enforceable. *See* J.R.D. Mgmt. Corp. v. Dulin, 883 So. 2d 314 (Fla. App. 2004) (enforcing severance pay clause in employment contract for at-will employee). This point is developed further in §2.10a, *supra,* on employee handbooks and §2.10b, *supra,* on employee covenants.

§7.17 n.66 p.377 In the second paragraph, add the following to the list after **"See generally"***:* Bales, Explaining the Spread of At-Will Employment as an Interjurisdictional Race to the Bottom of Employment Standards, 75 Tenn. L. Rev. 454 (2008) (and works cited therein).

§7.17 n.72 p.379 Add the following after the citation to **Mitford***:* , followed in Witt v. State Dep't of Corr., 75 P.3d 1030 (Alaska 2003) ("The subjective prong of the covenant is breached when an employer is motivated by the goal of depriving the employee of a benefit of the contract.").

§7.17 n.72 p.379 Add the following to the list after **"But see"***:* Kelly v. State Farm Mut. Auto. Ins. Co., 218 S.W.3d 517 (Mo. App. 2007) ("there can be no claim for the breach of an

implied covenant of good faith and fair dealing in the termination of an at-will employment relationship"); LoPresti v. Rutland Regional Health Servs., 865 A.2d 1102 (Vt. 2004) ("the covenant [of good faith and fair dealing] does not apply to at-will employment agreements when the plaintiff's argument amounts to no more than an objection to the other party's freedom to avail itself of the at-will arrangement by terminating the agreement for reasons that the other party does not accept").

***§7.17 n.73 p.379 Add the following to the list after* "Accord":** Mitchell v. Teck Cominco Alaska, 193 P.3d 751 (Alaska 2008) (good faith covenant includes a ban on employers terminating employees for the purpose of depriving the employee of the benefits of their contracts).

§7.17 n.75 p.381 In the first paragraph, add the following after the second sentence: *Cf.* Okpik v. City of Barrow, 230 P.3d 672 (Alaska 2010) ("'The objective prong of the covenant is breached when an employer fails to act in a manner that a reasonable person would consider fair, which includes treating similarly situated employees disparately, terminating employees on unconstitutional grounds, and terminating employees in violation of public policy.'") (quoting from Witt v. State Dep't of Corr., 75 P.3d 1030 (Alaska 2003)).

§7.17 n.75 p.381 Replace the second paragraph with the following: That federal law does not preempt actions under state law, *see* Lingle v. Norge Div. of Magic Chef, 486 U.S. 399 (1988) (Labor Management Relations Act), followed in Hawaiian Airlines v. Norris, 512 U.S. 246 (1994) (Railway Labor Act), and in Norcon, Inc. v. Kotowski, 971 P.2d 158 (Alaska 1999) (irrelevant that earlier cases involved tort rather than breach of covenant of good faith and fair dealing). *See generally* H. Perritt, Employee Dismissal Law and Practice §§2.39-2.47.

***§7.17 n.77 p.381 Add the following to the list after* "See":** Wesco Autobody Supply v. Ernest, 243 P.3d 1069 (Idaho 2010) (covenant found in all employment agreements; "[Determining] whether the covenant has been breached is an objective determination of whether the parties have acted in good faith in terms of enforcing the contractual provisions.").

§7.17a TERMINATION OF EMPLOYMENT AGREEMENTS

§7.17a n.1 p.381 In the second paragraph, add the following to the list: Finkin, Shoring Up the Citadel (At-Will Employment), 24 Hofstra Labor & Employment J. 1 (2006); Porter, The Perfect Compromise: Bridging the Gap Between At-Will Employment and Just Cause, 87 Neb. L. Rev. 63 (2008).

§7.17a n.2 p.382 In the first paragraph, delete the citations to **Maw** ***and to*** **Escalante.**

§7.17a n.2 p.382 In the first paragraph, add the following to the list after **"Accord"*:*** Reust v. Alaska Petrol. Contractors, 127 P.3d 807 (Alaska 2005) ("there is an actionable public policy tort in Alaska for retaliation against witnesses in legal proceedings"); Willard v. Khotol Servs. Corp., 171 P.3d 108 (Alaska 2007) ("firing an employee in retaliation for requesting safety equipment gives rise to a cause of action for breach of the implied duty of good faith and fair dealing"); Kearl v. Portage Envt'l, 205 P.3d 496 (Colo. App. 2008) ("Colorado has a clearly expressed public policy against terminating an employee in retaliation for the employee's good faith attempt to prevent the employer's participation in defrauding the government."), followed in Bonidy v. Vail Valley Ctr. for Aesthetic Dentistry, 232 P.3d 277 (Colo. App. 2010) (discharge for refusing to work hours prohibited by law); Jasper v. H. Nizam, Inc., 764 N.W.2d 751 (Iowa 2009) (administrative rule on minimum staffing requirements for child care facilities "supports a clear and well-defined public policy that gives rise to the tort of wrongful discharge"); Keveney v. Mo. Military Acad., 304 S.W.3d 98 (Mo. 2010) (discharge of teacher for reporting child abuse as required by state law).

§7.17a n.2 p.382 In the second paragraph, add the following to the list after **"Cf.":** Bonidy v. Vail Valley Ctr. for Aesthetic Dentistry, 232 P.3d 277 (Colo. App. 2010) ("[W]hen an employee objects to performing an act that [would violate public policy so as to yield] a claim for wrongful termination in violation of public policy and is immediately fired before having an opportunity to refuse to perform the directed act, the refusal element of the [wrongful discharge cause of action] is satisfied.").

§7.17a n.2 p.382 In the second paragraph, add the following to the list after **"But cf.":** Lamson v. Crater Lake Motors, 216 P.3d 852 (Or. 2009) (refusal to take part in business activity involving a firm that employed unfair trade practices inadequately linked to public policy against unfair trade practices).

§7.17a n.2 p.384 In the third paragraph, add the following to the list after **"see":** Okpik v. City of Barrow, 230 P.3d 672 (Alaska 2010) ("Constructive discharge satisfies the first element [of a cause of action for wrongful termination]"); Baker v. Tremco Inc., 917 N.E.2d 650 (Ind. 2009) ("We . . . conclude that a constructive retaliatory discharge falls within the ambit of the narrowly drawn public policy exception to the employment at will doctrine.").

§7.17a n.3 p.384 In the first paragraph, add the following to the list after **"Accord":** Dean v. Consol. Equities Realty #3, 914 N.E.2d 1109 (Ohio App. 2009) (no clear public policy against auto dealer's falsifying information on credit applications so that its customers could get credit); Swears v. R.M. Roach & Sons, Inc., 696 S.E.2d 1 (W. Va. 2010) (discharge for communicating evidence of possible criminal conduct to company principal).

§7.17a n.4 p.385 Add the following to the list after **"Accord":** Baker v. Tremco Inc., 917 N.E.2d 650 (Ind. 2009) ("The presumption of at-will employment is strong, and we are disinclined to adopt broad and ill-defined exceptions to the employment at will doctrine."); Berry v. Liberty Holdings, 803 N.W.2d 106 (Iowa 2011) (referring to "a narrow public-policy exception" encompassing only "a clearly defined and well-recognized public policy"; this does not include "alleged public

policies based in general and vague concepts of socially desirable conduct, internal employment policies, or private interests").

§7.17a n.5 p.386 In the second paragraph, add the following at the end: *Accord:* Byrd v. VOCA Corp., 962 A.2d 927 (D.C. 2008) (extending wrongful discharge action to contractual employees; "The duty giving rise to the tort remedy is not derived from the covenants of contract, but rather from the employer's obligation to conduct its affairs in conformity with fundamental public policy."; collecting cases); Keveney v. Missouri Military Acad., 304 S.W.3d 98 (Mo. 2010) (extending wrongful discharge action to contractual employees, because (1) "An employer's obligation to refrain from discharging an employee who refuses to participate in or conceal actions inconsistent with public policy does not depend on the terms and conditions of the employment contract."; (2) the remedies for wrongful discharge are distinct from those for breach of contract; and (3) "it is inconsistent to allow an at-will employee to pursue an action for wrongful discharge while denying a contract employee the same right."; collecting cases). *But see* Haynes v. Zoological Soc'y of Cincinnati, 652 N.E.2d 948 (Ohio 1995) (action in tort for wrongful discharge not available to employee who was member of union and not employee at-will).

§7.17a n.6 p.386 Add the following at the end of the second paragraph: These cases may, however, be less exceptional than once they were. Courts remain divided, but a respectably large body of caselaw now favors extending wrongful discharge to cover wrongful demotion. *See* Brigham v. Dillon Cos., 935 P.2d 1054 (Kan. 1997) (retaliatory demotion for filing workers' compensation claim); Trosper v. Bag 'N Save, 734 N.W.2d 704 (Neb. 2007) (retaliatory demotion for filing workers' compensation claim; collecting cases); Lawson v. AK Steel Corp., 699 N.E.2d 951 (Ohio App. 1997) (retaliatory demotion for whistleblowing). In light of the equally respectable body of caselaw to the contrary, though, it would be imprudent to proclaim a trend. *Cf.* Crowley v. Alaska Dep't of Health & Human Servs., 253 P.3d 1226 (Alaska 2011) ("A pattern of harassing conduct may breach the implied covenant, as constituting disparate treatment.").

§7.17a n.10 p.388 Add the following to the list after **"Accord"***:* Weaver v. Harpster, 975 A.2d 555 (Pa. 2009) (declining to apply public policy against sex discrimination beyond the range of employers covered by the pertinent statute; "Extending protections afforded by a statute beyond its explicit limitations would require the courts to act as a super-legislature.").

§7.17a n.12 p.388 Add the following to the list after **"Accord"***:* Jasper v. H. Nizam, Inc., 764 N.W.2d 751 (Iowa 2009) ("Administrative regulations have the potential to reflect legislative intent, satisfy our concern that public policy be derived from statutory sources, and can provide the same notice to employees and employers as a statute. . . . Consequently, we are satisfied that administrative regulations can be used as a source of public policy to support the tort of wrongful discharge when adopted pursuant to a delegation of authority in a statute that seeks to further a public policy."; collects cases), followed and limited in Ballalatak v. All Iowa Agric. Ass'n, 781 N.W.2d 272 (Iowa 2010) ("In all cases recognizing a public-policy exception, this court has relied on a statute or administrative regulation.").

§7.17a n.12 p.388 Add the following after the citation to **Green***:* , followed in Barbosa v. IMPCO Techs., 101 Cal. Rptr. 3d 923 (Ct. App. 2009) (duty to pay overtime wages a fundamental public policy as found in both statutes and common law; claim need not be rightful, as long as in good faith).

§7.17a n.13 p.389 Add the following to the list after **"Accord"***:* Kearl v. Portage Envt'l, 205 P.3d 496 (Colo. App. 2008) (deriving public policy against defrauding the government from a judicial opinion).

§7.17a n.13 p.389 Add the following after the citation to **Barker***:* and in Wilburn v. Mid. South Health Dev., 343 F.3d 1274 (10th Cir. 2003) (statutes "simply not sufficient to establish the 'clear mandate of public policy' necessary to state a *Burk* tort claim").

§7.17a n.14 p.389 Add the following to the list in the first sentence: Jasper v. H. Nizam, Inc., 764 N.W.2d 751 (Iowa 2009) ("The causal link essentially requires the discharge to be an actual cause of the injury and further requires the discharge to be a proximate cause of the injury."; damages for work done on premises not recoverable because the plaintiff "cannot establish those expenses would have been reimbursed if [the employer] would not have terminated her employment.").

§7.17a n.14 p.389 Add the following at the end: Many courts have tried to give structure to this seemingly inchoate body of law, with varying degrees of success. One of the sounder approaches comes from Ohio, which states the elements thus:

> "1. That clear public policy existed and was manifested in a state or federal constitution, statute or administrative regulation, or in the common law (the *clarity* element).
>
> 2. That dismissing employees under circumstances like those involved in the plaintiff's dismissal would jeopardize the public policy (the *jeopardy* element).
>
> 3. The plaintiff's dismissal was motivated by conduct related to the public policy (the *causation* element).
>
> 4. The employer lacked overriding legitimate business justification for the dismissal (the *overriding justification* element)."

Painter v. Graley, 639 N.E.2d 51, 57 n.8 (Ohio 1994). This test has been adopted elsewhere. *See* Berry v. Liberty Holdings, 803 N.W.2d 106 (Iowa 2011). Swears v. R.M. Roach & Sons, Inc., 696 S.E.2d 1 (W. Va. 2010). The Ohio court used a test laid out in an influential law review article on this tort action. Perritt, The Future of Wrongful Discharge Claims: Where Does Employer Self-Interest Lie?, 58 U. Cin. L. Rev. 397 (1989).

§7.17a n.19 p.391 Add the following at the end: but followed in Connolly v. Napoli, Kaiser & Bern, LLP, 817 N.Y.S.2d 872 (Sup. 2006) (*Wieder* applies to refusal to engage in misconduct, not just to insist misconduct be reported) and reaffirmed in Sullivan v. Harnisch, 969 N.E.2d 758 (N.Y. 2012) (*Wieder* the sole exception to the rule in *Murphy*; not extended to compliance officer in hedge fund who objected to improper trades, because his regulatory obligations and employment duties were not incapable of separation, particularly where, as here, compliance was only one aspect of the officer's employment). *See also* Trakis v. Manhattanville College, 859 N.Y.S.2d 453 (App. Div. 2008) ("There is no requirement that the employee be discharged in good faith."; collecting cases).

§7.17a n.21 p.391 Add the following after the citation to **Witt***:* , reaffirmed in Mitchell v. Teck Cominco Alaska, 193 P.3d 751 (Alaska 2008) ("The covenant does not have a precise definition but generally requires employers to treat like employees alike and act in a manner that a reasonable person would regard as fair.") and in turn followed in Crowley v. Alaska Dep't of Health & Human Servs., 253 P.3d 1226 (Alaska 2011) (duty of good faith contains both subjective and objective components; former asks whether the employer was "motivated by an improper or impermissible objective" and latter asks whether the employer has treated like employees alike or has terminated an employee on unconstitutional grounds or against public policy) (internal quotations omitted).

§7.17a n.21 p.391 Add the following after the citation to **Prout***:* distinguished in Tvedt v. Farmers Ins. Grp. of Cos., 91 P.3d 1 (Mont. 2004) (insurance company's termination of manager under provision allowing termination at will without cause was not violation of duty of good faith and fair dealing).

§7.17a n.22 p.392 Add the following to the list after **"Accord"***:* Vetromile v. JPI Partners, 706 F. Supp. 2d 442 (S.D.N.Y. 2010) ("'The implied covenant of good faith does not give rise to a contract action for the wrongful discharge of an at-will employee.'") (quoting from Arbeeny v. Kennedy Exec. Search, 893 N.Y.S.2d 39 (App. Div. 2010)); Cramer v. Fairfield Med. Ctr., 914 N.E.2d 447 (Ohio App. 2009) ("Ohio law does not recognize a good-faith-and-fair-dealing requirement in employment-at-will relationships.").

§7.17a n.22 p.392 Add the following after the citation to **Shell***:* , reaffirmed in Hatfield v. Health Mgmt. Assocs., 672 S.E.2d 395 (W. Va. 2008)

§7.17a n.22 p.392 Add the following at the end: *See generally* Apps, Good Faith Performance in Employment Contracts: A "Comparative Conversation" Between the U.S. and England, 8 U. Pa. J. of Labor & Employment L. 883 (2006).

§7.17b MEANING OF *GOOD FAITH*

§7.17b n.1 p.393 Add the following to the list in the first sentence: Littlejohn v. Parrish, 839 N.E.2d 49 (Ohio App. 2005) ("a party can be found to have breached its contract if it fails to act in good faith"). In the securities context, Holtz v. JPMorgan Chase Bank, NA, 846 F.3d 928 (7th Cir. 2017) involved an allegation that the bank's failure to disclose that its employees had incentives to recommend investment in bank-owned mutual funds constituted a breach of fiduciary duty. Desiring to represent a class of all other investors, the plaintiff styled the complaint as sounding in contract in order to avoid the Securities Litigation Uniform Standards Act, which creates a cause of action for "misrepresentation or omission of a material fact in connection with the purchase or sale of a covered security" but also prohibits class actions. 15 U.S.C. §78bb(f)(1)(A). Judge Easterbrook was concerned that "[t]he possibility that plain vanilla contract claims can proceed under state law creates an incentive to characterize all securities claims as 'contract' suits and avoid federal preemption." 846 F.3d at 931. It held that the plaintiff's (and would-be class members') claims were securities claims and subject to the class action limitations of federal law. "If she wants to pursue a contract or fiduciary-duty claim under state law, she has only to proceed in the usual way: one litigant against another." *Id.* at 934.

§7.17b n.8 p.394 In the third paragraph, add the following after the first sentence: For a comparative vantage, *see* Tetley, Good Faith in Contract: Particularly in the Contracts of Arbitration and Chartering, 35 J. Maritime L. & Com. 561 (2004).

§7.17b n.9 p.395 In the first paragraph, add the following to the list after **"Accord"***:* State Street Bank & Trust Co. v. Inversiones Errazuriz Ltda., 374 F.3d 158 (2d Cir. 2004) (if contract "allows a

bank to withhold consent for particular conduct and sets no express restrictions on the bank's right to do so, the bank is not prohibited from unreasonably or arbitrarily withholding such consent"); FAMM Steel, Inc. v. Sovereign Bank, 571 F.3d 93 (1st Cir. 2009) (no breach of covenant of good faith and fair dealing because of failure to extend loans or waive rights, where "plaintiffs pointed to no provision in the loan agreements that obligated Sovereign to take action[]"); Shawmut Bank v. Wayman, 606 N.E.2d 925 (Mass. App. 1993) (implied covenant of good faith and fair dealing "would require that the bank be honest in its dealings with [client] and that it not purposefully injure [its] right to obtain the benefit of the contract.").

§7.17b n.9 p.395 In the first paragraph, add the following after the third sentence: *Cf.* HSH Nordbank AG N.Y. Branch v. Street, 421 Fed. Appx. 70 (2d Cir. 2011) (no duty for loan syndicate seeking to invoke guaranties given by principals of debtor: syndicate did not frustrate performance by declining to fund advances, "for the simple reason that Nordbank had no obligation to fund any advances," and in any event the guaranties contained broad waivers of defenses).

§7.17b n.14 p.397 Add the following at the end: For a more recent version of Wyoming's definition, *see* Excel Constr. v. HKM Eng'g, 228 P.3d 40 (Wyo. 2010) ("The implied covenant imposes an obligation to act honestly in fact in the transaction, and to refrain from actions which would injure the rights of the other party to receive the benefit of its bargain."). This definition goes beyond that in *Wendling* by covering actions that interfere with or harm the other party, and thus may fit better with those discussed *infra*.

§7.17b n.16 p.397 Add the following at the end: One may doubt *Nolan*'s validity in light of sweeping pronouncements by the New Jersey Supreme Court. *See* Brunswick Hills Racquet Club v. Rte. 18 Shopping Ctr. Assocs., 864 A.2d 387 (N.J. 2005) (adopts Restatement Second §205; "A defendant may be liable for a breach of the covenant of good faith and fair dealing even if it does not violate an express term of a contract. . . . A plaintiff may be entitled to relief under the covenant if its reasonable expectations are destroyed when a defendant acts with ill motives and without any legitimate purpose.").

§7.17b n.17 p.398 Add the following at the end: *Accord:* Nemec v. Shrader, 991 A.2d 1120 (Del. 2010) ("Delaware's implied duty of good faith and fair dealing is not an equitable remedy for rebalancing economic interests after events that could have been anticipated, but were not, that later adversely affected one party to a contract."); Naqvi v. Saudi Arabian Airlines, Inc., 123 F. Supp. 3d 129 (D.D.C. 2016) (airline did not breach implied duty of good faith and fair dealing in failing to advise flyer in advance that the departure gate had been moved to a terminal at least five miles away or in failing to ensure access to drinking water and sanitary bathroom facilities in the terminal, where the airline had neither effective control over the terminal change nor the conditions in the terminal).

The duty of good faith and fair dealing cannot reverse or modify what is expressly in the contract. In Stokes v. DISH Network, LLC, 838 F.3d 948 (8th Cir. 2016), subscribers of satellite television sued when the provider ceased to carry Fox stations or provide compensation for the reduction in service. However, the contract provided that subscribers were "not entitled to any refund because of a deletion, rearrangement or change of any programming, programming packages or other Services." Applying Colorado law, the appellate court emphasized that "The duty of good faith and fair dealing 'will not contradict terms or conditions for which a party has bargained.' The duty 'does not obligate a party . . . to assume obligations that vary or contradict the contract's express provisions, nor does it permit a party to inject substantive terms into the contract.' " *Id.* at 953 (quoting Amoco Oil Co. v. Ervin, 908 P.2d 493, 498 (Colo. 1995) and ADT Sec. Servs., Inc. v. Premier Home Prot., Inc., 181 P.3d 288, 293 (Colo. App. 2007)). The Eighth Circuit criticized the district court for "improperly convert[ing] the covenant of good faith and fair dealing into an additional contract term. It allowed Plaintiffs to recover monetary relief for Services interruptions, a remedy that is unambiguously precluded by the express terms of the parties' contractual bargain." *Id.* at 955. The court also considered and rejected the suggestion that such broad discretion rendered the contract illusory, as discussed in §2.13, *supra*.

§7.17b n.18 p.398 Add the following at the end of the first sentence: , followed in Flood v. ClearOne Comm'ns, 618 F.3d 1110 (10th Cir. 2010) (quoting from and adopting Summers, *supra*).

§7.17b n.19 p.398 Add the following at the end: , followed by Estate of Draper v. Bank of Am., 205 P.3d 698 (Kan. 2009) (duty of good faith applies to prenuptial agreement that wife would, if she survived husband, leave at least three-fourths of her estate to husband's sons by a previous marriage, where widow put almost all assets into an irrevocable trust for the benefit of charities; "the promisor may not 'thwart the expectation of the promisee by squandering his assets irresponsibly or by making gifts of them to other persons. The promisor maintains his *power* to dispose of his assets, but he has no *right* to do so in a manner which will frustrate the purposes of his contract.' ") (quoting from Rheinstein, Critique: Contracts to Make a Will, 30 N.Y.U. L. Rev. 1224 (1955)). *Accord:* Landry v. Spitz, 925 A.2d 334 (Conn. App. 2007) ("To constitute a breach of [the implied covenant of good faith and fair dealing], the acts by which a defendant allegedly impedes the plaintiff's right to receive benefits that he or she reasonably expected to receive under the contract must have been taken in bad faith. . . . Bad faith in general implies both actual or constructive fraud, or a design to mislead or deceive another, or a neglect or refusal to fulfill some duty or some contractual obligation, not prompted by an honest mistake as to one's rights or duties, but by some interested or sinister motive. Bad faith means more than mere negligence; it involves a dishonest purpose. [B]ad faith may be overt or may consist of inaction, and it may include evasion of the spirit of the bargain.") (citations and internal quotation marks omitted); Livingston v. 18 Mile Point Drive, 972 A.2d 1001 (N.H. 2009) (quoting from Restatement Second §205 cmt. *d* ("Among the types of bad faith recognized by courts are evasion of the spirit of the bargain and failure to cooperate in the other's performance."); bad faith when seller did not notify potential buyer that his exercise of the option to buy was too early and not in writing, but rather remained silent until the time for exercise had passed).

§7.17b n.21 p.399 Add the following at the end: , in Waste Connections v. Ritchie Corp., 228 P.3d 429 (Kan. App. 2010) (party "acted in bad faith by attempting to maximize its profits to 'recapture opportunities foregone' through granting of the right of first refusal"; quoting from Burton, *supra*); Spencer Reed Grp. v. Pickett, 163 S.W.3d 570 (Mo. App. 2005) (covenant of good faith and fair dealing includes an "obligation imposed by law to prevent opportunistic behavior, that is, the exploitation of changing economic conditions to ensure gains in excess of those reasonably expected at the time of contracting") and in Wilson v. Amerada Hess Corp., 773 A.2d 1121 (N.J. 2001) (this "approach respects the express bargain of the parties that gave unilateral authority over price to one party alone"). *Accord:* County of La Paz v. Yakima Compost Co., 233 P.3d 1169 (Ariz. App. 2010) ("a party breaches [the covenant of good faith and fair dealing] by exercising discretion afforded under the contract for a reason beyond the risks assumed by the other party"; county's failure to perform its duties in a timely manner "merely to force a termination of the Agreement due to a change of heart regarding the wisdom of the Agreement" went beyond the risks assumed by the other party); Bak-A-Lum Corp. v. Alcoa Bldg. Prods., 351 A.2d 349 (N.J. 1976) (planned termination of distributor's exclusive territory withheld while distributor expanded its facilities and signed a long-term lease, both with the defendant's encouragement, in order to avoid cooling the plaintiff's interest in selling the products in the months before new distributors were in place; although there was no literal breach of the agreement's terms, the "defendant's selfish withholding from plaintiff of its intention" to terminate the exclusive distributorship, while knowing that the plaintiff continued to invest in its continuance, violated the covenant of good faith and fair dealing). *Cf. In re* Kaplan, 143 F.3d 807 (3d Cir. 1998) (covenant of duty of good faith and fair dealing entails the exercise of discretion "reasonably and with proper motive, . . . not . . . arbitrarily, capriciously, or in a manner inconsistent with the reasonable expectations of the parties") (internal quotations omitted), followed in Fishoff v. Coty Inc., 634 F.3d 647 (2d Cir. 2011) (*post hoc* revaluation of stock in order to lower the value of a former employee's stock options inconsistent with covenant).

§7.17b n.24 p.399 Add the following after the first sentence: *See also* Sanders v. FedEx Ground Package Sys., 188 P.3d 1200 (N.M. 2008) (quoting from Restatement Second, Burton).

§7.17b n.25 p.399 Add the following after the first sentence: *Accord:* Boland, Inc. v. Rolf C. Hagen (USA) Corp., 685 F. Supp. 2d 1094 (E.D. Cal. 2010) ("A party breaches this duty when it acts in a way that deprives another contracting party of benefits conferred by the contract."); Chokel v. Genzyme Corp., 867 N.E.2d 325 (Mass. 2007) ("The purpose of the implied covenant is to ensure that neither party interferes with the ability of the other to enjoy the fruits of the contract"); Ferrara v. Walters, 919 So. 2d 876 (Miss. 2005) ("The covenant imposes a duty not to prevent or hinder the other party's performance, but may also impose a duty 'to take some affirmative steps to cooperate in achieving those goals.' ") (quoting from Cenac v. Murry, 609 So. 2d 1257, 1272 (Miss. 1992)); City of St. Joseph v. Lake Contrary Sewer Dist., 251 S.W.3d 362 (Mo. App. 2008) ("When a contract provides a single party with discretion, that discretion is not unlimited; it must not be exercised to deprive the other party of the benefit of the contractual relationship or evade the spirit of the bargain."); Fleming v. Civil Serv. Comm'n, 792 N.W.2d 871 (Neb. 2011) ("[T]he scope of protection offered by the [covenant of good faith and fair dealing] is curtailed by the purposes and express terms of the contract. In other words, the nature and extent of the covenant's protections are measured by the justifiable expectations of the parties.") (citation omitted); 511 W. 232nd Owners Corp. v. Jennifer Realty Co., 773 N.E.2d 496 (N.Y. 2002) ("This covenant embraces a pledge that neither party shall do anything which will have the effect of destroying or injuring the right of the other party to receive the fruits of the contract.") (citations and internal quotations omitted), followed in Fishoff v. Coty Inc., 634 F.3d 647 (2d Cir. 2011) (duty breached when former employer cut its stock price by almost half in order to devalue a former employee's stock options) and in Forman v. Guardian Life Ins. Co., 908 N.Y.S.2d 27 (App. Div. 2010) (duty breached when the breaching party "frustrated the basic purpose of the parties' contracts"); Hometown Folks v. S & B Wilson, Inc., 643 F.3d 520 (6th Cir. 2011) (Tennessee law: "The duty of good faith and fair dealing requires parties to a contract to conduct themselves fairly and responsibly."); City of Gillette v. Hladky Constr., 196 P.3d 184 (Wyo. 2008) ("A breach of the implied covenant occurs when a party interferes with or fails to cooperate in the other party's performance.").

§7.17b n.26 p.399 Add the following to the end of the first paragraph: *Cf.* McAdams v. Mass. Mut. Life Ins. Co., 391 F.3d 287 (1st Cir. 2004) ("The core fiduciary obligation in this sort of context is a duty . . . to exercise any discretionary power . . . in good faith, with prudence and after serious consideration, and reasonably according to the purposes of the agreement and standard fiduciary principles."). For what may be called a quasi-fiduciary duty, see St. Paul Fire & Marine Ins. Co. v. Onvia, Inc., 196 P.3d 664 (Wash. 2008) ("The good faith duty between an insurer and an insured arises from a source akin to a fiduciary duty.").

***§7.17b n.27 p.400 Add the following to the list after* "See":** De La Concha of Hartford v. Aetna Life Ins. Co., 849 A.2d 382 (Conn. 2004) (rejecting argument that mall owner had obligation to make good faith efforts to promote and maintain mall because "economic viability of any one retail tenant of an enclosed mall . . . upon the occupancy rate of the entire mall," and holding that mall owner "was free to take appropriate action to reduce the losses it had incurred for many years").

§7.17b n.28 p.400 In the first paragraph, add the following at the end: It follows from this subjective aspect of good faith that behavior alleged to lack good faith be looked at in its full context, both of the contract at issue and other contracts the parties have or have had. Actions that by themselves seem nefarious may, when viewed as part of the ongoing relations of the parties, prove nothing of the sort. Metavante Corp. v. Emigrant Sav. Bank, 619 F.3d 748 (7th Cir. 2010) ("The obligations of the parties to perform the terms of a contract must be evaluated in the context of the totality of the business arrangement contemplated by the contract.").

§7.17b n.28 p.400 In the second paragraph, add the following to the list in the first sentence: Flood v. ClearOne Comm'ns, 618 F.3d 1110 (10th Cir. 2010) ("[T]he covenant is about securing to the parties the sort of good faith performance that, in the particular circumstances of the case at hand, they reasonably thought they were securing at the time they entered the bargain."); Potlatch Educ. Ass'n v. Potlatch Sch. Dist., 226 P.3d 1277 (Idaho 2010) (court is to undertake "an 'objective determination of whether the parties have acted in good faith in terms of enforcing the contractual provisions,' an inquiry wholly independent of the employer's subjective intent.") (quoting from Jenkins v. Boise Cascade Corp., 108 P.3d 380 (Idaho 2005)).

§7.17b n.28 p.400 In the second paragraph, replace the citation to* Leutdke *with the following: Luedtke v. Nabors Alaska Drilling, 834 P.2d 1220 (Alaska 1992).

§7.17b n.28 p.400 In the second paragraph, add the following after the citation to* Luedtke*: , amplified by Willard v. Khotol Servs. Corp., 171 P.3d 108 (Alaska 2007) ("Breach of the implied covenant may be either subjective or objective.") and Okpik v. City of Barrow, 230 P.3d 672 (Alaska 2010) ("An employer may breach the covenant objectively or subjectively."), and further clarified by Mitchell v. Teck Cominco Alaska, 193 P.3d 751 (Alaska 2008) ("The covenant has both a subjective and an objective component: the subjective component 'prohibits an employer from terminating an employee for the purpose of depriving the employee of the contract's benefits,' and the objective component 'prohibits the employer from dealing with the employee in a manner that a reasonable person would regard as unfair." (quoting from Belluomini v. Fred Meyer of Alaska, 993 P.2d 1009, 1013 (Alaska 1999))), in turn treated consistently with but without citation to *Luedtke, Willard, Mitchell,* or *Belluomini* in Anchorage Chrysler Ctr. v. DaimlerChrysler Motors Corp., 221 P.3d 977 (Alaska 2009) ("The covenant includes subjective and objective elements, both of which must be satisfied.") and expressly followed in Crowley v. Alaska Dep't of Health & Human Servs., 253 P.3d 1226 (Alaska 2011).

§7.17b n.28 p.400 Add the following at the end of the second paragraph: *Cf.* McAdams v. Mass. Mut. Life Ins. Co., 391 F.3d 287 (1st Cir. 2004) ("lack of good faith can be inferred from 'unreasonable[ness] under all the circumstances' ") (quoting from Nile v. Nile, 734 N.E.2d 1153 (Mass. 2000)).

§7.17b n.30 p.401 Add the following at the end: *Cf.* Goldman v. Capital City Mortg. Corp. (*In re* Nieves), 648 F.3d 232 (4th Cir. 2011) (adopting objective aspect of UCC definition for purposes of bankruptcy law: "[R]esorting to routine business practices to fashion a definition of good faith gives an industry wide latitude in which to operate, so long as it follows the very customs the industry itself has created.").

§7.17b n.32 p.402 Add the following at the end: *Accord:* Estate of Draper v. Bank of Am., 205 P.3d 698 (Kan. 2009) ("good faith and reasonableness are usually questions of fact"); City of Gillette v. Hladky Constr., 196 P.3d 184 (Wyo. 2008) ("Where the evidence establishes a material dispute as to whether a party's conduct went beyond the exercise of contract rights and amounted to self-dealing or a violation of community standards of decency, fairness or reasonableness, the issue is one for determination by the fact-finder.").

Another somewhat inchoate area is who carries the burden of proof of what. One prominent approach states that "There is no requirement that bad faith be shown; instead, the plaintiff has the burden of proving a lack of good faith." T.W. Nickerson, Inc. v. Fleet Nat'l Bank, 924 N.E.2d 696, 704 (Mass. 2010). The difference between the absence of good faith and the presence of bad faith is not always easy to see, particularly for courts employing the excluder approach to good faith. Normally proof of the lack of good faith would entail evidence that the other party acted in bad faith. If not, then there must exist some contractual purgatory in which behavior is neither in good faith nor in bad faith. (Indeed, even the *Nickerson* court wavers on this point; elsewhere in the opinion it states that "the plaintiff bears the burden of presenting evidence of bad faith or an absence of good faith." 924 N.E.2d at 706.) Alternatively, the problem may be whether certain acts or their absence are in good faith or in bad faith, not whether they occurred. That would make a real difference in the nature of proof. Proving that something fits within reasonable commercial standards of fair dealing, to use one definition of good faith, is not the same as proving that something is considered bad faith. That thing may be neither one nor the other — or, rather, may be one or the other depending on context, or on who opines on the matter.

§7.17c MEANING OF *BEST EFFORTS*

§7.17c n.12 p.405 Add the following after the second sentence: *Accord:* Questar Builders v. CB Flooring, 978 A.2d 651 (Md. 2009) (termination for convenience clause in construction subcontract subject to duty of good faith and fair dealing, so the promise "was required to act reasonably in ensuring that the Subcontract did not become inconvenient").

§7.17c n.12 p.405 Add the following at the end: , disavowed by Reyelt v. Danzell, 533 F.3d 28 (1st Cir. 2008) (the district judge "noted, but sensibly did not apply, our own conflation of [good faith and best efforts] in *Triple-A Baseball Club Assocs.*").

§7.17c n.13 p.405 Add the following to the list in the first sentence: Reyelt v. Danzell, 533 F.3d 28 (1st Cir. 2008) (requiring implied "reasonable efforts to secure the variance" beyond the express duty of good faith) (quoting from treatise); Samica Enters. v. Mail Boxes Etc. USA, 637 F. Supp. 2d 712 (C.D. Cal. 2008) (no claim for breach of best efforts clause because the plaintiffs "have not raised a genuine issue that [the parent company] would have acted any differently had [the franchisor] exerted greater effort."; quoting from treatise and Farnsworth, *supra* note 1); Mark Techs. Corp. v. Utah Res. Int'l, 147 P.3d 509 (Utah App. 2006) ("'best efforts' is primarily a subjective standard under which a party agrees to do the best that it can regardless of the capabilities of others. . . . Thus, compliance with a best efforts clause must be measured subjectively in the context of the particular facts and circumstances involved. . . . Neither success nor the single-minded pursuit of the objective is required.") (quoting from Carlson Dist. Co. v. Salt Lake Brewing Co., 95 P.3d 1171 (Utah App. 2004)) (quoting from treatise).

§7.17c n.13 p.405 Add the following after the first sentence: *Cf.* Hall v. Martin Eng'g Co., 597 F. Supp. 2d 651 (S.D.W. Va. 2009) ("A duty to use best efforts exists as an independent contractual duty and will only be implied in exceptional circumstances . . . The covenant of good faith and fair dealing, on the other hand, serves only as a guide to the construction of explicit terms in a contract; it is implied in every contract.").

§7.17c n.16 p.406 Add the following at the end: , reprinted and revised in V. Goldberg, Framing Contract Law ch. 6 (2006).

§7.17c n.27 p.409 Add the following to the list in the first sentence: Citri-Lite Co. v. Cott Beverages, 721 F. Supp. 2d 912 (E.D. Cal. 2010) ("commercially reasonable efforts" clause in distributorship contract "permits the performing party to consider its economic business interests" when setting its level of effort).

§7.17c n.27 p.409 Add the following after the citation to **Van Valkenburgh***:* followed in First Union Nat'l Bank v. Steele Software Sys. Corp., 838 A.2d 404 (Md. App. 2003) (best efforts "does not necessarily mean that the promisor is required to give all of its efforts" or "is prohibited from promoting competing products").

§7.17c n.30 p.410 Replace the citation to **Fontaine & De Ly** *with the following:* M. Fontaine & F. De Ly, Drafting International Contracts: An Analysis of Contract Clauses ch. 4 (2006).

CHAPTER 8

PERFORMANCE AND NONPERFORMANCE

§8.2 THE MEANING OF *CONDITION*

*§8.2 n.2 p.414 **Add the following at the end:*** *See generally* Kraus & Scott, Contract Design and the Structure of Contractual Intent, 84 N.Y.U. L. Rev. 1023 (2009).

*§8.2 n.7 p.416 **Add the following to the list after "Accord":*** Israel v. Chabra, 537 F.3d 86 (2d Cir. 2008) ("Over time, the law has come to recognize and enforce the use of linguistic conventions to create conditions precedent."; "provided that" creates a condition; quoting from treatise); Midam. Constr. Mgmt. v. MasTec N. Am., 436 F.3d 1257 (10th Cir. 2006) ("the Subcontract Agreement's failure to say all that it might have said is not enough to throw the intent of the contracting parties into doubt"), followed in BMD Contractors v. Fid. & Deposit Co. 679 F.3d 643 (7th Cir. 2012) (giving effect to pay-if-paid provision: "It is expressly agreed that owner's acceptance of subcontractor's work and payment to the contractor for the subcontractor's work are conditions precedent to the subcontractor's right to payments by the contractor."; "Although it's possible to reinforce the clarity of a pay-if-paid clause by using redundant language — e.g., 'in agreeing to this condition precedent, subcontractor assumes the risk of owner's insolvency' — additional language like this is not necessary if the meaning of the condition precedent is clear"); Mid-State Sur. Corp. v. Thrasher Eng'g, 575 F. Supp. 2d 731

(S.D.W. Va. 2008) ("Words such as 'provided that' and 'if,' when used to qualify a promise, are among the most commonly used expressions to create a condition precedent, but they are not the only words capable of doing so. . . . Thus, a condition precedent is more a matter of the intention of the parties than it is an issue of phrase or form."); Thedford Crossing v. Tyler Rose Nursery, 306 S.W.3d 860 (Tex. Civ. App. 2010) ("[W]hile certain terms such as 'if,' 'provided that,' 'on condition that,' or some other phrase ordinarily connote the parties' intent that there be a condition precedent, no particular words are necessary for the existence of such a condition.").

§8.2 n.7 p.416 Add the following at the end: *Cf.* Solar Applications Eng'g v. T.A. Operating Corp., 327 S.W.3d 104 (Tex. 2010) ("When no conditional language is used and another reasonable interpretation of the contract is possible, the terms will be construed as a covenant in order to avoid a forfeiture.") (internal quotes omitted).

§8.2 n.8 p.416 Add the following after the first sentence: This is sometimes called the *special funds doctrine*. *See* Jeschke v. Lamarr, 44 Cal. Rptr. 416 (Ct. App. 1965) (attorneys to be paid from proceeds of film, but film was never distributed and was a complete flop; attorneys therefore unable to collect fee because condition of payment did not occur), distinguished by Sunniland Fruit v. Verni, 284 Cal. Rptr. 824 (Ct. App. 1991) (loan for pre-harvest expenses, to be repaid from funds due the grower, did not create a special fund; "When the money claimed is an identifiable debt and there is no evidence establishing that the party advancing the monies assumed the risk inherent in the venture, identification of a particular pool of money as a source of payment does not limit or preclude recovery from other sources when the pool fails to materialize *unless* the agreement expressly so states."); Easton-Babcock & Assocs. v. Trivest, Inc., 983 So. 2d 595 (Fla. App. 2007) ("Easton-Babcock had an obligation to divide any development funds *which it received* to Trivest. The payment of development funds was thus a condition precedent of any division of money with Trivest.") (emphasis in original); Kaufmann v. Corp. Realty, 759 So. 2d 969 (La. App. 2000) ("The trial court did not err in dismissing Mrs. Kaufmann's suit, because she presented no

evidence that the buildings in fact generated the remaining funds to fulfill the conditional obligation to repay her advance. The right to enforce the obligation does not arise until the fulfillment of the . . . condition, and the obligation may not be enforced until the condition is met."); Young v. Wardley Corp., 182 P.3d 412 (Utah App. 2008) (selling broker agreed to pay agent part of the commission "after collection of such commissions"; "unless Wardley actually collects the commission amount from the seller, it has no obligation to pay Young her share of the commission.").

In the construction industry, a general contractor may make an unconditional promise to pay a subcontractor or only if the general contractor receives payment from the owner. If the owner's payment to the general contractor is clearly made a condition precedent to the obligation to the subcontractor, the courts will generally give effect to that provision. *See* Transtar Elec., Inc. v. A.E.M. Elec. Servs. Corp., 140 Ohio St. 3d 193, 200 (OH 2014) ("the term 'condition precedent' in the payment provision of a contract between a general contractor and a subcontractor clearly and unequivocally shows the intent of those parties to transfer the risk of the project owner's nonpayment from the general contractor to the subcontractor."); BMD Contrs., Inc. v. Fid. & Deposit Co. of Maryland, 679 F.3d 643, 650 (7th Cir.2012) ("provision means just what it says — that [the contractor's] duty to pay [the subcontractor] is expressly conditioned on its own receipt of payment — thus evincing the parties' unambiguous intent that each party assumes its own risk of loss if [the owner] becomes insolvent or otherwise defaults.").

This doctrine applies in somewhat diluted form when the federal government is the promisee. As a recent Supreme Court decision phrased it, "When a Government contractor is one of several persons to be paid out of a larger appropriation sufficient in itself to pay the contractor . . . the Government is responsible to the contractor for the full amount due under the contract, even if the agency exhausts the appropriation in service of other permissible ends." Salazar v. Ramah Navajo Chapter, 132 S. Ct. 2181, 2189 (2012). For the government contractor this qualifies as modified rapture. True, the government cannot stiff a contractor over and over, provided the agency appropriation could cover the government obligation. (Though one may imagine some practical difficulty in enforcing this right.) On the other hand, the

Court observed that this principle applies only to lump-sum appropriations; appropriations carrying legal restrictions may not be used for the purpose. It would thus be easy in principle for an agency never to pay a particular contractor because its appropriations were almost entirely subject to legal restrictions. So the special funds doctrine applies to the government as far as the funds appropriated are not marked for use elsewhere.

§8.2 n.9 p.416 Add the following to the list after **"Accord"***:* Westchester Fire Ins. Co. v. City of Brooksville, 731 F. Supp. 2d 1298 (M.D. Fla. 2010) (bonds required surety to pay city if developer failed to build infrastructure; court implied condition that development proceed before city could collect from surety, because the bonds were intended to make certain that new homes have access to city utilities, and bankruptcy of developer combined with collapse of Florida real estate market meant that no new homes would be built for several years), *aff'd*, 465 Fed. Appx. 851 (11th Cir. 2012), *aff'd*, 465 Fed. Appx. 851 (11th Cir. 2012).

§8.2 n.13 p.417 Add the following after the first sentence: *Accord:* Solymar Invs. v. Banco Santander, 672 F.3d 981 (11th Cir. 2012) ("[U]nder Florida law, whether a condition precedent is at issue is not relevant to contract formation," but rather is a defense of non-performance). *But see* Edelman Arts, Inc. v. Art Int'l (UK) Ltd., 841 F. Supp. 2d 810 (S.D.N.Y. 2012) ("New York law recognizes two types of conditions precedent: the first type 'describe[s] acts or events which must occur before a party is obliged to perform a promise made pursuant to an existing contract' and the second is a 'condition precedent to the formation or existence of the contract itself.' "), quoting from Oppenheimer & Co. v. Oppenheim, Appel, Dixon & Co. 660 N.E.2d 415 (N.Y. 1995); M W., Inc. v. Oak Park Mall, 234 P.3d 833 (Kan. App. 2010) ("Courts have recognized two types of conditions precedent: conditions precedent to *performance under an existing contract* and conditions precedent to the *formation of a contract*."; emphasis in original); Sharifi v. Steen Automotive, 370 S.W.3d 126 (Tex. Civ. App. 2012) ("A condition precedent may be either a condition to the formation of a contract or a condition to an obligation to perform an existing agreement."). The use of conditions to refer to

events that must occur before the parties to an agreement are bound is, as this opinion indicates, common, and shows no signs of abatement.

§8.2 n.13 p.417 Add the following at the end: For another use of the distinction, *see* Potter v. Patterson UTI Drilling Co., 234 P.3d 104 (N.M. App. 2010) (employment contract apparently made in New Mexico, but requiring that employee pass drug test at Pennsylvania work site before starting work; whether contract was formed in New Mexico or in Pennsylvania determined jurisdiction for workers' compensation claim; court held that contract formed in New Mexico when the parties manifested assent, and drug test was a condition subsequent, not a condition of formation).

***§8.2 n.19 p.419 Add the following to the list after* "See":** Nunez v. Simms, 341 F.3d 385 (5th Cir. 2003) ("condition subsequent is 'a condition referring to a future event upon the happening of which the obligation becomes no longer binding on the other party, if he chooses to avail himself of the condition' "); Capital City Ins. Co. v. Ringgold Timber Co., 898 So. 2d 680 (Miss. App. 2004) ("A contract that is conditioned to become void on a specified event is one subject to a condition subsequent."); Pointe Dev. v. Enterprise Bank & Trust, 316 S.W.3d 543 (Mo. App. 2010) (acknowledging, but not following, Restatement Second shift in vocabulary; "a condition subsequent presumes a valid contract, the performance of which is excused by the occurrence or non-occurrence of the condition"); Anna H. Cardone Revocable Trust v. Cardone, 8 A.3d 1 (N.H. 2010) (condition subsequent created in deed granting beneficiary ownership of condominium unless she used it as collateral or allowed a lien to be exercised against it).

§8.2 n.21 p.419 Add the following after the first sentence: *Accord:* Calce v. Dorado Exploration, 309 S.W.3d 719 (Tex. Civ. App. 2010) ("A party seeking to recover under a contract bears the burden of proving that all conditions precedent have been satisfied.").

§8.2 n.22 p.419 ***Add the following at the end:*** BJC Health Sys. v. Columbia Cas. Co., 478 F.3d 908 (8th Cir. 2007) ("defendants typically have the burden of proving the occurrence of conditions subsequent").

§8.2 n.23 p.419 ***Add the following at the end:*** *See also* BJC Health Sys. v. Columbia Cas. Co., *supra* note 22 (characterizing as condition subsequent a provision of an insurance policy that the insured had to maintain a particular incurred loss ratio in order to continue coverage, relying in particular on the perception that " 'subject to' language indicates a condition subsequent").

§8.2 n.24 p.420 ***Add the following to the list after "see":*** Capital City Ins. Co. v. Ringgold Timber Co., *supra* note 19 (characterizing notice requirement as condition subsequent).

§8.2 n.24 p.420 ***Add the following at the end:*** *Cf.* D & S Realty v. Markel Ins. Co., 789 N.W.2d 1 (Neb. 2010) (thorough treatment of conditions subsequent in insurance contracts).

A common source of conditions subsequent is the pre-employment drug test. Frequently this is characterized as a condition subsequent; the employment contract exists, but is terminated if the worker fails the test. *See* Potter v. Patterson UTI Drilling Co., 234 P.3d 104 (N.M. App. 2010). On the other hand, frequently this is characterized as a condition precedent; employment begins only if the worker passes the test. *See* Speer v. Sammons Trucking, 128 P.3d 984 (Kan. App. 2006). Courts trying to navigate these waters commonly ask when the parties manifested intent to be bound. This does a poor job of distinguishing one group from another, because both an agreement containing a condition precedent and an agreement containing a condition subsequent are contracts. It does a better job of distinguishing between agreements containing duties that may or may not arise — contracts with conditions — and agreements providing that some event must occur before the contract is formed. But conditions are by definition part of existing contracts; "conditions" to contract formation are better looked at as elements of the offer that must occur before acceptance. On the whole, the courts seem to reach reasonable results in these cases, so very possibly this topic contains more than its share of judicial reasoning backwards from a conclusion.

§8.2 n.27 p.421 Add the following to the list after* "See"*: Cedyco Corp. v. Petroquest Energy, 497 F.3d 485 (5th Cir. 2007) ("Confusion in terminology is somewhat common. . . . For this reason, perhaps the best approach is taken by the Restatement Second of Contracts . . ."); Flynn v. Hanna, 131 P.3d 844 (Or. App. 2006) ("This case illustrates the confusion generated by relying too heavily on labels such as 'condition precedent' and 'condition subsequent.' Indeed, the *Restatement (Second) of Contracts* has jettisoned the distinction . . ."; clause making transaction subject to securing the approval of an attorney).

§8.2 n.28 p.421 Add the following to the list in the second sentence: Corbin, Conditions in the Law of Contract, 28 Yale L.J. 739 (1919) ("The practice is almost universal of using these terms to describe the legal operation of some fact without mentioning or even clearly considering the particular legal relation to which the fact is being related in time. The result is most distressing; it leaves the reader confused and doubtful and it is a cause of conflict in decision, uncertainty of law, and actual injustice. In one case a fact will be called a condition precedent and in another case the same fact (or its nonexistence) will be called a condition subsequent, because in the first case it is being subconsciously related to the legal relations that follow it and in the other case to the legal relations that preceded it.").

§8.2 n.28 p.421 Add the following to the list in the fourth sentence: ; Potter v. Patterson UTI Drilling Co., 234 P.3d 104 (N.M. App. 2010) (referring to Restatement Second's abandonment of the term and noting the difficulty of distinguishing a condition precedent from a condition subsequent, but then using the older terminology).

§8.3 EFFECTS OF NONOCCURRENCE OF A CONDITION

§8.3 n.11 p.423 Add the following to the list after **"Accord"***:* Roberts v. Clark, 188 S.W.3d 204 (Tex. Civ. App. 2002) (payment due by May 1, but not available until May 2; alternative basis was that sellers demanded payment before they would sign deed and financers wanted the deed signed before they would advance funds).

§8.3 n.12 p.424 Add the following at the end of the first paragraph: *Cf.* Sun Secured Fin. v. ARCS Comm'l Mortg., 730 F. Supp. 2d 132 (D.D.C. 2010) (noting "some support for the proposition that notice provisions are generally understood to be conditions precedent to the exercise of power about which notice is being given").

§8.3 n.12 p.424 Add the following after the second paragraph: Warranties in insurance policies ordinarily must be complied with strictly. *See* Trishan Air v. Federal Ins. Co., 635 F.3d 422 (9th Cir. 2011) (incomplete training of co-pilot breached warranty in policy, so no coverage even if lack of training irrelevant to whether accident occurred). Courts have described these warranties in terms of conditions — that is, that "compliance with the terms of a warranty is a condition precedent to a right of recovery." Chase v. Nat'l Indem. Co., 278 P.2d 68 (Ct. App. 1954). The harshness of this rule is mitigated somewhat by its limited scope. The courts have drawn distinctions between warranties that go to basic coverage and warranties that go to the fundamental risk insured; the former may be subject to a substantial performance test, but the latter are, like ordinary conditions, subject to strict performance. *See* §8.3 n.13 & §§8.4-8.7 *infra*.

§8.3 n.18 p.427 Add the following at the end: *Cf.* Shaffer v. Bellows, 260 P.3d 1064 (Alaska 2011) (contract for sale of island effective only if the grantor decides to sell the property and the former owner chooses to go forward with the transaction).

§8.3 n.24 p.428 Add the following after the citation to **Ross***:* , followed in Colo. Structures v. Ins. Co. of the W., 106 P.3d 815 (Wash. App. 2005) ("When a contract provision is both a condition and a promise, the remedies available for its breach vary by whether the breach is 'material.' If the breach is 'material,' the promisee has an election: He or she may treat the breach as a failure of a condition that excuses further performance, and thus terminate the contract; or, he or she may waive the condition and allow performance to continue. Regardless of whether the breach is 'material,' the promisee can recover damages."). *Cf.* McArthur v. State Farm Mut. Auto. Ins. Co., 274 P.3d 981 (Utah 2012) (thorough treatment of differences between conditions and promises).

§8.4 INTERPRETATION AND CONDITIONS

§8.4 n.2 p.430 Add the following at the end: As with contract interpretation generally, determining whether a particular term is a condition or a promise "can be a mixed question of fact and law or simply a question of law," depending on whether there are disputes over material facts). Hatheway Farms Ass'n v. Hatheway Farms of Suffield, 43 A.3d 175 (Conn. App. 2012). *Accord:* Weisel v. Beaver Springs Owners Ass'n, 272 P.3d 491 (Idaho 2012) (determining whether a provision in a contract is a condition: "If the language is plain and unambiguous, interpretation is a matter of law, and this Court will give the contract as a whole its plain meaning. If the parties' intent cannot be determined from a contract's plain language, interpretation of the contract is a question of fact.") (citation omitted).

§8.4 n.9 p.431 In the second paragraph, add the following to the list after **"See"***:* Bestform, Inc. v. Herman, 804 N.Y.S.2d 80 (App. Div. 2005) (provision that buyer's "payment obligation . . . be 'conditioned upon' a confirmation by the buyer of plaintiff's merchandise that the goods shipped 'conform' to the buyer's purchase orders" "not subject to an express condition precedent," as it "neither stated that such compliance was required nor set forth the consequences of noncompliance"; moreover, doing this would "avoid a result that was absurd, commercially unreasonable and contrary to the reasonable expectations of the parties").

§8.4 n.12 p.432 Add the following to the list after **"Accord"***:* New York Bronze Powder Co. v. Benjamin Acquisition Corp., 716 A.2d 230 (Md. 1998) (applying "preferred construction" and holding that language "creates a covenant or contractual duty" rather than a condition); Mid-State Sur. Corp. v. Thrasher Eng'g, 575 F. Supp. 2d 731 (S.D. W. Va. 2008) ("When West Virginia courts recognize an implied provision in a contract, they may interpret it as either a condition or a covenant, but must choose the least burdensome of the two where both would effectuate the intent of the parties."); Mullany v. Munchkin Enters., 893 N.Y.S.2d 714 (App. Div. 2010) ("[A] contractual duty ordinarily will not be construed as a condition precedent absent clear language showing that the parties intended to make it a condition."); Boro Constr. v. Ridley Sch. Dist., 992 A.2d 208 (Pa. Commw. 2010) ("an event or act enumerated in a contract will not be construed as a condition precedent unless it clearly appears to have been the parties' intention").

§8.4 n.12 p.432 Add the following after the second sentence: *Cf.* Mumblow v. Monroe Broad., 401 F.3d 616 (5th Cir. 2005) ("Louisiana courts do not infer [conditions precedent] without very strong proof. . . . Indeed, they do so only when the express language of the contract 'compels' such a construction.").

§8.4 n.12 p.432 Add the following to the list after **"But cf."***:* Dinnerware Plus Holdings v. Silverthorne Factory Stores, 128 P.3d 245 (Colo. App. 2004) ("Provided all other retail tenants . . . are similarly obligated" construed as condition; effect is not forfeiture, but rather temporary inability to recover pass-through charges for lease); BSA 77 P St. v. Hawkins, 983 A.2d 988 (D.C. 2009) (presumption against condition weaker where the condition "was an event outside the parties' control"); Dove v. Rose Acre Farms, 434 N.E.2d 931 (Ind. App. 1982) (substantial performance not applicable to bonus agreement where employee knew employer's "strict policies and knew that any absence for any cause whatever worked a forfeiture of the bonus").

§8.4 n.24 p.435 Add the following after the first ***sentence:*** *Accord:* Edelman Arts, Inc. v. Art Int'l (UK) Ltd., 841 F. Supp. 2d 810 (S.D.N.Y. 2012) (bill of sale held inoperative until

funds received; the party proposing this term risked non-completion of the contract, so "the general interpretive preference against a condition precedent carries less weight"); Yost v. State Div. of Corps., Bus. & Prof'l Licensing, 234 P.3d 1264 (Alaska 2010) (invoking §227 to find rule favoring promise over condition inapplicable when the event constituting the condition was within the hands of one party); Perkins v. Cedar Mountain Sewer Improv. Dist., 199 S.W.3d 667 (Ark. 2004) (invoking §227 to find language in engineer's contract with improvement district a promise rather than a condition; otherwise, failure to construct the project would mean forfeiture by the engineer); Dinnerware Plus Holdings v. Silverthorne Factory Stores, *supra* note 12 (invoking §227 to find language conditional).

§8.4 n.29 p.437 Add the following at the end: , distinguished in Hugh O'Kane Elec. Co. v. Mastec N. Am., 797 N.Y.S.2d 45 (App. Div. 2005) ("the prohibition against pay-when-paid provisions is not a deeply rooted tradition of this state," so a Florida provision of this sort is enforceable in New York courts) and in turn affirmed in Welsbach Elec. Corp. v. MasTec N. Am., 859 N.E.2d 498 (N.Y. 2006) ("[W]e cannot say [pay-if-paid clauses] are 'truly obnoxious' so as to void the parties' choice of law."); Lehrer McGovern Bovis, Inc. v. Bullock Insulation, 197 P.3d 1032 (Nev. 2008) ("Because a pay-if-paid provision limits a subcontractor's ability to be paid for work already performed, such a provision impairs the subcontractor's statutory right to place a mechanic's lien on the construction project. . . . Therefore, we conclude that pay-if-paid provisions are unenforceable because they violate public policy."). *But see* BMD Contrs. v. Fid. & Deposit Co. 679 F.3d 643 (7th Cir. 2012) (Indiana law: pay-if-paid clauses do not violate state statutes and thus are not void as against public policy); Galloway Corp. v. S.B. Ballard Constr. Co., 464 S.E.2d 349 (Va. 1995) (upholding validity of pay-when-paid provision as condition precedent to payment). California, Nevada, and New York appear to be the only states to have voided pay-if-paid clauses as against public policy. Carney & Cizek, Payment Provisions in Construction Contracts and Construction Trust Fund Statutes: A Fifty-State Survey, Constr. Law, Fall 2004, at 5. Some jurisdictions have enacted statutes making unenforceable agreements that place the risk of non-payment by the owner on the subcontractor. Nev. Rev. Stat. §§624.624-.626; N.C. Gen. Stat. §22C-2; Wis. Stat. Ann. §779.135(1), (3).

§8.4 p.437 Add the following at the end of the third sentence: . . . sometimes a *pay-if-paid* provision.)[29a]

[29a] For a useful analysis of the difference, *see* Midam. Constr. Mgmt. v. MasTec N. Am., 436 F.3d 1257 (10th Cir. 2006).

***§8.4 n.30 p.437 Add the following to the list after* "Contra":** BMD Contractors v. Fid. & Deposit Co. 679 F.3d 643 (7th Cir. 2012) (language of condition precedent sufficient to create a pay-if-paid clause); Sloan & Co. v. Liberty Mut. Ins. Co., 653 F.3d 175 (3d Cir. 2011) ("Pennsylvania courts . . . construe clauses that condition payment to the subcontractor on the general contractor's receipt of payment from the owner as pay-if-paid clauses."); FaulknerUSA, LP, v. Alaron Supply Co., 322 S.W.3d 357 (Tex. Civ. App. 2010) ("Although . . . we should be hesitant to find a condition precedent in a construction contract, we cannot turn a blind eye when, as here, the provision is an express condition precedent"; provision was captioned "condition precedent," first sentence stated that payment by the owner is a condition precedent to payment to the subcontractor, clause states that "Subcontractor expressly assumes the risk of nonpayment by Owner," and ends with "This provision establishes a condition precedent, and it shall not be construed merely as a Time of Payment Clause."); Wellington Power Corp. v. CNA Sur. Corp., 614 S.E.2d 680 (W. Va. 2005) ("in a public construction project, a pay-if-paid condition precedent clause in a contract between a subcontractor and a contractor does not violate the public policy of this State").

§8.4 n.30 p.437 Add the following at the end: *See generally* Comment, Contracting Away an Honest Day's Pay: An Examination of Conditional Payment Clauses in Construction Contracts, 58 Ark. L. Rev. 353 (2005).

***§8.4 n.32 p.438 Add the following to the list after* "Accord":** Midam. Constr. Mgmt. v. MasTec N. Am., *supra* note 29a ("provided that, all payments to Subcontractor by Contractor are expressly contingent upon and subject to receipt of payment for the Work by Contractor from Owner"); Everett Painting Co. v. Padula & Wadsworth Constr., 856 So. 2d 1059 (Fla. App. 2003) (language of condition "is clear and unambiguous"); J.J. Shane, Inc. v. Aetna Cas. & Sur. Co., 723 So. 2d 302 (Fla. App. 1998) (language sufficient to "plainly and unambiguously make payment . . . a condition precedent"); Evans, Mechwart, Hambleton & Tilton, Inc. v. Triad Architects, 965 N.E.2d 1007 (Ohio App. 2011) ("If a payment provision fails to unequivocally evince an intent to create a condition precedent or shift the risk of the owner's nonpayment, then the majority of courts . . . will interpret the provision as a pay-when-paid, and not a pay-if-paid, provision."; collecting cases).

§8.4 n.32 p.438 Add the following after the citation to **Galloway Corp.:** , distinguished in Universal Concrete Prods. v. Turner Constr. Co., 595 F.3d 527 (4th Cir. 2010) (finding no ambiguity in clause stating that "The obligation of Turner to make a payment under this agreement, whether a progress or final payment, or for extras or change orders or delays to the Work, is subject to the express condition precedent of payment therefor by the Owner.").

§8.4 n.34 p.438 Add the following after the first sentence: Accord: Springs & Davenport, Inc. v. AAG, Inc., 683 S.E.2d 814 (S.C. App. 2009) (later agreement in pay-if-paid form did not supersede an agreement whose conditions were satisfied, so brokerage fee was already due; language that fee "shall be paid . . . 10% of all principal payments made by [buyer]" not clear enough to be a pay-if-paid clause). The court went on to suggest that the defendant "could have used language stating no commission was due unless payment was made by [the buyer]." 683 S.E.2d at 817.

§8.4 n.34 p.438 Add the following at the end: But the analogy to construction contracts may fall apart when we reach sales of goods. Calpine Producer Servs. v. Wiser Oil Co., 169 S.W.3d 783 (Tex. Civ. App. 2005) (enforcing clause setting payment date as "within five (5) business days of the date it receives payment from its customers"; distinguishing construction cases as depending

upon industry expectations of who bears the risk of non-payment by the owner, which was not the case here).

§8.4 n.35 p.439 Add the following to the list in the third sentence: Sloan & Co. v. Liberty Mut. Ins. Co., 653 F.3d 175 (3d Cir. 2011) ("When certainty is lacking . . . Pennsylvania courts tend to interpret payment provisions as pay-when-paid clauses.").

§8.4 n.42 p.441 Add the following to the list after **"Accord"*:*** RUS, Inc. v. Bay Indus., 322 F. Supp. 2d 302 (S.D.N.Y. 2003) (buyer to be "reasonably satisfied" with the results of an environmental assessment of property owned by subsidiary to be purchased), followed in Rohn Indus. v. Platinum Equity LLC, 911 A.2d 379 (Del. 2006) (New York has adopted Restatement Second §228; question "is whether it is possible to determine objectively whether a reasonable person in [the promisee's] position would have been satisfied by the protections against asbestos-related liability, as distinguished from whether [the promisor] itself in good faith concluded the protections were unnecessary"); Pearse Assocs. v. Perry, 960 A.2d 1166 (Me. 2008) ("When an obligor's duty to perform is conditioned on his or her satisfaction with respect to an act, the standard to be employed in determining if the condition was met is generally that of an objectively reasonable person.").

§8.4 n.43 p.441 Add the following after the second sentence: *Accord:* Flood v. ClearOne Comm'ns, 618 F.3d 1110 (10th Cir. 2010) (where firm had discretion whether to advance fees, "it bore a duty to do so only in good faith" and thus " 'the contract is not unenforceable *ab initio* for lack of mutuality of consideration.' ") (quoting from Res. Mgmt. Co. v. Weston Ranch & Livestock Co., 706 P.2d 1028, 1037 (Utah 1985)).

§8.4 n.44 p.441 Add the following after the citation to **Greenwood*:*** , distinguished in Christie's Inc. v. SWCA, Inc., 867 N.Y.S.2d 650 (Sup. 2008) (authenticity of Picasso sculpture; contract in *Greenwood* provided for "sole discretion," whereas here the contract conditioned approval upon "reasonable belief" and thus called for an objective test).

§8.4 n.44 p.441 Add the following to the list after **"Accord"***:* Sweet v. TCI MS, Inc., 47 So. 3d 89 (Miss. 2010) (buyer's obligations conditional upon its satisfaction; the provision "unambiguously sets forth that [buyer's] contractual obligations are contingent upon [buyer's] obtaining financing satisfactory to *it.* [The buyer] need only exercise good faith."); Sentco Constr. Co. v. Ross Grp. Constr. Corp., 172 P.3d 241 (Okla. Civ. App. 2007) ("[W]hen performance of a subcontract is contingent upon the approval of the contractor or owner, the contractor or owner's dissatisfaction must be based upon an honest, good faith reason, and there is no requirement to act as a reasonable person would have acted under the same or similar circumstances.").

§8.4 n.44 p.441 In the second paragraph, add the following to the list after **"See generally"***:* Kraus & Scott, Contract Design and the Structure of Contractual Intent, 84 N.Y.U. L. Rev. 1023 (2009).

§8.4 n.46 p.442 In the second paragraph, add the following after the citation to **Columbia Christian College***:* followed by Flynn v. Hanna, 131 P.3d 844 (Or. App. 2006) ("[W]e will not examine the true motives of a party who exercises rights under a contract in order to escape its legal obligations. . . . Even assuming that their motivation for [seeking their attorney's review] was the hope that their attorney would disapprove the agreement, their act ofseeking review was not a violation of their duty of good faith, because it was expressly permitted.").

§8.4 n.49 p.443 Add the following at the end: For an analysis of *Morin* based in formal logic, *see* Brewer, Satisfaction and Posner's *Morin* Opinion: *Aliquando Bonus Dormitat Posnerus?*, 120 Harv. L. Rev. 1123 (2007).

§8.4 n.55 p.444 In the first paragraph, add the following to the list after **"Accord"***:* Harbor Park Mkt. v. Gronda, 743 N.W.2d 585 (Mich. App. 2007) (agreement giving attorney complete discretion whether to approve sales contract did not prevent sellers from submitting other offers to attorney before he decided on the first one).

§8.4 n.55 p.444 Add the following at the end of the first paragraph: This reading may be more flexible still when the third party is an attorney, because close examination of the attorney's decisionmaking might require interfering with the attorney-client relation. Accordingly, even a loose duty of good faith may not constrain an attorney in this setting. Moran v. Erk, 901 N.E.2d 187 (N.Y. 2008) ("[W]here a real estate contract contains an attorney approval contingency providing that the contract is 'subject to' or 'contingent upon' attorney approval within a specified time period and no further limitations on approval appear in the contract's language, an attorney for either party may timely disapprove the contract for any reason or for no stated reason."). Presumably this latitude does not encompass unlawful reasons.

§8.4 n.56 p.445 In the first paragraph, add the following after the second sentence: *Accord:* Town of Plainfield v. Paden Eng'g Co., 943 N.E.2d 904 (Ind. App. 2011) ("An owner who fails to give contractually-required notice, upon receipt of a proper architect's certificate, may not rightfully rescind the contract and take charge of the work;" town's failure to procure an architect's certificate meant that it could not terminate its contract with a general contractor).

§8.5 EXCUSE OF CONDITION BY WAIVER

§8.5 n.2 p.447 Add the following at the beginning: Hovnanian Land Inv. Grp. v. Annapolis Towne Ctr., 25 A.3d 967 (Md. 2011) ("our case law does require mutual knowledge and acceptance, whether implicit or explicit, of the non-conforming action").

§8.5 n.3 p.447 Add the following after the first sentence: *Accord:* Crabby's, Inc. v. Hamilton, 244 S.W.3d 209 (Mo. App. 2008) (real estate contract with term making contract contingent upon the buyer obtaining financing; "Because such conditions are meant to protect the buyer, they are a condition of the buyer's duty, but not a condition of the seller's duty under the contract."); Burgess v. N. Bend Sch. Dist., 173 P.3d 1271 (Or. App. 2007) (requirement that buyer apply for loan within ten days of entering into the contract

if it needed to borrow was for the buyer's benefit; buyer was not required to obtain financing, and clause itself states that it is solely for the buyer's benefit).

§8.5 n.3 p.447 Add the following at the end: *Cf.* Hovnanian Land Inv. Grp. v. Annapolis Towne Ctr., 25 A.3d 967 (Md. 2011) ("a condition precedent usually benefits *one* of the two parties, and the benefited party's actions will weigh more heavily"); McGill v. Moore, 672 S.E.2d 571 (S.C. 2009) (requirement in land purchase contract that all owners sign before the closing occurs cannot be waived by the buyer; the clause also served the sellers' purpose of transferring all rights or none).

§8.5 n.4 p.447 Add the following at the beginning: Anderson Property Mgmt. v. H. Anthony Miller, Jr., LLC, 943 N.E.2d 1286 (Ind. App. 2011) (settlement agreement regarding division of property stated that "[t]he parties presume that existing building . . . except 3' encroachment, is located on Defendant's property as verified by survey," but survey showed that the building encroached by as much as 7.3 feet; because the presumption was by both parties, "the terms of their agreement were *contingent* on that presumption" and so both parties needed to waive the condition in order for the duties to arise).

§8.5 n.6 p.447 Add the following at the beginning: Dynamic Mach. Works v. Mach. & Elec. Consultants, 831 N.E.2d 875 (Mass. 2005) (quoting this treatise).

***§8.5 n.12 p.449 In the first paragraph, add the following to the list after* "Accord":** Jet Asphalt & Rock Co. v. Angelo Iafrate Constr., 431 F.3d 613 (8th Cir. 2005) ("a party may waive a breach of a condition set forth in a written contract by permitting the other party to proceed with performance of the contract after discovering the apparent breach"); Dayton Dev. Co. v. Gilman Fin. Servs., 419 F.3d 852 (8th Cir. 2005) (continued performance despite lack of notice operates "as a voluntary waiver of that contract term, rather than a 'modification' of the contract"); Carraway Methodist Health Sys. v. Wise, 986 So. 2d 387 (Ala. 2007) (condition that contract would not be replaced by newer contract until written notice given of termination of old contract;

performance in accord with new contract amounts to waiver of condition); Carr-Gottstein Foods Co. v. Wasilla, LLC, 182 P.3d 1131 (Alaska 2008) (relocation of store violated lease, but landlord assisted tenant in making the move; "This combination of acquiescence and assistance in the relocation, consciously declining to declare a breach, even upon request, and prejudice" results in waiver of right to claim a breach); Cinel v. Barna, 142 Cal. Rptr. 3d 329 (Ct. App. 2012) (party to arbitration that was terminated for non-payment of fees waived right to reopen arbitration); Bland v. Green Acres Grp., 12 So. 3d 822 (Fla. App. 2009) ("[A] party may waive a right to arbitrate after suit has been filed by actively participating in the suit."; entry of default sufficient), distinguished by Price v. Fax Recovery Sys., 49 So. 3d 835 (Fla. App. 2010) (answer and counterclaim did not waive arbitration where they asserted arbitration as an affirmative defense); Ball v. Maynard, 645 S.E.2d 890 (N.C. App. 2007) (closing date waived by vendor's continued attempts to effect performance); Citizens Nat'l Bank v. Bryce, 271 S.W.3d 347 (Tex. App. 2008) ("A party implicitly waives its arbitration rights when it substantially invokes the judicial process to the other party's detriment or prejudice.").

§8.5 n.12 p.449 Add the following at the end of the first paragraph: *Cf.* RUS, Inc. v. Bay Indus., 322 F. Supp. 2d 302 (S.D.N.Y. 2003) (treating waiver as modification and then rejecting the modification because of a no-oral-modifications clause, not discussing whether the NOM clause could itself be waived). However, performance while awaiting an act by a third party that would satisfy the condition does not constitute waiver, because those acts are consistent with an intent to perform only if the condition occurs. Demeritt v. Springsteed, 693 S.E.2d 719 (N.C. App. 2010) (where condition was approval of project by planning board, potential buyer's acts to secure approval and assurances that he intended to go through with the deal did not waive the condition, but rather were acts "in accordance with the written agreement").

§8.5 n.12 p.449 In the second paragraph, add the following after the first sentence: *Accord:* Hovnanian Land Inv. Grp. v. Annapolis Towne Ctr., 25 A.3d 967 (Md. 2011) ("Given the highly factual nature of the waiver inquiry, it is an uncommon case in which the issue can be resolved by summary judgment. . . . Occasionally, however, the waiver is so obvious that a ruling can be made as a matter of law."); Valspar Refinish v. Gaylord's, Inc., 764 N.W.2d 359 (Minn. 2009) ("Waiver generally is a question of fact, and '[i]t is rarely to be inferred as a matter of law.' ") (quoting from Farnum v. Peterson-Biddick Co., 234 N.W. 646, 647 (Minn. 1931)).

§8.5 n.12 p.449 In the second paragraph, add the following to the list after " **But see**"*:* Hugh O'Kane Elec. Co. v. MasTec N. Am., 797 N.Y.S.2d 45 (App. Div. 2005) (fact issue on estoppel raised "by evidence that . . . the general contractor . . . represented that the owner had the money to pay, although the owner was then in default of certain loans extended to the general contractor" but does not raise "an issue of fact as to waiver").

§8.5 n.12 p.449 Add the following at the end: Unlike course of performance, however, most jurisdictions require that waiver be specially pleaded. *See* Town of Stratford v. A. Secondino & Son, Inc., 38 A.3d 179 (Conn. App. 2012) (stating general principle, though finding exception where the pleadings contained the factual allegations needed to establish waiver).

§8.5 n.14 p.449 Add the following at the end: The increasing frequency of anti-waiver clauses has predictably led to litigation invoking their ability to prevent waiver of conditions. This argument has just as predictably led to the common failure of these clauses to prevent waiver; after all, as has often been observed, if any term in a contract can be waived, then anti-waiver clauses may themselves be waived. As one court has observed in the course of disregarding an anti-waiver clause, "[T]he freedom to contract is not limited to the contract as written. Instead, the freedom to contract includes the freedom to alter that contract." Hovnanian Land Inv. Grp. v. Annapolis Towne Ctr., 25 A.3d 967, 983 (Md. 2011). These clauses are not meaningless, though, because a party alleging waiver must establish not only waiver of the pertinent contract term but also waiver of the anti-waiver clause. *See* §7.6a *supra* (significance of anti-waiver clauses).

§8.5 n.16 p.450 Add the following to the list after **"Accord"***:* Richmond v. EBI, Inc., 53 So. 3d 859 (Miss. App. 2011) ("Although modification of an agreement that falls under

the statute of frauds must be in writing, a waiver is not required to be in writing"; consequently, waiver by holder of right of first refusal effective even though created by adamant refusal to meet the offered terms).

§8.5 n.16 p.450 Add the following to the end of the final sentence: Royster-Clark, Inc. v. Olsen's Mill, 714 N.W.2d 530 (Wis. 2006) (whether attempt at modification waives statute of frauds "closely related to the inquiry to determine whether there was a valid oral modification").

*§8.5 n.20 p.450 In the first paragraph add the following to the list after "**Cf.**":* Moe v. John Deere Co., 516 N.W.2d 332 (S.D. 1994) ("majority of states" . . . adhere to the general rule that "a secured party who has . . . accepted late payments as a matter of course," must before declaring default and repossessing, "give notice to the debtor . . . that strict compliance . . . will be demanded").

§8.5 n.20 p.450 Add the following at the end of the first paragraph: In contrast, a modification becomes part of the original contract and thus cannot be retracted without the assent of the other party. Dynamic Mach. Works v. Mach. & Elec. Consultants, *supra* note 6.

*§8.5 n.27 p.452 Add the following to the list after "**Accord**":* Mobile Airport Auth. v. Health STRATEGIES, 886 So. 2d 773 (Ala. 2004) (receipt of premiums and correspondence with the insured waives condition that insured must submit medical forms before coverage would take effect); McGraw v. Marchioli, 812 N.E.2d 1154 (Ind. App. 2004) (quoting this section of this treatise). Similarly, Pinnacle Props. Dev. Grp., LLC v. Daily, 59 N.E.3d 1101 (Ind. 2016) involved a lease that required written notice of damage to the property, but the landlord also provided an emergency telephone number and represented that it would respond to repeated instances of flooding. The court found that the landlord was "equitably estopped from asserting lack of written notice as a defense to its breach of the Lease" and further commented that it "can hardly imagine a more appropriate application of the equitable estoppel doctrine."

§8.5 n.28 p.452 In the second sentence of the first paragraph, add the following after the citation to* Lee*: , followed in Falkner v. Colony Woods Homes Ass'n, 198 P.3d 152 (Kan. App. 2008) ("Could the [Architectural Control Committee] withdraw and nullify its implied waiver of the condition to submit a timely approval request form? Yes, if promptly done, but not, as here, after the Falkners had relied on ACC's invitation to submit a tardy approval request form.").

§8.6 EXCUSE OF CONDITION BY BREACH

§8.6 n.3 p.454 Add the following to the list after* "Accord"*: Aarow Equip. & Servs. v. Travelers Cas. & Sur. Co., 417 Fed. Appx. 366 (4th Cir. 2011) ("Under the prevention doctrine, when a general contractor materially contributes to the failure of a condition limiting the duty to perform under a contract, the general contractor may not rely on that failure as a defense to its performance of its contractual obligations"; contractor instructed subcontractor to perform work without a change order and to bill for the work under fictitious headings, perhaps as a result of which government refused to pay contractor (and thus that contractor's surety refused to pay subcontractor because of a "pay-if-paid" clause in the contract between the contractor and the subcontractor)); Davis v. Key Gas Corp., 124 P.3d 96 (Kan. App. 2005) ("A party may not raise nonperformance of a condition as a bar to liability where its own action is the cause of the nonperformance."); Gupton v. Son-Lan Dev. Co., 695 S.E.2d 763 (N.C. App. 2010) ("[W]hen a party, whose obligation it is to fulfill a condition precedent contained in a contract, clearly repudiates his obligation to act in good faith and ensure that reasonable efforts are taken to fulfill the condition, the other party acquires rights under the contract and may sue to enforce those rights."); Orbisonia-Rockhill Joint Mun. Auth. v. Cromwell Township, 978 A.2d 425 (Pa. Commw. 2009) (township appealed state approval of its own water treatment plan, which was a condition to a contract with a water authority; "Township cannot claim that there was no Department approval when, in fact, there was tentative approval and it was only rescinded because of Township's appeal.").

§8.6 n.3 p.454 In the second sentence, add the following before **"159 F.2d 105":** Vanadium Corp. v. Fidelity & Deposit Corp.

§8.6 n.3 p.454 Add the following after the second sentence: Cf. RUS, Inc. v. Bay Indus., 322 F. Supp. 2d 302 (S.D.N.Y. 2003) ("actions that contributed to [the] non-occurrence" of a condition "will not constitute a breach of the party's duty of good faith . . . unless it has acted in a way that defeats the 'reasonable expectations' held by the parties when they entered into the contract.").

§8.6 n.3 p.454 Add the following after the third sentence: This principle is tested in Rockford Mut. Ins. Co. v. Pirtle, 911 N.E.2d 60 (Ind. App. 2009). There the insured claimed replacement value for a building destroyed by fire. The policy required that the repair or replacement be finished before the insurer would pay more than the actual cash value of the building. The insured neither repaired nor replaced the building but nevertheless sought the full replacement value, arguing that the insurer's delay in tendering the cash value made the replacement impossible. The court agreed, stating that "equitable principles win the day in this situation; otherwise, the repair or replacement endorsement paid for by Pirtle would be rendered illusory. Rockford had the ability to advance sums of money under that endorsement to assist in commencement of the rebuilding, and could have joined Pirtle in agreements entered into for repairs." The court's invocation of equity seems both dangerous and unnecessary; dangerous because it introduces uncertainty in a part of contract law characterized by fairly bright lines, and unnecessary because it should have been easy for Pirtle to show that he was unable to begin the repairs while the insurer dallied, and that it was impossible to do so by the time they delivered. The court's argument that the insurer could have done more to assist in the rebuilding is correct, but is also beside the point; the insured could have secured insurance that provided for that added degree of cooperation, but did not.

§8.6 n.5 p.455 Add the following after the first sentence: Cf. Semi-Tech Litigation v. Bankers Trust Co. (*In re* Bankers Trust Co.), 450 F.3d 121 (2d Cir. 2006) ("Because [the defendant] had a

duty . . . to examine the certificates, its failure to do so cannot excuse its failure to comply with the duty . . . to take action with respect to known defaults.").

§8.6 n.6 p.455 Add the following to the list after **"Accord":** Gen. Injectables & Vaccines v. Gates, 519 F.3d 1360 (Fed. Cir. 2008) (failure of condition that vaccine be approved by FDA excused because the lack of approval was caused by the vaccine's contamination; "failure of the 'condition precedent' was simply a consequence of that failure to perform"); *In re* Estate of Drake, 4 A.3d 450 (D.C. 2010) (failure of condition of settlement agreement that trustees obtain release of tax liens excused because trustees had not done so ten years after the settlement, with no attempts whatever made for the last four years); Dengler v. Hazel Blessinger Family Trust, 106 P.3d 449 (Idaho 2005) ("Where a party has control over the happening of a condition precedent he must make a reasonable effort to cause the condition to happen."); Ind. State Highway Comm'n v. Curtis, 704 N.E.2d 1015 (Ind. 1998) (clause in settlement agreement making provisions subject to approval by governor and Department of Transportation governed by duty of good faith, but obligation is only "to consider that approval in good faith").

§8.6 n.8 p.456 In the first paragraph, add the following to the list after **"Accord":** M W., Inc. v. Oak Park Mall, 234 P.3d 833 (Kan. App. 2010) (citing to treatise; "good-faith effort" along with "an implied condition on both parties to cooperate with each other in obtaining the goals of the contract").

§8.6 n.9 p.456 Add the following after the citation to **District-Realty Title Ins.:** , followed in King & King, Chartered v. Harbert Int'l, 436 F. Supp. 2d 3 (D.D.C. 2006) ("[I]f the contract explicitly or implicitly permits the promisor to take some action, and that action, in turn, prevents or hinders the occurrence of some condition precedent to the promisor's performance obligation, then the failure to meet that obligation will *not* constitute breach."; client thus allowed to discontinue pursuit of claim without liability to attorney under contingent fee agreement).

§8.6 n.9 p.456 Add the following to the list after **"Accord"*:*** Gilbert v. Nationwide Mut. Ins. Co., 275 S.W.3d 690 (Ky. 2009) (where subrogation clause in insurance policy required insured to "do nothing to prejudice" insurer's rights, no obligation on insured's part to act on insurer's behalf; thus, insured's "mere failure to [bring suit] within the limitations period cannot . . . be deemed a contract violation barring her recovery of collision benefits").

§8.6 n.12 p.457 Add the following after the citation to **Amies*:*** , distinguished in Semi-Tech Litigation v. Bankers Trust Co. (*In re* Bankers Trust Co.), *supra* note 5 (in *Amies* there was no promise "to take steps to enforce the . . . performance," so active frustration of the condition precedent would be necessary to excuse the condition; had there been a promise, failure to act would also suffice).

§8.6 n.14 p.458 In the first paragraph, add the following to the list after **"Accord"*:*** Boro Constr. v. Ridley Sch. Dist., 992 A.2d 208 (Pa. Commw. 2010) ("[A]n anticipatory repudiation by an obligor will discharge an obligee's duty to perform a condition precedent." (though note the unfortunate use of *duty* to refer to the performance of a condition)).

§8.6 n.16 p.458 Add the following to the list after **"Accord"*:*** Semi-Tech Litigation v. Bankers Trust Co. (*In re* Bankers Trust Co.), *supra* note 5 (requiring that the plaintiff show "that [the defendant's] breach of its duty . . . was a cause-in-fact of plaintiff's losses"); *In re* Estate of Drake, 4 A.3d 450 (D.C. 2010) (referring to Restatement Second §245; not necessary to show but-for causation, but rather only that the non-occurrence be "fairly attributable to the promisor's own conduct"); M W., Inc. v. Oak Park Mall, 234 P.3d 833 (Kan. App. 2010) (following Restatement Second §245); D & S Realty v. Markel Ins. Co., 816 N.W.2d 1 (Neb. 2012) ("The doctrine of prevention does not require proof that the condition would have occurred 'but for' the wrongful conduct of the promisor, but requires only that the promisor's conduct contributed materially to the nonoccurrence of the condition."); Flynn v. Hanna, 131 P.3d 844 (Or. App. 2006) (applying §255; the defendants' "allegedly repudiating actions did not directly or indirectly cause their attorney to disapprove the agreement and, thus, did not cause the condition to fail").

§8.6 n.17 p.459 Add the following at the end: The burden of proof in prevention cases can be the source of dispute. Naturally, the breached-against party must prove that the promisor did not perform its contractual duties. If those duties are subject to a condition, then the breached-against party must prove that the condition is no obstacle to enforcement. *See* §8.2 *supra* note 21. But what if the condition did not occur, but the promisee contends that the promisor prevented it from coming about? The best answer appears to be that the promisee has the initial burden of showing that the promisor's action or inaction was at least a partial cause of the failure of the condition. Once that is met, the promisor has the burden of establishing that any misfeasance or nonfeasance on its part did not contribute substantially to the non-occurrence of the condition. Shear v. Nat'l Rifle Ass'n, 606 F.2d 1251 (D.C. Cir. 1979), followed in *In re* Estate of Drake, 4 A.3d 450 (D.C. 2010). *Cf.* D & S Realty v. Markel Ins. Co., 816 N.W.2d 1 (Neb. 2012) ("[I]f the promisee could not or would not have performed the condition, or it would not have happened whatever had been the promisor's conduct, the condition is not excused."). Note also that, like impracticability, non-performance of a condition may be temporary. This most often happens when an insurer's non-performance stems from its good-faith denial of liability. If so, the insured's duties under the policy may be held in abeyance, rather than excused entirely. *See* D & S Realty v. Markel Ins. Co., 816 N.W.2d 1 (Neb. 2012) (collecting cases; citing to Restatement Second §245). *But see* Rockford Mut. Ins. Co. v. Pirtle, 911 N.E.2d 60 (Ind. App. 2009) (good-faith denial of liability permanently excuses performance of the condition). But "if the delay in determining the insurer's liability materially contributed to a situation where the insured can no longer perform the condition after the coverage dispute is resolved, then the condition will be absolutely excused." D & S Realty v. Markel Ins. Co., 816 N.W.2d 1, 18 (Neb. 2012).

§8.7 EXCUSE OF CONDITION TO AVOID FORFEITURE

§8.7 n.6 p.461 Add the following after the second sentence: *Accord:* Edelman Arts, Inc. v. Art Int'l (UK) Ltd., 841 F. Supp. 2d 810 (S.D.N.Y. 2012) ("Impossibility excuses the non-occurrence of a condition precedent if the occurrence of the condition is not a material part of the agreement and forfeiture would otherwise result."; applied to condition precedent to formation, where art dealer's requirement that a bill of sale be put in escrow was prerequisite to signing the bill of sale and thus of carrying on with the transaction was material and thus not excused because of impossibility).

§8.7 n.13 p.462 In the first paragraph, add the following after the first sentence: *Accord:* S. Tex. Elec. Co-op. v. Dresser-Rand Co., 575 F.3d 504 (5th Cir. 2009) (non-performance of condition excused if its performance " '(a) will involve extreme forfeiture or penalty, and (b) its existence or occurrence forms no essential part of the exchange for the promisor's performance' ") (quoting from Lesikar Constr. Co. v. Acoustex, Inc., 509 S.W.2d 877 (Tex. Civ. App. 1974)); Root v. Am. Equity Specialty Ins. Co., 30 Cal. Rptr. 3d 631 (Ct. App. 2005) (notice requirement in malpractice insurance policy waived where insured learned of claim made during coverage after last day and where insured had no opportunity to purchase an extended notice endorsement; "California's common law of contracts has traditionally allowed for the equitable excusal or remediation of non-occurrence of conditions precedent in contracts when such non-occurrence works a forfeiture."); Bray v. Bray, 978 A.2d 582 (Conn. Super. 2008) (rental agreement in separation decree, where ex-wife reduced rent payments by amount of ex-husband's failure to comply with divorce decree; court invokes "equitable doctrine of nonforfeiture" and applies test requiring that "(1) the tenant's breach was not willful or grossly negligent; (2) upon eviction the tenant will suffer a loss wholly disproportionate to the injury to the landlord; and (3) the landlord's injury is reparable," also "tak[ing] into consideration the tenant's actions after receiving notice by the landlord of the termination of the lease, looking favorably upon any actions by the tenant to cure the default or evidencing an intent to prevent the forfeiture.") (quoting from Cumberland Farms v. Dairy Mart, 627 A.2d 386 (Conn. 1993)); Jyurovat v. Univ. Prop. & Cas. Ins. Co., 84 So. 3d 1238 (Fla. App. 2012) ("An insured's refusal to comply with a presuit condition may be a willful and material breach of an insurance contract that precludes recovery as a matter of law. . . . However, if the insured cooperates to some degree or explains his failure to comply, whether the insured materially breached the policy remains a question for the fact finder."); Inman v. St. Paul Fire & Marine Ins. Co., 347 S.W.3d 569 (Mo. App. 2011) ("an insured, or one standing in the shoes of an insured, will not be barred from recovery based on the breach of these [notice] conditions unless the insurer can show that it has been prejudiced by the insured's non-compliance with such policy provisions"; insurer prejudiced where insured's failure to provide notice of an amended petition denied the insurer the chance to defend against liability at trial and seek to reduce any damages); Cortez v. Cortez, 203 P.3d 857 (N.M. 2009) (provision in marital settlement that if wife delinquent on mortgage, husband could pay amount due and take title, and wife sent payment within redemption period, but payment arrived after; "if the defaulting party substantially performed with reasonable diligence and in good faith, and 'the other party has suffered no damage by the delay, and particularly if the property has not materially enhanced in value during the time of the delay, a Court of Equity will not enforce the forfeiture.' ") (quoting from Steele v. Branch, 40 Cal. 3, 11 (1870)).

§8.7 n.14 p. 463 Add the following to the list after "Accord": *Ex parte* Keelboat Concepts, 938 So. 2d 922 (Ala. 2005) ("time is of the essence in an option contract and . . . option contracts are to be strictly construed"; attempt to exercise option nineteen days late therefore not effective); Thomson Learning v. Olympia Props., 850 N.E.2d 314 (Ill. App. 2006) ("[A] lessee seeking to exercise an option to cancel or extend a commercial lease must strictly comply with the terms of that option."); Prison Health Servs. v. Baltimore County, 912 A.2d 56 (Md. App. 2006) ("an option must be exercised precisely as its terms require . . . The parties must be able to know whether the continuing offer has been accepted and a new contract formed.";

enforcing terms where option expired on June 30 and renewal arrived July 1); Alexander's Land Co. v. M & M & K Corp., 703 S.E.2d 207 (S.C. 2010) (failure to close on purchase of business by date stated in option meant that right to exercise never came about), relying upon Faulkner v. Millar, 460 S.E.2d 378 (S.C. 1995) ("In equity, strict compliance with time limits contained in a contract will not ordinarily be enforced, except with regard to option contracts.").

§8.7 n.15 p.464 ***Add the following at the beginning:*** *See* Cotter v. James L. Tapp Co., 230 S.E.2d 715 (S.C. 1976) ("[T]he courts have recognized that harsh results in option cases are necessary to further more compelling considerations of public policy. When an individual grants an option he ties up his rights and property for a specified period of time without binding the other side. For this reason he is entitled to strict compliance with time limits and other terms of the option. Thus, if the optionee fails to comply with the terms of the option, even though he may have an excuse, he must bear the responsibility and not the optionor.").

§8.7 n.17 p.464 ***Add the following at the end:*** As with other conditions, if the seller's actions impede the buyer's attempted exercise of the option, the buyer's tardy exercise may be excused. *Ex parte* Keelboat Concepts, *supra* note 14; Chambers v. Hunt Petroleum Corp., 320 S.W.3d 578 (Tex. Civ. App. 2010) ("the failure of the optionee to comply strictly with the terms or conditions of the option will be excused when the failure is brought about by the conduct of the optionor"; optionor's refusal to respond to optionee's repeated requests to meet in order to exercise the option excuses optionee's failure to tender payment during the term of the option).

§8.7 n.19 p.464 ***Add the following after the citation to* J.N.A. Realty Corp.:** , followed in Vitarelli v. Excel Auto. Tech. Ctr., 811 N.Y.S.2d 689 (App. Div. 2006) (strict enforcement may be relieved through equity "if (1) the tenant in good faith made substantial improvements to the premises and would otherwise suffer a forfeiture, (2) the tenant's delay was the result of an excusable delay, and (3) the landlord was not prejudiced by the delay").

§8.7 n.19 p.464 Add the following to the list after **"Accord"***:* Tel-Towne Props. Grp. v. Toys "R" Us Del., 630 F. Supp. 2d 766 (E.D. Mich. 2007) ("State courts typically only grant such relief if: (1) the tenant's delay in renewing was slight and/or was the result of an honest mistake or other excusable fault; (2) the delay did not prejudice the landlord; and (3) failure to grant relief would cause a tenant to suffer unconscionable hardship."); Trinity Realty I v. Chazumba, LLC, 931 N.E.2d 510 (Mass. App. 2010) (exercise of option to renew lease permitted in spite of noncompliance with two lease covenants; the infractions were "inconsequential and immaterial" and were not "significant or prejudicial" to the lessor; although lease characterized the two covenants as a "major inducement" or a "material inducement" to the lessor, "boilerplate in this lease characterized *all* the tenant's obligations under the lease as 'material,' 'unique,' 'extraordinary,' and 'of the essence.' ").

§8.7 n.19 p.464 Add the following to the list after **"But cf."***:* Genesco, Inc. v. 33 N. LaSalle Partners, 889 N.E.2d 769 (Ill. App. 2008) (noting split within Illinois appellate courts; holding that cases permitting equitable relief "offer no basis in law upon which courts are purportedly empowered with a blanket ability to provide equitable relief" and "provide an unsupported theory of equitable power").

§8.7 n.19 p.464 Add the following after the citation to **Reynolds-Penland Co.***:* , firmly rejected in Valley Educ. Found. v. Eldercare Props. (*In re* Eldercare Props.), 568 F.3d 506 (5th Cir. 2009) (*Reynolds-Penland* inconsistent with controlling Texas Supreme Court authority permitting equitable intervention for *de minimis* departures from strict compliance with lease renewal option; one-month delay in exercising option excused where original lease term ten years with renewal of five, lessor was unable to prove any tangible harm resulting from the late notice, failing to allow the lessee to exercise its option would destroy its business, and lessor's "failure to raise the issue of renewal during the parties' ongoing, extensive discussions is a factor in the analysis of unconscionability") (O'Connor, Associate Justice, sitting by designation).

§8.7a PITFALLS IN DRAFTING POSED BY CONDITIONS

§8.7a n.4 p.467 ***Add the following at the beginning:*** And not just because unusual language may yield ambiguity. *See* Solar Applications Eng'g v. T.A. Operating Corp., 327 S.W.3d 104 (Tex. 2010) ("When no conditional language is used and another reasonable interpretation of the contract is possible, the terms will be construed as a covenant in order to avoid a forfeiture.") (internal quotes omitted).

For an instance of narrowly averted disaster, *see* Diesel Props S.r.l. v. Greystone Bus. Credit II, 631 F.3d 42 (2d Cir. 2011) (contract provided that agreement to pay would "only be applied to orders placed by [distributor] upon receipt of a purchase order for product"; distributor would provide copies of purchase orders to manufacturer and lender; manufacturer "agree[d] to provide [lender] with a copy of any invoice for its products delivered to [distributor]"; and the lender would be obligated to pay the manufacturer after the distributor supplied the lender with a copy of its invoice to a customer in the amount of the manufacturer's invoice; held unclear whether this created a condition or a promise, but parol evidence clarified that the requirement that purchase orders be supplied to the lender was a condition to the lender's payments to the manufacturer). The court here got to the right result, but in spite of drafting, not because of it. The various requirements that invoices be supplied were framed as promises to do something, exactly the opposite of what was likely intended. It would have been easy to reframe these requirements using the classic language of conditions — for example, "Lender will provide funds to manufacturer if/on condition that/provided that/subject to the following events . . ." Using the language of promise was dangerous, to say the least; it worked this time, but it is hard to see why one would choose to cross a river by a tightrope when a suspension bridge is next to it.

§8.7a n.9 p.468 ***Add the following at the beginning:*** BMD Contractors v. Fid. & Deposit Co. 679 F.3d 643 (7th Cir. 2012) (giving effect to pay-if-paid provision: "It is expressly agreed that owner's acceptance of subcontractor's work and payment to the contractor for the subcontractor's work are conditions precedent

to the subcontractor's right to payments by the contractor."; "Although it's possible to reinforce the clarity of a pay-if-paid clause by using redundant language — e.g., 'in agreeing to this condition precedent, subcontractor assumes the risk of owner's insolvency' — additional language like this is not necessary if the meaning of the condition precedent is clear"); Sloan & Co. v. Liberty Mut. Ins. Co., 653 F.3d 175 (3d Cir. 2011) (giving effect to pay-if-paid provision: "Final payment shall be made within thirty (30) days after the last of the following to occur, the occurrence of all of which shall be conditions precedent to such final payment"; among the named conditions were "[Owner] shall have accepted the Work and made final payment thereunder to [Contractor]" and "[Contractor] shall have received final payment from [Owner] for [Subcontractor's] Work."); FaulknerUSA, LP, v. Alaron Supply Co., 322 S.W.3d 357 (Tex. Civ. App. 2010) (giving effect to pay-if-paid clause; provision was captioned "condition precedent," first sentence stated that payment by the owner is a condition precedent to payment to the subcontractor, later portions state that "Subcontractor is entitled to payment only for that portion of the Subcontract Work for which [contractor] has been paid by Owner," "Subcontractor expressly assumes the risk of nonpayment by Owner," and "The Subcontract Amount includes compensation to Subcontractor for the assumption of this risk," and final sentence declared that "[t]his provision establishes a condition precedent, and it shall not be construed merely as a Time of Payment Clause.").

§8.7a n.20 p.470 Add the following to the list in the first sentence: Wis. Elec. Power v. Union Pac. R.R., 557 F.3d 504 (7th Cir. 2009) ("It is true that while nonwaiver clauses are no longer unenforceable, there is still some authority for treating them as themselves waivable. But if that notion were taken literally, no-waiver clauses would be worthless. Fortunately, it is not taken literally; the waiver of a no-waiver clause must be proved by clear and convincing evidence . . .) (citations omitted) (Posner, J.).

§8.8 PERFORMANCE AS DISCHARGE AND NONPERFORMANCE AS BREACH

§8.8 n.4 p.471 Add the following: Pacini v. Regopoulos, 665 N.E.2d 493 (Ill. App. 1996) (shopping center sale contract required 95% occupancy and 94.9953% was achieved).

§8.9 CONSTRUCTIVE CONDITIONS OF EXCHANGE

§8.9 n.15 p.475 Add the following to the list after **"Accord"***:* Kaufman v. Byers, 823 N.E.2d 530 (Ohio App. 2004) ("When possible, courts should construe promises in a bilateral contract as mutually dependent and concurrent, rather than one promise as a condition precedent to the other.").

§8.9 n.18 p.476 Add the following after the citation to **Coleman***:* , followed in Williams v. Habul, 724 S.E.2d 104 (N.C. App. 2012) (promise to dismiss litigation independent from promise to retain worker not party to litigation, so failure to retain worker did not justify failing to dismiss the case).

§8.9 n.20 p.477 Add the following after the first sentence of the second paragraph: *Accord:* Beaulieu Grp. v. S&S Mills, 664 S.E.2d 816 (Ga. App. 2008) (promise to pay for tufting yarn and promise to return unused materials independent covenants).

§8.9 n.26 p.478 Add the following at the end of the second paragraph: *Accord:* Adell Broadcasting Corp. v. Apex Media Sales, 708 N.W.2d 778 (Mich. App. 2005) (failure of consideration entails "the impossibility of performance of the consideration," which is "different from, and greater than, a mere breach of contract warranting an action for damages"); Quick v. Plastic Solutions, 270 S.W.3d 173 (Tex. Civ. App. 2008) ("Failure of consideration occurs when, because of some supervening cause after an agreement is reached, the promised performance fails.").

§8.10 CONCURRENT CONDITIONS

§8.10 n.7 p.481 Change the Restatement Second citation in the first sentence to: Restatement Second §238 cmt. *b.*

§8.10 n.11 p.481 Add the following to the list after "See": Erin Food Servs. v. Derry Motel, 553 A.2d 304 (N.H. 1988) (Souter, J.: invoking "the rule excusing formal tender to a party whose repudiation of a contract has previously indicated that tender would be a useless act"), followed in Glick v. Chocorua Forestlands Ltd. P'ship, 949 A.2d 693 (N.H. 2008) (rejecting argument that tender required even after an anticipatory repudiation of a sales contract); Frostar Corp. v. Malloy, 823 N.E.2d 417 (Mass. App. 2005) (obligation to tender excused if other party has frustrated attempts to perform).

§8.10 n.12 p.481 Add the following to the list after "Accord": Point S. Land Trust v. Gutierrez, 997 So. 2d 967 (Miss. App. 2008) ("where time was of the essence to the contract, and neither party was ready, willing, and able to perform the contractual duties on the closing date, the contract terminated"; citing to Restatement Second §238).

§8.11 ORDER OF PERFORMANCE

§8.11 n.4 p.484 Add the following at the end: *See also* Samra v. Shaheen Bus. & Inv. Grp., 355 F. Supp. 2d 483 (D.D.C. 2005) ("[W]here possible, simultaneous performance of contractual obligations is preferred."; "To say there may have been a lack of trust between the parties to this contract would be an understatement. An order of simultaneous performance with the Court as intermediary seems to accomplish each party's goal of securing a measure of protection against treachery by the other.").

§8.11 n.16 p.486 Add the following at the end: *See also* Nassau Beekman, LLC v. Ann/Nassau Realty, LLC, 105 A.D.3d 33, 960 N.Y.S.2d 70 (N.Y. App. Div. 2013) (finding breach and entitlement to retain $9 million down payment where seller failed to appear at closing, despite claim of oral agreement to reschedule and past practice of accepting such oral agreements, where contract required modifications to be by signed instrument.)

§8.12 SUBSTANTIAL PERFORMANCE AS A MEANS OF AVOIDING FORFEITURE

§8.12 n.12 p.490 Add the following to the list after **"Cf.":** Dexter v. Brake, 269 P.3d 846 (Kan. App. 2012) ("[T]he doctrine of substantial performance provides that the performance may still be considered complete if the essential purpose of the contract is accomplished and a party to the contract has made a good-faith attempt to comply with the terms of the agreement even though he or she fails to precisely meet the terms of the agreement.") (Note, however, that the performance actually is *not* considered complete, for even if performance is substantial there remains a cause of action for breach of the insubstantial and unperformed part.).

§8.12 n.22 p.492 Add the following to the list after **"Accord":** Curtis Constr. Co. v. Am. Steel Span, 707 N.W.2d 68 (N.D. 2005) (to qualify as substantial performance, "[t]he contractor's default must not be willful").

§8.12 n.22 p.492 Add the following at the end: *See generally* Kimel, The Morality of Contract and Moral Culpability in Breach, 21 King's L.J. 213 (2010).

§8.12 n.24 p.493 In the first paragraph, add the following to the list after **"See":** QualComm Inc. v. Tex. Instruments, 875 A.2d 626 (Del. 2005) (New York law: "The fact that [the breach] was intentional and motivated by self-interest does not make it material . . . [a]t most" the material breach rule "is somewhat relaxed" when the default is willful) (quoting from McGuire v. Rudy's Rail, 73 N.Y.S.2d 72 (Sup. Ct. 1947)).

§8.12 n.24 p.493 In the second paragraph, add the following to the list after* "See"*: Strategic Resources Grp. v. Knight-Ridder, Inc., 870 So. 2d 846 (Fla. App. 2003) (though newspaper "intentionally reduced the size of the advertisements, it did not intentionally breach the contract" because it "relied on contract language").

§8.12 n.26 p.493 Add the following at the end: For another instance of the use of strict performance rather than substantial performance, *see* Trishan Air v. Fed. Ins. Co., 635 F.3d 422 (9th Cir. 2011) (California law: "insurance warranties require strict performance to invoke coverage"; accordingly, failure of insured's co-pilot to fulfill all requirements for training results in loss of coverage, even if co-pilot's actual training sufficient or if lack of training had no effect on whether accident occurred).

§8.12 n.33 p.494 In the third paragraph, add the following to the list after* "See generally"*: Note, Good Faith Rejection of Goods in a Falling Market, 42 Conn. L. Rev. 611 (2009).

§8.12 n.33 p.494 Add the following at the end: It should be remembered that for any particular contract, *perfect tender* is defined by, among other things, the bargain made by the parties, a course of performance, a course of dealing, or a usage of trade. An apparently absolute term may thus have built-in leeways — leeways that may not be present in the language of the agreement, but that are there all the same. In addition, the parties are free to define what constitutes complete performance. If, for example, they want to make a substantial performance rule for themselves, they may do so. As with any other contract terms, of course, care must be taken to avoid creating a vague or ambiguous definition of performance. And to the extent performance entails the exercise of judgment, the UCC's duty of good faith and fair dealing will control that exercise. *See* Cavendish Farms v. Mathiason Farms, 792 N.W.2d 500 (N.D. 2010) (term allowing buyer to reject potatoes "at any time" until July 31 did not permit the buyer to withhold notice of its rejection until July 31, even though it had decided to reject at least some of the potatoes in February; the exercise of discretion afforded buyer on time of rejection was not in good faith).

§8.12 n.34 p.495 Add the following at the end: As to the effect on rejection of continued use of the goods, *see* Keller v. Inland Metals All Weather Conditioning, 76 P.3d 977 (Idaho 2003) (where seller had removed old dehumidifier, athletic club's failure to return new dehumidifier or turn it off to prevent damage due to humidity in pool area was not inconsistent with rejection).

§8.12 n.35 p.495 Add the following to the list after **"See"***:* *Cf.* Manassas Autocars v. Couch, 645 S.E.2d 443 (Va. 2007) (subjective test not universally applicable, but relevant where the buyers can show needs beyond the ordinary; here, done by showing particular value attached to having *new* car).

§8.12 n.38 p.495 Add the following at the end: *See generally* Bridge, Avoidance for Fundamental Breach of Contract under the UN Convention on Contracts for the International Sale of Goods, 59 Int'l & Comp. L.Q. 911 (2010); Ferrari, Fundamental Breach of Contract Under the UN Sales Convention – 25 Years of Article 25 CISG, 25 J.L. & Com. 489 (2005-2006); Lubbe, Fundamental Breach under the CISG: A Source of Fundamentally Divergent Results, 68 Rabels Zeitschrift für Ausländisches und Internationales Privatrecht 444 (2004).

§8.13 DIVISIBILITY AS A MEANS OF AVOIDING FORFEITURE

§8.13 n.6 p.497 Add the following to the list after **"See"***:* Stanley Works v. Wichita Falls Indep. Sch. Dist., 366 S.W.3d 816 (Tex. Civ. App. 2012) ("The divisible or indivisible nature of a contract cannot be ascertained by any one test or rule of law.").

§8.13 n.7 p.497 Add the following to the list after **"See"***:* Coady v. Wellfleet Marine Corp., 816 N.E.2d 124 (Mass. App. 2004) (following Restatement Second §240; in contract for lease of boat slip, "performances under the contract were implicitly divided by boating season," so the defendant was entitled to payment for last season even though in breach for present

season); Kornegay v. Aspen Asset Grp., 693 S.E.2d 723 (N.C. App. 2010) (promises to pay employee by different standards for different types of work divisible as "not interdependent in any way").

§8.13 n.8 p.497 Add the following to the list after "Accord": Stanley Works v. Wichita Falls Indep. Sch. Dist., 366 S.W.3d 816 (Tex. Civ. App. 2012) ("A contract is divisible when the performance by one party consists of several distinct and separate items and the price paid by the other party is apportioned to each item."; tax abatement agreement divisible when it referred to specific phases of the larger project and stated that if the taxpayer failed to make the promised improvements and additions, then it would repay all property tax revenue "insofar as such lost tax revenue related to the additions and improvements described in any particular Phase").

§8.13 n.10 p.498 Add the following to the list after "See": State v. Chambers, 256 P.3d 1283 (Wash. App. 2011) (plea agreement not divisible, even though it pairs individual cause numbers and sentences; "the agreed sentencing range for [one set of] crimes is discussed . . . with clear consideration of the sentencing ranges on the other cause numbers," and the plea agreement "explicitly states that Chambers's failure to accept the terms would result in filing of charges of felony murder"), *review granted*, 266 P.3d 879 (Wash. 2012).

§8.13 n.10 p.498 Add the following after the second sentence: *Cf.* Menorah Chapels v. Needle, 899 A.2d 316 (N.J. Super. App. Div. 2008) (although funeral services independently priced, not divisible because itemized pricing required by statute; "[e]ven when such apportionment is possible, however, the *Restatement* [§240] requires that a court look to the parties' intent to determine whether the value to the injured party of what he received is equivalent to its stated price or whether that value is materially diminished by the part performance.").

§8.13 p.498 In the first full paragraph, add the following after the final sentence: . . . the value to that party of full performance.[12a]

[12a] Restatement Second §240 cmt. *e*. *Cf.* Fid. & Dep. Co. v. Rotec Indus., 392 F.3d 944 (7th Cir. 2004) (Posner, J.) (questioning, in light of fairness analysis, whether divisibility increases certainty) (citing to hornbook).

§8.13 n.14 p.499 Add the following to the list after "Accord": Fid. & Dep. Co. v. Rotec Indus., *supra* note 12a ("the use of the contract price to determine entitlements when the contract has not been fully performed is defensible only when the contract itself can be said to specify the price for partial performance," so no divisibility here where "it is impossible to affirm that [the promisee] would have assented to any part [of the contract] unless [it] assented to all.") (quoting from Trapkus v. Edstrom's Inc., 489 N.E.2d 340 (Ill. App. 1986)).

§8.13 n.14 p.499 Add the following at the end: *Cf.* AMEC Civil v. Fla. Dep't of Transp., 41 So. 3d 235 (Fla. App. 2010) (construction contract to be regarded as entire, in light of its own claims procedure, for the purposes of determining whether the contractor could sue the owner for successive breaches of parts of the contract), disagreed with in Loveland Essential Grp. v. Grommon Farms, 2012 Colo. App. 22 (2012) (collecting cases; majority rule is that contract is not to be considered entire for the purposes of claim preclusion, so that only the breaches that occurred before the first action began would be precluded by that action).

§8.13 n.17 p.500 Add the following at the end: *See also* SunTrust Mortgage v. United Guar. Residential Ins. Co. of N.C., 806 F. Supp. 2d 872 (E.D. Va. 2011) (master contract between mortgage lender and insurer not divisible, even though individual contracts of insurance could be separated from the mass; rate factors on each loan inseparable from rate factors for the others, insurer's coverage obligation was linked, not to individual loans, but to the mass of loans in a pool, and the master contract refers to one contract of insurance); Jacobs v. CNG Transmission Corp., 332 F. Supp. 2d 759 (W.D. Pa. 2004) ("[T]he divisibility of the subject(s) of the contract is not controlling. . . . For example, an agreement calling for installment payments in correlation to the specific stages of building a house will not render a contract to build the entire home divisible.").

§8.13 p.500 In the first full paragraph, add the following at the end: . . . affects rights and duties as to all parts.[18a]

[18a] How this is to be determined — as a matter of fact or a matter of law — is unresolved in the courts. *See* Fid. & Dep. Co. v. Rotec Indus., *supra* note 12a (collecting cases). As Judge Posner suggests, perhaps the best way to deal with divisibility is in the same manner as other matters of contract interpretation. In most jurisdictions this means giving the matter to the judge in the first instance and, if resolving the ambiguity requires questions of fact, giving those to the finder of fact. *Id.*

§8.13 n.19 p.500 Add the following at the end: *Accord:* Raab v. Lander, 427 Fed. Appx. 182 (3d Cir. 2011) (joint agreement to purchase property indivisible, even though it called for different acts at different times, because the consideration was single; accordingly, the statute of limitations began running for the entire contract at the time of the initial breach). *Cf.* Wood v. Unified Govt. of Athens-Clarke Cnty., Ga., 818 F.3d 1244, 166 Lab. Cas. (CCH) P61, 697, 26 Fla. L. Weekly Fed. C 225 (11th Cir. 2016) (contract for health benefits between retired government employees and county was divisible because, although the county made a single promise, it could perform this promise only by successive performances (e.g., premium payments) and plaintiffs had no immediate claim for the entirety of the contract, as they would if the contract were entire; therefore, plaintiffs could pursue contract claims for each alleged breach occurring within the limitations period).

§8.14 RESTITUTION AS A MEANS OF AVOIDING FORFEITURE

§8.14 n.1 p.500 Add the following at the end: *Cf.* Menorah Chapels v. Needle, 899 A.2d 316 (N.J. Super. App. Div. 2008) (breaching party "may nonetheless be entitled to recovery of the value of its remaining services on a *quantum meruit* basis"; quoting from treatise). *But see* Swoger v. Rare Coin Wholesalers, 803 F.3d 1045 (9th Cir. 2015) (coin expert provided information that may have had some commercial value, but the parties had negotiated for payment for specific information, and thus his "claims for

relief depended upon the accuracy of his assertion that he had provided to Appellees proof that their Coin was the first legal-tender gold coin struck pursuant to an Act of Congress." Since the court found his information did not provide such proof, the expert "could not recover because he had not provided the information he alleged he was required to provide pursuant to the parties' agreement.")

§8.14 n.12 p.502 Add the following to the list after "Accord": Fid. & Deposit Co. v. Rotec Indus., 392 F.3d 944 (7th Cir. 2004) (Posner, J.) (breaching subcontractor "would nevertheless be entitled to claim compensation in a suit for quantum meruit for the value of the services that it had rendered to [the general contractor] before the breach, minus any damages that [the general contractor] suffered from the breach"); David M. Somers & Assocs. v. Busch, 927 A.2d 832 (Conn. 2007) ("if an attorney fails to perform fully under a contract that has been terminated because of his or her own disbarment, the disbarred attorney may recover, under the doctrine of unjust enrichment, for partial performance of services rendered in furtherance of the contract's objective, the measure of which is the benefit derived by the client").

§8.14 n.12 p.503 Add the following to the list after "Cf.": Strong v. Beydoun, 83 Cal. Rptr. 3d 632 (Ct. App. 2008) (*quantum meruit* recovery permitted by attorney against other attorney with whom she entered into a fee-sharing agreement, but not against the client who had hired only the other attorney; "Allowing an attorney to recover the reasonable value of his or her services from a client is premised on the services being requested by the client.").

§8.14 n.15 p.503 Substitute the following in place of the final sentence: This provision is anomalous from the vantage of the expectation remedy, though it has been defended variously as a statutory liquidated damages clause and as compensation for losses that are unprovable or too costly to prove. The courts have divided in its application, with some applying the statute as written and others omitting the statutory minimum. *Compare* Neri v.

Retail Marine Corp., 285 N.E.2d 311 (N.Y. 1972) (omitting statutory minimum) *with* R.E. Davis Chem. Corp. v. Diasonics, Inc., 826 F.2d 678 (7th Cir. 1987) (applying as written).

§8.14 n.16 p.504 Add the following after the citation to* Maxton Builders*: , in turn followed in Spirit Locker v. EVO Direct, 696 F. Supp. 2d 296 (E.D.N.Y. 2010) (no recovery of earnest money unless the buyer can establish unconscionability; speculating that "Perhaps because of the size of land transactions and the greater likelihood that the parties will take professional advice, New York law accords with the economic scholars' conclusions" that these clauses broadly be permissible).

§8.14 n.18 p.505 In the first paragraph, add the following to the list after* "Accord"*: Kuish v. Smith, 105 Cal. Rptr. 3d 475 (Ct. App. 2010) (in a rising market, a clause "precluding the return of plaintiff's deposit above and beyond any damages suffered by defendants as a result of plaintiff's breach would render that provision unenforceable"); Berggren v. Hill, 928 N.E.2d 1225 (Ill. App. 2010) (retaining deposit of 5% of purchase price "was reasonable at the time the parties signed the contract, and the fact that plaintiff subsequently sold the property for a lower price does not change that analysis").

§8.14 n.23 p.507 Add the following at the end: The Restatement (Third) of Restitution and Unjust Enrichment deals indirectly with the problem of willful breach. Like the Restatement Second, it rejects the absolute bar on willfulness found in some of the cases. As the commentary points out, though, "there remain many circumstances in which the quality of the claimant's breach will bar the claim." Restatement (Third) of Restitution and Unjust Enrichment §36 cmt. *b*. For example, the claimant may not recover in restitution for what is effectively a forced exchange — as might occur if a builder cuts corners on a job in order to increase profits, even if the resulting structure has the same value as if the builder had followed the plans. Restatement (Third) of Restitution and Unjust Enrichment §36 cmt. *f* & ill. 19. Nor must a claim in restitution succeed if it is grounded in "fraud or other inequitable conduct." Restatement (Third) of Restitution and Unjust Enrichment §36(4). And innocent recipients of nonreturnable benefits are liable in restitution "by the standard that yields the smallest liability in restitution," which "may not leave the recipient worse off (apart from the costs of litigation) than if the transaction giving rise to the liability had not occurred." Restatement (Third) of Restitution and Unjust Enrichment §50(2)(a) & (3).

§8.14 n.25 p.508 Add the following after the first sentence: *Accord:* Menorah Chapels v. Needle, *supra* note 1 ([the breaching party's] "damages cannot be measured solely by reference to the unit price of the goods and services actually provided"; quoting from Restatement Second §240 cmt. *e*).

§8.14 n.26 p.508 Add the following to the list after **"Accord":** Fid. & Dep. Co. v. Rotec Indus., 392 F.3d 944 (7th Cir. 2004) (Posner, J.) (breaching plaintiff suing in restitution "was entitled to the value of its performance and a court would look to the contract price as a guide to that value") (citing to hornbook).

§8.15 POWER TO SUSPEND PERFORMANCE AND TO TERMINATE THE CONTRACT

§8.15 n.2 p.509 Add the following before the last sentence: *See* United States v. Scruggs, 356 F.3d 539 (4th Cir. 2004) (following Uniform Commercial Code and Restatement Second terminology for "rescission" and "termination").

§8.15 n.13 p.512 Add the following at the end: *See* Fire Sprinklers v. Icon Contracting, 279 S.W.3d 230 (Mo. App. 2009) (quoting from treatise).

§8.15 n.17 p.512 Add the following at the end: Another term for partial breach is *incidental* breach. R.C. Hobbs Enters. v. J.G.L. Distrib., 104 P.3d 503 (Mont. 2004) (" 'incidental' breaches . . . only entitle the non-breaching party to sue for damages").

The decision whether to terminate the contract certainly affects the breached-against party's rights and remedies under the contract. It does not, however, amount to an independent breach. Termination is a right, not a duty; unless some independent contractual obligation requires that the breached-against party terminate a contract, it may choose whether to do so however it likes. *See* Norwood Promotional Prods. v. KustomKoozies, LLC, 835 F. Supp. 2d 685 (S.D. Ind. 2011) (dispatching argument that failure to terminate agreement promptly was a breach of contract).

§8.15 n.18 p.513 Add the following at the end: *See* Yankee Atomic Elec. Co. v. United States, 536 F.3d 1268 (Fed. Cir. 2008) ("In this partial breach case where the parties' performance obligations survive, the non-breaching party is not at this time responsible for obligations that must be performed later, when they mature.") (quoting from treatise).

§8.15 n.27 p.515 Add the following after the first sentence: *Accord:* Long Island Sav. Bank v. United States, 503 F.3d 1234 (Fed. Cir. 2007) (prior fraud by bank precludes its *Winstar* action against the government); Nutrisoya Foods v. Sunrich, LLC, 626 F. Supp. 2d 985 (D. Minn. 2009) ("The 'prior breach' doctrine recognizes that the non-performance of one party under a contract excuses the future contractual obligations of the other party.").

§8.15 n.27 p.515 In the first paragraph, add the following at the end: For an overenthusiastic rendition of this doctrine, see Profit Pet v. Arthur Dogswell, LLC, 603 F.3d 308 (6th Cir. 2010) ("Michigan law does not allow a party who was the first to substantially breach a contract to later sue on the same contract."). Leaving aside the conflation of substantial performance and material breach, the party committing the first material breach still has the right to sue for any prior breaches (presumably non-material) by the other party. It would be more accurate to say that the first material breacher may not sue for future non-performance of the contract by the other side, because that side has terminated the contract and with it its contractual duties.

§8.15 n.34 p.516 Add the following to the list after **"Accord"***:* Ambling Mgmt. Co. v. Univ. View Partners, 581 F. Supp. 2d 706 (D. Md. 2008) ("A party to a contract cannot engage in conduct that prevents the other party from performing, and then use that as an excuse for not performing.").

§8.16 MATERIAL BREACH AND SUSPENSION

§8.16 n.1 p.517 In the second paragraph, add the following after the second sentence: *Accord:* Reyelt v. Danzell, 533 F.3d 28 (1st Cir. 2008) ("contract case law . . . looks primarily at whether a breach caused harm of significantly impaired the value of the contract"; breach not material when zoning application granted within contractual time limit, despite significantly tardy filing of application) (quoting from treatise).

§8.16 n.1 p.517 Add the following at the end: Who carries the burden of proving materiality, or, as the case may be, nonmateriality has proved a tricky question. On the one hand, the promisor will assert either its own substantial performance or the promisee's lack of material performance as a defense. On the other, an aggrieved promisee must, as the plaintiff, take the laboring oar for all elements of its cause of action, presumably including the promisor's material breach if the plaintiff seeks rescission. Most courts place the burden of proving materiality on the promisee-plaintiff. *See* United States v. Castaneda, 162 F.3d 832 (5th Cir. 1998); Collins/Snoops Assocs. v. CJF, LLC, 988 A.2d 49 (Md. App. 2010). Along much the same lines, the courts generally require that a plaintiff who itself has performed prove that it substantially performed, rather than leave it to the defendant to assert as a defense that the plaintiff was the first to materially breach. *See* ESPN, Inc. v. Office of Comm'r of Baseball, 76 F. Supp. 2d 383 (S.D.N.Y. 1999); Hawkins v. Teeples & Thatcher, Inc., 515 P.2d 927 (Or. 1973). Usually this makes sense, but not always. If, for example, an insured sues an insurer for failure to pay a claim and the insurer asserts failure to comply with a covenant in the insurance policy as a defense, it would seem logical to put the burden of proving materiality on the insurer. The insured may not know what aspect of its performance is deficient in the eyes of the insurer, making proof of substantial performance at best difficult. In addition, whether a breach is material rests mainly on its effect on the promisee. Of the promisor and the promisee, the promisee seems better suited to proving how it was harmed.

§8.16 n.3 p.518 Add the following after the first sentence: See also Dexter v. Brake, 269 P.3d 846 (Kan. App. 2012) ("[S]ubstantial performance is in direct contrast to the concept of material breach. If a breach is material, substantial performance has not been rendered.") (citations omitted); Fire Sprinklers v. Icon Contracting, 279 S.W.3d 230 (Mo. App. 2009) (quoting from treatise).

§8.16 n.4 p.518 Add the following after the first sentence: Manassas Autocars v. Couth, 645 S.E.2d 443 (Va. 2007) (where the plaintiffs "intended to buy not only a means of transportation but a *new* vehicle," the appropriate value for determining substantial impairment is the new vehicle value to the plaintiffs).

§8.16 n.6 p.518 Add the following to the list in the final sentence of the first paragraph: M.M. Silta, Inc. v. Cleveland Cliffs, Inc., 572 F.3d 532 (8th Cir. 2009) (applying Restatement Second factors, and observing that "defendant's failure to give notice of the breach" is "certainly one factor to be considered in analyzing the materiality of the alleged breach"); Prima Tek II v. Klerk's Plastic Indus., 525 F.3d 533 (7th Cir. 2008) (citing to Restatement Second factors as applied in Rubloff CB Machesney v. World Novelties, 844 N.E.2d 462 (Ill. App. 2006) (slightly late payment by tenant a material breach when tenant, after history of noncompliance, had only recently agreed to comply strictly with terms of lease)); Qualcomm Inc. v. Tex. Instruments, 875 A.2d 626 (Del. 2005) (New York law: breach not material, focusing on forfeiture, lack of deprivation of benefit, and adequate compensation for loss); Burgess v. N. Bend Sch. Dist., 173 P.3d 1271 (Or. App. 2007) (applying Restatement Second criteria; breach of earnest money agreement's requirement that loan application, if needed, be made within ten days not material, because the clause was solely for the buyer's benefit, the seller would have been deprived of no benefit, there was ample time to secure a loan, and the buyer

acted in good faith); Int'l Diamond Importers v. Singularity Clark, L.P., 40 A.3d 1261 (Pa. Super. 2012) (landlord sought to evict tenant without the notice and cure rights provided in the lease, and argued that those duties were discharged because the tenant had already materially breached the lease by not operating a retail business at the site; genuine issue of material fact on material breach, given factual dispute about whether other tenants on that floor had also ceased operating retail businesses); Vanden Hoek v. Weber, 724 N.W.2d 858 (S.D. 2006) (plea agreement: emphasis on breach of the duty of good faith and fair dealing).

§8.16 n.6 p.518 Add the following after the citation to **Foundation Dev. Corp.***:* , followed in Maleki v. Desert Palms Prof'l Props., 214 P.3d 415 (Ariz. App. 2009) (a tenant's right to renew "may not be conditioned on perfect performance of a commercial lease, but may be forfeited only upon a material breach").

§8.16 n.7 p.519 Add the following at the end: ; Marion Fam. YMCA v. Hensel, 897 N.E.2d 184 (Ohio App. 2008) ("A 'material breach' of contract is a failure to do something that is so fundamental to a contract that the failure to perform defeats the essential purpose of the contract or makes it impossible for the other party to perform.").

§8.16 n.8 p.519 Add the following to the list after **"Accord"***:* Long Island Sav. Bank v. United States, 503 F.3d 1234 (Fed. Cir. 2007) (false certification of fundamental representations and warranties was material; in addition, "any degree of fraud is material as a matter of law") (quoting from Christopher Village, L.P. v. United States, 360 F.3d 1319 (Fed. Cir. 2004)); Dexter v. Brake, 269 P.3d 846 (Kan. App. 2012) (where "the main objective" of the contract was to ensure that every oil well was either producing or plugged, the failure to do either for three wells materially breached the contract); R.C. Hobbs Enters. v. J.G.L. Distrib., 104 P.3d 503 (Mont. 2004) ("A material breach is one that touches the fundamental purpose of the contract and defeats the object of the parties in making the contract.").

§8.17 CURE

§8.17 n.1 p.521 ***Add the following at the end:*** Cure may also be inappropriate, such as when the material breach is also willful or in bad faith. This issue comes up with some frequency when an insured refuses to perform its obligation to submit to an examination, but offers to do so after the time for performance has passed. *See* Hanover Ins. Co. v. Cape Cod Custom Home Theater, 891 N.E.2d 703 (Mass. App. 2008) (collecting cases).

§8.17 n.2 p.522 ***Add the following after the second sentence:*** *But see* Landis v. William Fannin Bldrs., 951 N.E.2d 1078 (Ohio App. 2011) (contractor replaced defective siding with conforming siding, arguing unsuccessfully that this cure vitiated its breach; "Fixing defective work may eliminate a nonbreaching party's injury, but it cannot negate the breach itself.").

§8.17 n.8 p.523 ***Add the following to the list after "Compare":*** Lile v. Kiesel, 871 N.E.2d 995 (Ind. App. 2007) (2-508 "pertains to a buyer's *rejection* of nonconforming goods upon delivery") (emphasis in original).

§8.17 n.16 p.524 ***Add the following at the end:*** It should, however, be added that the buyer's right to cure under CISG is severely limited by the doctrine of fundamental breach. For example, the cure right bars a declaration of fundamental breach where the buyer can sell the goods, have them repaired, or otherwise use them without great inconvenience. Bundesgericht 4C.179/1998/odi (Switz. Oct. 28, 1998) (no fundamental breach for shipment of meat that was too fatty and watery, with lowered value of 25.5%, because the meat could be resold at a lower price), available at http://cisgw3.law.pace.edu/cases/981028s1.html.

§8.18 TOTAL BREACH AND TERMINATION

§8.18 n.1 p.525 ***Add the following after the first sentence:*** *See* Queiroz v. Harvey, 204 P.3d 390 (Ariz. App. 2008), *vacated on other grounds*, 205 P.3d 1120 (Ariz. 2009) ("[T]he general rule is that a

party that has materially breached a contract is given a reasonable period of time in which to cure, even if the contract contains no express cure provision."; following Restatement Second §242; quoting from treatise); Frazier v. Mellowitz, 804 N.E.2d 796 (Ind. App. 2004) (comparing first and second Restatements).

§8.18 n.2 p.525 Add the following to the list after **"Accord"***:* Murphy Farrell Dev. v. Sourant, 272 P.3d 355 (Ariz. App. 2012) ("an uncured material breach of contract relieves the non-breaching party from the duty . . . too perform and can discharge that party from the contract"); LeTarte v. W. Side Dev., 855 A.2d 505 (N.H. 2004) ("Successive breaches of a continuing contract, while generally viewed as a series of partial breaches, can result in a total breach when there is a repudiation or a material failure of performance.").

§8.18 n.4 p.526 Add the following at the start: *See* Admiral Fin. Corp. v. United States, 378 F.3d 1336 (Fed. Cir. 2004) (*Winstar* case; no total breach where the breach "had no practical effect on [the plaintiff's] ability to find the necessary additional funding" and thus did not substantially impair the value of the contract).

§8.18 p.527 Add the following at the end of the carryover sentence: . . . breach is material in the first place.[6a]

[6a] *See* Volvo Trucks N. Am. v. Wis. Dep't of Transp., 779 N.W.2d 423 (Wis. 2010) ("Ordinarily, in contract law, whether the breaching party's conduct has cured the breach is a question of fact. But in contract law, if no material facts are in dispute and only one conclusion is to be drawn from the facts, whether the breaching party's conduct has cured the breach may be viewed as a question of law.") (citing to treatise).

§8.18 n.7 p.527 Add the following at the end: *See* Mustang Pipeline Co. v. Driver Pipeline Co., 134 S.W.3d 195 (Tex. 2004) (relying on §242 in concluding that pipeline's builder's failure to complete construction by deadline discharged pipeline owner). These factors are elaborated upon in Restatement Second §243. *See* Mobil Oil Exploration & Producing Se. v. United States, 530 U.S. 604 (2000) (quoting from and adopting Restatement analysis).

***§8.18 n.13 p.528 In the first paragraph, add the following to the list after* "But cf.":** Atlanta Jet v. Liberty Aircraft Servs., 866 So. 2d 148 (Fla. App. 2004) (contract for sale of airplane provided for closing on or before April 15, 1999, but "did not specify that time was of the essence").

***§8.18 n.15 p.529 Add the following to the list after* "Accord":** Reyelt v. Danzell, 533 F.3d 28 (1st Cir. 2008) ("Courts are often (although not necessarily) more forgiving of failures to meet time provisions in contracts than, say, of failures to pay the price agreed. . . . In a contract for the sale of land, a modest delay might be tolerable . . .") (quoting from treatise); Erin Food Servs. v. Derry Motel, 553 A.2d 304 (N.H. 1988) (Souter, J.: "[T]he party seeking enforcement must have been ready to perform within a reasonable time of the date specified, provided delay was not willful or harmful to the other party."); Mayfield v. Koroghli, 184 P.3d 362 (Nev. 2008) ("the time for performance under a contract is not considered of the essence unless the contract expressly so provides"); ADC Orange v. Coyote Acres, 857 N.E.2d 513 (N.Y. 2006) (a fixed date in a real estate sales contract "alone does not make time of the essence"; payment two weeks late not a material breach); Ball v. Maynard, 645 S.E.2d 890 (N.C. App. 2007) (for real estate contracts, without a time-is-of-the-essence clause the parties are allowed a reasonable time after the closing date to finish their deal); 1800 Smith Street Assocs. v. Gencarelli, 888 A.2d 46 (R.I. 2005) ("explicit time limits 'standing alone and without more do not indicate that the time[s] fixed for performance [are] intended by the parties to be a material or an essential part of their agreement. . . . the party contending that time is of the essence has the burden of proof thereon.' ") (quoting from Safeway Sys. v. Manuel Bros., Inc., 228 A.2d 851 (R.I. 1967)), followed in Empire Acquisition Grp. v. Atl. Mortg. Co., 35 A.3d 878 (R.I. 2012) ("absent explicit contractual language to the contrary . . . the parties were obliged to perform under the agreement only within a reasonable time of the contemplated performance dates").

§8.18 n.16 p.529 Add the following at the end: Even here, though, sometimes enough is enough. *See* Empire Acquisition

Grp. v. Atl. Mortg. Co., 35 A.3d 878 (R.I. 2012) (no communication from buyer between request for delayed closing date in November and the following June, when seller gave notice that the earlier agreements had expired; even though time not of the essence, "each party is bound to proceed reasonably and in good faith toward the completion of the contemplated performance," and here buyer provided no explanation for its "enigmatic silence," which was held unreasonable as a matter of law).

§8.18 n.17 p.530 Add the following after the second sentence: Sublime, Inc. v. Boardman's Inc., 849 So. 2d 470 (Fla. App. 2003) (though settlement agreement contained no provision stating that time was of the essence, any delay in payment was sheltered by grace period and "agreement clearly specified that upon default, the stated amount would be 'immediately' due and payable").

§8.18 n.20 p.531 In the second paragraph, add the following to the list in the second sentence: Command Sec. Corp. v. Moffa, 84 So. 3d 1097 (Fla. App. 2012) (as part of rationale for permitting late notice for receiving reduction in price for sale of assets).

***§8.18 n.21 p.531 Add the following to the list after* "Accord":** Queiroz v. Harvey, *supra* note 1 ("A cure period may be imposed even where a party has materially breached a contract that, like the one at issue here, provides that time is of the essence."; following Restatement Second §242 cmt. *d*).

***§8.18 n.22 p.531 Add the following to the list after* "See":** Advanced Bodycare Solutions v. Thione Int'l, 615 F.3d 1352 (11th Cir. 2010) (non-conformity of 20% of the goods in one shipment insufficient to breach the contract as a whole; value of order was $41,250 and whole contract was for almost $9 million).

§8.19 WAIVER AND ELECTION

§8.19 n.6 p.535 Add the following after the citation to **Fracassa***:* , followed in 1800 Smith Street Assocs. v. Gencarelli, 888 A.2d 46 (R.I. 2005) ("the mere occasion of continued deliberations with a mind toward reviving anything akin to the original agreements places this case squarely within our holding in *Fracassa*").

§8.19 n.6 p.535 Add the following to the list after **Accord:** Summit Apparel, Inc. v. Promo Nation, Inc., 25 N.Y.S.3d 773 (N.Y. App. Div. 2015) (delay in delivery could constitute failure to conform to the "ASAP" requirement in the contract, and acceptance of the delayed delivery of goods does not waive right to seek damages, per UCC 2-607; however, failure to object until several years after the delivery does not satisfy UCC requirement to notify the party within a reasonable time, so buyer was "barred from any remedy.");

§8.19 n.7 p.535 Add the following: Edwards v. Allied Home Mtg. Capital Corp., 962 So. 2d 194 (Ala. 2007) ("Where the parties have exchanged promises of performances . . . the injured party is not excused from performing his remaining duties if he continues the agreement with knowledge of the default by the breaching party."); Restatement Second §246.

§8.19 n.8 p.535 Add the following after the first sentence: Cf. Old Stone Corp. v. United States, 450 F.3d 1360 (Fed. Cir. 2006) (discussing different approaches to whether reliance is required for election).

§8.19 n.13 p.537 Add the following to the list after **"Accord"***:* Bayshore Ford Truck Sales v. Ford Motor Co., 380 F.3d 1331 (11th Cir. 2004) ("an agreement to waive the personal or mail delivery requirement can be inferred from the Dealers' conduct as inconsistent with an intent to demand strict performance"); Guidry v. Charter Comm'ns, 269 S.W.3d 520 (Mo. App. 2008) (apartment complex waived cable provider's breach of fee agreement "by continuously accepting less than twenty percent of [cable provider's] subscription fees over a period of 18 months

with full knowledge that [cable provider] was not fulfilling its obligations under the payment arrangement.").

§8.19 n.13 p.537 Add the following to the list after **"But cf.":** PNC Bank v. Branch Banking & Trust, 466 Fed. Appx. 766 (11th Cir. 2012) (even though joint lender agreed to extend loan with knowledge of debtor's breach, lender did not waive its right to sue joint lender for breach of their participation agreement; lender accompanied extension with "blistering letter . . . accusing [joint lender] of mismanagement and putting [joint lender] on notice that [lender] considered [joint lender] to be in default of the participation agreement," so it was reasonable to conclude that the extension was understood to be an accommodation to the debtor and not a waiver).

§8.19 n.14 p.537 Add the following at the end: An anti-waiver clause may prove an effective way to counter acceptance of the other side's performance. *See* Wis. Elec. Power v. Union Pac. R.R., 557 F.3d 504 (7th Cir. 2009) (giving effect to anti-waiver clause because party seeking to waive it could not establish waiver by the requisite clear and convincing evidence); Long Island Sav. Bank v. United States, 503 F.3d 1234 (Fed. Cir. 2007) (finding presence of anti-waiver clause conclusive in refuting claim of waiver); *Ex parte* Keelboat Concepts, 938 So. 2d 922 (Ala. 2005) (anti-waiver clause meant that the promisee's "failure to strictly enforce terms of the franchise agreement . . . could not amount to a waiver of the requirement that notice of the election to renew be timely given"); Town of Hempstead v. Village of Freeport, 790 N.Y.S.2d 518 (App. Div. 2005) (lack of enforcement of minimum requirements clause not waived where contract "contained a 'no waiver' clause which specifically provided that the failure of any party to insist upon strict performance of any of the terms of the agreement 'shall not be considered to be a waiver' of such terms"); Am. Safety Cas. Ins. Co. v. City of Olympia, 174 P.3d 54 (Wash. 2007) (anti-waiver assertion, even if not invariably made, is enough to make the conduct "*not* unequivocal, as is required for waiver"). However, the actions of the parties may vitiate an anti-waiver clause. Pollard v. Southdale Gardens, 698 N.W.2d 449 (Minn. App. 2005) ("Because a nonwaiver clause may be modified by subsequent conduct, the mere presence of a nonwaiver clause does not automatically bar a waiver claim.").

***§8.19 n.15 p.537 In the second paragraph, add the following to the list after* "See generally":** Davis, UCC Breach of Warranty and Contract Claims: Clarifying the Distinction, 61 Baylor L. Rev. 783 (2009); Note, Revocation of Tripartite Rolling Contracts: Finding a Remedy in the Twenty-First Century Usage of Trade, 66 Ohio St. L.J. 397 (2005).

***§8.19 n.16 p.538 Add the following to the list after* "See":** Peavey Elecs. Corp. v. Baan U.S.A., 10 So. 3d 945 (Miss. App. 2009) ("The notice requirement exists to prevent commercial bad faith, promote mitigation and cure, enable the seller to collect evidence while still fresh, and promote settlement."; where contract between merchants, necessary for the aggrieved party "to give reasonable and timely notice that it considered [the other party] to be in breach of the agreement and to provide [it] with an opportunity to cure or mitigate [the aggrieved party's] continuing damages."); Wilson v. Tuxen, 754 N.W.2d 220 (Wis. App. 2008) (timely notice of breach required, even though cure impossible; "[T]he purpose of a notice goes beyond simply triggering any right to cure . . . [T]he notice is intended to 'open the way for settlement through negotiation between the parties' and give the seller an opportunity to protect him or herself . . . [UCC 2-607] required a notice of breach when a business solution to this problem was most likely to still be available.") (quoting from Eastern Air Lines, *supra*).

§8.19 n.16 p.538 In the first paragraph, add the following at the end: This has occasionally been framed using the language of condition. *See* Mauk v. Pioneer Ford Mercury, 709 S.E.2d 353 (Ga. App. 2011) ("The condition precedent to a claim for damages due to the seller's failure to accept the buyer's contract revocation under [UCC 2-608] is that the buyer give the seller notice of the revocation within a reasonable time and before the condition of the goods changes substantially from unrelated causes."). The main point — that with no notice there is no right to damages — is strictly accurate, though somewhat misleading; the absence of notice means that the buyer has made an ineffective revocation, but does not necessarily mean that the buyer has no cause of action against the seller for damages under UCC 2-714. *But see* UCC 2-607(3)(a) (notice requirement for recovery of damages under any theory). It is, however, unusual to use *condition* to refer to a statutory requirement. CISG contains a similar rule, though with a default limit of two years for the giving of notice. CISG Art. 39.

§8.19 n.16 p.538 In the second paragraph, add the following to the list after* "See generally"*: Flechtner, Funky Mussels, a Stolen Car, and Decrepit Used Shoes: Non-Conforming Goods and Notice Thereof Under the United Nations Sales Convention ("CISG"), 26 B.U. Int'l L.J. 1 (2008).

§8.19 n.20 p.539 Add the following after the citation to* Deere & Co.*: , followed in SCD RMA, LLC v. Farsighted Enters., 591 F. Supp. 2d 1131 (D. Haw. 2008) (sale of weather stripping for louvers: "[I]f the defect in the weather stripping could not be revealed upon mere visual inspection, RMA may not be barred from revoking acceptance simply because they cut and installed the louvers.").

§8.19a SELF-HELP

§8.19a n.1 p.543 Add the following after the first sentence: *See* Principles of the Law of Software Contracts §4.03 (2010) (outlining rights of software licensor to engage in automated disablement).

§8.19a n.1 p.543 Add the following after the second sentence: Similarly, a bank may exercise its right of set-off against a customer by taking the amount as to which the customer is in default from the amount held on deposit by the bank. Winecoff v. Compass Bank, 876 So. 2d 1145 (Ala. Civ. App. 2003). *See also* UCC 9-340 (bank's right of set-off prevails over secured lender with claims on account, unless the lender has control over the account).

§8.19a n.3 p.543 ***Add the following after the first sentence:*** *Cf.* Wis. Elec. Power v. Union Pac. R.R., 557 F.3d 504 (7th Cir. 2009) (use of no-waiver clause promotes the "amicable adjustment of contingencies bound to arise" in the course of a long-term contract).

§8.19b DRAFTING IN AID OF SELF-HELP

§8.19b n.6 p.549 ***Add the following at the end:*** It is not uncommon to use these clauses in, for example, government contracts, permitting the government to terminate the contract at will — the *termination for convenience* clause. Questar Bldrs. v. CB Flooring, 978 A.2d 651 (Md. 2009) (detailed discussion). It should, however, be noted that termination clauses are, like any others, subject to the general duty of good faith and fair dealing. *Id.* On the enforceability of these clauses, *see* §2.14 *supra.*

The actual notice of termination should be prompt, unequivocal, and complete — complete in the sense of listing all relevant bases for termination, lest any be waived. Once a notice of termination goes out, it is important to make certain that all later communications be consistent with termination. Inconsistent messages frequently yield disputes over whether and when termination occurred. The result may well be that the initial notice of termination is vitiated, thus bollixing up attempts to act upon a termination. *See* Centrix Mgmt. Co. v. Valencia, 33 A.3d 802 (Conn. App. 2011) (after eviction notice served, property manager told tenant that they would try to work out a settlement and that he did not want to evict her; result was dismissal of summary eviction proceedings).

§8.19b p.549 ***Add the following after the second full paragraph:*** Another means of furthering self-help is by putting in place a contractual cure right. In contracts not governed by Article Two of the UCC, this has the salutary effect of eliminating uncertainty as to the nature and scope — indeed, the existence — of cure. By doing so, "it allow[s] the parties, in the event of breach, to correct their course and maintain the promises in their contract."[8a] These clauses are not, however,

impervious to attack; as observed by the Pennsylvania Supreme Court, "when there is a breach of contract going directly to the essence of the contract, which is so exceedingly grave as to irreparably damage the trust between the contracting parties, the non-breaching party may terminate the contract without notice, absent explicit contractual provisions to the contrary."[8b]

[8a] Raymond Weil, S.A. v. Theron, 585 F. Supp. 2d 473 (S.D.N.Y. 2008) (clause stating that "[n]o party shall have the right to terminate the Agreement or sue for breach of this Agreement until it gives written notice of the alleged breach to the [other] party and a period of five (5) business days (in the country where the breach occurred) to cure the breach and such period elapses without such cure, unless the breach is of a sort that it cannot be cured. In that case, termination or suit may proceed immediately.").

[8b] LJL Transp. v. Pilot Air Freight, 962 A.2d 639 (Pa. 2009) (franchisee of freight forwarding company routed shipments through other freight for warders, including its own affiliated company). The court went on to observe that "[s]uch a breach is so fundamentally destructive, it understandably and inevitably causes the trust which is the bedrock foundation and veritable life-blood of the parties' contractual relationship to essentially evaporate." LJL Transp. v. Pilot Air Freight, 962 A.2d 639, 652 (Pa. 2009).

§8.20 ANTICIPATORY REPUDIATION AS A BREACH

§8.20 n.9 p.552 In the second paragraph, add the following at the end of the first sentence: and Kraus & Triantis, Anticipatory Repudiation Reconsidered, 6 Va. J. 54 (2003).

§8.20 n.9 p.552 In the second paragraph, add the following at the end: On comparative aspects of anticipatory repudiation, see Saidov, Anticipatory Non-Performance and Underlying Values of the UNIDROIT Principles, 11 Uniform L. Rev. 795 (2006).

§8.20 n.12 p.553 In the first paragraph, add the following to the list after* "Accord"*: Alvarez v. Rendon, 953 So. 2d 702 (Fla. App. 2007) ("[U]nder some circumstances, the anticipatory b[r]each of a contract by one party may excuse the other party from performing a condition precedent to that contract. . . . While anticipatory repudiation obviates the requirement that the conditions be performed, it does not obviate the requirement that they be performable.").

§8.20 n.12 p.553 Add the following after the citation to **Huntington Mining Holdings***:* , extended in Pesa v. Yoma Dev. Grp., 965 N.E.2d 228 (N.Y. 2012) (in action for damages, breached-against buyers must "show that they would and could have closed the transaction if the seller had proceeded to a closing as the contract required).

§8.20 n.12 p.553 ***In the first paragraph, add the following to the list after*** **"Cf."***:* Alter v. Levine, 870 N.Y.S.2d 464 (App. Div. 2008) (breach of contract to sell apartment, where cooperative board subsequently refused to approve the application; "Inasmuch as the board's refusal to approve the defendants' application rendered performance of the contract an impossibility, the issue of whether the defendants anticipatorily repudiated the contract is academic. . . . Accordingly, the plaintiff is not entitled to retain the down payment, even if the defendants had anticipatorily repudiated the contract.").

§8.20 n.12 p.553 ***In the first paragraph, add the following after the citation to*** **American List Corp.***:* , explained in Pesa v. Yoma Dev. Grp., 965 N.E.2d 228 (N.Y. 2012) (*American List* addresses only contracts to be performed far into the future, so that a plaintiff "would not be forced to meet the perhaps impossible burden of showing what its financial condition would have been for many years to come").

§8.20 n.15 p.554 ***Add the following at the end:*** New Hampshire does the same. LeTarte v. W. Side Dev., 855 A.2d 505 (N.H. 2004) ("an immediate cause of action for the plaintiff's entire injury [is] proper because 'courts should be able to deal with such a situation as here exists so as to avoid endless delays and multiplicity of suits.' ") (quoting from Hoyt v. Horst, 201 A.2d 118 (N.H. 1964)).

§8.20 n.16 p.554 ***Add the following at the end:*** *Contra:* Combs v. International Ins. Co., 354 F.3d 568 (6th Cir. 2004) ("there is ample authority for the proposition that the promising party can

anticipatorily repudiate a unilateral contract" such as directors' and officers' liability policy).

§8.21 WHAT CONSTITUTES A REPUDIATION

§8.21 n.1 p.558 Add the following at the end: The parties may in their contract define the standards for anticipatory repudiation, just as they do for issues of contract performance. This sort of clause is routine in financial contracts, in which merely having reason to doubt whether the debtor will perform ordinarily entitles the lender to declare a breach and accelerate repayment. They appear in other contexts as well, sometimes with a contractual right for the promisor to provide adequate assurance, sometimes not. *See* Shelby Homes at Millstone v. Cullinane, 61 So. 3d 472 (Fla. App. 2011) (giving effect to clause in home purchase agreement).

§8.21 n.4 p.559 Add the following at the end of the first paragraph: Thus repudiation of only one part of a contract will, if serious, amount to a repudiation of the whole; accordingly, a partial repudiator cannot insist on enforcing the balance of the contract. Lorang v. Fortis Ins. Co., 192 P.3d 186 (Mont. 2008).

§8.21 n.4 p.559 Add the following after the citation to **Mobil Oil Exploration***:* , distinguished by Amber Resources Co. v. U.S., 538 F.3d 1358 (Fed. Cir. 2008) (in *Mobil* the government immediately put the statute into effect, while here "[n]ot only had the parties in this case been performing under the lease agreements for years before the 1990 CZMA amendments were enacted, but they continued to perform under the lease agreement for another 11 years after the enactment of the 1990 amendments on the assumption that the 1990 amendments did not apply to lease suspensions"; accordingly, "the 1990 enactment itself did not constitute either a breach or an anticipatory repudiation").

§8.21 n.8 p.559 Add the following to the list after **"Accord"***:* Ratliff v. Hardison, 199 P.3d 696 (Ariz. App. 2008) (sufficiently clear that buyer had repudiated when buyer said,

inter alia, " 'I'm not capable of closing,' '[w]e're just not capable,' 'if my property had . . . sold, I would have [been able to perform],' and, '[w]ell Buddy, I can't perform. That's — that's it.' "); Lorang v. Fortis Ins. Co., *supra* note 4 (repudiation "must be absolute and unequivocal"; quoting from treatise); Butler Block, LLC v. Tri-County Metro. Transp. Dist., 255 P.3d 665 (Or. App. 2011) (repudiation occurs when a promisor by "its conduct evinces a fixed purpose not to perform the contract"; that party must refuse its obligations " 'positively, unconditionally, unequivocally, distinctly and absolutely' ") (quoting Mohr v. Lear, 395 P.2d 117 (Or. 1964)); Boro Constr. Co. v. Ridley Sch. Dist., 992 A.2d 208 (Pa. Commw. 2010) (statement that "some unnamed representative of the [owner] indicated to [the COO of the contractor] that the [owner] would not tender final payment under the contracts unless he dropped his claims regarding payment for extra work outside of the contracts" "does not objectively constitute the required 'absolute and unequivocal refusal to perform or a distinct and positive statement of an inability to do so.' ") (quoting from 2401 Pa. Ave. Corp. v. Fed'n of Jewish Agencies, 489 A.2d 733 (Pa. 1985)).

§8.21 n.8 p.559 Add the following after the citation to* Lake Durango Water Co.*: , followed in Lawry v. Palm, 192 P.3d 550 (Colo. App. 2008) ("A repudiation of a contract must consist of a party's present, positive, unequivocal refusal to perform the contract, not a mere threat to abandon its obligations under the contract.").

§8.21 n.9 p.560 Add the following to the list after* "Accord"*: Lorang v. Fortis Ins. Co., *supra* note 4 (insurance claim denial stating that the policy does not provide coverage for that type of claim, but offering to conduct a review of the claim determination upon request, insufficiently absolute; "By expressly offering to reconsider its determination, Fortis left open the possibility that it would honor its contractual obligation to cover . . . future claims"); D.G. II, LLC v. Nix, 712 S.E.2d 335 (N.C. App. 2011) (after boat builder told buyer that it would not meet the contract date for completion, owner offered a compromise, one option of which had the builder paying damages for breach; owner's offer held not an anticipatory repudiation, because one can both pursue a lawful remedy for breach and seek performance under the contract); UT Med. Grp. v. Vogt, 235 S.W.3d 110 (Tenn. 2007) (physician sought to negotiate buy-out clause, which her employer treated as an anticipatory repudiation: "An indication that more negotiations are sought is not a total and unqualified refusal to perform.").

§8.21 n.11 p.561 Add the following to the list after **"Accord"***:* Langer v. Bartholomay, 745 N.W.2d 649 (N.D. 2008) (notice to terminate lease given after deadline in option contract, where landowner thought tenant was in breach; thus, "the landowners' repudiation constituted an anticipatory breach of the lease").

§8.21 n.11 p.561 Add the following to the list after **"But see"***:* Butler Block, LLC v. Tri-County Metro. Transp. Dist., 255 P.3d 665 (Or. App. 2011) (party's statement that it did not understand a term of the contract to mean that the other party was entitled to an extension, particularly when accompanied by statements that it was "willing to meet to discuss [the other party's] request for an extension" and that it was "prepared to consider a request for an extension").

§8.21 n.11 p.561 Add the following after the fourth sentence: Lorang v. Fortis Ins. Co., *supra* note 4 ("Although the parties dispute whether the denial was a mistake or an intentional act, that issue is not relevant in determining whether Fortis repudiated its contractual duty."; citing to treatise).

§8.21 n.13 p.562 Add the following to the list after **"See"***:* PAMI-FL11 Inc. v. EMB-NHC, L.L.C., 857 A.2d 998 (Del. Ch. 2004) (defendant "repudiated the partnership agreements by stating unequivocally that it would perform only on terms different than those required [under] those agreements. In doing so, [defendant] unilaterally sought to alter both the present and reasonably anticipated future relations created by the partnership agreements and tried to use its superior economic power to impose a noncontractual understanding in lieu of the agreement between the parties").

***§8.21 n.14 p.562 In the first paragraph, add the following to the list after* "Accord":** O'Connor v. Sleasman, 830 N.Y.S.2d 377 (App. Div. 2007) (where "not a single word or inference threatened non-performance under the contract if the suggested modifications were not accepted," there was no unequivocal refusal to perform, making "plaintiff's immediate termination of the contract wrongful") (quoting from treatise); Hunter v. PriceKubecka, PLLC, 339 S.W.3d 795 (Tex. Civ. App. 2011) (offer of settlement agreement does not show fixed intention to refuse to perform contract).

§8.21 n.14 p.562 In the second paragraph, add the following to the list in the first sentence: Landwehr v. FDIC, 734 F. Supp. 2d 161 (D.D.C. 2010) ("neither the filing of a declaratory judgment action nor the allegations made in support of such an action can form the basis of a claim for anticipatory repudiation"); Restatement Second §250 cmt. *d* ("Modern procedural devices, such as the declaratory judgment, may be used to mitigate the harsh results that might otherwise result from [anticipatory repudiation]"); Lauchle v. Keeton Grp., 768 F. Supp. 2d 757 (M.D. Pa. 2011) (request for declaratory judgment to determine whether mineral leases valid under Pennsylvania statute not an anticipatory repudiation).

***§8.21 n.16 p.563 Add the following after the citation to* Record Club of Am.:** , followed in Homeland Training Ctr. v. Summit Point Auto. Research Ctr., 594 F.3d 285 (4th Cir. 2010) ("The dispositive consideration . . . is whether [the promisor] objectively manifested an unwillingness to perform under the contract — not its actual, subjective intention.").

***§8.21 n.17 p.563 Add the following to the list after* "Accord":** Cinel v. Barna, 142 Cal. Rptr. 3d 329 (Ct. App. 2012) (distinguishing between express and implied repudiation; "Implied repudiation occurs where conduct of the promisor puts it out of his or her power to perform the contract, and consists of a voluntary act rendering the obligor without the capacity to perform without a total breach.").

§8.21 n.18 p.564 Add the following to the list after **"But cf."***:* Timmerman v. Grain Exch., 915 N.E.2d 113 (Ill. App. 2009) ("once Grain Exchange lost its license to deal in grain, the contracts were effectively repudiated").

§8.21 n.19 p.564 Add the following to the end of the first sentence: Stiles Family Ltd. P'ship, III, LLP v. Riggs & Stiles, Inc., 2016 W. Va. LEXIS 902 (W. Va. Nov. 18, 2016) (no anticipatory repudiation where lease was for use of the land to farm only and tenant applied for a permit for a music festival but withdrew it without ever holding a concert or ceasing farming operations; "[w]ithdrawal of the application demonstrated precisely the type of equivocation that showed that respondents lacked an absolute and positive intent to breach the lease").

§8.21 n.19 p.564 Add the following at the end: For an exploration of how repudiation by impossibility relates to the defense of impossibility, *see* Record v. Kempe, 928 A.2d 1199 (Vt. 2007).

§8.22 RESPONSES TO REPUDIATION

§8.22 n.5 p.565 Add the following to the list after **"Accord"***:* Carnes Co. v. Stone Creek Mech., 412 F.3d 845 (7th Cir. 2005) ("far from being a repudiation of the contract . . . the refusal to ship was a legally justifiable response to [the defendant's] repudiation of the contract").

§8.22 n.6 p.565 Add the following to the list after **"Accord"***:* Thomas v. Montelucia Villas, 275 P.3d 607 (Ariz. App. 2012) ("The law does not require the non-breaching party to prove it was able to perform . . . unless it is seeking damages."); Trinity Quadrille v. Opera Place, 42 So. 3d 884 (Fla. App. 2010) ("Trinity breached the instant contract . . . and this anticipatory repudiation obviated further performance by Opera. Nonetheless, a showing that Opera otherwise could have performed remained a prerequisite to Opera's ability to prevail on its breach of contract claim."); Erin Food Servs. v. Derry Motel, 553 A.2d 304 (N.H. 1988) (Souter, J.: "Derry Motel's repudiation on

December 20 thus left Erin free to seek enforcement so long as it could establish its readiness, willingness, and ability to perform its side of the bargain . . .").

§8.22 n.10 p.566 Add the following at the end: *See generally* Carter & Peden, Damages Following Termination for Repudiation: Taking Account of Later Events, 24 J. Contract L. 145 (2008).

***§8.22 n.11 p.567 In the second paragraph, add the following to the list after* "see":** Ratliff v. Hardison, 199 P.3d 696 (Ariz. App. 2008) ("Retractions of repudiations must be clear and unequivocal in order for both the repudiator and the injured party to be treated fairly in a dispute. . . . Additionally, allowing a less than clear and unequivocal statement to serve as a retraction of a repudiation could yield harsh results for both repudiators and injured parties. Anticipatory repudiators who express remorse for their prospective breaches could find themselves unwittingly re-bound to a contract under which they are incapable of performing and surprised by substantial damages from a party who did not act to mitigate losses . . . Similarly, injured parties who understand an ambiguous retraction to be a mere expression of remorse could find themselves in breach when they make other arrangements to cover the repudiator's breach.").

§8.22 n.13 p.567 Add the following at the end: On the other hand, accepting the repudiation or responding to the repudiation by a termination may amount to a material change of position and prevent the retraction of the repudiation. Cent. Valley Hosp. v. Smith, 75 Cal. Rptr. 3d 771 (Ct. App. 2008) (following Restatement Second §256 and quoting from comment c and illustration 4).

***§8.22 n.14 p.567 Add the following to the list after* "Accord":** Lawry v. Palm, 192 P.3d 550 (Colo. App. 2008) ("The filing of a lawsuit based on repudiation is generally considered to constitute a material change of position.").

***§8.22 n.15 p.568 Add the following to the list after* "Accord":** Bookworld Trade v. Daughters of St. Paul, 532 F. Supp. 2d 1350 (M.D. Fla. 2007) (book publisher terminated relationship with distributor without giving proper notice;

however, where distributor continued listing publisher's books in its catalog and continued to demand and sell publisher's books, the publisher "waived any anticipatory breach"); Hanson v. Boeder, 727 N.W.2d 280 (N.D. 2007) ("[a] retraction of an anticipatory repudiation after the injured party sues for enforcement of damages comes too late") (quoting from Glatt v. Bank of Kirkwood Plaza, 383 N.W.2d 473 (N.D. 1986)).

§8.22 n.19 p.569 Add the following after the citation to **Mobil Oil Exploration***:* , followed in Amber Resources Co. v. United States, 538 F.3d 1358 (Fed. Cir. 2008) ("[M]erely requesting assurance from the other party that it does not intend to breach the agreement does not constitute an election to continue performance and to forgo the right to sue the other party for breach."; citing to Restatement Second §257).

§8.22 n.20 p.569 Add the following to the list after **"Accord"***:* Highlands Ranch Univ. Park v. Uno of Highlands Ranch, 129 P.3d 1020 (Colo. App. 2005) ("A continued willingness of the injured party to receive performance after a repudiation is an indication that, if the repudiator will withdraw its renunciation, but not otherwise, the contract may proceed. However, the innocent party does not thereby forfeit its right to treat the renunciation as a breach . . . So long as the repudiating party refuses to retract and continues its repudiation, the nonbreaching party may still elect to treat such repudiation as a breach."); AG Props. v. Besicorp-Empire Dev. Co., 788 N.Y.S.2d 694 (App. Div. 2005) (continuing discussions after anticipatory breach "did not constitute an election, but only a willingness to proceed with the agreement in the event that plaintiff agreed to retract its repudiation").

§8.22 n.21 p.570 Add the following at the end: As a corollary to this principle, until the injured party chooses to treat a repudiation as a breach, the contract is not breached — hence the ability of the repudiating party to retract its repudiation. Profile Invs. No. 25 v. Ammons E. Corp., 700 S.E.2d 232 (N.C. App. 2010).

§8.22 n.22 p.570 Add the following to the list after **"See"***:* EastBanc v. Georgetown Park Assocs. II, 940 A.2d 996

(D.C. 2008) ("[T]he time for filing suit does not begin to run on the strength of the repudiation alone. . . . [After repudiation] EastBanc was entitled to elect whether to sue immediately or to wait until a breach occurred.").

§8.23 EFFECT OF INSECURITY AS TO RETURN PERFORMANCE

§8.23 n.3 p.572 Add the following at the end: Before the rise of adequate assurance doctrine, one way around this problem was for the parties to create a contractual right to adequate assurance. Clauses of this sort were universally found enforceable. *See* James B. Berry's Sons Co. v. Monark Gasoline & Oil Co., 32 F.2d 74 (8th Cir. 1929); Casinghead Gas Co., v. Osborn, 112 A. 469 (Pa. 1921). *See generally* Havighurst, Protecting the Seller against Impairment of the Buyer's Credit, 20 Minn. L. Rev. 367 (1936). Clauses of this sort are still common, especially in lending agreements. *Cf.* Shelby Homes at Millstone v. Cullinane, 61 So. 3d 472 (Fla. App. 2011) (contract provided that if "Buyer informs Seller in writing that Buyer intends to terminate this agreement, or may be unable or unwilling to close, Seller may treat same as an anticipatory breach by Buyer unless Buyer provides assurances reasonably satisfactory to Seller that Buyer has the financial ability to close and will close.").

§8.23 n.6 p.572 Add the following at the end: This right came into the common law through the use of an implied condition of solvency in credit contracts. If the buyer became insolvent, the failure of the condition meant that the seller was not under a duty to grant credit. (It is not clear from the cases whether this was a condition precedent to the granting of credit or a condition subsequent to the continuation of credit. Very likely both.) This condition applied only to the credit aspect of the agreement, though, "so the seller could demand cash payment, and the buyer could be held in breach if it failed to pay at the time set for performance. More importantly, this condition had effect both with stoppage in transit and before; a credit seller could thus demand cash payment before the goods left its hands." But this implied condition did not relieve the seller of its obligation to tender the goods, and thus could not mitigate its losses immediately upon learning of the buyer's insolvency. *See* Garvin, Adequate Assurance of Performance: Of Risk, Duress, and Cognition, 69 U. Colo. L. Rev. 71, 83 (1998) (traces origins of adequate assurance).

§8.23 n.10 p.573 Add the following at the end: *See generally* Nyer, Withholding Performance for Breach in International Transactions: An Exercise in Equations, Proportions or Coercion?, 18 Pace Int'l L.J. 29 (2006).

§8.23 n.11 p.573 Add the following at the end of the last sentence: , followed in Advanced Bodycare Solutions v. Thione Int'l, 615 F.3d 1352 (11th Cir. 2010) (" '[t]o hold otherwise would allow a party to avoid liability for breaching its contract by invoking 2-609' ") (quoting from Hope's Architectural Prods., *supra*).

§8.23 n.12 p.573 In the second paragraph, add the following to the list after* "See generally"*: Borden, The Promissory Character of Adequate Assurances of Performance, 76 Brook. L. Rev. 167 (2010).

§8.23 n.15 p.574 Add the following to the list after* "Accord"*: Sean Wood, L.L.C. v. Hegarty Grp., 29 A.3d 1066 (N.J. Super. App. Div. 2011) (insecure seller unilaterally added COD term to contract and refused to deliver on any other terms; refusal held an anticipatory repudiation; court pointed out that the seller "could have demanded adequate assurance of future performance").

§8.23 n.16 p.574 Add the following to the list after* "Accord"*: Spring Creek Holding Co. v. Shinnihon U.S.A. Co., 943 A.2d 881 (N.J. App. Div. 2008) ("Whether the obligee's asserted grounds to demand adequate assurance are 'reasonable,' and whether the obligor's response is 'adequate,' are ordinarily questions of fact for the jury.").

§8.23 n.16 p.574 Add the following after the second sentence: *Cf.* Brisbin v. Superior Valve Co., 398 F.3d 279 (3d Cir. 2005) ("For a court of appeals sitting in review of a district court, the inquiry of whether conduct was so egregious . . . as to allow a conclusion on adequate assurance as a matter of law is functionally the same as whether a district court's finding of fact was clearly erroneous."), followed in Rocheux Int'l of N.J. v. U.S. Merchants Fin. Grp., 741 F. Supp. 2d 651 (D.N.J. 2010) ("a number of courts have recognized that the reasonableness of a party's insecurity, the propriety of a demand of assurance, and the adequacy of assurance tendered present questions of fact to be resolved by the jury," but "in certain circumstances where 'reasonable persons could reach only one conclusion, taking all inferences in favor of the moving party,' courts have determined that these issues may be resolved at the summary judgment stage.") (quoting from Alaska Pac. Trading v. Eagon Forest Prods., 933 P.2d 417, 422 (Wash. App. 1997)).

§8.23 n.20 p.575 Add the following after the first sentence: *See* Wildwood Indus. v. Genuine Mach. Design, 587 F. Supp. 2d 1035 (N.D. Ind. 2008) ("A buyer's demand of adequate assurance need not be based on a term of the contract; the buyer is then entitled to something that the contract may not otherwise require the seller to give."). This statement contains a regrettable negative inference — namely, that if the basis for the demand *is* a term of the contract, then the buyer is entitled only to something that the contract requires the seller to give. That extrinsic grounds for insecurity will generally yield extrinsic grounds for adequate assurance is correct, but the Code nowhere limits the basis for adequate assurance when the grounds for insecurity are intrinsic, and it would be unfortunate were courts to seize upon this dictum.

§8.23 n.23 p.576 Add the following to the list after "Accord": Validsa, Inc. v. PDVSA Servs., 424 Fed. Appx. 862 (11th Cir. 2011) ("[W]hether any assurances offered are adequate under UCC 2-609 is ordinarily a question of fact, but may be resolved as a matter of law when the evidence presented is such that a rational trier of fact could only arrive at one conclusion as to the issue."); Rocheux Int'l of N.J. v. U.S. Merchants Fin. Grp., 741 F. Supp. 2d 651 (D.N.J. 2010) (in response to demand for assurances, "a buyer's refusal to perform except upon conditions not required by the contract constitutes repudiation"; response to demand for overdue payment that sought to extend the delivery period and potentially the time for payment, or, if the goods were delivered C.O.D., to get a discount not adequate as a matter of law).

§8.23 n.23 p.576 Add the following after the citation to* Creusot-Loire Int'l*: , followed in Rocheux Int'l of N.J. v. U.S. Merchants Fin. Grp., 741 F. Supp. 2d 651 (D.N.J. 2010) (demand for letter of credit not unreasonable, given buyer's continued failure to pay outstanding invoices, buyer's offer of C.O.D. hence inadequate).

§8.23 n.24 p.577 Add the following to the list after* "See"*: Validsa, Inc. v. PDVSA Servs., 424 Fed. Appx. 862 (11th Cir. 2011) (noting that if the promisor "gave adequate assurances and did not anticipatorily breach, then [the promisee] breached by wrongfully terminating [the] contracts . . ."); Spring Creek Holding Co. v. Shinnihon U.S.A. Co., 943 A.2d 881 (N.J. App. Div. 2008) (where "requests for assurance yielded contradictory claims" and in substance amounted to "predictions of success in [underlying] litigation or straight denials of any problem," the proffered assurances were not adequate).

§8.23 p.577 In the first paragraph, add the following at the end of the last sentence: . . . greater security than was provided for in the contract.[24a]

[24a] Brisbin v. Superior Valve Co., *supra* note 16 ("the requested assurance need not be due under the contract"), followed in Wildwood Indus. v. Genuine Mach. Design, *supra* note 20 ("A buyer's demand of adequate assurance of due performance need not be based on a term of the contract; the buyer is then entitled to something that the contract may not otherwise require the seller to give."). As stated *supra* note 20, linking the first part of the quoted sentence to the last part is unsound, in that the requested assurance can always be outside the contract (though as the assurance departs more and more from the cause of insecurity, the recipient of the demand will be more and more entitled to reject it as unreasonable or offer a substitute more closely related to the contract).

§8.23 n.27 p.577 Add the following at the end: , distinguished in Bank of N.Y. v. River Terrace Assocs., 804 N.Y.S.2d 728 (App. Div. 2005) (declining to extend *Norcon* to long-term construction loan agreement). *Cf.* Carolina Consulting Corp. v. Ajax Paving Indus., 86 So. 3d 502 (Fla. App. 2012) (declining to decide whether adequate assurance doctrine applies to construction contracts; even if it did, no basis for insecurity where subcontractor's fears of going unpaid by general contractor were unfounded, given the presence of a statutorily-required bond, so subcontractor's refusal to perform was a breach of contract).

§8.23 n.28 p.577 Add the following to the list in the second sentence: McNeal v. Lebel, 953 A.2d 396 (N.H. 2008) (construction contract).

§8.23a PROBLEMS OF PROSPECTIVE NONPERFORMANCE

§8.23a n.2 p.579 Add the following to the list: Drake v. Wickwire, 795 P.2d 195 (Alaska 1990) (lawyer did not act reasonably in treating statement as repudiation and instead "could have sought assurances of performance").

§8.23a n.7 p.579 Add the following to the list after **"Accord"***:* GFSI, Inc. v. J-Loong Trading, 505 F. Supp. 2d 935 (D. Kan. 2007) (oral demand for assurance inadequate, and seller's decision to terminate the contract after was a breach).

§8.23a n.8 p.580 Add the following to the list in the second sentence: Rocheux Int'l of N.J. v. U.S. Merchants Fin. Grp., 741 F. Supp. 2d 651 (D.N.J. 2010) ("Although neither message included the exact term 'adequate assurance,' courts have generally eschewed applying formalistic requirements for the demand of adequate assurance, instead opting for a case-specific approach that considers a party's demands in the context of its course of dealings with the adverse party."); Validsa, Inc. v. PDVSA Servs., 632 F. Supp. 2d 1219 (S.D. Fla. 2009) (seller's letter stating that receipt of buyer's internal e-mail ordering suspension "a serious situation," listing the seller's concerns with the e-mail, and requesting "a written explanation of the situation" qualifies as a request for adequate assurance; "there is no requirement that requests for assurance track the statute"), *aff'd in part, rev'd in part on other grounds*, 424 Fed. Appx. 862 (11th Cir. 2011).

CHAPTER 9

FAILURE OF A BASIC ASSUMPTION: MISTAKE, IMPRACTICABILITY AND FRUSTRATION

§9.1 NATURE OF THE PROBLEM

§9.1 n.2 p.584 Add the following at the end of the first paragraph: For an illustration of a very different typology — that of Scottish law, derived both from the common law and from Roman law — *see* Hogg, The Continuing Confused Saga of Contract and Error, 13 Edinburgh L. Rev. 286 (2009).

§9.1 n.11 p.586 Add the following to the list in the first sentence: Kim, Mistakes, Changed Circumstances and Intent, 56 U. Kan. L. Rev. 473 (2008).

§9.1a STRICT LIABILITY OR BEST EFFORTS

§9.1a n.1 p.586 Add the following at the end: But it is far from clear that Holmes's generalization remains accurate, or even was accurate when he uttered it. A recent symposium has examined fault from many different and fruitful vantages. Symposium, Fault in American Contract Law, 107 Mich. L. Rev. 1341-1599 (2009).

§9.1a n.5 p.587 In the first paragraph, add the following after the second sentence: *Cf.* Occidental Permian Ltd. v. Helen Jones Found., 333 S.W.3d 392 (Tex. Civ. App. 2011) (oil and gas leases contain implied covenant by the lessee to manage and administer the lease, which "places on the lessee the duty to market the oil and gas reasonably").

§9.1a n.6 p.588 Add the following at the end of the first paragraph: *See also* N. Ins. Co. v. Point Judith Marina, 579 F.3d 61 (1st Cir. 2009) (supplying implied warranty of workmanlike performance, which is "inherent in federal maritime law"); Speight v. Walters Dev. Co., 744 N.W.2d 108 (Iowa 2008) (implied warranty of workmanlike construction); Carlile v. Harbour Homes, 194 P.3d 280 (Wash. App. 2008) (implied warranty of habitability).

§9.2 TYPES OF MISTAKE

§9.2 n.1 p.589 Add the following at the end: *See generally* C. MacMillan, Mistakes in Contract Law (2010); Eisenberg, Mistake in Contract Law, 91 Cal. L. Rev. 1573 (2003); Gordley, Mistake in Contract Formation, 52 Am. J. Comp. L. 433 (2004); Kim, Mistakes, Changed Circumstances, and Intent, 56 U. Kan. L. Rev. 473 (2008).

§9.2 n.4 p.590 Add the following to the list after "Accord": McKeever v. Warden, 486 F.3d 81 (3d Cir. 2007) (dictum: pointing out in the course of rejecting a mutual mistake defense, "this Court notes that . . . the mistake was one of law, not fact"); Wheeler-Dealer, Ltd. v. Christ, 885 N.E.2d 350 (Ill. App. 2008) ("The mistake must be one of fact, not of law"); Burggraff v. Baum, 720 A.2d 1167 (Me. 1998) ("The rationale behind this rule is that the parties are presumed to know the law, or at least [are] capable of verifying it, whereas they cannot be expected to be acquainted with all factual matters, regardless of their diligence."); Janusz v. Gilliam, 947 A.2d 560 (Md. 2008) ("the mutual mistake of law made by the parties is not, as a matter of law, grounds for rescission"; "The rule that a mistake of law is not grounds for rescission is founded on the principle that ignorance of the law is no excuse."); Vestin Realty Mortgage I v. Pickwick Partners, 279 S.W.3d 536 (Mo. App. 2009) ("Missouri law generally does not afford a remedy to a party who acts under a mistake of law."); Admiral Ins. Co. v. Paper Converting Machine Co., 811 N.W.2d 351 (Wis. 2012) ("A mistake of law does not provide a basis for voiding a contractual obligation.")

§9.2 n.5 p.590 Add the following to the list after **"Accord":** Harding County v. Frithiof, 575 F.3d 767 (8th Cir. 2009) (rescission available "if there was (1) 'misapprehension of the law by all parties . . . making substantially the same mistake as to the law,' or (2) 'misapprehension of the law by one party of which the others are aware at the time of contracting.' " (quoting S.D. Codified Laws §53-4-10)); Dowling v. Farmers Ins. Exch., 145 Cal. Rptr. 3d 748 (Ct. App. 2012) ("A mistake of law vitiates consent only if (1) all contracting parties shared the same misunderstanding of the law; or (2) one party misunderstood the law, and the other contracting parties were aware of this and failed to rectify it."); Hearn v. Hearn, 936 A.2d 400 (Md. App. 2007) (mistake as to legal effect of benefits terms of annuity contract; "a mistaken belief regarding legal provisions is but one variety of mistake as to the facts"; quoting from treatise); *In re* Lemieux, 949 A.2d 720 (N.H. 2008) ("Modern contract law does not distinguish between mistakes of fact and mistakes of law, but treats both alike for purposes of equitable relief.") (quoting from treatise); Pugh's Lawn Landscape Co. v. Jaycon Dev. Corp., 320 S.W.3d 252 (Tenn. 2010) (mistake rests "on an erroneous conviction of law or fact"); Restatement Second §151 cmt. *b* ("The rules stated in this Chapter do not draw the distinction that is sometimes made between 'fact' and 'law.' They treat the law in existence at the time of the making of the contract as part of the total state of facts at that time.").

§9.2 n.5 p.590 Add the following after the third sentence: Cf. Johnson Family Ltd. P'ship v. White Pine Wireless, 761 N.W.2d 353 (Mich. App. 2008) (within mistakes of law, distinguishing between "mistakes regarding the legal effect of the contract actually made and mistakes in reducing the instrument to writing"; " 'In the former, . . . the contract actually entered into will seldom, if ever, be relieved against unless there are other equitable legal

features calling for the interposition of the court; but in the second class, where the mistake is not in the contract itself, but terms are used in or omitted from the instrument which give it a legal effect not intended by the parties, and different from the contract actually made, equity will always grant relief unless barred on some other ground, by correcting the mistake so as to produce a conformity of the instrument to the agreement.'") (quoting from Schmalzriedt v. Titsworth, 9 N.W.2d 24 (Mich. 1943)).

§9.2 n.6 p.591 Add the following to the list after **"Accord"***:* Mears v. Safeco Ins. Co., 888 F. Supp. 2d 1048 (D. Mont. 2012) ("parties are bound by their agreement if they merely underestimated the future severity of an injury or failed to predict a future event or condition"); Flintlock Constr. Servs. v. Am. Safety Risk Retention Grp., 819 F. Supp. 2d 1303 (N.D. Ga. 2011) (New York law: whether general liability insurer would indemnify a general contractor is a mistake as to a future fact, and thus does not justify rescission of an agreement between the general contractor and owner based on that assumption), *aff'd in part, rev'd in part on other grounds*, 710 F.3d 1221 (11th Cir. 2013); Simkin v. Blank, 968 N.E.2d 459 (N.Y. 2012) (marital settlement agreement was made before the Madoff Ponzi scheme was exposed; on its exposure, husband's assets declined significantly, and he sought to reform the contract because the parties were mistaken in their belief that they had an actual brokerage account and not a sham; no reformation, in part because "the mutual mistake must have existed at the time the agreement was executed," and when the agreement was executed it was still possible to redeem the investment); Deep Creek Ranch v. Utah State Armory Bd., 178 P.3d 886 (Utah 2008) ("To serve as a basis for voiding a contract, the mutual mistake must concern a past or existing fact, not a future contingency."), followed in Robinson v. Robinson, 232 P.3d 1081 (Utah App. 2010) (husband attempted to avoid property settlement because part of the property could not be refinanced and generated less income than expected; "These assumptions are simply expectations as to future events — that those events would not vary significantly from the current state of events — and therefore do not support the contractual defense of mutual mistake."); Ryan v. Ryan, 640 S.E.2d 64 (W. Va. 2006) ("A party's prediction or judgment as to events to occur in the future,

even if erroneous, is not a 'mistake' for the purpose of reforming a contract or making a contract voidable."), followed in Kruzich v. Old Republic Ins. Co., 188 P.3d 983 (Mont. 2008) ("parties to a contract make a mutual mistake of fact only if they are unconsciously ignorant or forgetful of a fact that existed *prior to or at the time of* settlement. Ignorance of a future event does not amount to a mistake of fact.") (emphasis in original); Restatement (Third) of Restitution and Unjust Enrichment §5(2) & cmt. *g* ("An invalidating mistake may be a misapprehension of either fact or law."; rejecting the distinction between law and fact "because it has always been theoretically unsound; because the two types of mistake are frequently impossible to distinguish as a practical matter; and because the distinction, even when it is possible, has no relevance to the real analysis by which restitution is either granted or withheld").

§9.2 n.8 p.592 In the first paragraph, add the following to the list after **"Cf."***:* Louis & Karen Metro Family, LLC v. Lawrenceburg Conservancy Dist., 616 F.3d 618 (7th Cir. 2010) (sale of land to district for use in a levee project included option to repurchase, but when the project was cancelled the district sold the land to another; latent ambiguity resolved through reformation for mutual mistake, because "at the time the agreement was signed there was a mutual mistake of present fact. The mutual mistake was that the project had reached the point beyond which cancellation was out of the question.").

§9.2 n.8 p.592 Add the following at the end of the first paragraph: The decision in *Metro Family* tests the boundaries of the fact-prediction distinction. What the court describes as a present fact about the likelihood of cancellation could at least as easily be described as a prediction regarding whether the project would be cancelled. But the courts have been willing to extend fact to include the likelihood of governmental action, so this decision at least has plentiful company. *See infra* §9.3 on the meaning of "basic assumption."

§9.2 n.12 p.594 Add the following to the list after **"Accord"***:* Alvarez v. Castellon, 55 A.3d 352 (Del. 2012) ("'[W]here parties have knowingly and purposely made an

agreement to compromise and settle a doubtful claim, whose character and extent are necessarily conditioned by future contingent events, it is no ground for the avoidance of the contract that the events happen very differently from the expectation, opinion, or belief of one or both of the parties.'"; no avoidance through mistake where insured knew that she had neck and back pain when she settled her claim and signed the release);

§9.2 n.14 p.595 Add the following at the end: *See also* Borden, Mistake and Disclosure in a Model of Two-Sided Informational Inputs, 73 Mo. L. Rev. 667 (2008); Harrison, Rethinking Mistake and Nondisclosure in Contract Law, 17 Geo. Mason L. Rev. 335 (2010); Kraus & Scott, Contract Design and the Structure of Contractual Intent, 84 N.Y.U. L. Rev. 1023 (2009).

§9.3 MUTUAL MISTAKE

§9.3 n.1 p.595 Add the following to the list in the first sentence: Johnson v. Conner, 260 S.W.3d 575 (Tex. Civ. App. 2008) (the parties interpreted a deed differently, but "[f]or a mutual mistake to exist, there must be the same mistaken belief or assumption in the minds of the grantors and grantees named in the deed. . . . Two separate unilateral mistakes in the minds of the grantors and grantees do not create a factual issue for a mutual mistake cause of action.").

***§9.3 n.1 p.595 Add the following to the list after* "Cf.":** Ill. Nat'l Ins. Co. v. Wyndham Worldwide Operations, 653 F.3d 225 (3d Cir. 2011) ("[T]he understanding of persons who were not contracting parties at the time of consummation of a contract is irrelevant.").

§9.3 n.1 p.595 Add the following at the end: Texas law oddly provides that "[u]nilateral mistake by one party, and knowledge of that mistake by the other party, is equivalent to mutual mistake." Davis v. Grammer, 750 S.W.2d 766, 768 (Tex. 1988), followed in Givens v. Ward, 272 S.W.3d 63 (Tex. Civ. App. 2008) ("the requisite mutual mistake consists of [the Givens's] unilateral mistake in signing a deed which did not conform to the parties' agreement and the Wards' knowledge that the deed did not conform"). Possibly this doctrine is a relic of the time when unilateral mistake yielded no remedy of avoidance. Whatever its origin, though, it surely is at best unnecessary today. If the unmistaken party knows of the other side's error, then the unilateral mistake provides a basis for relief if the mistake otherwise meets the basic requirements of relief for mutual mistake. Restatement Second §153(b); see *infra* §9.4 at notes 23-28 (unilateral mistake). Perhaps there is no harm in placing these cases under the mutual mistake rubric, but there is also no need.

§9.3 n.2 p.596 Add the following to the list after "See": Stockmeyer, To Err is Human, To Moo Bovine: The Rose of Aberlone Story, 24 T.M. Cooley L. Rev. 491 (2007).

§9.3 n.2 p.596 Add the following at the end: *See generally* Eisenberg, Mistake in Contract Law, 91 Cal. L. Rev. 1573 (2003); Gordley, Mistake in Contract Formation, 52 Am. J. Comp. L. 433 (2004).

§9.3 n.3 p.596 Add the following at the end: The Restatement Second approach is by no means uniformly adhered to, though most jurisdictions have adopted its approach either expressly or tacitly. *See, e.g.*, Oakes v. Holly, 268 P.3d 1084 (Alaska 2012) (noting adoption of Restatement Second §§152, 155). *But see* McEntee v. Davis, 861 A.2d 459 (R.I. 2004) (declining to adopt Restatement Second approach, instead looking at such things as the intent of the parties and the extent to which the mistake fails to reflect the understanding of both parties, proved by clear and convincing evidence), followed in Hazard v. Hazard, 45 A.3d 545 (R.I. 2012) (requires clear and convincing evidence; not present when merely different opinions by appraisers). For remarkable ecumenism on the standard of proof, see Bert Allen Toyota v. Grasz, 909 So. 2d 763 (Miss. App. 2005) ("the proof must establish mutual mistake beyond a reasonable doubt" and "the evidence must be clear and convincing"). Here as elsewhere, a stricter standard of proof may restrain the overuse of the mistake defense. *See* nVision Global Tech. Solutions v. Cardinal Health 5, LLC, 887 F. Supp. 2d 1240 (N.D. Ga. 2012) (obtaining equitable relief based on a mutual mistake requires "clear, unequivocal and decisive" evidence.).

§9.3 n.6 p.597 Add the following to the list after **"Accord"***:* Louis & Karen Metro Family, LLC v. Lawrenceburg Conservancy Dist., 616 F.3d 618 (7th Cir. 2010) (sale of land to district for use in a levee project included option to repurchase, but when the project was cancelled the district sold the land to another; latent ambiguity resolved through reformation for mutual mistake, because "at the time the agreement was signed there was a mutual mistake of present fact. The mutual mistake was that the project had reached the point beyond which cancellation was out of the question."); Anwar v. Fairfield Greenwich Ltd., 728 F. Supp. 2d 372 (S.D.N.Y. 2010) (investors in Madoff enterprises held basic assumption that their money was actually going to be invested); Merryman v. Cargile, 2012 Ark. App. 248, 413 S.W.3d 555 (2012) (reforming deeds because the settlement agreement that allocated land was based on a highly inaccurate assumption about the location of a road used as a benchmark).

§9.3 n.6 p.597 Add the following to the list after **"But cf."***:* United States v. Frownfelter, 626 F.3d 549 (10th Cir. 2010) (in plea agreement, government dismissed all but one count on the assumption that the remaining count was a felony, but it in fact was a misdemeanor; when the government sought to avoid the plea agreement, the court held that "nothing in the language of the plea agreement indicates that the distinction between misdemeanor and felony was a basic assumption of the plea agreement"); United States v. White, 597 F.3d 863 (7th Cir. 2010) (in plea agreement, government promised to recommend "safety valve" reduction in sentence if accused qualified, but ultimately accused did not; no mutual mistake because "both the plea agreement and the district court specifically addressed the contingency regarding safety valve treatment" and so "the mistake was not about an essential term of the agreement"); Landmark Inv. Grp. v. Chung Family Realty, 10 A.3d 61 (Conn. App. 2010) (absence of brownfields funding not grounds for rescission due to mutual mistake where contract already provided for that possibility).

***§9.3 n.11 p.599 Add the following to the list after* "See":** McKeever v. Warden, 486 F.3d 81 (3d Cir. 2007) (plea bargain: mutual mistake of law not material under the Restatement Second approach when the plaintiff stated "that had it not been for the mistake, he 'may, or may not, have pleaded guilty rather than risk trial' ").

§9.3 n.12 p.599 Add the following at the end: For a somewhat extravagant judicial expression of this view, *see* Kesling v. Kesling, 967 N.E.2d 66 (Ind. App. 2012) ("It is not enough that both parties are mistaken about any fact; rather, the mistaken fact complained of must be one that is of the essence of the agreement, the *sine qua non,* or, as is sometimes said, the efficient cause of the agreement, and must be such that it animates and controls the conduct of the parties.") (internal quotations omitted).

§9.3 n.25 p.603 Add the following to the list in the third sentence: State v. Codiga, 175 P.3d 1082 (Wash. 2008) ("a successful avoidance of an agreement based on mutual mistake depends upon a finding that the party seeking to avoid the agreement did not bear the risk of the mistake") (citing to treatise).

***§9.3 n.27 p.603 Add the following to the list after* "Accord":** Kroll v. United States, 107 Fed. Cl. 605 (Fed. Cl. 2012) (HUD's invitation to bid contained "numerous provisions . . . calling for due diligence by bidders in determining the value of the property" up for auction; buyer complaining of grossly inaccurate information supplied by HUD has no mutual mistake defense, because "[t]he Acknowledgment by Bidder clearly places the onus on Ms. Kroll to have determined an appropriate bid for the property."); Deep Creek Ranch v Utah State Armory Bd., 178 P.3d 886 (Utah 2008) (where seller "explicitly warranted its ability to cause the transfer of the surplus property . . . and neglect[ed] to make the contract contingent on approval from the GSA, Armory assumed the risk of being held liable if the GSA did not approve the transaction").

***§9.3 n.27 p.603 In the first paragraph, add the following after the citation to* Pairett:** and in Cherry v. McCall, 138 S.W.3d 35 (Tex. Civ. App. 2004) (there was "no evidence to support the . . . argument that the 'as is' provision was not freely negotiated").

§9.3 n.27 p.603 Add the following to the list after **"Accord"***:* Rawson v. UMLIC VP, L.L.C., 933 So. 2d 1206 (Fla. App. 2006) (where contract for sale of real property stated that the purchase was "in an 'as is, where is' condition 'with all faults,' " that the buyers did not rely on any representations made by the seller, and that it was the buyer's duty to verify any representations, "the risk of the mistake was clearly placed on the [buyer].").

§9.3 n.31 p.605 Add the following at the end: Cf. Coburn v. Auto-Owners Ins. Co., 938 N.E.2d 400 (Ohio App. 2010) ("mutual mistake is a full defense to a release if the parties did not intend to relinquish all future claims"; laying out seven-factor test for determining the intent of the parties, including whether the parties negotiated, whether the insured was "clearly liable," whether consideration was inadequate in light of the risk involved, whether the release was secured in haste, and whether the terms of the release exclude the injury in question).

§9.3 n.34 p.605 Add the following to the list after **"Accord"***:* BP Grp., Inc. v. Kloeber, 664 F.3d 1235 (8th Cir. 2012) (Florida law: "A party who is aware of a problem or uncertainty, but elects to ' "take a chance" and close,' waives its right to rescind"; mutual uncertainty whether aircraft could be transferred legally means that the parties "consciously accepted the risk of any mistake") (quoting from Rosique v. Windley Cove, Ltd., 542 So. 2d 1014, 1016 (Fla. App. 1989)); Std. Steam Trust LLC v. Windfall Minerals, 872 F. Supp. 2d 1207 (D. Colo. 2012) (Nevada law: geothermal energy firm knew that river ran through part of leased area and that the river would affect its ability to use the lands; "The fact that Standard Steam did not know the full extent of the restrictions . . . place[d] on the land due to the riparian zone does not mean that there was a mistake of fact at the time of formation of the Lease."); Leff v. Ecker, 972 So. 2d 965 (Fla. App. 2007) (following Restatement Second §154; "[P]laintiff went into the mediation conference without a clear picture of what the policy limits were for the incidents in question. . . . Notwithstanding this limited knowledge, plaintiff chose to go ahead with the

mediation and entered into an agreement at the end thereof. . . . The doctrine of mutual mistake was not created to relieve litigants of agreements entered into improvidently."); Thor Props. v. Chetrit Grp., 936 N.Y.S.2d 196 (App. Div. 2012) (settlement agreement hinged on governmental approval of development; "Because it was always uncertain whether the City would permit or deny further development of the property, any assumption about the ability to develop property could not have existed at the time the parties entered into the agreement.").

§9.3 n.35 p.606 Add the following at the end: Kentucky and Oregon take this approach as far as it will go, categorically rejecting the mutual mistake defense for personal injury releases. Coomer v. Phelps, 172 S.W.3d 389 (Ky. 2005) ("To retreat from this rule would cast great doubt on the finality of releases in this state and unnecessarily complicate settlement considerations."); Graves v. Tulleners, 134 P.3d 990 (Or. App. 2006) ("mutual mistake is not a basis on which to void a release agreement" because "'[c]ertainty and judicial economy are served when parties can negotiate settlement of their disputes with confidence that their settlement agreements will be upheld'") (quoting from Lindgren v. Berg, 772 P.2d 1336 (Or. 1989)).

§9.3 n.36 p.606 Add the following at the beginning: Cordovez v. High-Rise Installation, 46 So. 3d 1120 (Fla. App. 2010) (upholding settlement where "both parties knew Claimant suffered an injury to the head; they did not, however, know the full extent of that head injury," and distinguishing other decision because it involved the unknown consequence of an unknown injury).

§9.3 n.41 p.607 Add the following to the list after "Accord": Harrison v. Liberty Nw. Ins. Corp., 181 P.3d 590 (Mont. 2008) ("At the time of settlement . . . [employer and employee] did not believe [employee's] injury would require surgery and therefore the settlement terms did not include consideration of this possibility. As a result, the parties were operating under a material mistake of fact.").

§9.3 n.41 p.607 ***Add the following at the end:*** For an interesting variation on this theme, *see* Cheff v. BNSF Ry. Co., 243 P.3d 1115 (Mont. 2010). There the parties knew how the claimant had been injured, but did not know about a pre-existing condition that rendered the expected surgery impossible. The court found the unawareness of the pre-existing condition sufficient to invalidate a settlement agreement.

§9.3 n.43 p.608 ***Add the following at the end:*** In a reversal of these fact patterns, a liability insurance company and a victim of its insured settled a claim on the assumption that the policy provided for higher limits of coverage than it actually did. The insurer was denied rescission of the settlement agreement due to mutual mistake because "an insurance company must be presumed to know the terms of a policy of insurance it issues" and the company in any event relied upon the understanding of its agent rather than consult the policy itself, with the court applying Restatement Second §154(b). Farm Bureau Mut. Ins. Co. v. Buckallew, 685 N.W.2d 675 (Mich. App.), *vacated on other grounds*, 690 N.W.2d 93 (Mich. 2004). This is a bit strained. The court here conflates what the insurance company *knew*, which is covered in §154(b), with what it *should have known*, which is covered, if at all, under §154(c) *infra*.

§9.3 n.47 p.609 ***Add the following after the first sentence:*** *Accord:* United States v. Frownfelter, 626 F.3d 549 (10th Cir. 2010) (plea agreement in which the sole surviving count was thought to be a misdemeanor, but actually was a felony; "The mistake in this case — that the language of the statute meant what it said — is a risk the United States assumed when it drafted both the original indictment and the plea agreement."); Wasser & Winters Co. v. Ritchie Bros. Auctioneers, 185 P.3d 73 (Alaska 2008) (following Restatement; where neither creditor nor auctioneer of creditor's collateral aware of liens, creditor bore risk, because it "had a direct financial interest in the equipment itself" and placing the risk on the auctioneer "would expose [it] to liability far exceeding its possible interest, whereas placing the risk of mistake on [the creditor] would give [the creditor] essentially what it would have received had it known about the other liens."); Farm Bureau Mut. Ins. Co. v. Buckallew, 685 N.W.2d 675 (Mich. App.),

vacated on other grounds, 690 N.W.2d (Mich. 2004) (following Restatement; in alternative holding, court finds no mutual mistake where insurer and victim of insured misinterpreted the insured's policy to provide greater coverage than it actually did, because the insurer bore the risk that it would misread its own policy); Eldridge v. Shaw, 952 N.Y.S.2d 360 (App. Div. 2012) (parties to settlement agreement based borderline on survey that proved inaccurate; no rescission for mutual mistake, because "the intent of the parties can be gleaned from the stipulation, wherein they unambiguously agreed that the boundary line between their properties 'would be established as the line designated in the [defendants'] survey.'"); State v. Codiga, 175 P.3d 1082 (Wash. 2008) (in plea agreement, "if any additional criminal history is discovered, both the standard sentence range and the prosecuting attorney's recommendation may increase" held to place the risk of a factual error on criminal history on the defendant, which "is both fair and reasonable because the facts of his or her criminal history should be within the defendant's knowledge . . . In contrast, a defendant should *not* be charged with knowing the *legal* impact of his or her criminal history on the offender score.") (emphasis in original).

§9.3 n.49 p.609 Add the following to the list after "Accord": Czarobski v. Lata, 882 N.E.2d 536 (Ill. 2008) ("[A] mistake that results from a party's lack of due care may be insufficient to support a claim of mutual mistake."); Motorists Mut. Ins. Co. v. Columbus Fin., 861 N.E.2d 605 (Ohio App. 2006) (mutual mistake is "a ground for rescission only where the complainant is not negligent in failing to discover the mistake"; here the insurance company mixed up two claims and paid the wrong one, and was held negligent).

§9.3 n.49 p.609 Add the following after the second sentence: *Cf.* Keller v. Liberty N.W., Inc., 246 P.3d 434 (Mont. 2010) ("mutual mistake may still exist when parties know about a theory of injury, if that theory is disregarded, forgotten, or not considered even though raised as a possibility").

§9.3 n.52 p.610 Add the following after the second sentence: Indeed, it has even been held that mutual mistake as to the consequences of a choice of law provision that rendered part of the contract invalid would not warrant reformation, given the possibility that "a choice of Georgia law may have had its own undesirable implications"; reformation would be warranted only when the entire contract would as a result be invalid. CS-Lakeview at Gwinnett v. Simon Prop. Grp., 659 S.E.2d 359, 362 (Ga. 2008).

§9.3 n.52 p.610 Add the following at the end: However, reformation is available only where the mistake rests in the expression of the contract rather than in its formation. Nichols v. City of Evansdale, 687 N.W.2d 562 (Iowa 2004) ("When the mistake is in the expression of the contract, the proper remedy is reformation . . . When the mistake is in the formation of the contract, on the other hand, avoidance is the proper remedy."); George v. Veeder, 820 N.W.2d 731 (N.D. 2012) ("'A mutual mistake that will justify reformation requires that, at the time of the execution of the agreement, both parties intended to say something different from what was said in the document.'") (quoting from Arndt v. Maki, 813 N.W.2d 564, 569 (N.D. 2012)); Restatement Second §155 cmt. *b* ("If, however, the parties make a written agreement that they would not otherwise have made because of a mistake other than one as to expression, the court will not reform a writing to reflect the agreement that it thinks they would have made. The remedy in that case is avoidance."). Nor is reformation favored as a remedy for mutual mistake. To the contrary: "This doctrine, like the doctrine of scrivener's error, undermines the integrity and certainty of contracts; and a court will not reform a written agreement on those grounds unless there is clear and convincing evidence of mutual mistake." Tiger Fibers v. Aspen Specialty Ins. Co., 594 F. Supp. 2d 630, 643-644 (E.D. Va. 2009). On reformation, see *supra* §7.5.

The Federal Rules of Civil Procedure, and thus the procedure codes of most states, provide for relief from a judgment based on mistake. Fed. R. Civ. Pro. Rule 60(b). *See also* Oakes v. Holly, 268 P.3d 1084 (Alaska 2012) (applying rule as codified in Alaska).

British law takes a somewhat different turn. "Common mistake," its equitable counterpart to mutual mistake, makes a contract *void* rather than merely voidable. Great Peace Shipping v. Tsavliris Salvage (Int'l), [2002] 3 W.L.R. 1617. On the other hand, *Great Peace Shipping* also limits common mistake to circumstances verging on impossibility. *Great Peace Shipping* has not escaped criticism in Britain, nor should it. Edelman, An Uncommon Mistake?, 15 King's Coll. L.J. 128 (2004).

***§9.3 n.54 p.610 Add the following to the list after* "Accord":** Wright v. O'Daniel, 58 So. 3d 694 (Miss. App. 2011) (neither mutual nor unilateral mistake when party seeking reformation knew of error in deed, but did not seek to correct it for four years).

§9.3 n.55 p.610 Add the following at the end: *But see* Scott v. Zimmer, Inc., 889 F. Supp. 657 (D. Del. 2012) (Indiana law: rescinding party must fully restore the other party before she can assert rescission; insufficient that the defendant "has *offered* to return the money he was paid if the contract is rescinded, however, he has not returned the compensation as a condition precedent to this action"; misstates precedent, which provides that "a party wishing to avoid the effect of his release must restore the status quo by restoring *or tendering* the consideration received by him") (quoting from Prall v. Ind. Nat'l Bank, 627 N.E.2d 1374 (Ind. App. 1994) (emphasis added)).

§9.3 n.56 p.611 Add the following after the third sentence: For an imaginative but misguided attempt, see Louis & Karen Metro Family, LLC v. Lawrenceburg Conservancy Dist., 616 F.3d 618 (7th Cir. 2010) (sale of land to district for use in a levee project included option to repurchase, but when the project was cancelled the district sold the land to another; court reformed option to give the former owners time in which to exercise it, but appellate court reversed and ordered damages, because the land "now lies beneath a spaghetti-bowl of freeway lanes and is utterly inaccessible," making the option worthless whatever its duration).

§9.3 n.56 p.611 Add the following at the end: These equitable concerns apply only to the contracting parties. Whether rescission would harm a non-party is no bar to its use. Ill. Nat'l Ins. Co. v. Wyndham Worldwide Operations, 653 F.3d 225 (3d Cir.

2011) ("Reformation on the basis of mutual mistake can be granted even when it is to the disadvantage of a third party.").

§9.3a DRAFTING RELEASES

§9.3a n.11 p.613 Add the following after the citation to* Jefferson*: , followed in Marder v. Lopez, 450 F.3d 445 (9th Cir. 2006) (release of "each and every claim . . . of any kind or character which have arisen or are based in whole or in part on any matters occurring at any time prior to the date of this Release," accompanied by a release form claims "arising out of or in any way connected with, either directly or indirectly, any and all arrangements . . ." "exceptionally broad" and encompassing claims of copyright infringement).

§9.3a p.613 Add the following after the last sentence of the first full paragraph: . . . in the face of a claim of mutual mistake.[11a]

[11a] Properly drafted clauses may even vitiate claims of mistake induced by inaccurate statements by the other party. *See* Kroll v. United States, 107 Fed. Cl. 605 (Fed. Cl. 2012) (HUD's invitation to bid contained "numerous provisions . . . calling for due diligence by bidders in determining the value of the property" up for auction; buyer complaining of grossly inaccurate information supplied by HUD has no mutual mistake defense, because "[t]he Acknowledgment by Bidder clearly places the onus on Ms. Kroll to have determined an appropriate bid for the property.").

§9.4 UNILATERAL MISTAKE

§9.4 n.1 p.614 Add the following to the list after* "Accord"*: *In re* UAL Corp., 411 F.3d 818 (7th Cir. 2005) (Posner, J.) ("a unilateral mistake . . . is not a generally recognized excuse for failing to comply with the contract's terms") (citing to treatise); McEntee v. Davis, 861 A.2d 459 (R.I. 2004) ("'[A] unilateral mistake in the formation of a contract affords the errant no relief.'") (quoting from Boccarossa v. Watkins, 313 A.2d 135 (R.I. 1973)).

§9.4 n.1 p.614 Add the following at the end: For a positively rhadamanthine approach to unilateral mistake, *see* Brown v. Genesee County, 872 F.2d 169 (6th Cir. 1989) (Michigan law: "A unilateral mistake is not sufficient to allow the mistaken to limit or avoid the effect of an otherwise valid settlement agreement."), followed in Hill v. Ohio State Univ., 870 F. Supp. 2d 526 (S.D. Ohio 2012) (Ohio law: even if professor mistaken about how pension rights would be affected by his settlement agreement with the university, that would be a unilateral mistake and thus could not be used to rescind the agreement). Fortunately for Ohioans, the district court did not recite Ohio law accurately. *See* Ohio *ex rel.* BDFM Co. v. Ohio Dep't of Transp., 2013-Ohio-107 (Ohio Ct. App. 2013) (evaluating claim that settlement agreement voidable because of unilateral mistake). Unfortunately for Michiganders, the circuit court did recite Michigan law accurately. *See* Casey v. Auto-Owners Ins. Co., 729 N.W.2d 277 (Mich. App. 2006) ("A unilateral mistake is not sufficient to warrant reformation."). This former Michigander and current Ohioan is much relieved.

A slightly less rigid approach limits the scope of unilateral mistake to error induced by the other party's fraud. *See* Comiskey v. FH Partners, LLC, 373 S.W.3d 620 (Tex. Civ. App. 2012).

§9.4 n.2 p.614 Add the following to the list after* "See generally"*: Eisenberg, Mistake in Contract Law, 91 Calif. L. Rev. 1573 (2003); Gordley, Mistake in Contract Formation, 52 Am. J. Comp. L. 433 (2004).

§9.4 n.7 p.615 Add the following at the end: Some states have dealt with this problem by statute, commonly by allowing recovery of the bid bond where the error was material. Cal. Pub. Cont. Code §§5101 & 5103; Wis. Stat. §66.0901(5).

§9.4 n.13 p.617 Add the following at the end: A variation on this theme comes when the detrimental reliance proffered is not that of a contracting party. Thus, when a liability insurer was permitted to rescind its settlement with a victim, the court noted but left open whether the *insureds* would be able to prove detrimental reliance upon the settlement, and, if so, what relief they might have against their insurer. Villanueva v. Amica Mut. Ins. Co., 864 A.2d 428 (N.J. Super. App. Div. 2005). It is safe to say that an insured is a third-party beneficiary of a settlement agreement made between its insurer and a claimant. The rights of the parties to a contract to modify or abrogate the contract are restricted when the beneficiary either relies materially on the contract or, if asked to do so by either of the parties to it, assents to the change. *See infra* §10.8. It is thus possible that the insureds could enforce the settlement agreement against the insurer, though perhaps only to the extent of any reliance damages incurred — to say the least, an unsatisfactory result. The court sensibly noted that "it behooves an insurer to place its own insured on notice of any settlement entered into on the insured's behalf, as well as any action to enforce or vacate such a settlement."

§9.4 n.15 p.617 Add the following at the end: *Cf.* Shurgard Storage Ctrs. v. Lipton-U. City, LLC, 394 F.3d 1041 (8th Cir. 2005) (plaintiff pleaded that lease agreement unconscionable by alleging that it "would not have agreed to enter into the Lease Agreement" had it known of the error in expression and that the option to sell would "reflect[] only half of its true value").

§9.4 n.16 p.618 Add the following at the end: *But cf.* Sumerel v. Goodyear Tire & Rubber Co., 232 P.3d 128 (Colo. App. 2009) (error of $550,000 in settlement of approximately $2.7 million "oppressive and unconscionable" because it would be a "windfall" to the plaintiffs if upheld, and "avoiding the purported agreement and awarding plaintiffs only what the jury awarded works no hardship on plaintiffs.").

§9.4 n.17 p.618 Add the following to the list after "See": United States v. Talley Def. Sys., 393 F. Supp. 2d 964 (D. Ariz. 2005) (federal government cannot avoid contract that overpays a tax refund; "USA was the only party to know if a mistake were made, and so it bears the risk of mistake.").

§9.4 n.17 p.618 Add the following at the end: A special case of risk-bearing is the "voluntary payment rule," under which one who pays in the face of uncertainty as to the amount owing and with full knowledge of the facts may not seek rescission and restitution in the absence of fraud or duress. Under these circumstances, the payor is deemed to have borne the risk that it is overpaying. For a thorough review of the rule, see BMG Direct Mktg. v. Peake, 178 S.W.3d 763 (Tex. 2005) (doctrine applies to unenforceable late payment fees); *see also* Bishop v. Bishop, 250 S.W.3d 570 (Ark. App. 2007) (payments on automobile awarded to wife in divorce decree but financed in husband's name, made after wife abandoned paying; "The voluntary-payment rule puts the risk of loss on the one who pays because that person . . . is best able to avoid the loss by not paying, or by paying under protest, and seeking a prompt legal remedy in either event."); Anthony v. Am. Gen. Fin. Servs., 697 S.E.2d 166 (Ga. 2010) (declining to apply voluntary payment doctrine when contract at issue misrepresented a statutory limit on the amount of payment); Med. Recovery Servs. v. Carnes, 230 P.3d 760 (Idaho App. 2010) ("lack of knowledge concerning the law . . . does not render a payment involuntary"); Huch v. Charter Comm'ns, 290 S.W.3d 721 (Mo. 2009) (defense based on waiver, and more broadly the inequity of allowing the overpayer to seek restitution whenever it liked, short of the limitations period, and the uncertainty that results; doctrine does not serve as defense to consumer protection act, however, where waiver would be singularly inapt), distinguished in Roberts v. BJC Health Sys., 391 S.W.3d 433 (Mo. 2013) (voluntary payment doctrine did not apply when the payment was induced by fraud); Restatement (Third) of Restitution and Unjust Enrichment §6 cmt. *e* (voluntary payment rule overbroad, covering as it does negligence and inadvertence; better framed as "money voluntarily paid *in the face of a recognized uncertainty as to the existence or extent of the payor's obligation to the recipient* may not be recovered, on the ground of 'mistake,' merely because the payment is subsequently revealed to have exceeded the true amount of the underlying obligation.") (emphasis in original). Some courts do allow mistake as a defense to voluntary payment. Even there, though, commonly the claimant is held subject to the rule because of its failure to make a proper investigation, thus bearing the risk. Spivey v. Adaptive Mktg., 622 F.3d 816 (7th Cir. 2010) (O'Connor, J., sitting by designation).

§9.4 n.19 p.618 Add the following after the first sentence: *Accord: In re* UAL Corp., *supra* note 1 ("Cases . . . distinguish between an obvious error, such as an error in computation, and an 'error of judgment,' which if a ground of restitution would make every contract party a kind of fiduciary of the opposing party, end arm's length bargaining, and make contractual obligations radically uncertain.").

§9.4 n.21 p.619 Add the following to the list after **"Accord"***:* Urban Sites of Chicago v. Crown Castle USA, 979 N.E.2d 480 (Ill. App. 2012) (defendant, "an experienced landlord," could not assert unilateral mistake in the terms of a contract when it failed to read the contract); Cox v. Lehman Bros., Inc., 790 N.Y.S.2d 16 (App. Div. 2005) (inappropriate to grant relief for unilateral mistake "given no indications that the defendant lacked good faith or intentionally avoided making an inquiry it had reason to know would disclose the true facts").

§9.4 n.21 p.619 Add the following at the end of the first paragraph: *But see* Decision One Mortgage Co. v. Victor Warren Props., 696 S.E.2d 145 (Ga. App. 2010) (vendor set opening bid too low and sought avoidance through unilateral mistake; denied because "had reasonable diligence been employed *before* the foreclosure sale, the alleged unilateral mistake . . . would not have occurred." Georgia is an outlier on this issue, but this particular case would likely have come out the same way had the more usual test been applied; the opening bid was set at $27,750 when it should have been set at $333,000, which is so gross an error that even a mildly negligent vendor should have sensed that something was amiss).

§9.4 n.21 p.619 In the second paragraph, add the following after the second sentence: *Cf.* Sumerel v. Goodyear Tire & Rubber Co., 232 P.3d 128 (Colo. App. 2009) (party making erroneous settlement offer did not bear risk, because it sent its erroneous numbers to the other party asking for review and discussion, after the parties had discussed an apparent discrepancy).

§9.4 n.22 p.619 Add the following to the list after **"Accord"***:* Kingik v. State Dep't of Admin., 239 P.3d 1243 (Alaska 2010) (party not entitled to void mistaken waiver because she had not read the waiver form; "[i]f she did not read the waiver, she must have known she was acting with limited knowledge of the contents and meaning of the contract"), followed in Handle

Constr. Co. v. Norcon, Inc., 264 P.3d 367 (Alaska 2011) (subcontractor bore risk of mistake where its general manager failed to provide key information to its bid preparer because "he 'did not have knowledge of the project details' "); Flores v. W. Covina Auto Grp., 151 Cal. Rptr. 3d 481 (Ct. App. 2013) ("[T]he rule that a party cannot avoid a contract term because the party failed to read it before signing applies even to adhesion contracts, when the term is conspicuous and does not defeat the reasonable expectations of the parties . . . "); Stamato v. Stamato, 818 So. 2d 662 (Fla. App. 2002) (test is "inexcusable neglect"; present when party to settlement agreement entered into that agreement without first checking whether the court had ruled on her pending motion); Bert Allen Toyota v. Grasz, 909 So. 2d 763 (Miss. App. 2005) (seller failed to use reasonable care when he miscalculated the price of a truck by $2,000, even though he knew the cost of the vehicle and the profit margin); El Paso Field Servs. v. MasTec N. Am., 389 S.W.3d 802 (Tex. 2012) ("Sophisticated parties, like all parties to a contract, have 'an obligation to protect themselves by reading what they sign.' ") (quoting from Thigpen v. Locke, 363 S.W.2d 247, 253 (Tex. 1962)).

§9.4 n.23 p.620 Add the following at the end: *Cf.* Johnson Family Ltd. P'ship v. White Pine Wireless, 761 N.W.2d 353 (Mich. App. 2008) ("[A] contract may be reformed because of a unilateral mistake where the other party had knowledge of the mistake and concealed that knowledge."; restrictions in purchase agreement omitted in deed).

In Patterson v. CitiMortgage, Inc., 820 F.3d 1273 (11th Cir. 2016), the bank was negotiating a short sale, rejected offers of $371,000 and $412,000 and then, in responding to an offer for $444,000, replied that it would accept a payout amount of $113,968.45. The Eleventh Circuit held that this unilateral mistake should have been apparent to the mortgagee and new buyer and therefore prevented a valid contract from being formed. The court explained that "[i]t is true that Georgia courts will often refuse to save contracting parties from their own unilateral mistakes that could have been avoided through the exercise of due diligence. But it is equally true, if not more so, that Georgia courts will not permit a party to take unfair advantage of an offer that contains an obvious, unilateral mistake." *Id.* at 1276 (citing

Decision One Mortg. Co. v. Victor Warren Props., Inc., 304 Ga. App. 423, 696 S.E.2d 145, 147-48 (Ga. Ct. App. 2010); Frazier Assocs. Mfrs. Representatives, Inc. v. Dabbs & Stewart, 173 Ga. App. 304, 325 S.E.2d 914, 916 (1985)). Applying a 1903 decision, the Eleventh Circuit held that "Georgia courts will rescind or refuse to enforce a contract when 'one of the parties has, without gross fault or laches on his part, made a mistake,' the mistake 'was known, or ought to have been known, to the opposite party,' and 'the mistake can be relieved against without injustice.' " *Id.* at 1277, *quoting* Singer v. Grand Rapids Match Co., 117 Ga. 86, 43 S.E. 755, 757 (1903).

§9.4 n.24 p.620 ***Add the following at the end:*** *Accord:* Angel v. Powelson, 977 N.E.2d 434 (Ind. App. 2012) (permitting reformation if "one party makes a mistake accompanied by fraud or inequitable conduct by the other party"). But one does see stray and peculiar decisions to the contrary. *See* City of Lawrenceville v. Ricoh Elec., 370 F. Supp. 2d 1328 (N.D. Ga. 2005) (rejecting argument that "a customer who has been underbilled for natural gas [must] reimburse the provider if the consumer had reason to know that it was being underbilled," even though the customer was billed for only about one-tenth of the natural gas it consumed), *aff'd*, 174 Fed. Appx. 491 (11th Cir. 2006).

§9.4 n.25 p.620 ***Add the following after the second sentence:*** *Cf.* Shurgard Storage Ctrs. v. Lipton-U. City, LLC, *supra* note 15 (buyer should have known that contract was in error when the sales price was roughly half its estimated value).

§9.4 n.28 p.621 ***Add the following at the end:*** This naturally applies as well when the other party acted fraudulently or inequitably. Garvin v. Tidwell, 126 So. 3d 1224 (Fla. App. Oct. 24, 2012) (granting rescission where seller of dangerous horse did not disclose that the horse had a history of bucking and running away with riders or that the horse had been taking a calming dietary supplement; "misconduct in discovery must be discouraged by disallowing the settlement which is the fruit of such misconduct"); Carr Dev. Grp. v. Town of N. Webster, 899 N.E.2d 12 (Ind. App. 2008) (granting reformation for unilateral mistake "where one party to a contract undertakes to draw up the contract in

accordance with a previous understanding, but drafts the contract contrary to that understanding, and permits the other party to sign the same without informing him that the contract is not in conformity with the previous understanding"). These questions of fault edge into the law of misrepresentation. Indeed, most misrepresentation cases could be decided under the law of unilateral mistake, and the two doctrines are at times conflated. ABA Consulting v. Liffey Van Lines, 889 N.Y.S.2d 540 (App. Div. 2009) (no evidence that defendant was fraudulently induced "to enter into the settlement agreement upon the false representation that it would adjust its fees if additional taxes were found due, as required for a finding that the contract was the product of unilateral mistake"). *See generally* J. Cartwright, Misrepresentation ¶ 1.02 (2002) ("misrepresentation is really a sub-category of mistake: induced mistake"); Bridge, Innocent Misrepresentation in Contract, 57 Current Legal Probs. 277, 303 (2004) ("innocent misrepresentation leading to rescission is a blend of wrongdoing and vice of consent (like mistake and duress")).

§9.4 n.29 p.621 Add the following to the list after "Accord": *In re* UAL Corp., *supra* note 1 (debtor seeking relief from order allowing it to assume certain airplane leases); Shurgard Storage Ctrs. v. Lipton-U. City, LLC, *supra* note 15 (lessor/seller of real property mistakenly agreed to a price roughly half the actual value); City of Lawrenceville v. Ricoh Elecs., *supra* note 24 (city mistakenly billed customer for only one-tenth the price of the natural gas it supplied); Landers v. Sgouros, 224 S.W.3d 651 (Mo. App. 2007) (grantor mistakenly conveyed her interest in 370 acres of land for $500, believing that to be merely a down payment).

§9.4 n.31 p.621 Add the following to the list after "Cf.": Sumerel v. Goodyear Tire & Rubber Co., 232 P.3d 128 (Colo. App. 2009) (defendant in products liability action settled dispute using erroneous calculations of fault allocations).

§9.4 n.35 p.622 Add the following at the end: *Cf.* State v. Rodriguez, 775 N.W.2d 907 (Minn. App. 2009) (bail bondsman denied relief where accused stated real name as well as aliases and bondsman provided the bond on the assumption that the accused's name was one of the aliases; no ambiguity in the contract or fraud or misrepresentation by the accused or the state, so no avoidance).

§9.4 n.39 p.623 Add the following at the end: *Accord:* Landers v. Sgouros, 224 S.W.3d 651 (Mo. App. 2007) ("'[a]s a general rule, rescission of a contract does not merely terminate it, but abrogates it in toto. Consequently, rescission of a contract involves restoration of the status quo of the parties, unless the parties have agreed otherwise.'") (quoting from Dilts v. Lynch, 655 S.W.2d 118, 121 (Mo. App. 1983)). *Cf.* Restatement (Third) of Restitution and Unjust Enrichment §5 & cmt. *d* ("The distinction drawn in the law of contracts between mutual and unilateral mistake has no direct application to the law of restitution."; the recipient's awareness of the claimant's mistake may, however, be relevant in determining what remedy, if any, results from the mistake).

§9.5 GROWTH OF IMPOSSIBILITY AS AN EXCUSE

§9.5 n.1 p.624 Add the following at the end of the first paragraph: For a broad historical and comparative analysis of impossibility, see Gordley, Impossibility and Changed and Unforeseen Circumstances, 52 Am. J. Comp. L. 513 (2004).

§9.5 n.1 p.624 In the third paragraph, add the following to the list after* "See"*: Specialty Beverages v. Pabst Brewing Co., 537 F.3d 1165 (10th Cir. 2008) ("Under Oklahoma law, the defense of impossibility of performance is a common law doctrine . . . "); Miller v. Parker McCurley Props., 36 So. 3d 1234 (Miss. 2010) ("There are three circumstances where performance is excused: (1) a subsequent change in the law, rendering performance unlawful; (2) the destruction, from no fault of either party, of an object which has to exist for there to be performance; and (3) the illness or death of the promisor who contracted to render personal services.").

§9.5 n.3 p.625 Add the following to the list after **"Accord":** White v. J.M. Brown Amusement Co., 601 S.E.2d 342 (S.C. 2004) (contract to supply video poker machines discharged when referendum outlawed them). This case poses an interesting question: If the law that discharged the contract is voided as unconstitutional, is the contract revived? Unconstitutional statutes are generally treated as though they had never been, which would point toward revival. But then the parties to the discharged contract would not be able to plan on the assumption that the contract would remain discharged — hence the ruling in *White* that the ultimate unconstitutionality of the statute "did not breathe life back into the contract." One might ask, though, whether it would be more appropriate to allow revival until a party has materially relied upon the discharge of the promise, as is done with a retraction of repudiation.

§9.5 n.4 p.625 Add the following to the list after **"Accord":** Hart v. Arnold, 884 A.2d 316 (Pa. Super. 2005) (U.S. attorney threatened injunction to stop construction of dam).

§9.5 n.5 p.625 Add the following to the citation to **MG Refining***:* (Sotomayor, J.)

§9.5 n.8 p.626 Add the following to the list after **"Accord":** Crossman v. Life Care Ctrs. of Am., 738 S.E.2d 737 (N.C. App. 2013) (arbitration clause required that the arbitrators be selected from the American Arbitration Association; when the AAA stopped accepting cases of this type, the failure of this requirement amounted to "an integral and material provision of the Agreement" and so the contract was unenforceable as impossible);

§9.5 n.9 p.626 Add the following to the list after **"See":** Schwartz *ex rel.* Schwartz v. Schwartz, 183 P.3d 552 (Colo. 2008) (antenuptial agreement barring elective share remains binding on the estate after the death of one party; "In fact, the agreement provided for its post-mortem application, as it explicitly prohibited either spouse from obtaining a share of the other's estate without the express authorization of a subsequent will."); Di Scipio v. Sullivan, 816 N.Y.S.2d 576 (App. Div. 2006) (contract to

sell realty; "As this executory contract contains no provision to the contrary, and does not involve an obligation personal to the decedent, decedent's death did not terminate the contract."; citations omitted); *In re* Estate of Sheppard, 789 N.W.2d 616 (Wis. App. 2010) (services as flight instructor and pilot personal and thus impossible to perform after student's death).

§9.5 n.10 p.627 Add the following to the list in the first sentence: ; Crockett Homes v. Hamilton, 2012-Ohio-2162 (Ohio Ct. App. 2012) (participation in real estate development did not end on the death of one of the principals)

§9.5 n.10 p.627 Add the following at the end: At times, however, the death of a party to the contract or a third party is encompassed by the contract's risk allocation, so the death should not provide a defense to enforcement. *See* State *ex rel.* Gardner v. Allstar Bail Bonds, 983 So. 2d 1218 (Fla. App. 2008) (death of accused who had failed to appear for arraignment; "Jones' death did not prevent Allstar from performing its obligations. It simply prevented Allstar from being able to mitigate the consequences of its earlier failure to perform.").

§9.5 n.26 p.631 Add the following at the end: *Accord:* Specialty Beverages v. Pabst Brewing Co., 537 F.3d 1165 (10th Cir. 2008) ("'Where, from the nature of the contract, it is evident that the parties contracted on the basis of the continued existence of the person, thing, condition, or state of things, or of facts, to which it relates, the subsequent perishing of the person or thing, or cessation of existence of the condition or state will excuse the performance, or terminate the contract, a condition to that effect being implied, in spite of the fact that the promise may have been unqualified.'") (quoting from Kan. Okla. & Gulf Ry. Co. v. Grand Lake Grain Co., 434 P.2d 153, 157 (Okla. 1967)).

§9.6 A NEW SYNTHESIS: THE DOCTRINE OF IMPRACTICABILITY

§9.6 n.1 p.632 In the second paragraph, add the following to the list after **"See also"***:* R. Speidel, Contracts in Crises: Excuse Doctrine and Retrospective Government Acts (2007); Eisenberg, Impossibility, Impracticability, and Frustration, 1 J. Legal Analysis 207 (2009); Katsivela, Frust[r]ation and Impracticability under English, United States (US) and Canadian Common Law of Contracts, 44 Eur. Transp. L. 3 (2009); Katsivela, Contracts: Force Majeure Concept or Force Majeure Clauses?, 12 Unif. L. Rev. 101 (2007); Martin, Adapting U.C.C. §2-615 Excuse for Civilian-Military Contractors in Wartime, 61 Fla. L. Rev. 99 (2009); Page, The Development of the Doctrine of Impossibility of Performance, 18 Mich. L. Rev. 589 (1920); Rösler, Hardship in German Codified Private Law — In Comparative Perspective to English, French and International Contract Law, 15 Eur. Rev. Private L. 483 (2007).

§9.6 n.1 p.632 Add the following at the end of the second paragraph: For a comparative treatment of the UCC and CISG treatments of impracticability, see Spivack, Of Shrinking Sweatsuits and Poison Vine Wax: A Comparison of Basis for Excuse under U.C.C. §2-615 and CISG Article 79, 27 U. Pa. J. Int'l Econ. L. 757 (2006).

§9.6 n.1 p.632 In the third paragraph, add the following to the list after **"See also"***:* Smythe, Bounded Rationality, The Doctrine of Impracticability, and the Governance of Relational Contracts, 13 S. Cal. Interdisc. L.J. 227 (2004); Note, Rendered Impracticable: Behavioral Economics and the Impracticability Doctrine, 26 Cardozo L. Rev. 2184 (2005).

§9.6 n.8 p.634 Add the following at the end: Impracticability appears in one of our civilian jurisdictions under the name *rebus sic stantibus*. This goes somewhat beyond ordinary impracticability in that a court may reform the impracticable contract to cure it of its infirmity. William L. Bonnell Co. v. Gándara, 714 F. Supp. 2d 272 (D.P.R. 2010) (settlement agreement reformed to remove requirements portion, where supplies disrupted unforeseeably

and very detrimentally). Our other civilian jurisdiction has stuck with *pacta sunt servanda*, setting aside recent French inclinations to extend the doctrine of *imprévision* from government contracts to private contracts. St. Charles Ventures v. Albertsons, Inc., 265 F. Supp. 2d 682 (E.D. La. 2003). *See generally* Farnsworth, Comparative Contract Law, in Oxford Handbook of Comparative Law 899, 926-27 (M. Reimann & R. Zimmermann eds., 2006).

§9.6 n.13 p.635 ***Add the following after the second sentence:*** *See also* Ner Tamid Cong. v. Krivoruchko, 638 F. Supp. 2d 913 (N.D. Ill. 2009) (basis for impracticability an inability to secure the desired type of financing: "[T]he defendant must demonstrate that he has tried all practical, available alternatives to permit performance," and here the defendant sought financing from only two banks), followed in Great Lakes Gas Trans. Ltd. P'ship v. Essar Steel Minn., 871 F. Supp. 2d 843 (D. Minn. 2012) (pleadings insufficient to support the impracticability defense; although debtor stated that it sought financing diligently, it did not "sufficiently allege that it sought all reasonable alternatives in order to perform its obligations").

§9.6 n.17 p.636 ***Add the following at the end:*** *Cf.* Virginia Power Energy Mktg. v. Apache Corp., 297 S.W.3d 397 (Tex. Civ. App. 2009) (2-614 is gap-filler, so it does not apply where contract provided that seller would be excused from making delivery if *force majeure* prevented delivery because of problems with pipelines).

§9.6 n.19 p.636 ***Add the following at the end:*** Louisiana, with its largely civilian contract law, adheres to impossibility. Associated Acquisitions v. Carbone Props., 962 So. 2d 1102 (La. App. 2007) ("'a party is obliged to perform a contract entered into by him if performance be possible at all, and regardless of any difficulty he might experience in performing it'") (quoting from Picard Constr. Co. v. Bd. of Comm'rs, 109 So. 816 (La. 1926)). Oklahoma keeps one foot in the past and one in the present by maintaining an impossibility doctrine at common law and an impracticability doctrine under Article Two — but still carrying impossibility over to Article Two cases. Specialty Beverages v. Pabst Brewing Co., 537 F.3d 1165 (10th Cir. 2008) ("Under

Oklahoma law, the defense of impossibility of performance is a common law doctrine . . . however, the Oklahoma courts regularly consider this defense when analyzing contracts governed by the UCC. . . . Unlike impossibility of performance, impracticability is a UCC-based defense."). *See also* Ferguson v. Ferguson, 54 So. 3d 553 (Fla. App. 2011) (applying impossibility doctrine). Retaining impossibility is one thing — many jurisdictions do that, while defining impossibility to include impracticability. Keeping separate bodies of doctrine for impossibility and impracticability is quite another. It is difficult to make sense of this save as an excessive reverence for bygone doctrine.

§9.6 n.20 p.637 Add the following at the end: The apprehension must, however, be based on actual symptoms or risks. Merely thinking it unlikely the other party will perform may provide a basis for seeking adequate assurance of performance, but does not amount to impracticability. Record v. Kempe, 928 A.2d 1199 (Vt. 2007) (cancellation of land sale contract in the middle of the cure period "premature" when based only upon the impression that it "seemed unlikely" that the plaintiffs could perform).

§9.6 n.22 p.637 Add the following to the list after "Accord": Waddy v. Riggleman, 606 S.E.2d 222 (W. Va. 2004) (not impossible to secure release of deeds of trust where reason for failure was tardy efforts by the party asserting the defense).

§9.6 n.24 p.638 In the second paragraph, add the following to the list in the second sentence: Ner Tamid Cong. v. Krivoruchko, *supra* note 13 (inability to get the type of financing desired; "[The buyer] has, however, offered no evidence that he does not have the financial wherewithal to buy the property with his own funds. For all we know, he is Donald Trump in miniature."); YPI 180 N. LaSalle Owner v. 180 N. LaSalle II, 933 N.E.2d 860 (Ill. App. 2010) (unavailability of commercial financing not a basis for impossibility where the owner's current assets exceeded $1.6 billion).

§9.6 n.25 p.638 Add the following to the list after "Accord": EZ Green Assocs. v. Ga.-Pac. Corp., 734 S.E.2d 485 (Ga. App. 2012) (increased expenses not grounds for impracticability defense, especially where the party seeking rescission was responsible for part of those increased expenses); Associated Acquisitions v. Carbone Props., 962 So. 2d 1102 (La. App. 2007) (contract to convey share and undertake construction in luxury hotel development not impracticable even after Hurricane Katrina, barring absolute impossibility), followed in Payne v. Hurwitz, 978 So. 2d 1000 (La. App. 2008) ("Hurricane Katrina undoubtedly was a *force majeure*"; however, "if the fortuitous event prevents the obligor from performing his obligation in the manner contemplated at the time of contracting, he must pursue reasonable alternatives to render performance in a different manner before he can take advantage of the defense of impossibility."; accordingly, failure to close on house not excused even though owner was unable to make repairs in time).

§9.6 n.29 p.640 Add the following at the end: Judge Posner has observed that "this explanation leaves unexplained why parties to a contract would have assumed that a condition would not occur that has occurred. Was it just a lack of foresight? Or is the idea behind the doctrine, rather, that the parties, had they negotiated with reference to the contingency that has come to pass and has made performance infeasible or fearfully burdensome, would have excused performance? The latter is the more promising line of inquiry . . . " Wis. Elec. Power Co. v. Union Pac. R.R. Co., 557 F.3d 504, 505-506 (7th Cir. 2009).

Richardson v. Casher, 88 Mass. App. Ct. 1115, 41 N.E.3d 330 (2015), involved an allocation agreement for a $9 million settlement with Travelers Indemnity, intended to determine distributions to lead counsel, plaintiffs, multiple former counsel, and a nonprofit organization. However, Travelers rejected the allocation plan, instead insisting on paying the court "the full $9,000,000 anticipated by the settlement, but not in the manner set forth in the allocation agreement." The appeals court held that the defendants had no obligations under allocation agreement because the timely receipt of funds was a condition precedent.

§9.6 p.640 At the end of the first full paragraph, add the following: . . . no account is taken of one party's purely private assumptions.[29a]

[29a] Ner Tamid Cong. v. Krivoruchko, *supra* note 13 ("Mr. Krivoruchko may have been proceeding on the assumption that financing was the *sine qua non* of the deal, but he never conveyed that to Ner Tamid, and 'private intent counts only if it is conveyed to the other party and shared.' ") (quoting from Robbins v. Lynch, 836 F.2d 330 (7th Cir. 1988)).

§9.6 n.36 p.642 Add the following to the list after **"Accord"***:* Waddy v. Riggleman, *supra* note 22 (where "the inability to obtain the needed releases was brought about by the [promisors'] own neglect," the promisors would be at fault).

§9.6 n.37 p.642 Add the following to the list after **"Accord"***:* Am. Nat'l Red Cross v. Vinton Roofing Co., 629 F. Supp. 2d 5 (D.D.C. 2009) (roofer "left the work site prior to ensuring that the roof was watertight," in spite of being on notice that a chance of rain had been forecast; "[t]he affirmative defense does not protect individuals who, negligently or otherwise, subject others . . . to the effects of nature"); Allegheny Energy Supply Co. v. Wolf Run Mining Co., 53 A.3d 53 (Pa. Super. 2012) (failure to mine sufficient coal; rejecting *force majeure* defense because "the conditions leading to the breach of the Agreement were not beyond the reasonable control of Wolf Run and occurred due to Wolf Run's fault or negligence").

§9.6 n.38 p.642 Add the following at the end: For a regrettable misreading of this doctrine, see Huber v. Farmers Union Serv. Ass'n, 787 N.W.2d 268 (N.D. 2010) (quoting from Restatement Second §§261 & 264; holding that impracticability and frustration do not apply to an insurance agent contract even though the agent's license was revoked, because "the doctrines of frustration of purpose and impossibility of performance do not apply if the frustration or impossibility is caused by one of the contracting parties"). This would be true were "one of the contracting parties" changed to "promisor." For a party to a contract to claim impossibility because he had rendered performance impossible would take chutzpah on the part of the client and feckless optimism on the part of the lawyer. In *Huber*, impossibility resulted from the agent's misconduct, but the issue was whether the insurance company had to pay commissions. The insurance company was the promisor, not the promisee, so because the

impossibility had nothing to do with its behavior, the defense should have been available,

§9.6 n.40 p.643 Add the following to the list after **"Accord"***:* Wis. Elec. Power Co. v. Union Pac. R.R. Co., *supra* note 29 (Posner, J: "To defeat the application of the doctrine of impossibility the contract must state that the promisor must pay damages even if he commits a breach that could not have been prevented at a reasonable cost.").

§9.6 n.41 p.643 Add the following to the list after **"Accord"***:* Kilgore Pavement Maint. v. West Jordan City, 257 P.3d 460 (Utah App. 2011) (risk of price increase allocated to contractor by clause stating that "All duties, responsibilities, and obligations assigned to or undertaken by the Contractor shall be at its expense without change in the Contract Price.").

§9.6 n.45 p.644 Add the following to the list after **"Accord"***:* Specialty Beverages v. Pabst Brewing Co., *supra* note 19 ("[T]he defense is not available if a promisor was aware of a potential risk that could interfere with its performance and assumed that risk by not explicitly addressing it in the contract."); Gen. Injectables & Vaccines v. Gates, 527 F.3d 1375 (Fed. Cir. 2008) (construction of FAR 52.212-4(f), the federally mandated *force majeure* clause for government contracts; "[A]n unexcused default by a subcontractor does not excuse nonperformance by the prime contractor. . . . GIV bore the risk of not being able to perform unless it could show that the reason for its failure to perform fell within the causes set forth in the 'excusable delay' clause. It could not shift that risk to the government simply by subcontracting production of the vaccine to a third party."); Ferguson v. Ferguson, 54 So. 3d 553 (Fla. App. 2011) (drop in value of home not grounds for undoing marital settlement; "Economic downturns and other market shifts do not truly constitute unanticipated circumstances in a market economy."); Clean the Uniform Co. v. Magic Touch Cleaning, 300 S.W.3d 602 (Mo. App. 2009) ("An event that reasonably could have been anticipated at the time of contracting does not excuse the obligor's performance under [impossibility, impracticability, and frustration] because if the event reasonably could be foreseen and the contract does not

provide for performance to be excused if the event occurs, we presume that the parties intended the obligor to assume this risk."; possibility that one-year contract would not be renewed was reasonably foreseeable).

§9.6 n.45 p.644 Add the following after the citation to **Kel Kim Corp.***:* , followed in Thor Props. v. Chetrit Grp., 936 N.Y.S.2d 196 (App. Div. 2012) (settlement agreement hinged on governmental approval of development; "Because it was always uncertain whether the City would permit or deny further development of the property, any assumption about the ability to develop property could not have existed at the time the parties entered into the agreement. . . . The ability to secure favorable zoning rulings is a well known risk in any property development project, and if expansion of the property was the key to profitability, as defendants claim, they should have explicitly handled that contingency in the settlement agreement.");

§9.6 n.47 p.645 Add the following at the end: Cf. E. Capitol View Cmty. Dev. Corp. v. Robinson, 941 A.2d 1036 (D.C. 2008) (lack of funding no justification for early termination of employment contract, even when cause was failure of governmental agency to renew grant; "Though appellant maintained that the revocation of funding deprived the corporation of sufficient assets to continue paying its employees, it failed to include such a possibility as a condition precedent in the employment contract. . . . Robinson's employment contract was objectively capable of performance, and East Capitol did nothing to reallocate the risk of its own inability to pay.").

§9.6 n.48 p.645 Add the following at the end: Accord: Ner Tamid Congregation v. Krivoruchko, *supra* note 13 ("It is precisely because inability to obtain financing is a foreseeable (and significant) risk that can be readily guarded against in the parties' agreement that financing contingency provisions are common in both commercial and residential real estate contracts. . . . It is not for a court paternalistically to rewrite a party's agreement to include terms that they chose not to make a part of their agreement, . . . and there is a strong presumption against provisions that easily could have been included in the contract but were

not."), followed in YPI 180 N. LaSalle Owner v. 180 N. LaSalle II, 933 N.E.2d 860 (Ill. App. 2010) ("Even without the global credit crisis of 2008, it was foreseeable that a commercial lender might not provide [the purchasers] with the financing they sought."), both in turn followed in Great Lakes Gas Trans. Ltd. P'ship v. Essar Steel Minn., 871 F. Supp. 2d 843 (D. Minn. 2012) (2008 financial crisis does not itself support the impracticability defense; "[i]t was completely foreseeable that [Essar] might not secure the necessary financing," and it could have insisted upon a clause that made financing a condition precedent to performance). *But cf.* Bank of Am. v. Shelbourne Dev. Grp., 732 F. Supp. 2d 809 (N.D. Ill. 2010) (impracticability defense survives motion to strike; "The fact that performance becomes economically burdensome generally does not excuse performance," but here the lender had itself stated that economic conditions were unprecedented and unparalleled, and hence potentially unforeseeable; distinguishing *Ner Tamid Congregation, supra*).

§9.6 n.49 p.646 Add the following at the end: Miller v. Mills Constr. Co., 352 F.3d 1166 (8th Cir. 2003) (collapse of steel building was "unanticipated" by general contractor and subcontractor given assurance by supplier of steel "that nothing further needed to be done to protect the structure from collapse").

§9.6 n.51 p.646 Add the following at the end: For a critical discussion of "acts of God" clauses in an age of global climate change, *see* Myanna F. Dellinger, *An "Act of God"? Rethinking Contractual Impracticability in an Era of Anthropogenic Climate Change*, 67 U.C. Hastings L.J. 1527 (2016) (arguing that "it makes little logical or legal sense to continue to allow parties to escape liability for weather events that are in fact highly foreseeable given today's knowledge about the causes and effects of severe weather").

§9.6 n.56 p.648 Add the following at the end: *Accord:* Specialty Beverages v. Pabst Brewing Co., *supra* note 19 ("Under Oklahoma law, this type of 'subjective impossibility' falls outside of the scope of the defense of impossibility."); E. Capitol Cmty. Dev. Corp. v. Robinson, *supra* note 47 ("[C]ourts will generally only excuse non-performance where performance is objectively impossible — that is, the contract is incapable of performance by anyone — rather than instances where the party subjectively claims the inability to perform."). *Cf.* Evan Johnson & Sons Constr. v. Mississippi, 877 So. 2d 360 (Miss. 2004) (employing objective test, but treating subjective impossibility as a factor to be used when determining whether performance objectively impossible).

§9.6 n.57 p.648 Add the following to the list after "Accord": E. Capitol Cmty. Dev. Corp. v. Robinson, *supra* note 47 ("a party's alleged financial inability to perform a contract that it voluntarily entered will rarely, if ever, excuse non-performance; though a party can prove that it can no longer afford performance, it will be hard-pressed to prove that non-performance 'exist[s] in the nature of the thing to be done.' ") (quoting White Lakes Shopping Ctr. v. Jefferson Std. Life Ins. Co., 490 P.2d 609 (Kan. 1971)); Hampton Island, LLC v. HAOP, LLC, 702 S.E.2d 770 (Ga. App. 2010) (defendant's subjective "inability to pay . . . could not serve as a basis for its defense of impossibility").

§9.7 FRUSTRATION OF PURPOSE

§9.7 n.2 p.650 Add the following at the end: *See generally* Hunter, From Coronations to Sand Bans: Frustration and Force Majeure in the Twenty-First Century, 28 J. Contract L. 61 (2011); Katsivela, Frust[r]ation and Impracticability under English, United States (US) and Canadian Common Law of Contracts, 44 Eur. Transp. L. 3 (2009); Schwartz, A "Standard Clause Analysis" of the Frustration Doctrine and the Material Adverse Change Clause, 57 UCLA L. Rev. 789 (2010).

§9.7 n.5 p.651 Add the following to the list after "Accord": Wal-Mart Stores v. AIG Life Ins. Co., 872 A.2d 611 (Del. Ch. 2005) (retailer not excused from insurance contracts entered into as part of a failed tax-avoidance plan), *aff'd in part, rev'd in part on other grounds*, 901 A.2d 106 (Del. 2006); Eisenberg, Impossibility, Impracticability, and Frustration, 1 J. Legal Analysis 207 (2009).

§9.7 n.9 p.652 Add the following at the end: Nevertheless, the doctrines serve different purposes, and combining them may yield confusion. *See* U.S. Claims v. Yehuda Smolar, PC, 602 F. Supp. 2d 590 (E.D. Pa. 2009) (using commercial frustration and commercial impracticability interchangeably).

***§9.7 n.10 p.652 Add the following to the list after* "Accord":** Turbines Ltd. v. Transupport, Inc., 808 N.W.2d 643 (Neb. App. 2012) (buyer's plan to resell goods to a company that proved legally ineligible to buy them not a basic assumption of the contract, because seller knew only that its buyer intended to resell goods in Asia, not that it intended selling to this specific company), *aff'd on other grounds*, 825 N.W.2d 767 (Neb. 2013).

§9.7 n.10 p.652 Add the following after the second sentence: *Cf.* Step Plan Servs. v. Koresko, 12 A.3d 401 (Pa. Super. 2010) ("one party's wholly subjective expectations are insufficient to avoid an otherwise clear agreement"; quoting from Restatement Second §265 cmt. *a*).

§9.7 n.11 p.653 Add the following at the end: One recent decision uses fault as the basis of its fundamental misconstruction of the law of frustration. *See* America's Floor Source v. Joshua Homes, 946 N.E.2d 799 (Ohio App. 2010) ("Frustration of purpose occurs when one of the two parties to a contract creates a situation where the basis of the parties' contract essentially becomes moot. . . . [F]rustration of purpose could be described as a form of breach of contract. If a party to a contract creates a situation whereby it cannot fulfill its obligations under the contract, the party is in breach of contract."). The basic problem with this statement is that frustration is not a breach; it is a defense to an action for breach. No cause of action is created by frustration *qua* frustration. To be sure, if the obligor's failure to perform a contractual duty frustrates the underlying purpose of the obligee, one might simultaneously have frustrated purpose and breach. But even then, the frustrated purpose is not a *type* of breach; it is a *consequence* of breach.

This may stem from an error in logic. The law of frustration, like the law of many other defenses, requires that the events giving rise to the demand for excuse not be the fault of the party seeking to be excused. Restatement Second §265. But saying that the obligor must be without fault is not the same thing as saying that the obligee must have acted with fault; fault need not figure in frustration, and indeed seldom does. *Cf.* State v. Jones, 271 P.3d 1277 (Kan. App. 2012) (an accused's attempt to breach a plea agreement does not yield frustration if the attempt is rebuffed, whatever the intent of the accused might have been). The law of the excluded middle applies in contracts just as elsewhere.

It ultimately didn't matter whether this court properly framed its frustration analysis. It had already held that the contract was breached, and from the context materially so. The breached-against party was thus entitled to cease its own performance and sue for breach, as it did. Frustration was really a red herring. But on its way to a sound result, the court fouled up frustration — this in spite of quoting the relevant Restatement Second section at length. One hopes that future readers and courts will recognize the wayward aspects of this opinion and stick resolutely to the path of the law.

§9.7 n.13 p.653 Add the following to the list after "Accord": Wal-Mart Stores v. AIG Life Ins. Co., *supra* note 5 ("commercial frustration is a question of law that is to be determined by the court").

§9.7 p.653 In the first paragraph, add the following: . . . than on the ground of impracticability.[13a]

[13a] Wal-Mart Stores v. AIG Life Ins. Co., *supra* note 5 ("the defense of commercial frustration is very difficult to invoke, as courts have been extremely reluctant to allow parties to disavow obligations that they have agreed to").

§9.7 n.14 p.654 Add the following at the end: *See* PPF Safeguard v. BCR Safeguard Holding, 924 N.Y.S.2d 391 (App. Div. 2011) (quoting Restatement Second §265 cmt. *a*: "The doctrine applies 'when a change in circumstances makes one party's performance virtually worthless to the other, frustrating his purpose in making the contract.' "; indemnity contract entered into in order to induce buyer to purchase business not frustrated when business destroyed by Hurricane Katrina, because the basic sale of the business was unaffected); Hiriam Hicks, Inc. v. Synagro WWT, LLC, 867 F. Supp. 2d 676 (E.D. Pa. 2012) (reduced profit not sufficient basis for frustration).

§9.7 n.15 p.654 Add the following to the list after **"Accord"***:* United States v. Frownfelter, 626 F.3d 549 (10th Cir. 2010) (government's error in allowing plea bargain for what it thought was a felony, but in fact was a misdemeanor, is not at the root of the bargain; "[a]ny additional collateral consequences of a felony conviction . . . appear tangential to these core benefits [from a misdemeanor conviction] obtained by the government"); Am. Prairie Constr. Co. v. Hoich, 594 F.3d 1015 (8th Cir. 2010) (contract by debtor in chapter 11 bankruptcy proceeding agreed to purchase a party's claims against the estate, but then the bankruptcy converted to chapter 7; the debtor "can no longer purchase those class claims because, after the conversion, such classes ceased to exist," so "the conversion defeated [the debtor]'s entire purpose in negotiating with [the creditor]."); NPS, LLC v. Ambac Assur. Corp., 706 F. Supp. 2d 162 (D. Mass. 2010) (guarantor of bonds lost AAA rating, but "not shown that the principal purpose of the Agreement was to benefit from Ambac's strong credit rating," as opposed to obtaining financial guaranty insurance; preamble to contract did not mention the credit rating); Island Dev. Corp. v. District of Columbia, 933 A.2d 340 (D.C. 2007) (requirement that construction project comply with certain environmental regulations and that its land be subject to modest conditions did not render the project worthless, merely more difficult); Liggett Rest. Grp. v. City of Pontiac, 676 N.W.2d 633 (Mich. App. 2003) ("Frustration of purpose is generally asserted where 'a change in circumstances makes one party's performance virtually worthless to the other, frustrating his purpose in making the contract.' ") (quoting from Restatement Second §265 cmt. *a*), followed in City of Flint v. Chrisdom Props., 770 N.W.2d 888 (Mich. App. 2009) (frustration where city, the lender to a builder, withheld permits for over one year and refused to let any of the completed apartments to be sold free of the general mortgage).

§9.7 n.15 p.654 Add the following to the list after **"But see"***:* Norfolk S. Ry. Co. v. Reading Blue Mtn. & N. R.R. Co., 346 F. Supp. 2d 720 (M.D. Pa. 2004) (agreement to maintain communications system frustrated when system destroyed by weather; "a basic assumption of the contracting parties was that the existing communications system . . . would not deteriorate to the point where it could not be repaired"); *In re* Estate of Sheppard,

789 N.W.2d 616 (Wis. App. 2010) (basic assumption of contract for flying lessons and pilot services was continued life of obligee, so obligee's death frustrated the contract's purpose).

§9.7 n.15 p.654 Add the following at the end: As in impracticability, the court may use parol evidence when determining the principal purpose of the contract, however integrated the contract may be. (Indeed, that happened in *Krell v. Henry*, the fount of frustration doctrine.) Pieper, Inc. v. Land O'Lakes Farmland Feed, 390 F.3d 1062 (8th Cir. 2004).

§9.7 n.17 p.655 Add the following to the list after **"see"***:* ; Fairfield Harbour Prop. Owners Ass'n v. Midsouth Golf, LLC, 715 S.E.2d 273 (N.C. App. 2011) (owner of amenities in planned community closed a golf course in violation of restrictive covenants; covenants allocated risk to owner, and supervening judicial decision barring the collection of fees from many residents severable from balance of master deed)

§9.7 n.19 p.655 Add the following after the citation to **Gold***:* followed in Grenall v. United of Omaha Life Ins. Co., 80 Cal. Rptr. 3d 609 (App. Ct. 2008) (purchaser of annuity did not know at the time of contracting that she had terminal cancer that would result in her death four months later; "such risks are an inherent part of life annuity contracts, which reflect, at their essence, a longevity wager measured by average life expectancy").

§9.7 n.19 p.655 Add the following to the list after **"Accord"***:* NPS, LLC v. Ambac Assur. Corp., 706 F. Supp. 2d 162 (D. Mass. 2010) (non-occurrence of a reduction in guarantor's credit rating not a basic assumption on which the contract was based; "A credit rating is determined by external institutions, not the rated agency. . . . NPS was aware that these institutions could at some point alter their evaluation of the risks involved in Ambac's business model," which indeed the obligor disclosed to prospective bondholders); Wal-Mart Stores v. AIG Life Ins. Co., *supra* note 5 ("the doctrine of commercial frustration does not apply if at the time of contracting the supervening event was reasonably foreseeable, and could (and should) have been anticipated by the parties and provided for in the contract"; invalidation of tax deduction

foreseeable because the possibility of contrary IRS determinations comes with tax sheltering, some states had held that employers have no insurable interest in employees, and retailer had raised the possible risks in its application for the policies).

§9.7 n.19 p.655 Add the following after the citation to **Faulconer***:* and in Currituck Assocs. v. Hollowell, 601 S.E.2d 256 (N.C. App. 2004) (event dealt with in prior contract: "We are unconvinced that appellants could not reasonably foresee a condition in 2002 that they had prepared for in 1996."), *aff'd by an equally divided court*, 622 S.E.2d 493 (N.C. 2005).

§9.7 n.21 p.656 Add the following to the list after **"See also"***:* Step Plan Servs. v. Koresko, 12 A.3d 401 (Pa. Super. 2010) ("Foreseeability of the untoward event is just onc factor in the calculus of discharge by supervening frustration of purpose.").

§9.7 n.27 p.658 Add the following to the list after **"Accord"***:* WRI/Raleigh v. Shaikh, 644 S.E.2d 245 (N.C. App. 2007) (lessee was unable to install the size of grease trap he required for a restaurant, but no frustration where "the premises at issue still exist and at the time defendant refused to perform were in the same condition as when the contract was signed," and in any event the current tenants of the property were running a restaurant with a functioning grease trap).

§9.7 n.28 p.658 Add the following to the list after **"Accord"***:* WRI/Raleigh v. Shaikh, 644 S.E.2d 245 (N.C. App. 2007) (for lease executed in 2002, inability to install grease trap complying with city ordinance enacted in 1999 was reasonably foreseeable at the time of contracting).

§9.7 n.34 p.660 Add the following after the first sentence: Most circuits have held that the arbitration agreement is rendered unenforceable if the chosen forum is no longer available and the forum selection was "integral" to the agreement. Inetianbor v. CashCall, Inc., 768 F.3d 1346, 1349-51 & n.1 (11th Cir. 2014) (holding that the selection of Cheyenne River Sioux Tribal Nation was integral to the arbitration agreement and that the tribe's refusal to become involved rendered the arbitration

agreement unenforceable), citing *In re* Salomon Inc. S'holder's Derivative Litig. 91 Civ. 5500 (RRP), 68 F.3d 554, 561 (2d Cir. 1995); Khan v. Dell Inc., 669 F.3d 350, 354-57 (3d Cir. 2012); BP Exploration Libya Ltd. v. ExxonMobil Libya Ltd., 689 F.3d 481, 491 n.7 (5th Cir. 2012); National Iranian Oil Co. v. Ashland Oil Co., 817 F.2d 326, 333-35 (5th Cir. 1987); Reddam v. KPMG LLP, 457 F.3d 1054, 1059-61 (9th Cir. 2006), abrogation on other grounds recognized by Atlantic Nat'l Trust LLC v. Mt. Hawley Ins. Co., 621 F.3d 931, 940 (9th Cir. 2010); *but see* Green v. U.S. Cash Advance Ill., LLC, 724 F.3d 787, 790-92 (7th Cir. 2013) (criticizing and rejecting the integral provision rule). The issue remains relevant to consumer contracts that identified the National Arbitration Forum (NAF) as the designated arbitrator prior to the 2009 consent decree with Minnesota that prevents it from hearing consumer arbitration cases. Minnesota v. National Arbitration Forum, LLC, 2009 Minn. Dist. LEXIS 340 (July 28, 2009) (consent decree). In Moss v. First Premier Bank, 835 F.3d 260 (2d Cir. 2016), the Second Circuit applied the reasoning in *Salomon* and found that "the pervasive references to NAF in the agreement, and the absence of any indication that the parties would assent to arbitration before a substitute forum if NAF became unavailable" rendered the agreement unenforceable. It "acknowledge[d] that there is a difference of opinion among the circuits on this issue." *Id.* at 266, *comparing* Flagg v. First Premier Bank, 644 Fed. Appx. 893 (11th Cir. 2016) (unpublished opinion) (holding that "[b]ecause the choice of the NAF as the arbitral forum was an integral part of the agreement to arbitrate, we conclude that the district court properly denied First Premier's motion to compel arbitration and appoint a substitute for NAF"), and Ranzy v. Tijerina, 393 Fed. Appx. 174, 176 (5th Cir. 2010) (unpublished opinion) (following Salomon to conclude that district court properly denied motion to compel arbitration given NAF's unavailability), *with* Green v. U.S. Cash Advance Ill., LLC, 724 F.3d 787, 793 (7th Cir. 2013) (holding that Section 5 required court to appoint substitute arbitrator), and Khan v. Dell Inc., 669 F.3d 350, 356 (3d Cir. 2012) (finding Salomon "unpersuasive" and holding that NAF's unavailability constituted a lapse within the meaning of Section 5).

§9.8 EXISTING IMPRACTICABILITY AND FRUSTRATION

§9.8 n.4 p.661 Add the following to the list after **"Accord"***:* United States v. Frownfelter, 626 F.3d 549 (10th Cir. 2010) (government had reason to know "the then four-year-old statute under which [the defendant] was charged"); Lindner v. Meadow Gold Dairies, 515 F. Supp. 2d 1154 (D. Haw. 2007) (dairy and assignee "presumptively aware of . . . the provisions of the Clean Water Act from the commencement of their tenure on the land"); Alaskan Crude Corp. v. Alaska, 261 P.3d 412 (Alaska 2011) (government order antedated contract, but appeal not complete until contract executed; held not a *force majeure* event, because the order was known and the possibility that the appeal would be unsuccessful readily foreseeable); 1700 Rinehart, LLC v. Advance Am., 51 So. 3d 535 (Fla. App. 2010) (lease for purpose inconsistent with zoning not avoidable because of frustration; although lessee unable to use leased store, frustration inapplicable "in a case such as this one, in which the particular potential obstacle was not only foreseen by the parties, but as to which they specifically bargained, with the risks of its occurrence divided by and between the parties in the agreement itself"); Gulliver Schs., Inc. v. Snay, 137 So. 3d 1045, 1048 (Fla. App. 2014) (settlement agreement that provided that plaintiff would not disclose "any information whatsoever regarding the existence or terms of this Agreement" to anyone except his spouse, attorneys, and professional advisors was breached when plaintiff told his daughter the case "was settled and we were happy with the results" (prompting a Facebook post by the daughter). "The fact that Snay testified that he knew he needed to tell his daughter something did not excuse this breach. There is no evidence that he made this need known to the school or to his or its attorneys so that the parties might hammer out a mutually acceptable course of action in the agreement.").

§9.8 n.6 p.662 Add the following at the end: For a rejection of the Restatement approach in favor of a strict linkage between existing illegality and unenforceability, see Merry Homes v. Chi Hung Luu, 312 S.W.3d 938 (Tex. Civ. App. 2010) ("Although section 266 [of the Restatement Second] excuses performance as impracticable based upon a pre-existing condition 'of which [the party] has no reason to know,' we previously held that '[a] contract to do a thing which cannot be performed without a violation of the law is void, *whether the parties knew the law or not.*' ") (quoting from Peniche v. Aeroméxico, 580 S.W.2d 152, 156 (Tex. Civ. App. 1979)) (emphasis added by *Merry Homes* court).

§9.8 p.662 In the third paragraph, add the following at the end of the first sentence: . . . claim excuse on the ground of mistake.[8a]

[8a] United States v. Frownfelter, 626 F.3d 549 (10th Cir. 2010) (government asserts both frustration and mistake in a (failed) attempt to avoid an improvident plea agreement; court notes that "[f]or an agreement to be rescinded under the doctrine of mutual mistake, the party seeking rescission must satisfy a three part test similar to that for frustration of purpose . . . ").

§9.9 EFFECTS OF IMPRACTICABILITY AND FRUSTRATION

§9.9 n.1 p.664 Add the following at the end: A corollary is that the party asserting frustration or impracticability must not itself materially have breached the contract, for if it has, all remaining duties under the contract will likely be discharged and there will be nothing left for frustration or impossibility to excuse. Gen. Linen Servs. v. Smirnioudis, 897 A.2d 963 (N.H. 2006).

§9.9 n.2 p.664 Add the following at the end of the first paragraph: As a result, the contract is not rescinded, but the remaining duties under it are discharged. This is pertinent when the party asserting frustration or impossibility seeks to sue in restitution for the losses sustained as a result of the other party's behavior; if the contract remains in place, it stands in the way of a cause of action in restitution. Wal-Mart Stores v. AIG Life Ins. Co., 872 A.2d 611 (Del. Ch. 2005), *aff'd in part, rev'd in part on other grounds*, 901 A.2d 106 (Del. 2006).

§9.9 n.11 p.666 Add the following at the end: Hoosier Energy Rural Elec. Coop. v. John Hancock Life Ins. Co., 588 F. Supp. 2d 919 (S.D. Ind. 2008) ("Temporary commercial impracticability excuses performance until circumstances have changed, plus a reasonable time afterwards"), *aff'd*, 582 F.3d 721 (7th Cir. 2009).

§9.9 n.13 p.667 Add the following after the first sentence: *Cf.* GHS Health Maint. Org. v. United States, 536 F.3d 1293 (Fed. Cir. 2008) ("Where a contract provision is based upon a regulation, and the regulation is deemed to be invalid, reformation is appropriate.").

§9.9 n.14 p.667 Add the following to the list in the first sentence: Maudlin v. Pac. Decision Sciences Corp., 40 Cal. Rptr. 3d 724 (Ct. App. 2006) (following Restatement Second formulation; doctrine applies where payments under stock redemption agreement depend upon the presence of sufficient retained earnings (*quaere* whether the special funds doctrine might apply, *see supra* §8.2 n.8)).

§9.9 n.16 p.667 Add the following to the list after "Accord": Carabetta Enters. v. United States, 482 F.3d 1360 (Fed. Cir. 2007) (no partial impracticability in making loans when Congress provided lending alternatives to the program it had abolished) (citing to treatise).

§9.9 n.17 p.668 Add the following at the end: *Cf. In re* Dissolution of Marriage of Wood, 35 So. 3d 507 (Miss. 2010) (property settlement agreement provided for distributions exceeding the value of the fund; court reformed settlement agreement to divide the fund pro rata).

§9.9 n.22 p.669 Add the following at the end: One court has gone so far as to say that "Appellant is entitled to damages in the form of restitution to the extent his performance prior to Appellees' breach benefited Appellees, and his damages may go beyond mere restitution to include losses stemming from Appellant's reliance on the contract, even if those losses did not directly benefit Appellees . . . " Hart v. Arnold, 884 A.2d 316 (Pa. Super. 2005). It is not clear why reliance should be granted if the contract was avoided because of impracticability. If, on the other hand, the contract is divisible and was performed in part, then the breached-against party would presumably get the benefit of its bargain on the completed section and discharge on the uncompleted section.

§9.9 n.34 p.671 Add the following to the list after **"See generally"***:* Macaulay, The Real and the Paper Deal . . . , in Implicit Dimensions of Contract 51 (D. Campbell et al. eds. 2003).

§9.9 n.35 p.672 Add the following at the end: In Leisure Time Travel, Inc. v. Villa Roma Resort & Conference Ctr., 2017 N.Y. Misc. LEXIS 666, 2017 N.Y. slip op. 27055 (N.Y. Sup. Ct. Feb. 22, 2017), the parties contracted for annual use of a resort facility for a period of several years. When the facility burnt down, the resort retained the deposit and then refused to allow the events after it was rebuilt two years later. The court held that "the fire undoubtably rendered the performance of the contract impossible" and it was unjust enrichment to retain the deposit; "proper remedy for this situation is restitution." It also denied relief to the travel agency for damages in being unable to use the facility after it was rebuilt, holding that the fire rescinded the contract. Even though the facility was rebuilt, that did not occur for two years and it was not certain at the time of the fire if it would ever be rebuilt. Since the travel agency could not have been obligated to return to the facility if and when it was ever rebuilt, "there was no mutuality of obligation and the contract was rendered unenforceable."

§9.9a DRAFTING CLAUSES TO DEAL WITH CHANGED CIRCUMSTANCES

§9.9a n.1 p.673 In the first paragraph, add the following to the list in the third sentence: Robertson, Force Majeure Clauses, 25 J. Contract L. 62 (2009).

§9.9a n.1 p.673 Replace the citation to **Fontaine & De Ly** ***with the following:*** M. Fontaine & F. De Ly, Drafting International Contracts: An Analysis of Contract Clauses ch. 8 (2006).

§9.9a n.1 p.673 Insert the following at the end of the first paragraph: For a comparative discussion of *force majeure* clauses in civil law and common law jurisdictions, see Katsivela, Contracts: Force Majeure Concept or Force Majeure Clauses?, 12 Unif. L. Rev. 101 (2007).

§9.9a n.2 p.673 Add the following at the end: Of late financial contracts have often contained *material adverse change* clauses. These allow the lender to terminate the loan if there is some material adverse change in financial conditions that could impair the borrower's ability to repay the loan or the lender's ability to sell it. These clauses are more akin to standard termination clauses or definitions of default than they are to classic *force majeure* clauses, but they share an allocation of the risk of changed circumstances. For a representative clause of this sort and the headaches that result from giving it effect, see Capitol Justice v. Wachovia Bank, 706 F. Supp. 2d 23 (D.D.C. 2009). *See generally* Schwartz, A "Standard Clause Analysis" of the Frustration Doctrine and the Material Adverse Change Clause, 57 UCLA L. Rev. 789 (2010); Talley, On Uncertainty, Ambiguity, and Contractual Conditions, 34 Del. J. Corp. L. 755 (2009); Note, Efficiency and Certainty in Uncertain Times: The Material Adverse Change Clause Revisited, 43 Colum. J.L. & Soc. Probs. 333 (2010).

§9.9a p.674 Insert the following after the third sentence of the third paragraph: . . . of that performance that is to pay.[5a]

[5a] It may also be appropriate to think about whose acts other than those of the seller or supplier itself may be included as acts within the control of the seller or supplier. Hutton Contracting Co. v. City of Coffeyville, 487 F.3d 772 (10th Cir. 2007) (for the purposes of "causes beyond the control of or without the fault of [contractor]," "contractor" was held to include "those to whom it delegates its responsibilities under the contract").

***§9.9a n.9 p.675 Add the following to the list after* "Cf.":** Welsch v. Trivestco Energy Co., 221 P.3d 609 (Kan. App. 2009) (clause stating that "lessee shall not be liable for delays or defaults in its performance of any agreement or covenant hereunder due to force majeure" did not encompass failure to pay minimum royalties due even after the cessation of production; even though no purchasing and transportation services were available, the lessee could have paid the royalties from other funds, so the *force majeure* did not cause the default).

§9.9a n.11 p.676 ***Add the following at the end:*** ; *In re* Cablevision Consumer Litig., 864 F. Supp. 2d 258 (E.D.N.Y. 2012) (*force majeure* clauses "are construed narrowly and will generally only excuse a party's nonperformance if the event that caused the party's nonperformance is specifically identified").

§9.9a n.13 p.676 ***Add the following to the list after*** **"But see"*:*** Gen. Injectables & Vaccines v. Gates, 527 F.3d 1375 (Fed. Cir. 2008) (catch-all provision excused non-performance if "caused by an occurrence beyond the reasonable control of the Contractor and without its fault or negligence such as . . . " followed by customary list of excuses; held not to include failure of subcontractor to perform, because " '[I]t would seem that the very essence of the promise of a contract to deliver articles is to procure or make them. . . . [The contract] would have no sense or incentive, no assurance of fulfillment, otherwise; and a delay resulting from the absence of such ability is not of the kind enumerated in the contract — is not a cause extraneous to it and independent of the engagements and exertions of the parties.' ") (quoting from Carnegie Steel Co. v. United States, 240 U.S. 156, 164-66 (1916)); Clean the Uniform Co. v. Magic Touch Cleaning, 300 S.W.3d 602 (Mo. App. 2009) (*force majeure* clause that enumerated strikes and lockouts held through the use of *ejusdem generis* not to encompass non-renewal of a contract).

§9.9a n.13 p.676 ***Add the following to the list after the citation to*** **Kel Kim*:*** followed in Team Mktg. USA Corp. v. Power Pact, LLC, 839 N.Y.S.2d 242 (App. Div. 2007) (applying *ejusdem generis* to limit scope of *force majeure* clause).

§9.9a n.14 p.677 ***Add the following at the end:*** *See also* Sherwin Alumina v. AluChem, Inc., 512 F. Supp. 2d 957 (S.D. Tex. 2007) ("if a contract's force majeure clause concludes its 'litany of force majeure events by mentioning causes beyond [the seller's reasonable] control,' then 'the juxtaposition evince[s] an intent that the qualification regarding control apply to each of the foregoing force majeure events' ") (quoting from Sun Operating Ltd.

P'ship v. Holt, 984 S.W.2d 277, 288 (Tex. Civ. App. 1998)); Pillsbury Co. v. Wells Dairy, 752 N.W.2d 430 (Iowa 2008) (enumerated events "or any other cause that is beyond the reasonable control of that party" included; held that the final clause as to reasonable control modified all items in the clause, not merely the final one).

VOLUME III

PART IV

RIGHTS OF THIRD PARTIES

CHAPTER 10

CONTRACT BENEFICIARIES

§10.1 NATURE OF THE PROBLEM

§10.1 n.3 p.4 Add the following at the end: *Cf.* Shumate v. Twin Tier Hospitality, 655 F. Supp. 2d 521 (M.D. Pa. 2009) (action under 42 U.S.C. §1981 for racial discrimination in contracting; jury question whether fiancée and child of father had standing as third-party beneficiaries of his intended contract).

§10.1 n.7 p.4 Add the following to the list after **"Accord"***:* CDP Event Servs. v. Atcheson, 656 S.E.2d 537 (Ga. App. 2008) (injured concert patron could not enforce contract between security company and promoter); Lakew v. Mass. Bay Transp. Auth., 844 N.E.2d 263 (Mass. App. 2006) (robbed and injured employee of lessee could not enforce lease provision requiring lessor to supply security services); Verni v. Cleveland Chiropractic Coll., 212 S.W.3d 150 (Mo. 2007) (student could not enforce employment contract between instructor and college); Ronning v. Yellowstone Cnty., 253 P.3d 818 (Mont. 2011) (people seeking to adopt dogs could not enforce plea agreement between owner and state that required owner to place dogs for adoption); Murshed v. N.Y. Hotel Trades Council, 898 N.Y.S.2d 25 (App. Div. 2010) (health center visitor could not enforce contract between security company and health center).

§10.1 n.7 p.4 Add the following to the list after **"But cf."***:* Travelers Ins. Co. v. Securitylink from Ameritech, 995 So. 2d 1175 (Fla. App. 2008) (subrogated insurer of warehouse owner

an intended beneficiary of contract between alarm company and security company for the latter to respond to alarm calls at the warehouse).

§10.2 HISTORICAL DEVELOPMENT

§10.2 n.3 p.7 Add the following at the end: *See generally* V. Palmer, The Paths to Privity: A History of Third Party Beneficiary Contracts at English Law, 1550-1850 (1992).

§10.2 n.20 p.11 Add the following at the beginning: *See, e.g.*, Corbin, Contracts for the Benefit of Third Persons, 46 L.Q. Rev. 12 (1930); Corbin, Contracts for the Benefit of Third Persons in Connecticut, 31 Yale L.J. 489 (1922); Corbin, Contracts for Benefit of Third Persons, 27 Yale L.J. 1008 (1918).

§10.3 A MODERN RULE

§10.3 n.1 p.12 In the first paragraph, add the following at the end: *See also* Shumate v. Twin Tier Hospitality, 655 F. Supp. 2d 521 (M.D. Pa. 2009) (following *Guy*; applying Pennsylvania law to claim under 42 U.S.C. §1981).

§10.3 n.1 p.12 In the second paragraph, add the following to the list in the first sentence: Smallwood v. Central Peninsula Gen. Hosp., 151 P.3d 319 (Alaska 2006) ("We now conclude that in third-party beneficiary cases we should follow the approach of the Restatement (Second) of Contracts to the extent it focuses on the intent of the promisee."); Spinks v. Equity Residential Briarwood Apts., 90 Cal. Rptr. 3d 453 (Ct. App. 2009) (citing to Restatement approach when stating that "[t]hird parties . . . are classified as either intended or incidental beneficiaries of the contract"); Midwest Dredging Co. v. McAninch Corp., 424 N.W.2d 216 (Iowa 1988) ("Noting the experiences of other jurisdictions . . . we now find reason to adopt Restatement (Second) of Contracts §302 (1981) relating to third-party beneficiaries."); Eaton v. Hancock

County, 741 F. Supp. 2d 307 (D. Me. 2010) "Maine has adopted the provisions of §302 of the Restatement (Second) of Contracts").

§10.3 n.1 p.12 In the second paragraph, add the following after the citation to* Cretex*: , followed in Hickman v. Safeco Ins. Co., 695 N.W.2d 369 (Minn. 2005) (abandoning donee and creditor beneficiaries in favor of incidental beneficiaries).

§10.3 n.1 p.12 In the second paragraph, add the following after the first sentence: *Cf.* Lovell Land v. State Hwy. Admin., 969 A.2d 284 (Md. 2009) (retaining donee/creditor distinction, but otherwise following Restatement Second approach; "It appears that the change made in *Restatement (Second)* was not one of substance, but only of terminology."; citing to treatise); Verni v. Cleveland Chiropractic Coll., 212 S.W.3d 150 (Mo. 2007) (using intended/incidental terminology without referring to Restatement Second).

§10.3 n.1 p.12 In the second paragraph, add the following to the list after* "But see"*: Epitech, Inc. v. Kann, 139 Cal. Rptr. 3d 702 (Ct. App. 2012) (sticking with creditor/donee terminology).

§10.3 n.1 p.12 In the third paragraph, add the following to the list after* "See also"*: Privity: Private Justice of Public Regulation (P. Kincaid ed. 2001); Halson, Variation, Privity and Law Reform, in Exploring the Boundaries of Contract 83 (R. Halson ed. 1996).

§10.3 n.1 p.12 In the third paragraph, add the following to the list in the last sentence: Ius Quaesitum Tertio (E.J.H. Schrage ed. 2008); Farnsworth, Comparative Contract Law, in The Oxford Handbook of Comparative Law 899, 932-33 (M. Reimann & R. Zimmermann eds. 2006).

§10.3 n.4 p.13 Add the following at the end: Curiously, one court insists on linking the old terminology with the Restatement Second. Jou v. Dai-Tokyo Royal State Ins. Co., 172 P.3d 471 (Hawaii 2007) ("The *Restatement (Second)* approach contemplates two types of intended third-party beneficiaries: creditor beneficiaries and donee beneficiaries."). Texas courts appear not to take sides between old and new. *See* Tawes v. Barnes, 340 S.W.3d 419

(Tex. 2011) (citing to Restatement Second §315 and not referring to donee or creditor beneficiaries); Alvarado v. Lexington Ins. Co., 371 S.W.3d 417 (Tex. Civ. App. 2012) (carefully following *Tawes*, but using donee/creditor terminology); Maddox v. Vantage Energy, 361 S.W.3d 752 (Tex. Civ. App. 2012) (same). Presumably, Texas is large enough that it can comfortably house two sets of terminology.

§10.3 n.8 p.14 Add the following to the list after* "Accord"*: Golek v. St. Mary's Hosp., 34 A.3d 452 (Conn. App. 2012) (necessary to show that the parties "had intended to extend not only to benefit him, but also to extend contractual rights to him"; agreement between hospital and accrediting agency was intended to benefit residents, but the plaintiff did not show that the parties intended to create obligations to those residents) (Peters, J.); City of E. Chicago v. E. Chicago Second Century, 878 N.E.2d 358 (Ind. App. 2007), *aff'd in part, rev'd in part on other grounds*, 908 N.E.2d 611 (Ind. 2009) (the relevant intent is "an intent that the promising party or parties shall *assume a direct obligation* to the third party, and not a desire or purpose to *confer a particular benefit* on the third party") (emphasis in original).

§10.3 n.8 p.14 Add the following at the end: This requirement of an obligation necessarily requires as well that the benefit in question is a duty owed by the promisor to the promisee, not merely a right held by the promisee. For example, in *Doe I v. Wal-Mart Stores* the contract at issue was between Wal-Mart and its suppliers. It provided, among other things, that Wal-Mart would undertake on-site inspections and the like to ensure that the suppliers met Wal-Mart's code of conduct. A group of workers sued for breach of this provision, claiming third-party beneficiary status. The court rejected this claim. It first observed that Wal-Mart had assumed no duties to the suppliers; rather, it had reserved a right to inspect. With no promise made by Wal-Mart, there was no promise for which the plaintiffs could be beneficiaries. Similarly, the plaintiffs could not use promises by the suppliers to adhere to those standards as a basis for suit against Wal-Mart; Wal-Mart was the promisee, not the promisor. 572 F.3d 677 (9th Cir. 2009). Somewhat along the same lines, the benefit conferred must really be a benefit, rather than a white elephant, unless the third party ratifies the proffer. The principle is stated in Bybee v. Abdulla, 189 P.3d 40 (Utah 2008) (arbitration clause in agreement between physician and patient did not bind wife, despite its express mention of her; the wife did not herself derive benefit from the arbitration clause, and she was otherwise only an incidental beneficiary of the contract for her husband's medical treatment). *See also* Thompson v. Witherspoon, 12 A.3d 685 (Md. App. 2011) (beneficiaries of life insurance policy not bound by arbitration clause in agreement between insured and broker who procured policy; beneficiaries "may potentially gain some benefit from the financial advice given by [the broker,] but such possibilities are too attenuated for either concluding that appellants are third party beneficiaries of the [brokerage agreements] or otherwise enforcing the arbitration provisions against appellants"). See *infra* §10.9 (susceptibility of beneficiaries to defenses and claims).

§10.3 n.10 p.14 Add the following to the list after **"Accord"***:* Souza v. Westlands Water Dist., 38 Cal. Rptr. 3d 78 (Ct. App. 2006) ("'The contracting parties must have intended to confer a benefit on the third party.'") (quoting from Neverkovec v. Fredericks, 87 Cal. Rptr. 2d 856 (Ct. App. 1999)), both followed and contradicted by Spinks v. Equity Residential Briarwood Apts., *supra* note 1 (quoting from same material as above, but also stating that "[T]here is no requirement that 'both of the contracting parties must intend to benefit the third party. . . . Rather, 'it is sufficient that the promisor must have understood that the promisee had such intent.' ") (quoting from Schauer v. Mandarin Gems, 23 Cal. Rptr. 3d 233 (Ct. App. 2005) and Lucas v. Hamm, 364 P.2d 685 (Cal. 1961), respectively); City of E. Chicago v. E. Chicago Second Century, *supra* note 8 ("the intent of the contracting parties to benefit the third party is the controlling factor"); Lovell Land v. State Hwy. Admin., *supra* note 1 ("'[I]t must clearly appear that the parties intend[ed] to recognize [the putative third-party beneficiary] as the primary party in interest and as privy to the promise.'") (quoting from Mackubin v. Curtiss-Wright Corp., 57 A.2d 318, 321 (Md. 1948)); Allan v. Nersesova, 307 S.W.3d 564 (Tex. Civ. App. 2010) ("A third party . . . may sue to enforce a contract as a third-party beneficiary only if the contracting parties entered into the contract directly and primarily for the third party's benefit.").

§10.3 n.10 p.14 Add the following at the end: Strangely, by statute Michigan has placed the focus entirely on the *promisor*. Mich. Comp. Laws §600.1405 ("A promise shall be construed to have been made for the benefit of a person whenever the promisor of said promise had undertaken to give or to do or refrain from doing something directly to or for said person."). *See also* Shay v. Aldrich, 790 N.W.2d 629 (Mich. 2010) (applying statute).

***§10.3 n.11 p.14 Add the following to the list after* "Accord":** Souza v. Westlands Water Dist., *supra* note 10 ("A party need not show that it was intended to benefit as an individual and may prevail by showing that it is a member of a class the parties intended to benefit."); Estate of Willis v. Kiferbaum Constr. Corp., 830 N.E.2d 636 (Ill. App. 2005) ("It is not necessary that the contract specifically name the third-party beneficiary if it adequately defines a class of individual beneficiaries."); RLI Ins. Co. v. S. Union Co., 341 S.W.3d 821 (Mo. App. 2011) ("The fact that the third-party beneficiary is not identified by name in the contract does not bar that party from enforcing the terms of the contract, if the party fits into the identifiable class of persons [present in the contract]."; contracts between owner and contractors included future contractors in their waiver of subrogation clauses).

§10.3 n.12 p.15 Add the following at the beginning: *In re* Citgo Petroleum Corp., 248 S.W.3d 769 (Tex. Civ. App. 2008) ("Identification of an intended beneficiary is made at the time enforcement of the right is sought.").

§10.3 n.13 p.15 Add the following at the end: *See also* Martis v. Grinnell Mut. Reins. Co., 905 N.E.2d 920 (Ill. App. 2009) ("If a contract makes no mention of the plaintiff or the class to which he belongs, he is not a third-party beneficiary of the contract."); Lovell Land v. State Hwy. Admin., *supra* note 1 ("[A]lthough it is not necessary to the creation of third-party beneficiary status that an intended beneficiary be specifically mentioned in the contract . . . the lack of acknowledgment is certainly a factor to consider."; citing to Restatement Second §308); Maddox v. Vantage Energy, 361 S.W.3d 752 (Tex. Civ. App. 2012) ("The third-party beneficiary need not be specifically named in the contract but must be otherwise sufficiently described or designated."; individual landowners not intended beneficiaries of leasing agreement between gas company and homeowners' association, because the agreement did not identify any group to which the landowners belonged, and the landowners did not provide evidence that they were members of any group mentioned in the agreement). For a remarkable attempt to claim rights under a remote contract, *see* Protective Life Ins. Co. v. Hansen, 632 F.3d 388 (7th Cir. 2011) (contract between owner and beneficiary of life insurance policy to transfer ownership to beneficiary; beneficiary's own intended beneficiary not an intended beneficiary).

***§10.3 n.15 p.15 Add the following to the list after* "Accord":** Anwar v. Fairfield Greenwich Ltd., 728 F. Supp. 2d 372 (S.D.N.Y. 2010) (investor is direct third-party beneficiary of investment management agreement between fund and manager; a point of fund is to avoid individual contracts between investors and managers); Smallwood v. Central Peninsula Gen. Hosp., *supra* note 1 (putative beneficiary must show that "the parties to the contract intended that at least one purpose of the contract was to benefit the third party"), followed in Ennen v. Integon Indem. Corp., 268 P.3d 277 (Alaska 2012) (additional insured has cause of action against insurer for bad faith); Prouty v. Gores Tech. Grp., 18 Cal. Rptr. 3d 178 (Ct. App. 2004) ("[T]he contract need not be exclusively for the benefit of the third party. He does not need to be the sole or the primary beneficiary."); Advanced Concepts Chicago v. CDW Corp., 938 N.E.2d 577 (Ill. App. 2010) ("The promise does not have to be for the sole benefit of the third party as long as it is for its direct or substantial bargain."; subcontractor held intended beneficiary of contract between owner and general contractor stating that the general contractor would retain that subcontractor to perform specified work); Corbett v. Firstline Sec., 687 F. Supp. 2d 124 (E.D.N.Y. 2009) (husband of party to alarm services agreement a third-party beneficiary, because he benefitted from the services while he lived at their home, and was thus bound by its shortened limitations period); Risk v. Lumber One Wood Preserving, LLC, 792 F.3d 1331 (11th Cir. 2015) (reversing dismissal where "the complaint alleges that when Lumber One warranted that its wood was pressure-treated, Lumber

One intended to benefit remote purchasers like Mr. Lisk and the proposed class members").

§10.3 n.15 p.15 Add the following after the citation to **Stine***:* , followed in Doe v. Tex. Ass'n of Sch. Bds., 283 S.W.3d 451 (Tex. Civ. App. 2009) (tortfeasor's insurer a creditor beneficiary of settlement agreement between tortfeasor and tort victim) and distinguished in Tawes v. Barnes, 340 S.W.3d 419 (Tex. 2011) (although third-party beneficiary need not be the sole object of the contract, it must be referred to in the contract "with sufficient specificity to illustrate a clear intent" of the contracting parties to confer a benefit) and in turn followed in Stokes & Spiehler Onshore v. Ogle (*In re* Wave Energy), 467 Fed. Appx. 248 (5th Cir. 2012) (creditor not third-party beneficiary of joint operating agreement).

§10.3 n.15 p.15 Add the following at the end: As a corollary of this approach to mixed motives, the parties to a contract may choose to confer only some of the benefits created by it upon a third party. *See* Civix Sunrise v. Sunrise Rd. Maintenance Ass'n, 997 So. 2d 433 (Fla. App. 2008) (homeowners' associations sued lessee of adjoining property to enforce terms of lease; the associations were intended third-party beneficiaries of the lease, but not of the provision for fee-shifting, for "nothing in the lease indicates the parties intended for them to benefit from, or for that matter be subject to, the attorney's fee provision.").

Perhaps in an attempt to cabin this doctrine, many courts employ strict standards of proof when determining the status of a possible beneficiary. *See, e.g.*, Foundation Health v. Westside EKG Assocs., 944 So. 2d 188 (Fla. 2006) ("clear or manifest intent"); Abarca v. Scott Morgan Residential, 305 S.W.3d 110 (Tex. Civ. App. 2009) ("[A] contract does not confer third-party beneficiary rights unless: (1) the contract plainly expresses the third-party obligation of the bargain-giver, (2) it is unmistakable that a benefit to the third party is within the contemplation of the primary contracting parties, and (3) the primary parties contemplate that the third party would be vested with the right to sue for enforcement of the contract.").

§10.3 n.16 p.16 Add the following to the list after **"See also":** Martis v. Grinnell Mut. Reins. Co., *supra* note 13 (medical provider not third-party beneficiary of workers' compensation policy, though it would qualify if "the policy provide[d] for payment directly to medical providers"); Spring Valley IV Joint Venture v. Neb. State Bank, 690 N.W.2d 778 (Neb. 2005) (where "the evidence indicates that the Bank was under no obligation to disburse funds directly to the Partnerships, but, rather, was obligated to disburse funds to the individual borrower, who would then be able to invest the sums in the Partnerships . . . the Partnerships were at most incidental beneficiaries of the loan agreements"); Ehret v. Uber Tech., Inc., 2014 U.S. Dist. LEXIS 132125 at *36-41 (N.D. Cal. Sept. 17, 2014) (plaintiff consumer who used Uber to hire private driver and alleged that much of the "20% gratuity" did not go to the driver as advertised but rather was retained by Uber, had standing, and stated a cause of action under California Unfair Competition Law and Consumer Legal Remedies Act but was not a third-party beneficiary or otherwise able to advance breach of contract claim; "[w]hile tips or gratuities may be customary in the service industry, they are not binding obligations on the part of customers. Uber's failure to remit the 20% gratuity to the drivers does not leave Plaintiff or the putative class members liable to the drivers for any debt or amount. Accordingly, the drivers are properly considered donee beneficiaries.").

§10.3 n.16 p.16 Add the following at the end: A related concept is "direct benefit estoppel," in which "a non-signatory plaintiff seeking the benefits of a contract is estopped from simultaneously attempting to avoid the contract's burdens, such as the obligation to arbitrate disputes." *In re* Kellogg Brown & Root, 166 S.W.3d 732, 739 (Tex. 2005), followed in Stanford Dev. Corp. v. Stanford Condo. Owners Ass'n, 285 S.W.3d 45 (Tex. Civ. App. 2009) (homeowners' association suing developer for breach of contracts with individual homeowners bound by arbitration clause in the homeowners' contracts). *See also* Goldman v. KPMG LLP, 92 Cal. Rptr. 3d 534 (Ct. App. 2009) ("[I]f a plaintiff relies on the terms of an agreement to assert his or her claims against a nonsignatory defendant, the plaintiff may be equitably stopped from repudiating the arbitration clause of that very document."); Stalley v. Transitional Hosps. Corp., 44 So. 3d 627 (Fla. App. 2010)

("an individual who makes use of a contract as long as it works to his or her advantage is estopped from avoiding the contract's provisions concerning the forum in which any dispute should be resolved"; not relevant here because arbitration agreement and admissions agreement separate); Hemphill v. Ford Motor Co., 206 P.3d 1 (Kan. App. 2009) (applying estoppel; collecting cases); Scruggs v. Wyatt, 60 So. 3d 758 (Miss. 2011) (associate of law firm that was part of joint venture subject to its arbitration clause, where associate sought fees arising from the joint venture agreement); Cleveland-Akron-Canton Advertising Coop. v. Physician's Weight Loss Ctrs. of Am., 922 N.E.2d 1012 (Ohio App. 2009) ("The co-op knowingly accepted the benefits conferred by the franchise agreements and must endure its burdens."). More pithily, "A nonparty cannot both have his contract and defeat it too." *In re* Weekley Homes, 180 S.W.3d 127, 135 (Tex. 2005). The benefit must, as the name suggests, flow directly from the contract; it is not enough that the non-signatory benefits from the relations of the contracting parties but not the contract itself. Thompson v. Witherspoon, 12 A.3d 685 (Md. App. 2011). *Accord:* Carr v. Main Carr Dev., 337 S.W.3d 489 (Tex. Civ. App. 2011) ("A non-signatory cannot be compelled to arbitrate when claims merely 'touch matters' covered by a contract or 'are dependent upon, or inextricably bound up with,' a contract; instead, the claims must rely on the terms of the contract.") (quoting from Goldman v. KPMG LLP, 92 Cal. Rptr. 3d 534, 541 (Ct. App. 2009)).

This is a species of equitable estoppel rather than an application of third-party beneficiary law; the former looks to what happens after the contract is formed, while the latter looks to the intent of the parties before entering into the contract. *See* E.I. du Pont de Nemours & Co. v. Rhone Poulenc Fiber & Resin Intermediates, 269 F.3d 187 (3d Cir. 2001) ("Under the third party beneficiary theory, a court must look to the intentions of the parties at the time the contract was executed. Under the equitable estoppel theory, a court looks to the parties' conduct after the contract was executed. Thus, the snapshot this Court examines under equitable estoppel is much later in time than the snapshot for third party beneficiary analysis."), agreed with in part and disagreed with in part by Comer v. Micor, Inc., 436 F.3d 1098 (9th Cir. 2006) (Kozinski, C.J.) (making same distinction between third-party beneficiary and equitable estoppel theories, but finding the *du Pont* court's third-party beneficiary analysis wanting; "A third party beneficiary might in certain circumstances have the power to sue under a contract; it certainly cannot be *bound* to a contract it did not sign or otherwise assent to.") (emphasis in original). In contrast, a non-signatory defendant seeking to enforce an arbitration clause against a signatory plaintiff may not invoke equitable estoppel for this reason. Mundi v. Union Sec. Life Ins. Co., 555 F.3d 1042 (9th Cir. 2009), distinguished in Townsend v. Quadrant Corp., 268 P.3d 917 (Wash. 2012) (non-signatory plaintiffs equitably estopped from rejecting arbitration demanded by signatory defendants, where parents were signatories and the pleadings do not distinguish the parents from the children). *See also* §10.9 *infra* on the vulnerability of the third-party beneficiary to defenses and claims.

§10.3 n.17 p.16 Add the following to the list after "Accord": Locke v. Ozark City Bd. of Educ., 910 So. 2d 1247 (Ala. 2005) (contract between school district and athletic association "was intended to directly benefit umpires like [the plaintiff]"); Forest Hill Nursing Ctr. v. McFarlan, 995 So. 2d 775 (Miss. App. 2008) (resident of nursing home third-party beneficiary of contract between nursing home and patient's granddaughter; although resident not bound through agency, "[t]he benefits of residing at Forest Hill flow directly to McFarlan" and so "McFarlan's care was not incidental to the contract, but instead was the essential purpose of the agreement."); Allan v. Nersesova, 307 S.W.3d 564 (Tex. Civ. App. 2010) (third party has right to sue under contract "only if the contracting parties entered into the contract directly and primarily for the third party's benefit"; owner of condominium unit intended beneficiary of contract between owner of other unit and owners' association, where the incorporated rules of the association require owners to compensate other owners for damage caused to other units).

§10.3 n.17 p.16 Add the following after the citation to* XL Disposal Corp.*: , followed in Advanced Concepts Chicago v. CDW Corp., 938 N.E.2d 577 (Ill. App. 2010) ("if the promisee bargains with the promisor to render a performance directly to a third party, in nearly every case the promisee will have intended to benefit that third party").

§10.3 n.18 p.16 In the first paragraph, add the following to the list after* "Accord"*: Hickman v. Safeco Ins. Co., *supra* note 18 ("performance need not be rendered directly to the intended beneficiary"); Eisert v. Archdiocese of Santa Fe, 207 P.3d 1156 (N.M. App. 2009) (daughter was third-party beneficiary of burial contract made between mother and cemetery for father's burial where two years later cemetery buried mother above father; no citation to *Jaynes*).

§10.3 n.19 p.17 In the first paragraph, add the following to the list after* "Accord"*: Estate of Willis v. Kiferbaum Constr. Corp., 830 N.E.2d 636 (Ill. App. 2005) ("[I]f the terms of a promise for which the promisee bargained with the promisor are to render a performance directly to the third party, in nearly every case the third party who is to receive performance will be the party intended to be benefited.").

§10.3 n.19 p.17 In the first paragraph, add the following to the list after* "Contra"*: Bohan v. Dennis C. Jackson Co., 935 N.E.2d 900 (Ohio App. 2010) (intended beneficiary of trust amendment had no cause of action against law firm that failed to prepare the amendment before the settlor's death); Rydde v. Morris, 675 S.E.2d 431 (S.C. 2009) ("The imposition of a duty on an attorney to a prospective beneficiary of a nonexistent will would wreak havoc on the attorney's ethical duty of undivided loyalty to the client and force an impermissible wedge in the attorney-client relationship.").

§10.3 n.19 p.17 Add the following after the first paragraph: *Lucas v. Hamm* set forth factors to be used in this analysis. *Id.* at 687 ("[T]he determination whether in a specific case the defendant will be held liable to a third person not in privity is a matter of policy and involves the balancing of various factors, among which are the extent to which the transaction was intended to affect the plaintiff, the foreseeability of harm to him, the degree of certainty that the plaintiff suffered injury, the closeness of the connection between the defendant's conduct and the injury, and the policy of preventing future harm."), followed in McIntosh County Bank v. Dorsey & Whitney, LLP, 745 N.W.2d 538 (Minn. 2008) ("[T]he attorney must be aware of the client's interest to benefit the third party in order for the exception to be applicable. . . . Imposing on attorneys a duty toward beneficiaries of whom they are unaware would risk dampening their zealous advocacy on behalf of their clients, for fear of harming a third party to whom a duty might later be found to be owed."), in turn followed in Perez v. Stern, 777 N.W.2d 545 (Neb. 2010) (comprehensive analysis of attorney's liability to third party; attorney of estate subject to malpractice suit by next of kin, where she failed to prosecute a wrongful death claim on the estate's behalf until limitations period had run) and in Credit Union Cent. Falls v. Groff, 966 A.2d 1262 (R.I. 2009) (lender was intended beneficiary of contract between attorney and borrower-client where attorney failed to pay off prior mortgages with part of the proceeds of the loan, despite instructions from the lender to do exactly that).

§10.3 n.20 p.18 Add the following to the list after "Cf.": Estate of Schneider v. Finmann, 933 N.E.2d 718 (N.Y. 2010) ("privity, or a relationship sufficiently approaching privity, exists between the personal representative of an estate and the estate planning attorney. . . . [S]trict privity remains a bar against beneficiaries' and other third-party individuals' estate planning malpractice claims . . . [because] [r]elaxing privity . . . would produce undesirable results — uncertainty and limitless liability."); Shoemaker v. Gindlesberger, 887 N.E.2d 1167 (Ohio 2008) (attorneys "are not liable to a third party for the good-faith representation of a client, unless the third part is in privity with the client for whom the legal services were performed").

§10.3 n.20 p.18 At the end of the first paragraph, delete the citation to Viscardi.

§10.3 n.20 p.18 Add the following at the end of the first paragraph: The basic principle applies for other forms of professional liability. *See* Levine v. Harriton & Furrer, LLP, 940 N.Y.S.2d 334 (App. Div. 2012) (law firm not third-party beneficiary of contract between claimant and engineer hired as expert, and thus could not assert malpractice claims against engineer).

§10.3 n.24 p.20 Add the following to the list after **"Accord"***:* RPC Liquidation v. Iowa Dep't of Transp., 717 N.W.2d 317 (Iowa 2006) (term stating that the contract "is not intended by any of the provisions of any part of the contract documents to create in the public or any member thereof a third party beneficiary hereunder clearly expresses the intent of the parties to exclude anyone from having third-party beneficiary status," including the plaintiff); Cumis Ins. Soc'y v. BJ's Wholesale Club, 918 N.E.2d 36 (Mass. 2009) (clause in agreement between merchant and bank acquiring credit card receivables that "[t]his Agreement is for the benefit of, and may be enforced only by, [bank] and [merchant] and their respective successors and permitted transferees and assignees, and is not for the benefit of, and may not be enforced by, any third party" bars attempt to enforce agreement by issuing bank); Lesieur v. Fryar, 325 S.W.3d 242 (Tex. Civ. App. 2010) (real estate broker not intended beneficiary of realty sales contract; contract stated that "All obligations of the parties for payment of brokers' fees are contained in a separate written agreement.").

§10.3 n.24 p.20 Add the following at the end: *Cf. In re* Stone & Webster, Inc., 558 F.3d 234 (3d Cir. 2009) (though purchase agreement contained a no-third-party-beneficiary clause, the sale order approving the purchase agreement contained language protecting third-party rights, with the latter superseding the former; "'general, boilerplate language' prohibiting third-party actions 'must yield to the specific direction' of separate contractual provisions granting third parties enforceable rights in assumed liabilities") (quoting from Caldwell Trucking PRP v. Rexon Tech. Corp., 421 F.3d 234, 245 (3d Cir. 2005)).

§10.3 n.26 p.20 Add the following at the end: In Bozzio v. EMI Grp. Ltd., 811 F.3d 1144 (9th Cir. 2016), a band member sued a record label, asserting she was paid a lower royalty rate than contracted for. She was not a party to the contract, which was between the incorporated band and the label, and had executed a separate agreement that she would "look solely to [Missing Persons, Inc.] for the payment of [her] fees and/or royalties . . . , and will not assert any claims in this regard against Capitol." *Id.* at 1147. Applying California law, the Ninth Circuit found the plaintiff was an intended third party beneficiary because the

"Agreement expressly provides that Bozzio and her bandmates would incur obligations and receive benefits" and it "contemplates royalty payments to individual artists." *Id.* at 1152-53. The plaintiff asserted the "look to" clause "was intended to prohibit an artist from asserting a claim against Capitol only 'when there is a dispute among individual band members over the internal allocation and distribution of royalties that have already been properly accounted for and paid by the record label to the artists' musical group or loan-out corporation.'" *Id.* at 1153. The court found the language subject to that interpretation and "whether she forfeited the ability to sue as a third-party beneficiary is a fact-bound inquiry ill-suited to resolution at the motion to dismiss stage."

§10.3 n.27 p.21 Add the following after the citation to* Garcia*: , followed in Souza v. Westlands Water Dist., *supra* note 10 ("the court must read the contract in light of the circumstances in which the parties entered into it").

§10.3 n.27 p.21 In the first paragraph, add the following to the list after* "See"*: Mundi v. Union Sec. Life Ins. Co., *supra* note 16 (beneficiary's claim of bad-faith denial against life insurer not intertwined with loan agreement with separate entity for whose benefit the life insurance policy had been taken out); Astra Oil Co. v. Rover Navigation, 344 F.3d 276 (2d Cir. 2003) (Sotomayor, J.: in determining "the degree of 'intertwined-ness' that would be required to support an estoppel theory . . . such a finding should only be made after careful review of the relationship between the parties, the contracts they signed, and the issues that arose between them").

§10.3 n.27 p.21 In the first paragraph, add the following to the list after* "But see"*: Becker v. Crispell-Snyder, Inc., 763 N.W.2d 192 (Wis. App. 2009) ("we can use the totality of the circumstances to evaluate whether the contract (1) specifically conferred a direct benefit on the Beckers, (2) limited the benefit to a well-defined group of third parties, and (3) required the contractor to assume liability to third parties").

§10.3 n.27 p.21 In the first paragraph, add the following after the fourth sentence: *But cf.* Podraza v. New Century Physicians of Neb., 789 N.W.2d 260 (Neb. 2010) (looking first to four corners of the document, but if intent not "clearly manifest" therein then may look to all evidence, and becomes a question of fact).

§10.3 n.27 p.21 In the second paragraph, add the following to the list after* "See also"*: Podraza v. New Century Physicians of Neb., 789 N.W.2d 260 (Neb. 2010) (adopting the "intent rule," and also adopting "a rebuttable presumption that a release benefits only those specifically designated").

§10.3 n.28 p.21 Add the following to the list after* "Accord"*: CDP Event Servs. v. Atcheson, 656 S.E.2d 537 (Ga. App. 2008) ("Parol evidence cannot confer third-party beneficiary status where the contract itself fails to do so . . . "); Partout v. Harper, 183 P.3d 771 (Idaho 2008) ("The intent to benefit the third party must be expressed in the contract itself."); Williamson v. Mont. Pub. Serv. Comm'n, 272 P.3d 71 (Mont. 2012) ("A plaintiff cannot assume that he is an intended third-party beneficiary; rather, he must show from the face of the contract that it was intended to benefit him.").

§10.3 n.28 p.21 Add the following after the citation to* Radosevic*: , followed in Nat'l Labor Coll. v. Hillier Grp. Architecture N.J., 739 F. Supp. 2d 821 (D. Md. 2010) (rejecting proffered evidence of performance under the contract to support claim of intended beneficiary status).

§10.3 n.28 p.21 Replace the citation to* Republic Nat'l Bank *with the following: , Basic Capital Mgmt. v. Dynex Commercial, 348 S.W.3d 894 (Tex. 2011) ("'The intention to contract or confer a direct benefit to a third party must be clearly and fully spelled out or enforcement by the third party must be denied.'") (quoting from MCI Telecomms. Corp. v. Tex. Untils. Elec. Co., 995 S.W.2d 647 (Tex. 1999)).

§10.3 n.29 p.22 In the first paragraph, add the following at the end of the first sentence: , followed in Fishbein v. Miranda, 670 F. Supp. 2d 264 (S.D.N.Y. 2009).

§10.3 n.29 p.22 In the first paragraph, add the following after the first sentence: For a qualification of New York's law in this area, *see* Air Atlanta Aero Eng'g v. SP Aircraft Owner I, 637 F. Supp. 2d 185 (S.D.N.Y. 2009) (although courts may, when appropriate, look to surrounding circumstances, they may do so only if the actual agreement contains some expression of intent to benefit the third party, or at least make that intent clear to the promisor). Even as qualified, note the contrast between this fairly receptive attitude toward parol evidence and the famously narrow approach to parol evidence used generally in New York. See *supra* §7.12.

***§10.3 n.29 p.22 In the first paragraph, add the following to the list after* "Accord":** Golek v. St. Mary's Hosp., 34 A.3d 452 (Conn. App. 2012) (in the absence of express language regarding the parties' intent to benefit the plaintiff, a medical resident suing a hospital, a court may "examine[] the terms of the accreditation agreement to ascertain its purpose and scope.") (Peters, J.); Hickman v. Safeco Ins. Co., *supra* note 1 ("In ascertaining the parties' intent to benefit a third person, the contract is read in light of all the surrounding circumstances.").

***§10.3 n.30 p.22 Add the following to the list after* "Accord":** Lopez v. Taylor, 195 S.W.3d 627 (Tenn. App. 2005) (marital dissolution agreements regarding the payment of college expenses "are generally regarded as intended third-party beneficiary contracts because their purpose is to confer a benefit on the children covered by the agreement").

***§10.3 n.34 p.23 Add the following to the list after* "Accord":** Hickman v. Safeco Ins. Co., *supra* note 1 ("Where the intention of the parties is clear from the face of a contract, construction of the contract is a question of law for the court."); Basic Capital Mgmt. v. Dynex Commercial, 348 S.W.3d 894 (Tex. 2011) ("'[w]hen a contract is not ambiguous, the construction of the written instrument is a question of law for the court'"; finding party intended beneficiary as a matter of law) (quoting from MCI Telecomms. Corp. v. Tex. Untils. Elec. Co., 995 S.W.2d 647 (Tex. 1999)).

§10.3 n.37 p.24 Add the following to the list after* "Accord"*: Intergen N.V. v. Grina, 344 F.3d 134 (1st Cir. 2003) ("law requires 'special clarity' to support a finding 'that the contracting parties intended to confer a benefit' on a third party"); Nitro Dist. v. Dunn, 194 S.W.3d 339 (Mo. 2006) ("In cases where the contract lacks an express declaration of that intent [that the third party be an intended beneficiary], there is a strong presumption that the third party is not a beneficiary and that the parties contracted to benefit only themselves."), followed in Bank of Am. v. UMB Fin. Servs., 618 F.3d 906 (8th Cir. 2010) (parent corporation not third-party beneficiary of contract between employees of its subsidiary and their licensing group, where no language in contract granted beneficiary status and parent corporation derived no benefit from the contract).

§10.3 n.37 p.24 Add the following after the citation to* MCI Telecom. Corp.*: , followed in Tawes v. Barnes, 340 S.W.3d 419 (Tex. 2011) ("Traditionally, Texas courts have maintained a presumption against third-party beneficiary agreements. . . . Therefore, in the absence of a clear and unequivocal expression of the contracting parties' intent to directly benefit a third party, courts will not confer third-party beneficiary status by implication."), in turn followed in Maddox v. Vantage Energy, 361 S.W.3d 752 (Tex. Civ. App. 2012) ("A third party may enforce as a third-party beneficiary a contract it did not sign when the parties to the contract entered the agreement with the clear and express intention of directly benefitting the third party."), and

§10.3 n.38 p.25 In the first paragraph, add the following after the citation to* Grigerik*: , followed in Golek v. St. Mary's Hosp., 34 A.3d 452 (Conn. App. 2012) (medical resident must prove not just that he was intended to benefit from a contract between an accrediting agency and his hospital, but that the parties "intended to obligate themselves to him contractually").

§10.3 n.38 p.25 In the third paragraph, add the following at the end: *Accord:* Advanced Concepts Chicago v. CDW Corp., *supra* note 15 ("A nonparty is a third-party beneficiary if the contracting parties, or at least the promisee, intended to confer a benefit on that party."; subcontractor held intended beneficiary of contract between owner and general contractor stating that the general contractor would retain that subcontractor to perform specified work).

§10.3 n.43 p.26 Add the following at the end: *See* Spring Valley IV Joint Venture v. Neb. State Bank, *supra* note 16 (although "the purpose of the loans was to fund partnership interests," "the Bank was under no obligation to disburse funds directly to the Partnerships" and so no actual duty arose).

***§10.3 n.45 p.26 Add the following to the list after* "Accord":** Williams v. Univ. Med. Ctr. of S. Nev., 688 F. Supp. 2d 1134 (D. Nev. 2010) (requiring that "a promissory intent to benefit the third party must be clearly present, and the third party beneficiary's reliance thereon must be foreseeable"; physician was third-party beneficiary of contract between fellow physician and hospital that fellow physician would act in accord with the hospital's bylaws, because "it is in the physicians' mutual benefit to agree to the common understanding that the Bylaws control their relationship both with the hospital, and amongst themselves."); Brooks v. Trustees of Dartmouth Coll., 20 A.3d 890 (N.H. 2011) (dictum: quoting Restatement Second §302 cmt. *d* approvingly).

§10.3 n.45 p.26 Add the following at the end: Note, however, the exact language of the Restatement Second. The comment asks whether "the beneficiary would be reasonable in relying on the promise," not whether the beneficiary *has* relied. Actual reliance may well be evidence that the reliance was reasonable, as it is in other reliance-based parts of contract law, but it is not necessary. If a reasonable third-party beneficiary would have felt justified in relying on a promise, presumably the third-party beneficiary should be treated as an intended beneficiary, reliance or no.

§10.3a DRAFTING AND CONTRACT BENEFICIARIES

***§10.3a n.1 p.27 Add the following to the list after* "See":** Katz v. Pershing, LLC, 672 F.3d 64 (1st Cir. 2012) (New York law: giving effect to statement that the contract "is not intended to confer any benefits on third-parties including, but not limited to, customers of [the obligor]"); GECCMC 2005-C1 Plummer St. Office Ltd. P'ship v. JPMorgan Chase Bank, 671 F.3d 1027 (9th Cir. 2012) (federal common law: giving effect to clause in bank purchase and assumption agreement that "[e]xcept as otherwise specifically provided in this Agreement, nothing expressed or referred to in this Agreement is intended or shall be construed to give any Person other than the Receiver, the Corporation, and the Assuming Bank any legal or equitable right, remedy or claim under or with respect to this Agreement or any provisions contained herein, it being the intention of the parties hereto that this Agreement, the obligations and statements of responsibilities hereunder, and all other conditions and provisions hereof are for the sole and exclusive benefit of the Receiver, the Corporation and the Assuming Bank and for the benefit of no other person"); Balsam v. Tucows Inc., 627 F.3d 1158 (9th Cir. 2010) (giving effect to "This Agreement shall not be construed to create any obligation by either [contracting party] to any non-party to this Agreement, including any Registered Name Holder"); *In re* TJX Cos. Retail Sec. Breach Litig., 564 F.3d 489 (1st Cir. 2009) (contract between bank acquiring credit card receivables and retail merchant: "This Agreement is for the benefit of, and may be enforced only by, Bank and Merchant . . . and is not for the benefit of, and may not be enforced by any third party."); Advanced Ground Sys. Eng'g v. RTW Indus., 388 F.3d 1036 (7th Cir. 2004) (Indiana law: "This Agreement will be binding upon, inure to the benefit of and will be enforceable by Seller and Purchaser and their respective heirs, if applicable, legal representatives, successors and permitted assigns, if any, and no other person or entity will be deemed a third-party beneficiary of this Agreement." is effective, as "the general third-party beneficiary rule is a default rule, which can be altered by express agreement of the parties"); BNP Paribas Mortg. Corp. v. Bank of Am., 778 F. Supp. 2d 375 (S.D.N.Y. 2011) (depositary agreement; giving effect to "no Person not a party to this Agreement shall be deemed to be a third-party beneficiary hereof nor shall any Person be empowered to enforce the provisions of this Agreement" save certain specific entities and their successors); Speleos v. BAC Home Loans Servicing, 755 F. Supp. 2d 304 (D. Mass. 2010) (federal common law: giving effect to "These rights and remedies are for our benefit and that of our successors and assigns"); Penn. State Employees Credit Union v. Fifth Third Bank, 398 F. Supp. 2d 317 (M.D. Pa. 2005) (same term as in *In re* TJX Cos. Retail Sec. Breach Litig., 564 F.3d 489 (1st Cir. 2009); enforceable, because the law "recognizes the right of the contracting parties to exclude third parties from invoking the benefits of their agreement"); Venezia Lakes Homeowners Ass'n v. CSX Transp., 43 So. 3d 93 (Fla. App. 2010) (giving effect to the term: "Neither this Agreement nor any provision hereof or agreement or provision included herein by reference shall operate or be construed as being for the benefit of any third person."); RPC Liquidation v. Iowa Dep't of Transp., 717 N.W.2d 317 (Iowa 2006) (term stating that the contract "is not intended by any of the provisions of any part of the contract documents to create in the public or any member thereof a third party beneficiary hereunder clearly expresses the intent of the parties to exclude anyone from having third-party beneficiary status," including the plaintiff); Cumis Ins. Soc'y v. BJ's Wholesale Club, 918 N.E.2d 36 (Mass. 2009) (same clause as In re TJX Cos. Retail Sec. Breach Litig., 564 F.3d 489 (1st Cir. 2009); enforced as an "explicit and unambiguous disclaimer").

§10.3a n.1 p.27 ***Add the following at the end:*** Nor is it sufficient to insert a clause excluding putative beneficiaries. If there are other, more specific clauses that appear to create third-party rights, basic principles of contract interpretation would suggest that the more specific clauses will control. It is thus important to ensure that no provisions create third-party rights. Prouty v. Gores Tech. Grp., 18 Cal. Rptr. 3d 178 (App. Ct. 2004) (specific clause granting employees severance benefits prevails over general provision precluding third-party beneficiary status); *In re* Stone & Webster, Inc., 558 F.3d 234 (3d Cir. 2009) (boilerplate language prohibiting third-party actions superseded by specific language in associated contract granting specific third-party rights).

On the other hand, it is important for a putative third-party beneficiary not to put too much weight on a carve-out provision. If a contract states that there are no third-party rights except for any created in a particular subsection, it does not follow that the subsection does create rights, but rather that it may do so. *See* Carr v. Main Carr Dev., 337 S.W.3d 489 (Tex. Civ. App. 2011) (contract stated that "Except with regards to the provisions of section 3 above, no claim as a third party beneficiary under this agreement by any person shall be made, or valid, against [the parties]."; third-party claim rejected, because the section "relates only to the right to assert claims. . . . No rights are conferred upon [the putative beneficiary]."). For an instance where failure to think through whether variant contracts created or destroyed third-party rights, *see* RLI Ins. Co. v. S. Union Co., 341 S.W.3d 821 (Mo. App. 2011), discussed at length *infra* at §10.4 n.1.

§10.3a p.28 In the carryover paragraph, add the following at the end of the first full sentence: . . . leave the matter to inference.[3a]

[3a] On the importance of excluding unwanted beneficiaries explicitly, *see* Limbach Co., LLC v. City of Philadelphia, 905 A.2d 567 (Pa. Commw. Ct. 2006) (lease provided that city was third-party beneficiary of lease between industrial authority and airline; contractor sought to enforce its provisions, and court held that the pertinent provision "does not indicate that the City is the *only* potential third party beneficiary, or that the parties intended to prohibit any other entity, such as a construction contractor, from claiming third party beneficiary status" and thus that the contractor's claim should not be dismissed). This *expressio unius* approach does sometimes work. *See* Ahmad v. Wells Fargo Bank, 861 F. Supp. 2d 818 (E.D. Mich. 2012) (loan servicing agreement between lender and U.S. government under HAMP: third-party claims of borrower held excluded by "The Agreement shall inure to the benefit of and be binding upon the parties to the Agreement and their permitted successors-in-interest."); Envt'l Staffing Acquisition Corp. v. B & R Constr. Mgmt., 725 S.E.2d 550 (Va. 2012) (giving effect to "All rights under this Contract Agreement shall be for the benefit of DEVELOPER and its successors and assigns . . ."). All these provisions could easily have been written to exclude third parties expressly-for example, in the last case, something like ". . . shall be for the *sole* benefit of . . ." would suffice. Better still, this proposition could be framed explicitly, as in "No one else is granted any rights in this agreement, including rights as a third-party beneficiary, unless otherwise stated expressly in this writing or in any written amendments to it."). *See* Veolia Water Indianapolis v. Nat'l Trust Ins. Co., 973 N.E. 3 (Ind. App. 2012) (giving effect to a separate subsection stating "This Agreement is intended to be solely for the benefit of Company and Department and their successors and permitted assigns and is not intended to and shall not infer any rights or benefits on any third party not a signat[or] hereto, except as specifically set forth herein.").

§10.3a n.4 p.28 Add the following at the end: For an example of an agreement that creates limited third-party beneficiary status for shareholders but expressly excludes them from that status otherwise, *see* Consol. Edison v. Northeast Utilities, 426 F.3d 524 (2d Cir. 2005) ("This Agreement . . . except for the provisions of Article II and Article 5.08, [is] not intended to confer upon any person other than the parties any rights or remedies."), followed in BNP Paribas Mortg. Corp. v. Bank of Am., 778 F. Supp. 2d 375 (S.D.N.Y. 2011) (noteholders have third-party beneficiary status to sue under a security agreement, but not a custodial agreement, entered into as part of a single mortgage lending facility; "contracting parties may simultaneously elect to confer a benefit or right upon a third party and to limit that right, including by limiting the third party's enforcement powers," so provision of agreement barring enforcement by unidentified third parties is effective).

§10.3a n.5 p.28 Add the following at the end: Geier v. M-Qube Inc., 824 F.3d 797 (9th Cir. 2016) (terms of use agreement provided for waiver of claims against "any of Company's suppliers" and the agreement could be enforced by any supplier, as third-party beneficiaries; remanded to make findings regarding assent and whether party was a supplier).

§10.4 CONSTRUCTION CONTRACTS

§10.4 n.1 p.29 In the second paragraph, replace the citation to **Barry, Bett & Led Duke** ***with the following:*** Bovis Lend Lease LMB v. GCT Venture, 728 N.Y.S.2d 25 (App. Div. 2001) (agreement is designed to "allow contractors to bring an action against the owner on behalf of their subcontractors").

§10.4 n.1 p.29 In the second paragraph, add the following at the end: As to the possibility of a "pass-through" claim by a general contractor in the absence of agreement, *see* Interstate Contracting Corp. v. City of Dallas, 135 S.W.3d 605 (Tex. 2004) (following the "many states [that] have expressly or implicitly recognized pass-through claims"). As to a subcontractor claiming rights under the general contractor's agreement with the owner, *see* Esposito v. True Color Enters. Constr., 45 So. 3d 554 (Fla. App. 2010) (subcontractor an incidental beneficiary; "[n]othing in the [contractor-owner] contract demonstrates an intent to primarily and directly benefit [the subcontractor]").

§10.4 n.1 p.29 In the third paragraph, add the following after the citation to **Pelletier***:* *and* Abarca v. Scott Morgan Residential, 305 S.W.3d 110 (Tex. Civ. App. 2009) ("these provisions, when read together with all of the provisions of the Subcontract Agreement and its addendum, reflect [the general contractor]'s desire to protect itself from liability to any employees of [the subcontractor]'s or [the subcontractor]'s own subcontractors.").

§10.4 n.1 p.29 Add the following at the end: Another problem may come about when a contractor breaches its contract with the owner and the owner's insurer seeks subrogation damages from the contractor. Usually this is not a problem; presumably the insurer stands in the shoes of the subrogor for the purposes of pursuing damages, as commonly happens when insureds assign to the insurer their rights against those who caused the harm. But what if the owner made contracts with other contractors containing broad waivers of subrogation? There is no third-party beneficiary issue if the waiver appears in the contract between the owner and the breaching contractor. In the face of silence, however, the breaching contractor must invoke its third-party beneficiary status as to the other contracts. This issue arose in RLI Ins. Co. v. S. Union Co., 341 S.W.3d 821 (Mo. App. 2011), with perhaps surprising results. The court first dispensed with the insurer's *expressio unius* argument that the absence of a waiver of subrogation clause in the contractor's fully integrated agreement with the owner, when contrasted with the presence of that clause in contracts made by the owner with other contractors, meant that there could be no third-party rights to invoke the waiver clause in those other contracts. The court was unwilling to draw any conclusions from the absence of a waiver clause, barring an express negation of such a clause or contradictory provisions in other contracts between the owner and the contractor. *See* Restatement Second §309 cmt. *c*. Then it was easy for the court to fit the breaching contractor under the broad waivers in the other contracts between contractors and the owner, which provided that the owner and contractor agreed to waive their rights resulting from casualty "against each other and against the Construction Manager,

Architect, Owner's own Contractors and own forces." The breaching contractor was one of "Owner's own Contractors"; consequently, it was a fairly clear third-party beneficiary of the other contracts and was able to assert the waiver of subrogation clause against the owner's insurer.

Why this discussion? Partly because subrogation is almost inevitable when insurers are involved, and waivers of subrogation are extremely common in this field (including in the AIA forms used by the owner here, except in its contract with the breaching contractor). But the main reason is the ease of eliminating the ambiguity here, which resulted principally because the owner did not use the same form contract for all its contractors. Had the owner done that, the owner's insurer would have had no real response when the contractor invoked the waiver-of-subrogation clause. On the other side, if the owner really meant to except this contractor from the waivers present in all other contracts, it should have done so expressly rather than by silence. And if the owner had wanted to limit the scope of each waiver-of-subrogation clause to damages caused by that contractor's own fault, that too would have been easy to draft. The inconsistent contract forms, perhaps combined with a failure to read the variant forms together or a blithe assumption that omitting the waiver would suffice, yielded costly and time-consuming — and very avoidable — litigation.

***§10.4 n.5 p.31 Add the following to the list after* "Accord":** Nelson v. Anderson Lumber Co., 99 P.3d 1092 (Idaho App. 2004) (no cause of action by owner against subcontractor; the general contractor "would still be liable for a breach of the contract between himself and the [owner] even if the subsequent contracts were not fulfilled," and "there is no evidence that the negotiations between [the general contractor and the subcontractor] expressed an intent to benefit the [owner]"); Nat'l Labor Coll. v. Hillier Grp. Architecture N.J., 739 F. Supp. 2d 821 (D. Md. 2010) (Virginia law; owner not an intended beneficiary where contract does not clearly and definitely intend the contract to benefit him; quotes from Restatement Second §302(1) & ill. 19); Warner v. Design & Build Homes, 114 P.3d 664 (Wash. App. 2005) ("[A]ny benefit the [owners] could assert arises out of their contract with [the general contractor] to purchase the home.").

***§10.4 n.6 p.31 Add the following to the list after* "Accord":** J.G.B. Enters. v. United States, 497 F.3d 1259 (Fed. Cir. 2007) ("A subcontractor is a third party beneficiary to the government contract when the [contracting officer] knew or should have known that the government's payment on the contract was intended to directly benefit the subcontractor."); AgGrow Oils v. Nat'l Union Fire Ins. Co., 420 F.3d 751 (8th Cir. 2005) (where the subcontractor "dealt directly with [the owner] before [the general contractor] was retained" . . . "and both [the subcontractor] and [the general contractor] knew the production guarantees [in their contract] were critical to the economic success of the project," those production guarantees were enforceable by the owner against the subcontractor); Vanerian v. Charles L. Pugh Co., 761 N.W.2d 108 (Mich. App. 2008) (distinguishing between owners who are mentioned expressly in the contract between the general contractor and the subcontractor and those who are not; here, "Pugh was necessarily contracting with defendant for the purpose of directly benefiting plaintiff because Pugh had an obligation to see to it that the basement floor was repaired" and "plaintiff is referred to expressly in the contract.").

§10.5 PAYMENT BONDS

§10.5 n.2 p.32 Add the following at the end: For an example, see Elm Haven Constr. Ltd. P'ship v. Neri Constr., 376 F.3d 96 (2d Cir. 2004).

§10.5 n.7 p.33 Add the following at the end: The legislation may well have its limits, though; for a statute based on the Miller Act, the Nevada Supreme Court recently held that the trustees of employee-benefit trust funds, though third-party beneficiaries of the contract between the surety and the contractor, lacked standing to sue on the bond because of the statute's limits on the right to sue. The trust funds were, however, able to achieve standing as constructive assignees of the workers' rights. Hartford Fire Ins. Co. v. Trustees of Constr. Indus. & Laborers Health & Welfare Trust, 208 P.3d 884 (Nev. 2009).

***§10.5 n.11 p.35 Add the following to the list after* "Cf.":** City of Yorkville *ex rel.* Aurora Blacktop v. Am. S. Ins. Co., 654 F.3d 713 (7th Cir. 2011) (subcontractors are third-party beneficiaries of payment bonds "where an agreement contains language to the effect that the surety will be responsible to third parties if the contractor is unable to fulfill its obligation to them"; in contrast, and in this case, "subcontractors are generally not accorded third-party beneficiary status where the surety agreement does not contain language suggesting that the surety's obligation to pay runs to third parties").

§10.5a MORTGAGE ASSUMPTIONS WITH A BREAK IN THE CHAIN

§10.5a n.7 p.37 Add the following after the first sentence: *Accord:* Langman v. Alumni Ass'n of Univ. of Va., 442 S.E.2d 669 (Va. 1994) (grantee accepting a deed is bound by its provisions, including a promise to assume an existing mortgage).

§10.5a n.10 p.38 Add the following after the first sentence: *Accord:* Somers v. Avant, 261 S.E.2d 334 (Ga. 1979) ("[A] remote grantee who takes mortgaged real property by a deed in which he agrees to pay the debt is personally liable to the mortgagee even though his grantor or a predecessor in title took only subject to the debt and was not personally liable for that debt.").

§10.6 GOVERNMENT CONTRACTS

***§10.6 n.1 p.39 Add the following to the list after* "Accord":** Jama v. U.S. INS, 334 F. Supp. 2d 662 (D.N.J. 2004) (detainee not intended beneficiary of private company's contract with INS to operate detainment facility; "[M]embers of the public may not sue as third party beneficiaries of government contracts unless the contract contains specific language providing them with the right to do so."); S. Tex. Water Auth. v. Lomas, 223 S.W.3d 304 (Tex. 2007) (denying water customers a cause of action: "The mere description of a product's intended use cannot confer third-party-beneficiary status on intended users . . . [G]eneral beneficence does not create third-party rights, else every Texan could challenge or seek to enforce any government contract and the presumption against third-party-beneficiary agreements would disappear."); Lakew v. Mass. Bay Transp. Auth., 844 N.E.2d 263 (Mass. App. 2006) (robbed and injured employee of lessee not third-party beneficiary of lease provision requiring lessor to supply security services), followed in Masad v. Weber, 772 N.W.2d 144 (S.D. 2009) (food service worker injured on job in prison not third-party beneficiary of safety provision in contract between state and employer; "The primary purpose of the contract was to provide food services for the prisoners in the custody of the State. Plaintiffs have failed to show that the contract was entered into by the parties 'directly and primarily' for [the employee's] benefit." (quoting from Sisney v. State, *infra* note 3), in turn distinguished in Jennings v. Rapid City Regional Hosp., 802 N.W.2d 918 (S.D. 2011) (employees were third-party beneficiaries of payer agreement between their self-insured employer and a managed care association and of a hospital agreement between a managed care association and a hospital; irrelevant that other entities benefited, because primary beneficiaries were employees); Dallas Fire Fighters Ass'n v. Booth Research Grp., 156 S.W.3d 188 (Tex. Civ. App. 2005) (firefighters not third-party beneficiaries of contract between city and company preparing promotion examination).

§10.6 n.1 p.39 Add the following after the citation to* Klamath Water Users Protective Assn.*: , followed in GECCMC 2005-C1 Plummer St. Office Ltd. P'ship v. JPMorgan Chase Bank, 671 F.3d 1027 (9th Cir. 2012) (lessor not intended beneficiary of bank purchase and assumption agreement between FDIC and Chase; contract stated specifically that nothing in it "is intended or shall be construed to give any Person other than [the FDIC and Chase] and legal or equitable right, remedy or claim under or with respect to this Agreement"); Speleos v. BAC Home Loans Servicing, 755 F. Supp. 2d 304 (D. Mass. 2010) (borrowers not third-party beneficiaries of contract between Fannie Mae and their loan servicer; contract's enforcement provision stated that "[t]hese rights and remedies are for our benefit and that of our successors and assigns").

***§10.6 n.1 p.39 Add the following to the list after* "See generally":** Crowder, More Than Merely Incidental: Third-Party Beneficiary Rights in Urban Redevelopment Contracts, 17 Geo. J. on Poverty L. & Pol'y 287 (2010).

§10.6 n.2 p.39 Add the following at the end: *But cf.* Cnty. of Santa Clara v. Astra USA, 588 F.3d 1237 (9th Cir. 2009) ("Demonstrating third-party beneficiary status in the context of a government contract is a comparatively difficult task."), *rev'd on other grounds by* Astra USA v. Santa Clara Cnty., 131 S. Ct. 1342 (2011); Kremen v. Cohen, 337 F.3d 1024, 1029 (9th Cir. 2003) (a "more stringent test applies" to government contracts).

§10.6 n.3 p.39 Add the following at the end: *See also* Smallwood v. Central Peninsula Gen. Hosp., 151 P.3d 319 (Alaska 2006) ("government contracts create the risk of imposing liability that is disproportionately burdensome in relation to the benefit received"); Lake Almanor Assocs. v. Huffman-Broadway Grp., 101 Cal. Rptr. 3d 71 (Ct. App. 2009) (rejecting developer's right of enforcement of contract between county and dilatory environmental engineer; allowing such suits could undercut the goal of providing accurate information about the environmental effects of proposed projects "by compromising the independence and objectivity of environmental consultants," because subjecting them to liability "would create incentives to complete the report that could undermine the analysis of the relevant environmental issues, creating a conflict between the consultant's duty to the public and its financial self-interest"); Sisney v. State, 754 N.W.2d 639 (S.D. 2008) ("A private third-party right of enforcement is not properly inferred because of the potential burden that expanded liability would impose."; inmate not third-party beneficiary to contract between supplier and state for kosher meals). In contrast, the inmate in *Sisney v. State* was held to be an intended beneficiary of a settlement agreement between a former inmate and the prison system to supply the kosher meals, because the agreement stated that the Department of Corrections "agreed to provide a kosher diet . . . to all Jewish inmates who request it" and that "[i]nmates who request a kosher diet will receive kosher meals regardless of their custody status," and Sisney was a member of that class. Sisney v. Reisch, 754 N.W.2d 813 (S.D. 2008), followed in Jennings v. Rapid City Regional Hosp., 802 N.W.2d 918 (S.D. 2011) (like Sisney, employees were members of an identifiable group, and the intent of the agreements between employer and administrator and between administrator and hospital was to provide medical services to that group; thus, the members are third-party beneficiaries of the agreements).

***§10.6 n.9 p.41 Add the following to the list after* "Cf.":** Amaral v. Cintas Corp., 78 Cal. Rptr. 3d 572 (Ct. App. 2008) (employees intended beneficiaries of employer's agreement with city that employer would pay living wage; "Like the prevailing wage law, the [Living Wage Ordinance] is clearly intended to benefit employees by requiring the payment of higher wages."); City of Indianapolis v. Kahlo, 938 N.E.2d 734 (Ind. App. 2010) (public third-party beneficiary of contract between city and developer providing that a plaza "shall be accessible to the public" and that "The use of such area by the public . . . shall not be unreasonably withheld or delayed"); Becker v. Crispell-Snyder, Inc., 763 N.W.2d 192 (Wis. App. 2009) (developer was intended beneficiary of contract between city and engineering firm where city required that developer use this engineering firm, reviewed invoices, and paid them from the developer's credit line).

§10.6 n.12 p.41 Add the following at the end: *See also* Speleos v. BAC Home Loans Servicing, 755 F. Supp. 2d 304 (D. Mass. 2010) (following Restatement section; homeowners not third-party beneficiaries of contract between Fannie Mae and their loan servicer, where contract specifically limits scope of enforcement to the parties to the contract); Lake Almanor Assocs. v. Huffman-Broadway Grp., 101 Cal. Rptr. 3d 71 (Ct. App. 2009) (following Restatement section; developer not a third-party beneficiary of contract between county and environmental engineer providing for an environmental impact report for developer's planned project); Fort Lincoln Civic Ass'n v. Fort Lincoln New Town Corp., 944 A.2d 1055 (D.C. 2008) (following Restatement section; civic association not a third-party beneficiary of contract between developer and municipal agency providing, inter alia, for minority ownership and minority contracting).

§10.6 n.14 p.42 Add the following to the list after "Accord": Smallwood v. Central Peninsula Gen. Hosp., *supra* note 3 (contract between Medicaid provider and state stated that the provider must "accept as payment in full the amounts paid in accordance with Alaska statutes . . . and make no additional charge to the recipient").

§10.6 n.21 p.44 Add the following at the end: The Supreme Court addressed this question in Astra USA v. Santa Clara County, 131 S. Ct. 1342 (2011). There a county and its medical facilities sued pharmaceutical manufacturers for breach of the manufacturers' pricing agreements with the federal government. The statute providing for this program did not, however, provide for a private right of action. The county therefore sued as a third-party beneficiary of those contracts. The Court unanimously held that the county could not sue on a third-party beneficiary theory. It pointed out that the pricing agreements "simply incorporate statutory obligations and record the manufacturers' agreement to abide by them. . . . A third-party suit to enforce an HHS-drug manufacturer agreement, therefore, is in essence a suit to enforce the statute itself." 131 S. Ct. at 1348. This ruling does not put the kibosh on all third-party beneficiary suits intended to avoid the absence of a private right of action. Should the private party seek to enforce an aspect of the contract other than one arising directly from statutory obligations, the Court's decision in *Astra USA* would not apply, though it would be incautious to draw the negative inference that such suits are necessarily permissible. But the great majority of these suits center upon violations of statutory requirements, and these are clearly foreclosed. *See* Sioux Honey Ass'n v. Hartford Fire Ins. Co., 672 F.3d 1041 (Fed. Cir. 2012) (federal common law: domestic food producers not third-party beneficiaries of bond contracts between importers and private sureties under which sureties insured payment of duty deposits to government; contracts themselves state that the government is the beneficiary, and the benefit the producers would derive is at best indirect; in addition, the bond contracts are part of a complex statute that does not grant the producers a private cause of action to recover fees); Feingold v. John Hancock Life Ins. Co., 2013 U.S. Dist. LEXIS 117070 (D. Mass. Aug. 20, 2013), *aff'd*, 753 F.3d 55, 61 (1st Cir. 2014) (insurance beneficiaries are not third-party beneficiaries of Global Resolution Agreement (GRA) between insurance company and several state governments, which settled litigation regarding handling of unclaimed property; plaintiff "cannot circumvent the strong presumption against third-party beneficiaries in Illinois law and the Restatement by recasting an alleged violation of the GRA as a common law claim").

§10.7 RELATIVE RIGHTS OF BENEFICIARY AND PROMISEE

§10.7 n.1 p.44 Add the following after the first sentence: *Accord:* Cain v. Griffin, 849 N.E.2d 507 (Ind. 2006) ("[A] third-party beneficiary may sue the insurer directly to enforce the contract between the insurer and the insured.").

§10.7 n.1 p.44 Add the following at the end: Because the third-party beneficiary's rights are independent rather than derivative, it is possible that the third-party beneficiary may lack standing to sue where the promisee would have standing. For example, a statute may limit the range of claimants to those in privity with the promisor; though the third party would have a right to sue as an assignee, it would not as a third-party beneficiary. *See* Hartford Fire Ins. Co. v. Trustees of Constr. Indus. & Laborers Health & Welfare Trust, 208 P.3d 884 (Nev. 2009) (standing to bring suit under a payment bond; trustees lacked standing as third-party beneficiaries, but had it as "constructive assignees"). *Cf.* Fort Lincoln Civic Ass'n v. Fort Lincoln New Town Corp., 944 A.2d 1055 (D.C. 2008) (even if civic association were a third-party beneficiary of contract between developer and municipal agency, the contract specifically excluded rights of action except by those named, so plaintiffs "could not reasonably rely on the [contract] as conveying the parties' intent to confer upon them the right to file such an action."). *See generally* §10.6 *supra* on the relation between private rights of action and third-party beneficiary status.

§10.7 n.5 p.45 Add the following after the first sentence: *Accord:* Souza v. Westlands Water Dist., 38 Cal. Rptr. 3d 78 (Ct. App. 2006) ("a third-party beneficiary may not obtain a greater recovery than that which would have been available to the promisee"), followed in Spinks v. Equity Residential Briarwood Apts., 90 Cal. Rptr. 3d 453 (Ct. App. 2009) ("Given the nature of the parties' legal relationship, an intended beneficiary is not required to sue the promisee directly.").

§10.7 n.7 p.46 Add the following after the first sentence: *Accord:* Israel v. Chabra, 601 F.3d 57 (2d Cir. 2010) (New York law; "the general rule is that a surety's obligation is discharged if the creditor and the principal debtor agree to extend maturity of the debt, even for a few days . . . A surety may, however, consent to an agreement between the creditor and principal debtor to extend the time for payment and, if he does so, he is not relieved of his obligations as a guarantor."); Arlona Ltd. P'ship v. 8th of Jan. Corp., 857 N.Y.S.2d 208 (App. Div. 2008) ("an alteration of the contract to which the guaranty applies will serve to discharge the guarantor's obligation unless the guarantor has consented to the alteration").

§10.7 n.8 p.46 Add the following at the end: *See* Campbell v. Parkway Surgery Ctr., LLC, 354 P.3d 1172 (Idaho 2015) (collecting cases and finding that "the Restatement contemplates that in third-party beneficiary contracts involving a promise to pay another's debt, a promisee is entitled to damages in the amount of the debt if the promisor fails to pay that debt").

§10.8 VULNERABILITY OF BENEFICIARY TO DISCHARGE OR MODIFICATION

§10.8 n.1 p.47 Add the following at the beginning of the first paragraph: Karo v. San Diego Symphony Orchestra Ass'n, 762 F.2d 819 (9th Cir. 1985) ("[I]n the absence of terms in a third party beneficiary contract prohibiting change or modification of a duty to an intended beneficiary, the promisor and promisee retain power to discharge or modify the duty by subsequent agreement."); Restatement Second §311(1).

§10.8 n.1 p.47 Add the following at the end of the second paragraph: At the risk of stating the obvious, modification or discharge that would affect the rights of a third-party beneficiary requires the assent of both the promisor and the promisee, as would be true for any modification or discharge. *In re* Enron Corp., 292 B.R. 507 (S.D.N.Y. 2002) ("[I]f [the promisor] unilaterally and unlawfully repudiated the Merger Agreement . . . then the [third-party beneficiaries] . . . possess standing to sue for damages.").

Plea agreements are interesting applications of this basic idea. In essence, a plea agreement exists "for the sole purpose of settling a pending criminal charge, or charges, against the defendant." Ronning v. Yellowstone Cnty., 253 P.3d 818, 821 (Mont. 2011). But the agreement must be approved by the court, and it does not limit the court's discretion. Even an intended beneficiary of a plea agreement, then, will have no cause of action if the court alters or omits the terms that would benefit the third party. Nor would the plea agreement itself create a right of action, as long as the defendant and prosecutor do what they said they would do — viz., propose to the court a mix of guilty pleas, dismissals, recommended sentences, and the like. Consequently, "[t]he only possible way [the putative beneficiaries] could be intended third party beneficiaries is if the [sentencing court's] order named them as such." Ronning v. Yellowstone Cnty., 253 P.3d 818, 821 (Mont. 2011). Of course, plea agreements are rather special types of contracts, and statutes in particular may give third parties rights in the course of sentencing not present in the plea agreement itself.

§10.8 n.2 p.48 Add the following after the citation to* Tweeddale*: , followed in Becker v. Crispell-Snyder, Inc., 763 N.W.2d 192 (Wis. App. 2009) (where a contract between a city and an engineering firm imposed an obligation on the part of a third-party developer to pay the engineering firm's bills, the developer "becomes a third-party beneficiary and the contract immediately establishes a creditor-debtor relationship between the contractual parties and that third party.").

§10.8 n.2 p.48 Add the following to the list after **"Accord"***:* Vision Aviation v. Airport Auth., 33 So. 3d 423 (La. App. 2010) ("[W]hen a benefit in a contract is stipulated for a third party, the contract may not be dissolved without the beneficiary's agreement.").

§10.8 n.5 p.49 Add the following to the list after **"Accord"***:* Karo v. San Diego Symphony Orchestra Ass'n, *supra* note 1 ("[T]he power to modify terminates when the beneficiary materially changes position in justifiable reliance on the promise before receiving notification of the modification.").

§10.8 n.6 p.49 Add the following to the list after **"Accord"***:* Palm Lake Partners II v. C & C Powerline, 38 So. 3d 844 (Fla. App. 2010) (adopting quoted portion of Restatement Second §311(3); no vesting where reliance, in the form of not objecting to rezoning, occurred after the rezoning took place).

§10.8 n.6 p.49 In the first paragraph, add the following after the third sentence: *Cf.* Lunceford v. Houghtlin, 326 S.W.3d 53 (Mo. App. 2010) (agreeing with, but distinguishing, Restatement Second §311; reformation under Restatement Second §155 is available to a narrower group of third parties, but third party with rights under Restatement Second §311 but not §155 still has standing to challenge the sufficiency of the evidence supporting reformation).

§10.9 VULNERABILITY OF BENEFICIARY TO DEFENSES AND CLAIMS

§10.9 n.2 p.52 Add the following to the list after **"Accord"***:* J.G.B. Enters. v. United States, 497 F.3d 1259 (Fed. Cir. 2007) ("a third party beneficiary to a contract [is] . . . subject to all of the defenses the promisor would have against the original promisee") (citing to Schneider Moving & Storage Co. v. Prosser's Moving & Storage Co., 466 U.S. 364 (1984)).

§10.9 n.2 p.52 Add the following at the end: Lopez v. Taylor, 195 S.W.3d 627 (Tenn. App. 2005) (where child "actively participated in the fraud against his mother . . . he forfeited his right to have his college expenses paid" as the third-party beneficiary of the marital dissolution agreement).

§10.9 n.4 p.53 In the first paragraph, add the following to the list after* "Accord"*: LaSalle, Inc. v. Int'l Bhd. of Elec. Workers Local No. 665, 336 F. Supp. 2d 727 (W.D. Mich. 2004) ("A third-party beneficiary bringing a breach of contract claim is bound by all of the terms and conditions of the contract that it invokes."; arbitration clause thus governs action by third party); Souza v. Westlands Water Dist., 38 Cal. Rptr. 3d 78 (App. Ct. 2006) ("a third-party beneficiary may not obtain a greater recovery than that which would have been available to the promisee"); Olshan Found. Repair & Waterproofing v. Otto, 276 S.W.3d 827 (Ky. App. 2009) ("As a matter of equity, [the third-party beneficiaries] may not choose to accept the benefit of the contracts while simultaneously avoiding the dispute resolution mechanism set out in those same contracts."); Shay v. Aldrich, 790 N.W.2d 629 (Mich. 2010) (third-party beneficiary "stands in the shoes of the original promisee and only gains the same right that the original promisee would have had") (note use of assignment language, which is not strictly the case when the promisee retains its own right to enforce the contract); Bohl v. Hauke, 906 N.E.2d 450 (Ohio App. 2009) (third-party beneficiaries suing for breach of warranty sought to avoid forum selection clause; "[T]he Bohls seek to selectively enforce provisions of a contract as third-party beneficiaries. They cannot use this status to reap the benefits of the warranty and also to protect themselves from enforcement of the forum-selection clause."); *In re* Labatt Food Serv., 279 S.W.3d 640 (Tex. 2009) (wrongful death beneficiaries of employee bound by arbitration clause in occupational injury contract entered into by employer and employee), followed in Graves v. BP Am., 568 F.3d 221 (5th Cir. 2009) (same result as In re *Labatt,* but applying federal general common law of contract rather than Texas law).

§10.9 n.4 p.53 Add the following at the end of the first paragraph: As a corollary, whether the promisor has a defense against the beneficiary naturally hinges on whether the beneficiary is an intended beneficiary at all. This has proven important in the law of arbitration. Before a promisor may seek to arbitrate its dispute with a beneficiary, a court must determine whether the beneficiary is bound by the arbitration clause — that is, whether it is an intended beneficiary. *See* Lion Gables Realty v. Randall Mech., 65 So. 3d 1098 (Fla. App. 2011) (reversing trial court's referral of dispute to arbitration and remanding for that court to determine whether the plaintiff was an intended beneficiary of the contracts at issue). On the related topic of direct benefit estoppel, see §10.3 note 16 *supra*.

***§10.9 n.4 p.53 In the second paragraph, add the following to the list after* "But cf.":** R.J. Griffin & Co. v. Beach Club II Homeowners Ass'n, 384 F.3d 157 (4th Cir. 2004) (contractor not third-party beneficiary of contract between developer and buyer, and thus cannot invoke its arbitration clause in a dispute between it and the buyer); Monroe v. Bd. of Regents, 602 S.E.2d 219 (Ga. App. 2004) (disclaimer in contract between promisor and promise did not limit the ability of the beneficiary to sue, where the disclaimer did not expressly bar such a claim; "[E]ven though [the beneficiary] is limited to remedies that would be available to a promise under the contract, that does not mean that [the beneficiary] literally stands in the [promisee's] shoes for purposes of such a personal waiver of rights.").

§10.9 n.4 p.53 Add the following at the end of the second paragraph: For an interesting case in which the promisor sought to make the non-signatory a third-party beneficiary and the promisee resisted, *see* In re SSP Partners, 241 S.W.3d 162 (Tex. Civ. App. 2007) (parent did not bind children to arbitrate claims arising from injuries incurred under employment contract; "[t]he children's claims are separate and distinct from those asserted by [the parent] under the contract" and "are neither bringing claims in a lawsuit that seek direct benefits from the contract containing an arbitration clause, nor are they deliberately seeking and obtaining substantial benefits from the contract itself outside of litigation"). *See also* Thompson v. Witherspoon, 12 A.3d 685 (Md. App. 2011) (beneficiaries of life insurance policy not bound by arbitration clause in agreement between insured and broker who procured policy; beneficiaries "may potentially gain some benefit from the financial advice given by [the broker,] but such possibilities are too attenuated for either concluding that appellants are third party beneficiaries of the [brokerage agreements] or otherwise enforcing the arbitration provisions against appellants"); Bybee v. Abdulla, 189 P.3d 40 (Utah 2008) (arbitration clause in agreement between physician and patient did not bind wife, despite its express mention of her; the wife did not herself derive benefit from the arbitration clause, and she was otherwise only an incidental beneficiary of the contract for her husband's medical treatment). *But see* Forest Hill Nursing Ctr. v. McFarlan, 995 So. 2d 775 (Miss. App. 2008) (arbitration clause in agreement between nursing home and granddaughter of resident bound resident; the patient's care "was not incidental to the contract, but instead was the essential purpose of the agreement.").

§10.9 n.8 p.54 Add the following to the list after "Accord": Herd v. Am. Sec. Ins. Co., 556 F. Supp. 2d 992 (W.D. Mo. 2008) (beneficiary is subject to promisor's mutual mistake defense regarding the presence of other insurance coverage).

§10.9 n.10 p.54 Add the following at the end: For an interesting reversal of this pattern, *see* Greeling v. Abendroth, 813 N.E.2d 768 (Ill. App. 2004) ("Because a third-party beneficiary's rights extend no further than the contract, the promisor can assert against the beneficiary any contractual defense that the promisor could assert against the promise . . . including the promisor's right to unilaterally waive a condition that benefits the promisor . . . If, however, the condition benefits other parties beside the promisor, each one so benefitted must waive the condition."; bank waived the surrender of a certificate of deposit, but waiver ineffective as a defense where not all beneficiaries of the surrender right waived it) (citing to treatise).

§10.9 n.11 p.55 Add the following to the list after "Accord": Souza v. Westlands Water Dist., *supra* note 4 ("If the promisee breaches the contract, and the damages to the promisor equal or exceed the amount of the benefit the promisor was to confer on the third party, the third party cannot recover.").

§10.9 n.12 p.55 Add the following at the beginning: Kiesel Co. v. J & B. Props., 241 S.W.3d 868 (Mo. App. 2008) ("we have found no authority permitting suit *against* a beneficiary for breach of a contract to which it was not a party").

§10.9 n.12 p.55 Add the following at the end: *Cf.* Dickerson v. Longoria, 995 A.2d 721 (Md. 2010) ("a third-party beneficiary to an arbitration agreement cannot be required to arbitrate a claim unless the third party is attempting to enforce the contract containing the arbitration agreement").

§10.9 n.16 p.57 Add the following after the first sentence: , followed in Schneider Moving & Storage Co. v. Robbins, 466 U.S. 364 (1984) ("Where the language of the contract, or the circumstances under which it was executed, establish that the parties have provided that the right of the beneficiary is not to be affected by any defenses that the promisor might have against the promisee, the [usual] rule is inapplicable."; arbitration clause in collective bargaining agreement did not extend to contract between multiemployer trust fund and employer citing to Restatement Second §309).

§10.9 n.19 p.57 Add the following to the list after* "Accord"*: J.G.B. Enters. v. United States, 497 F.3d 1259 (Fed. Cir. 2007) ("the right of setoff is not a contract *defense*" . . . "Rather, setoff is a device that facilitates the efficient reconciliation of competing *claims* between the same parties. . . . Therefore, in order to rightfully claim a setoff here since the claim against the government is not a derivative claim, the government must itself have a valid *claim* against the party subject to the setoff . . ."); Oltman v. Holland Am. Line USA, 178 P.3d 981 (Wash. 2008) (wife's loss of consortium action arising from injury to husband on cruise not subject to forum selection clause of cruise contract to which wife not party; wife "asserts a separate, independent claim").

In Krist v. Pearson Educ., Inc., 2017 U.S. Dist. LEXIS 55667 (E.D. Pa. Apr. 12, 2017), a copyright holder granted a license and authority to sub-license certain photographs, but sued a sub-licensee he alleged was using his work outside the scope of the license. The sub-licensee sought to enforce a forum selection clause, but the court refused. There was no contract between the parties, and the plaintiff's claims sounded in copyright, not contract. The court distinguished cases where nonsignatories were held to a forum selection clause because those cases involved suits under the contract, while this suit would require "consideration of" the license agreement but did not arise under it.

CHAPTER 11

ASSIGNMENT AND DELEGATION

§11.1 TERMINOLOGY AND PRACTICAL BACKGROUND

§11.1 n.4 p.60 ***Add the following at the end:*** *See* Burnison v. Johnston, 764 N.W.2d 96 (Neb. 2009) ("a likely stumbling block here was the failure of our case law to consistently use the proper terminology to discuss the transfer of contractual rights and duties") (citing to treatise).

§11.1 n.10 p.62 ***Add the following at the end:*** *See* Donahue v. Multimedia, Inc., 608 S.E.2d 162 (S.C. App. 2005) ("The transfer of the stock of a corporation . . . does not constitute an assignment of a contract of that corporation.").

§11.2 HISTORICAL BACKGROUND AND CODE PROVISIONS

§11.2 n.1 p.63 ***Add the following at the end:*** For a particularly helpful overview of the law of assignment through the nineteenth century, see Sprint Commc'ns Co. v. APCC Servs., 554 U.S. 269, 275-85 & 292-98 (2008) (Breyer, J.).

§11.2 n.5 p.64 Substitute the following for the citation to **Dawson, Harvey & Henderson***:* J. Dawson, W. Harvey, S. Henderson & D. Baird, Contracts: Cases & Comment 873 (9th ed. 2008).

§11.2 n.6 p.64 Substitute the following for the citation to **Dawson, Harvey & Henderson***:* J. Dawson, W. Harvey, S. Henderson & D. Baird, Contracts: Cases & Comment 873 (9th ed. 2008).

§11.2 n.8 p.65 Add the following to the list after **"See"***:* R. Zimmermann, The Law of Obligations 58-67 (1992).

§11.2 n.15 p.66 Add the following after the first sentence: *Cf.* Associated Ins. Serv. v. Garcia, 307 S.W.3d 58 (Ky. 2010) ("As was the trend in the early twentieth century, the broad common law prohibition against assignment of claims receded."); *In re* FH Partners, 335 S.W.3d 752 (Tex. Civ. App. 2011) (principles of free assignability "date back to the English antecedents of Texas common law, and embody public policies favoring alienability and trade of legal rights to achieve economic benefit, in derogation of older concepts that rights are unique to particular parties and particular situations").

§11.2 n.16 p.66 Add the following to the list after **"See also"***:* Edens Technols. v. Kile Goekjian Reed & McManus, PLLC, 675 F. Supp. 2d 75 (D.D.C. 2009) (invalidating attempted assignment of legal malpractice claim to former litigation adversary because of "collusion and role-reversal concerns," among others); Stockman Bank of Mont. v. Mon-Kota, Inc., 180 P.3d 1125 (Mont. 2008) (agricultural lien not purely personal, so "the assignment of a claim for services performed or materials furnished will confer upon the assignee the right to perfect such claim").

§11.2 n.29 p.68 Add the following at the end: The receivables convention has been signed by the United States, but has not yet been ratified.

§11.3 EFFECTIVENESS OF AN ASSIGNMENT

§11.3 n.2 p.69 Add the following at the end: For a discussion of the differences between assignment and subrogation, see Continental Cas. Co. v. Ryan Inc. E., 974 So. 2d 368 (Fla. 2008).

§11.3 n.3 p.69 Add the following to the list after **"Accord"***:* People v. Adams, 243 P.3d 256 (Colo. 2010) ("No specific formality is required to execute a valid assignment, but the intent to make an assignment must be clearly reflected in the plain language of the parties' agreements."); Easton Bus. Opportunities v. Town Executive Suites-Eastern Marketplace, 230 P.3d 827 (Nev. 2010) ("The assignor must manifest a present intention to transfer its contract right to the assignee. . . . Absent some additional contract- or statute-based requirement, no particular formality in expressing that intention needs to be followed . . .") (quotes from Restatement Second §324).

§11.3 n.4 p.69 In the first paragraph, add the following to the list after* "Accord"*: La Belle Epoque v. Old Eur. Antique Manor, 958 A.2d 269 (Md. 2008) ("Contractual rights are assigned when the assignor manifests the intent to make the assignment."; quoting from treatise).

§11.3 n.4 p.69 In the first paragraph, add the following after the second sentence: *Cf.* Cal. Ins. Guarantee Ass'n v. Workers' Comp. Appeals Bd., 138 Cal. Rptr. 3d 24 (Ct. App. 2012) ("use of the word 'assign' is not conclusive").

§11.3 n.4 p.69 In the first paragraph, add the following to the list after* "see"*: People v. Adams, 243 P.3d 256, note 3 ("An assignment which appears to be absolute on its face may not be completely effective if parol evidence demonstrates an intent departing from the terms of the assignment."); Schoonmaker v. Lawrence Brunoli, Inc., 828 A.2d 64 (Conn. 2003) ("An assignment is a contract between the assignor and the assignee, and is interpreted or construed according to rules of contract construction."), followed in Sunset Gold Realty v. Premier Bldg. & Dev., 36 A.3d 243 (Conn. App. 2012); Rabius v. Brandon, 257 S.W.3d 641

(Mo. App. 2008) ("Assignments are interpreted according to their plain and ordinary meaning just as other contracts . . .").

***§11.3 n.4 p.69 In the second paragraph, add the following to the list after* "see":** Brandon Apparel Grp. v. Kirkland & Ellis, 887 N.E.2d 748 (Ill. App. 2008) (denying summary judgment on "whether a *de facto,* rather than a formal, assignment has occurred" in a receivership order).

§11.3 n.5 p.69 Add the following at the beginning: It thus follows that what is assigned is the assignor's interest only; one cannot transfer that which one does not have. The assignee of a breach of warranty right of action must therefore prove, not injury to itself, but injury to the assignor. Renaissance Leasing v. Vermeer Mfg. Co., 322 S.W.3d 112 (Mo. 2010) ("Because an assignee merely steps into the shoes of the assignor, an *assignee* must allege facts showing that the *assignor* would be entitled to relief.") (emphasis in original). On the other hand, the assignee need not prove any loss to itself, because it asserts the rights of the assignor. Cascades Dev. v. Nat'l Specialty Ins., 675 F.3d 1095 (8th Cir. 2012) ("When *A* assigns its right to indemnification to *B, B* receives the right to reimbursement from *C* for *A*'s loss as assignor, not *B*'s loss as assignee.").

§11.3 n.6 p.70 In the second paragraph, add the following to the list in the second sentence: Cal. Ins. Guarantee Ass'n v. Workers' Comp. Appeals Bd., 138 Cal. Rptr. 3d 24 (Ct. App. 2012) (contract giving collection agency the right to collect accounts on behalf of medical providers not an assignment, despite the use of "assign" and "assignment" in the contract; the providers remained the owners of the accounts, with considerable control over the terms of collection); People v. Adams, 243 P.3d 256, note 3 ("The assignments at issue were not effective because they did not wholly divest the purported assignors of any interest in their claims . . .").

§11.3 n.6 p.70 Add the following at the end: An interesting problem arises when the parties execute both a release of liability and an assignment of rights — for example, when employees release their employer from liability from their claims for breach of contract and the employer assigns to the employees any potential causes of action it might have against its insurers and insurance brokers. Does the release vitiate the assignment, in that the employees released the employer from all liability? Certainly having the assignment precede the release is better practice, but there is authority to the effect that the two can be simultaneous. Wachovia Ins. Servs. v. Toomey, 994 So. 2d 980 (Fla. 2008). *Cf.* DeMarco v. Travelers Ins. Co., 26 A.3d 585 (R.I. 2011) (tort victim released tortfeasor from all liability, but was assigned rights to pursue insurer for bad faith denial; assignment upheld in painstaking opinion).

***§11.3 n.8 p.70 Add the following to the list after* "Cf.":** *In re* Liquidation of Home Ins. Co., 953 A.2d 443 (N.H. 2008) (distinguishing between "absolute assignments and assignments for collection"; in the latter, the assignee is effectively a trustee or agent of the assignor, which retains equitable ownership).

§11.3 p.73 In the first paragraph, add the following after the second sentence: . . . only if the event that is the condition occurs.[20a]

[20a] Restatement Second §320; *see also* Amber Resources Co. v. United States, 538 F.3d 1358 (Fed. Cir. 2008) ("even if breach is regarded as a condition precedent to the existence of the right to seek contract enforcement, such a conditional right is considered to pass along with the assignment."); Briar Rd. v. Lezah Strenger Homes, 321 S.W.3d 488 (Mo. App. 2010) (giving effect to assignment subject to the exercise of an option). In contrast, an assignment of a future right — one depending on the making of a contract — is not itself an assignment, but rather merely a promise to assign. Restatement Second §321(2) ("a purported assignment of a right expected to arise under a contract not in existence operates only as a promise to assign the right when it arises and as a power to enforce it").

***§11.3 n.21 p.73 Add the following to the list after* "Accord":** Wachovia Bank Nat'l Ass'n v. EnCap Golf Holdings, 690 F. Supp. 2d 311 (S.D.N.Y. 2010) (New Jersey law; where debtor "absolutely and presently assign[ed]" rights under agreement subject to a license to use those rights until default, debtor had no further rights to convey after its default; irrelevant that assignment was in part to secure an obligation); Conerly Corp. v. Regions Bank, 668 F. Supp. 2d 816 (E.D. La. 2009) (contract claims assigned, not merely as a security interest; financing agreement provided for immediate assignment of claims and for assignee's right to enforce them "at [its] sole option"); First Fidelity Bank v. Eleven Hundred Metroplex Assocs., 190 B.R. 510 (S.D.N.Y. 1995) ("An absolute assignment and a license to the assignor may certainly be used to secure a note; they simply provide the creditor with a greater degree of security than a lien.") (Sotomayor, J.).

§11.3 n.21 p.73 Add the following after the second sentence: *Cf.* UCC 1-201(b)(35) (defining "security interest" as "an interest in personal property or fixtures which secures payment or performance of an obligation").

§11.3 n.22 p.73 Add the following at the end: *Cf.* Cincinnati Ins. Co. v. Am. Hardware Mfrs. Ass'n, 898 N.E.2d 216 (Ill. App. 2008) ("[T]he rule against partial assignments refers to the division of interest in a right among multiple persons or entities, not division of the right that was assigned.").

§11.3 n.24 p.74 Add the following to the list after "Accord": Cincinnati Ins. Co. v. Am. Hardware Mfrs. Ass'n, *supra* note 22 (insureds assigned rights to recover defense costs against one insurer to the other insurer, who had undertaken the actual defense, while retaining the right to indemnification; were this not permitted, "the purpose underlying the rule against partial assignments — avoidance of multiple suits — would be frustrated.").

§11.3 n.25 p.74 Add the following after the first sentence: *Accord:* Conerly Corp. v. Regions Bank, 668 F. Supp. 2d 816 (E.D. La. 2009) ("Under Louisiana law, when an incorporeal right is partially assigned, it must be enforced by both the assignor and assignee."; assignor thus joined as a necessary party under Fed. R. Civ. P. 19(a)(2)).

§11.3 n.26 p.74 Add the following after the first sentence: *Accord:* Chemetall GMBH v. ZR Energy, 320 F.3d 714 (7th Cir. 2003) (citing to Restatement: "an assignor may transfer some or all of its rights . . . and if only part of a right is transferred, that part may be enforced by the assignee as if it were a separate right"); Phillips v. Selecto Scientific, 707 S.E.2d 615 (Ga. App. 2011) (recognizing that former employee assigned his right to payment under his employment agreement, but retaining "his right, title, and interest" under that agreement; consequently, former employee remained the real party in interest in an action for breach of the employment contract).

***§11.3 n.26 p.74 Add the following to the list after* "See also":** Bain v. Fin. Sec. Life Ins. Co., 368 N.E.2d 1023 (Ill. App. 1977) (where holders of 119/120ths of the interests in a promissory note sued on the note but the holder of the remaining 1/120th did not wish to, "the ends of equity would not be adequately served by denying [the majority] an adjudication because the holder of 1/120th of that interest does not choose to join").

§11.3 n.27 p.75 Add the following at the end: The Patent Act is a prominent example of such a statute. 35 U.S.C. §251. Even here, though, the courts construe the statute narrowly to permit other oral methods of transfer. Sky Technologies v. SAP AG, 576 F.3d 1374 (Fed. Cir. 2009) (transfer by foreclosure does not require a writing); Akazawa v. Link New Technology Int'l, 520 F.3d 1354 (Fed. Cir. 2008) (passage of title through intestacy does not require a writing). *See also* Barefoot Architect v. Bunge, 632 F.3d 822 (3d Cir. 2011) (§204(a) of the Copyright Act requires a writing to make an assignment of a copyright effective).

§11.3a DRAFTING AN ASSIGNMENT

***§11.3a n.1 p.75 Substitute the following for the citation to* Fontaine & De Ly:** M. Fontaine & F. De Ly, Drafting International Contracts: An Analysis of Contract Clauses ch.11 (2006).

§11.3a p.76 Add the following at the end of the first full paragraph: . . . identification of the rights assigned identifies the obligors as well.[3a]

[3a] With assignments in bulk, actually proving when a particular account was assigned has proved a headache for some assignees. It is not sufficient to prove that an assignee acquired accounts from an assignor on a particular date; the assignee must prove that the account at issue was among them. This may be done either by showing actual notice of the transfer or, more commonly, by establishing that the particular account was in a class of account, *all* of which was assigned. For an example of overly general proof, *see* Porter v. AT & T Mobility, 35 A.3d 1002 (Vt. 2011).

§11.3a n.7 p.77 Add the following at the end: The current version of Article 9 removes the necessity of mentioning after-acquired property in order to perfect a floating lien. UCC 9-502 cmt. 2. But this is a litigator's provision; prudent drafters will insert a phrase like "now owned or hereafter acquired" to remove a potential point for dispute.

§11.4 LIMITATIONS ON ASSIGNABILITY

§11.4 n.1 p.78 In the first paragraph, add the following after the first sentence: *See, e.g.*, Applied Materials v. Advanced Micro-Fabrication Equip. (Shanghai) Co., 630 F. Supp. 2d 1084 (N.D. Cal. 2009) (barring employee's assignment of all inventions created for one year after employment, regardless of whether invention based on work done while employed, as an overly broad restraint on trade).

§11.4 n.1 p.78 Add the following to the list after* "Accord"*: Gurski v. Rosenblum & Filan, LLC, 885 A.2d 163 (Conn. 2005) (adopting case-by-case approach to permitting assignment of legal malpractice claims, but barring assignment to an adverse party in the underlying action; "This counterintuitive claim and reversal of roles, requiring the assignee to bring a claim for legal malpractice when she was the very party who benefited from that malpractice in the underlying litigation, would engender a perversion that would erode public confidence in the legal system. . . . [and] also creates the opportunity and incentive for collusion in stipulating to damages in exchange for an agreement not to execute on the judgment in the underlying litigation"), distinguished by Esposito v. CPM Ins. Servs., 922 A.2d 343 (Conn.

Super. 2006) (permitting assignment of claim for negligent advice by insurance agent by insured to estate of victims as settlement for wrongful death suits); Associated Ins. Serv. v. Garcia, 307 S.W.3d 58 (Ky. 2010) (assignment of legal malpractice claim barred, but assignment of malpractice claim against insurance agent permitted), followed in Davis v. Scott, 320 S.W.3d 87 (Ky. 2010) (assignment of proceeds of malpractice claim unenforceable where assignee gains control over the progress of the litigation); Taylor v. Babin, 13 So. 3d 635 (La. App. 2009) ("The mere threat of a malpractice claim being assigned would be detrimental to an attorney's duty of loyalty and confidentiality to his client, would promote collusion, and would increase a lawyer's reluctance to represent an underinsured or insolvent client."), followed in Conerly Corp. v. Regions Bank, 668 F. Supp. 2d 816 (E.D. La. 2009) (barring assignment of commercial tort claim); Scroggins v. Red Lobster, 325 S.W.3d 389 (Mo. App. 2010) (public policy prohibits the transfer of a personal injury claim, except when the transfer is of the proceeds of a potential claim and is granted to an existing creditor); Mut. of Omaha Bank v. Kassebaum, 814 N.W.2d 731 (Neb. 2012) (public policy permits the assignment of the unliquidated proceeds of a tort claim, provided the assignee has no control over the litigation; then "there is little or no concern of intermeddling" or of champerty and maintenance); W. Broad Chiropractic v. Am. Family Ins., 912 N.E.2d 1093 (Ohio 2009) (prohibited assignment of proceeds of personal injury claim, in part because "if an injured person executes multiple assignments to a variety of creditors, the third-party insurer may be faced with determining the priority of assignments and how to distribute settlement proceeds pro rata among numerous assignees if the debt exceeds the amount of the settlement," thus increasing the burden on the obligor); A. Unruh Chiropractic Clinic v. De Smet Ins. Co., 782 N.W.2d 367 (S.D. 2010) (assignment of personal injury claim or proceeds of personal injury claim both prohibited).

§11.4 n.1 p.78 Add the following after the citation to* Picadilly*: abrogated on other grounds by Liggett v. Young, 877 N.E.2d 178 (Ind. 2007) and explained in Rosby Corp. v. Townsend, Yosha, Cline & Price, 800 N.E.2d 661 (Ind. App. 2003) (rejecting argument "that *Picadilly* does not bar the assignment of a legal malpractice claim unless the assignment was to an adversary in the underlying action").

§11.4 n.1 p.78 Add the following after the citation to* MNC Credit Corp.*: , followed somewhat obliviously in Johnson v. Hart, 692 S.E.2d 239 (Va. 2010) (barring legal malpractice action by testamentary beneficiary to mother's estate against attorney who represented beneficiary in her capacity as executor, even though the beneficiary was the residuary legatee and the estate had been closed at the time of the action).

§11.4 n.1 p.78 Add the following to the list after the first* "Cf."*: Ondimar Transportes Maritimos v. Beatty St. Props., 555 F.3d 184 (5th Cir. 2009) (admiralty law: generally acknowledging assignment of tort actions, but prohibiting "the assignment of tort claims from the injured party to one tortfeasor permitting the settling defendant to proceed against a co-tortfeasor," because it would undermine the proportionate fault approach and would encourage partial, rather than total, settlement of claims), somewhat limited in Combo Maritime v. U.S. United Bulk Terminal, 567 F.3d 182 (5th Cir. 2009) (permitting assignment of unliquidated tort claim to one tortfeasor if the assignment discharges the plaintiff's entire claim; then the settling tortfeasor may bring a claim for contribution against the other possible tortfeasors) Edens Technols. v. Kile Goekjian Reed & McManus, PLLC, 675 F. Supp. 2d 75 (D.D.C. 2009) (barring assignment of legal malpractice claim to former litigation adversary; would yield a "disreputable and illogical role reversal" and would encourage collusion between the parties to "stipulate[e] to artificially inflated damages that could serve as the basis for unjustly high damages in the 'trial within a trial' phase of the subsequent malpractice action."); O'Grady v. Boldt (*In re* Estate of Molino), 81 Cal. Rptr. 3d 512 (Ct. App. 2008) (agreement to assign partial interest in estate to "heir hunter" unenforceable because it amounted to the illegal practice of law); Canal Indem. Co. v. Greene, 593 S.E.2d 41 (Ga. App. 2003) ("under Georgia law a right to punitive damages cannot be assigned"); Gremminger v. Missouri Labor & Indus. Relations Comm'n, 129 S.W.3d 399 (Mo. App. 2004) (whether tort is "personal tort or a property tort determines when a cause of action is assignable"); Trust for Certificate Holders of Merrill Lynch

Mortgage Invs. v. Love Funding Corp., 918 N.E.2d 889 (N.Y. 2009) ("[T]he champerty statute does not apply when the purpose of an assignment is the collection of a legitimate claim."), after certification, 591 F.3d 116 (2d Cir. 2010), applied in MVB Collision v. Allstate Ins. Co., 900 N.Y.S.2d 631 (Dist. Ct. Nassau Cnty. 2010) (repair shop that took assignments from customers and sued insurer in order to get higher labor rates not champertous; underlying dispute about labor rates legitimate, and acquisition of rights of action a plausible means of protecting repair shop's interests); PPG Indus. v. JMB/Houston Ctrs. Partners Ltd. P'ship, 146 S.W.3d 79 (Tex. 2004) (declining to permit the assignment of claims under the Deceptive Trade Practices Act as particularly personal and potentially "encourag[ing] some buyers to cooperate — if not collude — with a seller who may have been the one that actually misled them"); Jennings v. Farmers Mut. Ins. Co., 687 S.E.2d 574 (W. Va. 2009) ("a cause of action for personal injuries may not be assigned"); DNAML Pty., Ltd. v. Apple, Inc., 2015 U.S. Dist. LEXIS 168245, 2015-2 Trade Cas. (CCH) P79,439 (S.D.N.Y. Dec. 16, 2015) ("Courts of Appeals have fashioned a uniform rule for the assignment of a federal antitrust claim. To effect a transfer of the right to bring an antitrust claim, the transferee must expressly assign the right to bring that cause of action, either by making specific reference to the antitrust claim or by making an unambiguous assignment of causes of action in a manner that would clearly encompass the antitrust claim").

§11.4 n.1 p.78 Add the following to the list after **"Contra"***:* Associated Ins. Serv. v. Garcia, 307 S.W.3d 58 (Ky. 2010) (Kentucky has "narrow[ed] the class of unassignable claims through reference to the survival statute"; here, permits assignment of professional malpractice claim against insurance agent or broker); Adams v. Cossa, 294 S.W.3d 101 (Mo. App. 2009) ("Where a cause of action at law in tort suits for damages could or would survive the death of an assignor, it is assignable."); Carlile v. Harbour Homes, 194 P.3d 280 (Wash. App. 2008) ("The traditional test for whether a cause of action is assignable is whether the claim would survive to the personal representative of the assignor on death. If it would, the cause of action is assignable.").

§11.4 n.1 p.78 Add the following after the citation to* New Hampshire Ins. Co.*: , followed in Nova Assignments v. Kunian, 928 N.E.2d 364 (Mass. App. 2010) (fraud claim assignable).

§11.4 n.1 p.78 Add the following after the citation to* Forgione*: , followed in Wachovia Ins. Servs. v. Toomey, 994 So. 2d 980 (Fla. 2008) (distinguishing unassignable claims for medical malpractice or intentional infliction of emotional distress from assignable claim for breach of fiduciary duty).

§11.4 n.1 p.78 In the first paragraph, add the following to the list after the second* "Cf."*: DeMarco v. Travelers Ins. Co., 26 A.3d 585 (R.I. 2011) (permitting assignment of rights to bad faith claim as part of general release of tort claim).

§11.4 n.1 p.78 In the first paragraph, add the following to the list after* "See"*: YPI 180 N. LaSalle Owner v. 180 N. LaSalle II, 933 N.E.2d 860 (Ill. App. 2010) ("Because of the equitable and personal character of the right to sue for rescission, mere naked claims for rescission are generally not assignable.").

§11.4 n.1 p.78 Add the following at the end of the first paragraph: *But cf.* Webb v. Gittlen, 174 P.3d 275 (Ariz. 2008) (declining to extend the prohibition on assignment of legal malpractice claims to professional negligence claims against insurance agents); Learning Curve Int'l v. Seyfarth Shaw, LLP, 911 N.E.2d 1073 (Ill. App. 2009) (permitting assignment of rights to legal malpractice claims to shareholders of pre-merger corporation; "[T]he assignment formed a minor part of a transaction that encompassed a panoply of other rights and obligations. Learning Curve did not assign the claim to an unrelated third party; instead, Learning Curve assigned part of the claim to the persons who actually suffered the loss due to the alleged malpractice."); Cincinnati Ins. Co. v. Am. Hardware Mfrs. Ass'n, 898 N.E.2d 216 (Ill. App. 2008) (distinguishing assignment of rights to reimbursement of defense expenses from assignment of rights to legal malpractice claims); Carlile v. Harbour Homes, *supra* (state consumer protection act claims are assignable).

A special case of unenforceable assignments arises in the world of secured lending. Ordinarily a secured transaction, whether for personal or real property, entails the creation of a promissory note evidencing the right to payment and a security agreement or deed of trust evidencing the right to realize upon the collateral. If these are separated, the mortgagor will reap a windfall. The holder of the promissory note will lack the right to foreclose upon the collateral, and thus will effectively hold an unsecured obligation. The holder of the security agreement or deed of trust will have a right to foreclose, but, in the absence of the promissory note, will have no occasion to use it. As a result, both the common law and Article 9 provide that a transfer of the note also transfers the security interest or deed of trust, rendering the two inseparable and nullifying any attempted transfer of only one. The Restatement (Third) of Property (Mortgages) does, however, allow for the possibility of this division when unambiguously stated, which may be useful if the underlying obligation is bifurcated. UCC 9-203(g); Restatement (Third) of Property (Mortgages) §5.4 & cmt. *b*. *See also* Prime Fin. Servs. v. Vinton, 761 N.W.2d 694 (Mich. App. 2008) ("A mortgage is a mere security interest incident to an underlying obligation, and the transfer of a note necessarily includes a transfer of the mortgage with it."), followed in Livonia Prop. Holdings v. 12840-12976 Farmington Rd. Holdings, 717 F. Supp. 2d 724 (E.D. Mich) ("Thus, *when an assignee takes ownership of a note, the underlying mortgage transfers to it by operation of law.*") (emphasis in original), *aff'd*, 399 Fed. Appx. 97 (6th Cir. 2010). Bellistri v. Ocwen Loan Servicing, 284 S.W.3d 619 (Mo. App. 2009) (invalidating purported transfer of deed of trust when not accompanied by promissory note), unpersuasively distinguished in *In re* Tucker, 441 B.R. 638 (Bankr. W.D. Mo. 2010) (where deed of trust held by agent of note-holder, no split between note and deed of trust) and more persuasively in Nicdao v. Chase Home Fin., 839 F. Supp. 2d 1051 (D. Alaska 2012) (no split where foreclosing party is the servicing agent of the owner of the loan and actually holds the note). *Cf.* U.S. Bank v. Collymore, 890 N.Y.S.2d 578 (App. Div. 2009) (because "the mere assignment of the mortgage without an effective assignment of the underlying note is a nullity," a bank that could not prove its ownership of the note lacked the standing to bring a foreclosure action). This rule has come up of late because of the boom in foreclosures and the prior sloppiness with paperwork, as in *Bellistri, supra*. *But see In re* Mortgage Elec. Registration Sys. (MERS)

Litigation, 744 F. Supp. 2d 1018 (D. Ariz. 2010) (rule applies only for judicial foreclosures; deed need not be accompanied by note for non-judicial foreclosures).

§11.4 n.1 p.79 In the second paragraph, add the following at the end: *But see* People v. Adams, 243 P.3d 256 (Colo. 2010) (claim on mechanics' lien trust fund assignable if only compensatory damages are sought, but not if punitive damages or civil theft remedies are sought as well).

§11.4 n.1 p.79 In the third paragraph, add the following to the list after* "See generally"*: Radin, Maintenance by Champerty, 24 Cal. L. Rev. 48 (1936).

§11.4 p.79 In the first paragraph, add the following at the end of the first full sentence: . . . assignments in the public interest.[2a]

[2a] Neurodiagnostics, Inc. v. Ky. Farm Bureau Mut. Ins. Co., 250 S.W.3d 321 (Ky. 2008) (construing Kentucky statute forbidding the assignment of rights under the Motor Vehicle Reparations Act; "it is a more efficient, economical, and equitable system to keep the provider out of the reparations process and afford the insured the control of how his or her benefits are paid because there is only a certain amount of money available for payment"); Tex. Lottery Comm'n v. First State Bank of DeQueen, 325 S.W.3d 628 (Tex. 2010) (statute requiring judicial approval of the assignment of lottery prizes in their last two years rendered ineffective by UCC 9-406(f); purpose of statute, protecting lottery winners from being cheated into unfavorable assignments, outweighed by Article 9's goal of uniformity). *Contra:* Stone Street Capital v. Cal. State Lottery Comm'n, 80 Cal. Rptr. 326 (Ct. App. 2008) (UCC does not render state lottery statute ineffective).

§11.4 n.5 p.80 Add the following at the end: *See also* OfficeMax Inc. v. County Qwick Print, 709 F. Supp. 2d 100 (D. Me. 2010) (following Restatement Second §317(2)(a)); Easton Bus. Opportunities v. Town Executive Suites-Eastern Marketplace, 230 P.3d 827 (Nev. 2010) (following Restatement Second §317(2)(a)-(c)); Pilkington N. Am. v. Travelers Cas. & Sur. Co., 861 N.E.2d 121 (Ohio 2006) (following Restatement Second §317).

§11.4 n.8 p.80 Add the following after the first sentence: *Accord:* BDI Laguna Holdings v. Marsh, 689 S.E.2d 39 (Ga. App. 2009) (although employment contract with original employer was for personal services, it also provided for assignment to the employer's successors and thus required no additional consent for assignment).

§11.4 n.10 p.80 Add the following to the list after* "See also"*: Easton Bus. Opportunities v. Town Executive Suites-Eastern Marketplace, 230 P.3d 827 (Nev. 2010) ("'When the obligor's duty is to pay money, a change in the person to whom the payment is to be made is not ordinarily material . . .'") (quoting from Restatement Second §317 cmt. *d*); *In re* FH Partners, 335 S.W.3d 752 (Tex. Civ. App. 2011) (refusing to extend rule against delegating payment obligations to encompass assigning rights to payment) (invoking Restatement Second §317 cmt. *d*).

§11.4 n.11 p.81 Add the following at the end: *Accord:* Metroil, Inc. v. ExxonMobil Oil Corp., 724 F. Supp. 2d 70 (D.D.C. 2010) (assignment of retail gasoline franchise agreement effective, even though the assignee is a competitor of the obligor). *But see* Jones v. Stahr, 746 N.W.2d 394 (Neb. App. 2008) ("rights of first refusal are presumed to be personal and are not ordinarily construed as transferable or assignable unless the particular clause granting the right refers to successors or assigns or the instrument otherwise shows that the right was intended to be transferable or assignable"). *See generally* Comment, Can a Right of First Refusal Be Assigned?, 68 U. Chi. L. Rev. 985 (2001).

§11.4 n.12 p.81 Add the following after the first sentence: *Cf.* DeVenney v. Hill, 918 So. 2d 106 (Ala. 2005) (personal services contracts that "relate to services that involve special skills" are unassignable); People v. Adams, 243 P.3d 256 (Colo. 2010) (although claims under construction trust fund statute are assignable, claims for punitive damages under that statute are not).

§11.4 n.13 p.81 Add the following at the end: *Accord:* Roeder v. Ferrell-Duncan Clinic, 155 S.W.3d 76 (Mo. App. 2004) ("The attempted assignment of a personal services contract without the employee's consent is improper, illegal and void."; distinguishing this from the assignment of a covenant not to compete as part of a sale of a business); Traffic Control Servs. v. United Rentals Nw., 87 P.3d 1054 (Nev. 2004) ("When an employee enters into a covenant not to compete with his employer, he may consider the character and personality of his employer to determine whether he is willing to be held to a contract that will restrain him from future competition with his employer, even after termination of employment. This does not mean, however, that the employee is willing to suffer the same restriction with a stranger to the original obligation."). For one attempt to catalog unassignable rights, *see* Dittman v. Model Baking Co., 271 S.W. 75 (Tex. Comm'n App. 1925) (these rights or duties "arise on account of suretyship; technical guaranty; personal relationship, as between master and servant; personal skill or services, as in such a case, or that of an attorney for his client; personal terms of contract, as where a particular oblige is made the measure of performance, the agreement is to supply what he 'needs,' or he is to be 'satisfied'; or confidence or trust, as from lender toward borrower — it being everywhere conceded that in such instances a man has the right to choose the individuals with whom he will deal"), followed in *In re* FH Partners, 335 S.W.3d 752 (Tex. Civ. App. 2011) (change in identity of creditor not within these categories and thus freely assignable).

§11.4 n.14 p.81 Replace the entry for* Hess *with the following: Hess v. Gebhard & Co., 808 A.2d 912 (Pa. 2002) ("covenant not to compete in an employment contract is not assignable . . . to a purchaser of the assets of the employer's business" absent a specific assignability provision), distinguished in Zambelli Fireworks Mfg. Co. v. Wood, 592 F.3d 412 (3d Cir. 2010) (assignment permissible as part of stock transfer); OfficeMax Inc. v. County Qwick Print, 709 F. Supp. 2d 100 (D. Me. 2010) (consent clause that referred to a particular potential assignee extended to that assignee's own assignee; distinguished *Hess* as pertinent for asset purchases, but not for stock sales), Missett v. Hub Int'l Pa., LLC, 6 A.3d 530 (Pa. Super. 2010) (assignment permissible as part of transfer of equity membership rights in a limited liability company), and J.C. Ehrlich Co. v. Martin, 979 A.2d 862 (Pa. Super. 2009) (upholding noncompete agreement entered into by predecessor firm; distinguished *Hess* as pertinent for asset purchases, but not for stock sales).

§11.4 n.14 p.81 Add the following to the list after **"Accord":** Corp. Express Office Prods. v. Phillips, 847 So. 2d 406 (Fla. 2003) ("when a corporation's sale of its assets includes a personal service contract that contains a noncompete agreement, the purchaser can enforce its terms only with the employee's consent to an assignment."); Traffic Control Servs. v. United Rentals Nw., *supra* note 13 (employee's covenant not assignable in asset purchase absent arm's-length agreement or consent), limited in HD Supply Facilities Maint. v. Bymoen, 210 P.3d 183 (Nev. 2009) ("*Traffic Control*'s rule of nonassignability does not apply when a successor corporation acquires restrictive employment covenants as the result of a merger"; following *Corporate Express, supra*).

§11.4 n.14 p.81 Add the following to the list after **"Contra":** Fransmart, LLC v. Freshii Dev., 768 F. Supp. 2d 851 (E.D. Va. 2011) (exclusive contract for marketing and sales with restaurant franchisor assignable; "the Agreement is between two corporate entities, the Agreement lasts ten years, and the Agreement does not identify any individual as being material to performance").

§11.4 n.15 p.82 Add the following to the list after **"Accord":** OfficeMax Inc. v. County Qwick Print, 709 F. Supp. 2d 100 (D. Me. 2010) (consent clause that referred to a particular potential assignee extended to that assignee's own assignee, at least for a sale of stock); Bybee v. Isaac, 178 P.3d 616 (Idaho 2008) ("Generally, a non-compete covenant ancillary to the sale of a business is assignable and an express assignment of the covenant to the subsequent purchaser is unnecessary; the covenant is treated as part of the goodwill of the business sold."); Kegel v. Tillotson, 297 S.W.3d 908 (Ky. App. 2009) ("in an employer-employee situation, the successor employer may enforce the employee's restrictive covenant as an assignee of the original covenantee"; no evidence of any relation of personal confidence).

***§11.4 n.15 p.82 Add the following to the list after* "Contra":** Sogeti USA v. Scariano, 606 F. Supp. 2d 1080 (D. Ariz. 2009) (rejecting *Hess* and *Traffic Control Servs.*; "Arizona law . . . has a distinct focus, less concerned with the personal relationship between employer and employee and more concerned with protecting employees from overreaching or other unconscionable arrangements," . . . so "express consent of an employee is not required before an employer's rights can be assigned to, and enforced by, a successor company.").

§11.4 n.19 p.83 Add the following at the end: *Accord:* Metroil, Inc. v. ExxonMobil Oil Corp., 724 F. Supp. 2d 70 (D.D.C. 2010) (assignment of franchise agreement by franchisor not a material increase in burden; although assignee "raised the price charged for fuel, demanded payment in advance instead of cash on delivery and withdrawn excessive funds from its bank account," each of these rights was expressly permitted by the franchise agreement, so "[a] gasoline distributor's decision to assert the rights under a franchise agreement more fully than the refiner had before the agreement was assigned does not invalidate the assignment under the U.C.C."). *Cf.* Duncan Servs. v. ExxonMobil Oil Corp., 668 F. Supp. 2d 719 (D. Md. 2009) (assignment of franchise potentially invalid if it results in a violation of a statutory component of the franchise relation and thus materially impairs the burden or risk imposed by the contract; merely potential assignment, however, is not such an injury and does not amount to constructive termination). The *Metroil* court did observe in dictum that the duty of good faith still applied to the assignee's future acts. Metroil, Inc. v. ExxonMobil Oil Corp., 724 F. Supp. 2d 70, at 81 n.7.

***§11.4 n.20 p.83 Add the following to the list after* "Accord":** Fransmart, LLC v. Freshii Dev., 768 F. Supp. 2d 851 (E.D. Va. 2011) (exclusive marketing and sales agreement assignable to corporate successor; key employees of assignee and assignor identical, in particular the CEO and the main sales force regarding this agreement); Youtie v. Macy's Retail Holding, 626 F. Supp. 2d 511 (E.D. Pa. 2009) ("Whether there is a change in partnership personnel or structure, the incorporation of a previously unincorporated business, the dissolution of a corporation or a change in corporate structure, 'if there is no material change in the contract obligations and duties of the employee, there is no reason for the transfer of the rights from one entity or form to another to work an assignment putatively prohibited by the rule against assignment of personal service contracts.' ") (quoting from Alexander & Alexander, Inc. v. Koelz, 722 S.W.2d 311, 313 (Mo. App. 1986)).

§11.4 n.21 p.84 Add the following after the second sentence: *See* Renaissance Leasing v. Vermeer Mfg. Co., 322 S.W.3d 112 (Mo. 2010) (permitting the assignment of a right to damages for breach of warranty, barring a contrary agreement).

§11.4 n.23 p.84 Add the following after the third sentence: *See* Pilkington N. Am. v. Travelers Cas. & Sur. Co., *supra* note 5 (assignment ineffective if it would "materially increase the insurer's burden or risk under the contract, materially impair the insurer's chance of securing a return on performance, or materially reduce the contract's value"). *Cf.* Viking Pump v. Century Indem. Co., 2 A.3d 76 (Del. Ch. 2009) (Strine, V.C.) (anti-assignment clauses in insurance contracts enforceable before a loss but not enforceable after; "although insurers have a legitimate interest in protecting themselves against additional liabilities the insurer did not contract to cover, once the insured-against loss has occurred, there is no issue of an insurer having to insure against additional risk."). *But see* Keller Founds. v. Wausau Underwriters Ins. Co., 626 F.3d 871 (5th Cir. 2010) (collecting cases supporting majority view, but stating that "Texas courts, however, diverge from this majority and enforce non-assignment clauses even for assignments made post-loss."); *In re* Katrina Canal Breaches Consol. Litigation, 63 So. 3d 955 (La. 2011) ("There is no public policy in Louisiana which precludes an anti-assignment clause from applying to post-loss assignments. However, the anti-assignment clause must clearly and unambiguously express that it applied to post-loss assignments . . . [A]ny contradiction or ambiguity in the contract must be strictly construed against the insurer.").

§11.4 n.23 p.84 Add the following at the end: Similarly, the manufacturer of goods normally cannot avoid a warranty or a remedial promise because ownership of the goods passes from an assignor to an assignee. Renaissance Leasing v. Vermeer Mfg. Co.,

supra note 21 (takes as given that a repair or replace obligation may be assigned, pursuant to UCC §2-210(2); observes that "only Georgia and Alabama hold that an express warranty may not be assigned because it significantly alters the rights and duties of the contracting parties"). This is all subject to contrary agreement, of course, whether in the form of a standard anti-assignment clause or, more likely, in a disclaimer of warranty or limitation of remedy to the first owner.

§11.4 n.27 p.85 In the second paragraph, add the following to the list after* "See"*: Aurora Nat'l Life Assur. Co. v. Harrison, 462 F. Supp. 2d 951 (S.D. Iowa 2006) (giving effect to anti-assignment clause in annuity contract, though the clause did not limit the beneficiary's ability to assign payment streams from the annuity pursuant to the settlement agreement under which the annuity was purchased); Johnson v. Structured Asset Servs., 148 S.W.3d 711 (Tex. Civ. App. 2004) (factoring of annuity; "Anti-assignment clauses are enforceable unless rendered ineffective by a statute."), followed in Pagosa Oil & Gas v. Marrs & Smith P'ship, 323 S.W.3d 203 (Tex. Civ. App. 2010) (oil and gas lease).

§11.4 n.28 p.86 Add the following to the list after* "Cf."*: Khan v. Douglas Machine & Tool Co., 661 F. Supp. 2d 437 (S.D.N.Y. 2009) (adopting Restatement Second §317(2)'s "presumption in favor of the free assignment of contract rights"; rejecting anti-assignment by implication); Handex of Md. v. Waste Mgmt. Disposal Servs., 458 F. Supp. 2d 266 (D. Md. 2006) (limiting scope of anti-assignment clause in contract between owner and general contractor to exclude the surety, where surety bond contract lacked anti-assignment clause and standard practice was to permit assignment); Kohl v. Blue Cross & Blue Shield of Fla., 988 So. 2d 654 (Fla. App. 2008) ("Benefits will be paid directly to you" held "far short of creating a contractual bar to assignment" of insurance claims); Cincinnati Ins. Co. v. Am. Hardware Mfrs. Ass'n, *supra* note 1 (anti-assignment clause in insurance policy barred only assignments before loss, not assignments of the policy proceeds); Carlile v. Harbour Homes, *supra* note 1 ("Even general anti-assignment clauses in contracts, aimed at prohibiting the assignment of contractual performance, will not be construed to prohibit assignments of a breach of contract cause of action unless the contract contains specific language to the contrary."); Au New Haven v. YKK Corp., 210 F. Supp. 3d 549, 2016 U.S. Dist. LEXIS 134062 (S.D.N.Y. Sept. 28, 2016) (in patent infringement action, license agreement prohibiting assignment of "this Agreement or any interest hereunder, or . . . any of its rights or obligations hereunder, without the prior written consent of the other party" did not prohibit assignment of the underlying patent, and patent assignee had standing to sue. "The parties could have chosen to draft the provision to expressly reference the '214 Patent, but did not do so. Therefore, given the narrow reading applicable to anti-assignment clauses under New York law, the 2014 Assignment would be void *ab initio* only if the '214 Patent is an 'interest' under the licensing agreement (i.e., an 'interest hereunder'). The Court finds that it is not.").

§11.4 n.28 p.86 Add the following after the second sentence: For a rationale for these limits in one important context, see Pilkington N. Am. v. Travelers Cas. & Sur. Co., *supra* note 5 ("The negation of the anti-assignment clause does not produce an unjust result for the insurer. The idea that an insurer would have to defend both the transferor and the transferee for the same risk is not sound. If the right to a defense has been transferred to a successor, the transferor no longer has that right. The right cannot both be transferred and retained."). Note, however, that this is correct only for true assignments; assignments for the purposes of collection, for example, leave residual rights in the hands of the assignor and thus could expose the obligor to two suits over the same claim.

§11.4 n.29 p.86 Add the following to the list after "Cf.": Almeida Oil Co. v. Singer Holding Corp., 857 N.Y.S.2d 689 (App. Div. 2008) ("As the Throughput Agreement only contained a covenant not to assign, and did not provide that any assignment would be void or invalid, the assignment was not void, but only gives rise to a claim for damages against [the assignor] for violation of the covenant not to assign.").

§11.4 n.29 p.86 Add the following after the citation to Bel-Ray: disapproved in Travertine Corp. v. Lexington-Silverwood, 683 N.W.2d 267 (Minn. 2004) (declining to require "the use of specific language, such as 'void' or 'invalid' — as mandated . . . in *Bel-Ray*") and distinguished by Kohl v. Blue Cross & Blue Shield of Fla., 988 So. 2d 654 (Fla. App. 2008) ("'Benefits will be paid directly to you' " did not "clearly and effectively convey[] to laymen that an assignment of benefits to their providers would not be permitted.").

§11.4 n.29 p.86 Add the following after the citation to* Rumbin*: , followed in David Caron Chrysler Motors v. Goodhall's, Inc., 43 A.3d 164 (Conn. 2012) ("without express contractual language providing otherwise, a provision restricting the assignment of a contract will be construed to be a covenant like any other contractual covenant — a breach thereof will render the breaching party liable in damages but will not make the contract a nullity").

§11.4 n.29 p.86 Add the following at the end of the first paragraph: *Cf.* R.C. Hobbs Enters. v. J.G.L. Distrib., 104 P.3d 503 (Mont. 2004) (assignment in violation of anti-assignment clause not a material breach of the contract).

§11.4 n.31 p.87 Add the following to the list after* "But cf."*: 321 Henderson Receivables Origination v. Sioteco, 93 Cal. Rptr. 3d 321 (Ct. App. 2009) (UCC 9-408 "evidences a public policy against anti-assignment clauses in general"; "contractual anti-assignment provisions are generally ineffective in barring transfers of structured settlement payments").

§11.4 n.31 p.87 Add the following after the citation to* Singer Asset Fin. Co.*: , followed in W. Sur. Co. v. APAC-S.E., 691 S.E.2d 234 (Ga. App. 2010) (failure to comply with anti-assignment clause results in an anticipatory repudiation of the underlying contract).

§11.4 n.33 p.87 Add the following to the list after* "Accord"*: David Caron Chrysler Motors v. Goodhall's, Inc., 43 A.3d 164 (Conn. 2012) ("[P]rovisions requiring the consent of the landlord to the assignment of a lease are for the sole benefit of the lessor. . . . As such, an assignment in violation of a covenant against assignment is valid subject to the option of the landlord to terminate the lease.").

§11.4 n.35 p.88 Add the following to the list after ***"Accord":*** Winn v. Ameritítle, Inc., 731 F. Supp. 2d 1093 (D. Idaho 2010) (clauses "are subject to a reasonableness and good faith analysis"); Speedway Superam. v. Tropic Enters., 966 So. 2d 1 (Fla. App. 2007) (the lessor's prior written consent to any assignment is subject to "the implied obligation of good faith performance" in a way that "gives effect to the reasonable expectations of the contracting parties"); Van Sloun v. Agans Bros., Inc., 778 N.W.2d 174 (Iowa 2010) (for real property lease, "a landlord may only withhold consent under a reasonableness clause where a prudent person in the landlord's position exercising reasonable commercial responsibility has a good faith and reasonable objection to assignment of the lease or subletting").

§11.4a DRAFTING A PROHIBITION OF OR CONSENT TO ASSIGNMENT

§11.4a n.1 p.89 In the first paragraph, add the following to the list in the first sentence: Khan v. Douglas Machine & Tool Co., 661 F. Supp. 2d 437 (S.D.N.Y. 2009) (failure to list assignees as potential beneficiaries of contract "does not constitute clear and plain language prohibiting assignment, as is required to render a contract non-assignable"); Kohl v. Blue Cross & Blue Shield of Fla., 988 So. 2d 654 (Fla. App. 2008) ("Benefits will be paid directly to you" held "far short of creating a contractual bar to assignment" of insurance claims).

§11.4a n.1 p.89 In the second paragraph, add the following at the end of the first sentence: , followed in Easton Bus. Opportunities v. Town Executive Suites-Eastern Marketplace, 230 P.3d 827 (Nev. 2010) (quoting this portion of *Citibank*; [the no-oral-modification clause] "lacks the specific language prohibiting assignment that the law requires of a valid anti-assignment clause").

§11.4a n.2 p.89 In the first paragraph, add the following to the list in the first sentence: Swiss Reins. Am. Corp. v. SuperValu, Inc., 743 F. Supp. 2d 1050 (D. Minn. 2010) (no-oral-modification clause ineffective to prevent assignment; "As a sophisticated party to a commercial contract, SuperValu, unlike Humpty Dumpty, must say what it means in advance, not after the fact."); David Caron Chrysler Motors v. Goodhall's, Inc., 43 A.3d 164 (Conn. 2012) (provision in lease that no part of it " 'shall, by operation of law or otherwise, be assigned . . . without the prior written consent of Landlord, which consent shall not be unreasonably withheld,' . . . purports to limit the right to assign the lease, [but] it does not state that an assignment in breach of the provision will be deemed void, invalid or otherwise ineffective automatically"); Almeida Oil Co. v. Singer Holding Corp., 857 N.Y.S.2d 689 (App. Div. 2008) ("As the Throughput Agreement only contained a covenant not to assign, and did not provide that any assignment would be void or invalid, the assignment was not void, but only gives rise to a claim for damages against [the assignor] for violation of the covenant not to assign.").

§11.4a n.2 p.89 In the first paragraph, add the following to the list after* "See also"*: Pagosa Oil & Gas v. Marrs & Smith P'ship, 323 S.W.3d 203 (Tex. Civ. App. 2010) (clause giving lessor right to approve assignments of oil and gas lease "does not indicate an intent to limit the parties' rights to assign a cause of action arising from an alleged breach of the lease").

§11.4a n.2 p.89 In the first paragraph, add the following to the list after* "Contra"*: Marx v. Clear Channel Broad., 887 So. 2d 405 (Fla. App. 2004) (" 'No party, however, may assign its rights or obligations under this Agreement,' which provides rather clearly that no rights under the contract may be assigned"); Travertine Corp. v. Lexington-Silverwood, 683 N.W.2d 267 (Minn. 2004) ("the rights and obligations of Berkey/Lennon shall not be assignable" "satisfies the requirement that the parties include something in the terms of the contract manifesting the intention of the parties that it shall not be assigned"); Singer Asset Fin. Co. v. Wyner, 937 A.2d 303 (N.H. 2007) ("may not assign, anticipate, pledge or encumber said payments, and any attempt to do so shall not bind [the insurer]" "can only be seen as [the potential assignor's] surrender of the power to assign"). The increasing weight, or at least bulk, of these decisions suggests that the courts are more commonly giving effect to somewhat vague language barring assignment. This may be a comfort to the worried litigator, but should not encourage careless drafting; there is, after all, a reason these vague clauses are so often litigated.

§11.4a n.3 p.90 Add the following after the first sentence: Bioscience W., Inc. v. Gulfstream Prop. & Cas. Ins. Co., 185 So. 3d 638 (Fla. Dist. Ct. App. 2016) (agreement that "*Assignment of this policy* will not be valid unless we give our written consent" did not prohibit assignment of a specific claim, but only of the policy as a whole; contractor as assignee could sue to recover a specific financial benefit derived from that insurance policy).

§11.4a p.90 Add the following at the end of the carryover paragraph: Another way to limit assignment is by a *right of action* clause, which, to provide an illustration from the world of surety, provides that "no right of action shall accrue pursuant to this bond to any person or entity other than the owner or its heirs, assigns, administrators, or successors." For rights under this sort of contract to be assigned, the obligor's assent would be necessary, because effecting an assignment would require that the underlying contract be modified.[5a]

[5a] *See* Swiss Reins. Am. Corp. v. SuperValu, Inc., 743 F. Supp. 2d 1050 (D. Minn. 2010) (suggesting right of action clause as alternative to standard anti-assignment clause; citing to Tony & Leo, Inc. v. United States Fid. & Guar. Co., 281 N.W.2d 862 (Minn. 1979), in which a clause much like the one in the text was upheld).

§11.4a n.6 p.90 Add the following to the list in the first sentence: Duncan Servs. v. ExxonMobil Oil Corp., 722 F. Supp. 2d 640 (D. Md. 2010) (free assignment clause enforceable notwithstanding even a material change in benefits or burdens that would result); Donahue v. Multimedia, Inc., 608 S.E.2d 162 (S.C. App. 2005) (talk show host's contract for personal services, but "[e]ven a personal services contract . . . may be assigned if the contract provides for assignment").

§11.4a n.6 p.90 Add the following at the end: Some statutes require that specific types of assignments be made particularly clear. *See* Fla. Stat. Ann. §542.335(f)(2) (non-competition clauses may be assigned only where the contract "expressly authorizes enforcement by a party's assignee or successor"). And, of course, if there is any doubt about the potential validity of a transfer, the agreement should contain an express consent to transfer. *See* Metroil, Inc. v. ExxonMobil Oil Corp., 724 F. Supp. 2d 70 (D.D.C. 2010) (assignment of franchise agreement for retail gas station: "ExxonMobil may transfer or assign all or part of its rights or interest in this Agreement . . . without restriction, to any person or entity." held effective).

§11.4a n.7 p.91 Add the following to the list in the first sentence: Fransmart, LLC v. Freshii Dev., 768 F. Supp. 2d 851 (E.D. Va. 2011) (giving effect to provision with caption "Binding Agreement and Assignability" and text "The provisions of this agreement shall be binding upon and inure to the benefit of the parties hereto and to their successors and assigns"; collecting cases); BDI Laguna Holdings v. Marsh, 689 S.E.2d 39 (Ga. App. 2009) ("This Agreement shall inure to the benefit of . . . the Company [and] its Permitted Successors and Assigns . . .").

§11.4a n.7 p.91 Add the following at the end: For an example of a particularly thorough waiver of restrictions on assignability, see Johnson v. Structured Asset Servs., 148 S.W.3d 711, 724 (Tex. Civ. App. 2004).

§11.4a n.8 p. 91 Add the following to the list in the first sentence: La Belle Epoque v. Old Eur. Antique Manor, 958 A.2d 269 (Md. 2008) ("[W]hen a lessor accepts rent from a new entity with knowledge that the lease has been assigned to that entity, the lessor waives the ability to contest the assignment under a lease covenant that provides the lease may not be assigned without the lessor's written consent.").

§11.5 LIMITATIONS ON ASSIGNABILITY OF FUTURE OR AFTER-ACQUIRED RIGHTS

§11.5 n.3 p.92 Add the following to the list after "Accord": Amber Res. Co. v. United States, 538 F.3d 1358 (Fed. Cir. 2008) ("Even if breach is regarded as a condition precedent to the existence of the right to seek contract enforcement, such a conditional right is considered to pass along with the assignment."); Handex of Md. v. Waste Mgmt. Disposal Servs., 458 F. Supp. 2d 266 (D. Md. 2006) (conditional assignment effective as of the time the assignment is made, not the time the condition occurs); Restatement Second §320 ("The fact that a right is . . . conditional does not prevent its assignment before the condition occurs.").

§11.5 n.3 p.92 Add the following after the second sentence: *Cf.* Sunridge Dev. Corp. v. RB&G Eng'g, 230 P.3d 1000 (Utah 2010) (allowing recovery of damages incurred after assignment; "[t]he correct inquiry looks at the assignor's rights and liabilities under the contract, not solely whether a claim for damages arose before or after the date of the assignment.").

§11.5 n.8 p.93 Add the following to the list after* "Accord"*: *In re* M. Fabrikant & Sons, 385 B.R. 87 (Bankr. S.D.N.Y. 2008) (following Restatement; rights to reimbursement for attorney's fees incurred in subsequent litigation enforceable).

§11.5 n.9 p.94 Add the following at the end: *Accord:* Liberty Life Assur. Co. v. Gilbert, 507 F.3d 952 (6th Cir. 2007) (Virginia law: "one may only assign a future anticipated benefit or obligation that is presently owned, i.e., under contract").

§11.5 n.14 p.94 Add the following after the first sentence: *See* Tribeca Lending Corp. v. Real Estate Depot, 42 So. 3d 258 (Fla. App. 2010) (applying equitable lien theory where mortgagor's own mortgage tainted by a forged deed).

§11.5 n.15 p.94 Add the following at the end: Viking Pump v. Century Indem. Co., 2 A.3d 76 (Del. Ch. 2009) (using "equitable assignment" to refer to an assignment not specifically enumerated in the assignment clause).

§11.5 n.16 p.95 Add the following to the list: Liberty Life Assur. Co. v. Gilbert, *supra* note 9 ("a beneficiary of an annuity which the beneficiary does not own [] has no legal right in the annuity to assign"); W. Broad Chiropractic v. Am. Family Ins., 912

N.E.2d 1093 (Ohio 2009) (4-3) ("A person may not assign the right to the future proceeds of a settlement if the right to the proceeds does not exist at the time of the assignment."). The decision in *West Broad Chiropractic*, issued over a strong dissent, runs counter to the clear trend of modern authority and, indeed, to what one would have considered settled and unexceptionable law, including that in Ohio. *Id.* at 1099-1102 (Moyer, C.J., dissenting). One may hope that this attempt to keep pre-*Mitchell* doctrine alive proves transitory and obscure.

§11.5 n.17 p.95 Add the following to the list in the second sentence: Restatement Second §321(2).

§11.6 REVOCABILITY OF A GRATUITOUS ASSIGNMENT

§11.6 n.12 p.99 Add the following to the list after* "Accord"*: AAA Valley Gravel v. Totaro, 219 P.3d 153 (Alaska 2009) (following Restatement Second §332; gratuitous assignment of royalties enforceable and irrevocable where assignment made in signed and sealed letter delivered by the assignor to the assignee).

§11.6 n.12 p.99 Add the following after the fourth sentence: *Cf.* El Paso Healthcare Sys. v. Molina Healthcare of N.M., 683 F. Supp. 2d 454 (W.D. Tex. 2010) ("[A]s a matter of hornbook law, contractual rights may be assigned gratuitously . . . The difference is that a gratuitous assignment may be revoked absent certain formalities in its granting, while a non-gratuitous one cannot."; citing to Restatement Second §332).

§11.6 n.16 p.100 Add the following at the end: *Accord:* Cascades Dev. v. Nat'l Specialty Ins., 675 F.3d 1095 (8th Cir. 2012) (Minnesota law; follows Restatement Second §332).

§11.7 VULNERABILITY OF ASSIGNEE TO DISCHARGE OR MODIFICATION

§11.7 n.1 p.102 Add the following to the list after **"Accord"***:* Smith v. Mallick, 514 F.3d 48 (D.C. Cir. 2008) ("Although a valid assignment of a chose in action requires no notice to the obligor . . . the assignee takes it subject to all claims and defenses that accrued before the obligor had notice of the assignment.") (citations omitted).

§11.7 n.2 p.102 Add the following at the end: Cf. Winship v. Gem City Bone & Joint, 185 P.3d 1252 (Wyo. 2008) (plaintiff in personal action assigned right to payment to medical provider for the payment of medical bills, but attorney instead distributed funds to plaintiff, plaintiff's family, and plaintiff's attorneys; because attorney had notice of assignment, attorney is liable to assignee for medical bills).

§11.7 n.3 p.103 Add the following after the first sentence: Accord: Employers Ins. of Wassau v. Penn. Dep't of Transp., 865 A.2d 825 (Pa. 2005) ("an assignor retains his power to discharge or modify the duty of the obligor until the obligor receives notification that the right has been assigned and that performance is to be rendered to the assignee").

§11.7 n.6 p.103 Add the following at the end: For a representative case applying UCC 9-406, see Holloway-Houston, Inc. v. Gulf Coast Bank & Trust Co., 224 S.W.3d 353 (Tex. Civ. App. 2006).

§11.7 p.103 Add the following at the end of the second paragraph: . . . Article 9 does not literally apply.[9a]

[9a] First Bank of Marietta v. Roslovic & Partners, 712 N.E.2d 703 (Ohio 1999) (The assignee is entitled to exercise collection rights against the account debtor as long as the account debtor "receives (1) an indication that the account has been assigned, (2) a specific direction that the payment is to be made to the assignee rather than the assignor, and (3) a reasonable identification of the rights assigned.").

§11.7a DRAFTING A NOTICE

§11.7a n.2 p.106 Add the following after the first sentence: *Cf.* Holloway-Houston, Inc. v. Gulf Coast Bank & Trust Co., 224 S.W.3d 353 (Tex. Civ. App. 2006) (giving effect to notice from assignee stating that "[Assignor] will be assigning their accounts receivable to [assignee]. From this point forward, please continue to make all checks payable to [assignor], but for proper processing and credit please remit all payments to [assignee]" combined with invoice verification letters from assignee).

§11.7a n.4 p.106 Add the following at the end: Because notice to the obligor is for the obligor's benefit, only the obligor can assert insufficient notice in order to avoid the effect of the assignment. *See* Stilwell v. Am. Gen. Life Ins. Co., 555 F.3d 572 (7th Cir. 2009) (notice of reassignment titled "Release of Assignment," even if of itself invalid, could not support an objection to the reassignment by the original assignor); Novartis Animal Health US v. Earle Palmer Brown, LLC, 424 F. Supp. 2d 1358 (N.D. Ga. 2006) ("[L]ack of notice has no effect on the validity of the assignment or the legality of the factoring arrangement.").

Questions of notice have lately arisen because of recent economic difficulties and the resulting wave of foreclosures and collection actions on overdue accounts. In a surprisingly high percentage of cases, the creditor/lender/assignee lacks the necessary basis to warrant judicial action. One such area is the collection of credit-card receivables. In a recent case, the court held that an error in stating the *assignor's* name in a notice was sufficient to render an assignment ineffective. Hutto v. CACV, 707 S.E.2d 872 (Ga. App. 2011) (overdue account was with "J.P. Morgan Chase & Co.," whereas supporting affidavit in collection action stated that account was with "Chase Manhattan Bank").

***§11.7a n.6 p.107 Add the following to the list after* "But see":** Bldg. Materials Corp. v. Presidential Fin. Corp., 972 So. 2d 1090 (Fla. App. 2008) (notice to logistics manager in branch office ineffective; the assignee "sent the notice to a location and an individual other than those that [the obligor] designated for receipt of such information" and the manager's "receipt of the notice and execution of the acknowledgement were not part of his regular job duties and . . . he would not necessarily understand the significance of the notice or acknowledgement").

§11.8 VULNERABILITY OF ASSIGNEE TO OBLIGOR'S DEFENSES AND CLAIMS

***§11.8 n.1 p.108 Add the following to the list after* "Accord":** Amber Resources Co. v. United States, 538 F.3d 1358 (Fed. Cir. 2008) ("the new leaseholders 'stand in the shoes' of the original lessees"; citing to treatise); Olvera v. Blitt & Gaines, 431 F.3d 285 (7th Cir. 2005) ("the common law puts the assignee in the assignor's shoes, whatever the shoe size"); Quartz of S. Cal. v. Mullen Bros., 61 Cal. Rptr. 3d 54 (App. Ct. 2007) ("Mullen is Mohawk's assignee, thereby stepping into Mohawk's shoes"); Credigy Receivables v. Whittington, 689 S.E.2d 889 (N.C. App. 2010) (assigning a judgment confers upon the assignee all the rights conferred upon the assignor by the judgment, but does not give the assignee the right to subject to that judgment anyone not party to it).

§11.8 n.2 p.109 In the second paragraph, add the following after the second sentence: *Accord:* Trippe Mfg. Co. v. Niles Audio Corp., 401 F.3d 529 (3d Cir. 2005) (Alito, J.) ("when an assignee assumes the liabilities of an assignor, it is bound by an arbitration clause in the underlying contract"); Green Tree-AL v. White, 55 So. 3d 1186 (Ala. 2010) ("Generally, an assignee steps into the shoes of an assignor who was the signatory of an arbitration provision, thus allowing the assignee to enforce that arbitration provision.").

§11.8 n.2 p.109 In the second paragraph, add the following to the list in the third sentence: LPP Mtg. Ltd. v. Tucker, 48 So. 3d 115 (Fla. App. 2010) (assignee of mortgage from federal government acquires the federal government's unlimited time in which to foreclose on mortgaged property).

§11.8 n.3 p.109 Add the following after the first sentence: *Accord:* Corbett v. Firstline Sec., 687 F. Supp. 2d 124 (E.D.N.Y. 2009) (assignee subject to statute of limitations that would have applied to the assignor); LPP Mortgage v. Boutwell, 36 So. 3d 497 (Ala. 2009) (same); Portfolio Recovery Assocs. v. King, 927 N.E.2d 1059 (N.Y. 2010) (same).

§11.8 n.4 p.109 Add the following at the end: That an assignee is bound by the assignor's agreement to arbitrate, see Illinois Farmers Ins. Co. v. Glass Serv. Co., 683 N.W.2d 792 (Minn. 2004) (if insurer had right to demand no-fault arbitration against policyholders, "it would also have that right against . . . assignee of the policyholders' claims against" insurer).

§11.8 n.5 p.110 Add the following at the end: *Accord:* Day v. Case Credit Corp., 427 F.3d 1148 (8th Cir. 2005) (buyer of purchase agreements took subject to the assignor's obligation to prepare written purchase agreements in accord with the oral agreements; the assignor "breached that obligation when he falsified the written contracts and attempted to defraud the [obligors]"); Cirone v. Tower Ins. Co. of N.Y., 908 N.Y.S.2d 178 (App. Div. 2010) (because assignor had failed to comply with notice provision of assigned insurance contract, assignee was estopped from asserting bad faith refusal to settle).

§11.8 n.6 p.110 Add the following to the list after "Accord": Delacy Invs. v. Thurman, 693 N.W.2d 479 (Minn. App. 2005) ("It makes no difference whether the defense or claim accrues before or after the account debtor is notified of the assignment if the account debtor's defenses on an assigned claim arise from the transaction that gave rise to the contract with the assignor.") (citation omitted).

§11.8 n.8 p.110 Add the following at the end: Delacy Invs. v. Thurman, *supra* note 6 ("because the rights of [the assignee] are subject to *all* terms of the agreement between [the assignor and the obligor] . . . we conclude that [the assignee] cannot collect from [the obligor] because the commissions earned by [the obligor] as a result of [the assignor' s] sales do not exceed his past-due financial obligations to [the obligor]"); Peerless Ins. Co. v. Michael Beshara, Inc., 903 N.Y.S.2d 833 (App. Div. 2010) (obligor's claims "cannot effect an affirmative recovery against [assignee], but rather may be maintained against [assignee] in the present action only to the extent of setting off [obligor's] claim").

§11.8 n.9 p.110 Add the following after the first sentence: *Accord:* Headwaters Constr. Co. v. Nat'l City Mortg. Co., 720 F. Supp. 2d 1182 (D. Idaho 2010) (assignment of rights is presumed not to carry with it liability for third-party claims affecting the property or arising from the assignor's acts). *Cf.* Duck Creek Tire Serv. v. Goodyear Corners, 796 N.W.2d 886 (Iowa 2011) ("A sublease reserves a reversionary interest in the lessee, whereas an assignment is the transfer of the lessee's entire interest, without reserving any reversionary interest": consequently, when holder of sublease assigned its rights, it also assigned the reversionary interest in its own subleases as well as any benefits and burdens created by those sub-subleases).

§11.8 n.12 p.111 Add the following after the first sentence: *See* Novartis Animal Health US v. Earle Palmer Brown, LLC, 424 F. Supp. 2d 1358 (N.D. Ga. 2006) ("an account debtor . . . may assert a claim against an assignee . . . 'only to reduce the amount the account debtor owes.' ") (quoting UCC §9-404(b)).

§11.8 n.17 p.112 Add the following after the last sentence: *Accord:* IFC Credit Corp. v. Specialty Optical Sys., 252 S.W.3d 761 (Tex. Civ. App. 2008) (assignee not entitled to protections given holders in due course because it did not take in good faith and without notice of a defense, both required under UCC 9-403; assignee knew that assignor was not providing the contracted services and had no intention of doing so).

§11.8 n.34 p.116 Add the following after the first sentence: This right to setoff applies, if at all, when there has been a true assignment; if the claim to be set off against the personal debt is instead merely an assignment for the purposes of collection, no setoff is possible. In re Liquidation of Home Ins. Co., 953 A.2d 443 (N.H. 2008) ("this type of assignment . . . does not create mutuality between the assignee and the original debtor, and therefore does not permit setoff").

§11.8 n.37 p.118 Add the following after the first sentence: *Accord:* Kroeplin Farms Gen. P'ship v. Heartland Crop Ins., 430 F.3d 906 (8th Cir. 2005) ("an assignee's right is subject to a defense that the contract was voidable or unenforceable before the assignment . . . [but] is not subject to any defense by the obligor against the assignor that arises after notice of the assignment"); Estate of DeSela v. Prescott Unified Sch. Dist., 228 P.3d 938 (Ariz. App. 2010) (following Restatement Second §336(2); assignment of claim to minor before running of statute of limitations bars the use of that defense until tolling period applying to minor had run), *rev'd on other grounds*, 249 P.3d 767 (Ariz. 2011).

§11.8a DRAFTING A WAIVER-OF-DEFENSE CLAUSE

§11.8a n.1 p.118 Add the following at the end: *Cf.* ReliaStar Life Ins. Co. of N.Y. v. Home Depot U.S.A., 570 F.3d 513 (2d Cir. 2009) (waiver-of-defense clause valid under UCC 9-403(b), but defense of constructive eviction survives; "[C]onstructive eviction is similar to the defenses of fraud and duress in that it goes to the very essence of the agreement, rather than a failure to perform in accordance with the terms of the agreement."); Wells Fargo Bank v. B.C.B.U., 49 Cal. Rptr. 3d 324 (Ct. App. 2006) (under UCC 9-403, enforcing waiver of defenses clause against lessee claiming lack of mutual assent, failure of consideration, cancellation, and material alteration, as none of these is available against a holder in due course); Private Capital v. J & K Engine & Rig Repair, 984 So. 2d 929 (La. App. 2008) (under UCC 9-403(c) and 3-305(a) and (b), an agreement not to assert defenses against an assignee is enforceable except for the defenses available to a holder in due course, such as infancy, incapacity, fraud, duress, and illegality). This result squares with the equities. Given misconduct on the part of the assignor, which — the obligor or the assignee — should bear the risk? The *Wells Fargo* court, *supra*, dealt with this issue in a somewhat unusual setting. A lessee signed lease documents before it had reached complete agreement with the lessor. The lessor then assigned the rights to payment to a bank, which took them in good faith and for value. The lessee and lessor never reached agreement, though, and the lessor never delivered to the lessee the equipment described in the lease documents. The lease was in turn securitized, the lessee defaulted, and the assignee brought suit. The court held that of the obligor and assignee the obligor "is the one that had the ability to protect itself and prevent the instant loss. It took a substantial risk in signing documents that reflected a completed transaction when it was still negotiating for a deal that ultimately fell through. . . . [The assignee], on the other hand, had no way of knowing the lease and guaranty were other than what they appeared to be." As a result, the court held the obligor's protestations of relative innocence to be "not to put too fine a point on it — hogwash," adding that it found "unavailing [the obligor's] attempts at extrication from the swamp it so rashly entered by signing a document that fairly shouted 'Do not sign me.' "

§11.8b DRAFTING A WARRANTY OR DISCLAIMER

§11.8b n.6 p.120 ***Add the following to the list in the first sentence:*** Lifewise Master Funding v. Telebank, 374 F.3d 917 (10th Cir. 2004) ("even in a non-recourse assignment, there is still an implied warranty").

§11.9 VULNERABILITY OF ASSIGNEE TO COMPETING CLAIMS OF OWNERSHIP

§11.9 n.22 p.124 ***Add the following at the end:*** *See* Rentenbach Constrs. v. CM P'ship, 639 S.E.2d 16 (N.C. App. 2007) (earlier factor subordinate to later factor, where later factor perfected its security interest first).

§11.9 n.33 p.126 ***Substitute the following for the citation to*** **White & Summers:** J. White & R. Summers, Uniform Commercial Code ch. 32 (6th ed. 2010).

§11.10 DELEGABILITY OF PERFORMANCE

§11.10 n.4 p.127 Add the following to the list after **"Accord"***:* Quartz of S. Cal. v. Mullen Bros., 61 Cal. Rptr. 3d 54 (App. Ct. 2007) ("the non-assigning original party has a stake in the reliability of the person with whom he has closed the original contract, and is, therefore, entitled to due assurance that any delegated performance will be properly forthcoming") (quoting from UCC 2-210 cmt. 6).

§11.10 n.5 p.127 Add the following after the first sentence: Accord: PDG Los Arcos v. Adams (*In re* Mortgages Ltd.), 427 B.R. 780 (D. Ariz. 2010) ("duties are not implicitly delegated to an assignee where 'the circumstances indicate the contrary, as in an assignment for security' ") (quoting from Restatement Second §328(1)); Unterberger v. Red Bull N. Am., 75 Cal. Rptr. 3d 368 (Ct. App. 2008) ("'An assignment of rights under an executory contract does not impose upon the assignee the obligations of the assignor under the contract unless the assignee assumes these obligations.'") (quoting Heppler v. J.M. Peters Co., 87 Cal. Rptr. 2d 497 (Ct. App. 1999)); Shaw v. State Farm Fire & Cas. Co., 37 So. 3d 329 (Fla. App. 2010) ("Assignment of a right to payment under a contract does not eliminate the duty of compliance with contract conditions, but a third-party assignee is not liable for performance of any duty under a contract, unless he was a party to the agreement or has become a party by subsequent agreement.").

§11.10 n.7 p.127 Add the following to the list after **"Accord"***:* Transp. & Transit Assocs. v. Morrison Knudsen Corp., 255 F.3d 397 (7th Cir. 2001) (quoting treatise; calling attempts to avoid this doctrine "farfetched" and "feeble"); Glass v. Nw. Airlines, 761 F. Supp. 2d 734 (W.D. Tenn. 2011) ("the duty of the performance of a contract does not, unless the obligee agrees otherwise, discharge the liability of the delegating obligor to the obligee for breach of contract"); Sunset Gold Realty v. Premier Bldg. & Dev.,36 A.3d 243 (Conn. App. 2012) ("an assignor's obligations are not extinguished by an assignment"); Pope v. Winter Park Healthcare Grp., 939 So. 2d 185 (Fla. App. 2006) ("[A]bsent an agreement to the contrary, the *rights* accruing under a contract

can be freely given up by assignment, but *duties* assumed under a contract cannot be transferred to another.") (emphasis in original); Seagull Energy E & P v. Eland Energy, 207 S.W.3d 342 (Tex. 2006) ("a party who assigns his contractual rights and duties to a third party remains liable unless expressly or impliedly released by the other party to the contract"); Brew City Redev. Grp. v. Ferchill Grp., 714 N.W.2d 582 (Wis. App.) ("'if the obligor delegates the performance of an obligation, the obligor is not relieved of responsibility for fulfilling that obligation or of liability in the event of a breach'") (quoting Brooks v. Hayes, 395 N.W.2d 167 (Wis. 1986)), *aff'd*, 724 N.W.2d 879 (Wis. 2006).

§11.10 n.7 p.127 Replace the citation to* Knapp & Crystal *in the last sentence with the following: C. Knapp, N. Crystal & H. Prince, Problems in Contract Law 764 (6th ed. 2007).

§11.10 n.7 p.127 Add the following at the end: *But see* DeVenney v. Hill, 918 So. 2d 106 (Ala. 2005) ("as assignees and partners, Hill and Thomas assumed all of [the assignor's] duties").

***§11.10 n.21 p.131 Add the following to the list after* "See":** Nightingale v. Leach, 842 A.2d 1277 (Me. 2004) (management contract was for personal services, so duties under it were nondelegable); Kim v. Moffett, 234 P.3d 279 (Wash. App. 2010) (contract to perform architectural services, like contracts for other professional services, is personal and nonassignable).

§11.10 n.21 p.131 Add the following at the end: *Cf.* OfficeMax, Inc. v. County Qwick Print, 709 F. Supp. 2d 100 (D. Me. 2010) (although a duty to work under an employment contract normally is not delegable, a covenant not to compete normally is assignable); *In re* FH Partners, 335 S.W.3d 752 (Tex. Civ. App. 2011) (bar on delegating duties to pay is part of the general exception for personal trust; held not to be extended to assigning rights to collect, barring contractual language to that effect).

§11.10a TRANSFERABILITY OF OPTIONS

§11.10a p.135 In the second paragraph, add the following at the end of the second sentence: . . . is in some sense personal.[2a]

[2a] *See, e.g.,* Rozen v. Russ & Russ, P.C., 908 N.Y.S.2d 217 (App. Div. 2010) ("While options are, in general, 'freely assignable,' this rule does not apply when a contract contains 'express language to the contrary or terms which indicate that the seller is relying upon the credit of the optionee or other forms of personal performance.' ") (quoting Toroy Realty Corp. v. Ronka Realty Corp., 493 N.Y.S.2d 800 (App. Div. 1985)).

§11.11 ASSUMPTION AND NOVATION

§11.11 n.2 p.137 Add the following at the end: *Accord:* Shaw v. State Farm Fire & Cas. Co., 37 So. 3d 329 (Fla. App. 2010) ("[T]he assignee of a contract right owes no duty of performance to the obligor.").

§11.11 n.3 p.137 Add the following at the end: Perhaps obviously, the assuming delegate is both liable under the terms of the contract between the delegating party and the obligee and able to invoke the defenses and rights contained in that contract. *See* Stenzel v. Dell, Inc., 870 A.2d 133 (Me. 2005) (third-party service providers were both assigned Dell's rights to payment and delegated Dell's duties to provide repairs; consequently, the providers could invoke the arbitration clause in the contract between the delegator and the obligee).

§11.11 n.5 p.138 Add the following to the list after "Accord": Pope v. Winter Haven Healthcare Grp., 939 So. 2d 185 (Fla. App. 2006) ("*Performance* of the duties assumed under a contract [is] usually delegable, but, even if delegable, the delegation will not relieve the promisor of the duty to perform his obligation under the contract."; hospital thus potentially liable for malpractice committed by physician it hired as an independent contractor, where hospital had contracted with patient to provide medical care) (emphasis in original).

§11.11 n.13 p.139 Add the following at the end of the first paragraph: Naturally, an assignee cannot implicitly assume duties of which it is reasonably unaware. Unterberger v. Red Bull N. Am., 75 Cal. Rptr. 3d 368 (Ct. App. 2008) ("While an assumption of obligations may be implied from the acceptance of benefits under a contract, that is so only 'so far as the facts are known, or ought to be known, to the person accepting.' ") (quoting Cal. Civ. Code §1589).

§11.11 n.22 p.141 Add the following after the first sentence: For an instance of a court losing sight of this principle while distracted by lurid facts, *see* Williams v. Ormsby, 966 N.E.2d 255 (Ohio 2012) (there was no consideration supporting a substituted agreement-which it calls a novation-even though the second contract had different terms that were objectively part of a bargained-for exchange; instead focused on whether love and affection constituted consideration (no)).

***§11.11 n.25 p.141 Add the following to the list after* "Accord":** Nightingale v. Leach, 842 A.2d 1277 (Me. 2004) ("Even if the evidence establishes that [the obligee] knew [the delegate] was managing his apartments, and that he assented to the substituted performance, this does not create a novation.") (citing to Restatement Second §329 cmt. *b*).

§11.11 n.25 p.141 Add the following at the end: *Cf.* Craig J. Duchossois Revocable Trust v. CDX Labs., 495 F. Supp. 2d 869 (N.D. Ill. 2006) (a novation requires " 'a previous valid obligation, agreement of all parties to the new obligation, extinguishment of the old contract, and a valid new contract' ") (quoting from Wasserstrom v. Interstate Litho Corp., 495 N.Y.S.2d 217 (App. Div. 1985)).

§11.11 n.26 p.142 Add the following at the end: *Accord:* Robinson v. Guarantee Trust Life Ins. Co., 389 F.3d 475 (5th Cir. 2004) ("A 'novation may be implied where the facts and circumstances demonstrate that it was the intention of the parties to substitute one party for another.' . . . However, an implied novation 'requires substantial proof that the creditor impliedly accepted the new debtor in the place of the old and it must not appear that the creditor intended to hold both the new and old debtor for the obligation.' ") (quoting from First Am. Nat'l Bank v. Alcorn, Inc., 361 So. 2d 481 (Miss. 1978)).

§11.11 n.27 p.142 Add the following at the end: The parties to a contract may, however, provide that the obligee may accept performance without thereby creating a novation. They may, for instance, provide specific and exclusive methods for substituting a party. *See* 216 Jamaica Ave., LLC v. S & R Playhouse Realty Co., 540 F.3d 433 (6th Cir. 2008) (lease provided for novation either by the written consent of the owner or by satisfying outstanding promises, establishing express assumption, recording the instrument of assignment, and giving the lessor a period to review the proposed assignment).

§11.11a DRAFTING AN ASSUMPTION OR NOVATION

§11.11a n.2 p.142 Add the following to the list: 216 Jamaica Ave., LLC v. S & R Playhouse Realty Co., 540 F.3d 433 (6th Cir. 2008) (providing for novation upon lessor's written consent or by satisfying outstanding promises, establishing express assumption, recording the instrument of assignment, and giving the lessor a period to review the proposed assignment; if these are satisfied, "'all personal liability of the lessees upon this lease and for the performance of the covenants herein contained shall cease and determine upon an assignment thereof.' A permitted assignment, the contract makes clear, also operates as a permitted novation.").

PART V

ENFORCEMENT OF PROMISES

CHAPTER 12

REMEDIES

§12.1 PURPOSES OF REMEDIES

§12.1 n.1 p.148 In the third paragraph, add the following to the list after* "see"*: Farnsworth, Comparative Contract Law, in Oxford Handbook of Comparative Law 901, 928-32 (M. Reimann & R. Zimmermann eds. 2006).

§12.1 n.5 p.149 In the first paragraph, add the following to the list in the second sentence: John Thurmond & Assocs. v. Kennedy, 668 S.E.2d 666 (Ga. 2008) ("damages are intended to place an injured party, as nearly as possible, in the same position they would have been in if the injury had never occurred"); Nichols Constr. Corp. v. Va. Mach. Tool Co., 661 S.E.2d 467 (Va. 2008) ("the proper measure of unliquidated damages for breach of a contract 'is the sum that would put [the plaintiff] in the same position, as far as money can do it, as if the contract had been performed.' ") (quoting from Estate of Taylor v. Flair Prop. Assocs., 448 S.E.2d 413, 414 (Va. 1994)).

§12.1 n.5 p.149 In the second paragraph, add the following to the list after* "see"*: Triantis, The Evolution of Contract Remedies (And Why Do Contracts Professors Teach Remedies First?), 60 U. Toronto L.J. 643 (2010); Zamir, The Missing Interest: Restoration of the Contractual Equivalence, 93 Va. L. Rev. 59 (2007).

§12.1 n.5 p.149 ***Add the following at the end of the second paragraph:*** The Fuller & Perdue classification remains central to most discussions of damages, including the discussion in this treatise. But it is important to remember that these interests are not hermetically sealed compartments that are both separate and exhaustive. The cases are chock-full of cases that could be called, say, "expectation minus" or "restitution plus." *See* House of Flavors v. TFG Mich., 643 F.3d 35 (1st Cir. 2011) ("Remedy theories are more malleable than one might think. Notions of remedies in simple cases — rescission of a sale of a lame horse or damages from a fender-bender — may have to be adjusted in more complicated cases.").

§12.1 n.6 p.150 ***Add the following at the end:*** *See generally* H.L.A. Hart & T. Honoré, Causation and the Law (2d ed. 1985) (especially pp. 308-324 on causation in contract).

§12.1 n.7 p.150 ***Add the following after the first sentence:*** *Accord:* Exxon Co. v. Sofec, Inc., 517 U.S. 830 (1996) ("Although the principles of legal causation sometimes receive labels in contract analysis different from the 'proximate causation' label most frequently employed in tort analysis, these principles nevertheless exist to restrict liability in contract as well."); Nat'l Market Share v. Sterling Nat'l Bank, 392 F.3d 520 (2d Cir. 2004) ("as in tort, a plaintiff must prove that a defendant's breach *directly and proximately caused* his or her damages") (emphasis in original). *See also* LNC Invs. v. First Fid. Bank, 173 F.3d 454 (2d Cir. 1999) (Sotomayor, J.) ("Ordinarily, causation is required to recover damages for breach of contract.") (quoting from treatise). *Cf.* US Ecology v. California, 28 Cal. Rptr. 3d 894 (App. Ct. 2005) (promissory estoppel claims should be treated "the same as contract claims when the question is whether a plaintiff's damages are proximately caused by the defendant's breach"). This court draws an unduly sharp line between contract claims and promissory estoppel claims, though its reasoning seems sound. *Id.* ("Restatement section 349 merely states an alternative measure of damages for *contract* actions, not promissory estoppel claims.").

§12.1 n.7 p.150 ***Add the following at the end:*** On the type of causation required, *see* Barkan v. Dunkin' Donuts, 627 F.3d 34 (1st

Cir. 2010) (Rhode Island law: "the plaintiff must prove that the defendant's breach was the 'but for' cause of the alleged damages"); Yankee Atomic Elec. Co. v. United States, 536 F.3d 1268 (Fed. Cir. 2008) ("substantial factor test is not preferred" over "the more traditional 'but-for' test").

None of this is to suggest that causation in contract necessarily correlates with causation in tort, either in practice or in theory. To take an important illustration, loss causation for the purposes of determining insurance coverage rejects proximate cause, intervening cause, and the like in favor of direct causation. "Insurance-coverage cases are not concerned with the philosophical social-duty underpinnings of tort law. The action sounds in contract, and our task is to interpret the parties' agreement." First State Bank of Monticello v. Ohio Cas. Ins. Co., 555 F.3d 564, 570 (7th Cir. 2009), followed in Beach Cmty. Bank v. St. Paul Mercury Ins. Co., 635 F.3d 1190 (11th Cir. 2011) (referring to "the erroneous application of tort concepts of causation"). *See also* Bird v. St. Paul Fire & Marine Ins. Co., 120 N.E. 86 (N.Y. 1918) (Cardozo, J.) ("General definitions of a proximate cause give little aid. Our guide is the reasonable expectation and purpose of the ordinary business man when making an ordinary business contract. . . . The question is not what men ought to think of as a cause. The question is what they do think of as a cause.").

§12.1 n.10 p.151 Add the following to the list after "Accord": Amigo Broad. v. Spanish Broad. Sys., 521 F.3d 472 (5th Cir. 2008) ("need not 'negative entirely the possibility that [the defendants'] conduct was not a cause [of the revenue loss]'; rather, 'it is enough to introduce evidence from which reasonable persons may conclude that the [loss of revenue] was caused by [the defendants' departure].' ") (quoting from Havner v. E-Z Mart Stores, 825 S.W.2d 456 (Tex. 1992)); Ind. Mich. Power Co. v. United States, 422 F.3d 1369 (Fed. Cir. 2005) (requiring that "the breach is a substantial causal factor in the damages"); Cal. Fed. Bank v. United States, 395 F.3d 1263 (Fed. Cir. 2005) ("This is not to say that the breach must be the sole factor or sole cause in the loss of profits. The existence of other factors operating in confluence with the breach will not necessarily preclude recovery based on the breach."), followed in Anchor Sav. Bank v. United States, 597 F.3d 1356 (Fed. Cir. 2010) (quoting above; "a plaintiff may recover only for those losses that would not have occurred but for the breach"); Citri-Lite Co. v. Cott Beverages, 721 F. Supp. 2d 912 (E.D. Cal. 2010) ("[t]he requisite causation . . . is established when the plaintiff demonstrates that the defendant's breach was a 'substantial factor' in causing damage"); Strong Constr. v. City of Torrington, 255 P.3d 903 (Wyo. 2011) (rejecting extension of comparative fault doctrine to contract law).

§12.1 n.10 p.151 Add the following after the second sentence: *Cf.* City of Westminster v. Centric-Jones Constructors, 100 P.3d 472 (Colo. App. 2003) ("A liquidated damages clause addressing delay in a construction contract will not be enforced 'where [the] delay is due in whole or in part to the fault of the party claiming the clause's benefit.' " In addition, "the City failed to apportion the total delay between optional redesign and the necessary correction of [the defendant's] defective construction.") (quoting from Medema Homes v. Lynn, 647 P.2d 664 (Colo. 1982)); Doering Equip. Co. v. John Deere Co., 815 N.E.2d 234 (Mass. App. 2004) (damages not recoverable when "the damages were . . . caused by the bad bargain itself, not by the . . . breach").

§12.1 n.10 p.151 Add the following at the end: A different rule applies for liquidated damages. *See* §12.18 *infra*.

§12.1 n.11 p.151 Add the following to the list after "Accord": Nat'l Market Share v. Sterling Nat'l Bank, *supra* note 7 ("the 'intervening cause,' which the district court found had broken the causal link between [the breach and the damages], was an integral part of the proximate cause analysis").

§12.1 n.13 p.152 Add the following after the first sentence: This aspect of causation is important in wrongful discharge cases when the employer learns after discharge of employee misconduct that would have caused the employer to dismiss the employee had it known of the misconduct. The employer may use evidence of the misconduct to defend against the claim. *See* Ellsworth v. Pot Luck Enters., 624 F. Supp. 2d 868 (M.D. Tenn. 2009).

§12.1 n.14 p.152 Add the following to the list after **"Accord":** Yankee Atomic Elec. Co. v. United States, *supra* note 7 (the plaintiffs "can only sustain their damages claim if: '(1) the damages were reasonably foreseeable by the breaching party at the time of contracting; (2) *the breach is a substantial causal factor in the damages;* and (3) the damages are shown with reasonable certainty' ") (quoting from Ind. Mich. Power Co. v. United States, *supra* note 10) (emphasis added in *Yankee Atomic*); Fifth Third Bank v. United States, 518 F.3d 1368 (Fed. Cir. 2008) ("At times the Government couches [its argument that damages were not foreseeable] in terms of proximate causation . . . Since both arguments relate to the ability of the Government to contemplate at the time of the contract the nature of [the] injuries, we will address both in terms of foreseeability.").

§12.1 n.16 p.153 Add the following to the list after **"Accord":** Citri-Lite Co. v. Cott Beverages, 721 F. Supp. 2d 912 (E.D. Cal. 2010) (contract between manufacturer and distributor provided for termination upon 60 days' notice; accordingly, manufacturer could not recover lost royalties or goodwill damages based on performance beyond the notice period); Asamoah-Boadu v. Missouri, 328 S.W.3d 790 (Mo. App. 2010) (contract provided for 30 days of notice before termination without cause effective; although actual termination purported to be for cause but was not, the without-cause notice provision limited lost profits to 30 days) (but see Ahuja, J., concurring, who makes a cogent argument against presuming irrebuttably that the employer would have terminated the contract for convenience on the date of the wrongful discharge for cause).

§12.1 n.19 p.153 Add the following at the end: Accord: Stovall v. United States, 94 Fed. Cl. 336 (2010) (making same distinction; citing to treatise).

§12.2 TYPES OF REMEDIES

§12.2 p.156 Add the following at the end of the last sentence: . . . foreclosing on security.[4a]

[4a] Bankruptcy Code §546(c) (reclamation for credit sales); UCC §§2-511 (reclamation for cash sales), 2-702(1) (stoppage in transit) & 2-702(2) (reclamation for credit sales) and Art. 9 subpt. 1 (enforcement of security interest). For more on reclamation, *see* Garvin, Credit, Information, and Trust in the Law of Sales: The Credit Seller's Right of Reclamation, 44 UCLA L. Rev. 247 (1996); Kull, Restitution in Bankruptcy: Reclamation and Constructive Trust, 72 Am. Bankr. L.J. 265 (1998).

§12.3 ECONOMIC ASPECTS

***§12.3 n.1 p.157 Add the following to the list after* "See":** Adler, Efficient Breach Theory Through the Looking Glass, 83 N.Y.U. L. Rev. 1679 (2008); Avraham & Liu, Private Information and the Option To Not Sue: A Reevaluation of Contract Remedies, 28 J.L. Econ. & Org. 77 (2012); Barnes & Zalesne, The Shadow Code, 56 S.C.L. Rev. 93 (2004); Barnes & Zalesne, A Unifying Theory of Contract Damage Rules, 55 Syracuse L. Rev. 495 (2005); Parisi et al., Optimal Remedies for Bilateral Contracts, 40 J. Legal Stud. 245 (2011); Scott & Triantis, Embedded Options and the Case Against Compensation in Contract Law, 104 Colum. L. Rev. 1428 (2004); Sloof et al., Breach Remedies, Reliance and Negotiation, 26 Int'l Rev. L. & Econ. 263 (2006).

***§12.3 n.7 p.160 Add the following to the list after* "See also":** Al-Tawil, The Efficient Breach Theory: The Transparency Objection, 28 J. Contract L. 218 (2012); Al-Tawil, The Efficient Breach Theory: The False Assumptions and Reasons, 28 J. Contract L. 150 (2011); Jimenez, The Value of a Promise: A Utilitarian Approach to Contract Law Remedies, 56 UCLA L. Rev. 59 (2008); Markovits & Schwartz, The Myth of Efficient Breach: New Defenses of the Expectation Interest, 97 Va. L. Rev. 1939 (2011), responded to in Klass, To Perform or Pay Damages, 98 Va. L. Rev. 143 (2012); Oman, The Failure of Economic Interpretations of the Law of Contract Damages, 64 Wash. & Lee L. Rev. 829 (2007); Sidhu, The Immorality and Inefficiency of an Efficient Breach, 8 Transactions 61 (2006).

§12.3 n.7 p.160 Add the following at the end: For empirical analysis of a moral dimension to remedies, *see* Wilkinson-Ryan &

Baron, Moral Judgment and Moral Heuristics in Breach of Contract, 6 J. Empirical L. Studies 405 (2009).

§12.3 n.8 p.160 ***Add the following at the end:*** But efficient breach and moral judgment may not be inconsistent after all. Recent experimental work suggests that liquidated damages clauses shift the norms of the contracting parties toward self-interest, promoting efficient breach without affecting the underlying communal norms regarding contract. Wilkinson-Ryan, Do Liquidated Damages Clauses Encourage Breach? A Psychological Experiment, 108 Mich. L. Rev. 633 (2010).

§12.3 n.9 p.160 *Add the following at the end:* For comparative analyses, *see* Scalise, Why No "Efficient Breach" in the Civil Law?: A Comparative Assessment of the Doctrine of Efficient Breach of Contract, 55 Am. J. Comp. L. 721 (2007); Zhou, Is a Seller's Efficient Breach of Contract Possible in English Law?, 24 J. Contract L. 268 (2008).

§12.4 HISTORICAL DEVELOPMENT OF EQUITABLE RELIEF

§12.4 n.17 p.165 ***Add the following to the list after* "See":** Poff v. Brown, 288 S.W.3d 620 (Ark. 2008) (plaintiff not entitled to specific performance of land sales contract because of unclean hands: plaintiff, a real estate appraiser, "pressured Brown to meet before Brown could ascertain the value of the mineral rights," "told Brown that the mineral rights he sought from Brown had 'little or no value,' " "told Brown he was buying the mineral rights for his grandchildren when he was actually buying them for himself," "provided a preprinted contract . . . and there was disparity between the contract Brown signed and the contract attached to the complaint," and "Brown had little knowledge of mineral rights and natural gas while Poff had significant knowledge."); Landers v. Biwer, 714 N.W.2d 476 (N.D. 2006) (the defendants "came into court with unclean hands" and thus the court "did not abuse its discretion when it concluded that because of their misrepresentations, the [defendants] were not entitled to

the equitable remedy of specific performance"); Wachovia Bank v. Coffey, 698 S.E.2d 244 (S.C. App. 2010) (lending institution prepared legal documents connected with mortgage without supervision by attorney; as a result, its unclean hands barred it from foreclosing on that mortgage), ratified in Matrix Fin. Servs. Corp. v. Frazer, 714 S.E.2d 532 (S.C. 2011) ("a lender may not enjoy the benefit of equitable remedies when that lender failed to have attorney supervision during the loan process as required by law").

§12.4 n.17 p.165 Add the following at the end of the first paragraph: The moral blameworthiness contained within the unclean hands doctrine need not rest directly in the party seeking equitable relief; "a principal seeking specific performance may be bound by an agent's inequitable conduct." Queiroz v. Harvey, 205 P.3d 1120, 1122 (Ariz. 2009). On the other hand, the naughty behavior must "relate directly to the transaction at issue" in order to provide the basis for an unclean hands assertion. *See* Simpson v. Pendergast, 659 S.E.2d 716, 721 (Ga. App. 2008), followed in Hampton Island, LLC v. HAOP, LLC, 702 S.E.2d 770 (Ga. App. 2010) (plaintiffs' alleged attempt to induce a third party to avoid its independent obligation to the defendant irrelevant). And the behavior must transcend the merely annoying; "[t]he clean hands doctrine should not be applied unless the party asserting the doctrine has been seriously harmed and the wrong complained of cannot be corrected without the application of the doctrine." Paciwest, Inc. v. Warner Alan Props., 266 S.W.3d 559, 571 (Tex. Civ. App. 2008).

§12.4 n.18 p.165 Add the following to the list in the third sentence: Lamar Advertising of S.D. v. Heavy Constructors, 745 N.W.2d 371 (S.D. 2008) (where plaintiff knowingly failed to give notice of lease violation until third party had substantially completed its work, plaintiff's request for specific performance of lease was subject to the affirmative defense of laches).

§12.4 n.18 p.165 Add the following at the end: A maxim of special interest to plaintiffs faced with the prospect of a difference-splitting partial recovery is "'[e]quity delights to do justice and not by halves.'" Green v. Green, 16 So. 3d 298 (Fla. App. 2009) (quoting from Skillman v. Baker, 142 So. 2d 113 (Fla. App. 1962)).

§12.4 n.23 p.166 Add the following at the end of the first paragraph: More recent studies, however, call into doubt that generalization; even under CISG, specific performance is rarely sought, and likewise in the domestic law of leading civil-law nations. Lando & Rose, On the Enforcement of Specific Performance in Civil Law Countries, 24 Int'l Rev. L. & Econ. 473 (2004).

§12.5 FORMS: SPECIFIC PERFORMANCE AND INJUNCTION

§12.5 n.1 p.167 Add the following to the end: *Accord:* Restatement Second §357 cmt. *a*; Poland v. Twomey, 937 A.2d 934 (N.H. 2007) ("a decree of specific performance is intended to produce essentially the same effect as if the performance due under a contract were rendered"). This idea has even been used to craft an equitable remedy for breach of a preliminary agreement to sell a hotel. Because the parties had agreed on all material terms, and the Type II preliminary agreement provided that upon reaching agreement the parties *shall* sign, the trial court issued a decree ordering the recalcitrant party to sign the final agreement, a decree upheld on appeal. Stanford Hotels v. Potomac Creek Assocs., 18 A.3d 725 (D.C. 2011) (seller's refusal to sign held in bad faith; additionally, placing burden on seller to show that damages would be adequate, rather than on buyer to show that damages would be inadequate).

§12.5 n.2 p.167 Add the following to the list after **"Accord"*:*** Edge Grp. WAICCS v. Sapir Grp., 705 F. Supp. 2d 304 (S.D.N.Y. 2010) ("specific performance may be precluded by impossibility of performance either at the time of breach or at the time that court relief is sought"); Four Seasons Lakesites v. HRS Props., 317 S.W.3d 193 (Mo. App. 2010) (where vendor conveyed real property at issue to others while the litigation on the original contract proceeded, court would not grant specific performance to original buyer; performance was impossible, and "'an equity court should not grant a decree purporting to affect rights of persons not parties to the suit.'") (quoting Gulf Oil Corp. v. Ferguson, 509 S.W.2d 1 (Mo. 1974)).

***§12.5 n.2 p.167 Add the following to the list after* "But see":** Stafford v. S. Vanity Magazine, 231 S.W.3d 530 (Tex. Civ. App. 2007) ("Impossibility of performance is not available as a defense to a party which by its voluntary act created the impossibility," so "the trial court did not abuse its discretion in awarding appellant specific performance" to compel issuance of shares).

§12.5 n.5 p.168 Add the following after the first sentence: Fruit of the Loom, Inc. v. Zumwalt, 2015 U.S. Dist. LEXIS 161491 (E.D. Ky. Dec. 2, 2015) (granting preliminary injunction to enforce non-compete and non-solicitation agreement).

§12.5 n.7 p.169 Add the following after the second sentence: *See also* Swan, A New Tortious Interference with Contractual Relations: Gender and Erotic Triangles in Lumley v. Gye, 35 Harv. J.L. & Gender 167 (2012).

§12.5 p.170 Add the following after the first sentence in the first full paragraph: . . . as fully as is practicable.[13a]

[13a] The world of plea bargains offers a special illustration of this principle. *See* United States v. Ramsey, 503 F. Supp. 2d 554 (N.D.N.Y. 2007) (where government in breach of plea agreement and defendant performed fully, the defendant was entitled to specific performance — in this context, "to deem the government to have made a motion for a downward departure").

§12.5 p.170 In the first full paragraph, add the following at the end of the fourth sentence: . . . sought to be enforced.[13b]

[13b] Adams v. Adams, 131 P.3d 464 (Alaska 2006) (granting specific performance of reformed lease).

***§12.5 n.14 p.170 Add the following to the list after* "Accord":** 1631 Second Ave. N. v. Raine, 963 So. 2d 71 (Ala. 2007) (recognizing specific performance pro tanto, but affirming its denial where consequences would, inter alia, be a cotenancy between the party seeking specific performance and several strangers to it); Bermont Lakes, LLC v. Rooney, 980 So. 2d 580 (Fla. App. 2008) ("Where a seller contracts to sell land and thereafter discovers that he does not own a portion of the land to be sold, the buyer may nevertheless seek specific performance of that portion of the land the seller does own."); Paradiso v. Drake, 143 P.3d 859 (Wash. App. 2006) ("A buyer is entitled to specific performance even though the seller has a lesser quality title than that contracted for. . . . And the remedy is available where . . . the buyer does not seek to abate the purchase price.").

***§12.5 n.15 p.170 Add the following to the list after* "See":** Restatement Second §358 cmt. *c* & ill. 4; Versatile Housewares & Gardening Sys. v. Thill Logistics, 819 F. Supp. 2d 230 (S.D.N.Y. 2011) ("New York courts ordering specific performance have also allowed a plaintiff to recover such monetary damages [as added litigation costs for breach of forum selection clause] or their equivalent when the defendant's breach caused the plaintiff losses that would not be cured by the belated performance ordered by the court"); Aldridge v. Olive, 876 So. 2d 1130 (Ala. 2003) (noting "the general rule that a party cannot have specific performance of a contract and also damages for breach of the same contract," but noting as well that "this Court, in an appropriate case, has permitted the recovery of incidental damages when specific performance has been ordered"); County of La Paz v. Yakima Compost Co., 233 P.3d 1169 (Ariz. App. 2010) ("The court may award equitable damages when specific performance does not afford complete relief. . . . The nonbreaching party may also receive damages for the breaching party's failure to perform one part of the contract and also attain specific performance of the contract as a whole."); Mandel v. Hernandez, 936 N.E.2d 1079 (Ill. App. 2010) ("when a decree of specific performance does not provide complete relief, the injured party is entitled to those damages that will make him whole, including monetary damages incidental to and caused by a delay in performance"); Flowers v. 73rd Townhouse, LLC, 857 N.Y.S.2d 146 (App. Div. 2008) ("[T]here is no inconsistency in a plaintiff seeking both specific performance and an abatement in the contract price when the subject of the contract is not delivered in the completed form contemplated in the contract.").

§12.5 n.15 p.170 In the first paragraph, add the following after the second sentence: *Cf.* Kissman v. Panizzi, 891 So. 2d 1147 (Fla. App. 2005) ("Damages that flow from the grant of specific performance are limited to those which will return the parties to status quo at the time of breach.").

§12.5 n.15 p.170 ***Add the following at the end:*** Because both legal and equitable remedies may be available for a single breach of contract, the doctrine of election of remedies affects the timing of a remedial choice very little. It may once have been true that choosing a legal remedy at the start of litigation necessarily foreclosed equitable remedies, and vice versa, but "most jurisdictions today have abandoned this dimension of election of remedies doctrine." Homeland Training Ctr. v. Summit Point Auto. Res. Ctr., 594 F.3d 285, 293 (4th Cir. 2010). Doctrines such as judicial estoppel may, of course, prevent a plaintiff from changing positions after a court has ruled on a matter affecting the choice of remedy. In addition, if the defendant has materially changed its position in reliance upon the plaintiff's choice of remedy, the plaintiff may be prevented from choosing a different remedy. Restatement Second §378 & cmt. *a*.

§12.5 n.16 p.171 ***Add the following at the end:*** Mitigation raises interesting issues when damages and specific performance go together. For the purposes of damages, breached-against parties are ordinarily treated as though they had mitigated their losses from breach. *See infra* §12.12. When specific performance enters, though, it is more sensible to dispense with limits stemming from a failure to mitigate. First, a party seeking specific performance must show that it is prepared to carry out its part of the bargain should the decree issue. This is inconsistent with mitigation, which ordinarily involves stopping one's performance or preparations. Second, the breached-against party's attempts to mitigate might be frustrated by the possibility of specific performance. For example, a seller seeking specific performance presumably would mitigate the buyer's losses through a proper resale, but no sane buyer would pay a reasonable amount for property potentially subject to an equitable decree. Ash Park, LLC v. Alexander & Bishop, Ltd., 783 N.W.2d 294 (Wis. 2010) (no mitigation necessary when seller seeks interest in addition to specific performance).

§12.5 n.17 p.171 ***Add the following at the end:*** Restitution is also available to the breaching party as a sort of offset to specific performance. For example, if a vendor of real property fails to perform, it may nevertheless be able to recover in restitution for any taxes or fees it has paid or improvements it has made in the property while in wrongful possession. Because the improvements amount to a forced transfer, however, they may go uncompensated for, and in any event will be valued very parsimoniously. For a careful analysis of this problem, *see* Marioni v. Roxy Garments Delivery, 9 A.3d 607 (N.J. Super. App. Div. 2010). *See also* Restatement (Third) of Restitution & Unjust Enrichment §§10 (mistaken improvements), 36 & cmt. *f* (restitution to a party in breach), & 50 (amount of liability of innocent recipient).

§12.5 p.171 ***Add the following at the end of the fourth sentence:*** . . . against future harm.[19]

[19] These prophylactic injunctions are fairly common in Great Britain, where they are known as *Mareva* injunctions after the leading decision, *Mareva Compania Naviera SA v. International Bulkcarriers SA* [1975] 2 Lloyd's Rep. 509. They have made imperfect headway in the United States, as some courts are content to leave these matters to an ultimate damages action. *See* Coleman v. Retina Consultants, 687 S.E.2d 457 (Ga. 2009). Furthermore, the Supreme Court has held that Mareva injunctions fall outside the equitable powers of the federal courts. Grupo Mexicano de Desarrollo S.A. v. Alliance Bond Fund, 527 U.S. 308 (1999). On the other hand, some jurisdictions have preserved the bill *quia timet*, which is an action in equity for relief against an anticipated injury — as, for example, when a surety seeks to compel the principal to pay the debt when it has come due. Concorde Equity II v. Miller, 732 F. Supp. 2d 990 (N.D. Cal. 2010). The National Conference of Commissioners on Uniform State Laws has begun drafting a uniform act on *Mareva* injunctions, with a final version likely to issue in 2013.

§12.6 THE ADEQUACY TEST

§12.6 n.2 p.172 ***Add the following to the list after*** **"See generally"*:*** Eisenberg, Actual and Virtual Specific Performance, the Theory of Efficient Breach, and the Indifference Principle in Contract Law, 93 Calif. L. Rev. 975 (2005); Goldstein, The Efficiency of Specific Performance in Stock-for-Stock Mergers, 29

Del. J. Corp. L. 747 (2004); Listokin, The Empirical Case for Specific Performance: Evidence from the IBP-Tyson Litigation, 2 J. Empirical Legal Stud. 469 (2005); Shavell, Specific Performance Versus Damages for Breach of Contract: An Economic Analysis, 84 Tex. L. Rev. 831 (2006).

§12.6 n.4 p.173 Add the following at the end: *Cf.* Edge Grp. WAICCS v. Sapir Grp., 705 F. Supp. 2d 304 (S.D.N.Y. 2010) ("doubts about the adequacy of a damage remedy should be resolved in favor of awarding specific performance").

§12.6 n.5 p.173 Add the following at the end: One important exception is mitigation, which is not pertinent to a decision whether to grant equitable relief. Edge Grp. WAICCS v. Sapir Grp., 705 F. Supp. 2d 304 (S.D.N.Y. 2010) ("mitigation is not required in order to justify specific performance"). No party has a *duty* to mitigate damages. *See infra* §12.12. Even leaving that aside, mitigation is relevant to damages only as a limit to the promisor's liability. Whether the promisee mitigated its damages is important when calculating damages, but it is not important when deciding whether it would be possible to measure damages at all.

***§12.6 n.7 p.173 Add the following to the list after* "Accord":** Vacold LLC v. Cerami, 545 F.3d 114 (2d Cir. 2008) ("Although a liquidated damages provision precludes a party from recovering lost profits and other measures of *damages*, . . . it does not prevent a party from seeking specific performance, absent an express provision to this effect."; because specific performance possible, agreement bound parties to buy and sell stock and thus ended duties to disclose under Rule 10b-5), followed in Edge Grp. WAICCS v. Sapir Grp., 705 F. Supp. 2d 304 (S.D.N.Y. 2010) (mere receipt of deposit insufficient to preclude equitable relief); Houston v. Willis, 24 So. 3d 412 (Miss. App. 2009) (granting both specific performance and liquidated damages in contract for sale of real property; earnest money recharacterized as down payment, so "in effect, there was no earnest money remaining to serve as liquidated damages; thus, Willis had no other remedy available but to sue for specific performance"); Coizza v. 164-50 Crossbay Realty Corp., 900 N.Y.S.2d 416 (App. Div. 2010) (granting specific performance, liquidated damages, *and* additional damages; the liquidated damages clause addressed only some of the losses, so the rest were compensable by other means); Granite Broadway Dev. v. 1711 LLC, 845 N.Y.S.2d 10 (App. Div. 2007) ("the court properly granted both liquidated damages and specific performance, as the legal and equitable remedies redress specific injuries").

§12.6 n.7 p.173 Add the following after the second sentence: *Contra:* Perroncello v. Donahue, 859 N.E.2d 827 (Mass. 2007) ("the retention of a deposit as liquidated damages is an alternative to specific performance, not an additional remedy").

§12.6 n.8 p.173 Add the following to the list after "Accord": Palm Lake Partners II v. C & C Powerline, 38 So. 3d 844 (Fla. App. 2010) (clause providing that "if Grantee fails to commence construction by February 28, 2009, Grantee shall pay to Grantor . . . $350,000 and shall be released from the obligation to construct the Future Access Road" held to preclude specific performance); Coizza v. 164-50 Crossbay Realty Corp., 831 N.Y.S.2d 433 (App. Div. 2007) ("Since the contract did not limit the plaintiffs' damages to liquidated damages, the plaintiffs' action for specific performance is not precluded."), *aff'd as modified after remand*, 900 N.Y.S.2d 416 (App. Div. 2010) (upholding grant of specific performance plus damages; liquidated damages clause inapplicable because triggering contingency did not occur).

§12.6 n.10 p.174 Add the following after the first sentence: *Accord:* Houseman v. Dare, 966 A.2d 24 (N.J. Super. App. Div. 2009) (equitable relief available for breach of oral agreement to transfer possession of pet dog, where dog has "special subjective value . . . based on one party's sincere affection for and attachment to it," as opposed to "a sentiment assumed for the purpose of litigation out of greed, ill-will or other sentiment or motive similarly unworthy of protection in a court of equity").

§12.6 n.10 p.174 Add the following at the end: Plea bargaining creates a not unusual application of this point; one's freedom cannot readily be assigned a dollar value, making specific performance particularly appropriate. United States v. Ramsey, 503 F. Supp. 2d 554 (N.D.N.Y. 2007) (granting specific performance to enforce plea agreement by deeming the government to have made a promised motion to authorize a downward departure). The parties to a plea agreement may, however, waive their equitable rights in whole or in part, and the degree of discretion generally vouchsafed the government on how to perform a plea agreement undercuts claims for some specific action by the government. As a result, a criminal defendant offered a plea bargain should be wary of deals with a paucity of specifics, though those deals may be all that is on offer.

§12.6 n.12 p.174 Add the following to the list after "Accord": Haymarket LLC v. D.G. Jewellery of Can., 736 N.Y.S.2d 356 (App. Div. 2002) (affirming grant of specific performance where "trading in defendant's stock was so thin that plaintiff would be unable to purchase the number of shares to which it is entitled on the open market, and nearly half the outstanding shares were owned by insiders or members of their families"); Stafford v. S. Vanity Magazine, 231 S.W.3d 530 (Tex. Civ. App. 2007) ("when a closely-held corporation's stock has no ascertainable value, the party may seek specific performance to enforce a stock purchase agreement").

§12.6 n.16 p.175 Add the following to the list after "Accord": Union Oil Co. of Cal. v. Greka Energy Corp., 80 Cal. Rptr. 3d 738 (Ct. App. 2008) (vendor of oil field compelled to plug and abandon idle wells; "[A] party entitled to specific performance of a continuing duty should receive it whenever it is practically feasible. . . . Moreover, where a party, as here, commits multiple breaches, specific performance is preferred over the inadequate remedy of repetitive future damage actions.").

§12.6 n.20 p.176 Add the following to the list after "Accord": Houston v. Willis, *supra* note 7 (specific performance granted "unless [transaction costs] are so high that no voluntary exchange can take place"; courts "give lip service to the requirement of a demonstration of the inadequacy of the legal remedy") (quoting from Osborne v. Bullins, 549 So. 2d 1337 (Miss. 1989)); Crafts v. Pitts, 162 P.3d 382 (Wash. 2007) ("the injured party in a land conveyance dispute always has a choice between specific performance and money damages"), followed in Cornish Coll. v. 1000 Va. Ltd. P'ship, 242 P.3d 1 (Wash. App. 2010) ("because land is unique and difficult to value, specific performance is often the only adequate remedy for a breach of contract regarding real property"; property in question, already leased by college, is part of college's campus plan, and was uniquely situated for use as scene shops for theater across an alley); Ash Park v. Alexander & Bishop, Ltd., 783 N.W.2d 294 (Wis. 2010) ("In the context of contracts for land . . . Wisconsin law does not require a seller to demonstrate the inadequacy of a remedy at law as a prerequisite to an award of specific performance."). Indeed, Mississippi courts have gone so far as to state that "where a contracting party can feasibly be given what he bargained for, specific performance is the *preferred* remedy." Frierson v. Delta Outdoor, 794 So. 2d 220, 225-26 (Miss. 2001) (emphasis added).

§12.6 n.20 p.176 Add the following at the end: *See also* Cohen, The Relationship of Contractual Remedies to Political and Social Status: A Preliminary Inquiry, 32 U. Toronto L.J. 31 (1982) (relating special remedies for land to the connection of land and status).

§12.6 n.25 p.177 Add the following at the end of the first paragraph: *Cf.* Ash Park, LLC v. Alexander & Bishop, Ltd., 783 N.W.2d 294 (Wis. 2010) ("If the court determines that legal damages are perfectly adequate, the court may in its discretion choose to award damages at law rather than specific performance.").

§12.6 n.28 p.178 Add the following to the list after "Accord": Sherwin Alumina v. AluChem, Inc., 512 F. Supp. 2d 957 (S.D. Tex. 2007) (granting specific performance where "the current market for calcined alumina is very tight; . . . the calcined alumina products provided by Sherwin Alumina to AluChem are unique products, manufactured by very few entities; . . . AluChem absolutely needs these products to survive in its business . . . " and if Sherwin Alumina anticipatorily breached its supply agreement, "AluChem will not be able to obtain the calcined alumina products it requires for its business," in spite of "extensive efforts to secure an alternative supply.").

§12.6 n.28 p.178 Add the following after the citation to **Laclede Gas***:* , disagreed with by Exelon Gen. Co. v. Gen. Atomics Techs. Corp., 559 F. Supp. 2d 892 (N.D. Ill. 2008) (rejecting argument that specific performance of long-term supply contract appropriate where only alternative was buying at greater cost on the spot market; "it would seem that it would simply increase the amount recoverable as damages").

§12.6 n.28 p.178 Add the following after the citation to **Campbell Soup***:* , analyzed in V. Goldberg, Framing Contract Law ch. 9 (2006).

§12.6 n.33 p.179 Add the following at the end: Accord: Cornish Coll. v. 1000 Va. Ltd., 242 P.3d 1 (Wash. App. 2010) ("given [the seller's] purported financial condition, an award solely of money damages may be difficult or impossible for [the purchaser] to collect"); NML Capital Master, Ltd. v. Republic of Argentina, 699 F.3d 246, 262 (2d Cir. 2013) (ordering specific performance of *pari passu* provision that bonds at issue rank at least equally with other debt, because plaintiffs would have difficulty collecting a money judgment. "In light of Argentina's continual disregard for the rights of its FAA creditors and the judgments of our courts to whose jurisdiction it has submitted, its contention that bondholders are limited to acceleration is unpersuasive. Insofar as Argentina argues that a party's persistent efforts to frustrate the collection of money judgments cannot suffice to establish the inadequacy of a monetary relief, the law is to the contrary.").

§12.6 n.35 p.180 Add the following to the list after **"Accord"***:* DiGiuseppe v. Lawler, 269 S.W.3d 588 (Tex. 2008) (clause providing that specific performance is available to the buyer "grants DiGiuseppe only the right to 'seek to enforce' specific performance, leaving open the possibility that he may seek to enforce it, but be unable to do so").

§12.6 n.35 p.180 Add the following after the second sentence: Cf. DVD Copy Control Ass'n v. Kaleidescape, Inc., 97 Cal. Rptr. 3d 856 (Ct. App. 2009) ("[A] court must reject a stipulation contemplating an equitable remedy that is contrary to law

or public policy, such as where the evidence shows that an aggrieved party actually has an adequate remedy at law. Otherwise, the court should honor the parties' agreement and enforce the stipulation."; collecting cases); Ash Park, LLC v. Alexander & Bishop, Ltd., 783 N.W.2d 294 (Wis. 2010) ("The availability of specific performance as a remedy does not mean that the court will automatically grant specific performance upon a seller's request."; response to contract listing specific performance as remedy available to seller); CBM Geosols. v. Gas Sensing Tech. Corp., 215 P.3d 1054 (Wyo. 2009) ("It is proper for a court acting in equity to consider the remedies contemplated by the parties in reaching its conclusion on the equities."; confirming propriety of equitable relief for covenant not to compete).

§12.7 OTHER LIMITATIONS

§12.7 n.1 p.181 Add the following at the end: In some jurisdictions, however, the heightened level of proof required to secure equitable relief may make an action at law feasible where an action in equity is not. *See* Dittrick v. Chalfant, 948 A.2d 400 (Del. Ch.) (clear and convincing evidence of valid contract, ability to perform obligations, and favorable balance of equities), *aff'd mem.*, 935 A2d 255 (Del. 2007); Clements v. Weaver, 687 S.E.2d 602 (Ga. App. 2009) ("In order to specifically enforce a parol contract to make a will, the contract must be proved beyond a reasonable doubt."); Roberts v. City of St. Louis, 254 S.W.3d 280 (Mo. App. 2008) ("A party requesting specific performance of the agreement has the burden of proving the claim by clear, convincing, and satisfactory evidence."). *Cf.* National Music Museum v. Johnson, 2017 U.S. Dist. LEXIS 8632 (D.S.D. Jan. 23, 2017) (contract for purchase of guitar formerly owned by Elvis Presley was not completed before it was sold to third party and put on display at museum; UCC Article 2 provides that "title passes to the buyer at the time and place at which the seller completes performance with reference to the physical delivery of the goods," which never occurred; therefore, "Moss could have sought specific performance as a remedy for Johnson's breach of the February 2008 contract," but because he instead waited until 2014, after the title had already transferred to the museum, the court held that the museum was the owner of the guitar).

§12.7 n.2 p.181 Add the following to the list after* "Accord"*: Dittrick v. Chalfant, *supra* note 1 (court may not supplement agreement "through its own judicial discretion," though an incomplete contract may nevertheless support specific performance if the missing term "would not appear to be an essential term of the agreement"); Marshall v. Floyd, 664 S.E.2d 793 (Ga. App. 2008) (option to purchase real property; "Because a decree for specific performance operates as a deed, the contract pertaining to the sale of land must describe the property with the same degree of certainty as that required of a deed."); Schilling v. Stahl, 918 N.E.2d 1077 (Ill. App. 2009) (specific performance of sale of realty granted even though contract omits, among other things, "procedures and imposition of costs and fees in the event of foreclosure; grace period before default; maintenance of insurance; remedy for failure to pay taxes; rights under a condemnation proceeding; assignment of rents . . . "; these terms "are a list of 'what ifs' that could arise at some future date, not terms that are essential to the creation of [a mortgage]"); DuBois Dutch, LLC v. Guido, 977 A.2d 1225 (Pa. Commw. 2009) (contract to sell real property; "Specific performance will not lie . . . where the evidence is uncertain, inadequate, equivocal, ambiguous, or contradictory as to render findings or reasonable inferences mere conjecture."); Barham v. McGraw, 342 S.W.3d 716 (Tex. Civ. App. 2011) ("when the essential elements of a property's description are left to inference or to development by parol, the description is insufficient to support a suit for specific performance irrespective of whether the parties themselves understood what land formed the subject matter of the conveyance"; descriptions consisting only of names presumably associated with different parcels inadequate); Cytogenix, Inc. v. Waldroff, 213 S.W.3d 479 (Tex. Civ. App. 2006) (contract for licensing technology).

§12.7 p.182 Add the following at the end of the third sentence in the first paragraph: . . . specific performance or injunction.[3a]

[3a] *See* Alzate v. Lazaro, 992 So. 2d 424 (Fla. App. 2008) ("'[a] lesser degree of certainty is required to afford relief for damages than is necessary

to decree specific performance'") (quoting from Fox v. Sails at Laguna Club Dev. Corp., 403 So. 2d 456, 458 (Fla. App. 1981)).

§12.7 n.5 p.182 Add the following to the list after **"See"***:* Restatement Second §362 cmt. B; Dittrick v. Chalfant, *supra* note 1 ("[A] judicial determination that an agreement is incomplete should not, by itself, make specific performance unavailable when a statute directly addresses, and stands ready to supply, a missing or ambiguous term;" missing interest rate in installment land sale contract).

§12.7 n.5 p.182 Add the following at the end: For a vigorous use of these techniques to render a contract sufficiently definite, *see* Hurtubise v. McPherson, 951 N.E.2d 994 (Mass. App. 2011) (enforcing oral agreement to trade land even though the descriptions were very general (e.g., the land on which Hurtubise wanted to build a storage shed for part of the front of Hurtubise's property); McPherson saw the ongoing construction of the shed without objection, and at trial Hurtubise designated the part of his property from which the land in exchange would be taken; even though the area and exact location were not determined, the trial judge reasonably equated the two areas).

For a refusal to parse usages and course of dealing, *see* Lewis v. YouTube, LLC, 244 Cal. App. 4th 118 (2015). There, the plaintiff alleged that her YouTube account was wrongfully removed and sought to compel YouTube to restore her channel to its prior condition, including all videos, comments, and view counts. She argued that the Terms of Use references to the "Service," together with the fact that "[e]ach channel on the website includes the very features that [she] seeks to have restored," was sufficient for the court to grant specific performance. *Id.* at 127. But the California Court of Appeal disagreed and would look only to the agreement itself, holding that because there was no "provision of the Terms of Service that she seeks to have a court enforce, the remedy of specific performance is unavailable."

§12.7 n.8 183 Add the following after the first sentence: Accord: Osborn *ex rel.* Osborn v. Kemp, 991 A.2d 1153 (Del. 2010) ("We will order specific performance only if a party is ready, willing, and able to perform under the terms of the agreement.

Unless the contract provides that time is of the essence, we will permit the parties a reasonable time to obtain financing and conclude the transaction."); Landmark Inv. Grp. v. Chung Family Realty P'ship, 10 A.3d 61 (Conn. App. 2010) ("'It is well settled that a buyer seeking specific performance has the burden of proving that he or she is ready, willing and able to purchase the premises, even when a seller . . . has failed to satisfy a condition of the contract.'") (quoting from Jaramillo v. Case, 919 A.2d 1061 (Conn. App. 2007)); Clark v. Route, 951 A.2d 757 (D.C. 2008) (buyer seeking specific performance must show that she was ready, willing, and able to proceed and "must first demonstrate a strong interest in completing the transaction"; not shown where buyer chose to "call off the settlement, not have any contact with the sellers, cease her efforts to finalize financing, and file suit for specific performance"); Taylor v. Richards, 971 So. 2d 127 (Fla. App. 2007) (proof that ready, willing, and able "(1) If he has the needed cash in hand, or (2) if he is personally possessed of assets . . . and a credit rating which enable him with reasonable certainty to command the requisite funds at the required time . . . or (3) if he has definitely arranged to raise the necessary money — or as much thereof as he is unable to supply personally — by obtaining a binding commitment for a loan to him for that purpose by a financially able third party . . .") (quoting from Hollywood Mall v. Capozzi, 545 So. 2d 918, 920-21 (Fla. App. 1989)); Forsyth Cnty. v. Waterscape Servs., 694 S.E.2d 102 (Ga. App. 2010) (when one party repudiated contract, the other "was relieved of its duty to make a formal tender of payment"); Mayfield v. Koroghli, 184 P.3d 362 (Nev. 2008) (tender unnecessary if the buyer demonstrates that it is ready, willing, and able to perform); DiGiuseppe v. Lawler, 269 S.W.3d 588 (Tex. 2008) ("[W]hen a defendant refuses to perform or repudiates a contract, the plaintiff may be excused from actually tendering his or her performance to the repudiating party before filing suit for specific performance. In such a circumstance, a plaintiff seeking specific performance is excused from tendering performance pre-suit and may simply plead that performance would have been tendered but for the defendant's breach or repudiation. . . . However, even when pre-suit tender of performance is excused, a plaintiff is still obligated to plead and prove his readiness, willingness, and ability to perform at relevant times before specific performance may be awarded."; insufficient to show "by simply offering to perform in his pleadings as opposed to actually proving to the finder of fact that he is and was — in fact — ready, willing, and able to perform.").

§12.7 n.11 p.183 Add the following to the list after **"See":** Blue Paper v. Provost, 914 So. 2d 1048 (Fla. App. 2005) ("If mutuality of remedies is understood to mean that both parties to a contract must have the *same* remedy to enforce it, then the concept has 'largely disappeared from the law of American jurisdictions.' . . . [S]uch an absence of mutuality of remedies will not destroy an agreement's validity.") (quoting from LaBonte Precision v. LPI Indus. Corp., 507 So. 2d 1202 (Fla. App. 1987)).

§12.7 n.14 p.184 Add the following after the first sentence: Accord: Cytogenix, Inc. v. Waldroff, *supra* note 2 ("A court should not decree future contractual performance by requiring a party to perform a continuous series of acts, extending through a long period of time, over which the court exercises its supervision.").

§12.7 n.16 p.185 Add the following after the third sentence: But cf. Craven v. TRG-Boynton Beach, Ltd., 925 So. 2d 476 (Fla. App. 2006) ("Florida, like the vast majority of other jurisdictions, does not permit specific performance of a lease even in ordinary circumstances, because the court would be forced to undertake an excessive supervisory responsibility.").

§12.7 n.19 p.185 Add the following at the end: See generally Oman, Specific Performance and the Thirteenth Amendment, 93 Minn. L. Rev. 2020 (2009). *Cf.* Principles of the Law of Software Contracts §4.06(a) & (c) & cmt. *a* (2010) ("Specific performance is not available if it would require the performance of personal services . . . ").

§12.7 n.20 p.186 Add the following after the third sentence: Cf. J.C. Ehrlich Co. v. Martin, 979 A.2d 862 (Pa. Super. 2009) (noncompete agreement enforceable through injunctive relief, even though agreement made with an entity whose stock was purchased by the entity seeking to enforce the agreement).

§12.7 n.32 p.187 Add the following to the list in the first sentence: Ash Park, LLC v. Alexander & Bishop, Ltd., 783 N.W.2d 294 (Wis. 2010) ("Before ordering specific performance, the court must be satisfied that the claim is fair, just, reasonable, and not the product of an unconscionable or oppressive bargain.").

§12.7 n.32 p.187 Add the following at the end: Related is the defense of *equitable nonforfeiture*, which arises in response to a landlord's attempt to evict a tenant for nonpayment of rent using summary proceedings. A tenant may invoke this defense "'if: (1) the tenant's breach was not [willful] or grossly negligent; (2) upon eviction the tenant will suffer a loss wholly disproportionate to the injury to the landlord; and (3) the landlord's injury is reparable.'" 10 Perry St., LLC v. Unionville Water Co., 987 A.2d 1009, 1022 (Conn. 2010) (quoting from Cumberland Farms v. Dairy Mart, 627 A.2d 386 (Conn. 1993)). Thus, for example, a water company was allowed to remain in possession of a leased well field, conditioned upon its payment of back rent plus interest, when its nonpayment was caused by a good-faith misinterpretation of the lease and its loss of water would cause harm far out of proportion to the unpaid rent.

§12.7 n.34 p.188 Add the following to the list after **"Accord"***:* Poff v. Brown, 288 S.W.3d 620 (Ark. 2008) (specific performance of contract to purchase mineral rights denied where buyer misled seller as to value of rights and purpose for purchase, buyer's knowledge greatly exceeded that of seller, and the version of the preprinted contract signed by the seller was not the same as that attached to the complaint); Clements v. Weaver, *supra* note 1 ("'[A] court will be justified in refusing a decree of specific performance should inadequacy of price appear, or any other fact showing the contract to be unfair, or unjust, or against good conscience.'") (quoting from Bullard v. Bullard, 44 S.E.2d 770 (Ga. 1947)); Surman v. Blansett, 539 S.E.2d 890 (Ga. App. 2000) (in a claim for specific performance, the underlying contract must be "fair, just and not against good conscience. And whether the price was adequate and whether enforcement of the contract was equitable are questions for the trier of fact."); Kilarjian v. Vastola, 877 A.2d 372 (N.J. Sup. Ct. Ch. Div. 2004) (denying specific performance of contract to sell home when a seller's "health is

rapidly deteriorating and the further physical and mental exhaustion of the move may exacerbate her condition"; to do so would yield "great hardship").

§12.7 n.35 p.188 ***In the first paragraph, add the following to the list after*** **"Accord"*:*** FMB, Inc. v. Creech, 679 S.E.2d 410 (N.C. App. 2009) ("[M]inors cannot be compelled to specifically perform a contract as long as they remain under the age of eighteen.").

§12.7 n.35 p.188 ***In the second paragraph, add the following at the end:*** *Accord:* Lamar Advertising of S.D. v. Heavy Constructors, 745 N.W.2d 371 (S.D. 2008) (denying specific performance of contract to lease property for erecting billboards, where specific performance would require that a third party's billboard would have to be removed; "specific performance would result in unjust harm to an innocent third party . . . as Lamar would be attempting to enforce a remedy under a contract to which [the third party] was not a party.").

§12.8 BASIC PRINCIPLES OF DAMAGES

§12.8 n.1 p.189 ***In the first paragraph, add the following to the list after*** **"Accord"*:*** Bourgeois v. Hughes, 55 So. 3d 1195 (Ala. Civ. App. 2010) (nominal damages available for breach of contract where there is no actual damage; rationale in part that they recognize the invasion of the plaintiff's legal rights); Parham v. CIH Props., Inc., 208 F. Supp. 3d 116, 2016 U.S. Dist. LEXIS 123834 (D.D.C. Sept. 13, 2016) (defendant breached warranty of habitability, but was only entitled to $1 nominal damages because plaintiff produced no evidence of value of damaged property).

§12.8 n.1 p.189 ***Add the following at the end of the first paragraph:*** *But see* Stovall v. United States, 94 Fed. Cl. 336 (2010) ("this court lacks the authority to award nominal damages").

§12.8 n.2 p.190 ***Add the following to the list after*** **"Accord"*:*** City of Westminster v. Centric-Jones Constructors, 100 P.3d 472 (Colo. App. 2003) ("'In the absence of special

circumstances, the [failure to award nominal damages is] of no consequence . . . and courts will not reverse a judgment simply because nominal damages were not awarded.'") (quoting from Sill Props. v. CMAG, Inc., 33 Cal. Rptr. 155 (Ct. App. 1963)).

§12.8 n.2 p.190 Add the following after the first paragraph: Whether the plaintiff received nominal damages may affect whether it can recover attorney's fees under fee-shifting statutes. Intercontinental Grp. P'ship v. KB Home Lone Star, 295 S.W.3d 650 (Tex. 2009) (under fee-shifting statute and fee-shifting contract provision, plaintiff not a "prevailing party" where it received zero damages; "KB Home, while perhaps a 'nominal winner' in convincing the jury that it was 'wronged,' cannot be deemed a 'prevailing party' in any non-Pyrrhic sense."). *Cf.* Farrar v. Hobby, 506 U.S. 103 (1992) (attorney's fees recoverable under 42 U.S.C. §1988 when plaintiff awarded one dollar in damages; "A judgment for damages in any amount, whether compensatory or nominal, modifies the defendant's behavior for the plaintiff's benefit by forcing the defendant to pay an amount of money he otherwise would not pay.").

§12.8 n.4 p.190 Add the following at the end: In a relatively extreme factual setting, the Court of Claims held that the Drug Enforcement Administration (DEA) was liable for medical damages, including treatment for multiple sclerosis, for an informant who was kidnapped and held captive for months after the DEA breached its duty of good faith and fair dealing when it violated its own procedures and failed to protect her. SGS-92-X003 v. United States, 118 Fed. Cl. 492 (2014); for discussion of liability, see §7.17 *supra*. The court applied a "substantial factor" test and found the plaintiff's kidnapping was the proximate cause of the DEA's breach, that the resulting stress led to neurological problems and multiple sclerosis, and that the harm was foreseeable. 118 Fed. Cl. at 525-30. The court awarded damages for "the full amount of the life care plan, totaling $1,145,161.47," *Id.* at 530, but found that plaintiff had not demonstrated the costs associated with emotional distress with sufficient certainty, even if available given the physical harm suffered, *Id.* at 532.

***§12.8 n.5 p.190 In the first paragraph, add the following to the list after* "But cf.":** Perry v. Baptist Health, 243 S.W.3d 310 (Ark. 2006) (invoking Ark. Code §16-22-308 to award attorney's fees to the prevailing party); Morrison Homes v. Wade, 598 S.E.2d 358 (Ga. App. 2004) (invoking Ga. Code §13-6-11 to award attorney's fees where "the defendant has acted in bad faith in the underlying transaction"); Bank One v. Surber, 899 N.E.2d 693 (Ind. App. 2009) (affirming award of attorney's fees under "third party litigation exception," which arises when "(1) the plaintiff became involved in a legal dispute because of the defendant's breach of contract or other wrongful act; (2) the litigation was with a third party and not the defendant; and (3) the fees were incurred in the third-party litigation"); Med. City Dallas v. Carlisle Corp., 251 S.W.3d 55 (Tex. 2008) (invoking Tex. Civ. Prac. & Rem. Code §38.001 to award attorney's fees in breach of warranty action).

§12.8 n.5 p.190 In the first paragraph, add the following after the fourth sentence: The third-party-litigation exception in *Bank One* may be a fairly routine application of the law of consequential damages, especially because the court goes on to state that the bank is liable only for foreseeable damages. See §12.14 *infra* on litigation costs as consequential damages.

§12.8 n.5 p.190 In the second paragraph, add the following to the list in the first sentence: Bank One v. Surber, *supra* (affirming award of prejudgment interest; "An award of prejudgment interest is founded upon the theory that there has been a deprivation of the plaintiff's use of money or its equivalent and that unless interest is added, the plaintiff cannot be fully compensated for the loss suffered."); Glasstech, Inc. v. Chicago Blower Corp., 675 F. Supp. 2d 752 (N.D. Ohio 2009) (under Ohio Rev. Stat., §1343.03(A), prejudgment interest available if the aggrieved party would otherwise not be fully compensated); Brandywine Smyrna v. Millennium Builders, 34 A.3d 482 (Del. 2011) (under Delaware law, prejudgment interest in contract disputes "is awarded as a matter of right," with the interest accumulating from the date payment was due the plaintiff); Koppe v. Campbell, 318 S.W.3d 233 (Mo. App. 2010) (ordinarily prejudgment interest available only when the demand is liquidated, but prejudgment interest is available in claims sounding in quantum meruit for the reasonable value of services); Poole v. Union Planters Bank, 337 S.W.3d 771 (Tenn. Ct. App. 2010) (prejudgment interest awarded on the basis of fairness, taking into account the general desire of the law to compensate a plaintiff fully; as a result, "equity and fairness, in almost all cases, . . . now mandate full compensation for losses that the defendant caused, including economic loss stemming from the plaintiff's inability to earn interest on funds he should have received").

§12.8 n.5 p.190 In the second paragraph, add the following to the list after **"But cf."***:* Commonwealth v. AMEC Civil, 699 S.E.2d 499 (Va. 2010) (no prejudgment interest against state unless specifically authorized by statute).

§12.8 n.5 p.190 In the fourth paragraph, add the following at the end: Cf. Helpin v. Trustees of the Univ. of Pa., 10 A.3d 267 (Pa. 2010) (using "total offset method" to calculate damage award for future lost earnings; payment stream not reduced to present value because "as a matter of law, the future interest rate [is] presumed to offset totally the future interest rate").

§12.8 n.8 p.192 In the first paragraph, add the following after the third sentence: Indeed, in Florida the *Flureau* approach has received much criticism even as it is still followed. *See* Shakeshober v. Fla. Resort Dev. Corp., 492 So. 2d 816 (Fla. App. 1986) (Glickstein, J., concurring) ("I fully realize that this state follows the English rule, not the American rule, but write because of the poet's admonition that we not be the last to lay the old aside. To me, the American rule is consistent with the principle of accountability inherent in our way of doing things.") (referring to Pope, Essay on Criticism 67, 74, *in* The Works of Alexander Pope (Wordsworth 1995) (1711)).

§12.8 n.23 p.196 In the second paragraph, add the following to the list after **"see generally"***:* Rowan, Reflections on the Introduction of Punitive Damages for Breach of Contract, 30 Oxford J. Legal Stud. 495 (2010).

§12.8 n.23 p.196 Add the following at the end: For a comparative perspective, *see* Calleros, Punitive Damages, Liquidated

Damages, and *Clauses Pénales* in Contract Actions: A Comparative Analysis of the American Common Law and the French Civil Code, 32 Brook. J. Int'l L. 67 (2006); McCamus, Prometheus Bound or Loose Cannon? Punitive Damages for Pure Breach of Contract in Canada, 41 San Diego L. Rev. 1491 (2004); Tettenborn, Punitive Damages: A View from England, 41 San Diego L. Rev. 1551 (2004).

***§12.8 n.25 p.196 Add the following to the list after* "Accord":** Wilson v. Vanden Berg, 687 N.W.2d 575 (Iowa 2004) ("Although a breach of contract will ordinarily not support a punitive damage award, where the breach also constitutes an intentional tort committed maliciously, punitive damages may be awarded.").

***§12.8 n.25 p.196 Add the following after the citation to* Murphy:** , contradicted without reference in Ferrisburgh Realty Investors v. Schumacher, 992 A.2d 1042 (Vt. 2010) (affirming award of punitive damages for breach of contract where jury found "malice, namely that Schumacher opposed the project [to develop a golf course, which he was contractually obliged not to oppose] out of spite after his own requests to purchase a lot were denied").

§12.8 n.26 p.197 Add the following after the first sentence: *Accord:* Mickalowski v. Am. Flooring, 972 So. 2d 703 (Miss. App. 2007) (affirming punitive damages for breach of non-compete covenant in light of promisors' "flagrant violations," including that they "deliberately engaged in a course of misconduct" and "elected to totally disregard the covenant"); Saddleridge Estates v. Ruiz, 323 S.W.3d 427 (Mo. App. 2010) (lot owners liable to developer and broker for punitive damages for breach when the owners acted with "willful or reckless disregard of Respondents' rights"; owners failed to build house when promised, did not tell developer when they sold their existing home and bought one in a nearby subdivision, did not agree to list the lot at a reasonable price, and used the lot as collateral for lines of credit, all supporting the conclusion that the owners never intended to perform under the purchase agreement but instead sought to buy the lot purely for speculative purposes); Villeneuve

v. Beane, 933 A.2d 1139 (Vt. 2007) (landlord's illegal eviction, harassment, and cutting off electricity permit punitive damages because they were "intentional, unlawful, criminal in nature, and outrageous," thus satisfying the standard of "willful and wanton or fraudulent . . . or when the evidence indicates the breaching party acted with actual malice").

§12.9 GENERAL MEASURE OF DAMAGES

§12.9 n.3 p.204 Add the following at the end: How this is calculated may cause problems. Value, though not defined in the Code, is not necessarily the same as market price; both terms are used, so one should assume they have different meanings. It thus may be that a buyer who decides to sell the undesirable goods will get more than the ordinary market price, potentially relevant because UCC 2-714(2) provides that "the measure of damages for breach of warranty is the difference at the time and place of acceptance between the value of the goods accepted and the value they would have had if they had been as warranted. . . ." In any event, a later sale is but imperfect evidence of the earlier value. For an unusual application of this, *see* Mayberry v. Volkswagen of Am., 692 N.W.2d 226 (Wis. 2005) (price on resale exceeded fair market value; this does not bar the claim, but "may be probative as to the value of the vehicle with defects at the time and place of acceptance"), discussed in Rowley et al., Sales, 61 Bus. Law. 1545 (2006). *Accord:* Shoop v. DaimlerChrysler Corp. 864 N.E.2d 785 (Ill. App. 2007) (where buyer accepted defective auto but later traded it in at the fair market value, "the application of the ordinary rule of damages for breach of warranty was not changed or modified by the fact that the purchaser had resold the article at a profit.").

§12.9 n.5 p.205 In the second paragraph, add the following at the end: *See generally* Gotanda, Awarding Damages Under the United Nations Convention on the International Sale of Goods: A Matter of Interpretation, 37 Geo. J. Int'l L. 95 (2005).

§12.9 n.6 p.206 In the first paragraph, add the following after the citation to **Mieske***:* followed in Sherman v. Kissinger, 195 P.3d 539 (Wash. App. 2008) (death of pet dog; question of fact whether a market value for pet and if pet could be replaced, with damages for intrinsic value available only if no market value and no replacement). *Accord:* Davis v. Sweeney, 31 So. 3d 1184 (La. App. 2010) ("Damages for nonpecuniary loss may be recovered when a contract, because of its nature, is intended to gratify a nonpecuniary interest and, because of the circumstances surrounding the formation or the nonperformance of the contract, the obligor knew or should have known, that his failure to perform would cause that kind of loss. . . . When damages are insusceptible of precise measurement, much discretion is left to the court for the reasonable assessment of those damages."; damages upheld for loss of use and enjoyment of ski boat); Smith v. Univ. Animal Clinic, 30 So. 3d 1154 (La. App. 2010) (same test; awarding damages where clinic mistagged pet cat, resulting in its disappearance).

§12.9 n.6 p.206 In the first paragraph, add the following to the list after **"see"***:* Luff, The Market Value Rule of Damages and the Death of Irreparable Injury, 59 Clev. St. L. Rev. 361 (2011).

§12.9 n.6 p.206 Add the following at the end of the first paragraph: Non-market value is not confined to non-economic settings. A developer who is putting together a large parcel of land for an office building would attach greater value to a necessary plot of land than would someone interested in the land for its own sake. *See* SCI Cal. Funeral Servs. v. Five Bridges Found., 137 Cal. Rptr. 3d 693 (Ct. App. 2012) (breach of contract to reconvey easement necessary to allow the buyer to develop its servient property; "Where a particular buyer has a special need for property the buyer does not presently own, the value of the property to that buyer is a factor that may be considered in determining the fair market value of the property, even if no one else shares that buyer's peculiar position," so the easement's value can be measured in part by looking at "the potential uses to which the unencumbered property could be put").

§12.9 n.8 p.207 In the third paragraph, add the following after the citation to **Firwood***:* followed in turn in Stamtec, Inc. v. Anson Stamping Co., 346 F.3d 651 (6th Cir. 2003) (salvage and interest charges paid by jobber to manufacturer were not incidental damages).

§12.9 n.8 p.207 In the fourth paragraph, add the following at the end: The recent ALI Principles of the Law of Software Contracts makes no distinction between transferors and transferees. Principles of the Law of Software Contracts §4.05 & cmt. *f* (2010).

§12.9 n.8 p.207 In the fifth paragraph, add the following after the third sentence: *But cf.* Ner Tamid Cong. v. Krivoruchko, 660 F. Supp. 2d 927 (N.D. Ill. 2009) (vendor of land may, in addition to direct damages, recover its "carrying costs" if they "were within the reasonable contemplation of the contracting parties").

§12.9 n.9 p.208 Add the following at the end of the first paragraph: *But cf. In re* Hannaford Bros. Co. Customer Data Sec. Breach Litig., 4 A.3d 492 (Me. 2010) (time and effort spent to avoid or remedy harm from fraudulent charges caused by a breach in defendant's security system not recoverable as damages; "the time and effort expended by the plaintiffs here represent 'the ordinary frustrations and inconveniences that everyone confronts in daily life.' ") (quoting from *In re* Hannaford Bros. Co. Customer Data Sec. Breach Litig., 613 F. Supp. 2d 108, 134 (D. Me. 2009)). This seems too facile a judgment. First, anyone who has had to salvage his or her credit rating after identity theft knows full well that this task goes far beyond the ordinary frustrations and inconveniences that everyone confronts. Second, suppose the time and effort expended here is the same in kind as that which one experiences routinely. So what? If the plaintiffs would otherwise not spent their time and effort on this decidedly frustrating and annoying task, they presumably would have spent it on other, more valuable endeavors. That seems a real enough loss. And just because a harm is quotidian does not make it immaterial. The constant need to clean up after children is presumably an ordinary frustration and inconvenience; certainly it is in this author's household. But if the cleaning service hired to restore one's house to more or less pristine condition instead makes it

dirtier, it presumably is in breach, and it will not do to say in defense that the dirt is just an ordinary frustration and inconvenience of daily life. Third, the court here implicitly held that the time and effort expended by the plaintiffs here has no legally cognizable value. What if they had hired credit-repair consultants to do what was necessary? Would those expenses also be unrecoverable? If not, then the court has created a perverse incentive to hand annoyance to others for a fee; if so, then it is hard to see what role incidental damages would have in breach of contract actions.

§12.9 n.10 p.208 Add the following to the list after "Accord": Mitchell Family Dev. Co. v. Universal Textile Techs., 602 S.E.2d 878 (Ga. App. 2004) (recoverable incidental damages include costs of testing goods "in order to determine how to effect cover").

§12.9 p.209 Add the following at the end of the last sentence in the first paragraph: . . . however characterized, is recoverable.[11a]

[11a] This general principle may give way when the contract has a disclaimer that covers one sort of loss but not another. For an illustration, *see* Penncro Assocs. v. Sprint Spectrum, 499 F.3d 1151 (10th Cir. 2007) (disclaimer of "consequential damages" that "include, but are not limited to, lost profits, lost revenues and lost business opportunities" did not exclude lost profits as part of direct damages). *Cf.* Tractebel Energy Mktg. v. AEP Power Mktg., 487 F.3d 89 (2d Cir. 2007) ("when the non-breaching party seeks only to recover money that the breaching party agreed to pay under the contract, the damages sought are general damages . . . The damages may still be characterized as lost profits . . . ").

§12.9 n.13 p.209 Add the following at the end of the first paragraph: Similarly, when a contractor breaches the owner's cost avoided is ordinarily the unpaid balance on the breached contract. Fire Sprinklers v. Icon Contracting, 279 S.W.3d 230 (Mo. App. 2009) (quoting from treatise).

§12.9 n.14 p.210 In the second paragraph, add the following to the list in the third sentence: Citizens Prop. Ins. Corp. v. Ashe, 50 So. 3d 645 (Fla. App. 2010) ("we are constrained by precedent to apply the collateral source rule to contract actions . . . It seems to us that the better view is that the collateral source rule should not apply in pure contract actions. We suggest it may be time to revisit this issue.") (but see strong dissent by Van Nortwick, J.).

***§12.9 n.14 p.210 In the second paragraph, add the following to the list after* "But cf.":** Ferrisburgh Realty Investors v. Schumacher, 992 A.2d 1042 (Vt. 2010) (payment from plaintiff-debtor to creditor, where damages were the creditor's loss of use of funds; although collateral source rule applies to breach of contract actions, here the payment was partial performance of contractual obligations and so would be set off).

§12.9 n.14 p.211 Add the following at the end of the fourth paragraph: A not dissimilar circumstance arises when a lawyer is hired under a contingent fee contract, commits malpractice, and is sued by his client for the lost value of his personal injury claim. The lawyer has been held able to seek reduction of those damages by the amount he would have been paid had the claim yielded that value. Horn v. Wooster, 165 P.3d 69 (Wyo. 2007). *Contra:* Akin, Gump, Strauss, Hauser & Feld v. Nat'l Dev & Res. Corp., 232 S.W.3d 883 (Tex. Civ. App. 2007) ("To give the firm a credit for a contingency fee it failed to earn would be to reward its wrongdoing."), *rev'd on other grounds*, 299 S.W.3d 106 (Tex. 2009).

§12.10 SUPPLIER'S DAMAGES

***§12.10 n.5 p.214 In the second paragraph, add the following to the list after* "see":** G.M. Harston Constr. Co. v. City of Chicago, 371 F. Supp. 2d 949 (N.D. Ill. 2005) ("The total cost method has often been described as not favored. . . . [b]ut . . . it is necessary to use that methodology when the contractor is entitled to an adjustment but cannot prove the increased costs to which it is entitled to a mathematical certainty."); City of Westminster v. Centric-Jones Constructors, 100 P.3d 472 (Colo. App. 2003) ("Recovery under this so-called 'total cost' theory is disfavored . . . and has generally been rejected unless a 'basis appears for even an educated guess as to the increased costs suffered by plaintiffs due to that particular breach or breaches [by the defendant] as distinguished from those causes from which defendant is contractually exempt from responding in damages.' ") (quoting from Lichter v. Mellon-Stuart Co., 305 F.2d 216 (3d Cir. 1962)); City of Gillette v. Hladky Constr., 196 P.3d 184 (Wyo. 2008) (total cost method "is disfavored primarily because it attributes all responsibility to the owner without establishing a clear causal connection between the owner's breach and the increased costs". . . . However, where such precise itemization is not possible, use of the total cost method is permissible if the breach substantially affected performance . . . In addition, the contractor must prove that "(1) the nature of the losses made it impossible or highly impracticable to determine them with a reasonable degree of accuracy; (2) [the contractor's] bid or estimate was realistic; (3) [the contractor's] actual costs were reasonable; and (4) [the contractor] was not responsible for the added expenses.").

§12.10 n.5 p.214 In the second paragraph, add the following after the citation to* Amelco Elec.*: , followed in Dillingham-Ray Wilson v. City of Los Angeles, 106 Cal. Rptr. 3d 691 (Ct. App. 2010) (permitting proof of modified total cost damages; cites to *Amelco Elec.* without noting its grudging acceptance of this method).

§12.10 n.5 p.214 In the second paragraph, add the following after the first sentence: A variant of this is the "measured mile" approach, which "compares the cost of completing work not subject to delay or acceleration with costs of completing work during a period of impact, the difference representing the measure of damages." James Corp. v. N. Allegheny Sch. Dist., 938 A.2d 474 (Pa. Commw. 2007). This differs from the total cost method in that it compares actual cost with a hypothetical cost derived from normal performance, while the total cost method compares actual cost with the estimated cost under the actual contract. The measured mile approach thus does not assume that all inefficiencies were caused by the owner's breach. *See* Ibbs & Liu, Improved Measured Mile Analysis Technique, 131 J. Constr. Eng'g & Mgmt. 1249 (2005).

§12.10 n.7 p.215 Add the following to the list after* "Accord"*: Sea Byte v. Hudson Marine Mgmt. Servs., 565 F.3d 1293 (11th Cir. 2009) (federal maritime law: to calculate damages for partial completion of reef restoration, court is "to determine what percentage of the project's value Hudson provided under the contract as of [the date of breach], and multiply that percentage by the contract price").

§12.10 n.7 p.215 Add the following at the end: For a whimsical return to the nineteenth-century approach of *Kehoe,* see Restatement (Third) of Restitution and Unjust Enrichment §38 and ill. 6 (Tent. Draft No. 3, Mar. 22, 2004).

§12.10 n.10 p.216 In the second paragraph, add the following to the list after* "Accord"*: Piroschak v. Whelan, 106 P.3d 887 (Wyo. 2005) ("Although a subsequent sale of the same property may be evidence of market value, it is not conclusive, but rather the price received is only evidence of value and not the measure of damage."). White v. Farrell, 20 N.Y.3d 487, 495; 987 N.E.2d 244, 249 (2013) (adopting the time of breach rule, collecting cases, and noting that "[t]he four departments of the Appellate Division, however, have consistently endorsed the time-of-the-breach rule, although there are certainly cases where the standard used is not stated, or it is not made clear that the resale price is simply evidence of the property's fair market value at the time of the breach.").

§12.10 n.17 p.218 Add the following at the end of the second paragraph: *Accord:* Bitterroot Int'l Sys. v. W. Star Trucks, 153 P.3d 627 (Mont. 2007) (adopting for all contracts Harris approach to lost-volume sales as "neither new, nor novel"). *Cf.* Chicago Title Ins. Corp. v. Magnuson, 487 F.3d 985 (6th Cir. 2007) ("In order to qualify as a lost volume seller, Chicago Title must prove that it had access to sufficient supply to make both sales and that it would have completed the additional sale even if it made the first sale."); PurCo Fleet Servs. v. Koenig, 240 P.3d 435 (Colo. App. 2010) ("in order to recover damages for loss of use of a commercial chattel that is normally rented out for profit, its owner must demonstrate that it lost the opportunity to earn income from the chattel"; particularly thoughtful analysis).

An interesting variation on this theme arose in Sci. Components Corp. v. ISIS Surface Mounting, 539 F. Supp. 2d 653 (E.D.N.Y. 2008). There the seller provided electronic components to a subcontractor for an equipment manufacturer. The subcontract repudiated its contract because it no longer received orders from the general contractor. The seller resold the components to two other subcontractors, who used the components to manufacture what the original buyer had been under contract to manufacture. The court held that the seller lost no volume, because the later buyers "entered the picture not as additional purchasers to whom [the seller] also intended to make sales, but rather as substitutes for ISIS."

***§12.10 n.22 p.220 Add the following to the list after* "Accord":** Bitterroot Int'l Sys. v. W. Star Trucks, *supra* note 17 (because freight hauler established a high growth rate and the ability to contract with other haulers to handle excess volume, hauler was a lost volume seller).

***§12.10 n.22 p.220 In the second paragraph, add the following to the list after* "see":** Schwartz, Price Discrimination with Contract Terms: The Lost-Volume Problem, 12 Am. L. & Econ. Rev. 394 (2010).

§12.10 n.22 p.220 Add the following to the end of the second paragraph: *Cf.* Collins Entm't Corp. v. Coats & Coats Rental Amusement, 629 S.E.2d 635 (S.C. 2006) (recognizing lost volume lessor approach in UCC 2A-528(2); applying Harris test, *supra* note 17).

§12.10 n.24 p.222 Add the following to the end of the first paragraph: For a useful overview of different types of overhead and how they fit within the law of damages, see Kan. Gas & Elec. Co. v. United States, 95 Fed. Cl. 257 (2010), *aff'd* in part, rev'd in part, 685 F.3d 1361 (Fed. Cir. 2012).

§12.10 n.24 p.222 In the second paragraph, add the following after the second sentence: The formula has its roots in Eichleay Corp., ASBCA No. 5183, 60-2 BCA 2688, *aff'd on reconsideration*, 61-1 BCA 2894. First one determines the pro rata share of the contractor's total overhead allocable to the delayed contract. This is converted to an amount per day for the job as a whole. This daily figure is then multiplied by the number of days of delay caused by the breach.

***§12.10 n.24 p.222 In the second paragraph, add the following to the list after* "See":** Wickham Constr. Co. v. Fischer, 12 F.3d 1574 (Fed. Cir. 1994) (*Eichleay* formula is the exclusive means for calculating unabsorbed overhead costs on federal construction contracts), followed in Martin Cnty. v. Polivka Paving, 44 So. 3d 126 (Fla. App. 2010) (denying recovery for home office overhead incurred during an extended time for performance caused by county's faulty description of site; no suspension of work as required under *Eichleay* and its progeny, and in any case no portion of the home-office overhead could be directly attributed to the contract in question).

***§12.10 n.24 p.222 In the second paragraph, add the following after the citation to* Fairfax County Redev. & Hous. Auth.:** , followed in Commonwealth v. AMEC Civil, 699 S.E.2d 499 (Va. 2010) (contractor "did not meet its burden of proving that it could not reasonably recoup its home office overhead from other revenue-producing work"; model presented by contractor assumed this, and no independent evidence introduced).

§12.11 RECIPIENT'S DAMAGES

§12.11 n.4 p.224 In the first paragraph, add the following to the list in the second sentence: Midwest Hatchery & Poultry Farms v. Doorenbos Poultry, 783 N.W.2d 56 (Iowa App. 2010) (measuring damages for purchase of immature hens by estimating the net profits lost because of their time to maturity).

§12.11 n.4 p.224 Add the following at the end of the first paragraph: For a thoughtful application of this principle to the sale of real property, in particular when the property is subject to an encumbrance, see Loveland Essential Grp. v. Grommon Farms, 251 P.3d 1109 (Colo. App. 2010) (vendor breached warranty that property free from encumbrances; "[I]n the event of a breach of this covenant, where the purchaser has paid to remove an encumbrance or has the right to do so unilaterally, the necessary reasonable expense to cure the defect (not exceeding the amount the purchaser paid the covenantor for the property) is the proper measure of damages. But in the absence of such expense . . . the measure of damages is the diminution in the property's fair market value caused by the encumbrance's existence (again, not to exceed the purchase price). . . . [W]here the encumbrance at issue is a lease, the difference between the fair rental value and the rent under the lease, if any, may represent the diminution in the property's value where the lease is consistent with the highest and best use of the property. In such cases, this measure truly represents the loss in value. But where the existence of a lease precludes development of a property for some more profitable use . . . this measure may not adequately compensate the buyer for the loss in value. In these cases, the loss in value will be the difference between the fair market value of the property with the encumbrance and the fair market value without it.") (citations omitted).

§12.11 n.5 p.224 In the second paragraph, add the following at the end: *Accord:* 1st Fed. Lincoln Bank v. United States, 518 F.3d 1308 (Fed. Cir. 2008) ("The market value of income-generating property reflects the market's estimate of the present value of the chance to earn future income, discounted by the market's view of the lower future value of the income and the uncertainty of the occurrence and amount of any future [income]."); Schonfeld v. Hilliard, 218 F.3d 164 (2d Cir. 2000) ("When the defendant's conduct results in the loss of an income-producing asset with an ascertainable market value, the most accurate and immediate measure of damages is the market value of the asset at the time of breach-not the lost profits that the asset could have produced in the future.").

§12.11 n.9 p.226 Add the following to the list after* "But see"*: Capitol Justice v. Wachovia Bank, 706 F. Supp. 2d 23 (D.D.C. 2009) (where lender breached loan commitment agreement, damages are "the difference between the contract interest rate and the rate available at breach and any damages that were foreseeable at the time [] the contract was executed").

§12.11 n.11 p.226 Add the following to the list after "Accord": Elliott v. Normand, 976 So. 2d 738 (La. App. 2008) ("the trial judge abused his discretion in awarding $20,000 as new engines to replace the original engines that needed to be rebuilt").

§12.11 n.11 p.226 Add the following to the list after "Cf.": City of Westminster v. Centric-Jones Constructors, 100 P.3d 472 (Colo. App. 2003) ("[W]here the plaintiff's own evidence of damages includes advantage beyond the benefit of the bargain, the plaintiff must present more than an unitemized total cost of replacement.").

§12.11 n.12 p.227 Add the following after the citation to Chronister Oil: , in turn followed by Medinol Ltd. v. Boston Scientific Corp., 346 F. Supp. 2d 575 (S.D.N.Y. 2004) (setting up own manufacturing line not cover; "Proper cover . . . is effectuated through the 'purchase of or [through a] contract to purchase goods in substitution for those due from the seller,' not through procuring for oneself an alternative source of supply.").

§12.11 n.19 p.229 Add the following at the end: *But cf.* Nycomed US v. Abbott Labs., 542 F.3d 1129 (7th Cir. 2008) (buyer used defective goods to manufacture product, which had to be destroyed and replaced; buyer did so without losing sales, so was entitled to only the profit it would have received on the original sale, plus the cost of making the destroyed product, the cost of destroying that product, and the costs of making the replacement product, including overtime and other extraordinary costs).

§12.12 AVOIDABILITY AS A LIMITATION

§12.12 n.2 p.229 In the second paragraph, add the following after the fifth sentence: *Accord:* Brennan Assocs. v. OBGYN Specialty Grp., 15 A.3d 1094 (Conn. App. 2011) (lessor of commercial property need not mitigate in ordinary action for rent, but mitigation does arise when the lessor manifests an intent to terminate the tenancy); Allen v. Harkness Stone Co., 609 S.E.2d

647 (Ga. App. 2004) ("if a tenant abandons leased premises without authorization prior to the expiration of the term, the landlord is not required to mitigate damages by re-letting the premises" . . . but "[t]his rule applies . . . only if the landlord refuses to accept the tenant's offer of surrender and the lease remains in full force."), followed in Sirdah v. N. Springs Assocs., 696 S.E.2d 391 (Ga. App. 2010) ("The mere taking of keys to the leased premises by a landlord does not give rise to an inference that the landlord accepted surrender of the premises"; where the letter accepting the keys stated that the landlord was not terminating the lease, "North Springs neither expressly nor impliedly accepted Sirdah's surrender of the leased premises; rather, Sirdah unilaterally abandoned the premises"); Rios v. Carrillo, 861 N.Y.S.2d 129 (App. Div. 2008) ("a residential landlord is under no duty to mitigate damages where the terms of the lease do not indicate otherwise"); Sylva Shops Ltd. P'ship v. Hibbard, 623 S.E.2d 785 (N.C. App. 2006) ("If a party may . . . contract to insulate itself from liability for a failure to exercise due care, we can perceive no basis for precluding a party from contracting to relieve itself from a duty of due care to minimize its damages." . . . but "such a clause in a residential lease . . . presents an entirely different situation"); Arrowhead Ridge I, LLC v. Cold Stone Creamery, 800 N.W.2d 730 (S.D. 2011) ("Only a handful of states have explicitly retained the common-law rule that a landlord has no duty to mitigate damages."; suggesting that South Dakota would extend mitigation to landlords, but finding that unnecessary to reach because the lease expressly provided an obligation on the part of the landlord to mitigate its damages); Hoppenstein Properties v. Schober, 329 S.W.3d 846 (Tex. Civ. App. 2010) ("A landlord has a duty to make reasonable efforts to mitigate damages when the tenant breaches the lease and abandons the property"). *Cf.* Cleveland Motor Cars v. Bank of Am., 670 S.E.2d 892 (Ga. App. 2008) (validating contractual waiver of mitigation by bank in loan purchase agreement). *But cf.* Summers v. Crestview Apartments, 236 P.3d 586 (Mont. 2010) ("An accelerated rent provision in a lease agreement undermines a landlord's duty to mitigate damages" as a matter of law; because this provision was part of a contract of adhesion, it is both substantively and procedurally unconscionable and is therefore unenforceable).

§12.12 n.3 p.230 Add the following after the citation to **Travelers Indem. Co.***:* , followed by APL Co. v. Blue Water Shipping U.S., 592 F.3d 108 (2d Cir. 2010) ("[A]s the breaching party, Blue Water was not entitled simply to shift any expenses or costs associated with the cargo disposal delay to APL. If Blue Water had the same opportunity to avoid such costs, it had an obligation to do so.").

§12.12 n.6 p.231 Add the following at the end of the first sentence: , followed in Ner Tamid Cong. v. Krivoruchko, 638 F. Supp. 2d 913 (N.D. Ill. 2009) ("While the defense is often couched in the language of obligation, the formulation is somewhat misleading, because the plaintiff incurs no liability for his failure to act. Rather, the amount of loss that could reasonably have been avoided by stopping performance or making substitute arrangements is simply subtracted from the amount that would otherwise have been recoverable as damages.").

§12.12 n.8 p.231 In the first paragraph, add the following to the list after **"Accord"***:* LaSalle Bank Nat'l Ass'n v. Nomura Asset Capital Corp., 899 N.Y.S.2d 15 (App. Div. 2010) ("defendants had the burden of establishing not only that plaintiff failed to make diligent efforts to mitigate, but also the extent to which such efforts would have diminished plaintiff's damages"); Hoppenstein Props. v. Schober, 329 S.W.3d 846 (Tex. Civ. App. 2010) ("A tenant's assertion that a landlord failed to mitigate damages is an affirmative defense. Thus, the tenant properly bears the burden of proof to demonstrate that the landlord has failed to mitigate damages and the amount by which the landlord could have reduced its damages.").

§12.12 n.8 p.231 In the second paragraph, add the following to the list after **"see"***:* Prusky v. ReliaStar Life Ins. Co., 532 F.3d 252 (3d Cir. 2008) (determination that the plaintiffs "did not adequately mitigate losses and that reasonable efforts would have reduced their damages are findings of fact reviewed for clear error").

§12.12 n.10 p.232 Add the following to the list in the first sentence of the second paragraph: Ner Tamid Cong. v. Krivoruchko, *supra* note 6 ("a duty to mitigate damages does not arise until the plaintiff learns of the other party's breach of the underlying contract"); Orbisonia-Rockhill Joint Mun. Auth. v. Cromwell Township, 978 A.2d 425 (Pa. Commw. 2009) ("It is not until a breach of contract occurs . . . that a party is required to mitigate damages.").

§12.12 n.10 p.232 Add the following after the first sentence of the second paragraph: On the other hand, one may recover pre-breach damages incurred in anticipation of mitigation, though in doing so one must meet the usual requirements of "foreseeability, causation, and reasonableness." Ind. Mich. Power Co. v. United States, 422 F.3d 1369 (Fed. Cir. 2005).

§12.12 n.14 p.232 Add the following to the list after* "Accord"*: Prusky v. ReliaStar Life Ins. Co., *supra* note 6 (after breach of investment contract, "a reasonable substitute must be one with a similar risk-reward profile to that of the opportunity lost as a result of the breach," so putting funds hitherto invested in equities into money market accounts was a failure to mitigate); Simmons v. Erie Ins. Exch., 891 N.E.2d 1059 (Ind. App. 2008) (personal injury claim against insurer; applies reasonable person test to whether insured should have to submit to surgery in order to mitigate damages, taking into account "(1) the likelihood that the surgery will correct or improve the condition; (2) the risk involved in the surgery; (3) the pain or inconvenience caused by the surgery; and (4) the ability of the plaintiff to bear the cost of the surgery"); Orbisonia-Rockhill Joint Mun. Auth. v. Cromwell Township, *supra* note 10 (expenses incurred reasonable even though "there was much uncertainty as to the joint project," where incurred in good faith); Arrowhead Ridge I, LLC v. Cold Stone Creamery, 800 N.W.2d 730 (S.D. 2011) (unreasonable to expect landlord to mitigate damages caused by a tenant's breach by leasing the space to a tenant whose occupancy would breach an exclusivity provision in another lease).

§12.12 n.14 p.232 Add the following after the citation to **Yang Ming Marine***:* , followed in A.P. Moller-Maersk A/S v. Taiwan Glass USA Sales Corp., 663 F. Supp. 2d 1011 (D. Or. 2009) (expenditure of $90,000 for used shipping containers substantial in light of the $151,850 sought in late fees).

§12.12 n.15 p.233 Add the following to the list after **"Accord"***:* Ind. Mich. Power Co. v. United States, *supra* note 10 ("Mitigation is appropriate where a reasonable person, in light of the known facts and circumstances, would have taken steps to avoid damage." Therefore, the breached-against party is "'not precluded from recovery . . . to the extent that [it] has made reasonable but unsuccessful efforts to avoid loss.'") (quoting from Restatement Second §350(2)).

§12.12 n.16 p.234 Add the following after the citation to **Luten Bridge***:* , placed in historical context by Richman, Weinstock & Mehta, A Bridge, a Tax Revolt, and the Struggle to Industrialize: The Story and Legacy of *Rockingham County v. Luten Bridge Co.*, 84 N.C.L. Rev. 1841 (2006).

§12.12 n.20 p.235 Add the following to the list after **"Accord"***:* Performance Mach. Co. v. Yellowstone Mountain Club, 169 P.3d 394 (Mont. 2007) (lessor should have mitigated by repairing or replacing damaged truck returned by lessee; "Performance cannot simply choose not to repair or replace the truck and then collect rent in perpetuity").

§12.12 n.21 p.235 Add the following at the end: Cf. Morehouse Coll. v. McGaha, 627 S.E.2d 39 (Ga. App. 2005) (wrongful expulsion from college; "Because McGaha is obligated to mitigate his damages by returning to school and obtaining a degree, and no evidence was presented that he is unable to do so, it appears that McGaha cannot recover lost wages beyond the time necessary for him to complete his degree.").

§12.12 n.23 p.236 Add the following at the end of the first paragraph: A similar situation applies for sales of goods. Under UCC 2-709(2), if the aggrieved seller sues for the price it must hold the goods for the buyer and, if resale is possible, it *may* resell

them before it collects on the judgment, with the net proceeds to be credited to the buyer. The courts have held that the seller's decision whether to resell is wholly discretionary, untrammeled by the usual concerns about mitigation. *See* Far East Servs. Corp. v. Tracker Marine, 246 S.W.3d 486 (Mo. App. 2007). Mitigation is not a worry here, however, because of the situations in which UCC 2-709(2) might be applied. UCC 2-709(1) provides these — namely, if the buyer has accepted the goods, if conforming goods have been lost or damaged after the risk of loss has passed to the buyer, and if the seller is either unable to resell the goods at a reasonable price or the circumstances indicate that it will not be able to do so. In the first case, the buyer will usually possess the goods. In the second, the goods have been destroyed or damaged, so resale is ordinarily not an option. In the third, the goods have already proved unsalable at a reasonable price. What is left are cases of wrongful revocations of acceptance, salvage sales of damaged goods, and sales of conforming but ordinarily unsalable goods at steep discounts. It is hard to muster much sympathy for the breaching buyer in any of these instances. At some point the buyer must take responsibility for the goods. At that point, the seller's damages should be unaffected by whether it mitigates.

§12.12 n.24 p.236 Add the following to the list after "Accord": Bonidy v. Vail Valley Ctr. for Aesthetic Dentistry, 232 P.3d 277 (Colo. App. 2010) (wrongfully terminated employee may pursue self-employment if that constitutes reasonable diligence, in which case "the aggregate economic gain . . . constitutes the offset against the employee's back pay damages award"; collecting cases on what triggers the termination of the back pay period); Air Line Pilots Ass'n v. Trans States Airlines, 692 F. Supp. 2d 1105 (E.D. Mo. 2010) (search need only be reasonable, and may be satisfied by self-employment; here, unfairly discharged pilot operated his own business and did not seek alternative employment as a pilot because he reasonably believed that such a search would be unavailing); Alamo Cmty. Coll. Dist. v. Miller, 274 S.W.3d 779 (Tex. Civ. App. 2008) ("[A] wrongfully discharged employee must exercise reasonable diligence to mitigate damages by pursuing other employment . . . or else the employee is barred from recovering those damages that could have been avoided. . . . The duty to mitigate damages arises only if it can be done with 'trifling expense or with reasonable exertions' "; here, discharged employee "did not actively seek any employment opportunities," and thus failed to mitigate).

§12.12 n.25 p.236 Add the following after the first sentence: *Cf.* Al's Serv. Ctr. v. BP Prods. N. Am., 599 F.3d 720 (7th Cir. 2010) (Posner, J.) (franchisee's claim that franchisor terminated its franchise potentially barred because the franchisee failed to try to enforce an injunction against the franchisor; cites to hornbook).

§12.12 n.27 p.237 In the second paragraphs, add the following to the list after* "see"*: Hess Energy v. Lightning Oil Co., 338 F.3d 357 (4th Cir. 2003) ("better reading . . . is that an aggrieved buyer's damages against a repudiating seller are based on the market price on the date of performance").

§12.12 n.32 p.239 Add the following to the list after* "Accord"*: Ner Tamid Cong. v. Krivoruchko, 660 F. Supp. 2d 927 (N.D. Ill. 2009) (referring to "the rather hoary, undisputed principle of Illinois law that the measure of damages in a case involving breach of contract to purchase land is the difference between the fair market value at the time of the breach and the contract price").

§12.12 n.33 p.239 Add the following at the end: *Cf.* Lindon v. Dalton Hotel Corp., 49 So. 3d 299 (Fla. App. 2010) (where close corporation wrongfully redeemed shares belonging to a former employee, the date for fixing damages is not necessarily the time of breach, which effectively would affirm the wrongful redemption; rather, the owner may prove "that (a) if the stock had not been wrongfully redeemed, [the owner] would have tendered it for sale in accordance with [the shareholder agreement] on a date certain and the value of the stock on that date; (b) if the stock had not been wrongfully redeemed, [the owner] would have retained the stock until [the main shareholder] disposed of his shares and the value of the stock on that date, or (c) if the stock no longer exists (or the business has been sold), evidence of the proceeds ultimately received for the stock by [the principal shareholder or the employer]").

§12.12 n.34 p.240 In the second paragraph, add the following after the second sentence: *Accord:* Kuish v. Smith, 105 Cal. Rptr. 3d 475 (Ct. App. 2010) (where seller of real property profited on resale, its rights to retain the buyer's deposit would be reduced dollar for dollar by the amount of the profit).

§12.12 n.34 p.240 In the third paragraph, add the following to the list in the final sentence: Doral Steel v. Gray Metal Prods., 672 F. Supp. 2d 798 (N.D. Ohio 2009) (calculates market price at end of October in volatile market by taking the mean of the overall prices for October and November).

§12.12 n.37 p.241 Add the following at the end: *But see* Ind. Mich. Power Co. v. United States, *supra* note 10 (if the plaintiff is faced with a partial breach or chooses to treat a total breach as a partial breach, "he is entitled to maintain an action for damages sustained from breaches up to the time of the institution of the action, and the judgment does not preclude a further action by him for a breach occurring after that date") (quoting from Restatement Second of Judgments §26 cmt. *g*).

§12.12 n.40 p.242 Add the following to the second paragraph: *Allied Canners* has been criticized in V. Goldberg, Framing Contract Law ch. 11 (2006).

§12.12 n.41 p.242 Add the following at the end of the first paragraph: *See generally* V. Goldberg, Framing Contract Law ch. 11 (2006) (supporting the *Tongish* approach).

§12.12 n.44 p.244 Add the following after the citation to **Parker*:*** , criticized in V. Goldberg, Framing Contract Law ch. 15 (2006).

§12.12 n.44 p.244 Add the following to the list after **"Accord"*:*** Cromwell v. Victor Sch. Dist., 140 P.3d 487 (Mont. 2006) (job requiring a seventy-mile roundtrip not appropriate substitute; "The law does not require a wrongfully terminated employee to move to another locality to find employment.").

§12.12 n.46 p.244 Add the following after the second sentence of the first paragraph: *Contra:* DeRosier v. Utility Sy. of Am., 780 N.W.2d 1 (Minn. App. 2010) (surveying cases; "when one party to the contract defectively performs and subsequently offers to correct the breach through a new contract, the non-breaching party may generally decline the offer and still recover its full damages").

§12.12 n.46 p.244 Add the following after the first paragraph: It is not clear why a breaching party should be able to offer a less favorable contract as mitigation and get off without liability if the breached-against party rebels. The breached-against party would have to pay more and then sue to get the extra payment back, or accept less and then sue to get the amount due. This effectively requires the breached-against party to subsidize the breaching party's litigation costs. Consider, in contrast, the salutary rise of the constructive condition concurrent as a means of avoiding the early requirement that a breached-against party perform in full before it could sue for damages. Consider as well the role of fault. Although contract is commonly thought to embody strict liability, that does not accurately describe a significant group of cases, nor is it entirely consistent with many of the philosophical bases for contracting. *See generally* Symposium, Fault in American Contract Law, 107 Mich. L. Rev. 1341 (2009). The law might therefore eliminate the breached-against party's vulnerability to a less favorable offer by the breaching party, or at the least put the burden on the breaching party to show that its offer is in good faith and is not willful.

§12.12 n.47 p.245 Add the following after the citation to **Coppola***:* , followed in Ner Tamid Cong. v. Krivoruchko, *supra* note 6 (seller not expected to finance purchase of land when original transaction was for cash).

§12.13 AVOIDABILITY AND COST TO REMEDY DEFECT

§12.13 n.3 p.248 Add the following to the list after "Accord": State *ex rel.* Stovall v. Reliance Ins. So., 107 P.3d 1219 (Kan. 2005) (damages to which state was entitled for contractor's failure to install piping system for prison was cost to replace system with working system though this would be more expensive because prison was then occupied); Elkin v. Urarn Assocs., 899 N.Y.S.2d 312 (App. Div. 2010) (giving cost-to-cure damages rather than diminution in value damages where without completion of the extension of water to a building lot the lot "would essentially be valueless").

§12.13 n.4 p.249 Add the following after the first sentence: For discussion of *Jacob & Youngs,* see R. Danzig & G. Watson, The Capability Problem in Contract Law 95-118 (2d ed. 2004).

§12.13 n.5 p.250 Add the following at the end: For an American case using reasonableness, *see* Traco Steel Erectors v. Comtrol, Inc., 222 P.3d 1164 (Utah 2009) (affirming decision "taking into account the actual costs incurred to Comtrol with any evidence suggesting the actual costs presented were not reasonable").

§12.13 n.6 p.250 In the first paragraph, add the following to the list after "See": Glasstech, Inc. v. Chicago Blower Corp., 675 F. Supp. 2d 752 (N.D. Ohio 2009) (for accepted but nonconforming goods, "to make it whole, Glasstech is entitled to repair costs for fans that were not fully destroyed, or full replacement costs for fans that cannot be repaired"); John Thurmond & Assocs. v. Kennedy, 668 S.E.2d 666 (Ga. 2008) ("[D]amages for defective construction . . . are determined by measuring the cost of repairing or restoring the damage, unless the cost of repair is disproportionate to the property's probable loss of value.") (citing Restatement Second §348); Lewis Elec. Co. v. Miller, 791 N.W.2d 691 (Iowa 2010) (following Restatement Second §§347 & 348; where contractor did not substantially perform, recovery limited to unpaid contract price less the cost of completion or repair and other damages suffered by the owner, these not to exceed the benefit received by the owner); St. Louis, LLC v. Final Touch Glass &

Mirror, 899 A.2d 1018 (N.J. Super. App. Div. 2006) ("Damages for defective construction . . . are often determined by using the reasonable cost of remedying the defects unless that cost is clearly disproportionate to the property's probable loss in value."); GSB Contractors, Inc. v. Hess, 179 S.W.3d 535 (Tenn. App. 2005) ("the measure of damages will be the cost o[f] repair unless the repairs are not feasible or the cost is disproportionate to the diminution [sic] in value").

§12.13 n.6 p.250 Add the following at the end of the first paragraph: These measures sometimes may not be mutually exclusive. *See* John Thurmond & Assocs. v. Kennedy, *supra* ("Although unusual, it may sometimes be appropriate, in order to make the injured party whole, to award a combination of both measures of damages. In such cases, notwithstanding remedial measures undertaken by the injured party, there remains a diminution in value of the property, and an award of only the costs of remedying the defects will not fully compensate the injured party.").

***§12.13 n.6 p.250 In the second paragraph, add the following to the list after* "see":** John Thurmond & Assocs. v. Kennedy, *supra* "[T]he defendant has the burden to present any contradictory evidence challenging the reasonableness or proportionality of those damages and where appropriate, evidence of an alternative measure of damages . . ."); Cason v. King, 327 S.W.3d 543 (Mo. App. 2010) ("Plaintiffs were not obligated to present any evidence of diminution in value unless and until Defendant presented evidence that the cost of repairing or replacing the property [was] disproportionate to the diminution in value of the property") (internal quotation omitted); GSB Contractors, Inc. v. Hess, *supra* ("the defendant . . . had the burden of showing 'the difference between the value of the defective structure and that of the structure if properly completed' ") (quoting from Edenfield v. Woodlawn Manor, 462 S.W.2d 237 (Tenn. App. 1970)).

§12.13 n.6 p.250 Add the following after the third paragraph: *Cf.* Irmscher Suppliers v. Schuler, 909 N.E.2d 1040 (Ind. App. 2009) (limiting damages for defective windows to difference between contract price and salvage value; replacement cost was higher because replacement windows were better quality; court did not address the possibility of making money allowance for different quality).

§12.13 n.6 p.250 In the fourth paragraph, add the following to the list after **"See generally"***:* Schwartz & Scott, Market Damages, Efficient Contracting, and the Economic Waste Fallacy, 108 Colum. L. Rev. 1610 (2008); Wirtz, Cost of Performance or Difference in Value?, 59 Case W. Reserve L. Rev. 61 (2008).

§12.13 n.8 p.251 Add the following to the list after **"Accord"***:* O & G Indus. v. All Phase Enters., 963 A.2d 676 (Conn. App. 2009) (awarding cost of superior rubber roof instead of steel roof provided for in contract, where defects in steel roof installed would have required tearing down old roof; "[t]earing down the roof to start over . . . would have been economic waste . . . Quite simply, installing the rubber membrane was not an impermissible betterment. Rather, it was a reasonable and cost-effective way to remedy the defect in time for the upcoming hockey season.").

§12.13 n.9 p.251 Add the following at the end: For other unwelcome revivals of this term, *see* Naples v. Keystone Bldg. & Dev. Corp., 990 A.2d 326 (Conn. 2010) ("'For a breach of a construction contract involving defective or unfinished construction, damages are measured by computing either (i) the reasonable cost of construction and completion in accordance with the contract, if this is possible and does not involve unreasonable economic waste; or (ii) the difference between the value that the product contracted for would have had and the value of the performance that has been received by the plaintiff, if construction and completion in accordance with the contract would involve unreasonable economic waste.'") (quoting from Levesque v. D & M Builders, 365 A.2d 1216 (Conn. 1976)); Heine v. Parent Constr., 4 So. 3d 790 (Fla. App. 2009) (following first Restatement; giving diminution in value damages where house built at wrong elevation, because cost of tearing down and rebuilding house was $930,000 and lost value was $25,000); Stom v. St. Clair Corp., 153 S.W.3d 360 (Mo. App. 2005) ("when the cost of repair or replacement would constitute an economic waste, then the

proper measure of damages is the diminished value of the property because of the defective work"); Elkin v. Urarn Assocs., 899 N.Y.S.2d 312 (App. Div. 2010) (because building lot would be valueless without water service, cost of rendering service functional "did not constitute economic waste"). *See generally* Daniel & Marshall, Avoiding Economic Waste in Contract Damages: Myths, Misunderstanding, and Malcontent, 85 Neb. L. Rev. 875 (2007).

§12.13 n.17 p.254 Add the following after the second sentence: *See generally* Symposium, Fault in American Contract Law, 107 Mich. L. Rev. 1341 (2009).

§12.14 UNFORESEEABILITY AS A LIMITATION

§12.14 n.3 p.256 In the second paragraph, add the following after the citation to* Danzig*: , revised and reprinted in R. Danzig & G. Watson, The Capability Problem in Contract Law 48-94 (2d ed. 2004)

§12.14 n.3 p.256 In the second paragraph, add the following after the third sentence: Indeed, some American decisions well before *Hadley* had stated something approaching the *Hadley* rule. *See* McAlpin v. Lee, 12 Conn. 129 (1837) (claim for lost profits on resale by aggrieved buyer: "[W]e do not think the defendant would have been responsible for any collateral loss or damage not naturally resulting from the breach of contract complained of."); Masterson & Smith v. Mayor of Brooklyn, 7 Hill 61 (N.Y. Sup. Ct. 1845) (distinguishing between "profits or advantages which are the direct and immediate fruits of the contract entered into between the parties," which are readily recoverable, and profits from collateral engagements, which are not: "Besides the uncertain and contingent issue of such an operation in itself considered, it has no legal or necessary connection with the stipulations between the parties, and cannot therefore be presumed to have entered into their consideration at the time of contracting.").

§12.14 n.3 p.256 In the third paragraph, add the following to the list after* "See generally"*: Geis, Empirically Assessing *Hadley v. Baxendale*, 32 Fla. St. U.L. Rev. 897 (2005); Tettenborn,

Consequential Damages in Contract — The Poor Relation?, 42 Loy. L.A. L. Rev. 177 (2008).

§12.14 n.4 p.256 Add the following at the end: These damages are commonly called *direct* damages. *See, e.g.*, Kraft Foods N. Am. v. Banner Eng'g & Sales, 446 F. Supp. 551 (E.D. Va. 2006) (referring to direct and consequential damages, the former deriving from UCC 2-714(1), the latter from UCC 2-715(2)).

§12.14 n.5 p.257 In the first paragraph, add the following after the first sentence: Although lost profits may be quintessential consequential damages, lost profits are not necessarily consequential damages. If, for example, a buyer purchases goods for resale, the lost profit and the lost value may be identical. Thus a contractual exclusion of consequential damages will not bar recovery of lost profits as direct damages. *See* T.Co Metals v. Dempsey Pipe & Supply, 592 F.3d 329 (2d Cir. 2010) ("[A] buyer may recover the diminution in the value of the contractual goods as warranted even when there is a contractual exclusion of consequential damages"; as a result, benefit-of-the-bargain damages under UCC 2-714 are recoverable even though consequential damages under UCC 2-715(2) are not.).

§12.14 n.5 p.257 In the first paragraph, add the following after the second sentence: *See* Hoang v. Hewitt Ave. Assocs., 936 A.2d 915 (Md. App. 2007) (employing general and special terminology).

§12.14 n.5 p.257 Add the following at the end of the first paragraph: For an application of the general/special distinction in both the realm of pleading and the realm of damages, see DeRosier v. Utility Sys. of Am., 780 N.W.2d 1 (Minn. App. 2010).

§12.14 n.5 p.257 Add the following after the first paragraph: In damages more than in most parts of contract law, misleading vocabulary can impede analysis. Consider, for example, the court that distinguished among "three types of damages — actual, consequential, and benefit-of-the-bargain." Actual damages were the "loss or injury sustained as a direct result of the wrongful act." Consequential damages encompassed *both Hadley* rules. Benefit-of-the-bargain damages are "also called lost profits damages." It is hard to see how these overlapping and oddly defined terms advance the law in the slightest, and easy to see how they could obscure otherwise clear damages calculations. Catroppa v. Metal Bldg. Supply, 267 S.W.3d 812 (Mo. App. 2008), followed, alas, in Cason v. King, 327 S.W.3d 543 (Mo. App. 2010) (using *Catroppa*'s definitions of actual and consequential damages, but largely ignoring them in its actual analysis).

§12.14 n.8 p.258 Add the following at the end: It may be that the reign of *Hadley v. Baxendale*, at least in the rest of the common-law world, is coming to a close. In *Transfield Shipping v. Mercator Shipping [The Achilleas]*, the House of Lords set forth a new test for determining when damages for breach of contract are too remote to be recovered. [2008] UKHL 48, [2009] 1 A.C. 61 (appeal taken from Eng.) (U.K.). The *seriatim* opinions do not agree on any precise phrasing, but the lords in the majority set out somewhat similar language. Lord Hoffmann put it as "what would reasonably have been regarded by the contracting party as significant for the purposes of the risk he was undertaking." Transfield Shipping v. Mercator Shipping [The Achilleas], [2008] UKHL 48, [2009] 1 A.C. 61 [22] (appeal taken from Eng.) (U.K.). Lord Hope stated that the "question is whether the loss was a type of loss for which the party can be reasonably assumed to have assumed responsibility." Transfield Shipping v. Mercator Shipping [The Achilleas], [2008] UKHL 48, [2009] 1 A.C. 61 [32] (appeal taken from Eng.) (U.K.). Finally, Lord Walker put it in terms of the "need for the loss suffered to be within the horizon of the parties' contemplation," adding that "what is most important is the common expectation, objectively assessed, on the basis of which the parties are entering into their contract." Transfield Shipping v. Mercator Shipping [The Achilleas], [2008] UKHL 48, [2009] 1 A.C. 61 [78] (appeal taken from Eng.) (U.K.). Courts around the world have been puzzling over the opinions in *The Achilleas*, hoping to distill from them a single test that they can apply predictably. So far there has been no consensus. This U.S. lawyer initially read the opinions as reviving the old tacit agreement test, which one would have thought safely interred. On further reflection, the opinions seem on balance to favor something on the whole less stringent than the tacit agreement test. Whether a term is within the common expectation of the parties or is one as to which there was an assumption of responsibility encompasses not just what was fairly within the parties' contemplation, but what the parties would have considered significant *ex ante*. It remains to be seen whether this test will rest on actual or common contemplation of risks — something seldom engaged in, and only for the most salient risks — or whether it ultimately will yield a more hypothetical question of what the parties would have done had they contemplated the risk in question. For a trenchant critique of all the suggested approaches, including that in *Hadley, see* Harris, Fairness and Remoteness of Damage in Contract Law: A Lexical Ordering Approach, 28 J. Contract L. 122 (2011).

§12.14 n.10 p.258 Add the following at the end: *Globe Refining* was decided under the pre-*Erie* general federal common law. Its tacit agreement test seems not to have carried over into the special federal common law of, for example, government contracts. *See* Prudential Ins. Co. v. United States, 801 F.2d 1295 (Fed. Cir. 1986) ("for damages to be recoverable as consequential or special, they must be foreseeable by the [breaching party] at the time the contract is executed"; refers to *Globe Refining*, but states that this is "the better rule"). *See also* Spang Indus. v. Aetna Cas. & Sur. Co., 512 F.2d 365 (2d Cir. 1975) ("A second fiction, added as an embellishment to Hadley v. Baxendale by Mr. Justice Holmes as federal common law in Globe Ref. Co. . . . would require not only knowledge of the special circumstances but a tacit agreement on the part of the party sought to be charged to accept the liability imposed by the notice. This second test has generally been rejected by the courts and commentators."). For the rather surprising history of *Globe Refining, see* Garvin, *Globe Refining Co. v. Landa Cotton Oil Co.* and the Dark Side of Reputation, 12 Nev. L.J. 659 (2012) (part of a symposium on the worst Supreme Court decisions ever).

§12.14 n.11 p.258 In the first paragraph, add the following at the end of the third sentence: and in K.C. Props. v. Lowell Inv. Partners, 280 S.W.3d 1 (Ark. 2008) ("In order to recover consequential damages in a breach-of-contract case, a plaintiff must prove more than the defendant's mere knowledge that a breach of contract will entail special damages to the plaintiff. It must also appear that the defendant at least tacitly agreed to assume responsibility.").

§12.14 n.11 p.258 In the second paragraph, add the following to the first sentence: and in Bi-Economy Market v. Harleysville Ins. Co., 886 N.E.2d 127 (N.Y. 2008) ("It is not necessary for the breaching party to have foreseen the breach itself or the particular way the loss occurred; rather, '[i]t is only necessary that loss from a breach is foreseeable and probable.' ") (quoting from this treatise).

§12.14 n.11 p.258 In the second paragraph, add the following after the first sentence: For an interesting application of *Kenford,* see Lava Trading v. Hartford Fire Ins. Co., 365 F. Supp. 2d 434 (S.D.N.Y. 2005) (breach of contract for business interruption insurance after September 11 attack; insured allowed to recover loss of business income, but not "(1) costs to secure funding which should have been provided by Hartford; (2) damages resulting from the alleged loss of clients; and (3) damages resulting from the alleged loss of future business growth"; insurance contract provided that delay in payment was foreseeable, but "[n]othing in the Policy before me would lead either the insured or the insurer to understand that the insurer, in the event of breach, would be liable for [these items].").

***§12.14 n.14 p.259 In the first paragraph, add the following to the list after* "see":** Hoang v. Hewitt Ave. Assocs., *supra* note 5 (lost profits foreseeable for breach of contract to sell real property where "the appellant and the other defendants knew that [the plaintiff] was purchasing the parcels to construct a town house community.").

§12.14 n.18 p.261 Add the following after the first sentence: *Accord:* Fifth Third Bank v. United States, 518 F.3d 1368 (Fed. Cir. 2008) ("Fifth Third was not required to demonstrate that the Government could have foreseen at the time of contracting that the market conditions might be less than favorable when it later breached the contract. . . . [A]ll that was necessary was a showing that the need to raise capital in the event of a breach was foreseeable.").

§12.14 n.20 p.261 Add the following to the list after "Accord": Bi-Economy Market v. Harleysville Ins. Co., *supra* note 11 (claim against business interruption insurer for losses including demise of business "was reasonably foreseeable and contemplated by the parties").

§12.14 n.20 p.261 Add the following at the end: *But cf.* Lewis Jorge Constr. Mgmt. v. Pomona Unified Sch. Dist., 102 P.3d 257 (Cal. 2004) (owner could not "have reasonably contemplated that its breach of the contract would probably lead to a reduction of [the builder's] bonding capacity by its surety, which in turn would adversely affect [the builder's] ability to obtain future contracts").

§12.14 n.22 p.262 Add the following at the beginning: *See* Anchor Sav. Bank v. United States, 597 F.3d 1356 (Fed. Cir. 2010) (federal government's enactment of FIRREA foreseeably injured the plaintiff by depriving it of favorable treatment of goodwill, and the general magnitude of the claims was similarly foreseeable at the time of enactment; quoting from treatise).

§12.14 n.23 p.262 In the first paragraph, add the following at the end: This approach does not predominate for breaches of contracts to buy real property. In these, the vendor may recover incidental and consequential damages to the extent they pass the foreseeability and certainty tests. *See* Ner Tamid Cong. v. Krivoruchko, 660 F. Supp. 2d 927 (N.D. Ill. 2009) ("The question in such cases, as in other breach of contract cases, is whether additional damages may be said to have arisen from the breach and were within the reasonable contemplation of the contracting parties.").

§12.14 p.263 In the first paragraph, add the following at the end of the last sentence: . . . supplier instead of a seller.[24a]

[24a] Lewis Jorge Constr. Mgmt. v. Pomona Unified Sch. Dist., *supra* note 20 ("Because general damages are a natural and necessary consequence of a contract breach, they are often said to be within the contemplation of the parties, meaning that because their occurrence is sufficiently predictable the parties at the time of contracting are 'deemed' to have contemplated them.").

§12.14 n.29 p.265 In the first paragraph, add the following after the second sentence: Capitol Justice v. Wachovia Bank, 706 F. Supp. 2d 23 (D.D.C. 2009) (where cover lending transaction required that borrower give new lender part of the equity gain of the building purchased, but original transaction did not, borrower potentially entitled to recover the difference in value between the two deals).

§12.14 n.36 p.267 Add the following after the first sentence: *Cf.* Green Wood Indus. Co. v. Forceman Int'l Dev. Grp., 67 Cal. Rptr. 3d 624 (App. Ct. 2007) ("A plaintiff may not recover damages for an unpaid liability to a third party, unless the plaintiff proves to a reasonable certainty that the liability could and would be enforced by the third party against the plaintiff or that the plaintiff otherwise could and would satisfy the obligation.").

§12.14 n.37 p.267 Add the following after the first sentence: *Accord:* Glasstech, Inc. v. Chicago Blower Corp., 675 F. Supp. 2d 752 (N.D. Ohio 2009) (allowing recovery for costs of settlement with third-party consumer, where settlement caused by seller's breach of warranty; "third-party claims may cause buyers consequential damages for which the seller should bear ultimate responsibility"); Pulte Home Corp. v. Parex, Inc., 942 A.2d 722 (Md. 2008) ("[I]f the buyer enters into a good faith settlement with the third party in order to avoid the commencement or continuation of litigation, the buyer should be able to recover the cost of settlement from the breaching seller . . ."); Restatement Second §351 cmt. *c*.

§12.14 n.37 p.267 Add the following at the end: *Cf.* Sunstate Indus. v. VP Grp., 679 S.E.2d 824 (Ga. App. 2009) (recovery of full settlement amount unsound because "there is no evidence relating the amount paid for the defective [product] to the mediation settlement.").

§12.14 n.40 p.268 Add the following to the list after **"Accord"*:*** Kraft Foods N. Am. v. Banner Eng'g & Sales, *supra* note 4 (defective design and installation of pipe system in food processing plant resulted in foreseeable damage to spoiled food, including the manufacturing costs for the food, disposal costs, and testing costs; apparently no demand for lost profits).

§12.15 UNCERTAINTY AS A LIMITATION

§12.15 n.6 p.269 Add the following to the list after **"But cf.":** Blase Indus. Corp. v. Anorad Corp., 442 F.3d 235 (Fed. Cir. 2006) (no consulting fees recoverable for at-will employee, as it was impossible to determine how long he might work).

§12.15 p.270 Add the following at the end of the second full sentence: . . . other loss that it does prove.[8a]

[8a] *See* ERI Consulting Eng'rs v. Swinnea, 318 S.W.3d 867 (Tex. 2010) (although the evidence did not support the court's award of lost profits, it "is legally sufficient evidence to prove a lesser, ascertainable amount of lost profits with reasonable certainty. In this situation, such a discrepancy between two reasonably certain amounts will not defeat recovery . . . ").

§12.15 n.9 p.270 Add the following to the list after **"Accord":** Amigo Broad. v. Spanish Broad. Sys., 521 F.3d 472 (5th Cir. 2008) ("'[w]hile some uncertainty as to the amount of damages is permissible, uncertainty as to the fact of damages will defeat recovery'") (quoting from Blase Indus. Corp. v. Anorad Corp., *supra* note 6); Fifth Third Bank v. United States, 518 F.3d 1368 (Fed. Cir. 2008) ("[T]he 'reasonable certainty' standard [applies] only to the *fact* of damages, after which the court may 'make a fair and reasonable assessment of the damages.'") (emphasis in original) (quoting from Bluebonnet Sav. Bank v. United States, 266 F.3d 1348, 1356-57 (Fed. Cir. 2001)); Tractebel Energy Mktg. v. AEP Power Mktg., 487 F.3d 89 (2d Cir. 2007) ("[O]nce the fact of damage is established, the non-breaching party need only provide a 'stable foundation for a reasonable estimate [of damages]' before an award of general damages can be made.") (quoting from Freund v. Washington Square Press, 314 N.E.2d 419 (N.Y. 1974)); Denny Constr. v. City & Cnty. of Denver ex rel. Bd. Of Water Comm'rs, 199 P.3d 742 (Colo. 2009) ("[A]s long as the fact of future loss is certain, the amount of damages awarded may be an approximation."); City of Westminster v.

Centric-Jones Constructors, 100 P.3d 472 (Colo. App. 2003) ("[U]ncertainty in the amount of damages does not preclude recovery, but '[u]ncertainty as to the cause from which they proceed' supports rejection of a damage claim as 'too remote, or conjectural or speculative.' ") (quoting from Donahue v. Pikes Peak Auto. Co., 372 P.2d 443 (Colo. 1962)); Gary's Implement, Inc. v. Bridgeport Tractor Parts, 799 N.W.2d 249 (Neb. 2011) ("Uncertainty as to the fact of whether any damages were sustained at all is fatal to recovery, but uncertainty as to the amount is not.").

§12.15 n.9 p.270 Add the following at the end: The test has been put in less felicitous ways, including one that is at best ambiguous and at worst flatly opposed to the great mass of modern cases. County of La Paz v. Yakima Compost Co., 233 P.3d 1169 (Ariz. App. 2010) ("Because lost future profits are capable of proof approaching mathematical precision, the requirement of 'reasonable certainty' must be applied with added force to such damages."). The court then applied conventional analysis, affirming an award of lost future profits on the basis of an expert report where the expert's assumptions "had a basis in fact." As the court didn't apply its own test, perhaps the rest of us can safely ignore it as well.

§12.15 n.15 p.271 Add the following to the list after "Accord": Denny Constr. v. City & Cnty. of Denver, *supra* note 9 ("[A] plaintiff contractor may establish a reasonable basis for computing the amount of lost profits by presenting evidence of prior profitability."; rejecting view that the uncertainties inherent in estimating future damages necessarily bar their recovery as too speculative).

§12.15 n.19 p.272 Add the following at the end: Indeed, these defenses often converge, with courts pointing to uncertainty as a reason damages were not foreseeable. Lewis Jorge Constr. Mgmt. v. Pomona Unified Sch. Dist., 102 P.3d 257 (Cal. 2004) (lost profits on future construction jobs "were uncertain and speculative" and thus not "reasonably probable to result from the [owner's] breach,"), *distinguished by* BEGL Constr. Co. v. Los Angeles Unified Sch. Dist., 66 Cal. Rptr. 3d 110 (Ct. App. 2007) ("unequivocal" evidence of industry custom on bonding practice in construction and that owner knew of this custom). One may also see causation mixed in, with unforeseeability adduced from the extreme unlikelihood of the particular event yielding the actual outcome.

§12.15 n.22 p.273 Add the following to the list after **"Accord"***:* Jarreau v. Quakenbush, 687 F. Supp. 2d 606 (M.D. La. 2010) (no lost profits for failure to deliver horse for competitive rodeos; plaintiff did not establish "the amount that could be won in each event" and, because the plaintiff's daughter rode other horses, it would have been necessary to establish "that in each event more money would have been won, and plaintiff's goals for his daughter's career would have been achieved if she had ridden [the horse]").

§12.15 n.22 p.273 Add the following at the end: This problem may also arise with breaches of non-competition agreements. If injunctive relief is unavailable, or if the breach caused harm before the injunction took effect, measuring lost profits resulting from competition may prove vexing. One indirect method is to look at the profits earned by the breaching party because of the breaching activity — not as a disgorgement remedy in restitution, but as a means of estimating what the breached-against party would have earned absent breach. *See* TruGreen Cos. v. Mower Bros., Inc., 199 P.3d 929 (Utah 2008) ("Our adoption of a lost profits standard, however, does not prevent a non-breaching party from examining a defendant's profits in an attempt to assess its own economic loss."). *Accord:* Trilogy Network Sys. v. Johnson, 172 P.3d 1119 (Idaho 2007) ("The profits realized by the defendant may be considered by the trier-of-fact, if shown to correspond with the loss of the plaintiff.").

§12.15 n.23 p.273 Add the following at the end: *Cf.* Totaro, Duffy, Canova & Co. v. Lane, Middleton & Co., 921 A.2d 1100 (N.J. 2007) (breach of agreement not to solicit clients for four years; court allows damages equal to one year's profit because the clients would have learned of the defendant's departure in a non-breaching manner by then).

§12.15 n.24 p.273 In the first paragraph, add the following to the list after* "Accord"*: Vienna Metro v. Pulte Home Corp., 786 F. Supp. 2d 1076 (E.D. Va. 2011) (contractor failed to build property infrastructure on time; developer's damages for lost profits unrecoverable "because Vienna Metro (1) has no approved site plans, (2) has no design plans, (3) has no tenant, and (4) has no buyer. Vienna Metro cannot demonstrate any substantial revenue from the property because its potential profit is based entirely on groundless income projections.").

§12.15 n.25 p.274 Add the following to the list after* "Accord"*: Hoang v. Hewitt Ave. Assocs., 936 A.2d 915 (Md. App. 2007) (real estate development; "The case at bar is an example of evidence of track record and experience on the part of the non-breaching party sufficient to make the collateral lost profits damages sought reasonable certain and not speculative . . . ").

§12.15 n.27 p.275 Add the following at the end of the second sentence: and followed in Schonfeld v. Hilliard, 218 F.3d 164 (2d Cir. 2000) (affirming trial court's rejection of claim for lost profits from a new cable television venture; "the Channel was a new entertainment venture similar to the proposed stadium in *Kenford I*. The operating entity's profits, the court noted, 'were purely hypothetical, stemming from the sale of untested programming to a hypothetical subscriber base, sold to advertisers at a hypothetical price and supported by hypothetical investors and carriers.' . . . After reviewing the seemingly endless list of assumptions upon which Schonfeld's expert relied in determining lost profits, the [trial] court held that Schonfeld could establish neither the existence nor the amount of lost profits with reasonable certainty.").

§12.15 n.27 p.275 Add the following after the third sentence: *Cf.* Tractebel Energy Mktg. v. AEP Power Mktg., *supra* note 9 ("If it is true that projecting profits over twenty years is so absurdly speculative that economists can do no better than fortune tellers, it would have been imprudent for the parties to enter a contract for such a long period in the first place. The reality, however, is that long-term contracts are entered into regularly, and a degree of speculation is acceptable in the business community.").

§12.15 n.27 p.275 Add the following at the end: In contrast, it seems reasonable not to extend damages into periods covered by unexercised options. In light of the conflict between the parties that gave rise to a lawsuit, it seems unlikely that the breached-against party would exercise its option to renew or, if the option initially rests with the breaching party, to accept the renewal. Nor, if the breaching party's breach is material, would there even be an option for that party to exercise; the breached-against party would then have the right to terminate the contract, including any unexercised options. *See* E. Coast Res. v. Town of Hempstead, 707 F. Supp. 2d 401 (E.D.N.Y. 2010) (no damages for option period where breached-against party refused either to exercise the option or permit the other party to exercise it).

§12.15 n.28 p.275 Add the following to the list after **"Accord"***:* Tipton v. Mill Creek Gravel, 373 F.3d 913 (8th Cir. 2004) ("The general rule under Missouri law is that anticipated profits of a commercial business are too remote and speculative to warrant recovery. . . . They can only be recovered when they are made reasonably certain by proof of actual facts, with present data for a rational estimate of their amount. . . . [C]ompetent and substantial evidence is required to support an award of damages. Moreover, [s]peculation as to probable or expected lost business profits is spurned, and [a]n unsupported opinion or estimate of a loss of profits is generally held to be insufficient.") (internal citations omitted).

§12.15 n.28 p.275 Add the following after the citation to **American Road Equip. Co.***:* and in Gary's Implement, Inc. v. Bridgeport Tractor Parts, 799 N.W.2d 249 (Neb. 2011) ("The rule that lost profits from a [new] business are too speculative and conjectural to permit the recovery of damages is not a hard and fast one, and loss of prospective profits may nevertheless be recovered if the evidence shows with reasonable certainty both the loss and the extent thereof.").

§12.15 n.28 p.275 Replace the citation to **Teletron Energy Mgmt.** *with the following:* Texas Instruments v. Teletron Energy Mgmt., 877 S.W.2d 276 (Tex. 1994)

§12.15 n.28 p.275 Add the following after the citation to **Hiller***:* and in M & A Tech. v. iValue Grp., 295 S.W.3d 356 (Tex. Civ. App. 2009) ("Where there are no past profits because the plaintiff is embarking upon a new and unproven enterprise, lost profits are not recoverable. . . . Revenue forecasting as in a lost income analysis must be based on objective facts or data and established to a reasonable certainty.").

§12.15 n.28 p.275 Add the following at the end: and in Amigo Broad. v. Spanish Broad. Sys., *supra* note 9 (allowing lost profits where some evidence of prior profitability). *See generally* Lloyd, The Reasonable Certainty Requirement in Lost Profit Litigation: What it Really Means, 12 Transactions 11 (2010).

§12.15 n.29 p.276 Add the following after the citation to **Air Technology***:* , distinguished in Gemini Investors v. AmeriPark, Inc., 643 F.3d 43 (1st Cir. 2011) (in *Air Technology,* promisee had contractual right to be awarded the subcontract in question, subject to conditions; in this case, in contrast, the promisee "was at best deprived of a contractually guaranteed right to exclude others from negotiations with the promisor").

§12.15 n.29 p.276 Add the following to the list after **"Accord"***:* Gary's Implement, Inc. v. Bridgeport Tractor Parts, 799 N.W.2d 249 (Neb. 2011) (expert testimony used to determine losses resulting from breach of covenant not to compete; expert looked at financial summaries of comparable stores outside breaching party's catchment area to compute lost revenue).

§12.15 n.35 p.278 Add the following after the second sentence: *Cf.* Birmingham News Co. v. Horn, 901 So. 2d 27 (Ala. 2004) (no recovery for both lost franchise value and lost future profits where franchises were improperly terminated, but the plaintiffs may elect which to take), *overruled on other grounds*, Horton Homes v. Shaner, 999 So. 2d 462 (Ala. 2008).

§12.15 n.35 p.278 Add the following at the end: At times courts may press the limits of reasonable certainty. Consider, for example, breach of a contract under which a manufacturer was to pay a royalty to a technical consultant for the use of its process on

up to 3,000 probes, with a termination payment to be given if the manufacturer "discontinues or in any way abandons the process prior to the completion of the 3000th probe." The manufacturer refused to pay royalties, arguing that it did not use the consultant's process. It used the process on about 200 probes per year. The jury awarded damages based on using the process on 3000 probes over six years, and that was upheld on appeal. Acoustic Mktg. Research v. Technics, LLC, 198 P.3d 96 (Colo. 2008). Given the presence of a termination clause and a rate of use well under the jury's finding, it is hard to justify these damages as sufficiently based in fact.

***§12.15 n.36 p.279 Add the following to the list after* "Accord":** Lamar Advertising of S.D. v. Heavy Constructors, 745 N.W.2d 371 (S.D. 2008) (lessor of billboard breached covenant prohibiting the building of other billboards within 1,000 feet of the leased billboard; "In . . . cases involving actual leases, revenues and expenses, lost profits are a proper measure of damages for at least the period of the contract.").

§12.16 RELIANCE AS AN ALTERNATIVE MEASURE OF DAMAGES

***§12.16 n.1 p.280 Add the following to the list after* "Accord":** Am. Capital Corp. v. FDIC, 472 F.3d 859 (Fed. Cir. 2006) ("Essentially, the injured party may not be able to prove with reasonable certainty what it would have made if the contract was performed; however, it may be able to prove what expenditures it made in relying on the contract.").

***§12.16 n.2 p.280 In the first paragraph, add the following to the list after* "Accord":** Amoco Oil Co. v. Gomez, 379 F.3d 1266 (11th Cir. 2004) (expenditures incurred under trial franchise lease unrecoverable as reliance damages for breach of subsequent franchise agreements).

§12.16 n.2 p.280 Add the following at the end of the second paragraph: *Accord:* Westfed Holdings v. United States, 407 F.3d 1352 (Fed. Cir. 2005) (allowing pre-contractual expenditures where the defendant "knew by that point in time that [plaintiff] was incurring expenses in preparation for and reliance upon the contract").

§12.16 n.3 p.281 Add the following to the list after **"Accord"***:* St. Lawrence Factory Stores v. Ogdensburg Bridge & Port Auth., 918 N.E.2d 124 (N.Y. 2009) (where lost profits on real estate sale too speculative, plaintiff may recover reliance damages — not merely those ordinarily incurred in a real estate sale, but also "money allegedly spent in preparing for performance, including, among other things, efforts to arrange financing and obtain tenants for the shopping center" that the buyer had planned to develop).

§12.16 n.3 p.281 Add the following at the end: Reliance damages may also be available when expectation is precluded by statute or policy. This is often, but not invariably, seen in damages where the obligation or its enforcement depend on promissory estoppel. See §2.19 *supra*. One prominent case of this type is Sullivan v. O'Connor, 296 N.E.2d 183 (Mass. 1973), in which the court permitted only reliance damages for breach of a contract to "enhance [the patient's] beauty and improve her appearance." The background to *Sullivan* may be found in R. Danzig & G. Watson, The Capability Problem in Contract Law 5-47 (2d ed. 2004). *See also* Meccon, Inc. v. Univ. of Akron, 933 N.E.2d 231 (Ohio 2010) (expectation damages not available to disappointed bidder in breach of contract action against governmental entity, but reliance damages in the form of bid-preparation costs "may be recovered if the rejected bidder promptly sought but was denied a timely injunction to suspend the public-improvement project pending resolution of the dispute and a court later determines that the bidder was wrongfully rejected by the public authority but injunctive relief is no longer available because the project has already been started or is completed under a contract awarded to another bidder").

§12.16 n.8 p.282 Replace the citation to* Beefy Trail *with the following: Beefy Trail v. Beefy King Int'l, 267 So. 2d 853 (Fla. App. 1972).

§12.16 n.9 p.282 Add the following at the end: *Accord:* Westfed Holdings v. United States, *supra* note 2 (no reliance damages where "as a consequence of tax benefits from [an acquisition,] the 'purchase price was zero' ").

***§12.16 n.12 p.282 Add the following to the list after* "Accord":** Am. Capital Corp. v. FDIC, *supra* note 1 ("In order to recover reliance damages, the 'plaintiff's loss must have been foreseeable to the party in breach at the time of contract formation.' ") (quoting from Landmark Land Co. v. United States, 256 F.3d 1365 (Fed. Cir. 2001)); 24/7 Records v. Sony Music Entm't, 566 F. Supp. 2d 305 (S.D.N.Y. 2008) ("in order to prove reliance damages, plaintiff must show foreseeable expenses legitimately made for performance of the agreement").

§12.16 n.12 p.282 Add the following at the end: For a somewhat unusual application, *see* Hess v. Johnston, 163 P.3d 747 (Utah App. 2007) (breach of promise to marry; no damages for travel, gifts to the fiancée's son, or a vasectomy where these losses did not "flow naturally from a breach of promise to marry or were reasonably contemplated by the parties at the time they decided to wed").

***§12.16 n.15 p.282 Add the following to the list after* "Accord":** Westfed Holdings v. United States, *supra* note 2 ("Damages based on the injured party's reliance interest may be reduced by 'any loss that the party in breach can prove with reasonable certainty the injured party would have suffered had the contract been performed.' ") (quoting from Restatement Second §349); Bausch & Lomb v. Bressler, 977 F.2d 720 (2d Cir. 1992) ("[A] reliance recovery will be offset by the amount of any loss that the party in breach can prove with reasonable certainty the injured party would have suffered had the contract been fully performed.") (quoting from Restatement section *supra*).

§12.16 n.15 p.282 Add the following at the end of the first paragraph: For an example of a plaintiff hoist by its own petard, *see* Doering Equip. Co. v. John Deere Co., 815 N.E.2d 234 (Mass. App. 2004) ("In the instant case, Doering is seeking to recover expenditures made in preparation for performance or during performance, but has also demonstrated, through its own submissions, that the contract, as performed, had been a losing proposition since inception, separate and apart from the breach. In fact, the operating losses for the contract, while being performed by both parties, are exactly what Doering seeks to recover.").

§12.16 n.18 p.283 Add the following after the citation to **Autotrol***:* followed in Designer Direct v. DeForest Redev. Auth., 368 F.3d 751 (7th Cir. 2004) ("overhead expenses are recoverable as reliance damages" if claimant "can show that these expenses were properly allocated to the breached contract").

§12.16a COUNTING LOST OPPORTUNITIES IN RELIANCE DAMAGES

§12.16a n.9 p.287 Add the following to the list in the first sentence: Toscano v. Greene Music, 21 Cal. Rptr. 3d 732 (Ct. App. 2004) (employee who resigned job on promise of future employment "may on an appropriate showing recover the lost wages he would have expected to earn from his former employer but for the defendant's promise," even though former employment was at-will).

§12.17 OTHER LIMITATIONS, INCLUDING EMOTIONAL DISTURBANCE

§12.17 n.10 p.290 In the first paragraph, add the following to the list after **"See also"***:* M.M. Silta, Inc. v. Cleveland Cliffs, Inc., 572 F.3d 532 (8th Cir. 2009) (damages of over seven million dollars not disproportionate for breach of sales contract with price of $2,480; "Cliffs is a sophisticated commercial entity that entered

into hundreds of contracts like the one here."); Royal Indem. Co. v. Factory Mut. Ins. Co., 786 N.W.2d 839 (Iowa 2010) (inspection fee of $6,000 and liability of $30,000,000; "the parties could not have intended for such a small fee to cover the risk of such enormous liability").

§12.17 n.13 p.291 In the second paragraph, add the following to the list after* "Accord"*: Sherman v. Kissinger, 195 P.3d 539 (Wash. App. 2008) (veterinary care for pet).

§12.17 n.13 p.291 In the third paragraph, add the following to the list after* "see"*: Carraway Methodist Health Sys. v. Wise, 986 So. 2d 387 (Ala. 2007) (employment contract); John Hancock Mut. Life Ins. Co. v. Banerji, 858 N.E.2d 277 (Mass. 2006) (insurance contract); Rakylar v. Wash. Mut. Bank, 858 N.Y.S.2d 759 (App. Div. 2008) (loan refinancing).

§12.17 n.13 p.291 In the third paragraph, add the following after the citation to* Kwan*: , followed in Pedroza v. Lomas Auto Mall, 625 F. Supp. 2d 1156 (D.N.M. 2009) (sale of automobile; "emotional distress damages are generally not recoverable in a standard breach of warranty action under the UCC").

§12.17 n.13 p.291 In the third paragraph, add the following at the end: *Cf.* Alday v. Raytheon Co., 619 F. Supp. 2d 726 (D. Ariz. 2008) (ERISA preempts claims for emotional distress).

§12.17 n.13 p.291 In the fourth paragraph, add the following at the end: *Accord:* Univ. of S. Miss. v. Williams, 891 So. 2d 160 (Miss. 2004) ("the plaintiff must show (1) that mental anguish was a foreseeable consequence of the particular breach of contract, and (2) that he or she actually suffered mental anguish," taking into account "the nature of the incident"; granting them for preventing doctoral candidate from receiving her doctorate), followed in Morris Newspaper Corp. v. Allen, 932 So. 2d 810 (Miss. App. 2005) (allowing emotional distress damages for employee discharged after spurning sexual advances by superior); Menorah Chapels v. Needle, 899 A.2d 316 (N.J. Super. App. Div. 2006) (funeral home failed to comply with Orthodox Jewish ritual requirements; emotional distress damages "may be available upon breach of contract 'where the subject-matter of the contract is such as to make it certain or reasonably probable that the parties had in contemplation, at the time of the making of the contract, a pecuniary satisfaction for the anguish and distress of mind ensuing from a breach of its terms.' "; collecting cases) (quoting from Spiegel v. Evergreen Cemetery Co., 186 A. 585 (N.J. Super. 1936)), followed in Gupta v. Asha Enters., 27 A.3d 953 (N.J. Super. App. Div. 2011) (emotional or spiritual injury resulting from restaurant filling order from Hindu vegetarians for vegetarian samosas with meat-filled samosas recoverable in breach of warranty action under UCC 2-313 and 2-715).

§12.17 n.14 p.292 In the first paragraph, add the following after the citation to **Allen***:* , followed in Ross v. Forest Lawn Mem. Park, 203 Cal. Rptr. 468 (Ct. App. 1984) (undertaker breached contract to keep punk rockers from disrupting funeral and desecrating grave) and approved of by Christensen v. Super. Ct., 820 P.2d 181 (Cal. 1991) (emotional distress damages available to immediate family where mortuary mishandled decedents' remains).

§12.17 n.14 p.292 In the first paragraph, add the following to the list after **"Cf."***:* Sheely v. MRI Radiology Network, 505 F.3d 1173 (11th Cir. 2007) (dictum: "The frequency and acuteness with which discrimination spawns emotional distress in the victim suggest that emotional distress is a 'probable result,' of funding recipients' breach of their promise not to discriminate, and thus that recipients have fair notice that, in breaching, they may be subject to liability for emotional damages.") (quoting from treatise); Murphy v. Lord Thompson Manor, 938 A.2d 1269 (Conn. App. 2008) (wedding site cancelled the bride's contractual wedding date reservation; "A contract for wedding services creates a rigorous expectation for contractual performance," the wedding site was "in a position to see how clients react to a myriad of wedding related mishaps," and "the cancelling of an event that [the plaintiff] had been planning for two years would naturally and foreseeably cause her distress, particularly given the difficulty of moving the multi-day festivities . . . with only seven months' notice.").

§12.17 n.14 p.292 Add the following at the end of the first paragraph: Louisiana, not surprisingly, deals with emotional distress damages in a relatively civilian manner. La. Civ. Code. art. 1998 & cmt. (only pecuniary losses cognizable unless a contract is intended to "gratify a nonpecuniary interest" — in other words, "one intended to satisfy an interest of a spiritual order such as a contract to create a work of art, or a contract to conduct scientific research, or a contract involving matters of sentimental value").

§12.17 n.14 p.292 In the second paragraph, add the following after the citation to **B & M Homes***:* , followed in Baldwin v. Panetta, 4 So. 3d 555 (Ala. Civ. App. 2008) (no damages for mental anguish where defects largely cosmetic and home not the primary residence).

§12.17 n.14 p.292 In the second paragraph, add the following to the list after **"See also"***:* Matt v. Agro Distrib., 904 So. 2d 928 (La. App. 2005) (allowing emotional distress damages to farmers suing seed company and distributor for crop failure and resulting inability to get loans); Univ. of S. Miss. v. Williams, *supra* note 13 (looking to nature of contract in granting emotional distress damages for preventing doctoral student from receiving doctorate); Cabaness v. Thomas, 232 P.3d 486 (Utah 2010) (emotional distress or mental anguish damages recoverable "when such damages were both a foreseeable result of the breach of contract and *explicitly* within the contemplation of the parties at the time the contract was entered into"; potentially available in employment case where employment handbook specifically stated that the employer would not tolerate harassing or disruptive conduct).

§12.17 n.14 p.292 Add the following after the second paragraph: Another exception arises when a common carrier, hotelier, or restaurateur breaches a contract with a patron. Though the courts generally continue to reject damages for emotional distress absent some independent tort, they are willing to grant "inconvenience damages," apparently on the theory that common carriers and the like owe special duties to their patrons such that they can reasonably foresee non-economic harm arising from their breach. Stone v. Continental Airlines, 804 N.Y.S.2d 652 (N.Y. City Civ. Ct. 2005).

***§12.17 n.15 p. 293 Add the following to the list after* "Accord":** John Hancock Mut. Life Ins. Co. v. Banerji, *supra* note 13 (allowing emotional distress damages where they "are the result of intentional or reckless conduct of an extreme and outrageous nature"); Villeneuve v. Beane, 933 A.2d 1139 (Vt. 2007) (breach of lease where landlord trespassed, harassed the tenants, and unlawfully cut off their electricity, which displayed the requisite "outrageousness" to warrant emotional distress damages).

***§12.17 n.16 p.293 Add the following to the list after* "Accord":** Isle of Wight Cnty. v. Nogiec, 704 S.E.2d 83 (Va. 2011) (damages for emotional distress and the like available only if there is a tort present).

***§12.17 n.17 p.293 Add the following to the list after* "Cf.":** McKay v. Wilderness Dev., 221 P.3d 1184 (Mont. 2009) ("In the absence of physical injury, damages for emotional distress are not allowed in an action to enforce a contract.").

§12.17a ROLE OF WILLFULNESS

§12.17a n.4 p.295 Add the following at the end: *See generally* Anenson, Limiting Legal Remedies: An Analysis of Unclean Hands, 99 Ky. L.J. 63 (2011).

Pace Holmes, recent experimental work shows that people penalize intentional harm more than negligent harm and greed more than fear, and will set a lower damages figure before breach than after — all consistent with a moral component to contract remedies. *See* Wilkinson-Ryan & Baron, Moral Judgment and Moral Heuristics in Breach of Contract, 6 J. Empirical L. Studies 405 (2009); Wilkinson-Ryan & Hoffman, Breach Is for Suckers, 63 Vand. L. Rev. 1003 (2010).

***§12.17a n.12 p.297 Add the following after the citation to* Metropolitan Life:** , distinguished by Banc of Am. Secs. v. Solow Bldg. Co. II, 847 N.Y.S.2d 49 (App. Div. 2007) (the contract in *Noble Lowndes* was simply abandoned, whereas the defendant here sought to impose a new burden upon the lessee with no new consideration and through threat of declaring defaults).

§12.17a p.298 Add the following at the end of the carryover sentence: . . . which measure of damages is appropriate.[12a]

[12a] Particularly flagrant or egregious breaches may qualify the breaching party for punitive damages, not merely an especially generous expectation measure. *See supra* §12.8.

§12.17a n.15 p.298 Add the following at the end: *Accord:* Septembertide Pub. v. Stein & Day, Inc., 884 F.2d 675 (2d Cir. 1989) ("[B]efore rescission will be permitted the breach must be 'material and willful, or, if not willful, so substantial and fundamental as to strongly tend to defeat the object of the parties in making the contract.' ") (quoting from Callanan v. Powers, 92 N.E. 747 (App. Div. 1910)), followed in Raymond Weil, S.A. v. Theron, 585 F. Supp. 2d 473 (S.D.N.Y. 2008); (Curtis Constr. Co. v. Am. Steel Span, 707 N.W.2d 68 (N.D. 2005)) ("A contractor has not substantially performed when the 'defects are intentional, willful, or so serious as to deprive the property of its value or intended use.' ") (quoting from Merrill Iron & Steel v. Minn-Dak Seeds, 334 N.W.2d 652 (N.D. 1983)).

§12.17a n.16 p.298 Add the following at the end: *But see* Emerald Pointe Prop. Owners' Ass'n v. Commercial Constr. Indus., 978 So. 2d 873 (Fla. App. 2008) ("The contract price generally is the upper limit where the contractor sues in quantum meruit, but in the event the owner's breach is willful, the contractor may recover his outlay even if it exceeds the contract price.' ") (quoting from Ballard v. Krause, 248 So. 2d 233 (Fla. App. 1971)).

§12.18 LIQUIDATED DAMAGES, PENALTIES, AND OTHER AGREED REMEDIES

§12.18 n.1 p.300 Add the following after the second sentence: On the role of professional standards, *see* §5.5 *supra*.

§12.18 n.1 p.300 Add the following at the end: Liquidated damages clauses are distinct from termination clauses. Any fee levied for termination of a contract is in effect just another performance term; certainly a rightful invocation of a termination clause is not a breach. Liquidated damages clauses, on the other hand, are by definition pertinent only to *damages*; they thus are irrelevant to questions of performance. Las Vegas Sands Corp. v. ACE Gaming, 713 F. Supp. 2d 427 (D.N.J. 2010) ("ACE's payment of the termination fee is a means of performance, even though ACE's obligation to pay the fee happens to arise, under the specific facts presented here, upon ACE's breach").

§12.18 n.2 p.301 Add the following to the list after **"Accord"***:* Schroeder v. Partin, 259 P.3d 617 (Idaho 2011) (quoting this section of this treatise).

§12.18 n.2 p.301 Add the following at the end: A corollary of the importance of certainty is that a remedy clause that does not fix damages, either at a sum certain or at an amount determinable without regard to the loss actually incurred, is not a liquidated damages clause and does not face the same scrutiny. *See* Shin-Con Dev. Corp. v. I.P. Invs., 270 S.W.3d 759 (Tex. Civ. App. 2008) (clause requiring the return of all funds paid plus interest if the defendant breached is not a liquidated damages clause). *But cf.* Karimi v. 401 N. Wabash Venture, 952 N.E.2d 1278 (Ill. App. 2011) (clause allowing seller upon buyer's breach to retain the earnest money plus "all amounts paid or to be paid by Purchase to Seller for any other services or work performed or to be performed by Seller" a proper liquidated damages clause; at the time of contracting the parties knew how the amount would be determined). This last is questionable. After all, the parties know at the time of contracting how expectation damages would be calculated, but that does not make a clause reciting the usual expectation test into a liquidated damages provision. Still, some degree of variation is not only permissible, but desirable, such as assessing damages per item sold, in order that the clause not prove impermissibly invariant. In *Karimi*, one might thus defend the clause by arguing that the variable portion — payment for services to be rendered — is an amount easy for the promisor to determine and plan around. But it would be better to find some other way to state

the idea. Possibly the clause might be split, allowing the parties to recite that the amounts paid or to be paid for future work are reasonable in light of the anticipated damages, et cetera.

On a related note, a 2014 Ninth Circuit case, *In re* Late Fee & Over-limit Fee Litig., 741 F.3d 1022 (9th Cir. 2014), raised interesting constitutional and contract law issues in the context of fees under consumer credit card agreements. The primary argument was a constitutional one: that excessive fees, to the extent that they greatly exceed the harm actually suffered by the bank due to late payments or charging amounts over the credit limit, were so "analogous to punitive damages imposed in the tort context, and that they are therefore subject to the substantive due process limits described in BMW of N. Am., Inc. v. Gore, 517 U.S. 559, 116 S. Ct. 1589, 134 L. Ed. 2d 809 (1996), and subsequent cases." *Id.* at *3-4. The court found that these tort law limitations do not apply in the context of a banking services contract that complied with statutory and regulatory provisions. Judge Reinhardt agreed with that assessment of current Supreme Court precedent, but "reluctantly." *Id.* at *13. He wrote separately to urge that the Supreme Court "would be well advised to apply the same rule to prevent disproportionate penalties from being imposed on consumers when they breach contracts of adhesion." *Id.* Of interest to contracts practitioners, Judge Reinhardt wrote that "[s]ubstantive due process should, at the very least, bar judicial enforcement of contractual penalty clauses when such clauses are so disproportionate to the damage caused by the breach that the damages would be impermissible as civil penalties in the tort context." *Id.* at *22. In a particularly unusual move, Senior Circuit Judge Nelson, who authored the majority opinion, also wrote a one-sentence concurring statement: "I write separately to join Judge Reinhardt's concurrence, although I agree that the district court reached the correct result under currently applicable law and should be affirmed." *Id.* at *24.

***§12.18 n.4 p.302 Add the following to the list after* "But see":** Rainbow Country Rentals & Retail v. Ameritech Pub., 706 N.W.2d 95 (Wis. 2005) (treating limitation of liability clause as stipulated damages clause for the purpose of determining enforceability).

§12.18 n.5 p.302 In the first paragraph, add the following after the first sentence: *See generally* Zeller, Penalty Clauses: Are They Governed by the CISG?, 23 Pace Int'l L. Rev. 1 (2011).

§12.18 n.5 p.302 In the first paragraph, add the following at the end: In contrast, the recent tendency in Commonwealth nations, at least until recently, has been highly restrictive. *See* Carter & Peden, A Good Faith Perspective on Liquidated Damages, 23 J. Contract L. 157 (2007).

§12.18 n.8 p.303 In the first paragraph, add the following after the second sentence: In addition, Montana has abolished the distinction between liquidated damages clauses and other contract provisions. Highway Specialties v. Mont. Dep't of Transp., 215 P.2d 667 (Mont. 2009) ("[L]iquidated damages provisions are presumed enforceable and will be enforced unless the party opposing the provision has established that it is unconscionable . . . The clause will only be deemed unconscionable if it is a contract of adhesion *and* if the contractual terms were unreasonably favorable to the drafter, which is generally determined by whether the provision was within the reasonable expectations of, or unduly oppressive to, the weaker party.") (emphasis in original).

§12.18 n.8 p.303 In the first paragraph, add the following at the end: *Cf.* Carrothers Constr. Co. v. City of S. Hutchinson, 207 P.3d 231 (Kan. 2009) ("It is uniquely difficult to calculate damages to the general public interest caused by a contractor's breach of its agreement to provide public improvements. This should be an important consideration in such cases and weigh favorably in finding a liquidated damages provision to be reasonable.").

§12.18 n.8 p.303 In the second paragraph, add the following at the end: For a rethinking of *Lake River, see* Goldberg, Cleaning Up *Lake River,* 3 Va. L. & Bus. Rev. 427 (2008).

§12.18 n.8 p.303 In the third paragraph, add the following to the list after **"See also"***:* Crespi, Measuring "Actual Harm" for the Purpose of Determining the Enforceability of Liquidated Damages Clauses, 41 Hous. L. Rev. 1579 (2005); Scott & Triantis, Embedded Options and the Case Against Compensation in

Contract Law, 104 Colum. L. Rev. 1428 (2004); Walt, Liquidated Damages After Behavioral Law and Economics, 6 Va. J. 98 (2003).

***§12.18 n.8 p.303 In the third paragraph, add the following to the list after the second* "see":** Oman, Consent to Retaliation: A Civil Recourse Theory of Contractual Liability, 96 Iowa L. Rev. 529 (2011).

§12.18 n.8 p.303 Add the following at the end of the third paragraph: For an English perspective, *see* Chen-Wishart, Controlling the Power to Agree Damages, in Wrongs and Remedies in the Twenty-First Century 271 (P. Birks ed. 1996); Downes, Rethinking Penalty Clauses, in *id.* at 249; Gullifer, Agreed Remedies, in Commercial Remedies 191 (A. Burrows & E. Peel eds. 2003). For comparative perspectives, *see* Miller, Penalty Clauses in England and France — A Comparative Study, 53 Int'l & Comp. L.Q. 79 (2004); Solórzano, An Uncertain Penalty: A Look at the International Community's Inability to Harmonize the Law of Liquidated Damage and Penalty Clauses, 15 L. & Bus. Rev. of the Ams. 779 (2009). For the history, *see* George, Reimposable Discounts and Medieval Contract Penalties, 20 Loy. Cons. L. Rev. 50 (2007). For an unexpected and important experimental finding that liquidated damages clauses permit efficient breach, *see* Wilkinson-Ryan, Do Liquidated Damages Encourage Breach? A Psychological Experiment, 108 Mich. L. Rev. 633 (2010).

§12.18 n.9 p.304 In the first paragraph, add the following at the end: *Accord:* XCO Int'l v. Pac. Scientific Co., 369 F.3d 998 (7th Cir. 2004) (Posner, J.) ("The rule hangs on, but is chastened by an emerging presumption against interpreting liquidated damages clauses as penalty clauses."), followed in Cummings Props. v. Nat'l Commc'ns Corp., 869 N.E.2d 617 (Mass. 2007) (quoting from treatise); S. Brooke Purill, Inc. v. Vailes, 850 A.2d 1135 (D.C. 2004) (quoting this section of treatise); Coastal Leasing Corp. v. T-Bar S Corp., 496 S.E.2d 795 (N.C. App. 1998) (a liquidated damages clause "carries with it a consensual apportionment of the risks of the agreement that a court should be slow to overturn"). For some particularly vigorous criticism, *see* Smelkinson SYSCO v. Harrell, 875 A.2d 188 (Md. App. 2005) ("The Law of

Liquidate[d] Damages is one of the most ancient concepts in the law. . . . *Exodus* 22:1 provides: 'if a man shall steal an ox, or a sheep, and kill it, or sell it; he shall restore five oxen for an ox, and four sheep for a sheep.' After quite literally centuries of veneration of these concepts, like the camel's nose under the tent, once the concept of 'penalty' crept into this area, the law of liquidated damages became *sui generis* within the law of contracts by overtly insulting the freedom of parties to structure their own agreement[,] which is universally acknowledged to be at the heart of the law of contracts. Why should such clauses be treated differently than other contract provisions that may be equally unfair or one-sided?").

***§12.18 n.9 p.304 In the second paragraph, add the following to the list after* "see":** DynaSteel Corp. v. Black & Veatch Corp., 698 F. Supp. 2d 1170 (W.D. Mo. 2010) ("Most significantly, DynaSteel is a sophisticated business that freely negotiated its contract with B & V and agreed to the [liquidated damages clause]."); HH E. Parcel v. Handy & Harman, Inc., 947 A.2d 916 (Conn. 2008) ("In particular, we note that [the liquidated damages clause] was actively negotiated by the parties in an attempt to reach an agreement on the sale of the property."); Schroeder v. Partin, 259 P.3d 617 (Idaho 2011) (suggesting inherent plausibility of liquidated damages clause drafted by breached-against party; "a reasonable jury could find that the party who voluntarily and independently drafted a contract providing for liquidated damages in the event of breach would not impose upon himself an unreasonable or punitive means of assessing those damages"); Hendricks Prop. Mgmt. Corp. v. Birchwood Props. Ltd. P'ship, 741 N.W.2d 461 (N.D. 2007) ("where experienced parties and their attorneys had multiple opportunities to examine the contracts and discuss their terms, including the liquidated damages clauses, we conclude the evidence supports the district court's finding that the liquidated damages clauses were the result of reasonable endeavor by the parties to fix compensation").

§12.18 n.10 p.304 Add the following at the end of the first paragraph: As to the enforceability of the balance of the agreement, *see* JMD Holding Corp. v. Congress Fin. Corp., 828 N.E.2d 604 (N.Y. 2005) (quoting treatise).

§12.18 n.11 p.304 In the second paragraph, add the following to the list after* "see"*: Coizza v. 164-50 Crossbay Realty Corp., 900 N.Y.S.2d 416 (App. Div. 2010) (granting both specific performance for the conveyance of real property and liquidated damages for breach of the contract); Paradise Orchards Gen. P'ship v. Fearing, 94 P.3d 372 (Wash. App. 2004) ("a liquidated damages clause in a real estate purchase and sale contract does not foreclose the remedy of specific performance absent specific language in the contract").

§12.18 n.11 p.304 In the second paragraph, add the following at the end: *Cf.* Osborn v. Dennison, 768 N.W.2d 20 (Wis. 2009) (land sales contract provided that seller could either request the earnest money as liquidated damages or direct its return and sue for actual damages; seller could not both direct that the earnest money be held and sue for actual damages, so directing that the earnest money be held foreclosed suit for actual damages).

§12.18 n.12 p.305 Add the following to the list after* "see"*: Berggren v. Hill, 928 N.E.2d 1225 (Ill. App. 2010) (contractual right to retain earnest money upon buyer's breach was liquidated damages clause, which "precludes plaintiff's claim for actual damages"); Handex of the Carolinas v. County of Haywood, 607 S.E.2d 25 (N.C. App. 2005) ("[W]hile liquidated damages may still be awarded even if no actual damages arise from the breach, they cannot be awarded in addition to actual damages because this would constitute double recovery.").

§12.18 n.12 p.305 Add the following to the list after* "But cf."*: Comstock Potomac Yard v. Balfour Beatty Constr., 694 F. Supp. 2d 468 (E.D. Va. 2010) (damages sought for substandard performance "go beyond those contemplated by the liquidated damages clause" and thus were recoverable); Coizza v. 164-50 Crossbay Realty Corp., 900 N.Y.S.2d 416 (App. Div. 2010) (both liquidated damages and actual damages available because liquidated damages clause is not exclusive).

§12.18 n.14 p.305 Add the following to the list after* "See"*: Bd. of Educ. v. Heister, 896 A.2d 342 (Md. 2006) ("'one of the most difficult and perplexing inquiries encountered in the construction of written agreements'") (quoting from Willson v. Mayor & City Council of Baltimore, 34 A.774 (Md. 1896)).

§12.18 n.15 p.305 Add the following at the end: *Accord:* McQueen, Rains & Tresch, LLP v. Citgo Petroleum Corp., 195 P.3d 35 (Okla. 2008). The Connecticut Supreme Court has retained this formula with modest differences in wording. *See* HH E. Parcel v. Handy & Harman, Inc., *supra* note 9; Am. Car Rental v. Comm'r of Consumer Protection, 869 A.2d 1198 (Conn. 2005).

A variant of this test appears when liquidated damages clauses are attached to restrictive covenants in employment agreements. Although these covenants already have severe limits on their enforceability, associated liquidated damages clauses often are subject to their own stringent test. *See* Mattern & Assocs. v. Seidel, 678 F. Supp. 2d 256 (D. Del. 2010) (Pennsylvania law; "In this context, [a liquidated damages] provision will survive scrutiny if: (1) the damages would be wholly uncertain and incapable or very difficult of being ascertained; (2) a party binds himself not to carry on any particular trade, business, or profession, within certain limits or within a specified period of time; (3) the sum fixed as security for the performance must not be overbroad in that it applies to a number of stipulations of widely different importance; and (4) the covenant is for abstaining from acts that are not measurable by any exact pecuniary standard."). *But see* Mayer Hoffman McCann, P.C. v. Barton, 614 F.3d 893 (8th Cir. 2010) (Missouri law; applies standard liquidated damages analysis to clause in non-compete agreement).

***§12.18 n.16 p.305 Add the following to the list after* "See":** Rohlin Constr. Co. v. City of Hinton, 476 N.W.2d 78 (Iowa 1991) ("We often turn to Restatements of the Law and believe it is appropriate to do in this case.").

***§12.18 n.18 p.306 Add the following to the list after* "Accord":** RKR Motors v. Associated Uniform Rental & Linen Supply, 995 So. 2d 588 (Fla. App. 2008) ("because the . . . actual lost profits [are] $10,437, and $10,437 is clearly disproportionate to the liquidated damages of $102,309, such that it would be unconscionable to impose the liquidated damages in this case, the trial court must award lost profits"); Ann-Par Sanitation v. Town of Brookhaven, 804 N.Y.S.2d 758 (App. Div. 2005) (charge for misuse of truck "grossly disproportionate" to the standard fee charged; "[h]ad the damage amount been more reasonable in light of the actual economic damage sustained or had Brookhaven established a reasonable relationship between the amount of damages and the economic and non-economic injuries sustained by it and its residents as a result of the breach, the Supreme Court would have been correct in sustaining the penalties.").

§12.18 n.18 p.306 Add the following at the end: For a particularly thoughtful application of the academic literature to New York law, see Spirit Locker v. EVO Direct, 696 F. Supp. 2d 296 (E.D.N.Y. 2010) (allowing unjust enrichment claim where sums paid under unenforceable penalty clause).

§12.18 n.19 p.306 Add the following to the list after **"Accord"***:* Cuneo Law Grp. v. Joseph, 669 F. Supp. 2d 99 (D.D.C. 2009) (upholding clause where damages "would have been difficult, if not impossible to assess when the settlement agreement was executed"); Schroeder v. Partin, 259 P.3d 617 (Idaho 2011) ("as long as a liquidated damages clause is intended at the outset to reasonably compensate a party for potential damages resulting from a breach, rather than to deter or punish the breach, the clause will be enforceable"); Carrothers v. City of S. Hutchinson, *supra* note 8 (rejecting use of actual damages in determining validity; "The better test, we believe, is to determine the reasonableness of a liquidated damages clause as of the time the contract was executed, not with the benefit of hindsight."); Barrie Sch. v. Patch, 933 A.2d 382 (Md. 2007) (party challenging clause must show that "[t]he damages contemplated in the Agreement were neither grossly excessive nor out of all proportion to those which might have been expected at the time of contracting").

§12.18 n.21 p.307 Add the following after the citation to **Kelly***:* , followed in NPS, LLC v. Minihane, 886 N.E.2d 670 (Mass. 2008) ("we do not take a 'second look' at the actual damages after the contract has been breached").

§12.18 n.21 p.307 Add the following to the list after **"Accord"***:* Carrothers Constr. Co. v. City of S. Hutchinson, *supra* note 8 (liquidated damages clauses "allow contracting parties to protect themselves against the difficulty, uncertainty, and expenses that necessarily follow judicial proceedings when trying to ascertain actual damages").

§12.18 n.22 p.307 Add the following to the list after **"Accord"***:* Cuneo Law Grp. v. Joseph, 669 F. Supp. 2d 99 (D.D.C. 2009) (the defendant's "argument that the actual damages sustained by the plaintiffs was minimal, as compared to the actual liquidated damages amount, is irrelevant. The fact remains that the extent of the damages could not be reasonably calculated when the settlement agreement was executed . . . "); Barrie Sch. v. Patch, *supra* note 19 ("Such a defense negates the benefit of an agreed-upon or stipulated damages clause and deviates from our acceptance of the principle that the time of contract formation is the appropriate point from which to judge the reasonableness of a stipulated amount of damages. It would also breed uncertainty in the calculation of damages . . ."); Seven Seventeen HB Charlotte Corp. v. Shrine Bowl of the Carolinas, 641 S.E.2d 711 (N.C. App. 2007) (rejecting argument that trial court should have required proof of damages after it held that contract breached; "Once the liquidated damages provision was declared enforceable, the proper damages were conclusively established by contract."); UPS Store, Inc. v. Hagan, 2016 U.S. Dist. LEXIS 54115 (S.D.N.Y. Mar. 15, 2016) (liquidated damages clause for trademark licensing fees enforceable, despite suggestion that UPS could easily recoup losses by licensing new UPS stores in the Manhattan area where franchisee had operated; "a mere possibility that UPS ultimately recouped its lost royalties through other franchisees does not show that the liquidated-damages clause — which was designed to estimate any future lost royalties — was unreasonable when made").

§12.18 n.23 p.307 Add the following after the citation to **Norwalk Door Closer***:* , followed in HH E. Parcel v. Handy & Harman, Inc., *supra* note 9 (quoting from *Norwalk Door Closer*: "[I]f the damage envisioned by the parties never occurs, the whole premise for their agreed estimate vanishes, and, even if the

contract was to be construed as one for liquidated damages rather than one for a penalty, neither justice nor the intent of the parties is served by enforcement. To enforce it would amount in reality to the infliction of a penalty.").

***§12.18 n.23 p.307 Add the following to the list after* "Accord":** ADP Marshall v. Noresco, LLC, 710 F. Supp. 2d 197 (D.R.I. 2010) ("If no loss has been sustained as a result of the breach, a liquidated damages clause may amount to an unenforceable penalty"; quoting from Restatement Second §356 cmt. *e*); Nat'l Serv. Indus. v. Here to Serve Rests., 695 S.E.2d 669 (Ga. App. 2010) (holding liquidated damages clause unenforceable in part because breached-against party ultimately did not seek recovery of any actual damages, even in the alternative).

***§12.18 n.25 p.308 Add the following to the list after* "Accord":** Dominic Wenzell, D.M.D. P.C. v. Ingrim, 228 P.3d 103 (Alaska 2010) ("the validity of a liquidated damages clause is to be decided by the court"); Kunelius v. Town of Stow, 588 F.3d 1 (1st Cir. 2009) ("In Massachusetts, whether a liquidated damages clause is valid and enforceable is a question of law"); Valence Operating Co. v. Dorsett, 164 S.W.3d 656 (Tex. 2005) ("Whether a contract term is a liquidated damages provision is a question of law for the court to decide.").

§12.18 n.25 p.308 Add the following after the citation to* Wassenaar*: , followed in Willard v. Javier, 899 A.2d 940 (Md. App. 2006) ("A legal conclusion regarding the validity of a stipulated damages provision . . . is dependent upon factual determinations of the trial judge").

§12.18 n.26 p.308 In the first paragraph, add the following to the list after* "Accord"*: Hendricks Prop. Mgmt. Corp. v. Birchwood Props. Ltd. P'ship, *supra* note 9 ("A party seeking to enforce a contractual clause for liquidated damages has the burden of proof").

§12.18 n.26 p.308 In the first paragraph, delete the citation to **Vernitron Corp.**

§12.18 n.26 p.308 In the second paragraph, add the following at the end of the second sentence: , followed in La Quinta Corp. v. Heartland Props., 603 F.3d 327 (6th Cir. 2010) ("The party challenging the bargained-for contractual provision has the burden of proving facts which would justify non-enforcement of the liquidated damages clause.").

§12.18 n.26 p.308 In the second paragraph, add the following to the list after **"Accord"*:*** Hutton Contracting Co. v. City of Coffeyville, 487 F.3d 772 (10th Cir. 2007) ("'The burden of proving that a liquidated damages clause constitutes an unenforceable penalty rests with the person challenging the provision.'") (quoting from IPC Retail Shops v. Oriental Gardens, 86 P.3d 543, 548 (Kan. App. 2004)); Midwest Oilseeds v. Limagrain Genetics Corp., 387 F.3d 705 (8th Cir. 2004) (Iowa law: predicting that "the Iowa Supreme Court would assign the burden of proving the unenforceability of a liquidated damages clause to the party raising that defense"); El Centro Mall v. Payless ShoeSource, 94 Cal. Rptr. 3d 43 (Ct. App. 2009) ("[Defendant] had the burden of proof to demonstrate the liquidated damages provision . . . was not intended by the parties to be a reasonable estimate of damages, but was instead a penalty."); S. Brooke Purill, Inc. v. Vailes, *supra* note 9 (holding that burden was on party seeking "to establish that the liquidated damage clause was a penalty"); TAL Fin. Corp. v. CSC Consulting, 844 N.E.2d 1085 (Mass. 2006) ("Any reasonable doubt as to whether a provision constitutes a penalty or a legitimate liquidated damages clause should be resolved in favor of the aggrieved party."); Holloway Auto. Grp. v. Lucic, 35 A.3d 577 (N.H. 2011) ("The defendants, as the parties alleging that the liquidated amount is unreasonable, bear the burden of proof."); JMD Holding Corp. v. Congress Fin. Corp., *supra* note 10 ("The burden is on the party seeking to avoid liquidated damages . . . to show that the stated liquidated damages are, in fact, a penalty."); Seven Seventeen HB Charlotte Corp. v. Shrine Bowl of the Carolinas, 641 S.E.2d 711 (N.C. App. 2007) ("the burden falls on the party seeking to invalidate a liquidated damages provision"; surveying arguments); Boots, Inc. v. Singh, 649 S.E.2d 695

(Va. 2007) ("[t]he party challenging the validity of a liquidated damages clause has the burden of proof").

§12.18 n.26 p.308 Add the following at the end: California takes an intermediate position. By statute, in a non-consumer case a liquidated damages clause is enforceable unless the party seeking to avoid the clause "establishes that the provision was unreasonable under the circumstances existing at the time the contract was made." Cal. Civ. Code §1671(b). In contrast, for consumer contracts or residential leases such a provision "is void except that the parties to such a contract may agree therein upon an amount which shall be presumed to be the amount of damage sustained by a breach thereof, when, from the nature of the case, it would be impracticable or extremely difficult to fix the actual damage." Cal. Civ. Code §1671(d). On consumer cases, *see* UCAN v. AT&T Broadband, 37 Cal. Rptr. 3d 827 (Ct. App. 2006) (courts require both that "fixing the amount of actual damages had to be impracticable or extremely difficult" and that "the amount selected must 'represent a reasonable endeavor to estimate fair compensation for the loss sustained,' " taking into account "both (1) the motivation and purpose in imposing the charges, and (2) their effect.") (quoting from Rice v. Schmid, 115 P.2d 498 (Cal. 1941)). Somewhat similarly, Maryland allocates the burden of proof according to the relative bargaining power of the parties. As a result, "the ultimate question of the assignment of the burden of proof, in cases where gross inequality of bargaining power exists, ought to be resolved in favor of the non-proponent of the provision, because the stipulated damage may prove unreasonable a priori." Willard v. Javier, *supra* note 25, at 952.

§12.18 n.27 p.309 Add the following at the end: On UCC 2A-504, *see* Shrank & Yim, Liquidated Damages in Commercial Leases of Personalty — The Proper Analysis, 64 Bus. Law. 757 (2009).

§12.18 n.28 p.310 Add the following after the first sentence: *Accord:* Raisin Mem. Trust v. Casey, 945 A.2d 1211 (Me. 2008) (adopting Restatement Second §356; " 'if such provisions reflect the anticipated or actual loss caused by the default and are

not usurious or excessive so as to constitute a penalty, they will be enforced.'") (quoting from St. Hilaire & Assocs. v. Harbor Corp., 607 A.2d 905 (Me. 1992)).

***§12.18 n.28 p.310 Add the following to the list after* "see":** Thomas v. Scarborough, 977 So. 2d 393 (Miss. App. 2007) (applying UCC §2-718 by analogy to contract for the lease of real estate, but misreading it to require that the liquidated damages clause be reasonable in light of the actual damages incurred); Holloway Auto. Grp. v. Lucic, 35 A.3d 577 (N.H. 2011) ("If the stipulated sum is grossly disproportionate to easily ascertainable, actual damages, the provision is an unenforceable penalty, and the aggrieved party will be awarded no more than the actual damages."); Boots, Inc. v. Singh, *supra* note 26 ("a liquidated damages clause is invalid only when the actual damages contemplated at the time of the agreement are shown to be certain and not difficult to determine or the stipulated amount is out of all proportion to the actual damages").

§12.18 n.29 p.310 Add the following at the end: Of course, a clause that is excessive for every reasonably foreseeable breach would also be unenforceable. *See* Am. Car Rental v. Comm'r of Consumer Protection, *supra* note 15 ($150 charge for driving rental auto for more than two minutes at more than 79 miles per hour a penalty, where harm caused by operation for two minutes at 80 miles per hour was 37 cents).

***§12.18 n.30 p.310 Add the following after the citation to* Carr-Gottstein Properties:** , followed in Dominic Wenzell, D.M.D. P.C. v. Ingrim, 228 P.3d 103 (Alaska 2010) ("we note our concern that the amount of stipulated damages is the same regardless of the nature of the breach . . . which suggests that the parties made no attempt to forecast actual damages").

§12.18 n.30 p.310 Add the following at the end: One court has gone so far as to say that a breach "was immaterial and insufficient to trigger the liquidated damages clause." Sheehan & Sheehan v. Nelson Malley & Co., 117 P.3d 219, 225 (Nev. 2005). The clause did not specify that it would be triggered only by material breach. The court may well have been correct in choosing not to enforce this invariant clause, but its reason seems misplaced. It should be possible to provide for liquidated damages for all types of breaches, whether material or not, if the clause is drafted properly.

§12.18 n.31 p.311 Add the following to the fourth sentence: , in JMD Holding Corp. v. Congress Fin. Corp., *supra* note 10 (limiting presumed scope of liquidated damages clause to material breaches; quoting from *United Air Lines* and this treatise as well).

§12.18 n.31 p.311 Add the following to the list after **"Accord"***:* Cummings Props. v. Nat'l Commc'ns Corp., *supra* note 9 ("in the case of a commercial agreement between sophisticated parties containing a liquidated damages provision applicable to breaches of multiple covenants, it may be presumed that the parties intended the provision to apply only to those material breaches for which it may properly be enforced") (citing to treatise).

§12.18 n.32 p.311 Add the following at the end: This may yield difficulties when more than one party may have caused the damages — for example, when delays in a construction project were caused by both the contractor and the owner, and the liquidated damages clause provides for *per diem* damages. Ordinarily it may be difficult to apportion cause, though not in the case mentioned above. The better view, and one held by "a strong majority" of recent decisions, allows a court to apportion damages so that the liquidated damages clause may be enforced as to the losses caused by the contractor, but not those caused by the owner. Hutton Contracting Co. v. City of Coffeyville, *supra* note 26; *accord* Robinson v. United States, 261 U.S. 486 (1923) (Brandeis, J.) ("The fact that the government's action caused some of the delay presents no legal ground for denying it compensation for loss suffered wholly through the fault of the contractor."); Aetna Cas. & Sur. Co. v. Butte-Meade Sanitary Water Dist., 500 F. Supp. 193 (D.S.D. 1980) ("simply because Defendant contributed to the delay in the completion of the project, it should not be barred from recovering liquidated damages"); Stop Loss Ins. Brokers v. Brown & Toland Med. Grp., 49 Cal. Rptr. 3d 609 (App. Ct. 2006) ("Rejecting the prior all-or-nothing rule, [California] courts have

applied apportionment principles to allocate contractual liquidated damages where delays in construction projects have been caused both by the owner and by the contractor.").

§12.18 n.33 p.311 Add the following to the list after* "Accord"*: Midwest Oilseeds v. Limagrain Genetics Corp., *supra* note 26 ("Because the breach involves the release of [the plaintiff's] intellectual property to its competitors, damages are extremely difficult to determine in this case."); Dynasteel Corp. v. Black & Veatch Corp., 698 F. Supp. 2d 1170 (W.D. Mo. 2010) (upholding liquidated damages of 25% of direct costs for added work as an estimate of overhead and similar costs; "overhead, supervision, and administrative expenses are types of costs that can be particularly difficult to accurately estimate, and the 25% markup is a reasonable forecast of the expenses [the breached-against party] would incur by having to do corrective work"); Am. Car Rental v. Comm'r of Consumer Protection, *supra* note 15 (condition "that the expected damages resulting from breach are uncertain in amount or difficult to prove"); NPS, LLC v. Minihane, *supra* note 21 (breach of ten-year contract to purchase two luxury seats at football stadium; "to predict at the time of contract how long it would take NPS to resell the defendant's seat license would be extremely difficult, if not impossible").

§12.18 n.33 p.311 Add the following to the list after* "But cf."*: Greentree Fin. Grp. v. Execute Sports, 78 Cal. Rptr. 3d 24 (Ct. App. 2008) (settlement agreement to pay $20,000 in two installments, with damages for breach set at full amount sought by plaintiff plus costs, coming to $61,232.50; held an unenforceable penalty because it "bears no reasonable relationship to the range of actual damages the parties could have anticipated from a breach of the stipulation to settle the dispute for $20,000.").

§12.18 n.33 p.311 In the first paragraph, add the following after the third sentence: Easy and difficult elements of damages may coincide. In those cases, the aggregate uncertainty is the pertinent question. *See* El Centro Mall v. Payless ShoeSource, *supra* note 26 (value of lost rental payments "readily ascertainable," so "the liquidation provision, to the extent considered only as a basis for estimating percentage rental damages, is an unenforceable penalty"; however, "the anticipated loss of the synergy, goodwill, and patronage Payless provides" is "difficult to estimate" and thus may render the liquidated damages clause reasonable).

§12.18 n.34 p.312 Add the following to the list after "See": H & G Ortho v. Neodontics Int'l, 823 N.E.2d 718 (Ind. App. 2005) ("a liquidated damage provision is particularly well-suited to a covenant not to compete ancillary to the sale of a business"); Willard v. Javier, *supra* note 25 ("The specific context of a covenant not to compete presents a factual scenario in which stipulated damage provisions are generally enforceable, given that quantifying the amount of damages in such cases may be an elusive prospect.").

§12.18 n.35 p.312 Add the following after the first sentence: *Accord:* Jameson Realty Grp. v. Kostiner, 813 N.E.2d 1124 (Ill. App. 2004) ("When determining whether actual damages would be uncertain in amount and difficult to prove . . . courts must look to 'the time of contracting, not the time of breach.' ") (quoting from Restatement Second §356).

§12.18 n.37 p.313 Add the following at the end of the second sentence: and in La Quinta Corp. v. Heartland Props., 603 F.3d 327 (6th Cir. 2010) (upholding liquidated damages award to franchisor of three years of franchise fees; "Actual damages, in the hospitality industry, are difficult to quantify and not strictly monetary . . . ").

§12.18 n.37 p.313 Add the following to the list after "See": Midwest Oilseeds v. Limagrain Genetics Corp., *supra* note 26 ("Where the difficulty of proof is great, Iowa allows greater latitude in the approximation of the actual harm."); Hendricks Prop. Mgmt. Corp. v. Birchwood Props. Ltd. P'ship, *supra* note 26 (these "foundational requirements . . . are not mutually exclusive").

§12.18 n.38 p.313 Add the following to the list after "Accord": Fuqua Constr. Co. v. Pillar Dev., 667 S.E.2d 633 (Ga. App. 2008) ("'the parties must intend to provide for damages rather than a penalty'") (quoting from S.E. Land Fund v. Real

Estate World, 227 S.E.2d 340 (Ga. 1976)), followed in JR Real Estate Dev. v. Cheeley Inv., 709 S.E.2d 577 (Ga. App. 2011) (where contract said that earnest money "is a reasonable estimate of the damages" and "is liquidated damages," earnest money found to be liquidated damages rather than penalty); Erie Ins. Co. v. Winter Constr. Co., 713 S.E.2d 318 (S.C. App. 2010) (whether a clause is for liquidated damages or a penalty is mainly a question of the intent of the parties).

§12.18 n.39 p.313 Add the following at the end: This court has retreated from its foray into subjectivism. *See* Bates Adver. USA v. 498 Seventh, LLC, 850 N.E.2d 1137 (N.Y. 2006) ("[T]he prospect of damages in the event of breach may always be said to encourage parties to comply with their contractual obligations. Liquidated damages are not transformed into a penalty merely because they operate in this way as well . . .").

§12.18 n.43 p.314 Add the following to the list after* "Accord"*: Am. Car Rental v. Comm'r of Consumer Protection, *supra* note 15 (whether a clause is a liquidated damages clause or a penalty is "not controlled by the fact that the phrase liquidated damage or the word penalty is used."); Schroeder v. Partin, 259 P.3d 617 (Idaho 2011) ("Where a provision uses the words 'penalty' or 'liquidated damages,' courts uniformly look beyond the provision's plain language to determine its character.").

§12.18 n.43 p.314 Add the following after the second sentence: *But cf.* Jameson Realty Grp. v. Kostiner, *supra* note 35 ("Although exculpatory language in the contract stating that the liquidated damages provision is not a penalty does not control, it should be given some weight."); White Lakes Shopping Ctr. v. Jefferson Std. Life Ins. Co., 490 P.2d 609 (Kan. 1971) ("The use of the terms 'penalty' or 'liquidated damages' in the [contract] . . . is given weight and is ordinarily accepted as controlling unless the facts and circumstances impel a contrary holding.").

§12.18 n.44 p.314 Add the following to the list after* "Accord"*: Schwan-Stabilo Cosmetics GmbH & Co. v. PacificLink Int'l Corp., 401 F.3d 28 (2d Cir. 2005) ("where an alternative contract provides as one alternative the payment of a sum of money," the proper remedy is the money); NPS, LLC v. Ambac Assurance Corp., 706 F. Supp. 2d 162 (D. Mass. 2010) ("Guaranteed Premium" to guaranty insurer upon early payment of bonds not a liquidated damages clause, because early payment not a breach, and the contract containing this clause "merely establishes the terms of termination"); Minnick v. Clearwire US, 683 F. Supp. 2d 1179 (W.D. Wash. 2010) (termination fee in wireless Internet and telephone contract alternative performance; "At the time of contracting, both options provided plausibly beneficial outcomes for the consumer. Customers could elect to fulfill their contract . . . [either by] pay[ing] for service for the full term of the contract . . . or . . . pay[ing] the monthly fee for a shorter term plus the [early termination fee]."); Planned Pethood Plus v. KeyCorp, Inc., 228 P.3d 262 (Colo. App. 2010) ("Where a borrower exercises an alternative form of performance by invoking a prepayment privilege, the law of liquidated damages is inapplicable."; collecting cases).

§12.18 n.46 p.315 In the first paragraph, add the following to the list after* "Accord"*: Am. Teleconferencing Servs. v. Network Billing Sys., 668 S.E.2d 259 (Ga. App. 2008) (requirement that customer purchase a minimum volume of service, whether the service was needed or not, was not a liquidated damages clause; "it was simply a negotiated minimum usage commitment that allowed ATS the benefit of negotiating lower rates and that justified certain capital expenses on the part of Network" and "does not in any way connect ATS's obligation to pay the minimum monthly fee with any breach of the contract").

§12.18 n.46 p.315 Add the following at the end of the second paragraph: This approach to *Parker* is profitably analyzed in V. Goldberg, Framing Contract Law chs. 15 & 16 (2006).

§12.18 n.51 p.316 Add the following to the list after* "Accord"*: Midwest Hatchery & Poultry Farms v. Doorenbos Poultry, 783 N.W.2d 56 (Iowa App. 2010) (enforcing fee-shifting provision in contract for sale of goods).

§12.18 n.53 p.316 In the second paragraph, add the following to the list after* "See"*: Barrie Sch. v. Patch, *supra* note 19 ("Because mitigation of damages is part of a post-breach calculation of actual damages . . . there exists no duty to mitigate damages where a valid liquidated damages clause exists."); NPS, LLC v. Minihane, *supra* note 21 ("in the case of an enforceable liquidated damages provision, mitigation is irrelevant and should not be considered in assessing damages").

§12.18 n.53 p.316 Add the following at the end: This line of cases is not without its attractions. If the liquidated damages clause is a reasonable estimate of the anticipated damage at the time of contracting, then whether the breached-against party acts prudently or not is immaterial. If it does not, then it has wasted its own money — but the clause would still be enforceable. The issue becomes more complex when the actual damages are taken into account. If the breached-against party has failed to mitigate, a logical outcome would be for the clause's validity to be judged using the damages that would have been assessed had the plaintiff properly mitigated. Otherwise an excessive liquidated damages clause could be enforced solely because a feckless plaintiff squandered chances to mitigate. Still, if mitigation is pertinent to the validity of a liquidated damages clause, we would see an erosion of the certainty promoted by liquidated damages clauses. *Cf.* Lake River Corp. v. Carborundum Co., 769 F.2d 1284 (7th Cir. 1985) (Posner, J.) ("the point of a liquidated-damages clause is to substitute party assessment [for the default rules of damages]; and that point is blunted, and the certainty that liquidated-damages clauses are designed to give impaired, if a defendant can force the plaintiff to take less than the damages specified in the clause, on the ground that the plaintiff could have avoided some of them"); Radisson Hotels Int'l v. Majestic Towers, 488 F. Supp. 2d 953 (C.D. Cal. 2007) ("[O]ne of the very purposes of liquidated damages is to allow the parties to avoid the cost, difficulty, and delay of proving damages. Requiring Radisson to prove its mitigation efforts would wholly undermine the rationale for employing liquidated damages provisions in the first place.") (internal quotation marks and citation deleted); NPS, LLC v. Minihane, *supra* note 21 ("When parties agree in advance to a sum certain that represents a reasonable estimate of potential damages, they exchange the opportunity to determine actual damages after a breach, including possible mitigation, for the peace of mind and certainty of result afforded by a liquidated damages clause. In such circumstances, to consider whether a plaintiff has mitigated its damages not only is illogical, but also defeats the purpose of liquidated damages provisions.") (internal quotation marks and citation deleted).

§12.18 n.54 p.317 Add the following at the end: *See generally* Note, Why There Should Be a Duty to Mitigate Liquidated Damages Clauses, 38 Hofstra L. Rev. 285 (2009).

§12.18 n.57 p.318 Add the following at the end: The employer's entitlement to liquidated damages was upheld after the contract was analyzed on the same principles that applied in cases by employees in *Kent State Univ. v. Ford*, 26 N.E.3d 868 (Ohio Ct. App. 2015) (liquidated damages provision enforceable against basketball coach who terminated his employment contract prior to expiration, in amount of $1.2 million, representing annual salary times number of years remaining on terminated contract).

§12.18a DRAFTING LIQUIDATED DAMAGES AND OTHER AGREED REMEDY PROVISIONS

§12.18a n.2 p.319 Replace the citation to* Fontaine & De Ly *with the following: M. Fontaine & F. De Ly, Drafting International Contracts: An Analysis of Contract Clauses ch. 6 (2006).

§12.18a n.4 p.319 Add the following at the end: Though it is prudent to avoid clauses that are, in the words of one judge, "invariant to the gravity of the breach," it is similarly prudent to ensure that the clause covers all categories of breach for which the drafter thinks a liquidated damages clause desirable. Lake River Corp. v. Carborundum Co., 769 F.2d 1284 (7th Cir. 1985) (Posner, J.). For an example of overly narrow drafting, *see* United Dairymen v. Schugg, 128 P.3d 756 (Ariz. App. 2006) (exclusive dairy marketing agreement linked damages to failure to deliver milk "produced by dairy cows that [the defendant] owns, possesses or controls"; defendant avoided clause by selling cows and leasing dairy to children).

Liquidated damages clauses made variant by levying per diem charges may well be easier to enforce than their fixed-charge kin, but they create a new problem: determining the start and end of the period over which liquidated damages will be assessed. Often it is difficult to fix an exact date for substantial completion. Even if the parties devise some means, that means may fail. For example, in one case involving breach by a subcontractor in a building project, the result of which was delay, the contract provided that the benchmark for ending the accrual of liquidated damages was the issuance of certificates of substantial completion by the architect. But what if the contractual prerequisites for substantial completion were never met and thus the certificates never issued? The court in that case held that potentially infinite liquidated damages would amount to a penalty. It instead fixed the damages as of the date at which the contract stated that the performance would be substantially complete. Comstock Potomac Yard v. Balfour Beatty Constr., 694 F. Supp. 2d 468 (E.D. Va. 2010). This result seems sound. Those who drafted this contract might have been wise to set an ending date for liquidated damages, not when an act occurred that is outside the control of the parties, but when the factual predicate for that act occurred.

§12.18a n.5 p.319 Add the following at the end: For a useful discussion of the difference between late charges and default interest (increased interest rates charged after default), see Inland Bank & Trust v. Knight, 927 N.E.2d 777 (Ill. App. 2010) ("[D]efault interest serves to balance the risk of lending to a defaulted borrower whereas late charges are more akin to a one-time penalty for missing or delaying a scheduled payment.").

§12.18a n.6 p.320 In the first paragraph, add the following after the citation to* Catholic Charities*: , both more or less distinguished in Dallas v. Chicago Teachers Union, 945 N.E.2d 1201 (Ill. App. 2011) (in both *Grossinger Motorcorp* and *Catholic Charities* the clauses at issue set up the option for the breached-against party either to take liquidated damages or to pursue actual damages; here, the clause stated that damages would be at least $100,000, but gave no optional remedies for the plaintiff) (*Quaere* whether this is a distinction without a difference; whether stated as an option or not, the effect is to give the plaintiff the choice of $100,000 or actual damages, whichever is greater.).

§12.18a n.6 p.320 ***In the second paragraph, add the following at the end:*** These cases may be better understood as more or less plausible statements of the intent of the contracting parties. Ordinarily it seems odd for the parties to a contract to agree that any breach, however trifling, will yield a certain amount of damages. It is our common experience that the greater the injury, the greater the loss. But it is not difficult to devise a scenario when *any* breach would indeed cause significant but difficult-to-determine damages, making a minimum clause of the sort upheld in *Dallas, supra*, a clear and reasonable expression of the intent of the parties. The facts of *Dallas* are an example. There the contract was a settlement agreement between a former union officer and the union, part of which barred the defendants from making any statements concerning the plaintiff on pain of damages of at least $100,000. As the court observed, the plaintiff had held union offices paying more than $100,000 per year, and the bar on comments in the settlement agreement would help make it possible for the plaintiff to hold union posts in the future. Even an apparently modest lapse might have a significant effect, but one whose probability and magnitude could not easily be calculated *ex ante.* All this is to say that it is generally best to avoid minimum clauses; if they are best suited to stating the intent of the parties, then it is best to lay a factual foundation in the contract itself.

§12.18a n.7 p.320 ***Add the following to the list after "See":*** DynaSteel Corp. v. Black & Veatch Corp., 698 F. Supp. 2d 1170 (W.D. Mo. 2010) (upholding liquidated damages of 25% of extra costs incurred where contract stated that these damages were "for Purchaser's overhead, supervision, and administrative costs").

§12.18a n.7 p.320 ***Add the following at the end:*** In contrast, merely stating that damages would be difficult to measure or that the liquidated damages clause estimates damages reasonably is not likely to have much effect. These statements are too general to carry weight, save perhaps as a minor indication that the parties

did not think the clause penal. *See* Nat'l Serv. Indus. v. Here to Serve Rests, 695 S.E.2d 669 (Ga. App. 2010) (holding unenforceable liquidated damages clause with a similar recital, especially because the statements presented as evidence in support of the clause were themselves conclusory). *But see* JR Real Estate Dev. v. Cheeley Inv., 709 S.E.2d 577 (Ga. App. 2011) (giving weight to liquidated damages clause in land contract stating that "the parties have agreed that the actual damages suffered by Seller if this Agreement is terminated due to a default by Buyer would be extremely difficult or impracticable to ascertain. After negotiation, the parties have agreed that, considering all the circumstances existing on the date of this Agreement, the amount of the Earnest Money deposit is a reasonable estimate of the damages that Seller would incur in such an event and that the aforesaid payment of Earnest Money deposit is liquidated damages hereunder and not a penalty"; no discussion of *Nat'l Serv. Indus., supra*).

§12.18a n.14 p.322 Add the following to the list after "See": NPS LLC v. Ambac Assurance Corp., 706 F. Supp. 2d 162 (D. Mass. 2010) ("Guaranteed Premium" to guaranty insurer upon early payment of bonds not a liquidated damages clause, because early payment not a breach); Morris v. Redwood Empire Bancorp, 27 Cal. Rptr. 3d 797 (App. Ct. 2005) (termination fee not a liquidated damages provision; "the payment is considered merely an alternative to performance, and not a penalty"); Smelkinson SYSCO v. Harrell, 875 A.2d 188 (Md. App. 2005) (settlement agreement provided that breach would entitle the aggrieved party to recover damages including reimbursement of any sums paid as well as any other damages; not a liquidated damages provision because the parties did not agree "to either a pre-determined amount of damages, or to a formula for damage, in the event of a breach" and because the clause "was not a mandatory and binding stipulation fixing the amount of damages"); Berens & Tate, P.C. v. Iron Mt. Info. Mgmt., 747 N.W.2d 383 (Neb. 2008) ("a provision for payment of a specified sum as compensation for services already contemplated by the contract, as opposed to compensation for injury resulting from a breach of the contract, is neither a liquidated damages clause nor a penalty provision"; removal fee charged by information storage firm not appropriately analyzed thus); Valence Operating Co. v. Dorsett, 164 S.W.3d 656 (Tex. 2005) (provision to recoup costs of well equipment, drilling, and operation from non-consenting participants in oil and gas operating agreement, so that consenting parties are repaid first, is not a liquidated damages clause; "liquidated damages are recoverable only where there has been a failure to perform contractual obligations").

§12.18a n.17 p.322 Add the following after the first sentence: *Accord:* Di Scipio v. Sullivan, 816 N.Y.S.2d 578 (App. Div. 2006) ("absent a legally cognizable excuse for defendant's failure to perform the contract, plaintiff may retain the down payment").

§12.18a n.17 p.322 Add the following after the second sentence: *Accord:* Hot Devs. v. Willow Lake Estates, 950 So. 2d 537 (Fla. App. 2007) (looking to the deposit's percentage of the total contract price to help determine the unconscionability of the clause; 9.65% "is well within the range of liquidated damages approved by Florida courts"); Boots, Inc. v. Singh, 649 S.E.2d 695 (Va. 2007) (looking to the deposit's percentage of the purchase price to determine whether retaining it "would be out of all proportion to any probable loss"; upholding retention of 3.3% deposit, where earlier had upheld deposits of 4.6% and 10%).

§12.18a n.21 p.323 Add the following to the list: Coizza v. 164-50 Crossbay Realty Corp., 900 N.Y.S.2d 416 (App. Div. 2010) (clause granting liquidated damages if title failed to close did not foreclose either specific performance or additional damages, where the clause was not expressly exclusive and the additional damages came from other failures to perform); Paradise Orchards Gen. P'ship v. Fearing, 94 P.3d 372 (Wash. App. 2004) ("shall have the right" to repossess the property and "shall have no obligation" to refund the earnest money do not bar specific performance; "No language in the agreement states the remedies are exclusive.").

§12.19 RELATION TO RESTITUTION IN GENERAL

§12.19 n.17 p.325 Add the following to the list after **"Accord"***:* Petrucelli v. Palmer, 596 F. Supp. 2d 347 (D. Conn. 2009) (as part of rescission of contract to purchase real property, buyers are entitled to recover mortgage payments made after the closing, as well as legal fees incurred as part of negotiating purchase agreement, taxes paid on property, and the like; this does not violate rule permitting rescission or damages, but not both, because that rule "does not prohibit parties from seeking to be made whole, in equity, simply because that remedy would demand more than a mere reversal of the properties exchanged in the contract").

§12.19 n.17 p.325 Add the following at the end: See Restatement (Third) of Restitution and Unjust Enrichment §37 & cmt. *a* (2011) (where an injured party may treat the contract as rescinded, it has the option of proceeding in restitution or in contract).

§12.19 n.18 p.325 Add the following to the list after **"Accord"***:* Old Stone Corp. v. United States, 450 F.3d 1360 (Fed. Cir. 2006) (for partial breach "restitution is not available, and the non-breaching party must pursue a claim for damages instead"); Admiral Fin. Corp. v. United States, 378 F.3d 1336 (Fed. Cir. 2004) ("an injured party is entitled to rescission only if the defendant repudiated the contract or committed a total breach"); Harrington v. Trotman, 983 A.2d 342 (D.C. 2009).

§12.19 n.19 p.326 Add the following to the list after **"See also"***:* Restatement (Third) of Restitution and Unjust Enrichment §38(1) (allowing restitution as remedy for "material breach or repudiation").

§12.19 n.19 p.326 Add the following at the end: Another instance of repudiation is the use of a *termination for convenience* clause, common in construction contracts, which "gives the customer the power to cancel the contract without cause, an act that would normally constitute a breach, while affording the contractor some compensation but not a right to common law damages,"

but does not bar the other party from suing for damages incurred before the termination for convenience. Winmar, Inc. v. Al Jazeera Int'l, 741 F. Supp. 2d 165, 179 (D.D.C. 2010). Termination under such a clause has in common with material breach and repudiation that it definitely ends the contractual relation (in the case of anticipatory repudiation, of course, only when the party receiving the repudiation chooses to treat it as a breach). As one authority has observed, "damages by the alternative measures [of restitution] are available when the effect of the defendant's breach or repudiation is to discharge the plaintiff's remaining duties of performance — making the award of damages a full reckoning of the parties' contractual obligations." Restatement (Third) of Restitution and Unjust Enrichment §38 cmt. *a*. Restitution damages should therefore be available for breaches of contract occurring before the invocation of a termination for convenience clause. (Note, however, that the *Winmar* court makes a regrettable error in stating the general principle, saying that "restitution is available for partial performance by a plaintiff of services under an express contract which has been breached by the defendant." Winmar, Inc. v. Al Jazeera Int'l, 741 F. Supp. 2d 165, 180 (D.D.C. 2010). This is true only for material breaches. Partial breaches, as the phrase is normally used, are breaches not rising to the level of material breaches. Those do not give the breached-against party a discharge of its remaining duties under the contract. Quite the contrary. *See* §8.15 *supra*. Indeed, the authority cited to by the *Winmar* court says as much. Lee v. Foote, 481 A.2d 484 (D.C. 1984) ("When an express contract has been repudiated or materially breached by the defendant, restitution for the value of the non-breaching party's performance is available as an alternative to an action for damages on the contract."). Appropriately narrowed, the *Winmar* court's statement is unexceptionable; left as is, it is unsupportable.)

§12.19 n.20 p.326 Add the following after the citation to* Earthinfo*: , followed in Watson v. Cal-Three, LLC, 254 P.3d 1189 (Colo. App. 2011) (allowing disgorgement to developer after guarantor incorrectly declared a default, secured the appointment of a receiver, foreclosed on the property, and sold it; remanded, however, so that trial court could apportion the profits produced by each party and give credit to the guarantor for payment of loan).

An agreement between two insurance companies included both an arbitration agreement and a provision that "directs the arbitrators to consider each agreement as 'an honorable engagement rather than merely a legal obligation' and goes on to explain that the arbitrators are 'relieved of all judicial formalities and may abstain from following the strict rules of law.' " First State Ins. Co. v. National Cas. Co., 781 F.3d 7, 12 (1st Cir. 2015). When the arbitration panel fashioned a payment protocol that one party characterized as beyond the terms of the agreement and "plucked out of thin air and not derived from any contract term," *id.* at 11, the company sought to have the award set aside under the Federal Arbitration Act. However, the First Circuit found that the arbitrators were at least arguably interpreting the contract and, moreover, "an honorable engagement provision empowers arbitrators to grant forms of relief, such as equitable remedies, not explicitly mentioned in the underlying agreement," *id.* at 12.

§12.19 n.21 p.326 Add the following to the list after "Accord": United City of Yorkville v. Village of Sugar Grove, 875 N.E.2d 1183 (Ill. App. 2007) (impossible to rescind agreement not to annex land where intermediate annexations could not practicably be undone).

§12.19 n.21 p.326 Add the following at the end: If, however, the injured party is unable to make its own restitution at the time it seeks to sue, the courts probably will permit the suit to go forward, with that party's restitution coming only after judgment. Cal. Civ. Code §1691 ("[a] party who has received benefits by reason of a contract that is subject to rescission and who in an action or proceeding seeks relief based upon rescission shall not be denied relief because of a delay in restoring or in tendering restoration of such benefits before judgment unless such delay has been substantially prejudicial to the other party; but the court may make a tender of restoration a condition of its judgment."); Village Northridge Homeowners Ass'n v. State Farm Fire & Cas. Co., 237 P.3d 598 (Cal. 2010) (tracing history, collecting cases).

§12.19 n.22 p.327 Add the following at the end: *See generally* Kull, Rescission and Restitution, 61 Bus. Law. 569 (2006).

§12.19 n.27 p.327 Add the following after the second sentence: *Accord:* Henrietta Piping v. Antetomaso & Micca Grp., 816 N.Y.S.2d 663 (Sup. Ct. 2006) (following Restatement).

§12.20 AVAILABILITY FOR BREACH

§12.20 n.3 p.329 In the first paragraph, add the following to the list after* "See also"*: Beale, Exceptional Measures of Damages in Contract, in Wrongs and Remedies in the Twenty-First Century 217 (P. Birks ed. 1996); McGregor, Restitutionary Damages, in *id.* at 203.

§12.20 n.4 p.329 Add the following at the end: The Restatement (Third) of Restitution and Unjust Enrichment recognizes a right to disgorgement where the promisor breached the contract deliberately, the breach yielded the promisor a profit, and ordinary damages remedies will not adequately protect the promisee's entitlement under the contract. Restatement (Third) of Restitution and Unjust Enrichment §39(1). This is distinct from accounting for profits arising from a breach of fiduciary duty or a duty of confidentiality. Restatement (Third) of Restitution and Unjust Enrichment §§39 cmt. *d*, 42, & 43. Put generally, the disgorgement remedy, as set forth in the Restatement, seeks to make opportunistic breach unprofitable. Thus, for example, the right to disgorgement where "the plaintiff has (in effect) paid the defendant in advance for a performance that the defendant has failed to render." Restatement (Third) of Restitution and Unjust Enrichment §39 cmt. *d* & ills. 5-7. This remedy is naturally narrow; it requires that the breach be both deliberate and profitable, after all, and that routine damages will not adequately protect the promisee. Restatement (Third) of Restitution and Unjust Enrichment §39 cmt. *f*.

§12.20 n.8 p.330 Add the following after the second sentence: *Accord:* Watson v. Cal-Three, LLC, 254 P.3d 1189 (Colo. App. 2011) (allowing disgorgement to developer after guarantor incorrectly declared a default, secured the appointment of a receiver, foreclosed on the property, and sold it; remanded, however, so that trial court could apportion the profits produced by each party and give credit to the guarantor for payment of loan).

§12.20 n.14 p.332 Add the following at the end of the first paragraph: Under these circumstances, the restitution and reliance interests converge, the only possible exception being the relevance of losses on the contract. Westfed Holdings v. United States, 407 F.3d 1352 (Fed. Cir. 2005) ("This type of restitution is sometimes said to be 'more properly viewed as a form of reliance damages[,]' as distinguished from restitution based on the breaching party's return of the value of benefits conferred by the non-breaching party's performance.") (quoting from Hansen Bancorp v. United States, 367 F.3d 1297 (Fed. Cir. 2004)). Hence the observation that "restitution is not recoverable in addition to reliance damages for the same injury." Am. Capital Corp. v. FDIC, 472 F.3d 859, 870 (Fed. Cir. 2006).

§12.20 n.14 p.332 Add the following at the end: The Restatement (Third) of Restitution and Unjust Enrichment has allied itself firmly with the minority position, limiting restitution to the provable expectation. Restatement (Third) of Restitution & Unjust Enrichment §38 & cmt. *c*. Whether this will prove pioneering or quixotic remains to be seen. It would have the effect of removing a fault-based damage measure from the law of contract, which may or may not be an advantage. This limit would remove the anomaly discussed *infra* at notes 23-28, in which a plaintiff who has completed or all but completed performance is limited to the contract price, but one who falls short of that may recover more.

§12.20 n.18 p.334 Add the following at the end: Again, the new Restatement has embraced *Kehoe*, at least for those contracts for which it is possible to relate the amount of performance to a portion of the contract price. Restatement (Third) of Restitution & Unjust Enrichment §38 cmt. *c* & ill. 10. It is not clear how this approach in practice will differ from the more common method. As the Restatement points out, a strict *pro rata* share likely will be inaccurate; if the heavier expenses fall in the early or late parts of performance, the remedy would be adjusted appropriately. The main difference would come if the value of the partial performance exceeds the contract price.

§12.20 n.26 p.336 In the second paragraph, add the following to the list in the first sentence: DeLapaz v. SelectBuild Constr. Co., 917 N.E.2d 93 (Ill. App. 2009) ("A discharged attorney . . . is entitled to payment for the services rendered prior to discharge on a *quantum meruit* basis."; where case taken on contingent fee and some of the work was done by lawyers discharged before settlement, the contingent fee was awarded to the firm less a *quantum meruit* payment to the discharged lawyers).

§12.20 n.27 p.337 Add the following to the list after **"Accord":** Engelke v. Athle-Tech Computer Sys., 982 So. 2d 3 (Fla. App. 2008) (limiting damages to a prorated share of the proceeds).

§12.20 n.28 p.337 Add the following at the end of the first paragraph: For an intermediate position, *see* O'Brien & Gere Tech. Servs. v. Fru-Con/Fluor Daniel Joint Venture, 380 F.3d 447 (8th Cir. 2004) (Missouri law: "[R]ecovery in quantum meruit is generally limited to the agreed-upon price for the goods and services; the contract price does not limit recovery, however, where the parties abandon the contract."). *See also* Emerald Pointe Prop. Owners' Ass'n v. Commercial Constr. Indus., 978 So. 2d 873 (Fla. App. 2008) ("'The contract price generally is the upper limit where the contractor sues in quantum meruit, but in the event the owner's breach is willful, the contractor may recover his outlay even if it exceeds the contract price.'") (quoting from Ballard v. Krause, 248 So. 2d 233 (Fla. App. 1971)).

§12.20a BASES FOR A BROADER DISGORGEMENT PRINCIPLE

§12.20a n.3 p.339 Add the following after the citation to **Earthinfo***:* , followed in Watson v. Cal-Three, LLC, 254 P.3d 1189 (Colo. App. 2011) (allowing disgorgement to developer after guarantor incorrectly declared a default, secured the appointment of a receiver, foreclosed on the property, and sold it; remanded, however, so that trial court could apportion the profits produced by each party and give credit to the guarantor for payment of loan).

§12.20a n.16 p.344 Add the following to the list after **"see"***:* Botterell, Contractual Performance, Corrective Justice, and Disgorgement for Breach of Contract, 16 Legal Theory 135 (2010); Eisenberg, The Disgorgement Interest in Contract Law, 105 Mich. L. Rev. 559 (2006); Grosskopf & Medina, Remedies for Wrongfully-Issued Preliminary Injunctions: The Case for Disgorgement of Profits, 32 Seattle U. L. Rev. 904 (2009); Roberts, Restitutionary Disgorgement for Opportunistic Breach of Contract and Mitigation of Damages, 42 Loy. L.A. L. Rev. 131 (2008); Roberts, Restitutionary Disgorgement as a Moral Compass for Breach of Contract, 77 U. Cin. L. Rev. 991 (2009); Thel & Siegelman, You *Do* Have to Keep Your Promises: A Disgorgement Theory of Contract Remedies, 52 Wm. & Mary L. Rev. 1181 (2011).

§12.20a n.16 p.344 Add the following to the list after **"See also"***:* Engler & Heyman, The Missing Elements of Contract Damages, 84 Temp. L. Rev. 119 (2011) (proposing presumptive measure of out-of-pocket expenditures plus a reasonable risky rate of return for breaches of contract with an undetermined rate of return; discussed as a contrast to disgorgement).

§12.20a n.21 p.346 Add the following at the end: But see McMillian v. McMillian, 713 S.E.2d 920 (Ga. App. 2011) (disgorgement an appropriate remedy for breaches of fiduciary duty, but recovery of share of lost profits more appropriate for misappropriation by a partner of a business opportunity of the partnership).

§12.20a p.347 Add the following at the end of the first sentence of the second full paragraph: . . . that resulted from the breach of fiduciary duty.[27a]

[27a] *See* Peters v. N.M. Banquest Investors Corp., 188 P.3d 1185 (N.M. 2008) ("[A] causal connection must exist between the breach [of fiduciary duty] and the benefit sought to be disgorged."). The relation between the benefits derived by the breaching party that will be subject to disgorgement and the losses incurred by the breached-against party is indirect. Whether the breached-against party suffered a loss as a result of the breach of fiduciary duty seems germane to whether the breaching party will be obliged to disgorge and, if so, how much, but even if the breached-against party suffers no loss, the breaching party may nevertheless be obliged to disgorge its gains. *See* Bertelsen v. Harris, 537 F.3d 1047 (9th Cir. 2008) (not an abuse of discretion for court not to order disgorgement of attorney fees after attorney violated multiple rules of professional conduct, when the fee paid was reasonable, the results successful, and the evidence of resulting harm absent).

§12.20a n.41 p.351 Add the following to the list after "See": McKendrick, Breach of Contract, Restitution for Wrongs, and Punishment, in Commercial Remedies 93 (A. Burrows & E. Peel eds. 2003).

§12.20a p.353 Add the following at the end of the first full paragraph: . . . I must disgorge my entire $25 gain.[47a]

[47a] *See* Griffith v. Barnes, 560 F. Supp. 2d 29 (D.D.C. 2008) (disgorgement of entire gain from sale of property without owner's knowledge or consent; gain measured as entire proceeds less what had already been paid to the owner).

§12.20a n.59 p.356 Add the following at the end: *Cf.* Watson v. Cal-Three, LLC, 254 P.3d 1189 (Colo. App. 2011) (disgorgement of profits earned as a result of wrongfully foreclosing on and selling property).

§12.20a n.74 p.361 Add the following at the end: The disgorgement remedy may, however, be termed equitable when it is used to restore property wrongfully taken, as opposed to figuring damages for breach. *See* Great-W. Life & Annuity Ins. Co. v. Knudson, 534 U.S. 204 (2002) ("for restitution to lie in equity, the action generally must seek not to impose personal liability on the defendant, but to restore to the plaintiff particular funds or property in the defendant's possession"); followed in Buffalo Laborers Sec. Fund v. J.P. Jeanneret Assocs. (*In re* Beacon Assocs. Litig.), 818 F. Supp. 2d 697 (S.D.N.Y. 2011) (characterizing as equitable a claim for profits derived from investment adviser's participation in Madoff fraud).

§12.20a n.77 p.361 Add the following at the end: Another line of cases grants disgorgement to public entities "when the wrongdoer obtained the benefit as a direct result of bribing a public official." County of Essex v. First Nat'l Bank, 891 A.2d 600, 606 (N.J. 2006) ("Disgorgement in favor of the public entity serves as a harsh remedy against those who bribe a public official to secure a public contract and provides a deterrent to such unlawful activity.").

§12.20b DISGORGEMENT PRINCIPLE AND MARKET DAMAGES

§12.20b n.3 p.363 Add the following at the end of the first paragraph: More commonly the defendant's profit is used as a less than desirable means of calculating the plaintiff's loss, especially when proving a lost profit will be difficult, if not impossible. This often is true for breaches of covenants not to compete. *See* TruGreen Cos. v. Mower Bros., Inc., 199 P.3d 929 (Utah 2008) ("Our adoption of a lost profits standard, however, does not prevent a non-breaching party from examining a defendant's profits in an attempt to assess its own economic loss."). This is purely a way of measuring expectation, and not an incursion of unjust enrichment into the realm of contract. *Id.* ("By holding that lost profits is the appropriate measure of damages in suits concerning breaches of covenants not to compete . . . we are also holding that restitution or unjust enrichment is not an appropriate measurement in these actions.").

§12.20c LIMITED EXTENSION OF DISGORGEMENT PRINCIPLE

§12.20c n.8 p.374 Add the following after the first sentence: *But see* Hinz v. Neurosci., Inc., 538 F.3d 979 (8th Cir. 2008) (rejecting use of defendant's gain for damages from breach of settlement agreement not to market products; no evidence what fraction of the defendant's gain was due to non-breaching efforts).

BIOGRAPHICAL APPENDIX

p. 385 In the Cardozo biography, add the following at the end: *See generally* A. Kaufman, Benjamin Cardozo (1998).

p. 387 In the Easterbrook biography, add the following at the end: *See generally* Special Issue: Celebrating Judge Easterbrook's Twenty-Five Years On the Bench, 77 U. Chi. L. Rev. 959 (2010).

p. 387 After the Eisenberg biography, add the following: **Farnsworth.** E[dward] Allan Farnsworth (1928–2005) took his law degree at Columbia and shortly became a member of the faculty, teaching with great distinction for over fifty years. He was Reporter for the Restatement (Second) of Contracts, succeeding Robert Braucher, *supra,* and was an influential participant in many projects in international contract and commercial law. He wrote many articles, treatises, monographs, and casebooks in contracts and commercial law, with particularly important articles in contract interpretation, precontractual obligation, and remedies, a classic casebook in contracts, and this treatise. These, and in particular his later books on regret and mistake, display his lucid style, unrivalled command of the contracts literature, and breadth of mind. *See generally* In Memoriam: E. Allan Farnsworth, 105 Colum. L. Rev. 1417 (2005); Theory and Anti-Theory in the Work of Allan Farnsworth, 13 Tex. Wesleyan L. Rev. 1 (2006).

p. 387 In the Friendly biography, add the following at the end: *See generally* D. Dorsen, Henry Friendly: Greatest Judge of His Era (2012).

p. 388 In the Hand biography, add the following at the end: *See generally* G. Gunther, Learned Hand (1994).

p.388 In the Holmes biography, add the following at the end: *See generally* S. Novick, Honorable Justice (1989); G. White, Justice Oliver Wendell Holmes (1993).

p. 389 After the Kozinski biography, add the following: **Langdell.** Christopher Columbus Langdell (1826–1906) was a successful New York practitioner from 1855 to 1870, after which he joined the Harvard law faculty. He spent the next 36 years there, 25 of them as dean. Langdell is known best today for creating and popularizing the Socratic method of law teaching, in part through the first casebook, *A Selection of Cases on the Law of Contracts* (1870). In this, his contracts treatise, and a series of books and articles, Langdell did much to develop the concepts of consideration and contract formation, particularly the bargain theory of consideration and the distinction between unilateral and bilateral contract. Attacks by Holmes and the Legal Realists have cemented his reputation as an arch-formalist, not entirely unfairly. *See generally* B. Kimball, The Inception of Modern Professional Education: C.C. Langdell, 1826–1906 (2009); Grey, Langdell's Orthodoxy, 45 U. Pitt. L. Rev. 1 (1983); Wells, Langdell and the Invention of Legal Doctrine, 58 Buff. L. Rev. 551 (2010).

p. 389 In the Llewellyn biography, add the following at the end: N.E.H. Hull, Roscoe Pound and Karl Llewellyn: Searching for an American Jurisprudence (1997); W. Twining, Karl Llewellyn and the Realist Movement (1973).

p. 389 In the Posner biography, add the following at the end: *See generally* Commentaries: Twenty-Five Years of Richard Posner, the Judge, 120 Harv. L. Rev. 1141 (2007); Special Issue: Commemorating Twenty-Five Years of Judge Richard A. Posner, 74 U. Chi. L. Rev. 1641 (2007).

p.389 After the Posner biography, add the following: **Scott.** Robert E. Scott (1943–) is Allan Farnsworth's successor as Alfred McCormack Professor of Law at Columbia. Before that, he was a long-time member of the Virginia law faculty, where he served as dean from 1991 to 2001. He is one of the pioneers of the economic analysis of contract law — indeed, he remains perhaps its most important figure, thanks to a long series of articles, many written with Charles Goetz or Alan Schwartz. Professor Scott also heads Columbia's Center for Contract and Economic Organization.

p. 390 In the Story biography, add the following at the end: *See generally* R. Newmyer, Supreme Court Justice Joseph Story: Statesman of the Old Republic (1985).

p. 390 In the Traynor biography, add the following at the end: *See generally* B. Field, Activism in Pursuit of the Public Interest: The Jurisprudence of Chief Justice Roger J. Traynor (2003).

***p. 390 In the Williston biography, add the following to the list after* "See generally":** Movsesian, Rediscovering Williston, 62 Wash. & Lee L. Rev. 207 (2005).

TABLE OF CASES

References are to sections and footnote numbers in the 2016-3 supplement.

Smith v. Mallick, 514 F.3d 48 (D.C. Cir. 2008), 11.7 n.1
Smith v. Mountjoy, 694 S.E.2d 598 (Va. 2010), 2.17 n.8
Smith v. Sharpensteen, 521 P.2d 394 (Okla. 1974), 4.26 n.26
Smith v. Smith, 597 S.E.2d 250 (Va. 2004), 3.27 n.5
Smith v. Univ. Animal Clinic, 30 So. 3d 1154 (La. App. 2010), 12.9 n.6
Smith v. Wachovia Bank, 33 So. 3d 1191 (Ala. 2009), 2.4 n.10
Smith-Hunter Constr. Co. v. Hopson, 616 S.E.2d 419 (S.C. 2005), 7.6 n.10
Smith Trust, *In re*, 745 N.W.2d 754 (Mich. 2008), 3.23a n.18
Smurfit-Stone Container Enters. v. Zion Jacksonville Ltd. P'ship, 52 So. 3d 55 (Fla. App. 2010), 5.2 n.6
SN4, LLC v. Anchor Bank, fsb, 848 N.W.2d 559 (Minn. Ct. App. 2014), 6.8 n.6
Sniecinski v. Blue Cross & Blue Shield, 666 N.W.2d 186 (Mich. 2003), 2.10 n.24
Snyder v. Bronfman, 921 N.E.2d 567 (N.Y. 2009), 6.11 n.20
Snyder v. HSBC Bank, 873 F. Supp. 2d 1139 (D. Ariz. 2012), 6.5 n.28; 6.9 n.17
Soc'y of Lloyd's v. Reinhart, 402 F.3d 982 (10th Cir. 2005), 4.27 n.7
Softchoice Corp. v. MacKenzie, 636 F. Supp. 2d 927 (D. Neb. 2009), 5.3a nn.15, 39
Softchoice, Inc. v. Schmidt, 763 N.W.2d 660 (Minn. App. 2009), 2.10b n.5
Sogeti USA v. Scariano, 606 F. Supp. 2d 1080 (D. Ariz. 2009), 11.4 n.15
Solar Applications Eng'g v. T.A. Operating Corp., 327 S.W.3d 104 (Tex. 2010), 8.2 n.7; 8.7a n.4
Solomon v. U.S. Healthcare Sys., 797 A.2d 346 (Pa. Super. 2002), 7.16 n.21
Solymar Invs. v. Banco Santander, 672 F.3d 981 (11th Cir. 2012), 8.2 n.13
Somers v. Avant, 261 S.E.2d 334 (Ga. 1979), 10.5a n.10
Soncoast Cmty. Church v. Travis Boating Ctr., 981 So. 2d 654 (Fla. App. 2008), 7.8 n.21
Sony Ericsson Mobile Commc'ns USA v. Agere Sys., 672 S.E.2d 763 (N.C. App. 2009), 3.28 n.8
Sorenson v. Bridge Capital Corp., 861 N.Y.S.2d 280 (App. Div. 2008), 4.14 n.9
S. Brooke Purill, Inc. v. Vailes, 850 A.2d 1135 (D.C. 2004), 12.18 nn.9, 26
S. Cherry St., LLC v. Hennessee Grp LLC, 573 F.3d 98 (2d Cir. 2009), 6.4 nn.9, 30

Spinks v. Equity Residential Briarwood Apts., 90 Cal. Rptr. 3d 453 (Ct. App. 2009), 10.3 n.1; 10.7 n.5
Spirit Locker v. EVO Direct, 696 F. Supp. 2d 296 (E.D.N.Y. 2010), 8.14 n.16; 12.18 n.18
Spivey v. Adaptive Mktg., 660 F. Supp. 2d 940 (S.D. Ill. 2009), 4.26 n.35
Spivey v. Adaptive Mktg., 622 F.3d 816 (7th Cir. 2010), 9.4 n.17
Spreitzer v. Hawkeye State Bank, 775 N.W.2d 573 (Iowa 2009), 4.14 nn.1, 2
Spring Creek Holding Co. v. Shinnihon U.S.A. Co., 943 A.2d 881 (N.J. App. Div. 2008), 8.23 nn.16, 24
Springs & Davenport, Inc. v. AAG, Inc., 683 S.E.2d 814 (S.C. App. 2009), 8.4 n.34
Springs Window Fashions Div. v. Blind Maker, 184 S.W.3d 840 (Tex. Civ. App. 2006), 7.4 n.26
Spring Valley IV Joint Venture v. Neb. State Bank, 690 N.W.2d 788 (Neb. 2005), 10.3 nn.16, 43
Springwell Corp. v. Falcon Drilling Co., 16 F. Supp. 2d 300 (S.D.N.Y. 1998), 4.23a n.4; 6.10 n.20
Sprint Commc'ns Co. v. APCC Servs., 128 S. Ct. 2531 (2008), 11.2 n.1
Sprout v. Bd. of Educ. of County of Harrison, 599 S.E.2d 764(W. Va. 2004), 3.6 n.2
SR Int'l Bus. Ins. Co. v. World Trade Ctr. Props., 467 F.3d 107 (2d Cir. 2006), 7.13 nn.16, 17
S.r.l. Orintix v. NV Fabelta Ninove, No. 1998/AR/2613 (App. Ct. Nov. 24, 2004), 1.9b n.10
SS-II, LLC v. Bridge St. Assocs., 977 A.2d 189 (Conn. 2009), 6.7 n.37; 6.9 n.14
SSP Partners, *In re*, 241 S.W.3d 162 (Tex. Civ. App. 2007), 10.9 n.4
Stafford v. S. Vanity Magazine, 231 S.W.3d 530 (Tex. Civ. App. 2007), 12.5 n.2; 12.6 n.12
Stalley v. Transitional Hosps. Corp., 44 So. 3d 627 (Fla. App. 2010), 10.3 n.16
Stamato v. Stamato, 818 So. 2d 662 (Fla. App. 2002), 9.4 n.22
Stamtec, Inc. v. Anson Stamping Co., 346 F.3d 651 (6th Cir. 2003), 12.9 n.8
Starke v. Gilt Grpe, Inc., No. 13-CV-5497, 2014 U.S. Dist. LEXIS 58006, 2014 WL 1652225, at *2-3 (S.D.N.Y. Apr. 24, 2014), 3.7 n.1
Std. Steam Trust LLC v. Windfall Minerals, 872 F. Supp. 2d 1207 (D. Colo. 2012), 9.3 n.34
Stanford Dev. Corp. v. Stanford Condo. Owners Ass'n., 285 S.W.3d 45 (Tex. Civ. App. 2009), 10.3 n.16

Thedford Crossing v. Tyler Rose Nursery, 306 S.W.3d 860 (Tex. Civ. App. 2010), 8.2 n.7
Thermal Design v. M & M Bldrs., 698 S.E.2d 516 (N.C. App. 2010), 7.6 n.18
THI of New Mexico v. Patton, 741 F.3d 1162 (10th Cir. 2014), 4.28 n.47
Thibodeau v. Comcast Corp., 912 A.2d 874 (Pa. Super. 2006), 4.28 nn.26, 52
Thiesing v. Dentsply Int'l, 748 F. Supp. 2d 932 (E.D. Wis. 2009), 2.3 n.2; 2.10b n.6; 2.13 n.1; 5.3 n.28; 5.8 n.21
Thigpen v. Locke, 363 S.W.2d 247, 253 (Tex. 1962), 9.4 n.22
Third Story Music v. Waits, 48 Cal. Rptr. 2d 747 (Ct. App. 1995), 7.17 n.45
Thomas, *In re* Marriage of, 199 S.W.3d 847 (Mo. App. 2006), 2.11 n.4; 4.27 n.1
Thomas v. Montelucia Villas, 275 P.3d 607 (Ariz. App. 2012), 8.22 n.6
Thomas v. Scarborough, 977 So. 2d 393 (Miss. App. 2007), 12.18 n.28
Thomas & Wong Gen Contr. v. Lake Bank, 553 F.3d 650 (8th Cir. 2009), 6.2 n.14
Thomas J. Sibley, P.C. v. Brentwood Inv. Dev. Co., 356 S.W.3d 659 (Tex. Civ. App. 2011), 6.2 n.1; 6.8 n.1
Thompson, *In re* Estate of, 752 N.W.2d 624 (N.D. 2008), 6.9 n.24
Thompson, *In re* Marriage of, 48 Cal. Rptr. 2d 721 (Ct. App. 1996), 4.24 n.9
Thompson v. Allstate Ins. Co., 673 S.E.2d 227 (Ga. 2009), 2.3 n.8; 7.3 n.56
Thompson v. Bar-S Foods Co., 174 P.3d 567 (Okla. 2007), 2.14 n.2; 3.14a n.14
Thompson v. First Am. Nat'l Bank, 19 So. 3d 784 (Miss. App. 2009), 6.12 n.3
Thompson v. Floyd, 713 S.E.2d 883 (Ga. App. 2011), 3.26 n.40; 3.30 n.7
Thompson v. Gordon, 948 N.E.2d 39 (Ill. 2011), 7.12 n.13
Thompson v. Hi Tech Motor Sports, 945 A.2d 368 (Vt. 2008), 4.29a n.21; 5.2 n.25
Thompson v. Miles, 741 F. Supp. 2d 296 (D. Me. 2010), 7.17 n.3
Thompson v. Toll Dublin, 81 Cal. Rptr. 3d 736 (Ct. App. 2008), 4.26 n.19; 4.28 n.56
Thompson v. Witherspoon, 12 A.3d 685 (Md. App. 2011), 10.3 nn.8, 16
Thomson Learning v. Olympia Props., 850 N.E.2d 314 (Ill. App. 2006), 8.7 n.14

Wall Street Network v. N.Y. Times Co., 80 Cal. Rptr. 3d 6 (Ct. App. 2008), 1.9a n.11

TABLE OF UNIFORM COMMERCIAL CODE SECTIONS

References are to sections and footnote numbers in the 2016-3 supplement.

TABLE OF RESTATEMENTS OF THE LAW

References are to sections and footnote numbers in the 2016-3 supplement.

Principles of the Law of Software Contracts

Restatement (Second) of Contracts

Restatement (Second) of Judgments

Restatement (Third) of Employment Law

Restatement (Third) of the Law Governing Lawyers

Restatement (Third) of Property

Restatement (Third) of Property (Mortgages)

Restatement (Third) of Restitution and Unjust Enrichment

TABLE OF AUTHORITIES

References are to sections and footnote numbers in the 2016-3 supplement.

Pryor, Consideration in the Common Law of Contracts: A Biblical-Theological Critique, 18 Regent U.L. Rev. 1 (2005-2006), 2.8 n.24

Quint, A Restatement of Rabbinic Civil Law (1995), 2.16 n.3

Radin, Maintenance by Champerty, 24 Cal. L. Rev. 48 (1936), 5.2 n.7; 11.4 n.1

Rakoff, Contracts of Adhesion: An Essay in Reconstruction, 96 Harv. L. Rev. 1174 (1983), 4.26 n.40

Rakoff, Good Faith in Contract Performance: *Market Street Associates Ltd. Partnership v. Frey*, 120 Harv. L. Rev. 1187 (2007), 7.17 n.33

Ravdin L., Premarital Agreements: Drafting and Negotiation (2011), 5.4a n. 1

Raymond, Manner, Method, Receipt or Dispatch: The Use of Electronic Media is Nothing New to the Law, 52 Loy. L. Rev. 1 (2006), 3.22 n.12

Reich, A European Contract Law: Ghost or Host for Integration?, 24 Wisc. Int'l L.J. 425 (2006), 1.8a n.4

Reimann, The CISG in the United States: Why It Has Been Neglected and Why Europeans Should Care, 71 Rabels Zeitschrift für Ausländisches und Internationales Privatrecht 115 (2007), 1.9b n.7

Rendleman, Restating Restitution: The Restatement Process and Its Critics, 65 Wash. & Lee L. Rev. 933 (2008), 2.20 n.8

Reyes, Emily Alpert, L.A. Plan Would Demand Airbnb Hand Over Information So City Can Track Down Illegal Rentals, Los Angeles Times, Apr. 15, 2016., 5.6 n.20

Rheinstein, Critique: Contracts to Make a Will, 30 N.Y.U. L. Rev. 1224 (1955), 7.17b n.19

Ribstein & Kobayashi, An Economic Analysis of Uniform State Laws, 25 J. Legal Stud. 131 (1996), 1.9 n.1

Richman, Weinstock & Mehta, A Bridge, a Tax Revolt, and the Struggle to Industrialize: The Story and Legacy of *Rockingham County v. Luten Bridge Co.*, 84 N.C.L. Rev. 1841 (1006), 12.12. n.16

Ricks, The Death of Offers, 79 Ind. L.J. 667 (2004), 3.18 n.2

Roberts, CFPB's Assault on Arbitration Stuck Between Rock, Hard Place, Bloomberg Law, Mar. 7, 2017, https://www.bna.com/cfpbs-assault-arbitration- n57982084833/, 4.28 n.52

Roberts, Restitutionary Disgorgement as a Moral Compass for Breach of Contract, 77 U. Cin. L. Rev. 991 (2009), 12.20a n.16

Roberts, Restitutionary Disgorgement for Opportunistic Breach of Contract and Mitigation of Damages, 42 Loy. L.A. L. Rev. 131 (2008), 12.20a n.16

Schwartz & Scott, Contract Interpretation Redux, 119 Yale L.J. 926 (2010), 7.12 n.22
Schwartz & Scott, Contract Theory and the Limits of Contract Law, 113 Yale L.J. 541 (2003), 1.10 n.11; 7.12 n.22
Schwartz & Scott, Market Damages, Efficient Contracting, and the Economic Waste Fallacy, 108 Colum. L. Rev. 1610 (2008), 12.13 n.6
Schwartz & Scott, Precontractual Liability and Preliminary Agreements, 120 Harv. L. Rev. 661 (2007), 3.26 n.20
Schwenzer & Hachem, The CISG—Successes and Pitfalls, 57 Am. J. Comp. L. 457 (2009), 1.9b n.7
Scott, *Hoffman v. Red Owl Stores* and the Myth of Precontractual Reliance, 68 Ohio St. L.J. 71 (2007), 3.26 n.39
Scott, A Theory of Self-Enforcing Indefinite Agreements, 103 Colum. L. Rev. 1641 (2003), 3.27 n.1
Scott & Triantis, Embedded Options and the Case Against Compensation in Contract Law, 104 Colum. L. Rev. 1428 (2004), 12.3 n.1; 12.18 n.8
Shavell, Contractual Holdup and Legal Intervention, 36 J. Legal Stud. 325 (2007), 4.16 n.1
Shavell, Is Breach of Contract Immoral?, 56 Emory L.J. 439 (2006), 1.8 n.31
Shavell, Specific Performance Versus Damages for Breach of Contract: An Economic Analysis, 84 Tex. L. Rev. 831 (2006), 12.6 n.2
Sheldon & Carter, Unfair & Deceptive Acts & Practices (5th ed. 2001), 3.14 n.10; 4.26 n.28
Shiffrin, The Divergence of Contract and Promise, 120 Harv. L. Rev. 709 (2007), 1.8 n.29
Shiffrin, Must I Mean what You Think I *Should* Have Said?, 98 Va. L. Rev. 159 (2012), 1.8 n.29
Shrank & Yim, Liquidated Damages in Commercial Leases of Personalty—The Proper Analysis, 64 Bus. Law. 757 (2009), 12.18 n.27
Sidhu, The Immorality and Inefficiency of an Efficient Breach, 8 Transactions 61 (2006), 12.3 n.7
Silber, Observing Reasonable Consumers: Cognitive Psychology, Consumer Behavior and Consumer Law, 2 Loy. Consumer L. Rep. 69 (1990), 4.29 n.14
Silver-Greenberg, Jessica and Robert Gebeloff, "Arbitration Everywhere, Stacking the Deck of Justice," New York Times (Oct. 31, 2015), 4.28 n.47
Silver-Greenberg and Gebeloff, "In Arbitration, a 'Privatization of the Justice System,'" New York Times (Nov. 1, 2015), 4.28 n.47
Skoloff, Singer & Brown, Drafting Prenuptial Agreements (1994), 5.4a n.1
Slawson, Unilateral Contracts of Employment: Does Contract Law Conflict With Public Policy, 10 Tex. Wesleyan L. Rev. 9 (2003), 2.10a n.24

INDEX

References are to sections and footnote numbers in the 2016-3 supplement.